Teacher Edition • Volume 1

Developed by
The Children's Math Worlds Research Project

PROJECT DIRECTOR AND AUTHOR
Dr. Karen C. Fuson

This material is based upon work supported by the
National Science Foundation
under Grant Numbers
ESI-9816320, REC-9806020, and RED-935373.

Any opinions, findings, and conclusions, or recommendations expressed in this material are those of the author and do not necessarily reflect the views of the National Science Foundation.

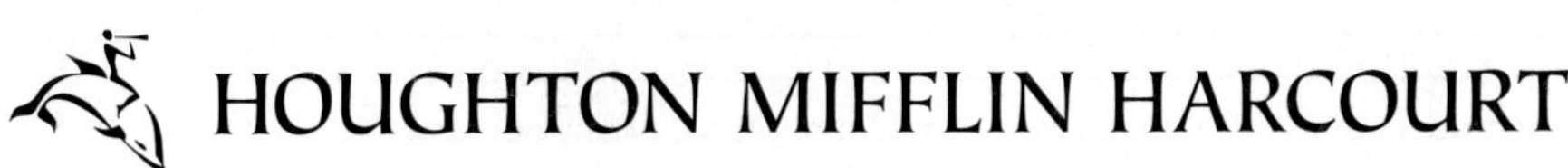

Teacher Reviewers

Kindergarten
Patricia Stroh Sugiyama
Wilmette, Illinois

Barbara Wahle
Evanston, Illinois

Grade 1
Sandra Budson
Newton, Massachusetts

Janet Pecci
Chicago, Illinois

Megan Rees
Chicago, Illinois

Grade 2
Molly Dunn
Danvers, Massachusetts

Agnes Lesnick
Hillside, Illinois

Rita Soto
Chicago, Illinois

Grade 3
Jane Curran
Honesdale, Pennsylvania

Sandra Tucker
Chicago, Illinois

Grade 4
Sara Stoneberg Llibre
Chicago, Illinois

Sheri Roedel
Chicago, Illinois

Grade 5
Todd Atler
Chicago, Illinois

Leah Barry
Norfolk, Massachusetts

Special Thanks
Special thanks to the many teachers, students, parents, principals, writers, researchers, and work-study students who participated in the Children's Math Worlds Research Project over the years.

Credits
(t) © Charles Cormany/Workbook Stock/Jupiter Images, (b) Noah Strycker/Shutterstock

Illustrative art: Robin Boyer/Deborah Wolfe, LTD; Dave Clegg, Geoff Smith, Tim Johnson
Technical art: Nesbitt Graphics, Inc.
Photos: Nesbitt Graphics, Inc.; Page 309 © Anna Clopet/Corbis; Page 366 (l) © David Hancock/Alamy, (c) © Halfdark/Getty Images, (r) © Brooke Fasani/Corbis.

Printed in China

ISBN: 978-0-547-05715-6

3 4 5 6 7 8 9 NPC 17 16 15 14 13 12 11 10 09

Introducing

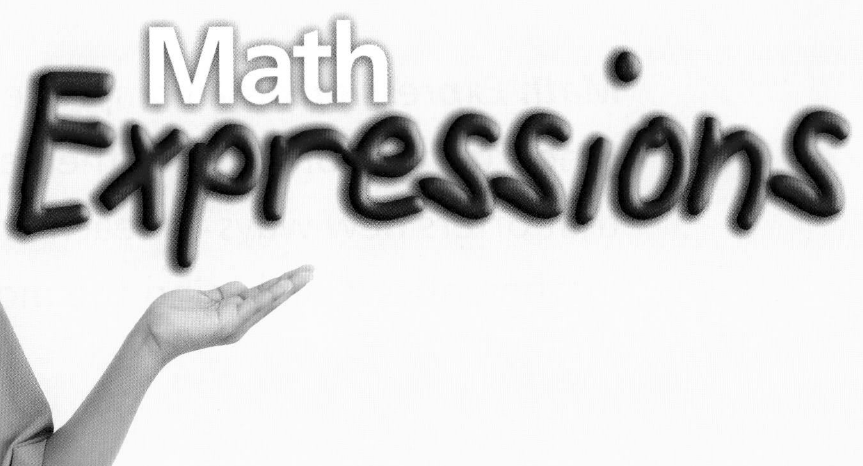

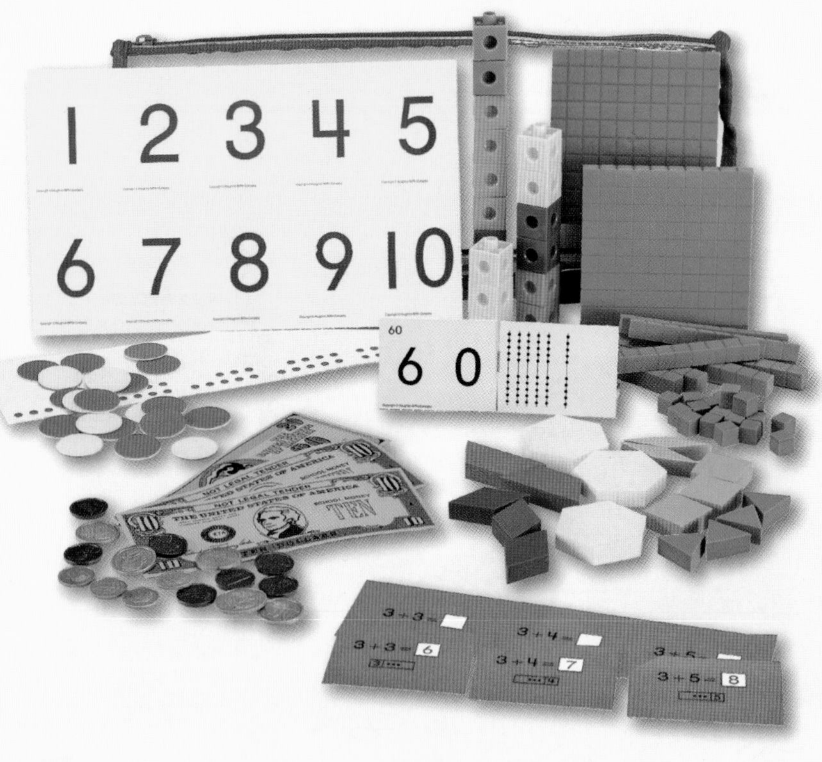

Helping Community Quick Practice Building Concepts Student Leaders Math Talk

A Fresh Approach to

Math Expressions is a comprehensive Kindergarten–Grade 5 mathematics curriculum that offers new ways to teach and learn mathematics. Combining the most powerful

Standards-Based Instruction

elements of standards-based instruction with the best of traditional approaches, ***Math Expressions*** uses objects, drawings, conceptual language, and real-world situations to help students build mathematical ideas that make sense to them.

Math Expressions implements state standards as well as the recommendations and findings from recent reports on math learning:

Curriculum Focal Points (NCTM, 2007)

Principles and Standards for School Mathematics (NCTM, 2000)

Adding It Up
(National Research Council, 2001)

How Students Learn Mathematics in the Classroom
(National Research Council, 2005)

Houghton Mifflin
Math Expressions

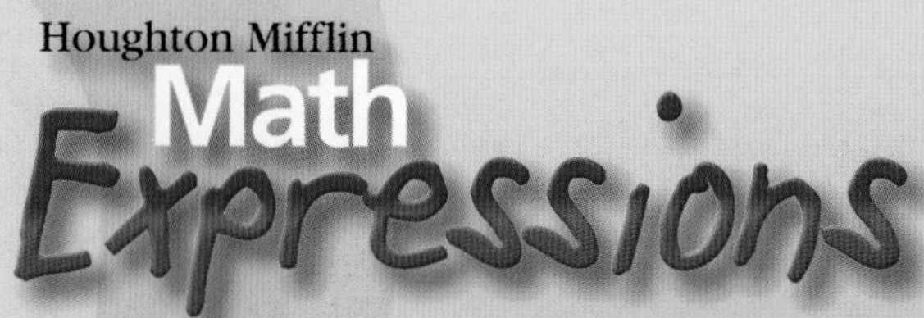

Focused on Understanding

In ***Math Expressions,*** teachers create an inquiry environment and encourage constructive discussion. Students invent, question, and explore, but also learn

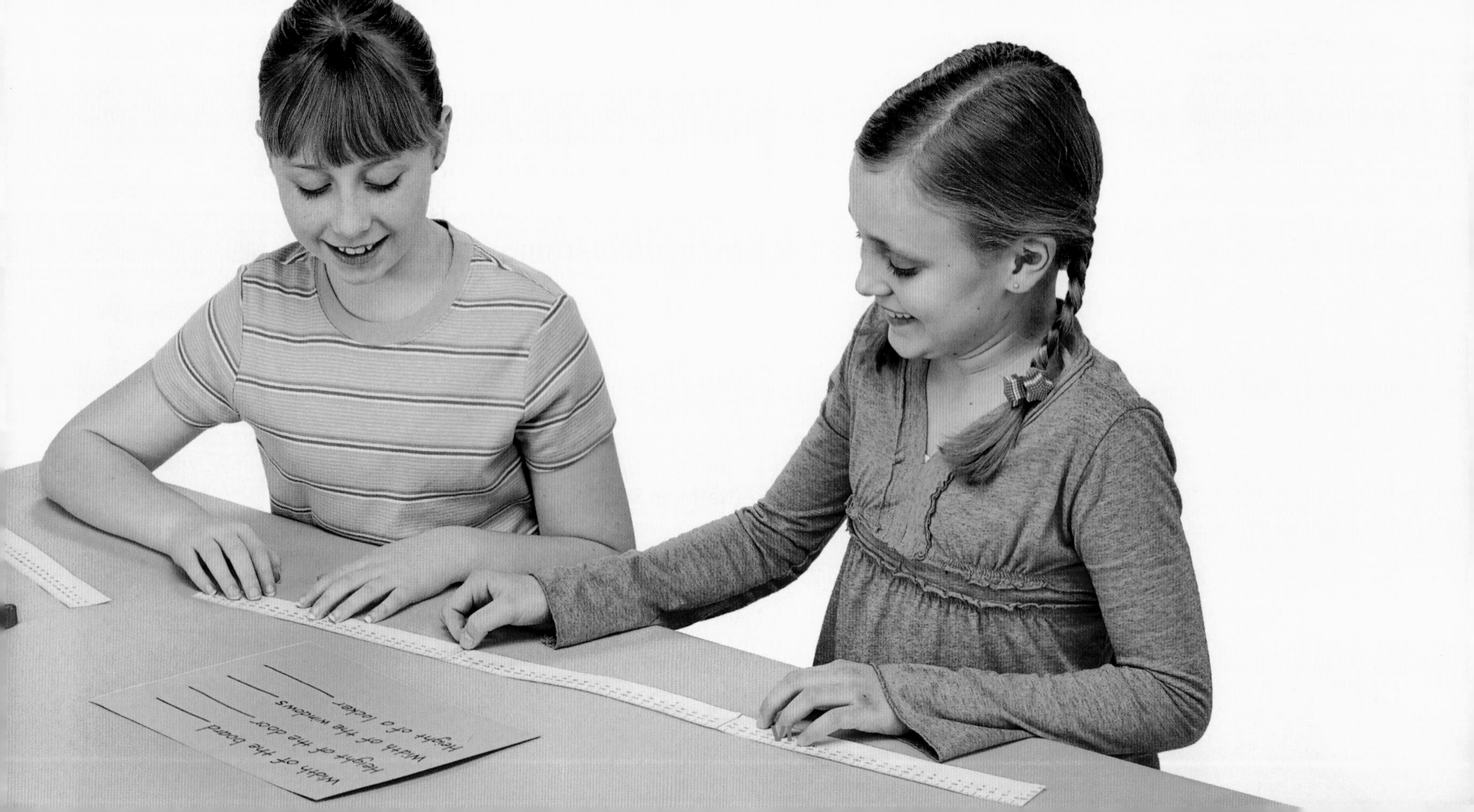

and Fluency

and practice important math strategies. Through daily Math Talk, students explain their methods and, in turn, become more fluent in them.

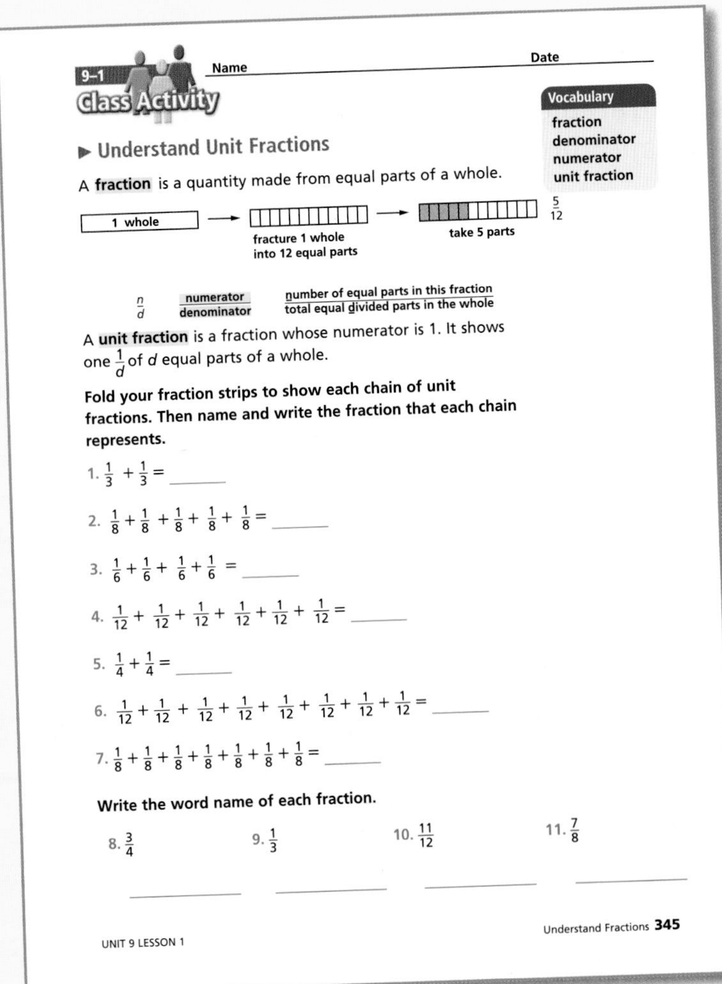

9–1 **Class Activity** Name ______ Date ______

Vocabulary
fraction
denominator
numerator
unit fraction

▶ **Understand Unit Fractions**

A **fraction** is a quantity made from equal parts of a whole.

1 whole → fracture 1 whole into 12 equal parts → take 5 parts $\frac{5}{12}$

$\frac{n}{d}$ $\frac{\text{numerator}}{\text{denominator}}$ $\frac{\text{number of equal parts in this fraction}}{\text{total equal divided parts in the whole}}$

A **unit fraction** is a fraction whose numerator is 1. It shows one $\frac{1}{d}$ of d equal parts of a whole.

Fold your fraction strips to show each chain of unit fractions. Then name and write the fraction that each chain represents.

1. $\frac{1}{3} + \frac{1}{3} =$ ______
2. $\frac{1}{8} + \frac{1}{8} + \frac{1}{8} + \frac{1}{8} + \frac{1}{8} =$ ______
3. $\frac{1}{6} + \frac{1}{6} + \frac{1}{6} + \frac{1}{6} =$ ______
4. $\frac{1}{12} + \frac{1}{12} + \frac{1}{12} + \frac{1}{12} + \frac{1}{12} + \frac{1}{12} =$ ______
5. $\frac{1}{4} + \frac{1}{4} =$ ______
6. $\frac{1}{12} + \frac{1}{12} + \frac{1}{12} + \frac{1}{12} + \frac{1}{12} + \frac{1}{12} + \frac{1}{12} + \frac{1}{12} =$ ______
7. $\frac{1}{8} + \frac{1}{8} + \frac{1}{8} + \frac{1}{8} + \frac{1}{8} + \frac{1}{8} + \frac{1}{8} =$ ______

Write the word name of each fraction.

8. $\frac{3}{4}$ ______ 9. $\frac{1}{3}$ ______ 10. $\frac{11}{12}$ ______ 11. $\frac{7}{8}$ ______

UNIT 9 LESSON 1 Understand Fractions **345**

"As Students are asked to communicate about the mathematics they are studying ... they gain insights into their thinking to others, students naturally reflect on their learning and organize and consolidate their thinking about mathematics"

- ***Principles and Standards for School Mathematics,*** **National Council of Teachers of Mathematics (2000), p. 120**

Organized for

Math Expressions is organized around five crucial classroom structures that allow children to develop deep conceptual

Quick Practice

Routines involve whole-class responses or individual partner practice

Math Talk

Students share strategies and solutions orally and through proof drawings

Building Concepts

Objects, drawings, conceptua language, and real-world situations strengthen mathematical ideas and understanding

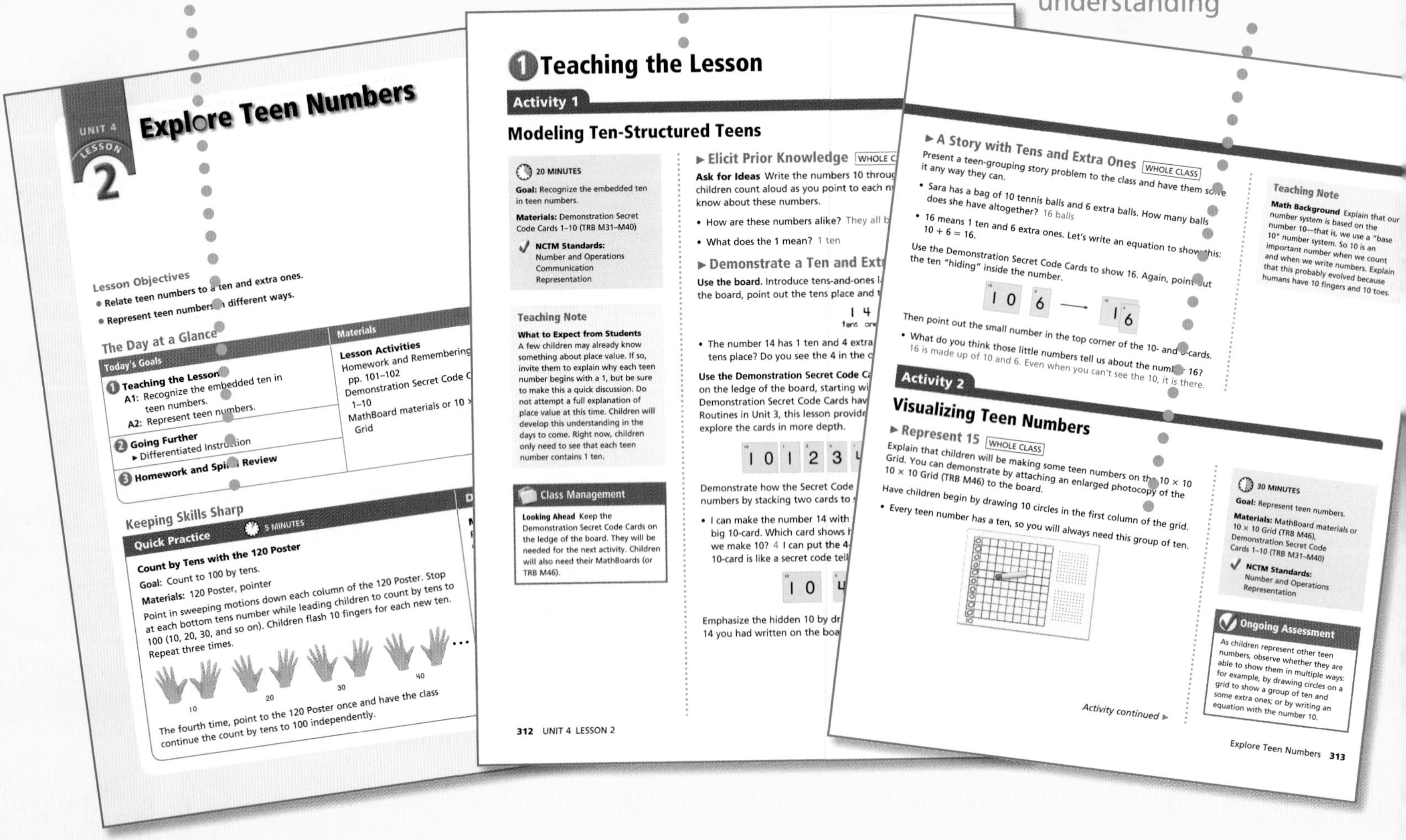

UNIT 4 LESSON 2

Explore Teen Numbers

Lesson Objectives

- Relate teen numbers to a ten and extra ones.
- Represent teen numbers in different ways.

The Day at a Glance

Today's Goals

1. Teaching the Lesson
   A1: Recognize the embedded ten in teen numbers.
   A2: Represent teen numbers.
2. Going Further
   ▸ Differentiated Instruction
3. Homework and Spiral Review

Materials

Lesson Activities
Homework and Remembering pp. 101–102
Demonstration Secret Code Cards 1–10
MathBoard materials or 10 × Grid

Keeping Skills Sharp

Quick Practice 5 MINUTES

Count by Tens with the 120 Poster

Goal: Count to 100 by tens.

Materials: 120 Poster, pointer

Point in sweeping motions down each column of the 120 Poster. Stop at each bottom tens number while leading children to count by tens to 100 (10, 20, 30, and so on). Children flash 10 fingers for each new ten. Repeat three times.

10 20 30 40 …

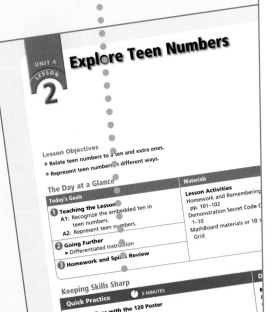

The fourth time, point to the 120 Poster once and have the class continue the count by tens to 100 independently.

1 Teaching the Lesson

Activity 1

Modeling Ten-Structured Teens

20 MINUTES

Goal: Recognize the embedded ten in teen numbers.

Materials: Demonstration Secret Code Cards 1–10 (TRB M31–M40)

✓ **NCTM Standards:**
Number and Operations
Communication
Representation

Teaching Note

What to Expect from Students
A few children may already know something about place value. If so, invite them to explain why each teen number begins with a 1, but be sure to make this a quick discussion. Do not attempt a full explanation of place value at this time. Children will develop this understanding in the days to come. Right now, children only need to see that each teen number contains 1 ten.

Class Management

Looking Ahead Keep the Demonstration Secret Code Cards on the ledge of the board. They will be needed for the next activity. Children will also need their MathBoards (or TRB M46).

▸ **Elicit Prior Knowledge** WHOLE C

Ask for Ideas Write the numbers 10 throu children count aloud as you point to each n know about these numbers.

- How are these numbers alike? They all b
- What does the 1 mean? 1 ten

▸ **Demonstrate a Ten and Ext**

Use the board. Introduce tens-and-ones l the board, point out the tens place and t

1 4
tens one

- The number 14 has 1 ten and 4 extra tens place? Do you see the 4 in the o

Use the Demonstration Secret Code Ca on the ledge of the board, starting wi Demonstration Secret Code Cards hav Routines in Unit 3, this lesson provide explore the cards in more depth.

1 0 1 2 3

Demonstrate how the Secret Code numbers by stacking two cards to

- I can make the number 14 with big 10-card. Which card shows we make 10? 4 I can put the 4 10-card is like a secret code tell

1 0

Emphasize the hidden 10 by dr 14 you had written on the boa

312 UNIT 4 LESSON 2

▸ **A Story with Tens and Extra Ones** WHOLE CLASS

Present a teen-grouping story problem to the class and have them solve it any way they can.

- Sara has a bag of 10 tennis balls and 6 extra balls. How many balls does she have altogether? 16 balls
- 16 means 1 ten and 6 extra ones. Let's write an equation to show this: $10 + 6 = 16$.

Use the Demonstration Secret Code Cards to show 16. Again, point out the ten "hiding" inside the number.

1 0 6 → 1 6

Then point out the small number in the top corner of the 10- and 6-cards.

- What do you think those little numbers tell us about the number 16? 16 is made up of 10 and 6. Even when you can't see the 10, it is there.

Teaching Note

Math Background Explain that our number system is based on the number 10—that is, we use a "base 10" number system. So 10 is an important number when we count and when we write numbers. Explain that this probably evolved because humans have 10 fingers and 10 toes.

Activity 2

Visualizing Teen Numbers

▸ **Represent 15** WHOLE CLASS

Explain that children will be making some teen numbers on the 10 × 10 Grid. You can demonstrate by attaching an enlarged photocopy of the 10 × 10 Grid (TRB M46) to the board.

Have children begin by drawing 10 circles in the first column of the grid.

- Every teen number has a ten, so you will always need this group of ten.

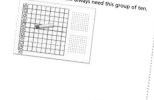

30 MINUTES

Goal: Represent teen numbers.

Materials: MathBoard materials or 10 × 10 Grid (TRB M46), Demonstration Secret Code Cards 1–10 (TRB M31–M40)

✓ **NCTM Standards:**
Number and Operations
Representation

Ongoing Assessment

As children represent other teen numbers, observe whether they are able to show them in multiple ways: for example, by drawing circles on a grid to show a group of ten and some extra ones; or by writing an equation with the number 10.

Activity continued ▸

Explore Teen Numbers 313

Classroom Success

understanding, and then practice, apply, and discuss what they know with skill and confidence.

Helping Community

A classroom in which everyone is both a teacher and a learner enhances mathematical understanding, competence, and confidence

Student Leaders

Teachers facilitate students' growth by helping them learn to lead practice and discussion routines

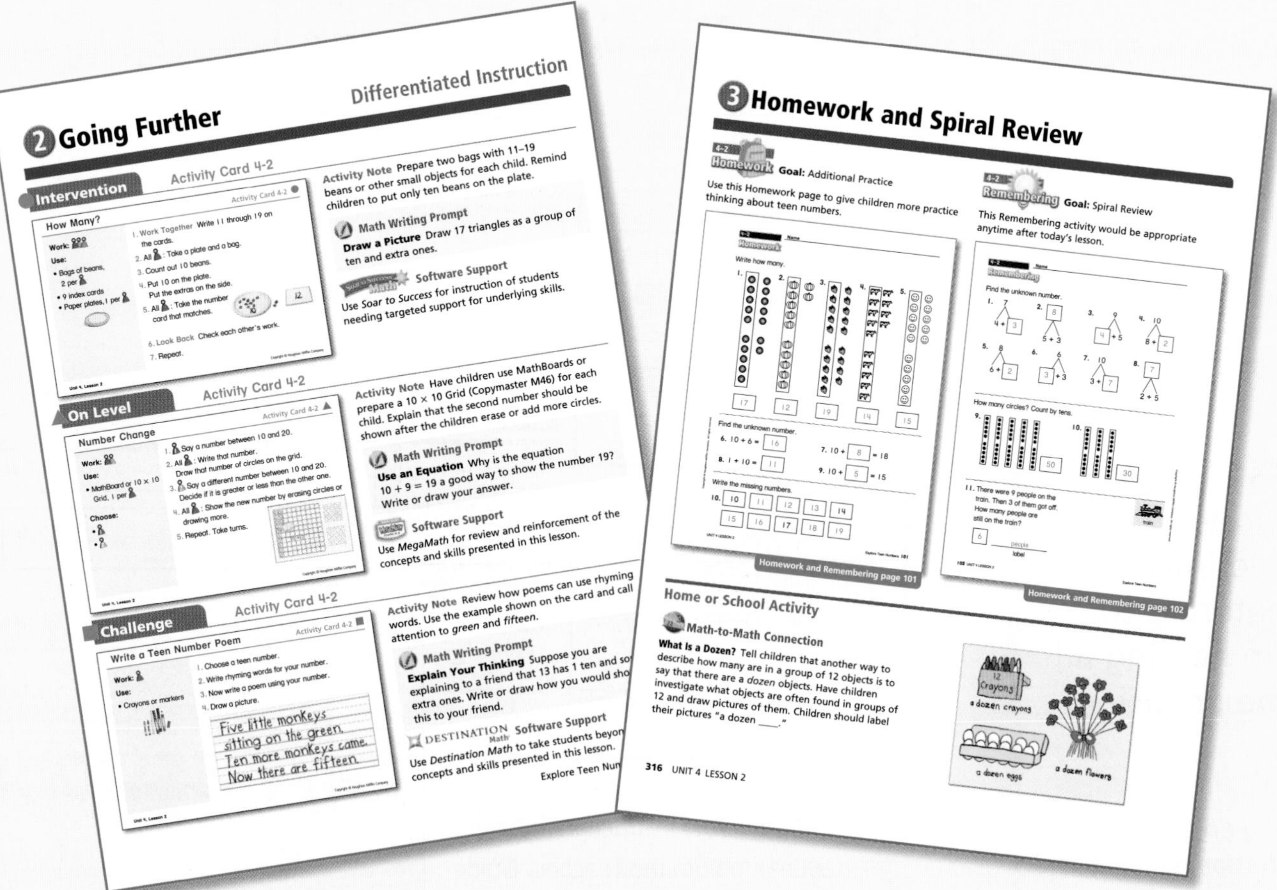

2 Going Further — Differentiated Instruction

Intervention — Activity Card 4-2

How Many?

Activity Note Prepare two bags with 11–19 beans or other small objects for each child. Remind children to put only ten beans on the plate.

Math Writing Prompt
Draw a Picture Draw 17 triangles as a group of ten and extra ones.

Software Support
Use Soar to Success for instruction of students needing targeted support for underlying skills.

On Level — Activity Card 4-2

Number Change

Activity Note Have children use MathBoards or prepare a 10 × 10 Grid (Copymaster M46) for each child. Explain that the second number should be shown after the children erase or add more circles.

Math Writing Prompt
Use an Equation Why is the equation 10 + 9 = 19 a good way to show the number 19? Write or draw your answer.

Software Support
Use *MegaMath* for review and reinforcement of the concepts and skills presented in this lesson.

Challenge — Activity Card 4-2

Write a Teen Number Poem

Five little monkeys
sitting on the green.
Ten more monkeys came.
Now there are fifteen.

Activity Note Review how poems can use rhyming words. Use the example shown on the card and call attention to *green* and *fifteen*.

Math Writing Prompt
Explain Your Thinking Suppose you are explaining to a friend that 13 has 1 ten and so extra ones. Write or draw how you would sho this to your friend.

DESTINATION Math Software Support
Use *Destination Math* to take students beyon concepts and skills presented in this lesson.

Explore Teen Num

3 Homework and Spiral Review

4-2 Homework **Goal:** Additional Practice

Use this Homework page to give children more practice thinking about teen numbers.

Homework and Remembering page 101

4-2 Remembering **Goal:** Spiral Review

This Remembering activity would be appropriate anytime after today's lesson.

Homework and Remembering page 102

Home or School Activity

Math-to-Math Connection

What Is a Dozen? Tell children that another way to describe how many are in a group of 12 objects is to say that there are a *dozen* objects. Have children investigate what objects are often found in groups of 12 and draw pictures of them. Children should label their pictures "a dozen ___."

a dozen crayons
a dozen eggs
a dozen flowers

316 UNIT 4 LESSON 2

Differentiated for

Every ***Math Expressions*** lesson includes intervention, on level, and challenge differentiation to support classroom needs. Leveled Math Writing Prompts provide opportunities for in–depth thinking and analysis, and help prepare students for high-stakes tests.

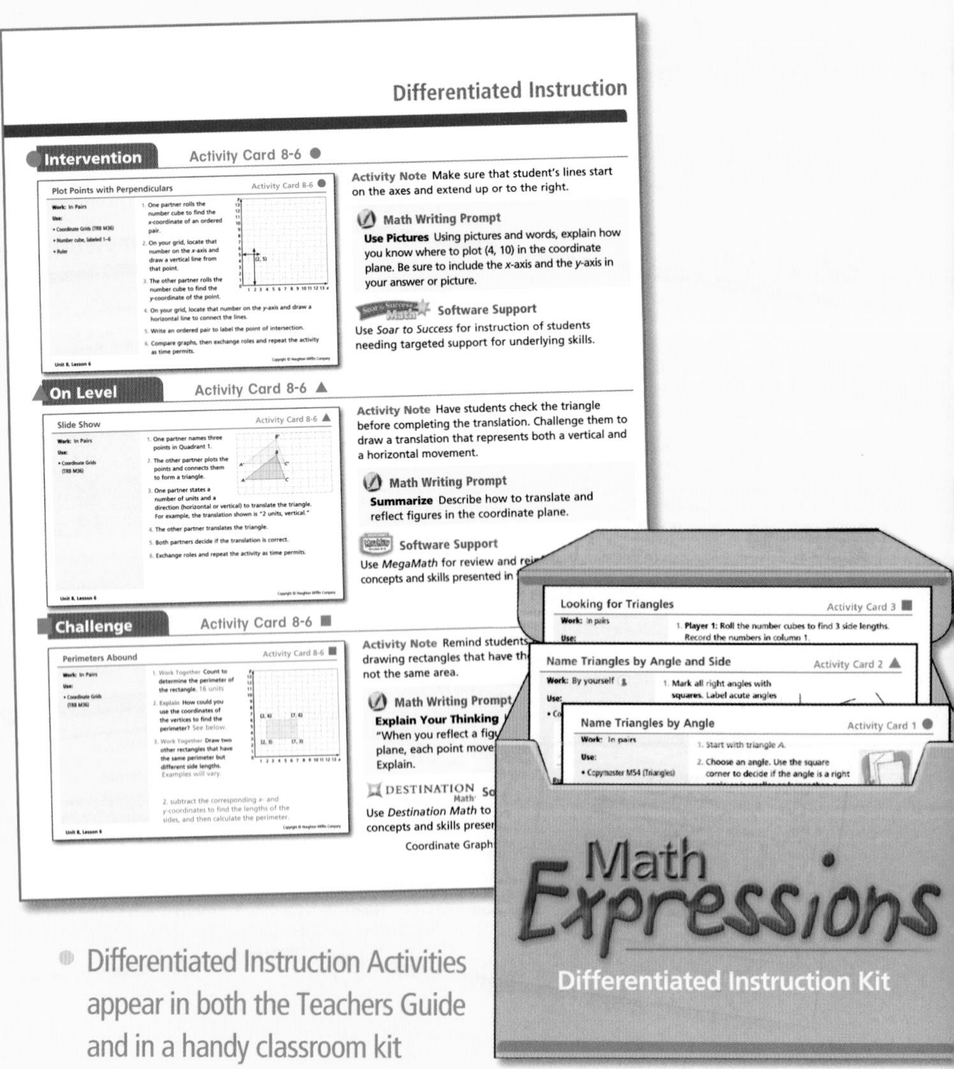

Differentiated Instruction Activities appear in both the Teachers Guide and in a handy classroom kit

> "Activities and strategies should be developed and incorporated into instructional materials to assist teachers in helping all students become proficient in mathematics"
>
> - *Adding It Up: Helping Children Learn Mathematics*, National Research Council (2001), p. 421

All Learners

Support for English Language Learners is included in each lesson. A special Challenge Math Center Easel, with activities, projects, and puzzlers, helps the highest math achievers reach their potential.

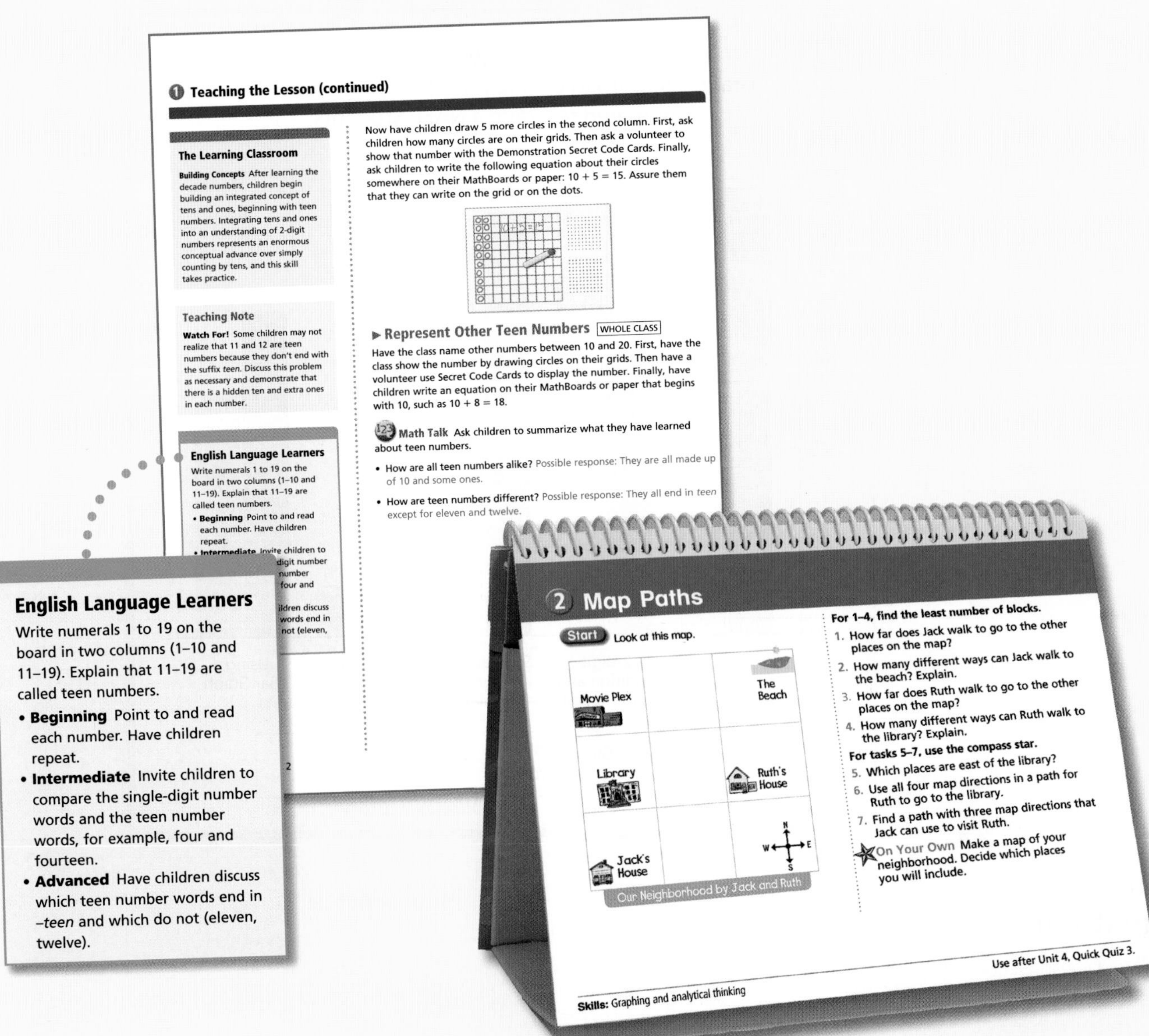

1 Teaching the Lesson (continued)

The Learning Classroom

Building Concepts After learning the decade numbers, children begin building an integrated concept of tens and ones, beginning with teen numbers. Integrating tens and ones into an understanding of 2-digit numbers represents an enormous conceptual advance over simply counting by tens, and this skill takes practice.

Teaching Note

Watch For! Some children may not realize that 11 and 12 are teen numbers because they don't end with the suffix *teen*. Discuss this problem as necessary and demonstrate that there is a hidden ten and extra ones in each number.

Now have children draw 5 more circles in the second column. First, ask children how many circles are on their grids. Then ask a volunteer to show that number with the Demonstration Secret Code Cards. Finally, ask children to write the following equation about their circles somewhere on their MathBoards or paper: 10 + 5 = 15. Assure them that they can write on the grid or on the dots.

▶ Represent Other Teen Numbers WHOLE CLASS

Have the class name other numbers between 10 and 20. First, have the class show the number by drawing circles on their grids. Then have a volunteer use Secret Code Cards to display the number. Finally, have children write an equation on their MathBoards or paper that begins with 10, such as 10 + 8 = 18.

Math Talk Ask children to summarize what they have learned about teen numbers.

- How are all teen numbers alike? Possible response: They are all made up of 10 and some ones.
- How are teen numbers different? Possible response: They all end in *teen* except for eleven and twelve.

English Language Learners

Write numerals 1 to 19 on the board in two columns (1–10 and 11–19). Explain that 11–19 are called teen numbers.

- **Beginning** Point to and read each number. Have children repeat.
- **Intermediate** Invite children to compare the single-digit number words and the teen number words, for example, four and fourteen.
- **Advanced** Have children discuss which teen number words end in *–teen* and which do not (eleven, twelve).

2 Map Paths

Start Look at this map.

For 1–4, find the least number of blocks.

1. How far does Jack walk to go to the other places on the map?
2. How many different ways can Jack walk to the beach? Explain.
3. How far does Ruth walk to go to the other places on the map?
4. How many different ways can Ruth walk to the library? Explain.

For tasks 5–7, use the compass star.

5. Which places are east of the library?
6. Use all four map directions in a path for Ruth to go to the library.
7. Find a path with three map directions that Jack can use to visit Ruth.

On Your Own Make a map of your neighborhood. Decide which places you will include.

Use after Unit 4, Quick Quiz 3.

Skills: Graphing and analytical thinking

Validated Through Ten

For twenty-five years, Dr. Karen Fuson, Professor Emeritus of Education and Psychology at Northwestern University, researched effective methods of teaching and learning mathematics.

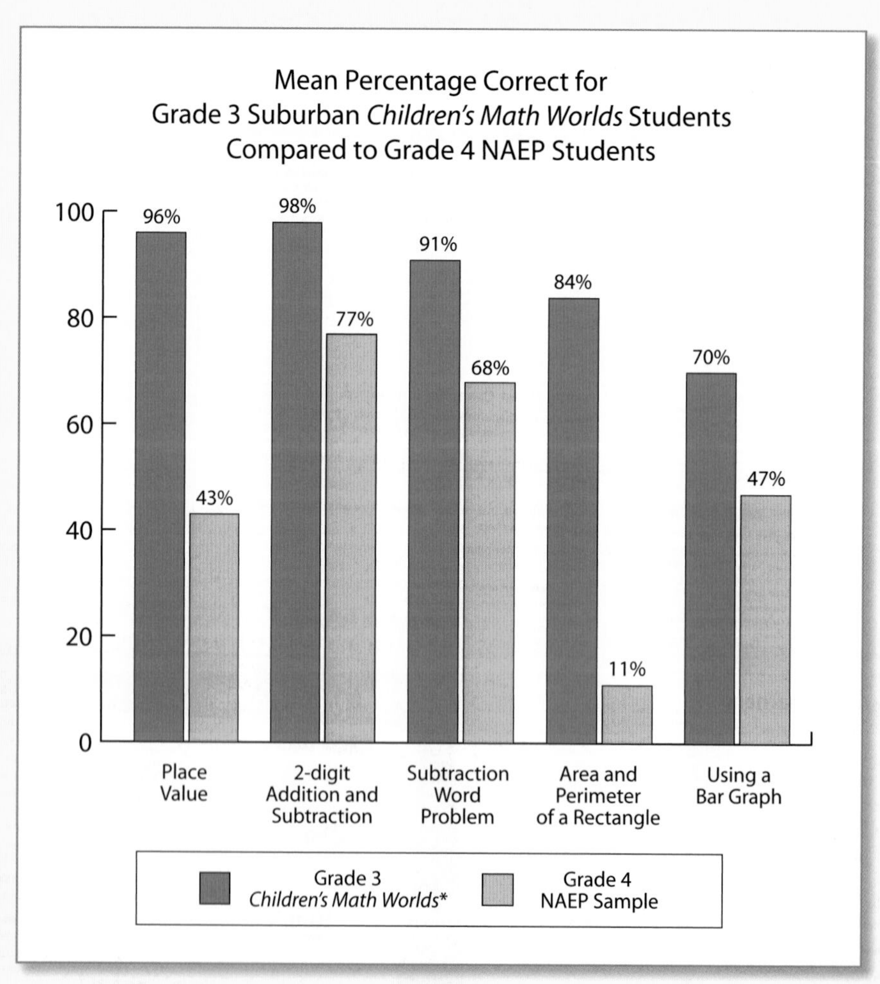

"I have many children who cheer when it's math time"
- Grade 2 Teacher

Years of Research

During the last ten years, with the support of the National Science Foundation for the Children's Math Worlds research Project, Dr. Fuson began development of what is now the ***Math Expressions*** curriculum in real classrooms across the country.

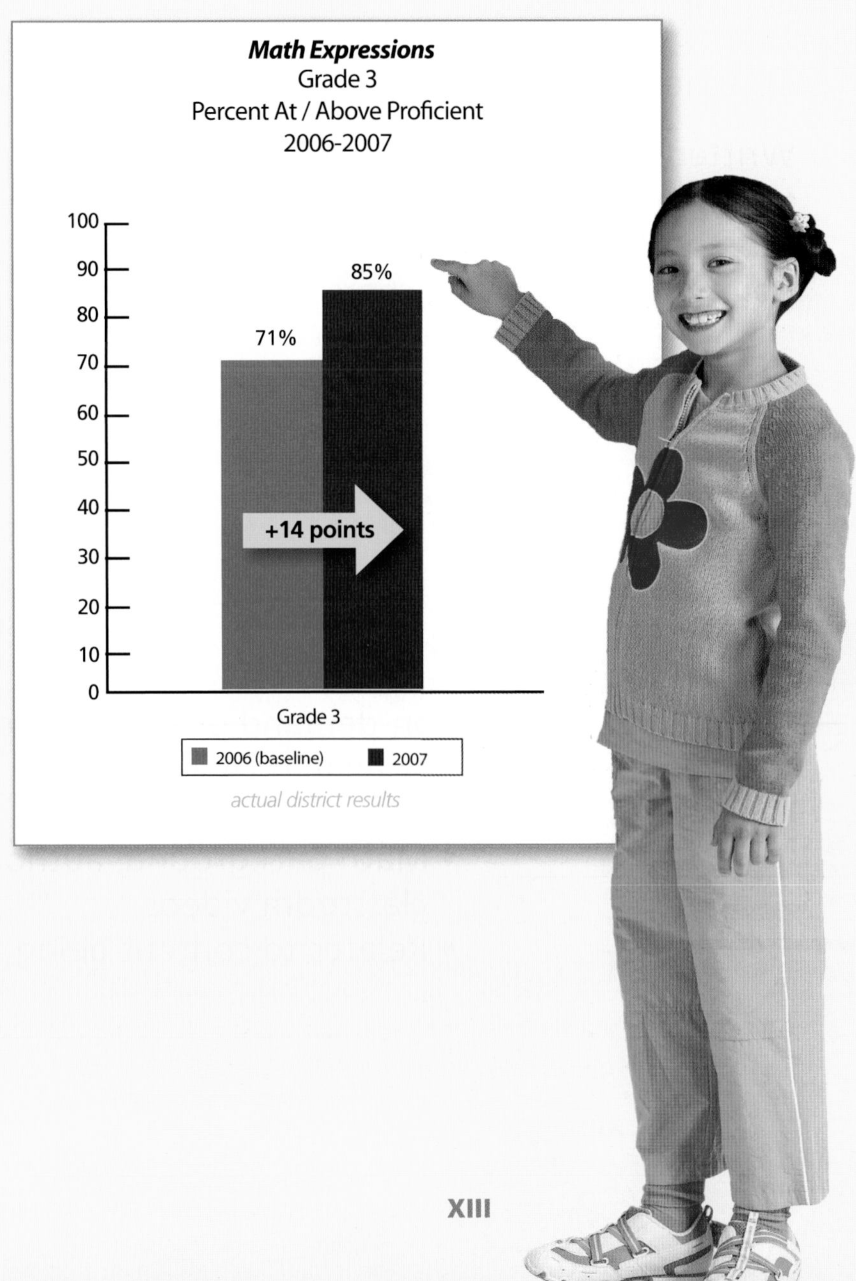

Powered by

Math Expressions is highly accessible by all teachers. To ensure the program gets off to the right start, our educational consultants are available to support districts implementing ***Math Expressions.*** Unique Teacher's Guide support and professional development options are also provided.

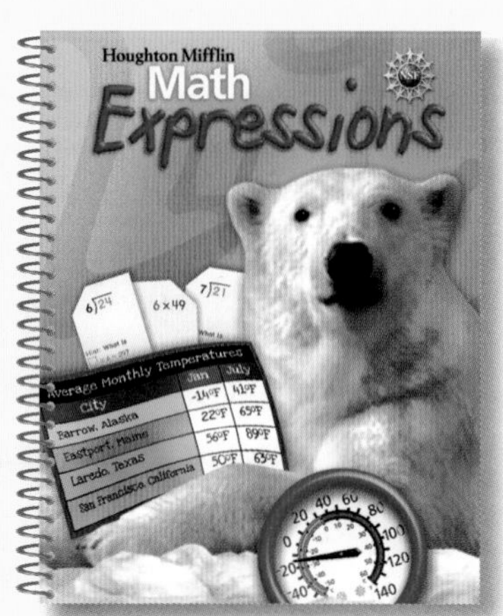

Teacher's Guide

Written in a learn while teaching style, math background and learning in the classroom resources are embedded at point of use in the Teachers Guide

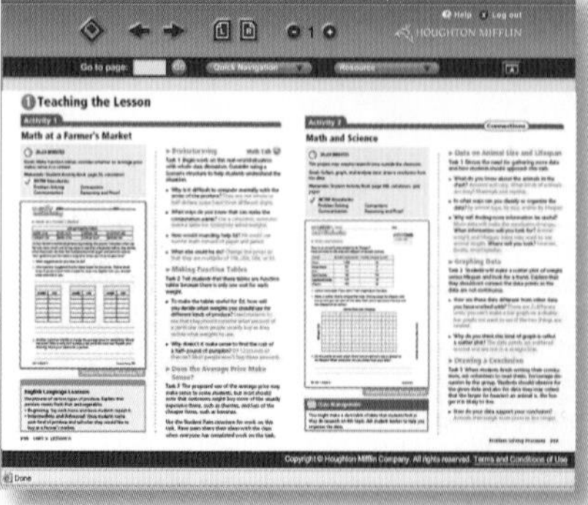

eTeacher's Guide

Offers on-demand professional development

- Available 24-7
- Direct links in the eTG
- Math background, author talks, and classroom videos
- Relates to content being taught

Professional Development

Special, in depth ***Math Expressions*** seminars are also available.

- **Administrator Institute**
  For administrators with school-based curriculum responsibilities

- **Level I Institute**
  For teachers who are new to ***Math Expressions***

- **Level II Institute**
  For teachers who have at least 6 months' experience teaching ***Math Expressions***

Components

New hardcover version Grades 3–5

	K	1	2	3	4	5
Core Components						
Teacher's Guide	•	•	•	•	•	•
Student Activity Book*	•	•	•	•	•	•
Homework and Remembering Book	•	•	•	•	•	•
Assessment Guide	•	•	•	•	•	•
Teacher Resource Book	•	•	•	•	•	•
MathBoards		•	•	•	•	•
Ready-Made Classroom Resources						
Individual Student Manipulatives Kit	•	•	•	•	•	•
Materials and Manipulatives Kit	•	•	•	•	•	•
Custom Manipulatives Kit	•	•	•	•	•	•
Challenge Math Center Easel	•	•	•	•	•	•
Hands-On Activity Workbook 3–5				•	•	•
Differentiated Instruction Activity Card Kit	•	•	•	•	•	•
Literature Library	•	•	•	•	•	•
Anno's Counting Book Big Book	•					
Technology						
eTeacher's Guide	•	•	•	•	•	•
eStudent Activity Book	•	•	•	•	•	•
Lesson Planner CD-ROM	•	•	•	•	•	•
ExamView Ways to Assess	•	•	•	•	•	•
Houghton Mifflin Online Assessment System	•	•	•	•	•	•
Mega Math	•	•	•	•	•	•
Destination Math	•	•	•	•	•	•
Soar to Success Math	•	•	•	•	•	•

*Grades K–5 available as consumable workbook; Grades 3–5 available as hardbound text

Materials and Manipulatives for Grade 2

The essential materials needed for teaching *Math Expressions* are provided in the Student Activity Book and/or can be made from Copymasters in the Teacher's Resource Book. However, many teachers prefer to use the more sturdy materials from the Materials and Manipulatives kits. This allows the students to take home the paper materials (from the Student Activity Book) or the cardstock materials (made from the Copymasters) to facilitate the connection between home and school.

Material or Manipulative in Grade 2	Pages in Student Activity Book	Copymasters in Teacher's Resource Book
Demonstration Secret Code Cards*		M7–M22
Secret Code Cards*	11–14	M3–M6
Count-On Cards*	27–28; 33–36	M25–M26; M29–M32
Make-a-Ten Cards*	39–42; 47–50	M35–M42
Math Mountain Cards	51–54	M43–M44
120 Poster*		M60–M61
Time Poster*		
Money Flip Chart*		Dime and Nickel Strips (M1), Dollar Bills (M67)
Pointer		
Math Expressions 25-cm ruler*		M47–M48
Math Expressions Inch Ruler*		M96
Play Coins (pennies, nickels, dimes, and quarters)	9–10; 271	M1, M73
Play Bills (1-dollar, 5-dollar, 10-dollar)	339, 385	M67–M68; M84, M89
Two-Color Counters		
Connecting Cubes		
Number Cubes		
Base Ten Blocks		
Pattern Blocks		M58
3-D Shapes		
Sticky Board		

* These materials were developed specifically for this program during the Children's Math Worlds Research Project.

Using Materials and Manipulatives for Each Unit

Material or Manipulative in Grade 2	Daily Routines	Unit													
		1	2	3	4	5	6	7	8	9	10	11	12	13	14
Demonstration Secret Code Cards	•	•				•				•		•			
Secret Code Cards		•		•		•				•		•			
Count-On Cards (red, yellow, and orange)		•		•		•									
Make-a-Ten Cards						•		•		•					
Math Mountain Cards				•				•				•			
120 Poster	•					•				•				•	
Time Poster	•						•								
Money Flip Chart	•														
Pointer	•	•	•	•	•	•	•	•	•	•	•	•	•	•	•
Math Expressions 25-cm ruler		•	•		•	•			•	•	•		•		
Math Expressions Inch Ruler															•
Play Coins (pennies, nickels, dimes, and quarters)	•	•				•		•		•		•	•	•	•
Play Bills (1-dollar, 5-dollar, 10-dollar)												•			
Two-Color Counters		•		•		•			•					•	
Connecting Cubes		•		•				•			•			•	
Number Cubes		•				•		•		•				•	
Base Ten Blocks			•			•				•		•	•		
Pattern Blocks					•						•				
3-D Shapes													•		
Sticky Board	•									•		•			

All materials for each unit (including those not in the kits) are listed in the planning chart for that unit.

Introduction

History and Development

Math Expressions is a K–5 mathematics program, developed from the Children's Math Worlds (CMW) Research Project conducted by Dr. Karen Fuson, Professor Emeritus at Northwestern University. This project was funded in part by the National Science Foundation.

The Research Project

The project studied the ways children around the world understand mathematical concepts, approach problem solving, and learn to do computation; it included ten years of classroom research and incorporated the ideas of participating students and teachers into the developing curriculum.

The research focused on building conceptual supports that include special language, drawings, manipulatives, and classroom communication methods that facilitate mathematical competence.

Curriculum Design

Within the curriculum, a series of learning progressions reflect recent research regarding children's natural stages when mastering concepts such as addition, subtraction, multiplication, and problem solving. These learning stages help determine the order of concepts, the sequence of units, and the positioning of topics.

The curriculum is designed to help teachers apply the most effective conceptual supports so that each child progresses as rapidly as possible.

During the research, students showed increases in standardized test scores as well as in broader measures of student understanding. These results were found for a wide range of both urban and suburban students from a variety of socio-economic groups.

Philosophy

Math Expressions incorporates the best practices of both traditional and reform mathematics curricula. The program strikes a balance between promoting children's natural solution methods and introducing effective procedures.

Building on Children's Knowledge

Because research has demonstrated that premature instruction in formalized procedures can lead to mechanical, unthinking behavior, established procedures for solving problems are not introduced until students have developed a solid conceptual foundation. Children begin by using their own knowledge to solve problems and then are introduced to research-based accessible methods.

In order to promote children's natural solution methods, as well as to encourage students to become reflective and resourceful problem solvers, teachers need to develop a helping and explaining culture in their classrooms.

Student Interactions

Collaboration and peer helping deepen children's commitment to values such as responsibility and respect for others. *Math Expressions* offers opportunities for students to interact in pairs, small groups, whole-class activities, and special scenarios.

As students collaboratively investigate math situations, they develop communication skills, sharpen their mathematical reasoning, and enhance their social awareness. Integrating students' social and cultural worlds into their emerging math worlds helps them to find their own voices and to connect real-world experiences to math concepts.

Main Concept Streams

Math Expressions focuses on crucially important core concepts. These core topics are placed at grade levels that enable students to do well on standardized tests. The main related concept streams at all grade levels are number concepts and an algebraic approach to word problems.

Breaking apart numbers, or finding the embedded numbers, is a key concept running through the number concept units.

- Kindergartners and first-graders find the numbers embedded within single-digit numbers and find the tens and ones in multi-digit numbers.
- Second- and third-graders continue breaking apart multi-digit numbers into ones and groups of tens, hundreds, and thousands. This activity facilitates their understanding of multi-digit addition and subtraction as well as solving word problems.
- Second-, third-, and fourth-graders work on seeing the repeated groups within numbers, and this awareness helps them to master multiplication and division.
- Fourth- and fifth-graders approach fractions as sums of unit fractions using length models. This permits them to see and comprehend operations on fractions.

Students work with story problems early in kindergarten and continue throughout the other grades. They not only solve but also construct word problems. As a result, they become comfortable and flexible with mathematical language and can connect concepts and terminology with meaningful referents from their own lives. As part of this process, students learn to make math drawings that enable teachers to see student thinking and facilitate communication.

Concepts and skills in algebra, geometry, measurement, and graphing are woven in between these two main streams throughout the grades. In grades two through five, geometry and measurement mini-units follow each regular unit.

Program Features

Many special features and approaches contribute to the effectiveness of ***Math Expressions.***

Quick Practice

The opening 5 minutes of each math period are dedicated to activities (often student-led) that allow students to practice newly acquired knowledge. These *consolidating activities* help students to become faster and more accurate with the concepts. Occasionally, *leading activities* prepare the ground for new concepts before they are introduced. Quick Practice activities are repeated so that they become familiar routines that students can do quickly and confidently.

Drawn Models

Special manipulatives are used at key points. However, students move toward math drawings as rapidly as possible.

These drawn models help students relate to the math situation, facilitate students' explanations of the steps they took to solve the problem, and help listeners comprehend these explanations.

The drawings also give teachers insight into students' mathematical thinking, and leave a durable record of student work.

Language Development

Math Expressions offers a wealth of learning activities that directly support language development. In addition to verbalizing procedures and explanations, students are encouraged to write their own problems and describe their problem-solving strategies in writing as soon as they are able.

Homework Assignments

To help students achieve a high level of mathematical performance, students complete homework assignments every night. Families are expected to identify a homework helper to be responsible for monitoring the student's homework completion and to help if necessary.

Daily Routines for Volume 1

See pages xvii and xviii for information about materials for Daily Routines.

THE MONEY ROUTINE

(Use throughout the Year)

Materials: 120 Poster, pointer, Money Flip Chart, sticky notes, MathBoard materials, Demonstration Secret Code Cards

The Money Routine reinforces fundamental money and multi-digit number concepts. It provides visual practice with these concepts that are built incrementally from day to day. This routine helps children learn to say 2- and 3-digit numbers, become skilled at counting, and helps them link money values with numeric values. This routine should be done every day while working on the numbered units and may be continued during the mini units as well. You should introduce the routine and lead it for 2 or 3 days and then help Student Leaders take over. Have more advanced and socially confident children lead first to act as models. Using four Student Leaders will help the routine move quickly.

Each day, a new total is created by adding a number from 5–9 to the total from the previous day. (The blue box below shows how the number to be added is determined.) The new total is then represented in various ways.

Plan for Using the Money Routine Throughout the Year

Cycle A (about 20 days)

- Begin at 0. Add 5, 6, or 7 (randomly chosen by a student volunteer or the teacher) each day until 120 is reached.
- Use pennies and dollars only.

Cycle B (about 30 days)

- Begin at 0 again. Add 7, 8, or 9 each day until 100 is reached.
- Then add 5, 6, 7, 8, or 9 each day until 240 is reached.
- Use pennies, dimes, and dollars.

Cycle C

- Begin at 0 again. Add 5, 6, 7, 8, or 9 each day until the end of the year.
- Use pennies, nickels, dimes, and dollars.

Using the 120 Poster

Student Leader 1 draws new circles on the 120 Poster to represent the number being added and, if there is a new ten, erases the circles on that ten and makes a bracket on the bottom of the column.

For example, if the previous total was 25 and 7 is being added:

- I am adding 7. So, 25 plus 7 is *(circling the numbers as saying them)* 26, 27, 28, 29, 30, 31, 32. I have a new ten, so I am going to erase all of the circles on these twenties and mark the ten at the bottom. *(Saying as writing this)* 32 = 30 + 2.

1	11	21	31	41	51	61	71	81	91	101	111
2	12	22	32	42	52	62	72	82	92	102	112
3	13	23	33	43	53	63	73	83	93	103	113
4	14	24	34	44	54	64	74	84	94	104	114
5	15	25	35	45	55	65	75	85	95	105	115
6	16	26	36	46	56	66	76	86	96	106	116
7	17	27	37	47	57	67	77	87	97	107	117
8	18	28	38	48	58	68	78	88	98	108	118
9	19	29	39	49	59	69	79	89	99	109	119
10	20	30	40	50	60	70	80	90	100	110	120

32 = 30 + 2

120 Poster

(Numbers 121–240 are on the back of the 120 Poster. This part of the routine is discontinued when the total *exceeds* 240.)

Count to the New Total Student Leader 1 then leads the class to count to the new total. If the total is ≤ 20, the class counts by ones. The Student Leader points to the numbers on the 120 Poster as the class counts. After 20, the children count by tens and ones. For example, to count to 32, children say 10, 20, 30, *freeze*, 31, 32. Children flash ten fingers all at once for each ten and show one finger for each one they count after that. Saying *freeze* helps children shift from counting by tens to counting by ones. You can stop when all children no longer need the signal.

Daily Routines for Volume 1 (Continued)

As the class counts, the Student Leader moves the pointer down each column as 10, 20, 30 are said and then points to each single number as 31, 32 are said.

Using the Money Flip Chart

Student Leader 2 directs the next part of the routine. On the first day, cover the 10 pennies in the first column using sticky notes. *(Keep all other columns covered with the flaps.)* Each day new pennies are uncovered to make the new total. When a new ten is made, another column of pennies and sticky notes is used.

- We have 25 pennies. I'm adding 7 pennies. Will I make a ten? Yes!! So, I'll flip over the covers on the next column so we can see the pennies. *(Flipping the covers)* 25 plus 5 is 30 *(takes off 5 sticky notes).* I have a new ten so I'll write it below *(erases the 5 below the 20s column and writes 10).* So, 25 plus 7 is 5 more to make 30 and 2 more from the 7 to make 32 *(pointing to the top 2 pennies in the fourth strip and writing + 2 below.)* I need to cover the rest of the pennies *(starts doing that with the sticky notes).* How many do I need to cover? 8
- So, my partners of 10 are 8 and 2 *(erases what was there and writes 8 + 2 to the right of the sticky note rectangles, pointing to the 8 empty rectangles and the 2 sticky notes).*
- Let's read the tens and ones. *(Pointing to the 10s written below the penny strips)* 10 plus 10 plus 10 plus 2. That's 3 tens and 2 ones equals 32. *(Writing 30 + 2 in vertical form in the upper right corner of the board)* 30 plus 2 is 32.

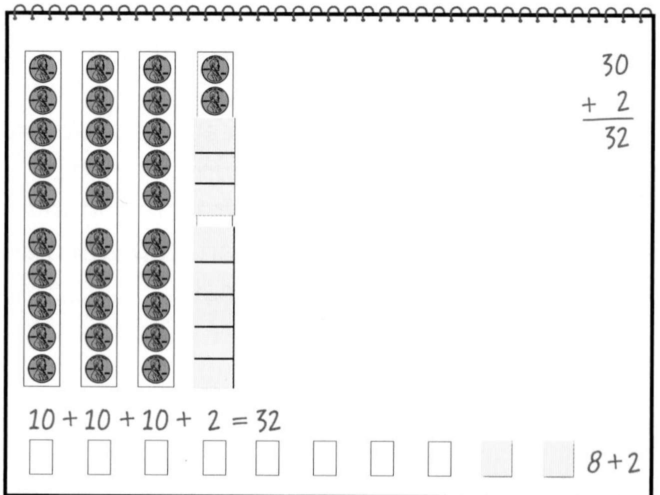

For numbers ≥ 100, the dollars are flipped to show dollar bills to the left of the Coin Strips. In Cycles B and C (see blue box), Dime Strips are flipped over to replace 10 pennies or 2 nickels and Nickel Strips are flipped over to replace 5 pennies.

Using the Number Path

Student Leader 3 leads the next part of the routine. Use a student MathBoard that can stay on display all day. Each day add the new number of circles on the Number Path. When a new ten is made, draw a line through all ten circles to show a 10-stick. (This part of the routine is discontinued when the total exceeds 100.)

Show the Addition Two Ways In the middle of the MathBoard, show in vertical form the addition of the previous day's total and today's new number resulting in today's new total. Then show the new total by adding sticks (Quick Tens) and circles to the drawing from the previous day and then redrawing the number if necessary just with Quick Tens. Be sure to show the 5-groups. (See page 307.)

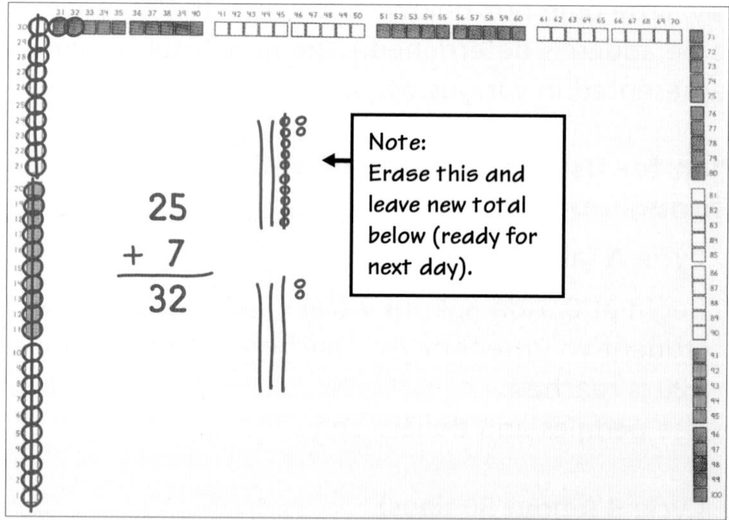

For numbers over 100, Quick Hundreds are also used; for example,

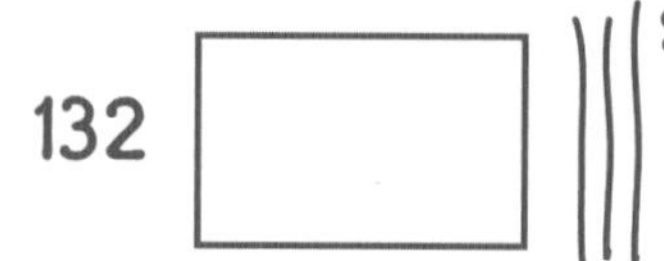

Using Secret Code Cards

Student Leader 4 shows the new total using the Demonstration Secret Code Cards.

- 30 *(shows 30 card)* plus 2 *(shows 2 card)*.
- *(Class responds)* 30 plus 2 makes *(puts 2 card over the 0)* 32.

Teaching Note

Some teachers choose to drop the Money Routine during Units 9 and 11 in order to focus more on the coin counting routines for those units. If you do this, you can return to this routine again during Unit 13.

COMPARING 2-DIGIT QUANTITIES

(Use with Units 3 and 4)

Materials: meter stick, sticky notes, MathBoard materials

This routine requires two Student Leaders. The routine begins with each Student Leader choosing a 2-digit number different from the total of the day (from the Money Routine), for example, 72 and 49.

Using a Meter Stick

Both Student Leaders mark their numbers on the meter stick with a sticky note.

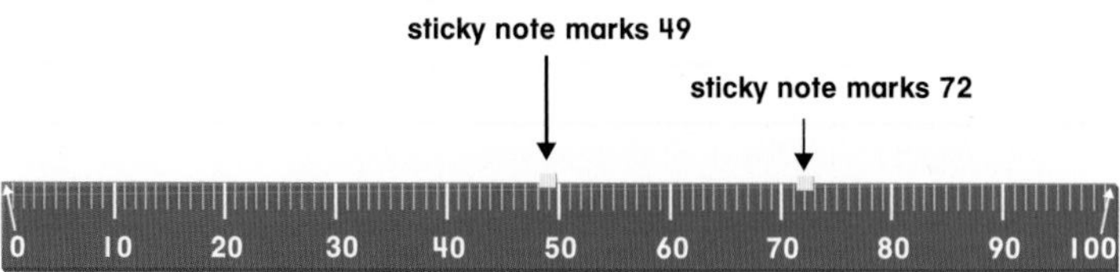

Using Number Flashes

Then they each lead the class to flash their numbers as tens and ones, saying the tens and ones at the same time.

49: 10, 20, 30, 40, 41, 42, 43, 44, 45, 46, 47, 48, 49
72: 10, 20, 30, 40, 50, 60, 70, 71, 72

Using the MathBoard

The leaders then write their numbers on a student MathBoard, one number above the other. They then draw sticks and circles and write tens and ones equations for their numbers as shown below.

Each Student Leader then writes the two numbers next to each other horizontally, leaving a space between them for the < and > symbols. One writes the greater number first; the other writes the lesser number first. They then insert the < and > symbols between the numbers. Watch to see that the symbols are oriented correctly. The point of the symbol points to the lesser number. The larger part of the symbol points to the greater number. The leaders then write "More" or "Less" under the appropriate numbers.

The class then reads the two number sentences. "72 is more than 49" and "49 is less than 72."

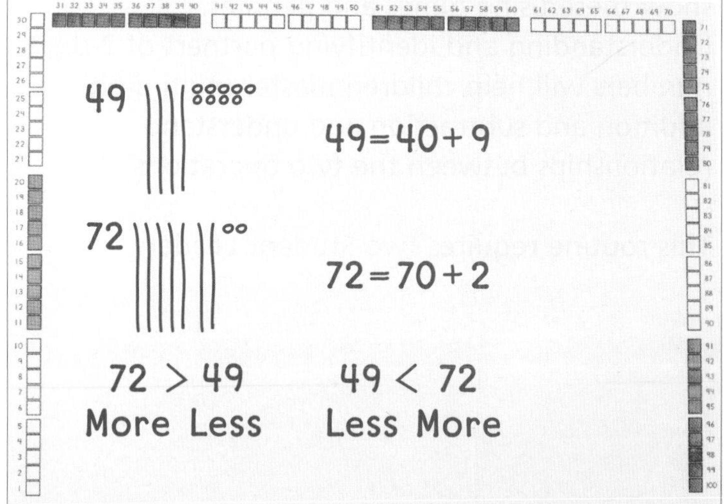

To complete the activity, the Student Leaders explain to the class how they decided which number was more and which was less. Encourage children to use the meter stick comparison, sticks and circles, and the tens and ones equations in their explanation. Leave the MathBoard on display all day if possible.

MATH MOUNTAINS FOR 100 or 2-DIGIT NUMBERS

(Use with Units 5 and 6)

Materials: MathBoard materials, sticky board (optional), play or real dimes and pennies

In this routine, children identify various partners of 100 or 2-digit numbers. Have them spend about 7 days breaking apart 100 into different partners, one pair of partners each day. On the first day, students can find decade partners to establish the routine (for example, 20 and 80). On days 2 through 7, they can work with other partners of 100 (for example, 62 and 38). After day 7, they should shift to breaking apart any 2-digit number (for example, 72 with partners 24 and 48).

Every day they draw Math Mountains to show the relationship between a total and partners and show these using dimes and pennies. Understanding and identifying partners of 2-digit numbers will help children master multi-digit addition and subtraction and understand relationships between the two operations.

This routine requires two Student Leaders.

Using the Math Board

Student Leader 1 gives the class the total (for example, 100) and one partner (for example, 62) and the class says the unknown partner (38). The leader then draws the Math Mountain and writes the 8 equations associated with it on the board. As the leader writes, the class says the equations, checking to be sure all are correct.

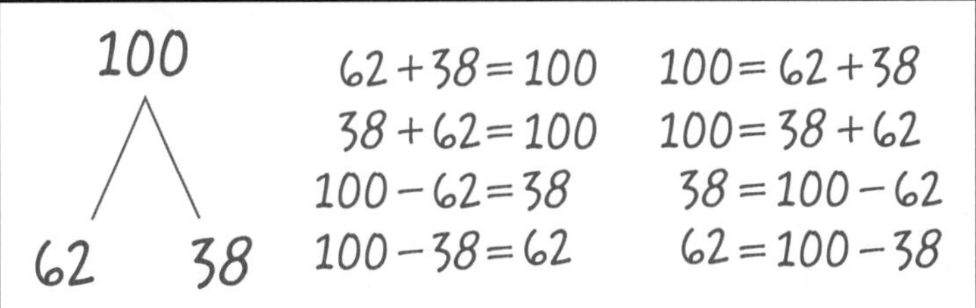

Using Dimes and Pennies

While Student Leader 1 is writing the equations, Student Leader 2 shows both partners using dimes and pennies. You can use a sticky board or tape coins to the board. Then Student Leader 1 writes the addition (see below) on a second student's MathBoard. Keep this board visible throughout the day and just erase and replace the numbers each day.

6 dimes + 2 pennies = 62¢

3 dimes + 8 pennies = 38¢

9 dimes + 10 pennies = 100¢

TELLING TIME
(Use with Units 7 and 8)

Materials: Demonstration clock or Time Poster and dry erase markers, pointer

This routine reinforces time concepts, the topic of Unit 6. This routine is intended to achieve the following goals for students: tell time to the hour, half hour, quarter hour, and 5 minutes; translate digital time to the analog clock; write the time shown on an analog clock in digital format; and link daily activities to times of the day.

Five Student Leaders lead this routine if you do all of the parts. Part 1 (Name the Hands) can be dropped after students have mastered the concepts. Telling time to 5-minute intervals can be added after the first week or so.

Name the Hands

Write 5, 10, 15 and so on around the outside of the clock on the Time Poster as shown. The class says the minute numbers as Student Leader 1 points to these 5-multiples.

The leader then asks the class to name the clock hands. "What hand is the short hand?" The class responds: "The short hand points to the hours." "What hand is the long hand?" The class responds: "The long hand points to minutes." Drop this part of the routine when all (or nearly all) students have mastered these concepts.

Telling Time on the Time Poster

Student Leader 2 draws hands to show an hour time (for example, 3:00) on the Time Poster. At a signal, the class says the time.

The leader then changes the placement of both the hour and minute hands to show the next half-hour (for example, 3:30). As the leader points (using a pointer) to the 5-minute marks, the class counts by 5s from the hour and to the new time: 5, 10, 15, 20, 25, 30—3:30! The leader sweeps the pointer from 3:00 to 3:30 and says: "The minute hand moved from the o'clock to the half-past time (or the half-hour time)."

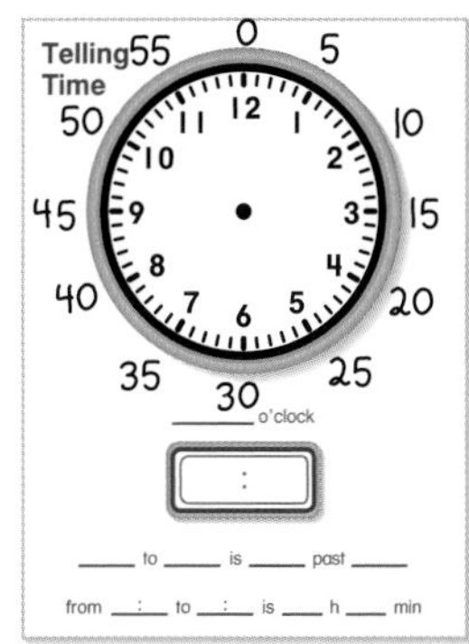

The leader then moves the minute hand back 15 minutes and moves the hour hand back a little bit to indicate 15 minutes past the hour. The leader then points to the 5-minute marks as the class counts by 5s from the hour to the new time: "5, 10, 15—3:15! 15 minutes past 3:00!" or "A quarter past 3!"

The leader then moves the hands ahead to show 45 minutes past the hour (for example, 3:45). The leader then points to the 5-minute marks as the class counts by 5s from the hour to the new time: "5, 10, 15, 20, 25, 30, 35, 40, 45—3:45! When you think the class is ready, they can also state the time as "15 minutes before 4!" and as "A quarter to 4!"

Student Leader 3 calls on Student Leaders 4 and 5 to show different times on the Time Poster. These should not be hour or half-hour times. Rather, they should show times to the 5 minutes such as 12:10, 3:40, or 7:35. Student Leader 4 draws hands on the Time Poster to show the time while Student Leader 5 writes the time on the digital clock on the poster.

Student Leader 5 then asks one or two classmates what they were doing at that hour, for example, "What were you doing at 7:35 this morning? Did you see the sun?" Later in the unit the leader can also ask classmates what they will be doing at some hour on a future day, for example, "What will you be doing at 7:35 P.M. two days from now?"

Volume 1 Contents

Unit 1 Understanding Addition and Subtraction

Big Idea Add and Subtract Using 10

Big Idea Relate Addition and Subtraction

Big Idea Understand Equations and Inequalities

MINI UNIT Unit 2 Measurement and Shapes

Big Idea Linear Measurement of 2-D Shapes

Unit 3 Solving Story Problems

Unit 5 Addition to 200

Big Idea Money, Sequences, and 100 Matrix

Big Idea Add 2-Digit Numbers

Unit 6 Time

Big Idea Bar Graphs, Circle Graphs, and Word Problems

Volume 2 Contents

Unit 8 Diagonals and Midpoints

Unit 9 Subtracting 2-Digit Numbers

Big Idea Multi-Digit Subtraction Strategies

Big Idea Relating Addition and Subtraction Strategies

Unit 11 3-Digit Addition and Subtraction

Unit 12 Metric Measurement and 3-D Shapes

Unit 13 Multiplication and Fractions

Unit 14 Non-Standard and Standard Units of Measure

Pacing Guide

Unit 1 is designed as a review of topics from Grade 1 but includes skills and understandings for Grade 2. Units 11 and 13 build strong conceptual development and skill fluency at a level often seen in the curricula of other countries that rank high in math performance. In the first year many classes may not cover all of the content of the later unit(s). But as more students experience *Math Expressions* in the previous grade(s) and teachers become familiar with *Math Expressions,* movement through the earlier units is more rapid and classes are able to do more of the later material in greater depth.

Some lessons in every unit, but especially the geometry and measurement mini-units, can be omitted if they do not focus on important state or district goals.

Be sure to do the Quick Practice activities with student leaders that begin each lesson, as they provide needed practice on core grade-level skills as well as support the growth of students as they lead these activities. Also be sure to do the Daily Routines on pages xxiii-xxvii to provide crucial grade-level practice for fluency with counting, place value, money, time, and other concepts.

	First Year		Later Years	
Unit	Pacing Suggestions	Days	Pacing Suggestions	Days
1	The first 2 lessons are introductory. Unit 1 focuses on numerical strategies, understanding partners, and teen numbers as tens and ones.	30	Many ideas are review for students who had Math Expressions in Grade 1. Move as quickly as you can while eliciting student ideas and building community.	20
2	Be sure that students understand these ideas.	6	These are important Grade 2 geometry concepts.	6
3	These are core Grade 2 topics for mastery except for two-step problems, which will continue in later units.	22	Unit 2 will go faster if students had Grade 1 Math Expressions story problem experiences.	14
4	These are important Grade 2 geometry concepts.	5	These are important Grade 2 geometry concepts.	4
5	Spend extra time for understanding these core concepts and use Math Talk with students on a regular basis.	29	Unit 3 will go faster with Grade 1 Math Expressions place-value experiences.	21
6	This introduction to time needs to be followed by the practice in the Daily Routines for mastery to occur.	6	This introduction to time needs to be followed by the practice in the Daily Routines for mastery to occur.	6
7	Do only important district and state goals. Comparison language is important but difficult.	18	Do only important district and state goals. Comparison language is important but difficult.	15
8	Do only important district and state goals.	2	Do only important district and state goals.	3
9	These are core Grade 2 topics for mastery. Be sure that students are able to explain ungrouping and the Ungroup First method.	25	Continue to focus on the core Grade 2 mastery topics of explaining ungrouping and the Ungroup First method.	20
10	Do only important district and state goals.	4	Do only important district and state goals.	4
11	Extend place-value ideas to 1,000 and money ideas through $10.00.	8	Finishing this unit will prepare students to move rapidly through Units 1 and 2 in Grade 3.	24
12	Do only important district and state goals.	2	Do only important district and state goals.	5
13	Lessons 1 and 4 will introduce multiplication.	2	Explore multiplication to 5 and unit fractions.	10
14	Do only important district and state goals.	1	Do only important district and state goals.	2
All Units	Total Days	160	Total Days	154

Correlation to NCTM Curriculum Focal Points and Connections for Grade 2

Grade 2 Curriculum Focal Points

1 *Number and Operations:* Developing an understanding of the base-ten numeration system and place-value concepts

Children develop an understanding of the base-ten numeration system and place-value concepts (at least to 1000). Their understanding of base-ten numeration includes ideas of counting in units and multiples of hundreds, tens, and ones, as well as a grasp of number relationships, which they demonstrate in a variety of ways, including comparing and ordering numbers. They understand multidigit numbers in terms of place value, recognizing that place-value notation is a shorthand for the sums of multiples of powers of 10 (e.g., 853 as 8 hundreds + 5 tens + 3 ones).

1.1 count in units	U1 L9, L10; U5 L17; U11 L1, L3
1.2 count in multiples of hundreds, tens, and ones	U5 L1; U11 L1, L3
1.3 compare and order numbers	U1 L21; U7 L2–4, L13
1.4 understand multidigit numbers in terms of place value	U1 L5, L11, L12; U5 L1–3, L5, L12; U11 L2, L4
1.5 recognize that place-value notation is a shorthand for the sums of multiples of powers of 10 (e.g., 853 as 8 hundreds + 5 tens + 3 ones)	U5 L1–3; U11 L2

2 *Number and Operations* and *Algebra:* Developing quick recall of addition facts and related subtraction facts and fluency with multidigit addition and subtraction

Children use their understanding of addition to develop quick recall of basic addition facts and related subtraction facts. They solve arithmetic problems by applying their understanding of models of addition and subtraction (such as combining or separating sets or using number lines), relationships and properties of number (such as place value), and properties of addition (commutativity and associativity). Children develop, discuss, and use efficient, accurate, and generalizable methods to add and subtract multidigit whole numbers. They select and apply appropriate methods to estimate sums and differences or calculate them mentally, depending on the context and numbers involved. They develop fluency with efficient procedures, including standard algorithms, for adding and subtracting whole numbers, understand why the procedures work (on the basis of place value and properties of operations), and use them to solve problems.

2.1 use understanding of addition to develop quick recall of basic addition facts and related subtraction facts	U1 L2, L3, L6–8, L13–19; U3 L1–13
2.2 solve problems by combining and separating sets	U1 L1, L2; U3 L3, L4, L8–13
2.3 solve problems by using a number line	U1 L17
2.4 solve problems by using place value	U5 L1–6, L9–12; U9 L3–6; U11 L2, L4, L5
2.5 solve problems by using properties of addition	U1 L3, L6, L22
2.6 use efficient, accurate, and generalizable methods to add multidigit whole numbers	U5 L5, L6, L9, L10, L12–15; U11 L9, L10, L12, L19, L21
2.7 use efficient, accurate, and generalizable methods to subtract multidigit whole numbers	U9 L3–13, L15; U11 L14, L15, L17–19, L21
2.8 select and apply appropriate methods to estimate sums and differences	U5 L11, L18; U9 L6, L11; U11 L4, L22

Grade 2 Curriculum Focal Points (cont.)	
2.9 calculate sums and differences mentally	U1 L13, L16, L20; U5 L4, L11, L12; U9 L12
2.10 develop fluency with efficient procedures including standard algorithms for adding whole numbers	U5 L5, L6, L9, L10, L12–15; U11 L9, L10, L12, L13, L19, L21
2.11 develop fluency with efficient procedures including standard algorithms for subtracting whole numbers	U9 L3–13, L15; U11 L14, L15, L17–19, L21

3 *Measurement:* Developing an understanding of linear measurement and facility in measuring lengths
Children develop an understanding of the meaning and processes of measurement, including such underlying concepts as partitioning (the mental activity of slicing the length of an object into equal-sized units) and transitivity (e.g., if object A is longer than object B and object B is longer than object C, then object A is longer than object C). They understand linear measure as an iteration of units and use rulers and other measurement tools with that understanding. They understand the need for equal-length units, the use of standard units of measure (centimeter and inch), and the inverse relationship between the size of a unit and the number of units used in a particular measurement (i.e., children recognize that the smaller the unit, the more iterations they need to cover a given length).

3.1 understand the concept of partitioning	U2 L1; U12, L1; U14, L1
3.2 understand the concept of transitivity	U12 L3
3.3 understand linear measure as an iteration of units	U2 L1; U12 L1; U14, L1
3.4 use rulers and other linear measurement tools	U2 L1, L3, L4; U4 L1; U5 L13; U8 L2; U12 L1–3; U14 L2
3.5 understand the need for equal-length units	U2 L1; U14 L1
3.6 use standard units of measure (centimeter and inch)	U2 L1, L3, L4; U5 L13; U8 L2; U12 L1–3; U14 L2
3.7 understand inverse relationship between the size of a unit and the number of units used in a particular measurement	U12 L2; U14 L2

Connections to the Focal Points

4 *Number and Operations:* Children use place value and properties of operations to create equivalent representations of given numbers (such as 35 represented by 35 ones, 3 tens and 5 ones, or 2 tens and 15 ones) and to write, compare, and order multidigit numbers. They use these ideas to compose and decompose multidigit numbers. Children add and subtract to solve a variety of problems, including applications involving measurement, geometry, and data, as well as nonroutine problems. In preparation for grade 3, they solve problems involving multiplicative situations, developing initial understandings of multiplication as repeated addition.

4.1 use place value and properties of operations to create equivalent representations	U5 L1–4, L9; U11 L1, L2, L4
4.2 use place value to write multidigit numbers	U5 L1–3; U11 L2
4.3 use place value to order and compare multidigit numbers	Daily Routines, Vol. 1, pp. xxv–xxvi; U1 L21; U3 L1–3
4.4 compose and decompose multidigit numbers	U5 L5, L9, L18; U9 L3–5, L12
4.5 add and subtract to solve measurement problems	U2 L3, L4; U5 L14, U10 L4; U12 L1, L3
4.6 add and subtract to solve geometry problems	U2 L3, L4; U5 L14; U10 L4

Correlation to NCTM Curriculum Focal Points and Connections for Grade 2 (cont.)

Connections to the Focal Points (cont.)	
4.7 add and subtract to solve data problems	U7 L1–5, L7–14
4.8 add and subtract to solve nonroutine problems	U3 L1, L4; U11 L13, L14
4.9 solve problems involving multiplicative situations	U13 L1–5
4.10 understand multiplication as repeated addition	U13 L1
5 *Geometry* and *Measurement:* Children estimate, measure, and compute lengths as they solve problems involving data, space, and movement through space. By composing and decomposing two-dimensional shapes (intentionally substituting arrangements of smaller shapes for larger shapes or substituting larger shapes for many smaller shapes), they use geometric knowledge and spatial reasoning to develop foundations for understanding area, fractions, and proportions.	
5.1 estimate length to solve problems	U8 L2; U12 L1, L2; U14 L2
5.2 measure length to solve problems	U2 L1, L3, L4; U5 L14
5.3 compute length to solve problems	U2 L1, L3, L4; U5 L14
5.4 compose and decompose two-dimensional shapes	U8 L1–3; U10 L1, L2
6 *Algebra:* Children use number patterns to extend their knowledge of properties of numbers and operations. For example, when skip counting, they build foundations for understanding multiples and factors.	
6.1 use number patterns, including skip counting	U1 L9; U5 L17; U6 L5; U11 L3; U13 L1–5; Extension L2

NCTM Standards and Expectations Correlation for Grade 2

Number and Operations Standard	
Understand numbers, ways of representing numbers, relationships among numbers, and number systems	
• count with understanding and recognize "how many" in sets of objects;	Unit 1, Lesson 2; Unit 5, Lesson 8; Lesson 16; Unit 6, Lesson 4; Unit 9, Lesson 1–Lesson 2; Unit 11, Lesson 1–Lesson 5; Lesson 7; Unit 13, Lesson 1–Lesson 4, Extension Lesson 2
• use multiple models to develop initial understandings of place value and the base-ten number system;	Unit 5, Lesson 1–Lesson 6; Unit 11, Lesson 1–Lesson 2; Lesson 5, Extension Lesson 1
• develop understanding of the relative position and magnitude of whole numbers and of ordinal and cardinal numbers and their connections;	Unit 1, Lesson 21; Unit 3, Lesson 14; Unit 6, Lesson 5; Unit 7, Lesson 3
• develop a sense of whole numbers and represent and use them in flexible ways, including relating, composing, and decomposing numbers;	Unit 1, Lesson 2; Lesson 4–Lesson 8; Unit 5, Lesson 1–Lesson 7; Lesson 15; Lesson 19; Unit 9, Lesson 1–Lesson 2; Unit 11, Lesson 2; Lesson 6; Lesson 24
• connect number words and numerals to the quantities they represent, using various physical models and representations;	Unit 1, Lesson 2; Lesson 4–Lesson 8; Unit 5, Lesson 1–Lesson 7; Lesson 15; Unit 7, Lesson 7; Unit 9, Lesson 1–Lesson 2; Unit 11, Lesson 1–Lesson 3
• understand and represent commonly used fractions, such as $\frac{1}{4}$, $\frac{1}{3}$, and $\frac{1}{2}$.	Unit 13, Lesson 9–Lesson 10; Lesson 13
Understand meanings of operations and how they relate to one another	
• understand various meanings of addition and subtraction of whole numbers and the relationship between the two operations;	Unit 1, Lesson 10; Lesson 14–Lesson 20; Unit 9, Lesson 3; Lesson 11–Lesson 14; Unit 11, Lesson 8; Lesson 14; Lesson 19
• understand the effects of adding and subtracting whole numbers;	Unit 1, Lesson 10; Lesson 14–Lesson 20; Unit 3, Lesson 1–Lesson 13; Unit 5, Lesson 9–Lesson 13; Unit 9, Lesson 3–Lesson 4; Lesson 7–Lesson 8; Lesson 11; Unit 11, Lesson 9, Lesson 19
• understand situations that entail multiplication and division, such as equal groupings of objects and sharing equally.	Unit 13, Lesson 1–Lesson 7

Number and Operations Standard (cont.)	
Compute fluently and make reasonable estimates	
• develop and use strategies for whole-number computations, with a focus on addition and subtraction;	Unit 1, Lesson 2; Lesson 9–Lesson 17; Lesson 19–Lesson 20; Lesson 22; Unit 3, Lesson 1–Lesson 13; Unit 5, Lesson 2; Lesson 4–Lesson 6; Lesson 9–Lesson 14; Lesson 16–Lesson 17; Lesson 19; Unit 7, Lesson 14; Unit 9, Lesson 3–Lesson 16; Unit 11, Lesson 5; Lesson 8–Lesson 10
• develop fluency with basic number combinations for addition and subtraction;	Unit 1, Lesson 2; Lesson 9–Lesson 17; Lesson 19–Lesson 20; Lesson 22; Unit 3, Lesson 1–Lesson 13; Unit 5, Lesson 13; Unit 7, Lesson 1–Lesson 5; Lesson 9–Lesson 13; Unit 9, Lesson 4–Lesson 5; Lesson 12; Unit 11, Lesson 10; Lesson 14
• use a variety of methods and tools to compute, including objects, mental computation, estimation, paper and pencil, and calculators.	Unit 1, Lesson 2; Lesson 9–Lesson 17; Lesson 19–Lesson 20; Lesson 22; Unit 3, Lesson 1–Lesson 13; Unit 5, Lesson 2, Lesson 4–Lesson 6; Lesson 9–Lesson 14; Lesson 16–Lesson 17; Lesson 19; Unit 7, Lesson 14; Unit 9, Lesson 3–Lesson 16; Unit 11, Lesson 5; Lesson 8–Lesson 22
Algebra Standard	
Understand patterns, relations, and functions	
• sort, classify, and order objects by size, number, and other properties;	Unit 3, Lesson 4; Unit 7, Lesson 10; Unit 10, Lesson 1
• recognize, describe, and extend patterns such as sequences of sounds and shapes or simple numeric patterns and translate from one representation to another;	Unit 1, Lesson 6; Lesson 23; Unit 5, Lesson 17; Unit 6, Lesson 5; Unit 11, Lesson 24
• analyze how both repeating and growing patterns are generated.	Unit 1, Lesson 6; Lesson 23; Unit 5, Lesson 17
Represent and analyze mathematical situations and structures using algebraic symbols	
• illustrate general principles and properties of operations, such as commutativity, using specific numbers;	Unit 1, Lesson 6; Lesson 20; Lesson 22
• use concrete, pictorial, and verbal representations to develop an understanding of invented and conventional symbolic notations.	Unit 1, Lesson 18; Unit 5, Lesson 1–Lesson 6; Unit 7, Lesson 1–Lesson 2; Unit 11, Lesson 14
Use mathematical models to represent and understand quantitative relationships	
• model situations that involve the addition and subtraction of whole numbers, using objects, pictures, and symbols.	Unit 1, Lesson 6–Lesson 11; Lesson 18; Lesson 20; Unit 5, Lesson 15; Unit 11, Lesson 14

NCTM Standards and Expectations Correlation for Grade 2 (cont.)

Algebra Standard (cont.)	
Analyze change in various contexts	
• describe qualitative change, such as a student's growing taller;	Unit 6, Lesson 5; Extension Lesson 3
• describe quantitative change, such as a student's growing two inches in one year.	Unit 6, Lesson 5; Unit 11, Lesson 11; Lesson 13–Lesson 14; Extension Lesson 3
Geometry Standard	
Analyze characteristics and properties of two- and three-dimensional geometric shapes and develop mathematical arguments about geometric relationships	
• recognize, name, build, draw, compare, and sort two- and three-dimensional shapes;	Unit 2, Lesson 2–Lesson 4; Unit 4, Lesson 1–Lesson 3; Unit 8, Lesson 1; Unit 10, Lesson 1–Lesson 3; Unit 12, Lesson 5–Lesson 6
• describe attributes and parts of two- and three-dimensional shapes;	Unit 2, Lesson 2–Lesson 4; Unit 4, Lesson 1–Lesson 3; Unit 8, Lesson 1; Unit 10, Lesson 1–Lesson 3; Unit 12, Lesson 5–Lesson 6
• investigate and predict the results of putting together and taking apart two- and three-dimensional shapes.	Unit 7, Lesson 16; Unit 8, Lesson 1–Lesson 3; Unit 10, Lesson 2; Unit 12, Lesson 6, Extension Lesson 4
Specify locations and describe spatial relationships using coordinate geometry and other representational systems	
• describe, name, and interpret relative positions in space and apply ideas about relative position;	Unit 5, Lesson 20; Unit 7, Lesson 12
• describe, name, and interpret direction and distance in navigating space and apply ideas about direction and distance;	Unit 7, Lesson 12
• find and name locations with simple relationships such as "near to" and in coordinate systems such as maps.	Unit 7, Lesson 12
Apply transformations and use symmetry to analyze mathematical situations	
• recognize and apply slides, flips, and turns;	Unit 10, Lesson 1; Lesson 3–Lesson 4
• recognize and create shapes that have symmetry.	Unit 8, Lesson 3; Unit 10, Lesson 3; Unit 13, Lesson 8

Geometry Standard (cont.)	
Use visualization, spatial reasoning, and geometric modeling to solve problems	
• create mental images of geometric shapes using spatial memory and spatial visualization;	Unit 4, Lesson 2; Unit 8, Lesson 2; Unit 12, Lesson 5
• recognize and represent shapes from different perspectives;	Unit 12, Lesson 5–Lesson 6
• relate ideas in geometry to ideas in number and measurement;	Unit 2, Lesson 3–Lesson 4; Unit 4, Lesson 1; Unit 5, Lesson 13; Unit 11, Lesson 24; Unit 12, Lesson 5
• recognize geometric shapes and structures in the environment and specify their location.	Unit 2, Lesson 3; Unit 4, Lesson 2; Unit 12, Lesson 5–Lesson 6

Measurement Standard	
Understand measurable attributes of objects and the units, systems, and processes of measurement	
• recognize the attributes of length, volume, weight, area, and time;	Unit 2, Lesson 2–Lesson 4; Unit 4, Lesson 2; Unit 3, Lesson 14; Unit 6, Lesson 1–Lesson 5; Unit 10, Lesson 1; Lesson 5; Unit 12, Lesson 1–Lesson 3; Lesson 5; Unit 14, Lesson 1–Lesson 3
• compare and order objects according to these attributes;	Unit 8, Lesson 1; Unit 10, Lesson 1; Lesson 5; Unit 14, Lesson 1; Lesson 3
• understand how to measure using non-standard and standard units;	Unit 2, Lesson 1–Lesson 4; Unit 10, Lesson 5; Unit 12, Lesson 1–Lesson 3; Unit 14, Lesson 1–Lesson 2
• select an appropriate unit and tool for the attribute being measured.	Unit 6, Lesson 4; Unit 10, Lesson 5; Unit 14, Lesson 1–Lesson 3
Apply appropriate techniques, tools, and formulas to determine measurements	
• measure with multiple copies of units of the same size, such as paper clips laid end to end;	Unit 2, Lesson 1; Unit 10, Lesson 5; Unit 12, Lesson 1–Lesson 2; Unit 14, Lesson 1
• use repetition of a single unit to measure something larger than the unit, for instance, measuring the length of a room with a single meterstick;	Unit 2, Lesson 1; Unit 14, Lesson 1–Lesson 2
• use tools to measure;	Unit 2, Lesson 1–Lesson 4; Unit 4, Lesson 1; Unit 6, Lesson 1; Lesson 2; Lesson 5; Unit 8, Lesson 2; Unit 10, Lesson 5; Unit 12, Lesson 1–Lesson 2; Unit 12, Lesson 1–Lesson 3
• develop common referents for measures to make comparisons and estimates.	Unit 6, Lesson 4; Unit 10, Lesson 5; Unit 12, Lesson 1–Lesson 4; Unit 11, Lesson 1–Lesson 3

NCTM Standards and Expectations Correlation for Grade 2 (cont.)

Data Analysis and Probability Standard	
Formulate questions that can be addressed with data and collect, organize, and display relevant data to answer them	
• pose questions and gather data about themselves and their surroundings;	Unit 7, Lesson 1–Lesson 2; Lesson 5–Lesson 6; Lesson 8; Lesson 16; Unit 12, Lesson 1–Lesson 2
• sort and classify objects according to their attributes and organize data about the objects;	Unit 3, Lesson 4; Unit 7, Lesson 10; Unit 10, Lesson 1; Extension Lesson 3
• represent data using concrete objects, pictures, and graphs.	Unit 3, Lesson 4; Unit 7, Lesson 1–Lesson 11; Lesson 13; Lesson 15–Lesson 16
Select and use appropriate statistical methods to analyze data	
• describe parts of the data and the set of data as a whole to determine what the data show.	Unit 1, Lesson 23; Unit 3, Lesson 4; Unit 7, Lesson 1–Lesson 5; Lesson 7–Lesson 15; Unit 13, Lesson 6; Lesson 13
Develop and evaluate inferences and predictions that are based on data	
• discuss events related to students' experiences as likely or unlikely.	Unit 13, Lesson 11–Lesson 13
Problem Solving Standard	
• build new mathematical knowledge through problem solving;	Unit 1, Lesson 1; Lesson 3; Lesson 23; Unit 3, Lesson 3; Lesson 7–Lesson 10; Lesson 14; Unit 5, Lesson 9–Lesson 10; Unit 7, Lesson 9; Lesson 14; Unit 5, Lesson 4; Lesson 12; Unit 11, Lesson 6; Unit 7, Lesson 1–Lesson 5, Lesson 12–Lesson 13
• solve problems that arise in mathematics and in other contexts;	Unit 1, Lesson 1–Lesson 3; Lesson 15; Unit 3, Lesson 1–Lesson 10; Unit 5, Lesson 9–Lesson 10; Unit 6, Lesson 4; Unit 4, Lesson 4; Lesson 9–Lesson 10; Lesson 14; Lesson 16; Unit 9, Lesson 4; Lesson 11–Lesson 17; Unit 11, Lesson 6–Lesson 8; Lesson 14; Lesson 24; Unit 13, Lesson 1–Lesson 5; Lesson 12–Lesson 13
• apply and adapt a variety of appropriate strategies to solve problems;	Unit 1, Lesson 1–Lesson 3; Lesson 15; Unit 3, Lesson 1–Lesson 10; Unit 5, Lesson 9–Lesson 10; Unit 7, Lesson 4; Lesson 9–Lesson 10; Lesson 14; Unit 9, Lesson 4; Lesson 11–Lesson 17; Unit 11, Lesson 6–Lesson 8; Lesson 14; Unit 13, Lesson 1–Lesson 5; Lesson 12
• monitor and reflect on the process of mathematical problem solving.	Unit 1, Lesson 1–Lesson 3; Lesson 15; Unit 3, Lesson 1–Lesson 10; Lesson 14; Unit 5, Lesson 9–Lesson 10; Lesson 20; Unit 7, Lesson 4; Lesson 9–Lesson 10; Lesson 14; Unit 9, Lesson 4; Lesson 11–Lesson 16; Unit 11, Lesson 6–Lesson 8; Lesson 14; Unit 7, Lesson 1–Lesson 5; Lesson 12

Reasoning and Proof Standard	
• recognize reasoning and proof as fundamental aspects of mathematics;	Unit 1, Lesson 1–Lesson 4; Lesson 8; Lesson 12; Unit 3, Lesson 1–Lesson 12; Unit 5, Lesson 2–Lesson 6; Lesson 9–Lesson 14; Lesson 19; Unit 9, Lesson 5–Lesson 6; Lesson 9; Lesson 16; Unit 11, Lesson 1–Lesson 2; Lesson 4–Lesson 5; Lesson 9–Lesson 10; Lesson 14–Lesson 17; Lesson 19–Lesson 22; Unit 13, Lesson 6; Lesson 8; Lesson 13
• make and investigate mathematical conjectures;	Unit 5, Lesson 9; Unit 7, Lesson 16; Unit 10, Lesson 1; Unit 9, Lesson 17; Unit 11, Lesson 24; Unit 13, Lesson 11
• develop and evaluate mathematical arguments and proofs;	Unit 3, Lesson 4, Unit 5, Lesson 20; Unit 13, Lesson 13
• select and use various types of reasoning and methods of proof.	Unit 1, Lesson 23; Unit 3, Lesson 4; Lesson 14; Unit 9, Lesson 17

Communication Standard	
• communicate their mathematical thinking coherently and clearly to peers, teachers, and others;	Unit 1, Lesson 1–Lesson 3; Lesson 22; Unit 3, Lesson 2–Lesson 7; Lesson 10–Lesson 14; Unit 4, Lesson 1; Lesson 3; Unit 5, Lesson 1–Lesson 2; Lesson 4; Lesson 6; Lesson 9; Lesson 15; Lesson 19; Unit 7, Lesson 1–Lesson 7; Lesson 16; Unit 8, Lesson 1–Lesson 3; Unit 9, Lesson 4; Lesson 6–Lesson 10; Lesson 13; Unit 11, Lesson 10; Lesson 12–Lesson 13; Lesson 19–Lesson 22; Lesson 24; Unit 12, Lesson 3; Unit 13, Lesson 6–Lesson 13
• analyze and evaluate the mathematical thinking and strategies of others;	Unit 1, Lesson 1–Lesson 3; Lesson 12–Lesson 13; Lesson 18; Lesson 22; Unit 3, Lesson 2–Lesson 3; Lesson 5-Lesson 7; Lesson 10–Lesson 13; Unit 5, Lesson 1–Lesson 2; Lesson 6; Lesson 9; Lesson 19; Unit 7, Lesson 1–Lesson 7; Unit 8, Lesson 2; Unit 9, Lesson 4; Lesson 6–Lesson 10; Unit 11, Lesson 10; Lesson 13; Lesson 19–Lesson 22; Unit 13, Lesson 8–Lesson 9; Lesson 11–Lesson 12
• use the language of mathematics to express mathematical ideas precisely.	Unit 1, Lesson 1–Lesson 3; Lesson 12–Lesson 13; Lesson 22; Unit 3, Lesson 3; Lesson 5–Lesson 6; Lesson 11; Lesson 13; Unit 5, Lesson 1–Lesson 2; Lesson 4–Lesson 6; Lesson 8; Lesson 17; Lesson 20; Unit 7, Lesson 1–Lesson 7; Unit 5, Lesson 3–Lesson 4; Lesson 6–Lesson 10; Lesson 13; Unit 11, Lesson 10; Lesson 12–Lesson 13; Lesson 17; Lesson 19–Lesson 22; Lesson 24; Unit 13, Lesson 8–Lesson 12

NCTM Standards and Expectations Correlation for Grade 2 (cont.)

Connections Standard	
• recognize and use connections among mathematical ideas;	Unit 1, Lesson 23; Unit 2, Lesson 1–Lesson 4; Unit 4, Lesson 2–Lesson 3; Unit 6, Lesson 1–Lesson 3; Unit 7, Lesson 9–Lesson 14; Unit 8, Lesson 1–Lesson 3; Unit 9, Lesson 11; Unit 10, Lesson 1; Lesson 5; Unit 12, Lesson 1–Lesson 2; Lesson 4; Lesson 6
• understand how mathematical ideas interconnect and build on one another to produce a coherent whole;	Unit 3, Lesson 14; Unit 7, Lesson 9-Lesson 14; Unit 5, Lesson 11; Unit 12, Lesson 1; Unit 14, Lesson 1–Lesson 2
• recognize and apply mathematics in contexts outside of mathematics.	Unit 1, Lesson 2–Lesson 5; Lesson 7–Lesson 8; Lesson 10–Lesson 15; Lesson 17–Lesson 22; Unit 3, Lesson 2–Lesson 3; Lesson 5–Lesson 13; Unit 5, Lesson 2–Lesson 6; Lesson 10–Lesson 15; Lesson 17; Lesson 19–Lesson 20; Unit 7, Lesson 2–Lesson 14; Unit 9, Lesson 1–Lesson 4; Lesson 6– Lesson 16; Unit 11, Lesson 2–Lesson 9; Lesson 11–Lesson 13; Lesson 15–Lesson 22; Unit 12, Lesson 3–Lesson 5; Unit 7, Lesson 1–Lesson 12
Representation Standard	
• create and use representations to organize, record, and communicate mathematical ideas;	Unit 1, Lesson 2; Lesson 23; Unit 2, Lesson 1–Lesson 3; Unit 4, Lesson 1; Unit 5, Lesson 4–Lesson 6; Lesson 10–Lesson 14; Lesson 15–Lesson 17; Lesson 19; Unit 7, Lesson 9–Lesson 14; Unit 9, Lesson 3–Lesson 4; Lesson 11–Lesson 12; Lesson 14–Lesson 16; Unit 10, Lesson 3; Unit 11, Lesson 2–Lesson 3; Lesson 6–Lesson 8; Lesson 14–Lesson 17; Lesson 22; Lesson 24; Unit 12, Lesson 6; Unit 13, Lesson 1–Lesson 5; Lesson 13
• select, apply, and translate among mathematical representations to solve problems;	Unit 1, Lesson 2; Unit 5, Lesson 4–Lesson 6; Lesson 10–Lesson 13; Lesson 15–Lesson 17; Lesson 19– Lesson 20; Unit 7, Lesson 9–Lesson 14; Unit 9, Lesson 3–Lesson 4; Lesson 11-Lesson 12; Lesson 14–Lesson 17; Unit 11, Lesson 2–Lesson 3; Lesson 6–Lesson 8; Lesson 14–Lesson 17; Lesson 22; Unit 13, Lesson 1–Lesson 5
• use representations to model and interpret physical, social, and mathematical phenomena.	Unit 5, Lesson 4–Lesson 6; Lesson 10–Lesson 13; Lesson 15–Lesson 17; Lesson 19; Unit 7, Lesson 16; Unit 9, Lesson 3–Lesson 4; Unit 11, Lesson 6; Lesson 8; Lesson 14– Lesson 15; Lesson 17; Lesson 22; Unit 12, Lesson 5–Lesson 6; Unit 13, Lesson 1–Lesson 5

Understanding Addition and Subtraction

THE GOAL OF UNIT 1 is to explore numbers to 18 by breaking apart each total into two smaller numbers called "partners." Understanding the concept of two partners embedded in a number is a precursor to adding and subtracting multi-digit numbers and to understanding the inverse relationships of addition and subtraction.

Skills Trace

Grade 1	Grade 2	Grade 3
• Represent and solve addition and subtraction story problems. • Represent and solve unknown partner story problems. • Write and solve addition and subtraction equations.	• Add 1-digit numbers (sums ≤ 18) and subtract 1-digit numbers from 18 or less. • Identify an unknown addend (sums ≤ 18). • Relate equations to story problems and to solution methods.	• Add and subtract whole numbers. • Write a related subtraction word problem for an addition problem and vice versa. • Solve a variety of word problems involving addition and subtraction.

Unit 1 Contents

Big Idea: Explore Addition and Subtraction Concepts

Big Idea: Break-Apart Numbers ≤ 10

Big Idea: Add and Subtract Using 10

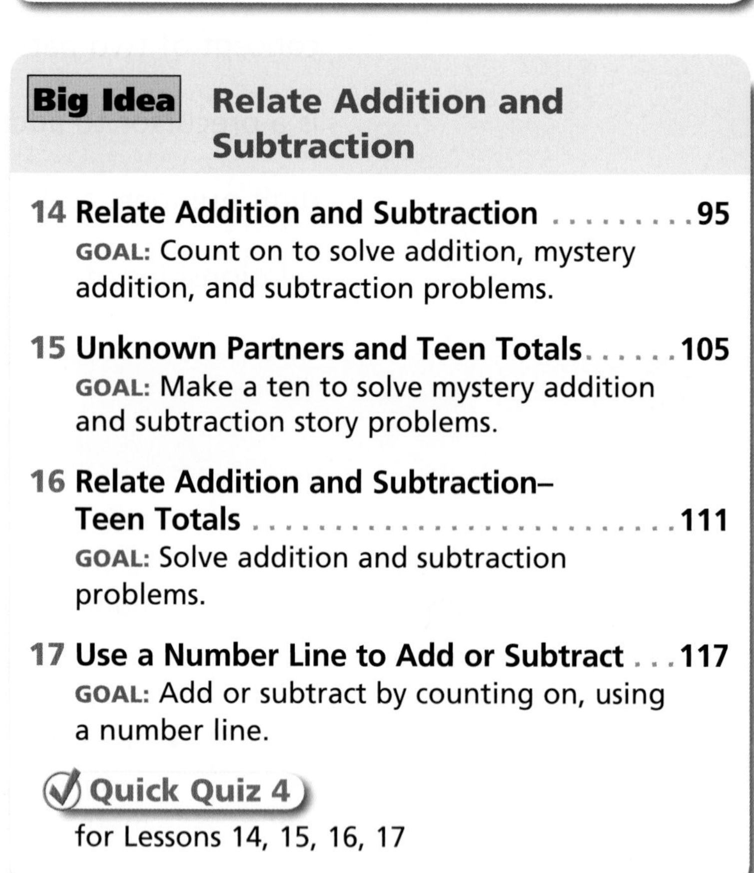

Big Idea: Relate Addition and Subtraction

Big Idea Understand Equations and Inequalities

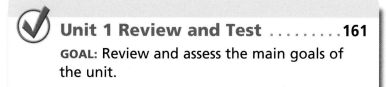

Planning Unit 1

Lesson/NCTM Standards	Resources	Materials for Lesson Activities	Materials for Going Further
1–1 **Introduce Stories and Drawings** NCTM Standards: 6, 8	TE pp. 1–6 SAB pp. 1–4 H&R pp. 1–2 AC 1-1		MathBoard materials Math Journals
1–2 **Practice with Stories and Drawings** NCTM Standards: 1, 6, 8, 10	TE pp. 7–12 SAB pp. 5–6 H&R pp. 3–4 AC 1-2		✓ Counters Index Cards MathBoard materials Math Journals
1–3 **Add or Subtract 0 or 1** NCTM Standards: 1, 6, 8	TE pp. 13–20 SAB pp. 7–8 H&R pp. 5–6 AC 1-3	MathBoard materials	*Oliver's Party* by Jenny Fry and Angela Jollife MathBoard materials Crayons ✓ Counters Bowl Math Journals
1–4 **Relationships in Numbers to 10** NCTM Standard: 1	TE pp. 21–26 SAB pp. 9–10 H&R pp. 7–8 AC 1-4	Coin Strips ✓ Real or play money Snack Bags	*Jelly Beans for Sale* by Bruce McMillan Scissors Coin Match-Up Cards (TRB M2) Coin Strips Index Cards Math Journals
1–5 **Teens, Tens, and Dimes** NCTM Standard: 1	TE pp. 27–36 SAB pp. 11–16 H&R pp. 9–10 AC 1-5 MCC 1-1 AG: Quick Quiz 1	✓ Secret Code Cards ✓ Real or play money ✓ Demonstration Secret Code Cards (TRB M7–M22) Coin Strips Snack Bags Chart Paper	Paper ✓ Counters Index cards ✓ Secret Code Cards Math Journals
1–6 **Break-Aparts of 10** NCTM Standards: 1, 2	TE pp. 37–44 SAB pp. 17–18 H&R pp. 11–12 AC 1-6	MathBoard materials	✓ Counters MathBoard materials Break-apart stick ✓ Game Cards (TRB M23) Math Journals
1–7 **Partners in Break-Aparts** NCTM Standards: 1, 7	TE pp. 45—50 SAB pp. 19–22 H&R pp. 13–14 AC 1-7	Counters MathBoard materials	Dot Cards Scissors Game Cards (TRB M23) ✓ Counters Break-apart stick ✓ Two-color counters Cup Index Cards Math Journals
1–8 **Partner Houses Through 10** NCTM Standards: 1, 9, 10	TE pp. 51–58 SAB pp. 23–24 H&R pp. 15–16 AC 1-8	MathBoard materials	✓ Connecting cubes Bowl ✓ Counters ✓ Number cubes Index cards Math Journals

Resources/Materials Key: TE: Teacher Edition SAB: Student Activity Book H&R: Homework and Remembering AC: Activity Cards MCC: Math Center Challenge AG: Assessment Guide ✓: Grade 2 kits TRB: Teacher's Resource Book

NCTM Standards Key: **1.** Number and Operations **2.** Algebra **3.** Geometry **4.** Measurement **5.** Data Analysis and Probability **6.** Problem Solving **7.** Reasoning and Proof **8.** Communication **9.** Connections **10.** Representation

Lesson/NCTM Standards	Resources	Materials for Lesson Activities	Materials for Going Further
1–9 **Count On to Find the Total** NCTM Standards: 1, 2, 7	TE pp. 59–66 SAB pp. 25–30 H&R pp. 17–18 AC 1-9	✓ Red Count-On Cards ✓ Demonstration Secret Code Cards (TRB M7–M22) ✓ Secret Code Cards Counters Snack bags	Reminder Sheet (TRB M24) Bowl ✓ Counters Spinners (TRB M27) Paper Clips ✓ Number cubes Math Journals
1–10 **Count On to Find the Partner** NCTM Standards: 1	TE pp. 67–74 SAB pp. 31–38 H&R pp. 19–20 AC 1-10 MCC 1-2 AG: Quick Quiz 2	✓ Yellow and Orange Count-On Cards ✓ Demonstration Secret Code Cards	✓ Connecting cubes ✓ Number cubes MathBoard materials Math Journals
1–11 **Use Tens** NCTM Standard: 1	TE pp. 75–82 H&R pp. 21–22 AC 1-11	Coin Strips Pennies Chart paper List of yard sale items Coin cover ✓ Two-color counters Ten Frame (TRB M33) ✓ Real or play money	Yard sale list Dime strips ✓ Real or play money Math Journals
1–12 **Make a Ten with Penny Strips and Fingers** NCTM Standards: 1, 8	TE pp. 83–88 H&R pp. 23–24 AC 1-12	Coin Strips Pennies Coin cover MathBoard materials	Game Cards (TRB M23) Look for Partners (TRB M34) Math Journals
1–13 **Practice Adding with Teen Totals** NCTM Standards: 1, 8	TE pp. 89–94 SAB pp. 39–42 H&R pp. 25–26 AC 1-13 AG: Quick Quiz 13	✓ Green Make-a-Ten Cards	✓ Two-color counters Ten Frame (TRB M33) Construction or other drawing paper Math Journals
1–14 **Relate Addition and Subtraction** NCTM Standards: 1, 8	TE pp. 95–104 SAB pp. 43–46 H&R pp. 27–28 AC 1-14	Count On Me Game Board MathBoard materials ✓ Counters ✓ Secret Code Cards Colored paper	MathBoard materials Sticky notes Index cards Math Journals
1–15 **Unknown Partners and Teen Totals** NCTM Standards: 1, 6	TE pp. 105–110 SAB pp. 47–50 H&R pp. 29–30 AC 1-15 MCC 1-3	✓ Blue Make-a-Ten Cards ✓ Counters	MathBoard materials ✓ Two-color counters Ten Frame (TRB M33) Math Journals
1–16 **Relate Addition and Subtraction—Teen Totals** NCTM Standards: 1	TE pp. 111–116 SAB pp. 51–56 H&R pp. 31–32 AC 1-16	✓ Math Mountain Cards Scissors Chart paper	Index cards ✓ Math Mountain Cards Chart paper Markers or crayons Math Journals

Manipulatives and Materials

- Essential materials for teaching *Math Expressions* are available in the Grade 2 kits. These materials are indicated by a ✓ in these lists. At the front of this Teacher Edition is more information about kit contents, alternatives for the materials, and use of the materials.

Lesson/NCTM Standards	Resources	Materials for Lesson Activities	Materials for Going Further
1–17 **Use a Number Line to Add or Subtract** NCTM Standards: 1, 8, 10	TE pp. 117–122 SAB pp. 57–58 H&R pp. 33–34 AC 1-17 AG: Quick Quiz 4		Large strips of paper Markers Index cards ✓ Two-color counters Spinners (TRB M27) Math Journals
1–18 **Equations and Equation Chains** NCTM Standards: 1, 2, 8	TE pp. 123–130 SAB pp. 59–60 H&R pp. 35–36 AC 1-18	MathBoard materials	Index cards Game Cards (TRB M23) Symbol Cards (TRB M45) MathBoard materials Strips of construction or drawing paper Tape Crayons or markers Math Journals
1–19 **Equations from Math Mountains** NCTM Standards: 1	TE pp. 131–137 SAB pp. 61–64 H&R pp. 37–38 AC 1-19	Colored paper	✓ Connecting cubes MathBoard materials Math Journals
1–20 **Stories from Math Mountains** NCTM Standards: 1, 2	TE pp. 138–142 SAB pp. 65–66 H&R pp. 39–40 AC 1-20 MCC 1-4	Large square sticky notes	*Splash!* by Ann Jonas Math Journals
1–21 **Compare and Order Numbers** NCTM Standards: 1	TE pp. 143–148 H&R pp. 41–42 AC 1-21	✓ Secret Code Cards MathBoard materials or Number Path (TRB M47)	✓ Secret Code Cards Index cards Math Journals
1–22 **Add Three Numbers** NCTM Standards: 1, 8	TE pp. 149–154 SAB pp. 67–68 H&R pp. 43–44 AC 1-22 AG: Quick Quiz 5	MathBoard materials	MathBoard materials
1–23 **Use Mathematical Processes** NCTM Standards: 6, 7, 8, 9, 10	TE pp. 155–160 SAB pp. 69–70 H&R pp. 45–46 AC 1-23	Calculators	Game Cards (TRB M46) ✓ Number cubes Math Journals
✓ **Unit Review and Test**	TE pp. 161–164 SAB pp. 71–72 AG: Unit 1 tests		

Manipulatives and Materials

Essential materials for teaching Math Expressions are available in the Grade 2 kits. These materials are indicated by a ✓ in these lists. At the front of this Teacher Edition is more information about kit contents, alternatives for the materials, and use of the materials.

Unit 1 Assessment

Unit Objectives Tested	Unit Test Items	Lessons
1.1 Identify numbers embedded in a larger number.	3	6–8
1.2 Add 1-digit numbers (sums ≤ 18).	4–7	3, 9–18, 22
1.3 Identify an unknown addend (sums ≤ 18).	8–11	10, 14–16
1.4 Subtract 1-digit numbers from 18 or less.	12–15	3, 10, 14–18
1.5 Add three numbers.	16	22
1.6 Compare and order numbers.	17–18	21
1.7 Relate equations to story problems and to solution methods.	19–20	1–3, 20

Assessment and Review Resources

Formal Assessment

Student Activity Book

- Unit Review and Test (pp. 71–72)

Assessment Guide

- Quick Quizzes (pp. A2, A3, A4)
- Test A–Open Response (pp. A5–A6)
- Test B–Multiple Choice (pp. A7–A10)
- Performance Assessment (p. A12)

Test Generator CD-ROM

- Open Response Test
- Multiple Choice Test
- Test Bank Items

Informal Assessment

Teacher Edition

- Ongoing Assessment (in every lesson)
- Quick Practice (in every lesson)
- Portfolio Suggestions (p. 163)

Math Talk

- The Learning Classroom (pp. 2, 9, 16, 24, 31, 41, 69, 101)
- Math Talk in Action (pp. 102, 114)
- Scenarios (p. 38)
- In Activities (pp. 29, 34, 47, 53, 56, 62, 77, 84, 97, 106, 124, 134, 145, 151)
- Solve and Discuss (p. 16)

Review Opportunities

Homework and Remembering

- Review of recently taught topics
- Cumulative Review

Teacher Edition

- Unit Review and Test (pp. 161–164)

Test Generator CD-ROM

- Custom Review Sheets

Independent Learning Activities

Ready-Made Math Challenge Centers

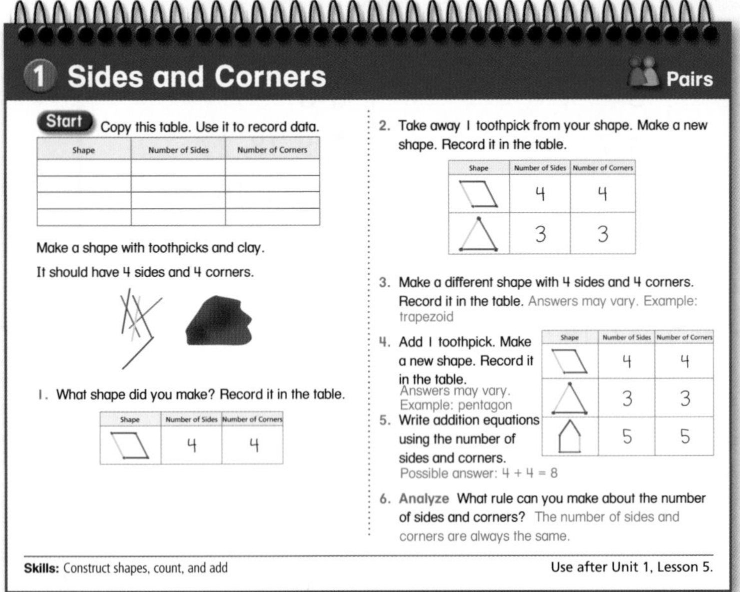

1 Sides and Corners — Pairs

Start Copy this table. Use it to record data.

Shape	Number of Sides	Number of Corners

Make a shape with toothpicks and clay.
It should have 4 sides and 4 corners.

1. What shape did you make? Record it in the table.

Shape	Number of Sides	Number of Corners
	4	4

2. Take away 1 toothpick from your shape. Make a new shape. Record it in the table.

Shape	Number of Sides	Number of Corners
	4	4
	3	3

3. Make a different shape with 4 sides and 4 corners. Record it in the table. Answers may vary. Example: trapezoid
4. Add 1 toothpick. Make a new shape. Record it in the table. Answers may vary. Example: pentagon

Shape	Number of Sides	Number of Corners
	4	4
	3	3
	5	5

5. Write addition equations using the number of sides and corners. Possible answer: 4 + 4 = 8
6. **Analyze** What rule can you make about the number of sides and corners? The number of sides and corners are always the same.

Skills: Construct shapes, count, and add — Use after Unit 1, Lesson 5.

Grouping Pairs

Objective Children construct figures with toothpicks, add and subtract 1 toothpick, then make new figures and count the number of sides and corners.

Materials Toothpicks, modeling clay

Connections Art and Geometry

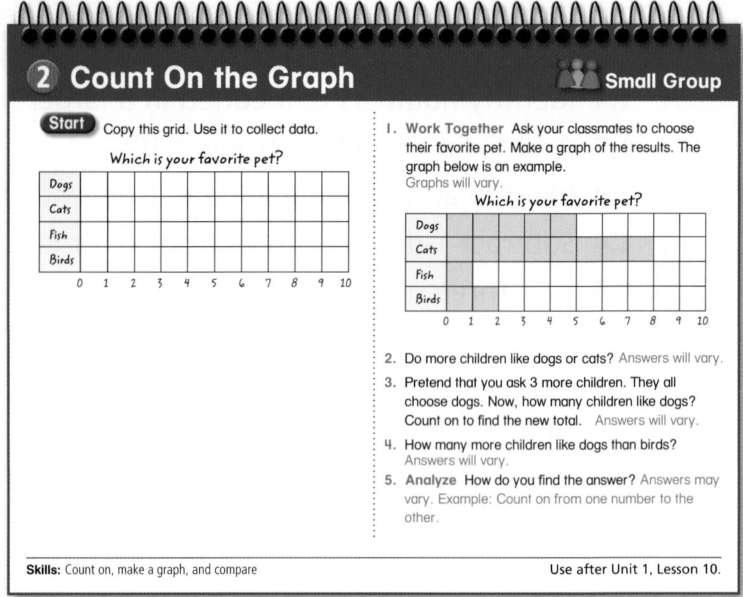

2 Count On the Graph — Small Group

Start Copy this grid. Use it to collect data.

Which is your favorite pet?

Dogs										
Cats										
Fish										
Birds										
	0 1	2	3	4	5	6	7	8	9	10

1. **Work Together** Ask your classmates to choose their favorite pet. Make a graph of the results. The graph below is an example. Graphs will vary.

   Which is your favorite pet? (Dogs, Cats, Fish, Birds; 0 1 2 3 4 5 6 7 8 9 10)
2. Do more children like dogs or cats? Answers will vary.
3. Pretend that you ask 3 more children. They all choose dogs. Now, how many children like dogs? Count on to find the new total. Answers will vary.
4. How many more children like dogs than birds? Answers will vary.
5. **Analyze** How do you find the answer? Answers may vary. Example: Count on from one number to the other.

Skills: Count on, make a graph, and compare — Use after Unit 1, Lesson 10.

Grouping Small Group

Objective Children represent their survey responses on a bar graph and then use counting and counting on to analyze the results.

Materials Inch Grid Paper (TRB M70), crayons

Connections Data and Representation

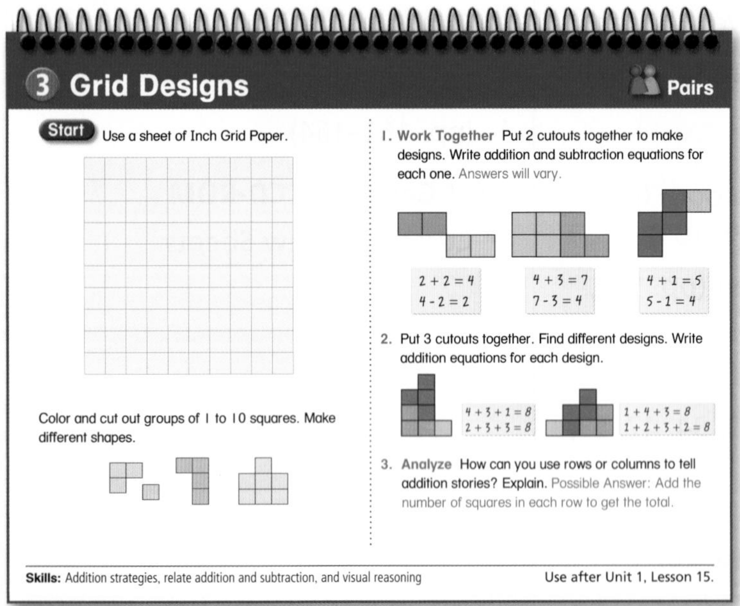

3 Grid Designs — Pairs

Start Use a sheet of Inch Grid Paper.

Color and cut out groups of 1 to 10 squares. Make different shapes.

1. **Work Together** Put 2 cutouts together to make designs. Write addition and subtraction equations for each one. Answers will vary.

   2 + 2 = 4, 4 − 2 = 2; 4 + 3 = 7, 7 − 3 = 4; 4 + 1 = 5, 5 − 1 = 4
2. Put 3 cutouts together. Find different designs. Write addition equations for each design.

   4 + 3 + 1 = 8, 2 + 3 + 3 = 8; 1 + 4 + 3 = 8, 1 + 2 + 3 + 2 = 8
3. **Analyze** How can you use rows or columns to tell addition stories? Explain. Possible Answer: Add the number of squares in each row to get the total.

Skills: Addition strategies, relate addition and subtraction, and visual reasoning — Use after Unit 1, Lesson 15.

Grouping Pairs

Objective Children create designs with cutouts from an inch grid, and they use numbers and equations to describe each design.

Materials Inch Grid Paper (TRB M70), crayons or markers

Connections Computation and Geometry

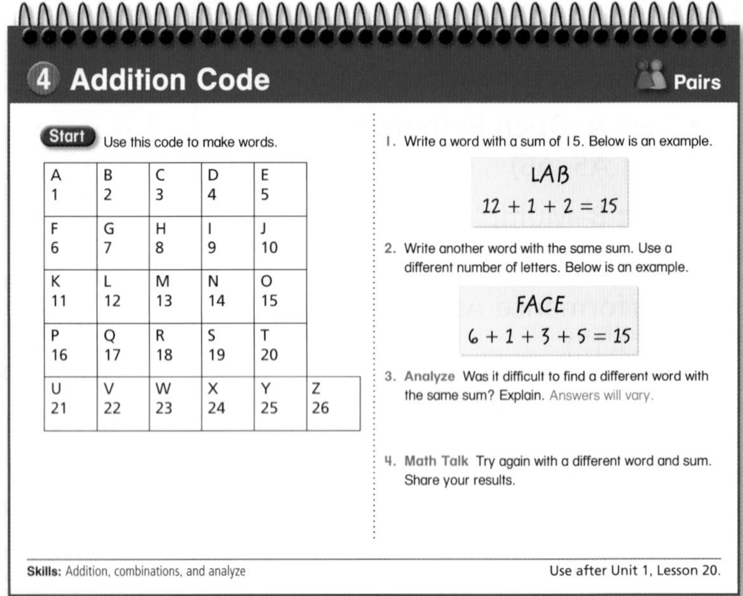

4 Addition Code — Pairs

Start Use this code to make words.

A 1	B 2	C 3	D 4	E 5	
F 6	G 7	H 8	I 9	J 10	
K 11	L 12	M 13	N 14	O 15	
P 16	Q 17	R 18	S 19	T 20	
U 21	V 22	W 23	X 24	Y 25	Z 26

1. Write a word with a sum of 15. Below is an example.

   LAB
   12 + 1 + 2 = 15
2. Write another word with the same sum. Use a different number of letters. Below is an example.

   FACE
   6 + 1 + 3 + 5 = 15
3. **Analyze** Was it difficult to find a different word with the same sum? Explain. Answers will vary.
4. **Math Talk** Try again with a different word and sum. Share your results.

Skills: Addition, combinations, and analyze — Use after Unit 1, Lesson 20.

Grouping Pairs

Objective Children create words, use a code to find the sum of the letters, and then create other words with the same sum.

Materials None

Connections Computation and Language Arts

Ready-Made Math Resources

Technology — Tutorials, Practice, and Intervention

Use activity masters and online, individualized intervention and support to bring students to proficiency.

Help students practice skills and apply concepts through exciting math adventures.

Extend and enrich students' understanding of skills and concepts through engaging, interactive lessons and activities.

Visit **Education Place**®
www.eduplace.com

Visit www.eduplace.com/mx2t/ and find family, teacher, and student materials, activities, games, and more.

Literature Links

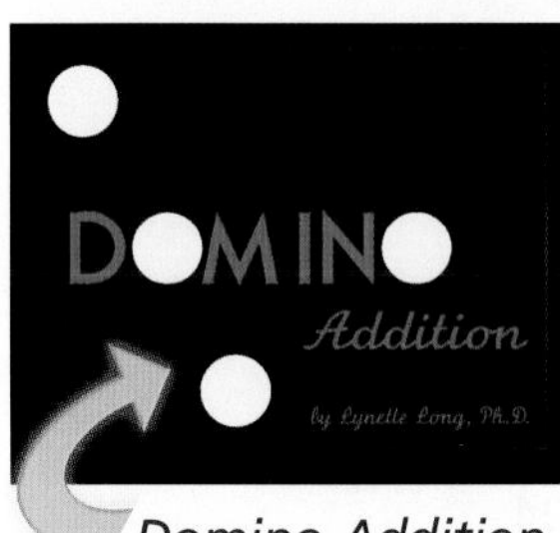

Domino Addition

Domino Addition
Dust off that box of dominoes for Lynette Long's book demonstrates how different domino dot combinations can be added together to achieve the same sum. This great introduction of basic addition and subtraction concepts will lead to multiple classroom activities.

Literature Connections

- *Oliver's Party*, by Jenny Fry and Angela Joliffe (Barron's Educational Series, Inc., 2002)
- *Jelly Beans for Sale*, by Bruce McMillan (Scholastic, 1996)

Unit 1 Teaching Resources

Differentiated Instruction

Individualizing Instruction		
Activities	Level	Frequency
	• Intervention • On Level • Challenge	All 3 in every lesson
Math Writing Prompts	Level	Frequency
	• Intervention • On Level • Challenge	All 3 in every lesson
Math Center Challenges	For advanced students	
	4 in every unit	

Reaching All Learners		
English Language Learners	Lessons	Pages
	1, 2, 3, 4, 5, 6, 7, 8, 9, 10, 11, 12, 13, 14, 15, 16, 17, 18, 19, 20, 21, 22, 23	2, 3, 4, 9, 15, 16, 23, 28, 39, 42, 47, 53, 60, 69, 76, 79, 84, 91, 96, 97, 107, 112, 119, 124, 133, 139, 144,145, 151
Extra Help	Lessons	Pages
	3, 4, 8, 9, 14, 18, 19, 21, 22	18, 23, 55, 62, 101, 125, 134, 146, 151
Advanced Learners	Lesson	Page
	19	132

Strategies for English Language Learners

Present this activity to all children. Offer different levels of support to meet children's levels of language proficiency.

Objective Identify relationship between addition as adding on or adding more.

Activity Show 4 cubes. Ask: **How many cubes?** 4 Add 2 more cubes. Ask: **How many cubes did I add?** 2 **What is 4 and 2 more?** 6

Newcomer

- Have children put the cubes into groups of 4 and 2. Have children count the cubes.
- Say: **Let's count the cubes.** Provide number words as needed.

Beginning

- Point and say: **There were 4 cubes. I added 2 more.** Now there are 6 cubes. Have children repeat.
- Write 4 + 2 on the board. Say: **4 + 2 = 6.**

Intermediate

- Ask: **How many cubes were there?** 4 **How many did I add?** 2 **How many cubes are there now?** 6
- Have children tell the addition fact that goes with the problem.

Advanced

- Have children tell their own addition story using the same or different addends.
- Ask children to name the addition fact for their story.

Connections

Music Connection
Lesson 8, page 58

Social Studies Connections
Lesson 15, page 110
Lesson 20, page 142
Lesson 22, page 154

Language Arts Connections
Lesson 5, page 36
Lesson 11, page 82
Lesson 14, page 104
Lesson 18, page 130
Lesson 19, page 136
Lesson 21, page 148

Technology Connection
Lesson 13, page 94

Physical Education Connection
Lesson 12, page 88

Real-World Connection
Lesson 23, page 160

Sport Connection
Lesson 2, page 12

Science Connections
Lesson 7, page 50
Lesson 17, page 122

Literature Connections
Lesson 3, page 20
Lesson 4, page 26

Math Background

Putting Research into Practice for Unit 1

From Our Curriculum Research Project: Exploring Break-Aparts and Counting Strategies

Children discover that numbers can be "embedded" in other numbers as they explore numbers through 18. We introduce this way of thinking about numbers to help children understand addition and subtraction concepts. As they see that partners are embedded in a larger number (a total), children can later see how partners and totals are related in addition and subtraction. Children can also recognize the inverse relationship between addition and subtraction.

For addition and subtraction, counting methods work well for children and help them to conceptualize adding and subtracting. Children will use counting on as a strategy to find the answers in a variety of addition and subtraction situations.

- They will count on from one addend to find the total.
- They will count on from a known addend to the known total to find the unknown addend, or partner.
- They will count on to subtract, finding the answer to exercises, such as $9 - 5 = \square$ and $15 - \square = 8$.

Children will also use the Make a Ten strategy when adding larger numbers. In this strategy, children will separate one number into partners so that they make a ten with the other number. For example, in the exercise $7 + 8 = \square$, 8 can be separated into the partners 3 and 5. The number 3 is added to 7 to make a ten. The exercise now becomes $10 + 5 = \square$.

–Karen Fuson, Author
Math Expressions

From Current Research: Accessible Methods for Single-Digit Addition

... substantial research from all over the world now indicates that children move through a progression of different [counting] procedures to find the sum of single-digit numbers.... First, children count out objects for the first addend, count out objects for the second addend, and count all of the objects (count all). This general counting-all procedure then becomes abbreviated, internalized, and abstracted as children become more experienced with it. Next, they notice that they do not have to count the objects for the first addend but can start with the addend in the first or the larger addend and count on the objects in the other addend.... With time, children recompose numbers into other numbers (4 is recomposed into 3 + 1) and use thinking strategies in which they turn an addition combination they do not know into one they do know (3 + 4 becomes 3 + 3 + 1).

National Research Council. *Adding It Up: Helping Children Learn Mathematics.* Washington, D.C.: National Academy Press, 2001. 187–188.

Other Useful References: Addition and Subtraction

National Council of Teachers of Mathematics. *Principles and Standards for School Mathematics.* Reston: NCTM, 2000.

O'Daffer, Phares, et al. 2nd edition. *Mathematics for Elementary School Teachers.* Boston: Addison-Wesley, 2002. 73–87.

Getting Ready to Teach Unit 1

Unit 1 starts with 3 days of story problems as a pre-assessment to help you see where your children are and as a way to get children talking about how they solve problems. Unit 2 is a deep systematic treatment of word problems in which we provide children with math tools to help with their solutions; in Unit 2 you can focus on mastery.

Representation

For Unit 1 the goal is to get your children making math drawings (simplified drawings of the situation) and talking about how they solved the problem. If we only give simple problems, Grade 2 children do not need to make drawings and they have little to discuss. That is why we include unknown addend and comparison problems for these first 3 days. We also want math to be situated in the real world and not just numbers in the classroom. These initial 3 days help children make these connections so that you can keep real-world links going during Unit 1, which focuses more on numerical relationships.

Exploring Break-Aparts Children explore numbers through 10 as they distribute counters in various ways onto two sections of a MathBoard. For example, they break apart the number 10 into 3 and 7. These smaller numbers are referred to as "partners" of 10. They are numbers *hiding inside* (embedded in) 10. We use a scenario of rabbits (represented by counters) playing in the carrot patch or in the lettuce patch of a garden.

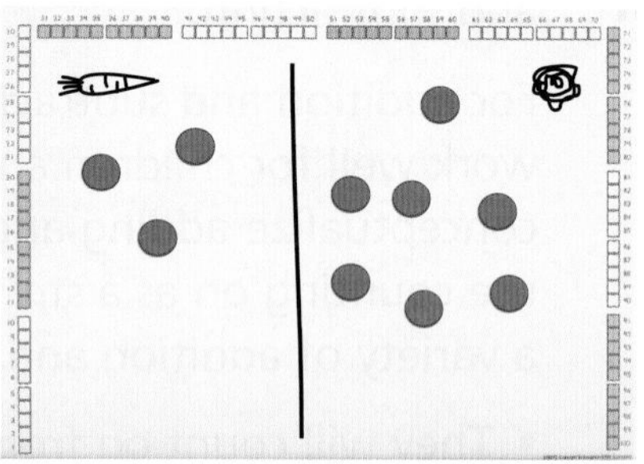

Children break apart numbers 11 through 18 by using their fingers, Penny Strips and coins, Math Mountains, and Secret Code Cards. For example, the Secret Code Cards below show that the numbers 10 and 3 are partners of the teen number, 13.

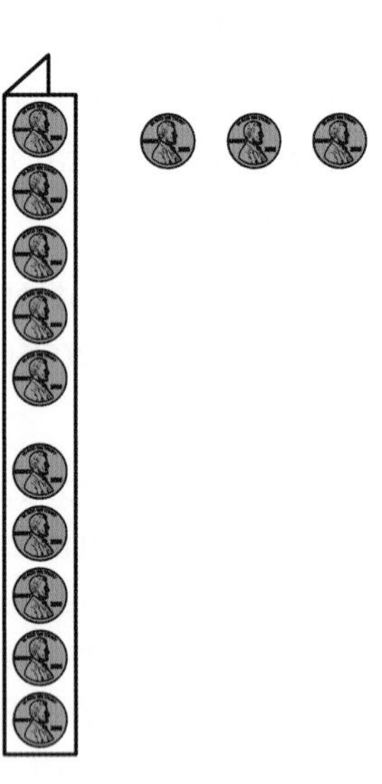

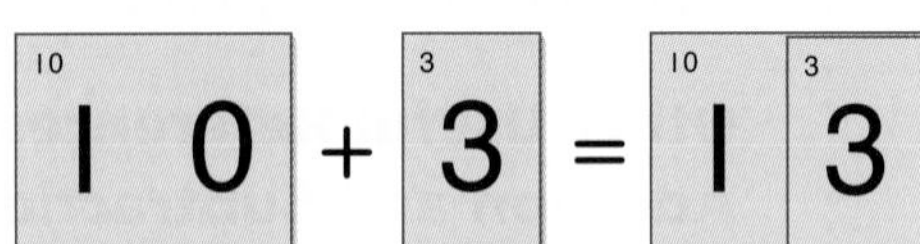

Using Partner Houses and Math Mountains to Show Break-Aparts Children see and draw pictorial representations of break-aparts of numbers with Partner Houses and Math Mountains.

Partner House

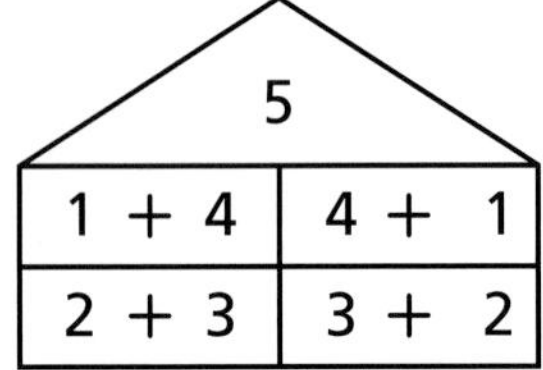

Math Mountains

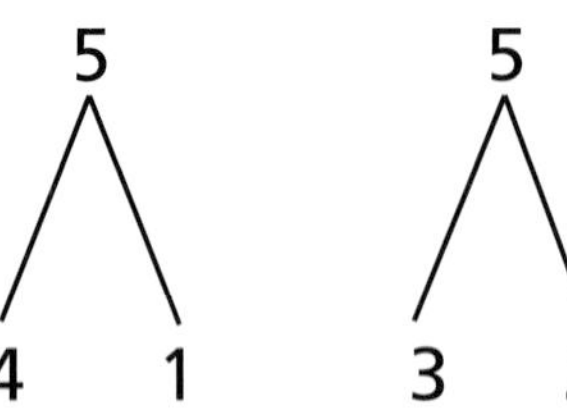

Count On Strategies for Addition and Subtraction

Counting methods help children conceptualize adding and subtracting and form the basis for strategies children can use to add and subtract.

Count On to Find the Total Children explore and use the strategy of counting on from one addend to find the total. This is a progression from the Count All strategy. Children also find that they can start their count from the larger addend.

$5 + 4 = \square$

Count All Using Pictures
Lesson 9

Children use the dot sides of the Secret Code Cards to count all.

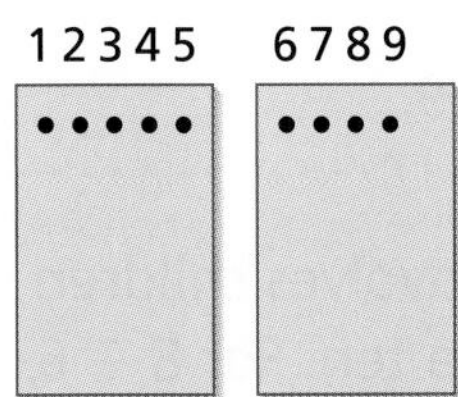

Count On Using a Number and Pictures
Lessons 9 and 11

Children use the numeral side of a Secret Code Card to say the first addend. They count on using the dot side of the second Secret Code Card.

Already 5 6 7 8 9

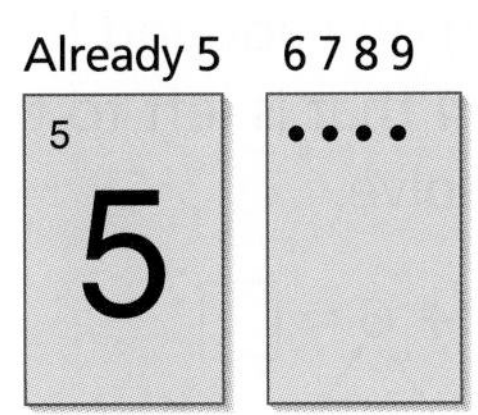

I know I already counted 5 for the first card, so I don't have to count those dots.

I count on 4 more. 6, 7, 8, 9

Count On Using Fingers
Lessons 9 and 11

Children count on using their fingers.

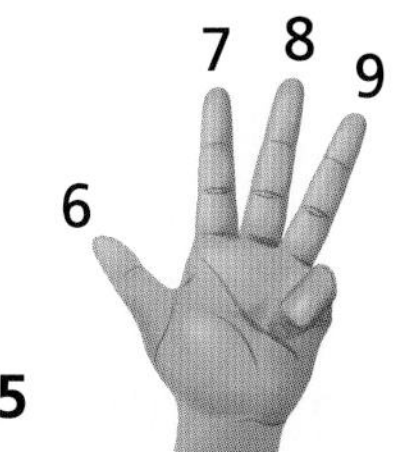

I pretend I already counted 5. Then I count on 6, 7, 8, 9.

Count On to Find the Partner This form of counting on is used to find the answer in mystery addition, such as $8 + \square = 14$, and in subtraction ($14 - 8 = \square$). Children count on from the known partner up to the total to find the other partner.

$5 + \square = 8$

Mystery Addition: Count On Using a Number and Pictures
Lessons 10, 14, 15

Children start from the partner they know. They count on until they reach the total.

$5 + 3$ more $= 8$

5	● ● ●
Already **5**	6 7 8

Mystery Addition: Count On Using Fingers
Lesson 10

Children start from the partner they know. They count on until they reach the total.

3 more to make 8

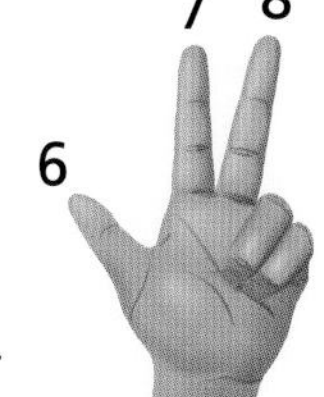

9 − 5 = □

Subtraction: Count On Using a Number and Pictures to Find the Partner
Lessons 10, 14, 15

Children start from the known partner. They count on to the known total.

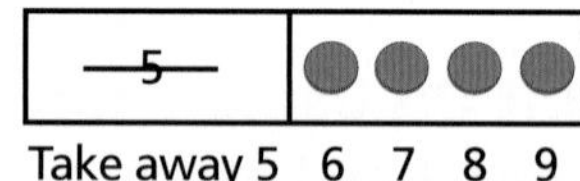

That was 4 more, so 9 − 5 = 4.

Subtraction: Count On Using Fingers to Find the Partner
Lesson 10

Children start from the known partner. They count on to the known total.

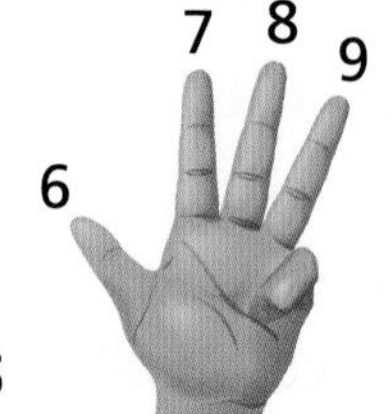

Take away **5**

4 more to make 9.

Make a Ten Strategy The link between the counting on and Make a Ten strategies involves children understanding that they can "give" numbers from one addend to the other to make a ten. For 8 + 6, they give 2 from the 6 to the 8 and then add the 4 that is left to the 10 they made. This changes the problem from 8 + 6 to 10 + 4, which is easier to solve.

8 + 6 = □

8 + 2 + 4

10 + 4 = 14

Children visualize this method by using their fingers or by using Dime Strips and pennies. At first children count on from 8 to 10 but may then just add on the 4 (left in the 6) instead of counting.

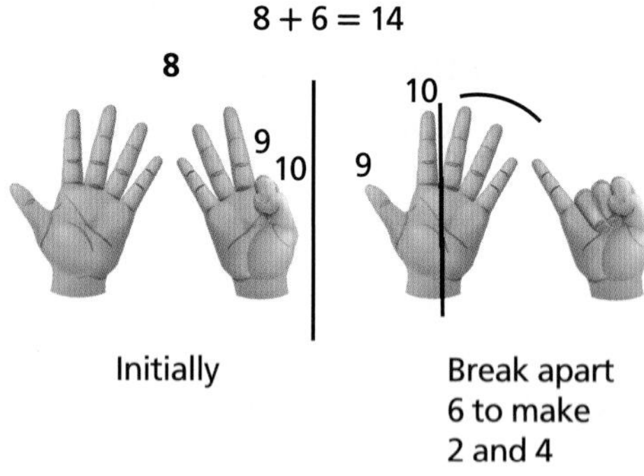

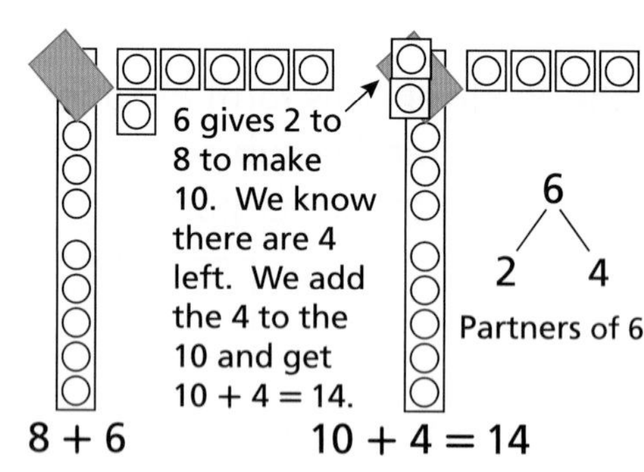

6 gives 2 to
8 to make
10. We know
there are 4
left. We add
the 4 to the
10 and get
10 + 4 = 14.
6
2 4
Partners of 6
8 + 6
10 + 4 = 14

Make a Ten with a Friend
Lesson 12

Two children use their fingers together. The first friend shows the first addend (8) and the second friend shows the second addend (6). The second friend with the smaller addend separates the 6 fingers to put enough to make ten with the first friend's 8 fingers.

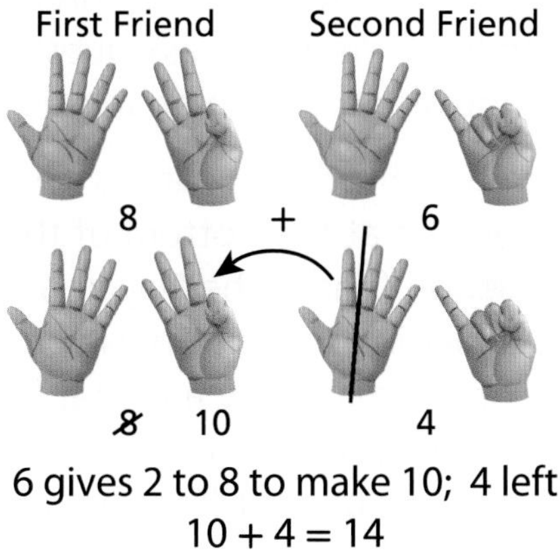

6 gives 2 to 8 to make 10; 4 left
$10 + 4 = 14$

Make a Ten with an Imaginary Friend
Lessons 13 and 15

This strategy is the same as the Make a Ten with a Friend strategy, only there is one child. The child must pretend a friend is present to whom he or she can "give" fingers. To indicate the friend, the child shows the first number in a physically different place than the second number and actually "moves" imaginary fingers to make the ten.

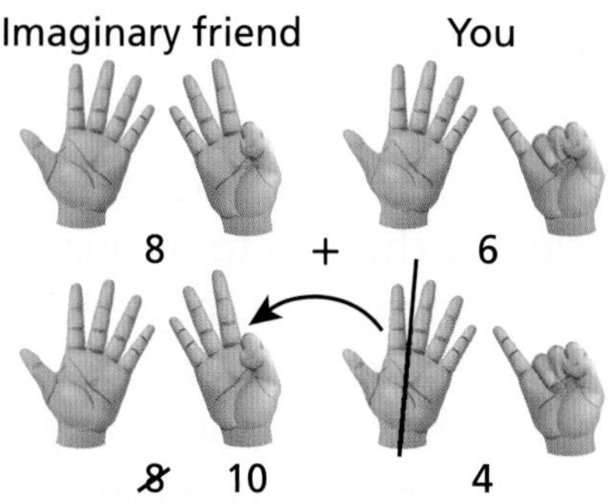

6 gives 2 to 8 to make 10; 4 left
$10 + 4 = 14$

Materials for Count On Strategies Children also use Count-On Cards, Make-a-Ten Cards, and Math Mountain Cards to practice addition, subtraction, and mystery partner addition. The cards make clear the relationships among the total and its partners and help children see how addition, subtraction, and mystery addition are related. Children learn that subtraction and mystery addition can be solved by the same process.

Count-On Cards
Lessons 9 and 10

$3 + 6 = \square$

$3 + 6 = \boxed{9}$

Make-a-Ten Cards
Lessons 13 and 15

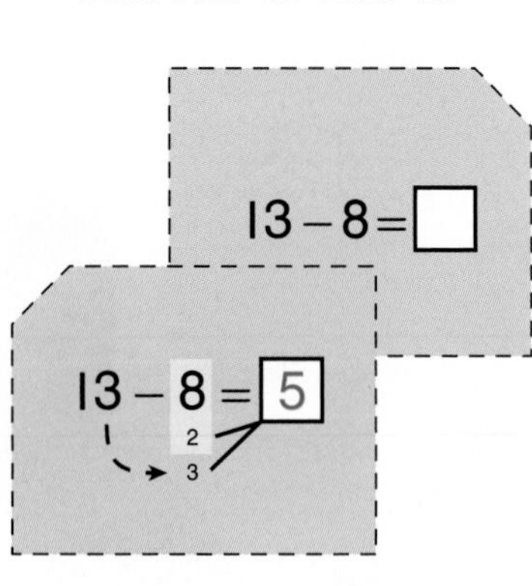

Math Mountain Cards
Lesson 16

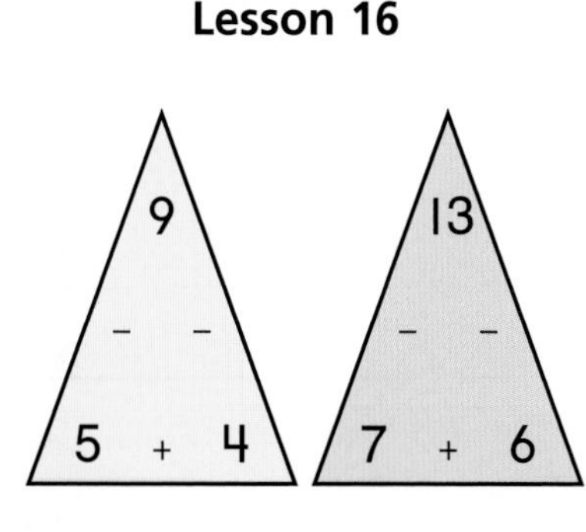

Communication

Using Math Talk

Throughout the unit, children learn to talk about math. Math talk can clarify children's thinking as well as expose the entire class to other approaches. Children are often asked to describe, explain, discuss, and defend their solution methods. They learn to talk to the class, listen to their classmates, and critically analyze their own work and the work of their peers. This will be a year-long goal for children—the development of their communication skills in mathematics.

Communicating through Story Problems This unit provides opportunities for children to tell math stories and explain their thinking as they solve problems. We help children from the onset to know the importance of speaking loudly and clearly to the class (not just to the teacher) as they share their stories, and how to listen carefully to their peers' stories. The teacher can move to the side or back of the classroom to encourage children to talk to the whole class.

Talking about Real Life This unit starts developing the connection of mathematics to the children's lives outside school. Various realistic scenarios are designed to help establish this connection. The teacher can encourage children to think about and share real-world connections.

Listening The classroom can be a place where all children listen to understand one another. Rather than just being quiet when someone is speaking, careful listening involves thinking about what a person is saying so the explanation can be repeated using different words. Children are always encouraged to listen carefully, ask questions, and help others understand an explanation of concepts.

Quick Practice and Student Leaders Quick Practice activities are located at the bottom of the first page of each lesson (under the Day at a Glance chart). You can begin class with these or do them at another time of the day. They are vital for building fluency. Student Leaders direct many of these activities; all students benefit from being Student Leaders.

Introduce Stories and Drawings

Lesson Objectives

- Paraphrase, represent, and solve story problems.
- Recognize math as a part of daily life.

Vocabulary

story problem	total
in all	zero
altogether	proof drawing

The Day at a Glance

Today's Goals	Materials	
1 Teaching the Lesson **A1:** Introduce *Math Expressions* and share number stories. **A2:** Solve story problems and discuss solutions.	**Lesson Activities** Student Activity Book pp. 1–4 (includes Family Letter) Homework and Remembering pp. 1–2	**Going Further** Activity Cards 1-1 MathBoard materials Math Journals
2 Going Further ▸ Differentiated Instruction		
3 Homework		

Use Math Talk today!

Keeping Skills Sharp

Quick Practice 5 MINUTES	Daily Routines
This section provides repetitive, short activities that either help children become faster and more accurate at a skill or help prepare ground for new concepts.	**Money Routine** Using the 120 Poster, Using the Money Flip Chart, Using the Number Path, Using Secret Code Cards (See pp. xxiii–xxv.) ▸ Led by teacher

1 Teaching the Lesson

Activity 1

Introduce *Math Expressions*

15 MINUTES

Goal: Introduce *Math Expressions* and share number stories.

NCTM Standards:
Problem Solving
Communication

The Learning Classroom

Math Talk As children respond to questions, try not to repeat what they say. You do not want children to rely on you to be their microphone. Model how to speak in a classroom voice and encourage children to do the same.

Aim for a classroom where all children listen to and understand one another. Explain to children that this is different than just being quiet when someone else is talking. This involves thinking about what a person is saying so that you can explain it yourself or help explain it more clearly. Also, children need to listen so that they can ask a question or help the explainer. Listening can also help children learn the concept better.

Differentiated Instruction

English Learners Sharing math stories is a good way to evaluate students' mastery of the English language. If students have difficulty telling their math story in front of the class, encourage them to draw their stories.

▶ Talk About Math WHOLE CLASS

Ask for Ideas Introduce math as a way to organize and count things and to put things together and take them apart. Invite children to share how they use math in their everyday lives. Emphasize that during math class, you and the children will focus on explaining, communicating, and helping. Assure children that everyone can learn math and that they can all help each other.

Share Math Stories Demonstrate the importance of math by inviting children to try and tell a story without numbers. After each story, point out the numbers "hiding" in the story. Invite children to help discover the hidden numbers too.

For example, after a story about a camping trip, you might ask:

- How many people went camping?
- How many days were you gone?
- Who can find other hidden numbers in the story?

If none of the questions asked have zero as an answer, ask a question such as:

- How many elephants went on the trip with you?
- How many skyscrapers did you take along?

Describe Math Class and Homework Talk about the class work for the coming year. Explain that there will be many opportunities to share math stories and make math drawings.

Tell children they will have homework every day and they will need to choose someone at home or nearby to be their special Homework Helper.

Explain to children that today they will take home a letter that explains this to their families. They should return the bottom part of the letter tomorrow. This will let you know whom each child has chosen to be the Homework Helper. The Family Letter is on Student Activity Book page 3.

Activity 2

Restate and Solve Story Problems

▶ Using the Story Problems in Lessons 1–3 WHOLE CLASS

Unit 1 starts with 3 days of word problems as a pre-assessment to help you see where your children are and as a way to get children talking about how they solve problems. Unit 2 is a deep systematic treatment of word problems in which we provide children with math tools to help with their solutions; in Unit 2 you will focus on mastery of word problems supported by the math tools in the *Math Expressions* Lessons.

In these first days of Unit 1 the goal is to get your children making math drawings (simplified drawings of the situation) and talking about how they solved the problem. If we only give simple problems, Grade 2 children do not need to make drawings and they have little to discuss. That is why we include unknown addend and comparison problems for these first 3 days, not for mastery, but to stimulate discussion and have children solving in different ways. Do not worry if some or even many children are not solving the unknown addend problems correctly. This unit will provide them with understanding of numerical relationships that will facilitate such solutions in Unit 2. We also started with word problems because we want math to be situated in the real-world and not just be numbers in the classroom. These initial 3 days help children make these connections so that you can keep real-world links going during the rest of Unit 1, which focuses more on numerical relationships.

Discuss with children that the picture beside the word problem does not always tell the word to be written in the label line (see 2 and 3). They need to read the question carefully to see what it is asking and then use the label in the question. You can make a game out of the trick problems where the picture is not the label of the answer. We provided the pictures to help English language learners, but we want to be sure that all children read the problem and especially the question carefully.

▶ Solve and Discuss Story Problems WHOLE CLASS

Read aloud the first story problem on Student Activity Book page 1. To help children find their place, ask them to look for the picture of a balloon.

Have children restate the problem, varying the language used, but preserving its numeric meaning.

- Andrew has 3 balloons. Erin has 6 balloons. How many balloons do they have in all?

Children will probably use math words and phrases such as *altogether, in all, total, now,* and so on. Be sure to elicit these different word meanings in story problems.

Activity continued ▶

 **35 MINUTES**

Goal: Solve story problems and discuss solutions.

Materials: Student Activity Book page 1

 **NCTM Standards:**
Problem Solving
Communication

Teaching Note

Research Studies indicate that using fingers (even in the upper grades) for addition and subtraction, especially with teen numbers, is fine as long as it is fast and accurate. Help children who are having difficulty, but be aware that individual children and diverse cultures may use their fingers in different ways. For example, some will start with the thumb, some with the little finger, and some with the index finger. Any method is fine as long as children understand what they are doing and show the right numbers. By the end of the school year, most children will be using mental math.

English Language Learners

Review *altogether, in all* and *total.* Draw Andrew and Erin's balloons.

- **Beginning** Point and say: **Andrew has 3 balloons. Erin has 6 balloons.** Circle all the balloons. Say: ***Altogether* they have 9 balloons.** Have children repeat. Continue with other problems. Use *in all* and *total.*
- **Intermediate** Have children count the balloons. Circle all the balloons. Say: ***Altogether* they have ___?** 9
- **Advanced** Circle all the balloons. Have children describe the total using *altogether, in all,* and *total.*

❶ Teaching the Lesson (continued)

Differentiated Instruction

English Learners The picture that appears with each story problem can be used to help children who are having difficulty with reading or children who are learning English. You may wish to pair children so that good readers can help others match the picture to a word in the problem. Discuss with children that the picture does not always tell the word to be on the label line (see problems 2 and 3).

The Learning Classroom

Building Concepts A Proof Drawing will help children communicate their thinking to the rest of the class. It can be a simple sketch of the situation. Children can make Proof Drawings, or label equations, or both. A Proof Drawing has the numbers or circles labeled as the things in the story.

Andrew's Erin's
OOO + OOOOOO
3 + 6 = 9
A E in all

Ongoing Assessment

- Watch children as they solve problems and explain their solutions. This will help you informally assess the math ability of individual children as well as the class as a whole.

Differentiated Instruction

English Learners The discussion aspect is particularly valuable to English Learners. Encourage their participation, and let them know that it is okay to ask for repetition or clarification of any topic throughout the year.

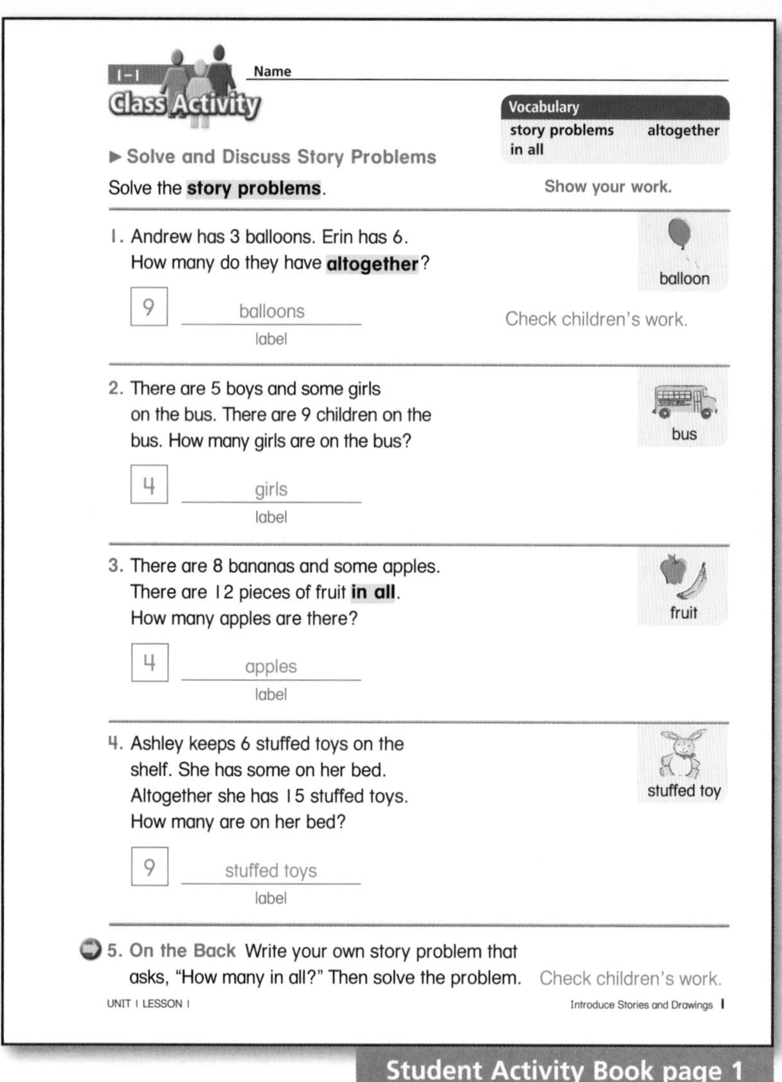

1-1 Class Activity Name

Vocabulary
story problems altogether
in all

► Solve and Discuss Story Problems

Solve the **story problems**. Show your work.

1. Andrew has 3 balloons. Erin has 6. How many do they have **altogether**?
   9 balloons
   label
   Check children's work.
   (balloon)

2. There are 5 boys and some girls on the bus. There are 9 children on the bus. How many girls are on the bus?
   4 girls
   label
   (bus)

3. There are 8 bananas and some apples. There are 12 pieces of fruit **in all**. How many apples are there?
   4 apples
   label
   (fruit)

4. Ashley keeps 6 stuffed toys on the shelf. She has some on her bed. Altogether she has 15 stuffed toys. How many are on her bed?
   9 stuffed toys
   label
   (stuffed toy)

5. On the Back Write your own story problem that asks, "How many in all?" Then solve the problem. Check children's work.

UNIT 1 LESSON 1 Introduce Stories and Drawings 1

Student Activity Book page 1

Introduce the Solve and Discuss Structure First, have several children demonstrate how to solve the problem on the board. (If you know that certain children would be good role models for the class, choose those children.) Ask the rest of the children to solve the problems at their desks.

Next, invite two children who are at the board to show and explain how they solved the problem using numbers, Proof Drawings, an equation, or any finger methods they may know.

This method of children solving problems at the board and explaining their work is known as the **Solve and Discuss** structure. It is an important component of Math Talk.

Invite a new group of children to the board. Continue as before until children have discussed several story problems. (Remember to have several children restate the problem in their own words before they solve it.) As time permits, encourage children to make up their own story problems for the class to solve.

2 Going Further

Differentiated Instruction

Intervention

Activity Card 1-1

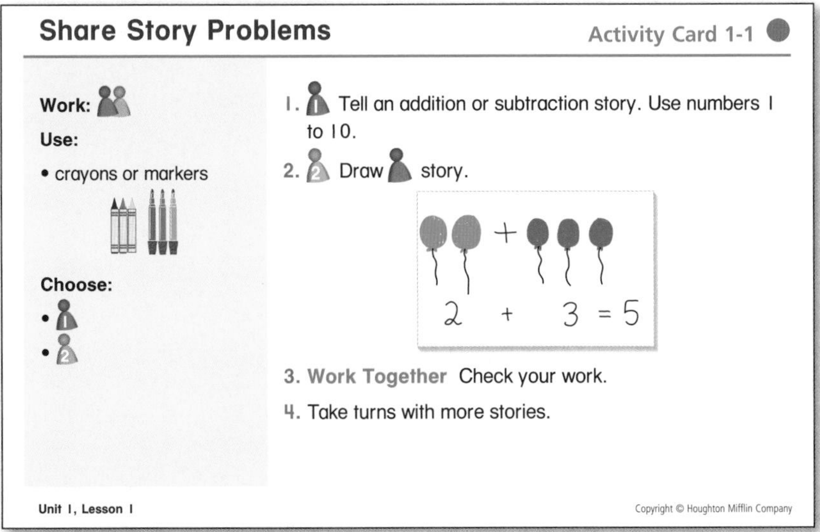
Share Story Problems — Activity Card 1-1 ●

Work: (pairs)
Use:
- crayons or markers

Choose:
- 1
- 2

1. (1) Tell an addition or subtraction story. Use numbers 1 to 10.
2. (2) Draw (1) story.

2 + 3 = 5

3. **Work Together** Check your work.
4. Take turns with more stories.

Unit 1, Lesson 1 — Copyright © Houghton Mifflin Company

Activity Note Remind children to listen carefully to their partner and draw what they hear. Have children check that they are using the right sign.

Math Writing Prompt

Write a Number Story Write a number story that uses the number 5.

Software Support

Use *Soar to Success* for instruction of students needing targeted support for underlying skills.

On Level

Activity Card 1-1

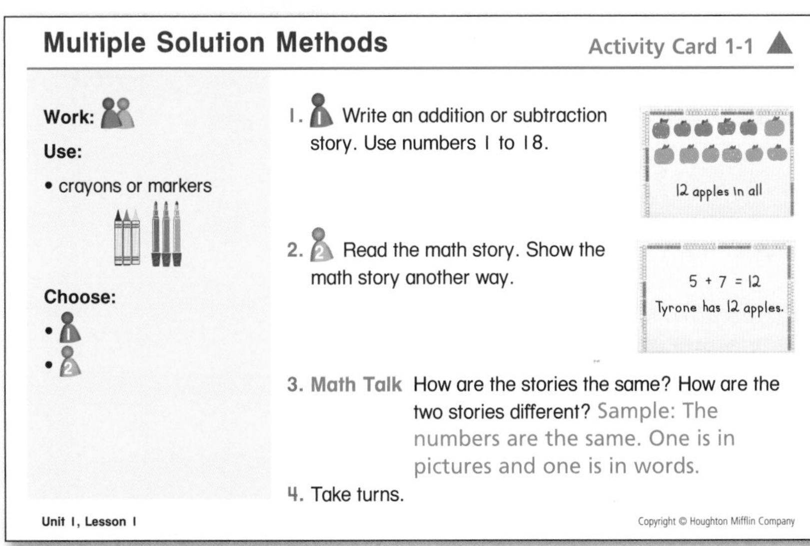
Multiple Solution Methods — Activity Card 1-1 ▲

Work: (pairs)
Use:
- crayons or markers

Choose:
- 1
- 2

1. (1) Write an addition or subtraction story. Use numbers 1 to 18.

12 apples in all

2. (2) Read the math story. Show the math story another way.

5 + 7 = 12
Tyrone has 12 apples.

3. **Math Talk** How are the stories the same? How are the two stories different? Sample: The numbers are the same. One is in pictures and one is in words.
4. Take turns.

Unit 1, Lesson 1 — Copyright © Houghton Mifflin Company

Activity Note Encourage children to use a different method to solve the story problem and discuss their methods.

Math Writing Prompt

Write a Story Problem Write an addition and a subtraction story problem using the numbers 9 and 7. Draw a picture to solve each problem.

Software Support

Use *MegaMath* for review and reinforcement of the concepts and skills presented in this lesson.

Challenge

Activity Card 1-1

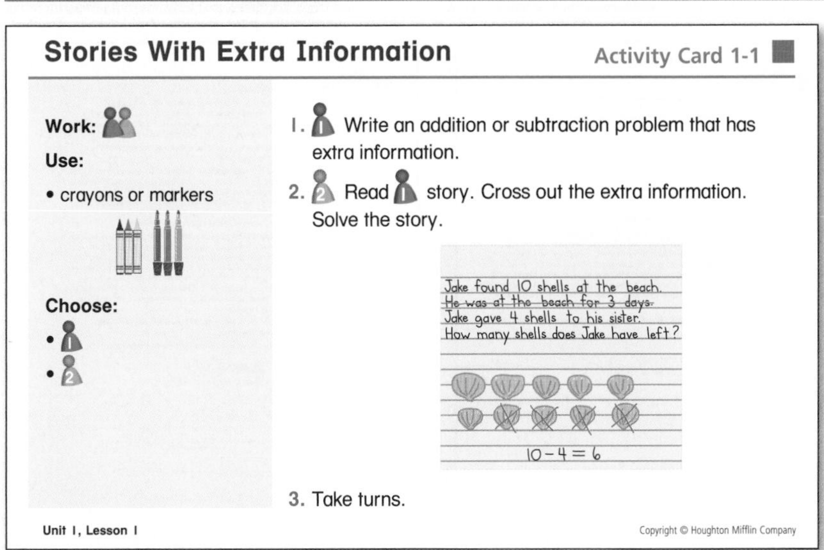
Stories With Extra Information — Activity Card 1-1 ■

Work: (pairs)
Use:
- crayons or markers

Choose:
- 1
- 2

1. (1) Write an addition or subtraction problem that has extra information.
2. (2) Read (1) story. Cross out the extra information. Solve the story.

Jake found 10 shells at the beach.
~~He was at the beach for 3 days.~~
Jake gave 4 shells to his sister.
How many shells does Jake have left?

10 − 4 = 6

3. Take turns.

Unit 1, Lesson 1 — Copyright © Houghton Mifflin Company

Activity Note Check that children are including extra information and that the partner correctly identifies the extra information.

Math Writing Prompt

No Zero? Write a story about what life would be like without the number 0.

Software Support

Use *Destination Math* to take students beyond the concepts and skills presented in this lesson.

3 Homework

Goal: Additional Practice

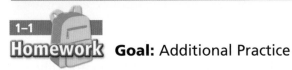

This Homework page provides practice in solving addition and subtraction story problems.

1-1 **Homework** Name ____________________

Solve the story problems. **Show your work.**

1. Spencer saw 8 frogs in the pond. Then he saw 5 more. How many frogs did Spencer see altogether?

frog

13 ___frogs___
label

Check children's work.

2. Beth has 5 red marbles and some blue marbles. Altogether she has 14 marbles. How many of the marbles are blue?

marbles

9 ___marbles___
label

3. Felix has 5 stamps from Mexico. The rest are from Canada. He has 8 stamps altogether. How many stamps are from Canada?

stamp

3 ___stamps___
label

4. Gary had 7 books. His mother gave him 3 more books. How many books does Gary have now?

book

10 ___books___
label

5. On the Back Write your own story problem. Then show how to solve it. Check children's work.

UNIT 1 LESSON 1 Introduce Stories and Drawings 1

Homework and Remembering page 1

Home and School Connection

Family Letter Have children take home the Family Letter on Student Activity Book page 3. This letter explains how concepts are developed in *Math Expressions.* It gives parents and guardians a better understanding of the learning that goes on in math class and creates a bridge between school and home. A Spanish translation of this letter is on the following page in the Student Activity Book.

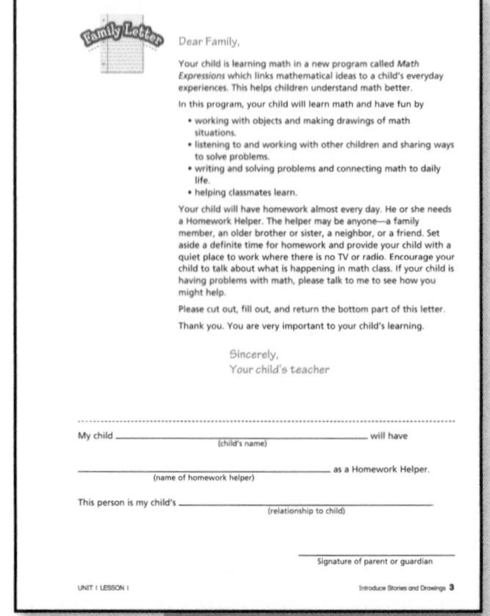

Family Letter

Dear Family,

Your child is learning math in a new program called *Math Expressions* which links mathematical ideas to a child's everyday experiences. This helps children understand math better.

In this program, your child will learn math and have fun by

- working with objects and making drawings of math situations.
- listening to and working with other children and sharing ways to solve problems.
- writing and solving problems and connecting math to daily life.
- helping classmates learn.

Your child will have homework almost every day. He or she needs a Homework Helper. The helper may be anyone—a family member, an older brother or sister, a neighbor, or a friend. Set aside a definite time for homework and provide your child with a quiet place to work where there is no TV or radio. Encourage your child to talk about what is happening in math class. If your child is having problems with math, please talk to me to see how you might help.

Please cut out, fill out, and return the bottom part of this letter.

Thank you. You are very important to your child's learning.

Sincerely,
Your child's teacher

My child ____________ (child's name) will have ____________ (name of homework helper) as a Homework Helper.

This person is my child's ____________ (relationship to child)

____________ Signature of parent or guardian

UNIT 1 LESSON 1 Introduce Stories and Drawings 3

Student Activity Book page 3

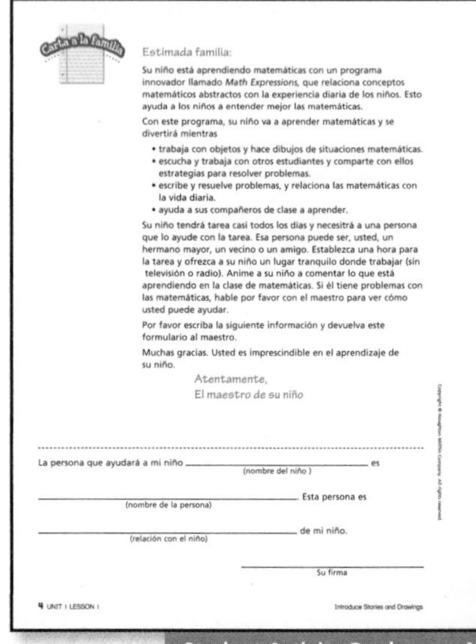

Carta a la familia

Estimada familia:

Su niño está aprendiendo matemáticas con un programa innovador llamado *Math Expressions,* que relaciona conceptos matemáticos abstractos con la experiencia diaria de los niños. Esto ayuda a los niños a entender mejor las matemáticas.

Con este programa, su niño va a aprender matemáticas y se divertirá mientras

- trabaja con objetos y hace dibujos de situaciones matemáticas.
- escucha y trabaja con otros estudiantes y comparte con ellos estrategias para resolver problemas.
- escribe y resuelve problemas, y relaciona las matemáticas con la vida diaria.
- ayuda a sus compañeros de clase a aprender.

Su niño tendrá tarea casi todos los días y necesitrá a una persona que lo ayude con la tarea. Esa persona puede ser, usted, un hermano mayor, un vecino o un amigo. Establezca una hora para la tarea y ofrezca a su niño un lugar tranquilo donde trabajar (sin televisión o radio). Anime a su niño a comentar lo que está aprendiendo en la clase de matemáticas. Si él tiene problemas con las matemáticas, hable por favor con el maestro para ver cómo usted puede ayudar.

Por favor escriba la siguiente información y devuelva este formulario al maestro.

Muchas gracias. Usted es imprescindible en el aprendizaje de su niño.

Atentamente,
El maestro de su niño

La persona que ayudará a mi niño ____________ (nombre del niño) es ____________ (nombre de la persona). Esta persona es ____________ (relación con el niño) de mi niño.

____________ Su firma

4 UNIT 1 LESSON 1 Introduce Stories and Drawings

Student Activity Book page 4

Practice with Stories and Drawings

Lesson Objectives

- Paraphrase, represent, and solve story problems.
- Create story problems.

Vocabulary

flash ten	proof drawing
story problem	matching picture
equation	number flash

The Day at a Glance

Today's Goals	Materials	
1 Teaching the Lesson **A1:** Use number flashes to count to 20. **A2:** Solve and discuss story problems involving numbers to 18.	**Lesson Activities** Student Activity Book pp. 5–6 Homework and Remembering pp. 3–4	**Going Further** Activity Cards 1-2 Counters Index Cards MathBoard materials Math Journals
2 Going Further ▸ Differentiated Instruction		
3 Homework and Spiral Review		

Use Math Talk today!

Keeping Skills Sharp

Quick Practice — 15 MINUTES	Daily Routines
Goal: Count to 20. For today's Quick Practice, use the first activity, Counting to 20. The usual amount of time set aside for Quick Practice is five minutes. However, in Unit 1, 10–15 minutes are allotted. This extra time allows children to learn the routines.	**Money Routine** Using the 120 Poster, Using the Money Flip Chart, Using the Number Path, Using Secret Code Cards (See pp. xxiii–xxv.) ▸ Led by teacher

1 Teaching the Lesson

Activity 1

Counting to 20

 15 MINUTES

Goal: Use number flashes to count to 20.

 **NCTM Standard:**
Number and Operations

The Learning Classroom

Student Leaders Once children see how a Quick Practice activity progresses, invite two children to serve as Student Leaders each day. Their job is to direct the Quick Practice.

For the first several sessions, select children who can take on the leadership role easily. They will serve as models for their classmates. After a few sessions, let other children volunteer for the leadership role. Since many Quick Practice activities call for two Student Leaders, ease the other children into the leadership role by pairing them with a strong student.

 Class Management

When demonstrating how to use fingers and hands, you should turn sideways to the class and hold your fingers so that children will see them positioned in the same way as their own fingers. Standing sideways allows you to see the class.

Keep in mind that some children will use different fingers than others. For example, some children will flash one using the thumb or pinky, while others may use the ring finger.

▶ Number Flashes WHOLE CLASS

This activity will be used as Quick Practice throughout this unit.

Invite children to count to 20 together. Children indicate each number by showing the appropriate number of fingers.

- Here's a way to count to 20 together. One. *Put up one finger.* Two. *Put up two fingers.* Three. *Put up three fingers, continuing to nine.*

When children reach ten, ask them to flash ten by opening and closing both hands to see the ten.

- We can flash ten when we reach the number 10. You can open and close your hands to show all 10 fingers. *Demonstrate.* This shows us the tens in the teen numbers.

Children can use number flashes for each teen number. First they flash ten, and then they show the ones.

- We can show 11 by flashing ten on the left and then putting up just one finger to the right. Eleven is ten and one.

11 = 10 + 1

Flash Ten Left → ***Flash One*** Right

- We can show 12 by flashing ten on the left and then putting up just two fingers to the right. Twelve is ten and two.

12 = 10 + 2

Flash Ten Left → ***Flash Two*** Right

Demonstrate as you call out the numbers 13–19. As you flash the extra ones, move your hands to the right so that you are not flashing "on top of" the ten you just flashed. Then flash ten twice for the number 20.

These finger flashes and words (thirteen equals ten and three) help children build their concept of teen numbers as a ten plus some ones.

Activity 2

Solve Story Problems

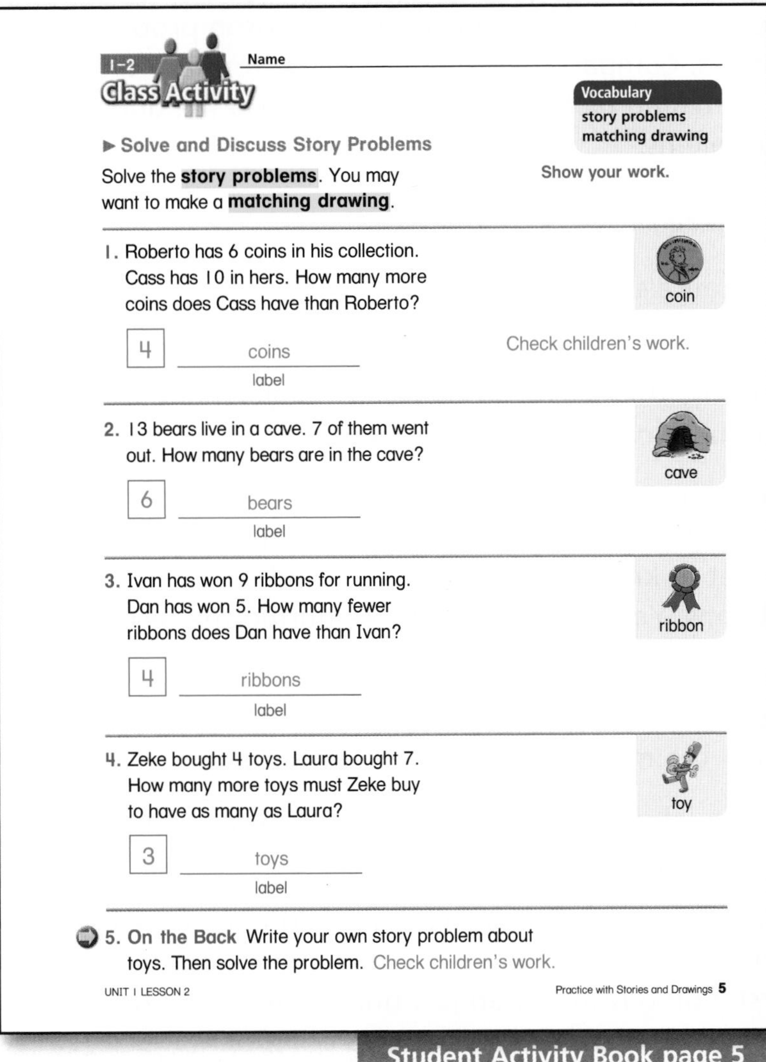

1-2 Class Activity

Name

Vocabulary
story problems
matching drawing

▶ Solve and Discuss Story Problems

Solve the **story problems**. You may want to make a **matching drawing**.

Show your work.

1. Roberto has 6 coins in his collection. Cass has 10 in hers. How many more coins does Cass have than Roberto?

coin

4 coins
label

Check children's work.

2. 13 bears live in a cave. 7 of them went out. How many bears are in the cave?

cave

6 bears
label

3. Ivan has won 9 ribbons for running. Dan has won 5. How many fewer ribbons does Dan have than Ivan?

ribbon

4 ribbons
label

4. Zeke bought 4 toys. Laura bought 7. How many more toys must Zeke buy to have as many as Laura?

toy

3 toys
label

5. **On the Back** Write your own story problem about toys. Then solve the problem. Check children's work.

UNIT 1 LESSON 2 Practice with Stories and Drawings 5

Student Activity Book page 5

▶ Solve and Discuss Story Problems WHOLE CLASS

Read aloud the first problem on Student Activity page 5 with the children. Then have several children retell the story problem in their own words.

Use the **Solve and Discuss** structure for the first problem. Encourage children to use equations, Proof Drawings, or other methods.

Invite new groups of children to the board for each remaining problem.

The next page and the Math Background for Unit 2 show different ways children might solve these problems.

Activity continued ▶

45 MINUTES

Goal: Solve and discuss story problems involving numbers to 18.

Materials: Student Activity Book page 5

✓ **NCTM Standards:**
Number and Operations
Problem Solving
Communication
Representation

The Learning Classroom

Math Talk When children explain their work, they need to stand beside their work and point to parts of it as they explain. Using a pointer that does not obscure any work enables watchers to see the part of the drawing or math symbols they are explaining at that moment.

English Language Learners

Model a *matching drawing* for problem 1. Draw the coins in two horizontal lines. Review *more,* and *fewer.*

- **Beginning** Say: **Robert has 6 coins. Cass has 10.** Gesture to show the difference. Say: **Cass has *more* coins. Robert has *fewer*.**
- **Intermediate** Ask: **Does Cass have *more* coins?** yes Count Cass's coins to 6. Gesture to the remaining coins. Ask: **How many more coins does Cass have?** 4
- **Advanced** Say: **This is a *matching drawing*.** Ask: **Who has more coins?** Cass **Fewer coins?** Robert

Teaching the Lesson (continued)

Ongoing Assessment

Have children retell this story problem in their own words, and then solve it.

▶ 12 children are on the playground. 5 of them go home. How many children are on the playground now?

Teaching Note

Homework Homework is very important in this program. If some Homework Helper forms are not returned today, keep trying to identify a Homework Helper for each child. Begin a homework check or homework collection routine that reinforces the idea to children that they are expected to finish their homework every day. Help children see homework as a usual part of the daily routine.

You may wish to go over homework as a class. Ask children if they have any questions about the homework. De-emphasize minor errors for now. Encourage children to see the homework as a learning experience and an opportunity to share ideas.

You might lead a classroom spot-check to assess whether most children seem to understand the concepts, rather than spending too much time checking every problem of the homework. Children who are having trouble will have opportunities in later activities and units to gain mastery.

Problems 1, 3, and 4 on Student Activity Book page 5 are comparison problems. Ask children to discuss the meanings of *more* and *fewer*.

Comparison Problems Problem 4 on Student Activity Book page 5 is a comparison problem. Some children may find comparison problems difficult to understand. Comparison problems will be formally taught in Unit 2. Drawing a *matching picture* helps children grasp the underlying concept in these problems.

Zeke's toys: ○ ○ ○ ○

Laura's toys: ○ ○ ○ ○ ○ ○ ○

1 2 3

- Laura has 3 more toys than Zeke. So Zeke must buy 3 more toys to have the same number of toys that Laura has.

Observe How Children Solve Problems Observe these aspects of your children's problem solving, retelling, and explaining. These 3 days will enable you to get to know a bit about your children's initial math strengths and problems. You can build on those during the next two units.

Retelling: Are children able to paraphrase problems? Note how well their retellings retain the meaning of the problem situation.

Labeling: Can children label their answers? Labeling helps them link the problem situation to the numbers.

Drawing: Do children represent the problem situation in a drawing and use the image to help determine the solution? Drawings can indicate if there is real understanding rather than just number manipulation.

Using Fingers: Do children count on their fingers to find solutions? If they do, do they count all the numbers or do they start with one number and count on to a total (for both subtraction and addition)? Children who count on are more advanced than children who count all.

Using Strategies: Does the children's work indicate that they apply appropriate strategies to solving problems? Question them in order to find out what they are doing.

Explaining Strategies: Are children able to explain what they do to solve problems? Using strategies and being able to explain them are not the same thing. Children who can explain their strategies are more advanced than children who simply apply algorithms to problems.

Using Mental Methods: Are children able to solve problems in their heads and explain what they did? Children will become more able to use mental math as the year progresses.

2 Going Further

Differentiated Instruction

Intervention — Activity Card 1-2

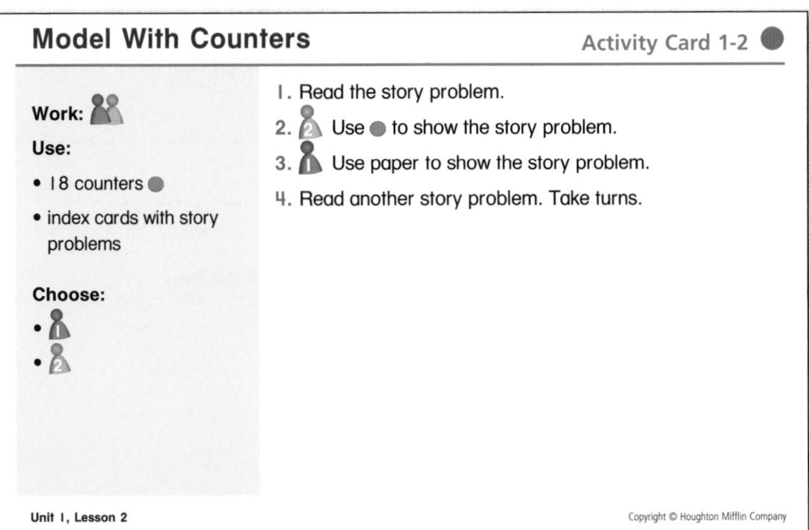

Model With Counters — Activity Card 1-2 ●

Work: pairs

Use:
- 18 counters ●
- index cards with story problems

Choose:
- 1
- 2

1. Read the story problem.
2. (2) Use ● to show the story problem.
3. (1) Use paper to show the story problem.
4. Read another story problem. Take turns.

Unit 1, Lesson 2

Activity Note Prepare index cards using the Homework problems as a model. Have pairs use counters.

Math Writing Prompt

More Than 10? Will the answer to this story problem be more or less than 10 bikes? Explain.

A store had 10 bikes. It sold 7 bikes. How many bikes does the store have now?

Software Support

Use *Soar to Success* for instruction of students needing targeted support for underlying skills.

On Level — Activity Card 1-2

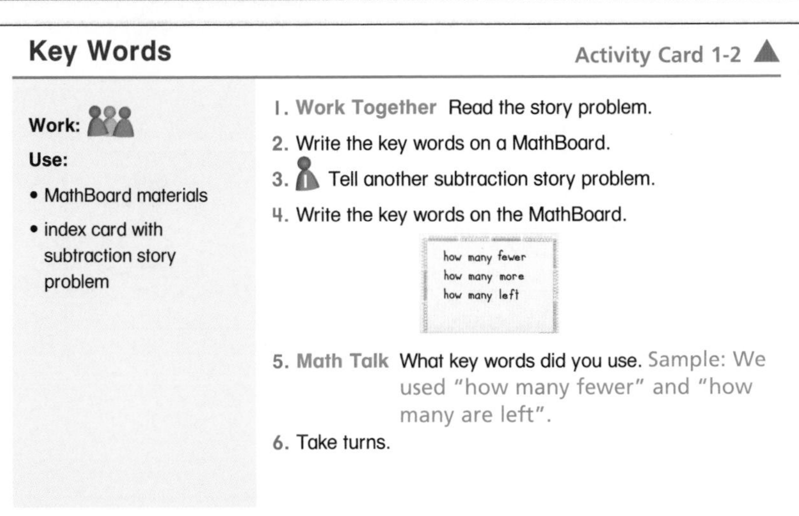

Key Words — Activity Card 1-2 ▲

Work: groups of three

Use:
- MathBoard materials
- index card with subtraction story problem

1. **Work Together** Read the story problem.
2. Write the key words on a MathBoard.
3. (1) Tell another subtraction story problem.
4. Write the key words on the MathBoard.

how many fewer
how many more
how many left

5. **Math Talk** What key words did you use. Sample: We used "how many fewer" and "how many are left".
6. Take turns.

Unit 1, Lesson 2

Activity Note Prepare story problems on index cards such as: Jay read 13 books. Lee read 8 books. How many fewer books did Lee read than Jay?

Math Writing Prompt

Write a Story Problem Draw this picture. Show 5 circles in the top row and 2 circles in the bottom row. Draw lines between the rows. Write a comparison story problem for the picture.

Software Support

Use *MegaMath* for review and reinforcement of the concepts and skills presented in this lesson.

Challenge — Activity Card 1-2

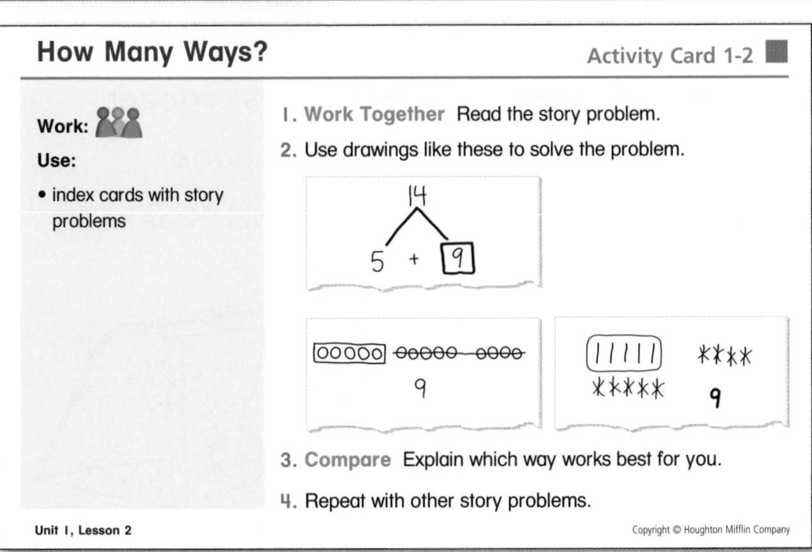

How Many Ways? — Activity Card 1-2 ■

Work: groups of three

Use:
- index cards with story problems

1. **Work Together** Read the story problem.
2. Use drawings like these to solve the problem.

14
5 + 9

9

9

3. **Compare** Explain which way works best for you.
4. Repeat with other story problems.

Unit 1, Lesson 2

Activity Note Prepare index cards with subtraction story problems. Have children show how they solved the problem in different ways.

Math Writing Prompt

Write a Sentence Look at the answer to one of the story problems you solved in your group. Write the answer to the problem in a full sentence.

DESTINATION Math

Software Support

Use *Destination Math* to take students beyond the concepts and skills presented in this lesson.

3 Homework and Spiral Review

Goal: Additional Practice

✓ Include children's completed Homework page as part of their portfolios.

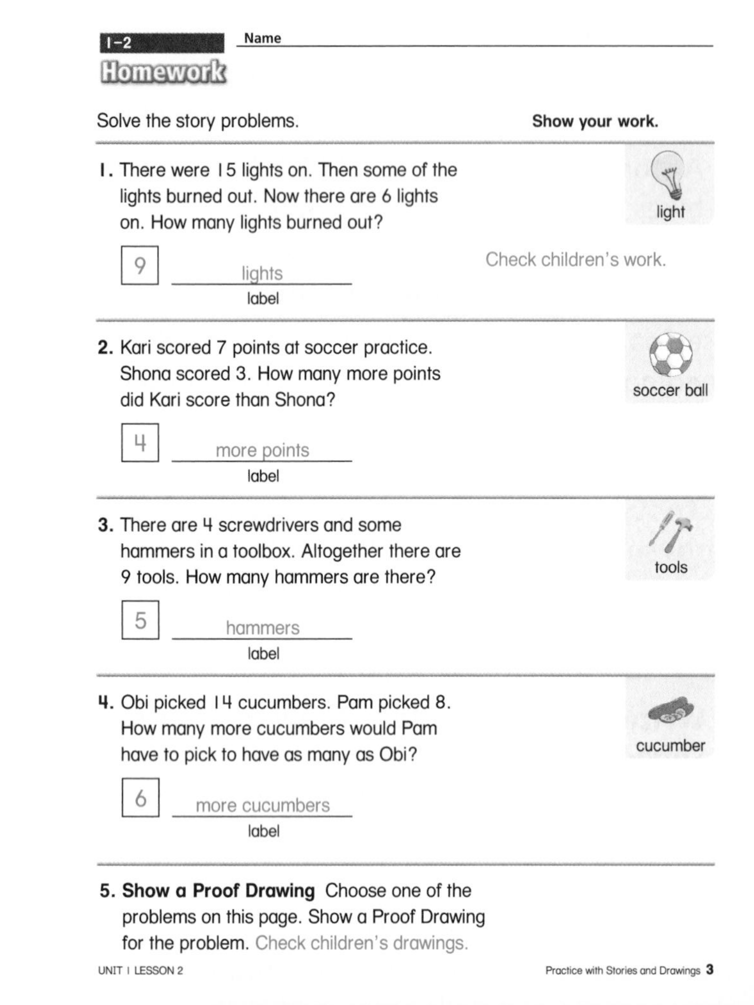

1–2 Homework Name ______

Solve the story problems. **Show your work.**

1. There were 15 lights on. Then some of the lights burned out. Now there are 6 lights on. How many lights burned out? light
9 lights
label
Check children's work.

2. Kari scored 7 points at soccer practice. Shona scored 3. How many more points did Kari score than Shona? soccer ball
4 more points
label

3. There are 4 screwdrivers and some hammers in a toolbox. Altogether there are 9 tools. How many hammers are there? tools
5 hammers
label

4. Obi picked 14 cucumbers. Pam picked 8. How many more cucumbers would Pam have to pick to have as many as Obi? cucumber
6 more cucumbers
label

5. **Show a Proof Drawing** Choose one of the problems on this page. Show a Proof Drawing for the problem. Check children's drawings.

UNIT 1 LESSON 2 Practice with Stories and Drawings 3

Homework and Remembering page 3

Goal: Spiral Review

This Remembering activity would be appropriate anytime after today's lesson.

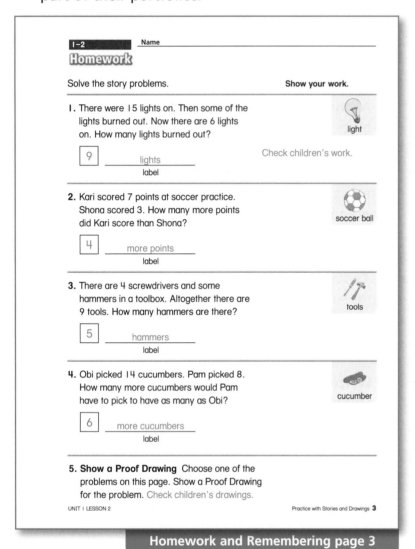

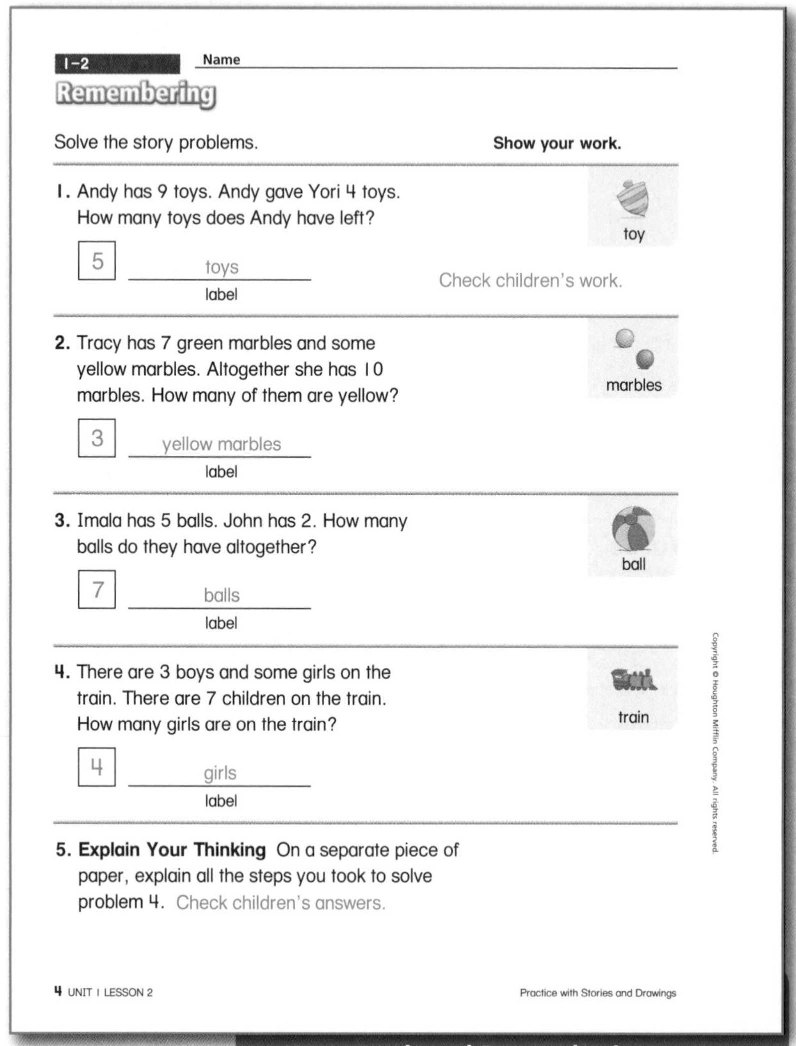

1–2 Remembering Name ______

Solve the story problems. **Show your work.**

1. Andy has 9 toys. Andy gave Yori 4 toys. How many toys does Andy have left? toy
5 toys
label
Check children's work.

2. Tracy has 7 green marbles and some yellow marbles. Altogether she has 10 marbles. How many of them are yellow? marbles
3 yellow marbles
label

3. Imala has 5 balls. John has 2. How many balls do they have altogether? ball
7 balls
label

4. There are 3 boys and some girls on the train. There are 7 children on the train. How many girls are on the train? train
4 girls
label

5. **Explain Your Thinking** On a separate piece of paper, explain all the steps you took to solve problem 4. Check children's answers.

4 UNIT 1 LESSON 2 Practice with Stories and Drawings

Homework and Remembering page 4

Home or School Activity

Sports Connection

Choose a Sport Have children write story problems about their favorite sport. As you review these, watch for good story problems. Have children rewrite them on cards and place them in a special file or math center where other children can use them for practice.

I scored 2 goals in Saturday's soccer game, and 3 goals in Sunday's game. How many goals did I score last weekend?

Add or Subtract 0 or 1

Lesson Objectives

- Solve addition and subtraction problems involving 0 or 1.
- Construct and verbalize rules for adding and subtracting 0 or 1.
- Explain how to solve story problems.

Vocabulary

zero	equation
minus	story problem
plus	number flash
flash ten	

The Day at a Glance

Today's Goals	Materials	
1 Teaching the Lesson A1: Solve story problems by adding or subtracting 0 or 1. Then verbalize the rules for adding or subtracting 0 and 1. A2: Discuss methods used for solving story problems.	**Lesson Activities** Student Activity Book pp. 7–8 Homework and Remembering pp. 5–6 MathBoard materials	**Going Further** Activity Cards 1-3 *Oliver's Party* by Jenny Fry and Angela Jollife MathBoard materials Crayons Counters Bowl Math Journals
2 Going Further ▶ Extra Practice ▶ Differentiated Instruction		
3 Homework		

Use Math Talk today!

Keeping Skills Sharp

Quick Practice — 10 MINUTES

Goal: Use number flashes to count to 20.

Number Flash: Counting to 20 If necessary, review the procedure for counting to 20 from Unit 1 Lesson 2. Invite two **Student Leaders** to lead the counting. Ask children to indicate the numbers by showing the appropriate number of fingers. For the teen numbers, they flash ten to the left and the extra ones to the right and say:

- Eleven is ten and one.
- Twelve is ten and two.
- Twenty is ten and ten.

Daily Routines

Money Routine Using the 120 Poster, Using the Money Flip Chart, Using the Number Path, Using Secret Code Cards (See pp. xxiii–xxv.)

▶ Led by teacher

1 Teaching the Lesson

Activity 1

Plus and Minus 0 and 1

15 MINUTES

Goal: Solve story problems by adding or subtracting 0 or 1. Then verbalize the rules for adding or subtracting 0 and 1.

Materials: MathBoard materials

NCTM Standards:
Problem Solving
Communication

The Learning Classroom

Helping Community Communicate often that the goal of the class is for everyone to understand the math they are studying. Praise children for learning to work together and help each other. Discuss why the math classroom is a place where children cooperate.

Create a safe classroom culture in which children are willing to try new things and to discuss their approaches. Discuss with children the importance of being careful when responding to their own and each other's errors. Talk about the motto, "Errors Help Us Learn," and invite children to make it their motto. Encourage children to see errors as an opportunity to learn rather than a reason to be criticized.

► Add and Subtract 0 WHOLE CLASS

Help children understand the concept of adding and subtracting 0 by solving the following problems.

Some children may find drawing pictures helpful.

- There are 8 bicycles in the rack. No one put in any more. How many bicycles are in the rack now? 8 bicycles

00000
000
8
\+ no more
8 + 0 = 8

- I have 6 grapes on a plate. I did not eat any of them. How many grapes do I have now? 6 grapes

00000
0
6 grapes
none eaten
6 - 0 = 6

Ask volunteers to suggest other story problems that show adding or subtracting with 0.

Rules for Adding and Subtracting 0 Help children see that adding or subtracting 0 from a number does not change that number.

- Who can make up a rule about adding 0 to a number? What is the general pattern? When you add 0 to a number, the number does not change.
- Who can make up a rule about subtracting 0 from a number? When you subtract 0 from a number, the number does not change.

You may wish to help children combine the rules they discovered into one general rule for adding and subtracting 0.

- Who can make up <u>one</u> rule about adding or subtracting 0? Adding or subtracting 0 does not change the number you started with.

▶ Add and Subtract 1 WHOLE CLASS

Follow the same procedure for adding and subtracting 1 as you did with adding and subtracting 0. Supply children with problems and have them write other problems on their own.

- I had 7 stickers. Then my friend gave me 1 more. How many stickers do I have now? 8 stickers

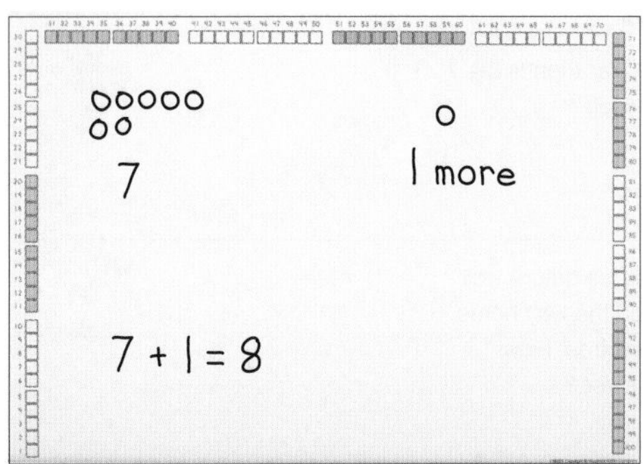

- I had 5 balloons. I popped 1. How many balloons do I have now? 4 balloons

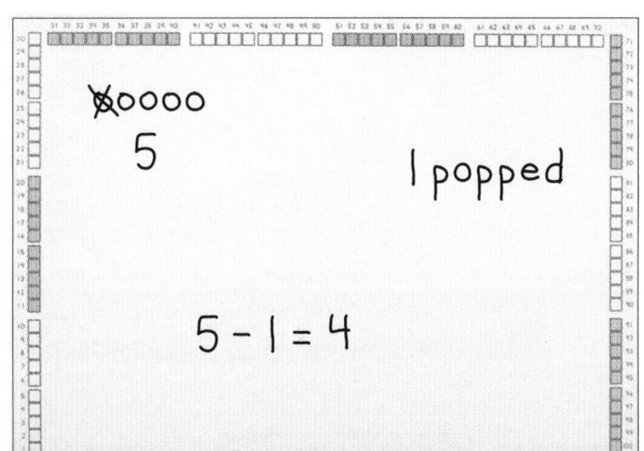

Rules for Adding and Subtracting 1 Help children see that adding 1 to any number means going to the next higher counting number and subtracting 1 from any number means going to the next lower counting number.

- What rule can we make up about adding 1 to any number? The answer is the next number we count, the next number "up," or the next number higher.
- What rule can we make up about subtracting 1 from any number? The answer is the number we count just before, the next number "down," or the next number lower.
- Does it make a difference if we add or subtract 0? No, the answer is always the number you started with.
- Does it make a difference if we add or subtract 1? Yes, the answer is not the number we started with. It's 1 more or 1 less than the number we started with—the next number we count or the number just before.

The Learning Classroom

Building Concepts Some children may want to create a general rule for adding and subtracting 1 as they did with adding and subtracting 0. If they can work out a principle that is not confusing to them, encourage them to do so. This will not work as well as it did with 0, however, because adding or subtracting 1 does change the result in different ways.

▶ Can you think of a rule for both adding or subtracting 1? The number is always 1 different. It is 1 up for addition or 1 down for subtraction.

English Language Learners

Model an *add* and a *subtract 1* problem. Draw the stickers on the board. Review *more* and *fewer.*

- **Beginning** Say: **I had 7 stickers. My friend gave me one more. 1 more means *add 1*.** Have children repeat.
- **Intermediate** Ask: **How many stickers did I have?** 7 **Does 1 more mean *add 1* or *subtract 1*?** add 1
- **Advanced** Say: **This is an *add 1* problem.** Ask: **How many stickers if I *add 1* more to 7?** 8 **What math did you do?** 7 + 1 = 8

Activity 2

Solve Story Problems

30 MINUTES

Goal: Discuss methods used for solving story problems.

Materials: Student Activity Book page 7

✓ **NCTM Standards:**
Problem Solving
Communication

Differentiated Instruction

English Learners Pair an English learner with a child who is fluent in English. It is important that the helping child be empathetic to children who are learning to speak English. The helping child should be fairly advanced in math concepts and understand that helping does not mean doing the work for the other child.

The Learning Classroom

Math Talk To help children understand what you mean when you say, "explain your thinking," solve one of the problems at the board as if you are the child. Be sure to discuss all parts of your problem and explain the thinking you used to solve it.

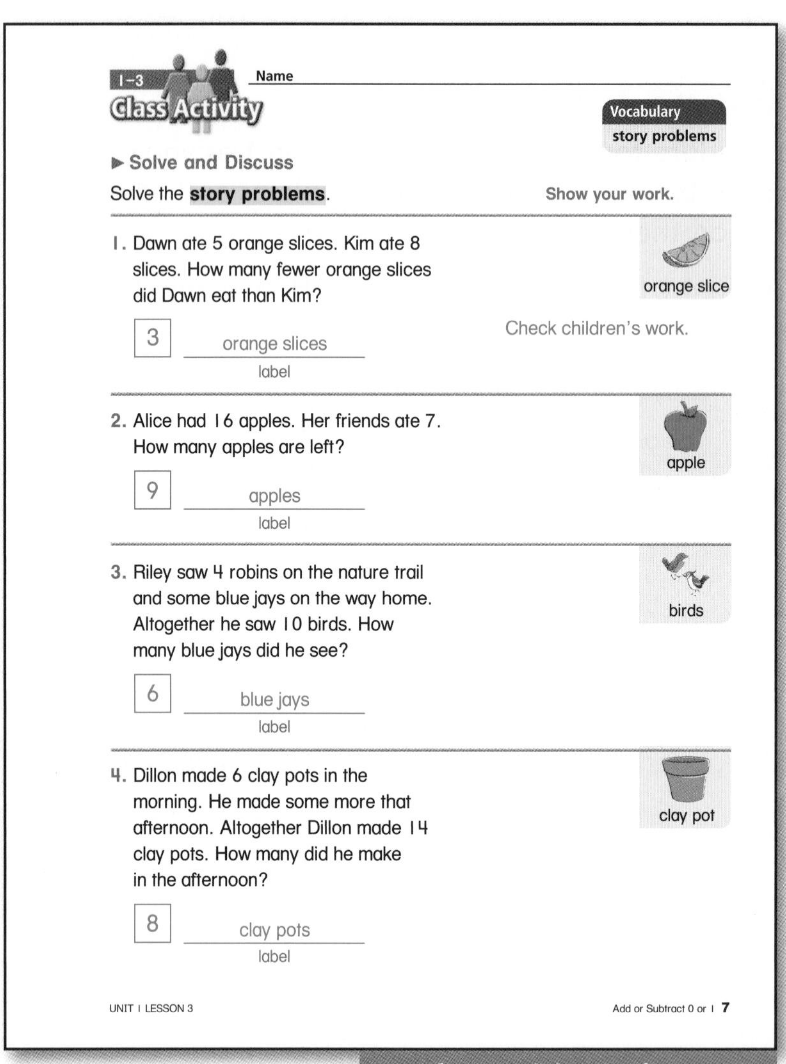

1–3 Class Activity Name ______

Vocabulary
story problems

▶ Solve and Discuss

Solve the **story problems**. Show your work.

1. Dawn ate 5 orange slices. Kim ate 8 slices. How many fewer orange slices did Dawn eat than Kim?
3 orange slices (label)
orange slice
Check children's work.

2. Alice had 16 apples. Her friends ate 7. How many apples are left?
9 apples (label)
apple

3. Riley saw 4 robins on the nature trail and some blue jays on the way home. Altogether he saw 10 birds. How many blue jays did he see?
6 blue jays (label)
birds

4. Dillon made 6 clay pots in the morning. He made some more that afternoon. Altogether Dillon made 14 clay pots. How many did he make in the afternoon?
8 clay pots (label)
clay pot

UNIT 1 LESSON 3 Add or Subtract 0 or 1 7

Student Activity Book page 7

▶ Solve and Discuss WHOLE CLASS

Math Talk 

Read aloud the first problem on Student Activity Book page 7 with the class. Then have a few children retell the story in their own words. Select as many children as will fit to solve the problem at the board. Then invite two or three of them to explain how they solved the problem.

This problem can be thought of in at least two ways in addition to making a matching drawing:

$5 + \square = 8$ Dawn fewer slices Kim	$8 - \square = 5$ Kim the difference Dawn

Children may also use different words and other ways of labeling the problem (such as using only letters instead of full names).

Encourage children to ask questions of each other if they need further clarification. Asking and answering questions will help them understand the solution process.

Invite children to practice explaining one another's work in their own words. They may do this from their seats, or they may go to the board and point to various parts of the first child's work.

Invite new children to the board to solve each of the problems on the student page. Remember to have some children restate the problem in their own words before the class solves it.

Encourage the children at the board to label their drawing or equation with items from the situation. Doing so will help them explain their thinking. They can use a word or a letter. For example, for problem 4 on Student Activity Book page 7, M can be used for *morning* and A can be used for *afternoon.*

Dillon made 6 clay pots in the morning. He made some more that afternoon. Altogether Dillon made 14 clay pots. How many did he make in the afternoon?

Method 1

6	+	□	=	14
M		A		altogether

Method 2

ooooooo | oooo oooo

m a 8

Children will also use other methods like counting on from 6 to 14 to find 8 more.

After children have completed the page, encourage them to make up story problems of their own for the class to solve, using numbers that total ≤ 18.

Class Management

Looking Ahead In the next lesson, children will use Penny Strips, Nickel Strips, and Dime Strips. These are on Student Activity Book page 9 and on Coin Strips (TRB M1).

Children can use the Coin Strips in the Student Activity Book, or they can take those home and you can make sturdy Coin Strips for classroom use by copying the copymaster onto card stock. Make sure and check that your copy machine has this capability. In either case, you may want to set aside a time before you begin the lesson for children to cut out the strips. See Student Activity Book page 9 for cutting instructions.

Ongoing Assessment

Observe children as they solve the story problems. Be sure to notice if any children are waiting until the problem is solved at the board before trying to solve it on their own. Try to find some time to work with those children individually.

2 Going Further

Extra Practice

 20 MINUTES

Goal: Practice adding or subtracting 0 and 1.

Materials: Student Activity Book page 8, crayons (yellow, red, green, and blue), counters, MathBoard materials

 **NCTM Standard:**
Number and Operations

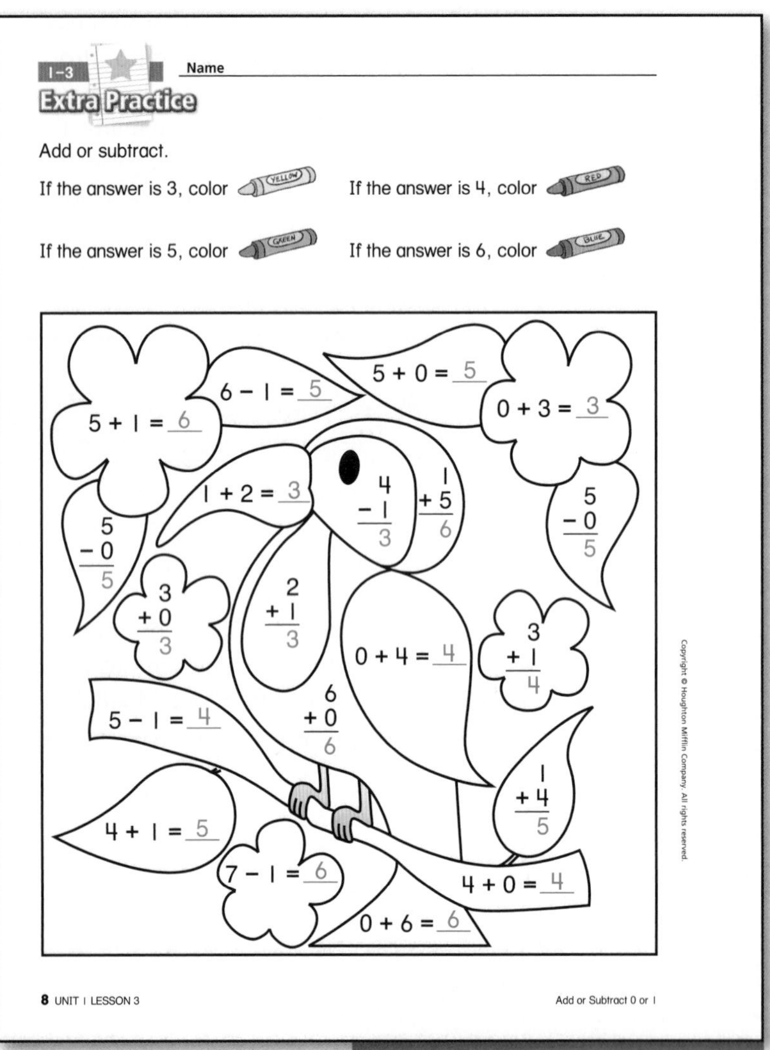
1-3 Name
Extra Practice

Add or subtract.

If the answer is 3, color YELLOW. If the answer is 4, color RED.

If the answer is 5, color GREEN. If the answer is 6, color BLUE.

8 UNIT 1 LESSON 3 Add or Subtract 0 or 1

Student Activity Book page 8

▶ Getting Started INDIVIDUALS

Have children complete the addition and subtraction exercises. Before children begin coloring Student Activity Book page 8, remind them to check their answers carefully. Encourage them to color lightly so they can read the answers to the exercises.

▶ Critical Thinking WHOLE CLASS

Use this critical thinking question for discussion after children complete the page.

- What do you notice about how the leaves in the picture are colored that could help you see if your answers are incorrect? Possible response: The total for the leaves should be 5, because the leaves of flowers are green.

Differentiated Instruction

Extra Help If children are experiencing difficulty with the exercises, have them use counters to model the addition and subtraction.

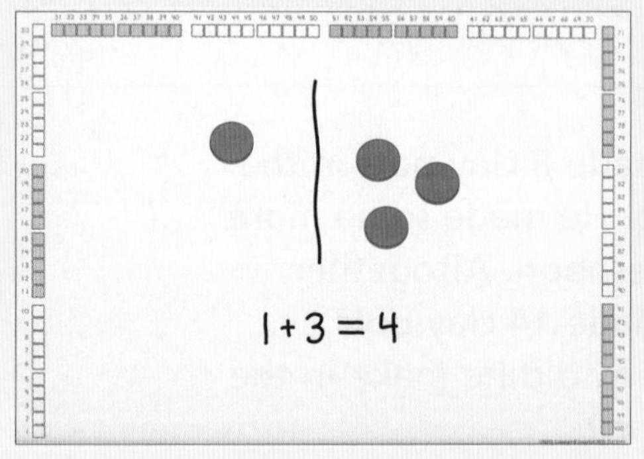

▶ Create Your Own PAIRS

Have children create their own hidden-picture practice pages. Pairs can exchange pages to complete and color.

Intervention — Activity Card 1-3

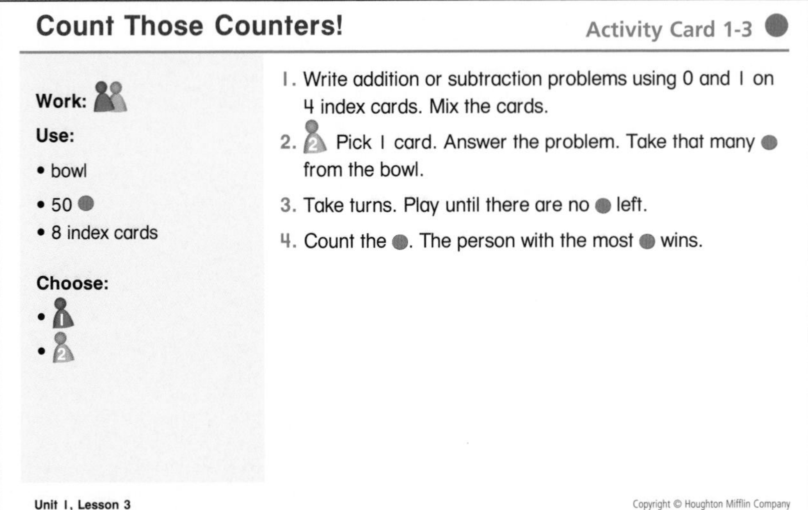

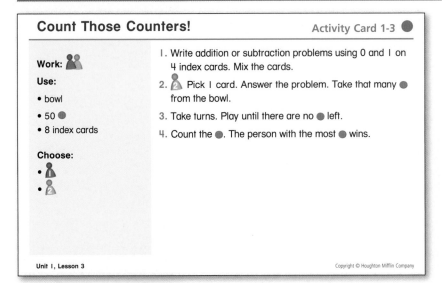

Count Those Counters! Activity Card 1-3 ●

Work: (pair)
Use:
- bowl
- 50 ●
- 8 index cards

Choose:
- (child 1)
- (child 2)

1. Write addition or subtraction problems using 0 and 1 on 4 index cards. Mix the cards.
2. Pick 1 card. Answer the problem. Take that many ● from the bowl.
3. Take turns. Play until there are no ● left.
4. Count the ●. The person with the most ● wins.

Unit 1, Lesson 3 — Copyright © Houghton Mifflin Company

Activity Note Put the counters in the bowl and have each child in the pair write four different exercises. Place the cards face down.

Math Writing Prompt

Draw a Picture Draw a picture to show the answer to each of the problems.

4 − 1 = __ 4 − 0 = __

4 + 1 = __ 4 + 0 = __

Software Support

Use *Soar to Success* for instruction of students needing targeted support for underlying skills.

On Level — Activity Card 1-3

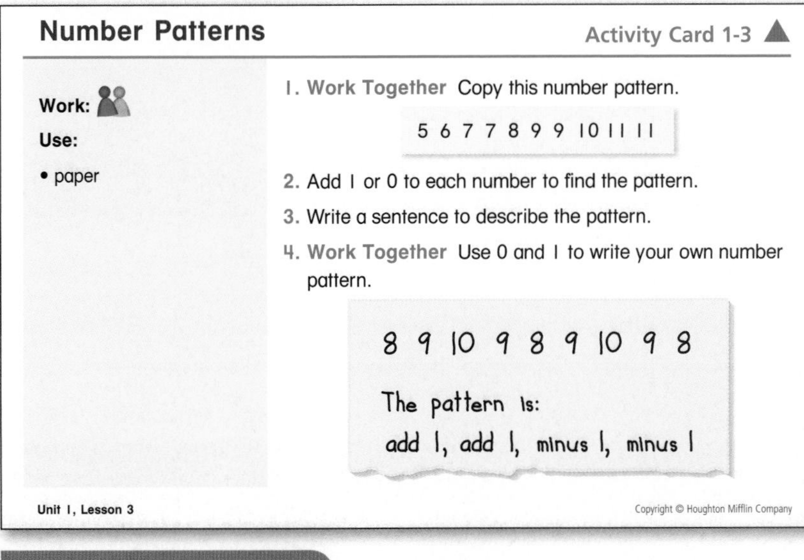

Number Patterns Activity Card 1-3 ▲

Work: (pair)
Use:
- paper

1. **Work Together** Copy this number pattern.

   5 6 7 7 8 9 9 10 11 11

2. Add 1 or 0 to each number to find the pattern.
3. Write a sentence to describe the pattern.
4. **Work Together** Use 0 and 1 to write your own number pattern.

   8 9 10 9 8 9 10 9 8

   The pattern is:
   add 1, add 1, minus 1, minus 1

Unit 1, Lesson 3 — Copyright © Houghton Mifflin Company

Activity Note Encourage children to describe the pattern they see. Have children share the patterns they write.

Math Writing Prompt

Write the Rule Write a rule for the following:

- adding 0
- subtracting 0
- adding 1
- subtracting 1

Software Support

Use *MegaMath* for review and reinforcement of the concepts and skills presented in this lesson.

Challenge — Activity Card 1-3

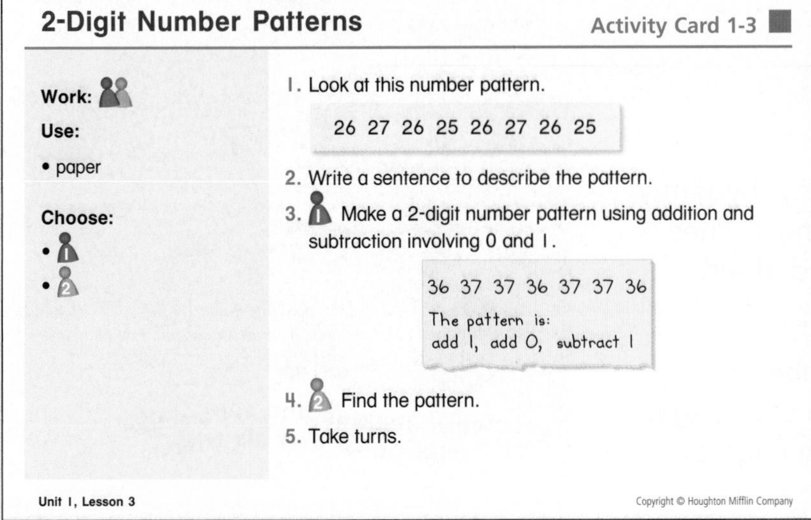

2-Digit Number Patterns Activity Card 1-3 ■

Work: (pair)
Use:
- paper

Choose:
- (child 1)
- (child 2)

1. Look at this number pattern.

   26 27 26 25 26 27 26 25

2. Write a sentence to describe the pattern.
3. Make a 2-digit number pattern using addition and subtraction involving 0 and 1.

   36 37 37 36 37 37 36

   The pattern is:
   add 1, add 0, subtract 1

4. Find the pattern.
5. Take turns.

Unit 1, Lesson 3 — Copyright © Houghton Mifflin Company

Activity Note Have children write a sentence to describe the pattern written by their partner.

Math Writing Prompt

Write About It Maria says that when you add 0 to 6 you get 60. Explain to Maria why this is not correct.

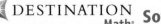

Software Support

Use *Destination Math* to take students beyond the concepts and skills presented in this lesson.

3 Homework

1–3 Homework **Goal:** Additional Practice

✓ Include children's completed Homework page as part of their portfolios.

1–3 Homework Name ____________

Add or subtract.

1. 7 + 1 = 8	5 − 0 = 5	0 + 1 = 1
2. 3 + 0 = 3	9 − 1 = 8	6 + 1 = 7
3. 0 + 7 = 7	2 − 0 = 2	4 + 1 = 5
4. 4 + 1 = 5	3 − 1 = 2	6 + 0 = 6
5. 9 + 0 = 9	5 − 1 = 4	9 + 1 = 10
6. 1 + 8 = 9	2 − 1 = 1	10 − 0 = 10
7. 1 + 3 = 4	4 − 0 = 4	8 − 0 = 8
8. 0 + 5 = 5	6 − 0 = 6	3 + 1 = 4
9. 5 + 1 = 6	7 − 1 = 6	6 − 1 = 5
10. 0 + 4 = 4	8 − 0 = 8	1 − 1 = 0

11. **On the Back** What happens when you add 0 to a number? Draw a picture to explain. Check children's drawings.

UNIT 1 LESSON 3 Add or Subtract 0 or 1 **5**

Homework and Remembering page 5

Home or School Activity

Literature Connection

Add and Subtract 1 Children can use the book *Oliver's Party,* by Jenny Fry and Angela Jolliffe, to practice adding 1 and subtracting 1. They can read this book on their own or it can be used as a read-aloud story.

If you read aloud the book, have children predict the number of children at the party before you read the last sentence on each page. Choose a volunteer to write the number sentence for each page as you finish reading it.

Relationships in Numbers to 10

Lesson Objectives

- **Show numbers in different ways.**
- **Represent numbers 6–10 as 5 and some more.**

Vocabulary

nickels
pennies
Penny Strips
Nickel Strips
number flash
Coin Strips

The Day at a Glance

Today's Goals	Materials	
1 Teaching the Lesson Show numbers from 6–10 as nickels and pennies (5s and 1s).	**Lesson Activities** Student Activity Book pp. 9–10 (includes Coin Strips) Homework and Remembering pp. 7–8 Real or play money Snack Bags	**Going Further** Activity Cards 1-4 *Jelly Beans for Sale* by Bruce McMillan Scissors Coin Match-Up Cards (TRB M2) Coin Strips Index cards Math Journals
2 Going Further ▸ Differentiated Instruction		
3 Homework and Spiral Review		

Use **Math Talk** today!

Keeping Skills Sharp

Quick Practice — 10 MINUTES

Goal: Use number flashes to count to 20

Number Flashes: Counting to 20 If necessary, review the procedure for counting to 20. (See Unit 1 Lesson 2.) Have two **Student Leaders** lead the counting. Children indicate each number by showing the appropriate number of fingers. For teen numbers, they flash ten to the left and extra ones to the right, saying each teen number in this form: *fourteen is ten and four.* They flash ten twice for the number 20.

Daily Routines

Money Routine Using the 120 Poster, Using the Money Flip Chart, Using the Number Path, Using Secret Code Cards (See pp. xxiii–xxv.)

▸ Led by **Student Leaders**

1 Teaching the Lesson

Activity

The Number Five and Nickels

 45 MINUTES

Goal: Show numbers from 6 to 10 as nickels and pennies (5s and 1s).

Materials: scissors (1 pair per child), Coin Strips (Student Activity Book page 9) (1 Nickel Strip per child), real or play money (5 pennies and 1 nickel per child), snack bags (1 per child)

NCTM Standard:
Number and Operations

Class Management

For this activity, each child will need 1 Nickel Strip, 1 loose nickel, and 5 loose pennies. If you wish, children can use the Nickel Strip and real or plastic coins instead of the paper coins. Store the other cut outs for later use. When you have finished the activity, have each child put their cut-out coins in a small bag. Collect and keep the bags. Children will use the coins at other times during the year.

The Learning Classroom

Building Concepts After the Quick Practice each day, ask a child to briefly summarize the main points of the previous day's work. This will help children remember what they learned and provide a transition into the new lesson.

▶ Cutting Coin Strips INDIVIDUALS

Have children cut out the Coin Strips on Student Activity Book page 9 or on TRB M1. Be sure they cut on the dotted lines.

Have children fold the Nickel Strips and Dime Strips lengthwise (on the solid lines) as shown below.

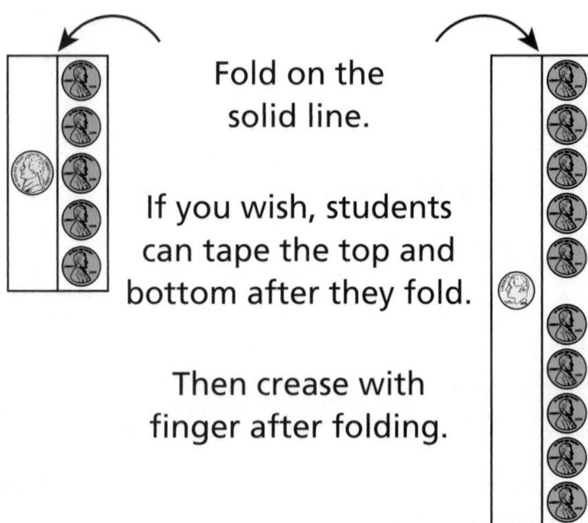

Fold on the solid line.
If you wish, students can tape the top and bottom after they fold.
Then crease with finger after folding.

▶ Show 8¢ with Coin Strips WHOLE CLASS

Penny Side of a Nickel Strip and Pennies Ask children to show 8¢ with a Nickel Strip (penny side up) and loose pennies.

- How can you make 8¢? 1 strip of 5 pennies and 3 loose pennies

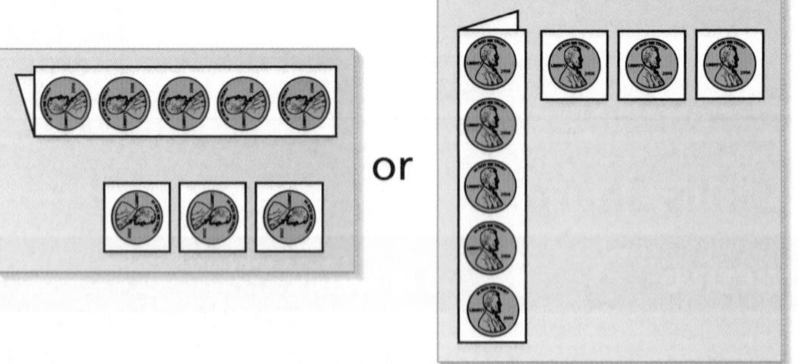

Then have children figure out how to show 6¢, 7¢, 9¢, and 10¢, using the penny side of the Nickel Strip and some loose pennies.

Nickel Strip and Pennies Ask children to show 8¢ again, this time using the nickel side of the Nickel Strip and loose pennies.

- Turn the Nickel Strip so that the nickel side is up. How can you make 8¢? 1 strip showing the nickel and 3 loose pennies

Then have the children figure out how to show 6¢, 7¢, 9¢, and 10¢, using the nickel side of the Nickel Strip and some loose pennies.

Nickel and Loose Pennies Now ask children to show the amounts using a nickel and pennies.

- Now let's use one of the nickels we cut out. We'll use that instead of the strip. How can we make 8¢ this time? 1 nickel and 3 loose pennies

Then have the children show 6¢, 7¢, 9¢, and 10¢, using the nickel and pennies.

Activity continued ▶

Differentiated Instruction

Extra Help If children are having difficulty using the Nickel Strip, you may wish to pair them with children that understand which side of the strip is supposed to be face up. Be sure the Student Helper only assists with the positioning of the Nickel Strip. This child should not be doing the work for the child needing help.

Ask questions such as:

- ▶ How many pennies do you need to show 7¢?
- ▶ How many nickels and pennies do you need to show 7¢?

English Language Learners

Model using the penny strip and loose pennies to make 8 cents. Have children turn to the nickel side of the strip.

- **Beginning** Say: **A *nickel* is 5 cents. A *nickel* and 3 pennies is 8 cents. 5, 6, 7, 8.** Have children repeat.
- **Intermediate** Ask: **What coin is this?** nickel **How many cents is a nickel?** 5 **How many cents is a nickel and 3 pennies?** 8 cents
- **Advanced** Ask: **What coins are these?** a nickel and 3 pennies **How many cents?** 8

 Teaching the Lesson (continued)

Class Management

Looking Ahead In the next lesson, children will use Secret Code Cards. These are on Student Activity pages 11–14 and on TRB M3–M6.

Children can use the cards on the Student Activity Book page, or they can take those home and you can make sturdy cards for classroom use by copying the copymaster onto card stock. In either case, you may want to set aside a time before you begin the lesson for children to cut out the Secret Code Cards.

If you have access to the *Math Expressions* materials kits, the Secret Code Cards are included, so you will not have to prepare these materials.

The Learning Classroom

Math Talk By discussing multiple strategies for math problems, children become aware of other children's thinking. As children better understand other children's thinking, they become better "helpers." Instead of showing how they would solve problems, they are able to look at another child's work to help them find the errors in their method.

▶ Show 8¢ with Fingers INDIVIDUALS

Now invite children to show the 8¢ with fingers as shown below.

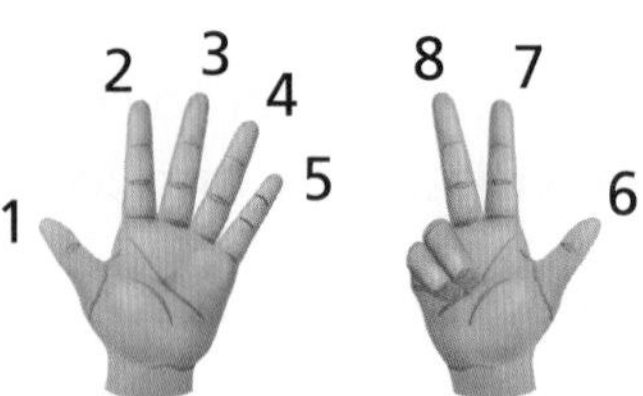

Then have them close one hand to hold 5 imaginary pennies (or a nickel), as shown below.

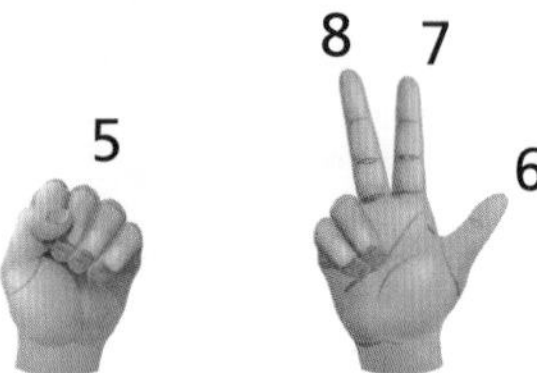

Now have children show 6¢, 7¢, 9¢, and 10¢, with their fingers.

▶ Show 8¢ with Circle Drawings INDIVIDUALS

Children can also make circle drawings of money values as shown below.

All Pennies

or

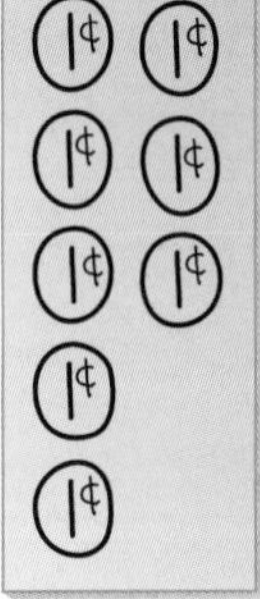

Nickel and Pennies

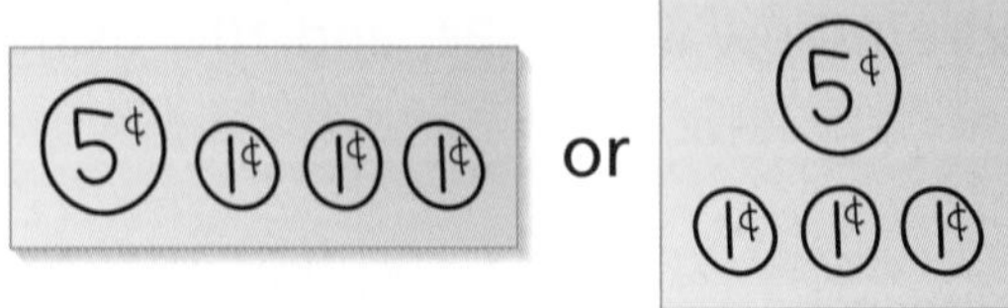

Notice that the pennies are shown in groups of 5 or less. Grouping objects in sets of 5 allows children to quickly count the number of objects in a set.

Continue having children make numbers between 5 and 10 with the nickel strips, nickels, fingers, and coin drawings to relate all of these visualizations.

2 Going Further

Intervention — Activity Card 1-4

Match Amounts — Activity Card 1-4 ●

Work:

Use:

- Coin Match-Up Cards
- scissors

Choose:

- 1
- 2

1. **Work Together** Cut the cards.
2. Mix the cards. Lay them face-down in equal rows.
3. Turn over 2 cards.

7¢

4. If the cards show the same amount, keep them. If not, turn the cards over.
5. Take turns.

Unit 1, Lesson 4

Activity Note Prepare 1 copy of Coin Match-Up cards (Teacher Resouce Book M2) for each pair. Guide children in playing the game.

Math Writing Prompt

Draw a Picture Draw a picture to show 9¢. Use 1 nickel and as many pennies as you need.

Software Support

Use *Soar to Success* for instruction of students needing targeted support for underlying skills.

On Level — Activity Card 1-4

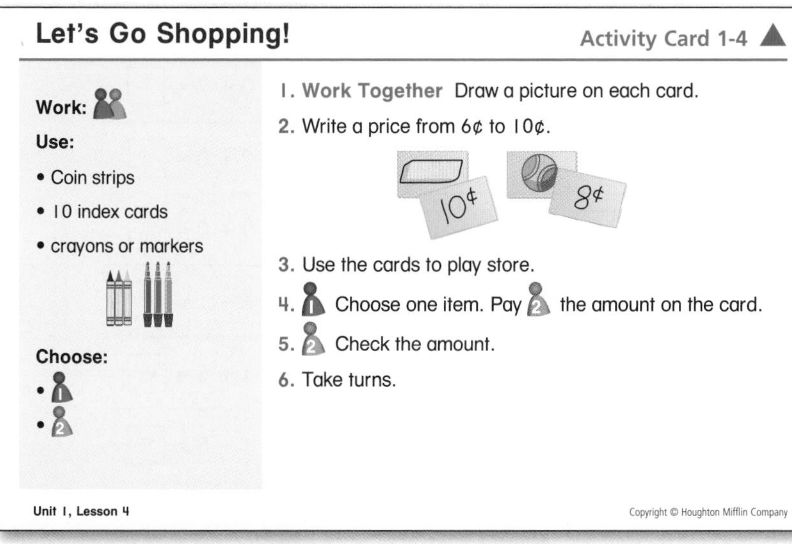

Let's Go Shopping! — Activity Card 1-4 ▲

Work:

Use:

- Coin strips
- 10 index cards
- crayons or markers

Choose:

- 1
- 2

1. **Work Together** Draw a picture on each card.
2. Write a price from 6¢ to 10¢.

10¢ 8¢

3. Use the cards to play store.
4. 1 Choose one item. Pay 2 the amount on the card.
5. 2 Check the amount.
6. Take turns.

Unit 1, Lesson 4

Activity Note Prepare 1 copy of Coin strips (Student Activity Book page 9) for each pair. Have children draw pencils, crayons, and small toys.

Math Writing Prompt

Write About It Use a nickel and pennies to describe two different ways to make 10¢.

Software Support

Use *MegaMath* for review and reinforcement of the concepts and skills presented in this lesson.

Challenge — Activity Card 1-4

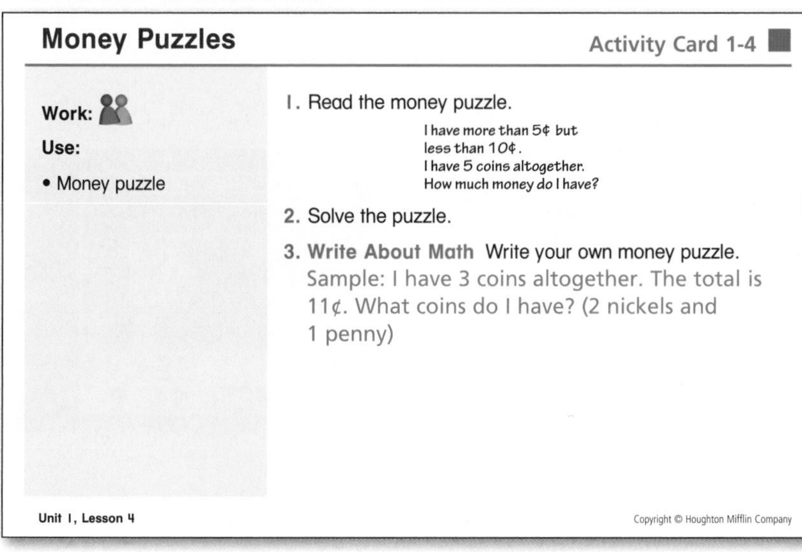

Money Puzzles — Activity Card 1-4 ■

Work:

Use:

- Money puzzle

1. Read the money puzzle.

   I have more than 5¢ but less than 10¢.
   I have 5 coins altogether.
   How much money do I have?

2. Solve the puzzle.
3. **Write About Math** Write your own money puzzle.
   Sample: I have 3 coins altogether. The total is 11¢. What coins do I have? (2 nickels and 1 penny)

Unit 1, Lesson 4

Activity Note Write a money puzzle using coins and amounts under 20¢. Have children solve each other's puzzles.

Math Writing Prompt

Explain Your Thinking Explain two ways to find 5 + 3.

Software Support

Use *Destination Math* to take students beyond the concepts and skills presented in this lesson.

3 Homework and Spiral Review

Goal: Additional Practice

This Homework page provides practice in solving addition and subtraction story problems.

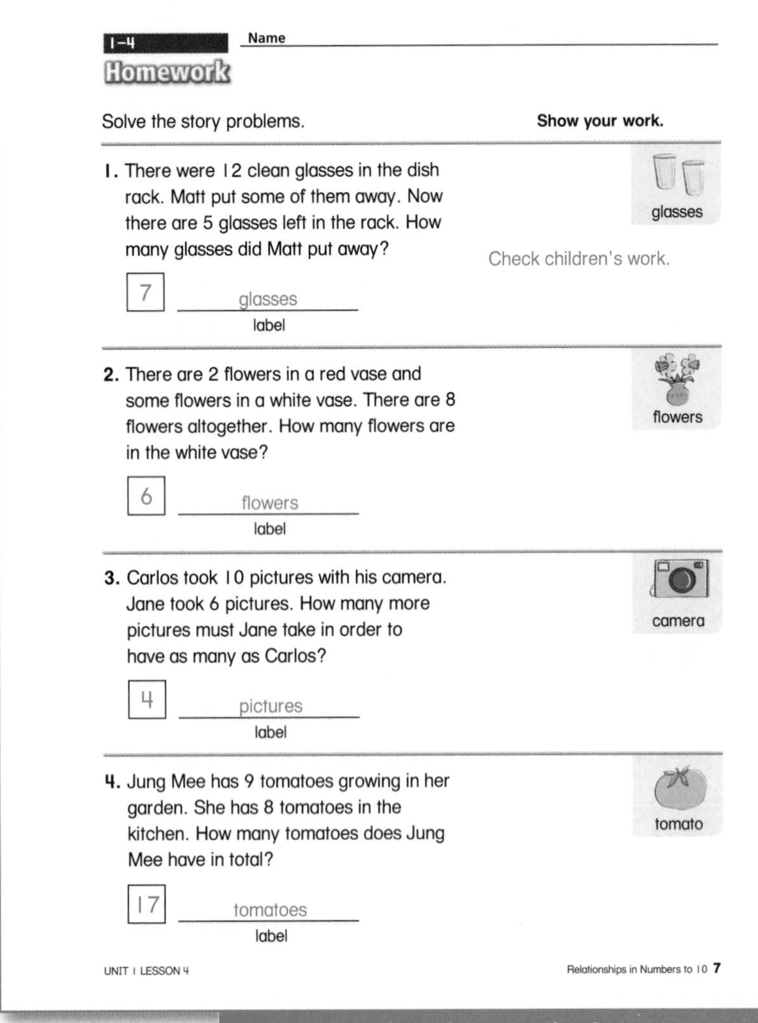

1-4 Name ____________

Homework

Solve the story problems. **Show your work.**

1. There were 12 clean glasses in the dish rack. Matt put some of them away. Now there are 5 glasses left in the rack. How many glasses did Matt put away?

glasses

Check children's work.

[7] glasses (label)

2. There are 2 flowers in a red vase and some flowers in a white vase. There are 8 flowers altogether. How many flowers are in the white vase?

flowers

[6] flowers (label)

3. Carlos took 10 pictures with his camera. Jane took 6 pictures. How many more pictures must Jane take in order to have as many as Carlos?

camera

[4] pictures (label)

4. Jung Mee has 9 tomatoes growing in her garden. She has 8 tomatoes in the kitchen. How many tomatoes does Jung Mee have in total?

tomato

[17] tomatoes (label)

UNIT 1 LESSON 4 Relationships in Numbers to 10 **7**

Homework and Remembering page 7

Goal: Spiral Review

This Remembering activity would be appropriate anytime after today's lesson.

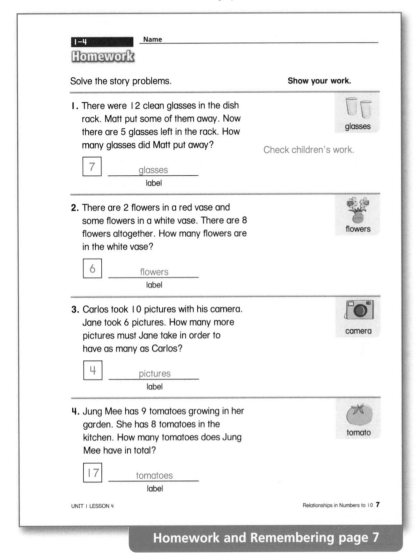

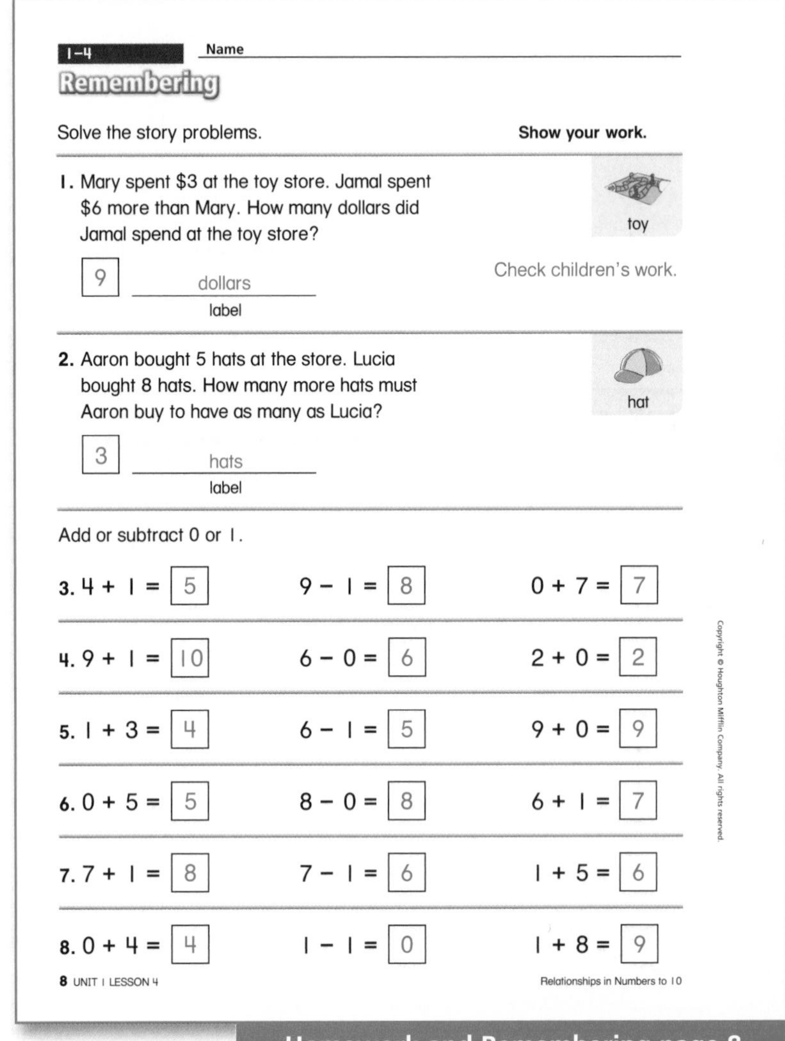

1-4 Name ____________

Remembering

Solve the story problems. **Show your work.**

1. Mary spent $3 at the toy store. Jamal spent $6 more than Mary. How many dollars did Jamal spend at the toy store?

toy

Check children's work.

[9] dollars (label)

2. Aaron bought 5 hats at the store. Lucia bought 8 hats. How many more hats must Aaron buy to have as many as Lucia?

hat

[3] hats (label)

Add or subtract 0 or 1.

3. 4 + 1 = [5]	9 − 1 = [8]	0 + 7 = [7]
4. 9 + 1 = [10]	6 − 0 = [6]	2 + 0 = [2]
5. 1 + 3 = [4]	6 − 1 = [5]	9 + 0 = [9]
6. 0 + 5 = [5]	8 − 0 = [8]	6 + 1 = [7]
7. 7 + 1 = [8]	7 − 1 = [6]	1 + 5 = [6]
8. 0 + 4 = [4]	1 − 1 = [0]	1 + 8 = [9]

8 UNIT 1 LESSON 4 Relationships in Numbers to 10

Homework and Remembering page 8

Home or School Activity

Literature Connection

Jelly Beans for Sale To review coin values and simple addition, read aloud Bruce McMillan's book *Jelly Beans for Sale* (Scholastic, 1996). This book illustrates buying different amounts of jelly beans with various combinations of coins. You may want to have children use real or play coins to model the transactions in the book.

Teens, Tens, and Dimes

Lesson Objectives

- Recognize teen numbers as a ten and some ones.
- Introduce word names for numbers to 20.

Vocabulary

teen numbers	dimes
tens	pattern
ones	Secret Code Cards
pennies	

The Day at a Glance

Today's Goals	Materials	
1 Teaching the Lesson **A1:** Represent teen numbers with pennies and Secret Code Cards. **A2:** Represent teen numbers, using money and Secret Code Cards. **A3:** Identify patterns in the word names for numbers to 20.	**Lesson Activities** Student Activity Book pp. 11–16 (includes Secret Code Cards) Homework and Remembering pp. 9–10 Quick Quiz 1 (Assessment Guide) Real or play money Demonstration Secret Code Cards (TRB M7–M22) Coin Strips Snack Bags Chart Paper	**Going Further** Activity Cards 1-5 Paper Counters Index cards Secret Code cards Math Journals
2 Going Further ▸ Differentiated Instruction		
3 Homework		

Use **Math Talk** today!

Keeping Skills Sharp

Quick Practice — 5 MINUTES

Goal: Use number flashes to count to 20

Number Flashes: Counting to 20 Have a **Student Leader** lead the count to 20. The children show fingers for each number. For the teen numbers, they flash ten to the left and extra ones to the right. (See Unit 1 Lesson 3.)

Daily Routines

Money Routine Using the 120 Poster, Using the Money Flip Chart, Using the Number Path, Using Secret Code Cards (See pp. xxiii–xxv.)

▸ Led by **Student Leaders**

1 Teaching the Lesson

Activity 1

The Secret Ten

 25 MINUTES

Goal: Represent teen numbers with pennies and Secret Code Cards.

Materials: real or play money (19 pennies per child), Secret Code Cards (Student Activity Book pages 11–14), Demonstration Secret Code Cards (TRB M7–M22)

 **NCTM Standard:**
Number and Operations

 **Class Management**

Work out a signal with the class to indicate when children should answer aloud. The signal should be obvious, such as dropping a raised arm or hand.

English Language Learners

Model setting up 14 pennies into a group of 10 and a group of 4.

- **Beginning** Say: **There are 10 pennies in this group. There are 4 pennies in this group. 10 plus 4 is 14.** Have children repeat.
- **Intermediate** Say: **There are 10 pennies in this group.** Ask: **How many pennies are in this group?** 4 **What is 10 and 4 more?** 14
- **Advanced** Ask: **How are the pennies grouped?** one group of 10, one group of 4 **What addition fact does this show?** 10 + 4 = 14

▶ Group 14 Pennies WHOLE CLASS

Tell children they are going to look at teen numbers today and use different ways to show the same number.

Have volunteers distribute 19 pennies to each group. Then have children count out 14 pennies. Then have them put 10 into one group and the remaining pennies into another group.

- You started with 14 pennies. You put 10 pennies in one group. How many pennies are in the second group? 4 pennies
- Let's say, *10 plus 4 is 14* together. (Give a hand signal of some kind so that all the children respond at the same time.) 10 + 4 is 14.

▶ Flash 14 Using Fingers WHOLE CLASS

Lead children in flashing 14 with their fingers. They should flash 10 fingers first (a bit to the left side) and then flash 4 fingers to the right side. As children flash 14 with their fingers, they say, "10 plus 4 is 14."

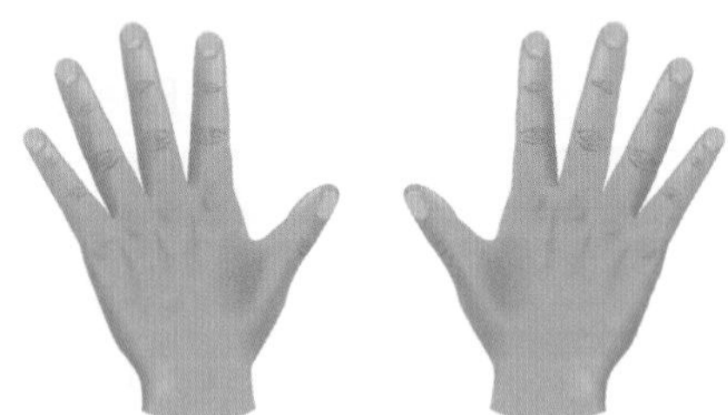

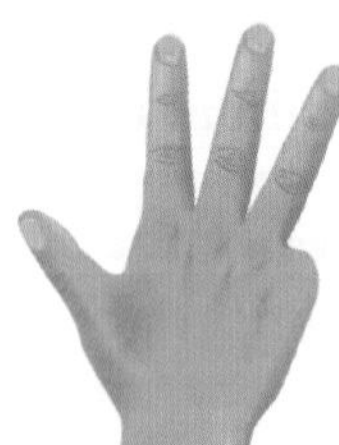

▶ Introduce Secret Code Cards WHOLE CLASS

Make sure each child has a set of Secret Code Cards for the numbers 1–10 or have them cut the cards out from Student Activity Book pages 11–12.

If the children already have Secret Code Cards to use in class they can use the ones on the student page to practice representing teen numbers at home with a family member.

The Demonstration Secret Code Cards needed for this activity can be cut out from TRB M7–M22.

Explain to children that these Secret Code Cards are special because they can show what teen numbers mean in another way. Point out that teen numbers really have a ten hiding inside.

- You just made the number 14 with pennies. You saw that 14 has 1 ten and 4 ones. You could also say that 14 is one group of ten and 4 extra ones.

Math Talk It is essential that you use "tens and ones" language and encourage children to do the same whenever you discuss numbers in terms of their place value.

Invite children to make 14 with their Secret Code Cards at their desks. Ask them to use the numbered side first. If a child figures out how to show 14 by putting the 4 on top of the 0 in the 10, encourage him or her to model this for the class. Have the child demonstrate with the small cards and then the large Demonstration Secret Code Cards.

Demonstrate how to show 14 if children do not figure it out on their own.

10 + 4 = 14

Activity continued ▶

Class Management

If children cut out the Secret Code Cards from Student Activity Book pages 11–14, you may wish to collect the cards for numbers 20–100 for later use. These cards will be used in the challenge activity on page 35.

If you have access to the *Math Expressions* materials kits, the Demonstration Secret Code Cards and Secret Code Cards are included, so you will not have to prepare these materials.

Teaching Note

Watch For! Some children may want to make 14 with the 1 and the 4 Secret Code Cards rather than with the 10 and the 4. Have children discuss whether it is all right to do this.

▶ What is the value of the digits in 14, 10 + 4 or 1 + 4?

The dots on the backs of the Secret Code Cards will help children avoid this error. The small numbers at the top left on the number side show the values of each of those digits.

Use this opportunity to discuss the small numbers in the upper left-hand corner of each Secret Code Card. The numbers allow children to see the value of each card even if it is partially covered by another.

In the case of the Secret Code Card for 10, the small numbers reinforce the idea that the 1 ten is really 10, not a single 1. Point out that the Secret Code Cards show the secret 10 that is hiding inside each teen number.

10 + 4 = 14

If no one thinks of it, you might suggest that children check their work by turning the cards over. The backs of the cards show that 10 dots plus 4 dots equals 14 dots.

Back of Cards

- Why do you think these are called Secret Code Cards? For 14 you only see the numbers 1 and 4, but really there is a 10 hiding inside. There is a secret or imaginary zero.

1 4 → 14

Have children continue using the loose pennies and Secret Code Cards to show other teen numbers as a ten and some ones. Relate each number to fingers: a ten flash and the ones number.

Activity 2

Show Teen Numbers

▶ Use Dime Strips and Pennies WHOLE CLASS

Be sure each child has a Dime Strip and 9 pennies.

Have children fold the Dime Strip lengthwise so the dime is on the underside and the pennies are on the top.

- How many pennies are on the strip? 10 pennies

Ask a child to name a teen number. Encourage the class to tell how they could make that number using the Dime Strip and some loose pennies.

Have children place the right amount of pennies near the Dime Strip to make the teen number. (See the illustration below for the number 16.)

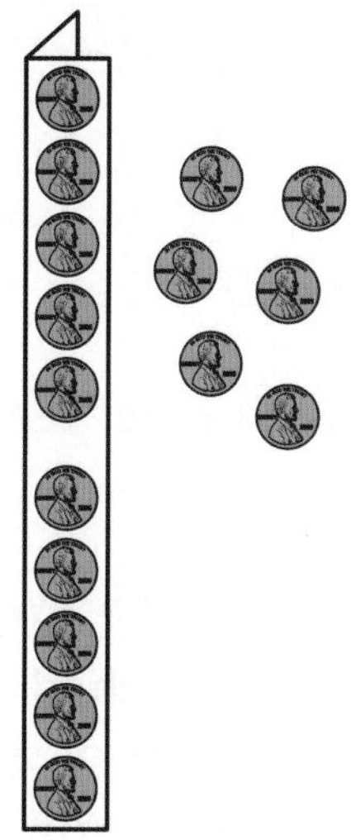

▶ Use Fingers WHOLE CLASS

Have children use their fingers to show the number. For example, to show the number 16, children should flash 10 fingers first to the left and then flash 6 fingers to the right. As they do this, on a given signal they say, "10 + 6 is 16."

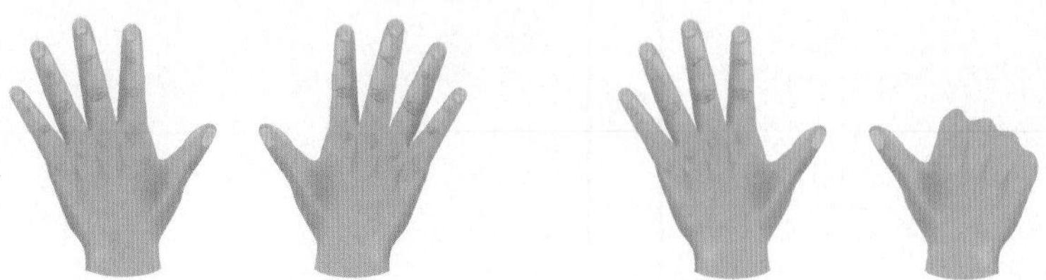

Activity continued ▶

 **15 MINUTES**

Goal: Represent teen numbers, using money and Secret Code Cards.

Materials: Coin Strips (from Unit 1 Lesson 4 or TRB M1) (1 Dime Strip per child), real or play money (1 dime, 9 pennies per child), Secret Code Cards 1–10 (Student Activity Book pages 11–12), Demonstration Secret Code Cards (TRB M7–M22)

 **NCTM Standard:**
Number and Operations

The Learning Classroom

Building Concepts This activity, which uses a Dime Strip showing 10 pennies and later showing one dime, helps children understand the value of a dime as 10 pennies.

The Learning Classroom

Math Talk Direct Math Talk in the classroom in order for it to be productive. Over time as children become more skilled at discussing their thinking and talking directly with each other, you can fade into the background. But you can continue to monitor, clarify, extend, and direct the math conversation so that it is productive for children.

The Learning Classroom

Building Concepts Seeing teen numbers as 1 ten and some ones is crucial for understanding math concepts in upcoming units. Children will practice this throughout the unit. By the end of the unit, most children should quickly be able to articulate the meaning of all teen numbers as 1 ten and some ones.

Children should understand that equations can be written in different ways. For example, 10 + 6 = 16 is the same as 16 = 10 + 6.

Class Management

Encourage children to store their Secret Code Cards in a snack bag after they have completed Activity 2 as they will need the cards for later lessons.

▶ Use Secret Code Cards WHOLE CLASS

Now have children make the number 16 with their Secret Code Cards. At the same time, have two **Student Leaders** make 16 with the Demonstration Secret Code Cards for the class to see.

Student Leaders show cards.

10 + 6 =

10 + 6 is ... (pause, then signal)

Student Leaders put cards together.

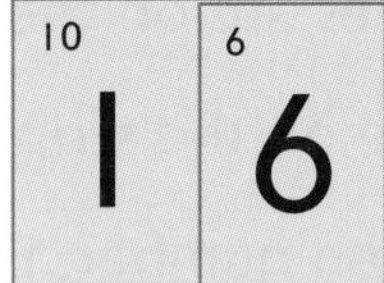

Class responds, "16."

Have the Student Leaders reverse the process.

16 =

16 is ... (pause, then signal)

10 + 6

Class responds, "10 and 6."

Continue in the same manner with other teen numbers. Be sure to work in both directions.

▶ Use Dime Strips and Dimes WHOLE CLASS

Dime Side of the Penny Strip Have children turn the Penny Strip over to the dime side and repeat the process of showing teen numbers. Select several teen numbers for them to show with money, Secret Code Cards, and fingers.

Here is an example for the number 16.

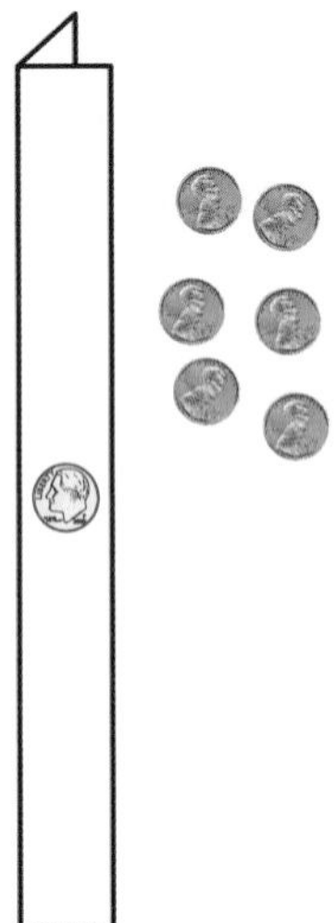

Real or Play Dime Repeat the above activity using coins.

Activity 3

Word Names for Numbers

▶ Discuss Patterns WHOLE CLASS

Give children a few minutes to look over Student Activity Book page 15.

1–5 Class Activity   Name

Vocabulary
patterns

▶ Discuss Patterns

Discuss the **patterns** you see.

1	one	11	eleven
2	two	12	twelve
3	three	13	thirteen
4	four	14	fourteen
5	five	15	fifteen
6	six	16	sixteen
7	seven	17	seventeen
8	eight	18	eighteen
9	nine	19	nineteen
10	ten	20	twenty

UNIT 1 LESSON 5   Teens, Tens, and Dimes 15

Student Activity Book page 15

- How are the numbers arranged on the page? The numbers 1 through 10 are written in the left column. The numbers 11 to 20 are written in the right column.

Be sure children understand which numbers are in the right column on the page and which numbers are in the left column.

- Look at the numbers 1 to 10 in the left column. What pattern do you notice? The numbers increase by one as they go down the page. Each number is one larger than the number above it.
- Look at the numbers 11 to 20 in the right column. What pattern do you notice? The numbers increase by one as they go down the page. Each number is one larger than the number above it.

Activity continued ▶

 15 MINUTES

Goal: Identify patterns in the word names for numbers to 20.

Materials: Student Activity Book pages 15–16, chart paper

 **NCTM Standard:**
Number and Operations

 **Ongoing Assessment**

On chart paper, create a list of the patterns that children identify. Keep adding to the list as children think of more patterns. At the end of the activity, have the class discuss the different patterns that were identified.

1 Teaching the Lesson (continued)

Teaching Note

What to Expect from Students How did your children explain their math thinking today? Children are often unfamiliar with this process; they are accustomed to providing math answers only. Encouraging children to talk more fully about their thinking will take repeated efforts. Expect this to be a building process that lasts for several weeks.

Early on, when a child provides an answer and then wants to sit down, try asking them to stay at the board and explain just one or two more things about the problem or math thinking first. For example, a child may be encouraged to tell more about a drawing they drew to solve a word problem or how they used the drawing to come up with an answer.

Math Talk Have children compare the numbers in the right and left columns. Ask them to describe any patterns.

- Each of the teen numbers in the right column has ten more dots (1 more ten-stick) than the number across from it in the left column.
- Each of the teen numbers in the right column is ten more than the number across from it in the left column.

Have children focus on the word names for the numbers, and encourage them to discuss any patterns they see.

- Which teen word names have the word *teen* in them? thirteen, fourteen, fifteen, sixteen, seventeen, eighteen, nineteen
- Which teen word names have the word name of another number in them? fourteen, sixteen, seventeen, eighteen, nineteen

▶ Word Names and Patterns INDIVIDUALS

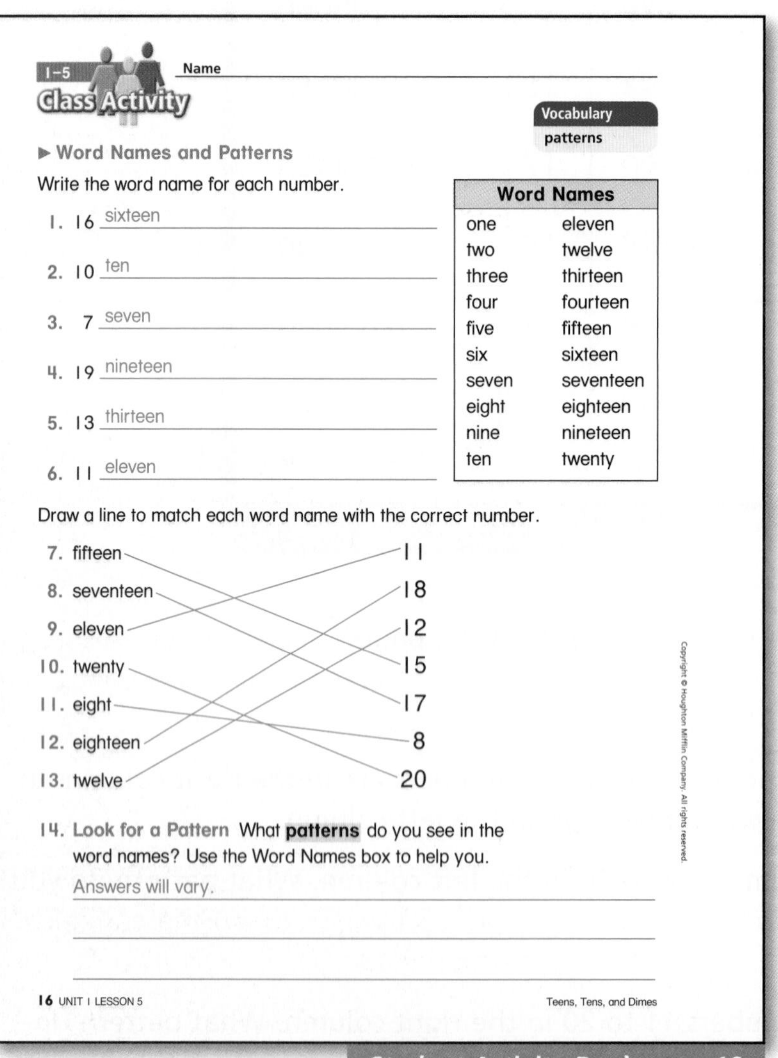

1-5 Class Activity

Name ____________

Vocabulary
patterns

▶ Word Names and Patterns

Write the word name for each number.

1. 16 sixteen
2. 10 ten
3. 7 seven
4. 19 nineteen
5. 13 thirteen
6. 11 eleven

Word Names	
one	eleven
two	twelve
three	thirteen
four	fourteen
five	fifteen
six	sixteen
seven	seventeen
eight	eighteen
nine	nineteen
ten	twenty

Draw a line to match each word name with the correct number.

7. fifteen — 11
8. seventeen — 18
9. eleven — 12
10. twenty — 15
11. eight — 17
12. eighteen — 8
13. twelve — 20

14. Look for a Pattern What **patterns** do you see in the word names? Use the Word Names box to help you.
Answers will vary.

Student Activity Book page 16

Quick Quiz

See Assessment Guide for Unit 1 Quick Quiz 1.

Intervention

Activity Card 1-5

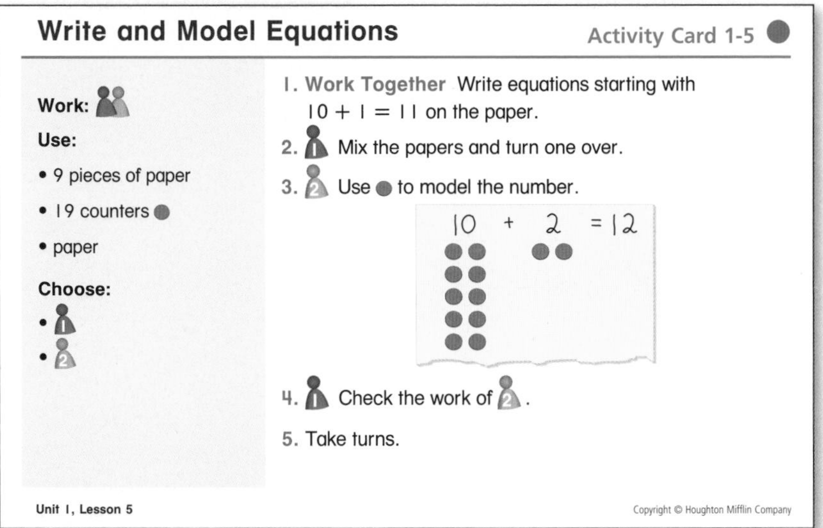

Write and Model Equations Activity Card 1-5

Work: (pair)

Use:
- 9 pieces of paper
- 19 counters
- paper

Choose:
- 1
- 2

1. **Work Together** Write equations starting with 10 + 1 = 11 on the paper.
2. (1) Mix the papers and turn one over.
3. (2) Use counters to model the number.

10 + 2 = 12

4. (1) Check the work of (2).
5. Take turns.

Unit 1, Lesson 5

Copyright © Houghton Mifflin Company

Activity Note Each pair needs 9 sheets of paper and 19 counters. Guide children to write equations 10 + 1 = 11 to 10 + 9 = 19 on paper.

Math Writing Prompt

Write About It Describe how the numbers 2 and 12 are the same. Then describe how they are different.

Software Support

Use *Soar to Success* for instruction of students needing targeted support for underlying skills.

On Level

Activity Card 1-5

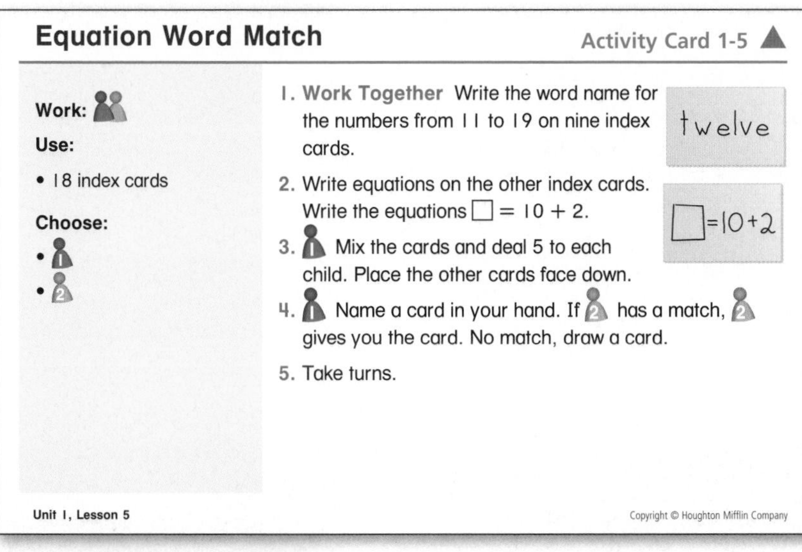

Equation Word Match Activity Card 1-5

Work: (pair)

Use:
- 18 index cards

Choose:
- 1
- 2

1. **Work Together** Write the word name for the numbers from 11 to 19 on nine index cards.
2. Write equations on the other index cards. Write the equations □ = 10 + 2.
3. (1) Mix the cards and deal 5 to each child. Place the other cards face down.
4. (1) Name a card in your hand. If (2) has a match, (2) gives you the card. No match, draw a card.
5. Take turns.

twelve

□=10+2

Unit 1, Lesson 5

Copyright © Houghton Mifflin Company

Activity Note Each pair needs 18 index cards. Check that children write the number words and equations on the index cards.

Math Writing Prompt

Compare the Numbers Which number is greater? Explain how you know.

1 ten + 5 ones = □

1 ten + 8 ones = □

Software Support

Use *MegaMath* for review and reinforcement of the concepts and skills presented in this lesson.

Challenge

Activity Card 1-5

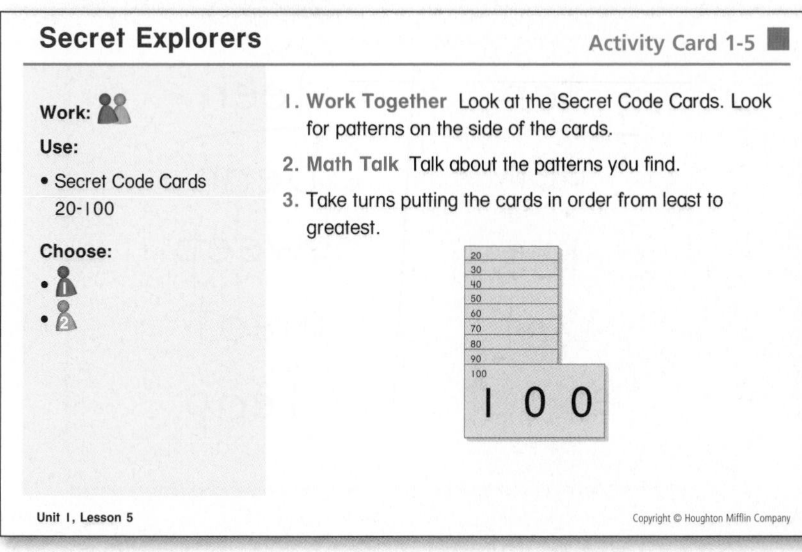

Secret Explorers Activity Card 1-5

Work: (pair)

Use:
- Secret Code Cards 20-100

Choose:
- 1
- 2

1. **Work Together** Look at the Secret Code Cards. Look for patterns on the side of the cards.
2. **Math Talk** Talk about the patterns you find.
3. Take turns putting the cards in order from least to greatest.

20 30 40 50 60 70 80 90 100

1 0 0

Unit 1, Lesson 5

Copyright © Houghton Mifflin Company

Activity Note Prepare Secret Code Cards 20–100 (Student Activity Book pp. 11–12) for each pair.

Math Writing Prompt

Explain Your Thinking Look at the Secret Code Cards for the numbers 20–100. Write three things you notice.

Software Support

Use *Destination Math* to take students beyond the concepts and skills presented in this lesson.

3 Homework

Goal: Additional Practice

This Homework page provides practice working with teen numbers.

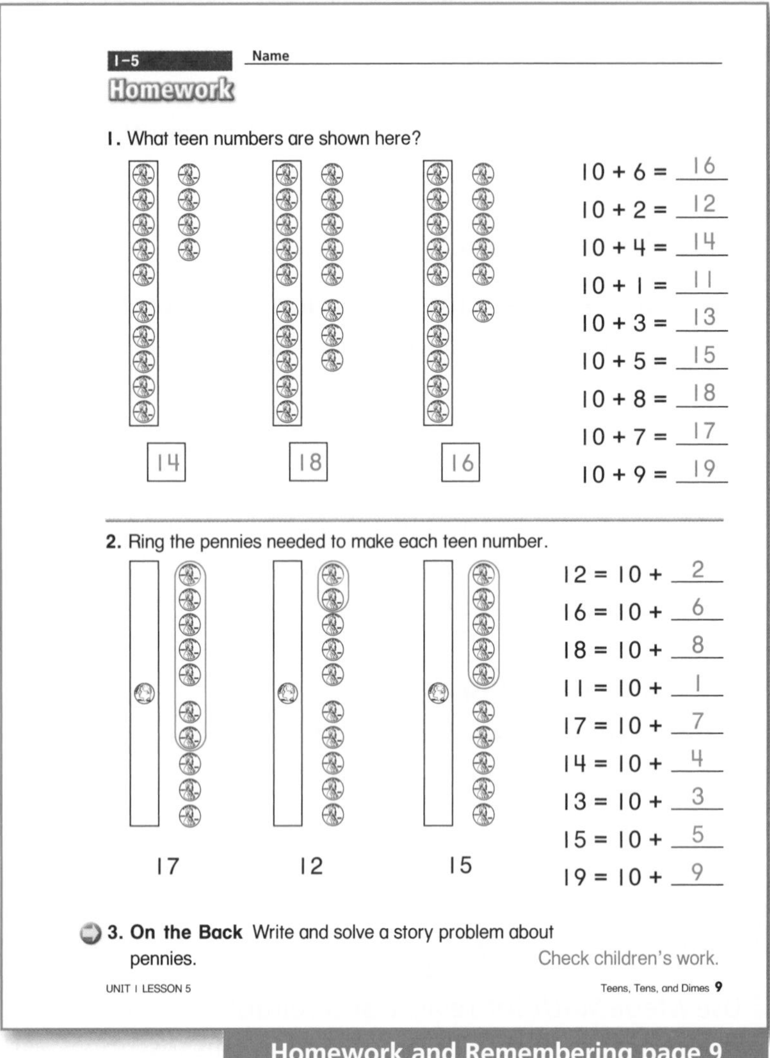

1–5 Homework Name ____________________

1. What teen numbers are shown here?

14 18 16

10 + 6 = 16
10 + 2 = 12
10 + 4 = 14
10 + 1 = 11
10 + 3 = 13
10 + 5 = 15
10 + 8 = 18
10 + 7 = 17
10 + 9 = 19

2. Ring the pennies needed to make each teen number.

17 12 15

12 = 10 + 2
16 = 10 + 6
18 = 10 + 8
11 = 10 + 1
17 = 10 + 7
14 = 10 + 4
13 = 10 + 3
15 = 10 + 5
19 = 10 + 9

3. **On the Back** Write and solve a story problem about pennies.

Check children's work.

UNIT 1 LESSON 5 Teens, Tens, and Dimes 9

Homework and Remembering page 9

Home or School Activity

Language Arts Connection

Short e, Long e Have children say the words *ten* and *teen* aloud. Both words have e as the vowel but the e makes a different sound in each word. *Ten* has a short e sound and *teen* has a long *e* sound. Have students make two lists—a list of short *e* words and a list of long *e* words.

ten	teen
pen	bean
let	sweep
wet	meat
swept	leap

Break-Aparts of 10

Vocabulary

break-aparts
partners
Math Mountain
switch the partners
equation
teen numbers

Lesson Objective

- **Identify the break-aparts of 10.**

The Day at a Glance

Today's Goals	Materials	
1 Teaching the Lesson **A1:** Find the break-aparts of 10. **A2:** Record the break-aparts of 10 using Math Mountains.	**Lesson Activities** Student Activity Book pp. 17–18 (includes Family Letter) Homework and Remembering pp. 11–12 MathBoard materials	**Going Further** Activity Cards 1-6 Counters MathBoard materials Break-apart stick Game Cards (TRB M23) Math Journals
2 Going Further ▸ Differentiated Instruction		
3 Homework and Spiral Review		

Use Math Talk today!

Keeping Skills Sharp

Quick Practice 5 MINUTES

Goal: Make and "unmake" teen numbers.

Materials: Demonstration Secret Code Cards

The Teen Machine Have **Student Leaders** show the 10 and 8 Demonstration Secret Code Cards and say, "10 and 8 is . . ." and give the signal. After the class responds, "18," the Student Leaders slide the cards together to make 18.

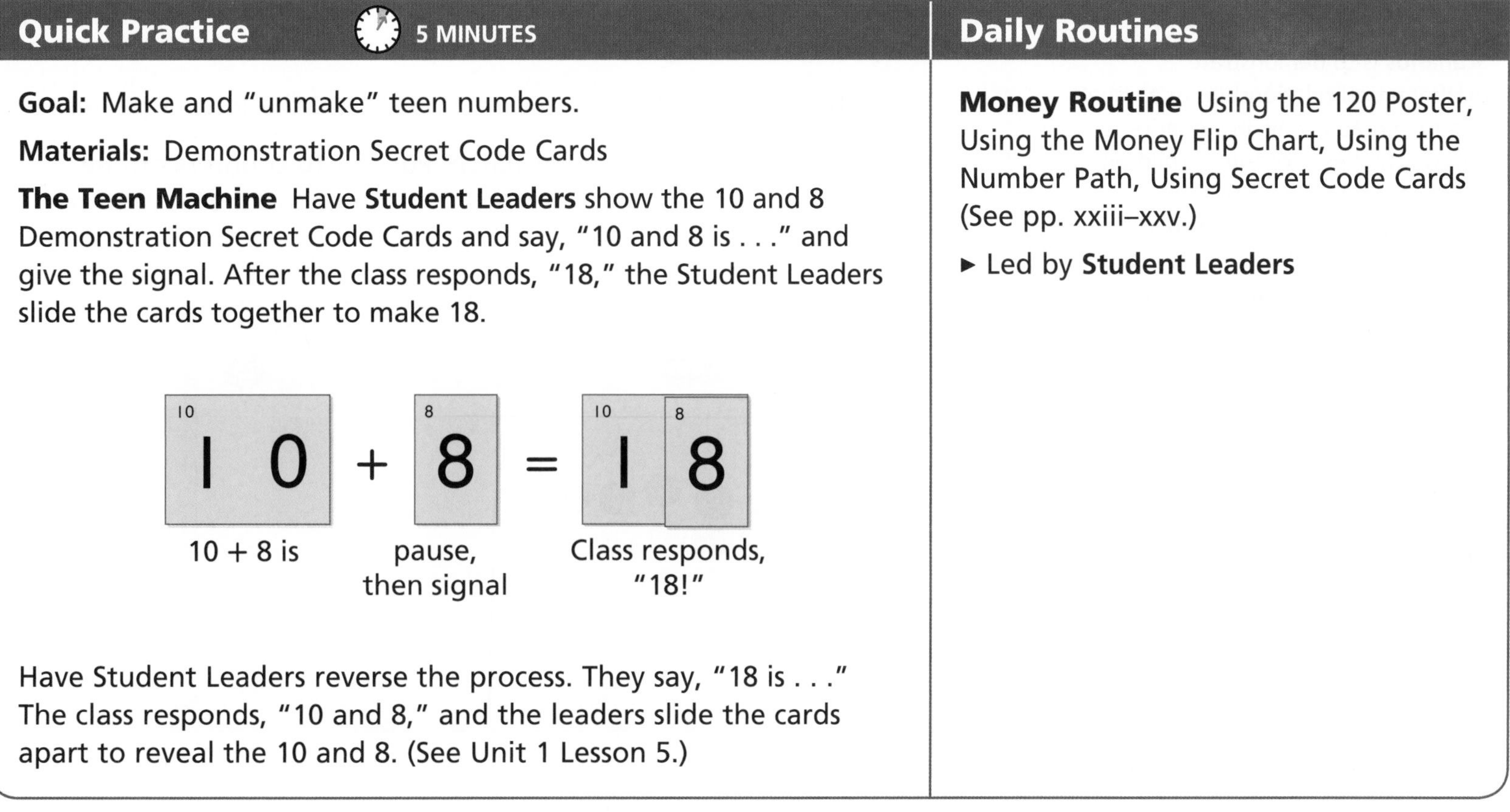

10 + 8 is — pause, then signal — Class responds, "18!"

Have Student Leaders reverse the process. They say, "18 is . . ." The class responds, "10 and 8," and the leaders slide the cards apart to reveal the 10 and 8. (See Unit 1 Lesson 5.)

Daily Routines

Money Routine Using the 120 Poster, Using the Money Flip Chart, Using the Number Path, Using Secret Code Cards (See pp. xxiii–xxv.)

▸ Led by **Student Leaders**

1 Teaching the Lesson

Activity

Break-Apart Scenario: Rabbits in the Garden

 30 MINUTES

Goal: Find the break-aparts of 10.

Materials: Counters (10 per child), MathBoard materials

 **NCTM Standards:**
Number and Operations
Algebra

 **Class Management**

If children used *Math Expressions* last year or are already familiar with the material presented in Lessons 6, 7, and 8, you may collapse the activities into two days instead of three. Be sure to include enough practice.

The Learning Classroom

Scenarios The main purpose of **Scenarios** is to demonstrate mathematical relationships in a visual and memorable way. In scenario-based activities, a group of children are called to the front of the classroom to act out a particular situation or they do so in story form. Scenarios are useful when a new concept is being introduced for the first time. They are especially valuable for demonstrating the physical reality that underlies such math concepts as embedded numbers (break-aparts) and regrouping. You can have 10 children act out the rabbits in the garden at any point during the lesson if you wish.

▶ Introduce the Garden Scenario WHOLE CLASS

Draw the "garden" pictured below on the classroom board. Sketch a carrot on one side of the garden and a head of lettuce on the other side. Ask children to draw the same garden on their MathBoards.

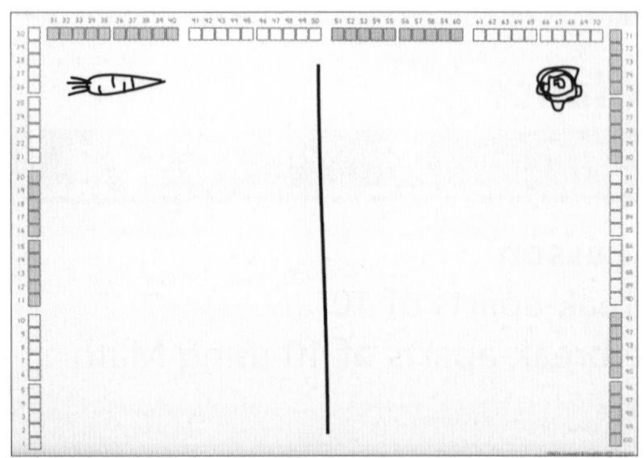

Be sure children position their boards as shown. Suggest they draw something long on the left side to represent the carrot and something round on the right side to represent the lettuce.

Use the classroom board to demonstrate and explain the activity to the class.

- Pretend your MathBoard is a garden. The 10 counters are 10 rabbits. They all live in the garden.
- The rabbits like to play in the carrot patch and the lettuce patch.
- Show the rabbits in the carrot patch. Put the 10 counters on the carrot side of the board. (Draw the 10 counters on the classroom board.)

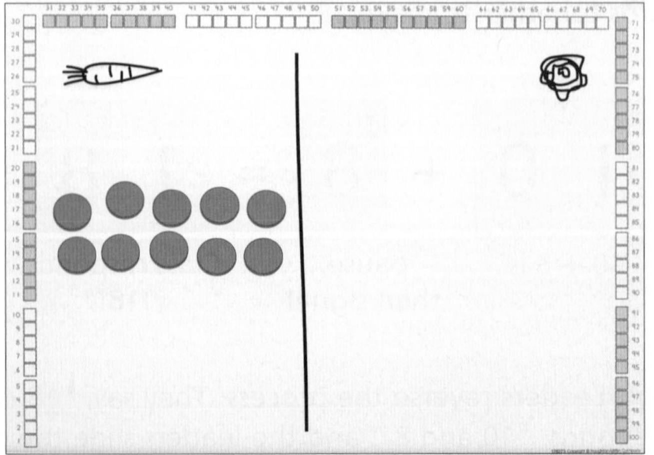

▶ Find a Break-Apart of 10 WHOLE CLASS

Have children use the MathBoards and counters to model the action of the rabbits.

- Let's find one way the 10 rabbits can play in the garden. Some will be in the carrot patch, and some will be in the lettuce patch.
- Move 1 of the counters from the carrot patch to the lettuce patch.

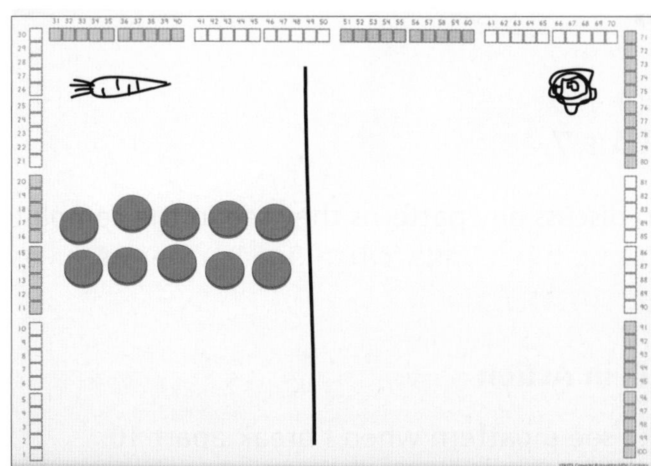

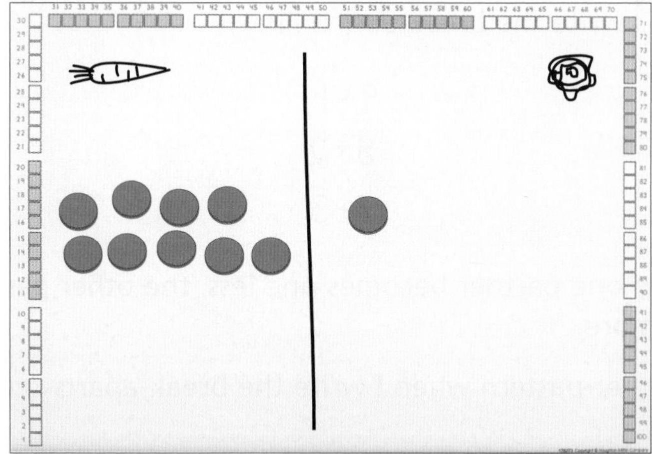

Move one counter from the carrot side, on the board, and draw it in on the lettuce side.

- Now how many rabbits are still in the carrot patch? 9
- How many are in the lettuce patch? 1
- How many rabbits are there altogether? 10

Write the break-apart on the board.

$$10 = 9 + 1$$

- 9 rabbits are in the carrot patch. 1 rabbit is in the lettuce patch.
- 9 and 1 are *partners* of 10.

Activity continued ▶

The Learning Classroom

Building Concepts It is important for children to see equations written in different ways so they understand equivalence. Write the break-aparts with the total first in the equation (10 = 9 + 1) because we are starting with the total (10) and breaking it into the parts (9 and 1).

Differentiated Instruction

English Learners Drawing or acting out scenarios is especially helpful to English Learners who will benefit from a visual representation of a concept.

English Language Learners

Set up math boards example with 9 rabbits in the carrot patch and 1 in the lettuce patch.

- **Beginning** Say: **10 rabbits are in the garden. One moved to the lettuce patch. 9 in the carrots + 1 in the lettuce is 10 rabbits.** Have children repeat.
- **Intermediate** Say: **10 rabbits are in the garden.** Ask: **How many in the carrot patch?** 9 **How many in the lettuce patch?** 1 **What is 9 + 1?** 10
- **Advanced** Ask: **How many rabbits are in the garden?** 10 **How do you know?** 9 in the carrots + 1 in the lettuce = 10

The Learning Classroom

Building Concepts The concept that a larger number can be broken apart into two smaller numbers (in this case, 1-digit "partners" of the larger number) is necessary for the Make a Ten addition strategies children will learn later in this unit. Children will use their knowledge of break-aparts to help understand related addition and subtraction. Understanding break-aparts also helps children solve more complex story problems.

Teaching Note

What to Expect from Students Children may suggest using 0 and 10 as break-aparts of 10. Zero is a partner of every number. It is important for children to learn the partners of numbers but including 0 in the lists interferes with learning the other partners. Share this with students. Yes, there is a nice pattern with $n = 0 + n$ and $n = n + 0$ for any number n. But our partner lists will not include these partners because it distracts us from learning the other partners.

▶ Record Break-Aparts of 10 WHOLE CLASS

Have children work as a class to discover the remaining break-aparts of the number 10 by breaking the ten rabbits apart into two groups. Update the drawing and write the break-aparts on the board.

Write the list of the break-aparts on the board as children suggest them. As you do, leave space so that the final list will be in order when it is complete.

$10 = 9 + 1$

$10 = 7 + 3$ — Spaces left for missing equations.

$10 = 4 + 6$
$10 = 3 + 7$

Ask children to discuss any patterns they see in the completed list of break-aparts. Sample response: When one partner becomes 1 less, the other partner becomes 1 more.

Math Talk in Action

Jeremy: I think I see a pattern when I break apart 10.

Ana: What is it?

Jeremy: When I write the break-aparts like,

$9 + 1$
$8 + 2$
$7 + 3$

I see that when one partner becomes one less, the other partner becomes one more.

Ana: I see another pattern when I write the break-aparts under each other like this:

$10 = 9 + 1$
$10 = 8 + 2$
$10 = 7 + 3$
$10 = 6 + 4$

I see that the first partner is counting backward.

Jeremy: And the other partner is counting forward!

▶ Switch the Partners WHOLE CLASS

Direct children to the completed list of break-aparts on the board.

- Can you name break-aparts that have the same partners but in a different order? Possible example: $10 = 1 + 9$ and $10 = 9 + 1$
- We call this *switching the partners* because the partners of 10, 1 and 9, are switched to make 9 and 1.

Draw a curved line to show the equations in which the partners were switched.

$$\begin{aligned} 10 &= 9 + 1 \\ 10 &= 8 + 2 \\ 10 &= 7 + 3 \\ 10 &= 6 + 4 \\ 10 &= 5 + 5 \\ 10 &= 4 + 6 \\ 10 &= 3 + 7 \\ 10 &= 2 + 8 \\ 10 &= 1 + 9 \end{aligned}$$

Ask children to name other equations (from this list) in which partners were switched and draw lines to match them.

Record the matching equations on the board.

$10 = 9 + 1$ and $10 = 1 + 9$
$10 = 8 + 2$ and $10 = 2 + 8$
$10 = 7 + 3$ and $10 = 3 + 7$
$10 = 6 + 4$ and $10 = 4 + 6$

Pay special attention to the $5 + 5 = 10$ break-apart.

- One of the equations does not have a match. Which one is it? $5 + 5 = 10$
- Why doesn't this equation have a match? If you switch the partners, it's still the same.

If there is extra time, do some oral practice with partners of 10. You give one partner and the class gives the other. Children can use fingers as necessary to see the partners of 10.

The Learning Classroom

Math Talk Elicit children's ideas when introducing a new topic. Children will become more engaged if they believe their contributions will be heard. You may want to allow for interruptions from children during the explanation of the content. When this occurs, decide what is important to continue exploring, but allow children to own new ideas or strategies. Children may volunteer to explain strategies that you are about to teach.

Record Break-Aparts as Math Mountains

20 MINUTES

Goal: Record the break-aparts of 10 using Math Mountains.

Materials: MathBoard materials

NCTM Standard:
Number and Operations

Differentiated Instruction

English Learners Help English learners understand Math Mountains.

- Invite children who speak another language to say Math Mountain in their home language or to make up their own term in their own language for Math Mountain.
- Make a Math Mountain poster for your room and have children refer to the poster.

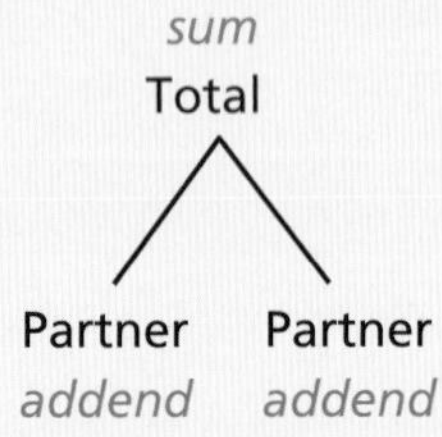

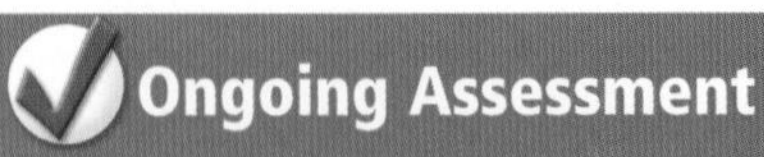

Ongoing Assessment

Draw Math Mountains with 10 as the total. Fill in one partner and ask children to find the missing partner.

▶ Introduce Math Mountains WHOLE CLASS

Erase the list of break-aparts from the previous activity.

Invite children to generate the first break-apart again.

- Put all of the rabbits on the carrot patch side. Then move 1 rabbit to the lettuce patch.

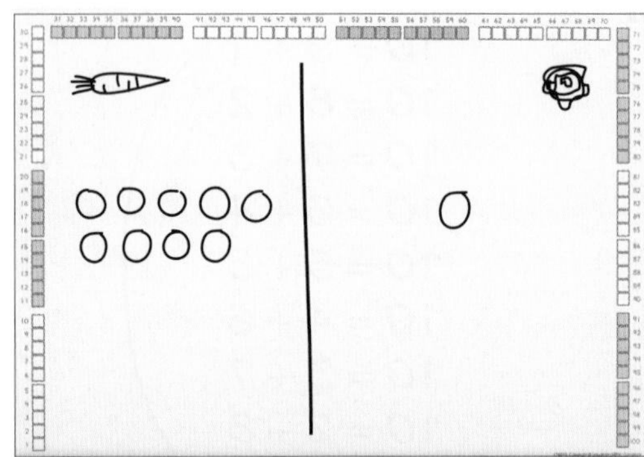

- What break-apart did you show? 10 = 9 + 1

Write the equation on the board and draw the Math Mountain next to the equation.

$10 = 9 + 1$

10
□ □

- Here's another way for us to think about this break-apart of 10. We can draw a Math Mountain with 10 at the top.
- Pretend that the 10 breaks apart into two partners. These partners roll down the mountain, one partner to one side and the other partner to the other side.
- What would the mountain look like now? What numbers would be at the bottom of the mountain? 9 and 1

Write the partners 9 and 1 in the boxes.

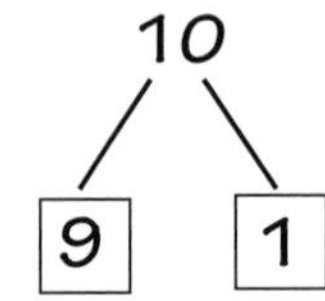

▶ Record Break-Aparts PAIRS

Invite children to work in pairs to generate the remaining break-aparts of 10. Have children draw the break-aparts as Math Mountains.

Circulate around the room to see that children are drawing the mountains correctly with the 10 at the top and the partners on the bottom.

2 Going Further

Differentiated Instruction

Intervention — Activity Card 1-6

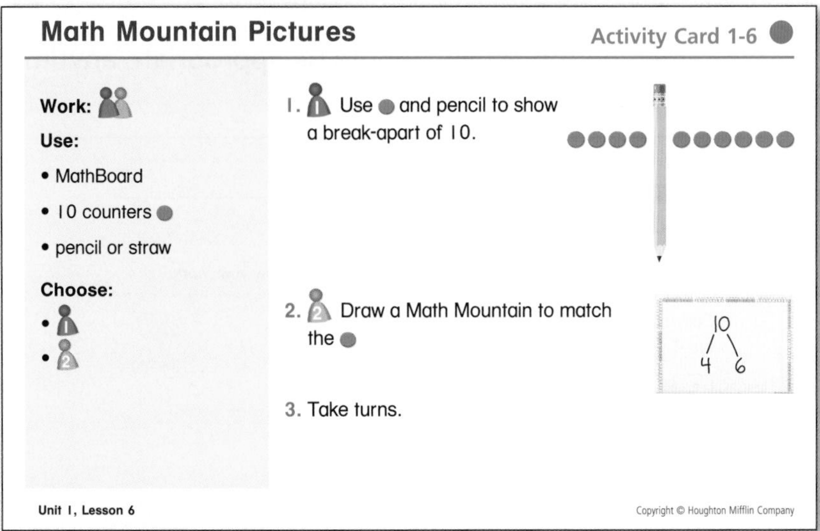

Math Mountain Pictures — Activity Card 1-6

Work: Use:
- MathBoard
- 10 counters
- pencil or straw

Choose:

1. Use ● and pencil to show a break-apart of 10.
2. Draw a Math Mountain to match the ●
3. Take turns.

Unit 1, Lesson 6 — Copyright © Houghton Mifflin Company

Activity Note Each pair needs 10 counters, a pencil or straw, and MathBoard Materials. Guide children to show a break-apart of 10.

Math Writing Prompt

Draw or Explain How can you use 10 counters to find two partners of 10? Use words or pictures to explain.

Software Support

Use *Soar to Success* for instruction of students needing targeted support for underlying skills.

On Level — Activity Card 1-6

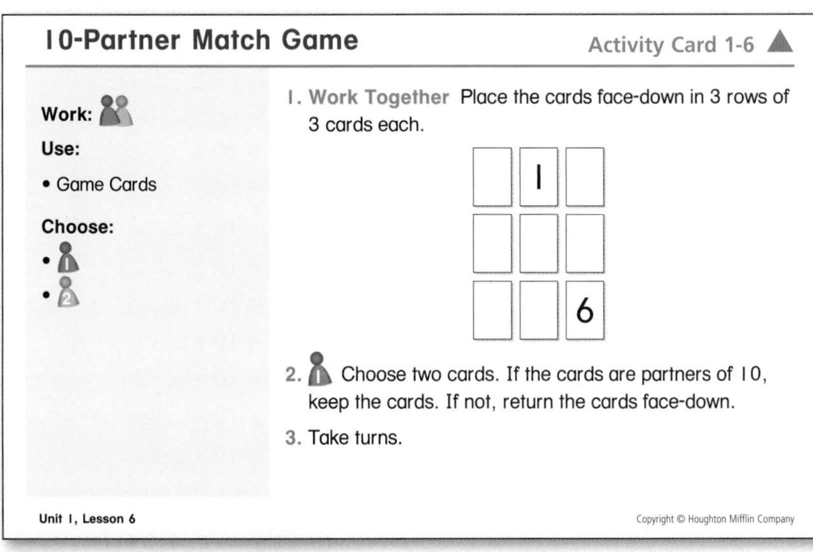

10-Partner Match Game — Activity Card 1-6

Work: Use:
- Game Cards

Choose:

1. Work Together Place the cards face-down in 3 rows of 3 cards each.
2. Choose two cards. If the cards are partners of 10, keep the cards. If not, return the cards face-down.
3. Take turns.

Unit 1, Lesson 6 — Copyright © Houghton Mifflin Company

Activity Note Prepare 1 set of Game Cards (TRB M23) per pair. Have partners check the work of each other as they look for partners of 10.

Math Writing Prompt

Find the Unknown Partner

$10 = 2 + \square$

Explain how to find the unknown partner of 10.

Software Support

Use *MegaMath* for review and reinforcement of the concepts and skills presented in this lesson.

Challenge — Activity Card 1-6

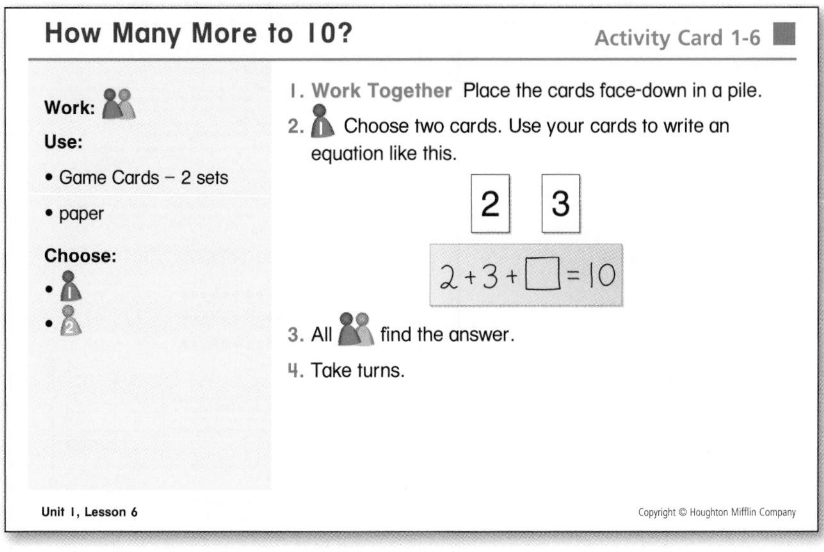

How Many More to 10? — Activity Card 1-6

Work: Use:
- Game Cards – 2 sets
- paper

Choose:

1. Work Together Place the cards face-down in a pile.
2. Choose two cards. Use your cards to write an equation like this.
3. All find the answer.
4. Take turns.

Unit 1, Lesson 6 — Copyright © Houghton Mifflin Company

Activity Note Prepare two sets of Game Cards (TRB M23) for each pair. Guide children to find a third number to equal 10 in all.

Math Writing Prompt

Compare Math Mountains Make all the Math Mountains for the number 10. Tell how they are alike and how they are different.

Software Support

Use *Destination Math* to take students beyond the concepts and skills presented in this lesson.

3 Homework and Spiral Review

Goal: Additional Practice

This Homework page provides practice in break-aparts and partners of 10.

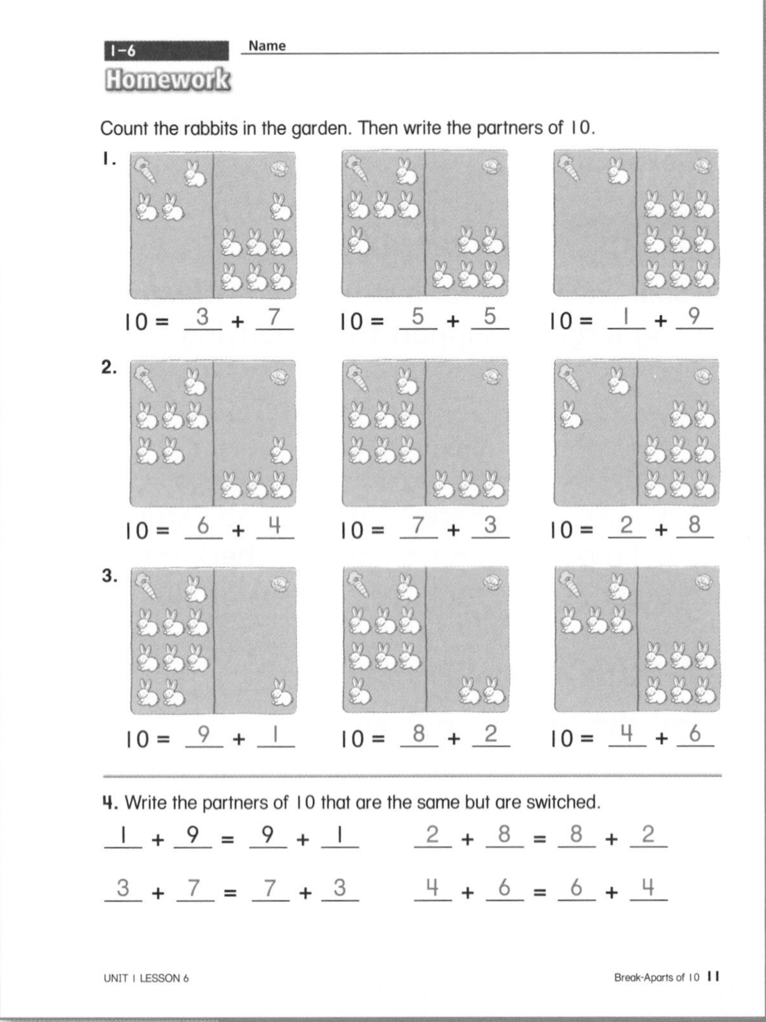

1-6 Name ______

Homework

Count the rabbits in the garden. Then write the partners of 10.

1. 10 = 3 + 7   10 = 5 + 5   10 = 1 + 9

2. 10 = 6 + 4   10 = 7 + 3   10 = 2 + 8

3. 10 = 9 + 1   10 = 8 + 2   10 = 4 + 6

4. Write the partners of 10 that are the same but are switched.

1 + 9 = 9 + 1   2 + 8 = 8 + 2

3 + 7 = 7 + 3   4 + 6 = 6 + 4

UNIT 1 LESSON 6   Break-Aparts of 10 11

Homework and Remembering page 11

Goal: Spiral Review

This Remembering activity would be appropriate anytime after today's lesson.

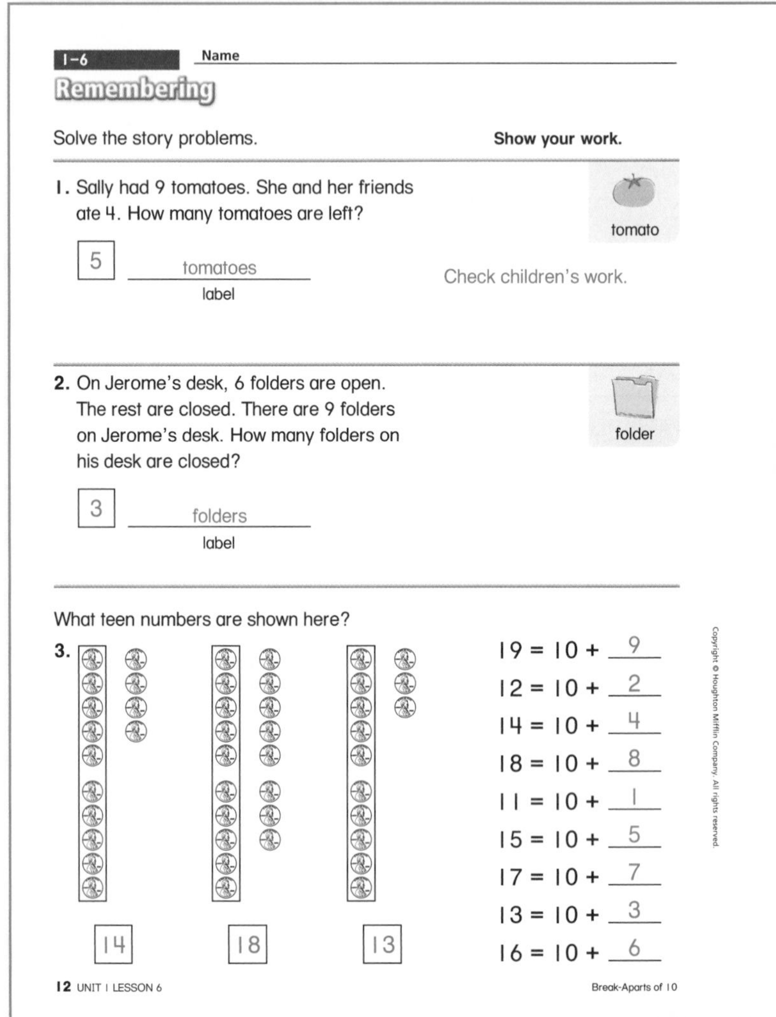

1-6 Name ______

Remembering

Solve the story problems. **Show your work.**

1. Sally had 9 tomatoes. She and her friends ate 4. How many tomatoes are left?

tomato

5 tomatoes (label)

Check children's work.

2. On Jerome's desk, 6 folders are open. The rest are closed. There are 9 folders on Jerome's desk. How many folders on his desk are closed?

folder

3 folders (label)

What teen numbers are shown here?

3. 14   18   13

19 = 10 + 9
12 = 10 + 2
14 = 10 + 4
18 = 10 + 8
11 = 10 + 1
15 = 10 + 5
17 = 10 + 7
13 = 10 + 3
16 = 10 + 6

12 UNIT 1 LESSON 6   Break-Aparts of 10

Homework and Remembering page 12

Home and School Connection

Family Letter Have children take home the Family Letter on Student Activity Book page 17. This letter explains some of the unique vocabulary used in *Math Expressions.* It gives parents and guardians a better understanding of the learning that goes on in math class and creates a bridge between school and home. A Spanish translation of this letter is on the following page in the Student Activity Book.

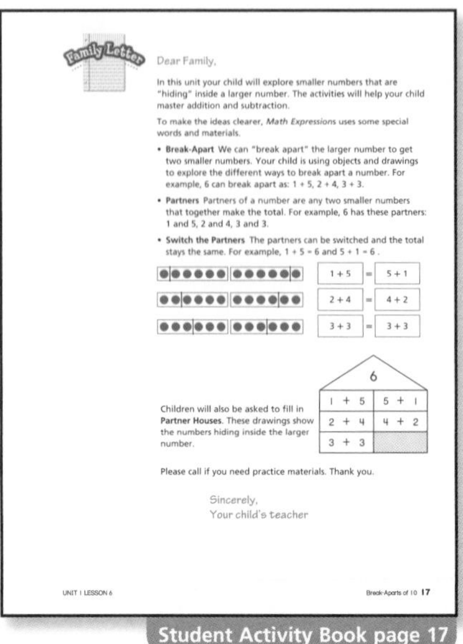

Family Letter

Dear Family,

In this unit your child will explore smaller numbers that are "hiding" inside a larger number. The activities will help your child master addition and subtraction.

To make the ideas clearer, *Math Expressions* uses some special words and materials.

- **Break-Apart** We can "break apart" the larger number to get two smaller numbers. Your child is using objects and drawings to explore the different ways to break apart a number. For example, 6 can break apart as: 1 + 5, 2 + 4, 3 + 3.
- **Partners** Partners of a number are any two smaller numbers that together make the total. For example, 6 has these partners: 1 and 5, 2 and 4, 3 and 3.
- **Switch the Partners** The partners can be switched and the total stays the same. For example, 1 + 5 = 6 and 5 + 1 = 6.

1 + 5 = 5 + 1
2 + 4 = 4 + 2
3 + 3 = 3 + 3

Children will also be asked to fill in **Partner Houses**. These drawings show the numbers hiding inside the larger number.

6	
1 + 5	5 + 1
2 + 4	4 + 2
3 + 3	

Please call if you need practice materials. Thank you.

Sincerely,
Your child's teacher

UNIT 1 LESSON 6   Break-Aparts of 10 17

Student Activity Book page 17

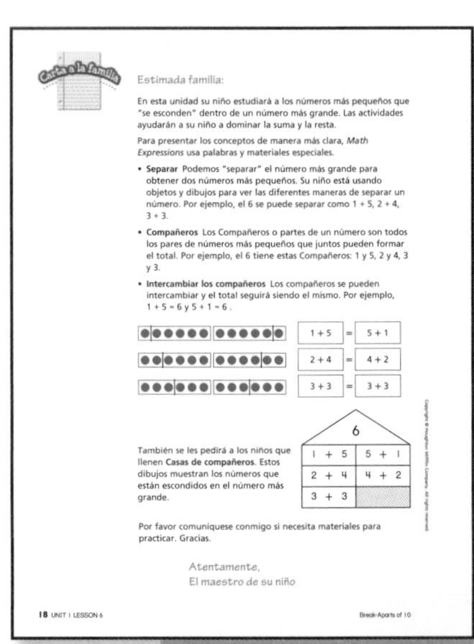

Carta a la familia

Estimada familia:

En esta unidad su niño estudiará a los números más pequeños que "se esconden" dentro de un número más grande. Las actividades ayudarán a su niño a dominar la suma y la resta.

Para presentar los conceptos de manera más clara, *Math Expressions* usa palabras y materiales especiales.

- **Separar** Podemos "separar" el número más grande para obtener dos números más pequeños. Su niño está usando objetos y dibujos para ver las diferentes maneras de separar un número. Por ejemplo, el 6 se puede separar como 1 + 5, 2 + 4, 3 + 3.
- **Compañeros** Los Compañeros o partes de un número son todos los pares de números más pequeños que juntos pueden formar el total. Por ejemplo, el 6 tiene estas Compañeros: 1 y 5, 2 y 4, 3 y 3.
- **Intercambiar los compañeros** Los compañeros se pueden intercambiar y el total seguirá siendo el mismo. Por ejemplo, 1 + 5 = 6 y 5 + 1 = 6.

1 + 5 = 5 + 1
2 + 4 = 4 + 2
3 + 3 = 3 + 3

También se les pedirá a los niños que llenen **Casas de compañeros**. Estos dibujos muestran los números que están escondidos en el número más grande.

6	
1 + 5	5 + 1
2 + 4	4 + 2
3 + 3	

Por favor comuníquese conmigo si necesita materiales para practicar. Gracias.

Atentamente,
El maestro de su niño

18 UNIT 1 LESSON 6   Break-Aparts of 10

Student Activity Book page 18

Partners in Break-Aparts

Vocabulary

break-aparts	Math Mountain
partners	teen numbers
total	Partner House
equation	

Lesson Objectives

- Identify the break-aparts of the numbers 2–9.
- Visualize various number groupings.

The Day at a Glance

Today's Goals	Materials	
1 Teaching the Lesson A1: Record break-apart partners as Math Mountains and equations. A2: Find partners and totals of groupings.	**Lesson Activities** Homework and Remembering pp. 13–14 Counters MathBoard materials	**Going Further** Activity Cards 1-7 Student Activity Book pp. 19–22 (includes Dot Cards) Scissors Game Cards (TRB M23) Counters Break-apart stick Two-color counters Cup Index cards Math Journals
2 Going Further ▸ Extension: Guess and Check ▸ Differentiated Instruction		
3 Homework and Targeted Practice		

Use Math Talk today!

Keeping Skills Sharp

Quick Practice — 5 MINUTES	Daily Routines
Goals: Count to 20. Make and "unmake" teen numbers. **Materials:** Demonstration Secret Code Cards **Number Flash: Counting to 20** The **Student Leader** leads the count to 20 as children show each number with their fingers. For the teen numbers, children flash ten on the left and the extra ones on the right. (See Unit 1 Lesson 2.) **The Teen Machine** Have two Student Leaders make and "unmake" teen numbers using the Demonstration Secret Code Cards. (See Unit 1 Lesson 6.)	**Money Routine** Using the 120 Poster, Using the Money Flip Chart, Using the Number Path, Using Secret Code Cards (See pp. xxiii–xxv.) ▸ Led by **Student Leaders**

1 Teaching the Lesson

Activity 1

Using the Garden Scenario Again

 30 MINUTES

Goal: Record break-apart partners as Math Mountains and equations.

Materials: counters (10 per child), MathBoard materials

 **NCTM Standard:**
Number and Operations

The Learning Classroom

Helping Community Some children may be hesitant to show their math work to others because they are afraid to be incorrect. Respond to errors as opportunities for learning. Model this for children as you make your own errors, saying, "Oh, that's OK, I see what I did." Fixing your errors models a positive approach for children.

Teaching Note

What to Expect from Students Some children may find the break-aparts systematically (1 + 6, 2 + 5, 3 + 4 for the number 7, for example). An advantage to working systematically is that it is easier to see if any of the break-aparts have been missed.

▶ Break-Aparts of 9 WHOLE CLASS

Have children draw a "garden" on their MathBoards as they did in Lesson 6.

- There is still a carrot patch and a lettuce patch where the rabbits like to play. This time, there are 9 rabbits in the garden. Put 9 counters on the carrot side.

Tell children that they can break apart other numbers the same way they broke apart the number 10.

Work as a class to find all the break-aparts of the number 9. List the equations for each break-apart on the board as children identify them. Write them in order, leaving space for the new ones. Invite children to identify the equations which "match," that is, have the same partners but the partners are switched.

$9 = 8 + 1$
$9 = 7 + 2$

$9 = 5 + 4$
$9 = 4 + 5$

▶ Break-Aparts of Numbers 2–8 SMALL GROUPS

Have groups of children find the break-aparts for the numbers 2–8. Assign each group a different number. Have children make Math Mountains and write the equations for each break-apart.

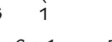

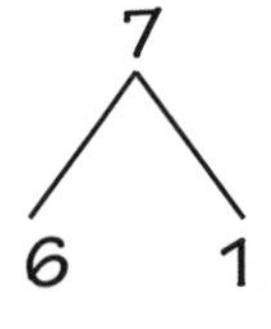

$7 = 6 + 1$

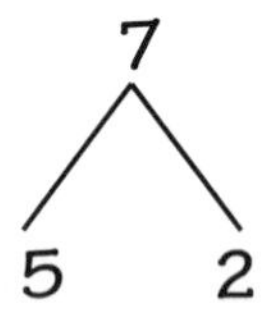

$7 = 5 + 2$

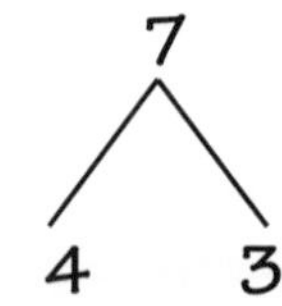

$7 = 4 + 3$

Ask children to relate the equations for which partners were switched. For example: $7 = 6 + 1$ and $7 = 1 + 6$; $7 = 5 + 2$ and $7 = 2 + 5$; $7 = 4 + 3$ and $7 = 3 + 4$.

Have the groups choose another number and repeat the process.

Activity 2

Circle Groupings: Seeing Numbers

▶ Visualize Partners and Totals WHOLE CLASS

Math Talk 

Help children visualize partners and totals for various numbers to 10. On the board draw a small group of circles separated by a line segment.

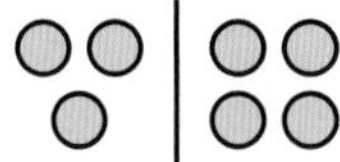

- What partners are shown here? 3 and 4
- What is the total? 7

Draw the Math Mountain for 7 to show the total and partners.

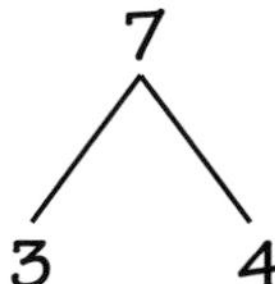

Then draw several other groupings on the board.

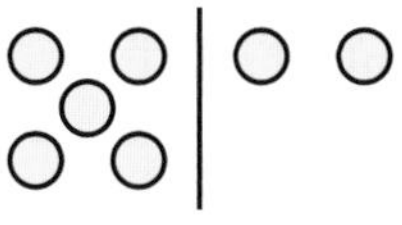

Partners: 5 and 2
Total: 7

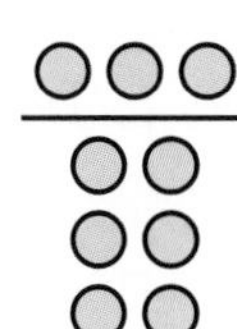

Partners: 3 and 6
Total: 9

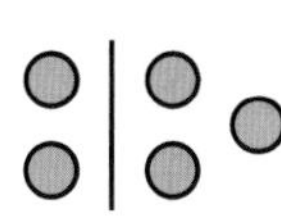

Partners: 2 and 3
Total: 5

Say, "partners," as you point to each group. The class should respond by naming the partners. Then say, "total." Ask the class to respond by giving the total.

As children work with pictures of partners and totals, ask questions such as:

- How do you know which are the partners?
- How do you find the total?

Encourage children to explain how to "see" each partner without counting. To help children visually, do not exceed 5 circles in a row. To get the total, children may add the partners or count on.

Draw the Math Mountain after children respond to each circle grouping.

 20 MINUTES

Goal: Find partners and totals of groupings.

 **NCTM Standard:**
Number and Operations

Teaching Note

Language and Vocabulary The word *partner* is used to refer to one of the two numbers in a break-apart. It is a meaningful term for *addend* and one that children can relate to and remember. Also, use the word *addend* sometimes and discuss with children that *addend* is the official math word for *partner.* It is important for children to know correct math vocabulary as well as the meaningful *Math Expressions* words.

English Language Learners

Draw the 8 grouping for partners 5 and 3 on the board.

- **Beginning** Say: **The partners are 5 and 3.** Draw the Math Mountain showing the partners only. Say: **5 and 3 is 8. The total is 8.** Write 8 on the mountain.
- **Intermediate** Ask: **What are the partners?** 5, 3 **What is the total?** 8 Draw a Math Mountain. Guide children to tell you where to write the partners and total.
- **Advanced** Ask: **What addition fact do the partners and total show?** $5 + 3 = 8$ Have children draw the math mountain.

2 Going Further

Extension: Guess and Check

Goal: Use the Guess and Check strategy to play the *Making Totals* game.

Materials: Scissors (1 pair per child), Student Activity Book pages 19–22

 **NCTM Standards:**
Number and Operations
Reasoning and Proof

Class Management

Going Further activities may be difficult for some students. These activities are intended to challenge students and to include mathematical topics required by state standards. Use these activities based on the individual needs of your students and/or according to specific state standards.

▶ *Making Totals* Game PAIRS

Playing the Game Have pairs of children each cut out the dot cards on Student Activity Book page 19 and combine the two sets to make 1 deck. Ask children to look at their dot cards and the recording sheet on Student Activity Book page 21.

To play, children shuffle the cards and deal three to each player. Players use two of their cards and find the total.

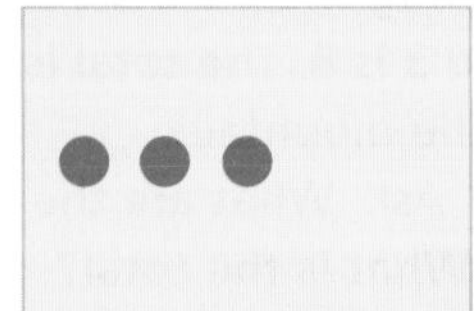

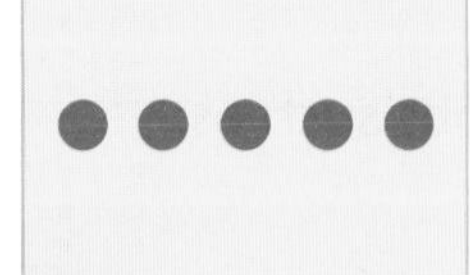

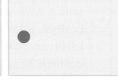

from Student Activity Book page 19

- Write the two partners you used to find each total on your recording sheet. If you choose the cards with 3 dots and 5 dots, you would write 3 and 5 in the "Total of 8" box on your recording sheet.

1–7 Name

▶ *Making Totals* Game

You need: Dot Cards for numbers 1–5 from Student Activity Book page 19

How to play:

1. Play with a classmate. Shuffle the cards and deal three to each player.
2. Each player chooses two of the three cards and finds the total.
3. Players record the partners for the total in the correct space on their sheet. Then they put the cards back in the deck and reshuffle.
4. The game continues until one player has found partners for all totals 2–10.

Write the partners you used for each total. Check children's answers.

Total of 2	Total of 3	Total of 4
___ and ___	___ and ___	___ and ___
Total of 5	**Total of 6**	**Total of 7**
___ and ___	___ and ___	___ and ___
Total of 8	**Total of 9**	**Total of 10**
___ and ___	___ and ___	___ and ___

UNIT 1 LESSON 7 Partners in Break-Aparts 21

Student Activity Book page 21

After children record the partners, they put the cards back in the deck and reshuffle. Play continues. At some point, players will not be able to record a response because the partners for the totals have already been written on their sheets in the spaces provided. The first player to fill in the partners for all of the totals wins the game.

More advanced children will use the **Guess and Check** problem-solving strategy to play this game. Before making the final choice, children mentally choose two numbers that they think will give one of the totals they need. If those numbers don't work, they try two other numbers.

Differentiated Instruction

Intervention — Activity Card 1-7

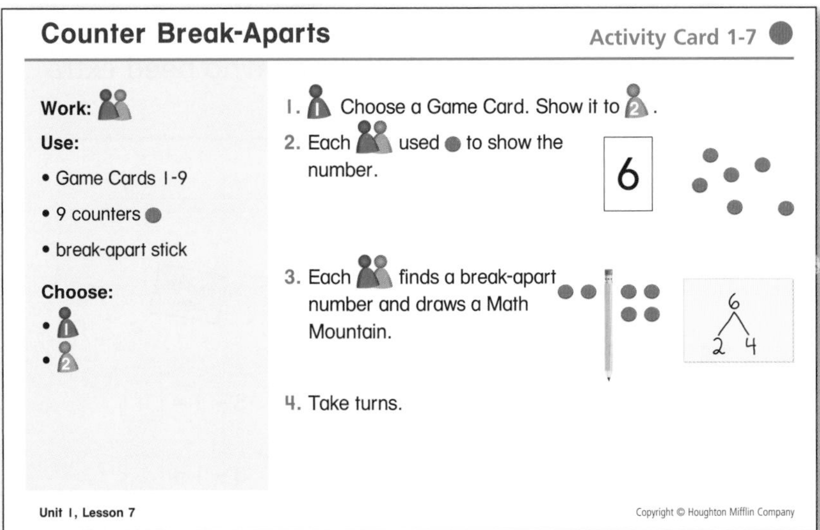

Activity Note Each pair needs Game Cards 1–9 (TRB M23), 9 counters, and a pencil or straw to use as a break-apart stick. Have each child show a different way to show the number.

Math Writing Prompt

Draw or Explain How can you use 6 counters to find partners for a total of 6?

Software Support

Use *Soar to Success* for instruction of students needing targeted support for underlying skills.

On Level — Activity Card 1-7

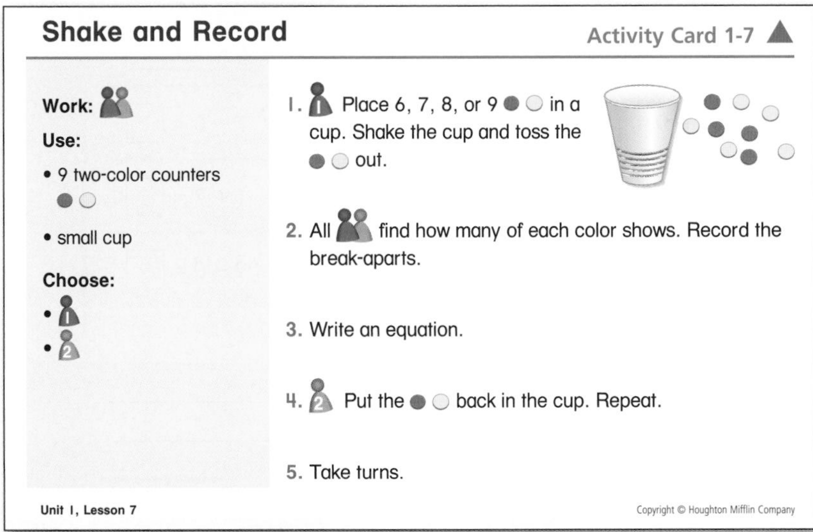

Activity Note Each pair needs 9 two-color counters and a small cup. After the pair records the break-aparts, make sure they write an equation for the counters.

Math Writing Prompt

Switch the Partners Explain how to switch the partners of 9 + 2 + 7 to make a new equation.

Software Support

Use *MegaMath* for review and reinforcement of the concepts and skills presented in this lesson.

Challenge — Activity Card 1-7

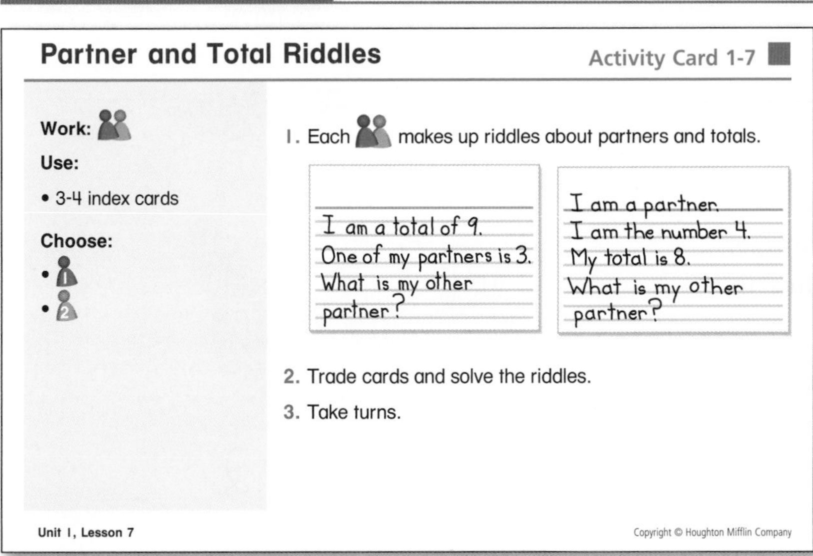

Activity Note Each pair needs 3–4 index cards. Have children write the answer on the back of the card and keep the cards in the math center for others to use.

Math Writing Prompt

Larger Totals Find two partners that have a total of 21. Explain your thinking.

Software Support

Use *Destination Math* to take students beyond the concepts and skills presented in this lesson.

 Homework and Targeted Practice

1-7 Homework **Goal:** Additional Practice

This Homework page provides practice in finding partners and totals.

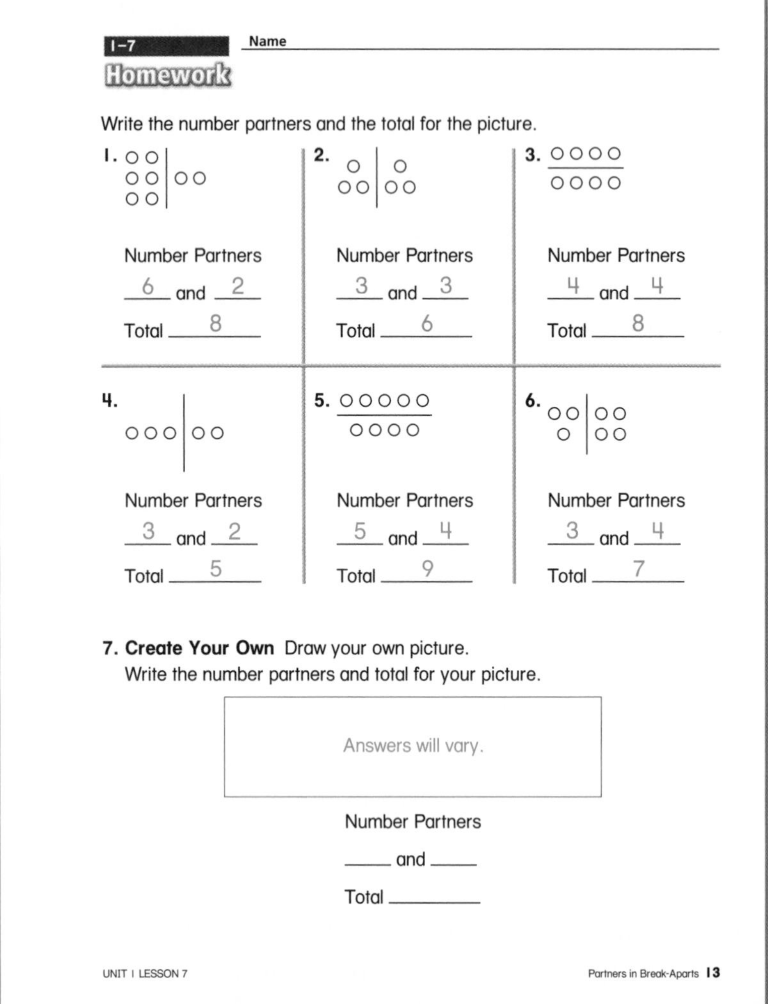

1-7 Name ______

Homework

Write the number partners and the total for the picture.

1. Number Partners 6 and 2 Total 8
2. Number Partners 3 and 3 Total 6
3. Number Partners 4 and 4 Total 8
4. Number Partners 3 and 2 Total 5
5. Number Partners 5 and 4 Total 9
6. Number Partners 3 and 4 Total 7

7. **Create Your Own** Draw your own picture. Write the number partners and total for your picture.

Answers will vary.

Number Partners ____ and ____

Total ______

UNIT 1 LESSON 7 Partners in Break-Aparts 13

Homework and Remembering page 13

1-7 Targeted Practice **Goal:** Add and subtract 0 and 1.

This page can be used with children who need extra practice adding and subtracting.

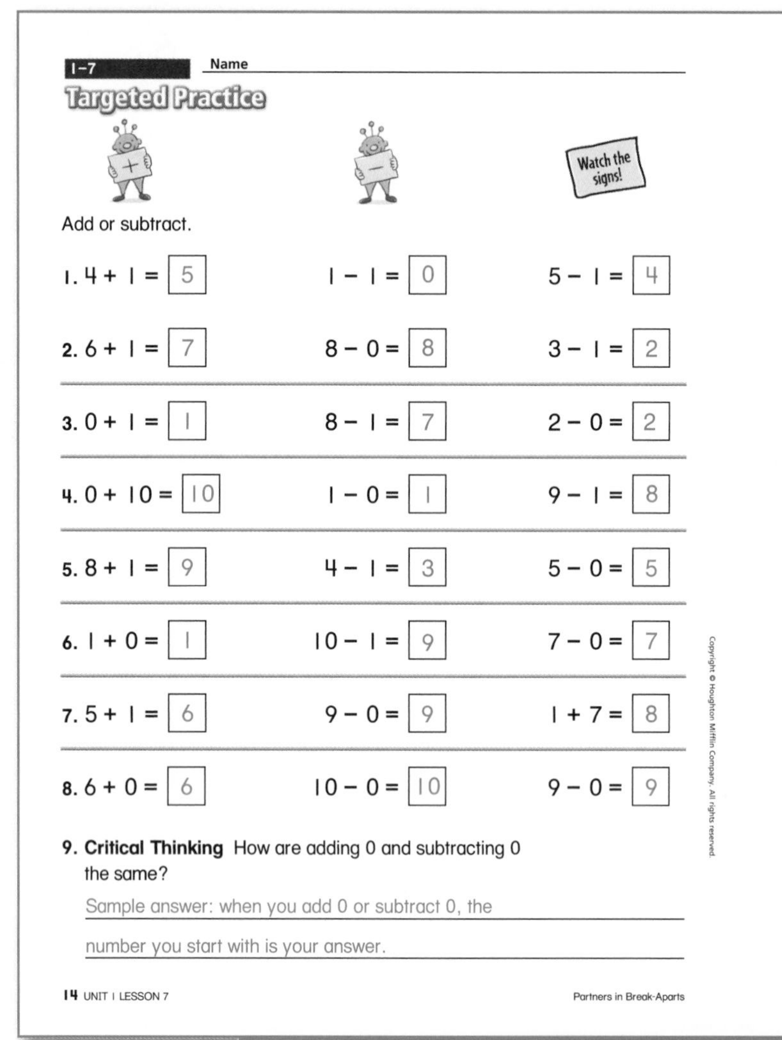

1-7 Name ______

Targeted Practice

Watch the signs!

Add or subtract.

1. 4 + 1 = 5	1 − 1 = 0	5 − 1 = 4
2. 6 + 1 = 7	8 − 0 = 8	3 − 1 = 2
3. 0 + 1 = 1	8 − 1 = 7	2 − 0 = 2
4. 0 + 10 = 10	1 − 0 = 1	9 − 1 = 8
5. 8 + 1 = 9	4 − 1 = 3	5 − 0 = 5
6. 1 + 0 = 1	10 − 1 = 9	7 − 0 = 7
7. 5 + 1 = 6	9 − 0 = 9	1 + 7 = 8
8. 6 + 0 = 6	10 − 0 = 10	9 − 0 = 9

9. **Critical Thinking** How are adding 0 and subtracting 0 the same?

Sample answer: when you add 0 or subtract 0, the number you start with is your answer.

14 UNIT 1 LESSON 7 Partners in Break-Aparts

Homework and Remembering page 14

Home or School Activity

 Science Connection

Animal Houses Discuss with children that just like we have different types of homes such as houses or apartments, animals also have different types of homes. Talk about how bees live in hives, birds make nests, bats live in caves, and so on.

Have children draw a picture of an animal family home. Ask them to show some of the animal family in their home and some of them outside the home. Tell children to write the break-apart for their picture.

Partner Houses Through 10

Vocabulary	
fair shares	partners
doubles	switch the partners
Partner House	Math Mountain
teen numbers	unknown partner

Lesson Objective

- Identify the break-aparts of numbers 2–10.

The Day at a Glance

Today's Goals	Materials	
1 Teaching the Lesson **A1:** Complete Partner Houses. Discuss doubles and fair shares. **A2:** Draw Math Mountains for numbers 2–10. **2 Going Further** ▸ Extension: Mayan Numbers ▸ Differentiated Instruction **3 Homework and Spiral Review**	**Lesson Activities** Student Activity Book p. 23 Homework and Remembering pp. 15–16 MathBoard materials	**Going Further** Activity Cards 1-8 Student Activity Book p. 24 Connecting cubes Bowl and counters Number cubes Index cards Math Journals

Use Math Talk today!

Keeping Skills Sharp

Quick Practice — 5 MINUTES

Goal: Find the unknown partners of 10.

Materials: Demonstration Secret Code Cards

Unknown Partner Invite children to review the break-aparts of 10 by playing Unknown Partner. Write the number 10 on the board. Call out any number from 1 to 9 to represent one partner of 10. For example, call out "6." Encourage the class to respond on a given signal, such as waving your hand. Children then hold up 4 fingers and call out "4," because 4 is the partner that goes with 6 to make 10. Continue rapidly for about 15 numbers, trying to cover all the partners of 10.

Daily Routines

Money Routine Using the 120 Poster, Using the Money Flip Chart, Using the Number Path, Using Secret Code Cards (See pp. xxiii–xxv.)

▸ Led by **Student Leaders**

1 Teaching the Lesson

Activity 1

Partner Houses

 40 MINUTES

Goals: Complete Partner Houses. Discuss doubles and fair shares.

Materials: Student Activity Book page 23

 **NCTM Standard:** Number and Operations

The Learning Classroom

Building Concepts Have children take turns summarizing the previous day's lesson at the beginning of math class. They can just say one or two sentences. An alternative may be to have one child summarize at the end of the lesson. Either way, if you do this regularly, children will get used to making mental summaries of the math concepts discussed and making conceptual connections.

Teaching Note

Starting with 1 With the garden scenario, the partners were listed beginning with 9 + 1. But it is easier for children to generate partners if they start from 1: 1 + 9. For the examples on Student Activity Book page 12 show 1 + 9 first. But children may fill in the Partner Houses in whatever order they prefer.

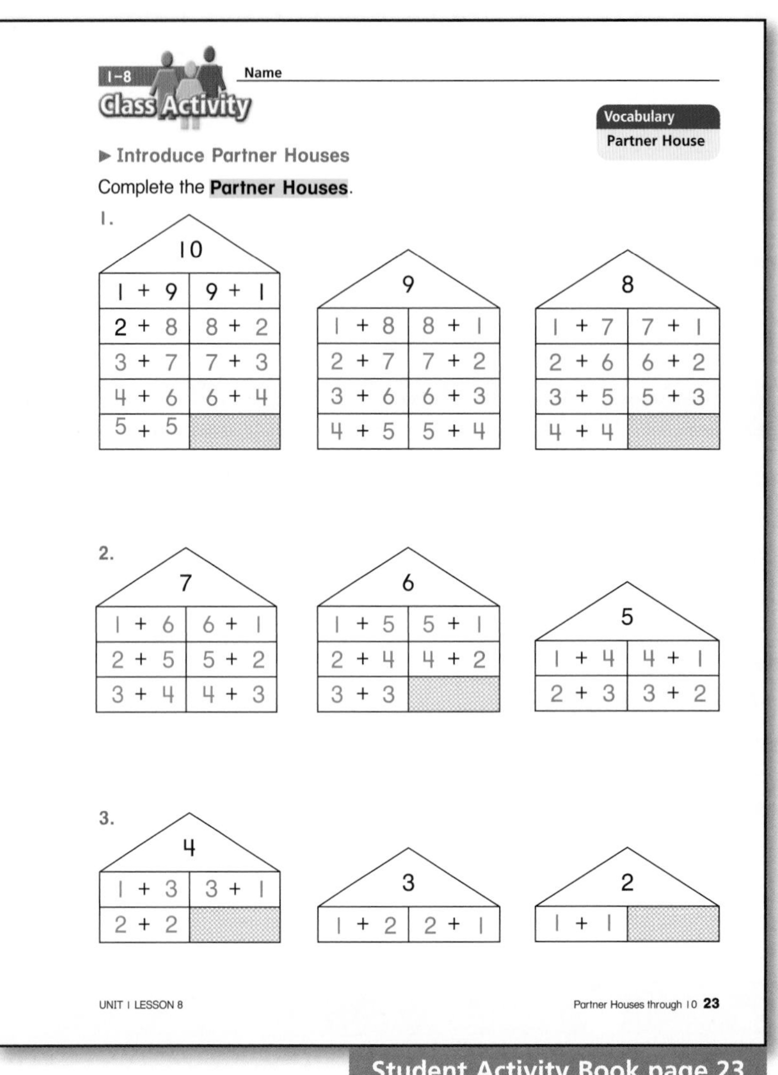

1–8 Class Activity Name

Vocabulary
Partner House

▶ Introduce Partner Houses

Complete the **Partner Houses**.

1.

10	
1 + 9	9 + 1
2 + 8	8 + 2
3 + 7	7 + 3
4 + 6	6 + 4
5 + 5	

9	
1 + 8	8 + 1
2 + 7	7 + 2
3 + 6	6 + 3
4 + 5	5 + 4

8	
1 + 7	7 + 1
2 + 6	6 + 2
3 + 5	5 + 3
4 + 4	

2.

7	
1 + 6	6 + 1
2 + 5	5 + 2
3 + 4	4 + 3

6	
1 + 5	5 + 1
2 + 4	4 + 2
3 + 3	

5	
1 + 4	4 + 1
2 + 3	3 + 2

3.

4	
1 + 3	3 + 1
2 + 2	

3	
1 + 2	2 + 1

2	
1 + 1	

UNIT 1 LESSON 8 Partner Houses through 10 **23**

Student Activity Book page 23

▶ Introduce Partner Houses WHOLE CLASS

Direct children's attention to the 10-house on Student Activity Book page 23. Help children determine why it is called a 10-house.

- Look at the first house. This is a picture of a 10-house. Look at the top floor of the house. What is in the top floor? The 1 + 9 partners of 10 and the switched partners, 9 + 1.
- What numbers do you think go in the next floor down? Another set of partners of 10 belongs there, such as 2 + 8 and 8 + 2.

Children may respond with any partners of 10. The partners do not have to be written in order.

Ask children to complete the 10-house and share their answers with the class.

Doubles or Fair Shares Ask children to look at the bottom floor of the 10-house.

- Why do you think the bottom floor has only one box instead of two? The partners 5 + 5 switched around are still 5 + 5.

Math Talk Use the following example and questions to discuss the concept of *doubles* and *fair shares.*

- Let's think about the number 10 a little more. Suppose I have 10 crackers and I want to share them with Ramona. If I keep 9 and give her 1, would that be fair? No, because you would have more than her.
- If I keep 8 and give her 2, is that fair? That is still not fair because she has fewer.
- Is there a way that we could both have the same amount of crackers? Yes. How many would we each get? 5
- So, if we split up the crackers into 5 and 5, we would each have a fair share. Some people call these *doubles* because they are the same number.

You may wish to draw pictures or use objects to explain, especially for English learners.

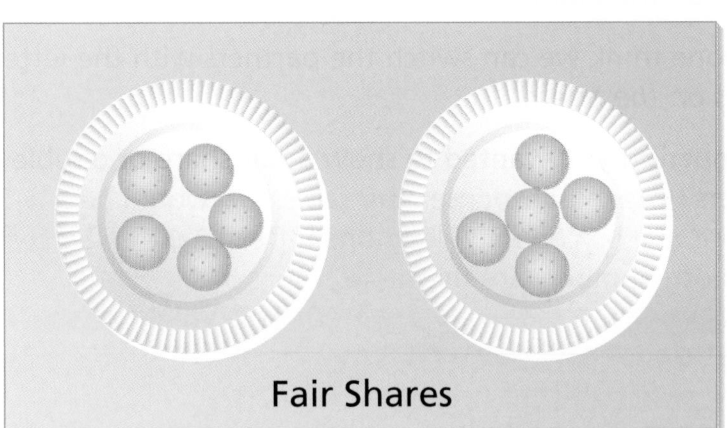
Fair Shares

Activity continued ▶

The Learning Classroom

Math Talk What types of questions are you asking the children? Are you asking questions that elicit a short answer, or do you probe to learn more about children's thinking as they tell about their work? If possible, make a video or audio recording of yourself leading a math lesson. Play it back and make notes about the types of questions you ask. Reflect on any changes you would like to make. Write a date in your planning book to do this again and see if you observe changes.

English Language Learners

Draw 2 empty plates on the board. Say: **I want to share 10 crackers with Ramona *fairly*.** Discuss ways that are not *fair* shares and draw 5 crackers on each plate.

- **Beginning** Say: **We both have 5 crackers. This is a *fair* share. *Fair* shares are doubles because the number is the same.** Have children repeat.
- **Intermediate** Ask: **How many crackers for me?** 5 **How many for Ramona?** 5 **Is this a *fair* share?** yes **Are these doubles?** yes
- **Advanced** Have children tell whether this is a *fair* share, or doubles.

Teaching Note

Research Studies have shown that even young children can understand and use variables to show general expressions and equations.

Ongoing Assessment

Circulate around the room while children are completing the Partner Houses and ask:

- How did you find the numbers for the 8-house?
- Which Partner House has a double? How do you know?

The Number Neighborhood Have children fill in the rest of the Partner Houses on Student Activity Book page 23. If you would like to tell a story about these exercises, suggest to children that the numbers live in houses in a number neighborhood.

When children are finished, have them share their answers with a classmate.

- Did anyone find any more *fair shares* or *doubles* in the Partner Houses? 2, 4, 6, 8, and 10 all have *fair shares* or *doubles* as one of the break-aparts.

Tell children that these *fair shares* are really easy to remember and can help when adding and subtracting.

▶ Use Letters and Algebra for Break-Aparts

WHOLE CLASS

Ask children to give you an example of partners for the number 10 and write them on the board (an example of 9 and 1 is used below). Explain to children that letters are sometimes used to stand for numbers. Write the letters *m* and *n* under the partners.

$$9 + 1$$
$$m + n$$

- What do you think the letter *m* stands for? 9
- What do you think the letter *n* stands for? 1
- Can anyone switch the partners for 9 + 1? 1 + 9
  Write this on the board.
- Does anyone think we can switch the partners with the letters? $n + m$
  Write this on the board.
- What happens if you wanted to show a fair share or double of 10 with only letters? Possible response: The fair share would be 5 + 5, so you could write $n + n$. You only need one letter to show *fair shares* because both numbers are the same.

Activity 2

Find Every Mountain

▶ Draw Math Mountains SMALL GROUPS

Relate Math Mountain drawings to the "floors" of the Partner Houses. Draw the sketch below on the board.

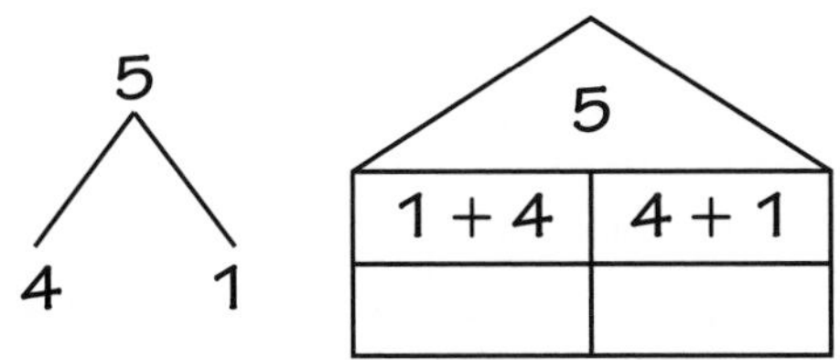

Children may notice that both the Partner Houses and Math Mountains are ways of showing the break-aparts of numbers.

Have children work in small groups to draw all the Math Mountains for one Partner House on a MathBoard. Some groups may be responsible for more than one Partner House since the lower numbers don't have as many break-aparts.

Groups may refer to Student Activity Book page 23 to help them find all the Math Mountains. Children do not have to draw separate mountains when they switch the partners.

Solve and Discuss Invite one child from each group to share observations and Math Mountain drawings with the class. As they share their drawings, ask questions about *fair shares* and *doubles.* Make sure all 25 Math Mountains are drawn. (These partners may be reversed or switched.)

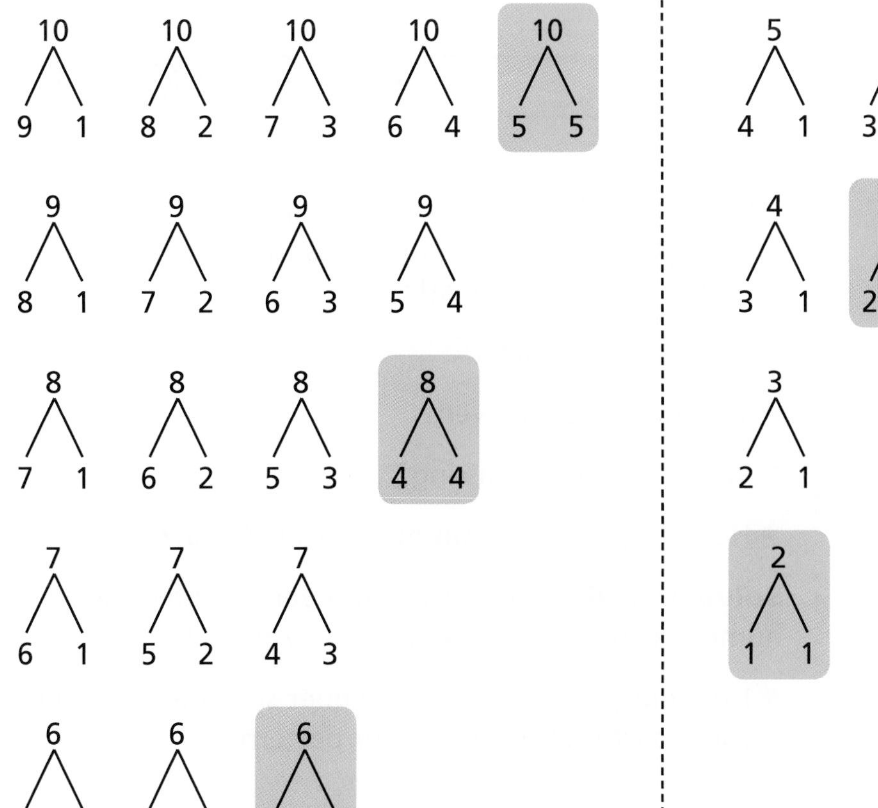

15 MINUTES

Goal: Draw Math Mountains for numbers 2–10.

Materials: MathBoard materials

NCTM Standard:
Number and Operations

Differentiated Instruction

Extra Help If some children are having difficulties with the break-aparts, you may want to group those children together and have them draw the Math Mountains for the lower numbered Partner Houses, 2, 3, and 4. There are fewer break-aparts in those Partner Houses.

Class Management

Looking Ahead In the next lesson, children will use the Red Count-On Cards (Addition). These are on Student Activity Book pages 27–28 and on TRB M25–M26. For classroom activities, children can use the cards provided in the Student Activity Book, or they can take those cards home. You can make sturdy cards specifically for classroom use by copying the copymasters onto card stock. In either case, you may want to set aside time before you begin the lesson for children to cut out the cards.

If you have access to the *Math Expressions* materials kits, the Red Count-On Cards are included, so you will not have to prepare these materials.

2 Going Further

Extension: Mayan Numbers

Goal: Explore Mayan numbers.

Materials: Student Activity Book page 24

✓ **NCTM Standards:**
Number and Operations
Connections
Representation

Teaching Note

Math Background The Mayan number system was one of the first to use zero and have a place value system. It was developed by the ancient Maya civilization of Central America.

▶ Explore Mayan Numbers WHOLE CLASS

Draw the first six Mayan numbers from Student Activity Book page 24 on the board. Explain to children that the ancient Mayan people of Central America had their own number system that was very different from ours. They used dots and bars for their numbers.

- What do you think each dot stands for? 1
- What do you think each bar stands for? 5
- How do you think the Mayans would have written the number 7?

Have several volunteers draw the number 7 on the board and explain how they made their drawing. Possible response: the bar stands for 5 and two dots equal 2. $5 + 2 = 7$

▶ Use Mayan Numbers INDIVIDUALS

Have children complete the Mayan number chart by looking for a pattern. Children should then try to complete the rest of the page on their own.

For the number 12, they will need to think of 12 as $10 + 2$.

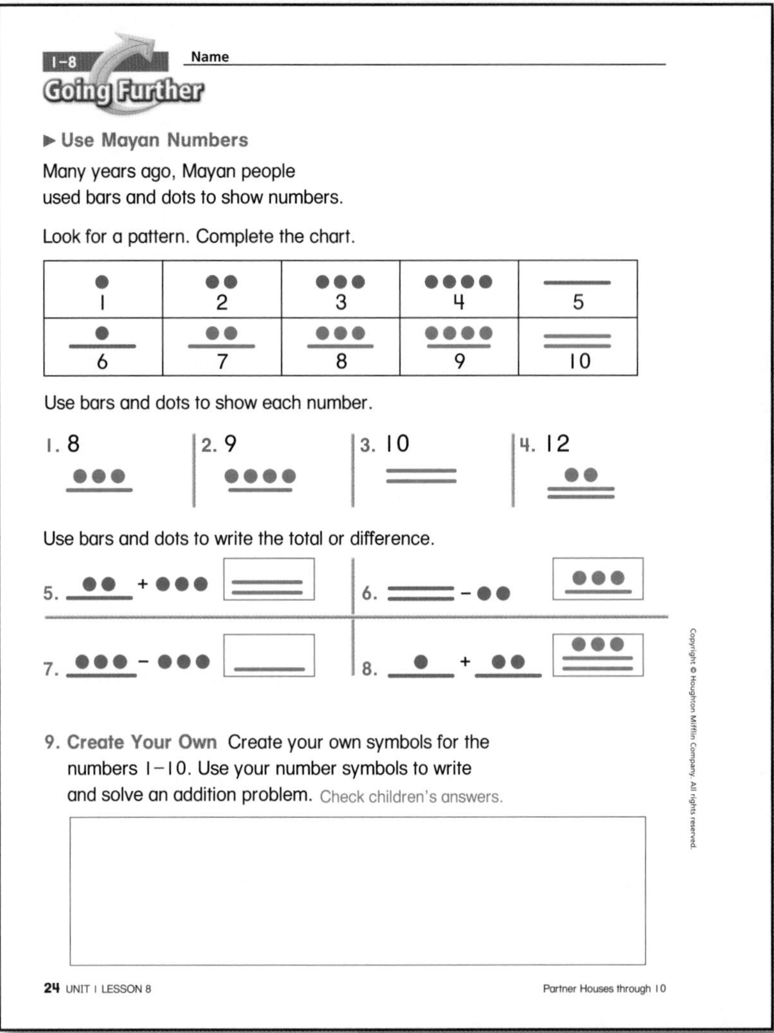

1–8 Going Further Name

▶ Use Mayan Numbers

Many years ago, Mayan people used bars and dots to show numbers.

Look for a pattern. Complete the chart.

• 1	•• 2	••• 3	•••• 4	— 5
• — 6	•• — 7	••• — 8	•••• — 9	— — 10

Use bars and dots to show each number.

1. 8 ••• —
2. 9 •••• —
3. 10 — —
4. 12 •• — —

Use bars and dots to write the total or difference.

5. •• — + ••• = — —
6. — — − •• = ••• —
7. ••• — − ••• = —
8. • — + •• — = ••• — —

9. **Create Your Own** Create your own symbols for the numbers 1–10. Use your number symbols to write and solve an addition problem. Check children's answers.

24 UNIT 1 LESSON 8 Partner Houses through 10

Student Activity Book page 24

Math Talk Encourage children to relate the break-aparts to whole numbers as they work on exercises 5–8. You may ask:

- What is the total?
- Which partner is given?
- Which partner is missing?
- How do you write that number in Mayan?

Solve and Discuss Invite volunteers to draw the number symbols they created for exercise 9.

- How did you create your number symbols? Did you use a pattern? Describe your pattern.

Intervention — Activity Card 1-8

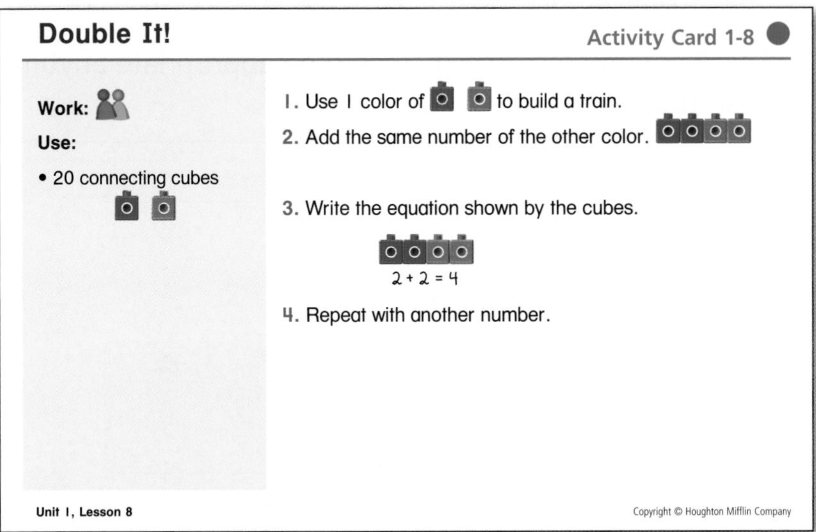
Double It! Activity Card 1-8

Work: (pair)
Use:
- 20 connecting cubes

1. Use 1 color of cubes to build a train.
2. Add the same number of the other color.
3. Write the equation shown by the cubes.
   2 + 2 = 4
4. Repeat with another number.

Unit 1, Lesson 8 — Copyright © Houghton Mifflin Company

Activity Note Each pair needs 20 connecting cubes, 10 of each color. Some children may find it easier to start with 1 cube and double it, then add 2, 3, and so on.

Math Writing Prompt

Draw or Explain Are you switching the partners when you add 4 + 5 and then add 5 + 3? Explain your thinking.

Software Support

Use *Soar to Success* for instruction of students needing targeted support for underlying skills.

On Level — Activity Card 1-8

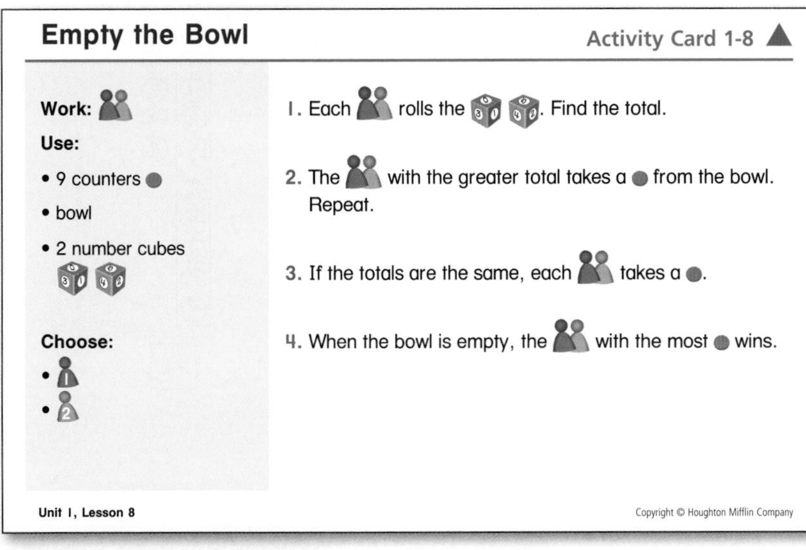
Empty the Bowl Activity Card 1-8

Work: (pair)
Use:
- 9 counters
- bowl
- 2 number cubes

Choose:
- 1
- 2

1. Each partner rolls the number cubes. Find the total.
2. The partner with the greater total takes a counter from the bowl. Repeat.
3. If the totals are the same, each partner takes a counter.
4. When the bowl is empty, the partner with the most counters wins.

Unit 1, Lesson 8 — Copyright © Houghton Mifflin Company

Activity Note Each pair needs 10 counters, a bowl, and two number cubes labeled 0–5. Each child rolls the number cubes and finds the total of the two numbers. The child with a greater total takes one counter.

Math Writing Prompt

8 Cars Write a story problem that has the answer "8 cars."

Software Support

Use *MegaMath* for review and reinforcement of the concepts and skills presented in this lesson.

Challenge — Activity Card 1-8

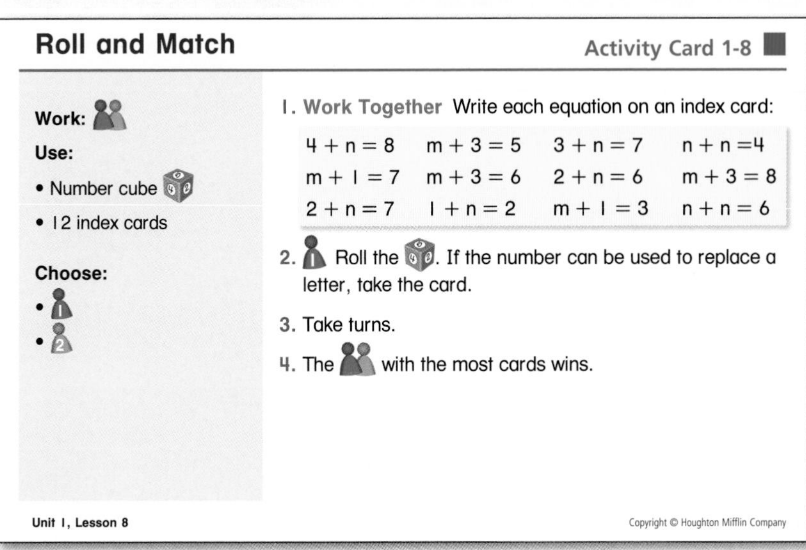
Roll and Match Activity Card 1-8

Work: (pair)
Use:
- Number cube
- 12 index cards

Choose:
- 1
- 2

1. **Work Together** Write each equation on an index card:

4 + n = 8	m + 3 = 5	3 + n = 7	n + n = 4
m + 1 = 7	m + 3 = 6	2 + n = 6	m + 3 = 8
2 + n = 7	1 + n = 2	m + 1 = 3	n + n = 6

2. Roll the number cube. If the number can be used to replace a letter, take the card.
3. Take turns.
4. The partner with the most cards wins.

Unit 1, Lesson 8 — Copyright © Houghton Mifflin Company

Activity Note Each pair needs a number cube with the numbers 1–6 and 12 index cards. Have children write the algebraic equations on the index cards and arrange the cards in rows.

Math Writing Prompt

Find the Number Explain how to find the number that n stands for in this equation.
$n + n = 8$

Software Support

Use *Destination Math* to take students beyond the concepts and skills presented in this lesson.

3 Homework and Spiral Review

Goal: Additional Practice

This Homework page provides practice in completing Partner Houses.

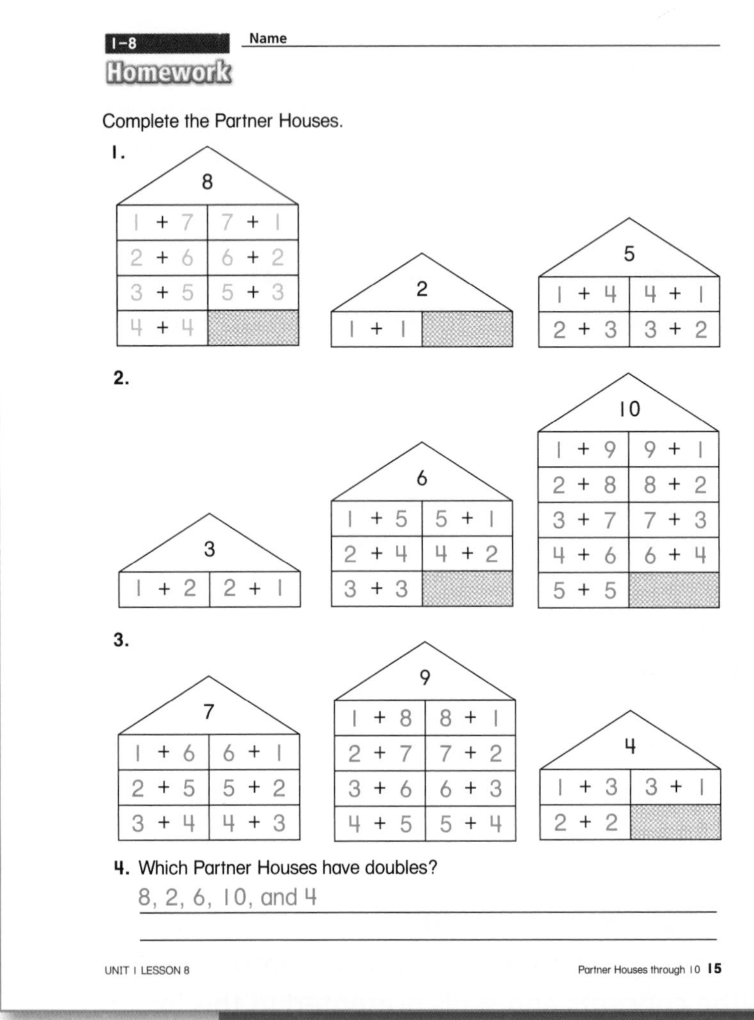

1-8 Homework Name ______

Complete the Partner Houses.

1.

8	
1 + 7	7 + 1
2 + 6	6 + 2
3 + 5	5 + 3
4 + 4	

2	
1 + 1	

5	
1 + 4	4 + 1
2 + 3	3 + 2

2.

3	
1 + 2	2 + 1

6	
1 + 5	5 + 1
2 + 4	4 + 2
3 + 3	

10	
1 + 9	9 + 1
2 + 8	8 + 2
3 + 7	7 + 3
4 + 6	6 + 4
5 + 5	

3.

7	
1 + 6	6 + 1
2 + 5	5 + 2
3 + 4	4 + 3

9	
1 + 8	8 + 1
2 + 7	7 + 2
3 + 6	6 + 3
4 + 5	5 + 4

4	
1 + 3	3 + 1
2 + 2	

4. Which Partner Houses have doubles?
8, 2, 6, 10, and 4

UNIT 1 LESSON 8 Partner Houses through 10 **15**

Homework and Remembering page 15

Goal: Spiral Review

This Remembering activity would be appropriate anytime after today's lesson.

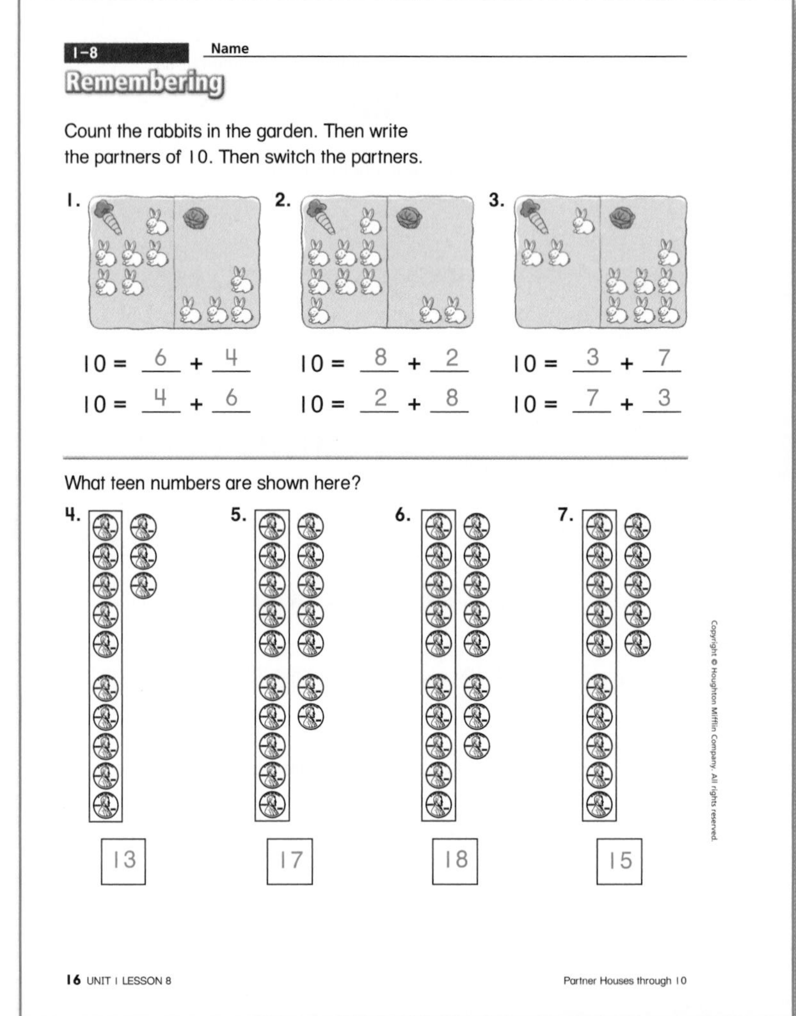

1-8 Remembering Name ______

Count the rabbits in the garden. Then write the partners of 10. Then switch the partners.

1. 10 = 6 + 4
10 = 4 + 6

2. 10 = 8 + 2
10 = 2 + 8

3. 10 = 3 + 7
10 = 7 + 3

What teen numbers are shown here?

4. 13

5. 17

6. 18

7. 15

Copyright © Houghton Mifflin Company. All rights reserved.

16 UNIT 1 LESSON 8 Partner Houses through 10

Homework and Remembering page 16

Home or School Activity

Music Connection

Ten Partners Have students listen to Ron Brown's *Intelli-Tunes* CD to help them become fluent with the partners of ten. You can also use the CD when teaching other math concepts, as the CD has 15 more original songs that teach other addition concepts.

Count On to Find the Total

Vocabulary	
count all	teen numbers
count on	partners
function	rule
equation	Count-On Cards

Lesson Objective

- Count on to add.

The Day at a Glance

Today's Goals	Materials	
1 Teaching the Lesson **A1:** Use Secret Code Cards and fingers to count on. **A2:** Practice counting on to find the total. **2 Going Further** ▶ Math Connection: Function Tables ▶ Differentiated Instruction **3 Homework and Targeted Practice**	**Lesson Activities** Student Activity Book pp. 25, 27–30 (includes Red Count-On Cards (Addition), Family Letter) Homework and Remembering pp. 17–18 Demonstration Secret Code Cards (TRB M7–M22) Secret Code Cards Counters Snack bags	**Going Further** Activity Cards 1-9 Reminder Sheet (TRB M24) Student Activity Book p. 26 Homework and Remembering p. 17 Bowl and counters Spinners (TRB M27) Paper Clips Number cubes Math Journals

Use Math Talk today!

Keeping Skills Sharp

Quick Practice — 5 MINUTES

Goal: Identify the break-aparts for 8.

Unknown Partner Have children review the break-aparts of 8 by playing Unknown Partner using 8 as the total. (See Unit 1 Lesson 8.)

For a silent version of Unknown Partner, children show their fingers only. For a more active version, play Prairie Dog. Children crouch near their desks like a prairie dog ready to jump out of a hole. When the first partner for the number is given, children wait for the signal and then jump up and call out the second partner as they hold up their fingers to show that number.

Repeated Quick Practice Use these Quick Practices from previous lessons.

- **Number Flash: Counting to 20** (See Unit 1 Lesson 3.)
- **The Teen Machine** (See Unit 1 Lesson 5.)

Daily Routines

Money Routine Using the 120 Poster, Using the Money Flip Chart, Using the Number Path, Using Secret Code Cards (See pp. xxiii–xxv.)

- Led by Student Leaders

1 Teaching the Lesson

Activity 1

Find the Total

 25 MINUTES

Goal: Use Secret Code Cards and fingers to count on.

Materials: Demonstration Secret Code Cards (TRB M7–M22), Secret Code Cards (from Unit 1 Lesson 5 or TRB M3–M4), counters, snack bags

 **NCTM Standard:**
Number and Operations

 **Class Management**

When children share their solutions make sure everyone is responsible for listening to one another. Be sure explainers talk loudly enough and that they are talking to the whole class, not just you. Move to the side or the back of the class so that children have to look at their classmates to see you. Have children pretend they are holding a microphone. The pretend situation reminds them to talk loudly and to look directly at their audience.

English Language Learners

Hold up the dot sides of cards 5 and 4. Repeat the problem. Have children count the dots to solve. Turn the 5 card to the numeral side.

- **Beginning** Say: **We know there are 5 boys. We can *count on* from 5 to solve. We *count on* 4 more. 5 plus 4 more is 9.**
- **Intermediate** Ask: **How many boys?** 5 Say: **We can *count on* from 5 to solve.** Ask: **How many more do we *count on*?** 4 **What is 5 plus 4 more?** 9
- **Advanced** Have children tell how to count on from 5 to solve the problem.

▶ Addition Story Problem WHOLE CLASS

Write the following story problem on the board for the children to solve.

Lisa invited 5 boys and 4 girls to her party.
How many children did Lisa invite?

- How would you solve this problem?

Have volunteers share their solution methods. If children do not discuss counting on as a method, ask if anyone can demonstrate the Counting On method to solve the problem.

Explain that today we will use and compare two methods for addition—Counting All and Counting On.

▶ Compare Counting All and Counting On WHOLE CLASS

Counting All Use the dot sides of the Demonstration Secret Code Cards as students use their Secret Code cards to count all (or have a child do this) to find the answer to 5 + 4.

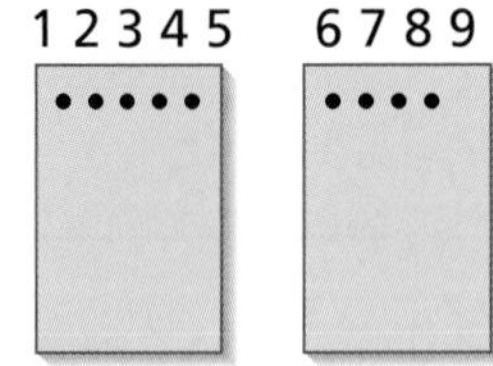

- There are 9 dots altogether.

Counting On with Secret Code Cards Use the numeral and dot sides of the Secret Code Cards to demonstrate counting on (or have a child demonstrate) to find the answer to the story problem.

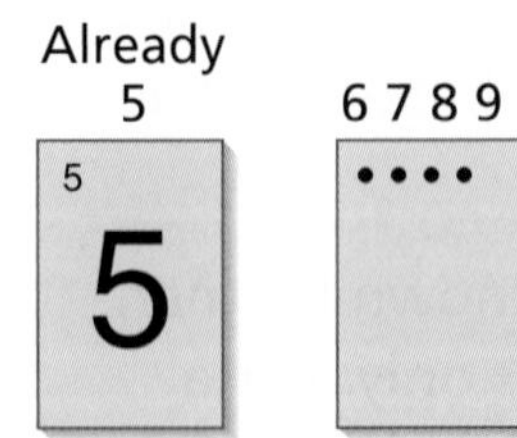

- I know I already counted 5 for the first card, so I don't have to count those dots.
- I count on 4 more. 6, 7, 8, 9. I get 9.

Counting On with Fingers Children can also count on using their fingers. Have the class solve 5 + 4 by counting on with their fingers.

- I pretend I already counted 5. Then count on 6, 7, 8, 9.

Already 5

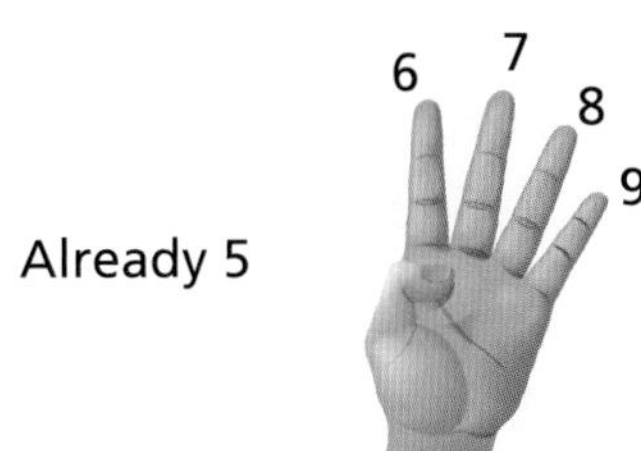

6 7 8 9

- Is it easier to count on or count all? Why do you think so? Possible response: Counting on is easier. You don't have to recount the first partner.

Have children try several more examples. They should do each example with Secret Code Cards and fingers. They can also count on into teen numbers.

$9 + 5 = \square$

Counting All

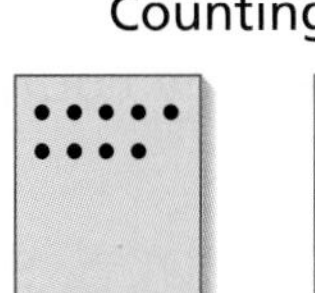

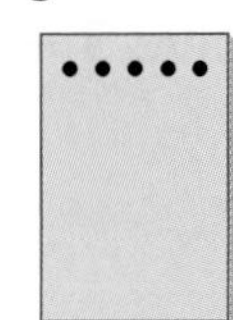

1, 2, 3, 4, 5, 6, 7, 8, 9, 10, 11, 12, 13, and 14

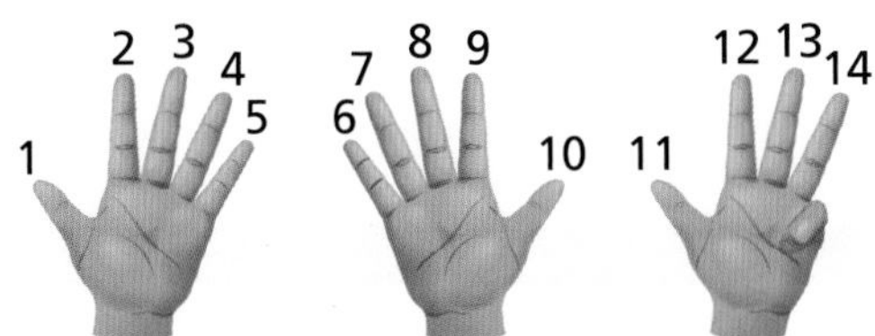

1 2 3 4 5 6 7 8 9 10 11 12 13 14

Counting On

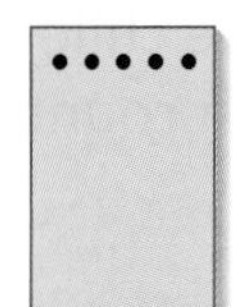

9 10 11 12 13 14

I pretend I already counted 9.

Already 9

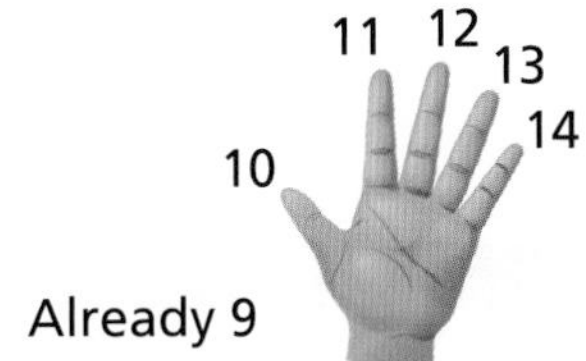

10 11 12 13 14

Activity continued ▶

Teaching Note

What to Expect from Students Children may suggest other strategies for solving addition problems. Some may use doubles. For example, they may say "I know that 4 + 4 = 8, so 5 + 4 is just one more. The answer must be 9." Others may decompose a related fact to find the answer, for example, "I know that 5 + 3 = 8, so 5 + 4 is just one more, or 9." Children may just know some answers. Encourage children who are still counting all to count on.

Teaching Note

Watch For! The main error children make when counting on is to begin counting fingers with the first addend. Children need to understand that saying the first number says how many are in that first group. It is helpful to put that group somewhere.

- ▶ Put 9 here (in my head—gesture—or on my shoulder or in my pocket).
- ▶ Now I can count on. Already 9 ... 10, 11, 12, 13, 14

9 ↑ voice emphasis — 10, 11, 12, 13, 14 fingers

"Already 9 ↑ I already counted these 9. — 10, 11, 12, 13, 14" fingers

Differentiated Instruction

Extra Help Some children may benefit from the Reminder Sheet (TRB M24), which can be laminated for ongoing use.

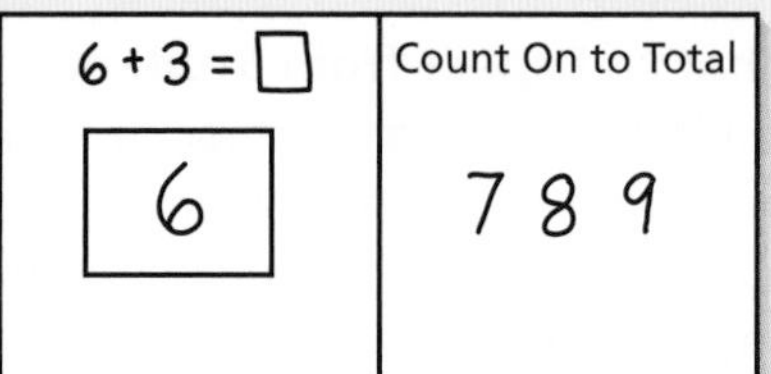

Suggest that children always write the greater partner in the box on the left and count on from there to find the total.

Visual Learners Some children may need more visual clues to remind them not to count all. For example, have children put all the counters for the first partner in a snack bag. They should see that they don't have to count them because they already know how many there are. Then, they should be able to count on the second partner to find the total.

▶ Count On from the Greater Number WHOLE CLASS

Write the following story problem on the board for the children to solve.

Lisa got 3 cards from her family and 6 cards from her friends. How many cards did Lisa get altogether?

Math Talk Ask volunteers to share their solution methods. Possible responses are below.

- I drew 3 dots for her family and 6 dots for her friends, and then counted all to find the total. She got 9 cards.
- I drew a Math Mountain with 3 and 6 as the partners on the bottom. The total at the top of the Mountain is 9. Lisa got 9 cards.
- You could use Secret Code Cards and count all the dots on the back sides of the cards.

In this problem, the smaller addend (3) is given first. Some children may start with it automatically. If you find that children do this and do not start counting on with the greater number, guide their discussion to find the advantages of beginning with the greater number.

- Did anyone begin with 6? Why do you think that is a good way to begin? Possible response: It is faster because there is less counting to do.

Have children demonstrate a faster way to solve 3 + 6 by counting on with counters, dots, and fingers.

Already 6 ○ ○ ○
7 8 9

Already 6

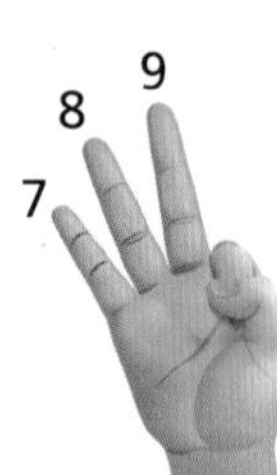

Activity 2

25 MINUTES

Goal: Practice counting on to find the total.

Materials: Student Activity Book pages 25, 27–30, Secret Code Cards (from Unit 1 Lesson 5 orTRB M3–M4), Red Count-On Cards

NCTM Standard:
Number and Operations

Practice Counting On

▶ Count On to Find the Total INDIVIDUALS

Have children practice counting on with Student Activity Book page 25. The first column has the greater addend first, the second column has the smaller addend first, and the last column is mixed. Some problems have teen totals. Children may use any solution method they prefer. The examples on the page remind children how to count on.

▶ Introduce the Red Count-On Cards INDIVIDUALS

Have children cut out the Red Count-On cards on Student Activity Book pages 27–28. (These cards are also on TRB M25–M26. If you wish, print the cards on card stock to have a set for children to use at home.)

Ask children to describe how the card fronts and backs are different. Have children place the cards to show the problem and not the answer by making sure that the cut corner of each card is in the upper right corner.

Explain to children how to use the cards to practice addition.

- Say the equation and the answer to yourself. Then turn the card over to see if you are correct. If you are incorrect, use the numbers and dots to help you see how to count on to find the total or use your fingers to count on. Then say the correct equation to yourself two times.
- Make three piles with the cards. In one pile, put the cards that you answer correctly and quickly. In a second pile, put the cards that you answer correctly and slowly. In a third pile, put the cards that you answer incorrectly.
- Practice the cards that you answered incorrectly or slowly.

Have children use the cards to practice addition.

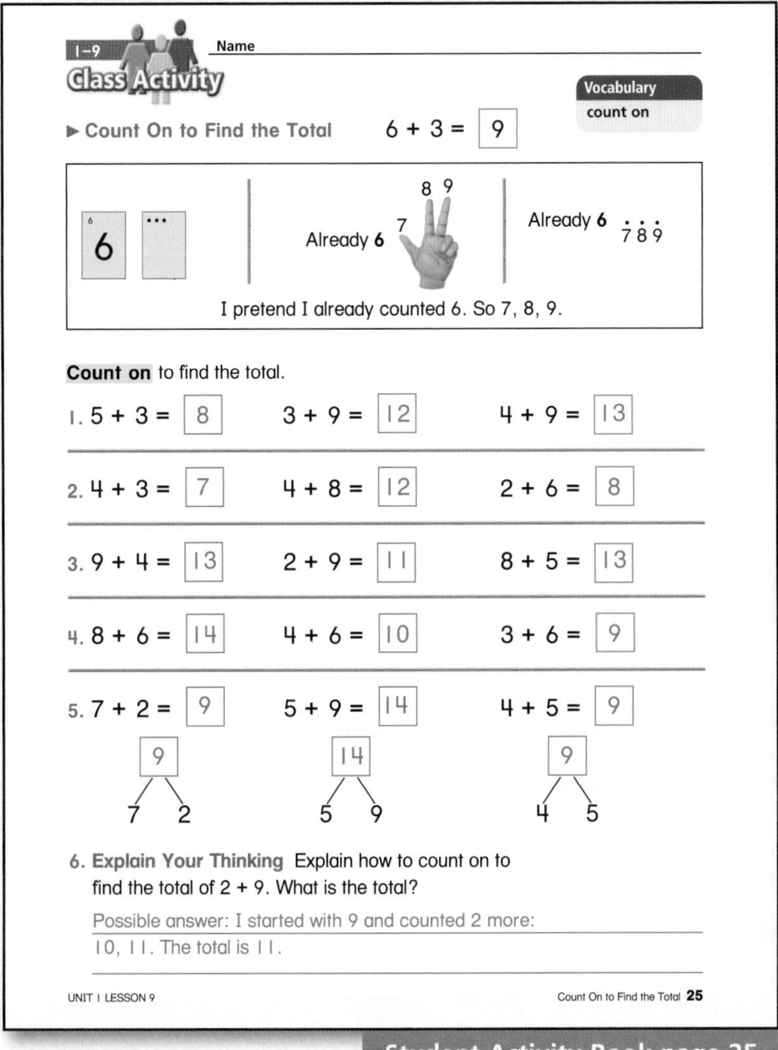

1–9 Class Activity Name

Vocabulary: count on

▶ Count On to Find the Total 6 + 3 = 9

Already 6 — 7 8 9

Already 6 — 7 8 9

I pretend I already counted 6. So 7, 8, 9.

Count on to find the total.

1. 5 + 3 = 8	3 + 9 = 12	4 + 9 = 13
2. 4 + 3 = 7	4 + 8 = 12	2 + 6 = 8
3. 9 + 4 = 13	2 + 9 = 11	8 + 5 = 13
4. 8 + 6 = 14	4 + 6 = 10	3 + 6 = 9
5. 7 + 2 = 9	5 + 9 = 14	4 + 5 = 9

9: 7, 2   14: 5, 9   9: 4, 5

6. **Explain Your Thinking** Explain how to count on to find the total of 2 + 9. What is the total?

Possible answer: I started with 9 and counted 2 more: 10, 11. The total is 11.

UNIT 1 LESSON 9 — Count On to Find the Total 25

Student Activity Book page 25

Red Count-On Cards

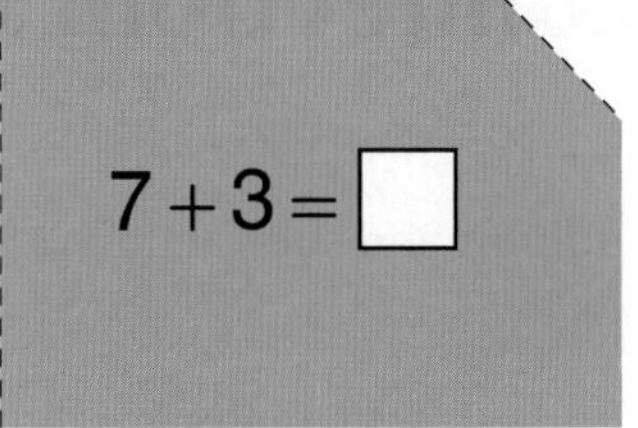

front of card

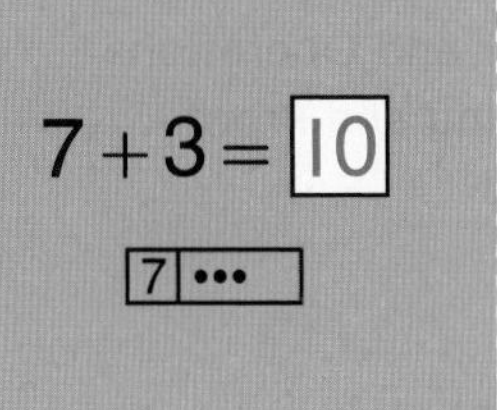

back of card

From Student Activity Book pages 27–28

Class Management

Looking Ahead In the next lesson, children will use the Yellow and Orange Count-On cards. These are on Student Activity Book pages 31–34 and on TRB M29–M32. For classroom activities, children can use the cards provided in the Student Activity Book, or they can take those cards home. You can make sturdy cards specifically for classroom use by copying the TRB onto card stock. In either case, you may want to set aside time before you begin the lesson for children to cut out the cards.

If you have access to the *Math Expressions* materials kits, the Yellow and Orange Count-On Cards are included, so you will not have to prepare these materials.

Ongoing Assessment

As children practice Counting On strategies, have them explain their work by asking questions such as:

- ▶ How can you use Secret Code Cards (or fingers) to find 4 + 2?
- ▶ Which number would you count on from to find 3 + 8? Why did you choose that number?

2 Going Further

Math Connection: Function Tables

Goal: Use addition and subtraction rules to complete a function table.

Materials: Student Activity Book page 26

NCTM Standards:
Number and Operations
Reasoning and Proof
Algebra

Teaching Note

Math Background A function is a relationship between two sets of numbers in which each number in the first set is paired with exactly one number in the second set.

▶ Introduce Function Tables WHOLE CLASS

Write the following equations on the board.

$0 + 3 = \square$
$1 + 3 = \square$
$2 + 3 = \square$
$3 + 3 = \square$

Ask children how the equations are alike and if they notice any patterns. Possible response: All the second partners are 3 and the first partners are in order from 0 to 3.

Have children find each total. Then point out that 3 was added to the first partner each time so we can use a table to show how the first partners and the total are related. We can think of "Add 3" as the rule.

$0 + 3 = 3$
$1 + 3 = 4$
$2 + 3 = 5$
$3 + 3 = 6$

Add 3.	
0	3
1	4
2	5
3	6

Complete the table with the children.

- "Add 3" is the rule for this table. The rule tells us what to do to each number in the first column to get the number in the second column.

Write the following table on the board.

Subtract 4.	
9	5
10	6
7	3
8	4

- What is the rule for this table? Subtract 4.
- What does the rule mean? Subtract 4 from each number in the first column.
- Complete the table with your class.

Have children complete Student Activity Book page 26.

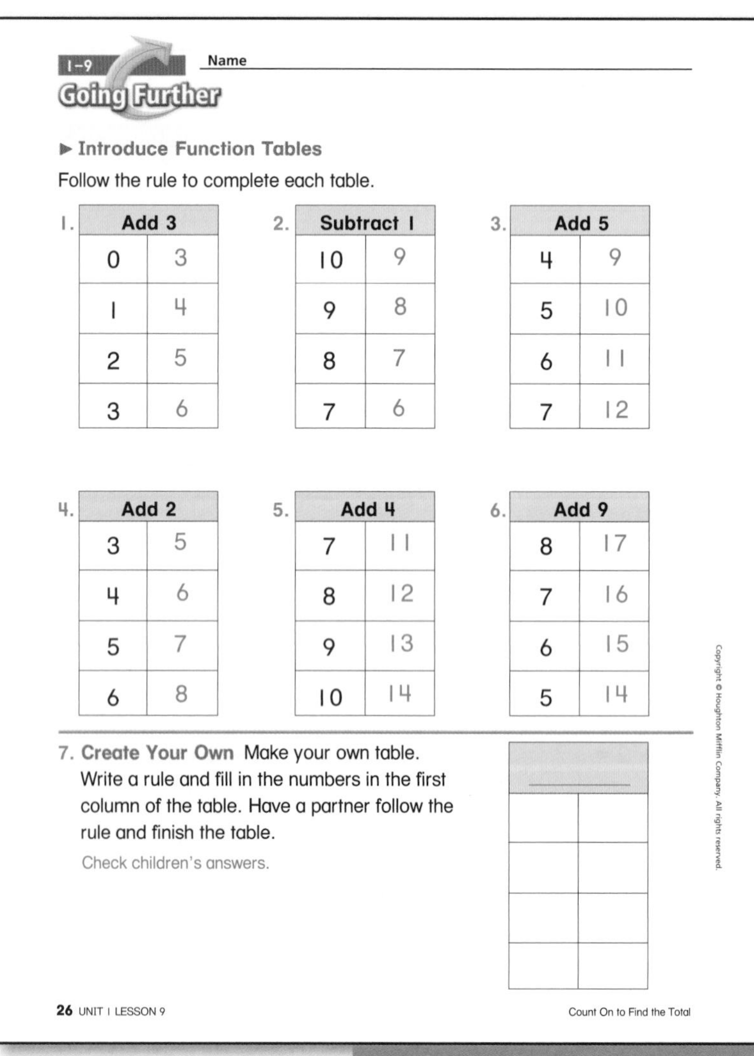

1-9 Going Further Name

▶ Introduce Function Tables

Follow the rule to complete each table.

1.

Add 3	
0	3
1	4
2	5
3	6

2.

Subtract 1	
10	9
9	8
8	7
7	6

3.

Add 5	
4	9
5	10
6	11
7	12

4.

Add 2	
3	5
4	6
5	7
6	8

5.

Add 4	
7	11
8	12
9	13
10	14

6.

Add 9	
8	17
7	16
6	15
5	14

7. **Create Your Own** Make your own table. Write a rule and fill in the numbers in the first column of the table. Have a partner follow the rule and finish the table.

Check children's answers.

26 UNIT 1 LESSON 9 Count On to Find the Total

Student Activity Book page 26

Intervention Activity Card 1-9

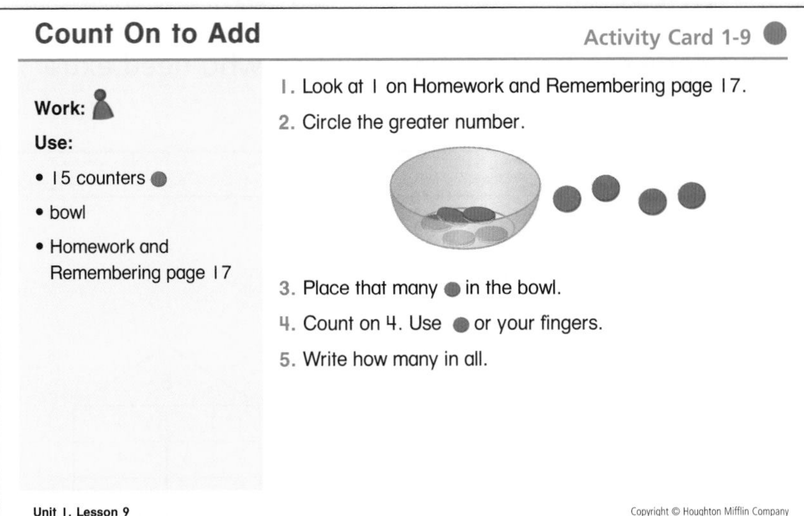

Count On to Add Activity Card 1-9

Work:

Use:

- 15 counters
- bowl
- Homework and Remembering page 17

1. Look at 1 on Homework and Remembering page 17.
2. Circle the greater number.
3. Place that many in the bowl.
4. Count on 4. Use or your fingers.
5. Write how many in all.

Unit 1, Lesson 9

Copyright © Houghton Mifflin Company

Activity Note Each child needs 15 counters, a bowl, and Homework and Remembering page 17. Have children count on to find each total.

Math Writing Prompt

Explain Your Thinking How can you use counting on to find the total of 3 + 4?

Software Support

Use *Soar to Success* for instruction of students needing targeted support for underlying skills.

On Level Activity Card 1-9

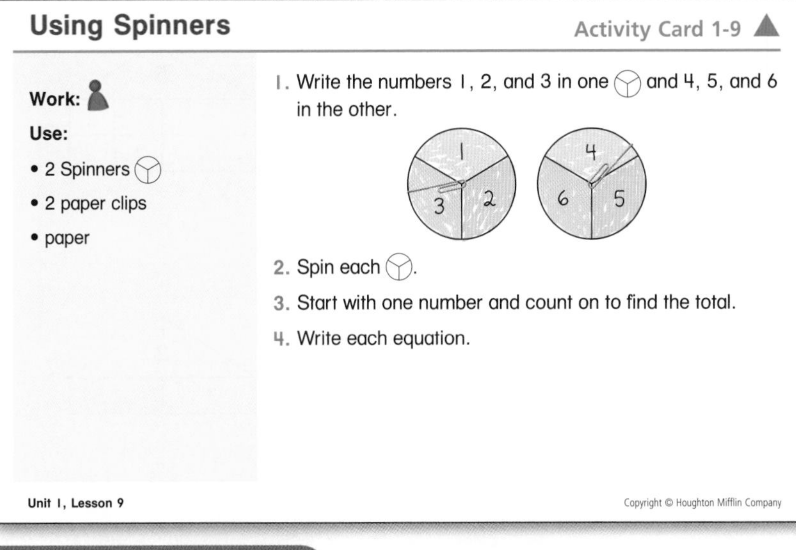

Using Spinners Activity Card 1-9

Work:

Use:

- 2 Spinners
- 2 paper clips
- paper

1. Write the numbers 1, 2, and 3 in one and 4, 5, and 6 in the other.
2. Spin each .
3. Start with one number and count on to find the total.
4. Write each equation.

Unit 1, Lesson 9

Copyright © Houghton Mifflin Company

Activity Note Each child needs 2 spinners (TRB M27), and paper clips. One spinner should have the numbers 1, 2, and 3 while the other one should have 4, 5 and 6.

Math Writing Prompt

You Decide Would you begin counting on from the 6 or the 4 to find the total of 4 + 6? Explain your answer.

Software Support

Use *MegaMath* for review and reinforcement of the concepts and skills presented in this lesson.

Challenge Activity Card 1-9

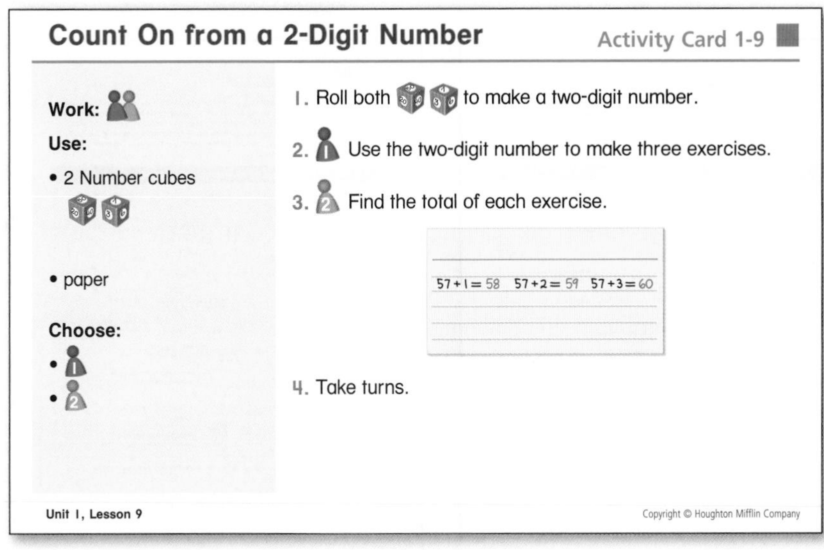

Count On from a 2-Digit Number Activity Card 1-9

Work:

Use:

- 2 Number cubes
- paper

Choose:

1. Roll both to make a two-digit number.
2. Use the two-digit number to make three exercises.
3. Find the total of each exercise.

57 + 1 = 58 57 + 2 = 59 57 + 3 = 60

4. Take turns.

Unit 1, Lesson 9

Copyright © Houghton Mifflin Company

Activity Note Each pair needs two number cubes (numbers 10, 20, 30, 40, 50, 60 and 3–8). One child rolls both number cubes to form a two-digit number. Then writes three exercises, such as 56 + 2.

Math Writing Prompt

Extend Your Thinking How can you use counting on to help add 67 + 4? Use drawings to help explain your answer.

Software Support

Use *Destination Math* to take students beyond the concepts and skills presented in this lesson.

Homework and Targeted Practice

1–9 Homework Goal: Additional Practice

Include children's completed Homework page as part of their portfolios.

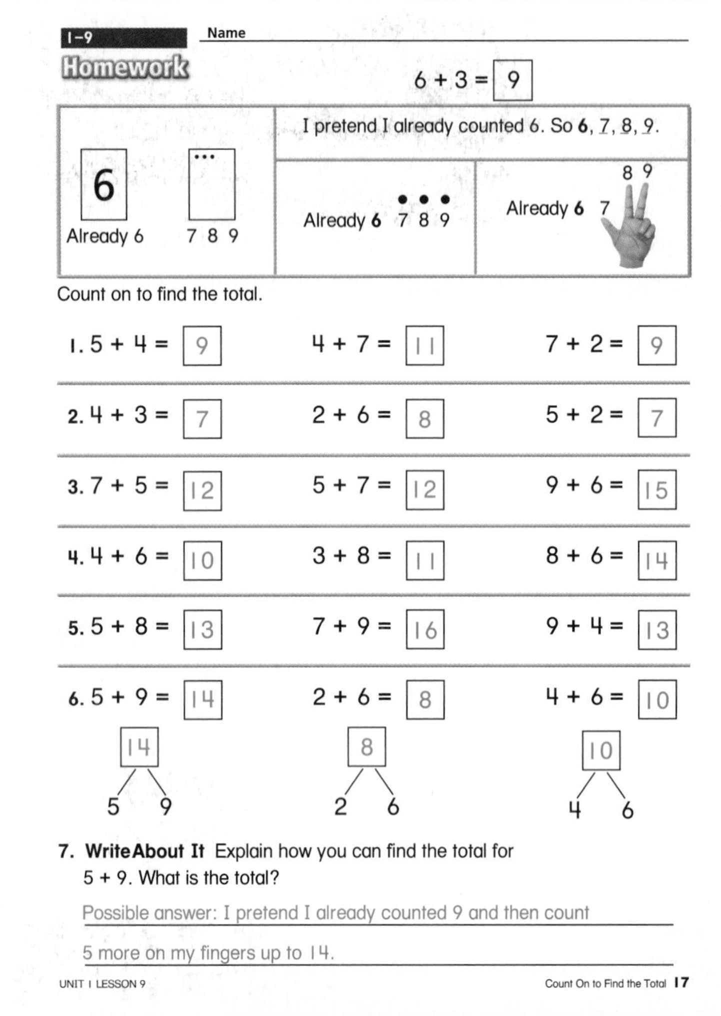

1–9 Homework Name ______

6 + 3 = 9

I pretend I already counted 6. So **6**, 7, 8, 9.

Already 6 — 7 8 9 | Already **6** 7 8 9 | Already **6** 7 8 9

Count on to find the total.

1. 5 + 4 = 9	4 + 7 = 11	7 + 2 = 9
2. 4 + 3 = 7	2 + 6 = 8	5 + 2 = 7
3. 7 + 5 = 12	5 + 7 = 12	9 + 6 = 15
4. 4 + 6 = 10	3 + 8 = 11	8 + 6 = 14
5. 5 + 8 = 13	7 + 9 = 16	9 + 4 = 13
6. 5 + 9 = 14	2 + 6 = 8	4 + 6 = 10
14 / 5 9	8 / 2 6	10 / 4 6

7. **Write About It** Explain how you can find the total for 5 + 9. What is the total?

Possible answer: I pretend I already counted 9 and then count 5 more on my fingers up to 14.

UNIT 1 LESSON 9 Count On to Find the Total **17**

Homework and Remembering page 17

1–9 Targeted Practice Goal: Complete Partner Houses.

This page can be used with children who need extra practice counting on.

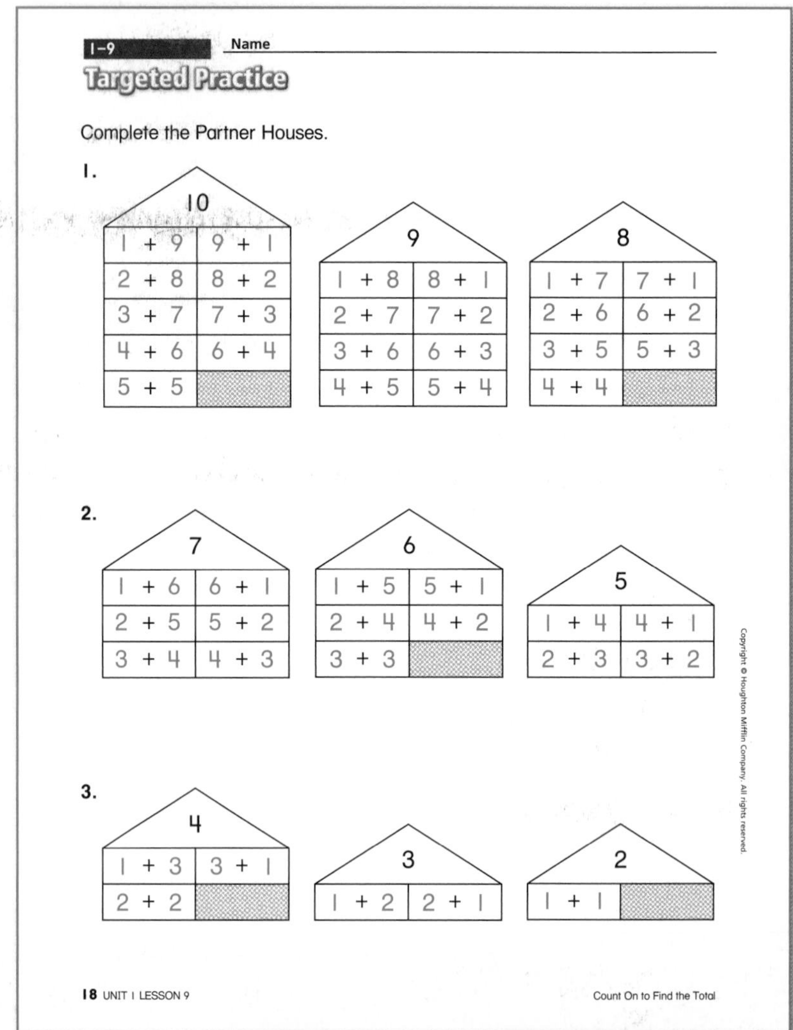

1–9 Targeted Practice Name ______

Complete the Partner Houses.

1.

10	
1 + 9	9 + 1
2 + 8	8 + 2
3 + 7	7 + 3
4 + 6	6 + 4
5 + 5	

9	
1 + 8	8 + 1
2 + 7	7 + 2
3 + 6	6 + 3
4 + 5	5 + 4

8	
1 + 7	7 + 1
2 + 6	6 + 2
3 + 5	5 + 3
4 + 4	

2.

7	
1 + 6	6 + 1
2 + 5	5 + 2
3 + 4	4 + 3

6	
1 + 5	5 + 1
2 + 4	4 + 2
3 + 3	

5	
1 + 4	4 + 1
2 + 3	3 + 2

3.

4	
1 + 3	3 + 1
2 + 2	

3	
1 + 2	2 + 1

2	
1 + 1	

18 UNIT 1 LESSON 9 Count On to Find the Total

Homework and Remembering page 18

Home and School Connection

Family Letter Have children take home the Family Letter on Student Activity Book page 29. This letter explains how the concept of addition is developed in *Math Expressions.* It gives parents and guardians a better understanding of the learning that goes on in math class and creates a bridge between school and home. A Spanish translation of this letter is on the following page in the Student Activity Book.

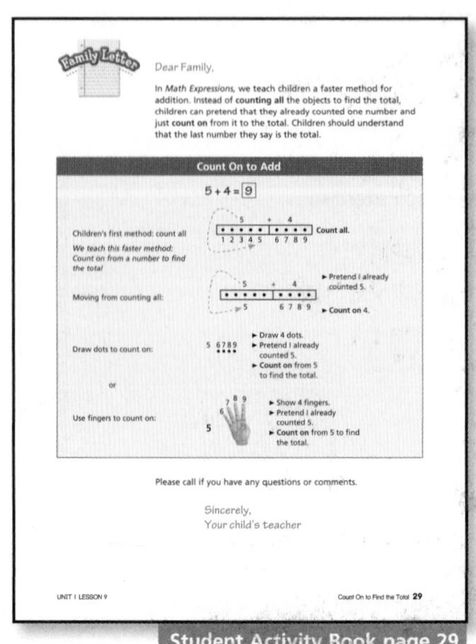

Family Letter

Dear Family,

In *Math Expressions*, we teach children a faster method for addition. Instead of **counting all** the objects to find the total, children can pretend that they already counted one number and just **count on** from it to the total. Children should understand that the last number they say is the total.

Count On to Add

5 + 4 = 9

Children's first method: count all — 1 2 3 4 5 6 7 8 9 **Count all.**

We teach this faster method: Count on from a number to find the total

Moving from counting all: 5 6 7 8 9 ► Pretend I already counted 5. ► **Count on** 4.

Draw dots to count on: 5 6789 ► Draw 4 dots. ► Pretend I already counted 5. ► **Count on** from 5 to find the total.

or

Use fingers to count on: 5 6 7 8 9 ► Show 4 fingers. ► Pretend I already counted 5. ► **Count on** from 5 to find the total.

Please call if you have any questions or comments.

Sincerely,
Your child's teacher

UNIT 1 LESSON 9 Count On to Find the Total **29**

Student Activity Book page 29

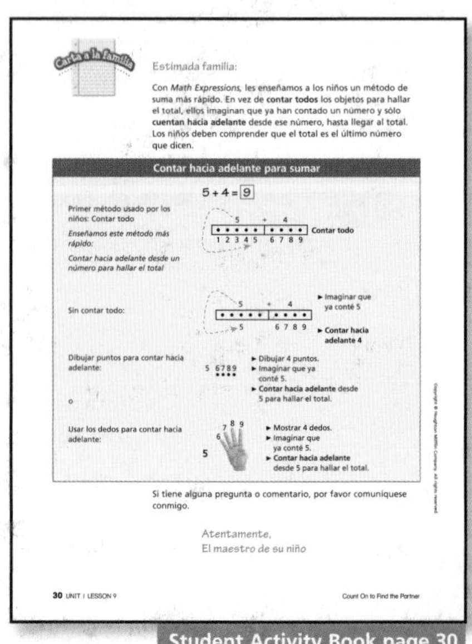

Carta a la familia

Estimada familia:

Con *Math Expressions*, les enseñamos a los niños un método de suma más rápido. En vez de **contar todos** los objetos para hallar el total, ellos imaginan que ya han contado un número y sólo **cuentan hacia adelante** desde ese número, hasta llegar al total. Los niños deben comprender que el total es el último número que dicen.

Contar hacia adelante para sumar

5 + 4 = 9

Primer método usado por los niños: Contar todo — 1 2 3 4 5 6 7 8 9 **Contar todo**

Enseñamos este método más rápido:

Contar hacia adelante desde un número para hallar el total

Sin contar todo: 5 6 7 8 9 ► Imaginar que ya conté 5 ► **Contar hacia adelante 4**

Dibujar puntos para contar hacia adelante: 5 6789 ► Dibujar 4 puntos. ► Imaginar que ya conté 5. ► **Contar hacia adelante** desde 5 para hallar el total.

o

Usar los dedos para contar hacia adelante: 5 6 7 8 9 ► Mostrar 4 dedos. ► Imaginar que ya conté 5. ► **Contar hacia adelante** desde 5 para hallar el total.

Si tiene alguna pregunta o comentario, por favor comuníquese conmigo.

Atentamente,
El maestro de su niño

30 UNIT 1 LESSON 9 Count On to Find the Partner

Student Activity Book page 30

Count On to Find the Partner

Vocabulary

partner
unknown partner
total
equation
proof drawing
count on
teen number

Lesson Objective

- Count on to solve mystery addition and subtraction problems.

The Day at a Glance

Today's Goals	Materials	
1 Teaching the Lesson **A1:** Explore counting on to solve mystery addition and subtraction equations. **A2:** Practice counting on to solve mystery addition and subtraction equations.	**Lesson Activities** Student Activity Book pp. 31, 33–38 (includes Yellow and Orange Count-On Cards, Family Letter) Homework and Remembering pp. 19–20 Quick Quiz 2 (Assessment Guide) Demonstration Secret Code Cards	**Going Further** Activity Cards 1-10 Student Activity Book p. 32 Connecting cubes Number cubes MathBoard materials Math Journals
2 Going Further ► Problem Solving Strategy: Reasoning ► Differentiated Instruction		
3 Homework and Spiral Review		

Keeping Skills Sharp

Quick Practice — 5 MINUTES

Goal: Add or subtract 0 or 1.

Stay or Go? Write the following exercises on the board.

7 + 1	3 + 0	8 + 1
7 − 0	3 − 0	8 − 0
7 + 0	3 + 1	8 − 1
7 − 1	3 − 1	8 + 0

The leader points to any exercise, pauses briefly, and then gives a signal for the class to respond together. The children give responses such as these.

7 + 1	Go on 1. 8		7 + 0	Stay. 7
7 − 1	Go back 1. 6		7 − 0	Stay. 7

Repeated Quick Practice Use these Quick Practices from previous lessons.

► **Unknown Partner or Prairie Dog** Use numbers 6 and 9. (See Unit 1 Lessons 8 and 9.)

► **The Teen Machine** (See Unit 1 Lesson 6.)

Daily Routines

Money Routine Using the 120 Poster, Using the Money Flip Chart, Using the Number Path, Using Secret Code Cards (See pp. xxiii–xxv.)

► Led by Student Leaders

1 Teaching the Lesson

Activity 1

Count On to Find the Partner

25 MINUTES

Goal: Explore counting on to solve mystery addition and subtraction equations.

Materials: Demonstration Secret Code Cards (TRB M7–M22)

NCTM Standard:
Number and Operations

Alternate Approach

Use Fingers Children have used fingers to count on to find the total. Demonstrate or ask a child to demonstrate how to use fingers to find an unknown partner.

5 + ☐ = 8

Already 5 +

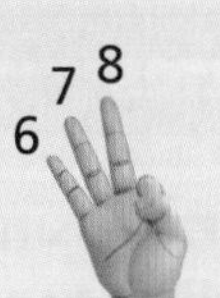

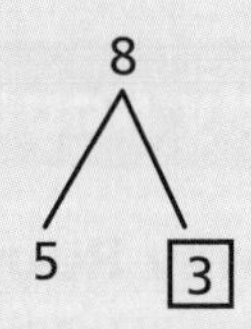

3 more to make 8.

5 + [3] = 8

When you use fingers to find the unknown partner, you stop when you hear the total you know and you look at your fingers to see the unknown partner.

▶ Finding an Unknown Partner WHOLE CLASS

Write the following story problem and equation on the board. Read the problem aloud.

We had 5 inches of snow this morning. We had some more snow this afternoon. Then the snow stopped. We had 8 inches of snow altogether. How much snow fell this afternoon?

5 + ☐ = 8

- The box stands for the unknown partner. We call this "mystery" addition because we have to find one of the numbers we are adding.
- How would you read this equation? 5 plus what number equals 8? 5 and how many more make 8?

Ask a few volunteers to explain how they would solve the problem. Accept various solutions.

▶ Count On to Find the Partner WHOLE CLASS

Use Secret Code Cards Display the Demonstration Secret Code Cards for 5 and 3, showing the number 5 and three dots.

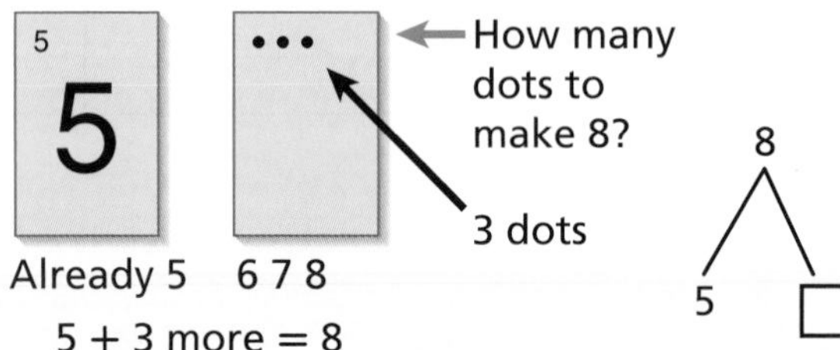

- Think about our snow problem. We know that we already have 5. We want to know how many more it takes to get to 8. Pretend we already counted 5. Then count on to find how many more dots to get to 8.

Remind children that 8 is the last number they say when they count; it is the total but not the answer. They need to go back and count the number of dots or fingers to get the answer 3. This is the unknown partner.

Show children that they counted up to 8: 6, 7, 8.

- How many dots did it take to get to 8? 3 3 inches of snow fell during the afternoon.
- We just used counting on to find the partner that we didn't know. In this problem, the partners 5 and 3 make a total of 8.

▶ Count On to Solve a Subtraction Problem

WHOLE CLASS

Write the story problem and the following equation on the board. Read the problem aloud.

Today 8 apples fell on the ground. Then squirrels took 5. How many apples are left on the ground?

$$8 - 5 = \square$$

Ask children how they would solve the problem. Accept various solutions.

If children do not discover it themselves, explain that the subtraction problem can be solved in the same way as a mystery addition problem. Both subtraction problems and mystery addition problems require you to find an unknown partner. You can count on from the partner you know to the total (T) to find the unknown partner (P).

$$\overset{T}{8} - 5 = \overset{P}{\square}$$

$$5 + \underset{P}{\square} = \underset{T}{8}$$

Children can subtract by pretending the 5 is there already as they did when finding the unknown partner in mystery addition.

$$5 + \square = 8$$

I took away 5 • • • 6 7 8 so 3 more to make 8

- We can solve the subtraction problem the same way we solved the mystery addition problem. How many did we subtract? 5 Count on to 8 to find the unknown partner: 6, 7, 8. That was 3 more, so 8 − 5 = 3.

Activity continued ▶

The Learning Classroom

Math Talk To continue to keep children in their seats engaged and to move this engagement to a deeper level, challenge them to listen carefully so that they might say the explainers' statements in their own words. Ask several children to "repeat" what has been explained by the child explainer in their own words.

Teaching Note

What to Expect from Students Many second graders count back to solve subtraction problems. These methods are slow, effortful, and prone to errors. It is faster and safer to count on for subtraction. Watch for children who count back for subtraction and make errors (they often are off by 1) and work with them to change to using counting on. Children can make this switch and find counting on to be much easier if they just think of the starting number as the amount taken away.

English Language Learners

Review the apple story problem. Write 8 − 5 = □ and 5 + □ = 8. Review *count on*.

- **Beginning** Say: **Subtract to solve. 8 − 5 = 3.** Have children repeat. Say: ***Count on* to 8 to solve. 6, 7, 8. That was 3 so 5 + 3 = 8.**
- **Intermediate** Say: **Subtract to solve.** Ask: **What is 8 − 5?** 3 Say: ***Count on* to 8 to solve. What number plus 5 is 8?** 3
- **Advanced** Have children tell how to use subtraction and counting on to solve.

Teaching the Lesson (continued)

Teaching Note

Watch For! Some children may get the wrong answer because they started counting from the total. Remind children to start counting on from the smaller number and count on to the larger number, raising a finger for each number spoken.

Use Fingers to Find the Partner Counting on to find the partner looks the same in subtraction and mystery addition. Remind children about the apple problem.

- We know that 8 apples fell from a tree to the ground. We know that squirrels took 5 of them. We want to find the other partner of 8 that goes with 5. That will tell us how many apples are left on the ground.

Start counting on with the smaller number (the known partner), and count on to the larger (the total), raising a finger for each number spoken.

- If we start at 5, how many more do we need to reach 8? Let's raise one finger for each new number we count on: 6, 7, 8.

5 +

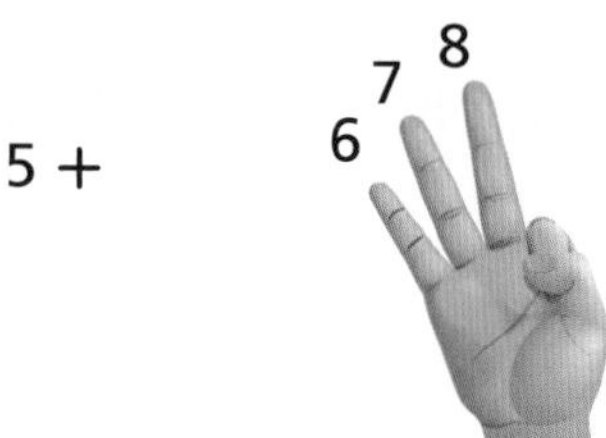

When the total is reached, look at or feel the number of fingers raised.

- Is 8 the answer? no We already know that 8 is the number of apples that fell to the ground.
- What is the answer? 3, the number of fingers we raised. There are 3 apples left on the ground.

Point out to children that they will be able to use what they learned today to help them when doing the Quick Practice activities Unknown Partner or Prairie Dog.

The Learning Classroom

Helping Community Encourage children who have success with this skill to help others who are having difficulty. Remind the class what a good helper does. For example, a good helper will lead someone through the process step by step but will not give the answer. Children may come up with a list of guidelines for good helping that can be posted in the classroom.

Activity 2

Practice Finding Unknown Partners

25 MINUTES

Goal: Practice counting on to solve mystery addition and subtraction equations.

Materials: Student Activity Book pages 31, 33–36, Yellow and Orange Count-On Cards

NCTM Standard:
Number and Operations

▶ Relate Addition and Subtraction WHOLE CLASS

Children can practice counting on by solving the equations on Student Activity Book page 31.

Have children demonstrate how they counted on for some of the more difficult problems. Stress that everyone is counting on today just to make sure everyone can count on because it is faster than counting all or taking away or counting down. On following days children can use other methods or may just "know the answer."

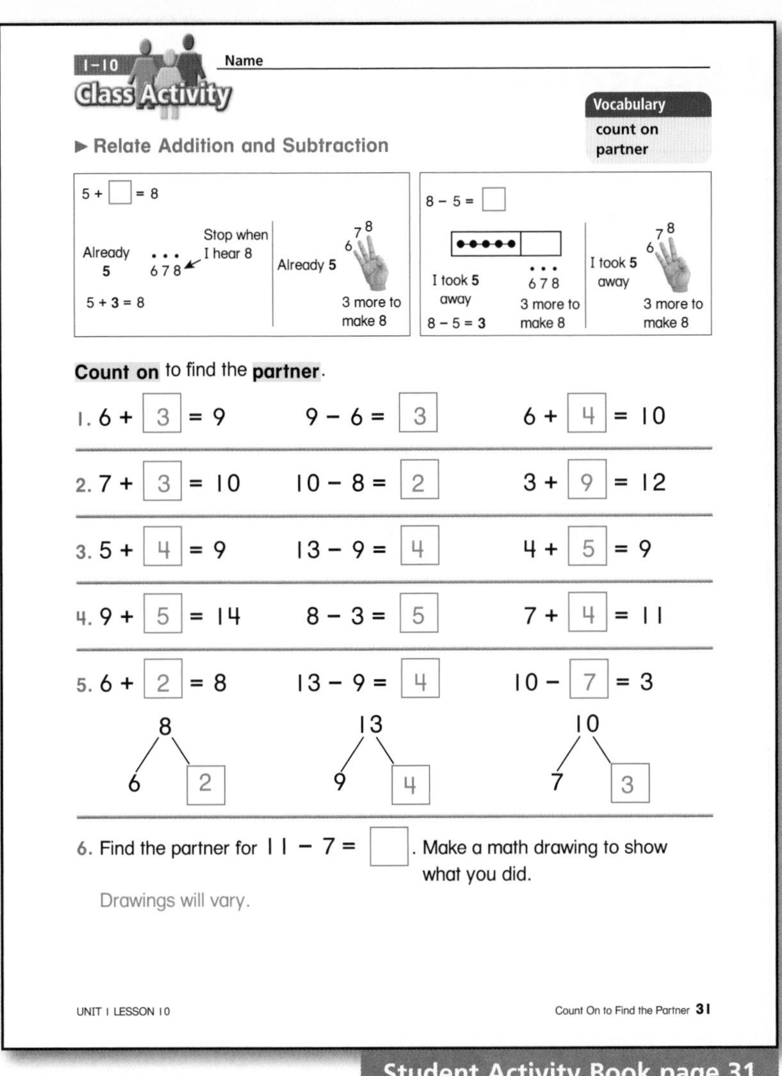

1-10 Class Activity

Name

Vocabulary
count on
partner

▶ Relate Addition and Subtraction

5 + ☐ = 8
Already 5 ... 6 7 8 Stop when I hear 8
5 + 3 = 8
Already 5 — 6 7 8 — 3 more to make 8

8 − 5 = ☐
I took 5 away ... 6 7 8 — 3 more to make 8
8 − 5 = 3
I took 5 away — 6 7 8 — 3 more to make 8

Count on to find the **partner**.

1. 6 + [3] = 9 9 − 6 = [3] 6 + [4] = 10
2. 7 + [3] = 10 10 − 8 = [2] 3 + [9] = 12
3. 5 + [4] = 9 13 − 9 = [4] 4 + [5] = 9
4. 9 + [5] = 14 8 − 3 = [5] 7 + [4] = 11
5. 6 + [2] = 8 13 − 9 = [4] 10 − [7] = 3

8: 6 and [2] 13: 9 and [4] 10: 7 and [3]

6. Find the partner for 11 − 7 = ☐. Make a math drawing to show what you did.

Drawings will vary.

UNIT 1 LESSON 10 Count On to Find the Partner 31

Student Activity Book page 31

▶ Introduce the Yellow and Orange Count-On Cards INDIVIDUALS

Have children cut out the Yellow and Orange Count-On Cards on Student Activity Book pages 33–36. (These cards are also on TRB M29–M32. If you wish, print the cards on card stock to have a set for children to use at home.) If you have access to the *Math Expressions* materials kits, the Orange and Yellow Count-On Cards are included, so you will not have to prepare these materials.

Point out that each card has a mystery addition or subtraction exercise on one side and the answer on the back. Have children place the cards so that the exercises are face up. Children can do this by making sure that the cut corner of each card is in the upper right corner.

Explain to children that they will use these cards in the same way they used the Red Count-On Cards. See page 63.

Ongoing Assessment

For both mystery addition equations and subtraction equations, check that children understand which numbers are partners and which are totals.

Quick Quiz

See Assessment Guide for Unit 1 Quick Quiz 2.

Yellow Count-On Cards

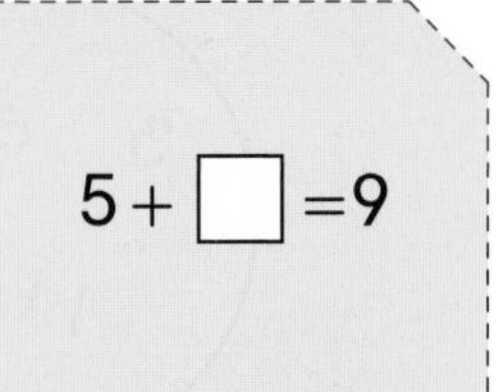

front of card

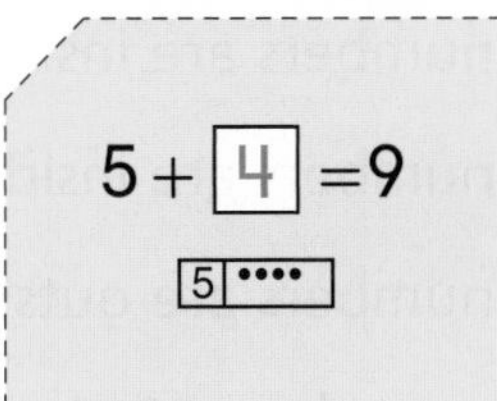

back of card

From Student Activity Book pages 33–34.

Orange Count-On Cards

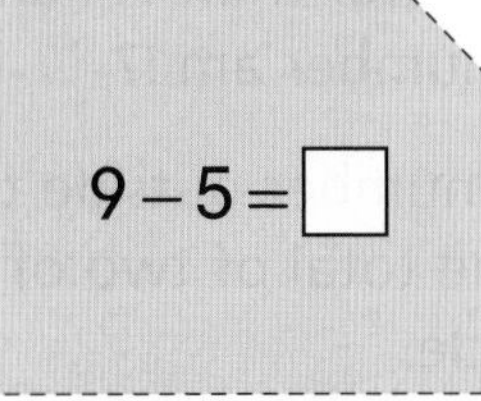

front of card

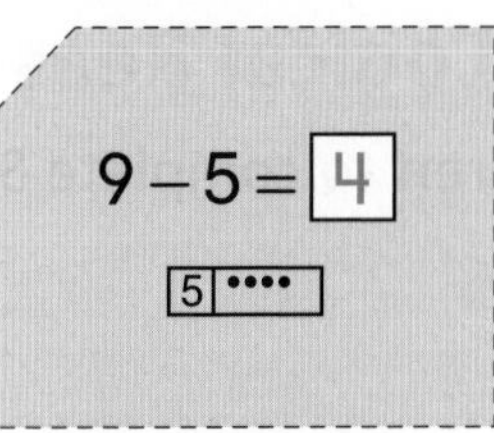

back of card

From Student Activity Book pages 35–36.

2 Going Further

Problem-Solving Strategy: Logical Reasoning

Goal: Use logical reasoning to solve problems.
Materials: Student Activity Book page 32

NCTM Standard:
Number and Operations

▶ Introduce Logical Reasoning

WHOLE CLASS

Draw the following on the board.

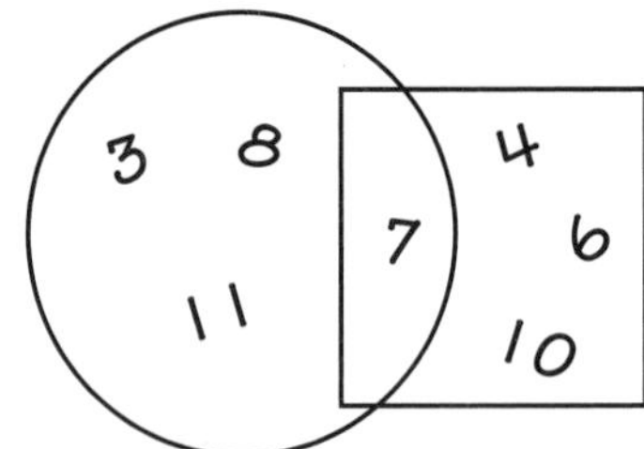

- Which numbers are inside the circle? 7, 3, 8, 11
- Which numbers are inside the square? 6, 4, 10, 7
- Which numbers are outside the square? 3, 8, 11
- Are any numbers inside *both* the circle and square? Yes; 7

Ask children to use the drawing to solve these number riddles.

- I am a number inside the circle.
  I am greater than 7. I am less than 11.
  What number am I? 8
- I am a number outside the circle.
  I am the total of two of the other numbers outside the circle.
  What number am I? 10

▶ Use Logical Reasoning

INDIVIDUALS

Ask children to complete Student Activity Book page 32.

1–10 Name ______

Going Further

▶ Use Logical Reasoning

Use logical reasoning to solve.

1. I am a number inside the circle.
   I am the total of two other numbers inside the circle.
   I am greater than 10. Which two numbers can I be? 11 or 17
2. I am a number inside the square.
   I am the total of two numbers outside the circle.
   I am less than 10. What number am I? 8
3. I am a number inside **both** the circle and the square.
   I am greater than 10. I am less than 15.
   What number am I? 12
4. I am a number outside the square.
   I am a total of two other numbers outside the square.
   What number am I? 9
5. **Write Your Own** Write your own number riddle for the picture. Make sure you can solve it.
   Check children's work.

Student Activity Book page 32

When children finish this page, go over the answers as a class. Have children share the clues they wrote. You may wish to have children share their responses in small groups or pairs. Create a problem bank of clues so the class can have the opportunity to solve all the number riddles.

The Learning Classroom

Helping Community When children finish their work early, let them work with others who may need additional help. Children like to take on this role and enjoy helping each other. This helps children who may otherwise become bored as they wait, to challenge themselves by explaining math content.

Differentiated Instruction

Intervention Activity Card 1-10

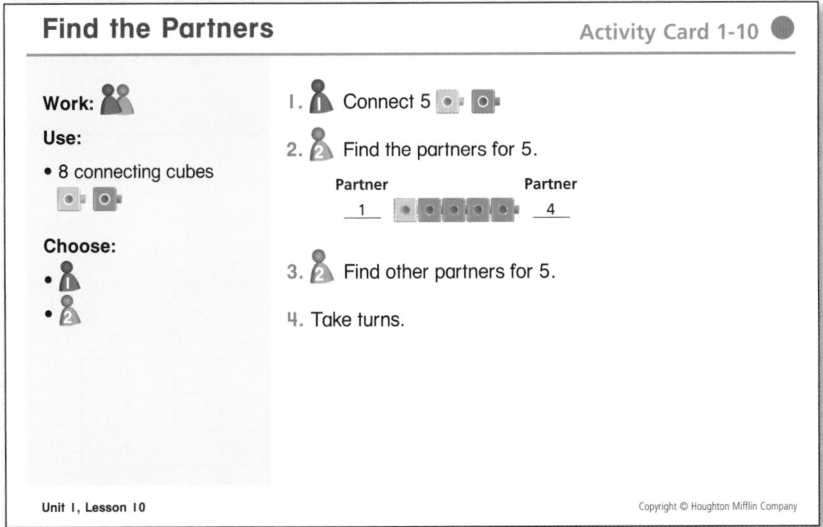

Find the Partners Activity Card 1-10

Work:

Use:

- 8 connecting cubes

Choose:

- 1
- 2

1. Connect 5
2. Find the partners for 5.

   Partner 1 / Partner 4

3. Find other partners for 5.
4. Take turns.

Unit 1, Lesson 10

Activity Note Each pair needs 8 connecting cubes, 4 of each color. One child makes a train with 5 cubes. The other child finds the partners.

Math Writing Prompt

Explain Your Thinking Explain how to count on to find the unknown partner. $6 + \square = 9$

Software Support

Use *Soar to Success* for instruction of students needing targeted support for underlying skills.

On Level Activity Card 1-10

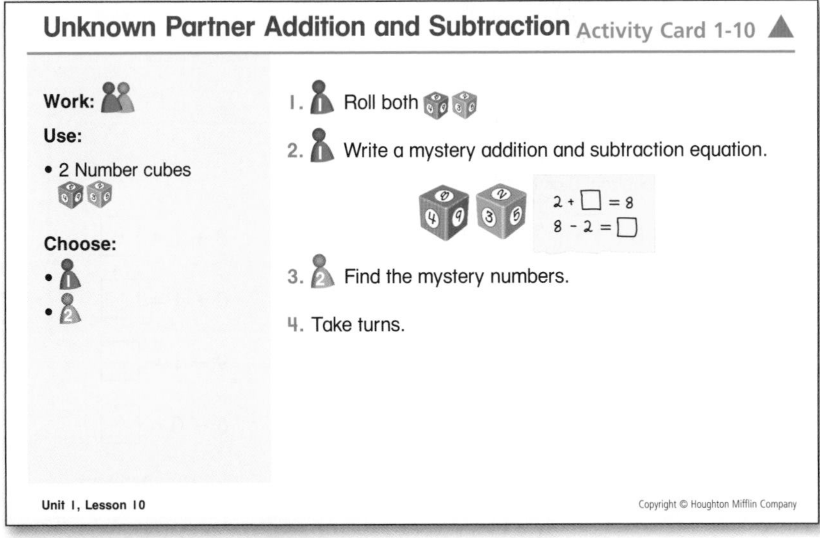

Unknown Partner Addition and Subtraction Activity Card 1-10

Work:

Use:

- 2 Number cubes

Choose:

- 1
- 2

1. Roll both
2. Write a mystery addition and subtraction equation.

   $2 + \square = 8$
   $8 - 2 = \square$

3. Find the mystery numbers.
4. Take turns.

Unit 1, Lesson 10

Activity Note Each pair needs 2 number cubes (numbers 1–6 and 4–9). One child rolls both cubes and uses the numbers to write two equations.

Math Writing Prompt

Investigate Math Carman had 15¢. After buying a pencil, she had 7¢. How much did the pencil cost?

Draw or write to explain how you solved the problem.

Software Support

Use *MegaMath* for review and reinforcement of the concepts and skills presented in this lesson.

Challenge Activity Card 1-10

Unknown Partner with Greater Numbers Activity Card 1-10

Work:

Use:

- paper

1. Write each of these on paper.

   $18 + \square = 22$ $\square + 14 = 17$
   $24 + \square = 28$ $\square + 32 = 37$

2. Find the missing number.
3. Draw or write to explain your answer.

Unit 1, Lesson 10

Activity Note Have children write each equation on paper. Ask children to explain what strategy they used to find the solution.

Math Writing Prompt

Write Your Own Write a mystery addition equation using the numbers 12 and 15. Write a story problem for your equation.

Software Support

Use *Destination Math* to take students beyond the concepts and skills presented in this lesson.

3 Homework and Spiral Review

1–10 Homework **Goal:** Additional Practice

✓ Include children's completed Homework page as part of their portfolios.

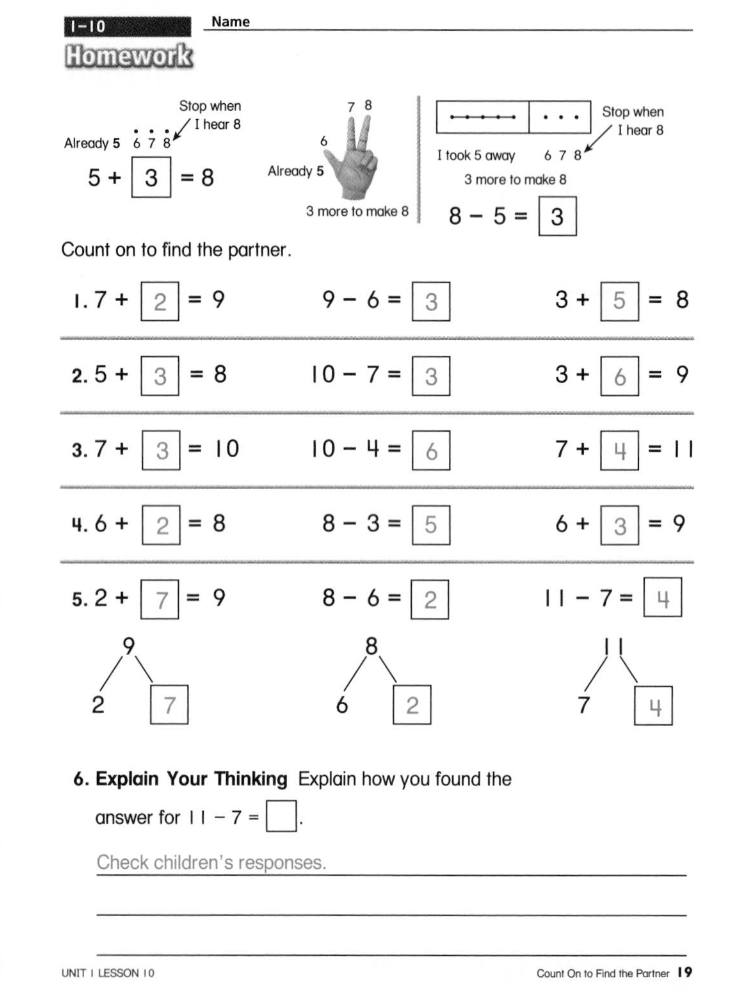

1-10 Homework Name ____________

Already 5 6 7 8 — Stop when I hear 8

5 + [3] = 8

Already 5, 6, 7 8 — 3 more to make 8

I took 5 away 6 7 8 — Stop when I hear 8 — 3 more to make 8

8 − 5 = [3]

Count on to find the partner.

1. 7 + [2] = 9 9 − 6 = [3] 3 + [5] = 8

2. 5 + [3] = 8 10 − 7 = [3] 3 + [6] = 9

3. 7 + [3] = 10 10 − 4 = [6] 7 + [4] = 11

4. 6 + [2] = 8 8 − 3 = [5] 6 + [3] = 9

5. 2 + [7] = 9 8 − 6 = [2] 11 − 7 = [4]

9: 2, [7] 8: 6, [2] 11: 7, [4]

6. **Explain Your Thinking** Explain how you found the answer for 11 − 7 = [ ].

Check children's responses.

UNIT 1 LESSON 10 Count On to Find the Partner **19**

Homework and Remembering page 19

1–10 Remembering **Goal:** Spiral Review

This Remembering activity would be appropriate anytime after today's lesson.

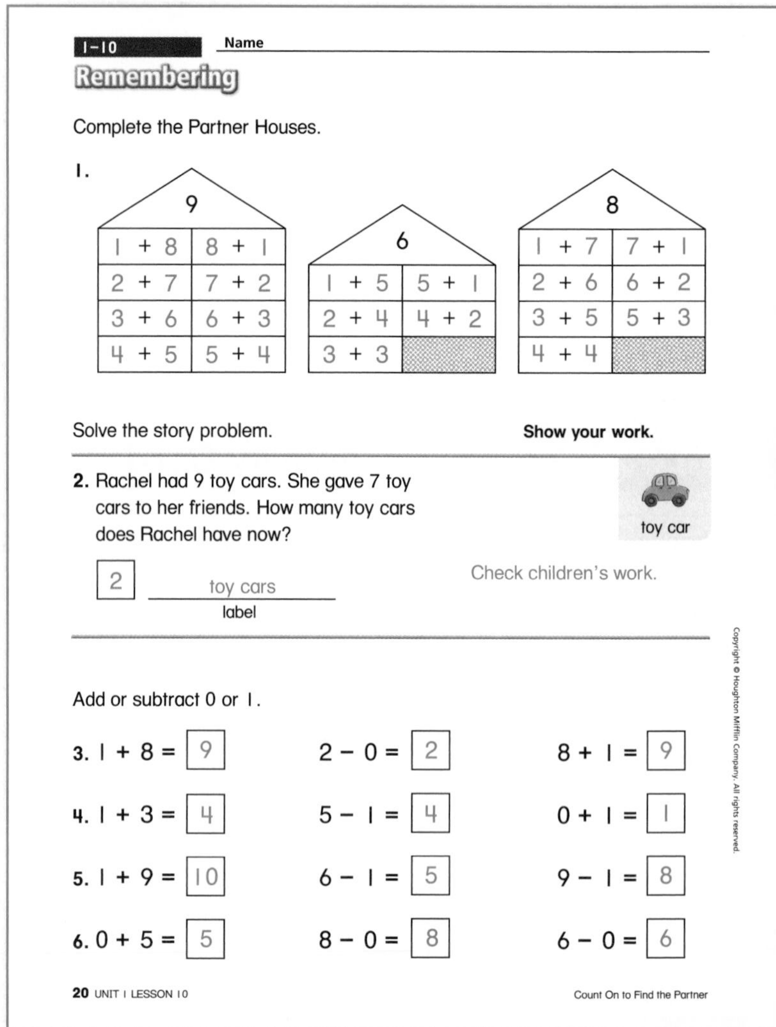

1-10 Remembering Name ____________

Complete the Partner Houses.

1.

9	
1 + 8	8 + 1
2 + 7	7 + 2
3 + 6	6 + 3
4 + 5	5 + 4

6	
1 + 5	5 + 1
2 + 4	4 + 2
3 + 3	

8	
1 + 7	7 + 1
2 + 6	6 + 2
3 + 5	5 + 3
4 + 4	

Solve the story problem. **Show your work.**

2. Rachel had 9 toy cars. She gave 7 toy cars to her friends. How many toy cars does Rachel have now?

toy car

[2] toy cars
label

Check children's work.

Add or subtract 0 or 1.

3. 1 + 8 = [9] 2 − 0 = [2] 8 + 1 = [9]

4. 1 + 3 = [4] 5 − 1 = [4] 0 + 1 = [1]

5. 1 + 9 = [10] 6 − 1 = [5] 9 − 1 = [8]

6. 0 + 5 = [5] 8 − 0 = [8] 6 − 0 = [6]

20 UNIT 1 LESSON 10 Count On to Find the Partner

Homework and Remembering page 20

Home and School Connection

Family Letter Have children take home the Family Letter on Student Activity Book page 37. This letter explains how the concept of counting on to find an unknown partner is developed in *Math Expressions.* This letter gives parents and guardians a better understanding of the learning that goes on in math class and creates a bridge between school and home. A Spanish translation of this letter is on the following page in the Student Activity Book.

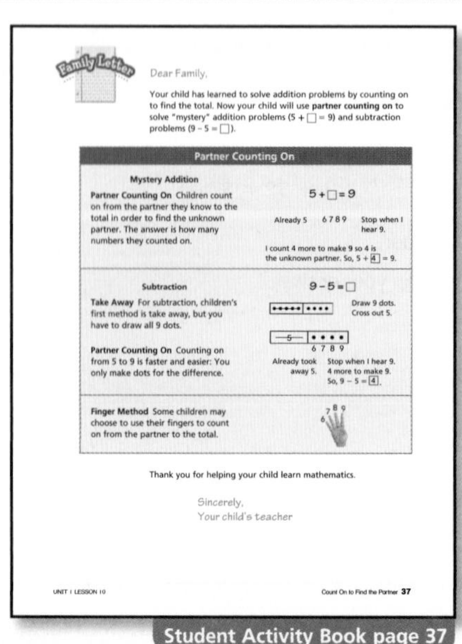

Family Letter

Dear Family,

Your child has learned to solve addition problems by counting on to find the total. Now your child will use **partner counting on** to solve "mystery" addition problems (5 + [ ] = 9) and subtraction problems (9 − 5 = [ ]).

Partner Counting On

Mystery Addition

Partner Counting On Children count on from the partner they know to the total in order to find the unknown partner. The answer is how many numbers they counted on.

5 + [ ] = 9

Subtraction

9 − 5 = [ ]

Take Away For subtraction, children's first method is take away, but you have to draw all 9 dots.

Partner Counting On Counting on from 5 to 9 is faster and easier: You only make dots for the difference.

Finger Method Some children may choose to use their fingers to count on from the partner to the total.

Thank you for helping your child learn mathematics.

Sincerely,
Your child's teacher

UNIT 1 LESSON 10 Count On to Find the Partner **37**

Student Activity Book page 37

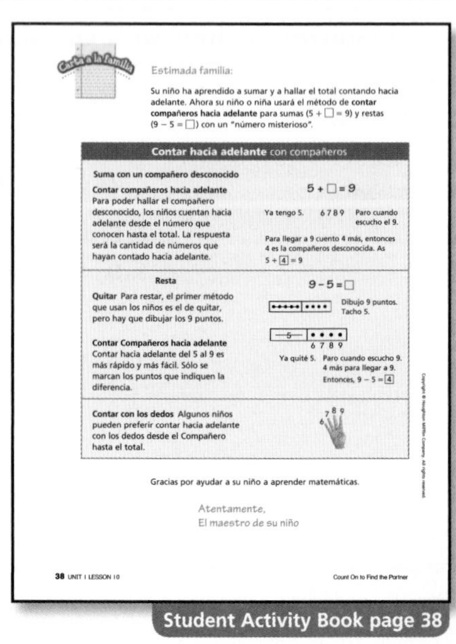

Carta a la familia

Estimada familia:

Su niño ha aprendido a sumar y a hallar el total contando hacia adelante. Ahora su niño o niña usará el método de **contar compañeros hacia adelante** para sumas (5 + [ ] = 9) y restas (9 − 5 = [ ]) con un "número misterioso".

Contar hacia adelante con compañeros

Suma con un compañero desconocido

5 + [ ] = 9

Resta

9 − 5 = [ ]

Contar con los dedos

Gracias por ayudar a su niño a aprender matemáticas.

Atentamente,
El maestro de su niño

38 UNIT 1 LESSON 10 Count On to Find the Partner

Student Activity Book page 38

Use Tens

Vocabulary
teen number
teen total
count on

Lesson Objectives
- Recognize that teen numbers are made up of a ten and some ones.
- Add numbers that make a teen total.

The Day at a Glance

Today's Goals	Materials	
1 Teaching the Lesson **A1:** Use Coin Strips to buy items (less than a dime) and make change. **A2:** Use Coin Strips and fingers to practice the Counting On and the Counting On to 10 strategies to find teen totals. **2 Going Further** ► Differentiated Instruction **3 Homework and Targeted Practice**	**Lesson Activities** Homework and Remembering pp. 21–22 Coin Strips Pennies Chart paper List of yard sale items Coin cover Two-color counters Ten Frame (TRB M33) Real or play money	**Going Further** Activity Cards 1-11 Yard sale list Dime strips Real or play money Math Journals

Use Math Talk today!

Keeping Skills Sharp

Quick Practice — 5 MINUTES

Goal: Add or subtract 0 and 1.

Materials: Pointer

Stay or Go? Write these exercises on the board.

9 + 1	1 + 0	5 + 1
9 − 0	1 − 0	5 − 0
9 + 0	1 + 1	5 − 1
9 − 1	1 − 1	5 + 0

Have a Student Leader point to an exercise, then give a signal for the class to respond together. Children give responses such as these.

9 + 1	Go on 1.	10	9 + 0	Stay.	9
9 − 1	Go back 1.	8	9 − 0	Stay.	9

Repeated Quick Practice Use this Quick Practice from a previous lesson.

- ► **Unknown Partner or Prairie Dog** Use numbers 7 and 10. (See Unit 1 Lessons 8 and 9.)

Daily Routines

Money Routine Using the 120 Poster, Using the Money Flip Chart, Using the Number Path, Using Secret Code Cards (See pp. xxiii–xxv.)

- ► Led by Student Leaders

1 Teaching the Lesson

Activity 1

Buy with a Dime

25 MINUTES

Goal: Use Coin Strips to buy items (less than a dime) and make change.

Materials: Coin Strips (from Unit 1 Lesson 4 or TRB M1) (1 Dime Strip, 1 Nickel Strip, and 9 pennies per child), chart paper

NCTM Standard:
Number and Operations

The Learning Classroom

Quick Practice The *Buy with a Dime* activity will continue as Quick Practice in lessons that follow. In these lessons just the children at the front of the class will use coins and Coin Strips. To keep the practice "quick," the other children will check the *Buy with a Dime* activity just with their fingers rather than with the coins and coin strips.

Class Management

Looking Ahead Keep the Yard Sale chart. You will need to use it again in future lessons.

Differentiated Instruction

English Learners Explain the double meaning of yard as both a unit of measurement and an outdoor area. Explain exactly what a "yard sale" is and have them write or draw examples of things one might find at a yard sale to ensure that they understand.

▶ Getting Prepared

Before this lesson, prepare this list on chart paper and display it in the classroom.

Yard Sale
baby rattle
pen
toy car

▶ Yard Sale Scenario WHOLE CLASS

Ask for Ideas Ask children if they have ever been to a yard sale. Have children who have bought or sold things at a yard sale (or in other situations) describe their experiences.

Direct children's attention to the chart paper and tell children that they are going to act out the Yard Sale scenario to practice making change from a dime.

- We will list some more items for sale on the list. What things would you want to sell or buy at the yard sale?

Record all acceptable answers on the chart paper. Help children price all the items between 1¢ and 10¢. You may want to suggest that they first choose an item that would cost 1¢, and then choose prices for other items that will cost more. Write a price next to each item.

Make Change with Coin Strips Invite six children to demonstrate the Yard Sale scenario. Assign roles: one child will be a Buyer, one will be a Seller, and four children will be Bookkeepers. Ask the Buyer and Seller to stand by the list of items for sale and have the Bookkeepers stand by the board.

Make sure that each child has a Dime Strip, a Nickel Strip, and 9 pennies.

Explain what the Buyer, Seller, and the four Bookkeepers should do.

- The Seller has a Nickel Strip and four pennies (you could also give nine pennies).
- The Buyer has a Dime Strip.
- After the Buyer chooses an item and completes the sale with the Seller, the four Bookkeepers record the change in different ways on the board.

Math Talk Help children go through a sales purchase.

Buyer: I'd like to buy the baby rattle for my baby brother. Here's my dime. (*Buyer hands his or her Dime Strip to the seller.*)

Seller: The baby rattle costs 1¢. So your change will be 9¢. 9¢ is 5¢ and 4¢, so I will give a Nickel Strip and 4 pennies for change. (*Seller hands a Nickel Strip and 4 pennies to the Buyer.*)

Have the four Bookkeepers draw and explain different ways to make 9¢ change.

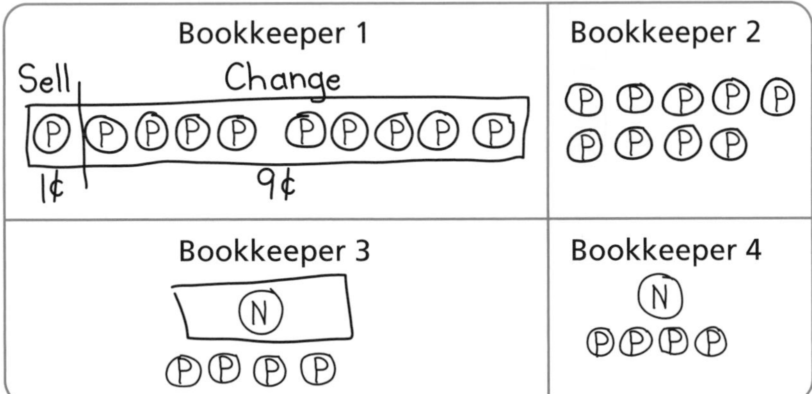

Ask the rest of the class to check the Buyer's, Seller's, and Bookkeepers' transactions with their Coin Strips and pennies. Make certain the whole class is participating by using their own Coin Strips and pennies.

Continue the scenario with other children acting as the Buyer, Seller, and Bookkeepers. As the children continue to play, encourage them to work at becoming faster at making change in different ways.

The Learning Classroom

Helping Community Children at the board may struggle at some time and they usually welcome help from other children at that point. Allowing other children to help instead of you will help them to assume responsibility for one another's learning. Ask the child who they would like to have help them. You can move on to another explainer while they redo the work. Of course, sometimes it is fine to go ahead and have the whole class help the child while you lead with questions.

Ongoing Assessment

As children work at their desks to model ways to show change, have them explain what they are doing. Encourage them to show the change in multiple ways by asking questions such as:

- How can you show the change using coins?
- Can you show the change using other coins?
- Can you use a Coin Strip to show the change?

Activity 2

Add to Get a Teen Number

 25 MINUTES

Goal: Use Coin Strips and fingers to practice the Counting On and the Counting On to 10 strategies to find teen totals.

Materials: Coin Strips (from Unit 1 Lesson 4 or TRB M1) (1 Dime Strip, and 6 Penny Strips per child), coin cover (index card, sticky note, or paper per child), two-color counters (10 per child), Ten Frame (TRB M33), real or play money

 **NCTM Standard:**
Number and Operations

The Learning Classroom

Building Concepts It is important to model the thinking for children and have them think aloud with you. Many children need concrete, visual support for symbolic representations.

Alternate Approach

Coins Some children may have difficulty using the individual pennies. For those children, you could use real or play money for the pennies.

▶ Counting On WHOLE CLASS

Children will use what they learned about the Counting On strategy to find teen totals.

Use Coin Strips Have children use their coin cover, 1 Dime Strip and 6 pennies to find the total of 8 + 6.

- We will use our Coins Strips to add two numbers to make a teen. Let's start with 8 + 6. Put your Dime Strip down and put the coin cover over the top two pennies so you can only see 8 pennies. Now put 6 more pennies next to your Dime Strip to show the 6 we are adding.

- To find the total of 8 and 6, we can count on.
- Imagine I already counted 8. Then count on your pennies. 9, 10, 11, 12, 13, 14.

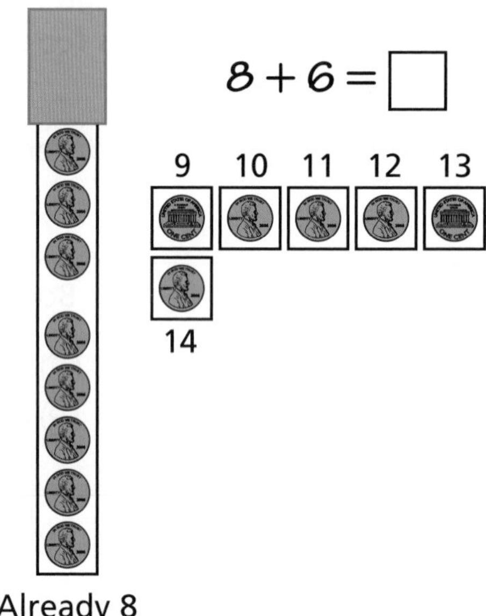

Use Fingers Have children also count on using their fingers. Have the class model how to find the teen total for 8 + 6.

- I pretend I already counted 8. Now I need to show the other number with my fingers. *(show 6 fingers)*

- Already 8 ... 9, 10, 11, 12, 13, 14. 8 + 6 equals 14.

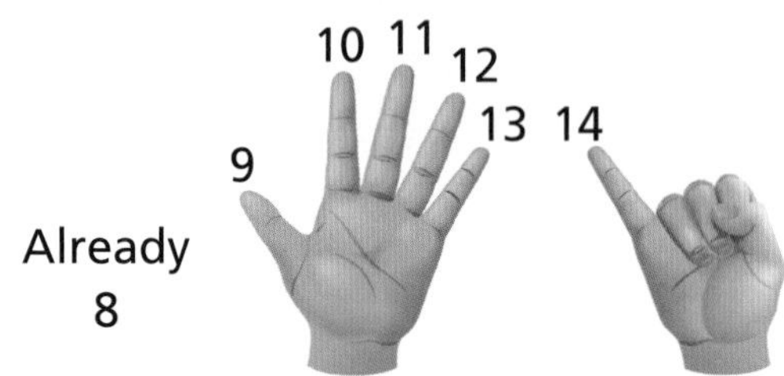

▶ Counting On to 10 WHOLE CLASS

Explain to children that using the Counting On strategy is fine, but there is another strategy that is faster, the Counting On to 10 strategy in which you count on but stop at 10 and look at your pennies or fingers and see the rest to make the total.

The Counting On to 10 strategy is transitional to the Make a Ten strategy explored in Lesson 12. There you chunk both numbers: the chunk to make ten and the chunk over ten. Today children will count on to 10 but then stop and look at their fingers or pennies to see how many to put with 10 to make the teen total.

Use Coin Strips Use the same example from before to model for your class how to use the Counting On to 10 strategy to find a teen total for 8 + 6.

- Put your Dime Strip down and put the coin cover over the top two pennies so you can only see 8 pennies. Now put 6 more pennies next to your Dime Strip to show the 6 we are adding.
- I already have 8. Now I'll count on to 10 and stop.
- I see and know there are 4 more. 10 + 4 = 14.

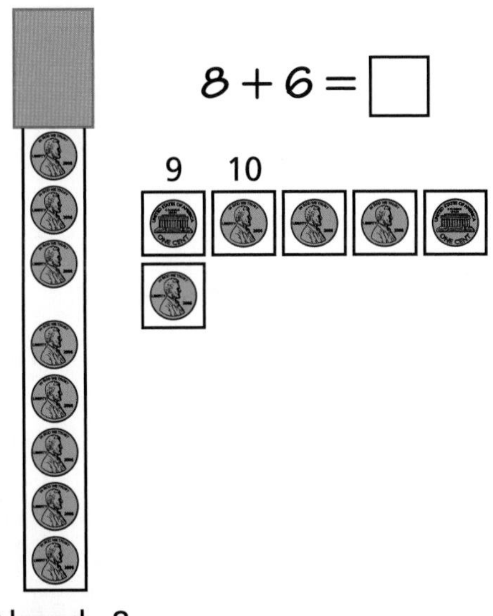

Use Fingers Tell children they can also count on to 10 using their fingers. Have the class model how to find the teen total for 8 + 6.

- I pretend I already counted 8. Now I need to show the other number with my fingers. (*show 6 fingers*)
- I have 8 ... 9, 10 (*stop*)
- I see 4 left, so we know that 10 + 4 = 14.

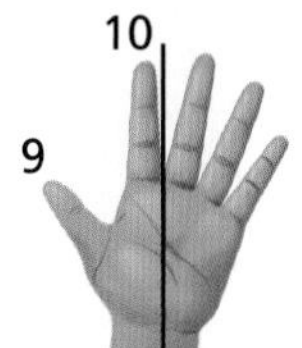

Activity continued ▶

Alternate Approach

Ten Frame Use Ten Frame (TRB M33) and two color counters to help children with the Counting On to 10 strategy. For example, to find the total of 8 and 5, children place 8 red counters in the ten frame and 5 yellow counters outside the ten frame. Then have children move yellow counters into the ten frame to make a 10. The total is 10 plus the counters outside the ten frame.

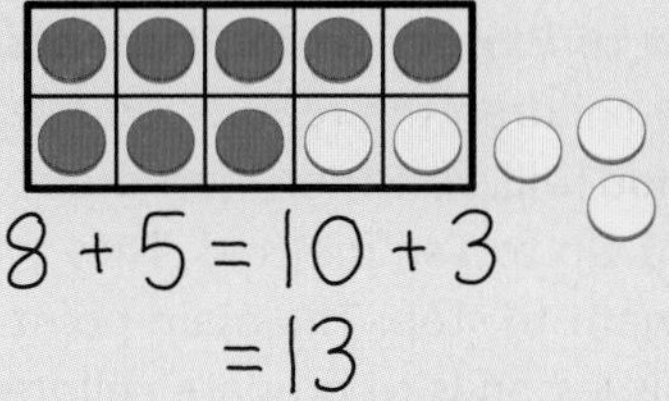

English Language Learners

Model 8 + 6 using the coin strips. Have children tell how to use their fingers to solve 8 + 6.

- **Beginning** Say: **I counted 8. Now I show 6.** Show 6 fingers. Say: **There are 8, 9, 10.** Ask: **How many more?** 4 **So 10 + 4 is 14.**
- **Intermediate** Say: **I counted 8.** Ask: **What do I show?** 6 Show 6 fingers. Say: **There are 8, 9, 10.** Ask: **How many more?** 4 **What is 10 + 4?** 14
- **Advanced** Have children tell how to use fingers to count on 6 more from 8.

1 Teaching the Lesson (continued)

Teaching Note

Math Background This lesson uses the Counting On and Counting On to 10 strategies. These strategies are the basis for the Make a Ten strategy they will learn in the next lesson. The emphasis is on teacher modeling so that children can understand the method.

Teaching Note

What to Expect from Students For many children the regular Count On method will be easier than the Count On to Ten method. They will not want to stop. The main point of this lesson is to prepare children conceptually to see that the second addend breaks into a chunk to make a ten and a chunk over ten that makes the teen answer. They will use this in the next lesson on the Make-a-Ten method. Some children do invent the Count On to Ten method, but we do not expect all children to use it. The Make-a-Ten method discussed in Lesson 12 is not for mastery by all at this time of the year, but many children will transition to using it during the year, especially once they begin multi-digit addition.

▶ Practice the Strategies WHOLE CLASS

Continue modeling the two strategies with other combinations like 7 + 6 until children understand what to do. Point out that children can count on to ten and then use the leftover ones to make a teen number. Have children relate the two strategies by using Coin Strips and fingers to count on to find teen totals.

$$7 + 6 = \square$$

Counting On

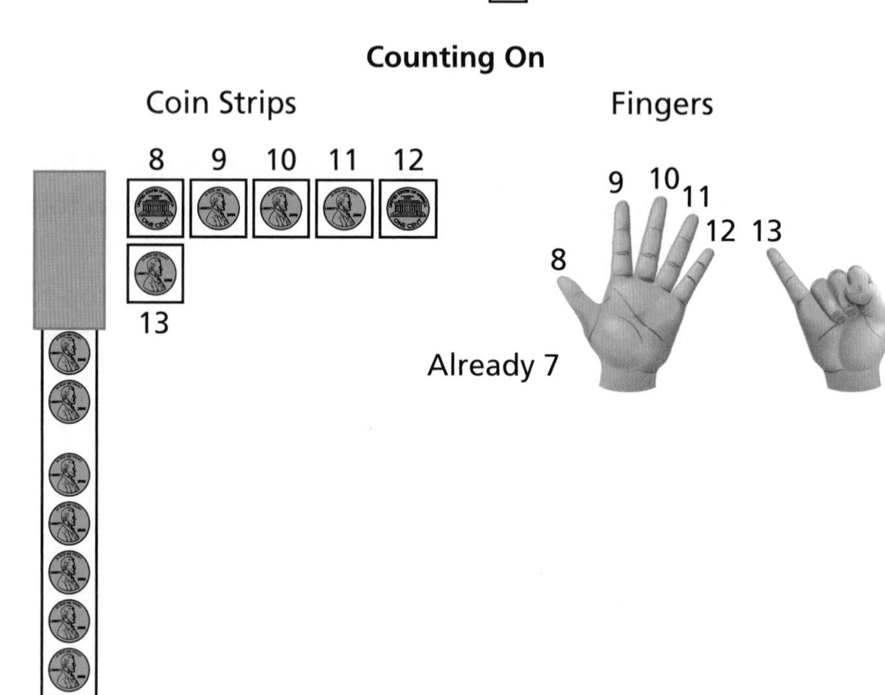

Counting On to 10

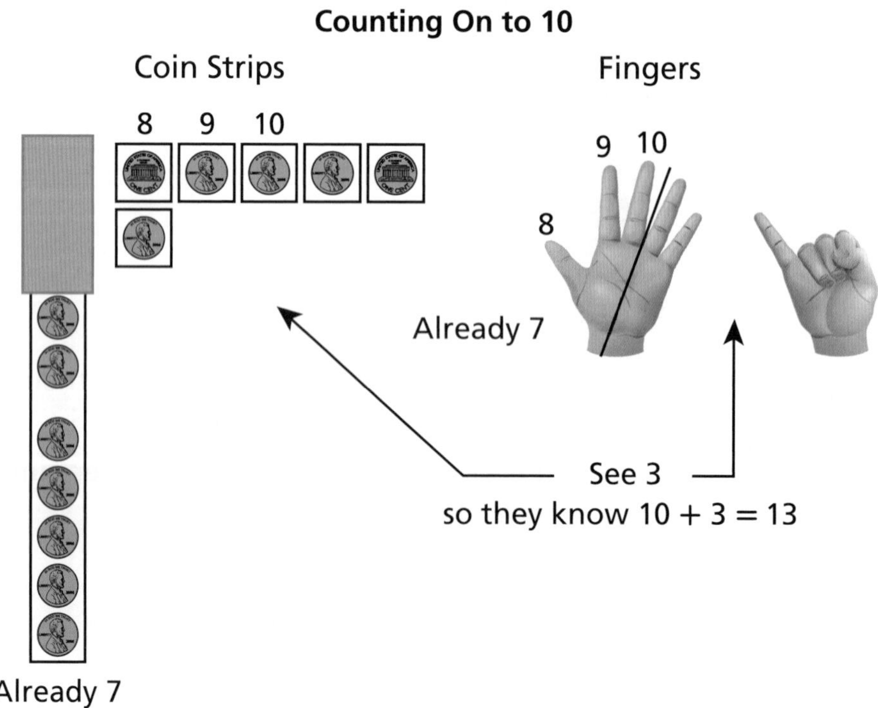

2 Going Further

Differentiated Instruction

Intervention — Activity Card 1-11

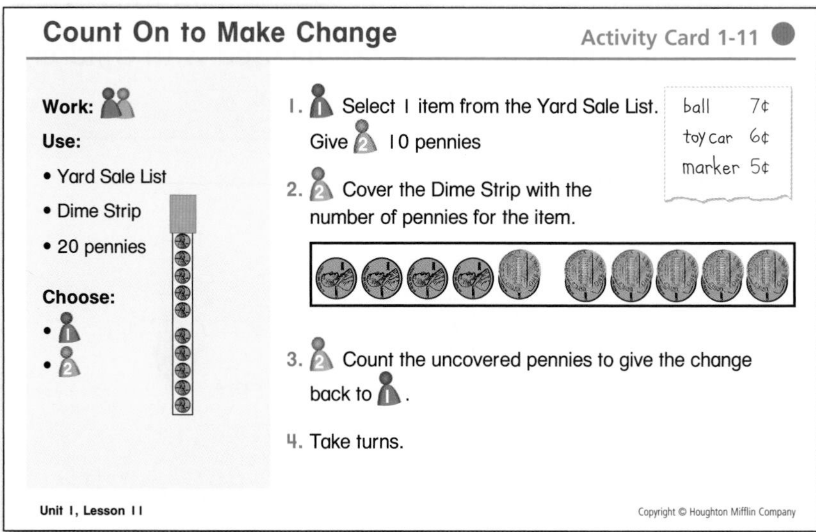

Count On to Make Change — Activity Card 1-11

Work: pairs

Use:
- Yard Sale List
- Dime Strip
- 20 pennies

Choose:
- 1
- 2

1. 1 Select 1 item from the Yard Sale List. Give 2 10 pennies
2. 2 Cover the Dime Strip with the number of pennies for the item.
3. 2 Count the uncovered pennies to give the change back to 1.
4. Take turns.

Activity Note Prepare a list of items under 10¢ for children to buy. Each pair needs 20 pennies and 2 Dime Strips (Teacher Resource Book, p. M1).

Math Writing Prompt

Explain Your Thinking You buy a pencil for 8¢ with a dime. Explain how you know how much change you'll get back.

Software Support

Use *Soar to Success* for instruction of students needing targeted support for underlying skills.

On Level — Activity Card 1-11

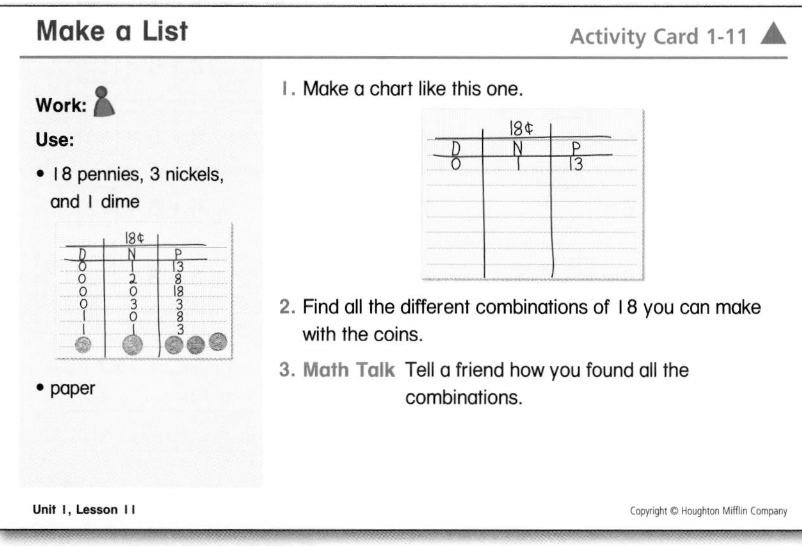

Make a List — Activity Card 1-11

Work: 1

Use:
- 18 pennies, 3 nickels, and 1 dime
- paper

1. Make a chart like this one.

18¢		
D	N	P
0	1	13

2. Find all the different combinations of 18 you can make with the coins.
3. **Math Talk** Tell a friend how you found all the combinations.

Activity Note Each child needs 18 pennies, 3 nickels, and 1 dime. Each child needs to make a chart to record the combinations of 18¢

Math Writing Prompt

Draw a Picture How can you tell when two numbers will total a teen number? Draw a picture to explain.

Software Support

Use *MegaMath* for review and reinforcement of the concepts and skills presented in this lesson.

Challenge — Activity Card 1-11

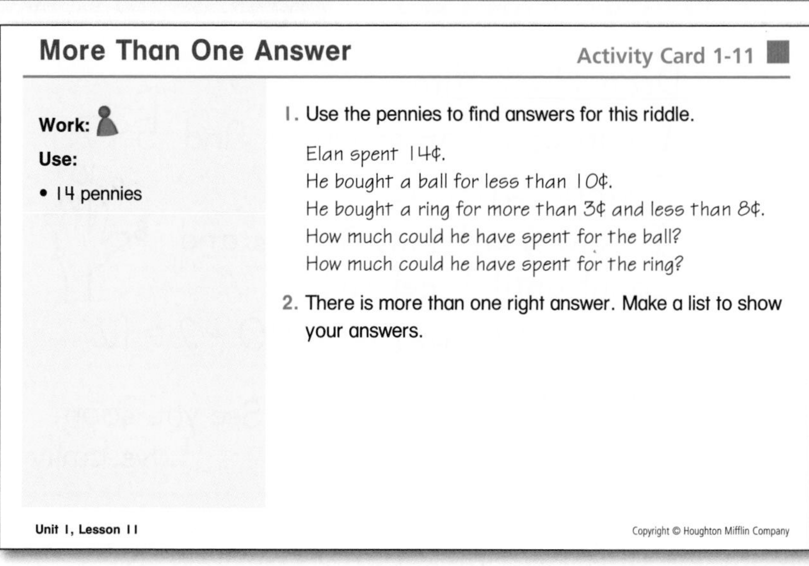

More Than One Answer — Activity Card 1-11

Work: 1

Use:
- 14 pennies

1. Use the pennies to find answers for this riddle.

   Elan spent 14¢.
   He bought a ball for less than 10¢.
   He bought a ring for more than 3¢ and less than 8¢.
   How much could he have spent for the ball?
   How much could he have spent for the ring?

2. There is more than one right answer. Make a list to show your answers.

Activity Note Each child needs 14¢. Point out to children that there is more than one correct answer to the riddle.

Math Writing Prompt

Multi-Step Story Problems You buy a crayon for 5¢ and a ball for 3¢. You pay with a dime. How much change will you get back? Explain the steps you took to find the answer.

Software Support

Use *Destination Math* to take students beyond the concepts and skills presented in this lesson.

3 Homework and Targeted Practice

1–11 Homework **Goal:** Additional Practice

This Homework page provides practice counting on or counting on to 10 to find the totals.

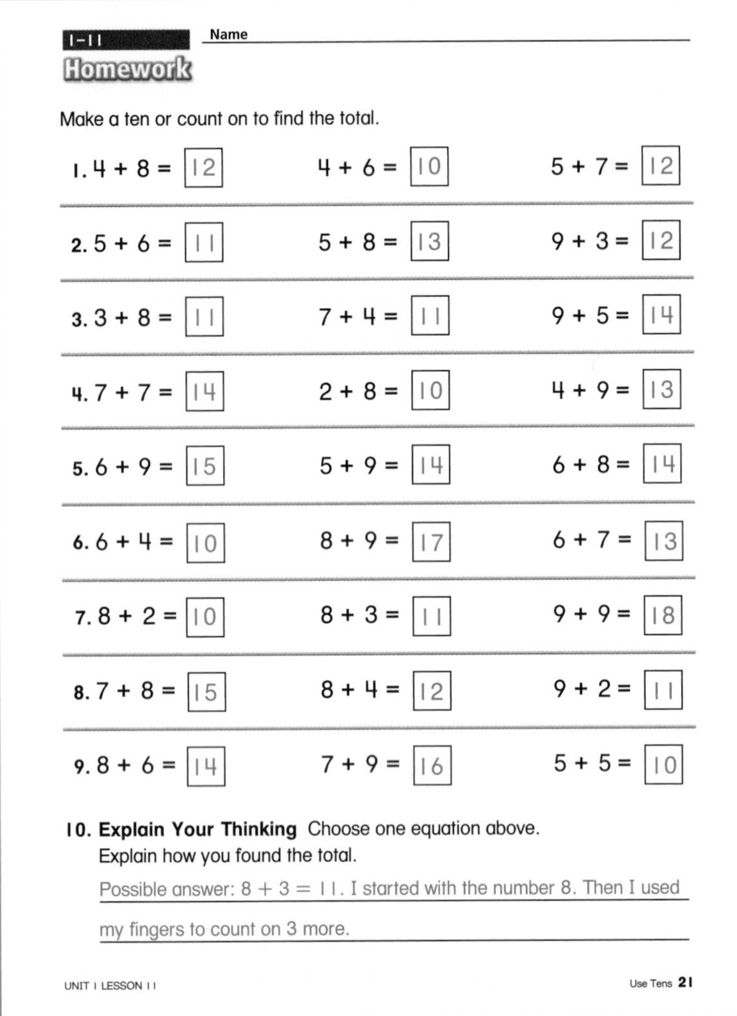

1–11 Homework Name ______________________

Make a ten or count on to find the total.

1. 4 + 8 = 12 4 + 6 = 10 5 + 7 = 12
2. 5 + 6 = 11 5 + 8 = 13 9 + 3 = 12
3. 3 + 8 = 11 7 + 4 = 11 9 + 5 = 14
4. 7 + 7 = 14 2 + 8 = 10 4 + 9 = 13
5. 6 + 9 = 15 5 + 9 = 14 6 + 8 = 14
6. 6 + 4 = 10 8 + 9 = 17 6 + 7 = 13
7. 8 + 2 = 10 8 + 3 = 11 9 + 9 = 18
8. 7 + 8 = 15 8 + 4 = 12 9 + 2 = 11
9. 8 + 6 = 14 7 + 9 = 16 5 + 5 = 10

10. **Explain Your Thinking** Choose one equation above. Explain how you found the total.

Possible answer: 8 + 3 = 11. I started with the number 8. Then I used my fingers to count on 3 more.

UNIT 1 LESSON 11 Use Tens 21

Homework and Remembering page 21

1–11 Targeted Practice **Goal:** Count on to add.

This Targeted Practice page can be used with children who need extra practice counting on.

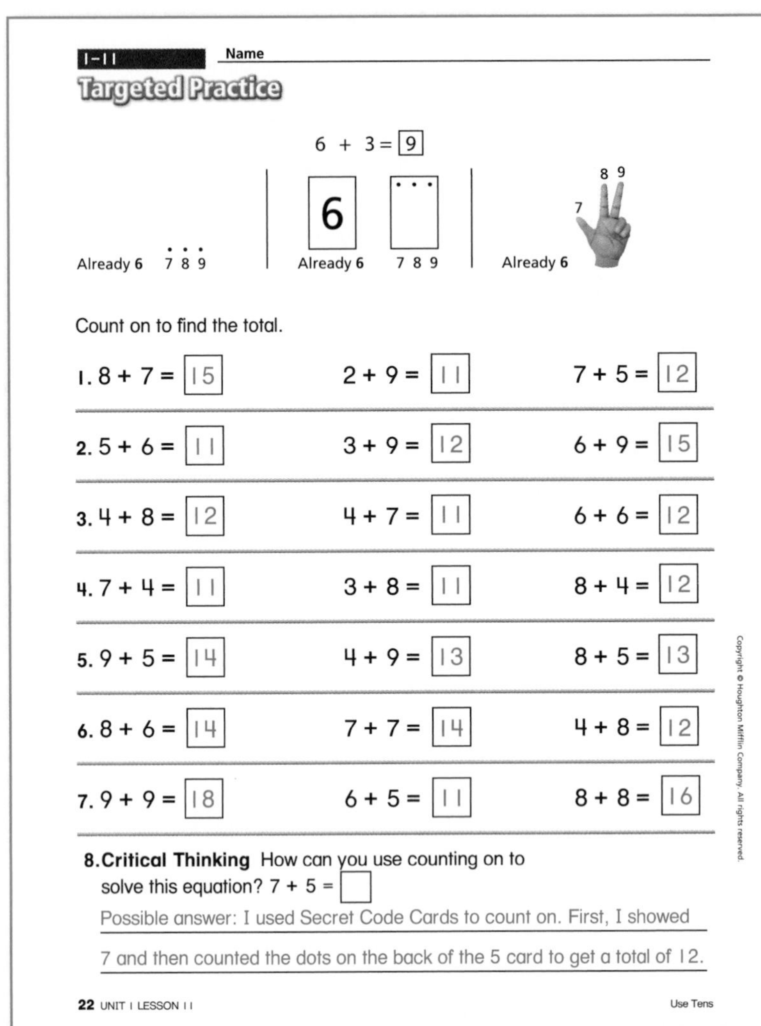

1–11 Targeted Practice Name ______________________

6 + 3 = 9

Already 6 7 8 9 | Already 6 7 8 9 | Already 6

Count on to find the total.

1. 8 + 7 = 15 2 + 9 = 11 7 + 5 = 12
2. 5 + 6 = 11 3 + 9 = 12 6 + 9 = 15
3. 4 + 8 = 12 4 + 7 = 11 6 + 6 = 12
4. 7 + 4 = 11 3 + 8 = 11 8 + 4 = 12
5. 9 + 5 = 14 4 + 9 = 13 8 + 5 = 13
6. 8 + 6 = 14 7 + 7 = 14 4 + 8 = 12
7. 9 + 9 = 18 6 + 5 = 11 8 + 8 = 16

8. **Critical Thinking** How can you use counting on to solve this equation? 7 + 5 = ☐

Possible answer: I used Secret Code Cards to count on. First, I showed 7 and then counted the dots on the back of the 5 card to get a total of 12.

22 UNIT 1 LESSON 11 Use Tens

Homework and Remembering page 22

Home or School Activity

Language Arts Connection

Write to Explain Have children write a letter to a family member explaining how to find the total of 5 + 7 using the Counting On to 10 strategy. Encourage children to use words and pictures in their letter.

Dear Aunt Kim,
I can count on to ten to find 5 + 7.
I start with 7.
I show 5 with my fingers and count until I get to 10.
I have 2 fingers left. 10 + 2 = 12
So, 5 + 7 = 12.

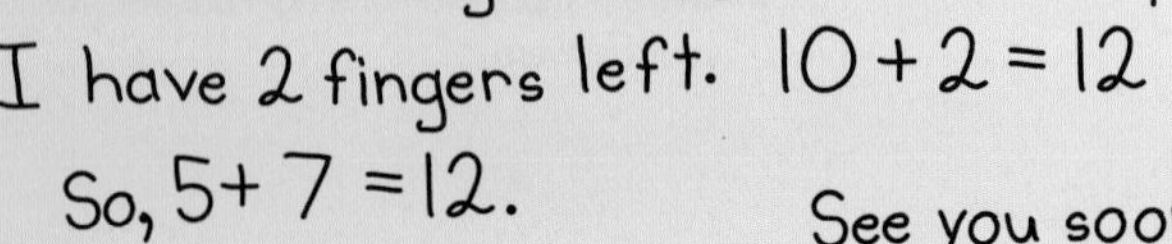

See you soon.
Love, Emily

Make a Ten with Penny Strips and Fingers

Lesson Objectives

- Add two numbers that make a teen total.
- Record the Make a Ten strategy in written form.

Vocabulary

teen number
teen total
proof drawing

The Day at a Glance

Today's Goals	Materials	
1 Teaching the Lesson **A1:** Introduce Make a Ten strategies to add two numbers to make a teen total. **A2:** Discuss Make a Ten strategies for adding two numbers to make a teen total.	**Lesson Activities** Homework and Remembering pp. 23–24 Coin Strips Pennies Coin cover MathBoard materials	**Going Further** Activity Cards 1-12 Game Cards (TRB M23) Look for Partners (TRB M34) Math Journals
2 Going Further ▶ Differentiated Instruction		
3 Homework and Spiral Review		

Use Math Talk today!

Keeping Skills Sharp

Quick Practice — 5 MINUTES

Goal: Practice making change from a dime.

Materials: List of yard sale items on chart paper (see Unit 1 Lesson 11), Coin Strips (from Unit 1 Lesson 4 or TRB M1) (1 Dime Strip and 9 pennies per child)

Buy with a Dime Invite six children to act out the Yard Sale scenario from Unit 1 Lesson 11. To make this a "quick" practice, ask children to check the work of the Buyer, Seller, and the Bookkeepers, using their fingers rather than the Coin Strips. Demonstrate how they should separate ten fingers to show cost and change. The Buyer and Seller can use Coin Strips and coins and the Bookkeepers can make drawings on the board. (See Unit 1 Lesson 11 Activity 1.)

Repeated Quick Practice Use these Quick Practices from previous lessons.

- ▶ **Unknown Partner or Prairie Dog** Use numbers 5 and 10. (See Unit 1 Lessons 8 and 9.)
- ▶ **Stay or Go?** Use numbers 2, 6, and 4. (See Unit 1 Lesson 10.)

Daily Routines

Money Routine Using the 120 Poster, Using the Money Flip Chart, Using the Number Path, Using Secret Code Cards (See pp. xxiii–xxv.)

- ▶ Led by Student Leaders

1 Teaching the Lesson

Activity 1

Make a Ten Strategies

 **30 MINUTES**

Goal: Introduce Make a Ten strategies to add two numbers to make a teen total.

Materials: Coin Strips (from Unit 1 Lesson 4 or TRB M1) (1Dime Strip and 8 pennies per pair), coin cover (index card, sticky note, or paper per pair)

 **NCTM Standards:**
Number and Operations
Communication

 **Class Management**

Looking Ahead In the next lesson, children will use the Green Make a Ten Cards. These are on Student Activity Book pages 39–42 and on TRB M35–M38.

English Language Learners

Tell children they will use dime strips, pennies, and coin covers to find 8 + 6.

- **Beginning** Point to the dime strip. Say: **We cover 2 to show 8. Then we move 2 from 6 to make a ten. Ten and 4 more is fourteen.**
- **Intermediate** Ask: **What do we cover to show 8?** 2 **What do we move from 6 to make a ten?** 2 **What is 10 + 4?** 14
- **Advanced** Have children tell how to use the dime strip, pennies, and coin covers to show how to find 8 + 6.

▶ Introduce Make a Ten PAIRS

Math Talk 

Use Dimes Strips and Pennies Have children sit in **Helping Pairs.** Explain that they will use their Dime Strips, pennies, and coin covers to see how to separate the second partner into a chunk to make ten and a chunk over ten that makes the teen number. Have children who have used the Make-a-Ten method on previous days show how they do it. Move through the steps below with the pennies, eliciting as much as possible from children.

- Shall we start adding with 8 or 6? 8 because it is larger.
- So let's cover 2 pennies to see 8 on our dime strip.
- Now let's add our 6 pennies and then see how we can make the 2 chunks to make a ten and then a teen number.
- How many pennies do we need to take from 6 and give to 8 to make 10? 2
- Peek under your coin cover or check your fingers to see that the 10-partner of 8 is 2.
- So move 2 pennies from your 6 and put them on top of the coin cover to make 10 pennies on the strip. 6 is giving 2 to 8 to change the 8 to be 10.
- How many are left in the 6 after it gives 2 to 8? 4

So we changed the problem 8 + 6 to be 10 + 4. Do you know the answer to 10 + 4 without counting? 14

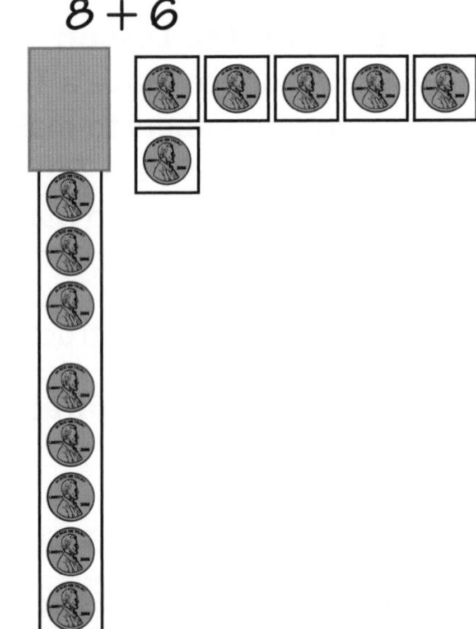

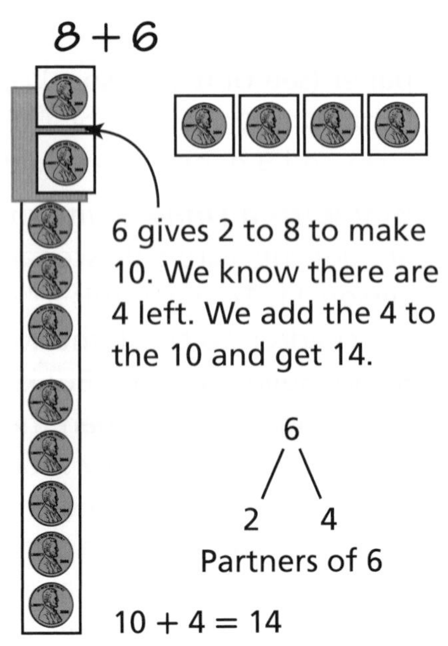

8 + 6
6 gives 2 to 8 to make 10. We know there are 4 left. We add the 4 to the 10 and get 14.
6
2 4
Partners of 6
10 + 4 = 14

Ask children to summarize what they did in the Make a Ten method. Have 2 or 3 children explain it in their own words. Then write on the board 8 + 6 and write 10 + 4 under it.

- We changed our 8 + 6 problem to an easier problem we know: 10 + 4.

If some children needed to count on 4 from 10 to find 14, use the Secret Code Cards to review how the teen numbers are all 10 and some ones (see Lesson 5).

Use Fingers Ask a child to demonstrate with fingers how to change 8 + 6 to be 10 + 4. There are several ways to do this. Ask other children if they have a different way. The easiest way is shown below, so demonstrate this method if a child doesn't show it.

- You start as if you are counting on by saying the larger partner. Show the smaller partner on your fingers, and separate the fingers into the amount to make ten with the number you said and the amount that will make the ones in the teen total (here 6 separates into 2 and 4).

Continue with other examples, as needed.

▶ Introduce Make a Ten with a Friend WHOLE CLASS

Explain that the Make a Ten with a Friend strategy is another way to make a teen total.

Invite two children to help you demonstrate how to find 8 + 6 using this new strategy. Have the first friend show 8 fingers. Then have the second friend show 6 fingers.

- Which friend should break apart his or her number to give their partner enough fingers to make a ten? The friend with fewer fingers (6), just as in counting on to make a 10.

Have the second friend separate the 6 fingers to put enough to make ten with the 8 fingers. Ask children how many fingers are needed to make 10. 2 So 2 fingers are put near the 8 and the other 4 fingers in the 6 are stretched apart.

Activity continued ▶

The Learning Classroom

Building Concepts Children have been practicing 10-flashes with the ten on the left and ones on the right (as viewed by the class). When children add by Making a Ten with a Friend, the friend on the left should show the greater number. To do this, children sit beside each other.

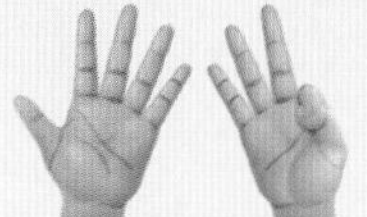
friend showing larger number (8)

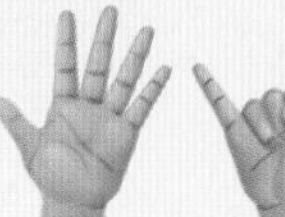
you showing smaller number (6)

However, if some children prefer making the ten above the ones, have the friend with the greater number place his or her hands above those of the friend with the lesser number.

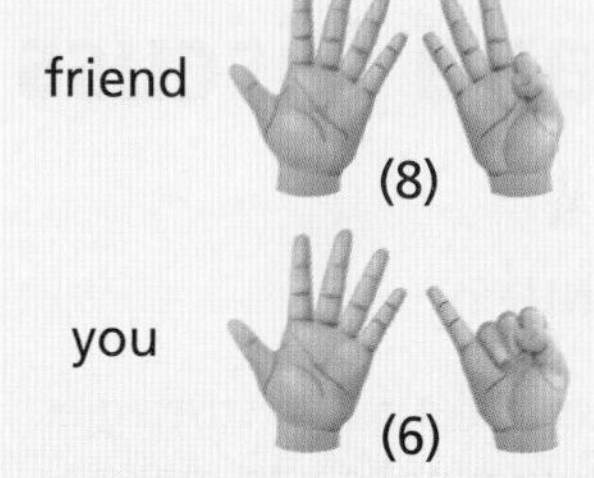

The Learning Classroom

Building Concepts Some children do not use the Make a Ten method or even need it, but for others, this is a transitional step they can use for the difficult part of making a ten: separating the smaller addend into the amount that makes ten (visualized as moving those fingers close to the friend's fingers) and the rest that will make the ones in the teen number. Japanese teachers use this with children who need the transition and have found that having children separate their fingers a little bit is enough for the child to shift their attention to the rest of the fingers.

1 Teaching the Lesson (continued)

The Learning Classroom

Building Concepts The written methods presented in this activity will eventually replace the method using a Dime Strip and pennies. However, it is important that children link these written methods to the money and the finger methods throughout the discussion. Children can later choose to use a written method or a finger method before they move to a mental method.

- How many fingers does the second friend have left? 4
- What do we see? 10 fingers and 4 fingers
- What is the answer to 8 + 6? 14
- How do you know? 10 plus the 4 left from the 6 is equal to 14.

Step 1 Friend shows 8 fingers. You show 6 fingers.

Step 2

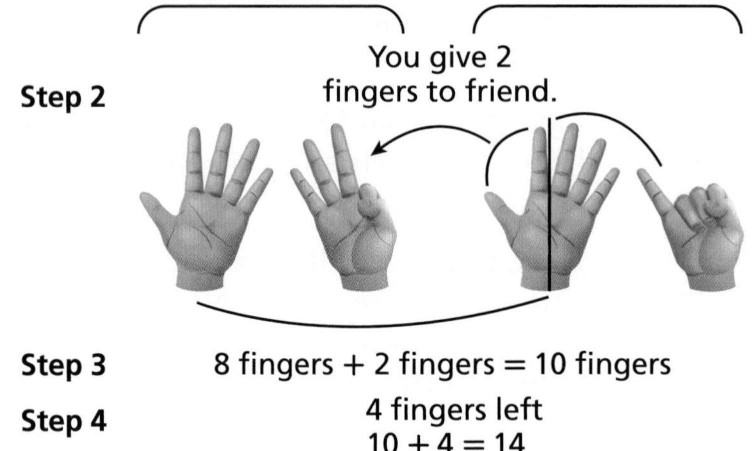

Step 3 8 fingers + 2 fingers = 10 fingers

Step 4 4 fingers left
10 + 4 = 14

Continue with other examples, as time allows. Be sure to link this strategy to using a Dime Strip and pennies.

Activity 2

Solve and Discuss

 **25 MINUTES**

Goal: Discuss Make a Ten strategies for adding two numbers to make a teen total.

Materials: MathBoard materials

 **NCTM Standards:**
Number and Operations
Communication

Ongoing Assessment

Ask the children to describe how to use a Make a Ten Strategy to solve various problems.

For example:

9 + 4 = □

7 + 8 = □

8 + 5 = □

▶ Ways to Record Make a Ten Methods WHOLE CLASS

Use **Solve and Discuss** to solve 8 + 6 = □. Ask children if they can show different ways to make a ten. The remaining children can show different ways on their MathBoards.

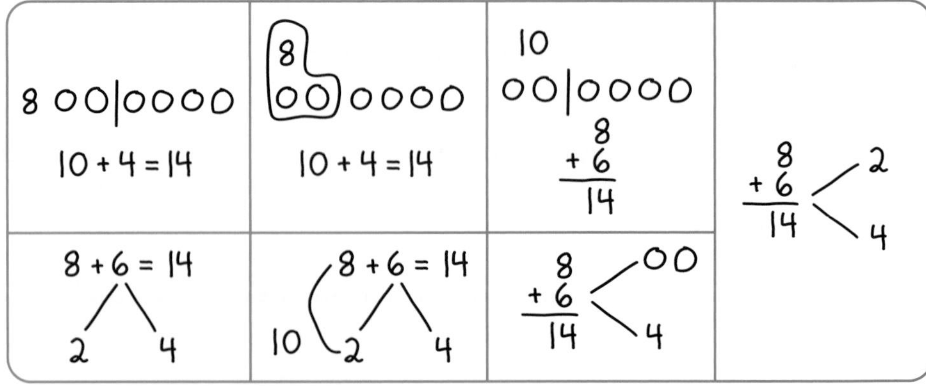

Encourage children to discuss the advantages and disadvantages of the various ways to show making a ten in written form. Some may use fingers as they do their written method.

2 Going Further

Differentiated Instruction

Intervention — Activity Card 1-12

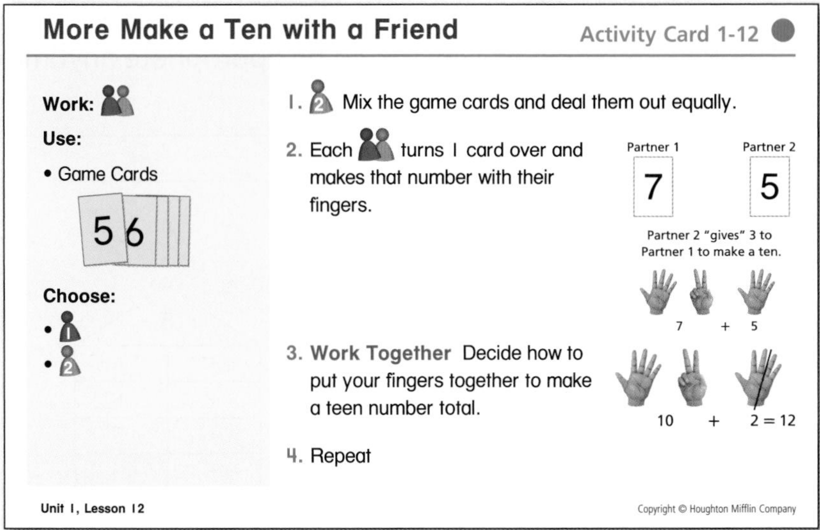

More Make a Ten with a Friend — Activity Card 1-12

Work: (2 children)

Use:

- Game Cards

Choose:

- 1
- 2

1. (1, 2) Mix the game cards and deal them out equally.
2. Each turns 1 card over and makes that number with their fingers.
3. **Work Together** Decide how to put your fingers together to make a teen number total.
4. Repeat

Unit 1, Lesson 12

Activity Note Each pair needs sets of Game Cards, 5–9 (TRB M23). Help children understand that they need to work together to make the answer.

Math Writing Prompt

Write About It You have 7 marbles. How many more do you need to have 10? How did you decide?

Software Support

Use *Soar to Success* for instruction of students needing targeted support for underlying skills.

On Level — Activity Card 1-12

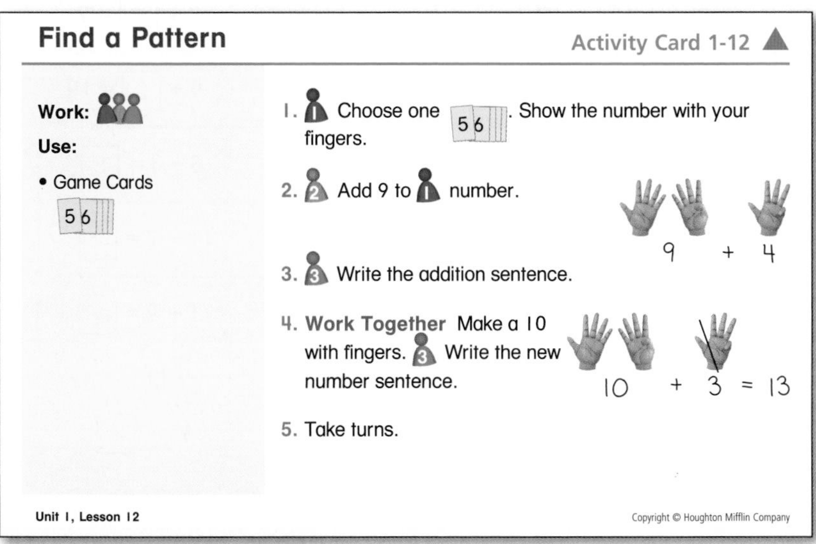

Find a Pattern — Activity Card 1-12

Work: (3 children)

Use:

- Game Cards

1. (1) Choose one (card). Show the number with your fingers.
2. (2) Add 9 to (1) number.
3. (3) Write the addition sentence.
4. **Work Together** Make a 10 with fingers. (3) Write the new number sentence.
5. Take turns.

Unit 1, Lesson 12

Activity Note Each group of three needs Game Cards 2–9 (TRB M23). Have children switch roles each time they play.

Math Writing Prompt

Create Your Own Write a story problem for 8 + 7. Draw a picture to show the answer.

Software Support

Use *MegaMath* for review and reinforcement of the concepts and skills presented in this lesson.

Challenge — Activity Card 1-12

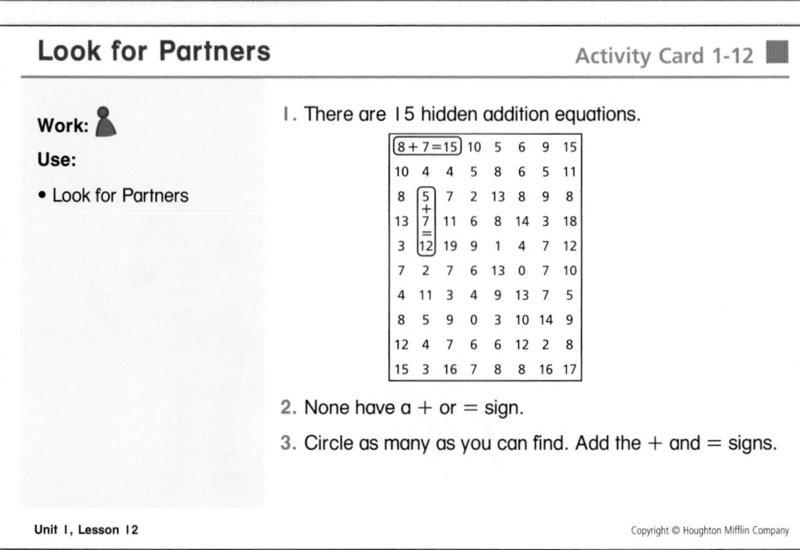

Look for Partners — Activity Card 1-12

Work: (1 child)

Use:

- Look for Partners

1. There are 15 hidden addition equations.

8 +	7 =	15	10	5	6	9	15
10	4	4	5	8	6	5	11
8	5 +	7	2	13	8	9	8
13	7 =	11	6	8	14	3	18
3	12	19	9	1	4	7	12
7	2	7	6	13	0	7	10
4	11	3	4	9	13	7	5
8	5	9	0	3	10	14	9
12	4	7	6	6	12	2	8
15	3	16	7	8	8	16	17

2. None have a + or = sign.
3. Circle as many as you can find. Add the + and = signs.

Unit 1, Lesson 12

Activity Note Each child needs the Look for Partners (TRB M34). Tell children that no number sentences overlap or criss-cross.

Math Writing Prompt

Explain Your Thinking Write a letter to a friend who was absent and explain what you did in math today. Use drawings to help explain your ideas.

Software Support

Use *Destination Math* to take students beyond the concepts and skills presented in this lesson.

3 Homework and Spiral Review

Goal: Additional Practice

This Homework page provides practice with the Make a Ten strategy.

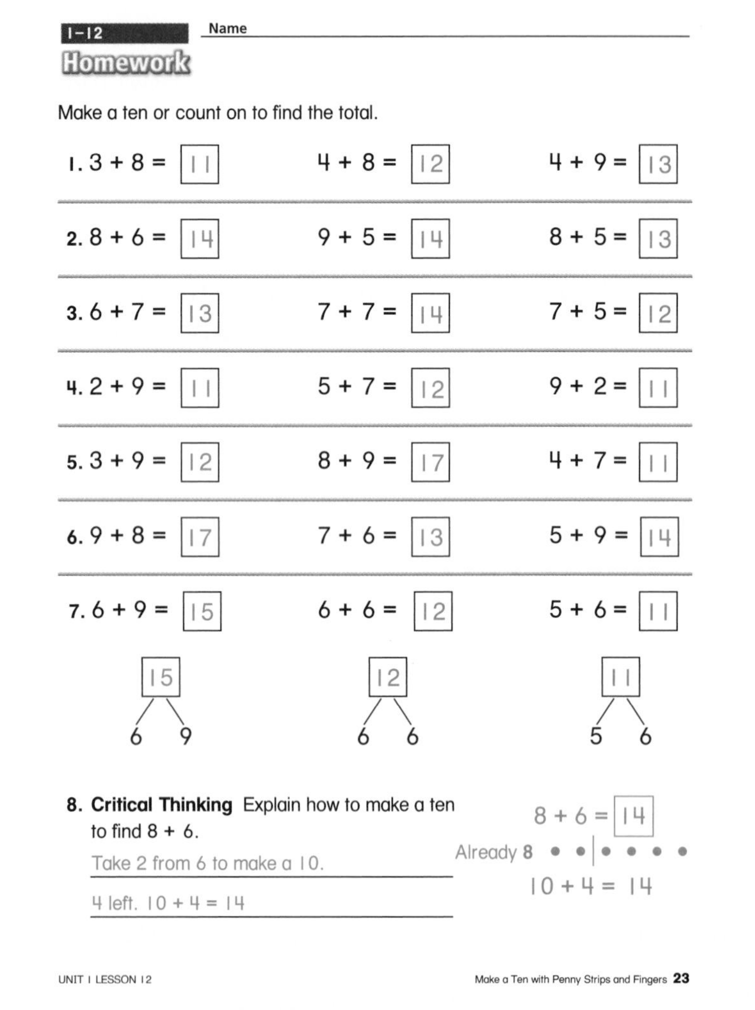

1–12 Name ______

Homework

Make a ten or count on to find the total.

1. 3 + 8 = 11 | 4 + 8 = 12 | 4 + 9 = 13
2. 8 + 6 = 14 | 9 + 5 = 14 | 8 + 5 = 13
3. 6 + 7 = 13 | 7 + 7 = 14 | 7 + 5 = 12
4. 2 + 9 = 11 | 5 + 7 = 12 | 9 + 2 = 11
5. 3 + 9 = 12 | 8 + 9 = 17 | 4 + 7 = 11
6. 9 + 8 = 17 | 7 + 6 = 13 | 5 + 9 = 14
7. 6 + 9 = 15 | 6 + 6 = 12 | 5 + 6 = 11

15: 6, 9 | 12: 6, 6 | 11: 5, 6

8. **Critical Thinking** Explain how to make a ten to find 8 + 6.

Take 2 from 6 to make a 10.
4 left. 10 + 4 = 14

8 + 6 = 14
Already 8 • • | • • • •
10 + 4 = 14

UNIT 1 LESSON 12 | Make a Ten with Penny Strips and Fingers 23

Homework and Remembering page 23

Goal: Spiral Review

This Remembering activity would be appropriate anytime after today's lesson.

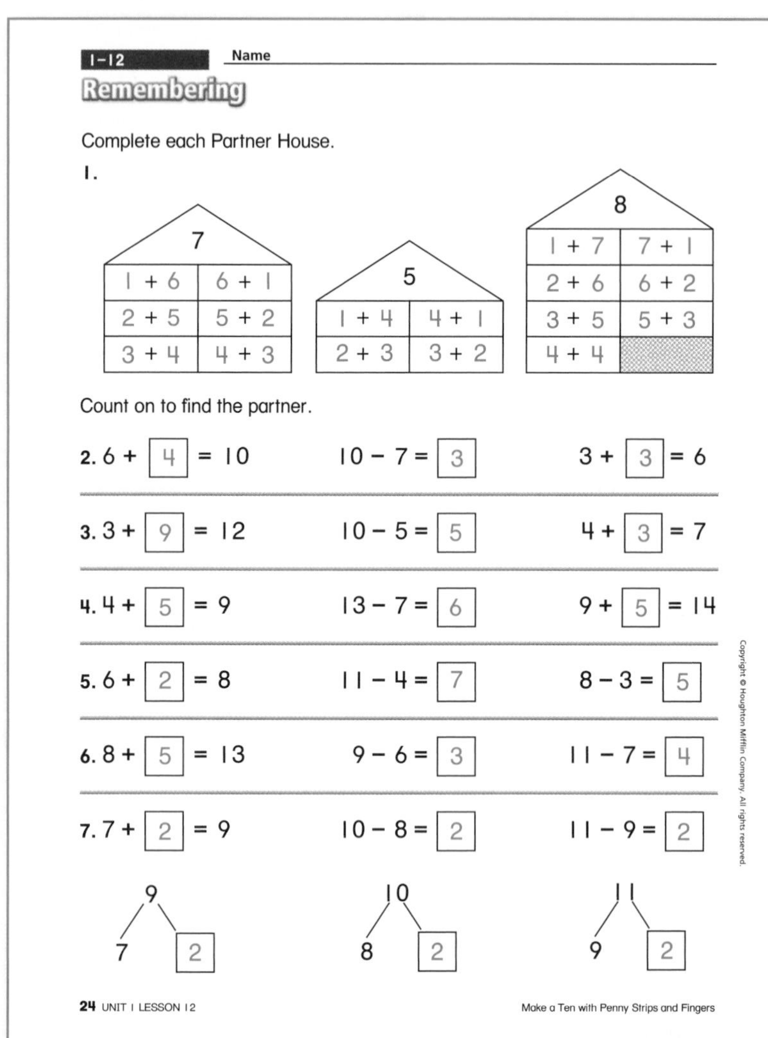

1–12 Name ______

Remembering

Complete each Partner House.

1.

7	
1 + 6	6 + 1
2 + 5	5 + 2
3 + 4	4 + 3

5	
1 + 4	4 + 1
2 + 3	3 + 2

8	
1 + 7	7 + 1
2 + 6	6 + 2
3 + 5	5 + 3
4 + 4	

Count on to find the partner.

2. 6 + 4 = 10 | 10 − 7 = 3 | 3 + 3 = 6
3. 3 + 9 = 12 | 10 − 5 = 5 | 4 + 3 = 7
4. 4 + 5 = 9 | 13 − 7 = 6 | 9 + 5 = 14
5. 6 + 2 = 8 | 11 − 4 = 7 | 8 − 3 = 5
6. 8 + 5 = 13 | 9 − 6 = 3 | 11 − 7 = 4
7. 7 + 2 = 9 | 10 − 8 = 2 | 11 − 9 = 2

9: 7, 2 | 10: 8, 2 | 11: 9, 2

24 UNIT 1 LESSON 12 | Make a Ten with Penny Strips and Fingers

Homework and Remembering page 24

Home or School Activity

Physical Education Connection

Jump to Ten Have pairs take turns using the Make a Ten strategy to make teen totals. Children begin with 7 + 5. One child says the greater number aloud, 7, giving the partner a signal to begin jumping. The child now says, "8, 9, 10," as the partner jumps. Pairs discuss how many jumps are still needed to solve the problem. The partner jumps 2 more times to make the teen total, 12. (Children may also hop, clap, do jumping jacks, or any other easily countable action.) Have children switch roles and add two different numbers that have a teen total.

Practice Adding with Teen Totals

Lesson Objectives

- **Make a ten to add two numbers that make a teen total.**
- **Compare finger, written, and mental strategies of making a ten to add numbers.**

Vocabulary
teen total
make a ten

The Day at a Glance

Today's Goals	Materials	
1 Teaching the Lesson **A1:** Practice using the Make a Ten with an Imaginary Friend strategy to add two numbers that make a teen total. **A2:** Discuss advantages and disadvantages of finger, written, and mental strategies of making a ten. **A3:** Practice making a ten to find a teen total.	**Lesson Activities** Student Activity Book pp. 39–42 (includes Green Make-a-Ten Cards) Homework and Remembering pp. 25–26 Quick Quiz 3 (Assessment Guide)	**Going Further** Activity Cards 1-13 Two-color counters Ten Frame (TRB M33) Construction or other drawing paper Math Journals
2 Going Further ▸ Differentiated Instruction		
3 Homework and Targeted Practice		

Use Math Talk today!

Keeping Skills Sharp

Quick Practice — 5 MINUTES

Goal: Practice making change from a dime.

Materials: List of yard sale items on chart paper (see Unit 1 Lesson 11), Coin Strips (from Unit 1 Lesson 4 or TRB M1)

Buy with a Dime Invite six children to act out the Yard Sale scenario from Lesson 11. To make this a "quick" practice, ask children to check the work of the Buyer, Seller, and Bookkeepers, using fingers. The Buyer and Seller can use Coin Strips and coins and Bookkeepers can draw on the board. (See Unit 1 Lesson 11 Activity 1.)

Repeated Quick Practice Use these Quick Practices from previous lessons.

- ▸ **Unknown Partner or Prairie Dog** Use numbers 6 and 10. (See Unit 1 Lessons 8 and 9.)
- ▸ **Stay or Go?** Use numbers 7, 5, and 3. (See Unit 1 Lesson 10.)

Daily Routines

Money Routine Using the 120 Poster, Using the Money Flip Chart, Using the Number Path, Using Secret Code Cards (See pp. xxiii–xxv.)

▸ Led by Student Leaders

1 Teaching the Lesson

Activity 1

Make a Ten with an Imaginary Friend

 20 MINUTES

Goal: Practice using the Make a Ten with an Imaginary Friend strategy to add two numbers that make a teen total.

 **NCTM Standard:**
Number and Operations

Teaching Note

What to Expect from Students It is important that all children are given the opportunity to practice and discuss the Make a Ten strategy for addition. However, do not expect all of them to master the strategy at this time. Some children will begin to use the strategy more when adding and subtracting multi-digit numbers. Others may continue to use counting on for both addition and subtraction throughout the year.

Teaching Note

Watch For! Some children may be confused about how many fingers to give to their imaginary friend.

Tell them to count on from the imaginary friend's number to the number 10. Then give that many fingers to the imaginary friend.

▶ Make a Ten with an Imaginary Friend WHOLE CLASS

In this activity children explore combinations for $n + 7$ to make a teen total. n can be 4, 5, 6, 7, 8, or 9.

Tell children that they will use their fingers and an imaginary friend to add two numbers to find a teen total. Ask a volunteer to help you model how to find 8 + 7 using this new strategy.

To add 8 and 7, have the child imagine that a friend is showing fingers for the greater number. Have the volunteer show what that would look like. (Help the child show 8 fingers above or to the left of him or herself, whichever they prefer.) Now ask the volunteer to put their fingers down and pretend the imaginary friend is still holding up 8 fingers.

- Now show the other addend with your fingers. What is that number? 7

Tell the volunteer to separate 7 fingers and give enough to the imaginary friend who has 8 to make 10.

- How many fingers do you give? 2
- How many fingers do you have left? 5
- You have 5 and your imaginary friend has 10. How many is that in all? 15
- 10 + 5 = 15, so 8 + 7 = 15.

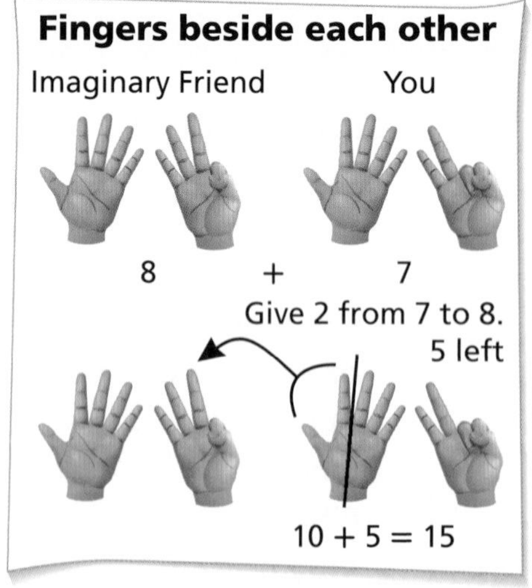

or

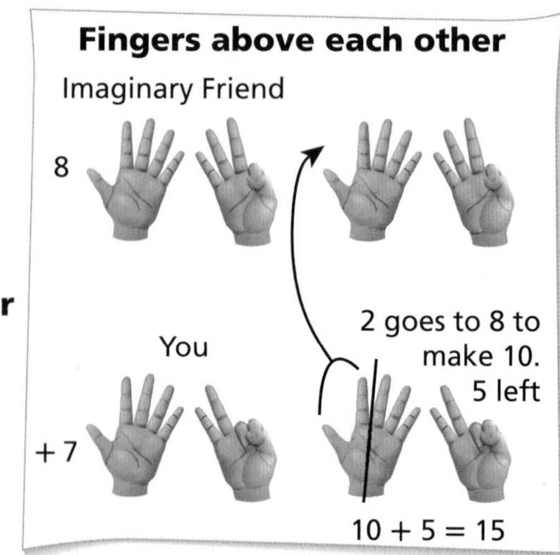

Continue modeling other examples, as needed.

Activity 2

Compare Different Methods of Making a Ten

▶ Invent and Compare Make a Ten Strategies WHOLE CLASS

Math Talk 

Invite several children to go to the board and add using written, finger, or mental methods that they learned in this lesson and Lesson 12. Encourage them to show any new method they think of.

Have children use any two 1-digit numbers with a total from 11 through 18, such as $6 + 8$ or $5 + 9$. As children work at the board, help children who are experiencing difficulty. If necessary, pair them with someone who understands the various Make a Ten strategies as you work through several problems together with the class.

Discuss advantages and disadvantages of the various methods. Record the children's responses on the board or chart paper. Use the table below as a guide, but let children suggest the advantages and disadvantages rather than telling them the ones listed in the table.

Advantages and Disadvantages of Different Methods

Strategies	Advantages	Disadvantages
Written Strategies	• Written work helps us keep track of what we're doing. • It helps us show and prove our work to others.	• Written work is slower than mental methods.
Using Fingers	• Fingers can help us really see how numbers can be broken apart and put together. • We always have fingers with us, unlike paper and pencils.	• Using your fingers can be slower than other strategies like mental math.
Mental Math	• We can use mental math anywhere, anytime. • Mental math will be the fastest.	• Using mental math is sometimes harder to picture or explain than written proofs or finger strategies.

 **15 MINUTES**

Goal: Discuss advantages and disadvantages of finger, written, and mental strategies of making a ten.

 **NCTM Standards:**
Number and Operations
Communication

Teaching Note

What to Expect from Students
Stress that the Make a Ten methods are just changing a problem we don't know to a problem we do know: $10 + n$. They all do that by using the break-apart partners of the smaller number to make 10 and n.

Some children need concrete strategies and may be confused by having to imagine a friend. Let them practice the strategies they are most comfortable with rather than having them learn all the strategies.

English Language Learners

Review different strategies of making a ten. Write *advantages* and *disadvantages* on the board.

- **Beginning** Say: ***Advantages* are good. I always have my fingers. I can always count on them. This is good. It's an *advantage*. *Disadvantages* are not good. Counting on my fingers is slow. That is a *disadvantage*.**
- **Intermediate and Advanced** Ask: **Which are positives?** advantages **Which are negatives?** disadvantages **What is an *advantage* of using fingers?** they are always there to use **What is a *disadvantage* to using fingers?** it can be slow

Activity 3

Practice Making a Ten

15 MINUTES

Goal: Practice making a ten to find a teen total.

Materials: Green Make-a-Ten Cards

NCTM Standard:
Number and Operations

▶ Introduce the Green Make-a-Ten Cards

INDIVIDUALS

Have children cut out the Green Make-a-Ten Cards on Student Activity Book pages 39–42. (These cards are also on TRB M35–M38 if you wish to print the cards on card stock or if you wish to have a set for children to use at home.) If you have access to the *Math Expressions* materials kits, the Green Make a Ten Cards are included, so you will not have to prepare these materials.

The Green Make-a-Ten Cards help children become fluent in the Make a Ten strategy for addition. This strategy requires three steps. Use the 7 + 8 = ☐ card and ask children to explain how the card shows to change 8 + 7 to 10 + 5.

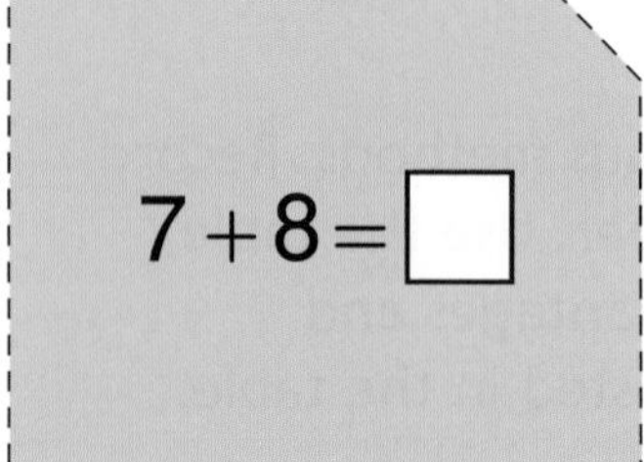

front of card

back of card

from Student Activity Book pages 39–42

- Find the 10-partner of the larger addend.
  On the card, the larger addend and its 10-partner are highlighted.

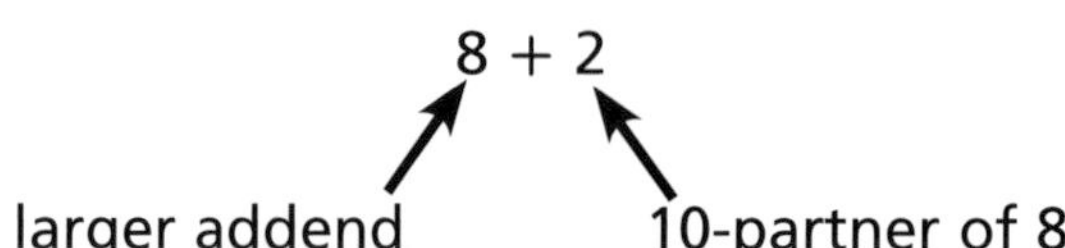

- Break apart the smaller addend into that 10-partner and the rest.
  On the card, dots and numbers show this break-apart.

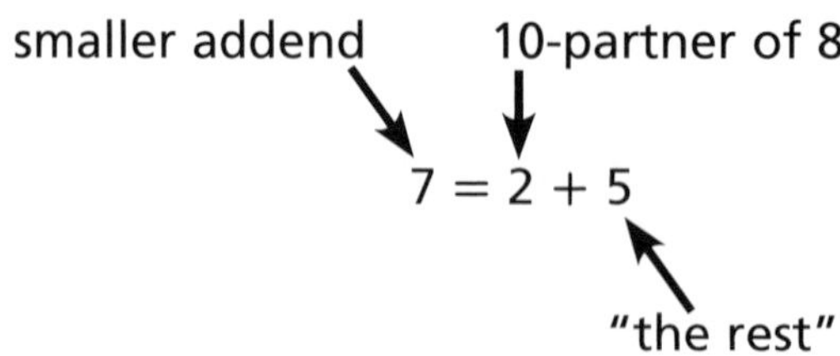

- Add "the rest" to 10 to make a teen number.

10 + 5 = 15

Some children may be able to do the first two steps mentally. Others will use fingers or just count on.

Explain to children that they will use these cards to practice addition in the same way they used the Count-On Cards. They will make three piles: the cards they answer quickly and correctly, the cards they answer correctly and slowly, and the cards they answer incorrectly.

Ongoing Assessment

Have children use any strategy they choose to find each total.

8 + 6 = ☐

5 + 7 = ☐

9 + 9 = ☐

Quick Quiz

See Assessment Guide for Unit 1 Quick Quiz 3.

Intervention Activity Card 1-13

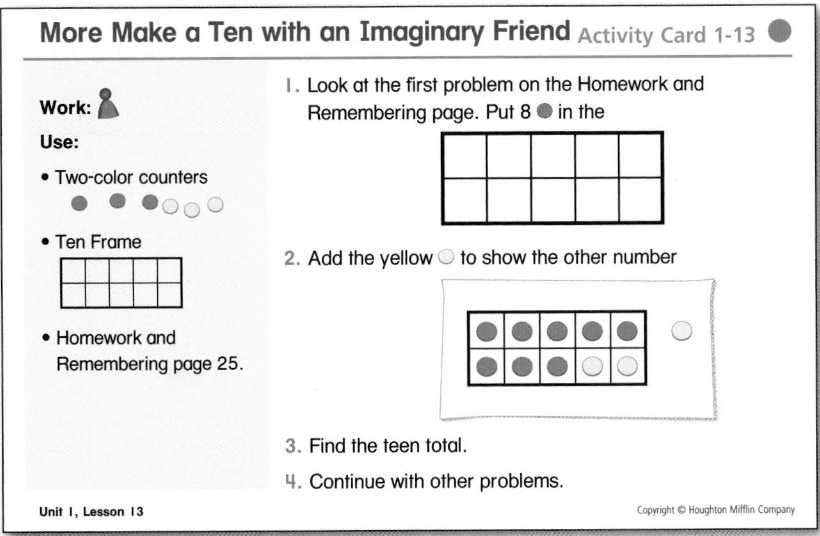
More Make a Ten with an Imaginary Friend Activity Card 1-13

Work:
Use:
- Two-color counters
- Ten Frame
- Homework and Remembering page 25.

1. Look at the first problem on the Homework and Remembering page. Put 8 in the
2. Add the yellow to show the other number
3. Find the teen total.
4. Continue with other problems.

Unit 1, Lesson 13

Copyright © Houghton Mifflin Company

Activity Note Each child needs 18 two-color counters sets, and a Ten Frame (TRB M33). Tell children to visualize an imaginary friend making part of the ten.

Math Writing Prompt

Explain Your Thinking What is a teen total? Explain it in your own words. Give examples.

Software Support

Use *Soar to Success* for instruction of students needing targeted support for underlying skills.

On Level Activity Card 1-13

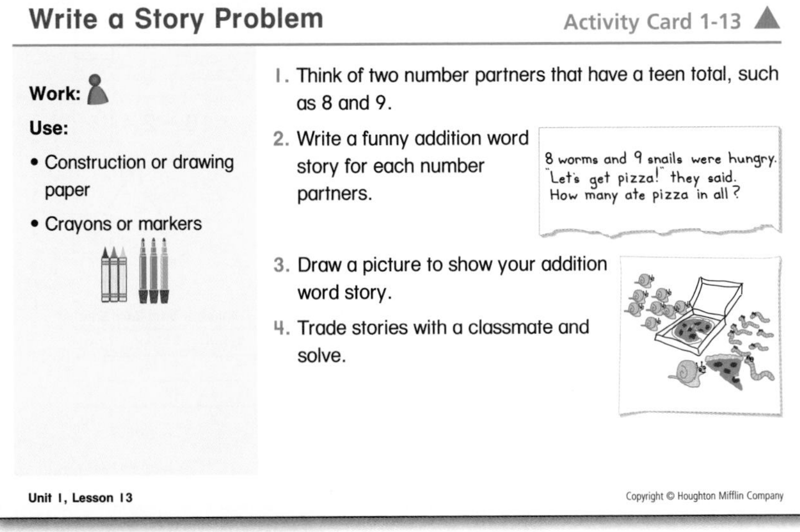
Write a Story Problem Activity Card 1-13

Work:
Use:
- Construction or drawing paper
- Crayons or markers

1. Think of two number partners that have a teen total, such as 8 and 9.
2. Write a funny addition word story for each number partners.

8 worms and 9 snails were hungry. "Let's get pizza!" they said. How many ate pizza in all?

3. Draw a picture to show your addition word story.
4. Trade stories with a classmate and solve.

Unit 1, Lesson 13

Copyright © Houghton Mifflin Company

Activity Note Suggest that children write a problem and illustrate it using number problems they want to remember.

Math Writing Prompt

Choose a Strategy Which is your favorite way to find teen totals? Explain why you use that strategy.

Software Support

Use *MegaMath* for review and reinforcement of the concepts and skills presented in this lesson.

Challenge Activity Card 1-13

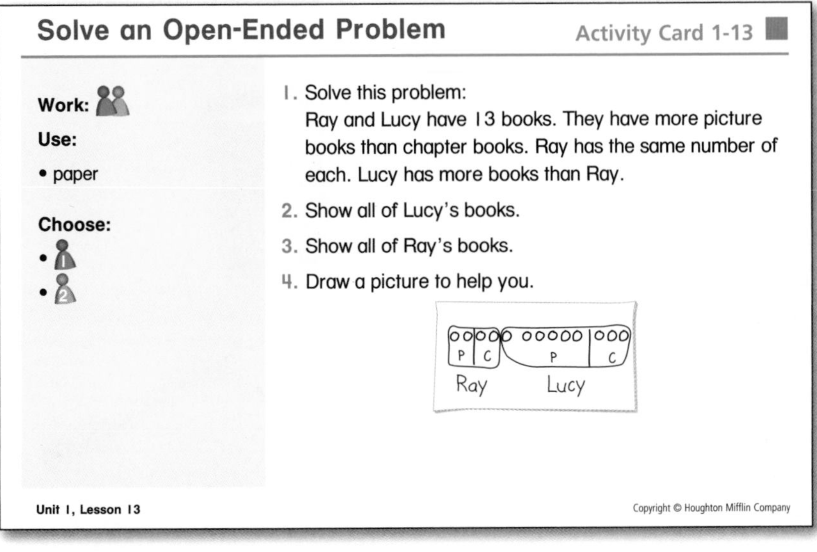
Solve an Open-Ended Problem Activity Card 1-13

Work:
Use:
- paper

Choose:

1. Solve this problem:
Ray and Lucy have 13 books. They have more picture books than chapter books. Ray has the same number of each. Lucy has more books than Ray.
2. Show all of Lucy's books.
3. Show all of Ray's books.
4. Draw a picture to help you.

P C P C
Ray Lucy

Unit 1, Lesson 13

Copyright © Houghton Mifflin Company

Activity Note Have children use any method they choose to solve the problem. Suggest that they use simple labels, such as P for picture books and C for chapter books.

Math Writing Prompt

Investigate Math How can you use the Make a Ten strategy to add 17 + 5?

Software Support

Use *Destination Math* to take students beyond the concepts and skills presented in this lesson.

Homework and Targeted Practice

1-13 **Homework** **Goal:** Additional Practice

This Homework page provides practice in using the Make a Ten or Counting On strategies to find a teen total.

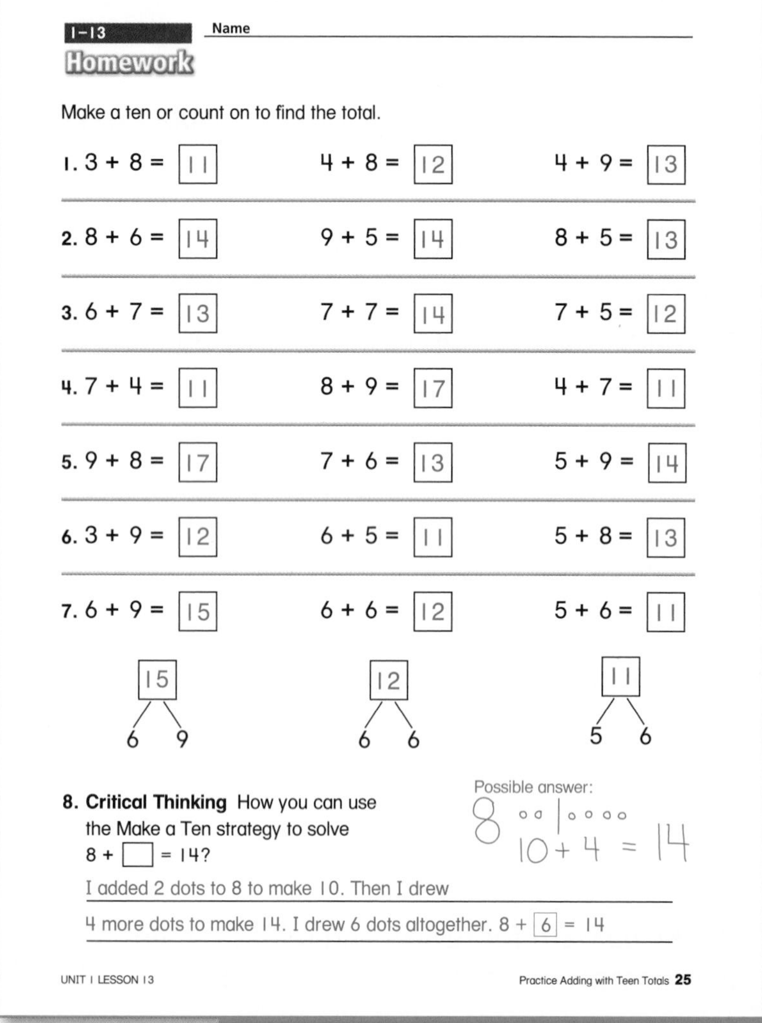

1-13 Name ______

Homework

Make a ten or count on to find the total.

1. 3 + 8 = 11 4 + 8 = 12 4 + 9 = 13
2. 8 + 6 = 14 9 + 5 = 14 8 + 5 = 13
3. 6 + 7 = 13 7 + 7 = 14 7 + 5 = 12
4. 7 + 4 = 11 8 + 9 = 17 4 + 7 = 11
5. 9 + 8 = 17 7 + 6 = 13 5 + 9 = 14
6. 3 + 9 = 12 6 + 5 = 11 5 + 8 = 13
7. 6 + 9 = 15 6 + 6 = 12 5 + 6 = 11

15: 6, 9 12: 6, 6 11: 5, 6

8. **Critical Thinking** How you can use the Make a Ten strategy to solve 8 + ☐ = 14?

Possible answer: 8 oo | oooo 10 + 4 = 14

I added 2 dots to 8 to make 10. Then I drew 4 more dots to make 14. I drew 6 dots altogether. 8 + 6 = 14

UNIT 1 LESSON 13 Practice Adding with Teen Totals 25

Homework and Remembering page 25

1-13 **Targeted Practice** **Goal:** Count on to subtract.

This Targeted Practice page can be used with children who need extra practice subtracting.

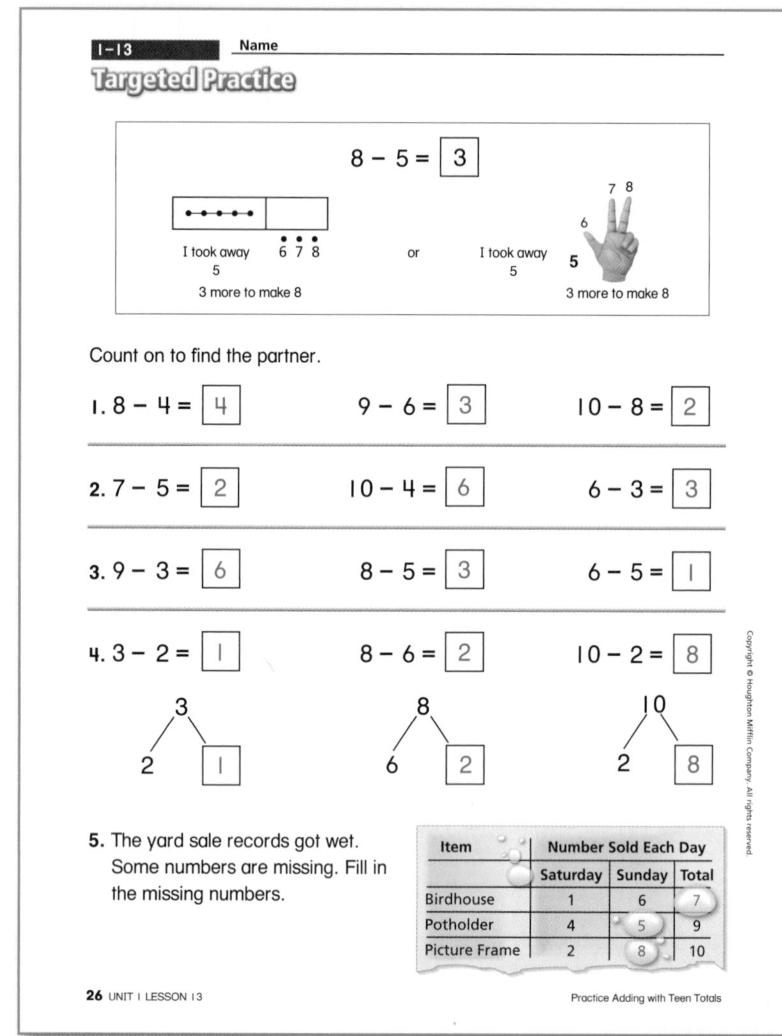

1-13 Name ______

Targeted Practice

8 − 5 = 3

I took away 5 6 7 8 3 more to make 8 or I took away 5 5 6 7 8 3 more to make 8

Count on to find the partner.

1. 8 − 4 = 4 9 − 6 = 3 10 − 8 = 2
2. 7 − 5 = 2 10 − 4 = 6 6 − 3 = 3
3. 9 − 3 = 6 8 − 5 = 3 6 − 5 = 1
4. 3 − 2 = 1 8 − 6 = 2 10 − 2 = 8

3: 2, 1 8: 6, 2 10: 2, 8

5. The yard sale records got wet. Some numbers are missing. Fill in the missing numbers.

Item	Number Sold Each Day		
	Saturday	Sunday	Total
Birdhouse	1	6	7
Potholder	4	5	9
Picture Frame	2	8	10

26 UNIT 1 LESSON 13 Practice Adding with Teen Totals

Homework and Remembering page 26

Home or School Activity

Technology Connection

Race the Calculator Have children work with a partner to play *Race the Calculator.* Players can use the first 4 rows of exercises on the homework page. To play, one player uses a calculator to find each total. The other player uses any other method (for example, fingers, pictures, or mental math). On a given signal, players race to complete the first 4 rows using their method. The player who finishes first wins the game. Have children discuss the advantages and disadvantages of their method.

Relate Addition and Subtraction

Vocabulary
partner
total
Math Mountain
equation

Lesson Objective

- Count on to solve addition, mystery addition, and subtraction problems.

The Day at a Glance

Today's Goals	Materials	
1 Teaching the Lesson **A1:** Compare addition and subtraction by working with Math Mountains and number equations. **A2:** Play the *Count on Me* game to practice counting on to find totals and partners.	**Lesson Activities** Student Activity Book p. 43, 45–46 (includes *Count On Me* Game Board) Homework and Remembering pp. 27–28 MathBoard materials Counters Secret Code Cards Colored paper	**Going Further** Activity Cards 1-14 Student Activity Book p. 44 MathBoard materials Sticky notes Index cards Math Journals
2 Going Further ▸ Math Connection: Match Story Problems and Equations ▸ Differentiated Instruction		
3 Homework and Spiral Review		

Use Math Talk today!

Keeping Skills Sharp

Quick Practice — 5 MINUTES	Daily Routines
Goals: Identify the break-aparts for the numbers 7 and 10. Buy with a dime and make change. **Materials:** Coin Strips (from Unit 1 Lesson 4 or TRB M1) **Unknown Partner and Prairie Dog** Have children review the break-aparts of the numbers 7 and 10 by playing Unknown Partner or Prairie Dog. (See Unit 1 Lessons 8 and 9.) **Buy with a Dime** Organize a new set of children to continue enacting the Yard Sale scenario begun in Unit 1 Lesson 11. To facilitate "*quick*" practice, ask children to check the work of the Buyer, Seller, and the Bookkeepers, using their fingers rather than the Coin Strips (separate ten fingers to show cost and change). The Buyer and Seller can use Coin Strips and coins and the Bookkeepers can make drawings on the board. (See Unit 1 Lesson 11 Activity 1.)	**Money Routine** Using the 120 Poster, Using the Money Flip Chart, Using the Number Path, Using Secret Code Cards (See pp. xxiii–xxv.) ▸ Led by Student Leaders

1 Teaching the Lesson

Activity 1

Addition and Subtraction

 25 MINUTES

Goal: Compare addition and subtraction by working with Math Mountains and number equations.

Materials: MathBoard materials, counters (10 per child)

 **NCTM Standard:**
Number and Operations

English Language Learners

Write the first Math Mountain example on the board.

- **Beginning** Say: **The number on top of mountain is the sum of the partners. The sum of 5 and 3 is 8. 8 goes on top.**
- **Intermediate** Ask: **How do you use the partners to find the number on top?** add them **What is 5 + 3?** 8 **Does 8 go on top?** yes
- **Advanced** Have children tell how to find the number on top of the mountain.

▶ Relate Math Mountains to Equations WHOLE CLASS

Have children draw these Math Mountains on their MathBoards as you draw them on the board.

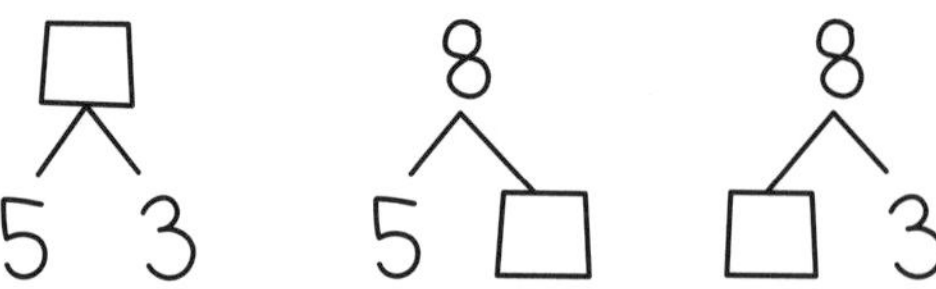

Tell children that they are going to write equations that go with each Math Mountain and later they will discuss story problems that go with each Math Mountain. They will see if they can write an addition equation, a subtraction equation, or a mystery addition equation (with an unknown partner) for each Math Mountain. Elicit as much from children as you can. Use the directive questions below only as necessary.

- What number belongs at the top of the first Math Mountain? 8
  How do you know? You add the two partners to get the total.
- We can use this *addition* equation to show the first Math Mountain.

$$5 + 3 = \square$$

- What is the *unknown partner* in the second mountain? 3

Ask for Ideas Ask what two kinds of equations children have solved to find an unknown partner.

One way: Think about how many numbers you need to count on from 5 to make 8. This way matches this *mystery addition* equation.

$$5 + \square = 8$$

Another way: Think about how many we get if we take away 5 from 8. This way matches this *subtraction* equation.

$$8 - 5 = \square$$

- What is the *unknown partner* in the third mountain? 5

Have children discuss the two ways to find the unknown partner.

Using this *mystery addition* equation:

$$\square + 3 = 8$$

Using this *subtraction* equation:

$$8 - 3 = \square$$

▶ Relate Math Mountains to Story Problems

WHOLE CLASS

Now ask children to give story problems for each Math Mountain. Use the problems below if children have difficulty coming up with a story problem.

Jake had 5 books. Marvin gave him 3 more books. How many books does Jake have now?

- Which Math Mountain shows this situation? the first one
- How do you solve the problem? You add 5 books and 3 books to get 8 books.

Now write and read this story problem.

Jake had 8 books. He gave 5 of them away. How many books does Jake have now?

- Which Math Mountain shows this situation? the second one
- How do you solve the problem? You count on from 5 to 8 to find the unknown partner.

Now write and read a third problem.

Jake had 5 books. Marvin gave him some more books. Now Jake has 8 books. How many books did Marvin give Jake?

- Which Math Mountain shows this situation? the second one
- How do you solve the problem? You count on from 5 to make 8 (or you subtract 5 books from 8 books) to see how many of all the books Marvin gave to Jake. Marvin gave Jake 3 books.

Story problems for the last Math Mountain will be like the last two problems except that 3 will be the known partner.

Math Talk Have volunteers make up other story problems that relate to one of the three Math Mountains. Challenge children to create a story problem for the third Math Mountain. Have children in the class decide whether the problem asks for a partner or a total and which Math Mountain each problem matches.

Activity continued ▶

Teaching Note

Watch For! When counting on, some children may have trouble understanding which number is the total and which number is the partner to find an unknown partner.

Children should remember to listen for the final number they say to find the total.

Children should remember to look at their fingers to see the unknown partner.

Draw circles to show taking away the first circles and discuss how subtracting is taking away one partner but you need to find the other partner. The other partner will be on their fingers when they count on.

Differentiated Instruction

English Learners Allow English Learners to draw their story problem first, then have them work with an English-speaking partner to write out their story problem. The visual/verbal pairing of drawing a story problem, writing it out, reading it with a partner, and creating a Math Mountain helps English Learners see the problem in various steps that all correlate to a math problem.

❶ Teaching the Lesson (continued)

Alternate Approach

Counters If children are having difficulties using mental math or fingers to find the total and partners, have them use counters.

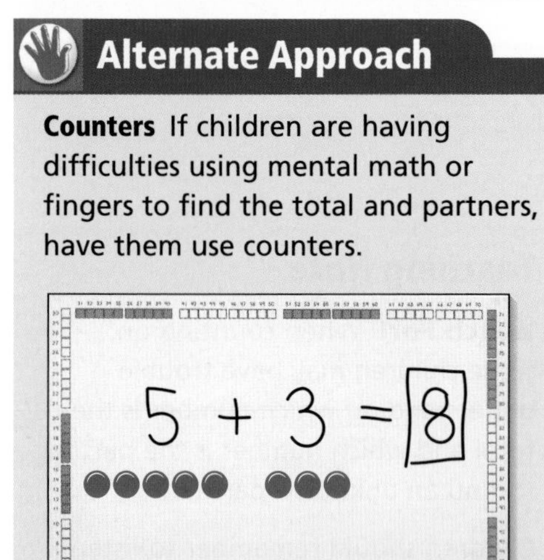

► Practice Finding Totals and Partners INDIVIDUALS

Leave the three Math Mountains on the board. Have children solve the equations on Student Activity Book page 43.

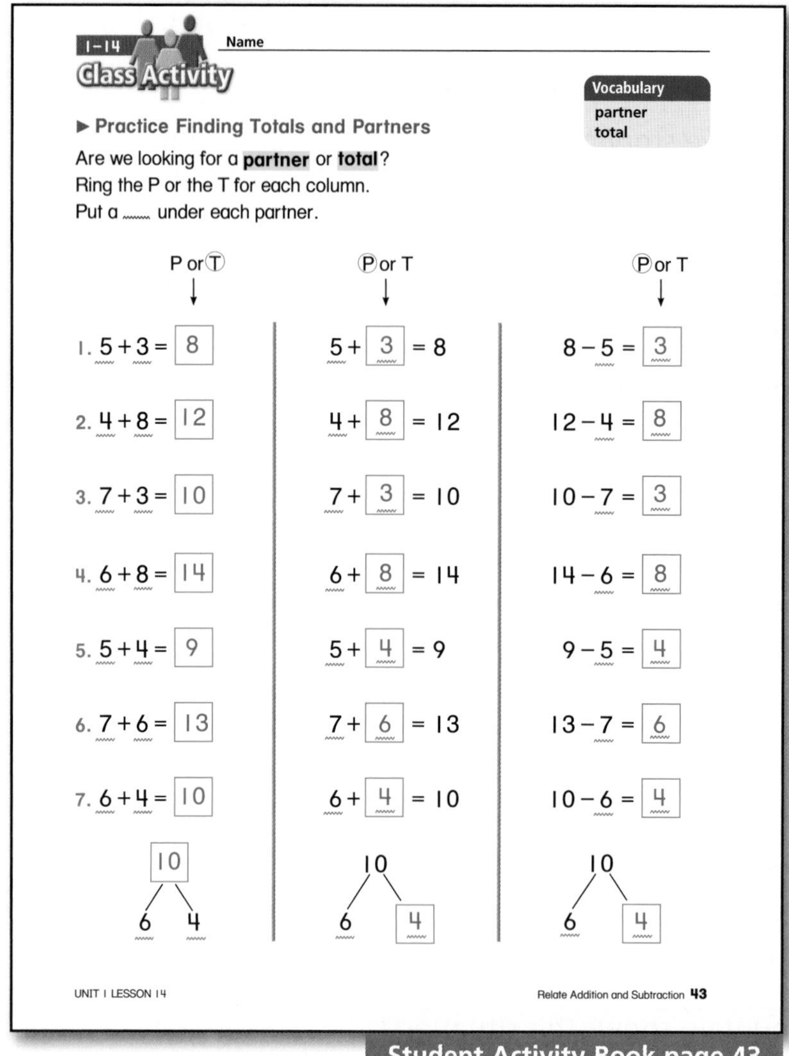

1–14 Class Activity

Name

Vocabulary
partner
total

► Practice Finding Totals and Partners

Are we looking for a **partner** or **total**?
Ring the P or the T for each column.
Put a ~~~ under each partner.

	P or (T)	(P) or T	(P) or T
1.	5 + 3 = 8	5 + 3 = 8	8 − 5 = 3
2.	4 + 8 = 12	4 + 8 = 12	12 − 4 = 8
3.	7 + 3 = 10	7 + 3 = 10	10 − 7 = 3
4.	6 + 8 = 14	6 + 8 = 14	14 − 6 = 8
5.	5 + 4 = 9	5 + 4 = 9	9 − 5 = 4
6.	7 + 6 = 13	7 + 6 = 13	13 − 7 = 6
7.	6 + 4 = 10	6 + 4 = 10	10 − 6 = 4
	10 / 6 4	10 / 6 4	10 / 6 4

UNIT 1 LESSON 14 Relate Addition and Subtraction 43

Student Activity Book page 43

Be sure children see that all the equations in a row have the same three numbers. The first column has addition equations, the second column has mystery addition equations, and the third column has subtraction equations. In the first column, children find a total, and in the second and third columns they find a partner. Help them recognize that the equations in column 2 and column 3 are solved using the same process.

Activity 2

The *Count on Me* Game

▶ Get Ready for the *Count on Me* Game PAIRS

Be sure each child has all the materials and have pairs sit next to each other while you go over the directions to the *Count on Me* game.

▶ How to Play the *Count on Me* Game

Directions for Addition

Children should fold their game board (Student Activity Book page 45) on the dotted line so only the + side shows and place it on their desks.

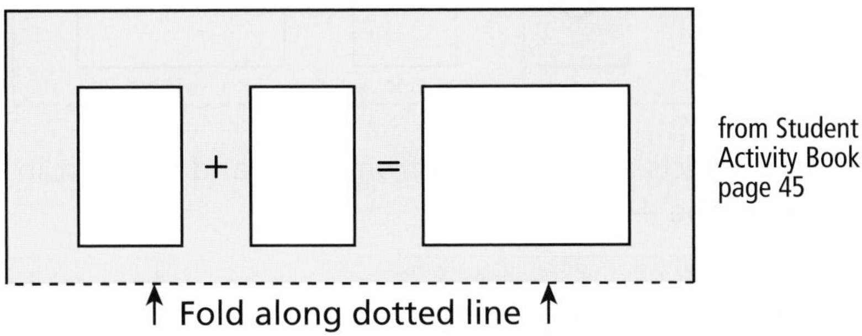

Have children decide who will be Player 1 and Player 2. Partners will rotate each round.

1. Spread one set of Secret Code Cards above the game board. This is Set 1.

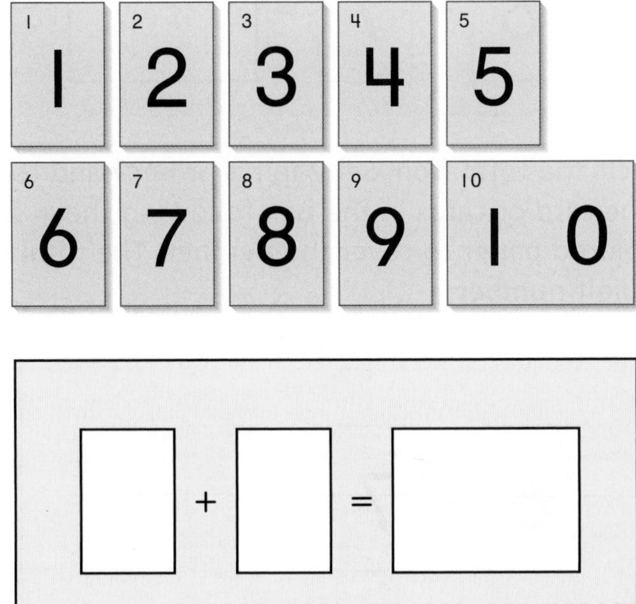

2. Player 2 holds another set of Secret Code Cards in his or her hand, so that all of the small numbers in the upper left can be seen. This is Set 2.

Activity continued ▶

 **30 MINUTES**

Goal: Play the *Count on Me* game to practice counting on to find totals and partners.

Materials: Secret Code Cards (from Unit 1 Lesson 5 or TRB M3–M4) (1 set per student), colored paper (2 pieces per child) (1 piece about the size of a 1-digit card, and the other piece about the size of a 2-digit card), *Count on Me* Game Board (Student Activity Book page 45)

 **NCTM Standard:** Number and Operations

 **Class Management**

While explaining the game to children, you may want to demonstrate with materials. While children play the game, circulate around the room and check to see that everyone is counting on or using a more advanced method. Help those who are still counting all to count on. Give them a Helping Partner who can continue to help them. If children disagree about whether or not an answer is correct, they can use the dots on the back of the cards to help them decide.

Class Management

Looking Ahead In the next lesson, children will use the Blue Make-a-Ten cards. These are on Student Activity Book pages 47–50 and on TRB M39–M42. For classroom activities, children can use the cards provided in the Student Activity Book, or they can take those cards home and you can make sturdy cards specifically for classroom use by copying the TRB onto card stock. In either case, you may want to set aside time before you begin the lesson for children to cut out the cards.

Ongoing Assessment

Circulate around the room while children are playing the *Count on Me* game and observe the strategies children are using. Help any that are still counting all to count on instead.

3. Player 1 chooses a 1-digit card from Set 1 on the table and places it number side up in the first box (to the left of the + sign).

6 + ☐ = ☐

4. Player 2 selects a 1-digit card from Set 1 and places it in the box following the + sign.

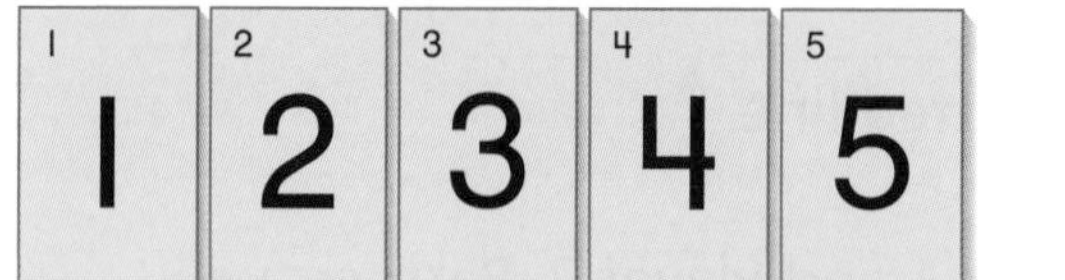

8 9 10

6 + 7 = ☐

5. Player 2 selects the total from Set 2 in his or her hand to show the total, puts the card or cards in the box following the = sign, and uses a piece of colored paper to cover the number. The total may be either a teen or 1-digit number.

6 + 7 =

6. Player 1 must say the total. Player 2 says "Correct" or "Try Again." When Player 1 gets the correct answer, players switch roles, and the game continues.

Directions for Mystery Addition

Steps 1, 2, and 3 are the same as for addition.

4. Player 1's card is on the board. Player 2 selects a card from Set 2 in his or her hand, places it in the box following the + sign, and covers it with a piece of colored paper. Player 2 makes the total from Set 1 and puts the card or cards in the box following the = sign.

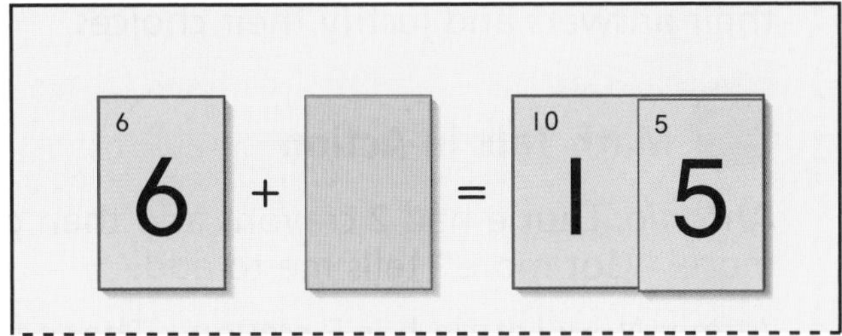

5. Player 1 must say the correct unknown partner. Player 2 says "Correct" or "Try Again." When Player 1 gets the correct answer, they switch roles, and the game continues.

Directions for Subtraction

Turn the game board so you can see the subtraction equation (– sign). Remember, Set 1 is on the table and Player 2 holds Set 2 in his or her hand.

1. Player 1 chooses the total from Set 1 and places the card or cards in the first blank space. This number is the total. Be sure the total is greater than 2.
2. Player 2 selects 2 cards from Set 2 in his or her hand that are partners of the total and places them in the remaining 2 boxes. Player 2 covers one of the partners with a piece of colored paper.

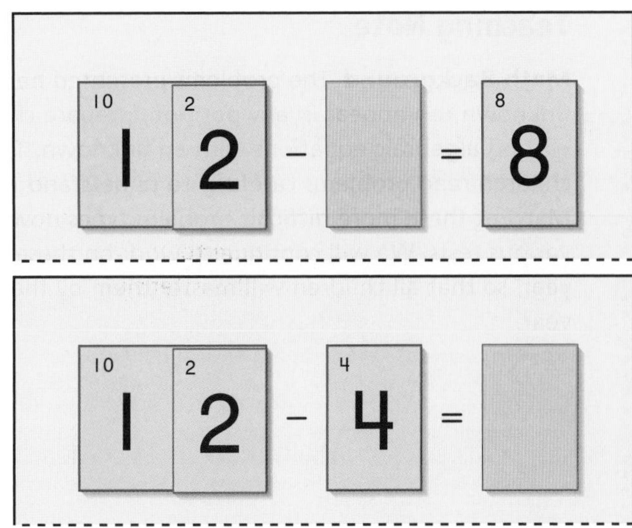

3. Player 1 must say the correct unknown partner. Player 2 says "Correct" or "Try Again." When Player 1 gets the correct answer, they switch roles, and the game continues.

Differentiated Instruction

Extra Help Playing all three games may be overwhelming for some children. In this case, have children play only 1 or 2 versions of the game at this time. Delay the more difficult versions, especially the subtraction version, until a later time.

The Learning Classroom

Math Talk After the game is over, elicit from children what they learned from playing the game. As children share, guide them to emphasize differences between addition, mystery addition, and subtraction.

Class Management

Looking Ahead Have children save their game boards for future use. If some children misplace their game boards and you need to make additional copies, use Copymaster M28.

2 Going Further

Math Connection: Match Problems and Equations

Goal: Match story problems and equations.

Materials: Student Activity Book page 44

NCTM Standards:
Number and Operations
Communication

The Learning Classroom

Building Concepts This activity introduces the idea of how to write equations. Any number in an equation can be the unknown. Children may have difficulty with some problem types, especially those with an unknown start or those that ask children to add or subtract an unknown. Have children try these problems; however, they are not expected to master them now.

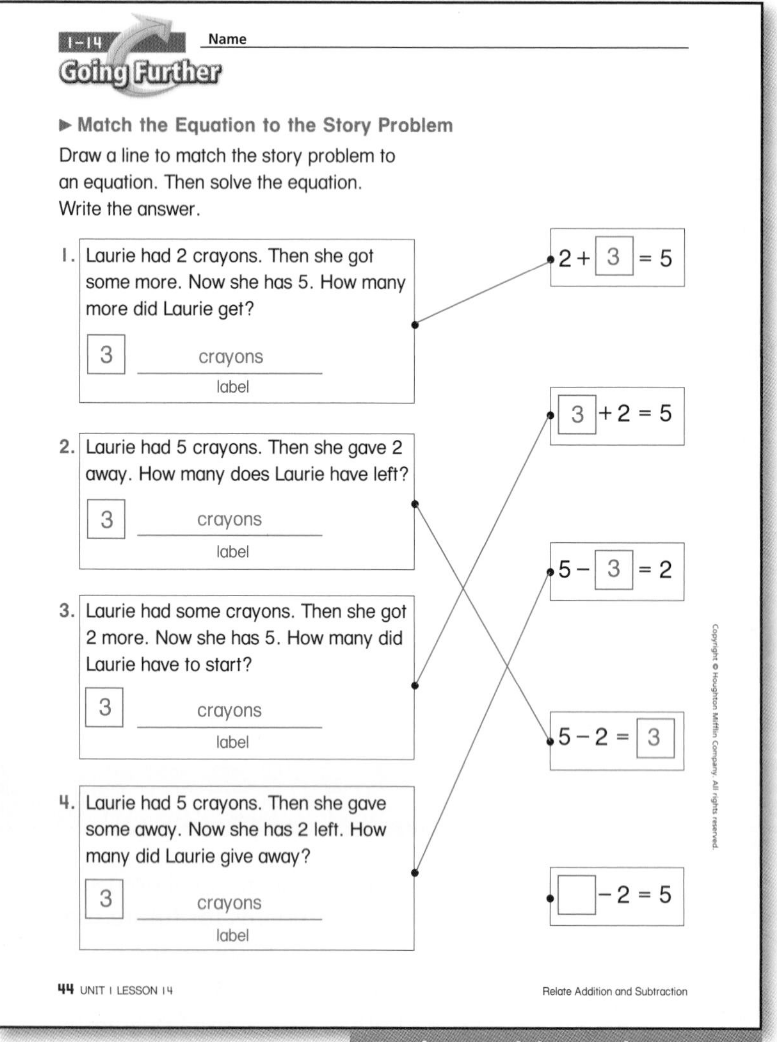

1–14 Going Further Name

▶ Match the Equation to the Story Problem

Draw a line to match the story problem to an equation. Then solve the equation. Write the answer.

1. Laurie had 2 crayons. Then she got some more. Now she has 5. How many more did Laurie get?
3 crayons
label

2. Laurie had 5 crayons. Then she gave 2 away. How many does Laurie have left?
3 crayons
label

3. Laurie had some crayons. Then she got 2 more. Now she has 5. How many did Laurie have to start?
3 crayons
label

4. Laurie had 5 crayons. Then she gave some away. Now she has 2 left. How many did Laurie give away?
3 crayons
label

$2 + \boxed{3} = 5$

$\boxed{3} + 2 = 5$

$5 - \boxed{3} = 2$

$5 - 2 = \boxed{3}$

$\boxed{} - 2 = 5$

Copyright © Houghton Mifflin Company. All rights reserved.

44 UNIT 1 LESSON 14 Relate Addition and Subtraction

Student Activity Book page 44

▶ Match the Equation to the Story Problem

Ask a volunteer to read problem 1. Then tell the children to look carefully at the five equations listed and to decide which equation *best* fits the story problem. Point to the points on the page. These dots will help children draw lines. Children should discuss their answers and justify their choices.

Math Talk in Action

Antonio: Laurie had 2 crayons and then got some more. "Got more" tells me to add.

Juana: Now Laurie has 5 crayons. That's the total. We can count on from 2 to get to 5: 3, 4, 5 [*keeps track on her fingers*]. That's three fingers.

Antonio: So, the 3 is the partner and it's the mystery number. I'll draw the Math Mountain. That will help us write the equation.

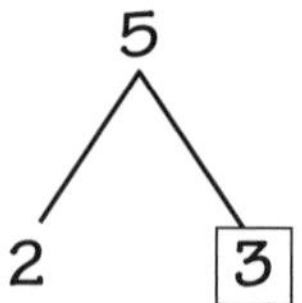

Juana: Is the equation $\square + 2 = 5$ or is it $2 + \square = 5$?

Antonio: I think the equation $2 + \square = 5$ because Laurie started with 2.

Teaching Note

Math Background The problems presented here, in which the unknown can appear in any position, prepare children for writing algebraic equations with an unknown. They also help children read problems carefully to understand the situation. Many of these more difficult problem types now appear on various tests. We will continue to work on these problems all year, so that all children will master them by the end of the year.

Intervention — Activity Card 1-14

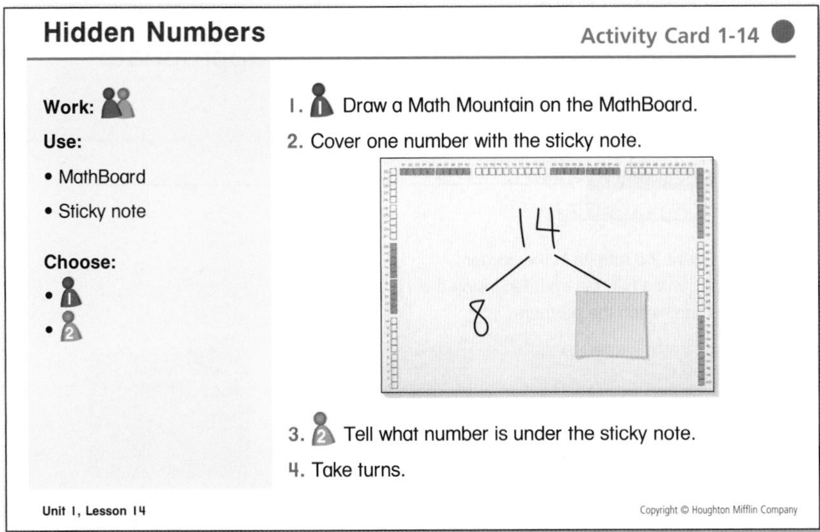

Hidden Numbers Activity Card 1-14

Work: Pairs

Use:
- MathBoard
- Sticky note

Choose:
- Partner 1
- Partner 2

1. Partner 1: Draw a Math Mountain on the MathBoard.
2. Cover one number with the sticky note.

3. Partner 2: Tell what number is under the sticky note.
4. Take turns.

Unit 1, Lesson 14

Activity Note One child in each pair will draw a Math Mountain and cover one number. The other child has to determine the missing number.

Math Writing Prompt

Count On Explain how to count on to solve this equation. 6 – 4 = □

Software Support

Use *Soar to Success* for instruction of students needing targeted support for underlying skills.

On Level — Activity Card 1-14

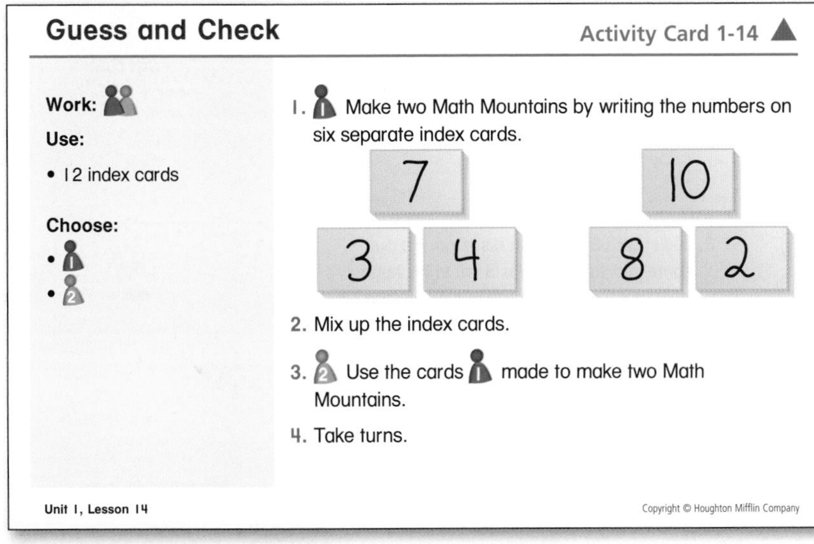

Guess and Check Activity Card 1-14

Work: Pairs

Use:
- 12 index cards

Choose:
- Partner 1
- Partner 2

1. Partner 1: Make two Math Mountains by writing the numbers on six separate index cards.

2. Mix up the index cards.
3. Partner 2: Use the cards Partner 1 made to make two Math Mountains.
4. Take turns.

Unit 1, Lesson 14

Activity Note Each child needs six index cards. Have each child use the cards to make two Math Mountains. Pairs trade cards and make the Math Mountains.

Math Writing Prompt

Write Your Own Write an equation using 17 as the total and 8 as a partner. Write a story problem to go with your equation.

Software Support

Use *MegaMath* for review and reinforcement of the concepts and skills presented in this lesson.

Challenge — Activity Card 1-14

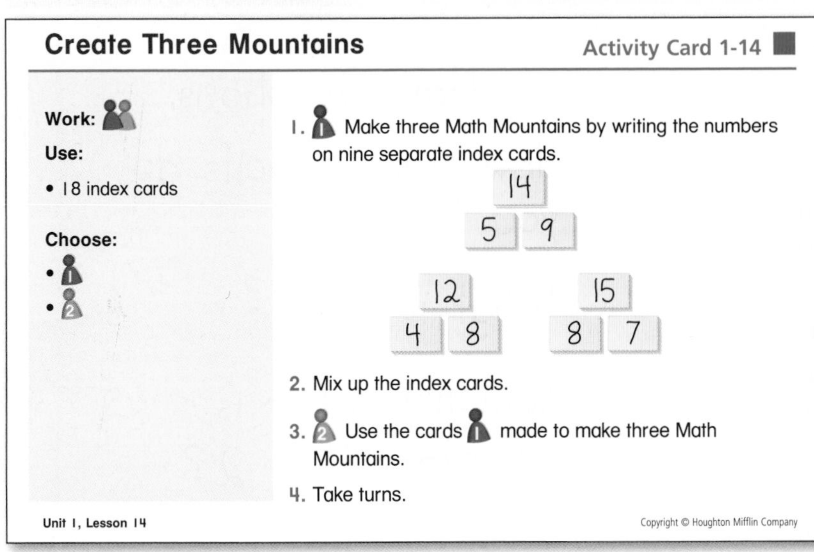

Create Three Mountains Activity Card 1-14

Work: Pairs

Use:
- 18 index cards

Choose:
- Partner 1
- Partner 2

1. Partner 1: Make three Math Mountains by writing the numbers on nine separate index cards.

2. Mix up the index cards.
3. Partner 2: Use the cards Partner 1 made to make three Math Mountains.
4. Take turns.

Unit 1, Lesson 14

Activity Note Each child needs nine index cards and uses the cards to make three Math Mountains. Pairs trade cards and make the Math Mountains.

Math Writing Prompt

Create a Math Mountain Create your own Math Mountain. Write and solve three equations that go with your mountain. What is the same about your equations? What is different?

DESTINATION Math®

Software Support

Use *Destination Math* to take students beyond the concepts and skills presented in this lesson.

Homework and Spiral Review

1–14 Homework **Goal:** Additional Practice

Include children's completed Homework page as part of their portfolios.

1–14 Remembering **Goal:** Spiral Review

This Remembering activity would be appropriate anytime after today's lesson.

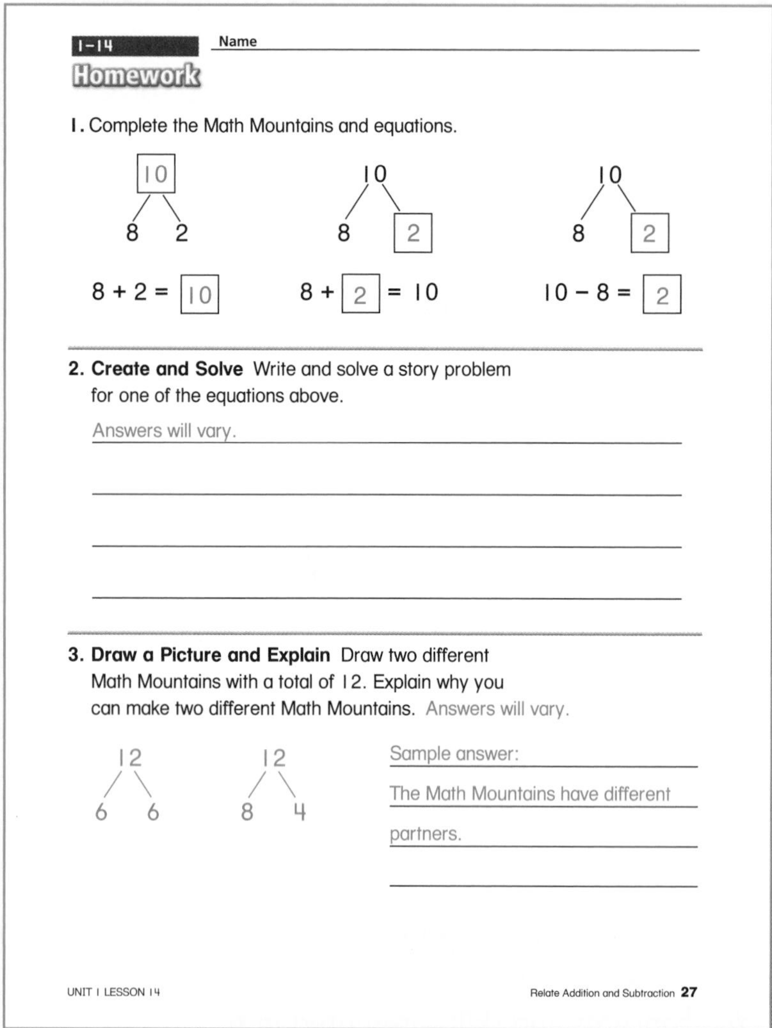

1–14 Name

Homework

1. Complete the Math Mountains and equations.

10 / 8, 2 — 8 + 2 = 10

10 / 8, 2 — 8 + 2 = 10

10 / 8, 2 — 10 − 8 = 2

2. **Create and Solve** Write and solve a story problem for one of the equations above.

Answers will vary.

3. **Draw a Picture and Explain** Draw two different Math Mountains with a total of 12. Explain why you can make two different Math Mountains. Answers will vary.

12 / 6, 6 — 12 / 8, 4

Sample answer: The Math Mountains have different partners.

UNIT 1 LESSON 14 — Relate Addition and Subtraction 27

Homework and Remembering page 27

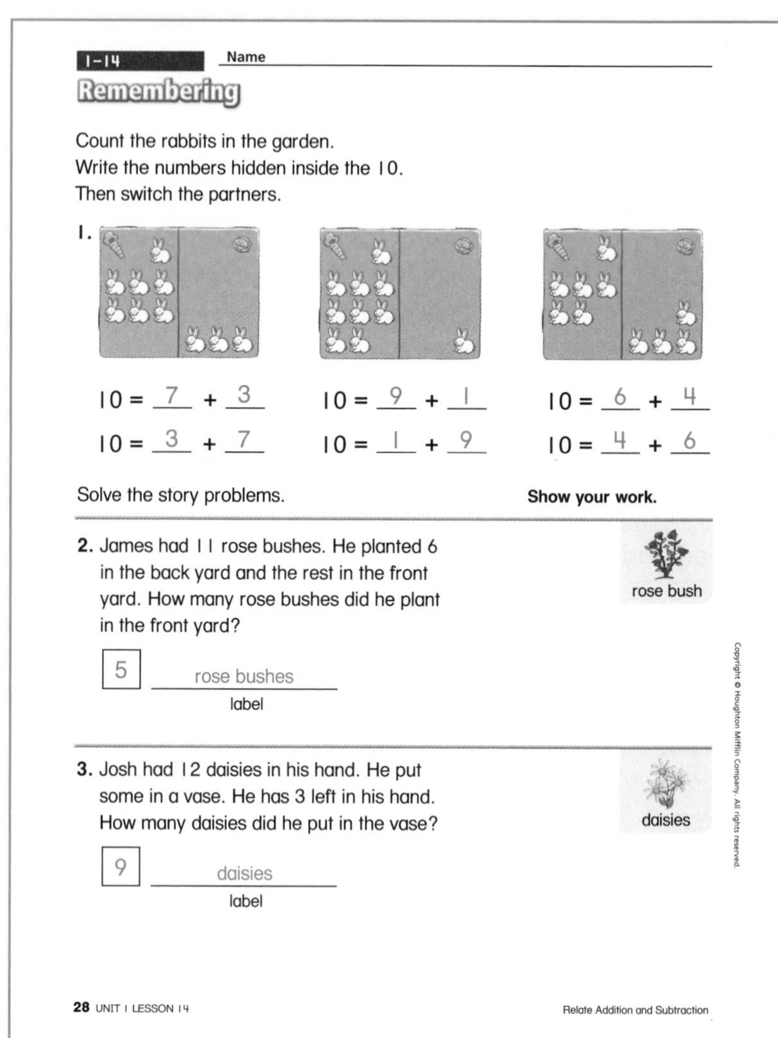

1–14 Name

Remembering

Count the rabbits in the garden.
Write the numbers hidden inside the 10.
Then switch the partners.

1.

10 = 7 + 3 — 10 = 9 + 1 — 10 = 6 + 4

10 = 3 + 7 — 10 = 1 + 9 — 10 = 4 + 6

Solve the story problems. **Show your work.**

2. James had 11 rose bushes. He planted 6 in the back yard and the rest in the front yard. How many rose bushes did he plant in the front yard?

rose bush

5 rose bushes (label)

3. Josh had 12 daisies in his hand. He put some in a vase. He has 3 left in his hand. How many daisies did he put in the vase?

daisies

9 daisies (label)

28 UNIT 1 LESSON 14 — Relate Addition and Subtraction

Homework and Remembering page 28

Home or School Activity

Language Arts Connection

What's a Question? Tell children they will be writing many math questions this year as they learn to write their own number story problems. Have children think about questions, reminding them that sometimes questions start with a question word like *who, which, how, what, where, when*, or *why*. Have children make a list of questions they might use in math. Remind them to end each question with a question mark.

Math Questions

How many pencils do you have?

What is 5 + 2?

Which number is greater, 4 or 2?

Unknown Partners and Teen Totals

Lesson Objective

- **Make a ten to solve mystery addition and subtraction story problems.**

Vocabulary
teen total
count on

The Day at a Glance

Today's Goals	Materials	
1 Teaching the Lesson **A:** Solve mystery addition and subtraction problems using the Make a Ten strategies.	**Lesson Activities** Student Activity Book pp. 47–50 (includes Blue Make-a-Ten Cards) Homework and Remembering pp. 29–30 Counters	**Going Further** Activity Cards 1-15 MathBoard materials Two-color counters Ten Frame (TRB M33) Math Journals
2 Going Further ▸ Differentiated Instruction		
3 Homework and Targeted Practice		

Use **Math Talk** today!

Keeping Skills Sharp

Quick Practice — 5 MINUTES

Goal: Practice making change from a dime.

Materials: Real or play money, Coin Strips (from Unit 1 Lesson 4 or TRB M1) (1 Dime Strip, 9 Penny Strips per child), Coin cover (index card, sticky note, or paper per pair), List of yard sale items on chart paper (see Unit 1 Lesson 11)

Buy with a Dime Invite six children to act out the Yard Sale scenario from Lesson 11. To make this a "quick" practice, ask children to check the work of the Buyer, Seller, and the Bookkeepers, using their fingers rather than the Coin Strips. The Buyer and Seller can use Coin Strips and coins and the Bookkeepers can make drawings on the board. (See Unit 1 Lesson 11 Activity 1.)

Repeated Quick Practice Use this Quick Practice from a previous lesson.

- ▸ **Unknown Partner or Prairie Dog** Use numbers 5 and 10. (See Unit 1 Lessons 8 and 9.)

Daily Routines

Money Routine Using the 120 Poster, Using the Money Flip Chart, Using the Number Path, Using Secret Code Cards (See pp. xxiii–xxv.)

- ▸ Led by Student Leaders

1 Teaching the Lesson

Activity

Using Make a Ten to Find the Unknown Partner

50 MINUTES

Goal: Solve mystery addition and subtraction problems using the Make a Ten strategies.

Materials: counters (18 per child)

NCTM Standards:
Problem Solving
Number and Operations

Teaching Note

Research The Make a Ten strategy for mystery addition and subtraction problems is similar to the Make a Ten strategy for addition. In both mystery addition and subtraction, children know one partner and the total so they will have to adapt Make a Ten methods for addition to find the unknown partner instead of the total. To solve, they find how much is needed to make ten and look at the teen total to see how much is left over ten. Children add those two numbers to make the other partner.

Mystery addition and subtraction Make a Ten strategies are easier than addition Make a Ten strategies because children can see one partner and the amount over 10 in the teen number. Children only have to find how much the known partner needs to make 10 and add it to the amount over 10. This is easy to develop from counting on, even though it looks complex.

$8 + \square = 14$

$8 + 2 + 4 = 14$

10 4

8 OO|OOOO

$2 + 4 = 6$

I have 8 9 10 4 make 14

$2 + 4 = 6$

6

8 OO 4

▶ Make a Ten to Solve Story Problems WHOLE CLASS

Math Talk

Have volunteers tell a story problem for each situation shown below. Be sure children understand that mystery addition situations are being discussed. Write the following on the board.

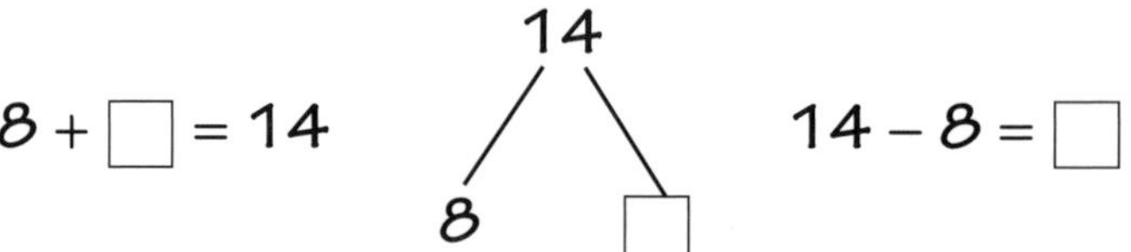

You can use the following problems if children have trouble making up story problems.

> Maria invited 14 children to her party. She already made 8 fruit cups. How many more fruit cups does Maria need to make so that every child at the party can have one fruit cup?

Invite children to solve the story problem using finger or written Make a Ten strategies they learned for addition, including Make a Ten with an Imaginary Friend. If they want to count on just to get started, they may. Explain to children that they should be ready to talk about the methods they used to solve the problem.

Have children solve the following subtraction problem using finger or written Make a Ten strategies, including Make a Ten with a Friend.

> Larry took 14 pencils to school. He gave 8 pencils to his friends. How many pencils did he have left?

Have children who used different strategies share their solutions. Help children see that they can think of this problem as taking away the first 8 and finding how many more to 14.

▶ Discuss and Compare Methods WHOLE CLASS

Have children describe how the methods work for mystery addition and subtraction and how they are similar and different.

▶ Make a Ten with a Friend to Find an Unknown Partner PAIRS

If children did not use the Make a Ten strategies earlier, have them use and then practice the method to find a partner for both mystery addition and subtraction. Have children sit in pairs so they can make a ten with a friend to solve the problems.

Write 8 + □ = 14 on the board.

- First let's make a ten to solve 8 + □ = 14. We need to find how many more fruit cups Maria needs to make for her party.
- What is the total? 14
- What partner do we know? 8

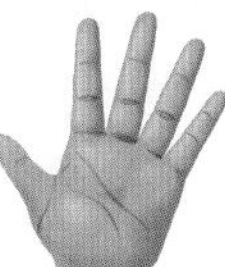
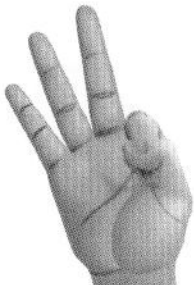

Have one friend show the known partner, 8.

- What do we want to find? The partner that goes with 8 to make 14.
- How many fingers does 8 need to make 10? 2
- How many more fingers to make 14? 4
- How many fingers does the second friend show all together? 6

2 fingers and 4 fingers are 6 fingers. Maria needs to make 6 more fruit cups.

8 + □ = 14

First Friend

Second Friend

put up 4 more in 14

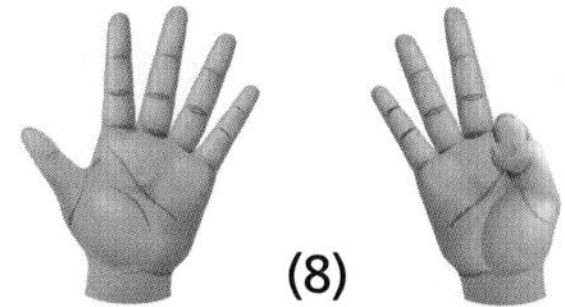
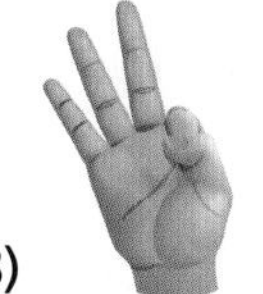

(8)

put up 2 to make 10

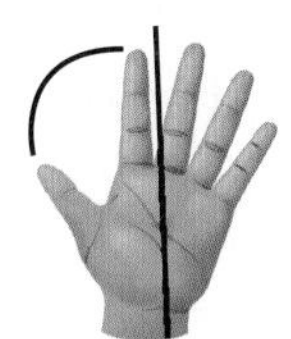

(6)

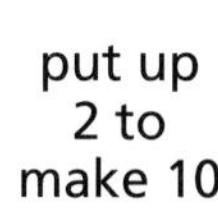

2 + 4 = 6 so 8 + 2 + 4 = 14

8 + [6] = 14

Write 14 − 8 = □ on the board. Repeat the process for the subtraction problem using the same strategy as above.

- How many pencils did Larry have left after he gave 8 pencils to his friends?

Activity continued ▶

The Learning Classroom

Building Concepts Constructing thoughtful questions and probing statements is often challenging for teachers while they are teaching lessons and juggling many thoughts. Here are some questions and statements that teachers have found useful. It is fine to use a few questions or statements repeatedly. Children will begin to predict your probes and grow more comfortable responding to them.

- ▶ So, what is this problem about?
- ▶ Tell us what you see.
- ▶ What would happen if . . . ?
- ▶ Is that true for all cases?
- ▶ How can we check to be sure that this is a correct answer?
- ▶ What did you mean when you said ____?
- ▶ What were you thinking when you decided to do ____?

English Language Learners

Write 8 + □ = 14 on the board. Have children work with a partner to solve.

- **Beginning** Say: **The total is 14. This partner is 8.** Point to the 8. Say: **Make a ten with your partner. 2 fingers make 10 along with 4 more fingers. 2 + 4 = 6.**
- **Intermediate and Advanced** Ask: **What is the total?** 14 **Which partner do we know?** 8 Say: **Make a ten with your partner.** Ask: **How many fingers make 10?** 2 **How many more fingers?** 4 **What is 2 + 4?** 6

Teaching the Lesson (continued)

Class Management

Looking Ahead In the next lesson, children will use Math Mountain Cards. These are on Student Activity Book pages 51–54 and on TRB M43–M44.

Children can use the cards in the Student Activity Book, or they can take those home and you can make sturdy cards for classroom use by copying the TRB onto card stock. In either case, you may want to set aside a time before you begin the lesson for children to cut out the Math Mountain Cards.

If you have access to the *Math Expressions* materials kits, the Math Mountain Cards are included, so you will not have to prepare these materials.

Ongoing Assessment

Circulate around the room while pairs are writing story problems. Ask children to explain how they could use the Make a Ten method to solve the problem.

Blue Make-a-Ten Cards

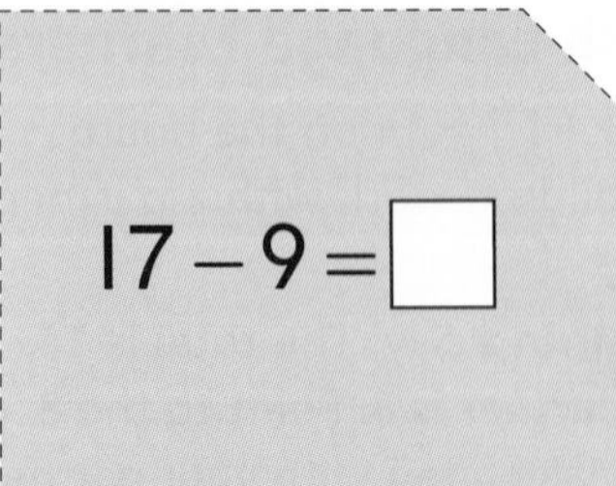

front of card

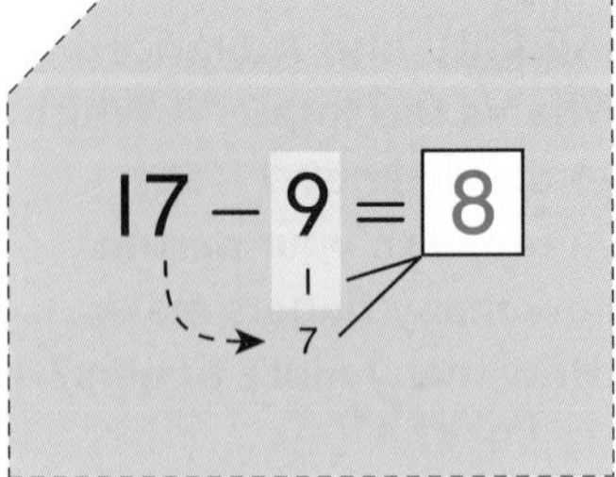

back of card

From Student Activity Book pages 47–50.

Have one friend show 8 fingers for the pencils Larry gave away. The other friend gives 2 fingers to make 10 and then shows the 4 fingers needed to reach the total of 14. Larry had 6 pencils left.

Do several more problems. Have children create a story problem for each equation below.

$9 + \square = 13$ $8 + \square = 15$ $7 + \square = 12$

$12 - 5 = \square$ $15 - 9 = \square$ $13 - 7 = \square$

When children seem to understand the method as they work in pairs, have them try some problems on their own. They can use the Make a Ten with an Imaginary Friend strategy.

Have children discuss how the strategy works for both types of problems, guiding them to see that the problem situations differ, but the solution process is the same for both.

▶ Introduce the Blue Make-a-Ten Cards INDIVIDUALS

Have children cut out the Blue Make-a-Ten Cards on Student Activity Book pages 47–50. (These cards are also on TRB M39–M42 if you wish to print the cards on cardstock, or if you wish to have a set for children to use at home.) If you have access to the *Math Expressions* materials kits, the Blue Make-a-Ten Cards are included, so you will not have to prepare these materials.

The Blue Make-a-Ten Cards help children become fluent in the Make a Ten strategy for subtraction. This strategy requires two steps. Use the $17 - 9 = \square$ card to discuss how the cards show the steps. Elicit as much of the explanation as possible from your children.

- Find the 10-partner of the known partner.
  On the card, the known partner (9 in the example) and its 10-partner (1 in the example) are highlighted.
- Add that 10-partner (1 in the example) to the ones in the teen number (7 in the example).

  $1 + 7 = 8$

Many children will find subtraction make a ten easier than addition make a ten because they just have to add 2 numbers: the partner to ten with the known addend and the ones they see in the teen number.

With this method, teen subtraction becomes a simple addition problem.

Explain to children that they will use these cards to practice subtraction in the same way they used the Count-On Cards and the Green Make-a-Ten Cards. They will make three piles: the cards they answer quickly and correctly, the cards they answer correctly and slowly, and the cards they answer incorrectly.

2 Going Further

Differentiated Instruction

Intervention

Activity Card 1-15

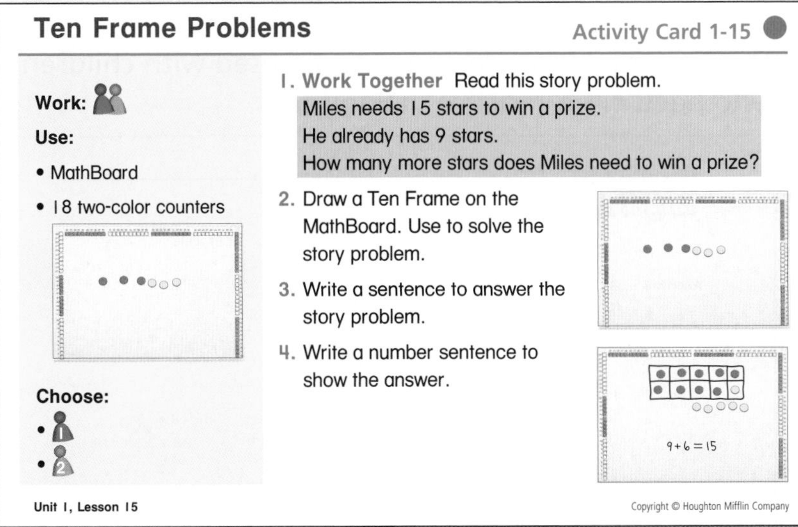

Ten Frame Problems Activity Card 1-15

Work:
Use:
- MathBoard
- 18 two-color counters

1. **Work Together** Read this story problem.
   Miles needs 15 stars to win a prize.
   He already has 9 stars.
   How many more stars does Miles need to win a prize?
2. Draw a Ten Frame on the MathBoard. Use to solve the story problem.
3. Write a sentence to answer the story problem.
4. Write a number sentence to show the answer.

9 + 6 = 15

Choose:
-
-

Unit 1, Lesson 15

Activity Note Each pair needs 18 two-counter counters. Pairs use the counters to solve a story problem. Ask children to explain how they found the answer.

Math Writing Prompt

Draw or Explain Explain how you can solve $8 + \square = 13$ using the Make a Ten strategy.

Software Support

Use *Soar to Success* for instruction of students needing targeted support for underlying skills.

On Level

Activity Card 1-15

Use a Table Activity Card 1-15

Work:
Use:
- paper

Choose:
-
-

1. Three child set a goal to read 14 books each. This table shows how many books each child read.

Book Club Goal: 14 Books Each

Name	Number of books	Number of books left to read
Sharon	6	
Linus	9	
Morgan	7	

2. Each copies the table and figures out how many books each child still has to read.
3. **Math Talk** Tell your partner how you found how many books each child still has to read.

Unit 1, Lesson 15

Activity Note Children need to copy the table and then complete it. Make sure children realize that each child story wants to read 14 books.

Math Writing Prompt

Explain Your Thinking Bob needs 14 points to win the game. He already scored 9 points. Explain how making a ten can help you find out how many points Bob needs to score to win the game.

Software Support

Use *MegaMath* for review and reinforcement of the concepts and skills presented in this lesson.

Challenge

Activity Card 1-15

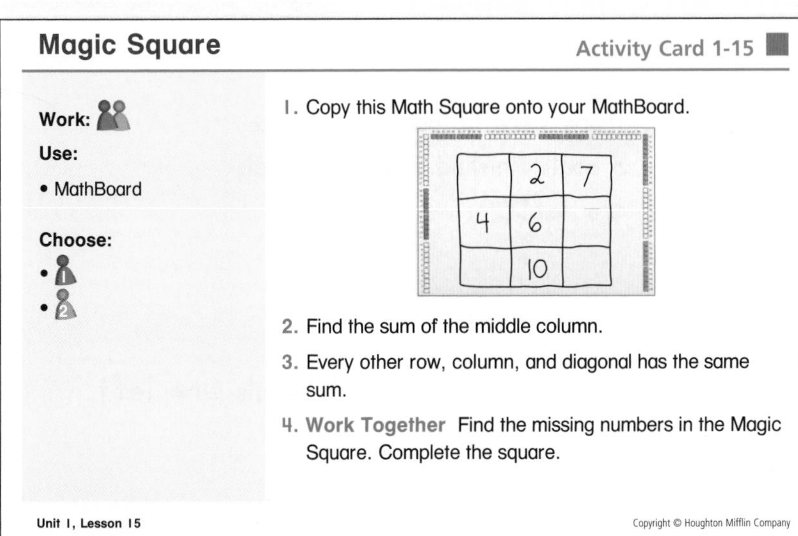

Magic Square Activity Card 1-15

Work:
Use:
- MathBoard

Choose:
-
-

1. Copy this Math Square onto your MathBoard.

	2	7
4	6	
	10	

2. Find the sum of the middle column.
3. Every other row, column, and diagonal has the same sum.
4. **Work Together** Find the missing numbers in the Magic Square. Complete the square.

Unit 1, Lesson 15

Activity Note Have each pair copy the Magic Square onto the MathBoard. Explain that the sum of the center column is called the Magic Total.

Math Writing Prompt

Explain Tell how mystery addition and subtraction are alike. Tell how they are different.

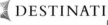

Software Support

Use *Destination Math* to take students beyond the concepts and skills presented in this lesson.

 Homework and Targeted Practice

1–15 Homework **Goal:** Additional Practice

This Homework page provides practice finding an unknown partner.

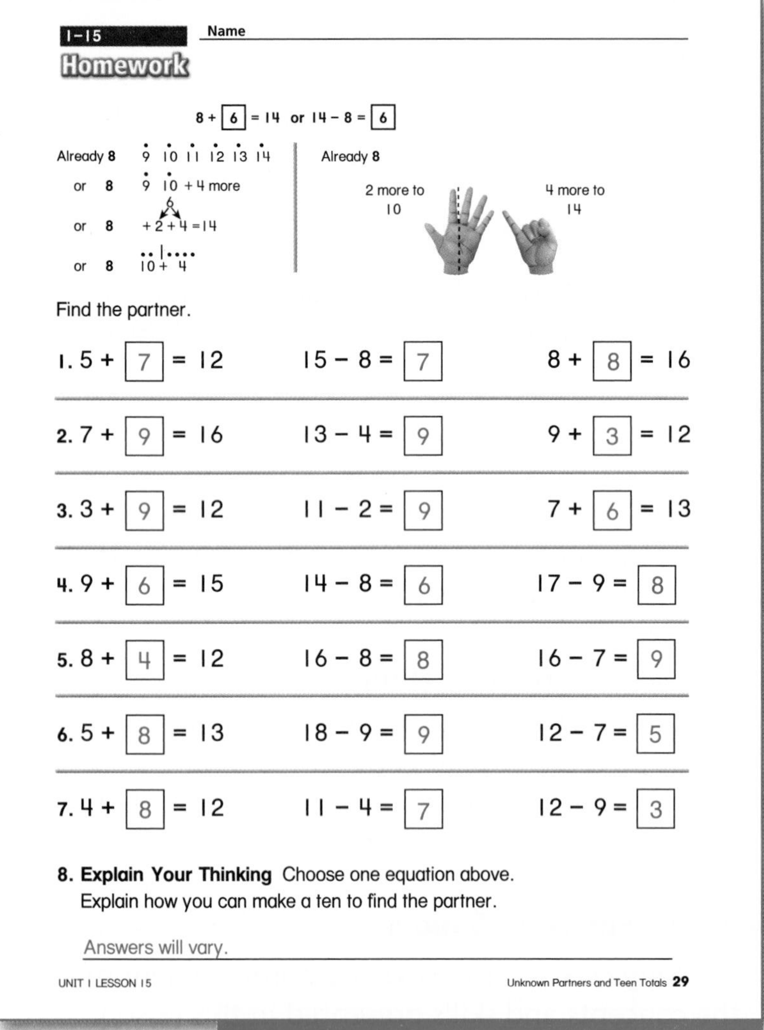

1–15 Homework Name

8 + [6] = 14 or 14 − 8 = [6]

Already 8: 9 10 11 12 13 14

or 8: 9 10 + 4 more

or 8: + 2 + 4 = 14

or 8: 10 + 4

Already 8: 2 more to 10, 4 more to 14

Find the partner.

1.	5 + [7] = 12	15 − 8 = [7]	8 + [8] = 16
2.	7 + [9] = 16	13 − 4 = [9]	9 + [3] = 12
3.	3 + [9] = 12	11 − 2 = [9]	7 + [6] = 13
4.	9 + [6] = 15	14 − 8 = [6]	17 − 9 = [8]
5.	8 + [4] = 12	16 − 8 = [8]	16 − 7 = [9]
6.	5 + [8] = 13	18 − 9 = [9]	12 − 7 = [5]
7.	4 + [8] = 12	11 − 4 = [7]	12 − 9 = [3]

8. **Explain Your Thinking** Choose one equation above. Explain how you can make a ten to find the partner.

Answers will vary.

UNIT 1 LESSON 15 Unknown Partners and Teen Totals 29

Homework and Remembering page 29

1–15 Targeted Practice **Goal:** Make a ten to add.

This Targeted Practice page can be used with children who need extra practice making tens.

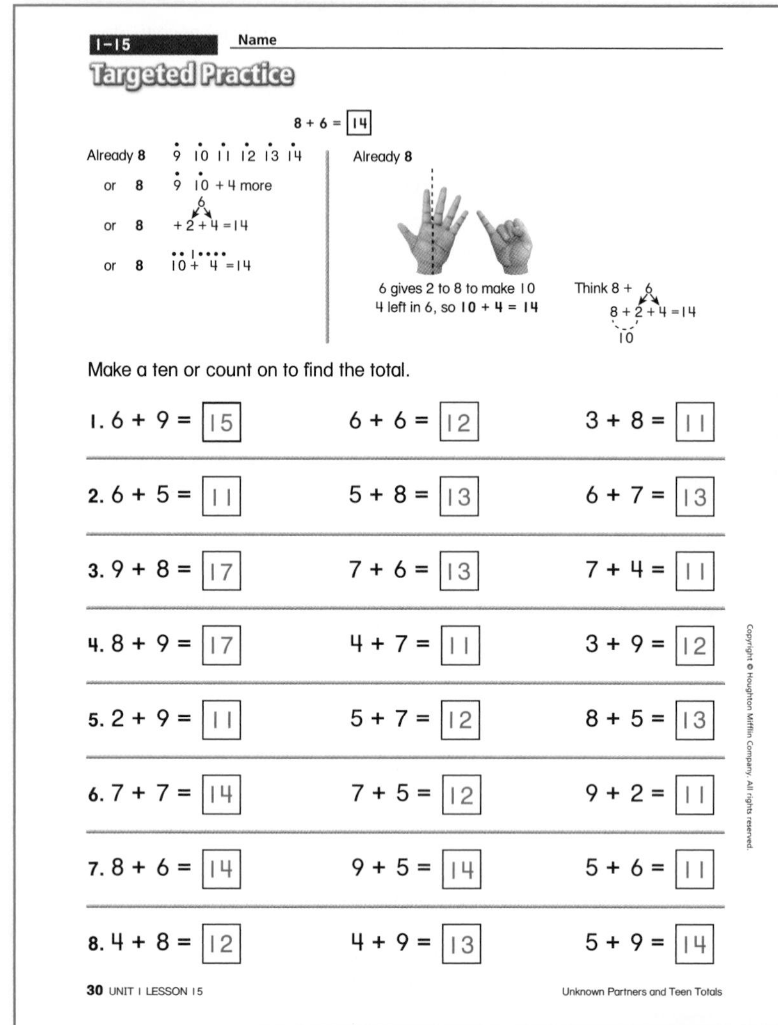

1–15 Targeted Practice Name

8 + 6 = [14]

Already 8: 9 10 11 12 13 14

or 8: 9 10 + 4 more

or 8: + 2 + 4 = 14

or 8: 10 + 4 = 14

Already 8

6 gives 2 to 8 to make 10. 4 left in 6, so 10 + 4 = 14

Think 8 + 6, 8 + 2 + 4 = 14, 10

Make a ten or count on to find the total.

1.	6 + 9 = [15]	6 + 6 = [12]	3 + 8 = [11]
2.	6 + 5 = [11]	5 + 8 = [13]	6 + 7 = [13]
3.	9 + 8 = [17]	7 + 6 = [13]	7 + 4 = [11]
4.	8 + 9 = [17]	4 + 7 = [11]	3 + 9 = [12]
5.	2 + 9 = [11]	5 + 7 = [12]	8 + 5 = [13]
6.	7 + 7 = [14]	7 + 5 = [12]	9 + 2 = [11]
7.	8 + 6 = [14]	9 + 5 = [14]	5 + 6 = [11]
8.	4 + 8 = [12]	4 + 9 = [13]	5 + 9 = [14]

30 UNIT 1 LESSON 15 Unknown Partners and Teen Totals

Homework and Remembering page 30

Home or School Activity

 Social Studies Connection

Transportation Stories Have children look for pictures of different modes of transportation. Discuss the different ways that people get around on land, water, and in the air. Display the pictures.

Ask children to create an addition or subtraction story problem about one of the pictures. Children can write their problems on cards with answers on the backs. Place the children's story problems in a box labeled "Transportation Story Problems" for classmates to read and solve.

There were 12 boats in the race. 8 boats finished. How many boats are left?

4 boats are left.

Relate Addition and Subtraction – Teen Totals

Lesson Objectives

- **Solve addition and subtraction problems.**
- **Apply the same solution methods to mystery addition and subtraction.**

Vocabulary

partners
Math Mountain
equation
Math Mountain Cards

The Day at a Glance

Today's Goals	Materials	
1 Teaching the Lesson **A1:** Practice addition and subtraction using Math Mountain Cards. **A2:** Solve mystery addition and subtraction problems and discuss how the solution procedures are the same.	**Lesson Activities** Student Activity Book pp. 51–56 (includes Math Mountain Cards, Family Letter) Homework and Remembering pp. 31–32 Scissors Chart paper	**Going Further** Activity Cards 1-16 Index cards Math Mountain Cards Chart paper Markers or crayons Math Journals
2 Going Further ▶ Differentiated Instruction		
3 Homework and Spiral Review		

Use Math Talk today!

Keeping Skills Sharp

Quick Practice 5 MINUTES	Daily Routines
Goal: Practice making change from a dime. **Materials:** Real or play money (1 dime, 9 pennies per child), Coin Strips (from Unit 1 Lesson 4 or TRB M1) (1 Dime Strip, 9 Penny Strips per child), Coin cover (index card, sticky note, or paper per pair), List of yard sale items on chart paper (see Unit 1 Lesson 11) **Buy with a Dime** Invite six children to act out the Yard Sale scenario from Unit 1 Lesson 11. To make this a "quick" practice, ask children to check the work of the Buyer, Seller, and the Bookkeepers, using their fingers rather than the Coin Strips.	**Money Routine** Using the 120 Poster, Using the Money Flip Chart, Using the Number Path, Using Secret Code Cards (See pp. xxiii–xxv.) ▶ Led by Student Leaders

1 Teaching the Lesson

Activity 1

Practice Addition and Subtraction

 20 MINUTES

Goal: Practice addition and subtraction using Math Mountain cards.

Materials: Math Mountain Cards (Student Activity Book pages 51 and 53), scissors

 **NCTM Standard:**
Number and Operations

The Learning Classroom

Quick Practice This activity will be used as a Quick Practice activity in future lessons.

Differentiated Instruction

English Learners Show pictures of mountains to English Learners to relate the shape of the Math Mountains to actual mountains.

English Language Learners

Write *Math Mountain Card* on the board above the example that was drawn.

- **Beginning** Say: **The *Math Mountain Card* shows partners for 5.** Point to 3 + 2, then 5. Say: **3 + 2 is 5.** Point to 5 – 3. Ask: **What is 5 – 3?** 2 Point to 5 – 2. Ask: **What is 5 – 2?** 3
- **Intermediate and Advanced** Ask: **What does the *Math Mountain Card* show?** partners for 5 Point to 3 + 2. Ask: **What does this show?** 3 + 2 = 5 Point to 5 – 3. Ask: **What does this show?** 5 – 3 = 2

▶ Introduce Math Mountain Cards WHOLE CLASS

Draw an example of a Math Mountain Card on the board.

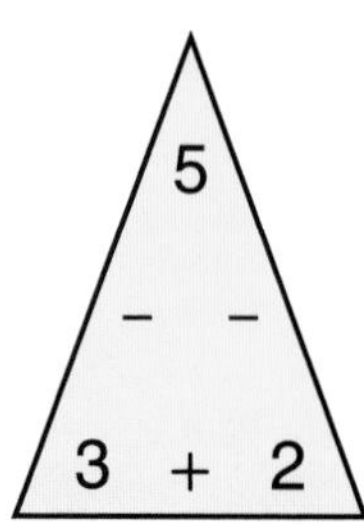

from Student Activity Book page 51

Ask children to describe what they notice about the cards. Then explain the different parts.

- What is the greatest number on the card? 5
- Where is it on the mountain? at the top
- What do you know about the numbers 3 and 2 at the bottom of the Math Mountain card? Possible answers: They are partners of 5. They can be added together to make 5.

Have children look at the Math Mountain Cards on Student Activity Book pages 51 and 53. If you have access to the *Math Expressions* materials kits, the Math Mountain Cards are included, so you will not have to prepare these materials. Discuss what children see on the cards. Possible responses: They are just like Math Mountains; the larger number is always at the top.

Direct children's attention to the sample card on the board again.

- Why is the plus sign on the bottom? It shows that the two numbers on the bottom can be added to make the total.
- Why are the minus signs on each side? They show that one partner can be subtracted from the total. The answer is the other partner.

▶ Addition and Subtraction with Math Mountain Cards WHOLE CLASS

Tell children they will use the Math Mountain Cards during the year to help them learn to add and subtract more quickly. The yellow cards have totals of 10 or less; the blue cards have teen totals.

Have children practice addition using the Math Mountain Cards. To add, tell children to cover the total (the greatest number) at the top of the card without looking. Then as quickly as they can, add the two lesser numbers together. Finally, children uncover the top number to see if their answer is correct.

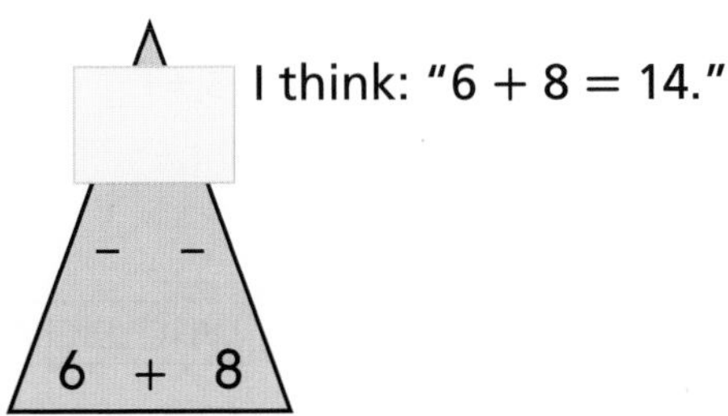

Allow children to practice addition for about five minutes. Have them place the cards they know really quickly in one pile, the cards they know but answered slowly in a second pile, and the cards they do not know in a third pile. Tell them to practice the ones they don't know or answered slowly.

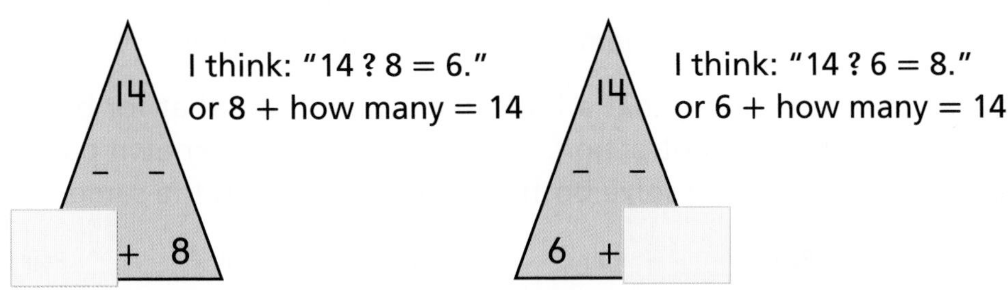

Let children practice subtraction using the Math Mountain Cards. To subtract, have them cover one of the lesser numbers (the partners). Then as quickly as they can, subtract the other partner from the total. Have children switch partners the next time they subtract.

Give children about 5 minutes to practice subtraction. Have them sort the cards the way they did for addition and practice the ones they don't know or answered slowly.

Class Management

Children can use a small piece of paper, a ruler, or the back of another Math Mountain Card to cover one of the numbers on the Math Mountain Card.

Ongoing Assessment

As children are practicing addition and subtraction with the Math Mountain Cards, ask questions such as:

- ▶ Are you adding or subtracting?
- ▶ What is the total? What partner do you know?
- ▶ How do you find the unknown partner?

Activity 2

Unknown Partners in Addition and Subtraction

30 MINUTES

Goal: Solve mystery addition and subtraction problems and discuss how the solution procedures are the same.

Materials: Chart paper

NCTM Standard:
Number and Operations

Math Talk in Action

Kim, how did you solve the first equation?

Kim: I made a ten and found out how many more up to the total.

9 0 | 0 0 0 0 0
10 | 11 12 13 14 15

How did you show that the solutions were the same?

Kim: I made a Math Mountain. A Math Mountain shows that you need to find a missing partner for both mystery addition and subtraction.

How did you solve the second equation?

Kim: I crossed out 9 and saw 1 more to make ten and 5 more so my unknown partner is 6.

▶ Unknown Partner Game SMALL GROUPS

Divide the class into 5 or 6 teams. Make sure that each team has a chance to go to the board.

Write a mystery addition and subtraction equation on the board. (See below.) Ask the first team to solve the first pair of equations at the board while the rest of the teams solve them at their seats. Ask 1 to 3 children to explain their solutions.

Continue playing the game until all teams have a chance to go to the board.

Pair A	Pair B	Pair C	Pair D	Pair E	Pair F
9 + ☐ = 15	8 + ☐ = 13	7 + ☐ = 13	5 + ☐ = 14	7 + ☐ = 15	6 + ☐ = 14
15 − 9 = ☐	13 − 8 = ☐	13 − 7 = ☐	14 − 5 = ☐	15 − 7 = ☐	14 − 6 = ☐

▶ Discuss Solution Processes WHOLE CLASS

Math Talk After all teams have had a turn at the board, ask children to explain how the solution processes for mystery addition and subtraction are the same. See the **Math Talk in Action** for a sample classroom discussion.

Continue the discussion until most children see that the solution procedures can be the same for the two problems even though different children may solve the problem situations in different ways.

Summarize by explaining that a Math Mountain shows that for both mystery addition and subtraction, you are finding an unknown partner. That is why the way you solve both kinds of problems is the same.

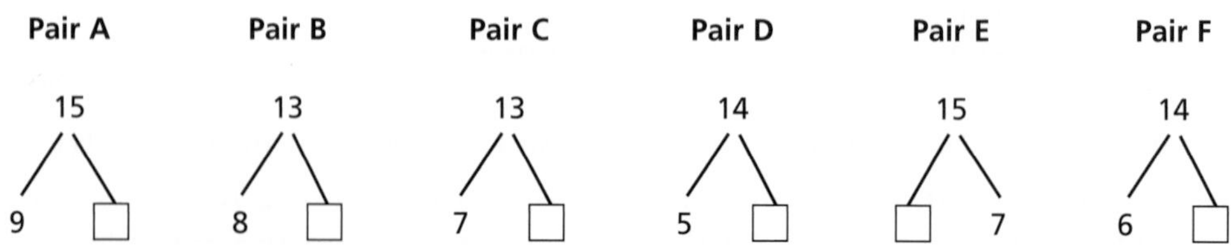

You may want to put some of the children's solutions on chart paper. Hang it in the room to show how subtraction and mystery addend solutions are alike.

Intervention Activity Card 1-16

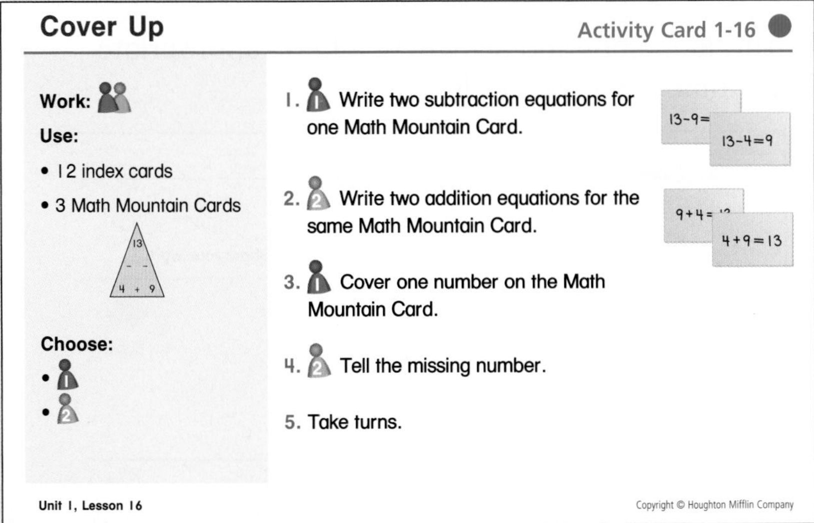

Cover Up Activity Card 1-16

Work: (pair)

Use:

- 12 index cards
- 3 Math Mountain Cards

Choose:

- (student 1)
- (student 2)

1. Write two subtraction equations for one Math Mountain Card.
2. Write two addition equations for the same Math Mountain Card.
3. Cover one number on the Math Mountain Card.
4. Tell the missing number.
5. Take turns.

13–9= 13–4=9

9+4= 4+9=13

Unit 1, Lesson 16 Copyright © Houghton Mifflin Company

Activity Note Each pair needs 12 index cards and 3 Math Mountain Cards with teen totals. (Student Activity Book, pp. 51–54)

Math Writing Prompt

Create Your Own Make your own Math Mountain Card for the number 17. Write how you knew what numbers to use and where to write them.

Software Support

Use *Soar to Success* for instruction of students needing targeted support for underlying skills.

On Level Activity Card 1-16

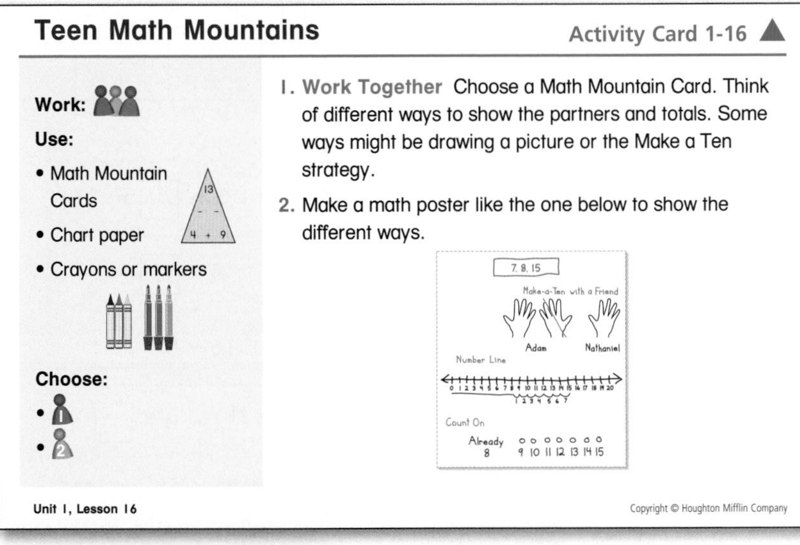

Teen Math Mountains Activity Card 1-16

Work: (group)

Use:

- Math Mountain Cards
- Chart paper
- Crayons or markers

Choose:

- (student 1)
- (student 2)

1. **Work Together** Choose a Math Mountain Card. Think of different ways to show the partners and totals. Some ways might be drawing a picture or the Make a Ten strategy.
2. Make a math poster like the one below to show the different ways.

Unit 1, Lesson 16 Copyright © Houghton Mifflin Company

Activity Note Each group needs 3–4 Math Mountain Cards with teen totals. (Student Activity Book, pp. 51–54). Groups make a math poster.

Math Writing Prompt

Explain Your Thinking Explain how a Math Mountain Card can work for mystery addition and subtraction. Use the words *partners* and *totals* when you write.

Software Support

Use *MegaMath* for review and reinforcement of the concepts and skills presented in this lesson.

Challenge Activity Card 1-16

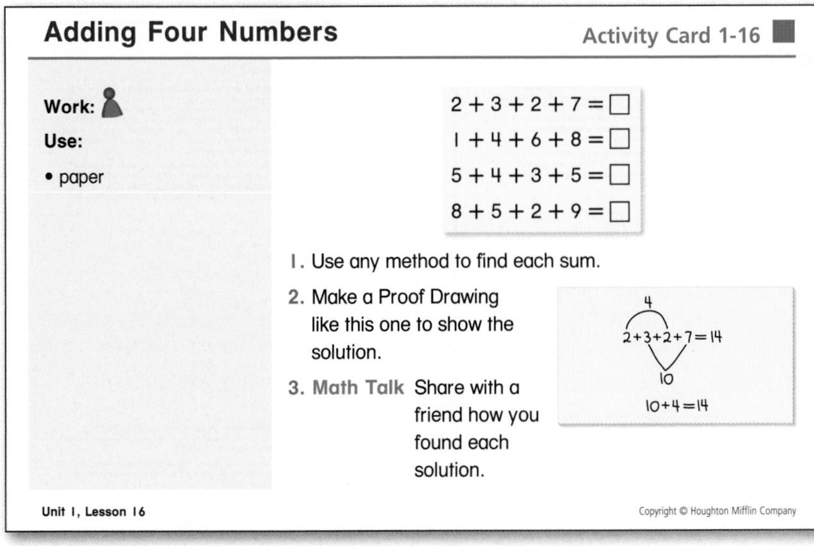

Adding Four Numbers Activity Card 1-16

Work: (individual)

Use:

- paper

2 + 3 + 2 + 7 = □
1 + 4 + 6 + 8 = □
5 + 4 + 3 + 5 = □
8 + 5 + 2 + 9 = □

1. Use any method to find each sum.
2. Make a Proof Drawing like this one to show the solution.
3. **Math Talk** Share with a friend how you found each solution.

2+3+2+7=14
10+4=14

Unit 1, Lesson 16 Copyright © Houghton Mifflin Company

Activity Note Have each child solve the four equations and make a Proof Drawing to show the solution. Have children share their work with the class.

Math Writing Prompt

Create Your Own Choose four numbers. Find the total of the four numbers. Write about the strategy you used.

Software Support

Use *Destination Math* to take students beyond the concepts and skills presented in this lesson.

3 Homework and Spiral Review

Goal: Additional Practice

This Homework page provides practice in mystery addition and subtraction.

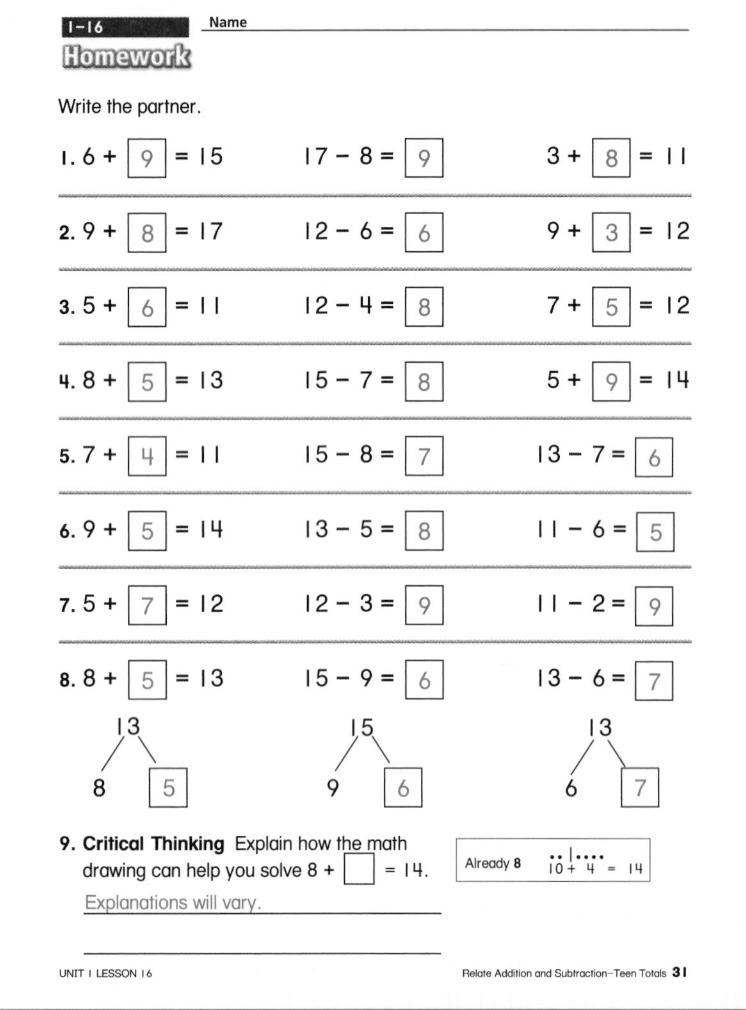

1-16 Name ____________

Homework

Write the partner.

1. 6 + 9 = 15	17 − 8 = 9	3 + 8 = 11
2. 9 + 8 = 17	12 − 6 = 6	9 + 3 = 12
3. 5 + 6 = 11	12 − 4 = 8	7 + 5 = 12
4. 8 + 5 = 13	15 − 7 = 8	5 + 9 = 14
5. 7 + 4 = 11	15 − 8 = 7	13 − 7 = 6
6. 9 + 5 = 14	13 − 5 = 8	11 − 6 = 5
7. 5 + 7 = 12	12 − 3 = 9	11 − 2 = 9
8. 8 + 5 = 13	15 − 9 = 6	13 − 6 = 7

13: 8, 5   15: 9, 6   13: 6, 7

9. **Critical Thinking** Explain how the math drawing can help you solve 8 + ☐ = 14.

Already 8 10 + 4 = 14

Explanations will vary.

UNIT 1 LESSON 16   Relate Addition and Subtraction–Teen Totals **31**

Homework and Remembering page 31

Goal: Spiral Review

This Remembering activity would be appropriate anytime after today's lesson.

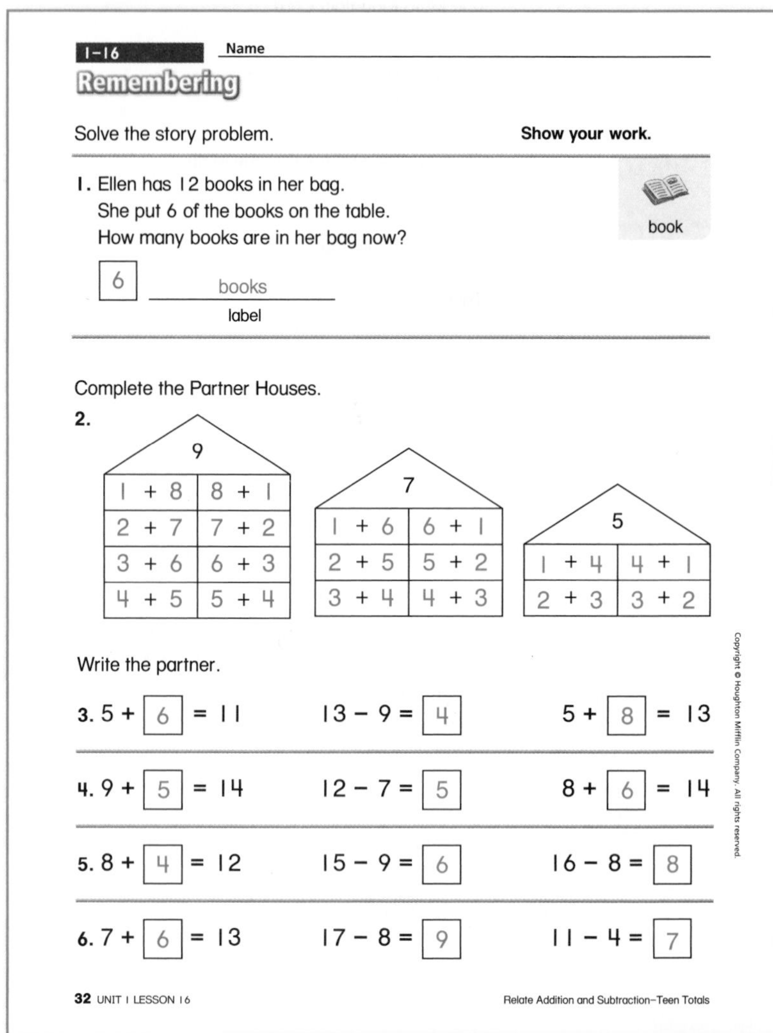

1-16 Name ____________

Remembering

Solve the story problem. **Show your work.**

1. Ellen has 12 books in her bag. She put 6 of the books on the table. How many books are in her bag now?

book

6 books
label

Complete the Partner Houses.

2.

9	
1 + 8	8 + 1
2 + 7	7 + 2
3 + 6	6 + 3
4 + 5	5 + 4

7	
1 + 6	6 + 1
2 + 5	5 + 2
3 + 4	4 + 3

5	
1 + 4	4 + 1
2 + 3	3 + 2

Write the partner.

3. 5 + 6 = 11	13 − 9 = 4	5 + 8 = 13
4. 9 + 5 = 14	12 − 7 = 5	8 + 6 = 14
5. 8 + 4 = 12	15 − 9 = 6	16 − 8 = 8
6. 7 + 6 = 13	17 − 8 = 9	11 − 4 = 7

32 UNIT 1 LESSON 16   Relate Addition and Subtraction–Teen Totals

Homework and Remembering page 32

Home and School Connection

Family Letter Have children take home the Family Letter on Student Activity Book page 55. This letter explains how the concept of addition and subtraction using Math Mountain Cards is developed in *Math Expressions.* It gives parents and guardians a better understanding of the learning that goes on in math class and creates a bridge between school and home. A Spanish translation of this letter is on the following page in the Student Activity Book.

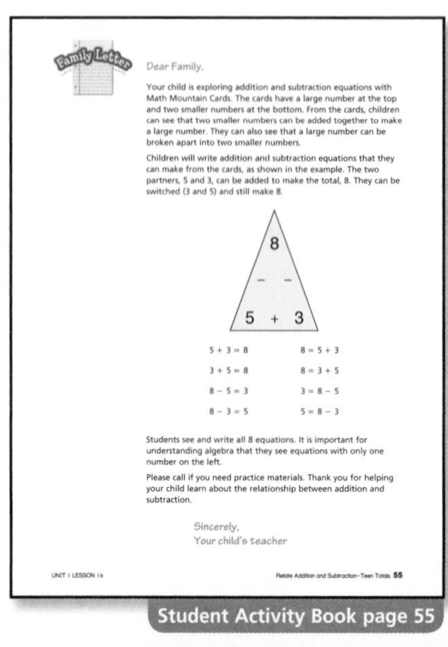

Family Letter

Dear Family,

Your child is exploring addition and subtraction equations with Math Mountain Cards. The cards have a large number at the top and two smaller numbers at the bottom. From the cards, children can see that two smaller numbers can be added together to make a large number. They can also see that a large number can be broken apart into two smaller numbers.

Children will write addition and subtraction equations that they can make from the cards, as shown in the example. The two partners, 5 and 3, can be added to make the total, 8. They can be switched (3 and 5) and still make 8.

8
5 + 3

5 + 3 = 8	8 = 5 + 3
3 + 5 = 8	8 = 3 + 5
8 − 5 = 3	3 = 8 − 5
8 − 3 = 5	5 = 8 − 3

Students see and write all 8 equations. It is important for understanding algebra that they see equations with only one number on the left.

Please call if you need practice materials. Thank you for helping your child learn about the relationship between addition and subtraction.

Sincerely,
Your child's teacher

UNIT 1 LESSON 16   Relate Addition and Subtraction–Teen Totals **55**

Student Activity Book page 55

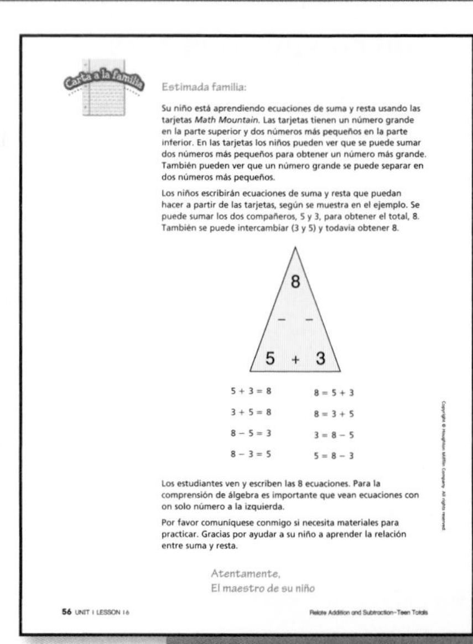

Carta a la familia

Estimada familia:

Su niño está aprendiendo ecuaciones de suma y resta usando las tarjetas *Math Mountain.* Las tarjetas tienen un número grande en la parte superior y dos números más pequeños en la parte inferior. En las tarjetas los niños pueden ver que se puede sumar dos números más pequeños para obtener un número más grande. También pueden ver que un número grande se puede separar en dos números más pequeños.

Los niños escribirán ecuaciones de suma y resta que puedan hacer a partir de las tarjetas, según se muestra en el ejemplo. Se puede sumar los dos compañeros, 5 y 3, para obtener el total, 8. También se puede intercambiar (3 y 5) y todavia obtener 8.

8
5 + 3

5 + 3 = 8	8 = 5 + 3
3 + 5 = 8	8 = 3 + 5
8 − 5 = 3	3 = 8 − 5
8 − 3 = 5	5 = 8 − 3

Los estudiantes ven y escriben las 8 ecuaciones. Para la comprensión de álgebra es importante que vean ecuaciones con on solo número a la izquierda.

Por favor comuníquese conmigo si necesita materiales para practicar. Gracias por ayudar a su niño a aprender la relación entre suma y resta.

Atentamente,
El maestro de su niño

56 UNIT 1 LESSON 16   Relate Addition and Subtraction–Teen Totals

Student Activity Book page 56

Use a Number Line to Add or Subtract

Vocabulary
number path
number line

Lesson Objective

- **Add or subtract by counting on, using a number line.**

The Day at a Glance

Today's Goals	Materials	
1 Teaching the Lesson **A1:** Add or subtract using a number path. **A2:** Count on to add or subtract using a number line.	**Lesson Activities** Student Activity Book pp. 57–58 Homework and Remembering pp. 33–34 Quick Quiz 4 (Assessment Guide)	**Going Further** Activity Cards 1-17 Large strips of paper Markers Index cards Two-color counters Spinners (TRB M27) Math Journals
2 Going Further ► Differentiated Instruction		
3 Homework and Targeted Practice		

Use **Math Talk** *today!*

Keeping Skills Sharp

Quick Practice — 5 MINUTES	Daily Routines
Goals: Identify the break-aparts for 3 and 8. Practice addition and subtraction. **Materials:** Yellow Math Mountain Cards (from Unit 1 Lesson 16 or TRB M43–M44) **Unknown Partner or Prairie Dog** Have children review the break-aparts for 3 and 8 by playing Unknown Partner or Prairie Dog. (See Unit 1 Lessons 8 and 9.) **Yellow Math Mountain Cards** Have children practice addition and subtraction with Math Mountain Cards using cards which have totals to 10. (See Unit 1 Lesson 16.)	**Money Routine** Using the 120 Poster, Using the Money Flip Chart, Using the Number Path, Using Secret Code Cards (See pp. xxiii–xxv.) ► Led by Student Leaders

1 Teaching the Lesson

Activity 1

Add or Subtract on a Number Path

 30 MINUTES

Goal: Add or subtract using a number path.

 **NCTM Standards:**
Number and Operations
Representation
Communication

Teaching Note

What to Expect from Students The number path is a bridge between counting using objects or fingers and counting using a number line. Young children of the same age can be at different developmental stages. Do not expect all children will be able to use the number path or the number line at this time. Some children may prefer to continue to use objects or fingers. This is acceptable. Allow children the time they need to move from one developmental stage to the next. The number line may be particularly difficult for some children at this time of the year. They may find it difficult to see the numbers as lengths rather than just as the numbered points. Circling these lengths during the lesson will be helpful to children to see the numbers involved.

▶ Introduce Number Paths WHOLE CLASS

Count On to Add Draw a number path by outlining ten squares, and writing the numbers 1–10 below each square. Then write $5 + 2 = \square$ beside the number path.

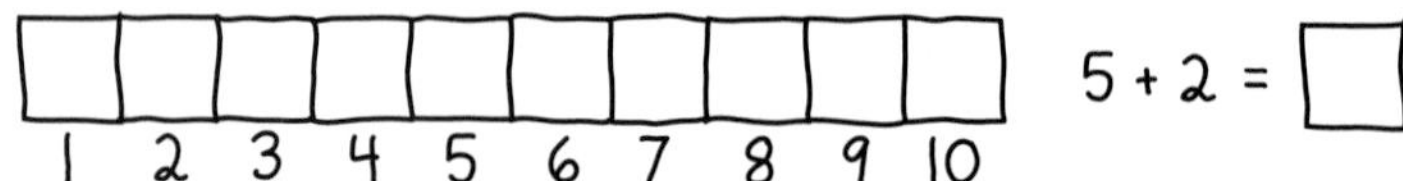

Tell children that they can use a number path to count on to solve the problem. Elicit responses from children as you demonstrate how to use the Number Path to count on.

- What number should we begin with to count on? 5 Why? Begin with the greater partner.

Point to the fifth square. (You may want to count the first five squares aloud, pointing to each square as you count.)

- What should we do next? Count on 2 more.

Count the next two squares aloud with children, saying, "one, two," as you move your finger along the number path, ending at 7.

- Where did we end on the number path? 7
- What is the total for 5 + 2? 7

Ask children to draw a number path to 10, and then, use their number paths to solve these equations.

$3 + 5 = \square$ $7 + 2 = \square$ $1 + 8 = \square$

Count On to Subtract Explain to children that they can also use a number path to subtract. Write on the board: $9 - 6 = \square$

- To count on to subtract, what number do we begin with? 6
- What number do we count on to? 9

Demonstrate the counting on process beginning at 6 and counting to 9 by saying, "1, 2, 3," as you move your finger along the number path.

- How many squares did we count? 3
- What is 9 − 6? 3

Ask children to use their number paths to solve these equations.

$10 - 7 = \square$ $8 - 5 = \square$ $9 - 2 = \square$

Activity 2

Add or Subtract on a Number Line

▶ Introduce Number Lines WHOLE CLASS Math Talk 

Count On to Add Draw the following number line on the board.

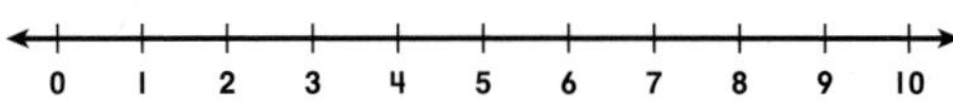

- What do you notice about the number line? Possible responses: The numbers go from 0 to 10. The numbers increase by 1 as they move to the right.

Tell children that they can use a number line to add and subtract. Write 6 + 3 = ☐ on the board.

- What number should we begin with to count on? 6 Why? Begin with the greater partner.
- What should we do next? Count on 3 more.

Start at the number 0 and slide your finger along the number line to the 6, saying, "siiiiix." Then draw three hops from 6 to 9, saying, "one, two, three." Have children keep track of the number of hops by using their fingers. Point out that your finger is now on the number 9, so 9 is the answer to 6 + 3.

6 + 3 = ☐

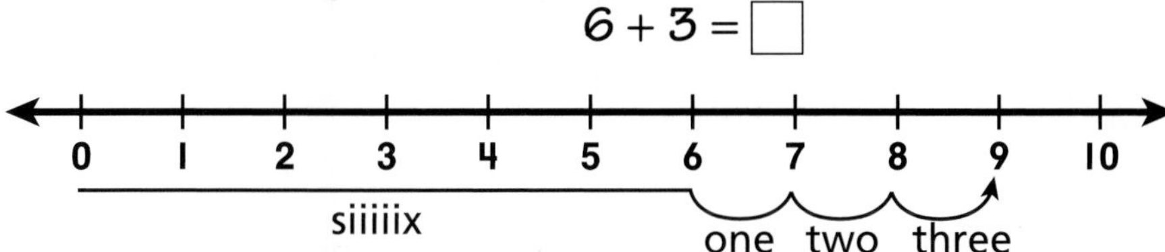

Count On to Subtract Draw another number line from 1 to 10. Write 9 – 6 = ☐ on the board.

Have children follow along as you demonstrate how to solve the problem.

- What number should we begin with to count on to subtract? 6

Slide your finger to the number 6, saying, "siiiiix." Tell children that you will count on until you reach the number 9. Draw 3 hops from 6 to 9, saying, "one, two, three."

9 – 6 = ☐

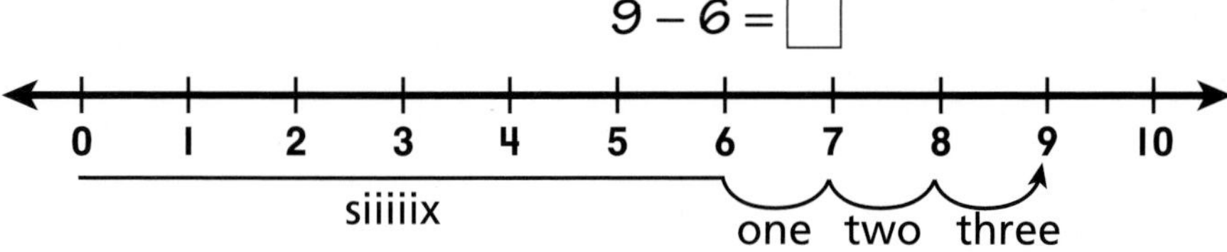

- How many hops did we draw? 3
- Since we made three hops, the answer to 9 – 6 is 3.

Activity continued ▶

 **25 MINUTES**

Goal: Count on to add or subtract using a number line.

 **NCTM Standards:**
Number and Operations
Communication

Teaching Note

Language and Vocabulary Saying the first addend in a stretched-out way will help children who are transitioning from counting all to counting on.

The Learning Classroom

Building Concepts The concept of a number line will be better understood as children work with rulers and bar graphs in future lessons.

English Language Learners

Use the number line from the example. Write 6 + 3 and 9 – 6 and *count on* and *count back* on the board.

- **Beginning** Say: **Add means *count on*. Start at 6. Count on 3.** Have children repeat. Say: **Subtract means *count back*. Start at 9. Count back 6.** Have children repeat.
- **Intermediate and Advanced** Ask: **What does add mean?** (count on) **Where do we start?** (6) **How many do we count on?** (3) **What does subtract mean?** (count back) **Where do we start?** (9) **How many do we count back?** (6)

Teaching the Lesson (continued)

Alternate Approach

Combine Number Paths and Number Lines Some children may have a difficult time making the transition to the number line. To help those children, use a number path and a number line together.

To solve $6 + 3 = \square$, have children draw six circles to represent the addend, 6. Then draw three more circles to represent the addend, 3. Have children count the circles to find the sum.

$$6 + 3 = \square$$

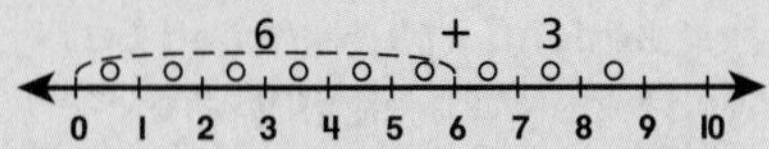

To solve $9 - 6 = \square$, have children draw nine circles to represent the total. Then have them draw a line through six circles. The number of circles remaining is the answer.

$$9 - 6 = \square$$

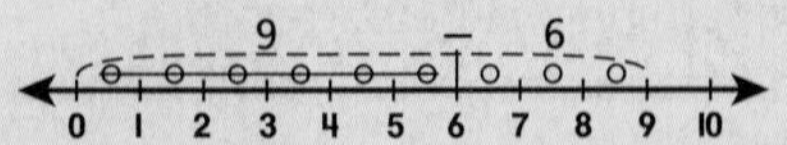

Ongoing Assessment

As children solve problems on their MathBoards, ask them to explain how to count on, using the number line to add or subtract.

Quick Quiz

See Assessment Guide for Unit 1 Quick Quiz 4.

Practice Addition and Subtraction Write the following addition and subtraction equations on the board for volunteers to complete while the class completes them at their seats.

$4 + 3 = \square$	$4 + 5 = \square$	$2 + 6 = \square$
$9 - 5 = \square$	$7 - 6 = \square$	$8 - 6 = \square$

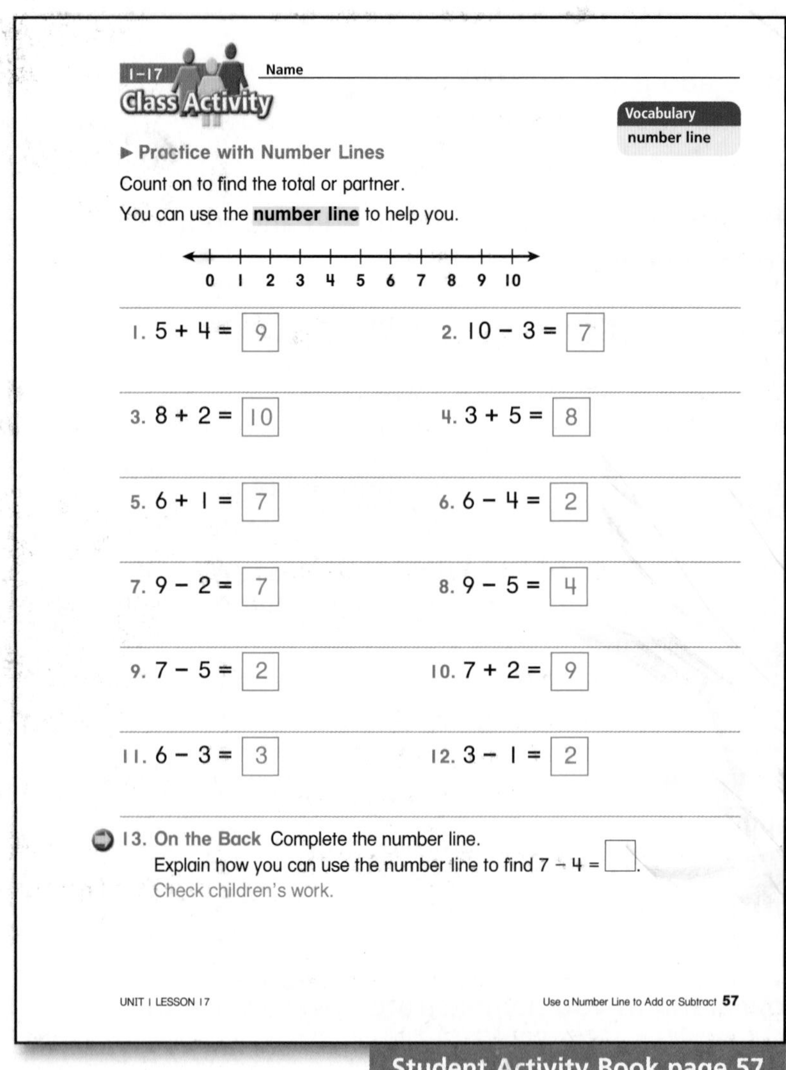

1-17 Class Activity Name

Vocabulary
number line

► Practice with Number Lines

Count on to find the total or partner.

You can use the **number line** to help you.

0 1 2 3 4 5 6 7 8 9 10

1. 5 + 4 = 9
2. 10 − 3 = 7
3. 8 + 2 = 10
4. 3 + 5 = 8
5. 6 + 1 = 7
6. 6 − 4 = 2
7. 9 − 2 = 7
8. 9 − 5 = 4
9. 7 − 5 = 2
10. 7 + 2 = 9
11. 6 − 3 = 3
12. 3 − 1 = 2
13. On the Back Complete the number line. Explain how you can use the number line to find 7 − 4 = ☐.
Check children's work.

UNIT 1 LESSON 17 Use a Number Line to Add or Subtract 57

Student Activity Book page 57

► Practice with Number Lines WHOLE CLASS

Have children complete Student Activity Book page 57. Invite volunteers to share their response for exercise 13.

2 Going Further

Differentiated Instruction

Intervention — Activity Card 1-17

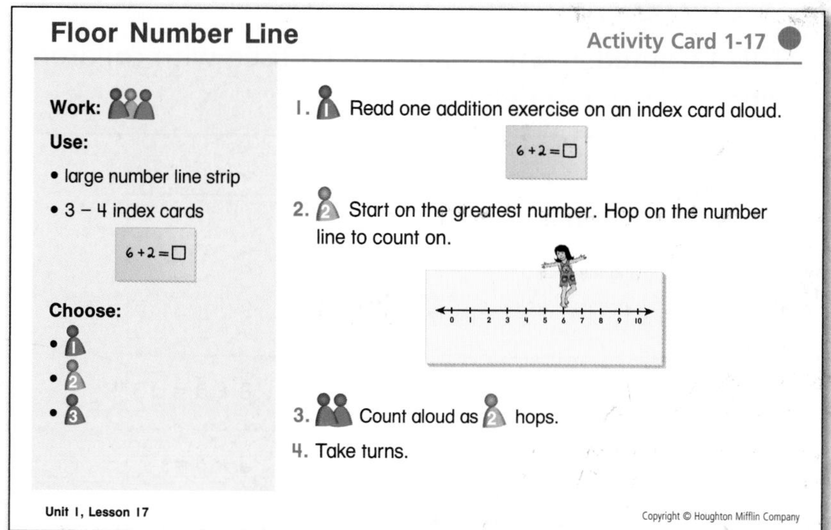

Floor Number Line — Activity Card 1-17

Work:

Use:

- large number line strip
- 3 – 4 index cards

6 + 2 = □

Choose:

- 1
- 2
- 3

1. Read one addition exercise on an index card aloud.

6 + 2 = □

2. Start on the greatest number. Hop on the number line to count on.
3. Count aloud as 2 hops.
4. Take turns.

Unit 1, Lesson 17

Copyright © Houghton Mifflin Company

Activity Note Each group needs a floor number line from 1–18 and 4 index cards with addition facts. Children start at the higher number and hop on.

Math Writing Prompt

You Decide Explain how to use a Number Path or a number line to count on to solve 5 + 2 = □.

Software Support

Use *Soar to Success* for instruction of students needing targeted support for underlying skills.

On Level — Activity Card 1-17

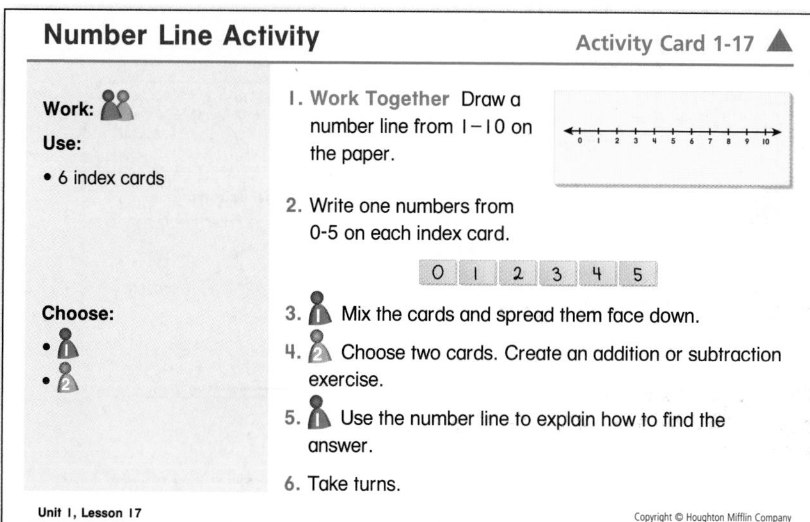

Number Line Activity — Activity Card 1-17

Work:

Use:

- 6 index cards

Choose:

- 1
- 2

1. **Work Together** Draw a number line from 1–10 on the paper.
2. Write one numbers from 0-5 on each index card.

0 1 2 3 4 5

3. Mix the cards and spread them face down.
4. Choose two cards. Create an addition or subtraction exercise.
5. Use the number line to explain how to find the answer.
6. Take turns.

Unit 1, Lesson 17

Copyright © Houghton Mifflin Company

Activity Note Each pair needs six index cards and paper to make a number line. Children use the number line to solve equations.

Math Writing Prompt

Explain Your Thinking Explain how you would use a number line to solve 8 – 5 = □.

Software Support

Use *MegaMath* for review and reinforcement of the concepts and skills presented in this lesson.

Challenge — Activity Card 1-17

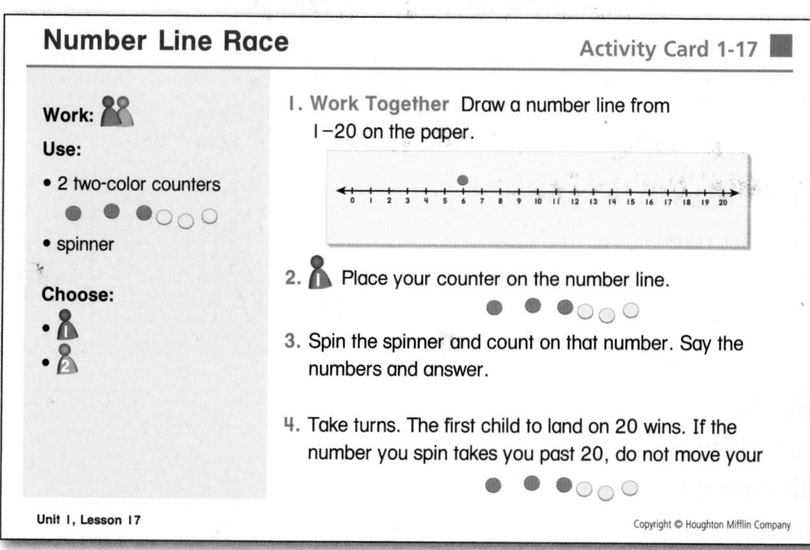

Number Line Race — Activity Card 1-17

Work:

Use:

- 2 two-color counters
- spinner

Choose:

- 1
- 2

1. **Work Together** Draw a number line from 1–20 on the paper.
2. Place your counter on the number line.
3. Spin the spinner and count on that number. Say the numbers and answer.
4. Take turns. The first child to land on 20 wins. If the number you spin takes you past 20, do not move your

Unit 1, Lesson 17

Copyright © Houghton Mifflin Company

Activity Note Each pair needs 2 two-color counters and spinner labeled 1–4 (TRB M27). Pairs use a number line to add. To win, a child must land on 20.

Math Writing Prompt

A Different Way to Subtract Describe two ways to find the answer to 8 – 5 = □ using a number line.

Software Support

Use *Destination Math* to take students beyond the concepts and skills presented in this lesson.

Homework and Targeted Practice

1–17 Homework **Goal:** Additional Practice

This Homework page provides practice adding and subtracting on a number line.

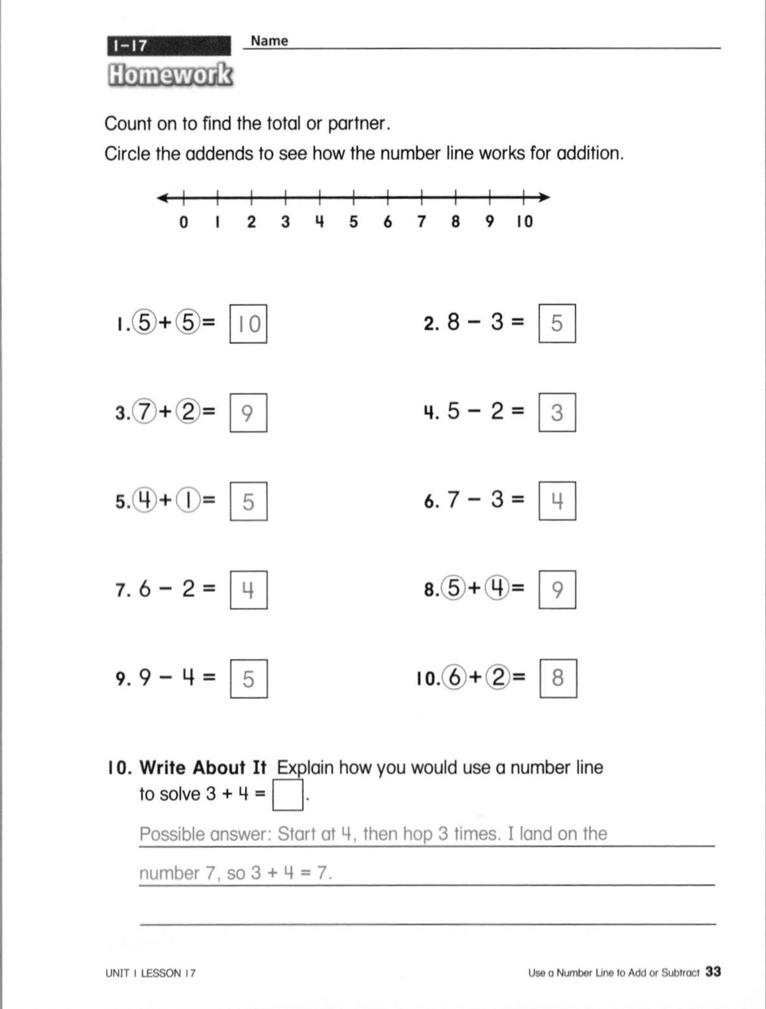

1–17 Homework Name

Count on to find the total or partner.

Circle the addends to see how the number line works for addition.

0 1 2 3 4 5 6 7 8 9 10

1. (5) + (5) = 10
2. 8 − 3 = 5
3. (7) + (2) = 9
4. 5 − 2 = 3
5. (4) + (1) = 5
6. 7 − 3 = 4
7. 6 − 2 = 4
8. (5) + (4) = 9
9. 9 − 4 = 5
10. (6) + (2) = 8

10. **Write About It** Explain how you would use a number line to solve 3 + 4 = ☐.

Possible answer: Start at 4, then hop 3 times. I land on the number 7, so 3 + 4 = 7.

UNIT 1 LESSON 17 — Use a Number Line to Add or Subtract 33

Homework and Remembering page 33

1–17 Targeted Practice **Goal:** Count on to add.

This Targeted Practice page can be used with children who need extra practice.

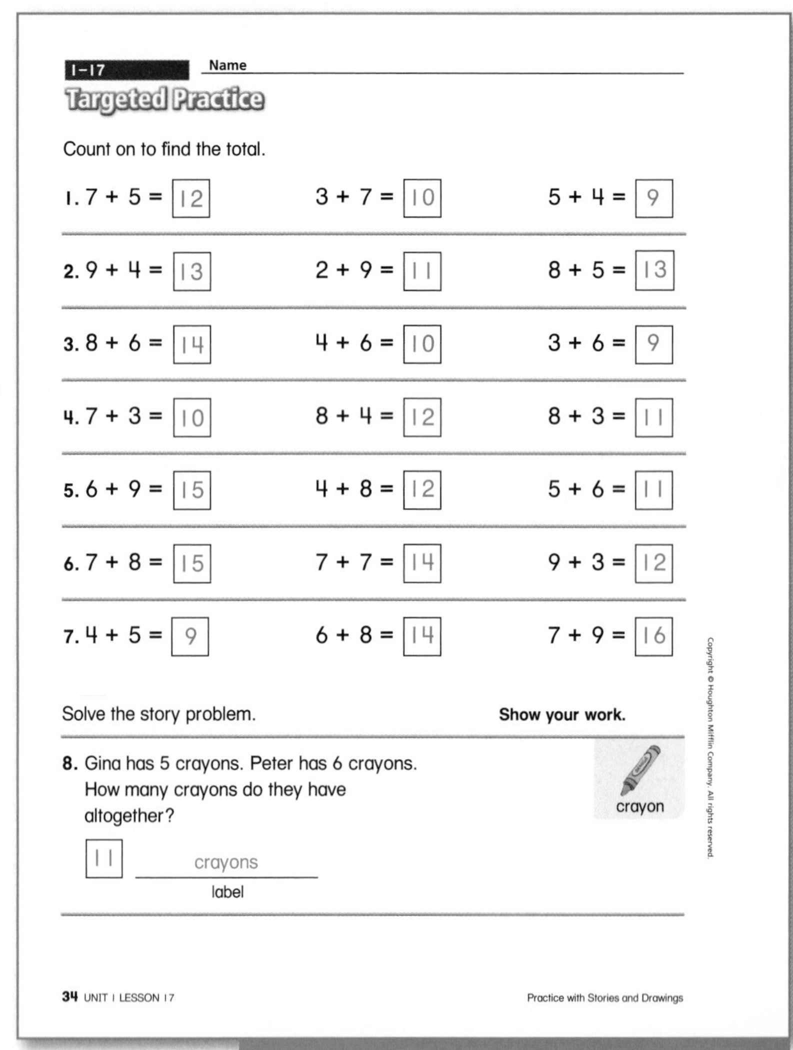

1–17 Targeted Practice Name

Count on to find the total.

1. 7 + 5 = 12   3 + 7 = 10   5 + 4 = 9
2. 9 + 4 = 13   2 + 9 = 11   8 + 5 = 13
3. 8 + 6 = 14   4 + 6 = 10   3 + 6 = 9
4. 7 + 3 = 10   8 + 4 = 12   8 + 3 = 11
5. 6 + 9 = 15   4 + 8 = 12   5 + 6 = 11
6. 7 + 8 = 15   7 + 7 = 14   9 + 3 = 12
7. 4 + 5 = 9   6 + 8 = 14   7 + 9 = 16

Solve the story problem. **Show your work.**

8. Gina has 5 crayons. Peter has 6 crayons. How many crayons do they have altogether?

11 crayons (label)

crayon

34 UNIT 1 LESSON 17 — Practice with Stories and Drawings

Homework and Remembering page 34

Home or School Activity

Science Connection

Thermometers and Number Lines Thermometers are used to measure how hot or cold something is. People in the United States often use thermometers that measure in degrees Fahrenheit. In many other countries, people often use thermometers that measure in degrees Celsius.

Use a real thermometer or a picture of one and tell whether it measures in degrees Celsius or degrees Fahrenheit. Then compare a thermometer to a number line. How are they the same? different? Help children record the temperature at different times of the day.

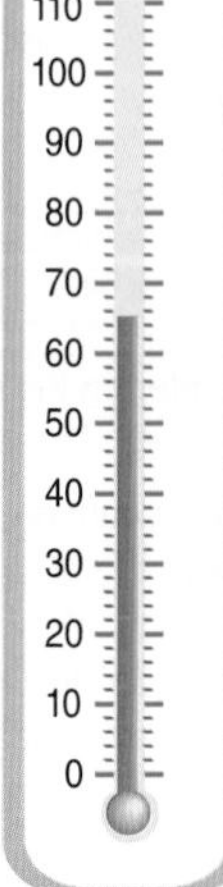

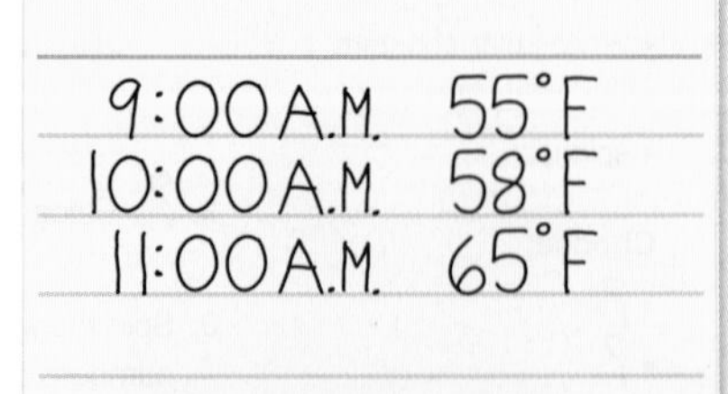

Equations and Equation Chains

Lesson Objectives

- **Understand what the equals sign means and recognize the symbol for "is not equal to."**
- **Write equation chains.**
- **Write equations in vertical form.**

Vocabulary
equation
equals sign
is not equal to
equation chain
vertical form
Math Mountain

The Day at a Glance

Today's Goals	Materials	
1 Teaching the Lesson A1: Define equation and introduce the "is not equal to" sign. A2: Write equation chains. A3: Introduce vertical form.	**Lesson Activities** Homework and Remembering pp. 35–36 MathBoard materials	**Going Further** Activity Cards 1-18 Student Activity Book pp. 59–60 Index cards Game Cards (TRB M23) Symbol Cards (TRB M45) MathBoard materials Strips of construction or drawing paper Tape Crayons or markers Math Journals
2 Going Further ▶ Extra Practice ▶ Differentiated Instruction		
3 Homework and Spiral Review		

Use **Math Talk** *today!*

Keeping Skills Sharp

Quick Practice 5 MINUTES		Daily Routines
Goal: Review the break-aparts for the numbers 4 and 7. **Unknown Partner or Prairie Dog** Have children review the break-aparts for the numbers 4 and 7 by playing Unknown Partner or Prairie Dog. Have the Student Leader write the number on the board as a reminder for the children as they play. (See Unit 1 Lessons 8 and 9.)	**Repeated Quick Practice** Use this Quick Practice from a previous lesson. ▶ **Yellow Math Mountain Cards** (See Unit 1 Lesson 16 Activity 1.)	**Money Routine** Using the 120 Poster, Using the Money Flip Chart, Using the Number Path, Using Secret Code Cards (See pp. xxiii–xxv.) ▶ Led by Student Leaders

1 Teaching the Lesson

Activity 1

Define Equation

 20 MINUTES

Goal: Define equation and introduce the "is not equal to" sign.

Materials: MathBoard materials

 **NCTM Standards:**
Algebra
Communication

 **Class Management**

Leave the list of equations that you write for Activity 1 on the board. The children will use them again to write equation chains in Activity 2.

English Language Learners

Point to and read all the examples of equations written on the board. Write the word *equation* above the examples.

- **Beginning** Say: **These are all *equations. Equations* all have an equal sign. And both sides of an *equation* must be equal.**
- **Intermediate** Ask: **What are these examples of?** (equations) **What do all equations have?** (an equal sign) **Do both sides of an equation have to be equal?** (yes)
- **Advanced** Have children tell what all equations have and what must be true of both sides.

▶ Discuss Prior Knowledge of Equations WHOLE CLASS

Ask for Ideas Elicit children's ideas about what an equation is. The discussion should include the fact that an equation is a true number sentence and has an equals sign.

Children's definitions will vary, but listen for the idea that the value of one expression is equal to, or the same as, the value of another expression. Children should understand that an equation will "say" that the values on both sides of the equals sign are the same.

Be sure children understand that the equals sign separates one side of the equation from the other side.

▶ Define an Equation WHOLE CLASS

Math Talk 

Write the equations below on the board. Then ask the children to decide whether each of these really is an equation. Remind them to check to see that the values on both sides of the equals sign are the same. They are all equations.

$5 = 5$	$1 + 4 = 4 + 1$
$5 = 2 + 3$	$6 - 1 = 4 + 1$
$3 + 2 = 5$	$1 + 4 = 5$
$5 - 3 = 2$	$2 + 3 + 1 = 8 - 2$
$5 - 3 = 1 + 1$	$20 - 10 = 2 + 2 + 2 + 2 + 2$

Ask children to describe equations. Children should understand that equations can have one or more numbers on a side, one or more plus and minus signs, and so on. If children have difficulty describing an equation, ask them a series of simple questions.

- Can an equation have more than one number on a side? yes
- Can an equation have a plus sign and a minus sign? yes
- What must every equation have? an equals sign
- Can an equation have just one number on each side? yes

▶ Write and Discuss Equations WHOLE CLASS

Have a few children write several different equations on the board while the rest of the class writes some equations on their MathBoards. Then discuss the equations that the children wrote on the board. Have everyone check that they are all equations.

▶ Introduce the *Is Not Equal To* Sign WHOLE CLASS

Explain to children that if two values are not equal, they can use a special sign to show this. Write the following on the board:

$$6 = 7$$

Explain that because 6 does not equal 7, and 7 does not equal 6, they cannot use an equals sign. Introduce the special sign they can use by drawing a line through the equals sign to make an "is not equal to" sign.

$$6 \neq 7$$

Ask children to suggest ways to remember the "is not equal to" sign. Responses will vary but children should realize that the equals sign is crossed out.

Ongoing Assessment

Have children tell whether they should use an equals sign or an "is not equal to" sign to complete each of these number sentences.

5 + 3 ◯ 10 − 2

5 + 1 ◯ 8 − 1

2 + 4 ◯ 3 + 4

10 + 8 ◯ 9 + 9

Activity 2

Equation Chains

▶ Write Equation Chains WHOLE CLASS

Have children look at the list of equations from Activity 1. Point out that many of the equations have both sides with a value of 5. Invite children to write the expressions that equal 5 as a chain. Ask all children to try to make more interesting entries on the chain using several numbers and/or bigger numbers as in the last two examples they saw earlier.

Ask a volunteer to start the chain on the board and then encourage the child to think of more expressions that equal 5. Have a few children do this on the board while the rest of the class writes the chain on their MathBoards.

$$5 = 2 + 3 = 3 + 2 = 1 + 4 = 4 + 1 = 6 - 1$$

If time permits, have children make an equation chain for the number 7.

$$7 = 3 + 4 = 8 - 1 = 5 + 2 = 10 - 3 = 6 + 1 = 12 - 5 = 8 - 1 = 7 + 0$$

This activity will be used as a Quick Practice activity in future lessons.

For students that may benefit from a visual representation of an equation chain, have them construct the paper chain with equations on each link shown on p. 129.

Emphasize having children being creative and making the most interesting pieces of their equation chain as they can. They may use forms like 5 − 2 − 2 or 1 + 3 − 2. These are fine as long as they are solved by moving left to right in order.

15 MINUTES

Goal: Write equation chains.

Materials: MathBoard materials

NCTM Standard: Algebra

Differentiated Instruction

Extra Help If children find it difficult to see all the expressions equal to 5, you may wish to draw a ring around each expression.

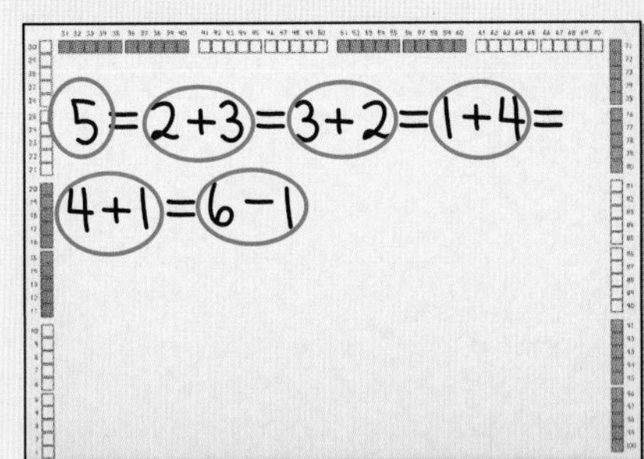

Advanced Learners To extend this activity, have children who are ready, create chains for larger numbers. Children can check each other's equation chains.

Activity 3

Vertical Form

 20 MINUTES

Goal: Introduce vertical form.

 **NCTM Standards:**
Algebra
Communication

▶ Discuss the Terms *Horizontal* and *Vertical*

WHOLE CLASS

Explain that when a line is *horizontal* it goes across like the horizon, the imaginary line where the sky and ground meet. Draw a horizontal line on the board.

Explain that a vertical line goes straight up and down. Draw a vertical line on the board.

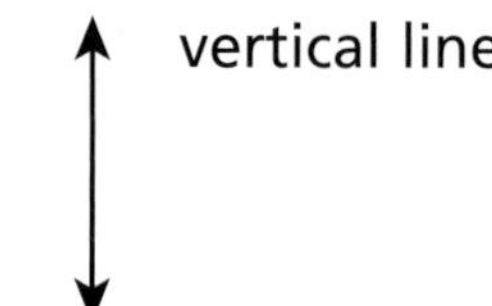

Draw the letter T on the board.

- Which part of the letter T is vertical? the bottom part of the T
- Which part of the letter T is horizontal? the top part of the T

▶ Vertical Form

WHOLE CLASS

Equations and Vertical Form Write the following on the board.

$9 + 4 = 13$

$$\begin{array}{r} 9 \\ +4 \\ \hline 13 \end{array}$$

- Which is written in horizontal form? the first
- Which is written in vertical form? the second

Help children see how the two forms are alike. Have two children go to the board. Ask the children to point to the partners, and then to the total. Help them see the relationship between the two forms.

Challenge children to relate the two forms to Math Mountains. Start by having the children discuss what they see for addition.

9 + 4 = □
P P T

9 P
+4 P
□ T

T
□
9 4
P P

Next, have children discuss what they see for mystery addition.

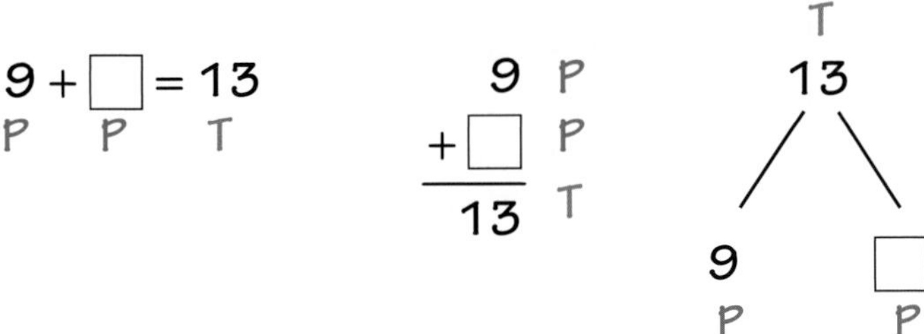

Finally, have children discuss what they see for subtraction.

13 − 9 = □
T P P

13 T
− □ P
9 P

T
13
9 □
P P

Show Three Ways Read the following questions aloud, one at a time. Ask a group of children to go to the board to write the equation, the vertical form, and the Math Mountain for each question. Children at their seats can do the same thing on paper or on their MathBoards.

- 8 and 5 make how many? 8 + 5 = □
- 7 and what number make 15? 7 + □ = 15
- 18 take away 8 equals what number? 18 − 8 = □
- 6 and 7 equal what number? 6 + 7 = □
- 5 and what number make 14? 5 + □ = 14
- 17 minus 8 makes what number? 17 − 8 = □

Allow time in between each, so that children can ask questions and discuss their work. Continue with as many examples as time allows.

The Learning Classroom

Helping Community You may wish to pair children experiencing difficulty with those who understand a concept. It is important to take some class time to discuss what *good helping* is all about. Children may come up with a list that can be posted in the classroom. It is important that they understand that good helping does not mean telling answers, but it means taking other children through steps so that they come up with the answer themselves.

2 Going Further

Extra Practice

Goal: Solve equations and make equation chains.

NCTM Standards:
Number and Operations
Algebra

▶ Use Equations to Make an Equation Chain INDIVIDUALS

Direct children's attention to Student Activity Book page 59. Read the directions aloud. Tell children to use any method they want to solve each equation. Children then use the answers to determine which blocks to color.

When children solve each equation and color, they will form the letter E.

Children then use the expressions that equal 8 to form the equation chain.

▶ Critical Thinking

- What other expressions could you add to your equation chain for the number 8? Sample answer: 15 − 7; 8 + 0
- Can you write an expression for the equation chain that has both a plus sign and a minus sign? Sample answer: 10 − 2 = 6 + 2

1-18  Name

Extra Practice

▶ Use Equations to Make an Equation Chain

1. Solve the equations.
If the answer is 8, color the block RED.

8 + 9 = 17	12 − 6 = 6	7 + 5 = 12
5 + 3 = 8	17 − 9 = 8	13 − 5 = 8
1 + 7 = 8	5 + 4 = 9	15 − 8 = 7
11 − 3 = 8	4 + 4 = 8	3 + 8 = 11
16 − 8 = 8	6 + 6 = 12	5 + 7 = 12
14 − 6 = 8	13 − 5 = 8	10 − 2 = 8

2. Use the blocks you colored to make an equation chain.

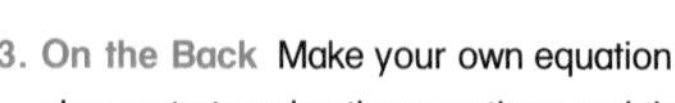

Sample answer: 5 + 3 = 17 − 9 = 13 − 5 = 1 + 7 = 11 − 3 = 4 + 4 = 16 − 8 = 14 − 6 = 13 − 5 = 10 − 2

3. On the Back Make your own equation puzzle. Ask a classmate to solve the equations and then write an equation chain. Answers will vary.

UNIT 1 LESSON 18 Equations and Equation Chains 59

Student Activity Book page 59

Class Management

As children complete the page, help those having difficulty. You can also invest time in helping children learn to help their classmates. Consider having Student Helpers work at the board with a small group of children. It is easier to see the work and it motivates children to try harder.

Intervention Activity Card 1-18

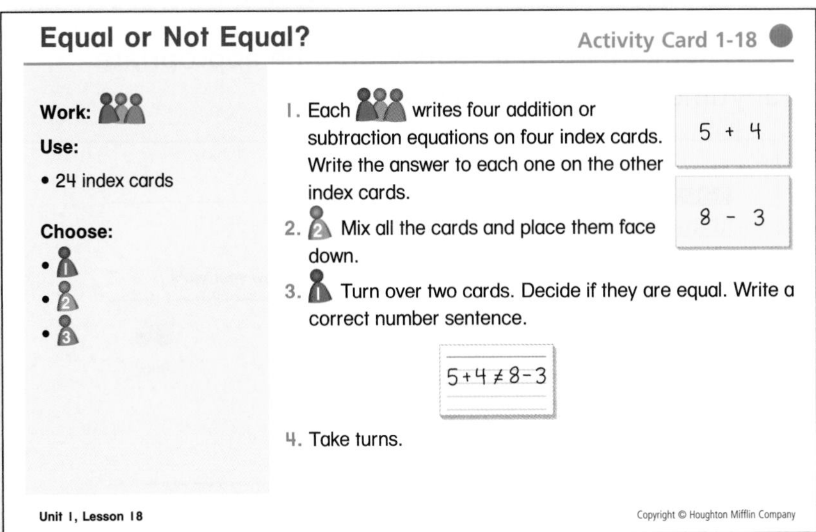
Equal or Not Equal? Activity Card 1-18

Work:
Use:
- 24 index cards

Choose:
- 1
- 2
- 3

1. Each writes four addition or subtraction equations on four index cards. Write the answer to each one on the other index cards.
2. Mix all the cards and place them face down.
3. Turn over two cards. Decide if they are equal. Write a correct number sentence.
4. Take turns.

5 + 4
8 − 3
5+4≠8−3

Unit 1, Lesson 18
Copyright © Houghton Mifflin Company

Activity Note You need 8 index cards per child. Children write equations on four index cards and the answers on the other four cards.

Math Writing Prompt

Summarize What is an equation? Explain it in your own words. Then give an example of a number sentence that is an equation and one that is not an equation.

Software Support

Use *Soar to Success* for instruction of students needing targeted support for underlying skills.

On Level Activity Card 1-18

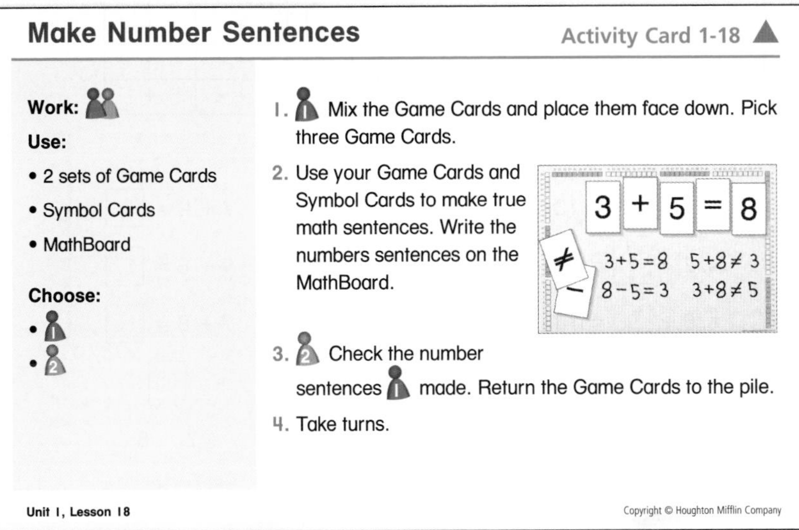
Make Number Sentences Activity Card 1-18

Work:
Use:
- 2 sets of Game Cards
- Symbol Cards
- MathBoard

Choose:
- 1
- 2

1. Mix the Game Cards and place them face down. Pick three Game Cards.
2. Use your Game Cards and Symbol Cards to make true math sentences. Write the numbers sentences on the MathBoard.
3. Check the number sentences made. Return the Game Cards to the pile.
4. Take turns.

3 + 5 = 8
3+5=8 5+8≠3
8−5=3 3+8≠5

Unit 1, Lesson 18
Copyright © Houghton Mifflin Company

Activity Note Each pair needs two sets of Game Cards (TRB M23), Symbol Cards (TRB M45), and MathBoard materials. Remind pairs to check each other's work.

Math Writing Prompt

Sides on an Equation Use words or a drawing to explain what the sides of an equation are.

Software Support

Use *MegaMath* for review and reinforcement of the concepts and skills presented in this lesson.

Challenge Activity Card 1-18

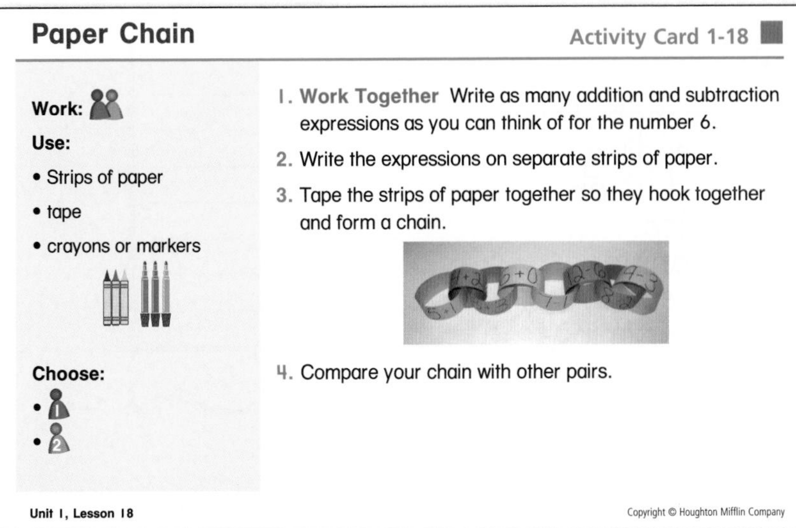
Paper Chain Activity Card 1-18

Work:
Use:
- Strips of paper
- tape
- crayons or markers

Choose:
- 1
- 2

1. **Work Together** Write as many addition and subtraction expressions as you can think of for the number 6.
2. Write the expressions on separate strips of paper.
3. Tape the strips of paper together so they hook together and form a chain.
4. Compare your chain with other pairs.

Unit 1, Lesson 18
Copyright © Houghton Mifflin Company

Activity Note See card for materials needed.

Math Writing Prompt

Greater Than or Less Than Ed says that you can always replace > (is greater than) or < (is less than) with a ≠ and still have a true sentence. Do you agree? Explain.

DESTINATION Math®

Software Support

Use *Destination Math* to take students beyond the concepts and skills presented in this lesson.

3 Homework and Spiral Review

Goal: Additional Practice

This Homework page provides practice solving vertical addition and subtraction problems.

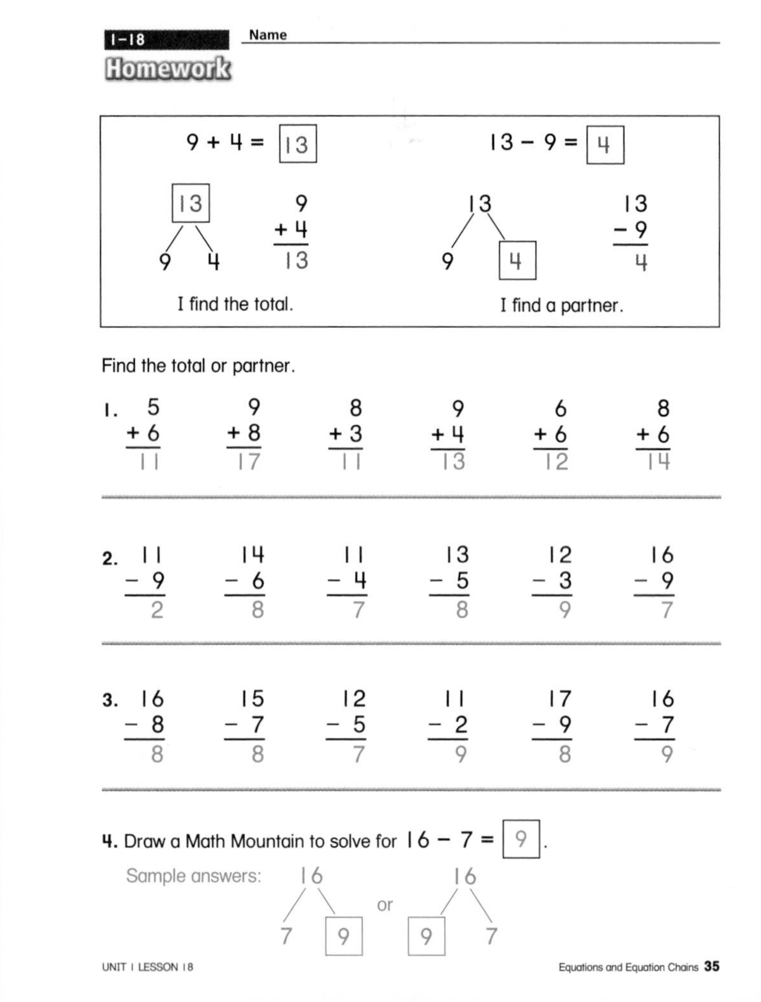

1-18 Homework Name ______

9 + 4 = 13 13 − 9 = 4

I find the total.	I find a partner.
13 → 9, 4; 9 + 4 = 13	13 → 9, 4; 13 − 9 = 4

Find the total or partner.

1. 5 + 6 = 11; 9 + 8 = 17; 8 + 3 = 11; 9 + 4 = 13; 6 + 6 = 12; 8 + 6 = 14

2. 11 − 9 = 2; 14 − 6 = 8; 11 − 4 = 7; 13 − 5 = 8; 12 − 3 = 9; 16 − 9 = 7

3. 16 − 8 = 8; 15 − 7 = 8; 12 − 5 = 7; 11 − 2 = 9; 17 − 9 = 8; 16 − 7 = 9

4. Draw a Math Mountain to solve for 16 − 7 = 9.

Sample answers: 16 → 7, 9 or 16 → 9, 7

UNIT 1 LESSON 18 Equations and Equation Chains 35

Homework and Remembering page 35

Goal: Spiral Review

This Remembering activity would be appropriate anytime after today's lesson.

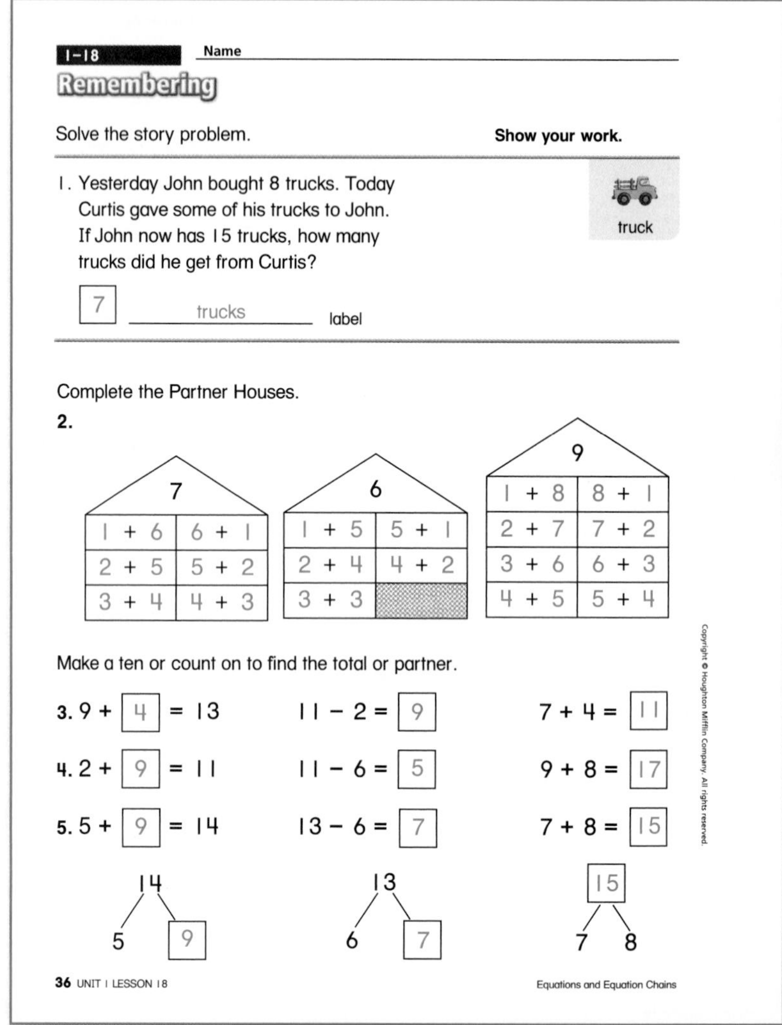

1-18 Remembering Name ______

Solve the story problem. **Show your work.**

1. Yesterday John bought 8 trucks. Today Curtis gave some of his trucks to John. If John now has 15 trucks, how many trucks did he get from Curtis? truck

7 trucks label

Complete the Partner Houses.

2.

7	
1 + 6	6 + 1
2 + 5	5 + 2
3 + 4	4 + 3

6	
1 + 5	5 + 1
2 + 4	4 + 2
3 + 3	

9	
1 + 8	8 + 1
2 + 7	7 + 2
3 + 6	6 + 3
4 + 5	5 + 4

Make a ten or count on to find the total or partner.

3. 9 + 4 = 13 11 − 2 = 9 7 + 4 = 11

4. 2 + 9 = 11 11 − 6 = 5 9 + 8 = 17

5. 5 + 9 = 14 13 − 6 = 7 7 + 8 = 15

14 → 5, 9 13 → 6, 7 15 → 7, 8

Copyright © Houghton Mifflin Company. All rights reserved.

36 UNIT 1 LESSON 18 Equations and Equation Chains

Homework and Remembering page 36

Home or School Activity

Language Arts Connection

Vertical Poems Have children write their names vertically. Then, for each letter, ask them to think of a word that begins with that letter and write the word. The words could describe themselves, something they like to do, something they like to eat, or someone important to them.

French fries
Reading
Addition
Nice
Caring
Ice skating
Swimming

Equations from Math Mountains

Vocabulary

equation
Math Mountain
partners
switch the partners
total
Parachute Drop

Lesson Objective

- Write equations involving a total and two partners.

The Day at a Glance

Today's Goals	Materials	
1 Teaching the Lesson **A1:** Practice addition, totals ≤ 10. **A2:** Write addition and subtraction equations for Math Mountains.	**Lesson Activities** Student Activity Book pp. 61–64 (includes Parachute Drop) Homework and Remembering pp. 37–38 Colored paper	**Going Further** Activity Cards 1-19 Connecting cubes MathBoard materials Math Journals
2 Going Further ▸ Differentiated Instruction		
3 Homework and Targeted Practice		

Use Math Talk today!

Keeping Skills Sharp

Quick Practice — 5 MINUTES	Daily Routines
Goals: Review the break-aparts for 9 and 5. Write equation chains for the number 14. **Unknown Partner or Prairie Dog** Have children review the break-aparts for the numbers 9 and 5 by playing Unknown Partner or Prairie Dog. Have the student leader write the number on the board as a reminder for the children as they play. (See Unit 1 Lessons 8 and 9.) **Equation Chains** Have three children write equation chains for the number 14 on the board. (See Unit 1 Lesson 18 Activity 2.)	**Money Routine** Using the 120 Poster, Using the Money Flip Chart, Using the Number Path, Using Secret Code Cards (See pp. xxiii–xxv.) ▸ Led by Student Leaders

1 Teaching the Lesson

Activity 1

Parachute Drop, Totals ≤ 10

10 MINUTES

Goal: Practice addition, totals $\leq$ 10.

Materials: Parachute Drop (Student Activity Book page 61), colored paper (1 thin strip) per child

NCTM Standard:
Number and Operations

Differentiated Instruction

Advanced Learners Have children who finish practicing the addition exercises early and are saying correct totals quickly practice the mystery addition exercises in the middle column.

The Learning Classroom

Quick Practice This activity will be used as a Quick Practice activity in future lessons. Have children save Student Activity Book page 61.
If some children misplace theirs and you need to make additional copies, use TRB M46.

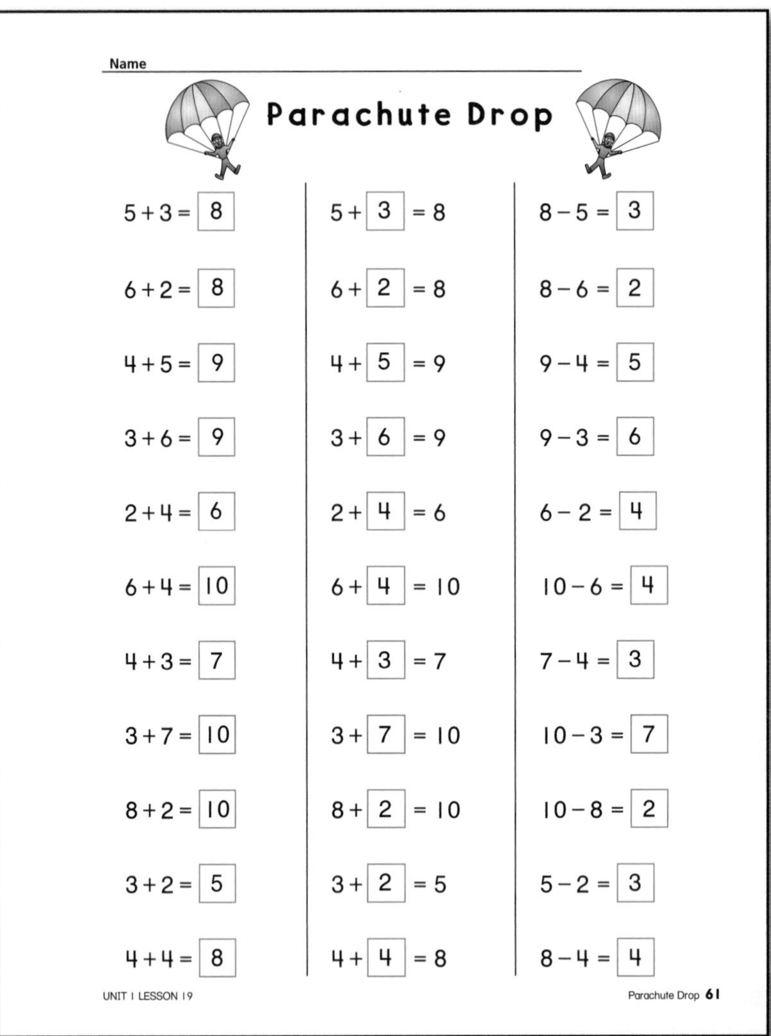

Name

Parachute Drop

5 + 3 = 8	5 + 3 = 8	8 − 5 = 3
6 + 2 = 8	6 + 2 = 8	8 − 6 = 2
4 + 5 = 9	4 + 5 = 9	9 − 4 = 5
3 + 6 = 9	3 + 6 = 9	9 − 3 = 6
2 + 4 = 6	2 + 4 = 6	6 − 2 = 4
6 + 4 = 10	6 + 4 = 10	10 − 6 = 4
4 + 3 = 7	4 + 3 = 7	7 − 4 = 3
3 + 7 = 10	3 + 7 = 10	10 − 3 = 7
8 + 2 = 10	8 + 2 = 10	10 − 8 = 2
3 + 2 = 5	3 + 2 = 5	5 − 2 = 3
4 + 4 = 8	4 + 4 = 8	8 − 4 = 4

UNIT 1 LESSON 19 Parachute Drop 61

Student Activity Book page 61

▶ Introduce Parachute Drop WHOLE CLASS

Have children turn to Student Activity Book page 61. Explain how to do the Parachute Drop activity.

For this activity, have children use a sheet of paper folded in half along the short length to cover the answers in a column. Today they will cover the answers in the first column. Tell them to start their plane ride up, saying the answers silently as they slowly move their paper up the column. If children miss one, they should silently say the whole problem two times. Children continue until they reach the top. Then they parachute back to the ground by saying all the answers again while sliding their strips of paper down the column. Tell children they should continue going up in the airplane and parachute down until the signal to stop is given.

Explain to children that they are practicing for an addition Secret Code Card Race in the next lesson.

Activity 2

Write Equations for Math Mountains

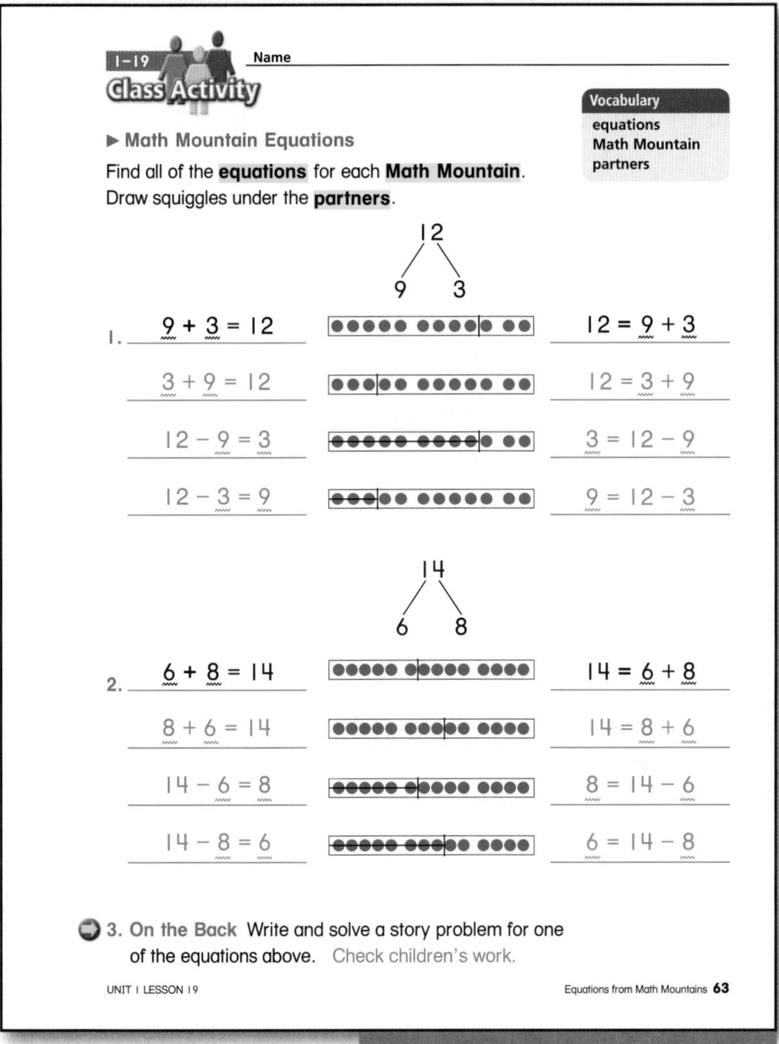

1-19 Class Activity Name ____________

Vocabulary
equations
Math Mountain
partners

▶ Math Mountain Equations

Find all of the **equations** for each **Math Mountain**. Draw squiggles under the **partners**.

12 / 9 3

1. 9 + 3 = 12 | 12 = 9 + 3
3 + 9 = 12 | 12 = 3 + 9
12 − 9 = 3 | 3 = 12 − 9
12 − 3 = 9 | 9 = 12 − 3

14 / 6 8

2. 6 + 8 = 14 | 14 = 6 + 8
8 + 6 = 14 | 14 = 8 + 6
14 − 6 = 8 | 8 = 14 − 6
14 − 8 = 6 | 6 = 14 − 8

3. On the Back Write and solve a story problem for one of the equations above. Check children's work.

UNIT 1 LESSON 19 Equations from Math Mountains 63

Student Activity Book page 63

▶ Math Mountain Equations WHOLE CLASS

Remind children that they have already solved addition and subtraction problems and found unknown partners by counting on. Explain that they will now talk about how the partners are related in addition and subtraction equations.

Have children look at Student Activity Book page 63. Sketch the first Math Mountain on the board. Ask children what numbers are in the Math Mountain. 12, 9, and 3

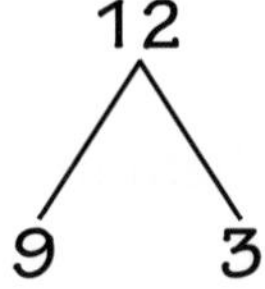

Now have children look at the first drawing of the box with circles inside.

Activity continued ▶

 35 MINUTES

Goal: Write addition and subtraction equations for Math Mountains.

Materials: Student Activity Book page 63

 **NCTM Standard:**
Number and Operations

The Learning Classroom

Building Concepts This activity can be used to model the process of correcting mistakes. As you write the equations, you might record an equation incorrectly. By noticing the error, asking what is wrong, then fixing the error, you can show children that mistakes can be corrected.

English Language Learners

Draw the first example on the board. Have children identify the partners and an equation.

- **Beginning** Point to 9 and 3. Say: **9 and 3 are the partners.** Point to the equation. Say: **9 + 3 = 12 is an equation of this Math Mountain.** Have children repeat.
- **Intermediate** Ask: **What are the partners?** (9 and 3) **What is an equation of this Math Mountain?** (9 + 3 = 12)
- **Advanced** Have children tell how to use the partners to write an equation for the Math Mountain.

1 Teaching the Lesson (continued)

Teaching Note

Language and Vocabulary *Switch the partners* is the term used in this program to teach children about the Commutative Property of Addition. Use this term because it is meaningful to children. As the drawings on Student Activity Book page 63 show, 3 + 9 has the same value as 9 + 3. Asking children to switch the partners can help them find different equations for the same Math Mountain.

Differentiated Instruction

Extra Help Some children may have trouble identifying and differentiating between the equations that can be written for a Math Mountain. You may wish to set up the problems as shown below. Explain that *P* stands for partner and *T* stands for total.

P + P = T	T = P + P
P + P = T	T = P + P
T − P = P	P = T − P
T − P = P	P = T − P

You may also wish to have children experiencing difficulty work with a helping partner.

Ongoing Assessment

As children write the equations for exercise 2 on Student Activity Book page 63, circulate around the room to monitor their progress. Note whether they are able to generate all eight equations, and have used squiggles to identify the partners. Ask them to explain how their equations relate to the pictures.

- What do you think the drawing shows? Sample response: The bar breaks apart the 12 into the partners 9 and 3.

Now find and write all of the equations for the Math Mountain on the board.

- Begin with the four equations that have one number on the right side of the equation. One has already been done. 9 + 3 = 12.
- The next row shows 3 + 9 = 12, which is the partner switch of 9 + 3 = 12. The last two rows show 12 − 9 = 3 and 12 − 3 = 9.

Ask children to write the 4 equations that have one number on the left. Write the equations on the board as children suggest them.

▶ Introduce "Squiggles" WHOLE CLASS

We found that putting squiggles under each partner in the equations helps children understand the equation forms and relate addition to subtraction. After children have put squiggles under all of the partners 9 and 3 (and you have them on your equations on the board), have children discuss how the equations are alike and different.

Write 12 − 9 = 3 and 12 − 3 = 9 on the board. Explain how squiggles can help children see the partner switches in subtraction.

- Which numbers should you write squiggles under? 3 and 9
- What do you think the squiggles mean? The smaller number is a partner of the larger number.

Put squiggles under the two numbers that are partners of 12. Tell children they can also write a "T" under the total to help them.

$$\underset{T}{12} - \underset{\sim}{9} = \underset{\sim}{3} \quad \text{and} \quad \underset{T}{12} - \underset{\sim}{3} = \underset{\sim}{9}$$

Explain that 12 and 9 cannot be switched because 9 − 12 ≠ 3, but they can switch the partners, and the equation will be true. 12 − 9 = 3 and 12 − 3 = 9 are both true.

Math Talk Have children complete Student Activity Book page 63, then write and solve story problems for each equation they wrote in exercise 2. For example:

- Will found 8 pennies. He put them in his pocket with the 6 he already had. How many pennies did he have in all? 14 pennies
- Julia wanted to give party favors to the 8 children that came to her birthday party. She had 14 bags of stickers. How many bags of stickers will she have left if everyone gets a bag? 6 bags

2 Going Further

Differentiated Instruction

Intervention — Activity Card 1-19

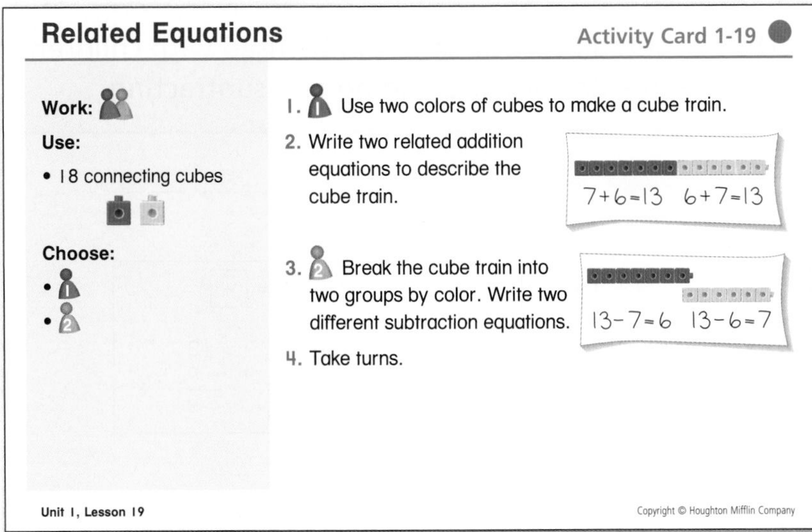

Related Equations — Activity Card 1-19

Work: (pair)

Use:
- 18 connecting cubes

Choose:
- (child 1)
- (child 2)

1. Use two colors of cubes to make a cube train.
2. Write two related addition equations to describe the cube train.

7+6=13 6+7=13

3. Break the cube train into two groups by color. Write two different subtraction equations.

13−7=6 13−6=7

4. Take turns.

Unit 1, Lesson 19

Copyright © Houghton Mifflin Company

Activity Note Each pair needs 18 connecting cubes in two different colors (nine each color.) Make sure children correctly record their trains.

Math Writing Prompt

Explain Your Thinking Look at this equation: 13 = 5 + 8. Write how you know which numbers are the partners and which number is the total.

Software Support

Use *Soar to Success* for instruction of students needing targeted support for underlying skills.

On Level — Activity Card 1-19

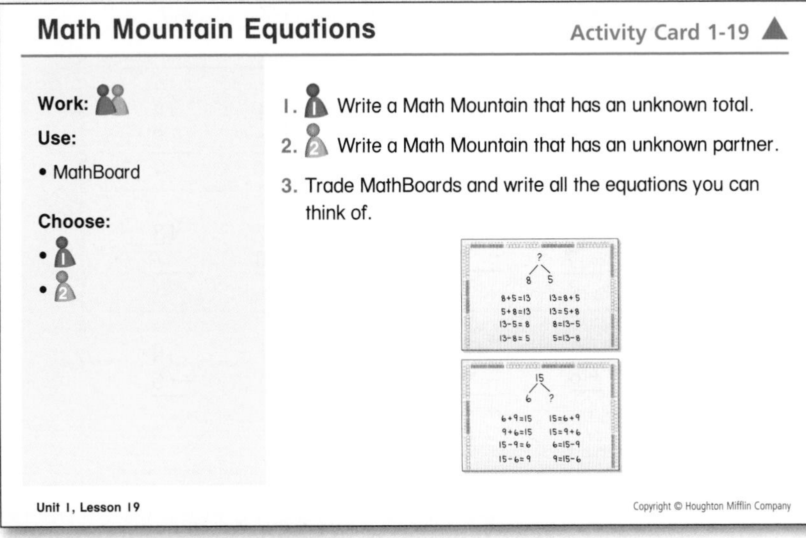

Math Mountain Equations — Activity Card 1-19

Work: (pair)

Use:
- MathBoard

Choose:
- (child 1)
- (child 2)

1. Write a Math Mountain that has an unknown total.
2. Write a Math Mountain that has an unknown partner.
3. Trade MathBoards and write all the equations you can think of.

Unit 1, Lesson 19

Copyright © Houghton Mifflin Company

Activity Note Check that one child has an unknown total and the other has an unknown partner. Suggest that children check each other's work.

Math Writing Prompt

Related Equations Tell how these equations are alike.

$5 + \square = 12$

$12 - 5 = \square$

Software Support

Use *MegaMath* for review and reinforcement of the concepts and skills presented in this lesson.

Challenge — Activity Card 1-19

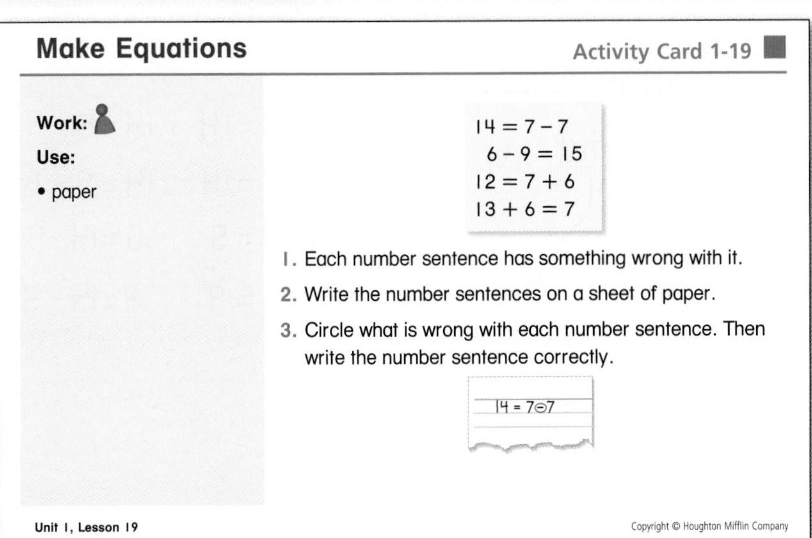

Make Equations — Activity Card 1-19

Work: (individual)

Use:
- paper

14 = 7 − 7
6 − 9 = 15
12 = 7 + 6
13 + 6 = 7

1. Each number sentence has something wrong with it.
2. Write the number sentences on a sheet of paper.
3. Circle what is wrong with each number sentence. Then write the number sentence correctly.

14 = 7 ⊖ 7

Unit 1, Lesson 19

Copyright © Houghton Mifflin Company

Activity Note Children identify what is wrong with each number sentence and write it correctly. It could be a sign or a number.

Math Writing Prompt

Justify Explain what it means to *switch the partners.* Tell why switching the partners does not change the total. Use pictures or words to explain.

Software Support

Use *Destination Math* to take students beyond the concepts and skills presented in this lesson.

Homework and Targeted Practice

1–19 Homework **Goal:** Additional Practice

Include children's completed Homework page as part of their portfolios.

1–19 Targeted Practice **Goal:** Add and subtract.

This Targeted Practice page can be used with children who need extra practice adding and subtracting.

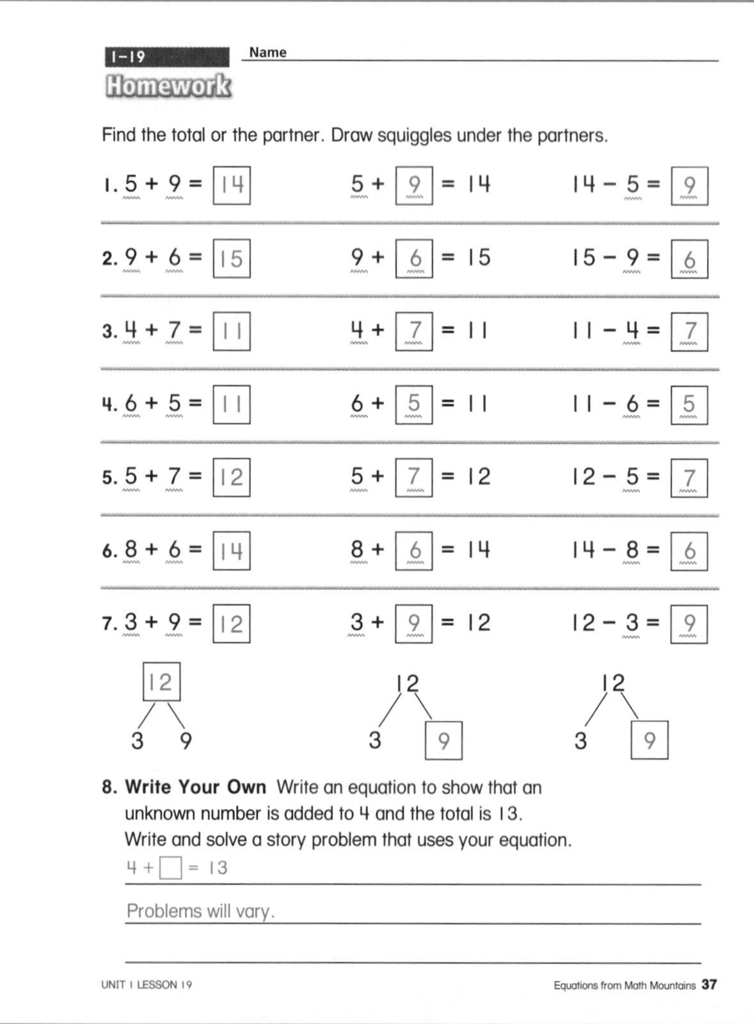

1–19 Name

Homework

Find the total or the partner. Draw squiggles under the partners.

1. 5 + 9 = [14] 5 + [9] = 14 14 − 5 = [9]
2. 9 + 6 = [15] 9 + [6] = 15 15 − 9 = [6]
3. 4 + 7 = [11] 4 + [7] = 11 11 − 4 = [7]
4. 6 + 5 = [11] 6 + [5] = 11 11 − 6 = [5]
5. 5 + 7 = [12] 5 + [7] = 12 12 − 5 = [7]
6. 8 + 6 = [14] 8 + [6] = 14 14 − 8 = [6]
7. 3 + 9 = [12] 3 + [9] = 12 12 − 3 = [9]

[12] / 3 9   12 / 3 [9]   12 / 3 [9]

8. **Write Your Own** Write an equation to show that an unknown number is added to 4 and the total is 13. Write and solve a story problem that uses your equation.

4 + [ ] = 13

Problems will vary.

UNIT 1 LESSON 19 Equations from Math Mountains **37**

Homework and Remembering page 37

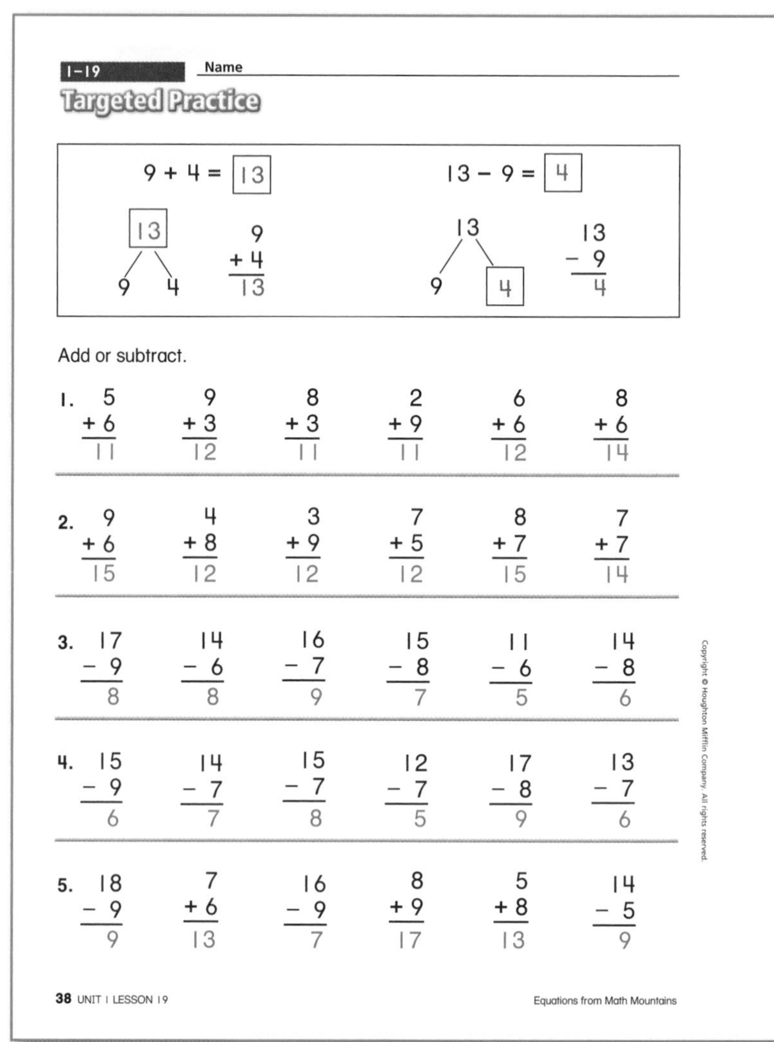

1–19 Name

Targeted Practice

9 + 4 = [13] 13 − 9 = [4]

[13] / 9 4 9 + 4 = 13 13 / 9 [4] 13 − 9 = 4

Add or subtract.

1.	5 + 6 = 11	9 + 3 = 12	8 + 3 = 11	2 + 9 = 11	6 + 6 = 12	8 + 6 = 14
2.	9 + 6 = 15	4 + 8 = 12	3 + 9 = 12	7 + 5 = 12	8 + 7 = 15	7 + 7 = 14
3.	17 − 9 = 8	14 − 6 = 8	16 − 7 = 9	15 − 8 = 7	11 − 6 = 5	14 − 8 = 6
4.	15 − 9 = 6	14 − 7 = 7	15 − 7 = 8	12 − 7 = 5	17 − 8 = 9	13 − 7 = 6
5.	18 − 9 = 9	7 + 6 = 13	16 − 9 = 7	8 + 9 = 17	5 + 8 = 13	14 − 5 = 9

38 UNIT 1 LESSON 19 Equations from Math Mountains

Homework and Remembering page 38

Home or School Activity

Language Arts Connection

Vowels and Consonants Ask children to write their first and last names and count the number of vowels and the number of consonants. Have them write a Math Mountain that shows the number of vowels, the number of consonants, and the total number of letters in all. Then have children write every possible equation for the Math Mountain.

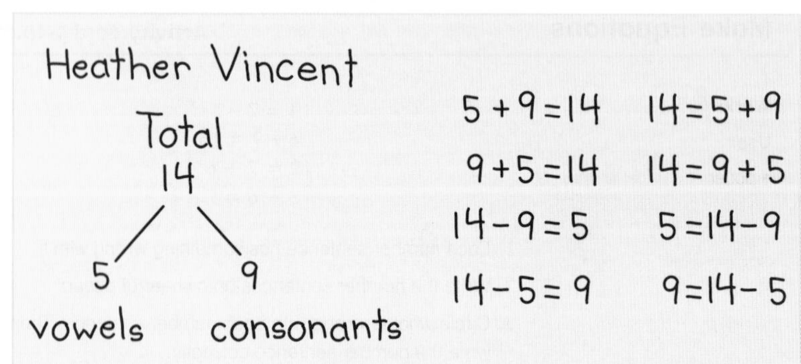

Stories from Math Mountains

Vocabulary
Math Mountain
equation
partners
total
difference

Lesson Objectives

- Create and solve story problems.
- Generate equations from Math Mountains.

The Day at a Glance

Today's Goals	Materials	
1 Teaching the Lesson **A1:** Write and use equations to create story problems with an unknown total or partner. **A2:** Match story problems and equations.	**Lesson Activities** Student Activity Book pp. 65–66 Homework and Remembering pp. 39–40 Large square sticky notes	**Going Further** Activity Cards 1-20 Student Activity Book p. 65 *Splash!* by Ann Jonas Math Journals
2 Going Further ▶ Differentiated Instruction		
3 Homework and Spiral Review		

123 Use Math Talk today!

Keeping Skills Sharp

Quick Practice — 5 MINUTES

Goal: Practice subtraction with totals of 10 or less.

Materials: Secret Code Cards (from Unit 1 Lesson 5 or TRB M3–M6) (1 set per student)

Addition Secret Code Card Race, Totals $\leq$ 10 Have children arrange the Secret Code Cards from 1 to 10 across their desks. Introduce the race by demonstrating what the Student Leader and the class should do. Then have leaders direct the race.

Leaders call out addition exercises reading from the bottom of the first column on the Parachute Drop page. As quickly as possible, children hold up a Secret Code Card to show the answer. Children race against themselves, trying to go more quickly and get more correct answers the next round.

Repeated Quick Practice
Use this Quick Practices from previous lessons.

- ▶ **Parachute Drop, Mystery Addition, Totals $\leq$ 10** Use the middle column. (See Unit 1 Lesson 19 Activity 1.)

Daily Routines

Money Routine Using the 120 Poster, Using the Money Flip Chart, Using the Number Path, Using Secret Code Cards (See pp. xxiii–xxv.)

- ▶ Led by Student Leaders

1 Teaching the Lesson

Activity 1

Create Problems from Math Mountains

 **40 MINUTES**

Goal: Write and use equations to create story problems with an unknown total or partner.

Materials: large square sticky notes (2 per child)

 **NCTM Standards:**
Number and Operations
Algebra

Teaching Note

Math Background This activity introduces the idea of an unknown and how to write an equation with an unknown number. Children should understand that any number in an equation can be the unknown. Some children may have difficulty with problems that start with an unknown, or those in which an unknown is added or subtracted. Mastery of these problems is not expected at this point; additional work with problems of this kind is provided in Unit 2.

▶ Addition Equations WHOLE CLASS

Draw a 12, 7, 5 Math Mountain on the board. Ask children to suggest an addition equation that can be written from the Math Mountain. Write the equation 5 + 7 = 12 on the board next to the Math Mountain.

▶ Story Problems for Addition Equations WHOLE CLASS

Unknown Totals Use a large sticky note to cover the total on the Math Mountain that is on the board. Cover the total in the equation 5 + 7 = 12 with another sticky note. Then write the equation with a box to represent the total.

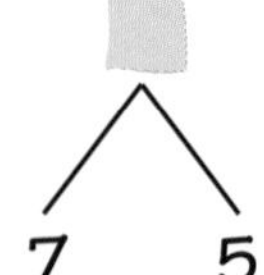

5 + 7 = ▢ ← Total covered with a sticky note

5 + 7 = □ ← Equation rewritten with a box

Have children suggest and solve story problems for the equation. They should generate problems in which the answer is the total, 12.

- I had 5 crayons. Then my friend gave me 7 more. How many crayons do I have now? 12 crayons

Unknown Partners Move the sticky note so that it covers the second number. Have children write the equation and draw squiggles under the partners. Have them suggest how to rewrite the equation with a box to represent the partner.

5 + ▢ = 12 5 + □ = 12

Have children suggest and solve story problems for the equation. Children should create problems in which the answer is the partner, 7.

- I had 5 crayons. Then my friend gave me some more. Now I have 12 crayons. How many crayons did my friend give me? 7 crayons

Move the sticky note again so that it covers the first number. Have children write the same equation and draw squiggles under the partners.

▢ + 7 = 12 □ + 7 = 12

Have children suggest and solve story problems for the equation. Children should create problems in which the answer is the partner, 5.

- I had some crayons. Then my friend game me 7 more. Now I have 12 crayons. How many crayons did I start with? 5 crayons

▶ Subtraction Equations WHOLE CLASS

Ask children to suggest and solve a subtraction equation for the Math Mountain on the board. Write the equation $12 - 5 = 7$ on the board.

▶ Story Problems for Subtraction Equations WHOLE CLASS

Unknown Partners Cover the last number in the equation with a sticky note. Then have students rewrite the equation with a box to represent the partner.

$12 - 5 = \blacksquare$ $\qquad$ $12 - 5 = \square$

Have children suggest and solve story problems for the equation. Children should generate problems in which the answer is the difference or partner, 7.

- I had 12 crayons. Then I gave 5 of them away. How many crayons do I have now? 7 crayons

Move the sticky note so that it covers the second number in the equation. Have children write the equation, draw squiggles under the partners, and rewrite the equation with a box.

$12 - \blacksquare = 7$ $\qquad$ $12 - \square = 7$

Have children suggest and solve story problems for the equation. Children should create problems in which the solution is the number being subtracted.

- I had 12 crayons. Then I gave some away. Now I have 7 crayons. How many crayons did I give away? 5 crayons

Unknown Totals Move the sticky note so that it covers the first number in the equation. Have children write the equation, draw squiggles under the partners, and rewrite the equation with a box.

$\blacksquare - 5 = 7$ $\qquad$ $\square - 5 = 7$

Have children suggest and solve story problems for the equation. Children should create problems in which the solution is the total, 12.

- I had some crayons. Then I gave 5 away. Now I have 7. How many crayons did I have to begin with? 12 crayons

Teaching Note

Research The types of problems presented in this lesson, in which the unknown can appear in any position, prepare children for writing algebraic equations with an unknown. They also help children develop the practice of reading a problem carefully in order to understand a given situation. This will aid children in mastering more difficult types of problems that often appear on tests.

English Language Learners

Write $12 - 5 = \square$ on the board. Write the word *unknown*.

- **Beginning** Point to the equation. Say: **12 minus 5 = □. The box means that number is *unknown*. The *unknown* is what you solve for.**
- **Intermediate** Ask: **What is the equation?** (12 – 5 = □) **What does the box mean?** (the number is unknown) **What do you solve for?** (the unknown)
- **Advanced** Have children tell what the box in the equation means and what you solve for.

Activity 2

Practice Connecting Story Problems with Equations

15 MINUTES

Goal: Match story problems and equations.

Materials: Student Activity Book page 65

NCTM Standards:
Number and Operations
Algebra

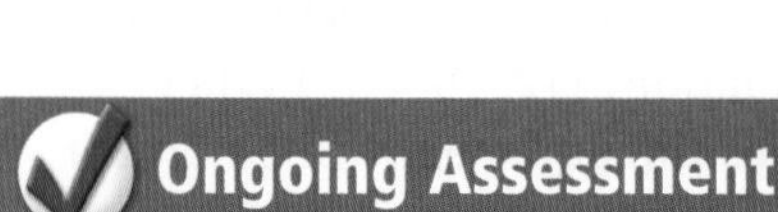

Write a 13, 6, 7 Math Mountain on the board. Have children write:

- an addition equation for the Math Mountain.
- an addition story problem in which the solution is one of the partners from the addition equation.

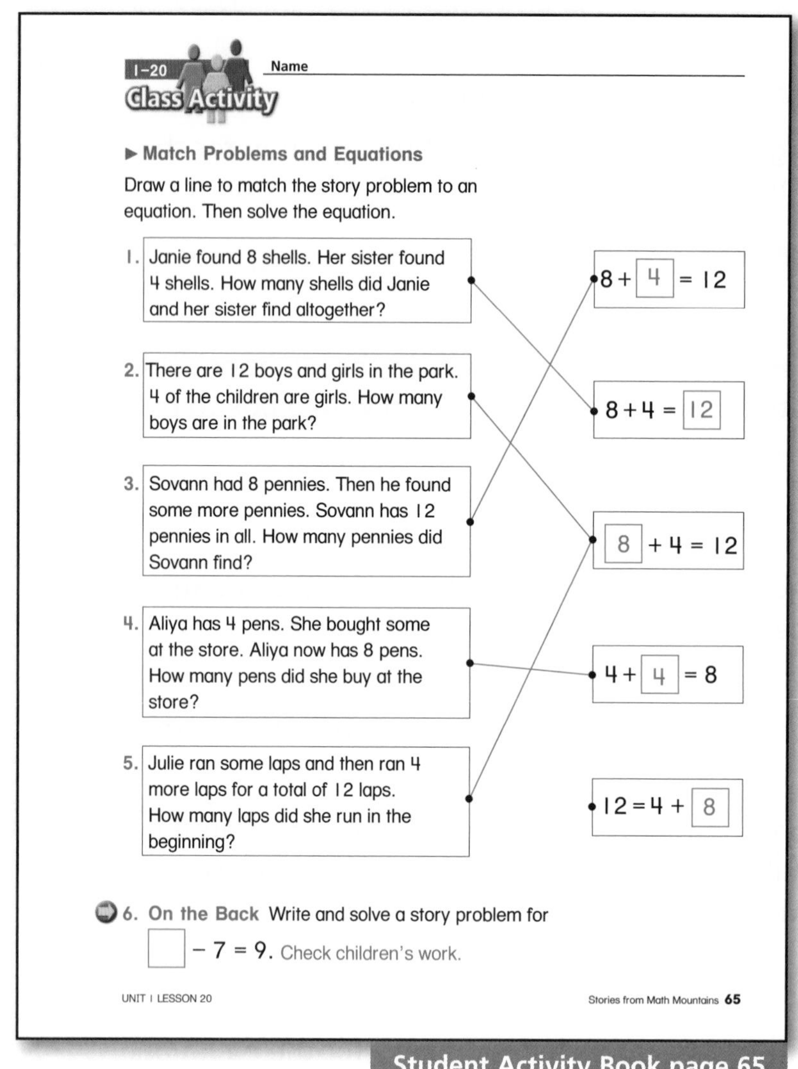

1-20 Class Activity Name

▶ Match Problems and Equations

Draw a line to match the story problem to an equation. Then solve the equation.

1. Janie found 8 shells. Her sister found 4 shells. How many shells did Janie and her sister find altogether?
2. There are 12 boys and girls in the park. 4 of the children are girls. How many boys are in the park?
3. Sovann had 8 pennies. Then he found some more pennies. Sovann has 12 pennies in all. How many pennies did Sovann find?
4. Aliya has 4 pens. She bought some at the store. Aliya now has 8 pens. How many pens did she buy at the store?
5. Julie ran some laps and then ran 4 more laps for a total of 12 laps. How many laps did she run in the beginning?

8 + [4] = 12

8 + 4 = [12]

[8] + 4 = 12

4 + [4] = 8

12 = 4 + [8]

6. On the Back Write and solve a story problem for [ ] − 7 = 9. Check children's work.

UNIT 1 LESSON 20 Stories from Math Mountains 65

Student Activity Book page 65

▶ Match Problems and Equations INDIVIDUALS

Math Talk

Have children complete Student Activity Book page 65 independently. Then discuss the answers as a class. Point out the points on the page. The dots will help children draw the lines.

Have several volunteers share the problems they wrote for exercise 6. Be sure children's problems reflect that the unknown is the total, not a partner. This problem could be one like 2 above where the total is separated into two subgroups, or it can be a change problem where 7 are taken away and 9 are left.

2 Going Further

Differentiated Instruction

Intervention — Activity Card 1-20

Draw the Mountain — Activity Card 1-20

Work:

Use:

- Student Activity Book, page 65

1. Read the first problem on Student Activity Book, page 65.
2. Draw a Math Mountain with one unknown to match the story.

1. □ / 8 4

3. Repeat for the rest of the problems.

Unit 1, Lesson 20

Activity Note Children draw Math Mountains for story problems on Student Activity Book, p. 65.

Math Writing Prompt

What's Wrong? How would you change the story problem below so that it matches this equation $3 + \square = 5$? Explain your answer.

Ed has 3 new balls. He has 5 old balls. How many balls does he have in all?

Software Support

Use *Soar to Success* for instruction of students needing targeted support for underlying skills.

On Level — Activity Card 1-20

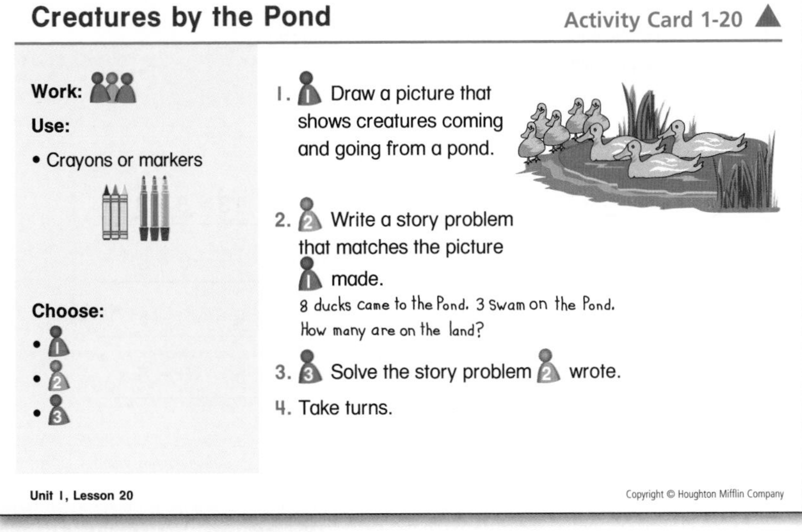

Creatures by the Pond — Activity Card 1-20

Work:

Use:

- Crayons or markers

Choose:

- 1
- 2
- 3

1. Draw a picture that shows creatures coming and going from a pond.
2. Write a story problem that matches the picture made.
   8 ducks came to the Pond. 3 swam on the Pond. How many are on the land?
3. Solve the story problem wrote.
4. Take turns.

Unit 1, Lesson 20

Copyright © Houghton Mifflin Company

Activity Note Check that children write a story problem to match the picture made by a group member. Have children exchange roles.

Math Writing Prompt

Explain Your Thinking Explain how you can solve a subtraction problem in which the unknown number is the total. For example, $\square - 6 = 9$

Software Support

Use *MegaMath* for review and reinforcement of the concepts and skills presented in this lesson.

Challenge — Activity Card 1-20

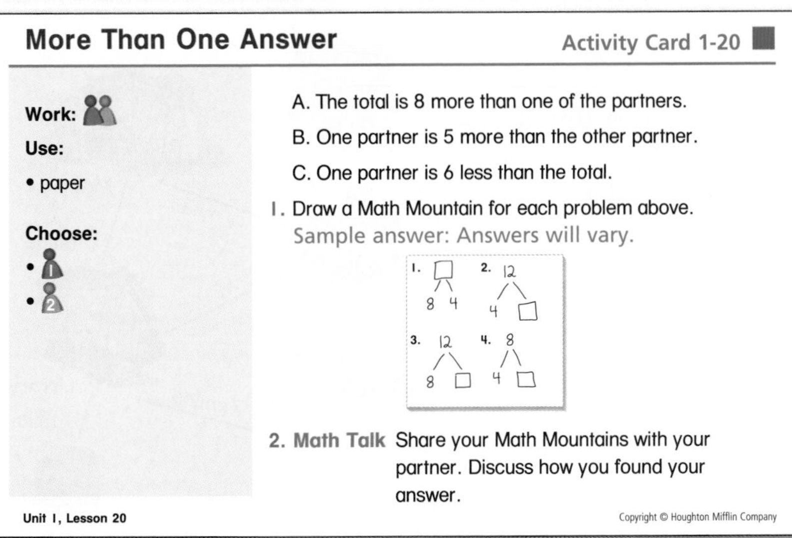

More Than One Answer — Activity Card 1-20

Work:

Use:

- paper

Choose:

- 1
- 2

A. The total is 8 more than one of the partners.
B. One partner is 5 more than the other partner.
C. One partner is 6 less than the total.

1. Draw a Math Mountain for each problem above.
   Sample answer: Answers will vary.
   1. □ / 8 4 2. 12 / 4 □ 3. 12 / 8 □ 4. 8 / 4 □
2. **Math Talk** Share your Math Mountains with your partner. Discuss how you found your answer.

Unit 1, Lesson 20

Copyright © Houghton Mifflin Company

Activity Note Children will make Math Mountains for each problem. Explain that there is more than one correct answer. Encourage pairs talk about how they found an answer.

Math Writing Prompt

Write a Story Problem Write a story problem that matches this equation. $\square - 7 = 8$

Software Support

Use *Destination Math* to take students beyond the concepts and skills presented in this lesson.

Homework and Spiral Review

1–20 Homework **Goal:** Additional Practice

This Homework page provides practice in addition and subtraction.

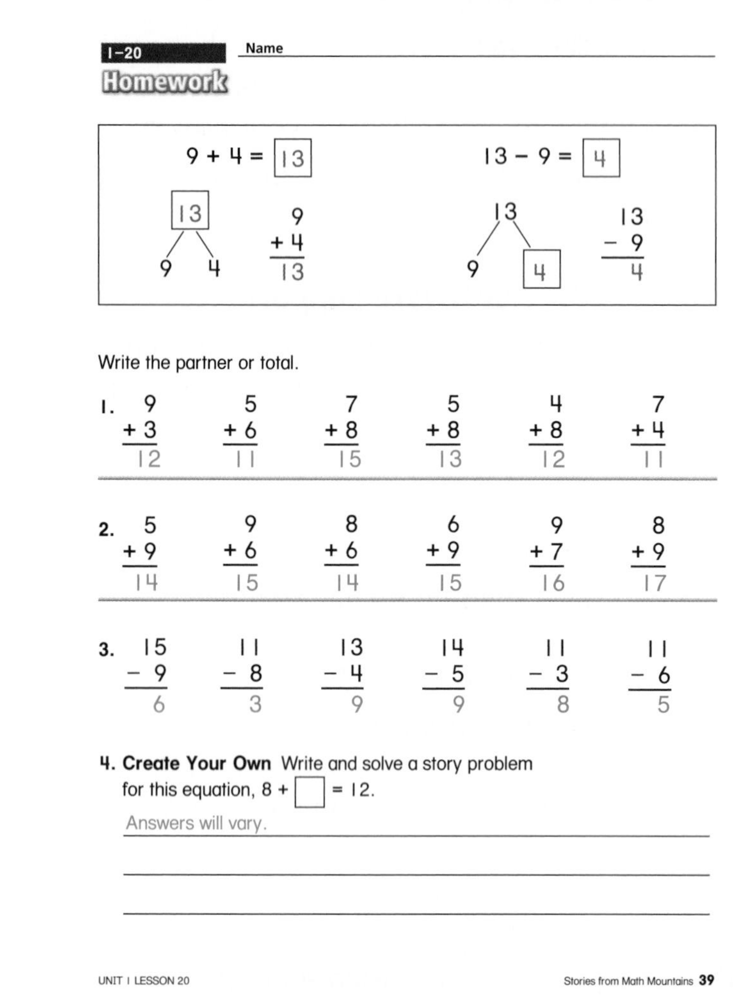

1–20 Homework

Name

9 + 4 = 13 13 − 9 = 4

13 / 9, 4 9 + 4 = 13 13 / 9, 4 13 − 9 = 4

Write the partner or total.

1. 9 + 3 = 12	5 + 6 = 11	7 + 8 = 15	5 + 8 = 13	4 + 8 = 12	7 + 4 = 11
2. 5 + 9 = 14	9 + 6 = 15	8 + 6 = 14	6 + 9 = 15	9 + 7 = 16	8 + 9 = 17
3. 15 − 9 = 6	11 − 8 = 3	13 − 4 = 9	14 − 5 = 9	11 − 3 = 8	11 − 6 = 5

4. **Create Your Own** Write and solve a story problem for this equation, 8 + ☐ = 12.

Answers will vary.

UNIT 1 LESSON 20 Stories from Math Mountains 39

Homework and Remembering page 39

1–20 Remembering **Goal:** Spiral Review

This Remembering activity would be appropriate anytime after today's lesson.

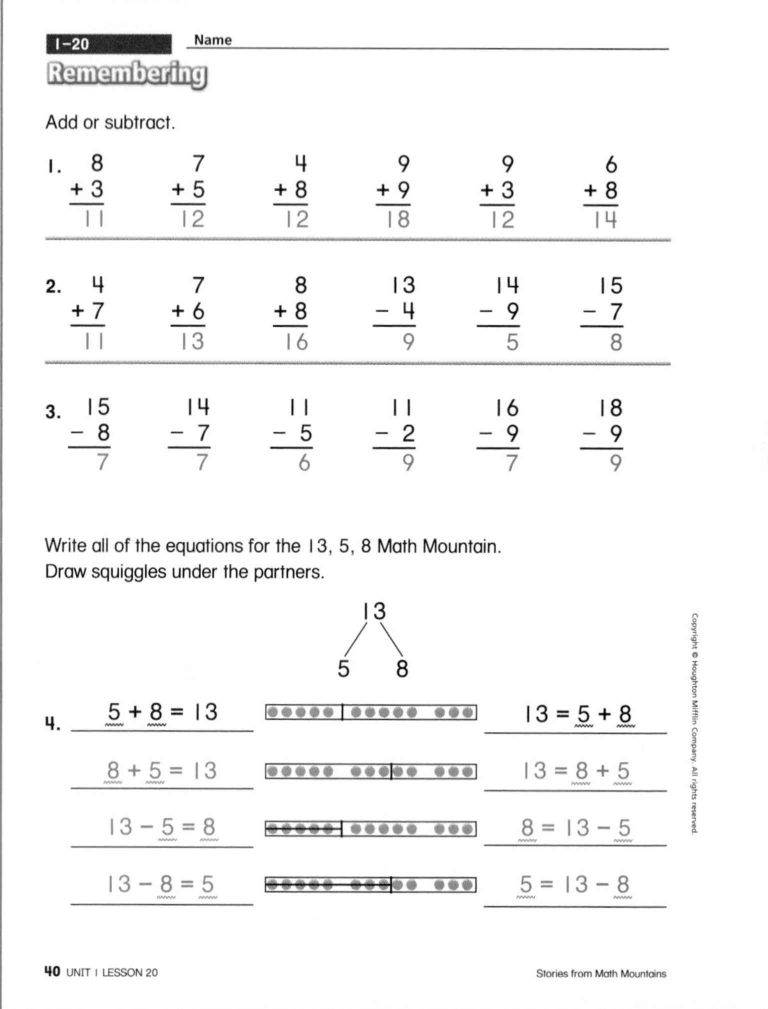

1–20 Remembering

Name

Add or subtract.

1. 8 + 3 = 11	7 + 5 = 12	4 + 8 = 12	9 + 9 = 18	9 + 3 = 12	6 + 8 = 14
2. 4 + 7 = 11	7 + 6 = 13	8 + 8 = 16	13 − 4 = 9	14 − 9 = 5	15 − 7 = 8
3. 15 − 8 = 7	14 − 7 = 7	11 − 5 = 6	11 − 2 = 9	16 − 9 = 7	18 − 9 = 9

Write all of the equations for the 13, 5, 8 Math Mountain. Draw squiggles under the partners.

13 / 5, 8

4. 5 + 8 = 13 13 = 5 + 8

8 + 5 = 13 13 = 8 + 5

13 − 5 = 8 8 = 13 − 5

13 − 8 = 5 5 = 13 − 8

40 UNIT 1 LESSON 20 Stories from Math Mountains

Homework and Remembering page 40

Home or School Activity

Social Studies Connection

Use a Map Provide children with a simple road map, preferably of the area surrounding the school. Ask children to use the numbers on the map to write and solve a story problem.

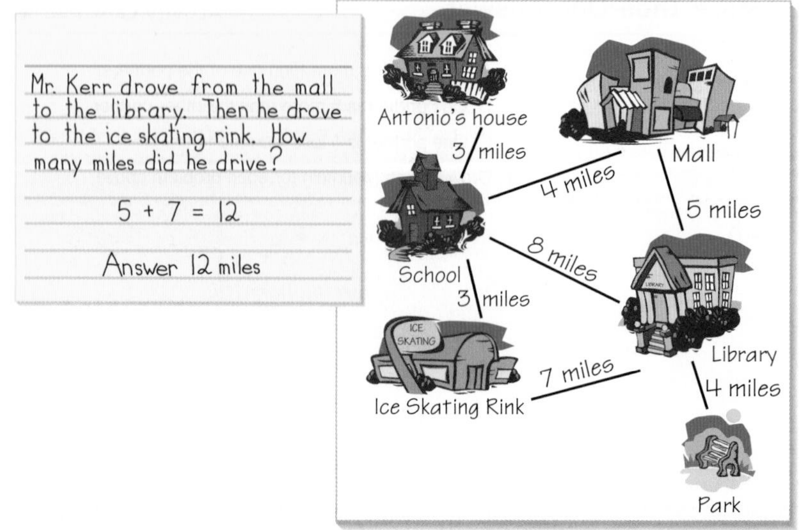

Compare and Order Numbers

Lesson Objectives

- Compare two numbers using the < or > symbol.
- Order three numbers.

Vocabulary	
equation	after
is less than	between
is greater than	least
before	greatest

The Day at a Glance

Today's Goals	Materials	
1 Teaching the Lesson **A1:** Compare two numbers using the < or > symbol. **A2:** Order three numbers.	**Lesson Activities** Homework and Remembering pp. 41–42 Secret Code Cards MathBoard materials or Number Path (TRB M47)	**Going Further** Activity Cards 1-21 Secret Code Cards Index cards Math Journals
2 Going Further ▸ Differentiated Instruction		
3 Homework and Targeted Practice		

Use Math Talk today!

Keeping Skills Sharp

Quick Practice — 5 MINUTES

Goals: Write equation chains for the number 15. Practice subtraction with totals of 10 or less.

Materials: Parachute Drop (from Unit 1 Lesson 19 or TRB M46)

Equation Chains Have three children write equation chains for the number 15 on the board. (See Unit 1 Lesson 18.)

Parachute Drop, Subtraction, Totals $\leq$ 10 Have children practice the subtraction exercises in the last column on Student Activity Book page 61. This will help them prepare for a Secret Code Card Race in the next lesson. (See Unit 1 Lesson 19 Activity 1.)

Daily Routines

Money Routine Using the 120 Poster, Using the Money Flip Chart, Using the Number Path, Using Secret Code Cards (See pp. xxiii–xxv.)

▸ Led by Student Leaders

1 Teaching the Lesson

Activity 1

"Is Less Than" and "Is Greater Than" Symbols

35 MINUTES

Goal: Compare two numbers using the < or > symbol.

Materials: MathBoard materials

NCTM Standard: Number and Operations

Teaching Note

What to Expect from Students Often children have difficulty remembering which symbol means *is less than* and which symbol means *is greater than.* Work with children to develop a way of easily distinguishing the two. One simple method is to remember that the small end of each symbol points to the smaller number, and the large end points to the greater number.

For example: Help children say both comparing statements.

$14 < 18$; 14 is less than 18
$18 > 14$; 18 is greater than 14

Differentiated Instruction

English Learners Use clothespins and posterboard to create this visual display to help English Learners to see the difference between the "is greater than" and "is less than" symbols.

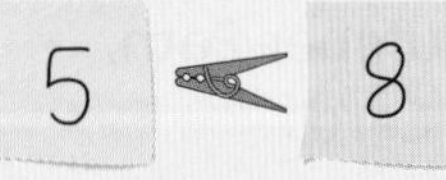

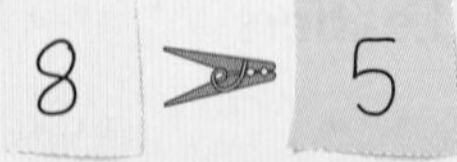

Have children write numbers on sticky notes and place them in the correct places.

▶ Inequality Statements and Symbols WHOLE CLASS

Recall with children that they have been writing equations to show that two expressions have the same value. Tell children they can also use special symbols to show that one value "is less than" or "is greater than" another value.

Invite volunteers to write the symbols for "equals," "is not equal to," "is less than," and "is greater than" on the board.

$=$	$\neq$	$<$	$>$
is equal to (equals)	is not equal to	is less than	is more than (is greater than)

▶ Discuss the "Is Less Than" Symbol WHOLE CLASS

- Let's say that Lydia has 14 dollars, and Harry has 14 dollars. What equation could we write to show that these numbers are the same?

Write the equation on the board.

$$14 = 14$$

Tell children that Lydia has 14 dollars, and Harry now has 18 dollars. Write both numbers on the board.

$$14 \qquad 18$$

Explain that the numbers are not equal anymore.

- Which number is less? 14

Write $14 < 18$ on the board while children write on their MathBoards.

Read the statement together: "14 is less than 18." Tell children to pretend they bent down the equal sign to point to the smaller number. This will help them remember that the small part of the symbol points to the lesser number.

$$14 < 18$$

small part of symbol

Erase the number 14. Invite volunteers to replace the 14 with other numbers less than 18. Have the class read each new statement together.

▶ Discuss the "Is Greater Than" Symbol WHOLE CLASS

Reverse the order of the numbers and have children state which number is greater.

- Suppose Lydia has 18 dollars and Harry has 14 dollars. Which number is greater? 18

Give children time to write 18 and 14 and draw in the "is greater than" symbol. Then write the numbers and symbol on the board. Have children check their work and fix their answer if they need to.

18 > 14

Read the statement together: "18 is greater than 14." Emphasize that any comparison can be written and said in two ways: 14 < 18 and 18 > 14.

▶ Compare Other Pairs of Numbers WHOLE CLASS

Math Talk Have the class generate and write more pairs of "is greater than" and "is less than" statements with other pairs of numbers. Be sure children write the pairs both ways and practice saying it both ways. For example, 15 and 12 can be written as 12 < 15 and 15 > 12.

Children should record responses on their MathBoards. Have children explain how they remember which symbol to use.

12 < 15
12 is less than 15

15 > 12
15 is greater than 12

English Language Learners

Write 11 > 9 and 9 < 11. Discuss how to read and the meaning of the > and < symbols.

- **Beginning** Say: **11 is *greater than* 9.** Point to the >. Say: **This means *greater than*.** Say: **9 is *less than* 11.** Point to the <. Say: **This means *less than*.**
- **Intermediate and Advanced** Ask: **What does this mean?** (11 is greater than 9) Point to the >. Ask: **Does this mean greater than?** (yes) Ask: **What does this mean?** (9 is less than 11) Point to the <. Ask: **Does this mean greater than?** (no)

Ongoing Assessment

As children are working through Activity 1, ask questions and present problems such as:

- ▶ Suppose Aliya has 6 apples and Liam has 8 apples. Who has more apples? How would you write a statement to show that 8 is more than 6?
- ▶ Write a statement that says 15 is less than 18.

Activity 2

Ordering Numbers

 20 MINUTES

Goal: Order three numbers.

Materials: Index cards (18 per pair), MathBoard materials or Number Path (TRB M47)

 **NCTM Standard:**
Number and Operations

Differentiated Instruction

Extra Help Use the class schedule to help children understand the concepts of before, after, and between. For example, you could use a sequence of events: reading may be before math, lunch is after math, and math is between reading and lunch. You may also use positions in line: Jenny is before Carlos.

Teaching Note

Language and Vocabulary Some concepts are more easily learned from examples, especially when a child is still developing a vocabulary. The meanings of before and after in this lesson ask for the number just before and the number just after the given number.

There are however, an infinite number of numbers before or after a given number. You may want to ask for other numbers that come before 5. The numbers 0, 1, 2, 3, and 4 are appropriate answers for this grade level, although some children may also mention fractions, decimals, or negative numbers.

► Before, After, and Between PAIRS

Have children write the numbers 1–18 on their Math Boards. Ask them to write and hold up the number that is just before the number 12. 11 Then ask them to write and hold up the number that is just after the number 12. 13 Finally, ask children to write and show the number that is between the numbers 11 and 13. 12 Children can circle numbers on the Number Path if they need help with these concepts.

Repeat the activity with other numbers as needed.

► Least to Greatest PAIRS

Have children count aloud from 1 to 10. Explain that the numbers are in order from least to greatest. Write the numbers 5, 9, 3 on the board.

Ask children if the numbers are in order from least to greatest? no Have them use their cards to show the numbers in order from least to greatest. If children are having difficulty, you may wish to have them ring the numbers on the Number Path on their MathBoards.

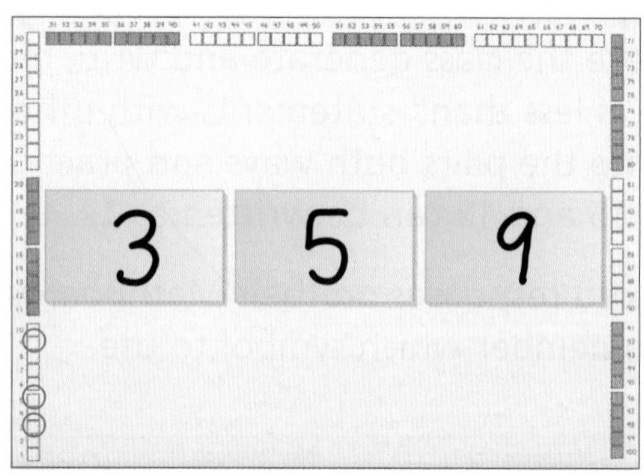

Repeat the activity with other numbers as needed.

► Greatest to Least PAIRS

Have children count backward from 10 to 1 aloud. Explain that the numbers are in order from greatest to least. Write the numbers 5, 9, 3 on the board.

Ask children if the numbers are in order from greatest to least? no Have children use their cards to show the numbers in order from greatest to least. Again, children may want to use the Number Path on their MathBoards.

Repeat the activity with other numbers as needed.

2 Going Further

Differentiated Instruction

Intervention

Activity Card 1-21

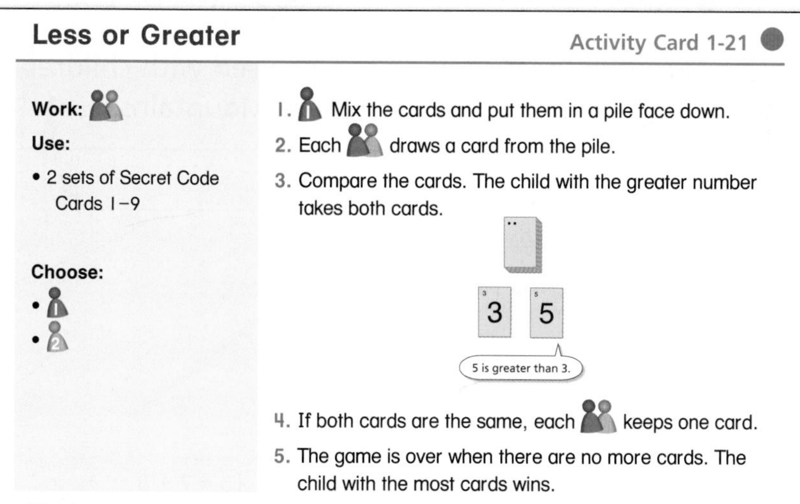

Less or Greater — Activity Card 1-21

Work: pairs
Use:
- 2 sets of Secret Code Cards 1–9

Choose:
- 1
- 2

1. Mix the cards and put them in a pile face down.
2. Each draws a card from the pile.
3. Compare the cards. The child with the greater number takes both cards.

4. If both cards are the same, each keeps one card.
5. The game is over when there are no more cards. The child with the most cards wins.

Unit 1, Lesson 21

Activity Note Prepare 2 sets of Secret Code Cards 1–9 for each pair (TRB M3–M4). Remind children to compare the numbers they turn up.

Math Writing Prompt

Draw a Picture Which number is greater, 6 or 4? Draw a picture to show how you know.

Software Support

Use *Soar to Success* for instruction of students needing targeted support for underlying skills.

On Level

Activity Card 1-21

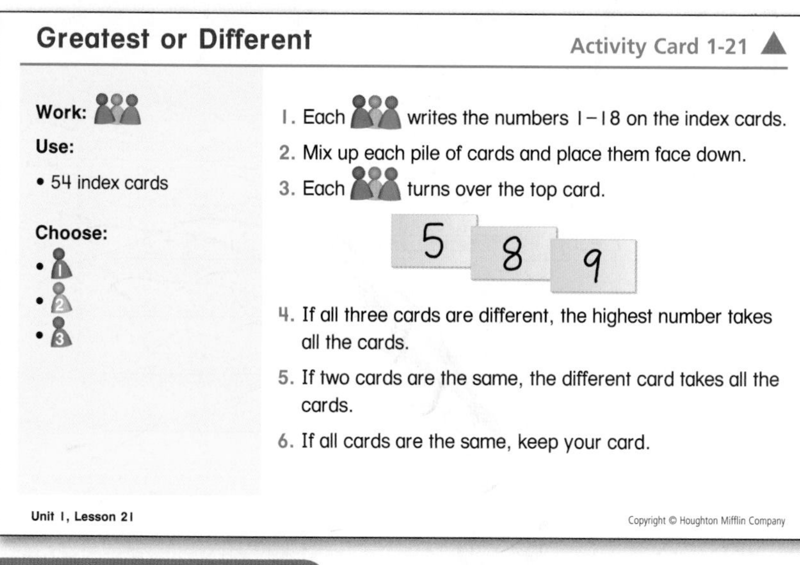

Greatest or Different — Activity Card 1-21

Work: groups of 3
Use:
- 54 index cards

Choose:
- 1
- 2
- 3

1. Each writes the numbers 1–18 on the index cards.
2. Mix up each pile of cards and place them face down.
3. Each turns over the top card.

4. If all three cards are different, the highest number takes all the cards.
5. If two cards are the same, the different card takes all the cards.
6. If all cards are the same, keep your card.

Unit 1, Lesson 21

Activity Note Each child needs 18 index cards. Children write numbers 1–18 on the cards. Remind children to follow the rules.

Math Writing Prompt

Compare
Alex has 7 pencils.
Gina has 9 pencils.
Show two different ways to compare the numbers. Explain your thinking.

Software Support

Use *MegaMath* for review and reinforcement of the concepts and skills presented in this lesson.

Challenge

Activity Card 1-21

More or Less Game — Activity Card 1-21

Work: pairs
Use:
- 2 sets of Secret Code Cards 1–9

Choose:
- 1
- 2

1. Mix the Secret Code Cards. Place them face down in a pile.
2. Each takes two cards.
3. Add the two cards together.
4. Compare the total with your partner. Record the totals using the < and > symbols.
5. The greater total takes all four cards.
6. If the totals are the same, each takes two cards.
7. Continue until all the cards are gone. The child with the most cards wins.

2 4 — $2 + 4 = 6$, $6 < 8$

5 3 — $5 + 3 = 8$, $8 > 6$

Unit 1, Lesson 21

Activity Note Prepare 2 sets of Secret Code Cards 1–9 for each pair (TRB M3–M4).

Math Writing Prompt

Compare and Explain Sophia has 3 stickers and bought 5 more. Joel had 9 stickers and gave 2 away.

Show two different ways to compare how many stickers each child has. Explain your thinking.

Software Support

Use *Destination Math* to take students beyond the concepts and skills presented in this lesson.

 Homework and Targeted Practice

1–21 Homework **Goal:** Additional Practice

This Homework page provides practice in comparing and ordering numbers.

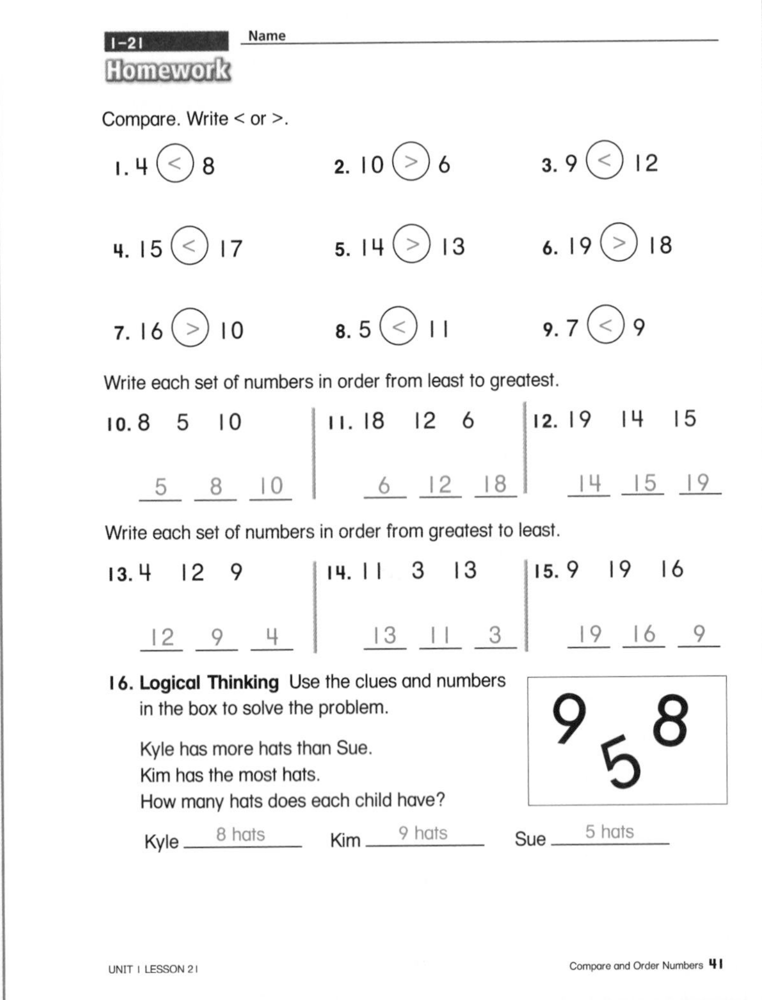

1–21 Homework Name ______

Compare. Write < or >.

1. 4 (<) 8
2. 10 (>) 6
3. 9 (<) 12
4. 15 (<) 17
5. 14 (>) 13
6. 19 (>) 18
7. 16 (>) 10
8. 5 (<) 11
9. 7 (<) 9

Write each set of numbers in order from least to greatest.

10. 8 5 10 — 5 8 10
11. 18 12 6 — 6 12 18
12. 19 14 15 — 14 15 19

Write each set of numbers in order from greatest to least.

13. 4 12 9 — 12 9 4
14. 11 3 13 — 13 11 3
15. 9 19 16 — 19 16 9

16. **Logical Thinking** Use the clues and numbers in the box to solve the problem.

9 5 8

Kyle has more hats than Sue.
Kim has the most hats.
How many hats does each child have?

Kyle 8 hats Kim 9 hats Sue 5 hats

UNIT 1 LESSON 21 Compare and Order Numbers 41

Homework and Remembering page 41

1–21 Targeted Practice **Goal:** Writing equations

This Targeted Practice page can be used with children who need extra practice with Math Mountains.

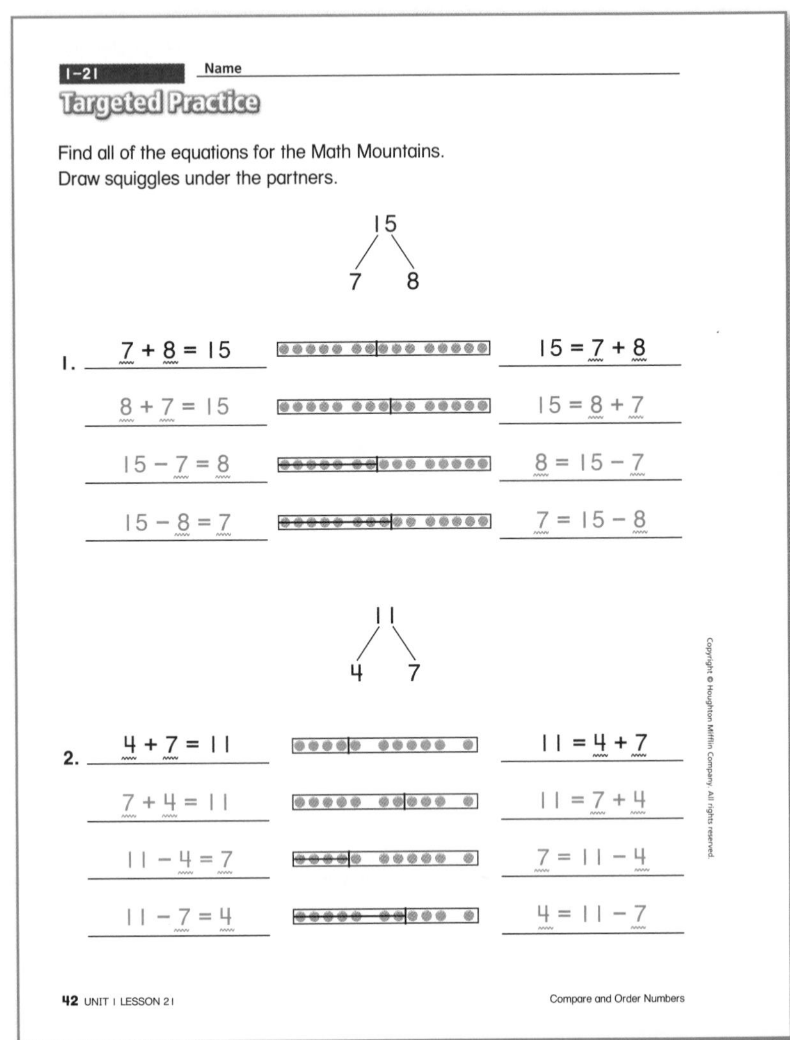

1–21 Targeted Practice Name ______

Find all of the equations for the Math Mountains.
Draw squiggles under the partners.

15
7 8

1. 7 + 8 = 15 | 15 = 7 + 8
8 + 7 = 15 | 15 = 8 + 7
15 − 7 = 8 | 8 = 15 − 7
15 − 8 = 7 | 7 = 15 − 8

11
4 7

2. 4 + 7 = 11 | 11 = 4 + 7
7 + 4 = 11 | 11 = 7 + 4
11 − 4 = 7 | 7 = 11 − 4
11 − 7 = 4 | 4 = 11 − 7

42 UNIT 1 LESSON 21 Compare and Order Numbers

Homework and Remembering page 42

Home or School Activity

 Language Arts Connection

Before, After, Between Have children write three sentences to describe different activities, using the words *before, after,* and *between.* For example, they could explain how to go to a friend's house or how they get ready for school.

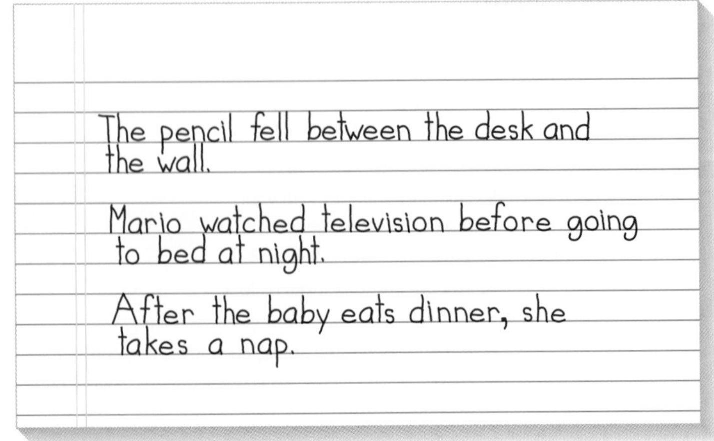

Add Three Numbers

Lesson Objectives

- Invent strategies for adding three numbers.
- Find and discuss teen Math Mountains.

Vocabulary

teen totals
teen numbers
Math Mountain
switch the partner

The Day at a Glance

Today's Goals	Materials	
1 Teaching the Lesson **A1:** Develop strategies to add three numbers. **A2:** Find and discuss teen Math Mountains.	**Lesson Activities** Student Activity Book pp. 67–68 Homework and Remembering pp. 43–44 MathBoard materials Quick Quiz 5 (Assessment Guide)	**Going Further** Activity Cards 1-22 Number cube Secret Code Cards Colored paper *Count On Me* Game Board MathBoard materials Math Journals
2 Going Further ▸ Differentiated Instruction		
3 Homework and Spiral Review		

Use Math Talk today!

Keeping Skills Sharp

Quick Practice — 5 MINUTES		Daily Routines
Goal: Practice subtraction for totals less than or equal to 10. **Materials:** Secret Code Cards (from Unit 1 Lesson 5 or TRB M3–M4) (1 set per child), Parachute Drop (from Unit 1 Lesson 19 or TRB M46) **Subtraction Secret Code Card Race, Totals ≤ 10** Have children arrange their Secret Code Cards across their desks. Have a Student Leader call out exercises starting from the bottom of the last column of the Parachute Drop page. As quickly as possible, children hold up a Secret Code Card to show the answer. (See Unit 1 Lesson 20.)	**Repeated Quick Practice** Use these Quick Practices from previous lessons. ▸ **Parachute Drop, Unknown Partner Addition** Use the middle column. (See Unit 1 Lesson 19.)	**Money Routine** Using the 120 Poster, Using the Money Flip Chart, Using the Number Path, Using Secret Code Cards (See pp. xxiii–xxv.) ▸ Led by Student Leaders

1 Teaching the Lesson

Activity 1

Add Three Numbers

 20 MINUTES

Goal: Develop strategies to add three numbers.

Materials: MathBoard materials, Student Activity Book pages 67–68

 **NCTM Standards:**
Number and Operations
Communication

Alternate Approach

Counters If some children have trouble understanding that the order in which you add does not affect the answer, have them use counters to model the addition in all three ways to show that the answer is the same in each case.

Teaching Note

Math Background The Associative Property of Addition states that addends can be grouped in any way and the sum will be the same.

So, $4 + 1 + 3 = (4 + 1) + 3 = 4 + (1 + 3)$

The Commutative Property of Addition states that you can change the order of two addends and the sum will be the same.

So, $4 + 1 = 1 + 4$

By using one or both properties, you can get any combination of the strategies discussed for these 3-addend problems.

▶ Add Three Numbers WHOLE CLASS

Totals Less than 10 Write an addition exercise with three addends, such as 3 + 2 + 4, on the board. The total of the numbers should be under 10. Ask children to share different ways to find the totals.

$$3 + 2 + 4 = \square$$

5 + 4	3 + 6	7 + 2
3 + 2 + 4 = 9	3 + 2 + 4 = 9	3 + 2 + 4 = 9

- Why do all of the methods result in the same answer? Possible responses: The numbers are just being added in different orders. The numbers can be combined to make different partners of 9.

Invite volunteers to the board to add the combinations of three numbers shown below, while the rest of the class does the addition on their MathBoards. Have children discuss which method is easiest for them. For example, they might say adding doubles or adding the 1 last.

4 + 1 + 4	1 + 3 + 5
5 + 3 + 1	2 + 5 + 1
4 + 2 + 3	6 + 2 + 1
3 + 2 + 3	1 + 4 + 4

Totals Greater than 10 Write 6 + 2 + 8 on the board. Ask children to add the numbers on their MathBoards. Encourage children to try different ways to add the numbers. As the children work, observe their strategies. Also use this time to help children who are experiencing difficulty.

$$6 + 2 + 8 = \square$$

8 + 8	6 + 10	14 + 2
6 + 2 + 8 = 16	6 + 2 + 8 = 16	6 + 2 + 8 = 16

Select three children who used the three different strategies to explain what they did. If no one used one of the solution strategies, ask children if they can find other ways to solve the problem. Encourage other children to comment and ask questions.

Math Talk Discuss why the three children got the same answer. The 16 things are just being counted in different orders. Be sure the children understand the strategies and know they can be generalized to other problems.

- What are some things you notice about the solutions? Possible responses: You can see whether two of the numbers make a ten, then add the third number to make a teen; You can add the two larger numbers, then count on the third number; You can see whether two of the numbers can make a double and then add the third number.
- Can you use these strategies with every problem? You can always add the two largest numbers, but some exercises won't have two numbers that make a ten and some won't have two numbers that make a double.

Have children complete Student Activity Book page 67. Discuss the answers as a class.

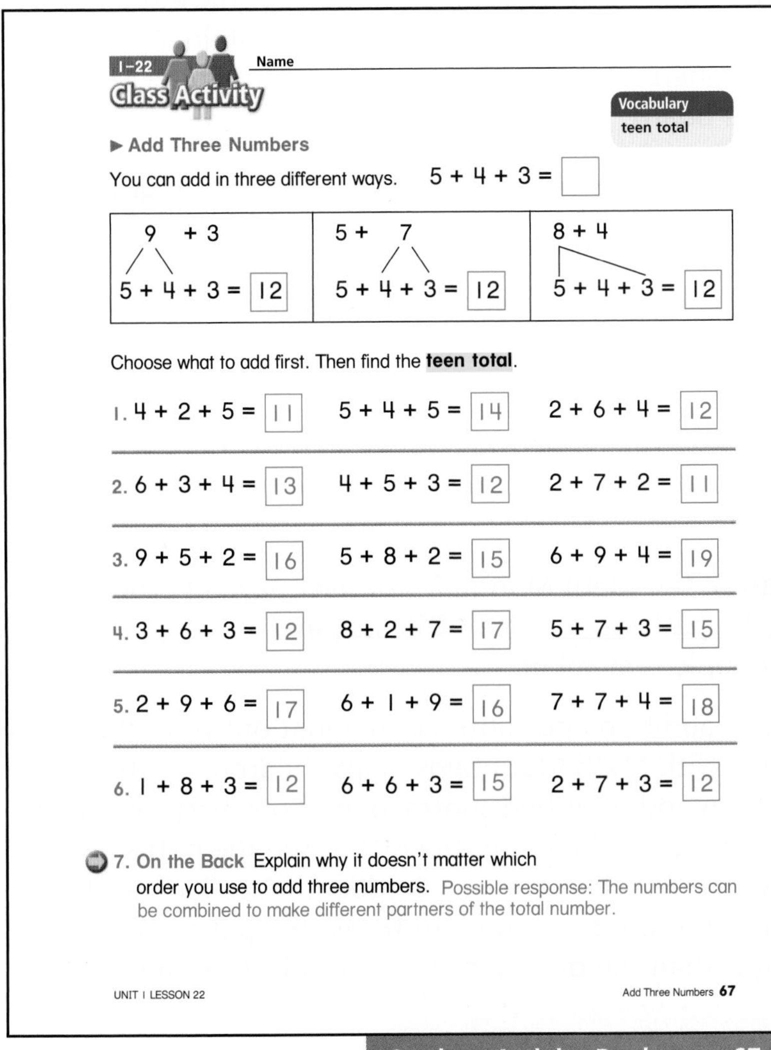

1–22 Class Activity Name ______

Vocabulary
teen total

▶ Add Three Numbers

You can add in three different ways. 5 + 4 + 3 = ☐

9 + 3	5 + 7	8 + 4
5 + 4 + 3 = 12	5 + 4 + 3 = 12	5 + 4 + 3 = 12

Choose what to add first. Then find the **teen total**.

1.	4 + 2 + 5 = 11	5 + 4 + 5 = 14	2 + 6 + 4 = 12
2.	6 + 3 + 4 = 13	4 + 5 + 3 = 12	2 + 7 + 2 = 11
3.	9 + 5 + 2 = 16	5 + 8 + 2 = 15	6 + 9 + 4 = 19
4.	3 + 6 + 3 = 12	8 + 2 + 7 = 17	5 + 7 + 3 = 15
5.	2 + 9 + 6 = 17	6 + 1 + 9 = 16	7 + 7 + 4 = 18
6.	1 + 8 + 3 = 12	6 + 6 + 3 = 15	2 + 7 + 3 = 12

7. **On the Back** Explain why it doesn't matter which order you use to add three numbers. Possible response: The numbers can be combined to make different partners of the total number.

UNIT 1 LESSON 22 Add Three Numbers 67

Student Activity Book page 67

Differentiated Instruction

Extra Help Solving the problem in three different ways may be overwhelming for some children. If necessary, allow children who are having difficulty to work with children who understand the concept. The child who is having difficulty can solve the problem one way while the other child solves the problem the other two ways.

English Language Learners

Write *teen total*. Review the teen numbers that will be the different answers to the equations.

- **Beginning** Point to the 9. Say: **You can add 5 + 4 first. Then add 9 + 3.** Point to the 7. Say: **You can add 4 + 3 first. Then add 5 + 7.** Point to the 8. Say: **You can add 5 + 3 first. Then add 8 + 4. The *teen total* is always 12.**
- **Intermediate and Advanced** Ask: **Which numbers can you add first?** 9 + 3 or 4 + 3 or 5 + 3 **Does it change the *teen total*?** no

Ongoing Assessment

As children work on Student Activity Book page 67, circulate around the room and have students explain what strategy they are using to solve each of the problems.

- ▶ Explain one way to solve 3 + 6 + 3.
- ▶ Explain how you would find 8 + 7 + 2.

Quick Quiz

See Assessment Guide for Unit 1 Quick Quiz 5.

Activity 2

Find and Discuss Teen Math Mountains

 30 MINUTES

Goal: Find and discuss teen Math Mountains.

Materials: MathBoard materials

 **NCTM Standards:**
Number and Operations
Communication

All 20 of the Teen Math Mountains

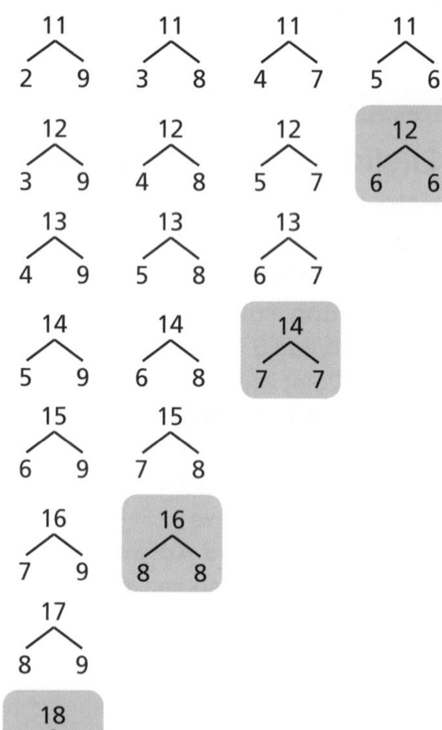

The Learning Classroom

Building Concepts Encourage children to find as many patterns as they can. If they do not mention these, explain the following:

- A single digit added to 9 will make a teen number 1 less than the single digit added to 10. For example, $9 + 4 = 13$.
- Doubles are easy to remember.
- The total 17 only has one pair of partners.
- The totals 15 and 16 only have two pairs of partners.

▶ Find Math Mountains with Teen Totals WHOLE CLASS

Invite children to suggest a Math Mountain that has a teen total. Tell them to find one with partners less than 10. Write the Math Mountain on the board.

Give children time to draw as many Math Mountains (with teen totals and partners less than 10) as they can think of on their MathBoards. Do not tell them how many Math Mountains there are altogether.

Remind them that switching the partners does not make a different mountain.

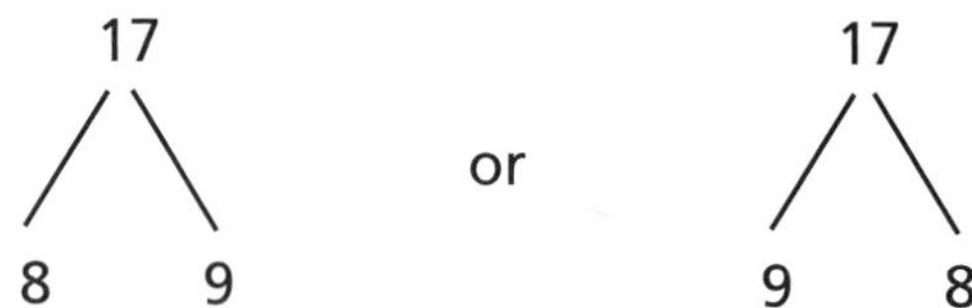

Share Teen Math Mountains Ask children to share the Math Mountains they made. Have children who have Math Mountains for 11 draw them on the board and say their mountain aloud. Have the rest of the class raise their hands if they found that same mountain. Repeat this procedure for the numbers 12 through 18 until all twenty teen Math Mountains are on the board.

▶ Discuss Patterns in Teen Math Mountains WHOLE CLASS

Discuss the Math Mountains with children.

- What patterns in the Math Mountains do you see? Possible responses: all have 9 as a partner, even numbers have doubles, larger numbers have fewer Mountains.
- What are some ways to remember them or to find them quickly? Accept children's responses, asking them to clarify their answers if needed.

If necessary, reorganize the Math Mountains or have several children reorganize so that the patterns are clear. Discuss patterns, emphasizing that patterns help people remember.

Have children suggest addition and subtraction equations from the Math Mountains. This work with Math Mountains helps children use these patterns in solving teen additions and subtractions. Look vertically at the 9 + Math Mountains (in the column on the left) to see the pattern of the teen ones being one less than the non-9 addend. Also look at the 8 + Math Mountains (in the second column) to see the pattern of the teen ones being 2 less than the ones in the teen total (for example, $8 + 3$ is $13 - 2 = 11$).

2 Going Further

Differentiated Instruction

Intervention

Activity Card 1-22

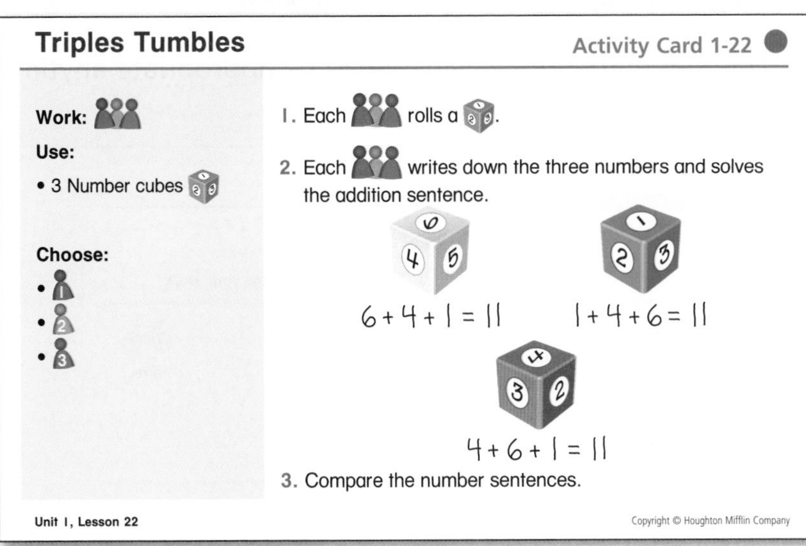

Triples Tumbles Activity Card 1-22 ●

Work:
Use:
- 3 Number cubes

Choose:
- 1
- 2
- 3

1. Each rolls a .
2. Each writes down the three numbers and solves the addition sentence.

6 + 4 + 1 = 11   1 + 4 + 6 = 11

4 + 6 + 1 = 11

3. Compare the number sentences.

Unit 1, Lesson 22 Copyright © Houghton Mifflin Company

Activity Note Prepare three number cubes labeled 1–6. Have children compare their number sentences to be sure they are correct.

Math Writing Prompt

Analyze Three number cubes are labeled 1–6. What is the greatest total you could get with three number cubes? What is the least number? Explain.

Software Support

Use *Soar to Success* for instruction of students needing targeted support for underlying skills.

On Level

Activity Card 1-22

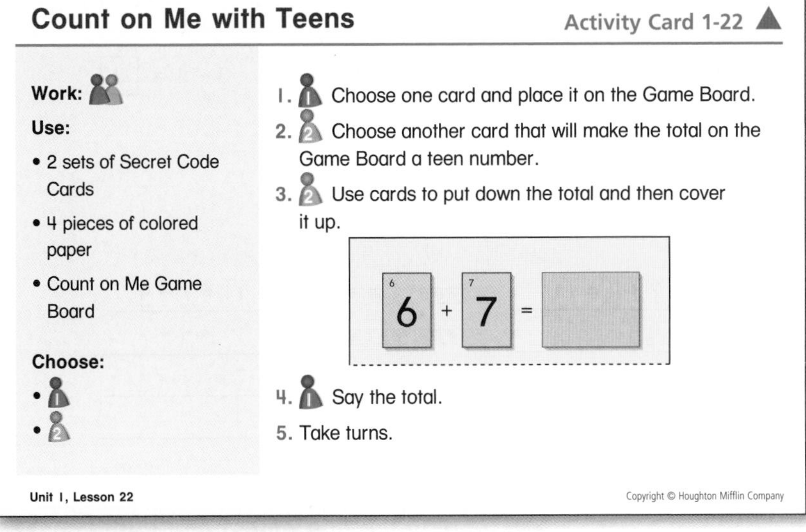

Count on Me with Teens Activity Card 1-22 ▲

Work:
Use:
- 2 sets of Secret Code Cards
- 4 pieces of colored paper
- Count on Me Game Board

Choose:
- 1
- 2

1. Choose one card and place it on the Game Board.
2. Choose another card that will make the total on the Game Board a teen number.
3. Use cards to put down the total and then cover it up.

6 + 7 =

4. Say the total.
5. Take turns.

Unit 1, Lesson 22 Copyright © Houghton Mifflin Company

Activity Note Prepare 2 sets of Secret Code Cards (TRB M3–M4), *Count on Me* Game Board, paper to cover the boxes on the game board.

Math Writing Prompt

Use Double to Add How can you use doubles to find the total of 3 + 1 + 3?

Software Support

Use *MegaMath* for review and reinforcement of the concepts and skills presented in this lesson.

Challenge

Activity Card 1-22

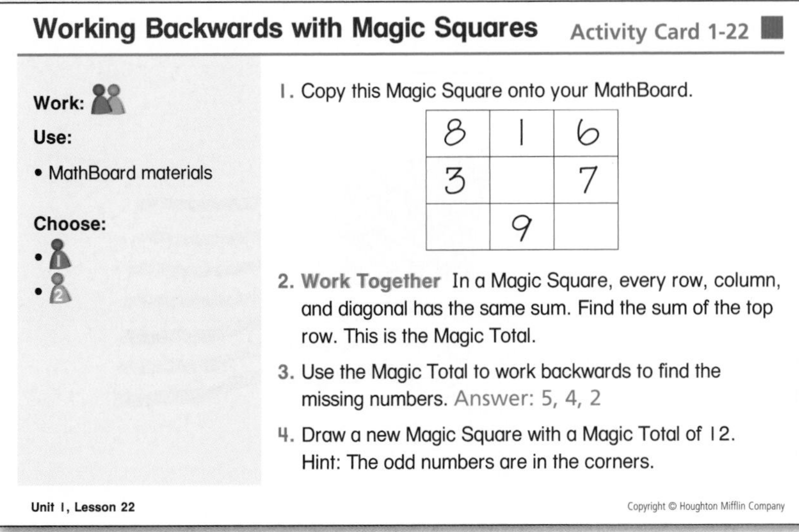

Working Backwards with Magic Squares Activity Card 1-22 ■

Work:
Use:
- MathBoard materials

Choose:
- 1
- 2

1. Copy this Magic Square onto your MathBoard.

8	1	6
3		7
	9	

2. **Work Together** In a Magic Square, every row, column, and diagonal has the same sum. Find the sum of the top row. This is the Magic Total.
3. Use the Magic Total to work backwards to find the missing numbers. Answer: 5, 4, 2
4. Draw a new Magic Square with a Magic Total of 12. Hint: The odd numbers are in the corners.

Unit 1, Lesson 22 Copyright © Houghton Mifflin Company

Activity Note Review with children what a Magic Square is and how to solve it. Ask children to share with partner how they found the answer.

Math Writing Prompt

Different Ways to Add Show two different ways to add 7 + 3 + 3. Which way is easier for you? Explain.

Software Support

Use *Destination Math* to take students beyond the concepts and skills presented in this lesson.

Homework and Spiral Review

1–22 Homework Goal: Additional Practice

This Homework page provides practice in adding three numbers.

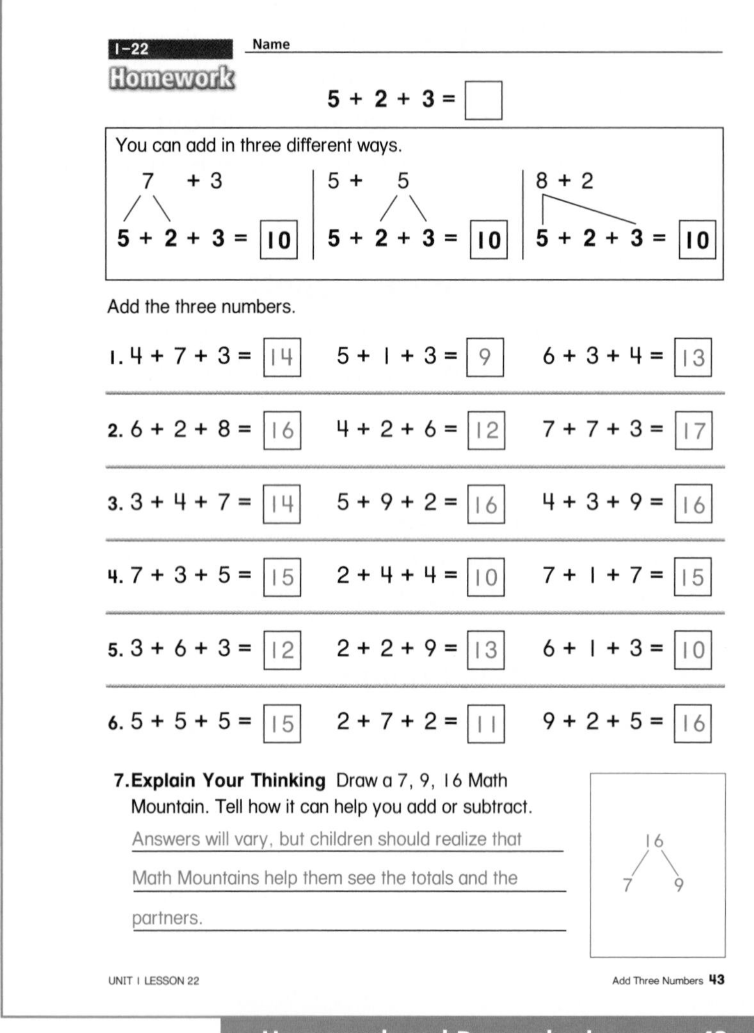

1–22 Name

Homework

5 + 2 + 3 = □

You can add in three different ways.

7 + 3	5 + 5	8 + 2
5 + 2 + 3 = 10	5 + 2 + 3 = 10	5 + 2 + 3 = 10

Add the three numbers.

1. 4 + 7 + 3 = 14   5 + 1 + 3 = 9   6 + 3 + 4 = 13
2. 6 + 2 + 8 = 16   4 + 2 + 6 = 12   7 + 7 + 3 = 17
3. 3 + 4 + 7 = 14   5 + 9 + 2 = 16   4 + 3 + 9 = 16
4. 7 + 3 + 5 = 15   2 + 4 + 4 = 10   7 + 1 + 7 = 15
5. 3 + 6 + 3 = 12   2 + 2 + 9 = 13   6 + 1 + 3 = 10
6. 5 + 5 + 5 = 15   2 + 7 + 2 = 11   9 + 2 + 5 = 16
7. **Explain Your Thinking** Draw a 7, 9, 16 Math Mountain. Tell how it can help you add or subtract.
   Answers will vary, but children should realize that Math Mountains help them see the totals and the partners.

16, 7, 9

UNIT 1 LESSON 22   Add Three Numbers 43

Homework and Remembering page 43

1–22 Remembering Goal: Spiral Review

This Remembering activity would be appropriate anytime after today's lesson.

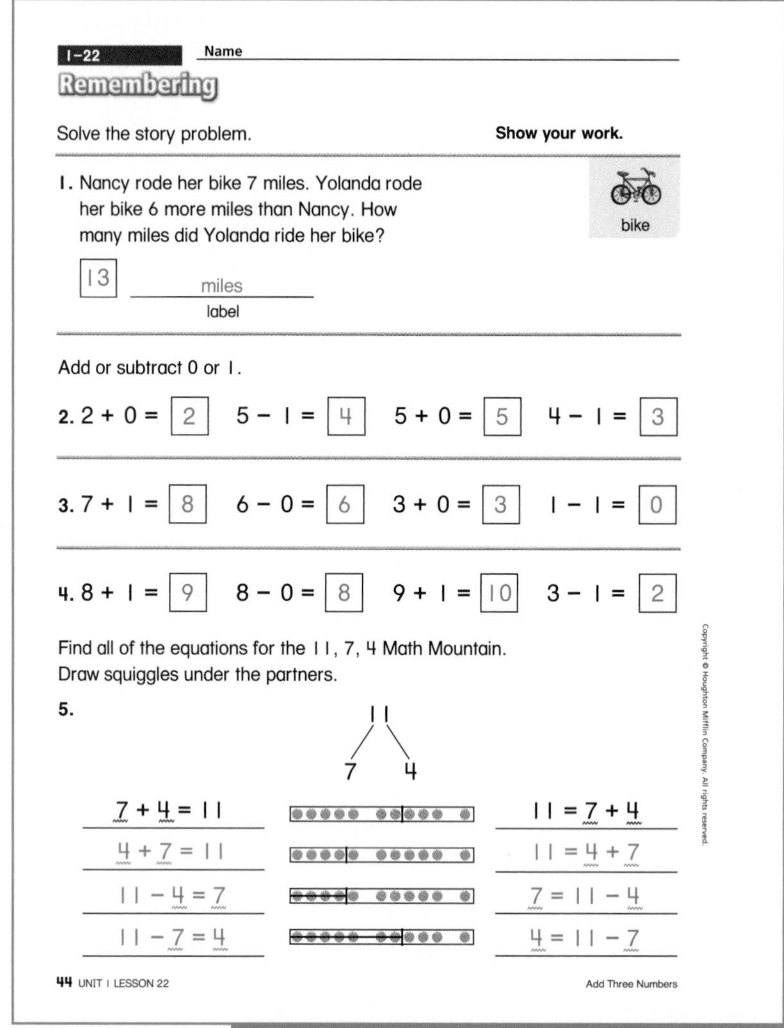

1–22 Name

Remembering

Solve the story problem. **Show your work.**

1. Nancy rode her bike 7 miles. Yolanda rode her bike 6 more miles than Nancy. How many miles did Yolanda ride her bike?
   bike
   13 miles (label)

Add or subtract 0 or 1.

2. 2 + 0 = 2   5 − 1 = 4   5 + 0 = 5   4 − 1 = 3
3. 7 + 1 = 8   6 − 0 = 6   3 + 0 = 3   1 − 1 = 0
4. 8 + 1 = 9   8 − 0 = 8   9 + 1 = 10   3 − 1 = 2

Find all of the equations for the 11, 7, 4 Math Mountain. Draw squiggles under the partners.

5. 11, 7, 4

7 + 4 = 11		11 = 7 + 4
4 + 7 = 11		11 = 4 + 7
11 − 4 = 7		7 = 11 − 4
11 − 7 = 4		4 = 11 − 7

44 UNIT 1 LESSON 22   Add Three Numbers

Homework and Remembering page 44

Home or School Activity

Social Studies Connection

Stars and Stripes Have children look at an American flag. Explain that the stars on the American flag stand for the 50 states in the United States. The 13 stripes stand for the number of original colonies that existed when the United States began. Have children make as many different Math Mountains as they can for the number 13. Then have them use the flag to find what number partners were used to design the stripes on the flag. 6 and 7

Use Mathematical Processes

Lesson Objectives

- **Solve a variety of problems using mathematical processes and skills.**
- **Use the mathematical processes of problem solving, connections, reasoning and proof, communication, and representation.**

The Day at a Glance

Today's Goals	Materials	
1 Teaching the Lesson **A1: Math Connections** Explore concrete models of vertex-edge graphs; organize data in a table; make predictions. **A2: Problem Solving** Complete tables; identify patterns in tables. **A3: Reasoning and Proof** Use reasoning to decide if the rules for two patterns are the same or different. **A4: Representation** Make drawings of different ways to represent amounts of money. **A5: Communication** Tell how to share objects between 2 people so each gets a fair share.	**Lesson Activities** Student Activity Book pp. 69–70 Homework and Remembering pp. 45–46 Calculators	**Other Activities** Activity Cards 1-23 Game Cards (TRB M6) Number cubes Math Journals
2 Going Further ► Differentiated Instruction		
3 Homework and Spiral Review		

123 Use Math Talk today!

Keeping Skills Sharp

Quick Practice	Daily Routines
No Quick Practice or Daily Routines are recommended. If you choose to do some, use those that provide extra practice that meets the needs of your class.	**Class Management** Use this lesson to provide more understanding of the NCTM process standards. Depending on how you choose to carry out the activities, this lesson may take two or more days of teaching.

1 Teaching the Lesson

Activity 1

Connections

Math and Games

 45 MINUTES

Goals: Explore concrete models of vertex-edge graphs; organize data in a table; make predictions.

Materials: Student Activity Book page 69

 **NCTM Standards:**
Problem Solving
Connections
Communication
Representation
Reasoning and Proof

1-23  Name

▶ Math and Games

Rules for the Game of Sprouts

A. Draw dots on a sheet of paper.
B. Take turns. Each time draw a line between two dots and place a dot on that line.
C. A line can be straight or curved but cannot cross itself or another line.
D. No more than 3 lines can be drawn from one dot.
E. The last player to draw a line wins.

Play Sprouts with 2 dots.

1. Make a table like this one on another piece of paper. Keep a record of each round.

Round Number	How Many Turns?	Who Won: First Player or Second Player?

2. Did every game have the same number of turns?
In most cases children will not always have the same number of turns.
3. Who won each time?
If children play the game correctly the first player should win each time.

Play Sprouts with 3 dots. Record the turns in a table.

4. Did every game have the same number of turns?
In most cases children will not always have the same number of turns.
5. Who won each time?
If children play the game correctly the second player should win each time.
6. **Predict** What do you think will happen when you play the game with 4 dots.
Answers will vary. Possible answer: I predict that the first player will always win.

UNIT 1 LESSON 23 69

Student Activity Book page 69

Teaching Note

Math Background Playing this game provides an informal way for children to explore vertex-edge graphs. The dots are vertices. The lines that connect dots are edges.

▶ Rules for Sprouts

Task 1 Go over the game rules with the class.

Ask a volunteer to help demonstrate a 2-Dot Game of Sprouts at the board. Play as many rounds as you need to ensure that children understand the rules.

▶ Play and Analyze the Sprouts Game

Math Talk 

Task 2 and 3 Have children play the 2-Dot Game of Sprouts and then the 3-Dot Game of Sprouts. Have them use tables to record the number of moves and who won for each round. Have them play the game at least 8 times and be sure that they play an even number of games. Discuss the exercises on the student page with the children.

Task 4 Point out that the game can start with any number of dots and that a new game could be invented by changing the rules. Ask:

- Do you think you could ever play a game that never ended? Allow children to share their ideas and explain why they think that way. In fact, games will always end. But what is most important here is to engage children in conversation about a mathematical idea.
- What are some ways you might change the rules? Suggest that children try playing with their own rules with a friend and let them make up new names for their games.

Activity 2

Problem Solving

The Bathtub Race

 **45 MINUTES**

Goals: Complete tables; identify patterns in tables.

Materials: Student Activity Book page 70

 **NCTM Standards:**
Problem Solving
Connections
Communication

1-23 Name ____________________

Problem Solving

▶ **The Bathtub Race**

A Bathtub Race takes place every year in Nanaimo, Canada. People like to buy souvenirs at the race.

Use a calculator to complete the tables.

1. The Bathtub Race poster costs $5.
   - How much will it cost to buy some posters?

1 poster	2 posters	3 posters	4 posters	5 posters	6 posters
$5	$10	$15	$20	$25	$30

   - What pattern do you see in the table?
   Answers may vary. Possible answer: There's a number with a 5 and then a number with a zero.

2. The 1978 Bathtub Race coin is worth $10.
   - What will be cost of buying some of these coins?

1 coin	2 coins	3 coins	4 coins	5 coins	6 coins
$10	$20	$30	$40	$50	$60

   - What pattern do you see in the table?
   Answers may vary. Possible answer: Each number is ten more.

3. The first place bathtub gets 50 points. Other places get 2 points less than the place before.
   - How many points does each place get?

1st Place	2nd Place	3rd Place	4th Place	5th Place	6th Place
50	48	46	44	42	40

   - What pattern do you see in the table?
   Answers may vary. Possible answer: Each number is 2 less.

70 UNIT 1 LESSON 23

Student Activity Book page 70

English Language Learners

Draw 3 people running to a finish line. Ask: **What are they doing?** running

- **Beginning** Ask: **Is this a *race*?** yes **Does the fastest person win?** yes
- **Intermediate and Advanced** Ask: **What kind of *race* is this?** running race Have children tell about other types of races. car, bicycle, swimming

▶ Brainstorm about a Bathtub Race

Ask for Ideas Elicit thoughts or knowledge about a Bathtub Race from the children.

▶ What do you think happens in a Bathtub Race? Most children will probably not have heard of or seen a bathtub race. Have them talk about what they think it would be like to race in a bathtub—how fast a bathtub might move, how a bathtub could be steered, and so on.

▶ Discuss Patterns

Math Talk

Tasks 1–3 Have children fill in the tables for exercises 1–3. Then ask children to discuss the patterns they see in their tables with a partner or in a small group. Summarize ideas about patterns with a whole-class discussion. Ask:

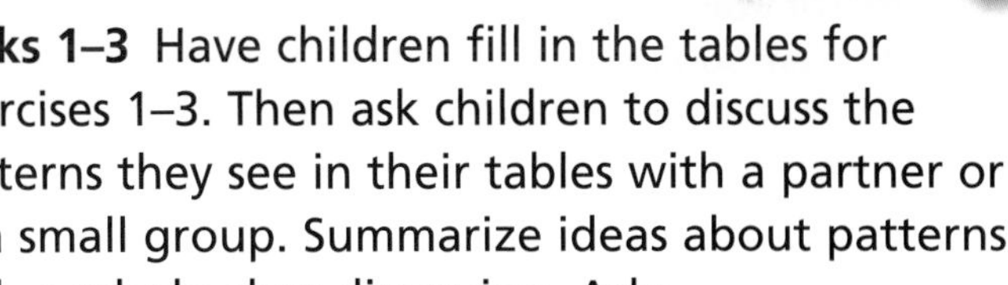

▶ What patterns did you see in the tables? Allow children to share their observations.

▶ How are the patterns in the tables the same? Answers will vary. Possible answer: In each table, the numbers change the same way.

▶ How are the patterns in the tables different? Answers will vary. Possible answer: Two tables have adding patterns; one has a subtraction pattern.

Activity 3

Reasoning and Proof

Same Rule or Different Rule?

 15 MINUTES

Goal: Use reasoning to decide if the rules for two patterns are the same or different.

 **NCTM Standards:**
Problem Solving
Communication
Reasoning and Proof

Write each pair of patterns on the board, one pair at a time.

1 4 7 10	2 5 8 11

2 6 10 14	2 5 8 11

For each pair, ask: Are the rules of these two patterns the same or different? First pair: same; second pair: different.

Then ask children to explain their thinking.

- How do you decide whether the rules are the same or different? Answers will vary. Possible answer: If they start with the same number and then have different numbers, the rules are different.
- If the rules are the same, why are there different numbers in the patterns? Answers will vary. Possible answer: The starting number is different in the two patterns.

Activity 4

Representation

Making 12¢

 15 MINUTES

Goal: Make drawings of different ways to represent a money amount.

 **NCTM Standards:**
Problem Solving
Connections
Representation

Draw pictures to show 2 or more different ways to make 12¢. Answers will vary. Check children's work.

Have children show different ways to make 12¢.

- What are some of the ways you found to make 12¢? Answers will vary. Possible answers: 12 pennies; 1 dime and 2 pennies; 2 nickels and 2 pennies; 1 nickel and 7 pennies

Repeat with other amounts less than 50¢.

Activity 5

Communication

Sharing Crackers

 15 MINUTES

Goal: Tell how to share objects between 2 people so each gets a fair share.

 **NCTM Standards:**
Problem Solving
Communication
Connections
Representation

Explain how to give 11 crackers to 2 people so each gets a fair share. Answers will vary. Possible answer: Give each person 5 crackers and then split the last cracker in half and give each person half of a cracker.

Have children share in a whole-class discussion how they solved this problem.

- How did you solve this problem? Answers will vary. Possible answers: Some children may have drawn pictures. Others may have used 11 pieces of paper to represent the crackers.

2 Going Further

Differentiated Instruction

Intervention — Activity Card 1-23

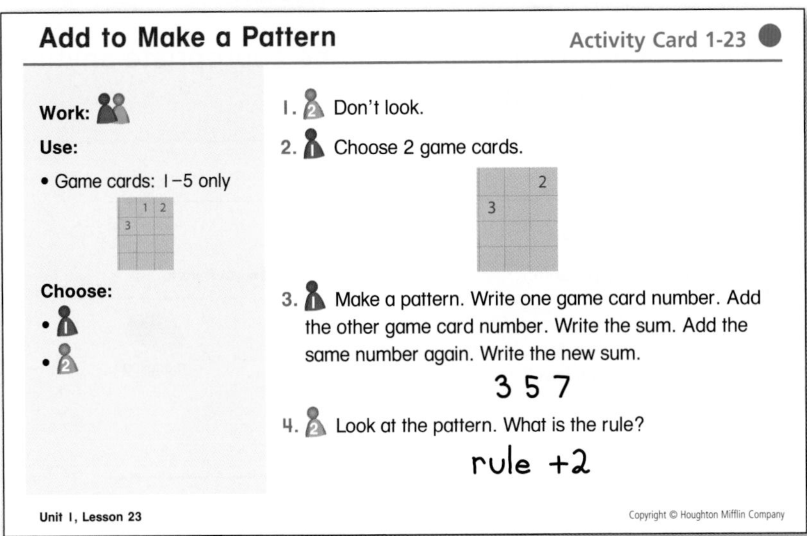

Add to Make a Pattern — Activity Card 1-23

Work: pairs
Use:
- Game cards: 1–5 only

Choose:

1. Don't look.
2. Choose 2 game cards.

3. Make a pattern. Write one game card number. Add the other game card number. Write the sum. Add the same number again. Write the new sum.

3 5 7

4. Look at the pattern. What is the rule?

rule +2

Unit 1, Lesson 23

Activity Note Depending on what needs for practice children have, you may assign different number cards for them to use.

Math Writing Prompt

Write a Pattern Write a pattern with numbers. Write the rule for your pattern.

Software Support

Use *Soar to Success* for instruction of students needing targeted support for underlying skills.

On Level — Activity Card 1-23

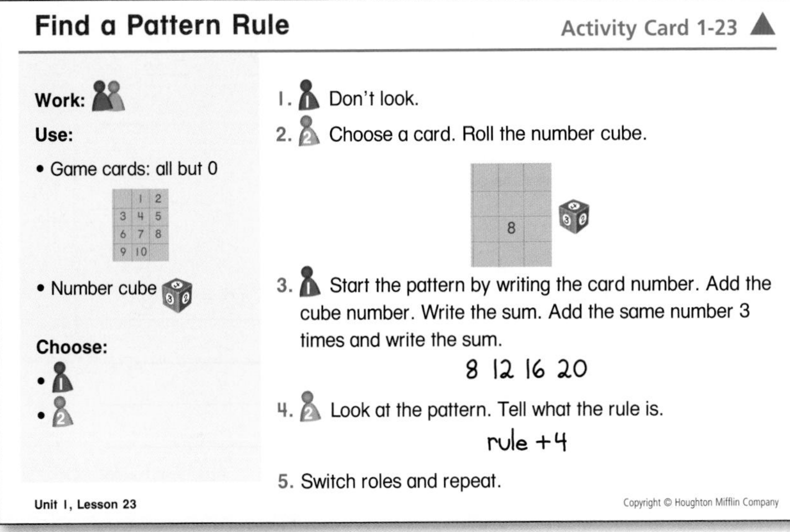

Find a Pattern Rule — Activity Card 1-23

Work: pairs
Use:
- Game cards: all but 0
- Number cube

Choose:

1. Don't look.
2. Choose a card. Roll the number cube.

3. Start the pattern by writing the card number. Add the cube number. Write the sum. Add the same number 3 times and write the sum.

8 12 16 20

4. Look at the pattern. Tell what the rule is.

rule +4

5. Switch roles and repeat.

Unit 1, Lesson 23

Activity Note If you do not have number cubes, have the child writing the pattern choose a number from 1 through 6 to use.

Math Writing Prompt

Patterns that Start with 3 Write 2 different patterns that start with 3. Write the rule for each pattern.

Software Support

Use *MegaMath* for review and reinforcement of the concepts and skills presented in this lesson.

Challenge — Activity Card 1-23

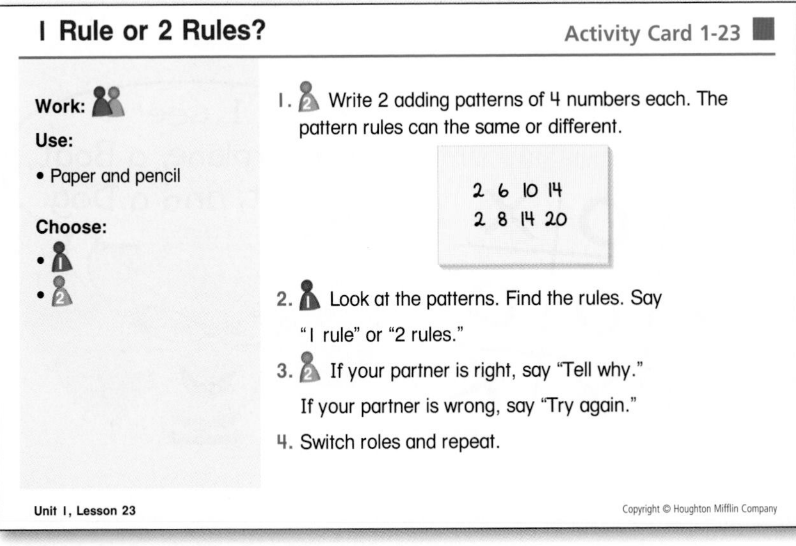

1 Rule or 2 Rules? — Activity Card 1-23

Work: pairs
Use:
- Paper and pencil

Choose:

1. Write 2 adding patterns of 4 numbers each. The pattern rules can the same or different.

2 6 10 14
2 8 14 20

2. Look at the patterns. Find the rules. Say "1 rule" or "2 rules."
3. If your partner is right, say "Tell why." If your partner is wrong, say "Try again."
4. Switch roles and repeat.

Unit 1, Lesson 23

Activity Note You may want to ask both children to write their patterns at the same time and then trade papers so that they can analyze each other's patterns at the same time.

Math Writing Prompt

Subtracting Pattern Write a pattern where you subtract. Write the rule for your pattern.

Software Support

Use *Destination Math* to take students beyond the concepts and skills presented in this lesson.

3 Homework and Spiral Review

Goal: Additional Practice

Include student's completed Homework page as part of their portfolios.

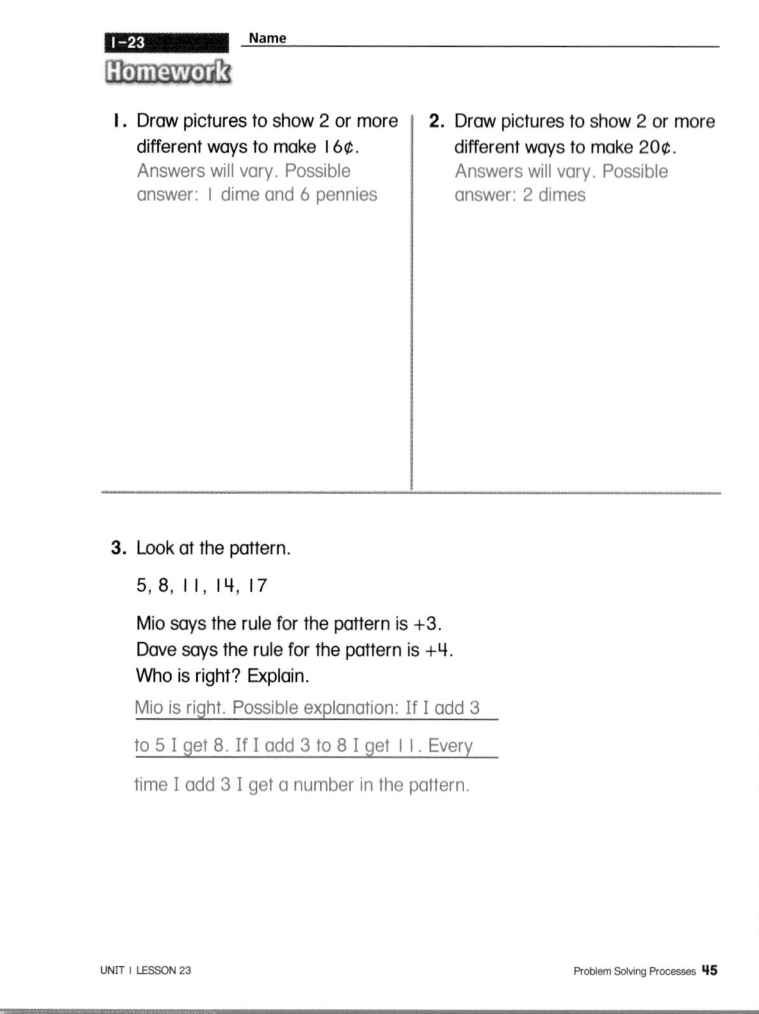

1-23 Homework Name

1. Draw pictures to show 2 or more different ways to make 16¢.
Answers will vary. Possible answer: 1 dime and 6 pennies

2. Draw pictures to show 2 or more different ways to make 20¢.
Answers will vary. Possible answer: 2 dimes

3. Look at the pattern.
5, 8, 11, 14, 17
Mio says the rule for the pattern is +3.
Dave says the rule for the pattern is +4.
Who is right? Explain.
Mio is right. Possible explanation: If I add 3 to 5 I get 8. If I add 3 to 8 I get 11. Every time I add 3 I get a number in the pattern.

UNIT 1 LESSON 23 Problem Solving Processes 45

Homework and Remembering page 45

Goal: Spiral Review

This Remembering page would be appropriate anytime after today's lesson.

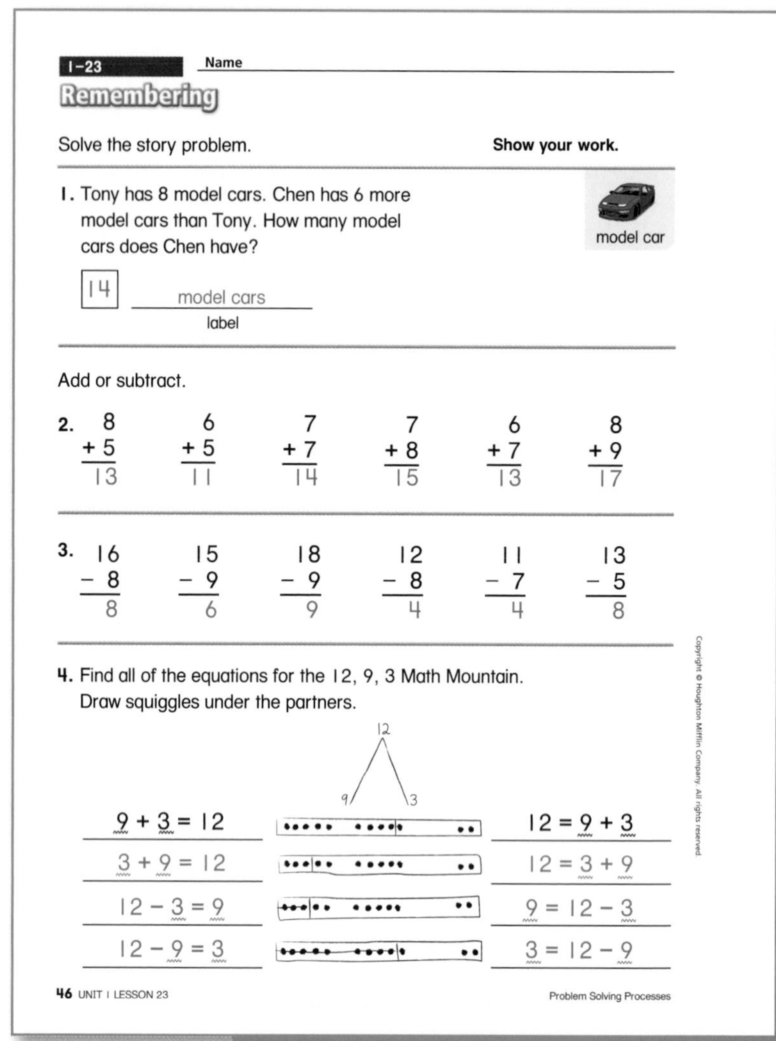

1-23 Remembering Name

Solve the story problem. **Show your work.**

1. Tony has 8 model cars. Chen has 6 more model cars than Tony. How many model cars does Chen have?
model car
14 model cars
label

Add or subtract.

2. 8 + 5 = 13; 6 + 5 = 11; 7 + 7 = 14; 7 + 8 = 15; 6 + 7 = 13; 8 + 9 = 17

3. 16 − 8 = 8; 15 − 9 = 6; 18 − 9 = 9; 12 − 8 = 4; 11 − 7 = 4; 13 − 5 = 8

4. Find all of the equations for the 12, 9, 3 Math Mountain. Draw squiggles under the partners.

9 + 3 = 12		12 = 9 + 3
3 + 9 = 12		12 = 3 + 9
12 − 3 = 9		9 = 12 − 3
12 − 9 = 3		3 = 12 − 9

46 UNIT 1 LESSON 23 Problem Solving Processes

Copyright © Houghton Mifflin Company. All rights reserved.

Homework and Remembering page 46

Home or School Activity

Real-World Connection

Thinking Games Ask children to play Sprouts at home with a parent or older relative. Have them ask the older person to tell them about thinking games they may have played when they were children. You might have children who learn about games share them with the class.

I see an Airplane, a Boat, a Cat, and a Dog.

Unit Review and Test

Lesson Objective

- **Assess children's progress on unit objectives.**

The Day at a Glance

Today's Goals	Materials
1 Assessing the Unit ▶ Assess children's progress on unit objectives. ▶ Use activities from unit lessons to reteach content. **2 Extending the Assessment** ▶ Use remediation for common errors. There is no homework assignment on a test day.	Unit 1 Test, Student Activity Book pages 71–72 Unit 1 Test, Form A or B, Assessment Guide (optional) Unit 1 Performance Assessment, Assessment Guide (optional)

Keeping Skills Sharp

Quick Practice — 5 MINUTES

Goal: Review any skills you choose to meet the needs of your children.

If you are doing a unit review day, use any of the Quick Practice activities that provide support for your students. If this is a test day, omit Quick Practice.

Review and Test Day You may want to choose a quiet game or other activity (reading a book or working on homework for another subject) for children who finish early.

1 Assessing the Unit

Assess Unit Objectives

 **45 MINUTES (more if schedule permits)**

Goal: Assess children's progress on unit objectives.

Materials: Student Activity Book pages 71–72; Assessment Guide (optional)

▶ Review and Assessment

If your children are ready for assessment on the unit objectives, you may use either the test on the Student Activity Book pages or one of the forms of the Unit 1 Test in the Assessment Guide to assess children's progress.

If you feel that children need some review first, you may use the test on the Student Activity Book pages as a review of unit content, and then use one of the forms of the Unit 1 Test in the Assessment Guide to assess children's progress.

To assign a numerical score for all of these test forms, use 5 points for each question.

You may also choose to use the Unit 1 Performance Assessment. Scoring for that assessment can be found in its rubric in the Assessment Guide.

▶ Reteaching Resources

The chart lists the test items, the unit objectives they cover, and the lesson activities in which the objective is covered in this unit. You may revisit these activities with children who do not show mastery of the objectives.

1-23 Name

▶ Math and Games

Rules for the Game of Sprouts

A. Draw dots on a sheet of paper.
B. Take turns. Each time draw a line between two dots and place a dot on that line.
C. A line can be straight or curved but cannot cross itself or another line.
D. No more than 3 lines can be drawn from one dot.
E. The last player to draw a line wins.

Play Sprouts with 2 dots.

1. Make a table like this one on another piece of paper. Keep a record of each round.

Round Number	How Many Turns?	Who Won: First Player or Second Player?

2. Did every game have the same number of turns?
In most cases children will not always have the same number of turns.
3. Who won each time?
If children play the game correctly the first player should win each time.

Play Sprouts with 3 dots. Record the turns in a table.

4. Did every game have the same number of turns?
In most cases children will not always have the same number of turns.
5. Who won each time?
If children play the game correctly the second player should win each time.
6. **Predict** What do you think will happen when you play the game with 4 dots. Answers will vary. Possible answer: I predict that the first player will always win.

UNIT 1 LESSON 23 69

Student Activity Book page 69

Unit Test Items	Unit Objectives Tested	Activities to Use for Reteaching
1–3	**1.1** Identify numbers embedded in a larger number.	Lesson 6, Activity 1 Lesson 8, Activity 2
4–7	**1.2** Add 1-digit numbers (sums ≤ 18).	Lesson 3, Activity 1 Lesson 11, Activity 2
8–11	**1.3** Identify an unknown addend (sums ≤ 18).	Lesson 10, Activity 1 Lesson 16, Activity 2
12–15	**1.4** Subtract 1-digit numbers from 18 or less.	Lesson 15, Activity 1

1 Unit Test

Name ____________

Write the total.

16. 6 + 3 + 4 = 13

Compare. Write < or >.

17. 10 (>) 7

Write the numbers in order from least to greatest.

18. 15 18 11   11 15 18

Ring the equation that matches the story problem.

19. Anwar bought 3 bananas. Lisa bought 8 bananas. How many bananas did Anwar and Lisa buy in all?

banana

(3 + 8 = ☐)   3 + ☐ = 8

20. **Extended Response** Make a drawing to solve this equation.

8 + 5 = 13

Check children's drawings.

*Item 20 also assesses the process skills of Representation and Reasoning.

Student Activity Book page 72

Unit Test Items	Unit Objectives Tested	Activities to Use for Reteaching
16	**1.5** Add three numbers.	Lesson 22, Activity 1
17–18	**1.6** Compare and order numbers.	Lesson 21, Activities 1–2
19–20	**1.7** Relate equations to story problems and to solution methods.	Lesson 1, Activity 2 Lesson 3, Activity 2 Lesson 20, Activity 1

▶ Assessment Resources

Free Response Tests

Unit 1 Test, Student Activity Book pages 69–70
Unit 1 Test, Form A, Assessment Guide

Extended Response Item

The last item in the Student Activity Book test and in the Form A test will require an extended response as an answer.

Multiple Choice Test

Unit 1 Test, Form B, Assessment Guide

Performance Assessment

Unit 1 Performance Assessment, Assessment Guide
Unit 1 Performance Assessment Rubric, Assessment Guide

▶ Portfolio Assessment

Teacher-selected Items for Student Portfolios:

- Homework, Lessons 2, 3, 9, 10, 14, and 19
- Class Activity work, Lessons 1, 6, 14, 17, 22, and 23

Student-selected Items for Student Portfolios:

- Favorite Home or School Activity
- Best Writing Prompt

2 Extending the Assessment

Common Errors

Activities for Remediation

Unit Objective 1.1

Identify numbers embedded in a larger number.

Common Error: Writes Incorrect Partners

The partners children write may not add to the given total.

Remediation Have children use cubes or fingers to model the addition, then count them to check that the numbers they added result in the correct total.

Unit Objective 1.2

Add 1-digit numbers (sums ≤ 18).

Common Error: Counts On from the Lesser Number

Some children may write incorrect totals when they begin counting on from the lesser number.

Remediation Remind children that it is easier to count on from the greater number.

Unit Objective 1.3

Identify an unknown addend (sums ≤ 18).

Common Error: Adds the Partner and the Total

Children may add the partner and the given total.

Remediation Remind children that the number they write for the unknown partner cannot be greater than the total.

Unit Objective 1.4

Subtract 1-digit numbers from 18 or less.

Common Error: Includes the Partner Number When Counting On to the Total

Children may include the given partner number when they count on to find how many more they need to reach the total.

Remediation Before beginning counting on from a partner, have them use a gesture (putting the partner on their shoulder or in a pocket) to emphasize the number that is "already counted," and to be sure they do not count it again.

Unit Objective 1.5

Add three numbers.

Common Error: Adds Only Two Addends

Children may only add two addends.

Remediation Remind children that they must add twice to find the sum of three numbers.

Have children check off the two addends they add first and write their sum next to or above the addends.

Unit Objective 1.6

Compare and order numbers.

Common Error: Confuses the Symbols $>$ and $<$

Children may use the wrong symbol to compare two numbers.

Remediation Provide children with cards that have pictures with the symbols as open mouths of animals. Tell children that the animal always eats the greater number. Have children use the symbol cards with number cards to compare.

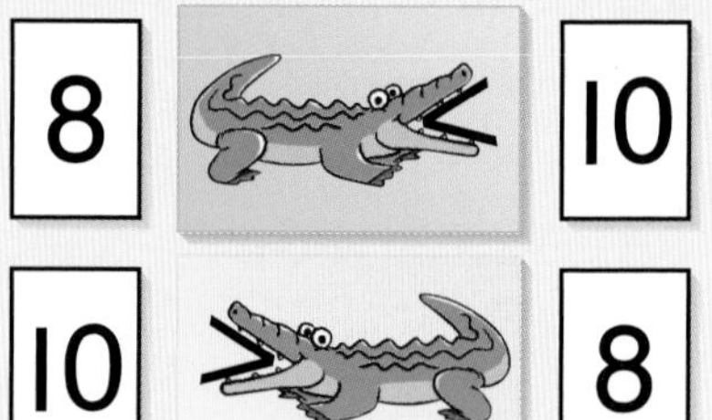

Unit Objective 1.7

Relate equations to story problems and to solution methods.

Common Error: Uses the Wrong Operation

Children may not understand when to add or subtract in a story problem.

Remediation Have children read or listen to the problem carefully and make a math drawing (Proof Drawing) to show the situation.

Unit 2 Overview

Measurement and Shapes

UNIT 2 BUILDS ON the conceptual understanding of linear measurement and properties of rectangles and triangles that children developed in previous grades. Children use rulers to measure and draw line segments and then apply their measuring skills to finding the perimeter of squares, rectangles, and triangles. In this unit, children also investigate the properties of squares, rectangles, and triangles and they are expected to draw these shapes using a ruler.

Skills Trace

Grade 1	Grade 2	Grade 3
• Measure and compare length to the nearest inch. • Relate shapes and numbers.	• Draw and measure line segments. • Draw squares, rectangles, and triangles. • Find perimeters of squares, rectangles, and triangles.	• Identify and classify quadrilaterals. • Use formulas for the area and perimeter of squares and rectangles.

Unit 2 Contents

Big Idea Linear Measurement of 2-D Shapes

Planning Unit 2

NCTM Standards Key: **1.** Number and Operations **2.** Algebra **3.** Geometry **4.** Measurement **5.** Data Analysis and Probability **6.** Problem Solving **7.** Reasoning and Proof **8.** Communication **9.** Connections **10.** Representation

Lesson/NCTM Standards	Resources	Materials for Lesson Activities	Materials for Going Further
2–1 **Use Rulers to Mark Centimeter Lengths** NCTM Standards: 4, 9, 10	TE pp. 165–172 SAB pp. 73–78 H&R pp. 47–48 AC 2–1 MCC 2–5	✓ 25-cm rulers or 25-cm Rulers (TRB M47–M48) ✓ Base-ten blocks MathBoard materials	✓ 25-cm rulers or 25-cm Rulers (TRB M47–M48) MathBoard materials Math Journals
2–2 **Observe and Draw Squares** NCTM Standards: 3, 4, 9	TE pp. 173–178 SAB pp. 79–82 H&R pp. 49–50 AC 2–2 MCC 2–6	MathBoard materials ✓ 25-cm rulers or 25-cm Rulers (TRB M47–M48)	MathBoard materials Geoboards and rubber bands Centimeter Dot Paper (TRB M49) Straw Scissors Math Journals
2–3 **Find Perimeters of Squares and Rectangles** NCTM Standards: 3, 4, 9, 10	TE pp. 179–184 SAB pp. 83–84 H&R pp. 51–52 AC 2–3 MCC 2–7	✓ 25-cm rulers or 25-cm Rulers (TRB M47–M48) MathBoard materials Digital camera (optional)	Centimeter Grid Paper (TRB M50) ✓ 25-cm rulers Math Journals
2–4 **Perimeters of Rectangles** NCTM Standards: 3, 4, 9	TE pp. 185–190 SAB pp. 85–86 H&R pp. 53–54 AC 2–4 MCC 2–8	✓ 25-cm rulers or 25-cm Rulers (TRB M47–M48) MathBoard materials Straws	*Racing Around,* by Stuart J. Murphy and Mike Reed Math Journals
✓ Unit Review and Test	TE pp. 191–194 SAB pp. 87–88 AG: Unit 2 tests		

Resources/Materials Key: TE: Teacher Edition SAB: Student Activity Book H&R: Homework and Remembering AC: Activity Cards MCC: Math Center Challenge AG: Assessment Guide ✓: Grade 2 kits TRB: Teacher's Resource Book

Manipulatives and Materials

- Essential materials for teaching *Math Expressions* are available in the Grade 2 kits. These materials are indicated by a ✓ in these lists. At the front of this Teacher Edition is more information about kit contents, alternatives for the materials, and use of the materials.

Unit 2 Assessment

Unit Objectives Tested	Unit Test Items	Lessons
2.1 Draw and measure line segments.	1, 2	1
2.2 Find partner lengths of line segments.	3	1
2.3 Learn properties of squares, rectangles, and triangles.	10	2
2.4 Draw squares, rectangles, and triangles.	4–6	2
2.5 Find perimeters of squares, rectangles, and triangles.	7–9	3, 4

Assessment and Review Resources

Formal Assessment

Student Activity Book

- Unit Review and Test (pp. 87–88)

Assessment Guide

- Test A-Open Response (pp. A14–A15)
- Test B-Multiple Choice (pp. A16–A18)
- Performance Assessment (pp. A19–A21)

Test Generator CD-ROM

- Open Response Test
- Multiple Choice Test
- Test Bank Items

Informal Assessment

Teacher Edition

- Ongoing Assessment (in every lesson)
- Quick Practice (in every lesson)
- Portfolio Suggestions (p. 193)

Math Talk

- In Activities (pp. 166, 169, 170, 182)

Review Opportunities

Homework and Remembering

- Review of recently taught topics
- Cumulative Review

Teacher Edition

- Unit Review and Test (pp. 191–194)

Test Generator CD-ROM

- Custom Review Sheets

Unit 2 Teaching Resources

Differentiated Instruction

Individualizing Instruction		
	Level	Frequency
Activities	• Intervention • On Level • Challenge	All 3 in every lesson
	Level	Frequency
Math Writing Prompts	• Intervention • On Level • Challenge	All 3 in every lesson
Math Center Challenges	For advanced students	
	4 in every unit	

Reaching All Learners		
English Language Learners	Lessons	Pages
	1, 2, 3, 4	165, 173, 179, 181, 185

Strategies for English Language Learners

Present this activity to all children. Offer different levels of support to meet children's levels of language proficiency.

Objective Familiarize children with the terms *measure, long,* and *length*.

Activity Line equal sized blocks along the length of a table and board. Hold up 1 block. Say: **1 block is 1 unit.**

Newcomer

- Gesture with your hands to show *long*. Say: **The table is *long*.**
- **Let's count the units.** Have children count. Say: **The table is ___ units *long*.**

Beginning

- Point to the table. Say: **Let's *measure* the table. *Measure* means count the units.**
- Have children count. Say: **The table is ___ units *long*.** Have children repeat. Continue with the board.

Intermediate

- Gesture as you say: **The table is *long*. The board is *long*. We *measure* to know exactly how *long*. *Measure* means count the units.**
- Have children count the blocks. Ask: **How *long* is the table? The board?**

Advanced

- Say: **We count units to *measure* how *long* things are.** Ask: **How *long* is the table? The board?**
- Say: ***Length* is how *long* something is.** Ask: **What is the *length* of the table? The board?**

Connections

Art Connection
Lesson 3, page 184

Social Studies Connection
Lesson 2, page 178

Literature Connection
Lesson 4, page 190

Independent Learning Activities

Ready-Made Math Challenge Centers

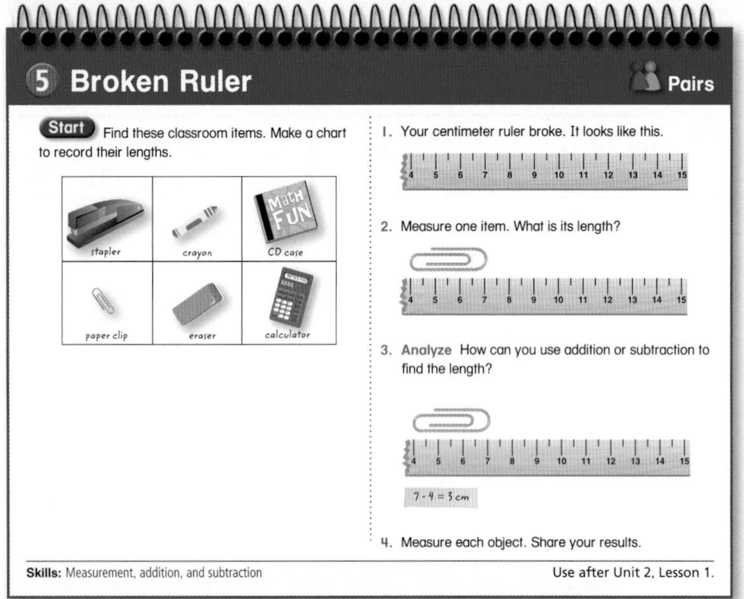

5 Broken Ruler — Pairs

Start Find these classroom items. Make a chart to record their lengths.

1. Your centimeter ruler broke. It looks like this.
2. Measure one item. What is its length?
3. **Analyze** How can you use addition or subtraction to find the length?
   7 - 4 = 3 cm
4. Measure each object. Share your results.

Skills: Measurement, addition, and subtraction — Use after Unit 2, Lesson 1.

Grouping Pairs

Objective Children measure classroom objects using a centimeter ruler that starts on 4 and not 0; they use computation to figure out each measurement.

Materials Stapler, crayon, CD case, paper clip, eraser, calculator, centimeter ruler, paper and pencil

Connections Computation and Measurement

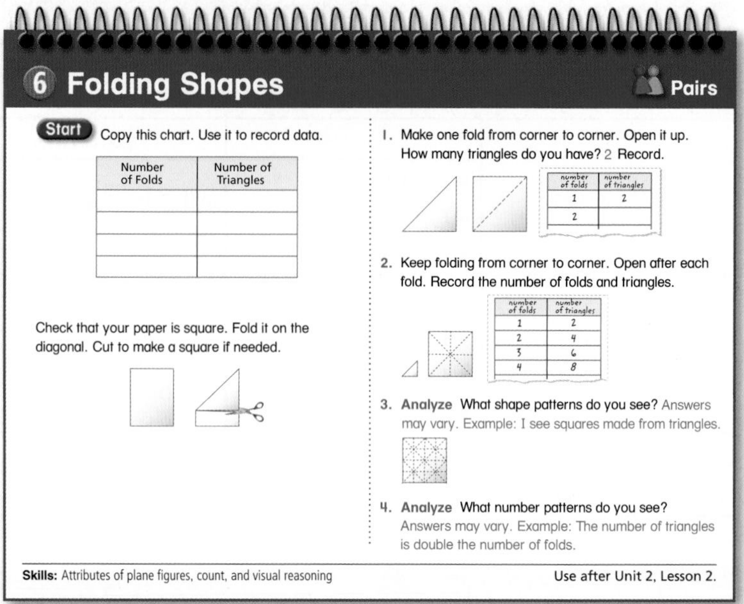

6 Folding Shapes — Pairs

Start Copy this chart. Use it to record data.

Number of Folds	Number of Triangles

Check that your paper is square. Fold it on the diagonal. Cut to make a square if needed.

1. Make one fold from corner to corner. Open it up. How many triangles do you have? 2 Record.

number of folds	number of triangles
1	2
2	

2. Keep folding from corner to corner. Open after each fold. Record the number of folds and triangles.

number of folds	number of triangles
1	2
2	4
3	6
4	8

3. **Analyze** What shape patterns do you see? Answers may vary. Example: I see squares made from triangles.
4. **Analyze** What number patterns do you see? Answers may vary. Example: The number of triangles is double the number of folds.

Skills: Attributes of plane figures, count, and visual reasoning — Use after Unit 2, Lesson 2.

Grouping Pairs

Objective Children fold a square piece of paper over and over to create triangles, and they identify number and shape patterns.

Materials Scissors

Connections Geometry and Algebra

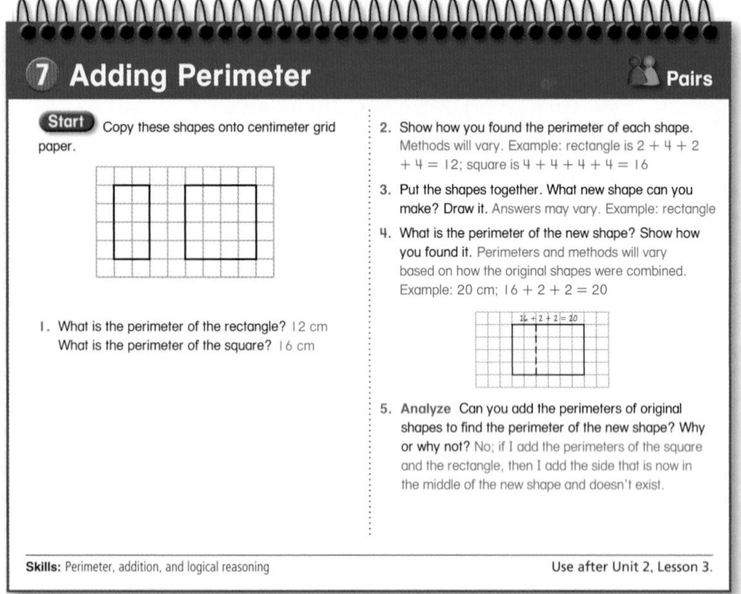

7 Adding Perimeter — Pairs

Start Copy these shapes onto centimeter grid paper.

1. What is the perimeter of the rectangle? 12 cm
   What is the perimeter of the square? 16 cm
2. Show how you found the perimeter of each shape. Methods will vary. Example: rectangle is 2 + 4 + 2 + 4 = 12; square is 4 + 4 + 4 + 4 = 16
3. Put the shapes together. What new shape can you make? Draw it. Answers may vary. Example: rectangle
4. What is the perimeter of the new shape? Show how you found it. Perimeters and methods will vary based on how the original shapes were combined. Example: 20 cm; 16 + 2 + 2 = 20
5. **Analyze** Can you add the perimeters of original shapes to find the perimeter of the new shape? Why or why not? No; if I add the perimeters of the square and the rectangle, then I add the side that is now in the middle of the new shape and doesn't exist.

Skills: Perimeter, addition, and logical reasoning — Use after Unit 2, Lesson 3.

Grouping Pairs

Objective Children find the perimeter of a square and a rectangle; they combine the figures to create a new figure and find the perimeter of the new figure.

Materials Centimeter Grid Paper (TRB M50), crayons or markers

Connections Representation and Geometry

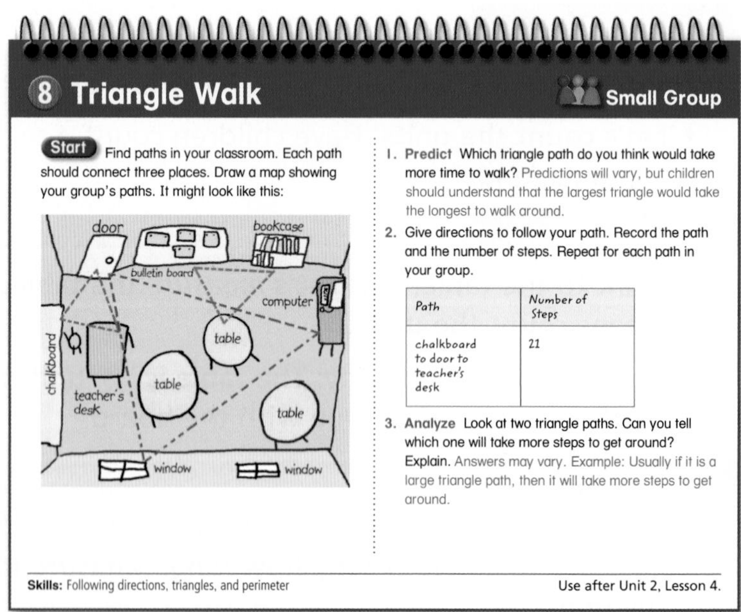

8 Triangle Walk — Small Group

Start Find paths in your classroom. Each path should connect three places. Draw a map showing your group's paths. It might look like this:

1. **Predict** Which triangle path do you think would take more time to walk? Predictions will vary, but children should understand that the largest triangle would take the longest to walk around.
2. Give directions to follow your path. Record the path and the number of steps. Repeat for each path in your group.

Path	Number of Steps
chalkboard to door to teacher's desk	21

3. **Analyze** Look at two triangle paths. Can you tell which one will take more steps to get around? Explain. Answers may vary. Example: Usually if it is a large triangle path, then it will take more steps to get around.

Skills: Following directions, triangles, and perimeter — Use after Unit 2, Lesson 4.

Grouping Small Group

Objective Children create and draw maps of triangular classroom paths, walk the paths to find the perimeters, and then compare length of the paths.

Materials Markers or crayons

Connections Social Studies and Real World

Ready-Made Math Resources

Technology — Tutorials, Practice, and Intervention

Use activity masters and online, individualized intervention and support to bring students to proficiency.

Help students practice skills and apply concepts through exciting math adventures.

Extend and enrich students' understanding of skills and concepts through engaging, interactive lessons and activities.

Visit **Education Place**®
www.eduplace.com

Visit www.eduplace.com/mx2t/ and find family, teacher, and student materials, activities, games, and more.

Literature Links

Keep Your Distance

Keep Your Distance

How far is not far enough when it comes to separating two rivaling sisters? Find out in Gail Herman's fascinating book on measurement.

Literature Connections

- *Racing Around,* by Stuart J. Reed, illustrated by Chuck Murphy (HarperTrophy, 2001)

Math Background

Putting Research into Practice for Unit 2

From Current Research:
The Importance of Measurement Instruction

Measurement is one of the most widely used applications of mathematics. It bridges two main areas of school mathematics—geometry and number. Measurement activities can simultaneously teach important everyday skills, strengthen students' knowledge of other important topics in mathematics, and develop measurement concepts and processes that will be formalized and expanded in later years.

Teaching that builds on students' intuitive understandings and informal measurement experiences helps them understand the attributes to be measured as well as what it means to measure. A foundation in measurement concepts that enables students to use measurement systems, tools, and techniques should be established through direct experiences with comparing objects, counting units, and making connections between spatial concepts and number.

National Council of Teachers of Mathematics. *Principles and Standards for School Mathematics.* Reston: NCTM, 2000. 103.

Between kindergarten and eighth grade, students must learn the attributes that they will be measuring (length, weight, capacity, and so on); what it means to measure, including an understanding of units of measure and how unit size affects measures; the selection and use of measurement instruments; systems of measurement (metric and customary); and formulas that can be used for determining measurements. Measurement is far more complex than we often realize.

Van de Walle, John A. "Developing Measurement Concepts." *Elementary and Middle School Mathematics: Teaching Developmentally.* 4th ed. New York: Addison, 2001. 277.

Other Useful References: Measurement, 2-D Shapes, Perimeter

Batista, Michael T. "Learning Geometry in a Dynamic Computer Environment." *Teaching Children Mathematics.* 8.6 (Feb. 2002): 333.

National Council of Teachers of Mathematics. *Principles and Standards for School Mathematics* (Number and Operations Standard for Grades 3–5). Reston: NCTM, 2000. 97, 103–105.

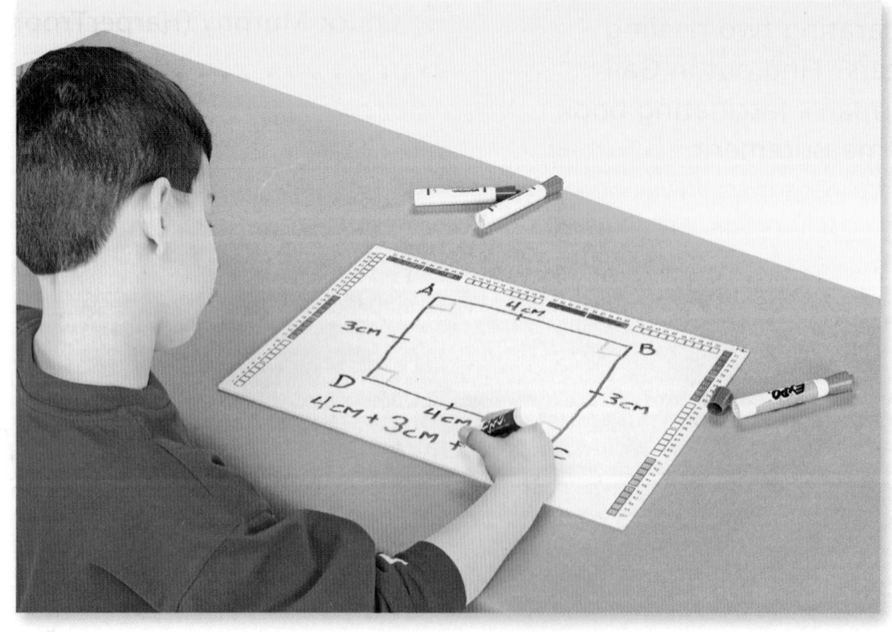

Math Expressions Vocabulary

As you teach this unit, emphasize understanding of these terms:

- partner lengths

See Glossary on pp. T7–T20.

Getting Ready to Teach Unit 2

In this unit, children build concepts and skills for linear measurement together, refine and extend their understanding of two-dimensional shapes, and develop informal ways of calculating perimeter of squares, rectangles, and triangles.

Linear Measurement

Lessons 1, 2, 3, and 4

Children will recreate rulers by drawing multiple copies of the same unit (1 cm) to form a line divided into 1-cm lengths. They will also divide and mark lines into 1-cm lengths and count the units to find the linear measure of the lines. These experiences will help children develop the basic idea of linear measurement as counting the number of times a standard unit fits along a length. Children will then move to using rulers where they will learn to accurately align the ruler, start counting units beginning at zero, and focus on the number of 1-cm units along the length rather than only reading the numbers on the ruler. The emphasis on measuring by counting repeating units rather than reading numbers occurs in subsequent geometry units in this program. This conceptual focus enables children to be flexible problem solvers and to understand length as being made of units.

Attributes of Shapes

Lessons 2, 3, and 4

Children will see that squares and rectangles have "square corners" and that squares are a special type of rectangle with four sides equal in length. Children will also explore triangles, drawing many examples and identifying that they have a range of side lengths and angle sizes. Children will use their own vocabulary to describe these two-dimensional shapes but will be encouraged to gradually use conventional terminology.

Perimeter

Lessons 3 and 4

For squares, class discussion will lead children to realize they only need to measure the length of one side to find the perimeter. For rectangles, children will be asked to share the various methods they developed for finding the perimeter. At this grade level, children are only expected to know that perimeter of a rectangle or a triangle is the sum of the side lengths; formulas will be introduced in subsequent years.

Rounding

Lesson 4

While finding perimeter, the concept of rounding is introduced. Children will learn to round their measures to the nearest number on their rulers.

Rulers, Lengths, and Partner Lengths

Vocabulary

length
centimeter
line segment
horizontal
vertical
partner lengths

Lesson Objectives

- Measure line segments by counting centimeter lengths.
- Break apart centimeter lengths into partner lengths.
- Measure line segments by reading numbers on a ruler.

The Day at a Glance

Today's Goals	Materials	
1 Teaching the Lesson **A1:** Explore rulers and measure line segments by marking and counting centimeter lengths. **A2:** Break apart centimeter lengths into partner lengths. **A3:** Measure line segments by reading centimeter marks and numbers on a ruler.	**Lesson Activities** Student Activity Book pp. 73–78 (includes Family Letter) Homework and Remembering pp. 47–48 25-cm rulers or 25-cm Rulers (TRB M47–M48) Base ten blocks MathBoard materials	**Going Further** Activity Cards 2-1 25-cm rulers or 25-cm Rulers (TRB M47–M48) MathBoard materials Math Journals
2 Going Further ▸ Differentiated Instruction		
3 Homework		

123 Use **Math Talk** today!

Keeping Skills Sharp

Daily Routines	English Language Learners
Money Routine: Using the 120 Poster, Using the Money Flip Chart, Using the Number Path, Using Secret Code Cards (See pp. xxiii–xxv.) ▸ Led by Student Leaders	Introduce *measure, length* and *centimeter* by describing the length of small objects in the classroom. Model 1 cm on a ruler. Hold up an eraser. • **Beginning** Say: **I want to know how long the eraser is. I can *measure* it with my ruler.** Model how to use the ruler to measure the eraser. Say: **The eraser is __ *centimeters* long. The *length* is __ *centimeters*.** Have children repeat. • **Intermediate** Say: **Let's *measure* the *length* of the eraser. *Length* is how long something is.** Model how to find the length in centimeters. Have children work in pairs to find the length of their pencils and other small objects. • **Advanced** Ask: **Is a *centimeter* big or small?** small Say: **We *measure* the *length* of small things in *centimeters*.** Have children brainstorm a few small things to measure then work in pairs to find the lengths in centimeters.

1 Teaching the Lesson

Activity 1

Use Rulers to Mark Centimeter Lengths

 **20 MINUTES**

Goal: Explore rulers and measure line segments by marking and counting centimeter lengths.

Materials: 25-cm rulers or 25-cm Rulers (TRB M47–M48), printed on card stock; Student Activity Book pages 73–74, base ten blocks

 **NCTM Standards:**
Measurement
Connections

▶ Explore Rulers WHOLE CLASS

Distribute two 25-cm rulers from TRB M47–M48, printed on card stock, to each child. If you have access to the *Math Expressions* materials kits, the 25-cm rulers are included, so you will not have to prepare these materials. Explain to children that they will keep one ruler at school to use for classroom math activities and the other ruler at home to use for homework. Throughout the year, provide children with new rulers as necessary.

Math Talk Hold up a ruler and ask children to describe it. Possible answers: It has straight edges; it has marks and numbers.

- What do people use rulers for? People use rulers to measure, to draw straight lines, and to draw lines of specific lengths.
- What else have you seen or used that looks like a ruler? Possible answers: inch ruler, yardstick, meter stick, measuring tape

Draw a 21-cm line segment on the board.

- If I measure this line with my pencil and tell you that it is two pencils long, will you know the length of the line in centimeters? No; we don't know the exact length of your pencil.

Invite children to compare the marks on their rulers with a classmate.

- Are the marks on your ruler the same as the marks on your classmate's ruler? yes
- If two children measure the same line with their rulers, will they find the same measurement? yes

Explain to the class that the lengths between the lines on their rulers are called *centimeters.*

Point out that centimeters are always the same length. If you measure the length of an object in centimeters, you can tell a friend the measurement and your friend will know the exact length of the object.

Inform children that some rulers have inches, some rulers have centimeters, and some rulers have both inches and centimeters.

▶ Count Centimeter Lengths WHOLE CLASS

Refer children to the 1-cm line segment on Student Activity Book page 73. Tell them that the "short way" to write centimeters is cm.

Next, to introduce the idea of marking line segments with 1-cm lengths, discuss how you can make a 6-cm line segment by pushing together six 1-cm line segments.

Hold up a copy of the Student Activity Book page. Demonstrate how to measure the marked 6-cm line segment by counting the 1-cm line segments.

You may wish to draw a 22-cm line segment on the board and demonstrate how to mark 1-cm lengths. Include marks on each end of the line segment. Measure the line segment by counting aloud the 1-cm lengths.

Ask children to complete exercises 1–3 on their own in order to practice measuring line segments by counting 1-cm lengths.

Teaching Note

Watch For! Some children may count the centimeter marks instead of the 1-cm lengths. For instance, a 6-cm line segment has seven marks, so children may say that the line segment is 7 cm long. Emphasize that they should count the centimeter lengths or spaces between the marks rather than the marks themselves.

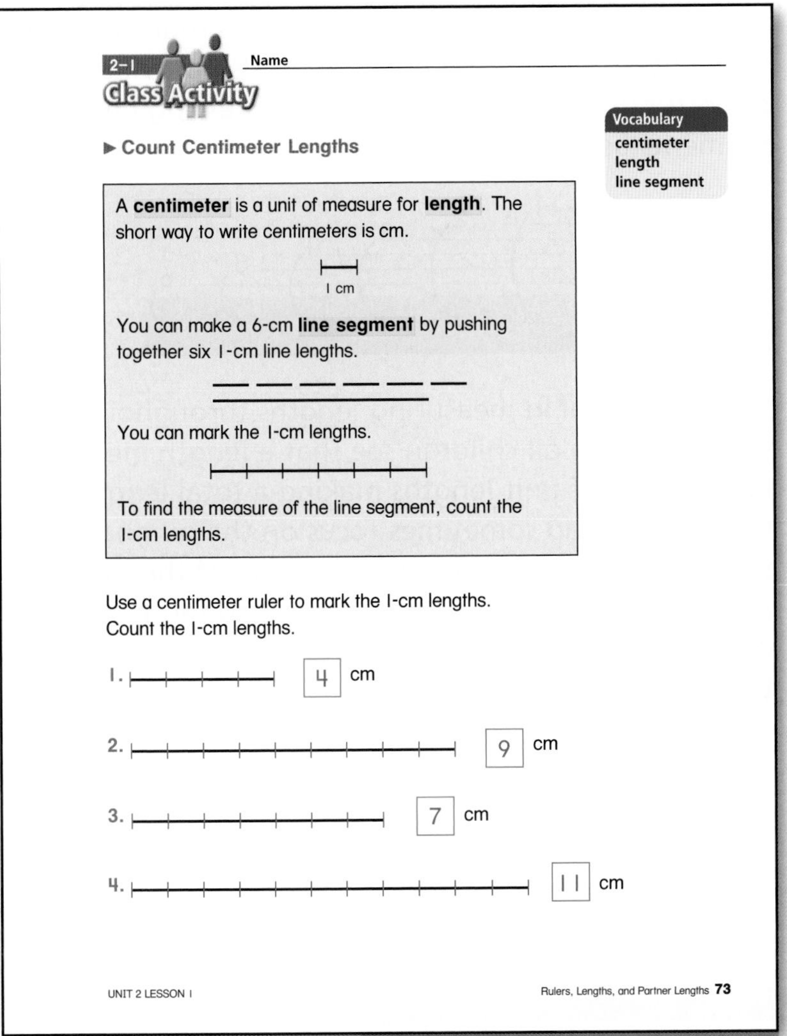

2-1 Class Activity

Name

▶ Count Centimeter Lengths

Vocabulary
centimeter
length
line segment

A **centimeter** is a unit of measure for **length**. The short way to write centimeters is cm.

1 cm

You can make a 6-cm **line segment** by pushing together six 1-cm line lengths.

You can mark the 1-cm lengths.

To find the measure of the line segment, count the 1-cm lengths.

Use a centimeter ruler to mark the 1-cm lengths. Count the 1-cm lengths.

1. 4 cm

2. 9 cm

3. 7 cm

4. 11 cm

UNIT 2 LESSON 1 Rulers, Lengths, and Partner Lengths 73

Student Activity Book page 73

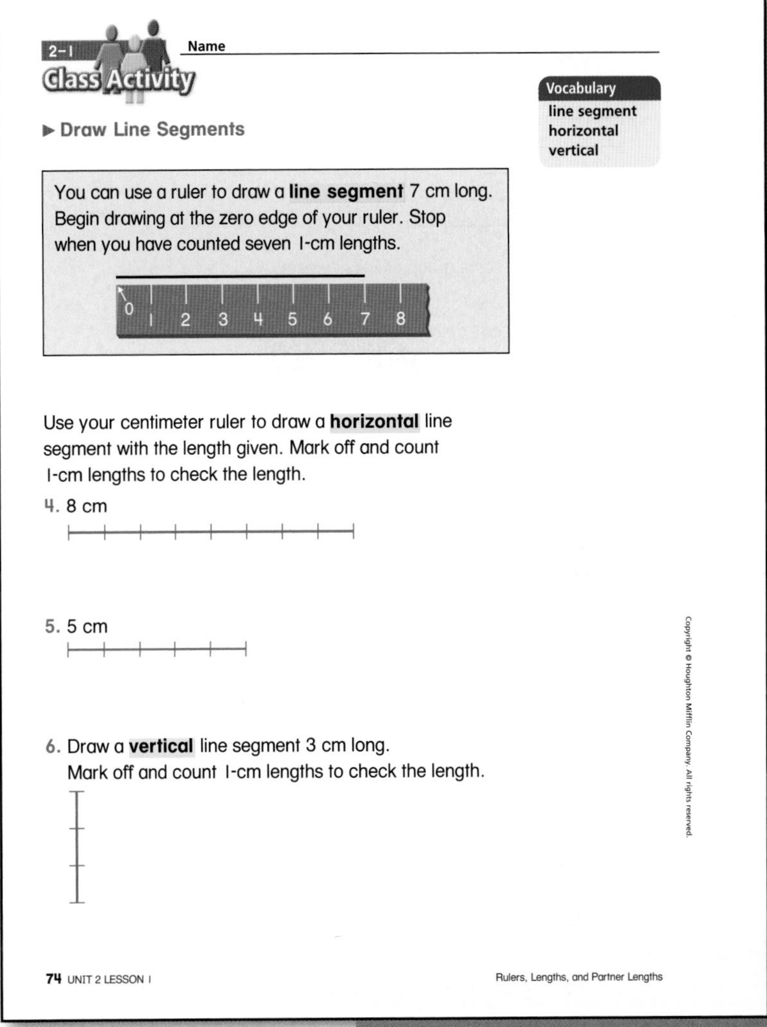

2-1 Class Activity

Name

▶ Draw Line Segments

Vocabulary
line segment
horizontal
vertical

You can use a ruler to draw a **line segment** 7 cm long. Begin drawing at the zero edge of your ruler. Stop when you have counted seven 1-cm lengths.

0 1 2 3 4 5 6 7 8

Use your centimeter ruler to draw a **horizontal** line segment with the length given. Mark off and count 1-cm lengths to check the length.

4. 8 cm

5. 5 cm

6. Draw a **vertical** line segment 3 cm long. Mark off and count 1-cm lengths to check the length.

74 UNIT 2 LESSON 1 Rulers, Lengths, and Partner Lengths

Student Activity Book page 74

Alternate Approach

Base Ten Blocks Children can use a ten to measure line segments. Explain that each unit cube is 1 cm long and 1 cm wide. The whole rod is 10 cm long. They can count centimeters by counting the number of unit cubes that make up the length of the line segment.

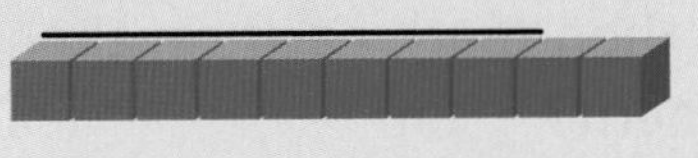

▶ Draw Line Segments INDIVIDUALS

Read aloud the explanation of how to draw a line segment using a ruler at the top of Student Activity Book page 74.

Refer children to exercises 4–6 for practice in drawing horizontal and vertical line segments. The children will mark the centimeters on their line segments and count the centimeters to check the length.

Activity continued ▶

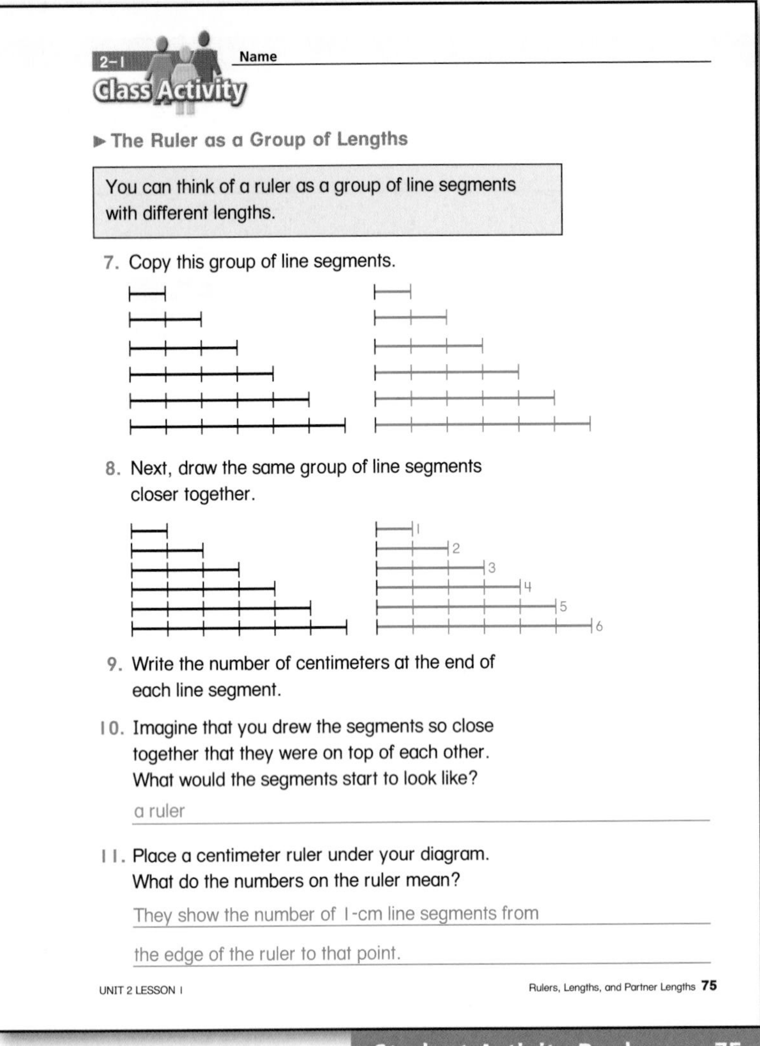

2-1 Class Activity Name

▶ The Ruler as a Group of Lengths

You can think of a ruler as a group of line segments with different lengths.

7. Copy this group of line segments.

8. Next, draw the same group of line segments closer together.

9. Write the number of centimeters at the end of each line segment.

10. Imagine that you drew the segments so close together that they were on top of each other. What would the segments start to look like?

a ruler

11. Place a centimeter ruler under your diagram. What do the numbers on the ruler mean?

They show the number of 1-cm line segments from the edge of the ruler to that point.

UNIT 2 LESSON 1 Rulers, Lengths, and Partner Lengths 75

Student Activity Book page 75

▶ The Ruler as a Group of Lengths

INDIVIDUALS

Work with children as they go through exercises 7–11 on Student Activity Book page 75. These exercises help children see that the numbers on rulers represent line segments of different lengths; they also provide an opportunity for children to practice drawing line segments using their rulers.

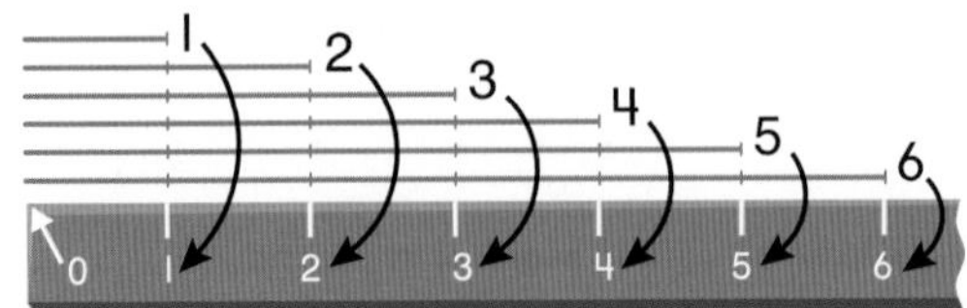

The major goal in measuring lengths throughout this year is helping all children see that a length measure is the number of unit lengths making a total length. Children instead sometimes focus on the number and think of that point instead of thinking of the number as telling the number of unit lengths so far. Numbers on number lines, ruler scales, and bar graph scales all tell the total length so far.

Activity 2

Draw Partner Lengths with Centimeter Rulers

 **20 MINUTES**

Goal: Break apart centimeter lengths into partner lengths.

Materials: Student Activity Book page 76, 25-cm rulers or 25-cm Rulers (TRB M47–M48) (1 ruler per child)

 **NCTM Standards:**

Measurement
Connections

▶ Explore Partner Lengths

WHOLE CLASS

Have each child turn to Student Activity Book page 76.

Guide children through the steps involved in finding the partner lengths of a 6-cm line segment.

- Look at the first line segment. Make a mark on the left end and then mark each centimeter. How long is the line segment? 6 cm
- Above the line segment, write the length: 6 cm.
- Now make the centimeter marks on the other two line segments. Label the length of each line segment.

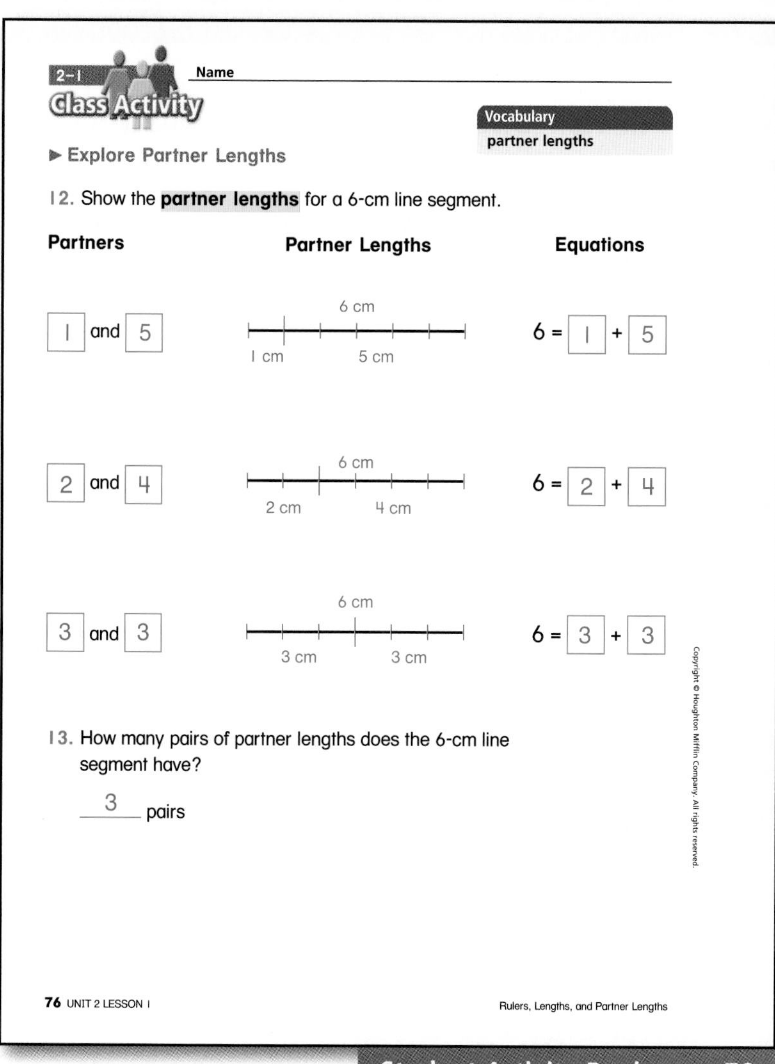

2-1 Class Activity

Name ______________________

Vocabulary
partner lengths

▶ Explore Partner Lengths

12. Show the **partner lengths** for a 6-cm line segment.

Partners	Partner Lengths	Equations
1 and 5	6 cm: 1 cm, 5 cm	6 = 1 + 5
2 and 4	6 cm: 2 cm, 4 cm	6 = 2 + 4
3 and 3	6 cm: 3 cm, 3 cm	6 = 3 + 3

13. How many pairs of partner lengths does the 6-cm line segment have?

3 pairs

76 UNIT 2 LESSON 1 Rulers, Lengths, and Partner Lengths

Student Activity Book page 76

- We will break apart each of these three line segments into partner lengths. What are some partners of 6? Use one of children's suggestions, for example, 1 and 5.
- Break apart the line segment into two parts: 1 cm and 5 cm. To do this, lengthen the mark at the end of the first centimeter. Label the 1-cm and 5-cm lengths below the line segment.
- Write the partners (1 and 5) and the equation (6 = 1 + 5).
- Now break apart the other two line segments to show other partners of 6. What are the other partners? 2 and 4, 3 and 3 Label the partner lengths.
- Write the partners and the equations for these two line segments.

Be sure children understand that they do not need to show 5 cm and 1 cm if they show 1 cm and 5 cm.

Ongoing Assessment

Ask children to draw all of the partner lengths for an 8-cm line segment. Remind them to include partners and equations with their partner lengths. Observe children as they work.

Activity 3

Measure Line Segments with a Ruler

20 MINUTES

Goal: Measure line segments by reading centimeter marks and numbers on a ruler.

Materials: 25-cm rulers or 25-cm Rulers (TRB M47–M48) (1 ruler per child), MathBoard materials

NCTM Standards:
Measurement
Representation

▶ Centimeter Marks and Centimeter Lengths WHOLE CLASS

Math Talk Lead a discussion with children on the relationship between marks and lengths on the ruler.

- Look closely at your ruler. What are the marks for? Possible response: They mark the beginning and end of a centimeter.
- Point to the 2 and 3 on your rulers. What do those numbers tell us? They tell us how many small centimeter lengths there are from the edge of the ruler to the mark.

Activity continued ▶

Draw Line Segments Draw four line segments on the board (4 cm, 7 cm, 11 cm, and 16 cm) and mark each 1-cm length. Your drawings can be freehand and larger so children can see how to count and draw them. Have children draw the line segments on their MathBoards, but make sure they use a ruler for their drawings.

Discuss Patterns While children continue drawing their line segments, set up this chart on the board.

Centimeters	Marks	1-cm Lengths
4		
7		
11		
16		

After children have finished, point to the 4-cm line segment and lead a discussion that will help children see the patterns between centimeter marks and lengths.

1 cm 1 cm 1 cm 1 cm

- How many marks are there altogether on a 4-cm line segment? 5, counting the edge
- How many 1-cm lengths are there on a 4-cm line segment? 4

Fill in the chart with the children's answers for the 4-cm line segment and have them try to find a pattern. Continue with as many examples until the pattern becomes clear. Fill in the rest of the chart.

Centimeters	Marks	1-cm Lengths
4	5	4
7	8	7
11	12	11
16	17	16

- Does anyone see a pattern? When you count the edge, the marks are one more than the number of 1-cm lengths. The number of 1-cm lengths is the same as the number of centimeters.
- When you measure a line segment, what do you have to count to know how long the line segment is? You have to count the spaces between the marks, not the marks.

Math Talk Discuss labeling a ruler with your class.

- Point to the zero edge on your ruler. How many centimeters are there? Zero; that is the beginning. There are no lengths yet.
- Point to the 1 on your ruler. How many centimeters are there now? 1 How do you know? The length between the zero edge and the 1 is 1 cm.
- How many marks are there? 2, counting the edge.
- Is this like the pattern in the chart? Yes; it's exactly the same pattern.

Explain to children that when you label rulers, you make the centimeter marks and then print the numbers that show how many centimeters there are. That is why some rulers don't show zero. Have children look at their rulers.

- How many marks are up to 1? 2, counting the edge
- What is the last number on your ruler? 25 How many lines are up to 25? 26, counting the edge

▶ Lengths between Numbers (Optional) WHOLE CLASS

Have children point to the 5-cm mark on their rulers with one finger.

- What does the 5 on your ruler tell you? There are five 1-cm lengths from the edge to the 5.

Have children point to the 9-cm mark on their rulers with another finger.

- What does the 9 on your ruler tell you? There are nine 1-cm lengths from the edge to the 9.
- How many centimeters are between the two marks? 4 cm How do you know? Possible responses: I counted four spaces or lengths between 5 and 9; I counted on from the 5 to the 9.

Class Management

Looking Ahead Children will be using these rulers throughout this unit, so have them readily available and stored in a safe place.

2 Going Further

Differentiated Instruction

Intervention — Activity Card 2-I

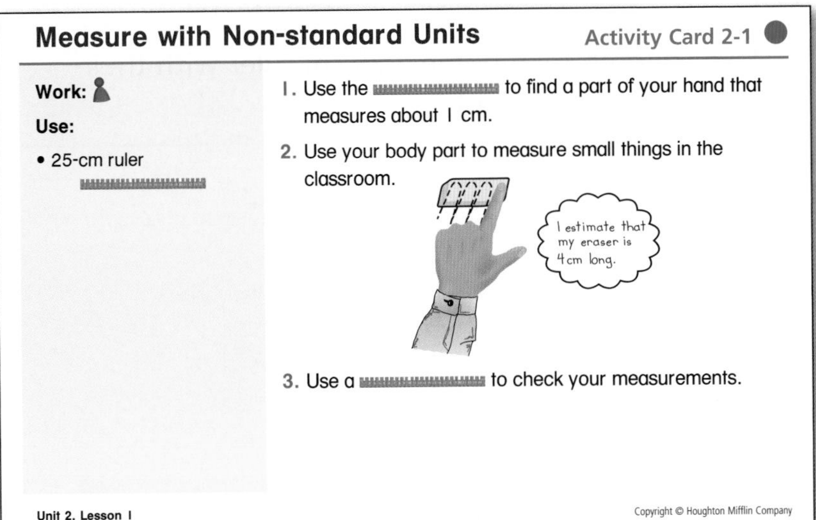

Measure with Non-standard Units — Activity Card 2-1 ●

Work: (individual)
Use:
- 25-cm ruler

1. Use the ____ to find a part of your hand that measures about 1 cm.
2. Use your body part to measure small things in the classroom.

I estimate that my eraser is 4 cm long.

3. Use a ____ to check your measurements.

Unit 2, Lesson 1 — Copyright © Houghton Mifflin Company

Activity Note Each child needs a 25-cm ruler or TRB M47–M48. Children find a part of their hand that measures about 1 cm.

Math Writing Prompt

You Decide Carlos places the 1-cm mark of a ruler at the beginning of a line segment. He then reads the number on the ruler at the end of the line segment. Will his measurement be correct? Explain.

Software Support

Use *Soar to Success* for instruction of students needing targeted support for underlying skills.

On Level — Activity Card 2-I

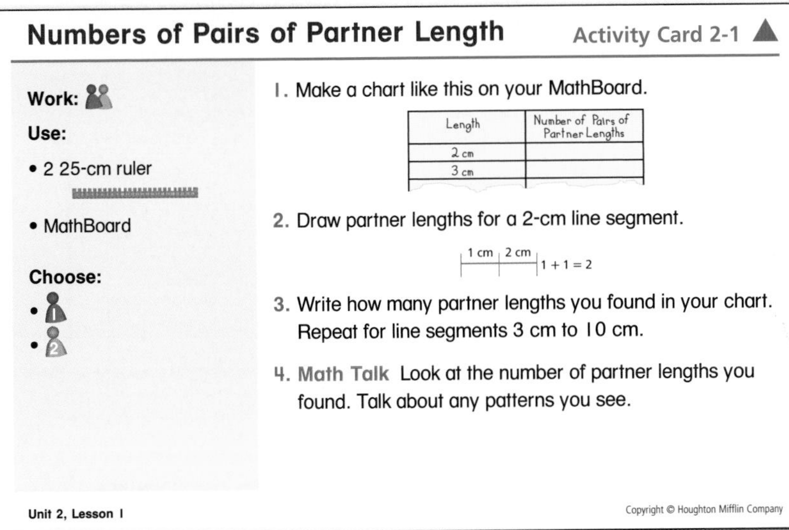

Numbers of Pairs of Partner Length — Activity Card 2-1 ▲

Work: (pairs)
Use:
- 2 25-cm ruler
- MathBoard

Choose: (1) (2)

1. Make a chart like this on your MathBoard.

Length	Number of Pairs of Partner Lengths
2 cm	
3 cm	

2. Draw partner lengths for a 2-cm line segment.

3. Write how many partner lengths you found in your chart. Repeat for line segments 3 cm to 10 cm.
4. **Math Talk** Look at the number of partner lengths you found. Talk about any patterns you see.

Unit 2, Lesson 1 — Copyright © Houghton Mifflin Company

Activity Note Each child needs a 25-cm ruler or TRB M47–M48 and MathBoard materials. Check that children create their charts.

Math Writing Prompt

Work Backward Break apart a line segment into partner lengths of 1 cm and 5 cm. What is the length of the line segment? Show a drawing and an equation in your answer.

Software Support

Use *MegaMath* for review and reinforcement of the concepts and skills presented in this lesson.

Challenge — Activity Card 2-I

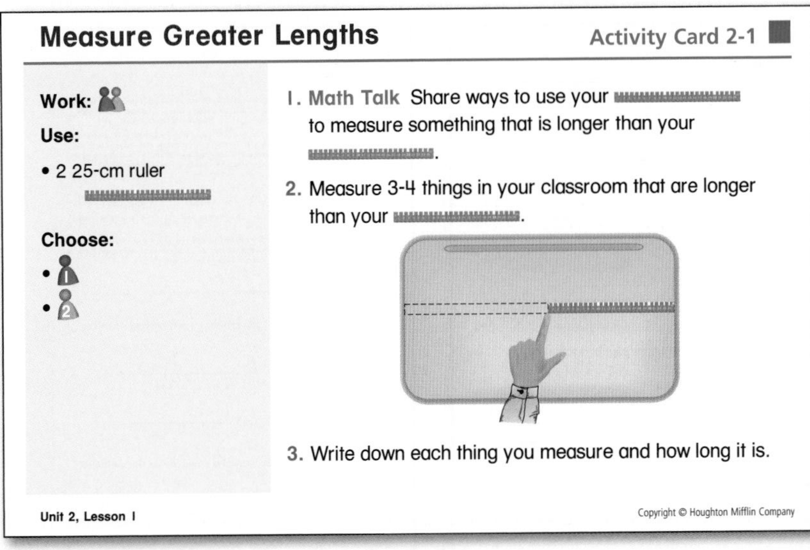

Measure Greater Lengths — Activity Card 2-1 ■

Work: (pairs)
Use:
- 2 25-cm ruler

Choose: (1) (2)

1. **Math Talk** Share ways to use your ____ to measure something that is longer than your ____.
2. Measure 3-4 things in your classroom that are longer than your ____.
3. Write down each thing you measure and how long it is.

Unit 2, Lesson 1 — Copyright © Houghton Mifflin Company

Activity Note Each child needs a 25-cm ruler or TRB M47–M48. Have children measure objects between 25 cm and 100 cm in length.

Math Writing Prompt

Explain How can you measure your height in centimeters using a 25-cm ruler?

DESTINATION Math® **Software Support**

Use *Destination Math* to take students beyond the concepts and skills presented in this lesson.

3 Homework

2-1 Homework **Goal:** Additional Practice

On this Homework page, children use their centimeter rulers to draw and measure line segments.

Have children take home a 25-cm ruler with their homework assignment.

2-1 Homework Name

1. Measure the horizontal line segment below by marking and counting 1-cm lengths.

6 cm

2. Draw a line segment 8 cm long. Mark and count 1-cm lengths to check the length.

Use your centimeter ruler to measure each vertical line segment.

3. 3 cm **4.** 5 cm **5.** 2 cm

6. On the Back Draw a 7-cm line segment. Draw all the partner lengths. Write the partners and the equation for each. Possible answers are shown on next page.

UNIT 2 LESSON 1 Rulers, Lengths, and Partner Lengths 47

Homework and Remembering page 47

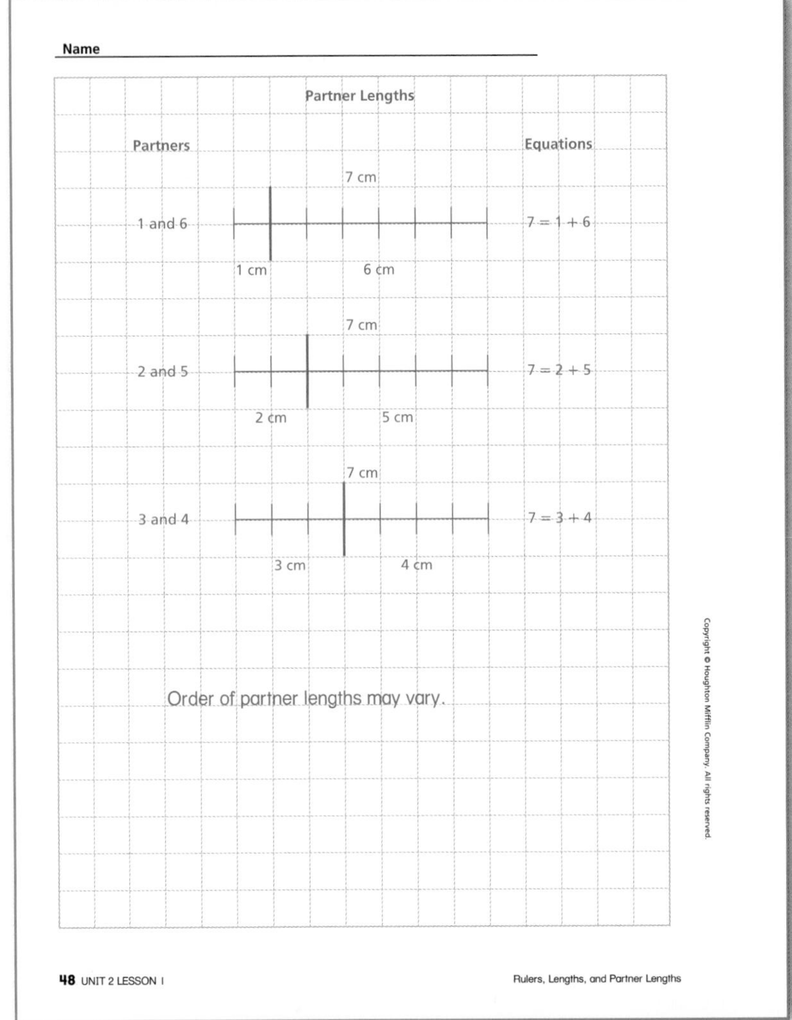
Name

Partner Lengths

Partners	Partner Lengths	Equations
1 and 6	7 cm: 1 cm, 6 cm	7 = 1 + 6
2 and 5	7 cm: 2 cm, 5 cm	7 = 2 + 5
3 and 4	7 cm: 3 cm, 4 cm	7 = 3 + 4

Order of partner lengths may vary.

Copyright © Houghton Mifflin Company. All rights reserved.

48 UNIT 2 LESSON 1 Rulers, Lengths, and Partner Lengths

Homework and Remembering page 48

Home and School Connection

Family Letter Have children take home the Family Letter on Student Activity Book page 77. This letter explains how the concept of partner lengths is developed in *Math Expressions.* It gives parents and guardians a better understanding of the learning that goes on in math class and creates a bridge between school and home. A Spanish translation of this letter is on the following page in the Student Activity Book.

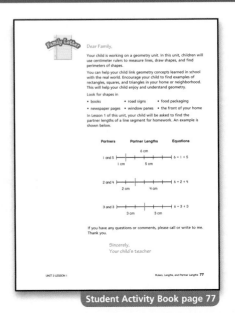

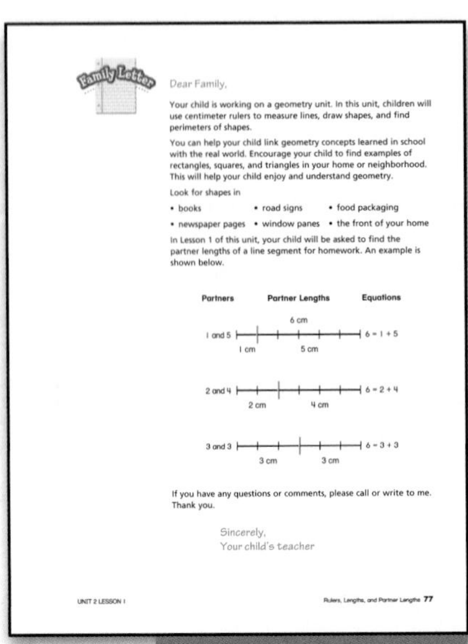
Family Letter

Dear Family,

Your child is working on a geometry unit. In this unit, children will use centimeter rulers to measure lines, draw shapes, and find perimeters of shapes.

You can help your child link geometry concepts learned in school with the real world. Encourage your child to find examples of rectangles, squares, and triangles in your home or neighborhood. This will help your child enjoy and understand geometry.

Look for shapes in

- books
- road signs
- food packaging
- newspaper pages
- window panes
- the front of your home

In Lesson 1 of this unit, your child will be asked to find the partner lengths of a line segment for homework. An example is shown below.

Partners	Partner Lengths	Equations
1 and 5	6 cm: 1 cm, 5 cm	6 = 1 + 5
2 and 4	2 cm, 4 cm	6 = 2 + 4
3 and 3	3 cm, 3 cm	6 = 3 + 3

If you have any questions or comments, please call or write to me. Thank you.

Sincerely,
Your child's teacher

UNIT 2 LESSON 1 Rulers, Lengths, and Partner Lengths 77

Student Activity Book page 77

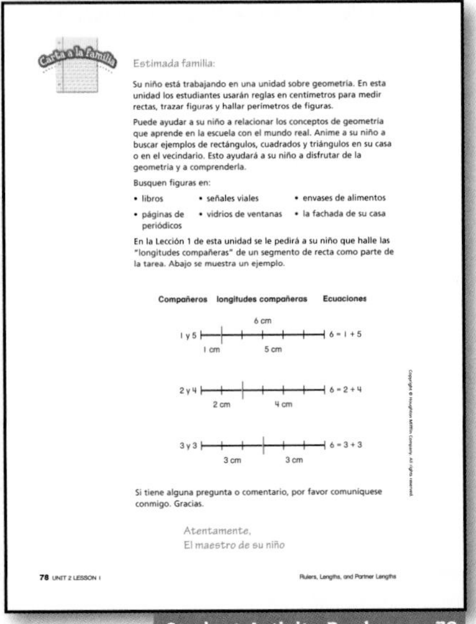
Carta a la familia

Estimada familia:

Su niño está trabajando en una unidad sobre geometría. En esta unidad los estudiantes usarán reglas en centímetros para medir rectas, trazar figuras y hallar perímetros de figuras.

Puede ayudar a su niño a relacionar los conceptos de geometría que aprende en la escuela con el mundo real. Anime a su niño a buscar ejemplos de rectángulos, cuadrados y triángulos en su casa o en el vecindario. Esto ayudará a su niño a disfrutar de la geometría y a comprenderla.

Busquen figuras en:

- libros
- señales viales
- envases de alimentos
- páginas de periódicos
- vidrios de ventanas
- la fachada de su casa

En la Lección 1 de esta unidad se le pedirá a su niño que halle las "longitudes compañeras" de un segmento de recta como parte de la tarea. Abajo se muestra un ejemplo.

Compañeros	longitudes compañeras	Ecuaciones
1 y 5	6 cm: 1 cm, 5 cm	6 = 1 + 5
2 y 4	2 cm, 4 cm	6 = 2 + 4
3 y 3	3 cm, 3 cm	6 = 3 + 3

Si tiene alguna pregunta o comentario, por favor comuníquese conmigo. Gracias.

Atentamente,
El maestro de su niño

Copyright © Houghton Mifflin Company. All rights reserved.

78 UNIT 2 LESSON 1 Rulers, Lengths, and Partner Lengths

Student Activity Book page 78

Squares, Rectangles, and Triangles

Vocabulary

square
rectangle
square rectangle
triangle

Lesson Objective

- **Describe properties of squares, rectangles, and triangles.**

The Day at a Glance

Today's Goals	Materials	
1 Teaching the Lesson **A1:** Discuss and draw squares. **A2:** Describe and draw rectangles. **A3:** Explore and draw triangles. **2 Going Further** ▶ Differentiated Instruction **3 Homework**	**Lesson Activities** Student Activity Book pp. 79–82 Homework and Remembering pp. 49–50 MathBoard materials 25-cm rulers or 25-cm Rulers (TRB M47–M48)	**Going Further** Activity Cards 2-2 MathBoard materials Geoboards and rubber bands Centimeter Dot Paper (TRB M49) Straw Scissors Math Journals

123 Use Math Talk today!

Keeping Skills Sharp

Daily Routines	English Language Learners
Money Routine: Using the 120 Poster, Using the Money Flip Chart, Using the Number Path, Using Secret Code Cards (See pp. xxiii–xxv.) ▶ Led by Student Leaders	Draw a square, rectangle, and triangle on the board. Name each shape. Have children repeat and draw the shapes in the air. Point to a side on the square. Say: **This is a side.** Point to a corner. Say: **This is a corner.** Have children repeat. • **Beginning** Ask: **How many sides does a square have?** 4 **How many corners?** 4 Continue with the rectangle and triangle. • **Intermediate** Have children count the sides and corners of each shape. Point to the square. Say: **All the sides are the same length.** Point to the rectangle. Ask: **Are all the sides the same length?** no Say: **A rectangle has 2 long sides and 2 short sides.** Have children repeat. • **Advanced** Have children describe the sides and corners of each shape. Ask: **What is similar about the square and rectangle?** 4 Sides, 4 corners **What is different about the triangle?** 3 Sides, 3 corners

1 Teaching the Lesson

Activity 1

Observe and Draw Squares

20 MINUTES

Goal: Discuss and draw squares.

Materials: MathBoard materials, 25-cm rulers or 25-cm Rulers (TRB M47–M48) printed on card stock (1 ruler per child); Student Activity Book page 79

NCTM Standards:
Geometry
Measurement
Connections

▶ Properties of Squares WHOLE CLASS

Draw four squares of various sizes on the board. Tell children that a small square drawn on a shape shows a square corner.

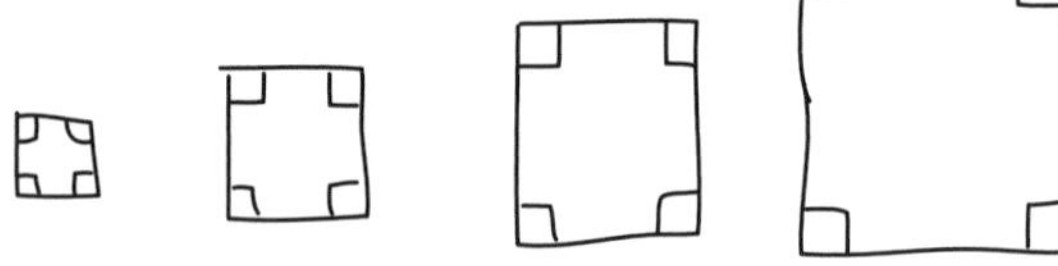

- What is the name of these shapes? They are squares.
- How many sides does a square have? 4
- How many corners does a square have? 4

Have children sketch several squares on their MathBoards, drawing freehand or using a centimeter ruler.

- How can you describe the sides of a square? Each side is a straight line; all sides are the same length.
- How can you describe the corners of a square? A horizontal line meets a vertical line at each corner; all four corners are square corners.

Leave the squares on the board for later reference.

Teaching Note

Language and Vocabulary Draw several examples of right angles on the board. You may choose to introduce the term *right angle* for the corner of a square, but children are not required to use this term yet.

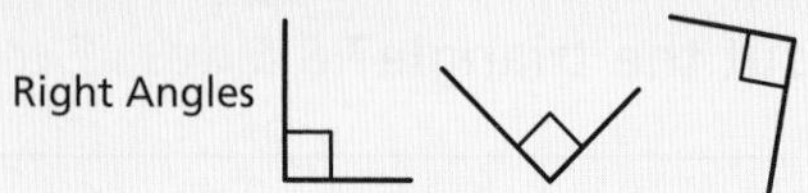

▶ Draw and Identify Squares PAIRS

Ask children to complete exercises 1–5 in pairs. When they are finished, discuss their answers as a class.

Teaching Note

Watch For! Some children think of a tilted square as a diamond and that is not still a square. To show them that a tilted square is still a square, have children place the corner of a sheet of paper or a ruler on the bottom corner of a tilted square. They will see that it is a square corner (right angle).

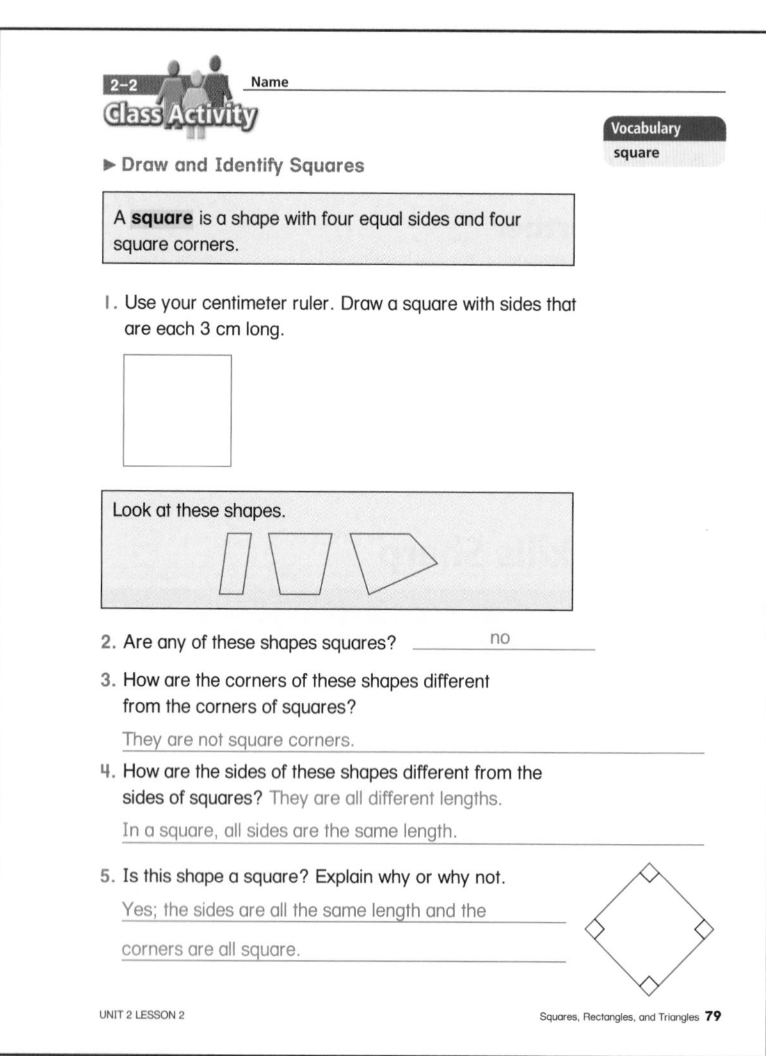

2–2 Class Activity

Name ____________________

Vocabulary
square

▶ Draw and Identify Squares

A **square** is a shape with four equal sides and four square corners.

1. Use your centimeter ruler. Draw a square with sides that are each 3 cm long.

Look at these shapes.

2. Are any of these shapes squares? no

3. How are the corners of these shapes different from the corners of squares?
They are not square corners.

4. How are the sides of these shapes different from the sides of squares? They are all different lengths.
In a square, all sides are the same length.

5. Is this shape a square? Explain why or why not.
Yes; the sides are all the same length and the corners are all square.

UNIT 2 LESSON 2

Squares, Rectangles, and Triangles 79

Student Activity Book page 79

Activity 2

Observe and Draw Rectangles

 **20 MINUTES**

Goal: Describe and draw rectangles.

Materials: MathBoard materials, 25-cm rulers or 25-cm Rulers (TRB M47–M48) printed on card stock (1 ruler per child), Student Activity Book page 80

 **NCTM Standards:**
Geometry
Measurement
Connections

▶ Properties of Rectangles WHOLE CLASS

Draw three rectangles of various sizes on the board.

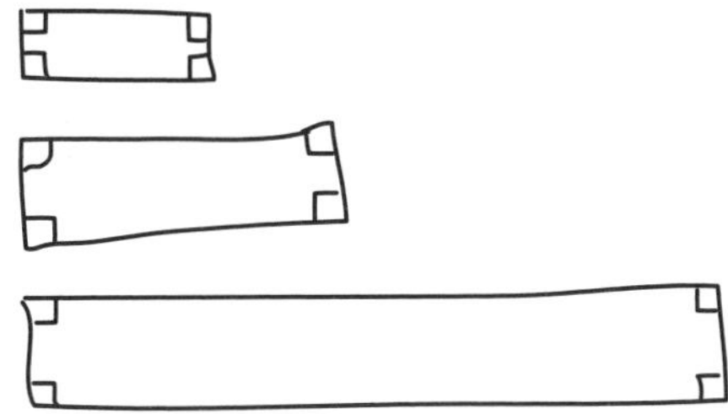

- What is the name of these shapes? rectangles
- How many sides does a rectangle have? 4
- How many corners does a rectangle have? 4

Have children sketch several rectangles on their MathBoards, drawing freehand or using a centimeter ruler.

- How can you describe the sides of a rectangle? Rectangles have 4 sides and the 2 sides opposite each other are equal in length.
- How can you describe the corners of a rectangle? Rectangles have square corners.

Ask children to tilt their MathBoards.

- If you tilt a rectangle, is it still a rectangle? yes

Have children compare the squares and rectangles on the board.

- How are rectangles like squares? They have 4 square corners and opposite sides of the same length.
- How are rectangles different from squares? All 4 sides don't have to be the same length.

▶ Draw and Identify Rectangles PAIRS

Ask children to work in pairs to complete exercises 6–8.

Discuss how a square is a special kind of rectangle: It has four square corners and opposite sides of equal length, so it is a rectangle. But it has all sides equal, so it is a special "square rectangle."

Ongoing Assessment

Challenge children to use their centimeter rulers to draw a square whose side lengths are all 5 cm and a rectangle that is 5 cm long and 2 cm wide.

2–2 Class Activity

Name ______

Vocabulary
rectangle

▶ Draw and Identify Rectangles

A **rectangle** is a shape with opposite sides that are equal in length and four square corners.

6. Use your centimeter ruler to draw a rectangle that is 6 cm long and 3 cm wide.
Answers may vary.
Possible answer:

Look at these shapes.

7. Are these shapes rectangles? Explain why or why not.
No; the corners are not square corners.

8. Is a square a rectangle? Explain why or why not.
Yes; the sides are all the same length, and the corners are square.

80 UNIT 2 LESSON 2 Squares, Rectangles, and Triangles

Student Activity Book page 80

Activity 3

Observe and Draw Triangles

 20 MINUTES

Goal: Explore and draw triangles.

Materials: MathBoard materials, 25-cm rulers or 25-cm Rulers (TRB M47–M48) printed on card stock (1 ruler per child), Student Activity Book page 81

 **NCTM Standards:**
Geometry
Measurement
Connections

▶ Properties of Triangles WHOLE CLASS

Draw three different triangles on the board.

  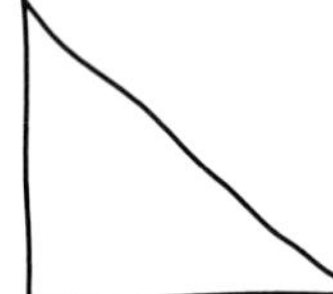

- What is the name of these shapes? They are triangles.
- How many sides does a triangle have? 3
- How many corners does a triangle have? 3

Invite children to sketch several triangles on their MathBoards, drawing freehand or using a centimeter ruler.

Ask children to tilt their MathBoards and look at their triangles again.

- If you tilt a triangle, is it still a triangle? yes

▶ Compare Lengths of Sides of Triangles INDIVIDUALS

Math Talk 

Have children complete exercises 9–11. When they are finished, discuss their findings as a class.

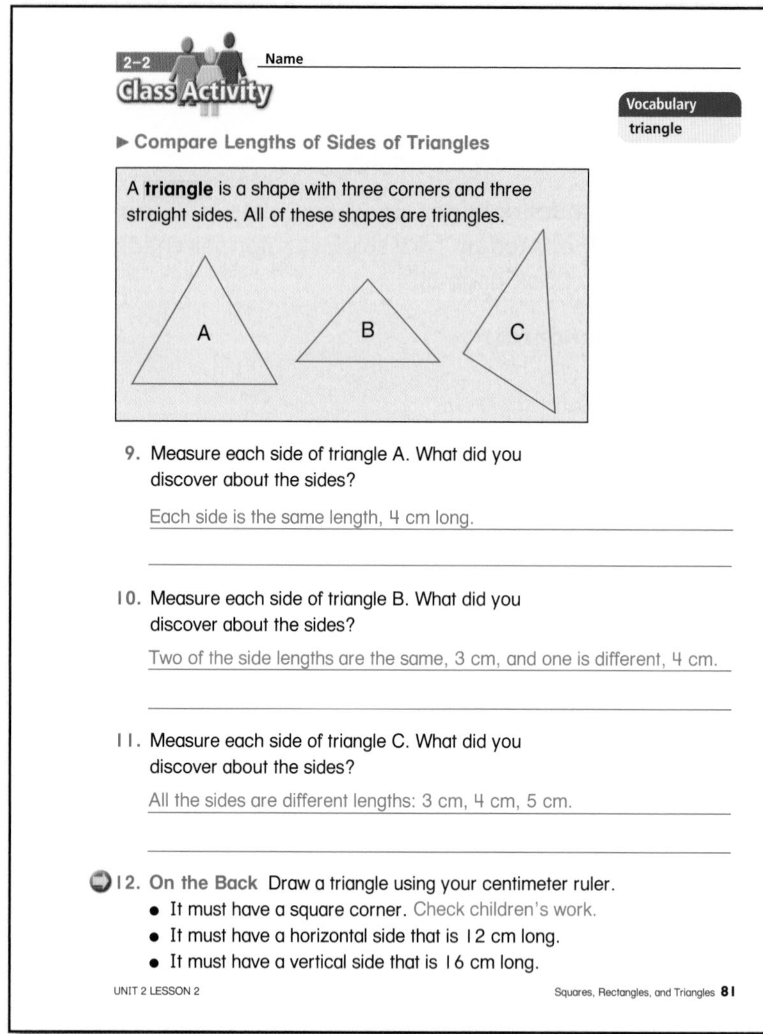

2-2 Class Activity Name

Vocabulary
triangle

▶ Compare Lengths of Sides of Triangles

A **triangle** is a shape with three corners and three straight sides. All of these shapes are triangles.

A B C

9. Measure each side of triangle A. What did you discover about the sides?
Each side is the same length, 4 cm long.

10. Measure each side of triangle B. What did you discover about the sides?
Two of the side lengths are the same, 3 cm, and one is different, 4 cm.

11. Measure each side of triangle C. What did you discover about the sides?
All the sides are different lengths: 3 cm, 4 cm, 5 cm.

12. On the Back Draw a triangle using your centimeter ruler.
- It must have a square corner. Check children's work.
- It must have a horizontal side that is 12 cm long.
- It must have a vertical side that is 16 cm long.

UNIT 2 LESSON 2 Squares, Rectangles, and Triangles 81

Student Activity Book page 81

On the Back On the board, demonstrate how to draw the triangle described in exercise 12. Draw a 12-cm horizontal line segment and a 16-cm vertical line segment that meet at a right angle. Then join them with a diagonal line segment.

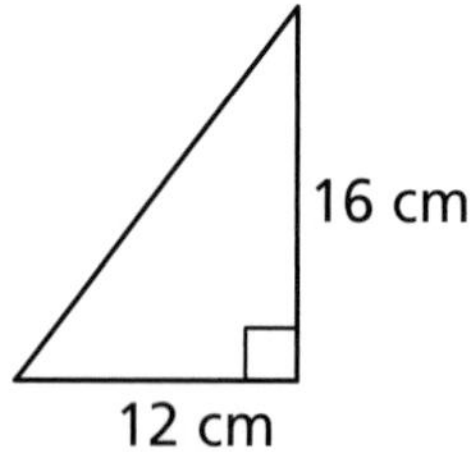

Children can use your drawing as a guide as they complete exercise 12.

2 Going Further

Differentiated Instruction

Intervention — Activity Card 2-2

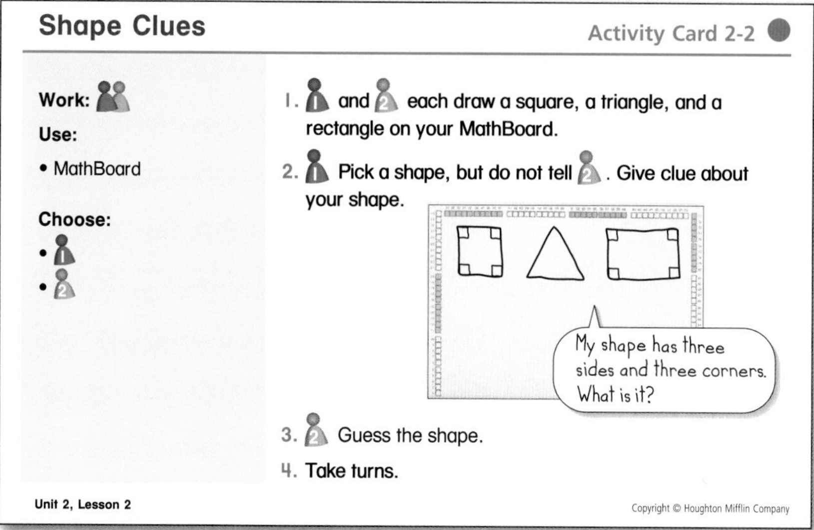

Shape Clues — Activity Card 2-2 ●

Work: (pair)

Use:

- MathBoard

Choose:

- 1
- 2

1. 1 and 2 each draw a square, a triangle, and a rectangle on your MathBoard.
2. 1 Pick a shape, but do not tell 2. Give clue about your shape.

My shape has three sides and three corners. What is it?

3. 2 Guess the shape.
4. Take turns.

Unit 2, Lesson 2

Activity Note Each child needs MathBoard materials. Have children describe the shapes from their MathBoards.

Math Writing Prompt

Compare Shapes How are triangles and squares alike? How are they different?

Software Support

Use *Soar to Success* for instruction of students needing targeted support for underlying skills.

On Level — Activity Card 2-2

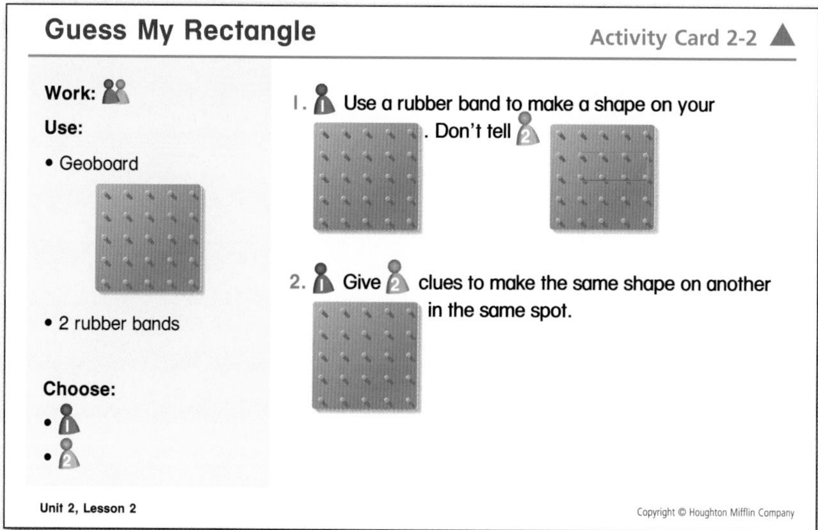

Guess My Rectangle — Activity Card 2-2 ▲

Work: (pair)

Use:

- Geoboard
- 2 rubber bands

Choose:

- 1
- 2

1. 1 Use a rubber band to make a shape on your [geoboard]. Don't tell 2.
2. 1 Give 2 clues to make the same shape on another [geoboard] in the same spot.

Unit 2, Lesson 2

Activity Note Each child needs a geoboard and rubber bands or Centimeter Dot Paper (TRB M49). The first child gives verbal clues about the shape and its position on the geoboard.

Math Writing Prompt

Explain Your Thinking Are all squares rectangles? Explain why or why not. Are all rectangles squares? Explain why or why not.

Software Support

Use *MegaMath* for review and reinforcement of the concepts and skills presented in this lesson.

Challenge — Activity Card 2-2

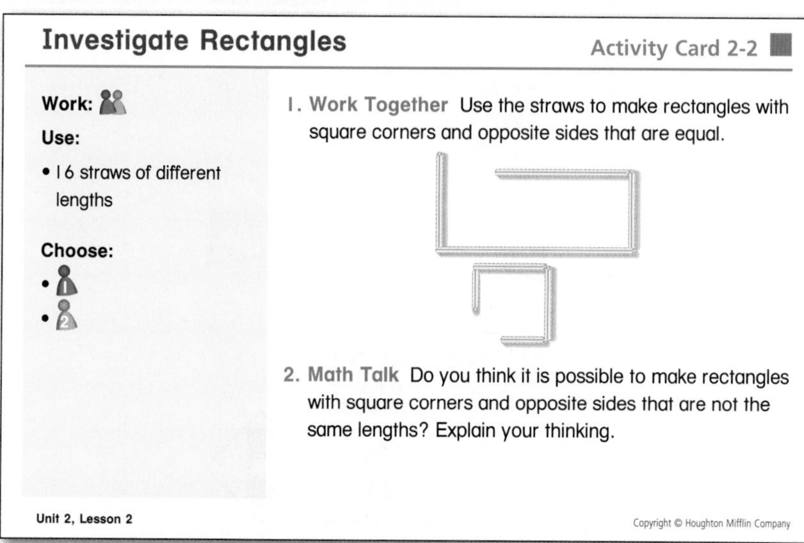

Investigate Rectangles — Activity Card 2-2 ■

Work: (pair)

Use:

- 16 straws of different lengths

Choose:

- 1
- 2

1. **Work Together** Use the straws to make rectangles with square corners and opposite sides that are equal.
2. **Math Talk** Do you think it is possible to make rectangles with square corners and opposite sides that are not the same lengths? Explain your thinking.

Unit 2, Lesson 2

Activity Note Each child needs eight straws of different lengths. Pairs try to make rectangles using the straws.

Math Writing Prompt

Investigate Math A shape has four square corners and four sides. Do you know for sure that the shape is a rectangle? Explain.

Software Support

Use *Destination Math* to take students beyond the concepts and skills presented in this lesson.

Homework

2-2 Homework **Goal:** Additional Practice

On this Homework page, children practice what they have learned about squares, rectangles, and triangles.

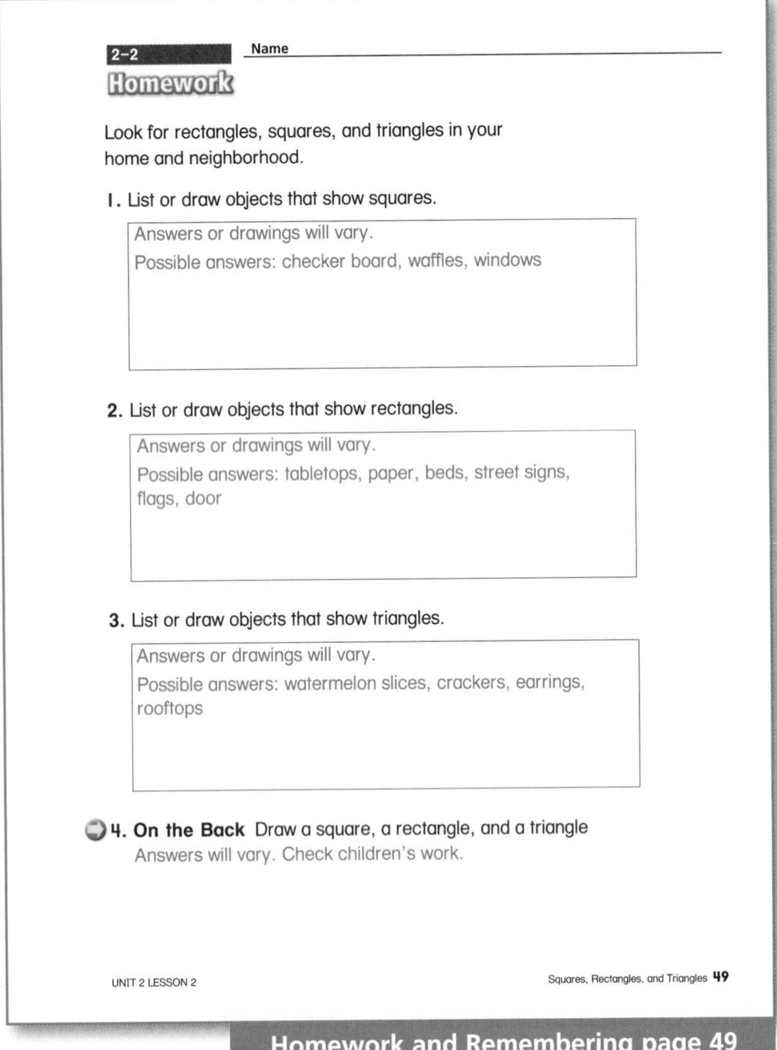

2-2 Homework Name

Look for rectangles, squares, and triangles in your home and neighborhood.

1. List or draw objects that show squares.

Answers or drawings will vary.
Possible answers: checker board, waffles, windows

2. List or draw objects that show rectangles.

Answers or drawings will vary.
Possible answers: tabletops, paper, beds, street signs, flags, door

3. List or draw objects that show triangles.

Answers or drawings will vary.
Possible answers: watermelon slices, crackers, earrings, rooftops

4. **On the Back** Draw a square, a rectangle, and a triangle
Answers will vary. Check children's work.

UNIT 2 LESSON 2 Squares, Rectangles, and Triangles 49

Homework and Remembering page 49

Home or School Activity

Social Studies Connection

Shapes in Signs The shape and color of road signs depend on their purpose. For example, signs that give information about parking are usually rectangles, while other types of signs may be squares or triangles.

Invite children to observe signs around the school and in their neighborhoods and to sketch those that are rectangles, squares, and triangles.

Perimeters of Squares and Rectangles

Lesson Objectives

- Label geometric shapes.
- Define and find perimeters of squares and rectangles.

Vocabulary
square
rectangle
perimeter

The Day at a Glance

Today's Goals	Materials	
1 Teaching the Lesson A: Draw, label, and find the perimeters of squares and rectangles.	**Lesson Activities** Student Activity Book pp. 83–84 Homework and Remembering pp. 51–52 25-cm rulers or 25-cm Rulers (TRB M47–M48) MathBoard materials Digital camera (optional)	**Going Further** Activity Cards 2-3 Centimeter Grid Paper (TRB M50) 25-cm rulers Math Journals
2 Going Further ▶ Differentiated Instruction		
3 Homework		

Use Math Talk today!

Keeping Skills Sharp

Daily Routines	English Language Learners
Money Routine: Using the 120 Poster, Using the Money Flip Chart, Using the Number Path, Using Secret Code Cards (See pp. xxiii–xxv.) ▶ Led by Student Leaders	Write *perimeter* on the board. Walk around a desk. Say: **I'm walking around the sides of the desk. I'm walking around the *perimeter*.** • **Beginning** Hold up a book. Trace the outside of it with a finger. Say: **All the sides together are the *perimeter*.** Have children trace the perimeter of different things with their fingers. desk, piece of paper, pencil case • **Intermediate** Draw a square with 10 cm sides. Say: **1 side is 10 cm long.** Ask: **Are all the sides 10 cm long?** yes Write 10 + 10 + 10 + 10 on the board. Say: **We add the sides to find the *perimeter*. The *perimeter* is 40 cm.** • **Advanced** Say: ***Perimeter* is the distance around the shape. We measure and add the 4 sides of a square or rectangle to get the *perimeter*.** Have children find the perimeter of their desks, a book, and a piece of paper.

1 Teaching the Lesson

Activity

Find Perimeters of Squares and Rectangles

 **60 MINUTES**

Goal: Draw, label, and find the perimeters of squares and rectangles.

Materials: 25-cm rulers or 25-cm Rulers (TRB M47–M48) (1 ruler per child); MathBoard materials, Student Activity Book pages 83–84, digital camera (optional)

 **NCTM Standards:**
Geometry
Measurement
Connections
Representation

Ask for Ideas Have children share their observations about squares, rectangles, and triangles that they see in their homes and neighborhoods. They may offer the following possible responses:

- The door on my house is a rectangle.
- I saw a yield sign on my way to school that was a triangle.
- The screen at the movie theater is a rectangle.
- The cushions on our couch are square.
- My sister baked cookies in the shape of triangles.

 **Alternate Approach**

Technology If time allows, take your class around the school and search for real-world examples of squares, rectangles, and triangles. Record their findings with a digital camera, or children can sketch the geometric shapes in their math journals.

▶ Label Squares and Rectangles

WHOLE CLASS

Label Shapes Demonstrate on the board how to label shapes in order to tell them apart.

Draw a square on the board. Start at the top left corner and proceed clockwise, placing an uppercase letter at each corner. Repeat with a rectangle.

Explain to children that when they label shapes, they can use any letters of the alphabet, but they should use the letters in sequential order.

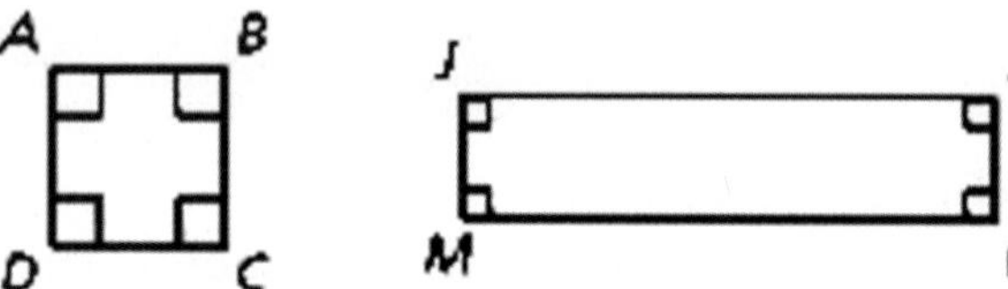

Have children draw two squares and two rectangles on their MathBoards, using centimeter rulers. Ask them to label each shape using letters.

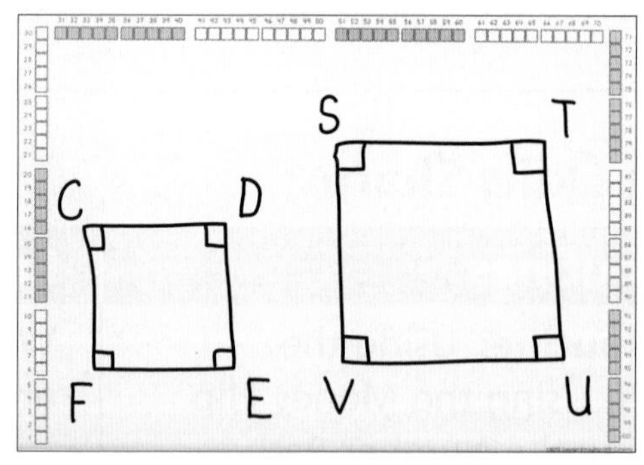

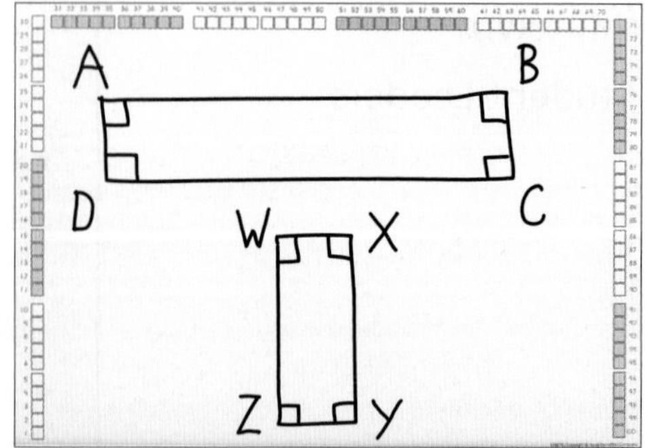

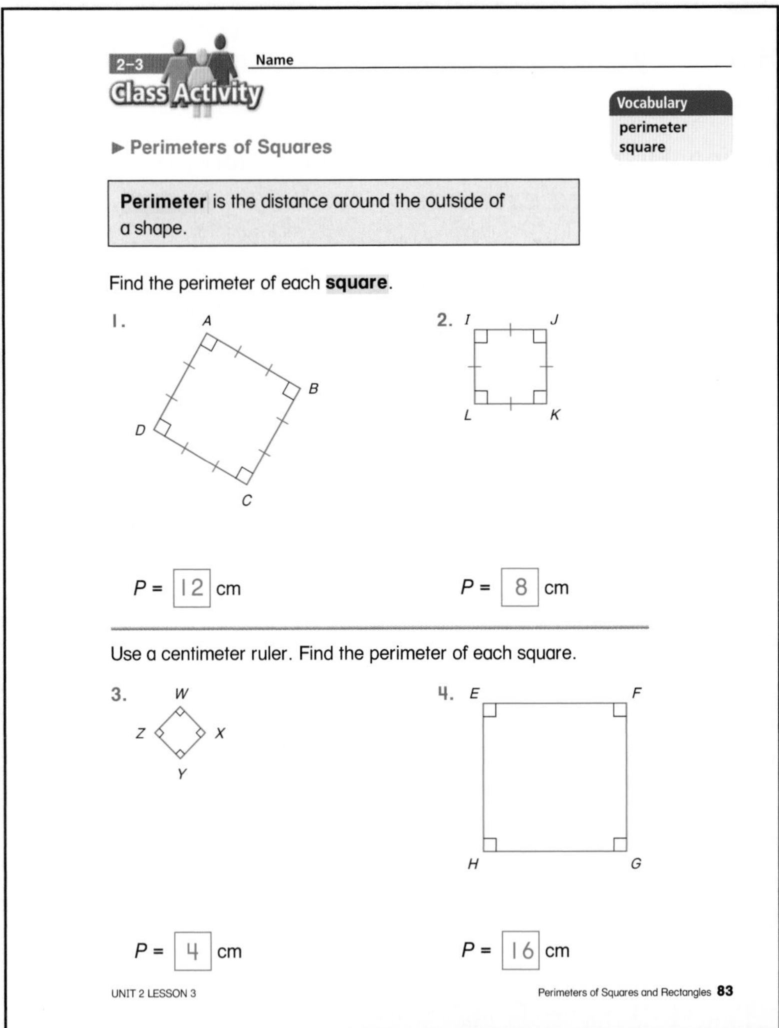
2-3 Class Activity

Name ______

Vocabulary
perimeter
square

► Perimeters of Squares

Perimeter is the distance around the outside of a shape.

Find the perimeter of each **square**.

1. A B C D

$P =$ 12 cm

2. I J K L

$P =$ 8 cm

Use a centimeter ruler. Find the perimeter of each square.

3. W X Y Z

$P =$ 4 cm

4. E F G H

$P =$ 16 cm

UNIT 2 LESSON 3

Perimeters of Squares and Rectangles **83**

Student Activity Book page 83

► Perimeters of Squares WHOLE CLASS

Together read the definition of perimeter on Student Activity Book page 83 and complete exercise 1.

- Why are there marks on the sides of the shape? They mark the centimeters.
- What is the length of the side between *A* and *B*? 3 cm

Ask children to label side *AB* as 3 cm to help them keep track of the measures.

- What is the length of the side between *B* and *C*? 3 cm

Ask children to label side *BC* as 3 cm. Continue the discussion until children have labeled all four sides.

- How many centimeters in total are there around the square? 12 cm
- What is the perimeter of the square? 12 cm

Have children complete exercises 2–4 on their own and assist those who are having difficulty.

When children are finished, discuss exercise 4 together, and have volunteers share ways to find the perimeter of the square. You can use these questions to help elicit the idea that you need to measure only one side of a square to find its perimeter.

- What is the length of the side between *E* and *F*? 4 cm
- Without measuring the other sides, do you know their lengths? yes
- How do you know the lengths of the three other sides? All four sides of a square are equal in length.
- Can you find the perimeter of a square by measuring just one side? yes
- Describe how you can find the perimeter of this square using the measure of one side. I can add four 4-cm lengths together.

Teaching Note

Language and Vocabulary You may want to define perimeter by explaining that *peri-* means "around" and *meter* means "measure," so the word *perimeter* means "the measure around."

Differentiated Instruction

English Learners Have students walk around the outside of a group of desks while saying "I am walking around the *perimeter* of the desks". This is a great way to help students, particularly English Learners, understand the definition of a new math term by acting it out.

Activity continued ►

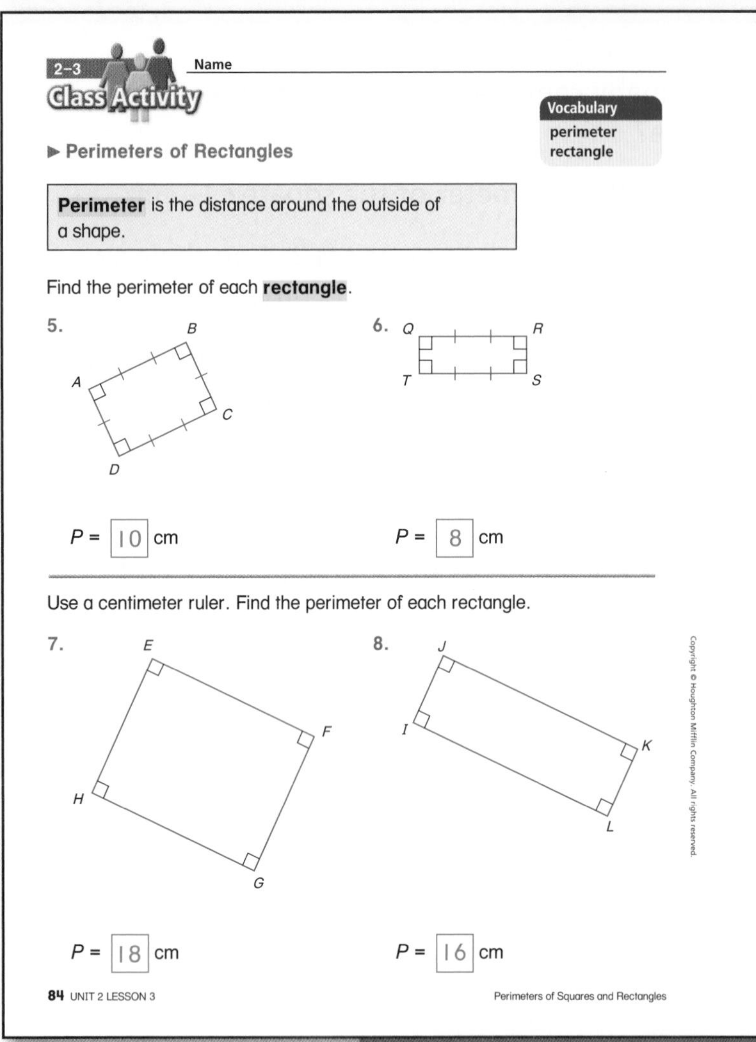

2-3 Class Activity Name

Vocabulary
perimeter
rectangle

▶ Perimeters of Rectangles

Perimeter is the distance around the outside of a shape.

Find the perimeter of each **rectangle**.

5. P = 10 cm

6. P = 8 cm

Use a centimeter ruler. Find the perimeter of each rectangle.

7. P = 18 cm

8. P = 16 cm

Copyright © Houghton Mifflin Company. All rights reserved.

84 UNIT 2 LESSON 3 Perimeters of Squares and Rectangles

Student Activity Book page 84

▶ Perimeters of Rectangles INDIVIDUALS

Have children look at the rectangle in exercise 5 and try to develop a way to find its perimeter. Invite volunteers to share and discuss the methods they used to find the shape's perimeter. Have them also compare finding the perimeters of rectangles and squares. See **Math Talk in Action** for an example of possible classroom discussion.

Then have children work independently to complete the page.

Ongoing Assessment

Ask children to draw a square and a rectangle with their centimeter rulers and to find the perimeter of each shape.

Math Talk in Action

How did you find the perimeter of the rectangle in exercise 5?

Janine: First I counted the centimeter lengths on each side and labeled each side.

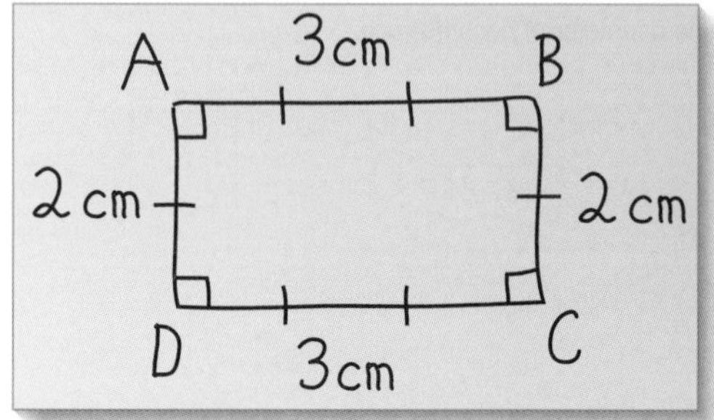

Then I found the total of all the lengths. The perimeter is 10 cm.

3 cm + 2 cm + 3 cm + 2 cm = 10 cm

Kyle: To find the perimeter of this rectangle, you only have to measure two sides. I found the perimeter like this:

3 cm + 2 cm = 5 cm
3 cm + 2 cm = 5 cm

5 cm
+ 5 cm
10 cm

Did anyone else have a different way to find the perimeter?

Sahil: I did it like this. I first found the total of the two short sides. Then I found the total of the two long sides. I added them together.

2 cm + 2 cm = 4 cm
3 cm + 3 cm = 6 cm

4 cm
+ 6 cm
10 cm

How is finding the perimeter of a square like finding the perimeter of a rectangle?

Brian: You need to find the distance around each shape. You need to find the total length of 4 sides.

2 Going Further

Differentiated Instruction

Intervention — Activity Card 2-3

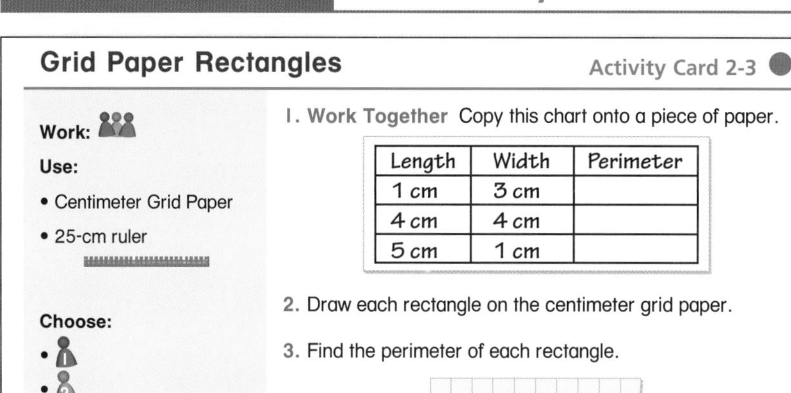

Grid Paper Rectangles

Activity Card 2-3

Work: [group]

Use:

- Centimeter Grid Paper
- 25-cm ruler

Choose:

- 1
- 2
- 3

1. **Work Together** Copy this chart onto a piece of paper.

Length	Width	Perimeter
1 cm	3 cm	
4 cm	4 cm	
5 cm	1 cm	

2. Draw each rectangle on the centimeter grid paper.
3. Find the perimeter of each rectangle.

Unit 2, Lesson 3

Activity Note Each child needs Centimeter Grid Paper (TRB M50) and 25-cm ruler or Copymaster M47–M48. The group works together to find the perimeter of each shape.

Math Writing Prompt

Perimeter of Shapes Tell two ways to find the perimeter of a square.

Software Support

Use *Soar to Success* for instruction of students needing targeted support for underlying skills.

On Level — Activity Card 2-3

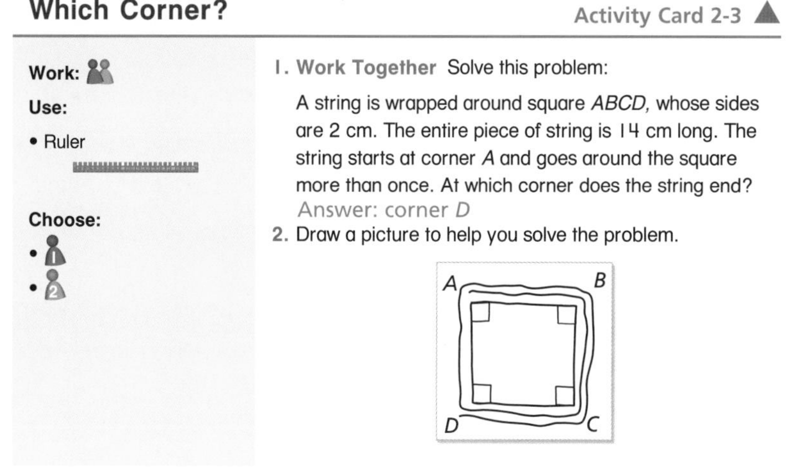

Which Corner?

Activity Card 2-3

Work: [pair]

Use:

- Ruler

Choose:

- 1
- 2

1. **Work Together** Solve this problem:

   A string is wrapped around square *ABCD*, whose sides are 2 cm. The entire piece of string is 14 cm long. The string starts at corner *A* and goes around the square more than once. At which corner does the string end?
   Answer: corner *D*
2. Draw a picture to help you solve the problem.

Unit 2, Lesson 3

Activity Note Each pair needs a 25-cm ruler or TRB M47–M48. Suggest pairs draw the details of the problem.

Math Writing Prompt

Perimeter of Rectangles Tell two ways to find the perimeter of a rectangle.

Software Support

Use *MegaMath* for review and reinforcement of the concepts and skills presented in this lesson.

Challenge — Activity Card 2-3

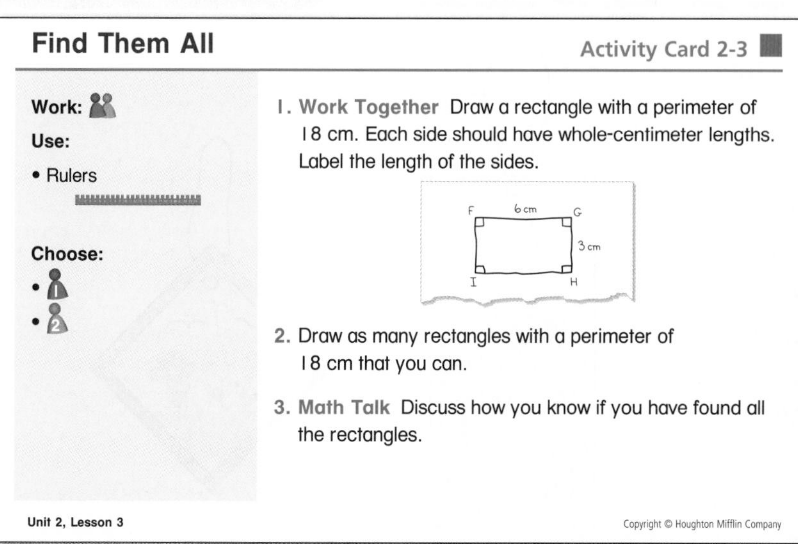

Find Them All

Activity Card 2-3

Work: [pair]

Use:

- Rulers

Choose:

- 1
- 2

1. **Work Together** Draw a rectangle with a perimeter of 18 cm. Each side should have whole-centimeter lengths. Label the length of the sides.

2. Draw as many rectangles with a perimeter of 18 cm that you can.
3. **Math Talk** Discuss how you know if you have found all the rectangles.

Unit 2, Lesson 3

Activity Note Each pair needs a 25-cm ruler or TRB M47–M48. Pairs should find four rectangles in total.

Math Writing Prompt

Explain Your Thinking Tim draws a square with a perimeter of 12 cm. He says that this is the only square with a perimeter of 12 cm that he can possibly draw. Do you agree? Explain your thinking.

DESTINATION Math®

Software Support

Use *Destination Math* to take students beyond the concepts and skills presented in this lesson.

3 Homework

Goal: Additional Practice

✓ Include children's completed Homework page as part of their portfolios.

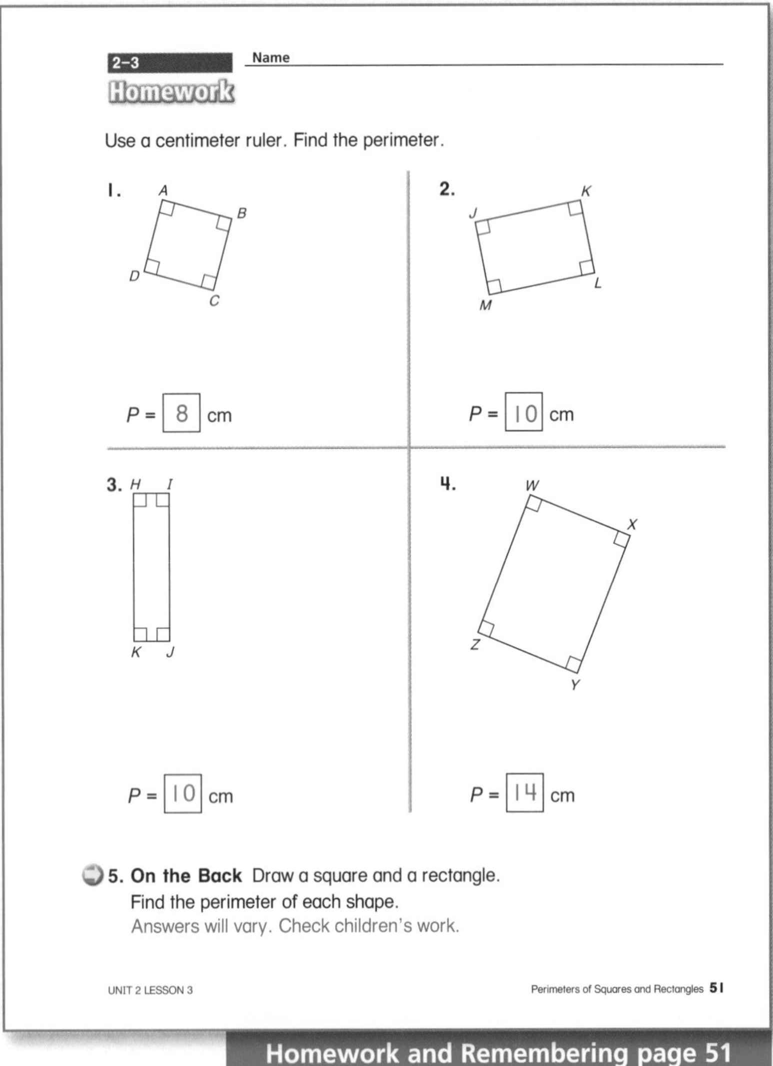

2-3 Homework Name

Use a centimeter ruler. Find the perimeter.

1. A B C D — $P =$ 8 cm

2. J K L M — $P =$ 10 cm

3. H I J K — $P =$ 10 cm

4. W X Y Z — $P =$ 14 cm

5. **On the Back** Draw a square and a rectangle. Find the perimeter of each shape.
Answers will vary. Check children's work.

UNIT 2 LESSON 3 Perimeters of Squares and Rectangles 51

Homework and Remembering page 51

Home or School Activity

Art Connection

Making Ornaments Children can make ornaments to decorate the classroom or a room in their home by cutting squares or rectangles from card stock. Ensure that the sides of each shape measure a whole number of centimeters. They can draw pictures or glue small objects, such as sequins or beads, onto the card stock. Children can then find the perimeter of each ornament to create a border using wool, felt, or ribbon.

Perimeters of Triangles

Lesson Objectives

- **Draw triangles.**
- **Find the perimeters of triangles.**
- **Draw angles of triangles.**

Vocabulary
triangle
perimeter
round
angle

The Day at a Glance

Today's Goals	Materials	
1 Teaching the Lesson **A1:** Draw and find the perimeters of triangles. **A2:** Draw and explore angles of triangles.	**Lesson Activities** Student Activity Book pp. 85–86 Homework and Remembering pp. 53–54 25-cm rulers or 25-cm Rulers (TRB M47–M48) MathBoard materials Straws	**Going Further** Activity Cards 2-4 *Racing Around* by Stuart J. Murphy and Mike Reed Math Journals
2 Going Further ▸ Differentiated Instruction		
3 Homework		

Use **Math Talk** today!

Keeping Skills Sharp

Daily Routines	English Language Learners
Money Routine: Using the 120 Poster, Using the Money Flip Chart, Using the Number Path, Using Secret Code Cards (See pp. xxiii–xxv.) ▸ Led by Student Leaders	Draw a right triangle on the board. Label the right angle A and the others B and C. • **Beginning** Point to A. Say: **This is a square corner.** Point to B and C. Ask: **Are these square corners?** no **Are they bigger or smaller than A?** smaller Say: **The size of the corner is the *angle*.** Have children repeat. • **Intermediate** Ask: **Which one is the square corner?** A **Are B and C square corners?** no Say: **They are different sizes. The size of the corner is the *angle*.** Have children repeat. • **Advanced** Ask: **What is corner A?** square corner Say: **The other corners are different sizes. The measurement of the corners is called the *angle*.** Have children use rulers or pencils to show different angles.

1 Teaching the Lesson

Activity 1

Find Perimeters of Triangles

 **40 MINUTES**

Goal: Draw and find the perimeters of triangles.

Materials: 25-cm rulers or 25-cm Rulers (TRB M47–M48) (1 ruler per child); MathBoard materials, Student Activity Book pages 85–86

 **NCTM Standards:**
Geometry
Measurement
Connections

▶ Draw Triangles WHOLE CLASS

Have children draw the triangle described below on their MathBoards.

- One side of your triangle should be 6 cm. Another side should be 5 cm. How do you draw the third side? Connect the two line segments with another line segment.

After the children have finished drawing, have them hold up their MathBoards so they can see and discuss the triangles.

- What do you notice about the triangles? Everyone's triangle is not the same.

Have children then draw a second triangle that looks different from the first one, but still has one side 6 cm long and one side 5 cm long.

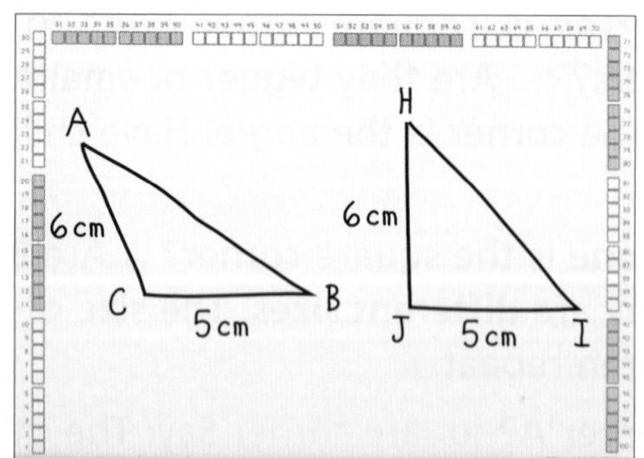

▶ Explore Perimeter PAIRS Math Talk 

Discuss how to find the perimeter of a triangle. Make sure children understand that you measure all three sides and add the measures together.

Then, have pairs of children find the perimeters of the triangles they drew on their MathBoards. You may want to have volunteers explain how they found the perimeter of their triangles.

Rounding Lengths Since many triangles have sides that are not whole centimeters, you need to discuss rounding with your class.

- Did anyone have trouble measuring the perimeter? Yes: I had trouble measuring the third side of my triangle.
- Can you explain what was difficult? I already knew one side was 6 cm and the other side was 5 cm. All I had to measure was the third side, but it was a little more than 3 cm.
- Was it closer to the 3 or the 4? The 3, so I just called it 3 cm.
- We call that rounding. Sometimes you may have to round all the sides of a shape to find the perimeter. How did you find the perimeter? I added 6 cm + 5 cm + 3 cm which equals 14 cm.

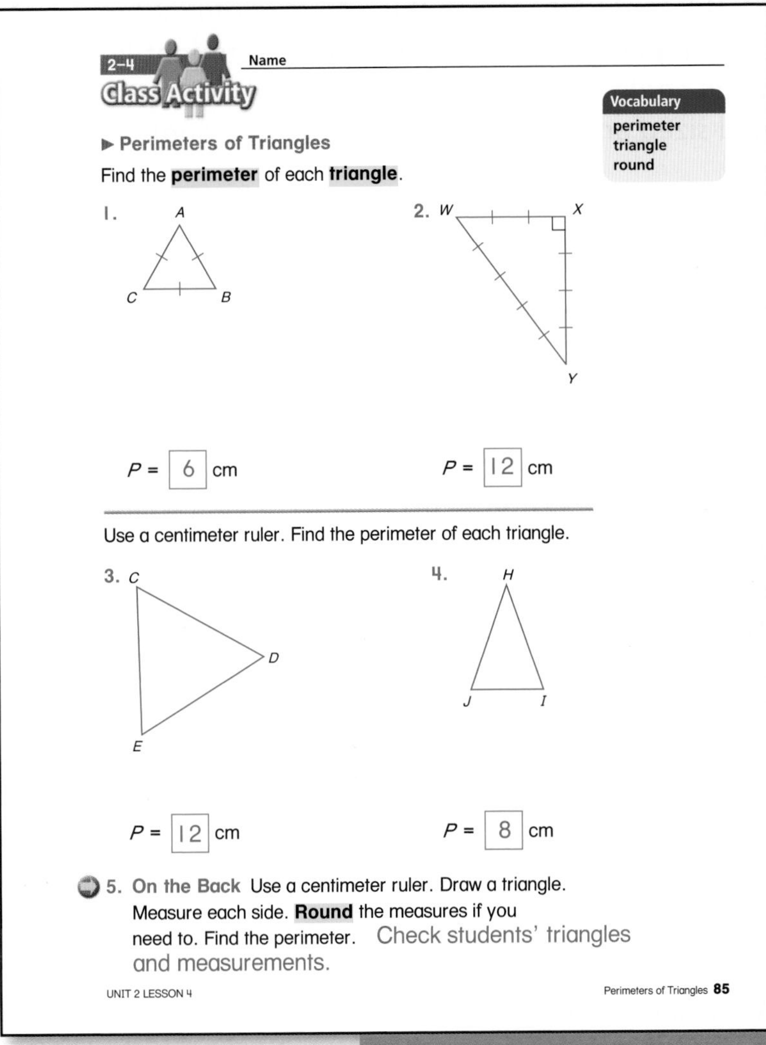

2-4 Class Activity

Name

Vocabulary
perimeter
triangle
round

▶ Perimeters of Triangles

Find the **perimeter** of each **triangle**.

1. A, C, B

$P =$ 6 cm

2. W, X, Y

$P =$ 12 cm

Use a centimeter ruler. Find the perimeter of each triangle.

3. C, D, E

$P =$ 12 cm

4. H, J, I

$P =$ 8 cm

5. **On the Back** Use a centimeter ruler. Draw a triangle. Measure each side. **Round** the measures if you need to. Find the perimeter. Check students' triangles and measurements.

UNIT 2 LESSON 4 Perimeters of Triangles 85

Student Activity Book page 85

▶ Perimeters of Triangles INDIVIDUALS

Refer children to the triangles on Student Activity Book page 85.

- How can you find the perimeter of each of these triangles? Possible answers: For the first two triangles, you can use the marks to count the centimeters. For the other triangles, you have to measure the lengths of the sides and add the measures.

Have children complete exercises 1–4 independently. For exercise 5, you may have to remind the class about rounding.

The Learning Classroom

Helping Community Children can work in pairs to complete exercise 5, and to assist each other in rounding the lengths of the sides and calculating perimeters.

Ongoing Assessment

Exercise 5 provides a good opportunity to informally assess children's understanding of perimeter. Circulate as children talk among themselves. Note those who appear to have mastered this concept and those who need extra support.

Activity 2

Explore Angles of Triangles

20 MINUTES

Goal: Draw and explore angles of triangles.

Materials: 25-cm rulers or 25-cm Rulers (TRB M47–M48) (2 rulers per child); MathBoard materials

NCTM Standards:
Geometry
Measurement

▶ Draw Angles WHOLE CLASS

Distribute a second 25-cm ruler to each child. Have children work in pairs if you don't have enough rulers. Demonstrate how to form an angle with two rulers. Explain to children that when two line segments meet at a point, they form an angle.

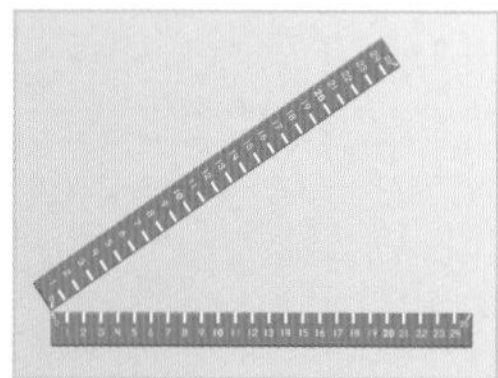

Slowly move the two rulers closer together and farther apart to emphasize how the angle changes from small (when the rulers are close together) to large (when the rulers are far apart). Invite children to do the same with their rulers.

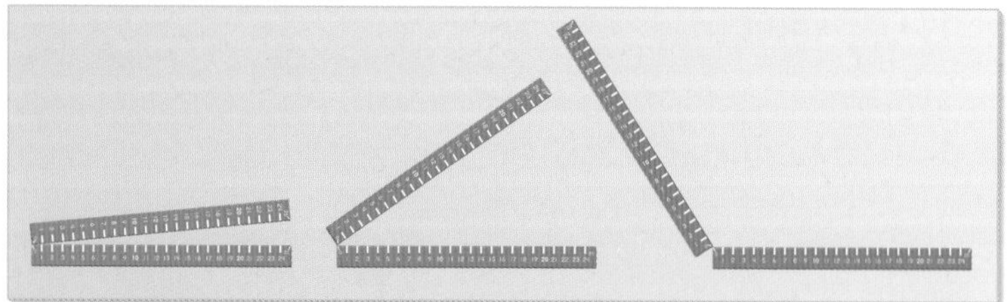

Demonstrate how to draw an angle on the board by tracing the inner edges of the two rulers.

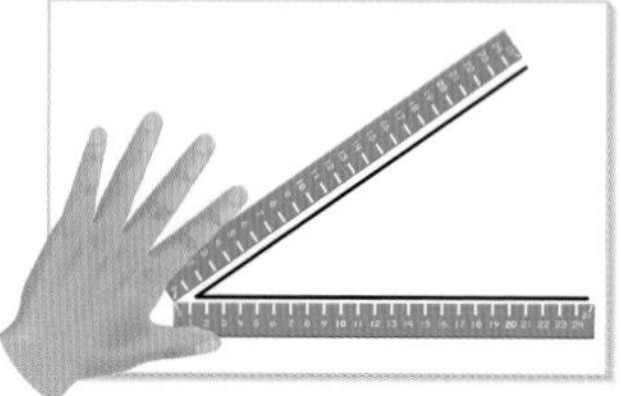

Practice Have children draw angles on their MathBoards. Encourage them to experiment by drawing large angles (approaching a straight line), small angles (approaching two lines that touch), and mid-sized angles (approaching a square angle).

▶ Explore Angles of Triangles (Optional) PAIRS

Demonstrate on the board how to draw a triangle from an angle by connecting the two sides of an angle with a line segment. Show children how it is possible to make several different triangles from the same angle by placing the line segment in different positions along the angle's sides.

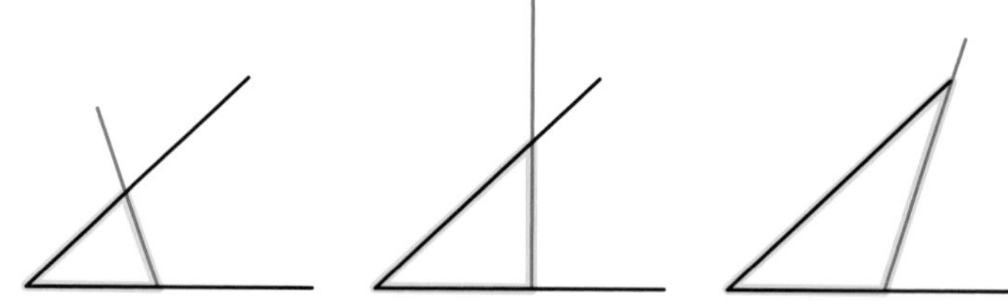

Ask children to use several of the angles they drew on their MathBoards and have them make triangles by connecting the two line segments with a third.

Challenge children to draw a triangle with one very small angle, a right angle, and a triangle with one very large angle.

- How many angles are in a triangle? three

Have children move their two rulers to each corner (vertex) of each triangle on their MathBoard to help them to visualize the three angles and to better understand why the shape is called a TRI-angle. See page 278 for the math words for triangles by angle in case you want to introduce them today.

2 Going Further

Differentiated Instruction

Intervention

Activity Card 2-4

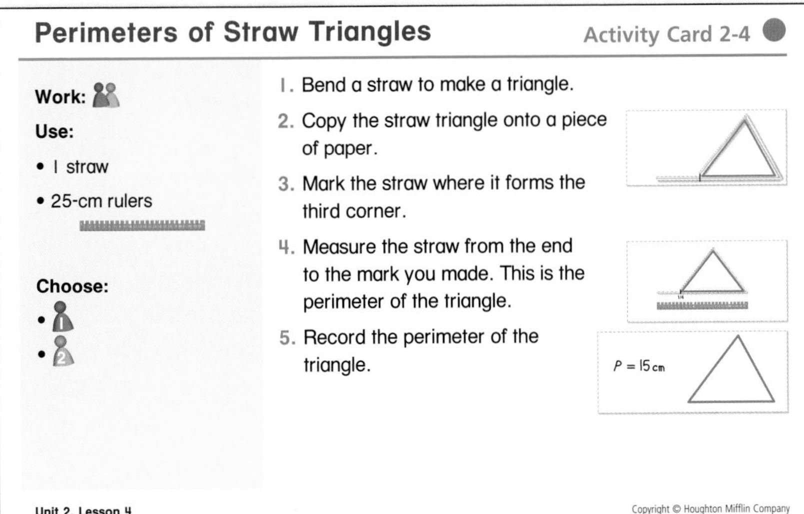

Perimeters of Straw Triangles Activity Card 2-4

Work: (pairs)
Use:
- 1 straw
- 25-cm rulers

Choose:
- (1)
- (2)

1. Bend a straw to make a triangle.
2. Copy the straw triangle onto a piece of paper.
3. Mark the straw where it forms the third corner.
4. Measure the straw from the end to the mark you made. This is the perimeter of the triangle.
5. Record the perimeter of the triangle.

P = 15 cm

Unit 2, Lesson 4

Copyright © Houghton Mifflin Company

Activity Note Each pair needs a drinking straw and 25-cm ruler or TRB M47–M48. The pair uses the straw to measure the perimeter of a triangle.

Math Writing Prompt

Write the Steps Write the steps you would use to find the perimeter of a triangle. Use words like *first, next,* and *then.*

Software Support

Use *Soar to Success* for instruction of students needing targeted support for underlying skills.

On Level

Activity Card 2-4

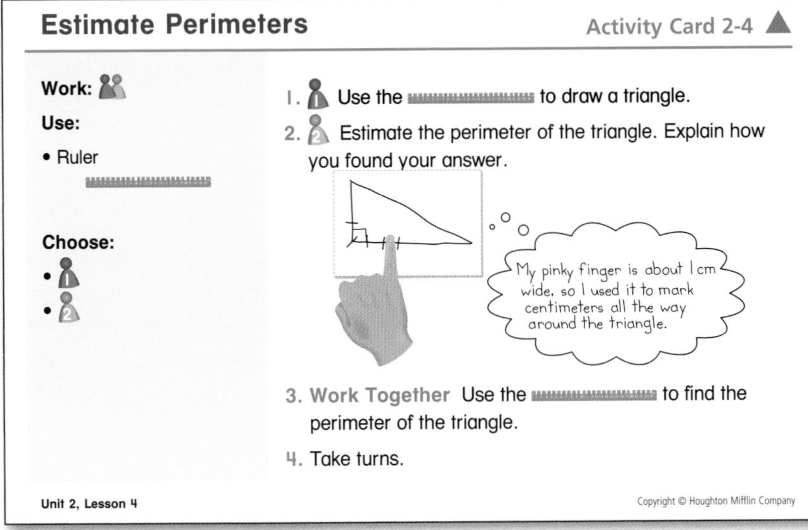

Estimate Perimeters Activity Card 2-4

Work: (pairs)
Use:
- Ruler

Choose:
- (1)
- (2)

1. (1) Use the ruler to draw a triangle.
2. (2) Estimate the perimeter of the triangle. Explain how you found your answer.

My pinky finger is about 1 cm wide, so I used it to mark centimeters all the way around the triangle.

3. Work Together Use the ruler to find the perimeter of the triangle.
4. Take turns.

Unit 2, Lesson 4

Copyright © Houghton Mifflin Company

Activity Note Each pair needs a 25-cm ruler or TRB M47–M48. Have children use a part of their hand to estimate the perimeter of the triangle.

Math Writing Prompt

Try It Can you draw a triangle with sides measuring 2 cm, 3 cm, and 6 cm? Explain your answer. Include a drawing.

Software Support

Use *MegaMath* for review and reinforcement of the concepts and skills presented in this lesson.

Challenge

Activity Card 2-4

The Longest Side of a Triangle Activity Card 2-4

Work: (individual)

Use:
- Rulers
- MathBoard

1. Draw one triangle on your MathBoard.
2. Measure the lengths of the all the sides of one triangle.
3. Add the sides the two shorter sides and compare the sum to the length of the longest side.

3+4=7
5 is less than 7
3 cm, 5 cm, 4 cm

4. Repeat Steps 1-3 six times.
5. Math Talk What do you notice about the sides of a triangle? Sample answer: The length of the longest side is always less than the sum of the lengths of the two shorter sides.

Unit 2, Lesson 4

Copyright © Houghton Mifflin Company

Activity Note Each child needs a 25-cm ruler or TRB M47–M48. Children draw six triangles and measure all sides.

Math Writing Prompt

Draw a Picture Adela found the perimeter of a triangle by measuring one side and adding it together three times. Her answer was correct. Draw a picture of the triangle.

Software Support

Use *Destination Math* to take students beyond the concepts and skills presented in this lesson.

3 Homework

2–4 Homework **Goal:** Additional Practice

On this Homework page, children find the perimeters of triangles.

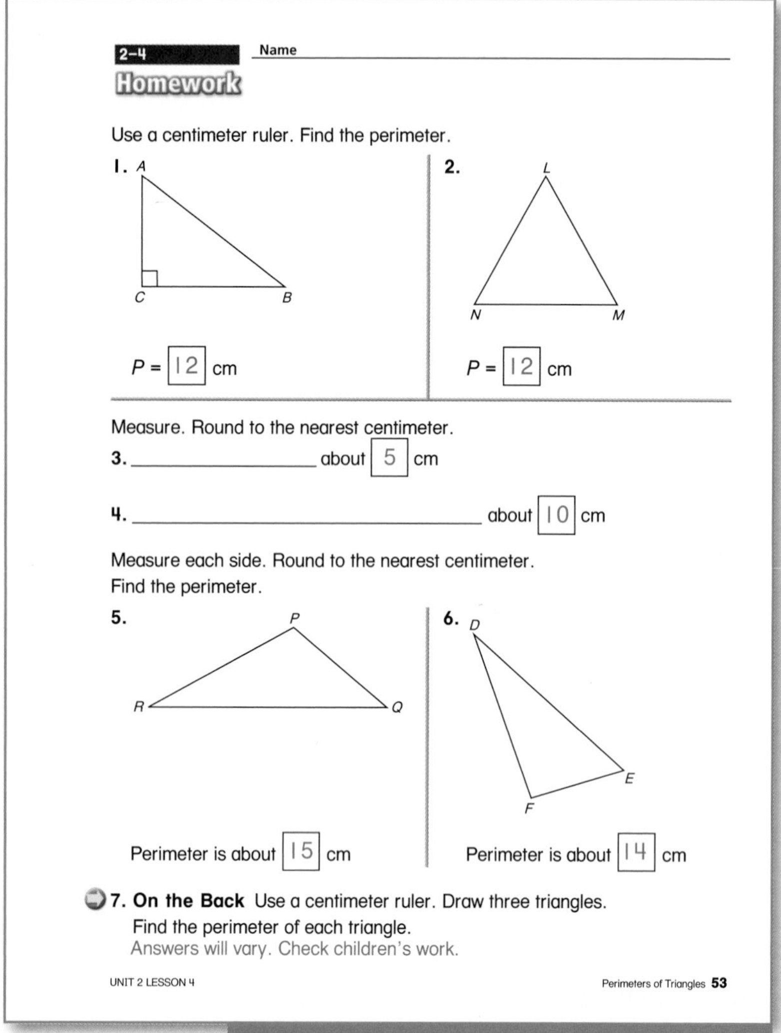

2–4 Homework Name

Use a centimeter ruler. Find the perimeter.

1. A, B, C

$P =$ 12 cm

2. L, M, N

$P =$ 12 cm

Measure. Round to the nearest centimeter.

3. ______________ about 5 cm

4. ______________________________ about 10 cm

Measure each side. Round to the nearest centimeter. Find the perimeter.

5. P, Q, R

Perimeter is about 15 cm

6. D, E, F

Perimeter is about 14 cm

7. **On the Back** Use a centimeter ruler. Draw three triangles. Find the perimeter of each triangle.
Answers will vary. Check children's work.

UNIT 2 LESSON 4 Perimeters of Triangles **53**

Homework and Remembering page 53

Home or School Activity

Literature Connection

Explore Perimeter Use the book *Racing Around* by Stuart J. Murphy and Mike Reed (HarperTrophy, 2001) to extend the idea of perimeter to other shapes and to introduce another unit of metric measurement, the kilometer.

You may want to have children read this book independently or you can use it as a read-aloud story. In this book, a young boy named Mike completes a bike race along a 15-kilometer circuit.

Explain to children that 15 kilometers is about 10 miles. Give them an example of a place that is about 15 kilometers from your school.

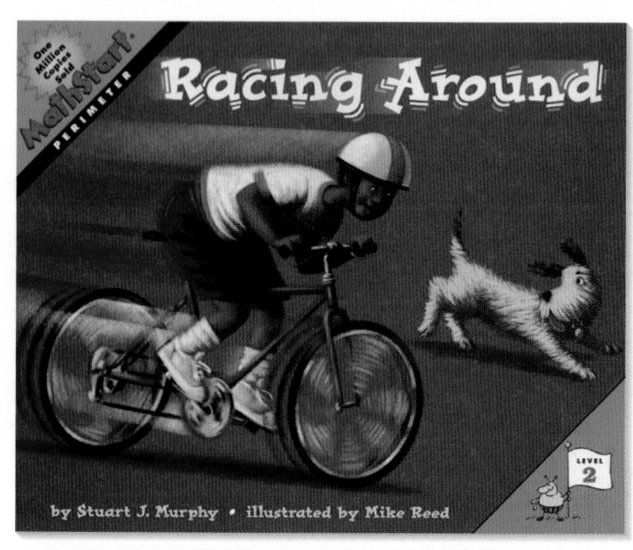

MathStart
PERIMETER
Racing Around
LEVEL 2
by Stuart J. Murphy • illustrated by Mike Reed

Unit Review and Test

Lesson Objectives

- Assess children's progress on unit objectives.

The Day at a Glance

Today's Goals	Materials
1 Assessing the Unit ▶ Assess children's progress on unit objectives. ▶ Use activities from unit lessons to reteach content. **2 Extending the Assessment** ▶ Use remediation for common errors. There is no homework assignment on a test day.	Centimeter Ruler Unit 2 Test, Student Activity Book pages 87–88 Unit 2 Test, Form A or B, Assessment Guide (optional) Unit 2 Performance Assessment, Assessment Guide (optional)

Keeping Skills Sharp

Daily Routines 5 MINUTES	
If you are doing a unit review day, go over the homework. If this is a test day, omit the homework review.	**Review and Test Day** You may want to choose a quiet game or other activity (reading a book or working on homework for another subject) for children who finish early.

1 Assessing the Unit

Assess Unit Objectives

 **45 MINUTES (more if schedule permits)**

Goal: Assess children's progress on unit objectives.

Materials: 25-cm ruler, Student Activity Book pages 87–88; Assessment Guide (optional)

▶ Review and Assessment

If your students are ready for assessment on the unit objectives, you may use either the test on the Student Activity Book pages or one of the forms of the Unit 2 Test in the Assessment Guide to assess student progress.

If you feel that students need some review first, you may use the test on the Student Activity Book pages as a review of unit content, and then use one of the forms of the Unit 2 Test in the Assessment Guide to assess student progress.

To assign a numerical score for all of these test forms, use 10 points for each question.

You may also choose to use the Unit 2 Performance Assessment. Scoring for that assessment can be found in its rubric in the Assessment Guide.

▶ Reteaching Resources

The chart lists the test items, the unit objectives they cover, and the lesson activities in which the objective is covered in this unit. You may revisit these activities with students who do not show mastery of the objectives.

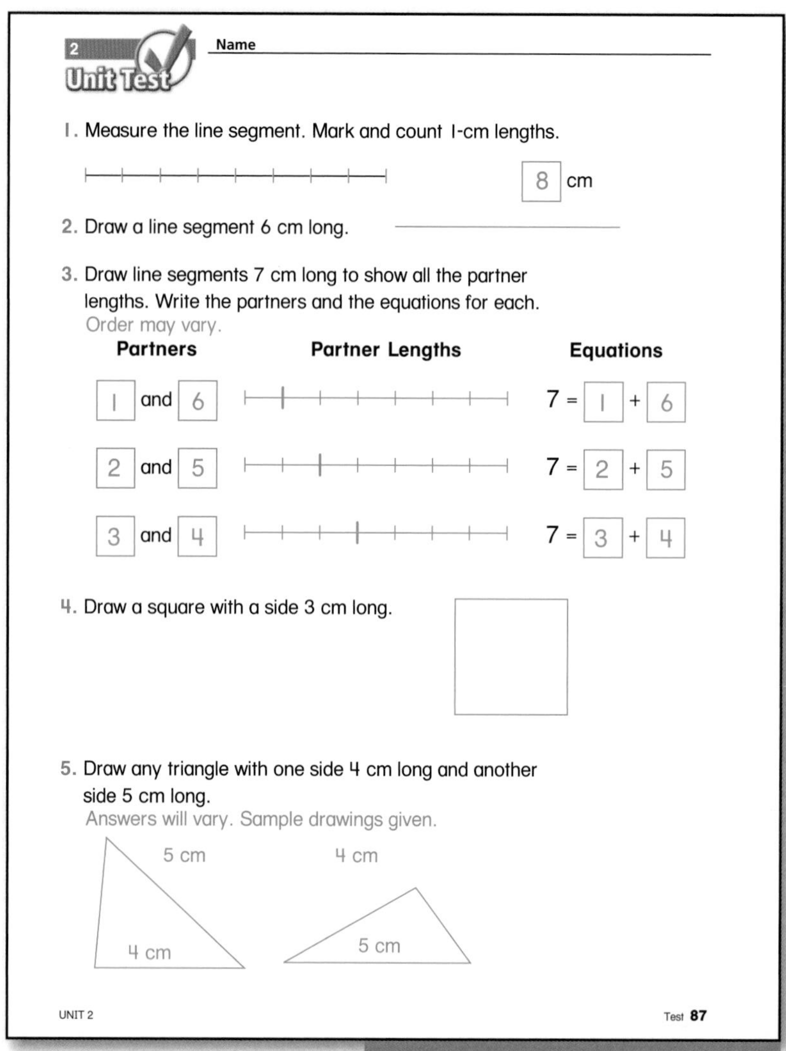
2 Unit Test

Name

1. Measure the line segment. Mark and count 1-cm lengths.

8 cm

2. Draw a line segment 6 cm long.

3. Draw line segments 7 cm long to show all the partner lengths. Write the partners and the equations for each.
Order may vary.

Partners	Partner Lengths	Equations
1 and 6		7 = 1 + 6
2 and 5		7 = 2 + 5
3 and 4		7 = 3 + 4

4. Draw a square with a side 3 cm long.

5. Draw any triangle with one side 4 cm long and another side 5 cm long.
Answers will vary. Sample drawings given.

UNIT 2 Test 87

Student Activity Book page 87

Unit Test Items	Unit Objectives Tested	Activities to Use for Reteaching
1, 2	**2.1** Draw and measure line segments.	Lesson 1, Activities 1 and 2
3	**2.2** Find partner lengths of line segments.	Lesson 1, Activity 2
10	**2.3** Learn properties of squares, rectangles, and triangles.	Lesson 2, Activities 1–3

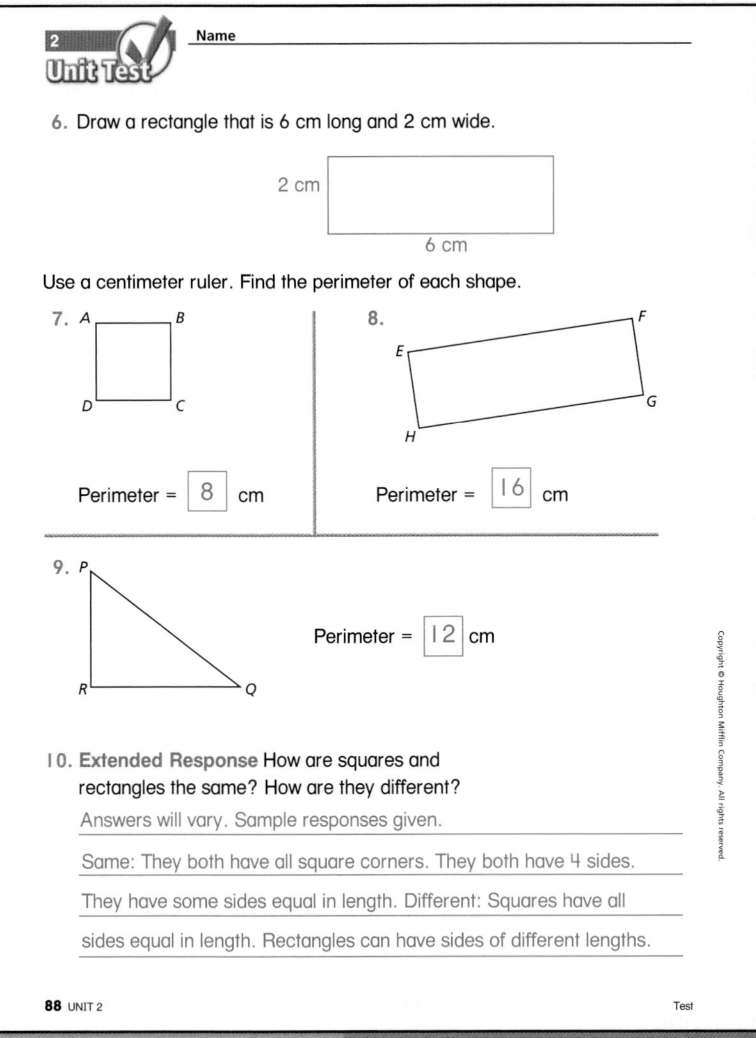

2 Unit Test

Name ____________

6. Draw a rectangle that is 6 cm long and 2 cm wide.

2 cm
6 cm

Use a centimeter ruler. Find the perimeter of each shape.

7. A B D C

Perimeter = 8 cm

8. E F G H

Perimeter = 16 cm

9. P R Q

Perimeter = 12 cm

10. **Extended Response** How are squares and rectangles the same? How are they different?

Answers will vary. Sample responses given.

Same: They both have all square corners. They both have 4 sides. They have some sides equal in length. Different: Squares have all sides equal in length. Rectangles can have sides of different lengths.

88 UNIT 2 Test

Student Activity Book page 88

Unit Test Items	Unit Objectives Tested	Activities to Use for Reteaching
4–6	**2.4** Draw squares, rectangles, and triangles.	Lesson 2, Activities 1–3
7–9	**2.5** Find perimeters of squares, rectangles, and triangles.	Lesson 3, Activity 1 Lesson 4, Activity 1

▶ Assessment Resources

Free Response Tests
Unit 2 Test, Student Activity Book pages 87–88
Unit 2 Test, Form A, Assessment Guide

Extended Response Item
The last item in the Student Activity Book test and in the Form A test will require an extended response as an answer.

Multiple Choice Test
Unit 2 Test, Form B, Assessment Guide

Performance Assessment
Unit 2 Performance Assessment, Assessment Guide
Unit 2 Performance Assessment Rubric, Assessment Guide

▶ Portfolio Assessment

Teacher-selected Items for Student Portfolios:

- Homework, Lesson 3
- Class Activity work, Lessons 2, 4

Student-selected Items for Student Portfolios:

- Favorite Home or School Activity
- Best Writing Prompt

2 Extending the Assessment

Common Errors

Activities for Remediation

Unit Objective 2.1

Draw and measure line segments.

Common Error: Uses a Ruler Incorrectly

When measuring with a ruler, some children may align the object with the incorrect position on their rulers.

Remediation Children must be familiar with the ruler they use in the classroom. The exact position of 0 may vary from one ruler to another. Make sure children know where the 0 indicator of their ruler is. If necessary, have them write a 0 on the ruler itself.

Unit Objective 2.2

Find partner lengths of line segments.

Common Error: Creates More Partner Lengths Than Necessary

When children are drawing partner lengths of a line segment, they may include partners that are the same but just switched.

Remediation Have children use two different colored connecting cubes to represent a line segment showing the partner lengths 1 cm and 6 cm. Show them that if you move the connecting cube representing the 1-cm length to the other side of the 6-cm cubes, the cubes show the partner lengths 6 cm and 1 cm. This will help them visualize that 6 + 1 is the same as 1 + 6.

Unit Objective 2.3

Learn properties of squares, rectangles, and triangles.

Common Error: Doesn't Recognize That a Square Is a Rectangle

When learning the properties of squares and rectangles, some children may not recognize that a square is a rectangle.

Remediation Reinforce the properties of a rectangle.

- opposite sides are the same length
- four square corners

Have children identify these properties in a square. Then explain that a square is a special rectangle having one additional property: all four sides are the same length.

Unit Objective 2.4

Draw squares, rectangles, and triangles.

Common Error: Doesn't Draw Square Corners Accurately

When drawing squares and rectangles, some children may not draw square corners accurately enough.

Remediation Have children use the corner of a sheet of paper or a corner at the end of their rulers to draw the square corners of their shapes.

Unit Objective 2.5

Find perimeters of squares, rectangles, and triangles.

Common Error: Includes the Same Length More than Once

In finding the perimeter of a shape, children may include the length of a side more than once.

Remediation Remind children that the perimeter is the distance around a shape so they only need to use the length of each side once. Suggest that they mark each side as they include it in the addends they are using to find the perimeter.

Common Error: Doesn't Include All the Side Lengths

In finding the perimeter of a shape, children may not include all of the side lengths of the shape.

Remediation Remind children that the perimeter is the distance around a figure so they need to include the length of each side in the perimeter. Have children count the number of sides in the shape and then the number of side lengths they added to find the perimeter.

Solving Story Problems

STORY PROBLEMS FORM an essential part of the *Math Expressions* curriculum as they connect the outside world with the classroom. In their own lives, children encounter mathematical situations that require them to understand the relationships between known and unknown quantities. Unit 3 encourages children to analyze the structure and language of story problems. Children are frequently asked to create their own story problems and to discuss the language in story problems. This unit can build literacy and communication skills for all children.

Skills Trace		
Grade 1	**Grade 2**	**Grade 3**
• Represent and solve addition and subtraction story problems. • Solve comparison story problems. • Solve story problems with extra information.	• Solve change plus and change minus story problems. • Solve collection and comparison story problems. • Solve story problems with extra or hidden information.	• Write equations and use comparison bars to represent and solve word problems. • Solve word problems with two steps, multi-steps, extra or hidden information, and identify problems with insufficient information.

Unit 3 Contents

Big Idea Addition and Subtraction Situations

Big Idea More Complex Situations

Big Idea Mixed Practice and Writing Story Problems

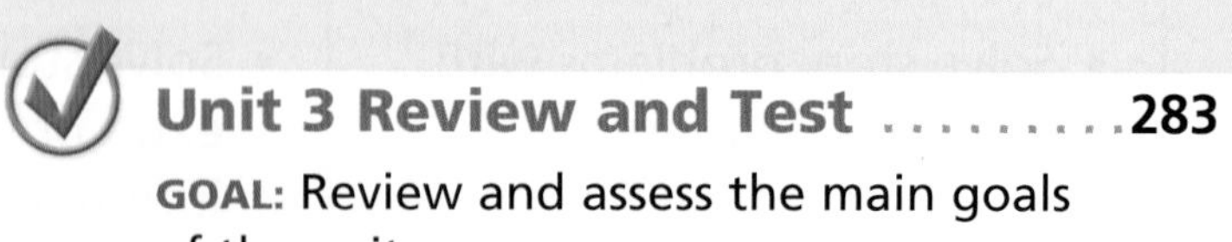

Unit 3 Assessment

Unit Objectives Tested	Unit Test Items	Lessons
3.1 Solve change plus and change minus story problems.	1–3	1–2, 7
3.2 Solve collection story problems.	4	3, 7
3.3 Solve comparison story problems.	5–6	5–7
3.4 Solve story problems with extra information.	7	8, 12
3.5 Solve story problems with hidden information.	8	9, 12
3.6 Solve two-step story problems.	9	10, 12
3.7 Write story problems.	10	2, 12

Assessment and Review Resources

Formal Assessment

Student Activity Book

- Unit Review and Test (pp. 123–126)

Assessment Guide

- Quick Quizzes (pp. A22, A23, A24)
- Test A–Open Response (pp. A25–A28)
- Test B-Multiple Choice (pp. A29–A32)
- Performance Assessment (pp. A33–A35)

Test Generator CD-ROM

- Open Response Test
- Multiple Choice Test
- Test Bank Items

Informal Assessment

Teacher Edition

- Ongoing Assessment (in every lesson)
- Quick Practice (in every lesson)
- Portfolio Suggestions (p. 286)

Math Talk

- Math Talk in Action (pp. 230, 236, 243, 262, 270)
- Solve and Discuss (pp. 197, 198, 204, 210, 217, 224, 229, 255, 274)
- In Activities (pp. 214, 248)

Review Opportunities

Homework and Remembering

- Review of recently taught topics
- Cumulative Review

Teacher Edition

- Unit Review and Test (pp. 283–286)

Test Generator CD-ROM

- Custom Review Sheets

Planning Unit 3

Lesson/NCTM Standards	Resources	Materials for Lesson Activities	Materials for Going Further
3–1 **Change Plus and Change Minus Story Problems** NCTM Standards: 1, 6	TE pp. 195–200 SAB pp. 89–92 H&R pp. 55–56 AC 3–1		Math Journals
3–2 **More Change Plus and Change Minus Story Problems** NCTM Standards: 1, 6, 8	TE pp. 201–206 SAB pp. 93–94 H&R pp. 57–58 AC 3–2	MathBoard materials	Equations and Math Mountains (TRB M52) Problems and Equations (TRB M53) Problems and Proof Drawings (TRB M54) Math Journals
3–3 **Collection Problems** NCTM Standards: 1, 6, 8	TE pp. 207–212 SAB pp. 95–96 H&R pp. 59–60 AC 3–3	MathBoard materials	✓ Two-color counters MathBoard materials Math Journals
3–4 **Story Problems with Group Names** NCTM Standards: 1, 5, 6, 7, 8	TE pp. 213–220 SAB pp. 97–100 H&R pp. 61–62 AC 3–4 MCC 3–9	MathBoard materials	Math Journals
3–5 **Comparison Story Problems** NCTM Standards: 1, 6, 8	TE pp. 221–226 SAB pp. 101–102 H&R pp. 63–64 AC 3–5		Math Journals
3–6 **More Comparison Story Problems** NCTM Standards: 1, 6, 8	TE pp. 227–232 SAB pp. 103–104 H&R pp. 65–66 AC 3–6	MathBoard materials	Math Journals
3–7 **Mixed Story Problems** NCTM Standards: 1, 6, 8	TE pp. 233–238 SAB pp. 105–108 H&R pp. 67–68 AC 3–7 MCC 3–10 AG Quick Quiz 1	✓ Secret Code Cards (TRB M3–M4) Colored paper *Count On Me* Game Board (TRB M28)	Mix and Match (TRB M56) Math Journals
3–8 **Problems with Not Enough or Extra Information** NCTM Standards: 1, 6	TE pp. 239–246 SAB pp. 109–112 H&R pp. 69–70 AC 3–8	✓ Counters MathBoard materials	Math Journals

Resources/Materials Key: TE: Teacher Edition SAB: Student Activity Book H&R: Homework and Remembering AC: Activity Cards MCC: Math Center Challenge AG: Assessment Guide ✓: Grade 2 kits TRB: Teacher's Resource Book

Lesson/NCTM Standards	Resources	Materials for Lesson Activities	Materials for Going Further
3–9 **Problems with Hidden Information and Mixed Practice** NCTM Standards: 1, 6	TE pp. 247–252 SAB pp. 113–114 H&R pp. 71–72 AC 3–9		Dictionary and other reference books ✓ Connecting cubes Index cards Math Journals
3–10 **Two-Step Story Problems** NCTM Standards: 1, 6, 8	TE pp. 253–258 SAB pp. 115–116 H&R pp. 73–74 AC 3–10 MCC 3–11		Highlighter or yellow marker Math Journals
3–11 **Strategies Using Doubles** NCTM Standards: 1, 8	TE pp. 259–266 SAB pp. 117–118 H&R pp. 75–76 AC 3–11 AG Quick Quiz 2	✓ Counters	*Even Steven and Odd Todd* by Kathryn Cristaldi and Henry Morehouse Index cards Math Journals
3–12 **Mixed Practice and Writing Story Problems** NCTM Standards: 1, 6, 8	TE pp. 267–272 SAB pp. 119–120 H&R pp. 77–78 AC 3–12		Chart paper Index cards Math Journals
3–13 **Mixed Practice** NCTM Standards: 1, 8	TE pp. 273–276 H&R pp. 79–80 AC 3–13 MCC 3–12	*Count On Me* Game Board (TRB M28) ✓ Secret Code Cards Colored paper	Math Journals
3–14 **Use Mathematical Processes** NCTM Standards: 6, 7, 8, 9, 10	TE pp. 277–282 SAB pp. 121–122 H&R pp. 81–82 AC 3–14 AG Quick Quiz 3		Math Journals
✓ Unit Review and Test	TE pp. 283–286 SAB pp. 123–126 AG: Unit 3 tests		

Resources/Materials Key: TE: Teacher Edition SAB: Student Activity Book H&R: Homework and Remembering AC: Activity Cards MCC: Math Center Challenge AG: Assessment Guide ✓: Grade 2 kits TRB: Teacher's Resource Book

Manipulatives and Materials

Essential materials for teaching *Math Expressions* are available in the Grade 2 kits. These materials are indicated by a ✓ in these lists. At the front of this Teacher Edition is more information about kit contents, alternatives for the materials, and use of the materials.

Independent Learning Activities

Ready-Made Math Challenge Centers

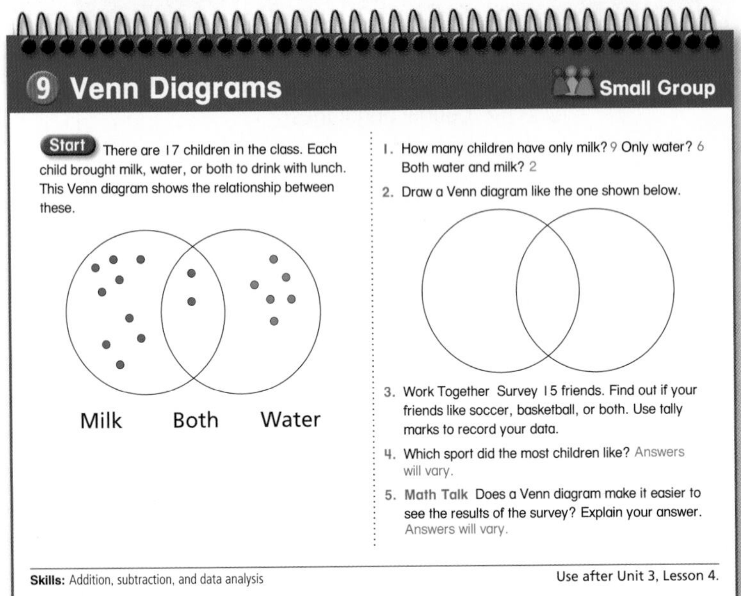

9 Venn Diagrams — Small Group

Start There are 17 children in the class. Each child brought milk, water, or both to drink with lunch. This Venn diagram shows the relationship between these.

1. How many children have only milk? 9 Only water? 6 Both water and milk? 2
2. Draw a Venn diagram like the one shown below.
3. Work Together Survey 15 friends. Find out if your friends like soccer, basketball, or both. Use tally marks to record your data.
4. Which sport did the most children like? Answers will vary.
5. Math Talk Does a Venn diagram make it easier to see the results of the survey? Explain your answer. Answers will vary.

Skills: Addition, subtraction, and data analysis — Use after Unit 3, Lesson 4.

Grouping Small Group

Materials None

Objective Children read information in a Venn diagram and then create their own Venn diagram based on collected data.

Connections Data and Reasoning

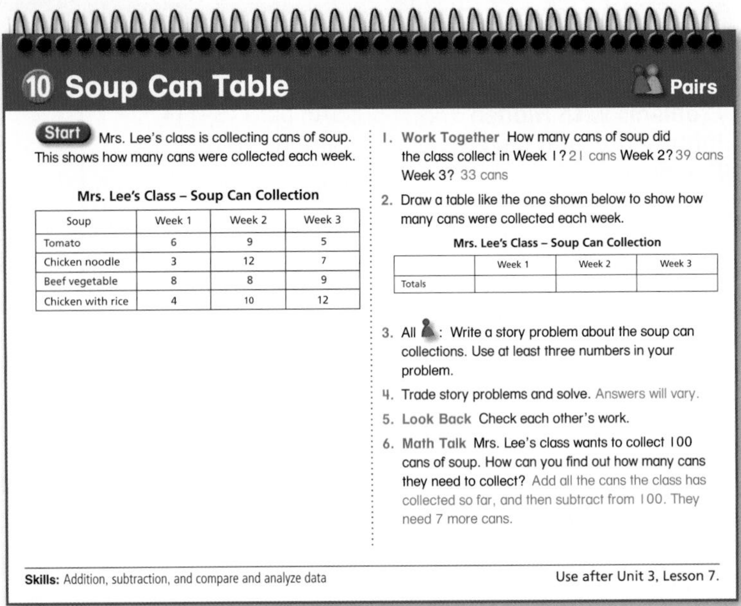

10 Soup Can Table — Pairs

Start Mrs. Lee's class is collecting cans of soup. This shows how many cans were collected each week.

Mrs. Lee's Class – Soup Can Collection

Soup	Week 1	Week 2	Week 3
Tomato	6	9	5
Chicken noodle	3	12	7
Beef vegetable	8	8	9
Chicken with rice	4	10	12

1. Work Together How many cans of soup did the class collect in Week 1? 21 cans Week 2? 39 cans Week 3? 33 cans
2. Draw a table like the one shown below to show how many cans were collected each week.

Mrs. Lee's Class – Soup Can Collection

	Week 1	Week 2	Week 3
Totals			

3. All: Write a story problem about the soup can collections. Use at least three numbers in your problem.
4. Trade story problems and solve. Answers will vary.
5. Look Back Check each other's work.
6. Math Talk Mrs. Lee's class wants to collect 100 cans of soup. How can you find out how many cans they need to collect? Add all the cans the class has collected so far, and then subtract from 100. They need 7 more cans.

Skills: Addition, subtraction, and compare and analyze data — Use after Unit 3, Lesson 7.

Grouping Pairs

Materials None

Objective Children interpret data in a table and write story problems.

Connections Problem solving and Real world

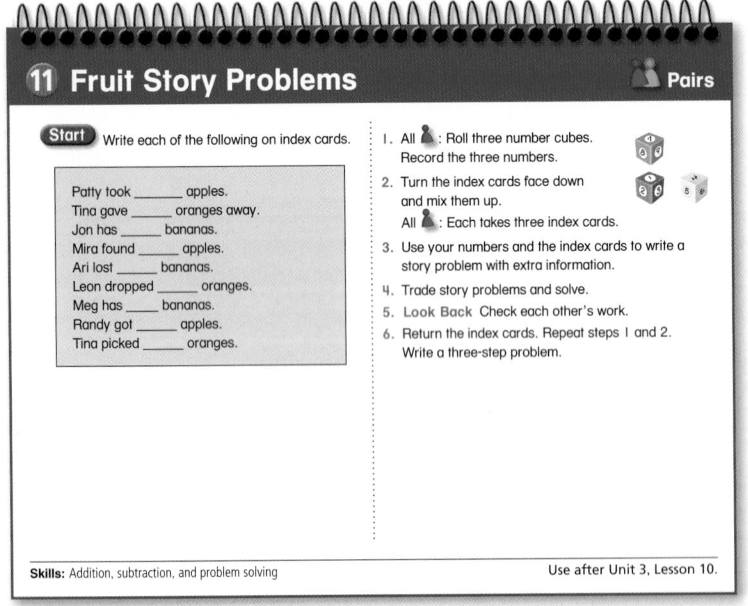

11 Fruit Story Problems — Pairs

Start Write each of the following on index cards.

Patty took _____ apples.
Tina gave _____ oranges away.
Jon has _____ bananas.
Mira found _____ apples.
Ari lost _____ bananas.
Leon dropped _____ oranges.
Meg has _____ bananas.
Randy got _____ apples.
Tina picked _____ oranges.

1. All: Roll three number cubes. Record the three numbers.
2. Turn the index cards face down and mix them up. All: Each takes three index cards.
3. Use your numbers and the index cards to write a story problem with extra information.
4. Trade story problems and solve.
5. Look Back Check each other's work.
6. Return the index cards. Repeat steps 1 and 2. Write a three-step problem.

Skills: Addition, subtraction, and problem solving — Use after Unit 3, Lesson 10.

Grouping Pairs

Materials Index cards, 3 number cubes: 1 with numbers 7, 8, 9 and 2 with numbers 1–6

Objective Children write story problems with extra information and three-step problems.

Connections Problem solving and Science

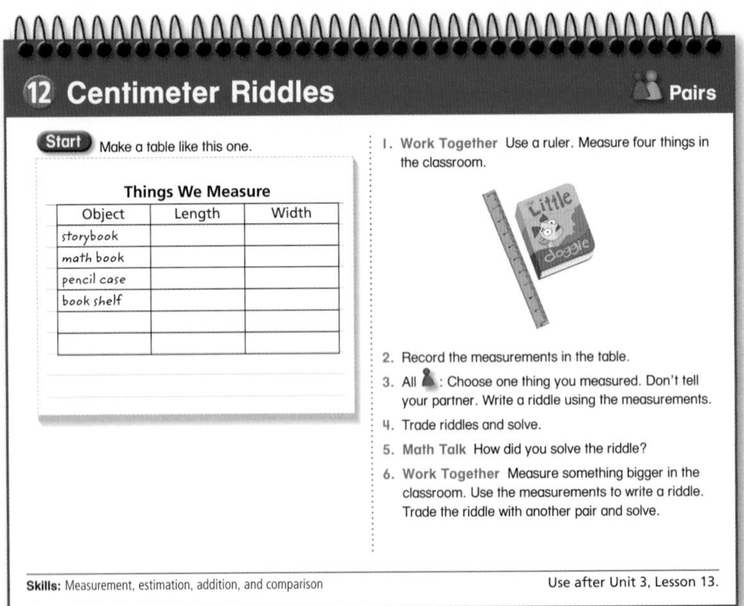

12 Centimeter Riddles — Pairs

Start Make a table like this one.

Things We Measure

Object	Length	Width
storybook		
math book		
pencil case		
book shelf		

1. Work Together Use a ruler. Measure four things in the classroom.
2. Record the measurements in the table.
3. All: Choose one thing you measured. Don't tell your partner. Write a riddle using the measurements.
4. Trade riddles and solve.
5. Math Talk How did you solve the riddle?
6. Work Together Measure something bigger in the classroom. Use the measurements to write a riddle. Trade the riddle with another pair and solve.

Skills: Measurement, estimation, addition, and comparison — Use after Unit 3, Lesson 13.

Grouping Pairs

Materials Centimeter ruler, books and other classroom objects

Objective Children measure objects in the classroom and write riddles about the object.

Connections Measurement and Reasoning

Ready-Made Math Resources

Technology — Tutorials, Practice, and Intervention

Use activity masters and online, individualized intervention and support to bring students to proficiency.

Help students practice skills and apply concepts through exciting math adventures.

Extend and enrich students' understanding of skills and concepts through engaging, interactive lessons and activities.

Visit **Education Place**®
www.eduplace.com

Visit www.eduplace.com/mx2t/ and find family, teacher, and student materials, activities, games, and more.

Literature Links

Count on Pablo

Count on Pablo

Pablo and his grandmother have a big problem. No one seems interested in buying their farm produce. Like many problems we all must solve in life, the solution to the problem is creative! Offer tortilla chips!

Literature Connections

- *Even Steven and Odd Todd*, by Kathryn Cristaldi, illustrated by Henry Morehouse (Cartwheel, 1996)

Unit 3 Teaching Resources

Differentiated Instruction

Individualizing Instruction		
Activities	Level	Frequency
	• Intervention • On Level • Challenge	All 3 in every lesson
Math Writing Prompts	Level	Frequency
	• Intervention • On Level • Challenge	All 3 in every lesson
Math Center Challenges	For advanced students	
	4 in every unit	

Reaching All Learners		
English Language Learners	Lessons	Pages
	1, 2, 3, 4, 5, 6, 7, 8, 9, 1, 11, 12, 13, 14,	196, 197, 203, 209, 210, 214, 217, 224, 229, 234, 241, 248, 254, 260, 268
Extra Help	Lessons	Pages
	3, 5, 7, 8, 9	209, 224, 236, 241, 243, 248
Advanced Learners	Lesson	Page
	11	264

Strategies for English Language Learners

Present this problem to all students. Offer the different levels of support to meet children's levels of language proficiency.

Objective Help children become comfortable with telling story problems.

Activity Have children work in pairs. Give 1 partner 7 blocks. Have those children give 4 blocks to their partners. Say: **Let's tell a story problem.**

Newcomer

- Have the first partners repeat. Say: **The teacher gave me 7 blocks.** Pause, then say: **I gave my partner 4 blocks.** Pause, then ask: **How many blocks do I have now?** Have the partners answer.

Beginning

- Say: **The teacher gave one student ___.** 7 blocks **The student gave a friend ___.** 4 blocks
- Say: **Now we ask: How many blocks does the student have now?** Have children repeat and answer.

Intermediate

- Ask questions to help children tell the story. Ask: **What did I do? What did the first partner do?**
- Say: **We finish the story with a question. We ask: How many blocks does the first partner ___?** have now

Advanced

- Have each pair tell the problem story. Have volunteers share the stories.

Connections

Language Arts Connections
Lesson 6, page 232
Lesson 9, page 252
Lesson 10, page 258
Lesson 14, page 282

Multicultural Connection
Lesson 2, page 206

Science Connection
Lesson 8, page 246

Social Studies Connection
Lesson 5, page 226

Sports Connection
Lesson 7, page 238

Technology Connections
Lesson 3, page 212
Lesson 12, page 272
Lesson 13, page 276

Literature Connection
Lesson 11, page 266

Putting Research into Practice for Unit 3

From Our Curriculum Research Project: Analyzing the Structure and Language of Story Problems

In this unit, children analyze a variety of story problem structures: "change plus," "change minus," "collection," and "comparison." They also analyze problems with not enough information, problems with extra information, problems with hidden information, and problems that require two steps to solve.

- "Change plus" and "change minus" problems provide a quantity which is modified by a change—something is added or subtracted—which results in a new quantity.
- "Collection" problems have all of the quantities of objects present from the start and nothing is introduced or removed.
- "Comparison" problems involve someone or something that has more or less of something than someone or something else.

Throughout, children model, draw, or act out the actions or relations presented in the story problems as a strategy for understanding and solving them.

–Karen Fuson, Author
Math Expressions

From Current Research: Accessible Methods for Multi-Digit Addition

Since children intuitively solve word problems by modeling the actions and relations described in them, it is important to distinguish among the different types of problems that can be represented by adding or subtracting. . . . One useful way of classifying problems is to heed the children's approach and examine the actions and relations described. This examination produces a taxonomy of problem types distinguished by the solution method children use and provides a framework to explain the relative difficulty of problems.

Four basic classes of addition and subtraction problems can be identified: problems involving (a) joining, (b) separating, (c) part-part-whole relations, and (d) comparison relations. Problems within a class involve the same type of action or relation, but within each class several distinct types of problems can be identified depending on which quantity is the unknown.

National Research Council: Developing Proficiency with Whole Numbers. *Adding It Up: Helping Children Learn Mathematics,* Washington, D.C.: National Academy Press, 2001. 184.

Other Useful References: Addition and Subtraction

Carpenter, Thomas P., Fennema, E., Franke, M.L., Empson, S.B., & Levi, L.W. *Children's Mathematics: Cognitively Guided Instruction.* Portsmouth, NH: Heinemann, 1999.

Carpenter, Thomas P. "Learning to add and subtract: An exercise in problem solving." *Teaching and Learning Mathematical Problem Solving: Multiple Research Perspectives,* E.A. Silver (Ed.). Hillsdale, NJ: Erlbaum, 1985. 17–40.

Getting Ready to Teach Unit 3

Throughout the unit, children will see a variety of story problems, which are systematically presented.

Math Expressions Vocabulary

As you teach this unit, emphasize understanding of these terms:

- change problem
- collection problem
- comparison problem
- hidden information
- two-step problem

See Glossary on pp. T7–T20.

Understanding Situations in Story Problems

All Lessons

Our research-based focus on story problems gives children a chance to recognize a type of problem by understanding the underlying situation presented. If children truly understand the situation, they will be less likely to perform rote computation steps that do not fit into the problem situation. Rather, they will think about the situation and try to comprehend it, before attempting to solve it.

Talking About Story Problems Children read story problems carefully and rephrase them in their own language. This helps them analyze what information is given and what is being asked. Children discuss the problems with one another and share ideas about the meaning of the situations. They share ideas about how they might solve the problems.

Representing Story Problems Throughout the unit, emphasis is placed on understanding, and then representing any story problem. Children use what they know from reading and talking about the problems to draw representational diagrams, Math Mountains, number boxes, and equations. Children label math drawings to link them to the problem situations and to show their thinking.

Story Problem Types

Extensive research from all over the world has identified the types of word problems described on the following pages. Children's solutions vary with the type of problem and with which quantity is unknown. Children need experience with all types in order to become good problem solvers.

Change Plus Problems

Lessons 1, 2, 7, 12, and 13

Change plus problems begin with a given quantity, which is then modified by a change—something is added—which results in a new quantity.

Joe had 9 toy cars. Then he got 3 more. How many toy cars does he have now?

$9 + 3 = \square$

had got now

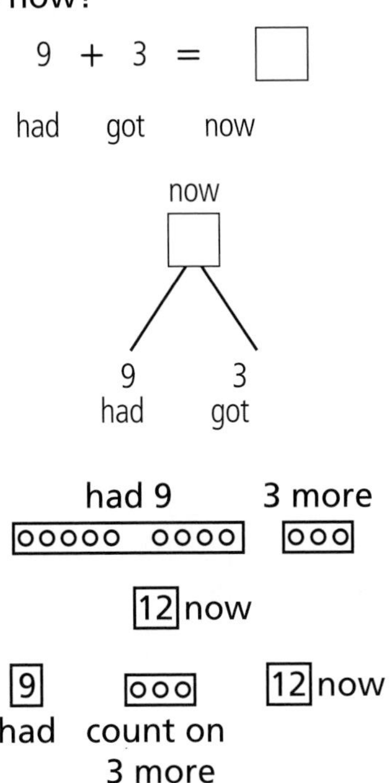

Joe had 9 toy cars. Then he got some more. Now he has 12. How many toy cars did he get?

$9 + \square = 12$

had got now

now
12
9
had
got

9 ooo 3
had got
12 now

Joe had some toy cars. Then he got 3 more. Now he has 12. How many toy cars did he have to start?

$\square + 3 = 12$

had got now

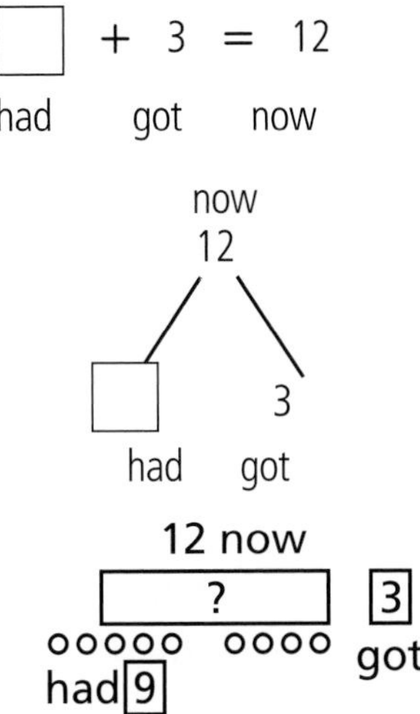

Change Minus Problems

Lessons 1, 2, 7, 12, and 13

Change minus problems begin with a given quantity, which is then modified by a change—something is subtracted—which results in a new quantity.

Sue had 12 books. Then she loaned her friend 9 books. How many books does Sue have now?

$12 - 9 = \square$

had loaned now

had
12
9
loaned now

had 12
9 o o o
loaned 10, 11, 12
3 now

Sue had 12 books. Then she loaned her friend some books. Now she has 3 books. How many books did she loan her friend?

$12 - \square = 3$

had loaned now

had
12
3
loaned now

had 12
ooooo oooo ooo
loaned 9 3
now

Sue had some books. Then she loaned her friend 9 books. Now she has 3 books. How many books did she have to start?

$\square - 9 = 3$

had loaned now

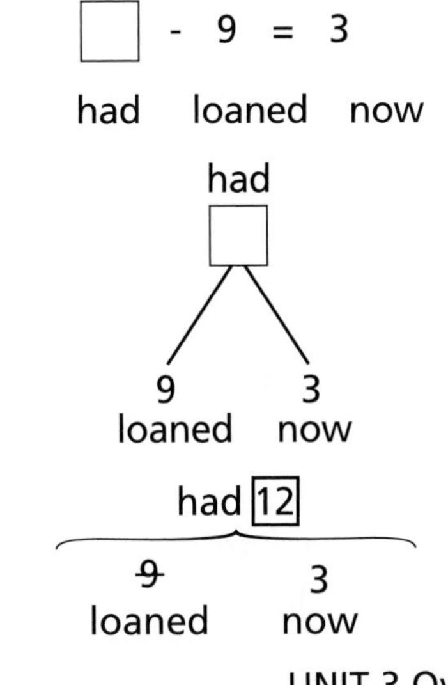

Collection Problems: Put Together or Take Apart

Lessons 3, 7, 12, and 13

All objects are present from the start, and nothing is introduced or removed. The situations involve conceptually putting objects together or taking them apart.

Ann had some tomato vines. She planted 8 in the front yard and 6 in the back yard. How many vines did she have?

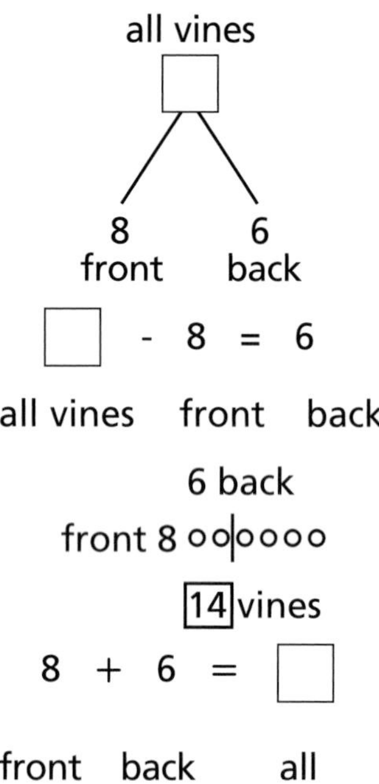

Ann had 14 tomato vines. She planted 8 in the front yard and some in the back yard. How many vines did she plant in the back yard?

all vines
14
8 front
☐ back

14 - 8 = ☐

all vines front back

[6] back
front 8 oo|oooo
[14] vines

8 + ☐ = 14

front back all

Ann had 14 tomato vines. She planted some in the front yard and 6 in the back yard. How many vines did she plant in the front yard?

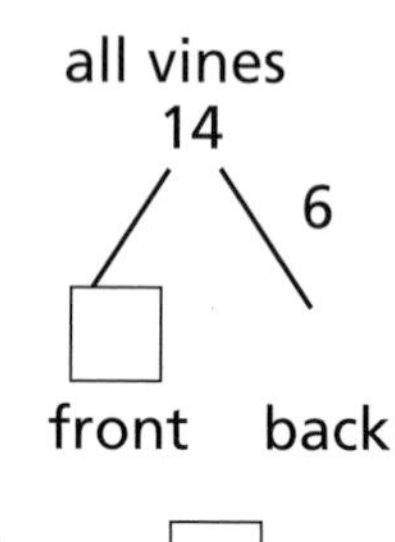

14 - ☐ = 6

all vines front back

front [8]
back 6 oooo|oooo
14 vines

6 + ☐ = 14

back front all

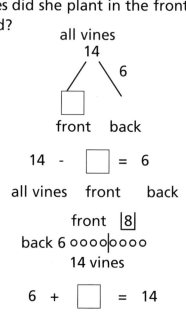

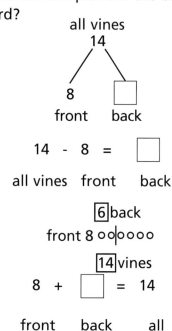

Collection Problems: Static/No Action

Lessons 3, 7, 12, and 13

These problems involve no change. All objects are present from the start, and nothing is introduced or removed. The situations describe groupings within a total.

7 children were on the swings. 8 were on the slides. How many children were playing altogether?

7 + 8 = ☐

swings slides altogether

playing
☐
7 swings
8 slides

swings 7
8 slides
ooo|ooooo
[15] playing

7 children were on the swings. Some were on the slides. 15 were playing altogether. How many children were on the slides?

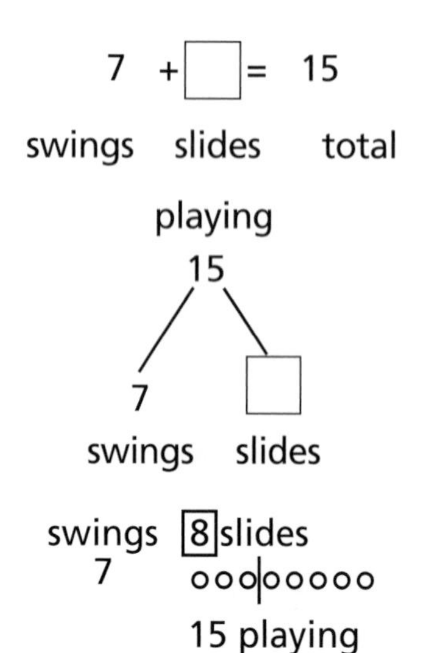

Some children were on the swings. 8 were on the slides. 15 were playing altogether. How many children were on the swings?

☐ + 8 = 15

swings slides in all

playing
15
swings
8 slides

slides 8
swings [7]
oo|ooooo
15 playing

Group Name Problem

Lessons 4, 7, 12, and 13

Group name problems are just a special case of collection problems that require the use of a new category name. For example, 8 daisies + 4 roses = 12 flowers. Or, for example, boys and girls can be grouped together as children; apples and oranges can be classified as fruits. Using drawings and Venn diagrams, children can develop an understanding that larger classifications can contain specific examples.

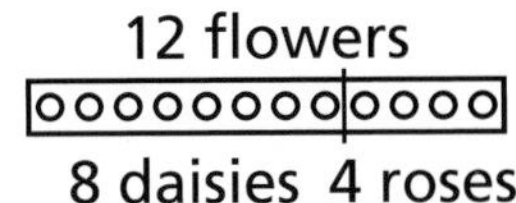

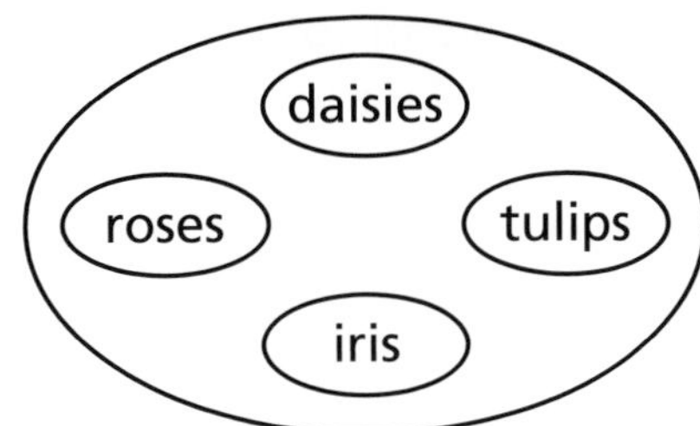

Comparison Problems

Lessons 5, 6, 7, 12, and 13

Comparison problems involve finding how many more or less one quantity is than another quantity. Children draw number boxes (or Comparison Bars) and match items between groups to help compare. Children can see which has more or less, and how many more or less.

Sue has 5 balloons.

Mike has 7 balloons.

Sue's balloons — 2 fewer balloons

Mike's balloons — "extra" items — 2 more balloons

Comparison language is difficult, and children need a lot of practice saying both forms of the comparing question.

- How many *fewer* balloons does Sue have than Mike?
- How many *more* balloons does Mike have than Sue?

} two forms of comparison questions

- How many *more* balloons does Sue need to have as many as Mike?
- How many balloons does Mike need to give away to have as many as Sue?

} using equalizing language

More-advanced children can draw Comparison Bars.

Comparison Bars

S [5] ○ ← [2] extra

M [7] difference is 2

Not Enough Information

Lessons 8, 12, and 13

Occasionally, children will encounter story problems that cannot be solved because they do not contain enough information. Children use Math Mountains, equations, and drawings to determine what might be wrong with the problem. Occasionally, children will be asked to supply missing information to help them solve the problem.

Sam has 8 pretzels. His friend Lydia has some too. How many pretzels do they have in total?

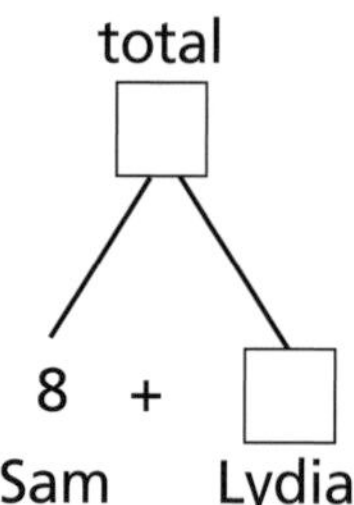

8 + □ = □

S L T

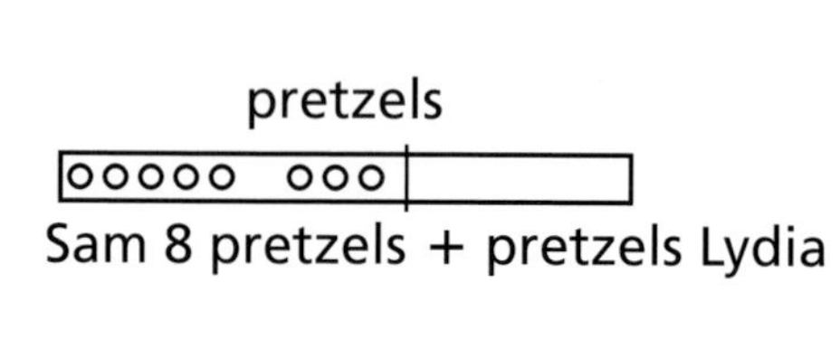

Extra Information

Lessons 8, 12, and 13

Problems with extra information have more information than is needed to solve the problem. Children may find it helpful to cross out the unnecessary information in the problem. They use drawings, equations, and Math Mountains to represent the needed information to solve.

The zoo had 8 elephants ~~and 7 zebras.~~ Last month 3 baby elephants were born. How many elephants are there at the zoo now?

ooooo oo
7 zebras

□ elephants now
ooooo ooo|oo o
8 elephants + 3 baby elephants

8 + 3 = □

e be e

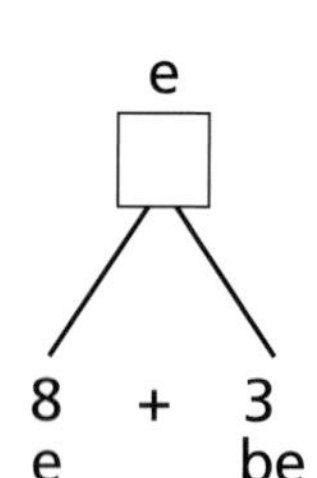

Hidden Information

Lessons 9, 12, and 13

Problems with hidden or implied information use special quantity words, instead of numbers, to present information. For example, a dozen, a pair, a week, the wheels of a bicycle. Children solve the problems by writing in numbers for the implied information. They may also draw pictures to help.

12
Holly bought ~~a dozen~~ eggs. She used 5 of them to make breakfast. How many eggs does she have left?

$12 - 5 = 7$ *eggs*

Rob's yard is shaped like a rectangle. He planted a tree in each corner. Theresa's yard is shaped like a triangle. She planted a tree in each corner. How many trees did Rob and Theresa plant in all?

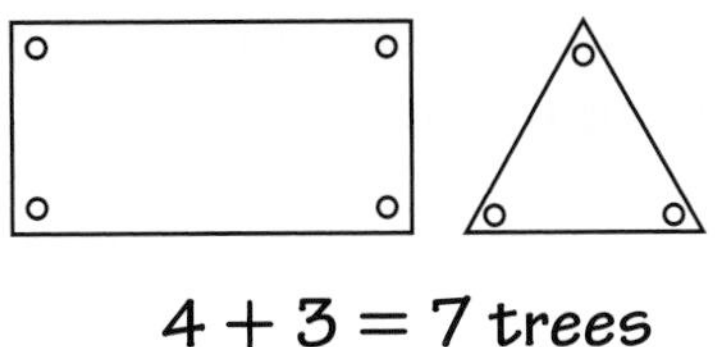

$4 + 3 = 7$ *trees*

Two-Step Problems

Lessons 8, 12, and 13

Two-step problems require two steps to solve. For these types of problems, it can be especially useful for children to read and rephrase the story problem and to ask themselves what the problem is asking. Children use drawings, equations, and Math Mountains to represent the problems. They analyze what steps they can use to solve, and make a drawing.

Kate counted 5 fish, 3 turtles, and some frogs in the pond. She counted 14 animals altogether. How many frogs are in the pond?

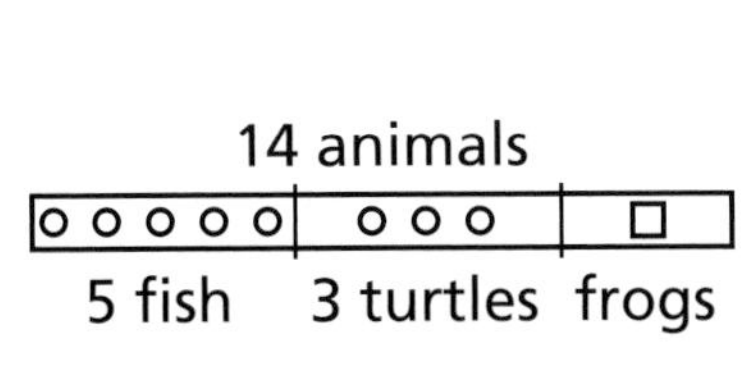

f t fg
$5 + 3 + \square = 14$

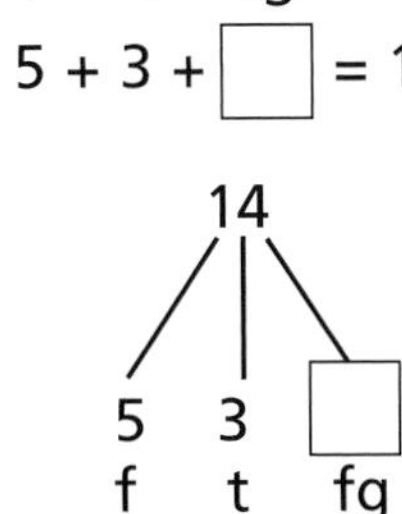

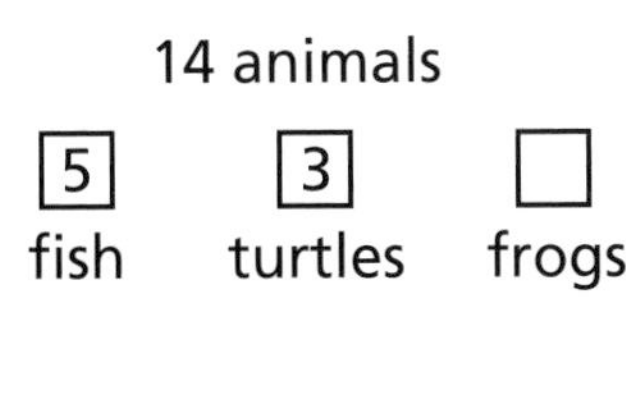

Situation Equations and Solution Equations

Lessons 2, 3, 4, 5, 7 and 8

Children often write situation equations like $5 + 3 + \square = 14$ that show relationships within the problem situation. They usually solve that equation without writing a solution equation like $14 - 8 = \square$. This is appropriate with such small numbers. With large numbers, children may wish to write solution equations after they have written situation equations.

Problem Solving

In *Math Expressions* a research-based, algebraic problem-solving approach that focuses on problem types is used: understand the situation, represent the situation with a math drawing or an equation, solve the problem, and see that the answer makes sense. Throughout the unit, children solve a variety of problems using the graphing and comparison skills being taught in this unit.

Using Mathematical Processes

Lesson 14

The mathematical process skills of problem solving, reasoning and proof, communication, connections, and representation are pervasive in this program and underlie all the children's mathematical work. Lessons that concentrate on developing and applying process skills can be found in every unit. In this unit, Lesson 14 has activities that focus on all of the process skills. Each of these activities, and its main process skill and goal, are listed below.

Activity	Process Skill	Goal
Math and Social Studies	Connections	Learn about the origins and importance of zero.
Pedro's Party Favors	Problem Solving	Understand that some problems may have multiple solutions or no solution at all.
What Am I Thinking of?	Reasoning and Proof	Decide whether enough information is given to find the answer to a problem.
Use a Diagram	Representation	Use Venn diagrams to sort.
Giving Directions	Communication	Give and follow directions for drawing a simple figure.

Change Plus and Change Minus Story Problems

Lesson Objective

- **Represent and solve change plus and change minus story problems.**

Vocabulary

change plus story problem
change minus story problem

The Day at a Glance

Today's Goals	Materials	
1 Teaching the Lesson A: Represent and discuss solution methods for change plus and change minus story problems. **2 Going Further** ▸ Differentiated Instruction **3 Homework and Spiral Review**	**Lesson Activities** Student Activity Book pp. 89–92 (includes Family Letter) Homework and Remembering pp. 55–56	**Going Further** Activity Cards 3-1 Math Journals

Use **Math Talk** today!

Keeping Skills Sharp

Quick Practice — 5 MINUTES

Goals: Write equation chains for 13. Make a ten when adding a number to 9. Find totals ≤ 10.

Materials: Red Count-On Cards (addition) (from Unit 1 Lesson 9 or TRB M25–M26)

Equation Chains Have three children write equation chains for the number 13 on the board. (See Unit 1 Lesson 18.)

Class Make a Ten Do this while **Student Leaders** pass out the Count-On Cards. Write the $9 + n$ list (left column) on the board. Do each row in turn. At the end, all rows will have a make a ten solution written (for example, $9 + 4 = 9 + 1 + 3 = 10 + 3 = 13$).

Red Count-On Cards (Addition) Children practice with the Red Count-On Cards (addition) individually or with a partner. Explain that they are practicing for a Secret Code Card addition race in Unit 3 Lesson 3.

Class Make a Ten

Student Leader 1 points to and says	Student Leader 2 shows fingers and says	Class says and Student Leader 2 writes = and
9 + 4	4 makes 1 and 3	9 + 1 + 3 = 10 + 3 = 13
9 + 8	8 makes 1 and 7	9 + 1 + 7 = 10 + 7 = 17
9 + 6	6 makes 1 and 5	9 + 1 + 5 = 10 + 5 = 15
9 + 3	3 makes 1 and 2	9 + 1 + 2 = 10 + 2 = 12
9 + 7	7 makes 1 and 6	9 + 1 + 6 = 10 + 6 = 16
9 + 5	5 makes 1 and 4	9 + 1 + 4 = 10 + 4 = 14
9 + 2	2 makes 1 and 1	9 + 1 + 1 = 10 + 1 = 11
9 + 9	9 makes 1 and 8	9 + 1 + 8 = 10 + 8 = 18

Daily Routines

Comparing 2-Digit Quantities Using a Meter Stick, Using Number Flashes, Using the MathBoard (See pp. xxv–xxvi.)

▸ Led by teacher

Money Routine Using the 120 Poster, Using the Money Flip Chart, Using the Number Path, Using Secret Code Cards (See pp. xxiii–xxv.)

▸ Led by Student Leaders

1 Teaching the Lesson

Activity

Represent Story Problems

 **55 MINUTES**

Goal: Represent and discuss solution methods for change plus and change minus story problems.

Materials: Student Activity Book pages 89–90

 **NCTM Standards:**
Number and Operations
Problem Solving

Differentiated Instruction

English Learners Some story problems have words or phrases that can be difficult or confusing. For example, some children think the word *altogether* means *each.* Other problem words include *then, some, rest, left,* and *each.* Identify words that cause difficulty for children. Have volunteers explain these words. As you discuss the words with the class, use math language that children might already know, such as *all, in all,* and *total.*

Teaching Note

Math Drawings Drawings help students understand and represent problem situations. A proof drawing is always done with a numerical method. It is not a method. It is a way to help students understand or check a numerical method. Each step in a proof drawing must be related to the corresponding step in the numerical method. That is how each numerical step takes on quantitative meaning. Eventually the drawings are not needed. In this unit, math drawings are sometimes called proof drawings. During our field testing, we learned that some teachers and students liked the name *proof drawings* for math drawings, so we used both.

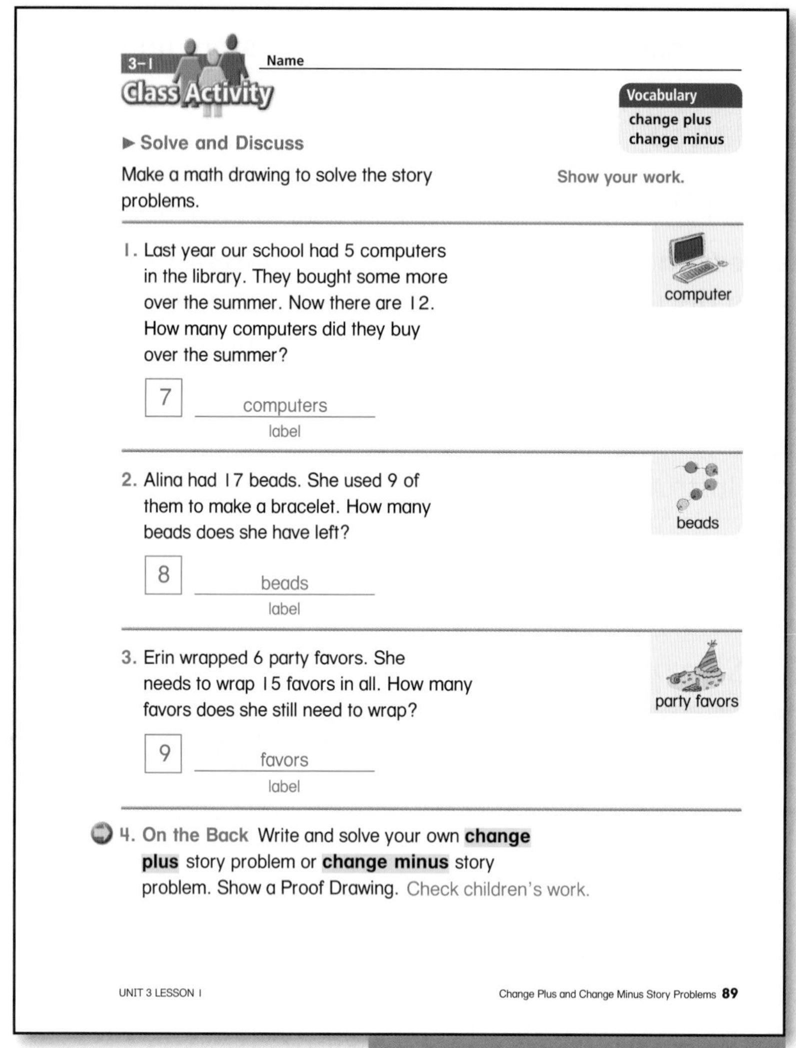
3–1 Class Activity   Name ______

Vocabulary
change plus
change minus

► Solve and Discuss

Make a math drawing to solve the story problems.   Show your work.

1. Last year our school had 5 computers in the library. They bought some more over the summer. Now there are 12. How many computers did they buy over the summer?   computer

7 computers (label)

2. Alina had 17 beads. She used 9 of them to make a bracelet. How many beads does she have left?   beads

8 beads (label)

3. Erin wrapped 6 party favors. She needs to wrap 15 favors in all. How many favors does she still need to wrap?   party favors

9 favors (label)

4. On the Back Write and solve your own **change plus** story problem or **change minus** story problem. Show a Proof Drawing. Check children's work.

UNIT 3 LESSON 1   Change Plus and Change Minus Story Problems 89

Student Activity Book page 89

► Solve and Discuss WHOLE CLASS

Change Plus Problems *A change plus problem begins with a given quantity which is then modified by a change—something is added—that results in a new quantity.*

Have children look at the first problem on Student Activity Book page 89 while a volunteer reads it aloud. Then have several children retell the problem in their own words, keeping its original meaning.

Children can change the order of the sentences and use different wording. For example:

- The school library had 5 computers last year. In the summer they bought more computers. Now there are 12. How many computers did they buy during the summer?

Math Talk Using the **Solve and Discuss** structure, invite three to six children to go to the board to solve the first problem using drawings and numbers. The rest of the class should work at their seats.

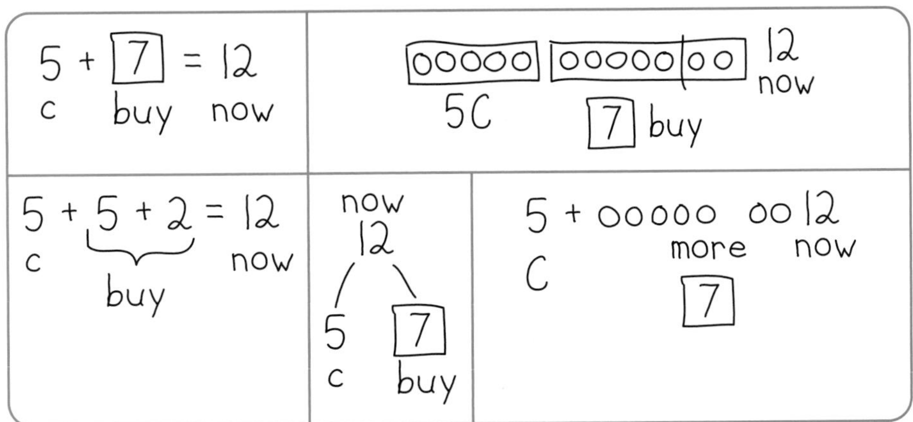

Ask two or three children to discuss their solutions with the class. Encourage children at their desks to ask questions and assist their classmates in understanding.

- How did you get 7 more?
- Why did you start with 5?
- Why did you put the 12 there?
- How did you know 7 was a partner?
- How did you know 12 was the total?
- Where did you get 5 + 2?

Activity continued ▶

The Learning Classroom

Math Talk Discussion in which children describe their thinking is a core part of teaching for understanding. Children will be more attentive listeners if they have an active role, either as a questioner or as someone who rephrases or elaborates upon a concept. To encourage this type of participation, you can ask children to say in their own words what someone else has said. To develop children's abilities to formulate questions, you can model good questions in each unit.

English Language Learners

Read Solve and Discuss problem 1 aloud. Help children identify words that tell them it is a change plus problem. Model how to write the equation 5 + □ = 12. Continue with other problems.

- **Beginning** Say: **The school *had* 5 computers. We start with 5. They *bought more* computers. Buy means add. This is a change plus.**
- **Intermediate** Say: **The school *bought more* computers.** Ask: **Do we add or subtract?** add Say: **This is a change ___.** plus
- **Advanced** Ask: **What word means the school got more computers?** bought **Is this a change plus or change minus problem?** change plus

❶ Teaching the Lesson (continued)

Change Minus Problems *A change minus problem begins with a given quantity which is then modified by a change—something is subtracted—that results in a new quantity.*

Math Talk Have children look at problem 2 on Student Activity Book page 89 while a volunteer reads it aloud. Then have several children retell the problem in their own words. Using the **Solve and Discuss** structure, encourage children to think in terms of a 17-partner.

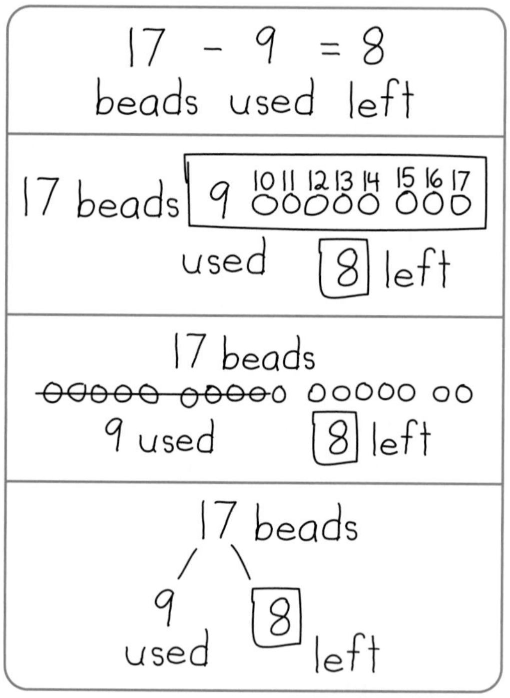

17 − 9 = 8
beads used left

17 beads | 9 10 11 12 13 14 15 16 17
used 8 left

17 beads
~~00000 00000~~ 00000 00
9 used 8 left

17 beads
9 used
8 left

Have children finish Student Activity Book page 89. Note that problem 3 has an unknown partner addend.

Ongoing Assessment

Circulate around the room as children complete problems 3 and 4. Ask children to explain their drawings, equations, and solution methods.

Differentiated Instruction

Intervention

Activity Card 3-I

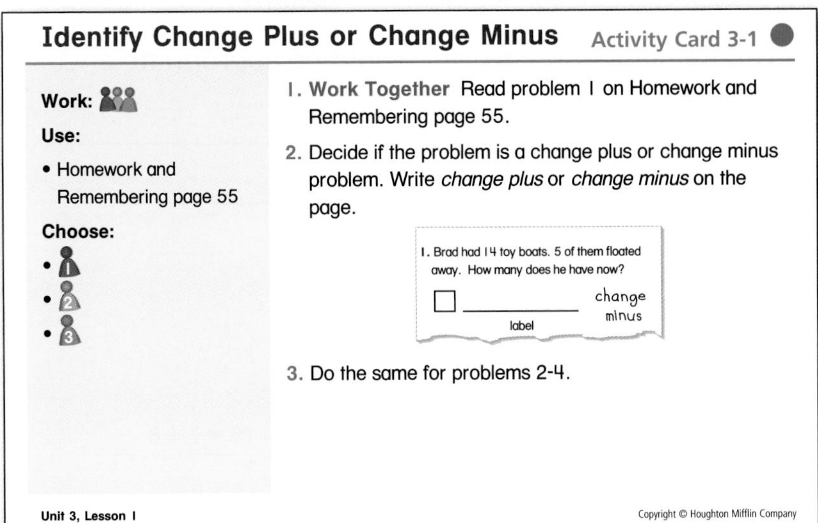
Identify Change Plus or Change Minus — Activity Card 3-1

Work: (pairs)
Use:
- Homework and Remembering page 55

Choose:
- 1
- 2
- 3

1. **Work Together** Read problem 1 on Homework and Remembering page 55.
2. Decide if the problem is a change plus or change minus problem. Write *change plus* or *change minus* on the page.

3. Do the same for problems 2-4.

Unit 3, Lesson 1

Activity Note Each child needs Homework and Remembering p. 55. Check children's work before they complete the page.

Math Writing Prompt

Explain Your Thinking Myra had 8 stuffed animals. Her aunt gave her 4 more. How many does she have now? Draw a picture to explain.

Software Support

Use *Soar to Success* for instruction of students needing targeted support for underlying skills.

On Level

Activity Card 3-I

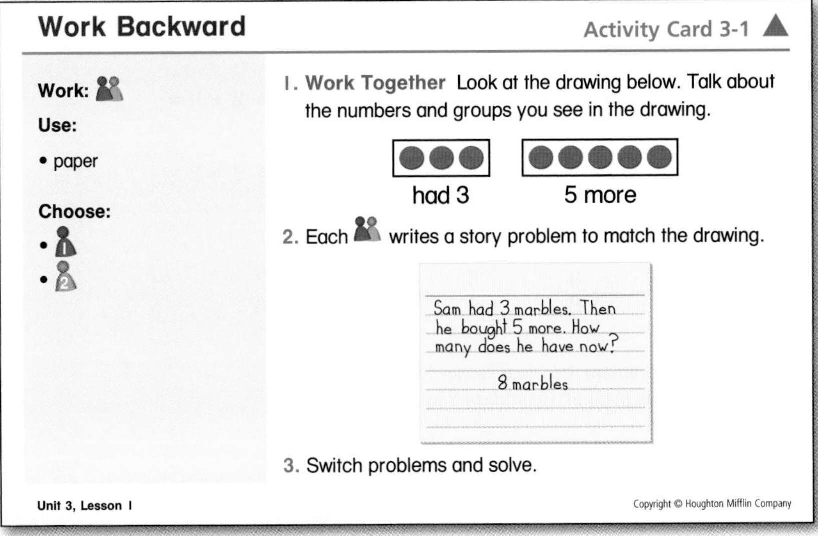
Work Backward — Activity Card 3-1

Work: (pairs)
Use:
- paper

Choose:
- 1
- 2

1. **Work Together** Look at the drawing below. Talk about the numbers and groups you see in the drawing.

2. Each (pair) writes a story problem to match the drawing.

3. Switch problems and solve.

Unit 3, Lesson 1

Activity Note Guide children to notice the two groups of dots and the words underneath. Then have children write and solve their own problems.

Math Writing Prompt

Write Your Own Write a change plus story problem to match $2 + 4 = 6$.

Software Support

Use *MegaMath* for review and reinforcement of the concepts and skills presented in this lesson.

Challenge

Activity Card 3-I

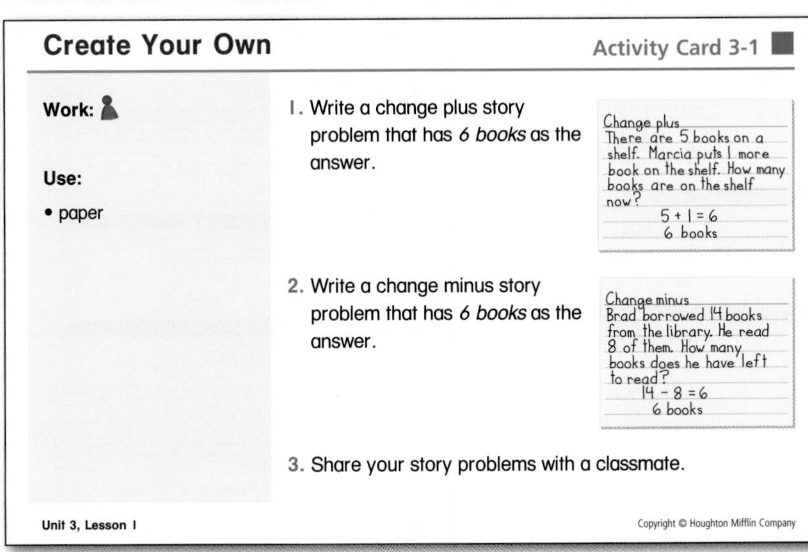
Create Your Own — Activity Card 3-1

Work: (individual)
Use:
- paper

1. Write a change plus story problem that has *6 books* as the answer.

Change plus
There are 5 books on a shelf. Marcia puts 1 more book on the shelf. How many books are on the shelf now?
5 + 1 = 6
6 books

2. Write a change minus story problem that has *6 books* as the answer.

Change minus
Brad borrowed 14 books from the library. He read 8 of them. How many books does he have left to read?
14 - 8 = 6
6 books

3. Share your story problems with a classmate.

Unit 3, Lesson 1

Activity Note Each child needs to write two story problems. The answer to each problem is *6 books*. Encourage children to write more problems.

Math Writing Prompt

Summarize Explain in your own words what a change minus story problem is. Give an example.

Software Support

Use *Destination Math* to take students beyond the concepts and skills presented in this lesson.

3 Homework and Spiral Review

3–1 Homework **Goal:** Additional Practice

Include children's completed Homework page as part of their portfolios.

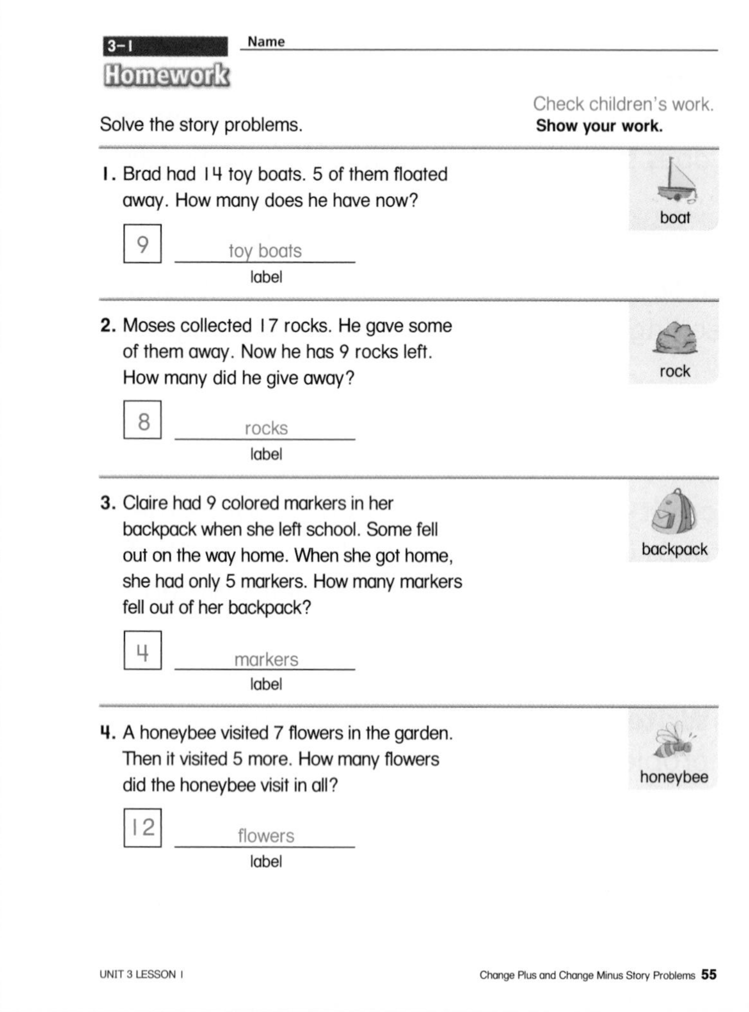

3–1 Name

Homework

Solve the story problems.

Check children's work.
Show your work.

1. Brad had 14 toy boats. 5 of them floated away. How many does he have now?

   boat

   9 toy boats
   label

2. Moses collected 17 rocks. He gave some of them away. Now he has 9 rocks left. How many did he give away?

   rock

   8 rocks
   label

3. Claire had 9 colored markers in her backpack when she left school. Some fell out on the way home. When she got home, she had only 5 markers. How many markers fell out of her backpack?

   backpack

   4 markers
   label

4. A honeybee visited 7 flowers in the garden. Then it visited 5 more. How many flowers did the honeybee visit in all?

   honeybee

   12 flowers
   label

UNIT 3 LESSON 1 — Change Plus and Change Minus Story Problems 55

Homework and Remembering page 55

3–1 Remembering **Goal:** Spiral Review

This Remembering activity would be appropriate anytime after today's lesson.

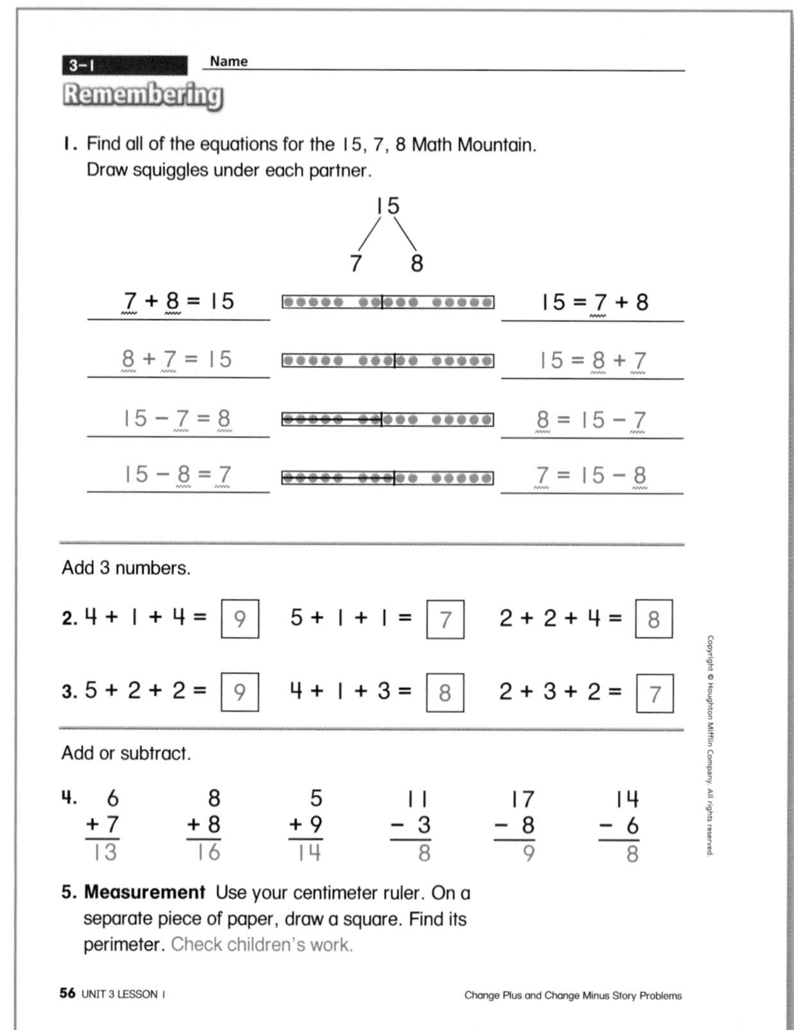

3–1 Name

Remembering

1. Find all of the equations for the 15, 7, 8 Math Mountain. Draw squiggles under each partner.

15
7 8

7 + 8 = 15	●●●●● ●●●●● ●●●●●	15 = 7 + 8
8 + 7 = 15	●●●●● ●●●●● ●●●●●	15 = 8 + 7
15 − 7 = 8	●●●●● ●●●●● ●●●●●	8 = 15 − 7
15 − 8 = 7	●●●●● ●●●●● ●●●●●	7 = 15 − 8

Add 3 numbers.

2. 4 + 1 + 4 = 9 5 + 1 + 1 = 7 2 + 2 + 4 = 8

3. 5 + 2 + 2 = 9 4 + 1 + 3 = 8 2 + 3 + 2 = 7

Add or subtract.

4.

6	8	5	11	17	14
+ 7	+ 8	+ 9	− 3	− 8	− 6
13	16	14	8	9	8

5. **Measurement** Use your centimeter ruler. On a separate piece of paper, draw a square. Find its perimeter. Check children's work.

56 UNIT 3 LESSON 1 — Change Plus and Change Minus Story Problems

Homework and Remembering page 56

Home and School Connection

Family Letter Have children take home the Family Letter on Student Activity Book page 91. This letter explains how the concept of change plus and change minus story problems is developed in *Math Expressions.* It gives parents and guardians a better understanding of the learning that goes on in math class and creates a bridge between school and home. A Spanish translation of this letter is on the following page in the Student Activity Book.

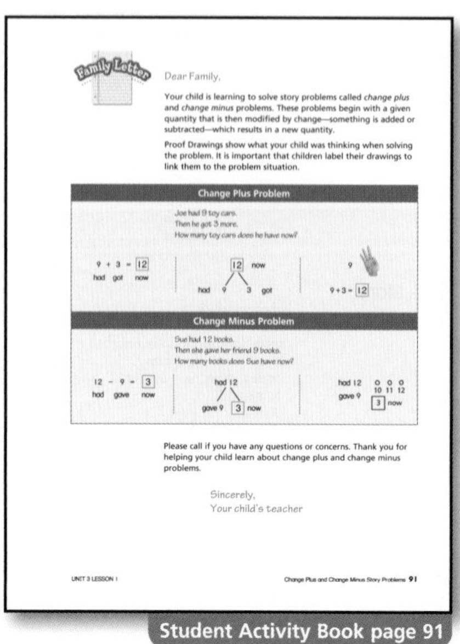

Family Letter

Dear Family,

Your child is learning to solve story problems called *change plus* and *change minus* problems. These problems begin with a given quantity that is then modified by change—something is added or subtracted—which results in a new quantity.

Proof Drawings show what your child was thinking when solving the problem. It is important that children label their drawings to link them to the problem situation.

Change Plus Problem

Joe had 9 toy cars.
Then he got 3 more.
How many toy cars does he have now?

9 + 3 = 12 (had, got, now) | 12 now; had 9, 3 got | 9; 9 + 3 = 12

Change Minus Problem

Sue had 12 books.
Then she gave her friend 9 books.
How many books does Sue have now?

12 − 9 = 3 (had, gave, now) | had 12; gave 9, 3 now | had 12, gave 9; 10 11 12; 3 now

Please call if you have any questions or concerns. Thank you for helping your child learn about change plus and change minus problems.

Sincerely,
Your child's teacher

UNIT 3 LESSON 1 — Change Plus and Change Minus Story Problems 91

Student Activity Book page 91

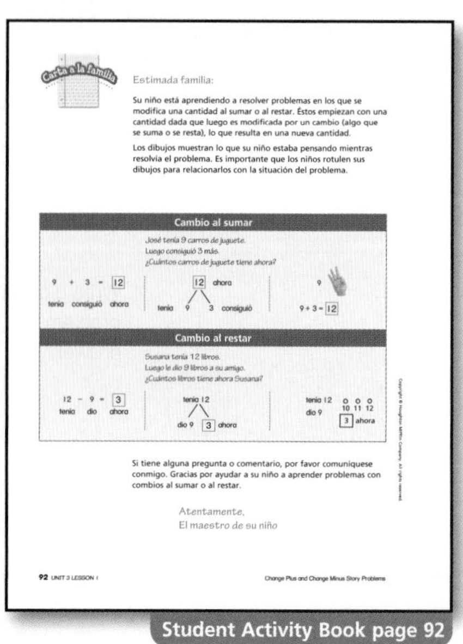

Carta a la familia

Estimada familia:

Su niño está aprendiendo a resolver problemas en los que se modifica una cantidad al sumar o al restar. Éstos empiezan con una cantidad dada que luego es modificada por un cambio (algo que se suma o se resta), lo que resulta en una nueva cantidad.

Los dibujos muestran lo que su niño estaba pensando mientras resolvía el problema. Es importante que los niños rotulen sus dibujos para relacionarlos con la situación del problema.

Cambio al sumar

José tenía 9 carros de juguete.
Luego consiguió 3 más.
¿Cuántos carros de juguete tiene ahora?

9 + 3 = 12 (tenía, consiguió, ahora) | 12 ahora; tenía 9, 3 consiguió | 9; 9 + 3 = 12

Cambio al restar

Susana tenía 12 libros.
Luego le dio 9 libros a su amigo.
¿Cuántos libros tiene ahora Susana?

12 − 9 = 3 (tenía, dio, ahora) | tenía 12; dio 9, 3 ahora | tenía 12, dio 9; 10 11 12; 3 ahora

Si tiene alguna pregunta o comentario, por favor comuníquese conmigo. Gracias por ayudar a su niño a aprender problemas con combios al sumar o al restar.

Atentamente,
El maestro de su niño

92 UNIT 3 LESSON 1 — Change Plus and Change Minus Story Problems

Student Activity Book page 92

More Change Plus and Change Minus Story Problems

REAL WORLD Problem Solving

Lesson Objectives

- Create and represent change plus and change minus story problems from equations and Math Mountains.
- Solve and discuss change plus and change minus story problems.

Vocabulary

change plus story problem
change minus story problem
situation equation

The Day at a Glance

Today's Goals	Materials	
1 Teaching the Lesson **A1:** Create and represent change problems. **A2:** Solve and discuss change story problems.	**Lesson Activities** Student Activity Book pp. 93–94 Homework and Remembering pp. 57–58 MathBoard materials	**Going Further** Activity Cards 3-2 Equations and Math Mountains (TRB M52) Problems and Equations (TRB M53) Problems and Proof Drawings (TRB M54) Math Journals
2 Going Further ▸ Differentiated Instruction		
3 Homework and Targeted Practice		

Use Math Talk today!

Keeping Skills Sharp

Quick Practice — 5 MINUTES

Goals: Write equation chains for 14. Make a ten when adding a number to 9. Find totals ≤ 10.

Materials: Red Count-On Cards (addition) (from Unit 1 Lesson 9 or TRB M25–M26)

Equation Chains Have three children write equation chains for the number 14 on the board. (See Unit 1 Lesson 18.)

Class Make a Ten Write the 9 + *n* list (left column) on the board. Do each row in turn.

Red Count-On Cards (Addition) Children practice with Red Count-On Cards (addition) individually or with a partner.

Class Make a Ten

Student Leader 1 points to and says	Student Leader 2 shows fingers and says	Class says and Student Leader 2 writes = and
9 + 5	5 makes 1 and 4	9 + 1 + 4 = 10 + 4 = 14
9 + 2	2 makes 1 and 1	9 + 1 + 1 = 10 + 1 = 11
9 + 3	3 makes 1 and 2	9 + 1 + 2 = 10 + 2 = 12
9 + 7	7 makes 1 and 6	9 + 1 + 6 = 10 + 6 = 16
9 + 4	4 makes 1 and 3	9 + 1 + 3 = 10 + 3 = 13
9 + 6	6 makes 1 and 5	9 + 1 + 5 = 10 + 5 = 15
9 + 8	8 makes 1 and 7	9 + 1 + 7 = 10 + 7 = 17
9 + 9	9 makes 1 and 8	9 + 1 + 8 = 10 + 8 = 18

Daily Routines

Comparing 2-Digit Quantities Using a Meter Stick, Using Number Flashes, Using the MathBoard (See pp. xxv–xxvi.)

▸ Led by teacher

Money Routine Using the 120 Poster, Using the Money Flip Chart, Using the Number Path, Using Secret Code Cards (See pp. xxiii–xxv.)

▸ Led by Student Leaders

1 Teaching the Lesson

Activity 1

Create Change Story Problems

 **30 MINUTES**

Goal: Create and represent change problems.

Materials: MathBoard materials

 **NCTM Standards:**
Number and Operations
Problem Solving

Teaching Note

Connect to Prior Knowledge Activity 1 begins with a review of Unit 1, Lesson 20. You can look there for more details. Children will vary the unknown in the equation and in the Math Mountain. Then they will make up change plus and change minus problems and make any other kind of drawing they want to represent the problem.

Teaching Note

Math Background Change plus and change minus problems begin with a given quantity, which is then modified by a change. An amount is either added or subtracted to the given quantity, which results in a new quantity. Math Mountains are a useful representation for showing whether the unknown is a partner or a total, but they do not show the actual change that is occurring.

▶ Create Change Plus Story Problems WHOLE CLASS

Choose an equation and then write it three ways, varying the position of the unknown. Have children give a Math Mountain for each equation as you draw it on the board. Then challenge them to create and modify the same story problem to go with each equation. Sample problems are provided below, but encourage your children to make up their own problems. Tell children to record their work on their MathBoards.

Situation Equations and Math Mountains

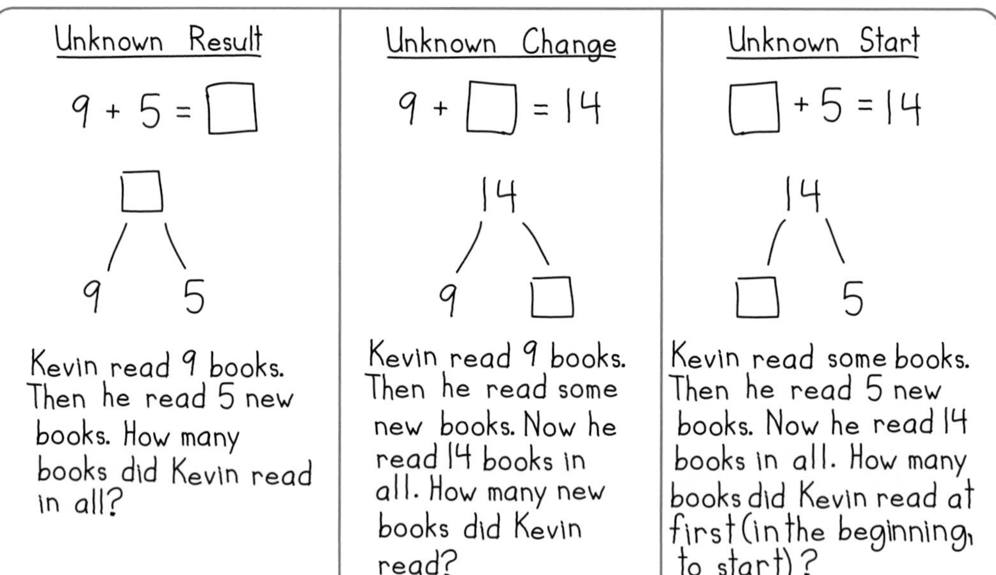

Now have children make drawings to represent the problems. Some children may draw all 14 objects. Encourage them to make drawings that use numbers instead. Some children may need extra time. Remind all children to label their drawings.

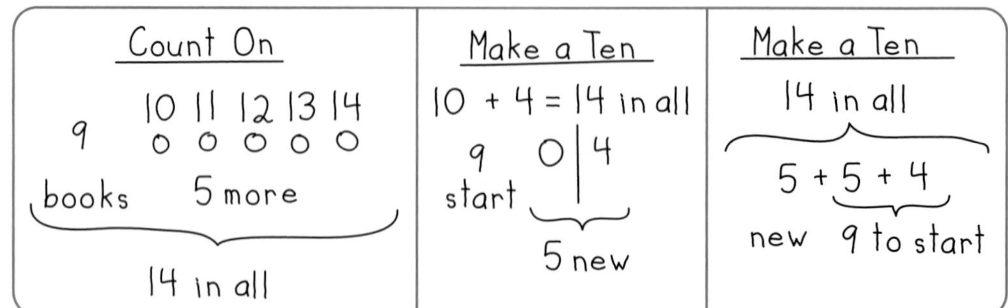

▶ Create Change Minus Story Problems WHOLE CLASS

Have children create change minus story problems using the same procedure as they did with the change plus problems. Remind children to label their drawings.

Situation Equations and Math Mountains

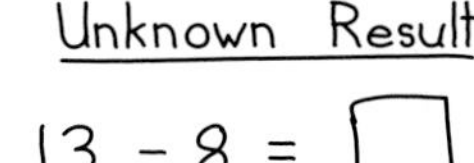

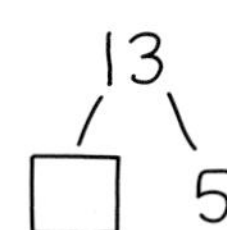

Unknown Result	Unknown Change	Unknown Start
13 – 8 = ☐	13 – ☐ = 5	☐ – 8 = 5
13 / 8, ☐	13 / ☐, 5	☐ / 8, 5
13 birds were at the feeder. Then 8 flew away. How many birds are at the feeder now?	13 birds were at the feeder. Then some flew away. Now 5 birds are at the feeder. How many birds flew away?	Some birds were at the feeder. Then 8 flew away. Now 5 birds are at the feeder. How many birds were at the feeder at first?

13 to start
00000 000(00 000)
Count On 8 flew [5]

5
8 0 0 0 0 0
9 10 11 12 13
so [13] to start
Count On

13 to start
8 00000
flew away [5] now
Count On

13 = 5 + 5 + 3
[8] flew

13 to start
00000 000(00 000)
[8] flew away 5 left

8 + 2 + 3 = [13] to start
flew away 5 now
Make a Ten

The Learning Classroom

Building Concepts Encourage all children to label their work. Labeling has benefits for both the children and for you, the teacher. It is easier for children to follow an explanation when the parts or steps are labeled. Labels also help children ask specific questions about particular aspects of the work. Finally, labels can help you assess children's understanding of the underlying concept.

Differentiated Instruction

English Learners For English Learners that are having difficulty writing out story problems, allow them to draw the problem and explain verbally what mathematical equation their drawing represents or have them work in pairs to help with the *left, gone, came,* etc. language.

English Language Learners

Model a change minus story problem for 8 – 5 = ☐. Say: **There were 8 cookies. Jo ate 5.** Point to the ☐. Ask: **How many cookies are left?**

- **Beginning** Say: **We start with 8. We take away 5. 8 – 5 = ___.** 3 **There are 3 cookies left.** Change the unknown and continue.
- **Intermediate** Write 8 – ☐ = 3. Say: **The story is different. Now we don't know how many Jo ate. We say: Jo ate *some*. Now there are 3 cookies left.**
- **Advanced** Write 8 – ☐ = 3. Have children work in pairs to tell the new story. Have volunteers share their stories with the class.

Activity 2

Solve Change Story Problems

 25 MINUTES

Goal: Solve and discuss change story problems.

Materials: MathBoard materials, Student Activity Book pages 93–94

 **NCTM Standards:**
Number and Operations
Problem Solving
Communication

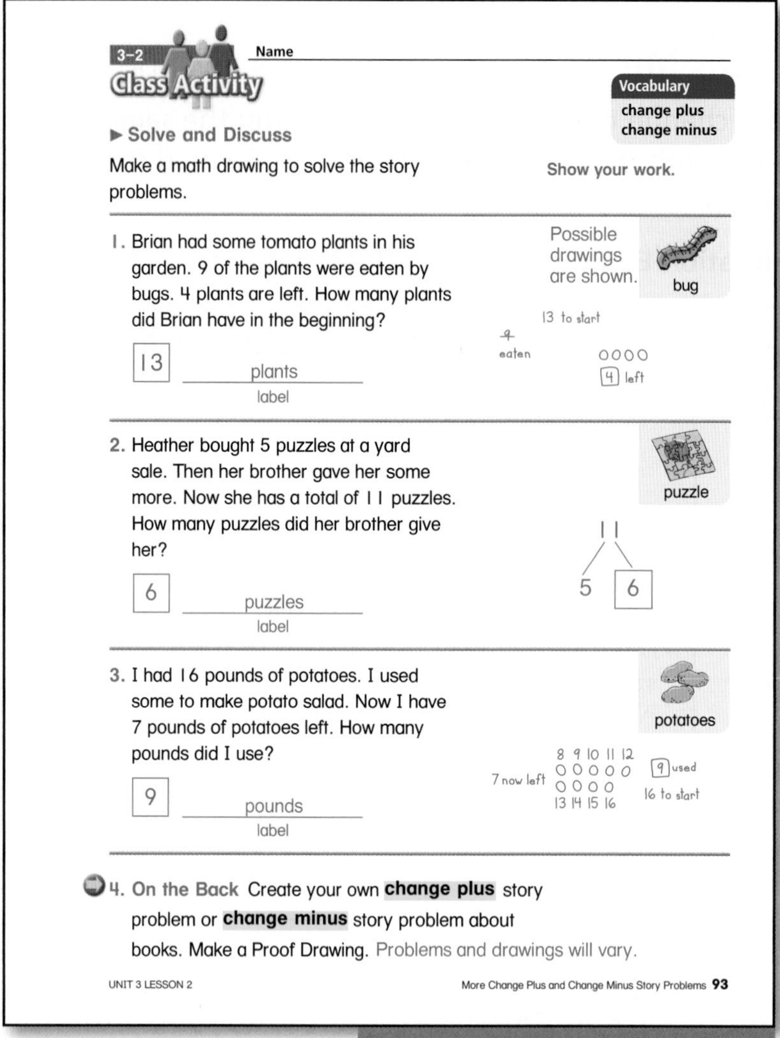

3-2 Class Activity Name

Vocabulary
change plus
change minus

▶ Solve and Discuss

Make a math drawing to solve the story problems.

Show your work.

1. Brian had some tomato plants in his garden. 9 of the plants were eaten by bugs. 4 plants are left. How many plants did Brian have in the beginning?

13 plants
label

Possible drawings are shown.

bug

13 to start
9 eaten
0000
4 left

2. Heather bought 5 puzzles at a yard sale. Then her brother gave her some more. Now she has a total of 11 puzzles. How many puzzles did her brother give her?

6 puzzles
label

puzzle

11
5 6

3. I had 16 pounds of potatoes. I used some to make potato salad. Now I have 7 pounds of potatoes left. How many pounds did I use?

9 pounds
label

potatoes

8 9 10 11 12
00000
7 now left
0000
13 14 15 16
9 used
16 to start

4. On the Back Create your own **change plus** story problem or **change minus** story problem about books. Make a Proof Drawing. Problems and drawings will vary.

UNIT 3 LESSON 2 More Change Plus and Change Minus Story Problems 93

Student Activity Book page 93

▶ Solve and Discuss WHOLE CLASS

Have children look at Student Activity Book page 93.

Math Talk Use the **Solve and Discuss** structure for problems 1–2. Ask several children to share their representations and invite other children to comment and ask questions.

Then ask children to solve problem 3 independently. As you circulate around the room encourage children to substitute numbers for parts of their diagrams whenever possible. You may wish to help any children who are experiencing difficulty or have them work with Helping Partners.

▶ Create Your Own INDIVIDUALS

Once children have completed problems 1–3, challenge them to complete problem 4 on the back of the page. After children have finished, invite a few to share their story problems and show their solution methods.

Ongoing Assessment

As children work on Student Activity Book page 93, circulate around the room asking individual children to explain their drawings and solutions. Ask children to identify whether they have solved a change plus or a change minus problem.

2 Going Further

Differentiated Instruction

Intervention

Activity Card 3-2

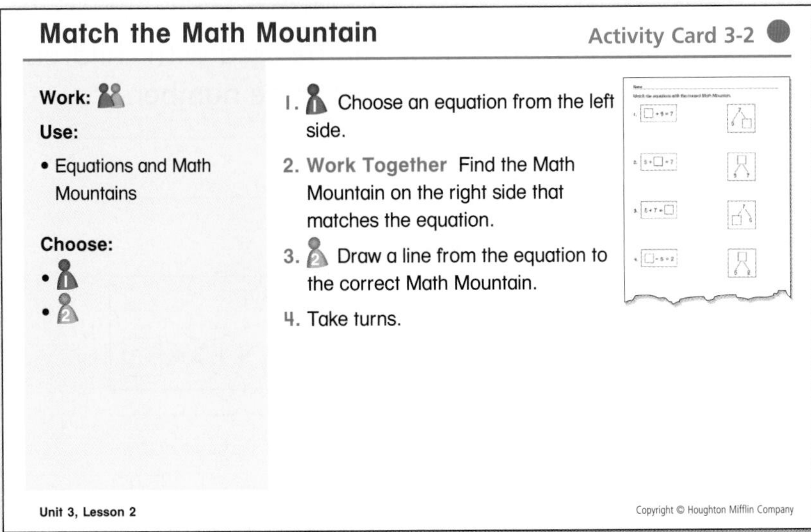

Match the Math Mountain — Activity Card 3-2 ●

Work:
Use:
- Equations and Math Mountains

Choose:
- 1
- 2

1. Choose an equation from the left side.
2. **Work Together** Find the Math Mountain on the right side that matches the equation.
3. Draw a line from the equation to the correct Math Mountain.
4. Take turns.

Unit 3, Lesson 2 — Copyright © Houghton Mifflin Company

Activity Note Each pair needs Equations and Math Mountains (TRB M52). Children work together to match the equations to the Math Mountains.

Math Writing Prompt

Draw Your Own Draw a Math Mountain that matches 3 + □ = 9. Explain your thinking.

Software Support

Use *Soar to Success* for instruction of students needing targeted support for underlying skills.

On Level

Activity Card 3-2

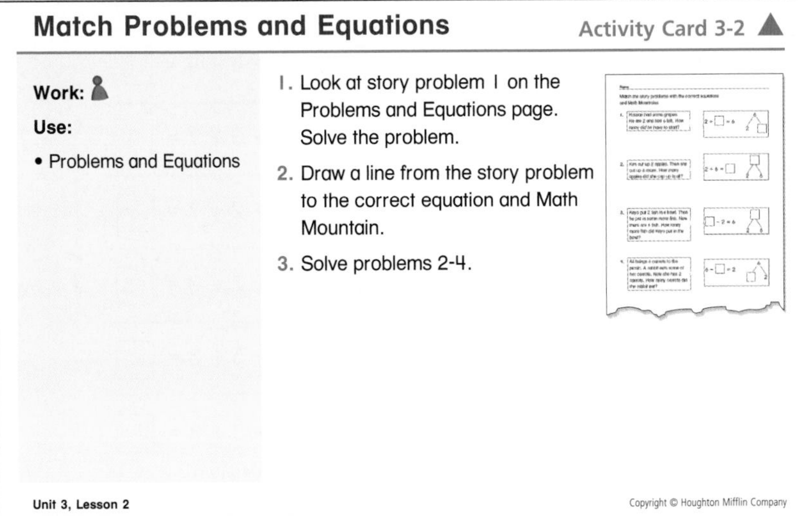

Match Problems and Equations — Activity Card 3-2 ▲

Work:
Use:
- Problems and Equations

1. Look at story problem 1 on the Problems and Equations page. Solve the problem.
2. Draw a line from the story problem to the correct equation and Math Mountain.
3. Solve problems 2-4.

Unit 3, Lesson 2 — Copyright © Houghton Mifflin Company

Activity Note Each child needs Problems and Equations (TRB M53). Remind children to read the problems carefully.

Math Writing Prompt

Explain Your Thinking Draw a Math Mountain. Write an equation to match. Explain how you know that they match.

Software Support

Use *MegaMath* for review and reinforcement of the concepts and skills presented in this lesson.

Challenge

Activity Card 3-2

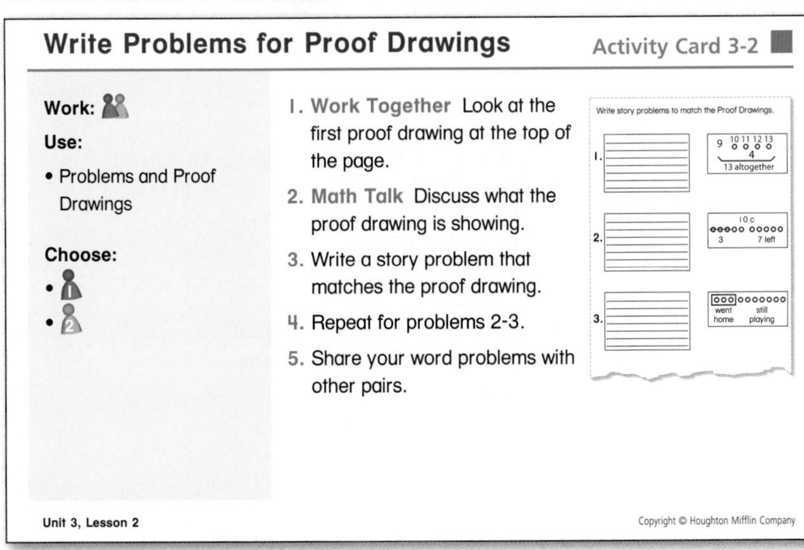

Write Problems for Proof Drawings — Activity Card 3-2 ■

Work:
Use:
- Problems and Proof Drawings

Choose:
- 1
- 2

1. **Work Together** Look at the first proof drawing at the top of the page.
2. **Math Talk** Discuss what the proof drawing is showing.
3. Write a story problem that matches the proof drawing.
4. Repeat for problems 2-3.
5. Share your word problems with other pairs.

Unit 3, Lesson 2 — Copyright © Houghton Mifflin Company

Activity Note Each pair needs Problems and Proof Drawings (TRB M54). Pairs need to write story problems to match the proof drawings.

Math Writing Prompt

Explain Your Thinking Explain the difference between a change plus and a change minus story. Use examples.

Software Support

Use *Destination Math* to take students beyond the concepts and skills presented in this lesson.

3 Homework and Targeted Practice

3–2 Homework **Goal:** Additional Practice

This Homework page provides practice solving change plus and change minus problems.

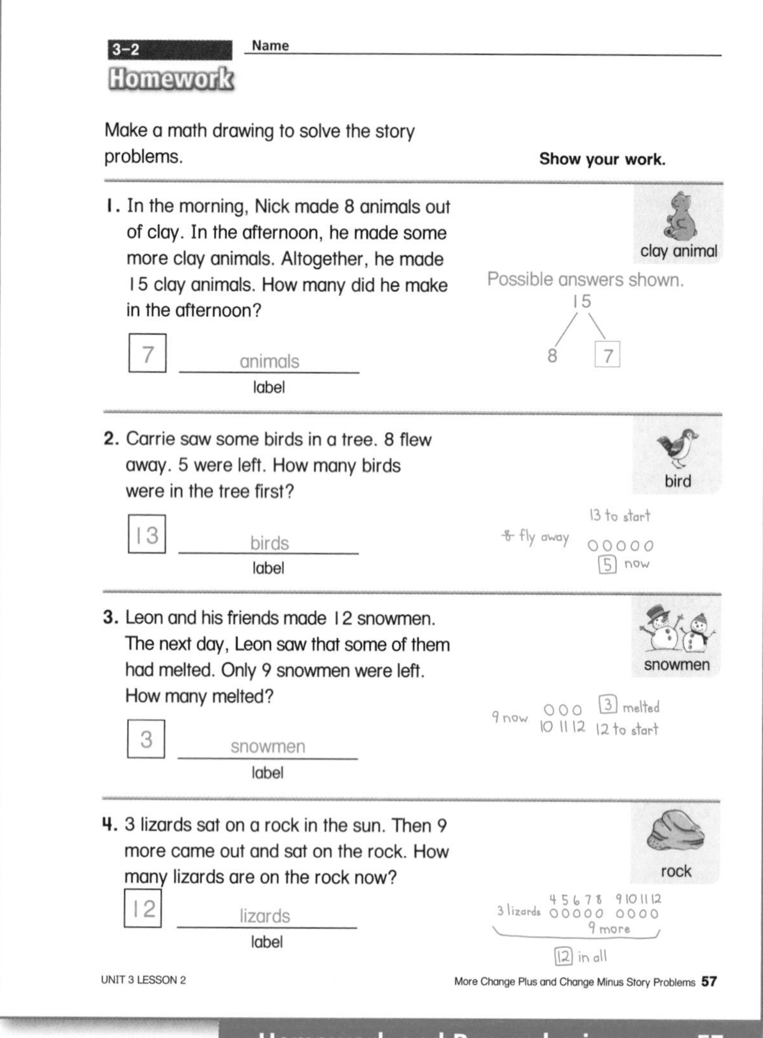

3–2 Name

Homework

Make a math drawing to solve the story problems. **Show your work.**

1. In the morning, Nick made 8 animals out of clay. In the afternoon, he made some more clay animals. Altogether, he made 15 clay animals. How many did he make in the afternoon?

   7 animals (label)

   clay animal

   Possible answers shown.

   15 / 8, 7

2. Carrie saw some birds in a tree. 8 flew away. 5 were left. How many birds were in the tree first?

   13 birds (label)

   bird

   13 to start; 8 fly away; 5 now

3. Leon and his friends made 12 snowmen. The next day, Leon saw that some of them had melted. Only 9 snowmen were left. How many melted?

   3 snowmen (label)

   snowmen

   9 now; 10 11 12; 3 melted; 12 to start

4. 3 lizards sat on a rock in the sun. Then 9 more came out and sat on the rock. How many lizards are on the rock now?

   12 lizards (label)

   rock

   3 lizards; 4 5 6 7 8 9 10 11 12; 9 more; 12 in all

UNIT 3 LESSON 2 — More Change Plus and Change Minus Story Problems 57

Homework and Remembering page 57

3–2 Targeted Practice **Goal:** Add three numbers.

This Targeted Practice page can be used with children who need extra practice adding three numbers.

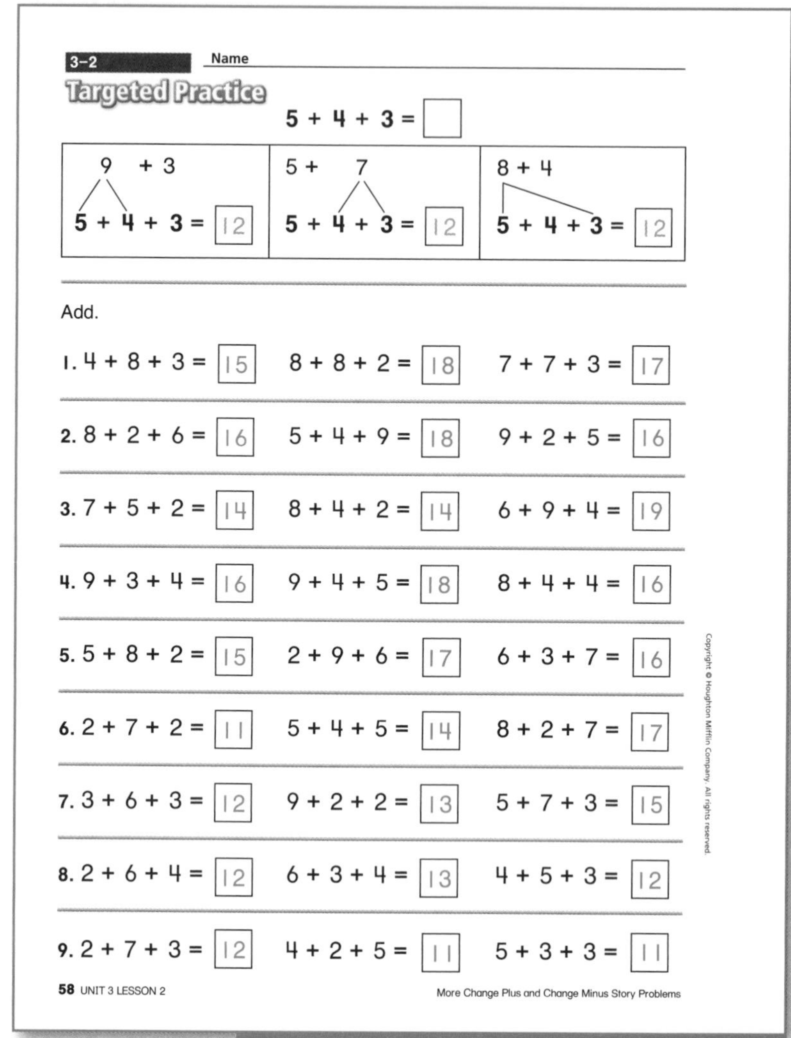

3–2 Name

Targeted Practice

5 + 4 + 3 = ☐

9 + 3	5 + 7	8 + 4
5 + 4 + 3 = 12	5 + 4 + 3 = 12	5 + 4 + 3 = 12

Add.

1.	4 + 8 + 3 = 15	8 + 8 + 2 = 18	7 + 7 + 3 = 17
2.	8 + 2 + 6 = 16	5 + 4 + 9 = 18	9 + 2 + 5 = 16
3.	7 + 5 + 2 = 14	8 + 4 + 2 = 14	6 + 9 + 4 = 19
4.	9 + 3 + 4 = 16	9 + 4 + 5 = 18	8 + 4 + 4 = 16
5.	5 + 8 + 2 = 15	2 + 9 + 6 = 17	6 + 3 + 7 = 16
6.	2 + 7 + 2 = 11	5 + 4 + 5 = 14	8 + 2 + 7 = 17
7.	3 + 6 + 3 = 12	9 + 2 + 2 = 13	5 + 7 + 3 = 15
8.	2 + 6 + 4 = 12	6 + 3 + 4 = 13	4 + 5 + 3 = 12
9.	2 + 7 + 3 = 12	4 + 2 + 5 = 11	5 + 3 + 3 = 11

58 UNIT 3 LESSON 2 — More Change Plus and Change Minus Story Problems

Homework and Remembering page 58

Home or School Activity

Multicultural Connection

Ethnic Foods Have children choose a food that originated in a country other than the United States. Have them write a description of the food and a change plus or change minus story problem about that food.

Children can exchange problems to solve or take turns sharing their problems and having everyone solve them.

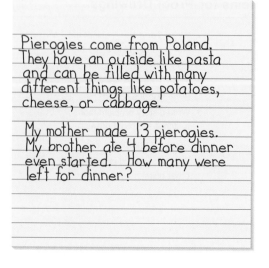

> Pierogies come from Poland. They have an outside like pasta and can be filled with many different things like potatoes, cheese, or cabbage.
>
> My mother made 13 pierogies. My brother ate 4 before dinner even started. How many were left for dinner?

Collection Problems

Lesson Objectives

- Differentiate between "change" and "collection" situations.
- Solve collection story problems.

Vocabulary
collection story problem

The Day at a Glance

Today's Goals	Materials	
1 Teaching the Lesson A1: Introduce collection story problems. A2: Solve collection story problems.	**Lesson Activities** Student Activity Book pp. 95–96 Homework and Remembering p. 59 MathBoard materials	**Going Further** Activity Cards 3-3 Homework and Remembering p. 59 Two-color counters MathBoard materials Math Journals
2 Going Further ▶ Differentiated Instruction		
3 Homework and Spiral Review		

Use Math Talk today!

Keeping Skills Sharp

Quick Practice — 5 MINUTES

Goals: Write equation chains for 16. Make a ten when adding a number to 9. Find totals ≤ 10.

Materials: Secret Code Cards 1–10, Parachute Drop (from Unit 1 Lesson 19 or TRB M46)

Equation Chains Have three children write equation chains for the number 16 on the board. (See Unit 1 Lesson 18.)

Secret Code Card Addition Race, Totals ≤ 10 Have children arrange their Secret Code Cards 1–10 across their desks. Then have a Student Leader call out problems starting from the bottom of column 1 of Parachute Drop. Other children use their Secret Code Cards to show the answer. (See Unit 1 Lesson 20.)

Class Make a Ten Write the 9 + *n* list (left column) on the board. Do each row in turn.

Class Make a Ten

Student Leader 1 points to and says	Student Leader 2 shows fingers and says	Class says and Student Leader 2 writes = and
9 + 3	3 makes 1 and 2	9 + 1 + 2 = 10 + 2 = 12
9 + 7	7 makes 1 and 6	9 + 1 + 6 = 10 + 6 = 16
9 + 8	8 makes 1 and 7	9 + 1 + 7 = 10 + 7 = 17
9 + 5	5 makes 1 and 4	9 + 1 + 4 = 10 + 4 = 14
9 + 2	2 makes 1 and 1	9 + 1 + 1 = 10 + 1 = 11
9 + 9	9 makes 1 and 8	9 + 1 + 8 = 10 + 8 = 18
9 + 4	4 makes 1 and 3	9 + 1 + 3 = 10 + 3 = 13
9 + 6	6 makes 1 and 5	9 + 1 + 5 = 10 + 5 = 15

Daily Routines

Comparing 2-Digit Quantities Using a Meter Stick, Using Number Flashes, Using the MathBoard (See pp. xxv–xxvi.)

▶ Led by teacher

Money Routine Using the 120 Poster, Using the Money Flip Chart, Using the Number Path, Using Secret Code Cards (See pp. xxiii–xxv.)

▶ Led by Student Leaders

1 Teaching the Lesson

Activity 1

Introduce Collection Problems

 25 MINUTES

Goal: Introduce collection story problems.

Materials: MathBoard materials

 **NCTM Standards:**
Number and Operations
Problem Solving
Communication

Teaching Note

Math Background Collection problems can involve actively putting things together (for example, putting two kinds of flowers in a vase) or they can involve separating a collection of things (putting some books on a shelf and some on a desk). Collection problems can also be static, where no action occurs (for example, some windows open, some windows closed).

▶ Collection Problems: Put Things Together WHOLE CLASS

Unknown Total Write the problem on the board and read it aloud.

Jason put 4 large plates and 8 small plates on the table. How many plates are on the table in all?

- Does anything change in the problem? No. Is anything added or taken away? Jason always had the plates. Nothing is added or taken away.
- What question does the problem ask? How many plates in all?
- Are we looking for a total or a partner? a total How do you know? He already has big plates and small plates. We have to find out how many of both sizes he has.

Have four to six children draw and solve the problem on the board while others draw and solve it on their MathBoards.

4 + 8 = [12] L S in all	[12] in all 4 8 L S	8 oo|oo S L [12]

Unknown Partner Have children discuss, draw, and solve this unknown partner problem.

Jason put 4 large plates and some small plates on the table. Altogether he has 12 plates. How many plates are small?

- Does anything change in this problem? No; Jason has 12 plates. He does not get more plates or give any away.
- What do we have to find out? How many small plates Jason has.
- Are we looking for a total or a partner? a partner How do you know? We know how many total plates Jason has. We know how many of them are large. We don't know how many are small.

4 + [8] = 12 L S Altogether	4 ooooo o|oo L 8 S
12 All 4 [8] L S	4 + 6 + 2 8

▶ Collection Problems: Separate Things WHOLE CLASS

Vary the previous problem to illustrate a separating situation.

> 12 large and small plates were on the table. Jason put the 4 large plates on a shelf and the small plates on the counter. How many small plates are on the counter?

- Is anything different about this situation? Yes; Jason's plates are in two different places.
- Is anything else different? No; Jason has 12 plates. Some are large and some are small. He does not get more plates or give any away.
- What do we have to find out? How many small plates Jason has on the table, just as we did with the previous problem.

Have four to six children draw and solve the problem on the board while others do the same on their MathBoards. Children's drawings and solution processes should look the same as those done for the putting together collection problem with an unknown partner.

▶ Collection Problems: No Action WHOLE CLASS

Present and discuss this problem to illustrate no action occurring.

> Dave has 9 fruit bars and 4 cereal bars. How many bars does he have in total?

- Is anything different about this situation? Yes; the bars were not put together or taken apart. They were just there.

Explain that in many collection problems, nothing at all happens. No one puts anything together or takes anything apart.

9 + 4 = □
FB CB in total

9 o|ooo
FB CB □ in total

□ in total
/\
9 4
FB CB

▶ Summarize Collection Story Problems WHOLE CLASS

Explain that the problems children have solved are called *collection problems.* They are special because we don't add anything or take anything away. We just move things around or talk about them. Sometimes two kinds of things are put together. Sometimes two kinds of things are taken apart. Sometimes nothing is moved at all.

Differentiated Instruction

Extra Help If you notice that some children are experiencing difficulty with their drawings, suggest that they try drawing Math Mountains to represent the situation, as Math Mountains depict collection situations very clearly.

English Language Learners

Have 3 boys and 2 girls stand in front of the class. Say: **There are 3 boys and 2 girls in this group.** Ask: **How many children in all?** 5

- **Beginning** Say: **This is an addition story problem. But it is not a change plus problem. We did not change the group.**
- **Intermediate** Ask: **Was this an addition or subtraction problem?** addition **Did we change the group?** no Say: **This is a collection problem.**
- **Advanced** Ask: **Did we add to the group or take away from the group?** no **Was this a collection problem or a change problem?** collection

Activity 2

Solve Collection Story Problems

 20 MINUTES

Goal: Solve collection story problems.

Materials: MathBoard materials, Student Activity Book pages 95–96

 **NCTM Standards:**
Number and Operations
Problem Solving
Communication

Differentiated Instruction

English Learners Have children who understand story problem language work with English learners who may find the language difficult. Encourage children to focus on language rather than on solving the problems.

Ongoing Assessment

Ask children to discuss similarities and differences in these two problems.

- Janet has 6 red hats and 7 blue hats. How many hats does she have?
- Janet has 13 hats. 6 of them are red. How many are blue?

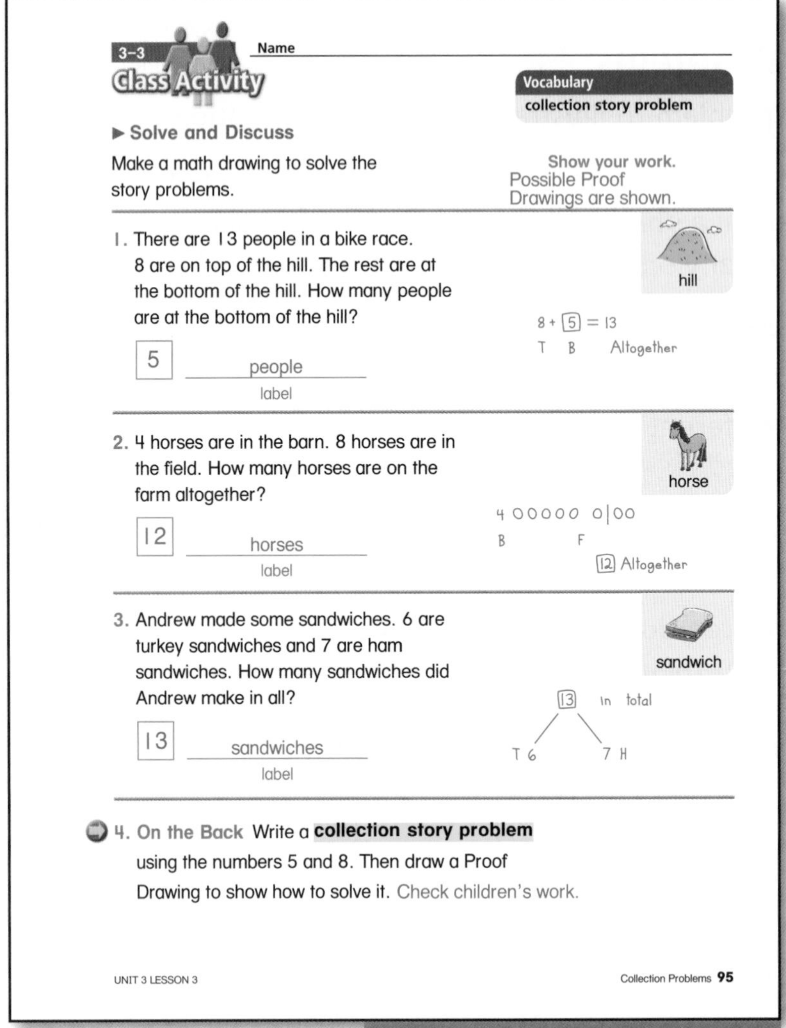

3-3 Class Activity Name

Vocabulary
collection story problem

▶ Solve and Discuss

Make a math drawing to solve the story problems.

Show your work.
Possible Proof Drawings are shown.

1. There are 13 people in a bike race. 8 are on top of the hill. The rest are at the bottom of the hill. How many people are at the bottom of the hill?

5 people
label

2. 4 horses are in the barn. 8 horses are in the field. How many horses are on the farm altogether?

12 horses
label

3. Andrew made some sandwiches. 6 are turkey sandwiches and 7 are ham sandwiches. How many sandwiches did Andrew make in all?

13 sandwiches
label

4. On the Back Write a **collection story problem** using the numbers 5 and 8. Then draw a Proof Drawing to show how to solve it. Check children's work.

UNIT 3 LESSON 3 Collection Problems 95

Student Activity Book page 95

▶ Solve and Discuss WHOLE CLASS

Direct children's attention to Student Activity Book page 95.

Math Talk Use the **Solve and Discuss** structure for problems 1–3. Children should explain the problem in their own words and tell how they got the answer. Encourage other children to comment and ask questions.

▶ Create Your Own INDIVIDUALS

Once children have discussed and solved problems 1–3, have them work on problem 4 independently. Ask a few children to share their stories and show their solutions.

2 Going Further

Differentiated Instruction

Intervention — Activity Card 3-3

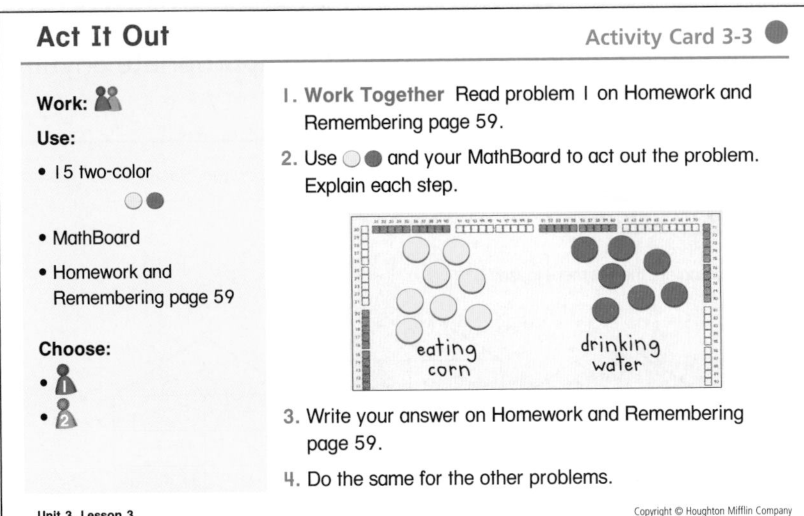
Act It Out — Activity Card 3-3

Work: (pair)
Use:
- 15 two-color counters
- MathBoard
- Homework and Remembering page 59

Choose:
- 1
- 2

1. **Work Together** Read problem 1 on Homework and Remembering page 59.
2. Use counters and your MathBoard to act out the problem. Explain each step.

3. Write your answer on Homework and Remembering page 59.
4. Do the same for the other problems.

Unit 3, Lesson 3

Activity Note Each pair needs 15 two-color counters, MathBoard materials, and Homework and Remembering p. 59.

Math Writing Prompt

Explain the Plan Explain how you could use counters to act out this problem.

Maria bought 2 red shirts and 3 blue shirts. How many shirts did she buy in all?

Software Support

Use *Soar to Success* for instruction of students needing targeted support for underlying skills.

On Level — Activity Card 3-3

Work Backward — Activity Card 3-3

Work: (individual)
Use:
- paper

1. Look at this equation and labeled drawing.

   7 + 5 = □
   baseballs footballs Altogether

   ooooo oo ooo|oo
   baseballs footballs

2. **Math Talk** Describe the labeled drawing. What do you see? Children should mention that the drawing includes a group of baseballs and a group of footballs.
3. Write a collection story problem to match the drawing.
4. Share your story with a classmate. Solve your classmate's problem.

Unit 3, Lesson 3

Activity Note Review the equation and drawing before children write their own collection story problems.

Math Writing Prompt

No Action Problems Explain why there is no action in this collection story problem.

A vase holds 6 red roses and 6 yellow roses. How many roses are there in all?

Software Support

Use *MegaMath* for review and reinforcement of the concepts and skills presented in this lesson.

Challenge — Activity Card 3-3

Multiple Strategies — Activity Card 3-3

Work: (group)
Use:
- MathBoard
- Homework and Remembering page 59

Choose:
- 1
- 2
- 3

1. **Work Together** Read problem 3 on Homework and Remembering page 59. Think about different ways to solve the problem.
2. Record different ways to solve the problem on the MathBoard.

   3 + [8] = 11
   B R Altogether

   11 All
   3 [8]
   blue red

3. **Math Talk** Share with other groups how you solved the problem.

Unit 3, Lesson 3

Activity Note Each group needs MathBoard materials and Homework and Remembering p. 59. Tell groups that the art on the card is an example of possible ways to solve problems.

Math Writing Prompt

Explain Your Thinking Ann solved a story problem using the equation 4 + □ = 13. Write a collection story problem that she may have solved.

Software Support

Use *Destination Math* to take students beyond the concepts and skills presented in this lesson.

3 Homework and Spiral Review

Goal: Additional Practice

This Homework page provides practice solving collection story problems.

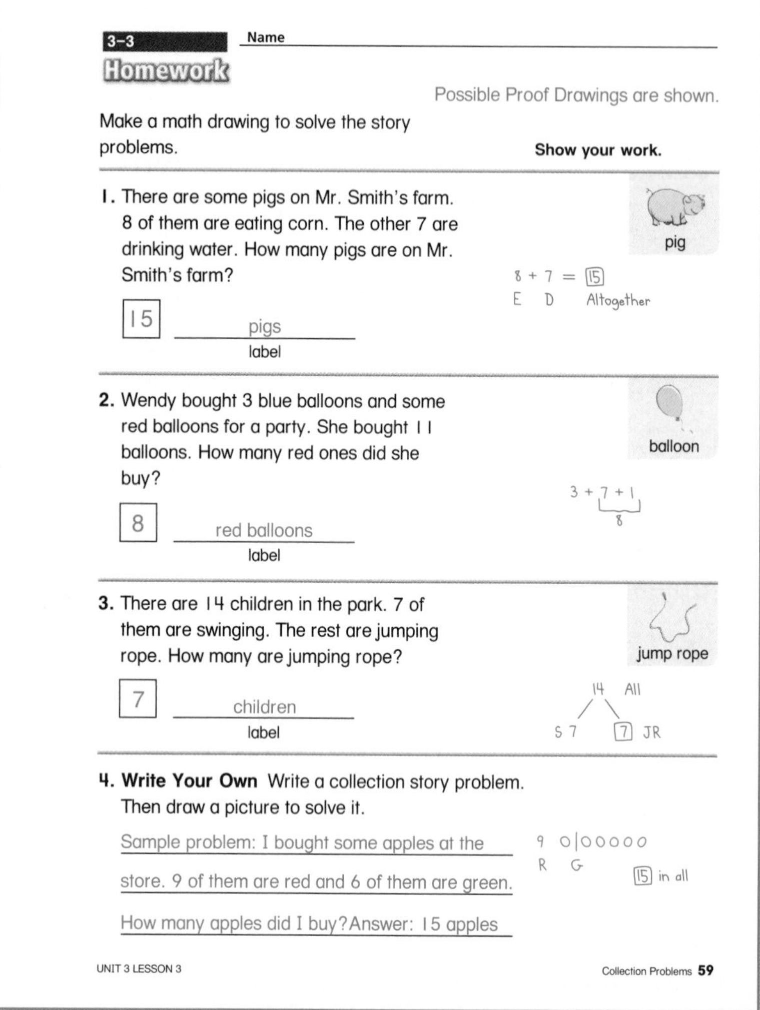

3-3 Homework — Name ______

Possible Proof Drawings are shown.

Make a math drawing to solve the story problems. **Show your work.**

1. There are some pigs on Mr. Smith's farm. 8 of them are eating corn. The other 7 are drinking water. How many pigs are on Mr. Smith's farm?

   pig

   8 + 7 = 15
   E D Altogether

   15 pigs
   label

2. Wendy bought 3 blue balloons and some red balloons for a party. She bought 11 balloons. How many red ones did she buy?

   balloon

   3 + 7 + 1
   8

   8 red balloons
   label

3. There are 14 children in the park. 7 of them are swinging. The rest are jumping rope. How many are jumping rope?

   jump rope

   14 All
   S 7 7 JR

   7 children
   label

4. **Write Your Own** Write a collection story problem. Then draw a picture to solve it.

   Sample problem: I bought some apples at the store. 9 of them are red and 6 of them are green. How many apples did I buy? Answer: 15 apples

   9 o|ooooo
   R G
   15 in all

UNIT 3 LESSON 3 — Collection Problems **59**

Homework and Remembering page 59

Goal: Spiral Review

This Remembering activity would be appropriate anytime after today's lesson.

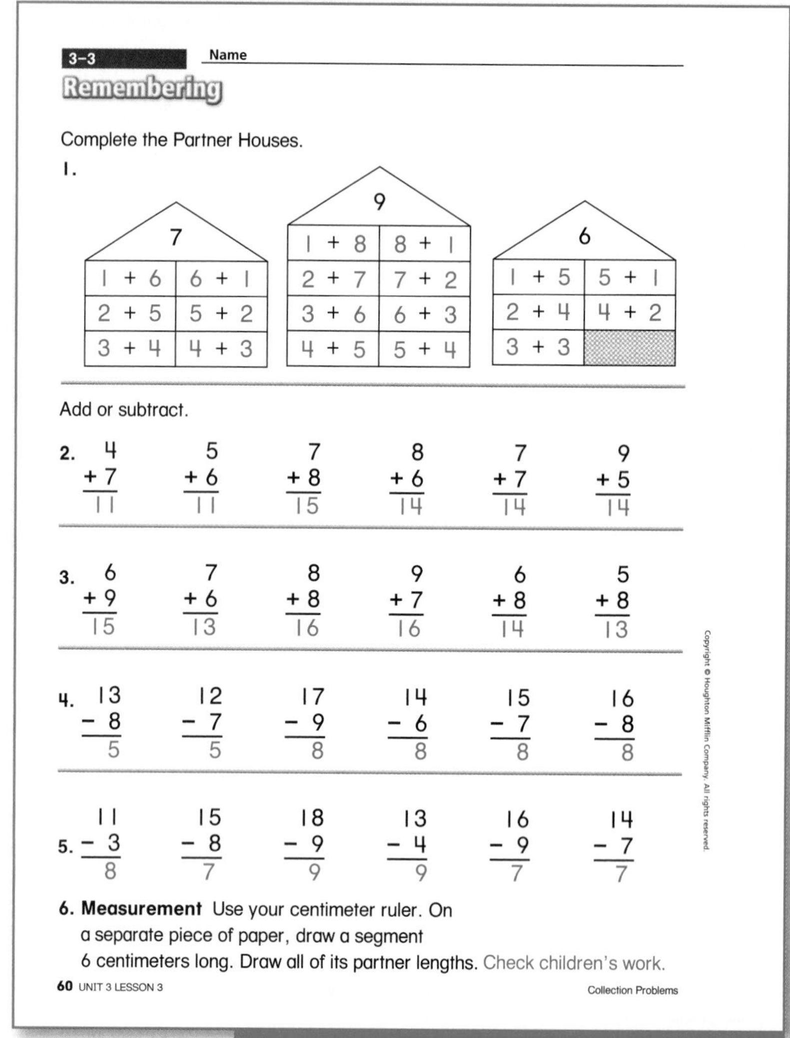

3-3 Remembering — Name ______

Complete the Partner Houses.

1.

7	
1 + 6	6 + 1
2 + 5	5 + 2
3 + 4	4 + 3

9	
1 + 8	8 + 1
2 + 7	7 + 2
3 + 6	6 + 3
4 + 5	5 + 4

6	
1 + 5	5 + 1
2 + 4	4 + 2
3 + 3	

Add or subtract.

2.	4 + 7 = 11	5 + 6 = 11	7 + 8 = 15	8 + 6 = 14	7 + 7 = 14	9 + 5 = 14
3.	6 + 9 = 15	7 + 6 = 13	8 + 8 = 16	9 + 7 = 16	6 + 8 = 14	5 + 8 = 13
4.	13 − 8 = 5	12 − 7 = 5	17 − 9 = 8	14 − 6 = 8	15 − 7 = 8	16 − 8 = 8
5.	11 − 3 = 8	15 − 8 = 7	18 − 9 = 9	13 − 4 = 9	16 − 9 = 7	14 − 7 = 7

6. **Measurement** Use your centimeter ruler. On a separate piece of paper, draw a segment 6 centimeters long. Draw all of its partner lengths. Check children's work.

60 UNIT 3 LESSON 3 — Collection Problems

Homework and Remembering page 60

Home or School Activity

Technology Connection

Illustrate a Problem Have children create and illustrate a collection story problem or choose a collection story problem from Student Activity Book page 95.

Have children type the story problem using a word processor and illustrate the problem using clip art.

Franny has 3 black cats and 2 white cats. How many cats does she have in all?

Story Problems with Group Names

Lesson Objectives

- Classify objects.
- Paraphrase and solve story problems containing group names.

Vocabulary
Venn diagram
group name

The Day at a Glance

Today's Goals	Materials	
1 Teaching the Lesson **A1:** Categorize objects. **A2:** Introduce Venn diagrams. **A3:** Solve story problems with group names. **A4:** Categorize objects and recognize classifications.	**Lesson Activities** Student Activity Book pp. 97–100 (includes Family Letter) Homework and Remembering pp. 61–62 MathBoard materials	**Going Further** Activity Cards 3-4 Math Journals
2 Going Further ▸ Differentiated Instruction		
3 Homework and Targeted Practice		

123 Use Math Talk today!

Keeping Skills Sharp

Quick Practice — 5 MINUTES

Goals: Make a ten when adding a number to 8. Subtract, totals ≤ 10.

Materials: Yellow and Orange Count-On Cards (from Unit 1 Lesson 10 or TRB M29–M32)

Class Make a Ten Write the $8 + n$ list (left column) on the board. Do each row in turn. (See Unit 3 Lesson 1.)

Yellow and Orange Count-On Cards Children practice with the Yellow (unknown addend) and Orange (subtraction) Count-On Cards individually or with a partner. Explain that they are practicing for a Secret Code Card subtraction race in Unit 3 Lesson 6.

Class Make a Ten

Student Leader 1 points to and says	Student Leader 2 shows fingers and says	Class says and Student Leader 2 writes = and
8 + 3	3 makes 2 and 1	8 + 2 + 1 = 10 + 1 = 11
8 + 7	7 makes 2 and 5	8 + 2 + 5 = 10 + 5 = 15
8 + 5	5 makes 2 and 3	8 + 2 + 3 = 10 + 3 = 13
8 + 8	8 makes 2 and 6	8 + 2 + 6 = 10 + 6 = 16
8 + 4	4 makes 2 and 2	8 + 2 + 2 = 10 + 2 = 12
8 + 6	6 makes 2 and 4	8 + 2 + 4 = 10 + 4 = 14

Daily Routines

Comparing 2-Digit Quantities Using a Meter Stick, Using Number Flashes, Using the MathBoard (See pp. xxv–xxvi.)

▸ Led by Student Leaders

Money Routine Using the 120 Poster, Using the Money Flip Chart, Using the Number Path, Using Secret Code Cards (See pp. xxiii–xxv.)

▸ Led by Student Leaders

1 Teaching the Lesson

Activity 1

Discuss Group Names

 10 MINUTES

Goal: Categorize objects.

 **NCTM Standards:**
Data Analysis and Probability
Communication

Differentiated Instruction

English Learners Visual examples of the different flowers can help English learners increase their vocabulary and solve the story problems.

English Language Learners

Show a picture of a daisy and a rose. Ask: **What are these?** flowers

- **Beginning** Hold up each picture. Say: **This is a daisy. This is a rose.** Have children repeat. **They are different flowers.**
- **Intermediate** Ask: **Do they look the same?** no **Are they different flowers?** yes
- **Advanced** Identify the flowers and have children describe how they are similar and different.

▶ Add Like Things WHOLE CLASS

Math Talk

Write the following sentences on the board.

I had 8 daisies. Then I picked 4 more.

- You have seen story problems that begin like this. What question could we ask to make this an addition story problem? How many daisies do I have now?
- We add daisies to daisies. How many daisies do I have now? 12 daisies

▶ Add Different Things WHOLE CLASS

Math Talk 

Write the following sentences on the board.

I had 8 daisies. Then I picked 4 roses.

- Suppose we want to make this into an addition story problem. Should we ask for the total number of daisies? No. The total is not all daisies.
- Should we ask for the total number of roses? No. The total isn't all roses.

Explain to children the idea of thinking about items as part of a larger classification or group.

- We have to think about daisies and roses for this story problem. What group name can we give to both daisies and roses? flowers
- What question could we use to make our story a problem? How many flowers do I have now?
- What would the answer be? 12 flowers

Activity 2

Use Venn Diagrams

 15 MINUTES

Goal: Introduce Venn diagrams.

Materials: Student Activity Book page 97

 **NCTM Standards:**
Data Analysis and Probability
Reasoning and Proof

▶ Introduce Venn Diagrams WHOLE CLASS

Draw the first Venn diagram from Student Activity Book page 97 on the board. Use it to illustrate the idea that both daisies and roses are members of a larger classification: flowers.

- Here are the daisies. Only daisies go in this circle.
- Here are the roses. Only roses go in this circle.
- Both daisies and roses are flowers. The big circle holds every kind of flower, but only flowers. Drawings like this are called Venn diagrams.

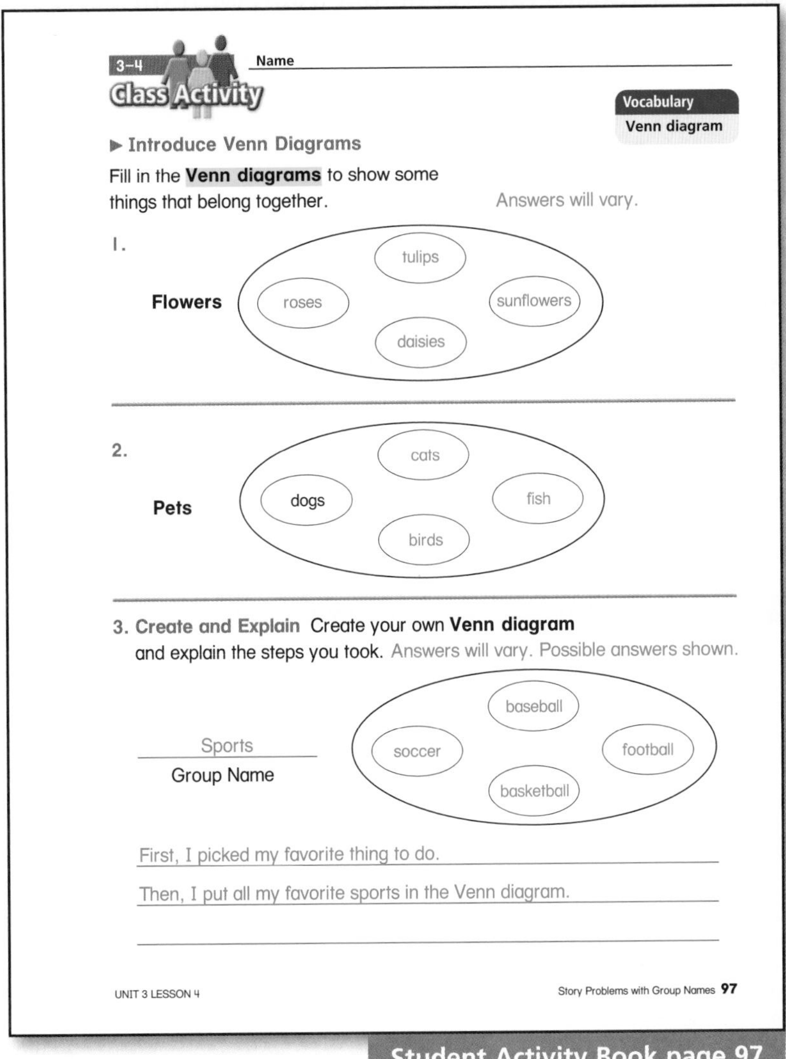

3–4 Class Activity

Name

Vocabulary
Venn diagram

▶ Introduce Venn Diagrams

Fill in the **Venn diagrams** to show some things that belong together. Answers will vary.

1. **Flowers**: tulips, roses, sunflowers, daisies

2. **Pets**: cats, dogs, fish, birds

3. **Create and Explain** Create your own **Venn diagram** and explain the steps you took. Answers will vary. Possible answers shown.

Sports
Group Name

baseball, soccer, football, basketball

First, I picked my favorite thing to do.

Then, I put all my favorite sports in the Venn diagram.

UNIT 3 LESSON 4 — Story Problems with Group Names 97

Student Activity Book page 97

Ask for Ideas Encourage children to think of other members of the same classification. Add these to the Venn diagram on the board as children fill in their pages. You can fill more than four ovals.

Have children contribute to the second Venn diagram by recording the class responses on their page. Be sure they start with the larger category and fill it with specific examples.

- Let's try another one. This time the group will be "Pets." One space is already filled in for us. Dogs are pets. Who can think of another pet someone might have? Possible response: cats

The Learning Classroom

Building Concepts Some story problems that children will encounter ask them to group various items together into an all-inclusive classification. We call these "group name" problems because the group has a special name that is different from the separate objects. For example, apples and oranges can be classified as *fruit.*

The difficulty of these problems lies in the language of categories. Having children group and then classify everyday objects is helpful for both math and language development. Make sure to use familiar objects when giving class examples.

Teaching Note

Math Background A Venn diagram is a pictorial way to represent relationships between sets. The Venn diagram used in this lesson may be different from others you have seen in which shapes intersect. The diagrams in this lesson show subsets of a set, that is, different items that are part of the same group. For example, zinnias, tulips, and roses are subsets of the larger set, *flowers.* So, the smaller ovals are contained within the larger oval.

Math Expressions revisits Venn diagrams in Volume 2 in lessons on sorting 3-D shapes.

Activity continued ▶

Ongoing Assessment

- On chart paper, create a list of group names and members of each group. Keep adding to it as children think of more items. Try to add to the list every day in this unit. At the end of the unit, have the class discuss the groups they listed.

Have children create their own Venn diagrams at the bottom of their page. Encourage children to share their Venn diagrams with the class.

If children find it difficult to think of group names, here is a list to get them started:

Fruit	apples, bananas, pears, and so on
Drinks	juice, water, milk, and so on
Fish	goldfish, angelfish, catfish, and so on
Toys	board games, stuffed animals, blocks, and so on

Activity 3

Solve Group Name Problems

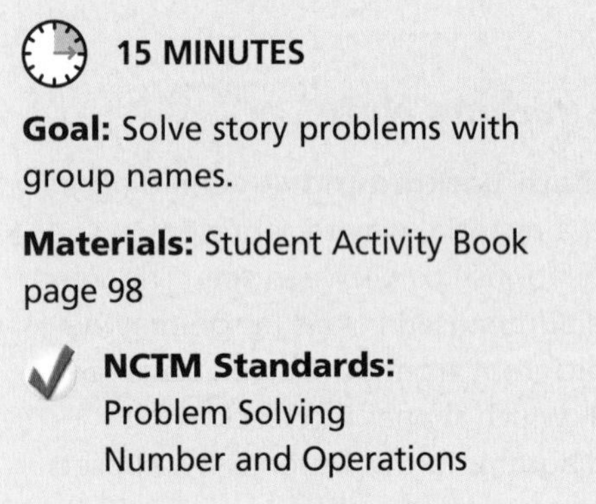
15 MINUTES

Goal: Solve story problems with group names.

Materials: Student Activity Book page 98

NCTM Standards:
Problem Solving
Number and Operations

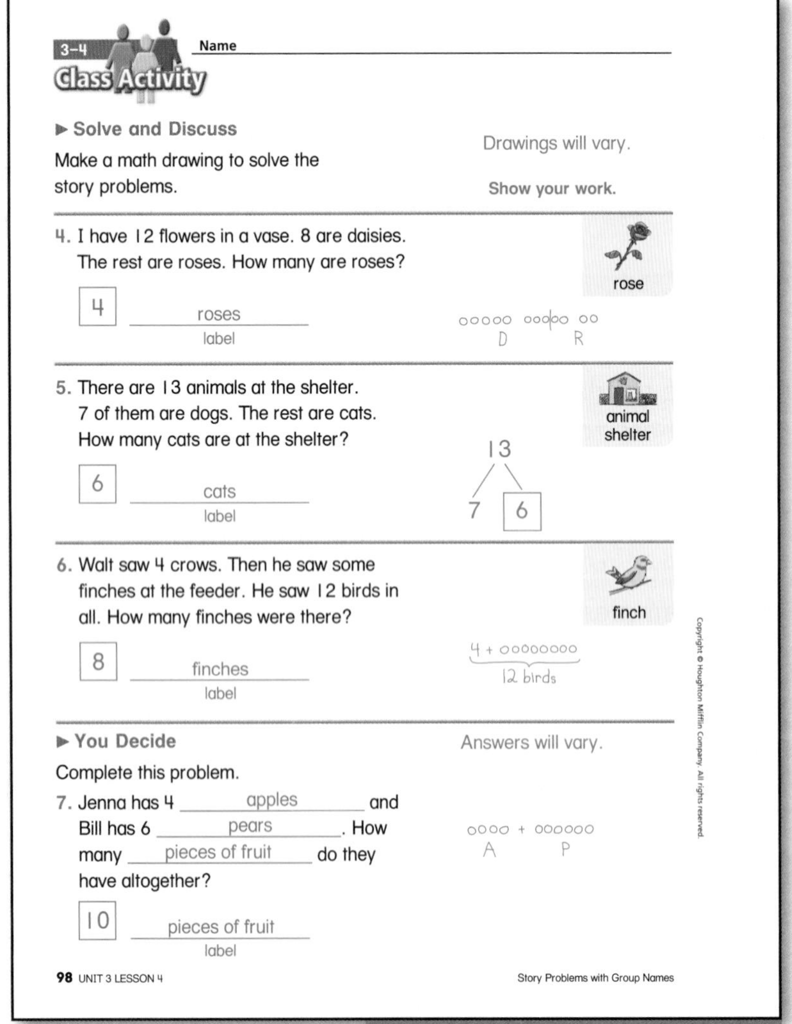
3-4 Class Activity Name

▶ Solve and Discuss

Make a math drawing to solve the story problems.

Drawings will vary.

Show your work.

4. I have 12 flowers in a vase. 8 are daisies. The rest are roses. How many are roses?

4 roses (label)

rose

5. There are 13 animals at the shelter. 7 of them are dogs. The rest are cats. How many cats are at the shelter?

6 cats (label)

animal shelter

6. Walt saw 4 crows. Then he saw some finches at the feeder. He saw 12 birds in all. How many finches were there?

8 finches (label)

finch

▶ You Decide

Answers will vary.

Complete this problem.

7. Jenna has 4 apples and Bill has 6 pears. How many pieces of fruit do they have altogether?

10 pieces of fruit (label)

98 UNIT 3 LESSON 4 Story Problems with Group Names

Copyright © Houghton Mifflin Company. All rights reserved.

Student Activity Book page 98

▶ Solve and Discuss WHOLE CLASS

Have children look at the first problem on Student Activity Book page 98. Several children should retell the problem in their own words. This allows children to learn basic paraphrasing skills and it reinforces the idea that children need to understand what's being asked of them in story problems.

They can change the order of the sentences and use different wording.

- I have 12 flowers in a vase. 8 are daisies. The others are roses. How many roses do I have in all?

Math Talk Use the **Solve and Discuss** structure for problem 4. Invite three to six children to go to the board and solve the problem with diagrams and numbers. The rest of the class should work at their seats. Encourage children to use numbers whenever possible and remind them to label their work.

D R F 8 + [2 + 2 / 4] = 12	8 + [0000 R 4] D 12 F
F 12 8 [4] ●●●● D R	12 Flowers 00000 000 | 0000 8D 4R 8 + [4] = 12 D R F

Then have two or three children present their solutions to the class for questions and discussion. Encourage children at their desks to ask questions and to assist their classmates in their understanding. As part of the discussion, elicit the idea that 8 and 4 are 12-partners. Continue the **Solve and Discuss** structure with the next two problems on Student Activity Book page 98.

▶ You Decide INDIVIDUALS

Once children have discussed problems 4–6, have them work on problem 7. Children fill in their own information to complete the story problem.

As a class, you may want to brainstorm a list of categories and objects to help children experiencing difficulty. Children can decide to use words from that list or create their own categories. Once children have finished, ask a few Student Leaders to share their story problems and show their solution methods.

Differentiated Instruction

English Learners Have student helpers, who understand story problem language, work with English learners who may find the language difficult. These helpers should focus on language rather than on solving the problem.

The Learning Classroom

Helping Community Doing work at the board reveals multiple methods of solving a problem, makes comparisons possible, and communicates to children that different methods are acceptable. When children work next to each other at the board, spontaneous helping frequently occurs. This approach allows children to help each other with math and allows errors to be identified in a supportive environment.

Ongoing Assessment

Ask questions such as:

- ▶ What items from the classroom can we group together?
- ▶ How could you name the groups?

Activity 4

The *Group Loop* Game

 15 MINUTES

Goal: Categorize objects and recognize classifications.

 **NCTM Standards:**
Data Analysis and Probability
Reasoning and Proof

Class Management

If children are interested in a competitive game for versions 2 and 3, the class can be divided into two or more teams. The score for each round is the number of items each team is able to name correctly.

▶How to Play WHOLE CLASS

Version 1:

One child draws a large circle (the "loop") on the board. This represents the category. He or she then names two or more objects that belong to the same category (a recorder can write the examples in the loop as they are named). Other children may suggest more objects, which are either accepted if they fit the category or rejected if they do not. The class then attempts to guess the category to which all of the objects belong. For example, collies and poodles belong to the category "dogs."

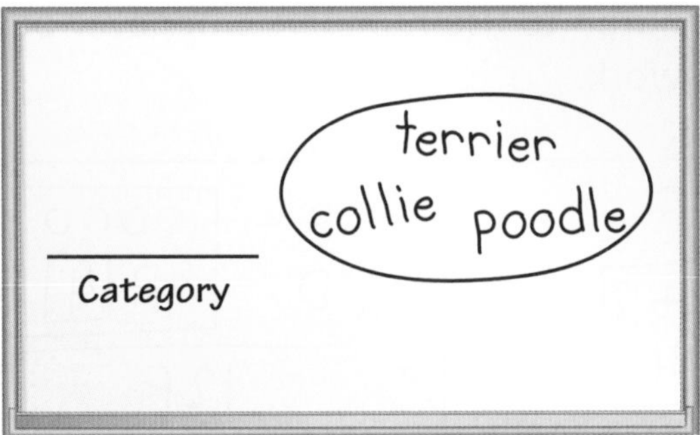

Version 2:

One child names a category (for example, vegetables). Another child gives a letter of the alphabet and supplies the first example (*b* for beans). Other children must supply as many examples beginning with the same letter as they can (broccoli, Brussels sprouts, and so on).

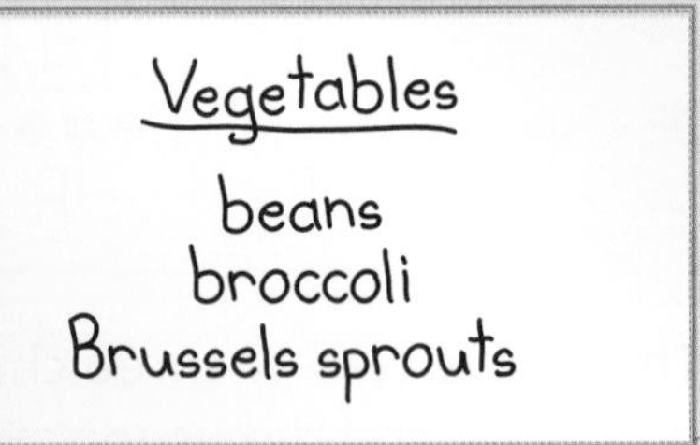

Version 3:

One child names a category (for example, fruit). Another child names an example beginning with the letter *a* (apples). The class then works its way through the alphabet. If no examples can be thought of for a letter, the class skips it and moves on to the next letter.

Fruit
apples
bananas
figs
grapes

2 Going Further

Differentiated Instruction

Intervention — Activity Card 3-4

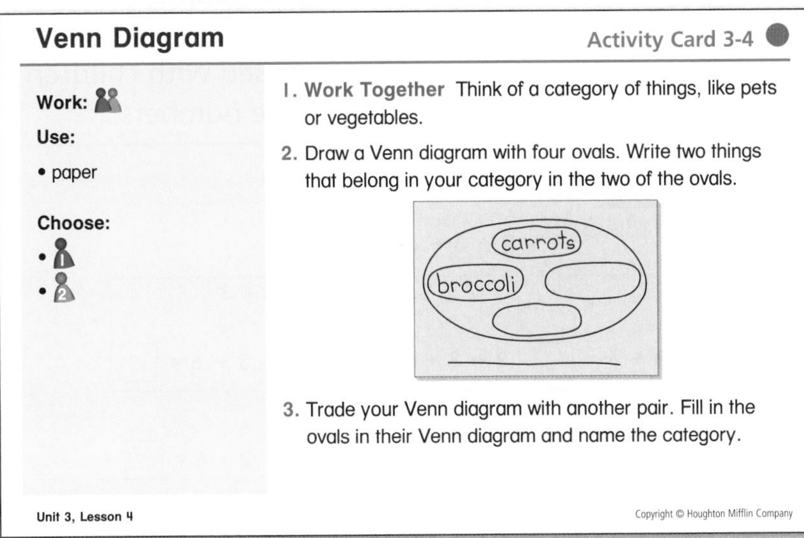
Venn Diagram Activity Card 3-4 ●

Work: (pairs)
Use:
- paper

Choose:
- (student 1)
- (student 2)

1. **Work Together** Think of a category of things, like pets or vegetables.
2. Draw a Venn diagram with four ovals. Write two things that belong in your category in the two of the ovals.

3. Trade your Venn diagram with another pair. Fill in the ovals in their Venn diagram and name the category.

Unit 3, Lesson 4 — Copyright © Houghton Mifflin Company

Activity Note Have children share their categories with you before they make their Venn diagrams.

Math Writing Prompt

What's Wrong? What's wrong with the story problem? How could you fix it?

Tom ate 6 apples after school. Norah ate 5 bananas. How many apples did they eat in all?

Software Support

Use *Soar to Success* for instruction of students needing targeted support for underlying skills.

On Level — Activity Card 3-4

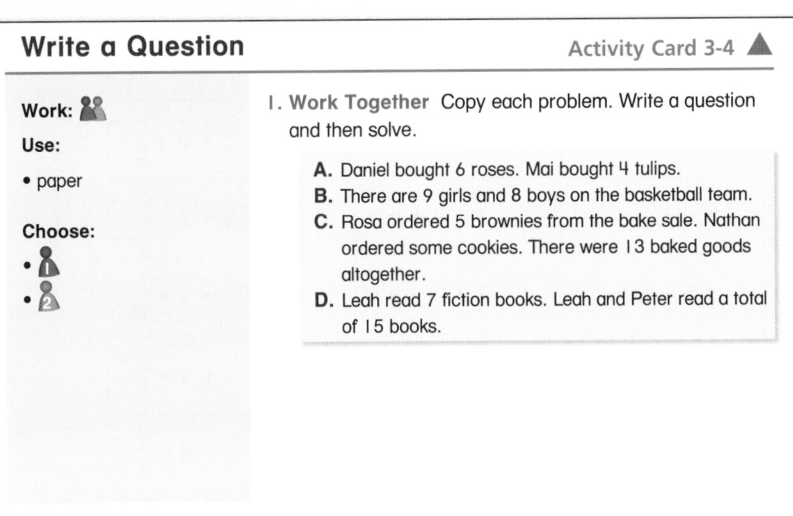
Write a Question Activity Card 3-4 ▲

Work: (pairs)
Use:
- paper

Choose:
- (student 1)
- (student 2)

1. **Work Together** Copy each problem. Write a question and then solve.

A. Daniel bought 6 roses. Mai bought 4 tulips.
B. There are 9 girls and 8 boys on the basketball team.
C. Rosa ordered 5 brownies from the bake sale. Nathan ordered some cookies. There were 13 baked goods altogether.
D. Leah read 7 fiction books. Leah and Peter read a total of 15 books.

Unit 3, Lesson 4 — Copyright © Houghton Mifflin Company

Activity Note Encourage pairs to explain how they decided what question to ask for each problem.

Math Writing Prompt

Write Your Own Create your own "group name" story problem. Draw a picture to solve your problem.

Software Support

Use *MegaMath* for review and reinforcement of the concepts and skills presented in this lesson.

Challenge — Activity Card 3-4

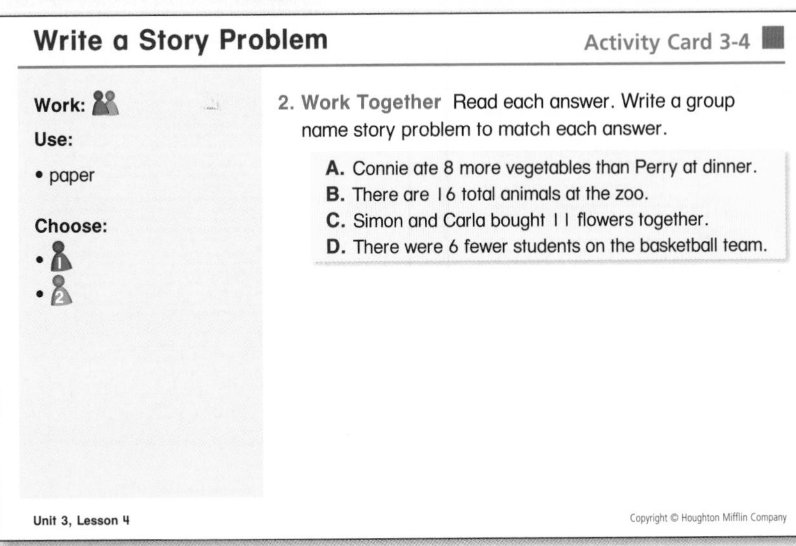
Write a Story Problem Activity Card 3-4 ■

Work: (pairs)
Use:
- paper

Choose:
- (student 1)
- (student 2)

2. **Work Together** Read each answer. Write a group name story problem to match each answer.

A. Connie ate 8 more vegetables than Perry at dinner.
B. There are 16 total animals at the zoo.
C. Simon and Carla bought 11 flowers together.
D. There were 6 fewer students on the basketball team.

Unit 3, Lesson 4 — Copyright © Houghton Mifflin Company

Activity Note Have pairs share their group name story problems with other groups. Check that the answers match the story problems.

Math Writing Prompt

Explain Dan placed an apple in a bag labeled "fruit." Shauna told him to put the apple in a bag labeled "snacks." Who is correct? Explain your thinking.

Software Support

Use *Destination Math* to take students beyond the concepts and skills presented in this lesson.

Homework and Targeted Practice

3-4 Homework **Goal:** Additional Practice

✓ Include children's completed Homework page as part of their portfolios.

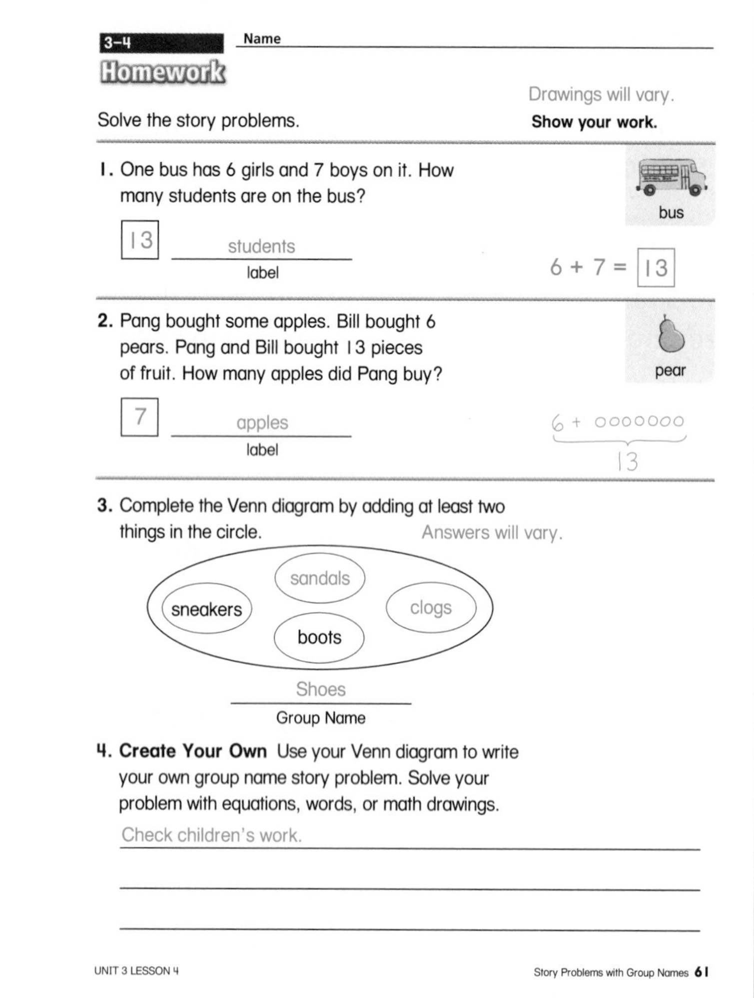

3-4 Homework Name

Solve the story problems.

Drawings will vary. **Show your work.**

1. One bus has 6 girls and 7 boys on it. How many students are on the bus?

13 students (label)

6 + 7 = 13

2. Pang bought some apples. Bill bought 6 pears. Pang and Bill bought 13 pieces of fruit. How many apples did Pang buy?

7 apples (label)

6 + 0000000 = 13

3. Complete the Venn diagram by adding at least two things in the circle. Answers will vary.

Shoes (Group Name)

4. **Create Your Own** Use your Venn diagram to write your own group name story problem. Solve your problem with equations, words, or math drawings.

Check children's work.

UNIT 3 LESSON 4 — Story Problems with Group Names 61

Homework and Remembering page 61

3-4 Targeted Practice **Goal:** Practice addition.

This Targeted Practice page can be used with children who need extra practice adding three numbers.

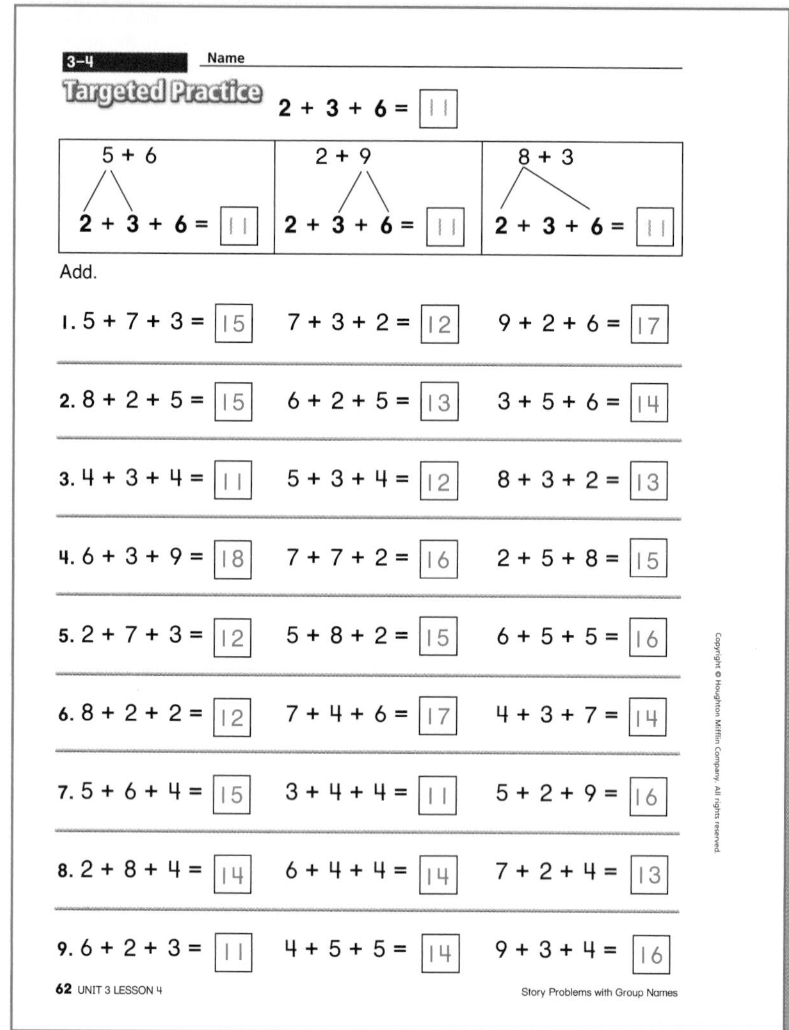

3-4 Targeted Practice Name

2 + 3 + 6 = 11

5 + 6	2 + 9	8 + 3
2 + 3 + 6 = 11	2 + 3 + 6 = 11	2 + 3 + 6 = 11

Add.

1. 5 + 7 + 3 = 15	7 + 3 + 2 = 12	9 + 2 + 6 = 17
2. 8 + 2 + 5 = 15	6 + 2 + 5 = 13	3 + 5 + 6 = 14
3. 4 + 3 + 4 = 11	5 + 3 + 4 = 12	8 + 3 + 2 = 13
4. 6 + 3 + 9 = 18	7 + 7 + 2 = 16	2 + 5 + 8 = 15
5. 2 + 7 + 3 = 12	5 + 8 + 2 = 15	6 + 5 + 5 = 16
6. 8 + 2 + 2 = 12	7 + 4 + 6 = 17	4 + 3 + 7 = 14
7. 5 + 6 + 4 = 15	3 + 4 + 4 = 11	5 + 2 + 9 = 16
8. 2 + 8 + 4 = 14	6 + 4 + 4 = 14	7 + 2 + 4 = 13
9. 6 + 2 + 3 = 11	4 + 5 + 5 = 14	9 + 3 + 4 = 16

62 UNIT 3 LESSON 4 — Story Problems with Group Names

Homework and Remembering page 62

Home and School Connection

Family Letter Have children take home the Family Letter on Student Activity Book page 99. This letter explains how problem solving is developed in *Math Expressions.* It gives parents and guardians a better understanding of the learning that goes on in math class and creates a bridge between school and home. A Spanish translation of this letter is on the following page in the Student Activity Book.

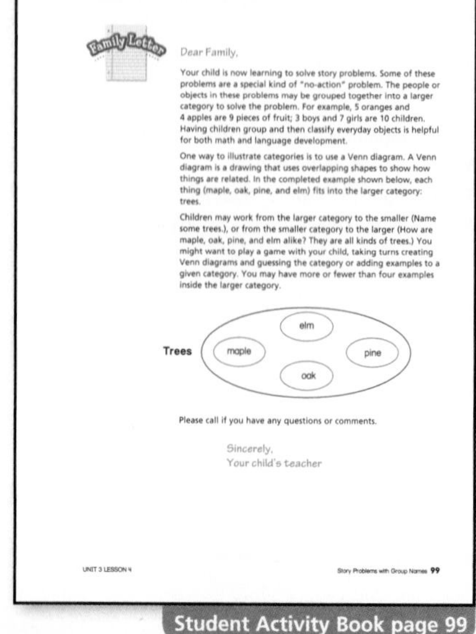

Family Letter

Dear Family,

Your child is now learning to solve story problems. Some of these problems are a special kind of "no-action" problem. The people or objects in these problems may be grouped together into a larger category to solve the problem. For example, 5 oranges and 4 apples are 9 pieces of fruit; 3 boys and 7 girls are 10 children. Having children group and then classify everyday objects is helpful for both math and language development.

One way to illustrate categories is to use a Venn diagram. A Venn diagram is a drawing that uses overlapping shapes to show how things are related. In the completed example shown below, each thing (maple, oak, pine, and elm) fits into the larger category: trees.

Children may work from the larger category to the smaller (Name some trees.), or from the smaller category to the larger (How are maple, oak, pine, and elm alike? They are all kinds of trees.) You might want to play a game with your child, taking turns creating Venn diagrams and guessing the category or adding examples to a given category. You may have more or fewer than four examples inside the larger category.

Please call if you have any questions or comments.

Sincerely,
Your child's teacher

UNIT 3 LESSON 4 — Story Problems with Group Names 99

Student Activity Book page 99

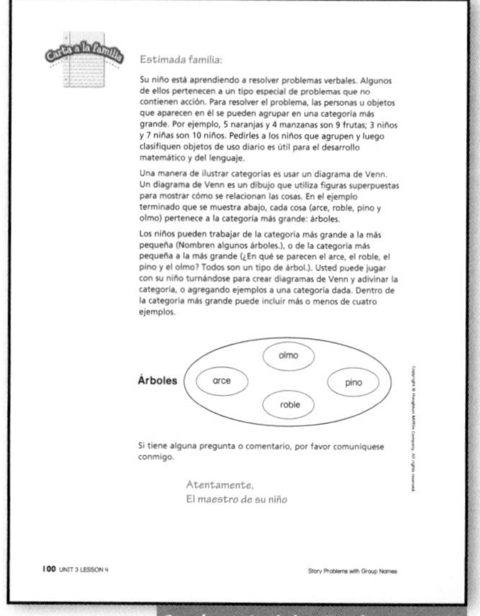

Carta a la familia

Estimada familia:

Su niño está aprendiendo a resolver problemas verbales. Algunos de ellos pertenecen a un tipo especial de problemas que no contienen acción. Para resolver el problema, las personas u objetos que aparecen en él se pueden agrupar en una categoría más grande. Por ejemplo, 5 naranjas y 4 manzanas son 9 frutas; 3 niños y 7 niñas son 10 niños. Pedirles a los niños que agrupen y luego clasifiquen objetos de uso diario es útil para el desarrollo matemático y del lenguaje.

Una manera de ilustrar categorías es usar un diagrama de Venn. Un diagrama de Venn es un dibujo que utiliza figuras superpuestas para mostrar cómo se relacionan las cosas. En el ejemplo terminado que se muestra abajo, cada cosa (arce, roble, pino y olmo) pertenece a la categoría más grande: árboles.

Los niños pueden trabajar de la categoría más grande a la más pequeña (Nombren algunos árboles.), o de la categoría más pequeña a la más grande (¿En qué se parecen el arce, el roble, el pino y el olmo? Todos son un tipo de árbol.). Usted puede jugar con su niño turnándose para crear diagramas de Venn y adivinar la categoría, o agregando ejemplos a una categoría dada. Dentro de la categoría más grande puede incluir más o menos de cuatro ejemplos.

Si tiene alguna pregunta o comentario, por favor comuníquese conmigo.

Atentamente,
El maestro de su niño

100 UNIT 3 LESSON 4 — Story Problems with Group Names

Student Activity Book page 100

Comparison Story Problems

Lesson Objectives

- Use comparison language appropriately.
- Solve comparison story problems.

Vocabulary

comparison story problem
matching drawing
comparison bars

The Day at a Glance

Today's Goals	Materials	
1 Teaching the Lesson A: Represent, solve, and discuss comparison story problems.	**Lesson Activities** Student Activity Book pp. 101–102 Homework and Remembering p. 63	**Going Further** Activity Cards 3-5 Homework and Remembering p. 63 Comparison Drawings (TRB M55) Two-color counters MathBoard materials Math Journals
2 Going Further ▶ Differentiated Instruction		
3 Homework and Spiral Review		

Use Math Talk today!

Keeping Skills Sharp

Quick Practice — 5 MINUTES

Goals: Write equation chains for 15. Make a ten when adding a number to 8. Subtract, totals $\leq$ 10.

Materials: Yellow and Orange Count-On Cards (from Unit 1 Lesson 10 or TRB M29–M32)

Equation Chains Have three children write equation chains for 15 on the board. (See Unit 1 Lesson 18.)

Class Make a Ten Write the $8 + n$ list (left column) on the board. Do each row in turn.

Yellow and Orange Count-On Cards Children practice with the Yellow (unknown addend) and Orange (subtraction) Count-On Cards individually or with a partner. Explain that they are practicing for a Secret Code Card subtraction race in Unit 3 Lesson 6.

Class Make a Ten

Student Leader 1 points to and says	Student Leader 2 shows fingers and says	Class says and Student Leader 2 writes = and
8 + 3	3 makes 2 and 1	8 + 2 + 1 = 10 + 1 = 11
8 + 6	6 makes 2 and 4	8 + 2 + 4 = 10 + 4 = 14
8 + 8	8 makes 2 and 6	8 + 2 + 6 = 10 + 6 = 16
8 + 5	5 makes 2 and 3	8 + 2 + 3 = 10 + 3 = 13
8 + 7	7 makes 2 and 5	8 + 2 + 5 = 10 + 5 = 15
8 + 4	4 makes 2 and 2	8 + 2 + 2 = 10 + 2 = 12

Daily Routines

Comparing 2-Digit Quantities Using a Meter Stick, Using Number Flashes, Using the MathBoard (See pp. xxv–xxvi.)

▶ Led by Student Leaders

Money Routine Using the 120 Poster, Using the Money Flip Chart, Using the Number Path, Using Secret Code Cards (See pp. xxiii–xxv.)

▶ Led by Student Leaders

1 Teaching the Lesson

Activity

Represent and Solve Comparison Problems

 **30 MINUTES**

Goal: Represent, solve, and discuss comparison story problems.

Materials: Student Activity Book pages 101–102

 **NCTM Standards:**
Number and Operations
Problem Solving
Communication

Teaching Note

Language and Vocabulary Children often find comparison problems more difficult to understand and solve than other types of story problems because of the language. Thus, instruction should focus on helping children understand the language of these problems before they try to solve them.

The underlying meaning of comparison story problems involves someone or something that has "more" or "less" of something than someone or something else. The comparison statement or question has two key pieces of information: *Who has more?* and *How much more?* Asking themselves these two key questions will help children understand the situation and decide whether to add or subtract, especially if they also make a drawing.

Another key skill is being able to reverse the comparing statement, which may lead children to an easier solution method. The comparison can be stated in two ways: *How many more does B have than A?* and *How many fewer does A have than B?*

Comparison problems can be represented by matching drawings or with comparison bars and ovals.

▶ Represent a Comparison Problem WHOLE CLASS

Write the following problem on the board and read it aloud.

Jane and Ernie have some apples. Jane has 6 apples and Ernie has 9 apples. Who has more apples? How many more?

- What is this problem about? Jane's and Ernie's apples
- What are the two questions? Who has more? How many more?
- How many apples does Jane have? 6 apples Ernie? 9 apples
- Who has more apples? Ernie
- Who has fewer apples? Jane

Now use the **Solve and Discuss** structure for students to solve this problem. Everyone should make a labeled math drawing. Be sure that matching solutions like this are shown and discussed as part of the Math Talk.

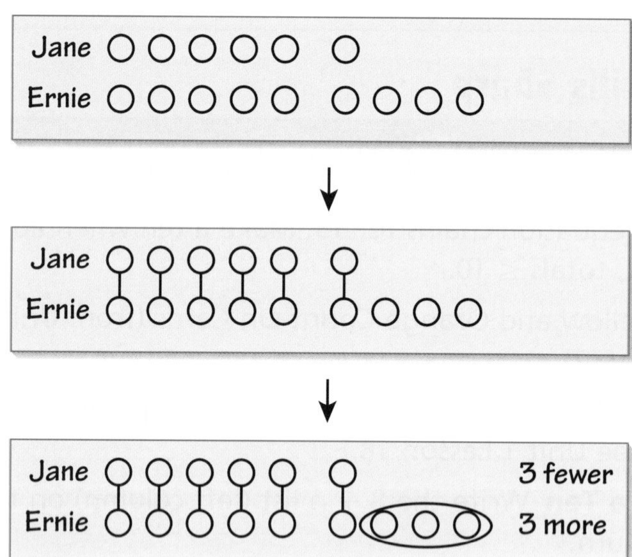

Be sure children can use the drawing to answer these questions.

- How many more apples does Ernie have than Jane? 3 more apples
- How many fewer apples does Jane have than Ernie? 3 fewer apples

Tell children they can also use bars and ovals, called comparison bars, to represent story problems. Sketch the following example on the board.

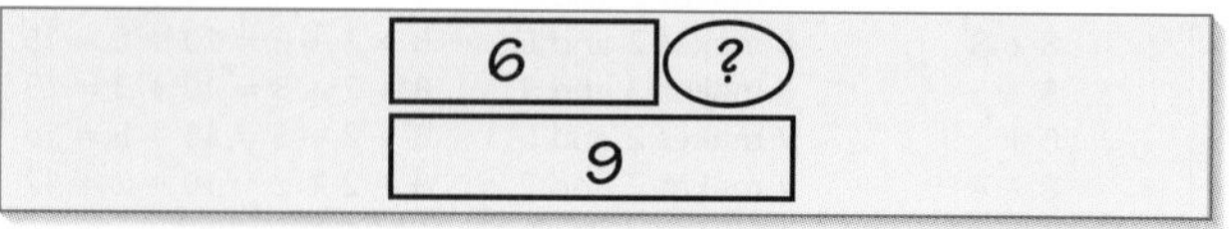

Explain that the longer rectangle is the total, the shorter rectangle is one of the partners, and the oval is the unknown partner. Have children discuss how this drawing is similar to and different from the matching drawings.

Some children may be ready to replace the matching drawings with the comparison bars, while other children may need to see the matching drawing to understand the situation.

▶ Solve and Discuss WHOLE CLASS

Have children look at the first problem on Student Activity Book page 101 while you or a volunteer read it aloud. Then ask two children to rephrase the problem in their own words.

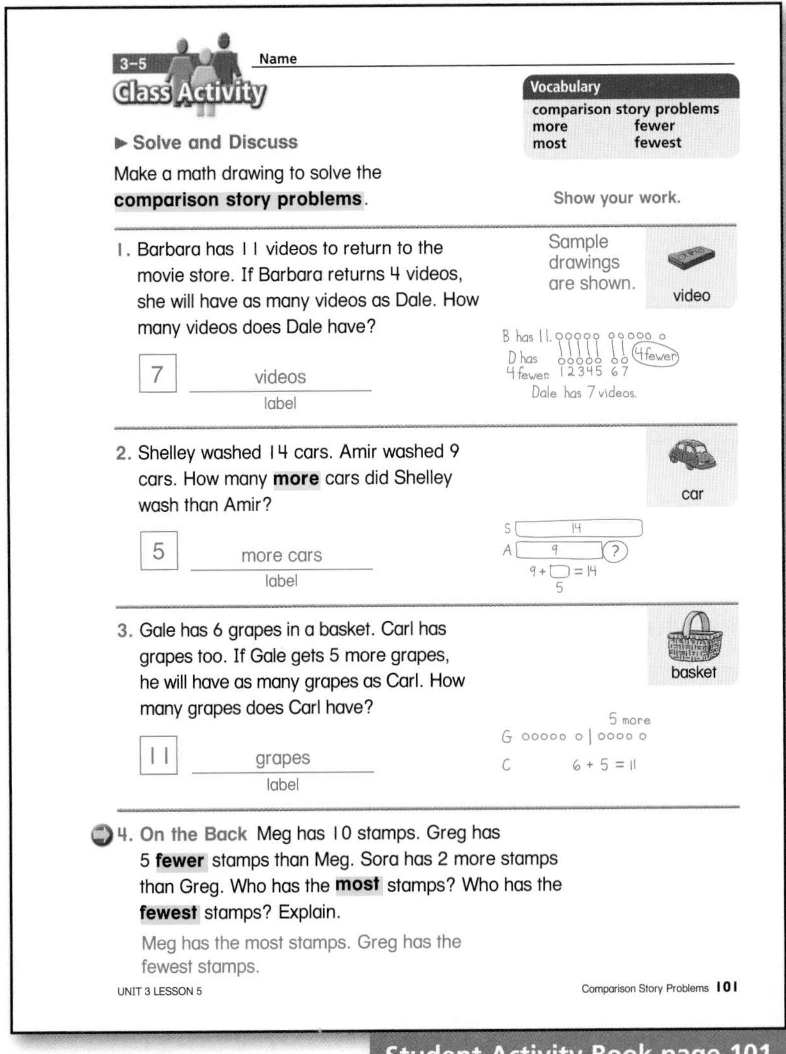

3-5 **Class Activity** Name ____

Vocabulary
comparison story problems
more fewer
most fewest

▶ Solve and Discuss

Make a math drawing to solve the **comparison story problems**.

Show your work.

1. Barbara has 11 videos to return to the movie store. If Barbara returns 4 videos, she will have as many videos as Dale. How many videos does Dale have?

Sample drawings are shown.

7 videos (label)

B has 11. ooooo ooooo o
D has ooooo oo (4 fewer)
4 fewer 12345 67
Dale has 7 videos.

2. Shelley washed 14 cars. Amir washed 9 cars. How many **more** cars did Shelley wash than Amir?

5 more cars (label)

S [14]
A [9] (?)
9 + □ = 14
5

3. Gale has 6 grapes in a basket. Carl has grapes too. If Gale gets 5 more grapes, he will have as many grapes as Carl. How many grapes does Carl have?

11 grapes (label)

5 more
G ooooo o | oooo o
C 6 + 5 = 11

4. **On the Back** Meg has 10 stamps. Greg has 5 **fewer** stamps than Meg. Sora has 2 more stamps than Greg. Who has the **most** stamps? Who has the **fewest** stamps? Explain.

Meg has the most stamps. Greg has the fewest stamps.

UNIT 3 LESSON 5 Comparison Story Problems 101

Student Activity Book page 101

Activity continued ▶

Teaching Note

Math Background Some comparison problems use more/fewer language and some use equalizing language. Examples of each are shown below.

Problems Using More/ Fewer Language

Manny has 5 roses. Asha has 8 roses. How many more roses does Asha have than Manny?
M [5](?)
A [8]

Manny has 5 roses. Asha has 3 more roses than Manny. How many roses does Asha have?
M [5](3)
A [?]

Asha has 8 roses. Manny has 3 fewer roses than Asha. How many roses does Manny have?
M [?](3)
A [8]

Problems Using Equalizing Language

Manny has 5 roses. Asha has 8 roses. How many roses does Manny have to get to have the same as Asha?
M [5](?)
A [8]

Manny has 5 roses. Manny has to get 3 roses to have the same as Asha. How many roses does Asha have?
M [5](3)
A [?]

Asha has 8 roses. She has to give away 3 roses to have the same as Manny. How many roses does Manny have?
M [?](3)
A [8]

① Teaching the Lesson (continued)

Differentiated Instruction

Extra Help If children are experiencing difficulty with comparison story problems, remind them to first focus on deciding who has more and who has less. Once they have determined that, they can make a labeled drawing to represent the situation and then either add or subtract to solve the problem.

Ongoing Assessment

Ask children to draw comparison drawings and solve the following problem.

► Carla has 8 stamps. Frank has 5 stamps. Who has more stamps? How many more?

► Who has fewer stamps? How many fewer?

English Language Learners

Draw a cookie, slice of cake, and sundae on the board. Help children compare them. Emphasize the form used when comparing 2 things or 3 or more things. Gesture and say: **The cake is *bigger* than the cookie.**

- **Beginning** Say: **The sundae is *bigger* than the cake.** Circle the sundae. Say: **The sundae is the *biggest*.** Have children repeat. Compare the desserts using *more* and *most* delicious.
- **Intermediate** Ask: **Is the sundae *bigger* or *smaller* than the cake?** bigger Say: **We compared 2 things. We added *er* to *big*.** Ask: **Of all 3, which is the *biggest?*** sundae Continue with more and most delicious.
- **Advanced** Ask: **How many desserts did I compare?** 2 **What's *bigger* than the cake?** sundae **What's the *biggest* dessert of all 3?** sundae **Now how many desserts did we compare?** 3

Math Talk Use the **Solve and Discuss** structure for problem 1.

As children work at the board, look for representations such as the following:

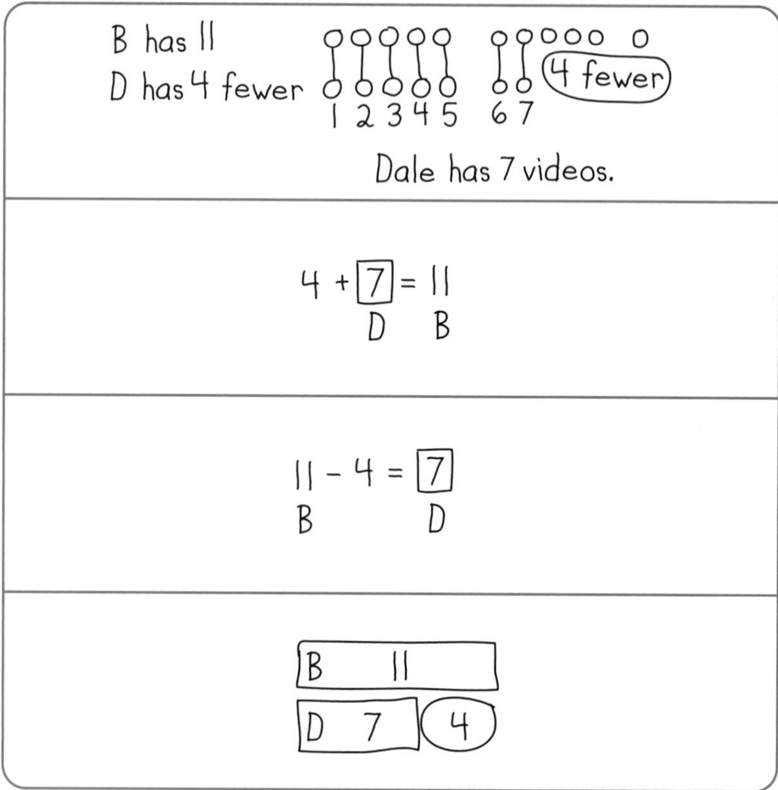

Have children work independently or in **Helping Pairs** to solve the rest of the problems on the page or do the whole page with the class if many children are still having difficulty.

Discuss the language *most* and *fewest* in problem 4. Be sure that children understand that we use the comparative -er forms *fewer* and *more* with 2 amounts and we use *most* and *fewest* with 3 or more amounts. Have children give situations where they use these different words.

2 Going Further

Differentiated Instruction

Intervention — Activity Card 3-5

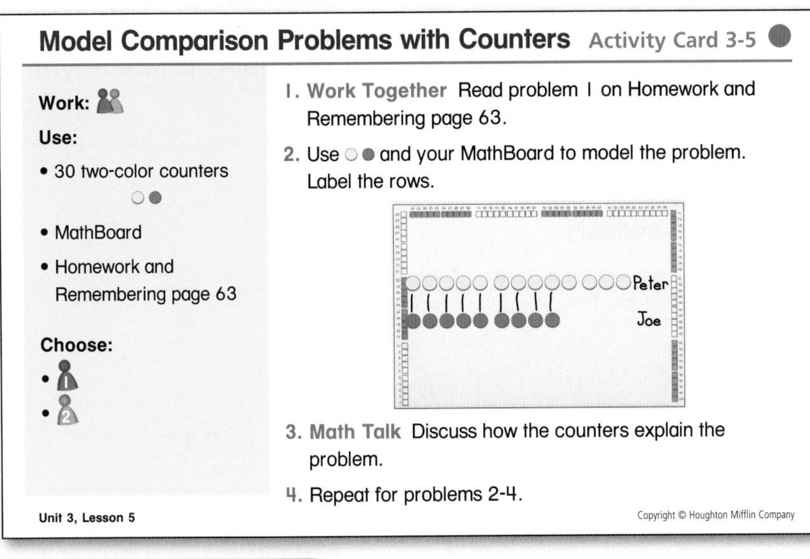

Model Comparison Problems with Counters Activity Card 3-5 ●

Work: (pair)

Use:
- 30 two-color counters
- MathBoard
- Homework and Remembering page 63

Choose:
- (1)
- (2)

1. **Work Together** Read problem 1 on Homework and Remembering page 63.
2. Use counters and your MathBoard to model the problem. Label the rows.

3. **Math Talk** Discuss how the counters explain the problem.
4. Repeat for problems 2-4.

Unit 3, Lesson 5

Activity Note Each pair needs 30 two-color counters, MathBoard materials, and Homework and Remembering, p. 63.

Math Writing Prompt

Write Your Own Write a comparison story problem that you could model using 4 red counters and 7 yellow counters.

Software Support

Use *Soar to Success* for instruction of students needing targeted support for underlying skills.

On Level — Activity Card 3-5

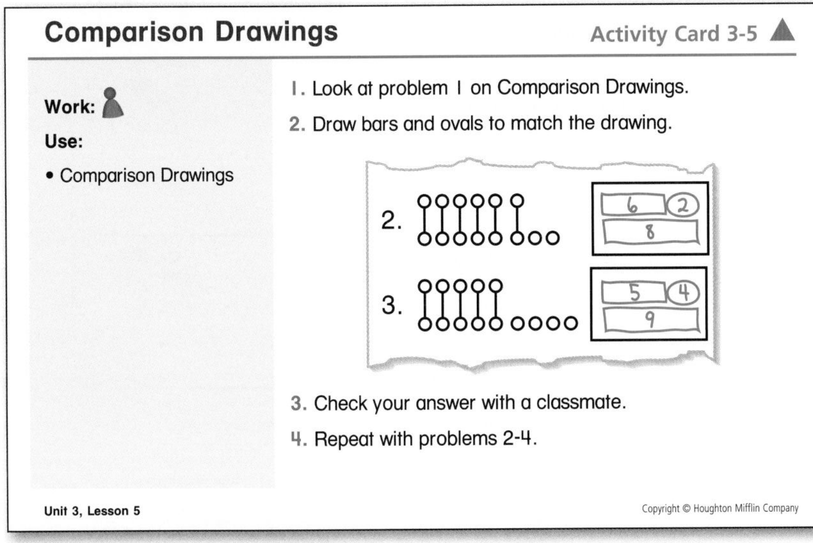

Comparison Drawings Activity Card 3-5 ▲

Work: (individual)

Use:
- Comparison Drawings

1. Look at problem 1 on Comparison Drawings.
2. Draw bars and ovals to match the drawing.

3. Check your answer with a classmate.
4. Repeat with problems 2-4.

Unit 3, Lesson 5

Activity Note Each child needs Comparison Drawings (TRB M55). Have children compare their drawings with a classmate.

Math Writing Prompt

Work Backward Write a comparison story problem that has the answer *3 pears*.

Software Support

Use *MegaMath* for review and reinforcement of the concepts and skills presented in this lesson.

Challenge — Activity Card 3-5

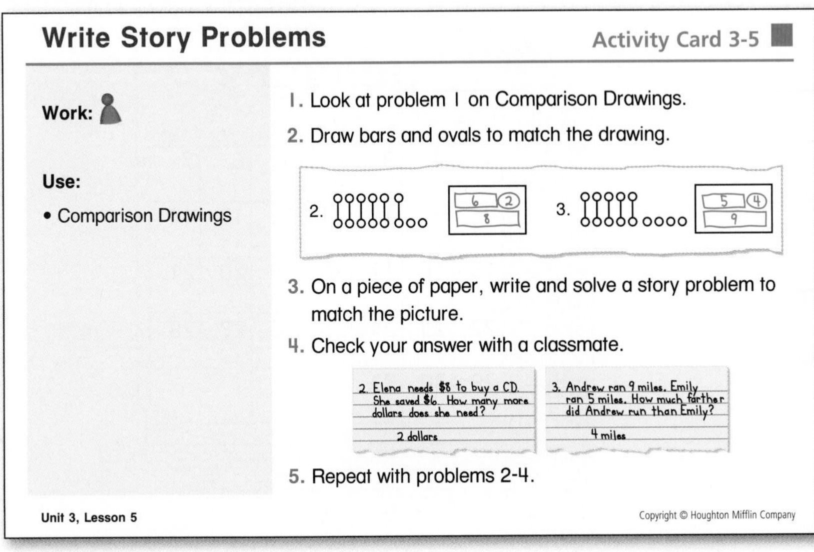

Write Story Problems Activity Card 3-5 ■

Work: (individual)

Use:
- Comparison Drawings

1. Look at problem 1 on Comparison Drawings.
2. Draw bars and ovals to match the drawing.

3. On a piece of paper, write and solve a story problem to match the picture.
4. Check your answer with a classmate.

5. Repeat with problems 2-4.

Unit 3, Lesson 5

Activity Note Each pair needs Comparison Drawings (TRB M55). Encourage classmates to check each other's problems.

Math Writing Prompt

More Than One Way Write a comparison story problem. Show two different drawings that could help you solve the problem.

Software Support

Use *Destination Math* to take students beyond the concepts and skills presented in this lesson.

3 Homework and Spiral Review

Goal: Additional Practice

This Homework page provides practice in solving comparison story problems.

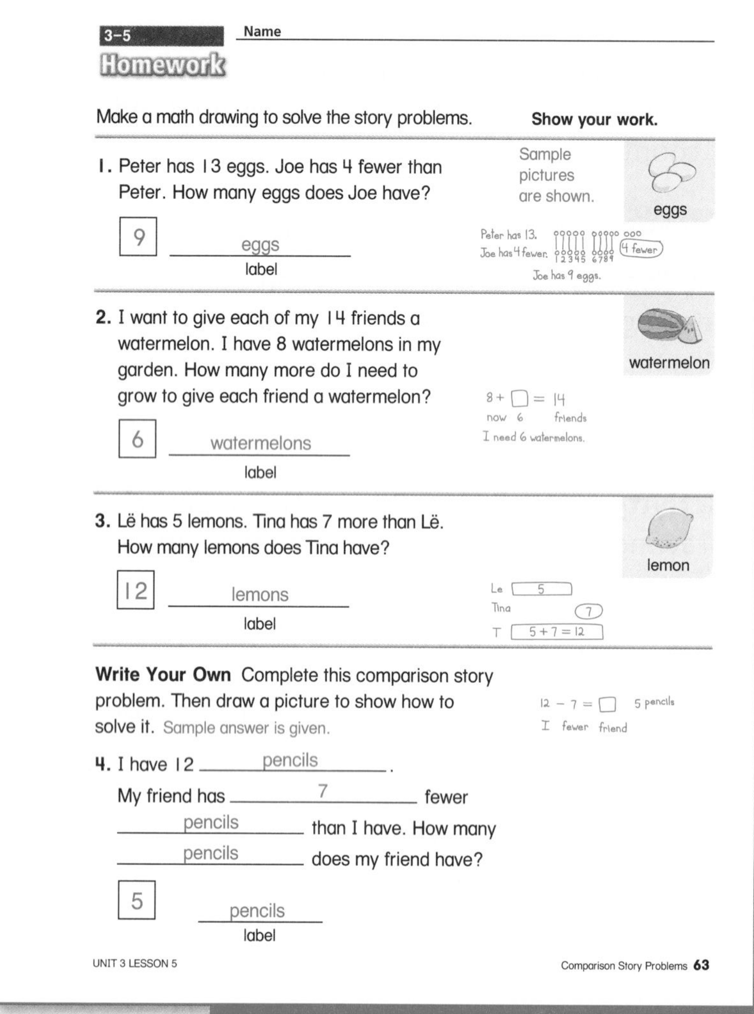

3-5 Homework Name

Make a math drawing to solve the story problems. **Show your work.**

Sample pictures are shown.

1. Peter has 13 eggs. Joe has 4 fewer than Peter. How many eggs does Joe have?

   eggs

   9 eggs
   label

   Peter has 13. Joe has 4 fewer. 4 fewer. Joe has 9 eggs.

2. I want to give each of my 14 friends a watermelon. I have 8 watermelons in my garden. How many more do I need to grow to give each friend a watermelon?

   watermelon

   6 watermelons
   label

   8 + ☐ = 14
   now 6 friends
   I need 6 watermelons.

3. Lë has 5 lemons. Tina has 7 more than Lë. How many lemons does Tina have?

   lemon

   12 lemons
   label

   Le 5
   Tina 7
   T 5 + 7 = 12

Write Your Own Complete this comparison story problem. Then draw a picture to show how to solve it. Sample answer is given.

4. I have 12 pencils.
   My friend has 7 fewer pencils than I have. How many pencils does my friend have?

   12 − 7 = ☐ 5 pencils
   I fewer friend

   5 pencils
   label

UNIT 3 LESSON 5 Comparison Story Problems **63**

Homework and Remembering page 63

Goal: Spiral Review

This Remembering activity would be appropriate anytime after today's lesson.

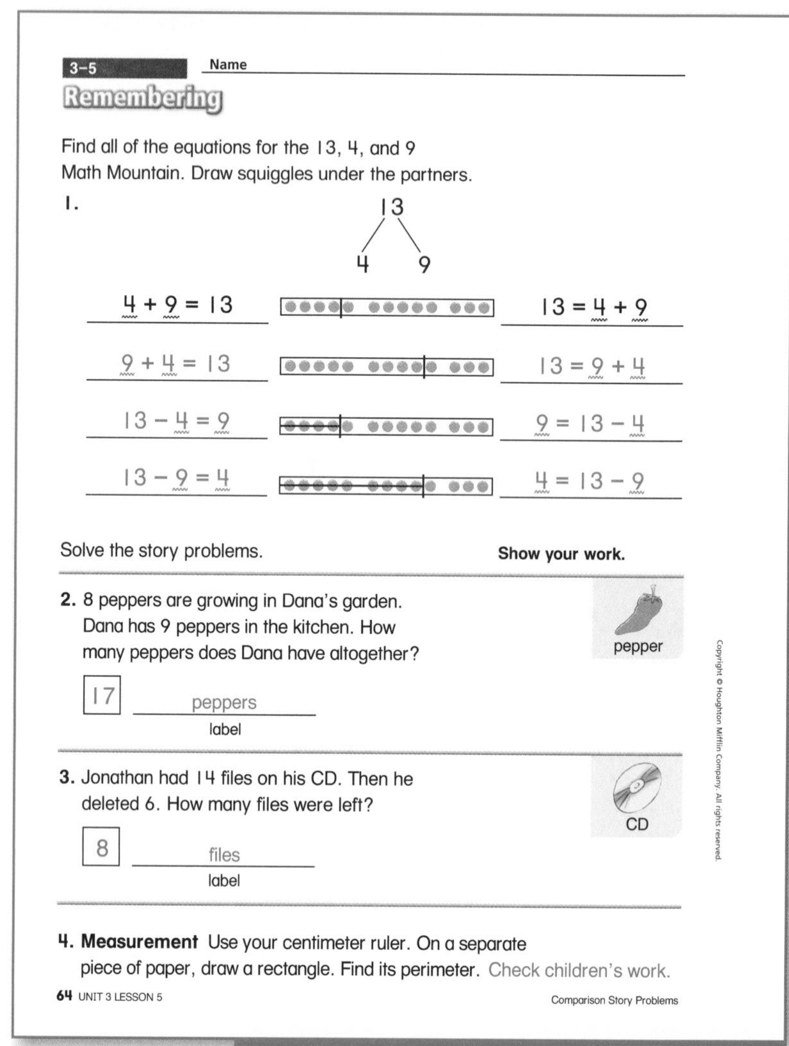

3-5 Remembering Name

Find all of the equations for the 13, 4, and 9 Math Mountain. Draw squiggles under the partners.

1.

13
4 9

4 + 9 = 13	●●●●│●●●●● ●●●●	13 = 4 + 9
9 + 4 = 13	●●●●● ●●●●│●●●●	13 = 9 + 4
13 − 4 = 9	●●●●│●●●●● ●●●●	9 = 13 − 4
13 − 9 = 4	●●●●● ●●●●│●●●●	4 = 13 − 9

Solve the story problems. **Show your work.**

2. 8 peppers are growing in Dana's garden. Dana has 9 peppers in the kitchen. How many peppers does Dana have altogether?

   pepper

   17 peppers
   label

3. Jonathan had 14 files on his CD. Then he deleted 6. How many files were left?

   CD

   8 files
   label

4. **Measurement** Use your centimeter ruler. On a separate piece of paper, draw a rectangle. Find its perimeter. Check children's work.

64 UNIT 3 LESSON 5 Comparison Story Problems

Homework and Remembering page 64

Home or School Activity

Social Studies Connection

Calendar Quest Have children use a calendar to find answers to the following comparison questions.

- How many more days are there in March than in September?
- How many more months begin with J than begin with D?

More Comparison Story Problems

Lesson Objectives

- Paraphrase and solve comparison story problems.
- Create comparison story problems.

Vocabulary
comparison story problem

The Day at a Glance

Today's Goals	Materials	
1 Teaching the Lesson **A1:** Paraphrase and solve comparison problems. **A2:** Create and solve comparison problems.	**Lesson Activities** Student Activity Book p. 103 Homework and Remembering pp. 65–66 MathBoard materials	**Going Further** Activity Cards 3-6 Student Activity Book pp. 103–104 Math Journals
2 Going Further ► Problem-Solving Strategy: Logical Reasoning ► Differentiated Instruction		
3 Homework and Targeted Practice		

Use Math Talk today!

Keeping Skills Sharp

Quick Practice — 5 MINUTES

Goals: Subtract, totals $\leq$ 10. Make a ten when adding a number to 6 or 7.

Materials: Secret Code Cards 1–10 (from Unit 1 Lesson 5 or TRB M3–M4), Parachute Drop (from Unit 1 Lesson 19 or TRB M46)

Secret Code Card Race, Totals $\leq$ 10 Have children arrange their Secret Code Cards across their desks. Have a Student Leader call out problems starting from the bottom of column 3 on Parachute Drop. The other children use their Secret Code Cards to show the answer. (See Unit 3 Lesson 3.)

Class Make a Ten Write the $m + n$ list (left column) on the board. Do each row in turn.

Class Make a Ten

Student Leader 1 points to and says	Student Leader 2 shows fingers and says	Class says and Student Leader 2 writes = and
7 + 4	4 makes 3 and 1	7 + 3 + 1 = 10 + 1 = 11
7 + 6	6 makes 3 and 3	7 + 3 + 3 = 10 + 3 = 13
7 + 5	5 makes 3 and 2	7 + 3 + 2 = 10 + 2 = 12
7 + 7	7 makes 3 and 4	7 + 3 + 4 = 10 + 4 = 14
6 + 5	5 makes 4 and 1	6 + 4 + 1 = 10 + 1 = 11
6 + 6	6 makes 4 and 2	6 + 4 + 2 = 10 + 2 = 12

Daily Routines

Comparing 2-Digit Quantities Using a Meter Stick, Using Number Flashes, Using the MathBoard (See pp. xxv–xxvi.)

► Led by Student Leaders

Money Routine Using the 120 Poster, Using the Money Flip Chart, Using the Number Path, Using Secret Code Cards (See pp. xxiii–xxv.)

► Led by Student Leaders

1 Teaching the Lesson

Activity 1

Solve Comparison Story Problems

 35 MINUTES

Goal: Paraphrase and solve comparison problems.

Materials: Student Activity Book page 103

 **NCTM Standards:**
Number and Operations
Problem Solving
Communication

The Learning Classroom

Building Concepts If children can state the comparison both ways, comparison problems will be easier for them to solve. In Unit 3 we will solve more difficult comparison problems for which it will be helpful to say the other sentence. Comparing language is very difficult in English. Even native speakers have difficulty learning these forms. Continue modeling correct usage, and have the whole class repeat the correct comparing sentences or questions often. Having individual children give the reverse comparing sentence or question is excellent practice in learning these language forms. For some children it may take months to be totally correct on these forms.

Ongoing Assessment

If children are having difficulties solving the problems, have them make matching drawings. Observing children as they draw can help you assess their understanding of the problem.

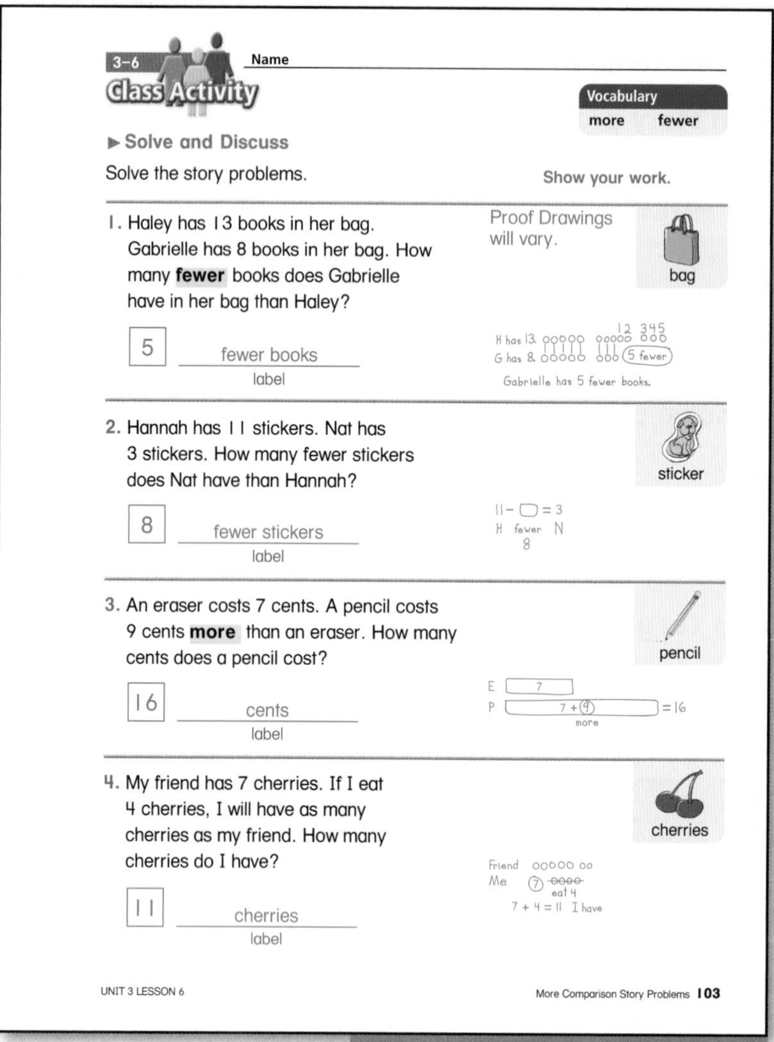
3–6 Class Activity   Name ____________

Vocabulary: more, fewer

▶ Solve and Discuss

Solve the story problems.   Show your work.

1. Haley has 13 books in her bag. Gabrielle has 8 books in her bag. How many **fewer** books does Gabrielle have in her bag than Haley?
5 fewer books (label)
Proof Drawings will vary.
H has 13 ooooo ooooo ooo
G has 8 ooooo ooo (5 fewer)
Gabrielle has 5 fewer books.
bag

2. Hannah has 11 stickers. Nat has 3 stickers. How many fewer stickers does Nat have than Hannah?
8 fewer stickers (label)
11 − ☐ = 3
H fewer N
8
sticker

3. An eraser costs 7 cents. A pencil costs 9 cents **more** than an eraser. How many cents does a pencil cost?
16 cents (label)
E [7]
P [7 + (9)] = 16
more
pencil

4. My friend has 7 cherries. If I eat 4 cherries, I will have as many cherries as my friend. How many cherries do I have?
11 cherries (label)
Friend ooooo oo
Me (7) oooo eat 4
7 + 4 = 11 I have
cherries

UNIT 3 LESSON 6   More Comparison Story Problems 103

Student Activity Book page 103

▶ Solve and Discuss WHOLE CLASS

Have children look at the first problem on Student Activity Book page 103 while you, a volunteer, or the class read it aloud. Ask a few children to rephrase the problem in their own words.

- Haley has 13 books and Gabrielle has 8. How many fewer books does Gabrielle have?

Have children say the two opposite comparison statements:

- How many fewer books does Gabrielle have than Haley?
- How many more books does Haley have than Gabrielle?

If children can say the problem both ways, it means they really understand the problem. Also, sometimes saying the comparison the other way helps solve the problem.

Math Talk Use the **Solve and Discuss** structure to solve the problem (see the box below). Children restate the comparing sentence or question in two ways (see the box below). Encourage the other children to comment and ask questions.

Problem 3	Problem 4
• A pencil costs 9¢ more than an eraser. • An eraser costs 9¢ less than a pencil.	• I have 4 more cherries than my friend. • My friend has 4 fewer cherries than I.

Children can use drawings or just explain their solutions in their own words. Encourage the use of varied drawings including matching circles, comparison bars, equations, and even Math Mountains. Be sure these are labeled to connect them to the problem situation.

English Language Learners

Draw a proof drawing for Solve and Discuss problem 1. Help children make comparison sentences with *more* and *fewer*.

- **Beginning** Point to the proof. Say: **13 is bigger than 8. Haley has *more* books. Gabrielle has *fewer* books.** Have children repeat.
- **Intermediate** Ask: **Which number is bigger?** 13 **Who has *more* books?** Haley **Fewer?** Gabrielle
- **Advanced** Have children work in pairs to restate the comparing sentence in two ways. Have volunteers share their sentences with the class.

Activity 2

Create and Practice Comparison Story Problems

▶ Create and Solve Comparison Story Problems

PAIRS

Review the structure of comparison problems. They are situations in which some amount is more or less than some other amount. Then ask children to write comparison problems. They can work individually, in pairs, or in small groups. Have children exchange problems to solve them.

As you circulate around the room, check that children are writing comparison story problems and not other kinds of story problems. You may need to interrupt the writing and do some brainstorming together to model some problems before continuing the writing process.

 **20 MINUTES**

Goal: Create and solve comparison problems.

 **NCTM Standards:**
Number and Operations
Problem Solving
Communication

2 Going Further

Problem-Solving Strategy: Logical Reasoning

Goal: Solve story problems using logical reasoning.

Materials: Student Activity Book page 102

NCTM Standard:
Problem Solving

Teaching Note

Math Background The ability to reason and think critically is essential as children progress in mathematical content and understanding. Some of the strategies children might use to help them reason logically include drawing a picture, creating a list, making a table, or acting out a problem using manipulatives. These strategies can help children organize facts as they solve reasoning problems.

▶ Use Logical Thinking PAIRS

Math Talk The problems on Student Activity Book page 102 provide a good opportunity for children to work cooperatively in pairs. See **Math Talk in Action** for an example of two children working together on problem 1.

Problem 1 can be solved by making a drawing similar to the comparison drawings children have used before. However, in this case, the drawing will have three rows. If children are having difficulty representing the information in the problem, tell them to first represent the green cars, then the blue cars, and finally, the red cars.

For problems 2 and 4, no actual amounts are given. Children can draw bars of different lengths to represent the cost of each toy and the height of each child. They can then match up the bars to the appropriate price tags in problem 2 and list the children in order from shortest to tallest in problem 4.

In Problem 3 the only two books that have a price difference of $2 are the *Dogs* book and the *Birds* book. Since the *Dogs* book cost $2 more than the *Birds* book, Craig bought the *Dogs* book and Orna bought the *Birds* book.

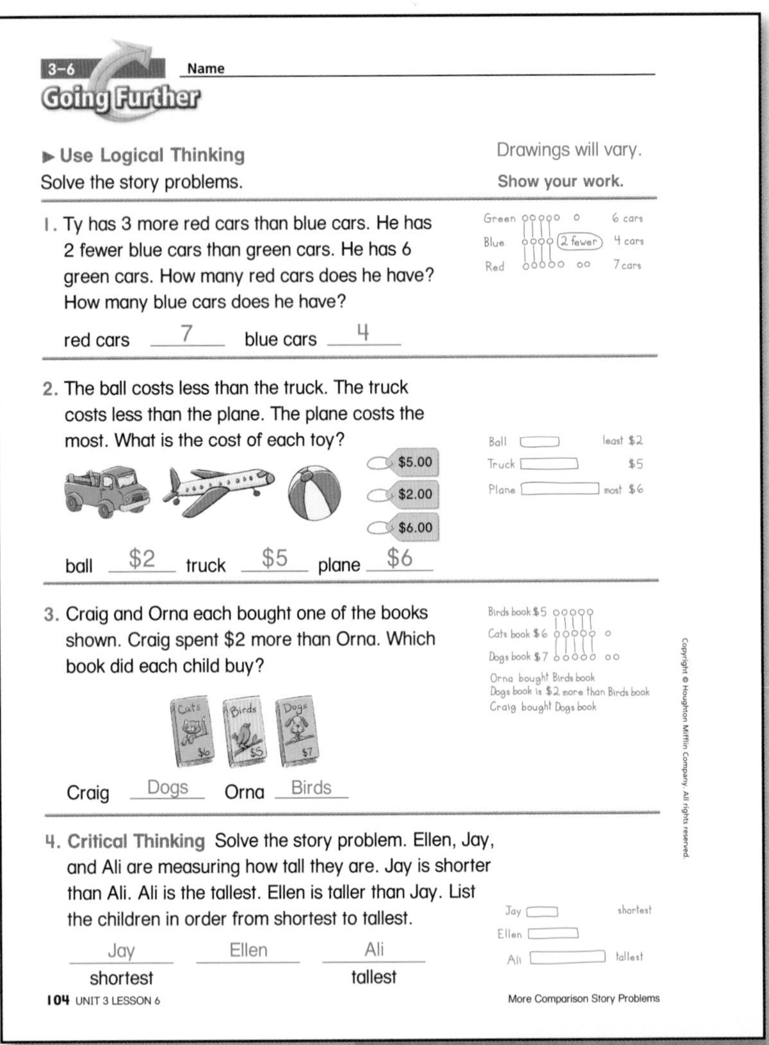

3–6 Name

Going Further

▶ Use Logical Thinking

Solve the story problems.

Drawings will vary.
Show your work.

1. Ty has 3 more red cars than blue cars. He has 2 fewer blue cars than green cars. He has 6 green cars. How many red cars does he have? How many blue cars does he have?

red cars 7 blue cars 4

2. The ball costs less than the truck. The truck costs less than the plane. The plane costs the most. What is the cost of each toy?

$5.00 $2.00 $6.00

ball $2 truck $5 plane $6

3. Craig and Orna each bought one of the books shown. Craig spent $2 more than Orna. Which book did each child buy?

Craig Dogs Orna Birds

4. **Critical Thinking** Solve the story problem. Ellen, Jay, and Ali are measuring how tall they are. Jay is shorter than Ali. Ali is the tallest. Ellen is taller than Jay. List the children in order from shortest to tallest.

Jay Ellen Ali
shortest tallest

Student Activity Book page 104

Math Talk in Action

Janeen: Let's draw a picture to help us solve the first problem. Ty has six green cars.

Sidney: I can draw six green circles.

Janeen: Ty has two fewer blue cars than green cars.

Sidney: So, two cars fewer than six cars is four cars. I can draw four blue circles.

Janeen: Ty has three more red cars than blue cars.

Sidney: Three plus four is seven. I can draw seven red circles.

Janeen: So, now we know that Ty has six green, seven red, and four blue cars.

Intervention Activity Card 3-6

Create a Similar Problem

Activity Card 3-6

Work: 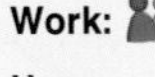
Use:
- Student Activity Book page 103

Choose:
-
-

1. **Work Together** Look at problem 1 on Student Activity Book page 103.
2. Circle all the numbers in the problem. Write a new number in each place.

1. Haley has 13 books in her bag. Gabrielle has 6 books in her bag. How many fewer books does Gabrielle have in her bag than Haley?

3. Rewrite the problem using the new numbers.
4. Solve the new problem.
5. Repeat for problem 2.

Unit 3, Lesson 6

Activity Note Each pair needs Student Activity Book, p. 103. Explain that pairs should change the numbers and solve the new problem.

Math Writing Prompt

Same and Different Sam has 6 fewer pencils than Maria.

Write a sentence that has the same meaning but uses the word *more* instead of *fewer*.

Software Support

Use *Soar to Success* for instruction of students needing targeted support for underlying skills.

On Level Activity Card 3-6

Rewrite Story Problems

Activity Card 3-6

Work:
Use:
- Student Activity Book page 103

Choose:
-
-

1. Read problem 3 on Student Activity Book page 103. Change the numbers to make a new story problem.

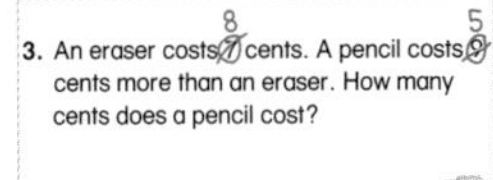

3. An eraser costs 7 cents. A pencil costs 9 cents more than an eraser. How many cents does a pencil cost?

2. Give the new story problem to .
3. Solve problem.
4. Read problem 4 on Student Activity Book page 103. Change the numbers to make a new story problem.
5. Give the new story problem to .
6. Solve problem.

Unit 3, Lesson 6

Activity Note Each pair needs Student Activity Book, p. 103. Have each child change one problem and then trade with their partner.

Math Writing Prompt

Compare and Contrast How are a collection story problem and a comparison story problem alike? How are they different?

Software Support

Use *MegaMath* for review and reinforcement of the concepts and skills presented in this lesson.

Challenge Activity Card 3-6

Greater Than 20

Activity Card 3-6

Work:
Use:
- Student Activity Book page 103

1. Look at problem 4 on Student Activity Book page 103.
2. Circle all the numbers in the problem. Change each number in the problem to a number greater than 20.

4. My friend has 7 cherries. If I eat 4 cherries, I will have as many cherries as my friend. How many cherries do I have?

3. Rewrite the problem using the new numbers.
4. Solve the new problem.
5. Repeat for problem 3.
6. **Math Talk** Discuss how you solved the new problem.

Unit 3, Lesson 6

Activity Note Each child needs Student Activity Book, p. 103.

Math Writing Prompt

Solve and Explain Explain how you solved.

Jim and Brad have 15 cards altogether. Jim has 3 fewer cards than Brad. How many cards do they each have?

Software Support

Use *Destination Math* to take students beyond the concepts and skills presented in this lesson.

Homework and Targeted Practice

3–6 Homework Goal: Additional Practice

This Homework page provides practice solving comparison story problems.

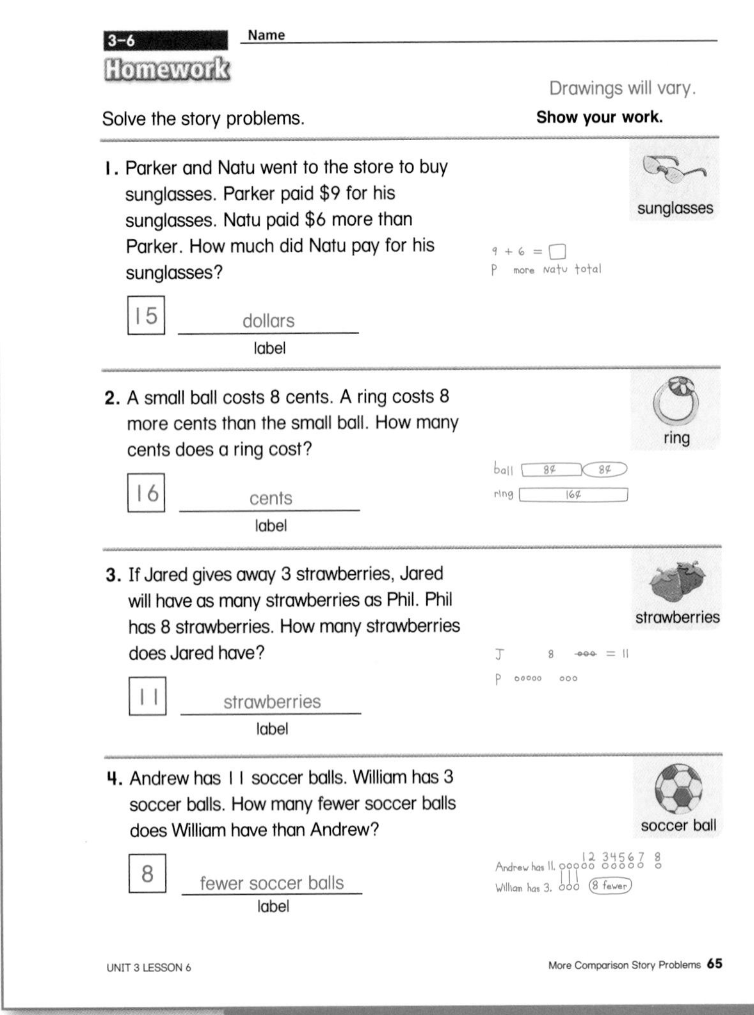

3–6 Homework Name

Drawings will vary.

Solve the story problems. **Show your work.**

1. Parker and Natu went to the store to buy sunglasses. Parker paid $9 for his sunglasses. Natu paid $6 more than Parker. How much did Natu pay for his sunglasses?

sunglasses

9 + 6 = ☐
P more Natu total

15 dollars
label

2. A small ball costs 8 cents. A ring costs 8 more cents than the small ball. How many cents does a ring cost?

ring

ball 8¢ 8¢
ring 16¢

16 cents
label

3. If Jared gives away 3 strawberries, Jared will have as many strawberries as Phil. Phil has 8 strawberries. How many strawberries does Jared have?

strawberries

J 8 ooo = 11
P ooooo ooo

11 strawberries
label

4. Andrew has 11 soccer balls. William has 3 soccer balls. How many fewer soccer balls does William have than Andrew?

soccer ball

Andrew has 11. 12 345678
William has 3. (8 fewer)

8 fewer soccer balls
label

UNIT 3 LESSON 6 More Comparison Story Problems 65

Homework and Remembering page 65

3–6 Targeted Practice Goal: Practice Venn diagrams.

This Targeted Practice page can be used with children who need extra practice with Venn diagrams.

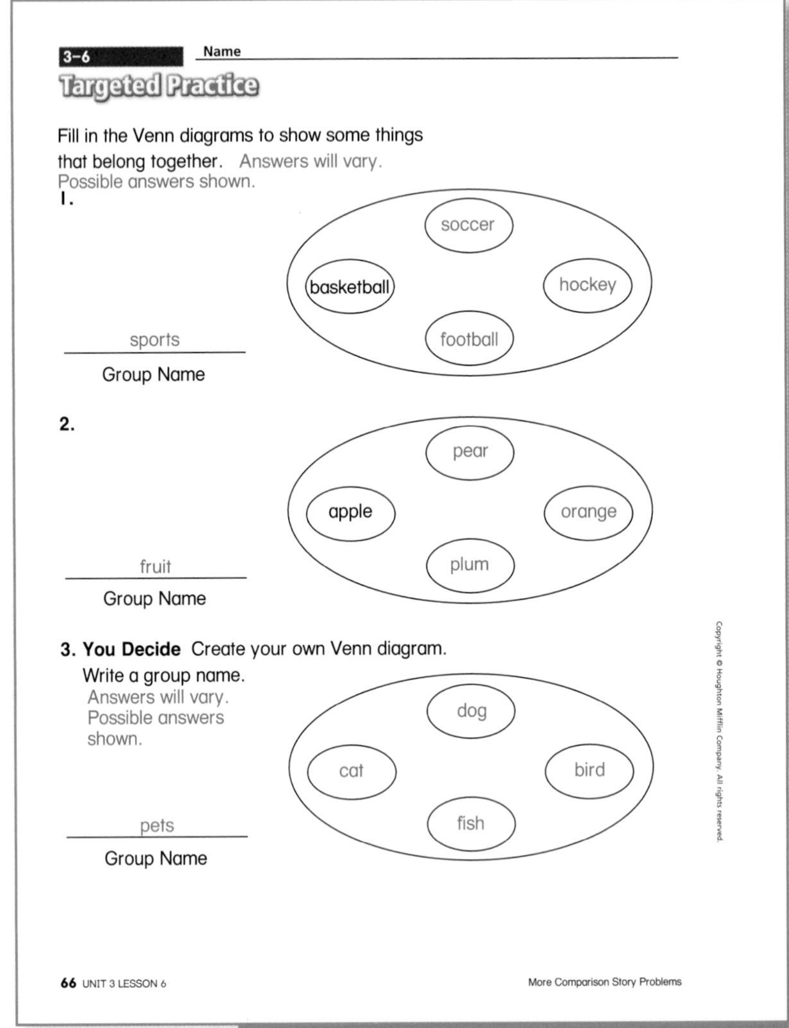

3–6 Targeted Practice Name

Fill in the Venn diagrams to show some things that belong together. Answers will vary. Possible answers shown.

1. soccer, basketball, hockey, football

sports
Group Name

2. pear, apple, orange, plum

fruit
Group Name

3. **You Decide** Create your own Venn diagram. Write a group name. Answers will vary. Possible answers shown.

dog, cat, bird, fish

pets
Group Name

Copyright © Houghton Mifflin Company. All rights reserved.

66 UNIT 3 LESSON 6 More Comparison Story Problems

Homework and Remembering page 66

Home or School Activity

Language Arts Connection

Exploring Antonyms Have children read the following sentences.

Juan has **more** *pencils that Sonia.*
Sonia has **fewer** *pencils than Juan.*

Tell them that *more* and *fewer* are opposites. Words that mean the opposite are called **antonyms**. Ask children to make a list of other words that are opposites or antonyms.

Antonyms: Words that mean the opposite

add	subtract
more	fewer
long	short
big	small
hot	cold
left	right

Mixed Story Problems

Vocabulary
- teen total
- partner
- Math Mountain
- equation

Lesson Objectives

- Count on or make a ten to solve addition and subtraction problems.
- Solve a variety of story problems.

The Day at a Glance

Today's Goals	Materials	
1 Teaching the Lesson **A1:** Play *Count on Me* to reinforce subtraction and mystery addition with teen totals. **A2:** Represent and solve mixed story problems.	**Lesson Activities** Student Activity Book p. 107 Homework and Remembering pp. 67–68 Secret Code Cards (TRB M3–M4) Colored paper *Count On Me* Game Board (TRB M28) Quick Quiz 1 (Assessment Guide)	**Going Further** Activity Cards 3-7 Student Activity Book p. 108 Homework and Remembering p. 67 Mix and Match (TRB M56) Math Journals
2 Going Further ► Extension: Use a Table ► Differentiated Instruction		
3 Homework and Spiral Review		

Use Math Talk today!

Keeping Skills Sharp

Quick Practice — 5 MINUTES

Goals: Add with teen totals. Make a ten when adding a number to 6 or 7.

Materials: Secret Code Cards 1-10 (from Unit 1 Lesson 5 or TRB M3–M4), Parachute Drop–Teen Totals (Student Activity Book page 105)

Class Make a Ten Write the $m + n$ list (left column) on the board. Do each row in turn.

Parachute Drop—Teen Totals This activity is like the Parachute Drop activity (see Unit 1 Lesson 19); however, this activity uses teen totals. Have children practice addition exercises in the first column on Student Activity Book page 105. Children who finish early may practice the mystery addition exercises in the middle column.

Student Leader 1 points to and says	Student Leader 2 shows fingers and says	Class says and Student Leader 2 writes = and
7 + 4	4 makes 3 and 1	7 + 3 + 1 = 10 + 1 = 11
7 + 6	6 makes 3 and 3	7 + 3 + 3 = 10 + 3 = 13
7 + 5	5 makes 3 and 2	7 + 3 + 2 = 10 + 2 = 12
7 + 7	7 makes 3 and 4	7 + 3 + 4 = 10 + 4 = 14
6 + 5	5 makes 4 and 1	6 + 4 + 1 = 10 + 1 = 11
6 + 6	6 makes 4 and 2	6 + 4 + 2 = 10 + 2 = 12

Daily Routines

Comparing 2-Digit Quantities Using a Meter Stick, Using Number Flashes, Using the MathBoard (See pp. xxv–xxvi.)

► Led by Student Leaders

Money Routine Using the 120 Poster, Using the Money Flip Chart, Using the Number Path, Using Secret Code Cards (See pp. xxiii–xxv.)

► Led by Student Leaders

1 Teaching the Lesson

Activity 1

Count on Me Game—Teen Totals

30 MINUTES

Goal: Play *Count on Me* to reinforce subtraction and mystery addition with teen totals.

Materials: Secret Code Cards 1–10 (from Unit 1 Lesson 5 or TRB M3–M4), colored paper (cut to cover a 1-digit secret code card), *Count on Me* game board (from Unit 1 Lesson 14 or TRB M28)

NCTM Standards:
Number and Operations
Communication

Class Management

Circulate around the room to be sure that children understand how to play the subtraction version of *Count on Me* with teen totals. Then once everyone is playing the game successfully, work with any children who need extra help representing and solving story problems.

English Language Learners

Draw partner houses for 11 through 19 to review teen totals. Start with 11.

- **Beginning** Ask: **1 + what = 11?** 10 Write 1+10 on the top floor. Complete the left side. Have children restate the equations for the right side.
- **Intermediate** Write 1 through 6 on the left side. Ask: **1 and what number are partners of 11?** Continue with the left side. Have children work in pairs to complete the right side.
- **Advanced** Have children work in pairs. One completes the left side. The other completes the right side. Then they compare answers.

▶ Play *Count on Me* PAIRS

Have children fold the game board so only the subtraction side shows. Then have children place the board on their desks. Tell them to place one set of Secret Code Cards above the gameboard. The other set of Secret Code Cards should be held by Player 2.

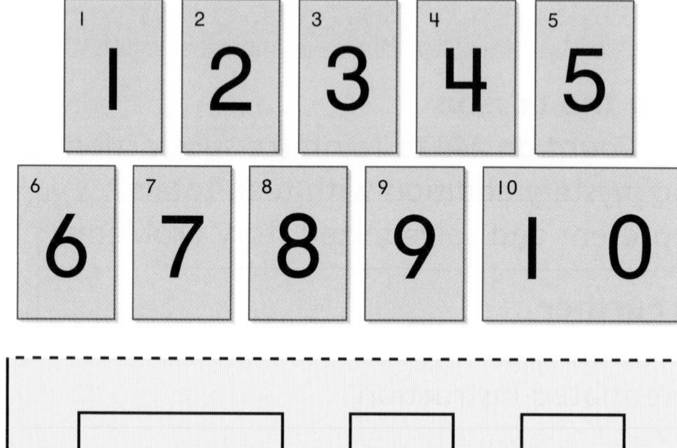

Game board from Unit 1 Lesson 14 or Copymaster M28

Player 1 chooses a teen total from the Secret Code Cards above the game board and places the cards in the first blank space. Remind children that they have to use the 10 card and another card in order to make a teen total.

Player 2 selects two partners of the teen total from the Secret Code Cards in his or her hand and places them in the remaining two boxes, being sure to cover one of the partners with a piece of colored paper.

12 – ▢ = 8 12 – 4 = ▢

Player 1 must identify the unknown partner. Remind children to count on, make a ten, or use their addition knowledge to identify the unknown partner. When Player 1 gets the right answer, partners switch roles, and the game continues.

After children have played a few rounds of the subtraction version, have them play the mystery addition version of the game using the addition side of the game board and covering one addend (see Unit 1 Lesson 14).

Activity 2

Solve Story Problems

▶ Solve and Discuss PAIRS

3–7 Class Activity Name ______________

▶ **Solve and Discuss**

Solve the story problems.

Drawings will vary.

Show your work.

1. Erica has 13 colored pencils. She has 8 at home and some at school. How many are at school?

   pencil

   5 pencils
   label

2. Joan has 15 toy guitars. Delia has 7 toy guitars. How many fewer toy guitars does Delia have than Joan?

   guitar

   8 fewer toy guitars
   label

3. Alvin had 14 puppets. He gave some to his brother. Now Alvin has 5 puppets left. How many puppets did Alvin give to his brother?

   puppet

   9 puppets
   label

4. Yolanda has a box of tennis balls. Eddie took 7 of them. Now Yolanda has 5 left. How many tennis balls did Yolanda have in the beginning?

   tennis ball

   12 tennis balls
   label

UNIT 3 LESSON 7 Mixed Story Problems 107

Student Activity Book page 107

Have children work in **Helping Pairs** to complete Student Activity Book page 107. You may also wish to use the **Solve and Discuss** structure for some problems.

Encourage children to explain each problem to their partner before solving. Have them make proof drawings and remind them to label their drawings and answers. Challenge children to write a Math Mountain and an equation for each of the problems.

Children who finish early can write story problems for other children to solve. Then have children add to their list of groups.

25 MINUTES

Goal: Represent and solve mixed story problems.

Materials: Student Activity Book page 107

✓ **NCTM Standards:**
Number and Operations
Problem Solving
Communication

Ongoing Assessment

Circulate around the room and ask children to label and explain their drawings and solutions. Encourage any children who are still drawing all the objects to try and use numbers in their drawings.

Quick Quiz

See Assessment Guide for Unit 3 Quick Quiz 1.

2 Going Further

Extension: Use a Table

Goal: Use information in a table to solve story problems.

Materials: Student Activity Book page 108

✓ **NCTM Standards:**
Problem Solving
Communication

Teaching Note

Math Background Children need to be able to collect, organize, and display information in order to interpret the data. This process of data analysis is facilitated through the use of a variety of data displays. A table is among the simplest of these displays. Children will be exposed to the use of tables throughout their studies, not only in mathematics, but also in science, social studies, and other subject areas.

▶ Find Information in a Table WHOLE CLASS

Discuss the table at the top of Student Activity Book page 108. Explain that the table shows the number of children who get to school in four different ways. Review the meaning of rows and columns. Tell children that when they read a table, they should read across the row.

Have children work independently to answer problems 1–5. When children have completed the problems, ask volunteers to explain their answers. Encourage other children to ask questions or make comments.

▶ Number Sense WHOLE CLASS

Challenge children to complete problems 6–8. When they have completed the section, ask volunteers to explain the thinking they used to complete each sentence.

Math Talk Have children write one or two story problems using the information in the table. Then ask volunteers to share their problems and solutions with the class. Encourage other children to ask questions and make comments.

Collect all children's problems and have volunteers come to the board to show how they would solve them.

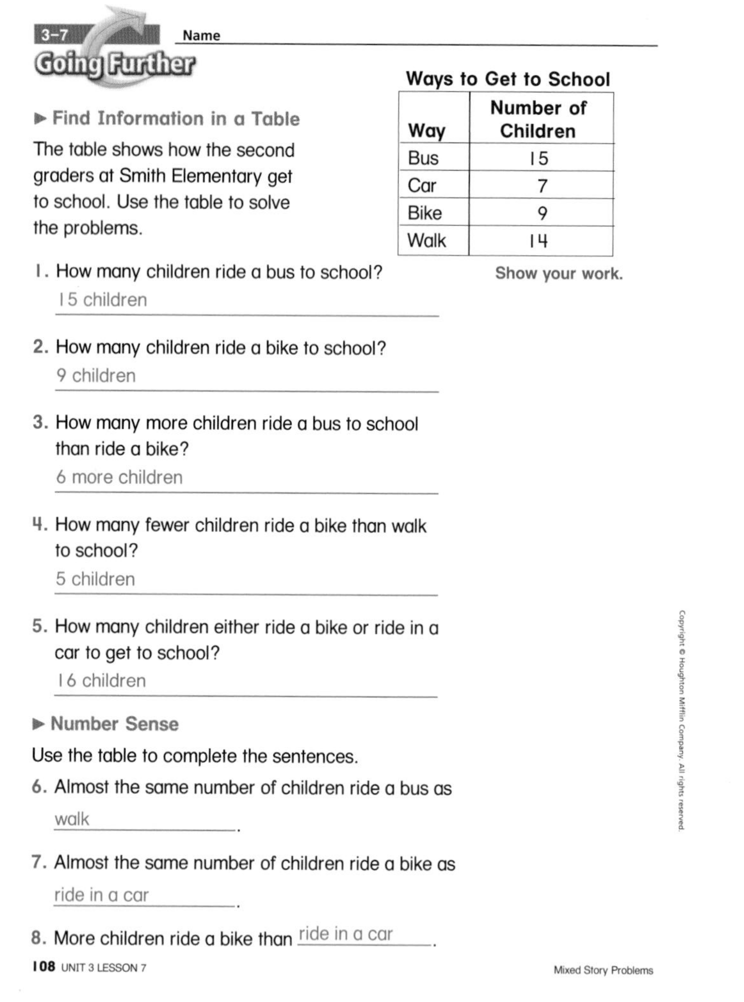
3-7 Going Further Name

▶ Find Information in a Table

The table shows how the second graders at Smith Elementary get to school. Use the table to solve the problems.

Ways to Get to School

Way	Number of Children
Bus	15
Car	7
Bike	9
Walk	14

Show your work.

1. How many children ride a bus to school? 15 children
2. How many children ride a bike to school? 9 children
3. How many more children ride a bus to school than ride a bike? 6 more children
4. How many fewer children ride a bike than walk to school? 5 children
5. How many children either ride a bike or ride in a car to get to school? 16 children

▶ Number Sense

Use the table to complete the sentences.

6. Almost the same number of children ride a bus as walk.
7. Almost the same number of children ride a bike as ride in a car.
8. More children ride a bike than ride in a car.

108 UNIT 3 LESSON 7 Mixed Story Problems

Student Activity Book page 108

Differentiated Instruction

Extra Help Circulate around the room as children work, providing help as needed. If some children are having difficulty keeping track of columns and rows, show them how to use a piece of paper to keep their place in the table.

The Learning Classroom

Helping Community Some children are initially reluctant to explain their thinking at the board. As you respond positively to children's efforts to talk about their thinking, the class will realize that there is an expectation in the math community to respond positively to one another. Eventually, more children will desire to make their math thinking the center of discussion. Some children will prefer to take a friend with them to the board. It is also fine for children to work at the board in pairs.

Intervention — Activity Card 3-7

Mix and Match

Activity Card 3-7

Work:

Use:

- Mix and Match
- Homework and Remembering page 67

Choose:

1. **Work Together** Read the story problem 1 on the Homework and Remembering page 67.
2. Look at the proof drawings on Mix and Match. Find the one that matches story problem 1. Write problem 1 next to the matching proof drawing.

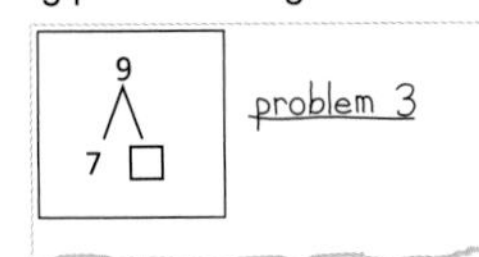

3. Match the rest of the story problems to the proof drawings.

Unit 3, Lesson 7

Activity Note Each pair needs Mix and Match (TRB M56) and Homework and Remembering p. 67.

Math Writing Prompt

Show Your Work Solve this story problem. Show your work and explain each step.

Jasmine can fit 8 pictures on each page of her album. One page has 6 photos. How many more photos does she need to fill the page?

Software Support

Use *Soar to Success* for instruction of students needing targeted support for underlying skills.

On Level — Activity Card 3-7

Investigate Math

Activity Card 3-7

Work: 

Use:

- Homework and Remembering page 67

Choose:

1. **Work Together** Read problem 1 on Homework and Remembering page 67. Solve the problem.
2. Choose a number and add that number to every number in problem 1. Solve the new problem.
3. Write the new answer on the page.

1. Susan rode her bicycle for 14 blocks. Awan rode his bicycle for 8 blocks. How many fewer blocks did Awan ride than Susan?

16 10 add 2 6 fewer blocks

6 fewer blocks
label

4. **Math Talk** Look at the answers to the two problems. What do you notice about the answers?
5. Repeat with problem 2 and check what you noticed.

Unit 3, Lesson 7

Activity Note Each group needs Homework and Remembering p. 67. Children should realize the answer does not change even when the numbers change.

Math Writing Prompt

Explain Your Thinking Choose one of the problems from today's Student Activity Book page 105. Explain the steps you used to solve the problem.

Software Support

Use *MegaMath* for review and reinforcement of the concepts and skills presented in this lesson.

Challenge — Activity Card 3-7

Investigate Further

Activity Card 3-7

Work:

Use:

- Homework and Remembering page 67

Choose:

1. **Work Together** Read problem 1 on Homework and Remembering page 67. Solve the problem.
2. Choose a number and add that number to every number in problem 1. Solve the new problem.
3. Write the new answer on the page.
4. **Math Talk** Look at the answers to the two problems. What do you notice about the answers?
5. Write a story problem for which the pattern does not work.

1. Susan rode her bicycle for 14 blocks. Awan rode his bicycle for 8 blocks. How many fewer blocks did Awan ride than Susan?

16 10 add 2 6 fewer blocks

6 fewer blocks
label

Yolanda has a box of tennis balls. Eddie took 2 of the tennis balls. Now Yolanda has 3 left. How many tennis balls did Yolanda have in the beginning?

Unit 3, Lesson 7

Activity Note Each group needs Homework and Remembering p. 67.

Math Writing Prompt

Guess and Check Solve and discuss.

The length of a rectangle is 2 centimeters longer than its width. It's perimeter is 16 cm. What are the length and width of the rectangle?

DESTINATION Math®

Software Support

Use *Destination Math* to take students beyond the concepts and skills presented in this lesson.

3 Homework and Spiral Review

Goal: Additional Practice

This Homework page provides practice in solving a variety of story problems.

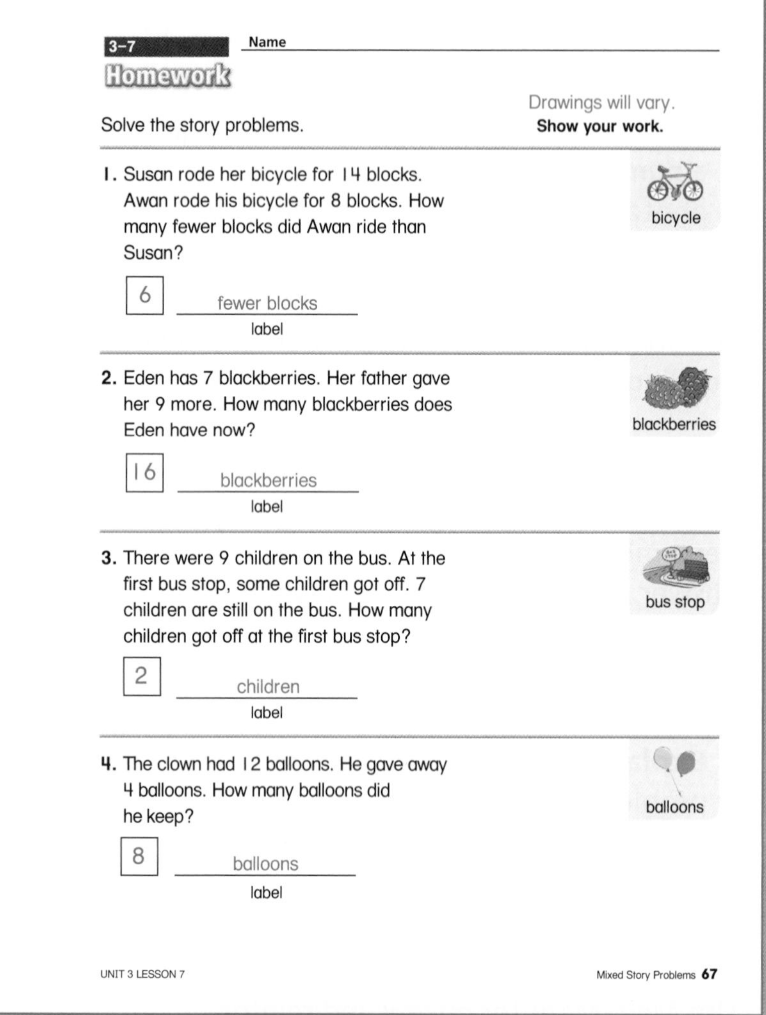

3–7 Homework Name ____________

Solve the story problems.

Drawings will vary.
Show your work.

1. Susan rode her bicycle for 14 blocks. Awan rode his bicycle for 8 blocks. How many fewer blocks did Awan ride than Susan?

bicycle

[6] fewer blocks
label

2. Eden has 7 blackberries. Her father gave her 9 more. How many blackberries does Eden have now?

blackberries

[16] blackberries
label

3. There were 9 children on the bus. At the first bus stop, some children got off. 7 children are still on the bus. How many children got off at the first bus stop?

bus stop

[2] children
label

4. The clown had 12 balloons. He gave away 4 balloons. How many balloons did he keep?

balloons

[8] balloons
label

UNIT 3 LESSON 7 Mixed Story Problems **67**

Homework and Remembering page 67

Goal: Spiral Review

This Remembering activity would be appropriate anytime after today's lesson.

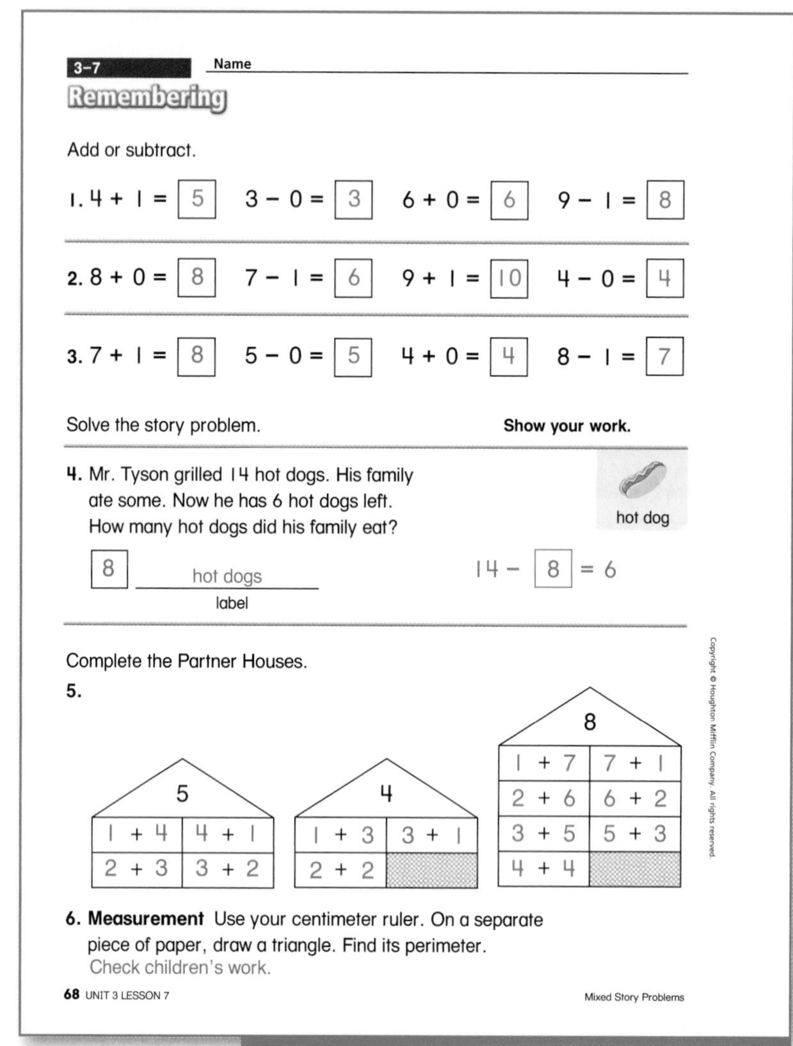

3–7 Remembering Name ____________

Add or subtract.

1. 4 + 1 = [5] 3 − 0 = [3] 6 + 0 = [6] 9 − 1 = [8]

2. 8 + 0 = [8] 7 − 1 = [6] 9 + 1 = [10] 4 − 0 = [4]

3. 7 + 1 = [8] 5 − 0 = [5] 4 + 0 = [4] 8 − 1 = [7]

Solve the story problem. **Show your work.**

4. Mr. Tyson grilled 14 hot dogs. His family ate some. Now he has 6 hot dogs left. How many hot dogs did his family eat?

hot dog

[8] hot dogs
label

14 − [8] = 6

Complete the Partner Houses.

5.

5	
1 + 4	4 + 1
2 + 3	3 + 2

4	
1 + 3	3 + 1
2 + 2	

8	
1 + 7	7 + 1
2 + 6	6 + 2
3 + 5	5 + 3
4 + 4	

6. **Measurement** Use your centimeter ruler. On a separate piece of paper, draw a triangle. Find its perimeter.
Check children's work.

68 UNIT 3 LESSON 7 Mixed Story Problems

Homework and Remembering page 68

Home or School Activity

Sports Connection

What Is Your Favorite Team? Have children share the names of one of their favorite sports teams. Then have them find out how many players are on that team. They should also find out how many of those players were on that team the previous year. Have children use the information to write a story problem.

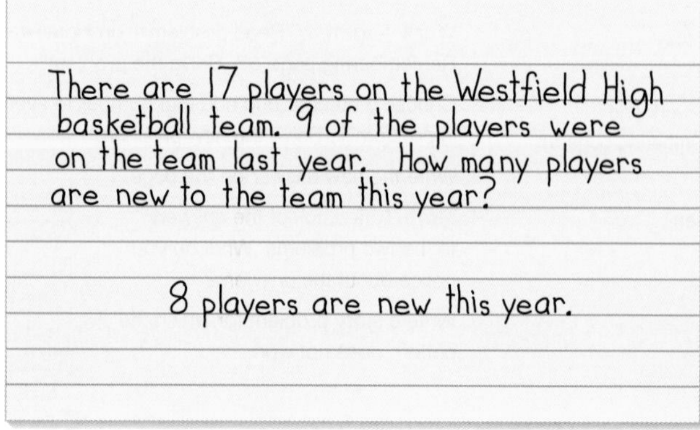

There are 17 players on the Westfield High basketball team. 9 of the players were on the team last year. How many players are new to the team this year?

8 players are new this year.

Problems with Not Enough or Extra Information

Lesson Objectives

- **Recognize when problems do not have enough or have extra information.**
- **Solve problems with not enough information by adding information.**
- **Fix and solve problems that have extra information.**

The Day at a Glance

Today's Goals	Materials	
1 Teaching the Lesson **A1:** Solve problems with not enough information by adding information. **A2:** Solve story problems with extra information.	**Lesson Activities** Student Activity Book pp. 109–110 Homework and Remembering pp. 69–70 Counters MathBoard materials	**Going Further** Activity Cards 3-8 Student Activity Book p. 111 Homework and Remembering p. 69 Math Journals
2 Going Further ► Extension: Use Information from a Story ► Differentiated Instruction		
3 Homework and Targeted Practice		

Use Math Talk today!

Keeping Skills Sharp

Quick Practice — 5 MINUTES

Goals: Addition with teen totals. Make a ten when adding a number to 6 or 7.

Materials: Parachute Drop–Teen Totals (from Unit 3 Lesson 7 or TRB M57)

Class Make a Ten Write the $m + n$ list (left column) on the board. Do each row in turn. (See Unit 3 Lesson 1.)

Parachute Drop—Teen Totals Have children practice the addition exercises in the first column of Parachute Drop–Teen Totals. Explain that they are practicing for a Secret Code Card addition race in the next lesson. (See Unit 3 Lesson 7.)

Student Leader 1 points to and says	Student Leader 2 shows fingers and says	Class says and Student Leader 2 writes = and
7 + 4	4 makes 3 and 1	7 + 3 + 1 = 10 + 1 = 11
7 + 6	6 makes 3 and 3	7 + 3 + 3 = 10 + 3 = 13
7 + 7	7 makes 3 and 4	7 + 3 + 4 = 10 + 4 = 14
7 + 5	5 makes 3 and 2	7 + 3 + 2 = 10 + 2 = 12
6 + 5	5 makes 4 and 1	6 + 4 + 1 = 10 + 1 = 11
6 + 6	6 makes 4 and 2	6 + 4 + 2 = 10 + 2 = 12

Daily Routines

Comparing 2-Digit Quantities Using a Meter Stick, Using Number Flashes, Using the MathBoard (See pp. xxv–xxvi.)

► Led by Student Leaders

Money Routine Using the 120 Poster, Using the Money Flip Chart, Using the Number Path, Using Secret Code Cards (See pp. xxiii–xxv.)

► Led by Student Leaders

1 Teaching the Lesson

Activity 1

Problems with Not Enough Information

 30 MINUTES

Goal: Solve problems with not enough information by adding information.

Materials: Student Activity Book page 109, counters

 **NCTM Standards:**
Number and Operations
Problem Solving

Teaching Note

Watch For! Children are not used to problems that do not have all the information they need to solve. In this lesson children have to decide what needs to be figured out and what information they need to do it. Children are asked to add their own information to make a story problem that has a solution. Be sure children realize that they should not add information to problems unless they are specifically directed to do so.

▶ Introduce Problems with Not Enough Information

WHOLE CLASS

Occasionally, children will encounter story problems that cannot be solved because they do not contain enough information. Write the following story problem on the board and read it aloud.

Bryce has 8 pretzels. His friend Lydia has some too. How many pretzels do they have in all?

Have children determine what is wrong with the problem.

- Can you solve the problem with the information given? No. Why? There isn't enough information to solve it. We don't know how many pretzels Lydia has, and we don't know the total.

Math Talk Begin a discussion of how much information is needed to solve a story problem. Suggest that children try to solve the problem by drawing Math Mountains or writing equations.

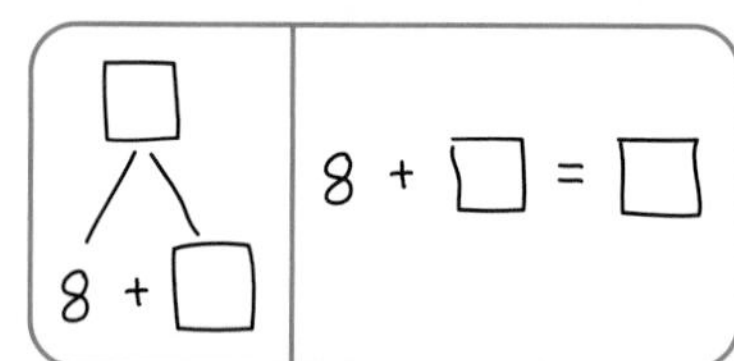

- Who would like to try to solve this problem at the board by making a drawing? Let's see what happens.

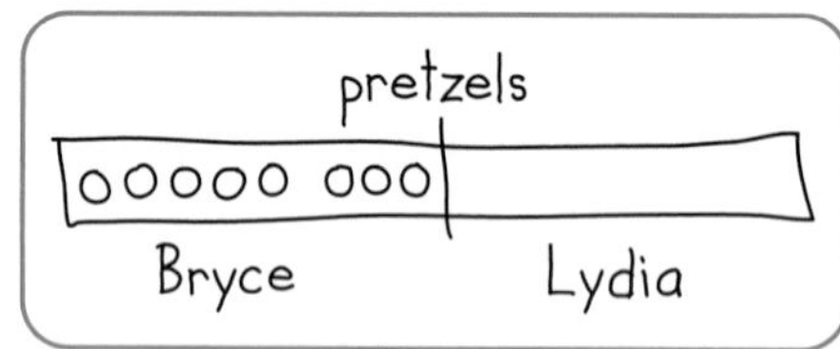

Ask children to add their own information to make a story problem that has a solution.

- What should we put in the story problem that is now missing? The number of pretzels that Lydia has.
- Choose an amount of pretzels for Lydia. Who can say the new problem? Bryce has 8 pretzels. Lydia has 7. How many pretzels do they have in all?
- What is the answer to the new problem? 15 pretzels

- What if the problem were:

  Bryce has 8 pretzels. His friend Lydia has some too. How many does she have?

- How could we fix this problem? Tell the total number of pretzels both children have.
- Choose an amount for how many pretzels they both have. Who can say the new problem? Bryce has 8 pretzels. Lydia has some too. Together they have 15 pretzels. How many pretzels does Lydia have?
- What is the answer to the problem? 7 pretzels

▶ Complete and Solve Story Problems PAIRS

Direct children's attention to the first problem on Student Activity Book page 109. Have them work independently or in **Helping Pairs** to add the information needed and then solve the problem. Ask children to share their problems with the class. Do the same with problems 2 and 3. Then ask children to make up problems of their own to share.

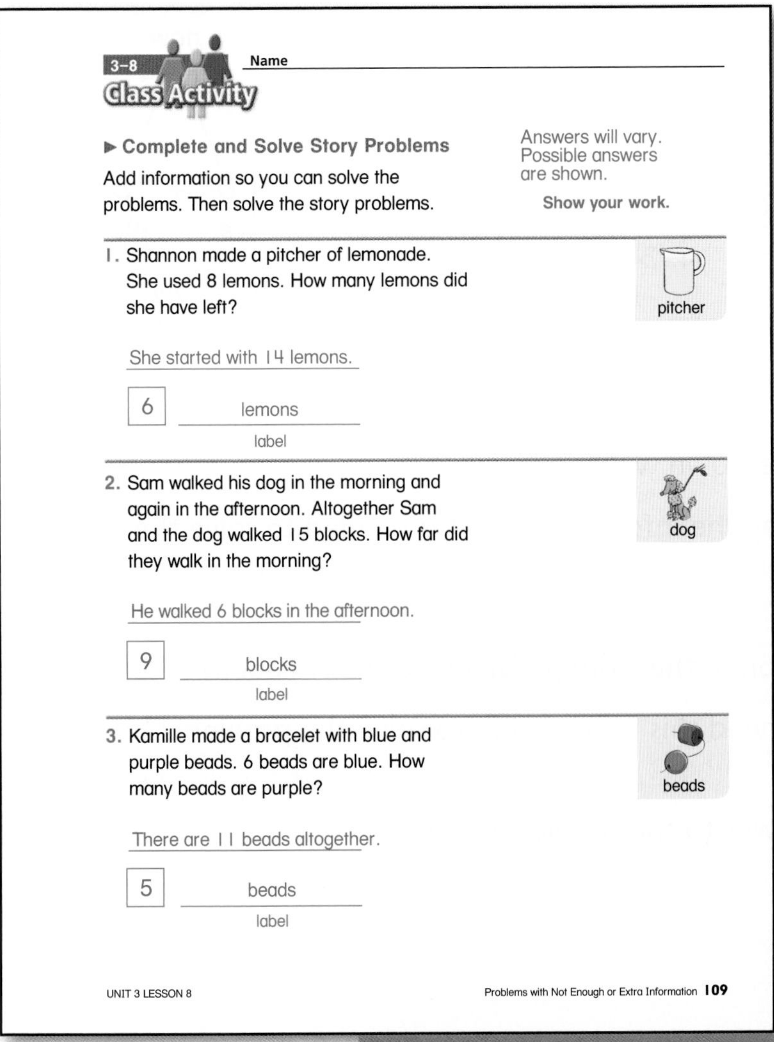

3-8 Class Activity Name

▶ **Complete and Solve Story Problems**

Add information so you can solve the problems. Then solve the story problems.

Answers will vary. Possible answers are shown.

Show your work.

1. Shannon made a pitcher of lemonade. She used 8 lemons. How many lemons did she have left?

   pitcher

   She started with 14 lemons.

   6 lemons
   label

2. Sam walked his dog in the morning and again in the afternoon. Altogether Sam and the dog walked 15 blocks. How far did they walk in the morning?

   dog

   He walked 6 blocks in the afternoon.

   9 blocks
   label

3. Kamille made a bracelet with blue and purple beads. 6 beads are blue. How many beads are purple?

   beads

   There are 11 beads altogether.

   5 beads
   label

UNIT 3 LESSON 8 Problems with Not Enough or Extra Information 109

Student Activity Book page 109

Differentiated Instruction

Extra Help If children need more practice, present them with the following problems.

▶ Amber has some crayons. She put 5 in a box and some on her desk. How many crayons does Amber have?

▶ Jholan bought 12 pieces of fruit. Some of them were oranges. The rest of them were bananas. How many oranges did she buy?

English Language Learners

Make sure children understand the word *enough*. Write and say:
A soccer ball costs $10. Carlo has $12. Kendra has $10. Jon has $9.

- **Beginning** Ask: **Can Kendra buy a soccer ball?** yes **Can Carlo?** yes **Can Jon?** no Say: **Kendra and Carlo have *enough* money. Jon does not have *enough* money.**
- **Intermediate** Ask: **Who can buy a soccer ball?** Carlo, Kendra Say: **Jon has less than $10. He does not have *enough* money.**
- **Advanced** Ask: **Who has *enough* money to buy a soccer ball?** Carlo, Kendra

Activity 2

Problems with Extra Information

 25 MINUTES

Goal: Solve story problems with extra information.

Materials: Student Activity Book page 110

 **NCTM Standards:**
Number and Operations
Problem Solving

Teaching Note

Research Some children find it helpful to cross out the unnecessary information in the written problem or at least to cross out the number they do not need.

▶ Introduce Problems with Extra Information

WHOLE CLASS

Math Talk 

Write the following story problem on the board and read it aloud to the class.

There were 8 elephants and 7 zebras at the zoo. Then 3 more elephants were born. How many elephants are there at the zoo now?

- There may be *more* information than we need to solve this problem. Let's try to figure out what information we need and what information is extra.

Tell children that they can make a drawing of the problem to see if there is any information that is not needed. Discuss what to draw as a class.

Draw the problem on the board while children draw it at their seats. Three sample drawings are shown below.

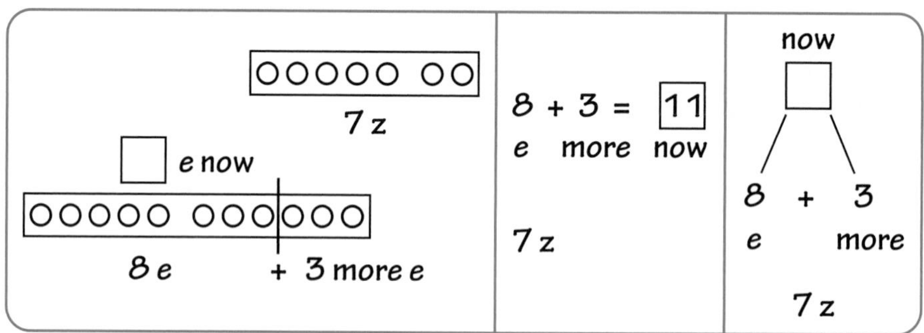

Have children identify both the information that is necessary to solve the problem and the information that is extra. Ask several children to retell the problem in their own words.

- This time, just say the information that is needed to solve the problem. There were 8 elephants at the zoo. Last month 3 baby elephants were born. How many elephants are there at the zoo now?
- What information in the story problem was not needed? 7 zebras
- Why didn't we need this information to solve the problem? The question was only about the number of elephants at the zoo.
- What is the answer to the problem? 11 elephants

▶ Solve Problems with Extra Information WHOLE CLASS

3–8 Class Activity Name ____________________

▶ Solve Problems with Extra Information

Show your work.

Cross out the extra information. Solve.

1. The dentist had 8 red toothbrushes ~~and 6 green ones.~~ Then she bought 9 more red ones. How many red toothbrushes does she have now?

   toothbrush

   17 red toothbrushes
   label

2. Jory walked 9 miles around the lake. Then he walked 4 miles around the pond. ~~He usually bicycles 18 miles a day.~~ How many miles did he walk today?

   pond

   13 miles
   label

3. Pam had ~~7 long ribbons and~~ 9 short ribbons. She gave away 5 short ones. How many short ribbons does Pam have now?

   ribbon

   4 short ribbons
   label

4. On Friday, Mr. Lopez rescued 5 animals. On Saturday, he rescued 8 animals. ~~He drove 7 miles.~~ How many animals did he rescue in all?

   animals

   13 animals
   label

Student Activity Book page 110

Have children look at the first problem on Student Activity Book page 110. Ask them to decide whether or not all of the information given is necessary for solving the problem. Have a few children solve the problem at the board. See **Math Talk in Action** for a discussion of this problem.

Ask children to cross out the information they do not need in the other problems and then solve them. You may wish to have some children solve the problems at the board.

If time permits, have children make up story problems of their own that contain extra information. Encourage them to make funny contributions if they wish. For example, "I have 5 roses, 7 daisies, and 6 pickles in a vase. How many flowers do I have?" Have children share their problems with the class.

Math Talk in Action

Sean: I added 8 and 9. The answer is 17.

Kamille: What does the answer mean? 17 what?

Sean: The dentist has 17 toothbrushes.

Kamille: Why didn't you add 6?

Sean: 6 *green* toothbrushes is extra information. The question asks how many *red* toothbrushes.

Kamille: Then why did you say your answer means the dentist has 17 toothbrushes?

Sean: I should have said the dentist has 17 *red* toothbrushes.

Differentiated Instruction

Extra Help If children need more practice, present them with the following problems.

- ▶ There are 9 boys and 8 girls in math class. 2 girls left to go to the library. How many girls are still in math class?
- ▶ Dad baked 7 muffins, 6 loaves of wheat bread, and some loaves of rye bread. Altogether he baked 15 loaves of bread. How many loaves of rye bread did he bake?

Ongoing Assessment

Present children with this problem and have them tell what information is extra.

- ▶ Michael jogs 8 miles around the park. Then he jogs 3 miles to get home. He drives 5 miles to work. How many miles does he jog in all?

2 Going Further

Extension: Use Information from a Story

Goal: Use reference books to find information.

Materials: Student Activity Book pages 111–112

NCTM Standards:
Number and Operations
Problem Solving

▶ Find Information in a Story PAIRS

Direct children's attention to the story at the top of Student Activity Book page 111. Read it aloud as the children follow along.

- What is the story about? A boy went to the zoo with his class.
- Who wrote the story? Robbie
- What did Robbie see at the zoo? animals
- What animals did Robbie see at the zoo? elephants, tigers, monkeys, penguins, and giraffes
- How many of each animal did Robbie see? Robbie saw 4 elephants, 5 tigers, 8 monkeys, and 13 penguins.
- How else could we show the information about the animals Robbie saw? Answers will vary. Possible answers: in a table, chart, list, or graph.

Explain to the class that they will use the information in the story to solve problems. Then have pairs work together to solve problems 1 and 2. When they have finished, discuss the answers and have pairs share their solutions. Then have children write another question based on the story. Ask volunteers to read their questions and ask additional volunteers to solve them.

▶ Write Stories and Problems PAIRS

If time allows, children can work in pairs to write their own story and two problems to go with it. Discuss different themes children can use for their stories.

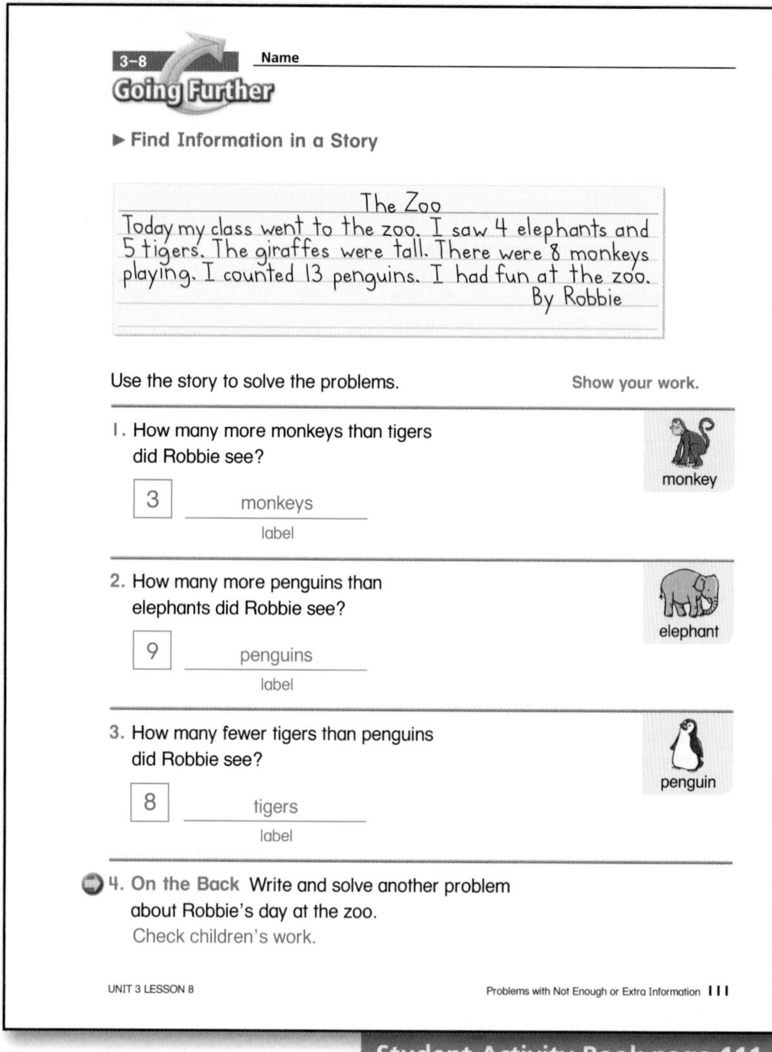
3-8 Going Further Name

▶ Find Information in a Story

The Zoo
Today my class went to the zoo. I saw 4 elephants and 5 tigers. The giraffes were tall. There were 8 monkeys playing. I counted 13 penguins. I had fun at the zoo.
By Robbie

Use the story to solve the problems. Show your work.

1. How many more monkeys than tigers did Robbie see?
3 monkeys
label

2. How many more penguins than elephants did Robbie see?
9 penguins
label

3. How many fewer tigers than penguins did Robbie see?
8 tigers
label

 4. On the Back Write and solve another problem about Robbie's day at the zoo.
Check children's work.

UNIT 3 LESSON 8 Problems with Not Enough or Extra Information 111

Student Activity Book page 111

Class Management

Walk around the room and observe children as they write their own stories. Provide assistance in spelling words. Watch for children who do not put any numbers in the story. Remind children to write two story problems that can be solved using the information they put in their story.

After children complete their story and problems, have them switch papers with their partner and solve each other's problems. Pairs can discuss their work and revise their stories and problems as needed. Use the revised stories to create a story bank and have children read and solve other children's stories and problems.

Intervention — Activity Card 3-8

Extra or Not Enough? Activity Card 3-8

Work: 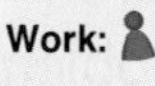

Use:

- Homework and Remembering page 69

1. Read story problem 1 on Homework and Remembering page 69.
2. Decide if the problem has extra information or not enough information. Write "extra" if there is extra information. Write "not enough" if the story has too little information.

1. There are 14 children in music class. Some children left the class to go to the library. How many children are still in music class?
not enough

3. If there is too much information, cross out the extra information.
4. Repeat with the rest of the problems.

Unit 3, Lesson 8

Activity Note Each child needs Homework and Remembering p. 69. Ask children to share how they know if there is too much or too little information.

Math Writing Prompt

Write Your Own Write a story problem about sandwiches. Include one piece of extra information.

Software Support

Use *Soar to Success* for instruction of students needing targeted support for underlying skills.

On Level — Activity Card 3-8

Write Your Own Activity Card 3-8

Work: 

Use:

- Homework and Remembering page 69

Choose:

- 1
- 2

1. **Work Together** Read story problem 1 on Homework and Remembering page 69.
2. Decide if the problem has extra information or not enough information. Write "extra" if there is extra information. Write "not enough" if the story has too little information.
3. If there is not enough information, rewrite the problem to have extra information.
4. If the problem has too much information, rewrite the problem so that the problem does not have enough information.
5. Repeat for problems 2-3.

1. There were 14 children in music class. 6 children were playing the piano. 5 children left the class to go to the library. How many children are still in music class?

Unit 3, Lesson 8

Activity Note Each pair needs Homework and Remembering p. 69. Ask pairs to trade new problems and check that problems.

Math Writing Prompt

Write Your Own Write a story problem about 5 hippos and 7 giraffes that does not have enough information.

Software Support

Use *MegaMath* for review and reinforcement of the concepts and skills presented in this lesson.

Challenge — Activity Card 3-8

Zoo Animals Activity Card 3-8

Work:

Use:

- paper

Choose:

- 1
- 2

1. Write a story problem about zoo animals that has extra information.
2. Read the story problem. Cross out the extra information. Then solve the problem.
3. Take turns.
4. Put your story problems and solutions on the bulletin board.

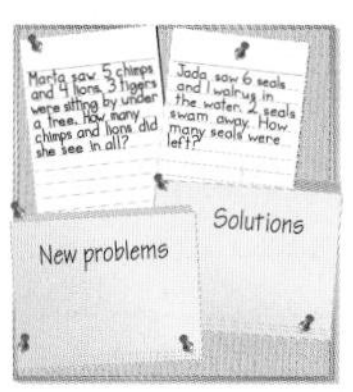

Unit 3, Lesson 8

Activity Note Prepare a bulletin board display for the problems. Include folders for "New Problems" and "Solutions."

Math Writing Prompt

Write a Definition Explain in your own words what "extra information" in a story problem is. How do you know when you have extra information?

Software Support

Use *Destination Math* to take students beyond the concepts and skills presented in this lesson.

3 Homework and Targeted Practice

Goal: Additional Practice

This Homework page provides practice in solving story problems with not enough or extra information.

3–8 Targeted Practice **Goal:** Solve story problems.

This Targeted Practice page can be used with children who need extra practice with comparison story problems.

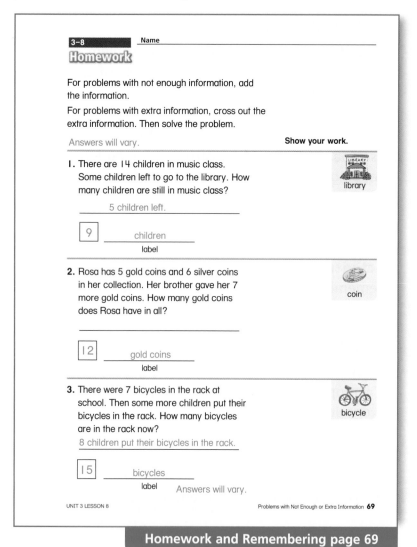

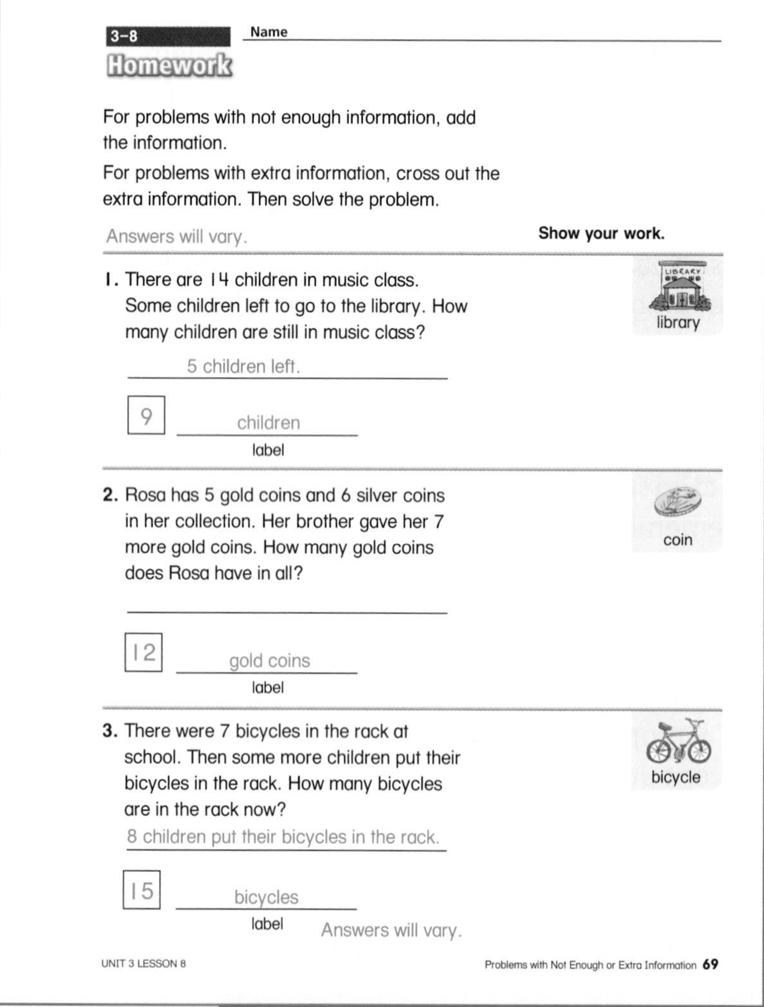

3–8 Name

Homework

For problems with not enough information, add the information.

For problems with extra information, cross out the extra information. Then solve the problem.

Answers will vary. **Show your work.**

1. There are 14 children in music class. Some children left to go to the library. How many children are still in music class?

   5 children left.

   9 children (label)

   library

2. Rosa has 5 gold coins and 6 silver coins in her collection. Her brother gave her 7 more gold coins. How many gold coins does Rosa have in all?

   12 gold coins (label)

   coin

3. There were 7 bicycles in the rack at school. Then some more children put their bicycles in the rack. How many bicycles are in the rack now?

   8 children put their bicycles in the rack.

   15 bicycles (label) Answers will vary.

   bicycle

UNIT 3 LESSON 8 Problems with Not Enough or Extra Information 69

Homework and Remembering page 69

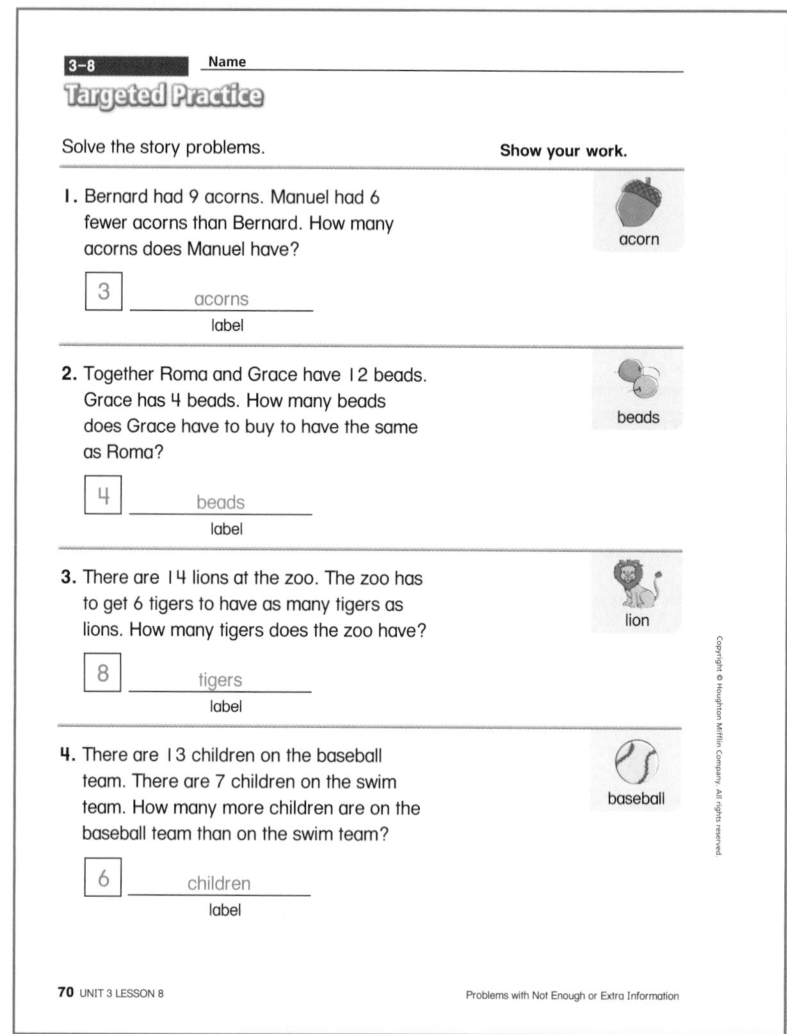

3–8 Name

Targeted Practice

Solve the story problems. **Show your work.**

1. Bernard had 9 acorns. Manuel had 6 fewer acorns than Bernard. How many acorns does Manuel have?

   3 acorns (label)

   acorn

2. Together Roma and Grace have 12 beads. Grace has 4 beads. How many beads does Grace have to buy to have the same as Roma?

   4 beads (label)

   beads

3. There are 14 lions at the zoo. The zoo has to get 6 tigers to have as many tigers as lions. How many tigers does the zoo have?

   8 tigers (label)

   lion

4. There are 13 children on the baseball team. There are 7 children on the swim team. How many more children are on the baseball team than on the swim team?

   6 children (label)

   baseball

Copyright © Houghton Mifflin Company. All rights reserved.

70 UNIT 3 LESSON 8 Problems with Not Enough or Extra Information

Homework and Remembering page 70

Home or School Activity

Science Connection

Too Much or Too Little? Have children brainstorm what they know about plants and what plants need to live. Children will probably suggest water, air, space, and sunlight. Have children write and draw what happens to a plant if it gets extra or not enough of these necessities.

A plant with too much water.
A plant with not enough water.
A plant with enough water.

Problems with Hidden Information and Mixed Practice

Lesson Objectives

- **Solve story problems with hidden information by figuring out what that information is.**
- **Solve story problems with not enough information by adding information to the problem.**
- **Solve problems with extra information by crossing out the extra information.**

Vocabulary
hidden information

The Day at a Glance

Today's Goals	Materials	
1 Teaching the Lesson **A1:** Find hidden numbers in story problems. **A2:** Practice solving problems with hidden information, not enough information, and extra information.	**Lesson Activities** Student Activity Book p. 113 Homework and Remembering pp. 71–72	**Going Further** Activity Cards 3-9 Student Activity Book p. 114 Dictionary and other reference books Connecting cubes Index cards Math Journals
2 Going Further ► Extension: Look It Up ► Differentiated Instruction		
3 Homework and Spiral Review		

Use Math Talk today!

Keeping Skills Sharp

Quick Practice — 5 MINUTES

Goal: Add with teen totals.

Materials: Secret Code Cards (1–10), Parachute Drop–Teen Totals (from Unit 3 Lesson 7 or TRB M57)

Secret Code Card Addition Race–Teen Totals Have **Student Leaders** call out addition problems from the Parachute Drop page. As quickly as possible, children hold up the Secret Code Cards for the answer.

Repeated Quick Practice
Use these Quick Practices from previous lessons.

- ► **Equation Chains** Use 17. (See Unit 1 Lesson 18.)
- ► **Class Make a Ten** (See Unit 3 Lesson 8.)

Daily Routines

Comparing 2-Digit Quantities
Using a Meter Stick, Using Number Flashes, Using the MathBoard (See pp. xxv–xxvi.)

- ► Led by Student Leaders

Money Routine Using the 120 Poster, Using the Money Flip Chart, Using the Number Path, Using Secret Code Cards (See pp. xxiii–xxv.)

- ► Led by Student Leaders

1 Teaching the Lesson

Activity 1

Problems with Hidden Information

 25 MINUTES

Goal: Find hidden numbers in story problems.

 **NCTM Standards:**
Number and Operations
Problem Solving

English Language Learners

Review the word *hidden*. Hold up a ball. Say: **Now you can see the ball. Close your eyes. I'm hiding the ball. Open your eyes. Now the ball is *hidden*.**

- **Beginning** Ask: **Can you see the ball?** no Say: **The ball is *hidden*. You cannot see it.**
- **Intermediate** Ask: **Do you know where the ball is?** no **Is it hidden?** yes
- **Advanced** Ask: **What did I do?** hid the ball Say: **It is ___.** hidden

Differentiated Instruction

Extra Help If children are having difficulty finding the answers to these types of story problems, substitute numbers for the key words, especially for English Learners.

> 12
> Holly bought ~~a dozen~~ eggs. She used 5 of them to make breakfast. How many eggs does she have left?

▶ Introduce Problems with Hidden Information

WHOLE CLASS

Math Talk

Present the following story problem, which contains a "hidden" or implied number.

> I have a pair of beautiful lamps. I bought another pair at a flea market. How many lamps do I have now?

Explain to children that some problems have hidden numbers that need to be figured out before the problem can be solved.

- Notice that you don't see any numbers in this problem. But there is a number that is "hidden." What is that number? 2 How is it hidden? The word *pair* means 2.

Give children time to solve the problem.

- How did you solve the problem and label the answer? 2 lamps + 2 lamps = 4 lamps

Now present the following story problem, which contains a different hidden number.

> Holly bought a dozen eggs. She used 5 of them to make breakfast. How many eggs does she have left? 7 eggs, because *dozen* means 12 and 12 − 5 = 7

Give children a few more problems of this type, and have them discuss hidden numbers. Encourage children to make sketches if it will help them.

> Sarah had $4 to spend at the school fair. Lita had double that amount to spend. How much money did Lita have to spend? $8, because *double that amount* means *that amount twice* and 4 + 4 = 8

> Rob's yard is shaped like a rectangle. He planted a tree in each corner. Theresa's yard is shaped like a triangle. She planted a tree in each corner. How many trees did Rob and Theresa plant in all? 7 trees, because rectangles have 4 corners, triangles have 3 corners, and 4 + 3 = 7

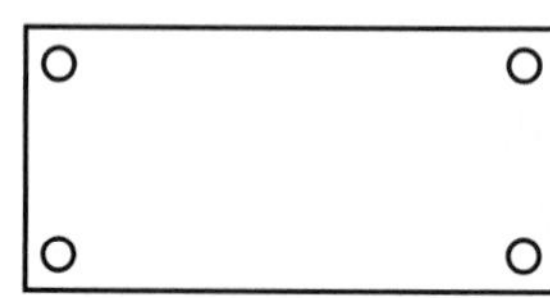

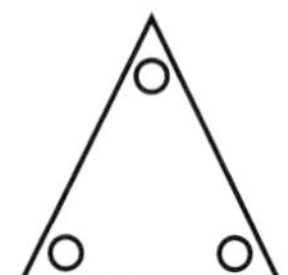

Activity 2

Mixed Practice

▶ Practice Solving Story Problems PAIRS

3-9 Class Activity Name

Vocabulary
hidden information

▶ Practice Solving Story Problems

Cross out extra information or write missing or **hidden information**. Solve the problems.

Answers will vary.

Show your work.

1. Chris washed some cars at the car wash. His friend Kelly washed some cars at the car wash. They washed a total of 16 cars. How many cars did Kelly wash?

car wash

Chris washed 8 cars.

8 cars
label

2. Shanna put 13 markers ~~and 6 crayons~~ in her book bag. When she got to school, she gave 4 of the markers to her friend. How many markers does Shanna have left?

marker

9 markers
label

3. There are 9 children and a set of triplets in the library. How many children are in the library?

library

Triplet means 3.

12 children
label

UNIT 3 LESSON 9 Problems with Hidden Information and Mixed Practice 113

Student Activity Book page 113

Children may work alone or in **Helping Pairs** to complete Student Activity Book page 113. Have some children work at the board and present their solutions to the class. Allow time for discussion and clarification.

If time permits, have children make up their own problems with hidden information.

30 MINUTES

Goal: Practice solving problems with hidden information, not enough information, and extra information.

Materials: Student Activity Book page 113

NCTM Standards:
Number and Operations
Problem Solving

Teaching Note

What to Expect from Students
Some children can solve the *not enough information, extra information,* and *hidden information* problems now. Others will need more experience with these problems. They will appear on Remembering pages and Targeted Practice pages. Also, collect problems children make up, edit them as needed, and use them in various ways (learning centers, extra work, helping partners).

Ongoing Assessment

As children solve the problems ask questions such as:

- ▶ What are you asked to find?
- ▶ What information do you need to solve the problem?
- ▶ Are there any hidden numbers?

2 Going Further

Extension: Look It Up

Goal: Use reference books to find information.

Materials: Student Activity Book page 114, dictionary and other reference materials

NCTM Standards:
Number and Operations
Measurement
Problem Solving
Communication
Connections

Teaching Note

Math Background Children have already begun to learn that numbers may be represented in various ways. For example, they know that another name for 5 cents is 1 nickel, and they know that 1 ten is the same as 10 ones. Using different numerical units, whether units of measurement or words that contain an implied number, will help children develop number sense.

▶ Research Information SMALL GROUPS

Discuss the various kinds of reference books people use to find information, such as a dictionary, almanac, and encyclopedia. Show children a dictionary or another reference book. Explain that reference books are used to find information that we might not know. Ask children to think of something they would like to find out more about. Have children give you a word they want to know the meaning of and show them how to look it up in the dictionary.

- Where else can you go to look up information about something? Possible answers: Ask an adult, use an encyclopedia, look it up on the computer.

If you have access to a computer in your classroom, show children how to search for information on a specific topic.

Then direct children's attention to the top of Student Activity Book page 114. Read aloud the directions and the first exercise.

- What do you have to do to complete the first exercise? Find the number in the box that tells the number of days in a week.

3-9 Going Further Name

▶ Research Information

Use the numbers below for exercises 1–7.

3	7	12	24	31	60	100

1. Number of days in a week 7
2. Number of months in a year 12
3. Number of seconds in a minute 60
4. Number of hours in a day 24
5. Number of feet in a yard 3
6. Number of days in July 31
7. Number of yards on a football field 100

Solve the problem.

8. Suzanne was on vacation for two weeks. How many days was Suzanne on vacation?

14 days
label

114 UNIT 3 LESSON 9 Problems with Hidden Information and Mixed Practice

Student Activity Book page 114

- What if you don't know the number of days in a week? How can you find that information? Possible responses: look on a calendar, in my math book, in the dictionary, or ask someone I think will know.

Have children work in small groups to complete the exercises. Provide reference materials for groups to use to look up information. As groups explain how they found the answers, have children make any corrections to their papers.

Use the **Solve and Discuss** structure to complete problem 8. Discuss how children used the information they found in the first exercise to solve the story problem.

Intervention Activity Card 3-9

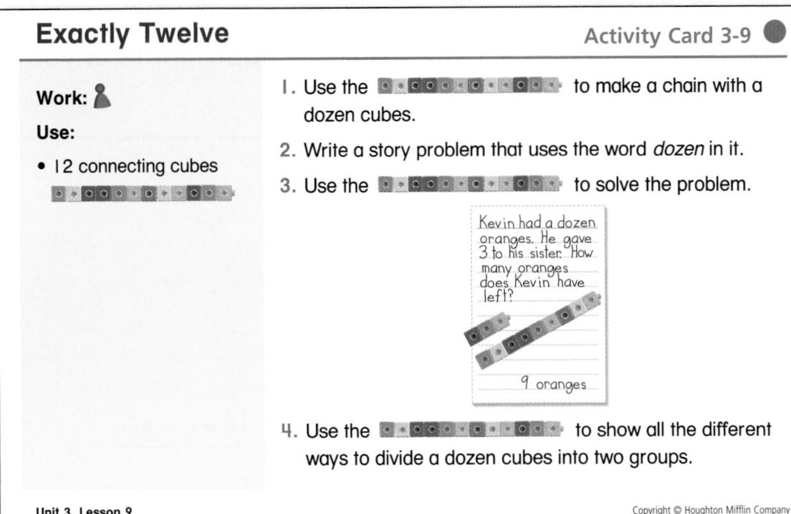
Exactly Twelve — Activity Card 3-9

Work: (individual)
Use:
- 12 connecting cubes

1. Use the (cubes) to make a chain with a dozen cubes.
2. Write a story problem that uses the word *dozen* in it.
3. Use the (cubes) to solve the problem.

Kevin had a dozen oranges. He gave 3 to his sister. How many oranges does Kevin have left?
9 oranges

4. Use the (cubes) to show all the different ways to divide a dozen cubes into two groups.

Unit 3, Lesson 9

Activity Note Each child needs 15 connecting cubes. Remind children what *dozen* means. Check that children start with 12 cubes.

Math Writing Prompt

Days in a Week Write a story problem with hidden information—the number of days in a week.

Soar to Success
Math

Software Support

Use *Soar to Success* for instruction of students needing targeted support for underlying skills.

On Level Activity Card 3-9

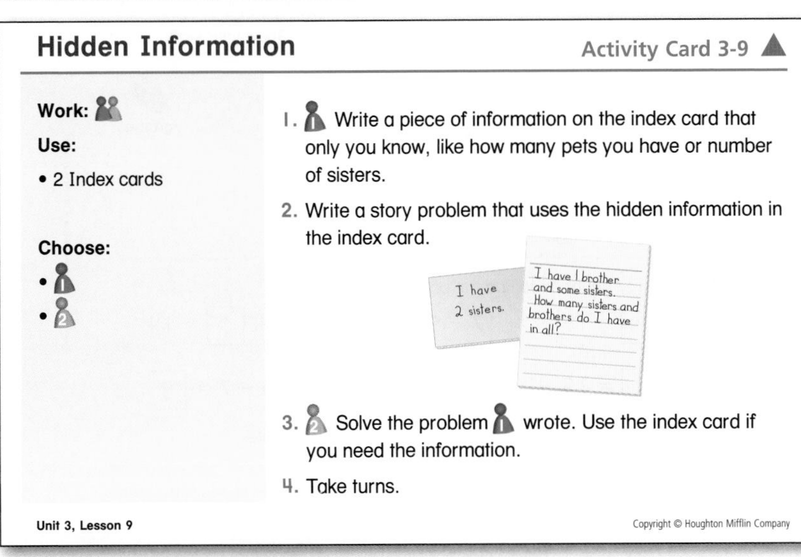
Hidden Information — Activity Card 3-9

Work: (pairs)
Use:
- 2 Index cards

Choose:
- (student 1)
- (student 2)

1. (Student 1) Write a piece of information on the index card that only you know, like how many pets you have or number of sisters.
2. Write a story problem that uses the hidden information in the index card.

I have 2 sisters.
I have I brother and some sisters. How many sisters and brothers do I have in all?

3. (Student 2) Solve the problem (student 1) wrote. Use the index card if you need the information.
4. Take turns.

Unit 3, Lesson 9

Activity Note Each child needs an index card. Have pairs trade their problems with other pairs for extra practice.

Math Writing Prompt

Coins Write a story problem with hidden information—the number of cents in a nickel, dime, or quarter.

HARCOURT
MegaMath
Grades K-6

Software Support

Use *MegaMath* for review and reinforcement of the concepts and skills presented in this lesson.

Challenge Activity Card 3-9

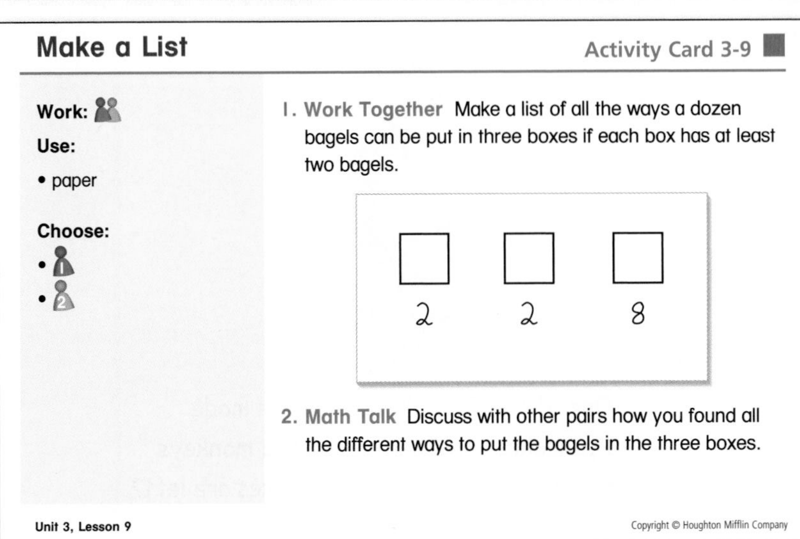
Make a List — Activity Card 3-9

Work: (pairs)
Use:
- paper

Choose:
- (student 1)
- (student 2)

1. **Work Together** Make a list of all the ways a dozen bagels can be put in three boxes if each box has at least two bagels.

2
2
8

2. **Math Talk** Discuss with other pairs how you found all the different ways to put the bagels in the three boxes.

Unit 3, Lesson 9

Activity Note The seven ways to put the bagels in the boxes are 2,2,8; 2,3,7; 2,4,6; 2,5,5; 3,3,6; 3,4,5; and 4,4,4.

Math Writing Prompt

Write Your Own Write and solve a story problem that uses the words *pair*, *dozen*, and *triplet*.

DESTINATION
Math

Software Support

Use *Destination Math* to take students beyond the concepts and skills presented in this lesson.

3 Homework and Spiral Review

Goal: Additional Practice

This Homework page provides practice in solving problems with hidden, not enough, or extra information.

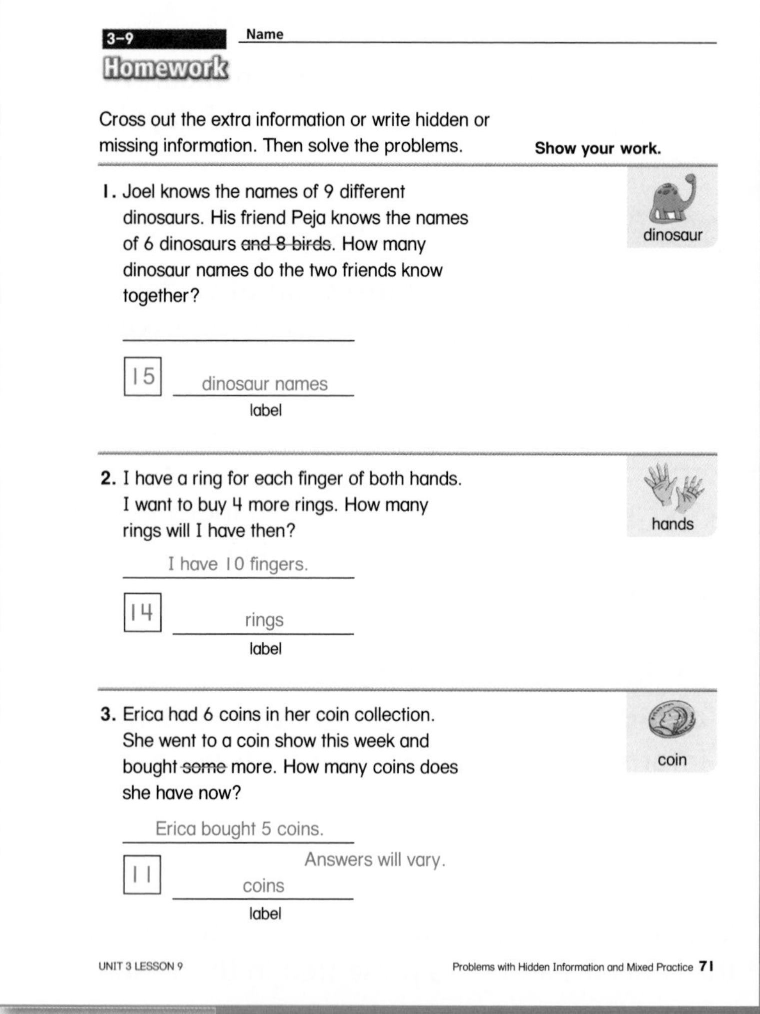

3–9 Homework Name

Cross out the extra information or write hidden or missing information. Then solve the problems. **Show your work.**

1. Joel knows the names of 9 different dinosaurs. His friend Peja knows the names of 6 dinosaurs ~~and 8 birds~~. How many dinosaur names do the two friends know together?

   dinosaur

   15 dinosaur names
   label

2. I have a ring for each finger of both hands. I want to buy 4 more rings. How many rings will I have then?

   hands

   I have 10 fingers.

   14 rings
   label

3. Erica had 6 coins in her coin collection. She went to a coin show this week and bought ~~some~~ more. How many coins does she have now?

   coin

   Erica bought 5 coins.

   11 coins
   label
   Answers will vary.

UNIT 3 LESSON 9 Problems with Hidden Information and Mixed Practice 71

Homework and Remembering page 71

Goal: Spiral Review

This Remembering activity would be appropriate anytime after today's lesson.

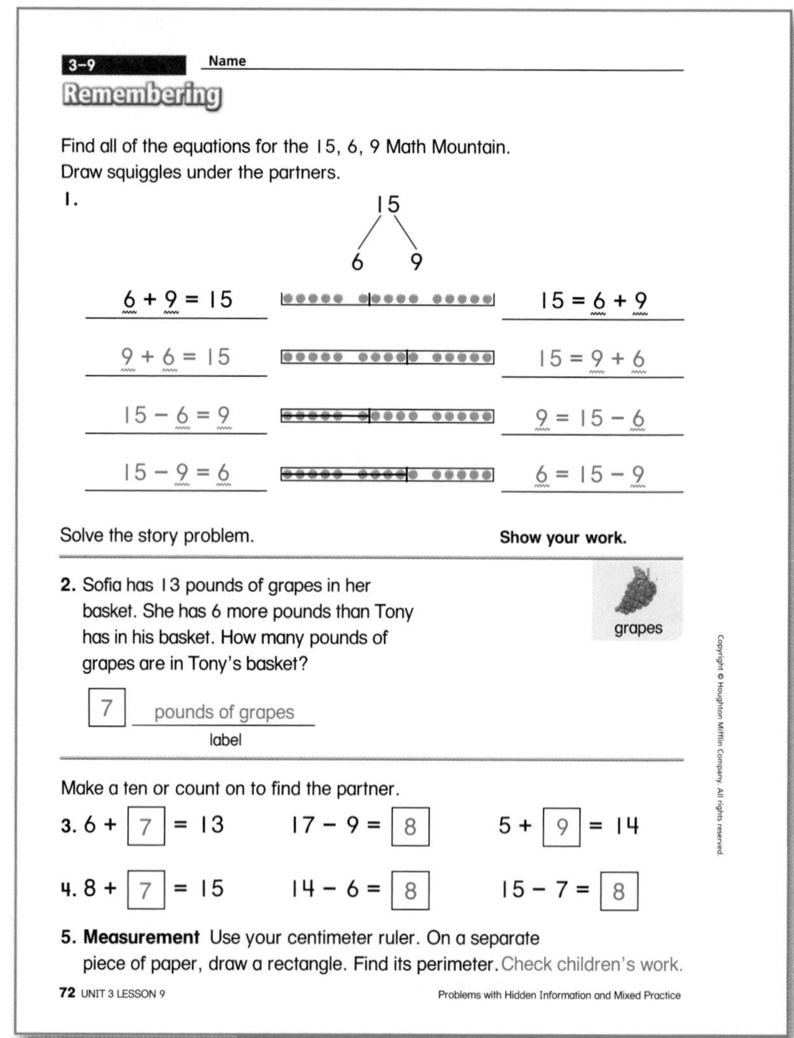

3–9 Remembering Name

Find all of the equations for the 15, 6, 9 Math Mountain. Draw squiggles under the partners.

1. 15 / 6 9

6 + 9 = 15		15 = 6 + 9
9 + 6 = 15		15 = 9 + 6
15 − 6 = 9		9 = 15 − 6
15 − 9 = 6		6 = 15 − 9

Solve the story problem. **Show your work.**

2. Sofia has 13 pounds of grapes in her basket. She has 6 more pounds than Tony has in his basket. How many pounds of grapes are in Tony's basket?

   grapes

   7 pounds of grapes
   label

Make a ten or count on to find the partner.

3. 6 + 7 = 13 17 − 9 = 8 5 + 9 = 14

4. 8 + 7 = 15 14 − 6 = 8 15 − 7 = 8

5. **Measurement** Use your centimeter ruler. On a separate piece of paper, draw a rectangle. Find its perimeter. Check children's work.

72 UNIT 3 LESSON 9 Problems with Hidden Information and Mixed Practice

Copyright © Houghton Mifflin Company. All rights reserved.

Homework and Remembering page 72

Home or School Activity

Language Arts Connection

Favorite Character Have children discuss their favorite characters from stories they have read or heard. Ask children to write and illustrate a story problem about the character. Encourage them to try to include hidden information in the problem.

One of the Five Little Monkeys made 13 pancakes. Another one of the monkeys ate 7 pancakes. How many pancakes are left?

Two-Step Story Problems

Lesson Objective

- Solve problems requiring more than one solution step.

Vocabulary

two-step story problem

The Day at a Glance

Today's Goals	Materials	
1 Teaching the Lesson A: Paraphrase and solve two-step story problems.	**Lesson Activities** Student Activity Book p. 115 Homework and Remembering pp. 73–74	**Going Further** Activity Cards 3-10 Student Activity Book p. 116 Homework and Remembering p. 73 Highlighter or yellow marker Math Journals
2 Going Further ▸ Problem-Solving Strategy: Reasonable Answers ▸ Differentiated Instruction		
3 Homework and Targeted Practice		

Use Math Talk today!

Keeping Skills Sharp

Quick Practice — 5 MINUTES

Goals: Write equation chains for 13. Add and subtract, totals ≤ 10. Make a ten when adding a number to 8 or 9.

Materials: Yellow Math Mountain Cards (≤ 10) (from Unit 1 Lesson 16 or TRB M43–M44)

Equation Chains Have three children write equation chains for the number 13 on the board. (See Unit 1 Lesson 18.)

Math Mountains (≤ 10) Have children practice addition and subtraction with the Yellow Math Mountain Cards.

Class Make a Ten Write the $m + n$ list (left column) on the board. Do each row in turn. (See Unit 3 Lesson 1.)

Class Make a Ten

Student Leader 1 points to and says	Student Leader 2 shows fingers and says	Class says and Student Leader 2 writes = and
9 + 7	7 makes 1 and 6	9 + 1 + 6 = 10 + 6 = 16
9 + 4	4 makes 1 and 3	9 + 1 + 3 = 10 + 3 = 13
8 + 4	4 makes 2 and 2	8 + 2 + 2 = 10 + 2 = 12
8 + 6	6 makes 2 and 4	8 + 2 + 4 = 10 + 4 = 14
9 + 3	3 makes 1 and 2	9 + 1 + 2 = 10 + 2 = 12
8 + 8	8 makes 2 and 6	8 + 2 + 6 = 10 + 6 = 16
8 + 5	5 makes 2 and 3	8 + 2 + 3 = 10 + 3 = 13

Daily Routines

Comparing 2-Digit Quantities Using a Meter Stick, Using Number Flashes, Using the MathBoard (See pp. xxv–xxvi.)

▸ Led by Student Leaders

Money Routine Using the 120 Poster, Using the Money Flip Chart, Using the Number Path, Using Secret Code Cards (See pp. xxiii–xxv.)

▸ Led by Student Leaders

1 Teaching the Lesson

Activity

Two-Step Story Problems

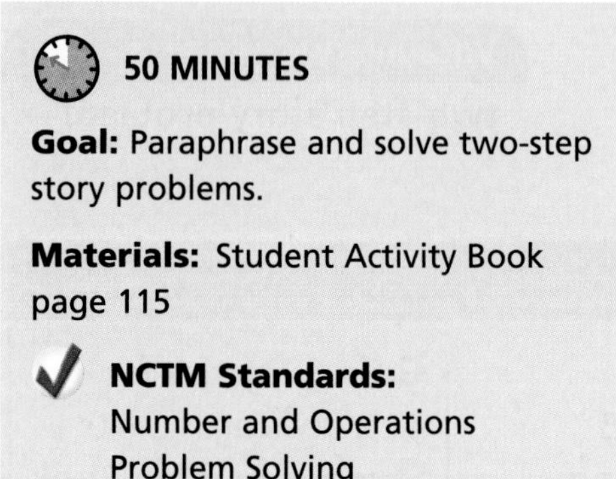

50 MINUTES

Goal: Paraphrase and solve two-step story problems.

Materials: Student Activity Book page 115

NCTM Standards:
Number and Operations
Problem Solving
Communication

Teaching Note

Math Background One of the principal reasons children have difficulty solving story problems is that they do not pay enough attention to the situation expressed in the problem, especially for **English Learners** who may feel overwhelmed by the amount of information presented. Instead they tend to focus on the numbers and some key word or phrase when they choose a solution strategy. This activity will help children listen carefully to story problems, retell the problem, and think before answering.

English Language Learners

Read Solve and Discuss problem 1 aloud. Help children find steps. Write *First* and draw the Math Mountain 9 + ☐ = 17. Write *Then* and ☐ + 2.

- **Beginning** Point to each number. Say: **There were 9 sheep and 17 animals in all.** Ask: **9 + what is 17?** 8 Say: **There were 8 horses. Lana gets 2 more horses. 8 + 2 = ___.** 10
- **Intermediate and Advanced** Have children work in pairs to retell the story using the equations, find the unknown, and the answer.

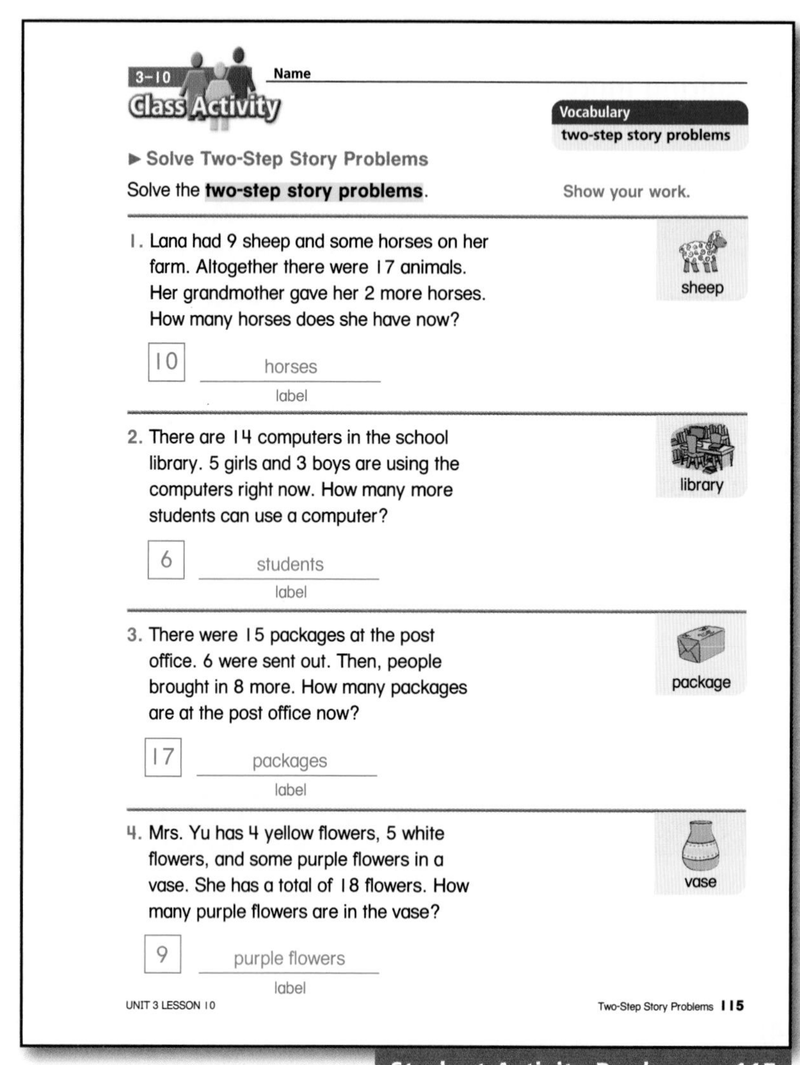

3–10 Class Activity Name ____________

Vocabulary
two-step story problems

▶ Solve Two-Step Story Problems

Solve the **two-step story problems**. Show your work.

1. Lana had 9 sheep and some horses on her farm. Altogether there were 17 animals. Her grandmother gave her 2 more horses. How many horses does she have now?

10 horses
label

2. There are 14 computers in the school library. 5 girls and 3 boys are using the computers right now. How many more students can use a computer?

6 students
label

3. There were 15 packages at the post office. 6 were sent out. Then, people brought in 8 more. How many packages are at the post office now?

17 packages
label

4. Mrs. Yu has 4 yellow flowers, 5 white flowers, and some purple flowers in a vase. She has a total of 18 flowers. How many purple flowers are in the vase?

9 purple flowers
label

UNIT 3 LESSON 10 Two-Step Story Problems 115

Student Activity Book page 115

▶ Retell Two-Step Story Problems WHOLE CLASS

Direct children's attention to Student Activity Book page 115. Have children read the first story problem aloud. Tell them not to answer the problem yet, but to focus on understanding what they read. This problem is more difficult than those they have encountered previously because it requires two steps to solve. Ask a volunteer to retell the problem in his or her own words. Other children can also retell the problem.

▶ Solve Two-Step Story Problems

WHOLE CLASS

Math Talk 

Use the **Solve and Discuss** structure for problem 1 on Student Activity Book page 115. Have children make their labeled drawing or equation at their seats while three to six children solve it on the board.

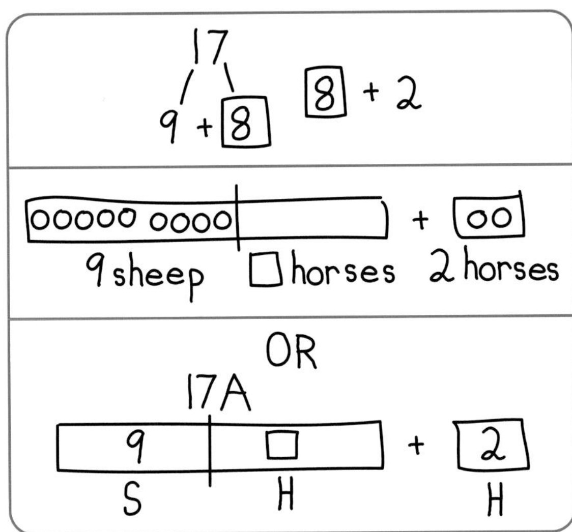

- What is the first step in the problem? Possible response: The first step in the problem is mystery addition. I know 9 sheep, so I need 8 more horses to get to 17.
- What is the second step in the problem? Possible response: Add. 8 horses plus 2 more is 10 horses.
- How else could you solve the story problem? Possible response: By adding first, then subtracting: 17 total animals plus 2 horses is 19. 19 minus 9 sheep is 10 horses.

Next have children read and solve the second story problem on Student Activity Book page 115. After the problem is read, some children can retell it in their own words. Then ask two children to explain their drawings and solutions and answer questions posed by the class.

Continue the process of reading, retelling, solving, asking questions, and discussing story problems with the remaining problems on the page.

For problem 2, some students may also want to write a 2-step subtraction equation ($14 - 5 - 3 = \square$) to solve this problem.

When children have completed the page, you may wish to have them write and solve their own two-step story problems.

Alternate Approach

Act It Out You may want to consider having children act out the story problem presented here. Acting out scenarios for two-step story problems would be particularly beneficial for English Learners. Select 9 children to be sheep, and have them go to the front of the class. Add enough "horses," one at a time, to make a total of 17 animals. (Children may imitate the actions of these animals.) The "sheep" can now sit down. Two more children can be the horses from Lana's grandmother, joining the children at the front of the class. Other two-step problems may be solved in this way, as well as by drawings, equations, or Math Mountains.

Ongoing Assessment

As children solve the two-step problems, ask questions such as:

- ▶ What do you have to find?
- ▶ What steps do you need to take to solve the problem?
- ▶ Could you do the steps in a different way to solve the problem?

2 Going Further

Problem-Solving Strategy: Reasonable Answers

Goal: Choose the most reasonable answer for a story problem.

Materials: Student Activity Book page 116

NCTM Standards:
Number and Operations
Problem Solving

Teaching Note

Math Background Being able to recognize if an answer is reasonable is a vital component to achieving competency in problem solving. Problem solving is more than just finding the right answer; it involves the ability to find and classify information in a form that makes it relevant to the problem being solved. Identifying reasonable answers is integral to this process.

▶ Discuss Reasonable Answers WHOLE CLASS

Write the following story problem on the board and read it to the class.

Claire has 8 red pencils. She has more blue pencils than red pencils. How many blue pencils could Claire have?

- Is 3 a reasonable answer for the problem? Why? Possible response: No, 3 is less than 8 and she has more than 8 blue pencils.
- What would be a reasonable answer to the problem? Possible response: 9, or any number larger than 8.

Discuss how you decide if an answer is reasonable. Explain to children that it is important to understand the situation of the story problem to decide if the answer would be reasonable.

Then write this story problem on the board and read it aloud.

Paige saw 3 goats, 7 pigs, and some horses at the fair. She saw 15 animals altogether. How many horses did Paige see?

- Is 16 a reasonable answer for the problem? Why? Possible response: No, because Paige only saw a total of 15 animals. 16 is greater than 15.

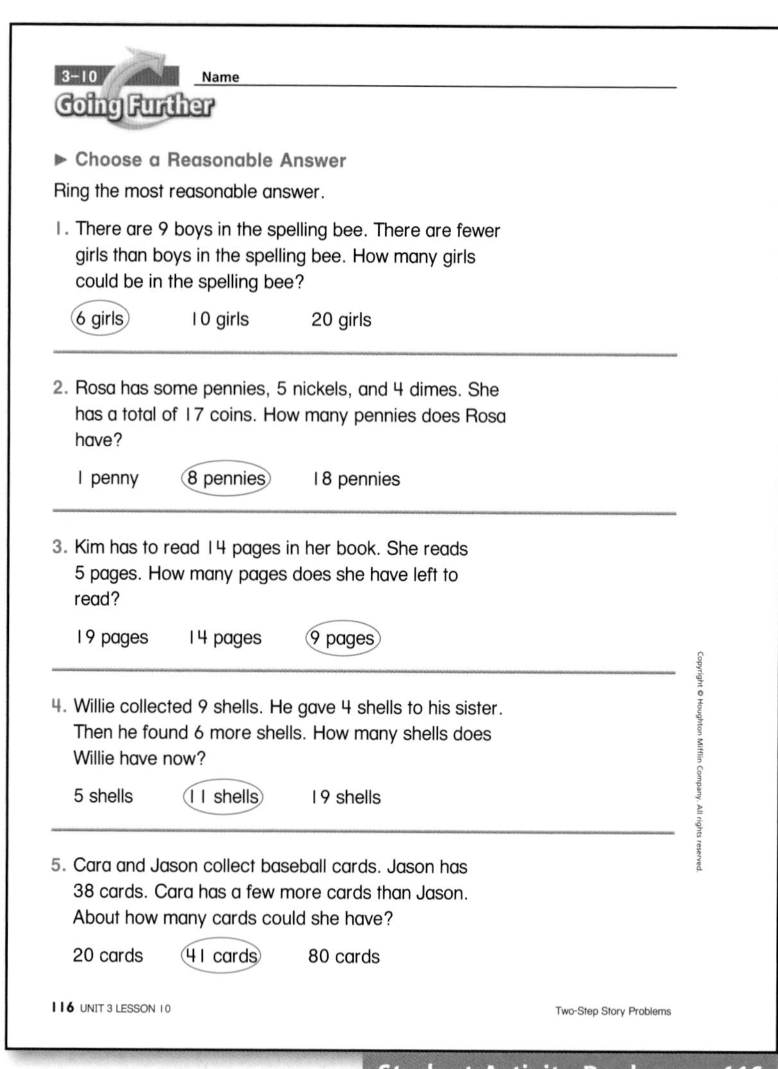

3-10 Going Further Name

▶ Choose a Reasonable Answer

Ring the most reasonable answer.

1. There are 9 boys in the spelling bee. There are fewer girls than boys in the spelling bee. How many girls could be in the spelling bee?

(6 girls) 10 girls 20 girls

2. Rosa has some pennies, 5 nickels, and 4 dimes. She has a total of 17 coins. How many pennies does Rosa have?

1 penny (8 pennies) 18 pennies

3. Kim has to read 14 pages in her book. She reads 5 pages. How many pages does she have left to read?

19 pages 14 pages (9 pages)

4. Willie collected 9 shells. He gave 4 shells to his sister. Then he found 6 more shells. How many shells does Willie have now?

5 shells (11 shells) 19 shells

5. Cara and Jason collect baseball cards. Jason has 38 cards. Cara has a few more cards than Jason. About how many cards could she have?

20 cards (41 cards) 80 cards

116 UNIT 3 LESSON 10 Two-Step Story Problems

Student Activity Book page 116

▶ Choose a Reasonable Answer PAIRS

Direct children's attention to Student Activity Book page 116.

Read the directions and explain that they need to ring the most reasonable answer. Explain that there are 3 possible choices for each story problem. Have children work in pairs to complete the page.

When children are done, have pairs share their answers and strategies for choosing each reasonable answer.

If time permits, you may wish to have children create their own story problems with 3 reasonable answer choices.

Intervention — Activity Card 3-10

Work — Activity Card 3-10 ●

Work: 1 child

Use:

- Highlighter or yellow marker
- Homework and Remembering page 73

1. Read problem 1 on Homework and Remembering page 73.
2. Highlight the last sentence of the problem. Ring the key word or words that identify the label for the answer.

1. Bessie counted 5 fish, 3 turtles, and some frogs in the pond. She counted 14 animals altogether. How many (frogs) are in the pond?

☐ frogs
label

3. Write the ringed word on the label line.
4. Repeat for each problem.

Unit 3, Lesson 10

Activity Note Each child needs a highlighter or yellow marker and Homework and Remembering p. 73. Have children share their work with classmates.

Math Writing Prompt

Hidden Questions Two-step problems have a hidden question. Choose one of the problems from the Class Activity page and tell what the hidden question is.

Software Support

Use *Soar to Success* for instruction of students needing targeted support for underlying skills.

On Level — Activity Card 3-10

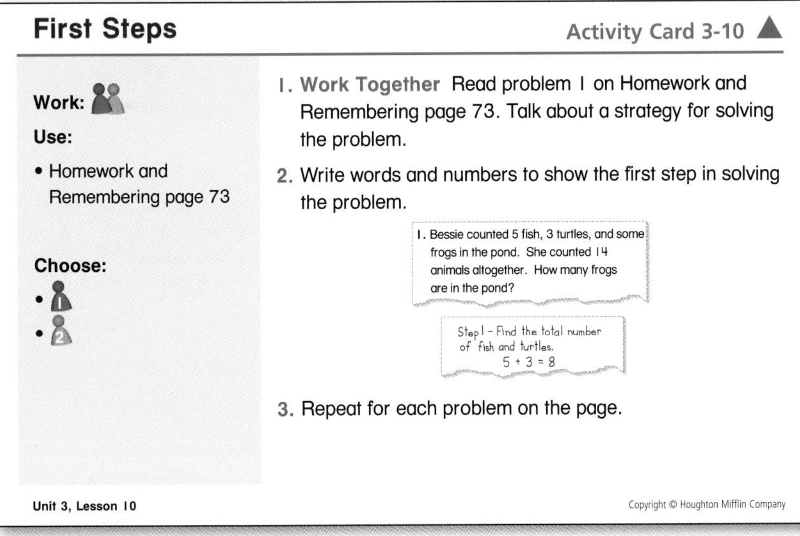

First Steps — Activity Card 3-10 ▲

Work: pairs

Use:

- Homework and Remembering page 73

Choose:

- 1
- 2

1. **Work Together** Read problem 1 on Homework and Remembering page 73. Talk about a strategy for solving the problem.
2. Write words and numbers to show the first step in solving the problem.

1. Bessie counted 5 fish, 3 turtles, and some frogs in the pond. She counted 14 animals altogether. How many frogs are in the pond?

Step 1 – Find the total number of fish and turtles.
5 + 3 = 8

3. Repeat for each problem on the page.

Unit 3, Lesson 10

Copyright © Houghton Mifflin Company

Activity Note Each pair needs Homework and Remembering p. 73. Check pair's work before they answer the problem.

Math Writing Prompt

Write Your Own Make your own two-step problem. Then write down the first question that you need to answer to solve the problem.

Software Support

Use *MegaMath* for review and reinforcement of the concepts and skills presented in this lesson.

Challenge — Activity Card 3-10

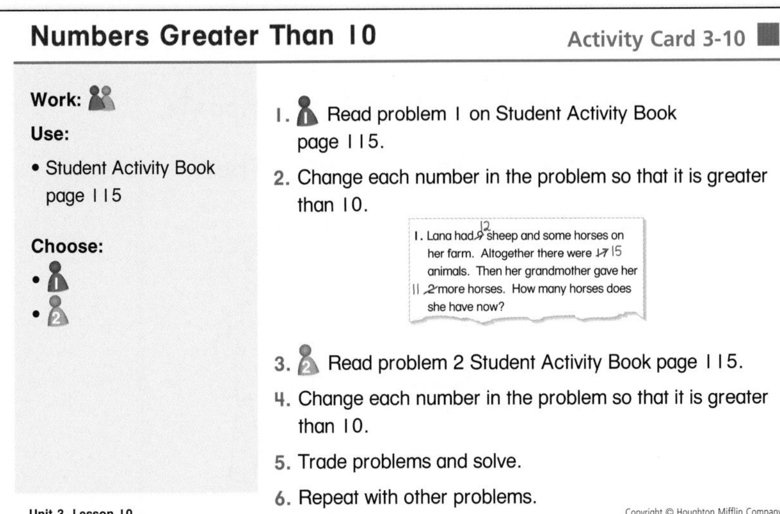

Numbers Greater Than 10 — Activity Card 3-10 ■

Work: pairs

Use:

- Student Activity Book page 115

Choose:

- 1
- 2

1. 1 Read problem 1 on Student Activity Book page 115.
2. Change each number in the problem so that it is greater than 10.

1. Lana had ~~9~~ 12 sheep and some horses on her farm. Altogether there were ~~17~~ 15 animals. Then her grandmother gave her 11 ~~2~~ more horses. How many horses does she have now?

3. 2 Read problem 2 Student Activity Book page 115.
4. Change each number in the problem so that it is greater than 10.
5. Trade problems and solve.
6. Repeat with other problems.

Unit 3, Lesson 10

Copyright © Houghton Mifflin Company

Activity Note Each pair needs Student Activity Book p. 115. Have each child change a different problem and than switch to solve.

Math Writing Prompt

Seven Elephants Write a two-step problem that has the answer *7 elephants*.

Software Support

Use *Destination Math* to take students beyond the concepts and skills presented in this lesson.

3 Homework and Targeted Practice

3–10
Homework

Goal: Additional Practice

This Homework page provides practice in solving problems with two steps.

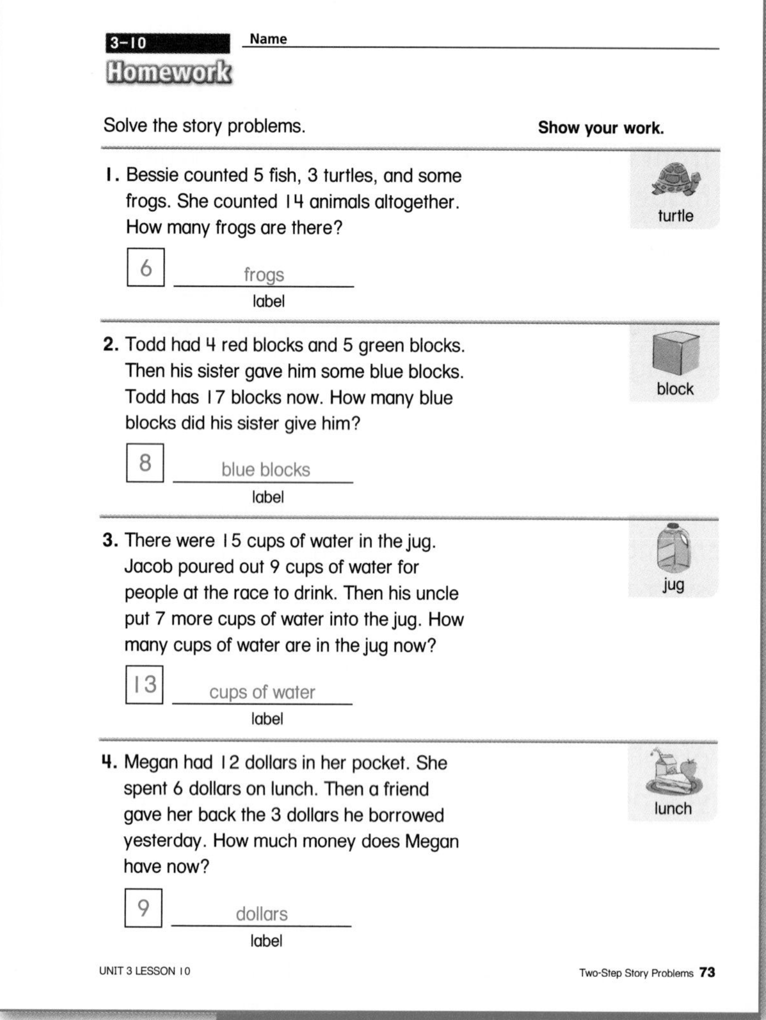

3–10 **Homework** Name ____________

Solve the story problems. **Show your work.**

1. Bessie counted 5 fish, 3 turtles, and some frogs. She counted 14 animals altogether. How many frogs are there?

turtle

6 frogs
label

2. Todd had 4 red blocks and 5 green blocks. Then his sister gave him some blue blocks. Todd has 17 blocks now. How many blue blocks did his sister give him?

block

8 blue blocks
label

3. There were 15 cups of water in the jug. Jacob poured out 9 cups of water for people at the race to drink. Then his uncle put 7 more cups of water into the jug. How many cups of water are in the jug now?

jug

13 cups of water
label

4. Megan had 12 dollars in her pocket. She spent 6 dollars on lunch. Then a friend gave her back the 3 dollars he borrowed yesterday. How much money does Megan have now?

lunch

9 dollars
label

UNIT 3 LESSON 10 Two-Step Story Problems **73**

Homework and Remembering page 73

3–10 **Targeted Practice** **Goal:** Solve story problems.

This Targeted Practice page can be used with children who need extra practice finding hidden information.

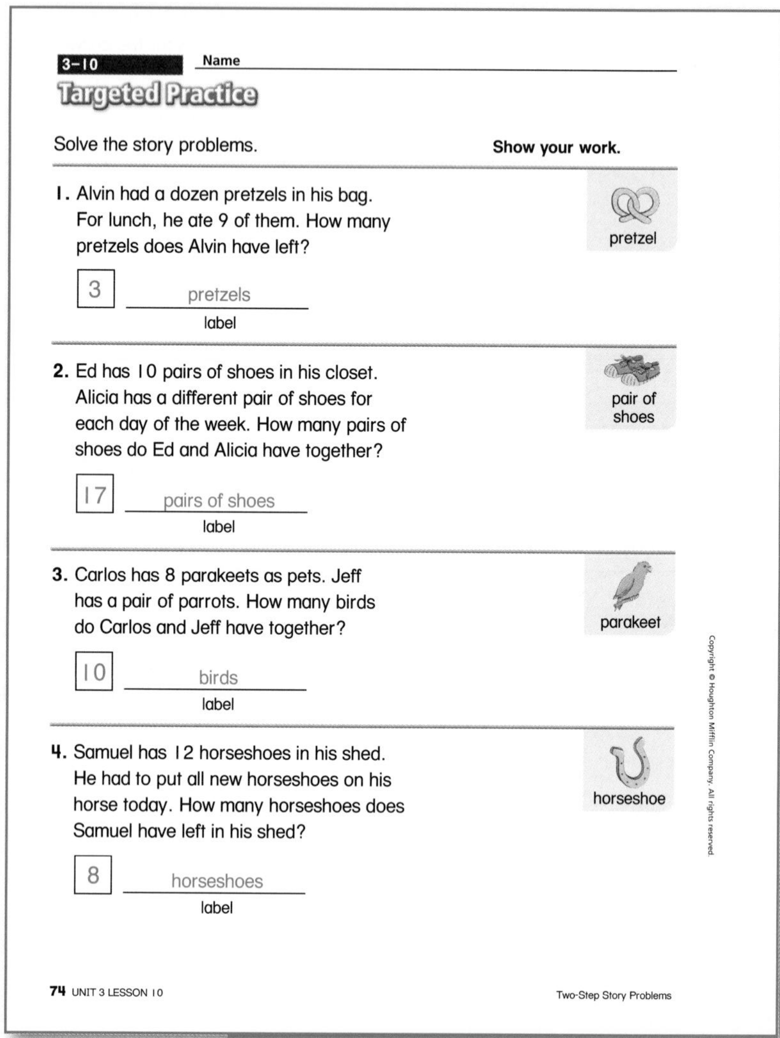

3–10 **Targeted Practice** Name ____________

Solve the story problems. **Show your work.**

1. Alvin had a dozen pretzels in his bag. For lunch, he ate 9 of them. How many pretzels does Alvin have left?

pretzel

3 pretzels
label

2. Ed has 10 pairs of shoes in his closet. Alicia has a different pair of shoes for each day of the week. How many pairs of shoes do Ed and Alicia have together?

pair of shoes

17 pairs of shoes
label

3. Carlos has 8 parakeets as pets. Jeff has a pair of parrots. How many birds do Carlos and Jeff have together?

parakeet

10 birds
label

4. Samuel has 12 horseshoes in his shed. He had to put all new horseshoes on his horse today. How many horseshoes does Samuel have left in his shed?

horseshoe

8 horseshoes
label

74 UNIT 3 LESSON 10 Two-Step Story Problems

Homework and Remembering page 74

Home or School Activity

Language Arts Connection

What Comes First? Have children practice sequencing events by thinking about the words *first* and *then.* Ask children to make a list of things that have to be done first before something else can happen. For example, a child might say, "First, I have to put toothpaste on my toothbrush and then I can brush my teeth." Or, "First my grandmother cooks the chicken and then we eat it for dinner." After children make a list, have them illustrate the two steps.

First, I have to put toothpaste on my toothbrush and then I can brush my teeth.

Strategies Using Doubles

Vocabulary
double
odd
even
Doubles Plus 1
Doubles Minus 1
two-step story problem

Lesson Objectives

- Find totals using the Doubles Plus 1 or the Doubles Minus 1 strategy.
- Understand that even numbers are those that can make two equal groups.

The Day at a Glance

Today's Goals	Materials	
1 Teaching the Lesson A1: Use doubles to solve addition and subtraction. A2: Solve two-step story problems.	**Lesson Activities** Student Activity Book p. 117 Homework and Remembering pp. 75–76 Counters Quick Quiz 2 (Assessment Guide)	**Going Further** Activity Cards 3-11 Student Activity Book p. 118 *Even Steven* and *Odd Todd* by Kathryn Cristaldi and Henry Morehouse Index cards Math Journals
2 Going Further ▸ Extra Practice ▸ Differentiated Instruction		
3 Homework and Spiral Review		

Use Math Talk today!

Keeping Skills Sharp

Quick Practice — 5 MINUTES

Goals: Write equation chains for 11. Add and subtract, totals ≤ 10. Make a ten when adding a number to 7, 8, or 9.

Materials: Yellow Math Mountain Cards (≤ 10) (from Unit 1 Lesson 16 or TRB M43–M44)

Equation Chains Have three children write equation chains for 11 on the board. (See Unit 1 Lesson 18.)

Math Mountains (≤ 10) Have children practice addition and subtraction with the Yellow Math Mountain Cards. (See Unit 3 Lesson 10.)

Class Make a Ten Write the $m + n$ list (left column) on the board. Do each row in turn. (See Unit 3 Lesson 1.)

Class Make a Ten

Student Leader 1 points to and says	Student Leader 2 shows fingers and says	Class says and Student Leader 2 writes = and
8 + 7	7 makes 2 and 5	8 + 2 + 5 = 10 + 5 = 15
8 + 3	3 makes 2 and 1	8 + 2 + 1 = 10 + 1 = 11
7 + 5	5 makes 3 and 2	7 + 3 + 2 = 10 + 2 = 12
7 + 7	7 makes 3 and 4	7 + 3 + 4 = 10 + 4 = 14
9 + 3	3 makes 1 and 2	9 + 1 + 2 = 10 + 2 = 12
7 + 6	6 makes 3 and 3	7 + 3 + 3 = 10 + 3 = 13
9 + 9	9 makes 1 and 8	9 + 1 + 8 = 10 + 8 = 18

Daily Routines

Comparing 2-Digit Quantities Using a Meter Stick, Using Number Flashes, Using the MathBoard (See pp. xxv–xxvi.)

▸ Led by Student Leaders

Money Routine Using the 120 Poster, Using the Money Flip Chart, Using the Number Path, Using Secret Code Cards (See pp. xxiii–xxv.)

▸ Led by Student Leaders

1 Teaching the Lesson

Activity 1

Doubles Plus 1 or Doubles Minus 1

 **40 MINUTES**

Goal: Use doubles to solve addition and subtraction.

Materials: Counters (10 per child)

 **NCTM Standards:**
Number and Operations
Communication

English Language Learners

Write *addition double* and *subtraction double* on the board. Write 1 + 1 = 2 on the board.
Say: ***Double* means the partners are the same.**

- **Beginning** Ask: **What are the partners?** 1 and 1 **Are they the same?** yes Write 2 − 1 = 1. Ask: **Are the partners the same?** yes Say: **This is a *subtraction double.***
- **Intermediate** Have children tell the addition doubles for 2 through 10. Have children work in pairs to tell and write the subtraction doubles.
- **Advanced** Ask: **What is the *subtraction double* with 1?** 2 − 1 = 1

▶ Review Addition and Subtraction Doubles

WHOLE CLASS

Remind children that addition or subtraction with the same partners is called *doubles.* This is because the total is double the partner (two times as big as the partner).

Write the addition doubles shown below on the board and have children give the totals.

Discuss the patterns children see in the addition doubles. Then ask them to help you build the subtraction equations that are related to each of the addition equations.

Addition Doubles	Subtraction Doubles
1 + 1 = 2	2 − 1 = 1
2 + 2 = 4	4 − 2 = 2
3 + 3 = 6	6 − 3 = 3
4 + 4 = 8	8 − 4 = 4
5 + 5 = 10	10 − 5 = 5
6 + 6 = 12	12 − 6 = 6
7 + 7 = 14	14 − 7 = 7
8 + 8 = 16	16 − 8 = 8
9 + 9 = 18	18 − 9 = 9
10 + 10 = 20	20 − 10 = 10

Leave this on the board for the next activity.

▶ Relate Odd and Even to Doubles WHOLE CLASS

Encourage children to discuss what they know about even numbers. Review that even numbers can form two equal, or even, groups with none left over.

Ask for Ideas Ask children how they might decide if 6 is an even or odd number. Here is one example: Draw two empty ovals on the board. Inside each oval draw 3 empty small circles. As you count with the children from 1 to 6, write 1 inside the first small circle in the first oval, 2 in the first small circle in the second oval, 3 in the second small circle of the first oval, 4 in the second, and so on. When you reach 6, ask children if there are 2 equal groups. yes Point out that 6 is an *even* number, because there are two equal, or even, groups.

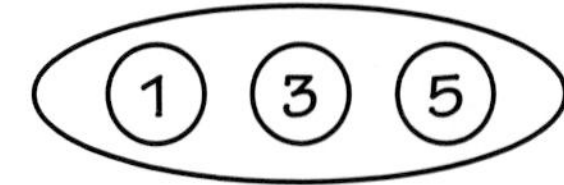

Ask how many numbers are in each group. 3 Relate those numbers to a doubles discussion: $3 + 3 = 6$, or $6 = 3 + 3$.

Allow time for partners or small groups to discuss whether 7 is an even number. Count and place the numbers in two ovals as you did for the number 6. Children should observe that because the first oval has one more number than the second oval, the number 7 is not even. Highlight the 7 and point out that it has no match in the second oval or group. Conclude that 7 is an *odd* number.

- Does this set of ovals show addition of doubles? No, because there are 4 in one group and 3 in the other group.

Repeat the activity for the numbers 8 through 18. Have students predict for each number whether it will be odd or even and relate the even numbers to doubles.

Activity continued ▶

Alternate Approach

Counters If children have difficulty sorting numbers into two ovals, have them use counters instead. For example, to determine if the number 6 is even, have children sort 6 counters into two equal groups. Children can also divide the counters into pairs; if there are no counters left over, the number is even.

Alternate Approach

Have students predict for each number whether it will be odd or even and relate their matching drawings to the rectangle of addition and subtraction doubles you wrote on the board earlier.

If you wish, you can ask students to extend the patterns they are finding (every other number is even, numbers that end in 0, 2, 4, 6, 8 are even) to somewhat larger numbers. Or you could have this discussion later in Unit 3 after all children understand numbers to 200.

1 Teaching the Lesson (continued)

Teaching Note

Watch For! Remind children that when they use the Doubles Plus 1 strategy, they only increase one of the addends in the doubles fact.

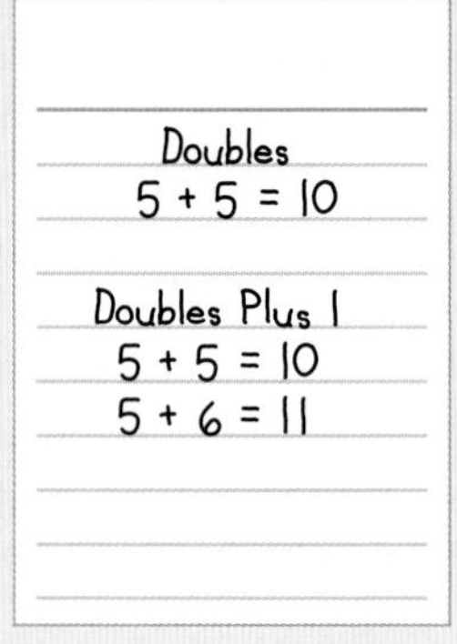

Doubles
5 + 5 = 10
Doubles Plus 1
5 + 5 = 10
5 + 6 = 11

▶ Discover Doubles Plus 1 and Doubles Minus 1 Strategies WHOLE CLASS

Ask children how they might use doubles to solve this problem:

$$7 + 6 = \square$$

Children may suggest:

Using a Double Plus 1	or	Using a Double Minus 1
6 + 6 = 12, so		7 + 7 = 14, so
7 + 6 = 13, 1 more than 12		7 + 6 = 13, 1 less than 14

Then have children try these. Possible responses:

$$7 + 8 = \square$$

7 + 7 = 14, so

7 + 8 = 15, 1 more than 14

8 + 8 = 16, so

7 + 8 = 15, 1 less than 16

$$6 + 5 = \square$$

5 + 5 = 10, so

6 + 5 = 11, 1 more than 10

6 + 6 = 12, so

6 + 5 = 11, 1 less than 12

$$8 + 9 = \square$$

8 + 8 = 16, so

8 + 9 = 17, 1 more than 16

9 + 9 = 18, so

8 + 9 = 17, 1 less than 18

See **Math Talk in Action** for a sample classroom discussion on solving this equation.

123 Math Talk in Action

Keisha: We have to find 8 + 9.

Jeremy: Let's start with 8 + 8. That's 16.

Keisha: So, 8 + 9 must be 1 more than 16. That's 17. 8 + 9 = 17

Jeremy: What if we try it by starting with 9 + 9?

Keisha: 9 + 9 = 18, so 8 + 9 is 1 less, 17.

Activity 2

Practice Two-Step Story Problems

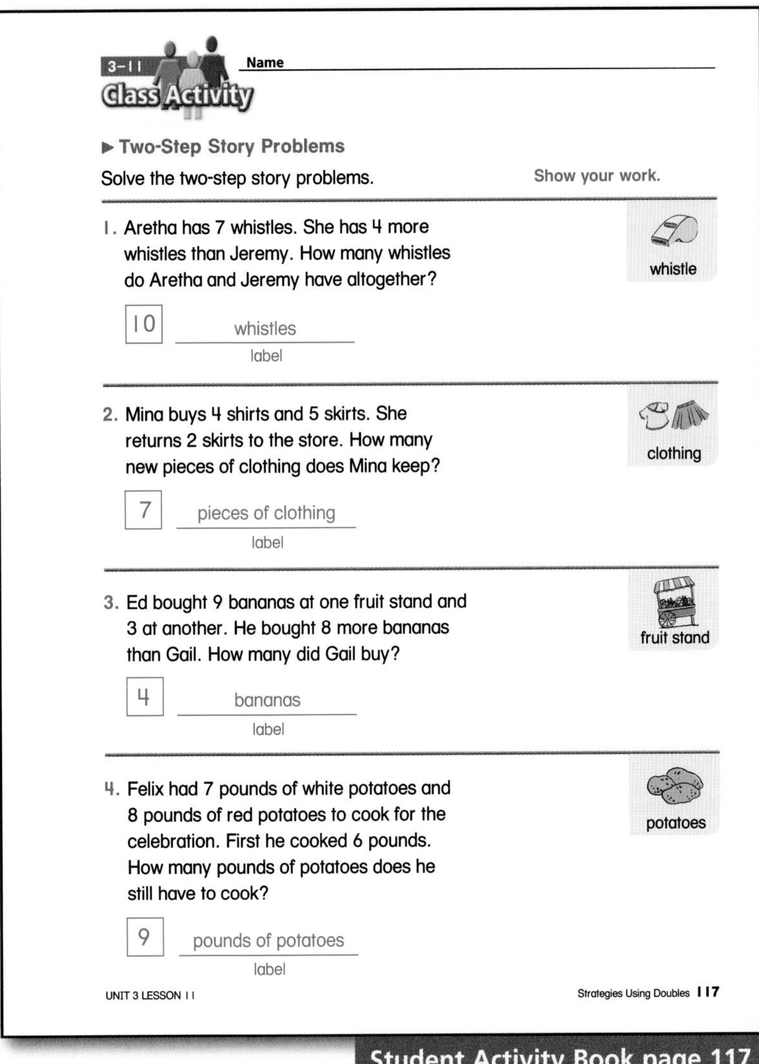

3-11 Class Activity

Name

▶ Two-Step Story Problems

Solve the two-step story problems. Show your work.

1. Aretha has 7 whistles. She has 4 more whistles than Jeremy. How many whistles do Aretha and Jeremy have altogether?

10 whistles
label

2. Mina buys 4 shirts and 5 skirts. She returns 2 skirts to the store. How many new pieces of clothing does Mina keep?

7 pieces of clothing
label

3. Ed bought 9 bananas at one fruit stand and 3 at another. He bought 8 more bananas than Gail. How many did Gail buy?

4 bananas
label

4. Felix had 7 pounds of white potatoes and 8 pounds of red potatoes to cook for the celebration. First he cooked 6 pounds. How many pounds of potatoes does he still have to cook?

9 pounds of potatoes
label

UNIT 3 LESSON 11 Strategies Using Doubles 117

Student Activity Book page 117

▶ Two-Step Story Problems PAIRS

Have children work in Helping Pairs to solve each story problem on Student Activity Book page 117. Encourage them to use a variety of strategies to solve each problem and to show their work.

Use this time to provide extra help to children who are experiencing difficulty. You might want to work with a group of children at the board.

15 MINUTES

Goal: Solve two-step story problems.

Materials: Student Activity Book page 117

NCTM Standards:
Number and Operations
Communication

Ongoing Assessment

Ask children to show or explain how they would answer these questions:

- ▶ Is 8 an even number?
- ▶ What is 6 + 7?
- ▶ What is 9 + 8?

Quick Quiz

See Assessment Guide for Unit 3 Quick Quiz 2.

2 Going Further

Extra Practice

Goal: Add using the Doubles Plus 1 and the Doubles Minus 1 strategies.

Materials: Student Activity Book page 118

NCTM Standard:
Number and Operations

▶ Add Using Doubles Plus 1 and Doubles Minus 1 Strategies WHOLE CLASS

Direct children's attention to the first section of Student Activity Book page 118. Use **Solve and Discuss** or have students solve independently and/or in **Helping Partners** or small groups.

▶ Solve the Riddle INDIVIDUALS

Direct children's attention to the riddle. Read it aloud and discuss possible answers. Explain that children can find the answer by using the lines and numbers below the riddle. Help children match the first line and number (9) with the letter A in Part 1 and write "A" on the first line. When children match all of the numbers, they should find that the answer is "a towel."

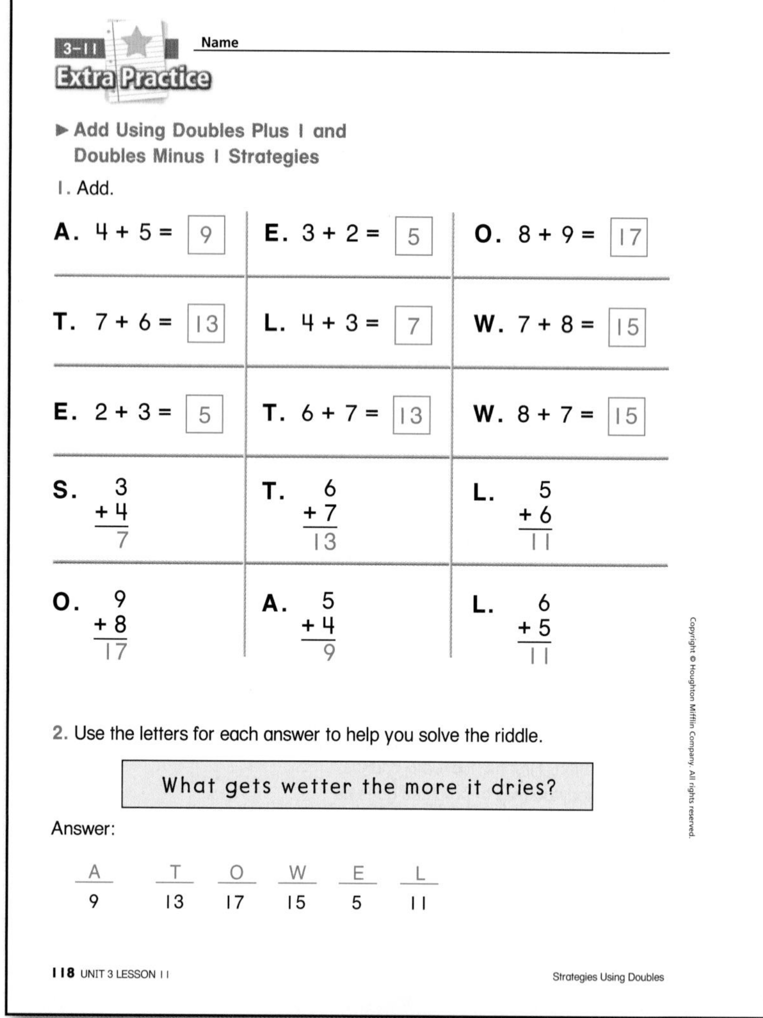

3-11 Extra Practice Name

▶ Add Using Doubles Plus 1 and Doubles Minus 1 Strategies

1. Add.

A. 4 + 5 = 9	E. 3 + 2 = 5	O. 8 + 9 = 17
T. 7 + 6 = 13	L. 4 + 3 = 7	W. 7 + 8 = 15
E. 2 + 3 = 5	T. 6 + 7 = 13	W. 8 + 7 = 15
S. 3 + 4 = 7	T. 6 + 7 = 13	L. 5 + 6 = 11
O. 9 + 8 = 17	A. 5 + 4 = 9	L. 6 + 5 = 11

2. Use the letters for each answer to help you solve the riddle.

What gets wetter the more it dries?

Answer:

A	T	O	W	E	L
9	13	17	15	5	11

118 UNIT 3 LESSON 11 Strategies Using Doubles

Student Activity Book page 118

Differentiated Instruction

Advanced Learners To extend the activity, children can use the letters on the page to create their own riddle. Remind children to number the lines for their answer correctly. Have children give their riddle to a classmate to solve.

Intervention Activity Card 3-11

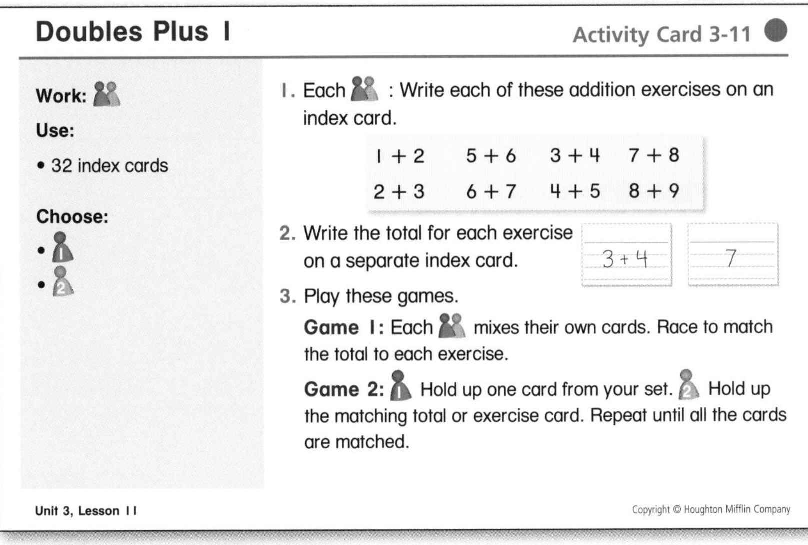

Doubles Plus 1 Activity Card 3-11

Work: pairs
Use:
- 32 index cards

Choose:
- 1
- 2

1. Each pair: Write each of these addition exercises on an index card.

1 + 2	5 + 6	3 + 4	7 + 8
2 + 3	6 + 7	4 + 5	8 + 9

2. Write the total for each exercise on a separate index card. 3 + 4 | 7
3. Play these games.
   Game 1: Each pair mixes their own cards. Race to match the total to each exercise.
   Game 2: 1 Hold up one card from your set. 2 Hold up the matching total or exercise card. Repeat until all the cards are matched.

Unit 3, Lesson 11

Activity Note Each pair needs 32 index cards. Each child writes the problems and sums on an index card. Review how to play each game with children.

Math Writing Prompt

Explain Explain how to use Double Plus 1 to find the total of 6 and 7.

Software Support

Use *Soar to Success* for instruction of students needing targeted support for underlying skills.

On Level Activity Card 3-11

Even or Odd? Activity Card 3-11

Work: individual
Use:
- paper

1. Copy and then complete the chart. Use a method to decide if each number is even or odd.

Number	Odd or Even?
18	
35	
22	
13	
89	

2. Math Talk How did you decide if each number was even or odd? Explain your thinking.

Unit 3, Lesson 11

Activity Note Each child has to copy the chart on the activity card. Have children share how they decided if a number was even or odd.

Math Writing Prompt

Explain Your Thinking How do you know that 17 is an odd number?

Software Support

Use *MegaMath* for review and reinforcement of the concepts and skills presented in this lesson.

Challenge Activity Card 3-11

Make a Rule Activity Card 3-11

Work: individual
Use:
- paper

1. Copy and then complete the chart. Use a method to decide if each number is even or odd.

Number	Odd or Even?
18	
35	
22	
13	
89	

2. Math Talk How did you decide if each number was even or odd? Explain your thinking.
3. Find a rule that you can quickly use to determine if a number is even or odd. Explain your rule to others.

Unit 3, Lesson 11

Activity Note Each child has to copy the chart on the activity card. Have children make a rule to determine if a number is even or odd.

Math Writing Prompt

Investigate Math If I add two odd numbers, will the total be even or odd? Explain.

Software Support

Use *Destination Math* to take students beyond the concepts and skills presented in this lesson.

3 Homework and Spiral Review

Goal: Additional Practice

This Homework page provides practice solving two-step story problems.

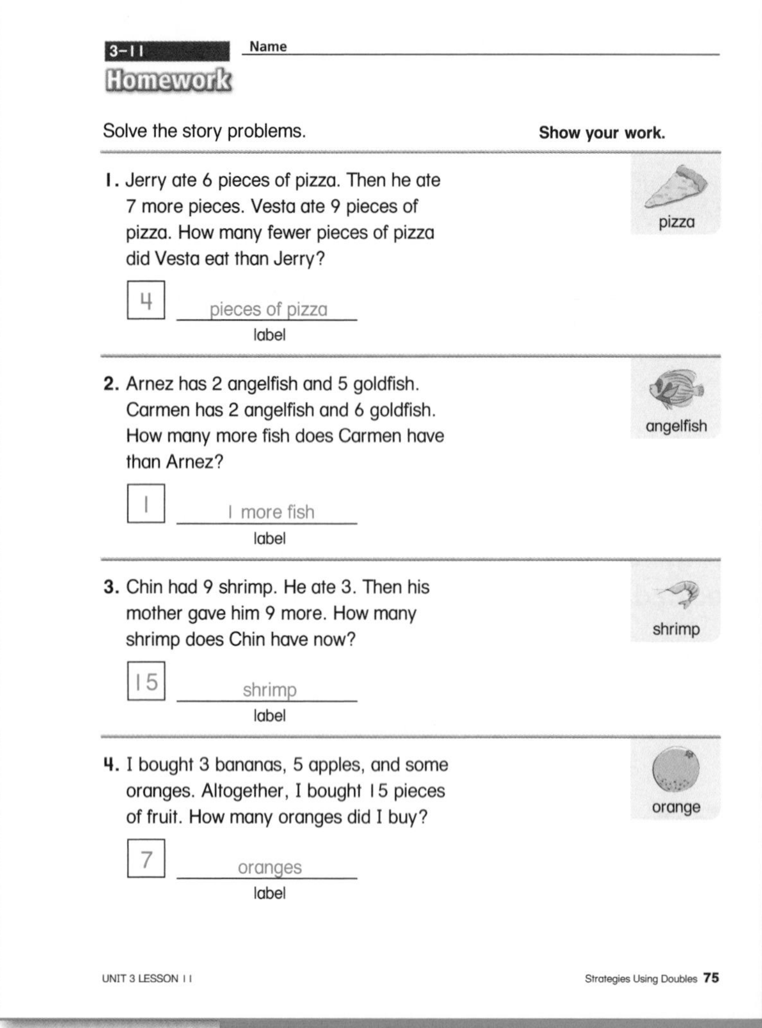

3-11 Homework   Name

Solve the story problems.   **Show your work.**

1. Jerry ate 6 pieces of pizza. Then he ate 7 more pieces. Vesta ate 9 pieces of pizza. How many fewer pieces of pizza did Vesta eat than Jerry?

pizza

4 pieces of pizza
label

2. Arnez has 2 angelfish and 5 goldfish. Carmen has 2 angelfish and 6 goldfish. How many more fish does Carmen have than Arnez?

angelfish

1 I more fish
label

3. Chin had 9 shrimp. He ate 3. Then his mother gave him 9 more. How many shrimp does Chin have now?

shrimp

15 shrimp
label

4. I bought 3 bananas, 5 apples, and some oranges. Altogether, I bought 15 pieces of fruit. How many oranges did I buy?

orange

7 oranges
label

UNIT 3 LESSON 11   Strategies Using Doubles 75

Homework and Remembering page 75

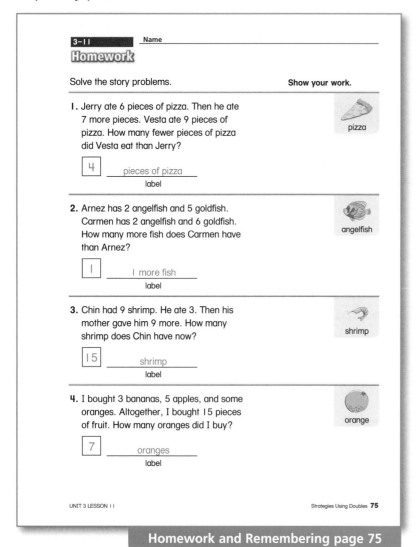

Goal: Spiral Review

This Remembering activity would be appropriate anytime after today's lesson.

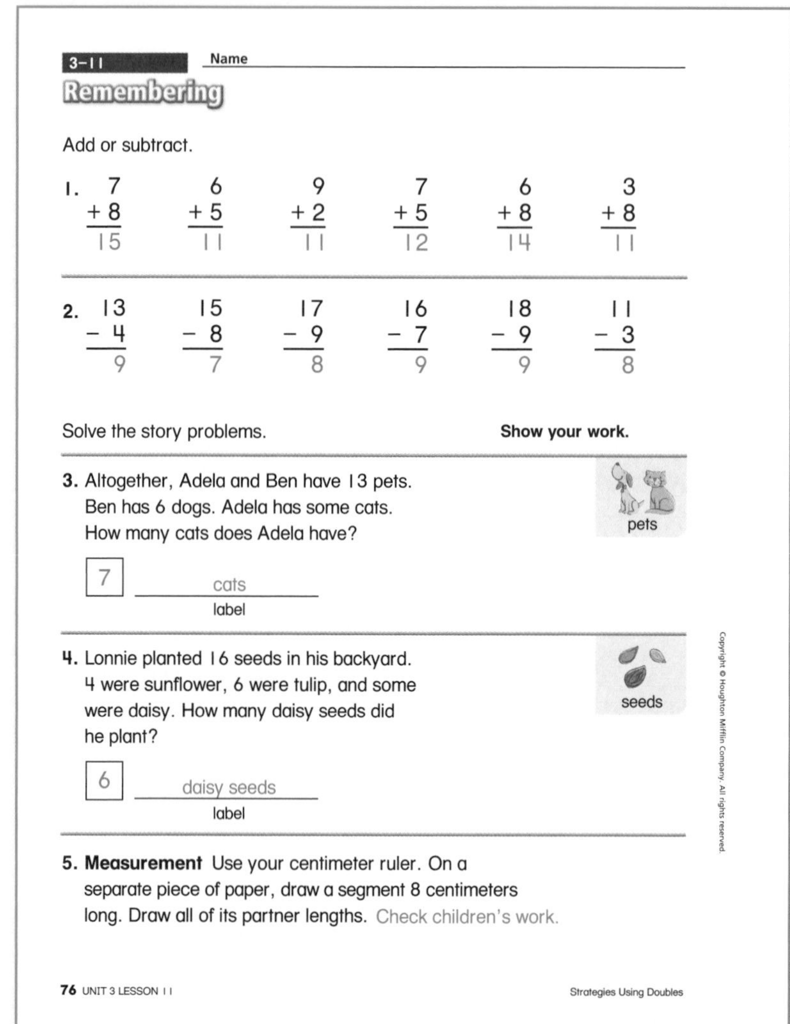

3-11 Remembering   Name

Add or subtract.

1. $7 + 8 = 15$ $6 + 5 = 11$ $9 + 2 = 11$ $7 + 5 = 12$ $6 + 8 = 14$ $3 + 8 = 11$

2. $13 - 4 = 9$ $15 - 8 = 7$ $17 - 9 = 8$ $16 - 7 = 9$ $18 - 9 = 9$ $11 - 3 = 8$

Solve the story problems.   **Show your work.**

3. Altogether, Adela and Ben have 13 pets. Ben has 6 dogs. Adela has some cats. How many cats does Adela have?

pets

7 cats
label

4. Lonnie planted 16 seeds in his backyard. 4 were sunflower, 6 were tulip, and some were daisy. How many daisy seeds did he plant?

seeds

6 daisy seeds
label

5. Measurement Use your centimeter ruler. On a separate piece of paper, draw a segment 8 centimeters long. Draw all of its partner lengths. Check children's work.

76 UNIT 3 LESSON 11   Strategies Using Doubles

Homework and Remembering page 76

Home or School Activity

Literature Connection

Odd and Even Numbers *Even Steven and Odd Todd* by Kathryn Cristaldi and Henry Morehouse (Cartwheel, 1996) reinforces the concept of even and odd numbers. This book tells an amusing story about two boys, Steven and Todd. Steven likes everything even and Todd likes everything odd.

Read this book aloud or have children read it independently. As children listen to or read the story, have them make a list of the even numbers in the story, and another list of the odd numbers in the story.

Mixed Practice and Writing Story Problems

Vocabulary

change problem
collection problem
comparison problem
hidden information
two-step problem

Lesson Objectives

- Create story problems.
- Solve story problems.

The Day at a Glance

Today's Goals	Materials	
1 Teaching the Lesson **A1:** Write story problems for classmates to solve. **A2:** Solve story problems.	**Lesson Activities** Student Activity Book p. 119 Homework and Remembering pp. 77–78	**Going Further** Activity Cards 3-12 Student Activity Book p. 120 Chart paper Index cards Math Journals
2 Going Further ▶ Extra Practice ▶ Differentiated Instruction		
3 Homework and Targeted Practice		

Use Math Talk today!

Keeping Skills Sharp

Quick Practice — 5 MINUTES

Goals: Subtract with teen totals. Make a ten when adding a number to 6, 7, 8, or 9.

Materials: Parachute Drop—Teen Totals (from Unit 3 Lesson 7 or TRB M57)

Class Make a Ten Write the $m + n$ list (left column) on the board. Do each row in turn. (See Unit 3 Lesson 1.)

Parachute Drop—Teen Totals Review how to do the Parachute Drop activity and explain that today children will just practice column 3. Tell children they are practicing for a Secret Code Card subtraction race in the next lesson. Children who finish early may practice the mystery addition problems in the middle column.

Class Make a Ten

Student Leader 1 points to and says	Student Leader 2 shows fingers and says	Class says and Student Leader 2 writes = and
6 + 7	7 makes 4 and 3	6 + 4 + 3 = 10 + 3 = 13
9 + 2	2 makes 1 and 1	9 + 1 + 1 = 10 + 1 = 11
9 + 6	6 makes 1 and 5	9 + 1 + 5 = 10 + 5 = 15
8 + 3	3 makes 2 and 1	8 + 2 + 1 = 10 + 1 = 11
7 + 7	7 makes 3 and 4	7 + 3 + 4 = 10 + 4 = 14
9 + 7	7 makes 1 and 6	9 + 1 + 6 = 10 + 6 = 16
8 + 5	5 makes 2 and 3	8 + 2 + 3 = 10 + 3 = 13

Daily Routines

Comparing 2-Digit Quantities Using a Meter Stick, Using Number Flashes, Using the MathBoard (See pp. xxv–xxvi.)

▶ Led by Student Leaders

Money Routine Using the 120 Poster, Using the Money Flip Chart, Using the Number Path, Using Secret Code Cards (See pp. xxiii–xxv.)

▶ Led by Student Leaders

1 Teaching the Lesson

Activity 1

Write Story Problems

 35 MINUTES

Goal: Write story problems for classmates to solve.

 **NCTM Standards:**
Number and Operations
Communication

The Learning Classroom

Building Concepts Children may have difficulty generating ideas for story problems. You may want to list the types of problems (collection, two-step, etc.) on the board.

Types of problems:
Change plus problems
Change minus problems
Collection problems
Comparison problems
Problems with not enough, extra, or hidden information
Two-step problems

English Language Learners

Have children suggest things they added and subtracted in previous lessons. Model how to write story problems on the board.

- **Beginning** Write and label examples of each type of story problem. Have children choose one and rewrite it with new numbers.
- **Intermediate** Write the steps. *1. Choose a type of problem. 2. Decide what your story is about. 3. Decide what your total and partners are.*
- **Advanced** Have children work in pairs to write their stories. Walk around and help children having trouble.

▶ Brainstorm Ideas for Story Problems WHOLE CLASS

Ask for Ideas Have children begin by brainstorming ideas for story problems. Tell children that they can use these ideas to write story problems or they can make up something new.

As children generate specific examples, (such as giving pencils away, needing some amount more of beads, grouping daisies and roses into a vase of flowers), list them on the board and write down the kind of problem it is.

Help the class create 1 or 2 problems together. Leave the problems on the board while the children write their own problems.

▶ Writing Story Problems INDIVIDUALS

Have children write their own story problems that you can collect.

Explain that writing an interesting problem is more important than spelling correctly. Remind them to write problems that are difficult. Emphasize to children that they can make problems more difficult by writing a difficult problem type, not by using big numbers. Tell children that tomorrow they will solve some of the problems they have written today.

Collect children's problems. Choose a variety of problems for children to solve in the next lesson.

Activity 2

Solve Story Problems

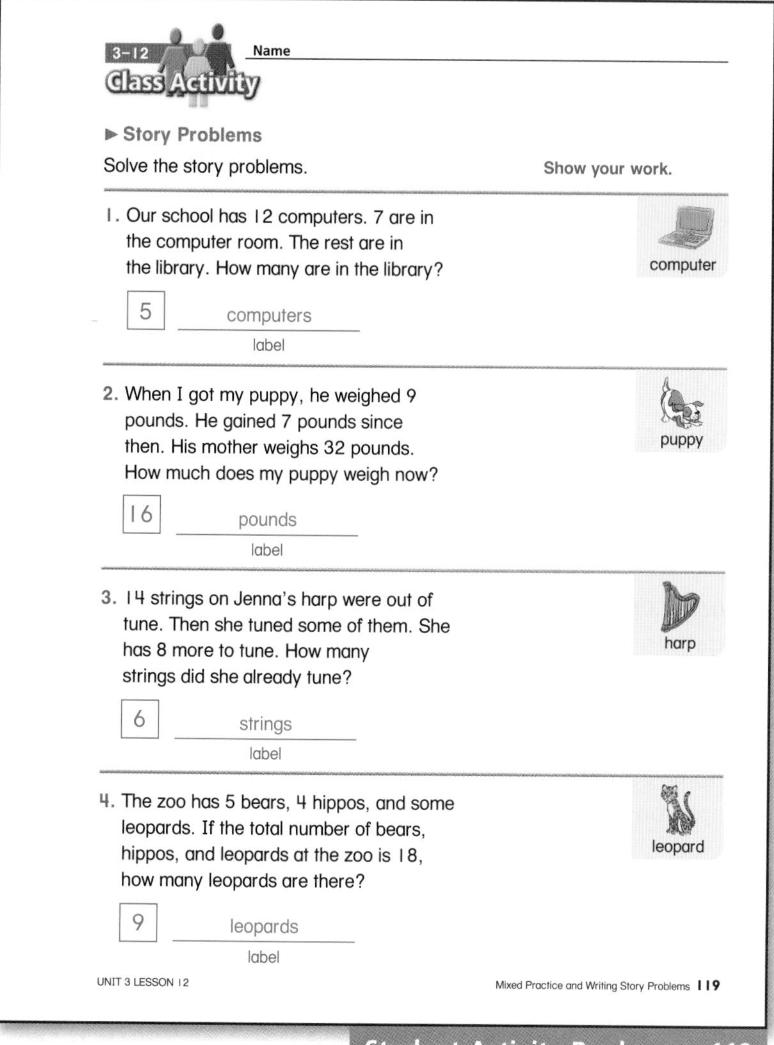

3–12 Class Activity

Name

▶ Story Problems

Solve the story problems. Show your work.

1. Our school has 12 computers. 7 are in the computer room. The rest are in the library. How many are in the library?

computer

5 computers
label

2. When I got my puppy, he weighed 9 pounds. He gained 7 pounds since then. His mother weighs 32 pounds. How much does my puppy weigh now?

puppy

16 pounds
label

3. 14 strings on Jenna's harp were out of tune. Then she tuned some of them. She has 8 more to tune. How many strings did she already tune?

harp

6 strings
label

4. The zoo has 5 bears, 4 hippos, and some leopards. If the total number of bears, hippos, and leopards at the zoo is 18, how many leopards are there?

leopard

9 leopards
label

UNIT 3 LESSON 12 Mixed Practice and Writing Story Problems 119

Student Activity Book page 119

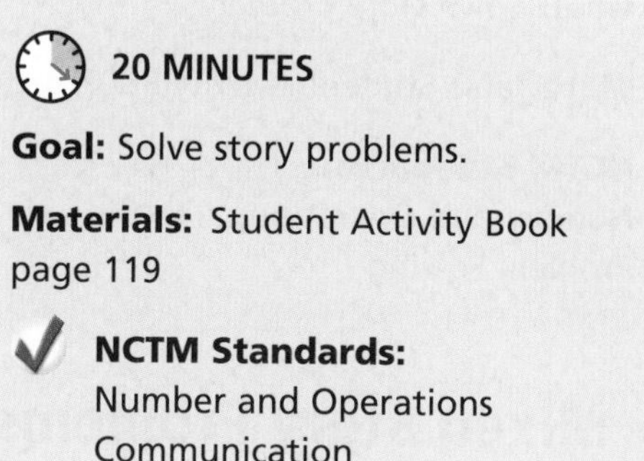

20 MINUTES

Goal: Solve story problems.

Materials: Student Activity Book page 119

NCTM Standards:
Number and Operations
Communication

▶ Story Problems WHOLE CLASS

Use the **Solve and Discuss** structure to work through the problems on Student Activity Book page 119. Have three to six children solve a few problems at the board while the others solve problems at their seats.

Remind the class to be good listeners and to ask questions.

Ongoing Assessment

Ask children to choose a problem on Student Activity Book page 119 and tell which operation or operations they used to solve the problem and explain why.

2 Going Further

Extra Practice

Goal: Solve story problems.

Materials: Student Activity Book page 120

NCTM Standards:
Number and Operations
Problem Solving

▶ Mixed Story Problems INDIVIDUALS

Direct children's attention to Student Activity Book page 120. Have children solve independently, or in **Helping Partners**, or use **Solve and Discuss**. If you use the former two, identify children to go to the board to put up their solutions while the rest of the class is working. This will save time. Children can also write solutions to share on their MathBoard or on overhead projector film.

3-12 Extra Practice

Name ____________

▶ Mixed Story Problems

Solve the story problems. Show your work.

1. There were 7 bicycles in the rack. 5 were red and 2 were blue. Then 6 more children put their bicycles in the rack. How many bicycles are in the rack now? bicycle

13 bicycles
label

2. Corey has 6 books in his bag. He has 6 more books in his bag than Angela has in her bag. How many books are there in the two bags altogether? book

6 books
label

3. The ice cube tray holds 14 ice cubes. Kacey and Riley put some ice cubes in their glasses. Kacey put 5 cubes in her glass. 3 cubes were left in the tray. How many cubes did Riley put in his glass? ice cube

6 cubes
label

4. The cook is making a dozen toasted cheese sandwiches. He has made 7. How many more does he have to make? cheese

5 sandwiches
label

120 UNIT 3 LESSON 12 Mixed Practice and Writing Story Problems

Student Activity Book page 120

See **Math Talk in Action** for possible class discussion of exercise 3.

Math Talk in Action

Anthony, how did you find the answer to exercise 3?

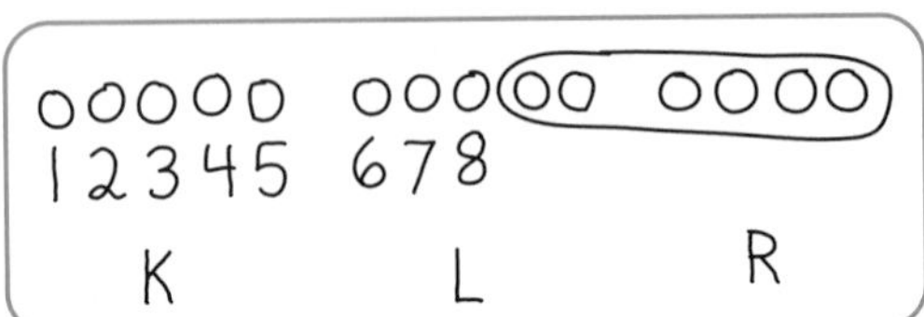

Anthony: First I made 14 circles. Then I counted 5 because Kacey had 5 ice cubes. Then I counted the 3 that were left. The circles left over show how many ice cubes Riley had in his glass.

Larisa: Why did you make 14 circles?

Anthony: I made 14 circles because there are 14 ice cubes altogether.

Larisa: In your drawing, you counted, 6, 7, 8. Can you explain that?

Anthony: I already counted 5. I needed to count 3 more, so I counted on 3 more from 5.

Did anyone solve this problem a different way?

Renee: I used the numbers in the problem to write an equation.

$$\begin{array}{r} 14 \\ -\ 8 \\ \hline 6 \end{array}$$

Galo: Why did you use the number 8?

Renee: I added 5 plus 3 to get 8.

Galo: How did you know to add 5 and 3?

Renee: I knew that there were 14 ice cubes in all. Kacey had 5, Riley had some, and there were 3 left over. So, 5 plus 3 plus another number equals 14. I added 5 plus 3 to get 8.

Dominique: Why did you subtract?

Renee: 14 is the total. 8 is a partner. I knew if I subtracted 8, I would find the other partner.

Intervention — Activity Card 3-12

Types of Story Problems
Activity Card 3-12 ●

Work: 
Use:
- Chart paper

Choose:
- 1
- 2
- 3

There are 6 red apples in the bowl.
There are 4 green apples in the bowl.

1. **Work Together** Use the sentences above to write a collection problem.
2. Use the sentences above to write a comparison problem.
3. Share your problems with another group. Solve the problems.

Unit 3, Lesson 12

Activity Note Each group needs chart paper. Have groups check their work with other groups to make sure there are two different types of problems.

Math Writing Prompt
Key Words What are some key words that can help you write a comparison problem?

Software Support
Use *Soar to Success* for instruction of students needing targeted support for underlying skills.

On Level — Activity Card 3-12

Yard Sale Problems
Activity Card 3-12 ▲

Work: 
Use:
- paper

Choose:
- 1
- 2
- 3

Yard Sale	
Item	Price
Books	10¢ each
Buttons	2¢ each
Pencils	3¢ each
Crayons	1¢ each
Marbles	9¢ each

1. Use the information in the table above to write and solve a two-step problem.
2. Use the information in the table above to write and solve a problem with extra information.
3. Trade your problems with another group. Solve the new problems.

Unit 3, Lesson 12

Activity Note Review items and costs in the yard sale table. Have groups write two problems using the information in the table.

Math Writing Prompt
Compare and Contrast How are problems with hidden information like problems with not enough information? How are they different?

Software Support
Use *MegaMath* for review and reinforcement of the concepts and skills presented in this lesson.

Challenge — Activity Card 3-12

Write Your Own
Activity Card 3-12 ■

Work: 
Use:
- Index cards

Choose:
- 1
- 2
- 3

1. Use the information in the table to the right to write and solve a three-step problem.
2. Use the information in the table to the right to write and solve a problem that requires adding three numbers.
3. Use the information in the table above to write and solve a problem with hidden information.

Yard Sale	
Item	Price
Books	10¢ each
Buttons	2¢ each
Pencils	3¢ each
Crayons	1¢ each
Marbles	9¢ each

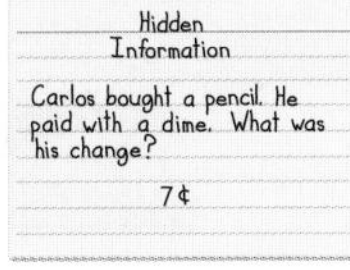

Hidden Information
Carlos bought a pencil. He paid with a dime. What was his change?
7¢

Unit 3, Lesson 12

Activity Note Review items and costs in the yard sale table. Have groups write three problems using the information in the table. Have groups trade and solve the problems.

Math Writing Prompt
Write Your Own Write a two-step problem with hidden information that has the answer *5 cents*.

DESTINATION Math®

Software Support
Use *Destination Math* to take students beyond the concepts and skills presented in this lesson.

3 Homework and Targeted Practice

3-12 Homework **Goal:** Additional Practice

This Homework page provides practice in solving a variety of story problems.

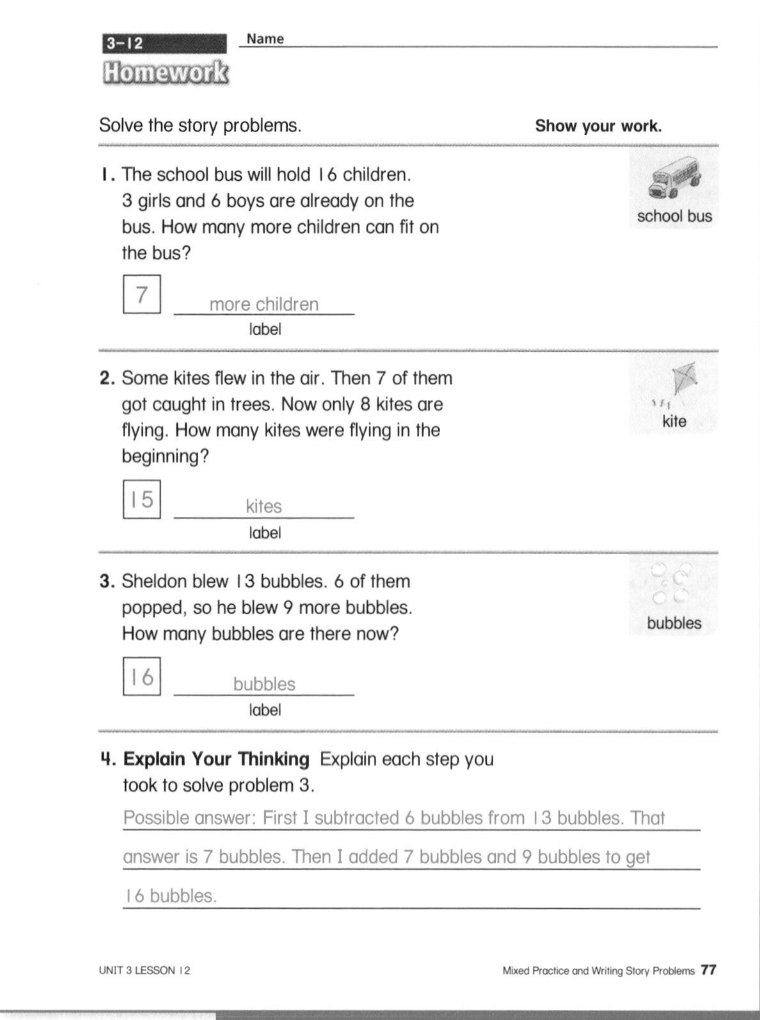

3-12 Name

Homework

Solve the story problems. **Show your work.**

1. The school bus will hold 16 children. 3 girls and 6 boys are already on the bus. How many more children can fit on the bus?

   school bus

   7 more children
   label

2. Some kites flew in the air. Then 7 of them got caught in trees. Now only 8 kites are flying. How many kites were flying in the beginning?

   kite

   15 kites
   label

3. Sheldon blew 13 bubbles. 6 of them popped, so he blew 9 more bubbles. How many bubbles are there now?

   bubbles

   16 bubbles
   label

4. **Explain Your Thinking** Explain each step you took to solve problem 3.

   Possible answer: First I subtracted 6 bubbles from 13 bubbles. That answer is 7 bubbles. Then I added 7 bubbles and 9 bubbles to get 16 bubbles.

UNIT 3 LESSON 12 Mixed Practice and Writing Story Problems 77

Homework and Remembering page 77

3-12 Targeted Practice **Goal:** Solve story problems.

This Targeted Practice page can be used with children who need extra practice in solving story problems.

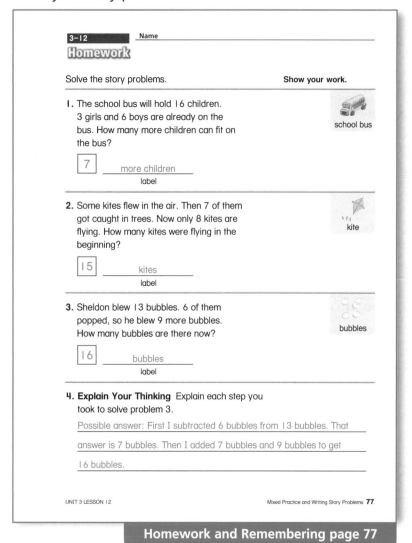

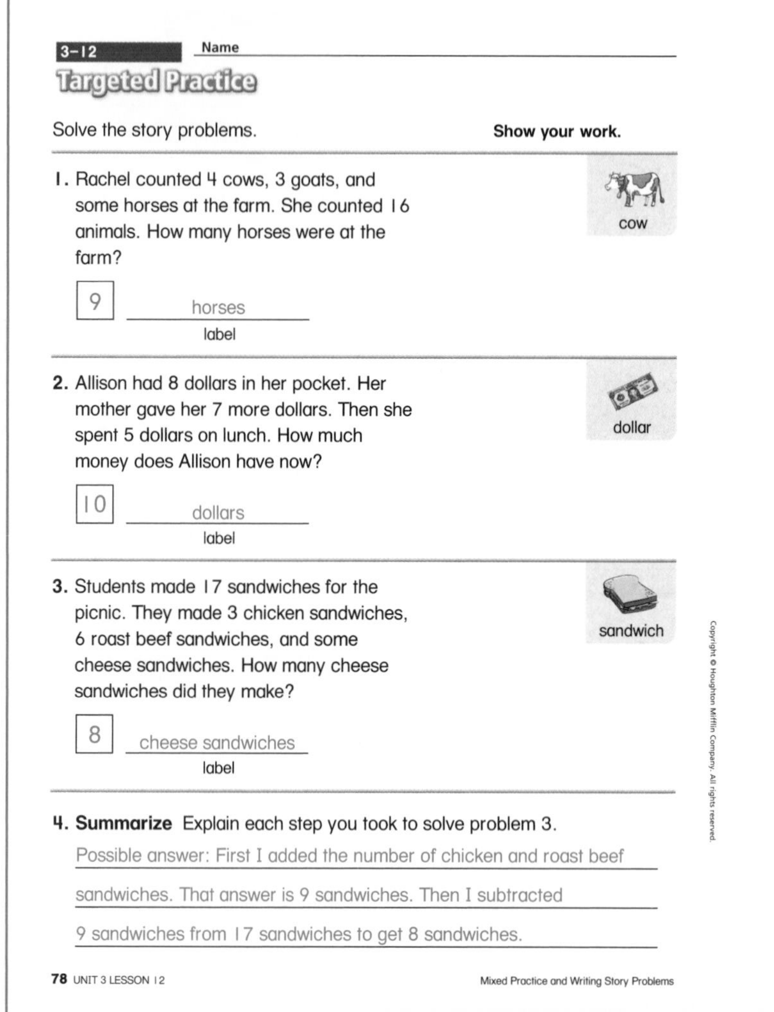

3-12 Name

Targeted Practice

Solve the story problems. **Show your work.**

1. Rachel counted 4 cows, 3 goats, and some horses at the farm. She counted 16 animals. How many horses were at the farm?

   cow

   9 horses
   label

2. Allison had 8 dollars in her pocket. Her mother gave her 7 more dollars. Then she spent 5 dollars on lunch. How much money does Allison have now?

   dollar

   10 dollars
   label

3. Students made 17 sandwiches for the picnic. They made 3 chicken sandwiches, 6 roast beef sandwiches, and some cheese sandwiches. How many cheese sandwiches did they make?

   sandwich

   8 cheese sandwiches
   label

4. **Summarize** Explain each step you took to solve problem 3.

   Possible answer: First I added the number of chicken and roast beef sandwiches. That answer is 9 sandwiches. Then I subtracted 9 sandwiches from 17 sandwiches to get 8 sandwiches.

78 UNIT 3 LESSON 12 Mixed Practice and Writing Story Problems

Homework and Remembering page 78

Home or School Activity

Technology Connection

Search for Information Have children use approved Internet resources to find information such as the following:

- the number of cups in a quart
- the number of legs on a ladybug
- the number of letters in President John F. Kennedy's middle name

Then have children write and solve story problems using the information they found.

1. My mother bought 2
quarts of ice cream.
How many cups is that?

Mixed Practice

Vocabulary

change problem
collection problem
comparison problem
hidden information
two-step problem

Lesson Objectives

- Solve challenging story problems.
- Review addition, mystery addition, and subtraction (teen totals).

The Day at a Glance

Today's Goals	Materials	
1 Teaching the Lesson **A1:** Solve story problems written by classmates. **A2:** Practice addition, mystery addition, and subtraction with teen totals.	**Lesson Activities** Homework and Remembering pp. 79–80 *Count On Me* game board Secret Code Cards Colored paper Quick Quiz 3 (Assessment Guide)	**Going Further** Activity Cards 3-13 Math Journals
2 Going Further ▸ Differentiated Instruction		
3 Homework and Spiral Review		

Use Math Talk today!

Keeping Skills Sharp

Quick Practice — 5 MINUTES

Goals: Subtract from teen numbers. Make a ten when adding a number to 6, 7, 8, or 9.

Materials: Secret Code Cards 1–10 (from Unit 1 Lesson 5 or TRB M3–M4), Parachute Drop–Teen Totals (from Unit 3 Lesson 7 or TRB M57)

Secret Code Card Subtraction Race–Teen Totals Have children arrange their Secret Code Cards across their desks. Have a **Student Leader** call out exercises starting from the bottom of the last column on the Parachute Drop (Student Activity Book page 105 or TRB M57). As quickly as possible, children hold up a Secret Code Card to show the answer.

Class Make a Ten Write the $m + n$ list (left column) on the board. Do each row in turn. (See Unit 3 Lesson 1.)

Class Make a Ten

Student Leader 1 points to and says	Student Leader 2 shows fingers and says	Class says and Student Leader 2 writes = and
7 + 4	4 makes 3 and 1	7 + 3 + 1 = 10 + 1 = 11
6 + 7	7 makes 4 and 3	6 + 4 + 3 = 10 + 3 = 13
7 + 6	6 makes 3 and 3	7 + 3 + 3 = 10 + 3 = 13
9 + 7	7 makes 1 and 6	9 + 1 + 6 = 10 + 6 = 16
8 + 3	3 makes 2 and 1	8 + 2 + 1 = 10 + 1 = 11
7 + 7	7 makes 3 and 4	7 + 3 + 4 = 10 + 4 = 14
9 + 2	2 makes 1 and 1	9 + 1 + 1 = 10 + 1 = 11

Daily Routines

Comparing 2-Digit Quantities Using a Meter Stick, Using Number Flashes, Using the MathBoard (See pp. xxv–xxvi.)

▸ Led by Student Leaders

Money Routine Using the 120 Poster, Using the Money Flip Chart, Using the Number Path, Using Secret Code Cards (See pp. xxiii–xxv.)

▸ Led by Student Leaders

1 Teaching the Lesson

Activity 1

Solve Story Problems Written by Classmates

 25 MINUTES

Goal: Solve story problems written by classmates.

 **NCTM Standards:**
Number and Operations
Communication

 **Quick Quiz**

See Assessment Guide for Unit 3 Quick Quiz 3.

▶ Solve Story Problems WHOLE CLASS

Math Talk 

Problems Written by Classmates Choose four problems from Unit 2 Lesson 12 for children to solve. Try to select the more difficult problems. You know which problems are difficult by looking for the problem type that children write with the least frequency. In other words, if most children write certain kinds of problems, it probably means that they have mastered those types.

Write two of the problems on the board. Read the problems aloud with children or have the authors read them. Have two to four children work at the board while the rest of the class works at their seats.

Use the **Solve and Discuss** structure and have children explain their solution methods. Invite listeners to ask questions and make helpful and supportive comments.

Continue using different story problems as time allows.

Activity 2

The *Count on Me* Game

 25 MINUTES

Goal: Practice addition, mystery addition, and subtraction with teen totals.

Materials: *Count on Me* game board (from Unit 1 Lesson 14 or Copymaster M28), Secret Code Cards, colored paper

 **NCTM Standard:**
Number and Operations

 **Ongoing Assessment**

Circulate around the room while children are playing the *Count on Me* game and have children:

- Select a different number for one of their totals or partners and solve the new equation.
- Draw a Math Mountain for one of their equations.

▶ *Count on Me*—Teen Totals PAIRS

Remind children how to play the *Count on Me* game. (See Unit 1 Lesson 14.) For this version of the game all of the totals will be teen numbers. Have children play whichever version they need practice in the most: addition, subtraction, or mystery addition.

Distribute the materials needed to play the game to children. While children play, help those who may need extra practice with story problems.

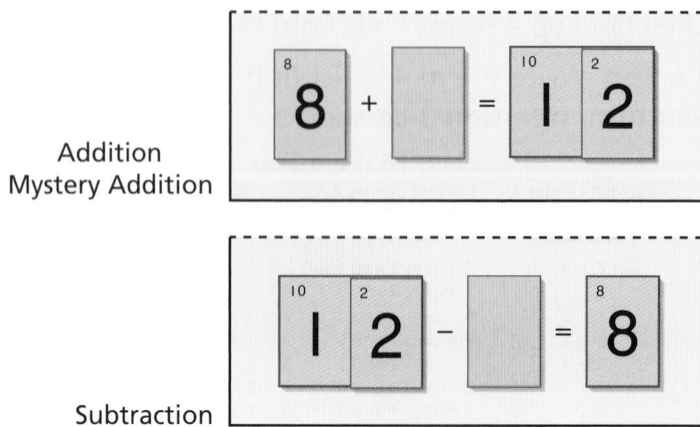

Intervention Activity Card 3-13

Change Plus and Change Minus

Activity Card 3-13

Work:
Use:
- paper

1. Write a change plus problem that has the answer *8 balloons.* Label your problem "change plus."

Change Plus
Kayla has 6 balloons.
She buys 2 more.
How many balloons does she have now?
Answer: 8 balloons

2. Write a change minus problem that also as the answer *8 balloons.* Label your problem "change minus."
3. Trade problems with a friend. Solve your friend's problems.

Unit 3, Lesson 13

Activity Note Have children trade and solve problems. Display problems on a bulletin board.

Math Writing Prompt

Change Plus or Change Minus? Is this a change plus or change minus problem? Explain.

Mia had 13 books. She loaned Yuri 9 books. How many books does Mia have now?

Software Support

Use *Soar to Success* for instruction of students needing targeted support for underlying skills.

On Level Activity Card 3-13

Comparison and Collection

Activity Card 3-13

Work:
Use:
- paper

1. Write a collection problem that has the answer *8 balloons.* Label your problem "collection."

Collection
Anita has 5 red balloons and 3 blue balloons. How many balloons does she have in all?
Answer: 8 balloons

2. Write a comparison problem that also has the answer *8 balloons.* Label your problem "comparison."
3. Trade problems with a friend. Solve your friend's problems.

Unit 3, Lesson 13

Activity Note Display completed problems on the bulletin board.

Math Writing Prompt

What Kind of Problem? Is this problem a collection problem or comparison problem? Explain.

Ari has 2 dogs and 3 cats. How many pets does he have?

Software Support

Use *MegaMath* for review and reinforcement of the concepts and skills presented in this lesson.

Challenge Activity Card 3-13

Two-Step and Hidden Information

Activity Card 3-13

Work:
Use:
- paper

1. Write a two-step problem with hidden information that has the answer *8 balloons.* Label your problem "Two-Steps and Hidden Information."

Two-Steps
Hidden Information
Maria has 1 yellow balloon, 3 blue balloons, and some red balloons. She has a dozen balloons in all. How many red balloons does Maria have?
Answer: 8 balloons

2. Trade your problem with a friend. Solve your friend's problem.
3. Math Talk Explain how you decided to write your problem.

Unit 3, Lesson 13

Activity Note Have children check that each problem uses two steps and has hidden information. Display problems on a bulletin board.

Math Writing Prompt

Explain Your Thinking What kind of problem is the most difficult for you to write? Tell why.

DESTINATION Math®

Software Support

Use *Destination Math* to take students beyond the concepts and skills presented in this lesson.

3 Homework and Spiral Review

Goal: Additional Practice

This Homework page provides practice solving collection story problems.

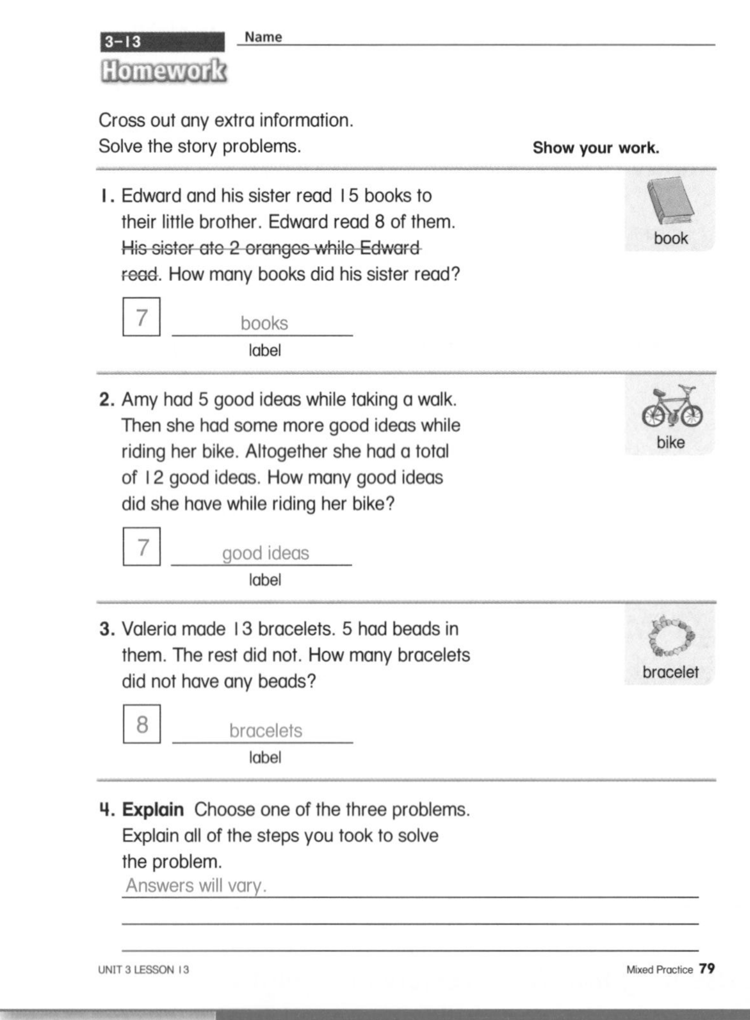

3–13 Homework Name

Cross out any extra information.
Solve the story problems. **Show your work.**

1. Edward and his sister read 15 books to their little brother. Edward read 8 of them. ~~His sister ate 2 oranges while Edward read.~~ How many books did his sister read? book

7 books label

2. Amy had 5 good ideas while taking a walk. Then she had some more good ideas while riding her bike. Altogether she had a total of 12 good ideas. How many good ideas did she have while riding her bike? bike

7 good ideas label

3. Valeria made 13 bracelets. 5 had beads in them. The rest did not. How many bracelets did not have any beads? bracelet

8 bracelets label

4. **Explain** Choose one of the three problems. Explain all of the steps you took to solve the problem.
Answers will vary.

UNIT 3 LESSON 13 Mixed Practice **79**

Homework and Remembering page 79

Goal: Spiral Review

This Remembering activity would be appropriate anytime after today's lesson.

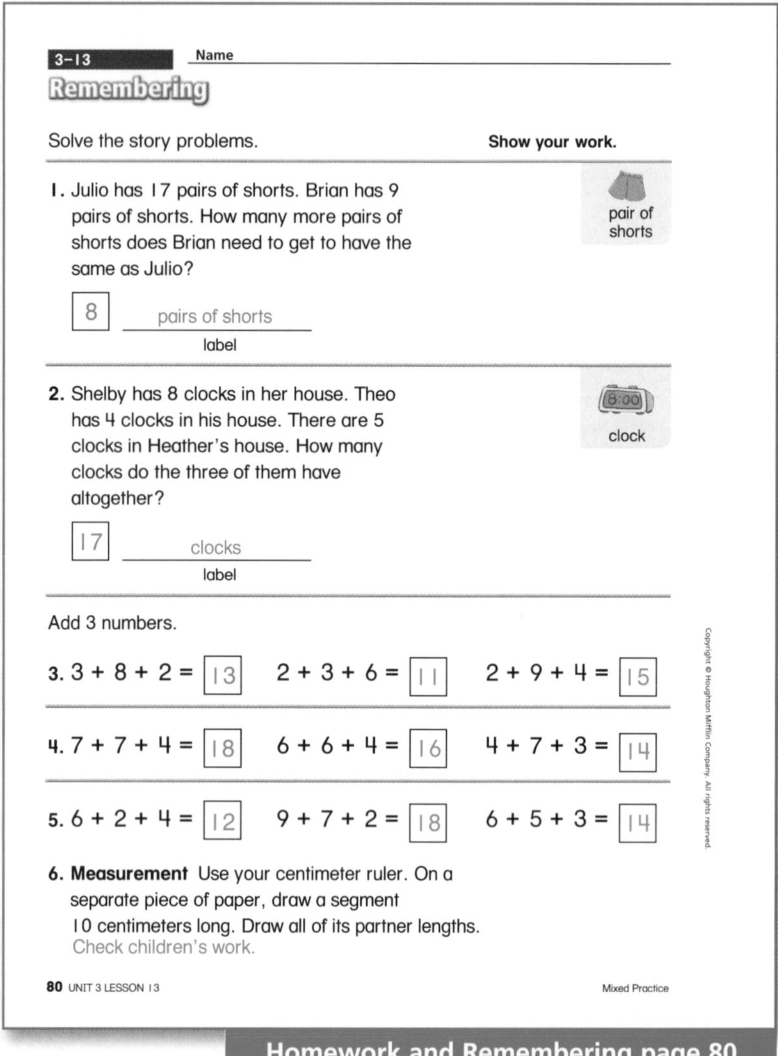

3–13 Remembering Name

Solve the story problems. **Show your work.**

1. Julio has 17 pairs of shorts. Brian has 9 pairs of shorts. How many more pairs of shorts does Brian need to get to have the same as Julio? pair of shorts

8 pairs of shorts label

2. Shelby has 8 clocks in her house. Theo has 4 clocks in his house. There are 5 clocks in Heather's house. How many clocks do the three of them have altogether? clock

17 clocks label

Add 3 numbers.

3. 3 + 8 + 2 = 13 2 + 3 + 6 = 11 2 + 9 + 4 = 15

4. 7 + 7 + 4 = 18 6 + 6 + 4 = 16 4 + 7 + 3 = 14

5. 6 + 2 + 4 = 12 9 + 7 + 2 = 18 6 + 5 + 3 = 14

6. **Measurement** Use your centimeter ruler. On a separate piece of paper, draw a segment 10 centimeters long. Draw all of its partner lengths.
Check children's work.

80 UNIT 3 LESSON 13 Mixed Practice

Homework and Remembering page 80

Home or School Activity

Technology Connection

Search for Information Have children use approved Internet resources (or other resources) to find information such as the following:

- the number of feet in a yard
- the number of legs on an ant
- the number of letters in the name of the capital of Iowa

Then have children write and solve story problems using the information they found.

1. Martha bought 2 yards of ribbon. How many feet of ribbon did she buy?

Use Mathematical Processes

Lesson Objectives

- **Solve a variety of problems using mathematical concepts and skills.**
- **Use mathematical processes in the context of problem solving, connections, reasoning and proof, communication, and representation.**

The Day at a Glance

Today's Goals	Materials	
1 Teaching the Lesson A1: **Math Connection** Explore the history of zero; describe imaginary situations without zero. A2: **Problem Solving** Understand that a problem can have multiple solutions or no solution. A3: **Reasoning and Proof** Decide whether enough information is given to solve a problem. A4: **Representation** Use a diagram to sort according to two rules. A5: **Communication** Give and follow directions for drawing a simple figure.	**Lesson Activities** Student Activity Book pp. 121–122 Homework and Remembering pp. 81–82	**Going Further** Activity Cards 3-14 Math Journals
2 Going Further ▸ Differentiated Instruction		
3 Homework and Spiral Review		

123 Use Math Talk today!

Keeping Skills Sharp

Quick Practice/Daily Routines	
No Quick Practice or Daily Routines are recommended. If you choose to do some, use those that provide extra practice that meets the needs of your class.	**Class Management** Use this lesson to provide more understanding of the NCTM process standards. Depending on how you choose to carry out the activities, this lesson may take two or more days of teaching.

1 Teaching the Lesson

Activity 1

Connections

Math and Social Studies

 **45 MINUTES**

Goals: Explore the history of zero; describe imaginary situations without zero.

Materials: Student Activity Book page 121

 **NCTM Standards:**

Problem Solving	Connections
Communication	Representation

3–14 Name ____________

▶ **Math and Social Studies**

Before zero was invented, people left a space in a number to show that a place had no value, but that was confusing. Then long ago, people invented zero. These are some symbols that have been used for zero.

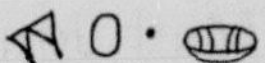

1. Make up your own symbol for zero. Write a number using your zero symbol.
   Answers may vary.

Imagine you saw this on TV one day. What if there was no zero? Answer the questions.

News Flash! Zero has disappeared. We can no longer use zero.

2. How would you write the number three hundred?
   Answers may vary. Possible answers: I can't think of a way to do it; I could write 299 + 1.
3. How would you give the answer to 6–6?
   Answers may vary. Possible answer: I could say nothing is left.
4. How would you use a number to say how many real elephants are in your classroom?
   Answers may vary. Possible answer: I could use another symbol for zero like *, but then I'd still be using zero.
5. Math Journal Write a story titled A Day Without Zero. Let it tell what might happen if there is no zero.
   Answers will vary. Check children's work.

UNIT 3 LESSON 14 Use Mathematical Processes 121

Student Activity Book page 121

Teaching Note

Math Background The first recorded use of zero was in Mesopotamia around 3 B.C.E. The Mayans independently invented the use of zero around 4 C.E. Zero was first used in India in the fifth century but is believed to have been introduced from Mesopotamia. After that, zero found its way to the Middle East (Arabia) and finally was used in Europe in the 12th Century.

▶ The History of Zero

Math Talk

Discuss what children know about zero and its importance in mathematics.

- ▶ Why is zero important? Answers may vary. Possible answer: It helps us understand place value.
- ▶ What does the zero in 20 mean? There are no ones in the number.
- ▶ What does the zero in 202 mean? There are no tens in the number.

Explain that we didn't always have zero. Many, many years ago, a group of people called the Babylonians who had been using empty spaces to show that there was no value in that place began using a symbol for a place with no value. Gradually people started using symbols for zero in other parts of the world.

The symbols (from left to right) shown on the student page were used in ancient Babylonia, China, India, and Central America.

Task 1 Have students invent and share symbols for zero and show how they used their symbols.

▶ Imagining Life Without Zero

Math Talk 

Have children look at the picture of the reporter and read the news flash.

- ▶ What would life be like without zero? Allow children to share their ideas.

Tasks 2–5 Discuss exercises 2–4 with the class before children write their responses. Then ask children to think about what they have learned about zero to write their A Day Without Zero stories. Finally let volunteers share their stories with the class.

Activity 2 — Problem Solving

Pedro's Party Favors

45 MINUTES

Goals: Understand that a problem can have multiple solutions or no solution.

Materials: Student Activity Book page 121

NCTM Standards:
Problem Solving
Communication
Connections

Name ______

▶ Pedro's Party Favors

Pedro owns a party favor company.
Baseball party favors are in packages of 4 and 9.

1. Can Pedro put packages together so he can ship exactly 13 baseball party favors? If so, how?
   Yes. 4 and 9
2. Can he ship exactly 11 baseball party favors? If so, how?
   No.

Rainbow party favors are in packages of 2 and 8.

3. Can Pedro ship an odd number of rainbow party favors? Why?
   No, because he can only make even numbers of packages.
4. Can Pedro ship rainbow party favors for orders with any even number of items? Why?
   Yes, he can ship any even number of items.

Fiesta favors are in packages of 2, 3, and 4.

5. Complete the table to show at least 3 different ways to fill each order.

Number of Fiesta Favors in an Order	Ways to Fill Order
6	2, 2, and 2; 3 and 3; 4 and 2
8	2, 2, 2, and 2; 4 and 4; 4, 2, and 2
12	Answers may vary. Possible answers: 2, 2, 2, 2, 2, and 2; 4, 4, and 4; 3, 3, 3, and 3
15	Answers may vary. Possible answers: 4, 4, 2, 2, and 3; 3, 3, 3, 3, and 3; 4, 4, 4, and 3

122 UNIT 3 LESSON 14 — Use Mathematical Processes

Student Activity Book page 122

English Language Learners

Write *party favor* on the board.

- **Beginning** Say: **These are *party favors.*** Ask: **Are they small gifts you get at a party?** yes
- **Intermediate and Advanced** Say: ***Party favors* are small __.** gifts **You get them at a __.** party

▶ Buying Party Favors in Packages

Ask for Ideas Begin by eliciting information about party favors.

▶ Did you ever get a favor at a party? Have you ever given away favors at a party? How do stores package party favors? Encourage children to share their experiences.

Task 1 Be sure children understand that party favors usually come in packages of more than one item. Have children complete exercises 1 through 5. Point out that Pedro never ships individual party favors.

▶ Party Favor Problems **Math Talk** 

Hold a class discussion of the party favor problems. Use questions like those below, and point out that some problems can be solved in more than one way and some problems do not have a solution.

▶ Why can Pedro ship exactly 13 baseball party favors but not exactly 11 baseball party favors? Since the favors only come in packages of 4 and 9, he can put 4 and 9 together to get 13 but he can't put 4 and 9 together to get 11.

▶ Why can't Pedro ever ship an odd number of rainbow party favors? Both packages of favors have an even number in them, so you can't put the packages together to get an odd number of favors.

▶ Why can Pedro fill the fiesta favor orders in different ways? Answers may vary. Possible answer: Bigger numbers have more different partners so there are many ways to fill these orders.

Have children share different ways they could fill the fiesta favor orders.

Activity 3

Reasoning and Proof

What Am I Thinking of?

 **15 MINUTES**

Goal: Decide whether enough information is given to solve a problem.

 **NCTM Standards:**

Problem Solving
Communication
Reasoning and Proof

Write the following problem on the board.

I am thinking of a number. It is even. It is greater than 20. It is less than 30. What is the number?

Ask whether anyone can solve the problem. Children will not be able to find a number.

Hold a whole-class discussion of the problem.

- Why can't you solve this problem? Answers may vary. Possible answer: There is not just one possible number.
- What even numbers are greater than 20 and less than 30? 22, 24, 26, 28
- What else do you need to know? Answers may vary. Possible answer: how to choose one of those numbers
- Add another sentence to the problem so that it can be answered and tell the answer. Answers may vary. Possible answer: It is 4 more than 24. 28

Activity 4

Representation

Use a Diagram

 **15 MINUTES**

Goal: Use a diagram to sort by two rules.

 **NCTM Standards:**

Problem Solving
Communication
Representation

Draw the following diagram on the board.

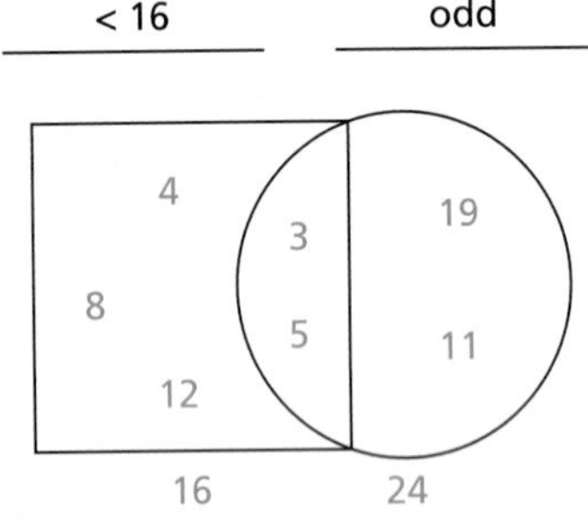

Tell children that you want to sort some numbers by two rules: 1. Are they odd? 2. Are they less than 16?

Explain that a number is placed in the circle if it is odd, in the square if it is less than 16, in the overlap space if it is both odd and less than 16, and outside the circle and the square if it is neither odd nor less than 16.

The numbers are 3, 4, 5, 8, 11, 12, 16, 19, and 24. For each number, ask a volunteer to go to the board, write the number in the diagram, and tell why it was placed there.

Activity 5

Communication

Giving Directions

 **15 MINUTES**

Goal: Give and follow directions for drawing a simple figure.

 **NCTM Standards:**

Problem Solving
Representation
Communication

Have children work in pairs. Ask each child to draw a simple figure. Tell them to take turns giving directions for their figure to their partner so the partner can draw the figure. When both have followed directions to draw the other's figure, let them compare the drawings and discuss how clear the directions were. Ask several pairs to share their experiences.

2 Going Further

Differentiated Instruction

Intervention

Activity Card 3-14

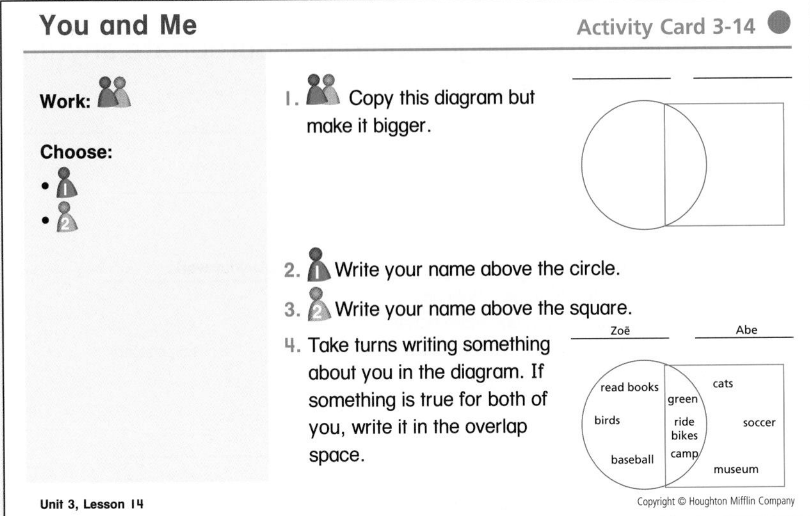

You and Me — Activity Card 3-14

Work: (pairs)

Choose:
- 1
- 2

1. Copy this diagram but make it bigger.
2. (1) Write your name above the circle.
3. (2) Write your name above the square.
4. Take turns writing something about you in the diagram. If something is true for both of you, write it in the overlap space.

Unit 3, Lesson 14

Activity Note If the overlapping diagram is hard for children to use, have them make separate diagrams and then look for things that are the same in both diagrams.

Math Writing Prompt

Add and Subtract with Zero What happens to a number when you add or subtract zero?

Software Support

Use *Soar to Success* for instruction of students needing targeted support for underlying skills.

On Level

Activity Card 3-14

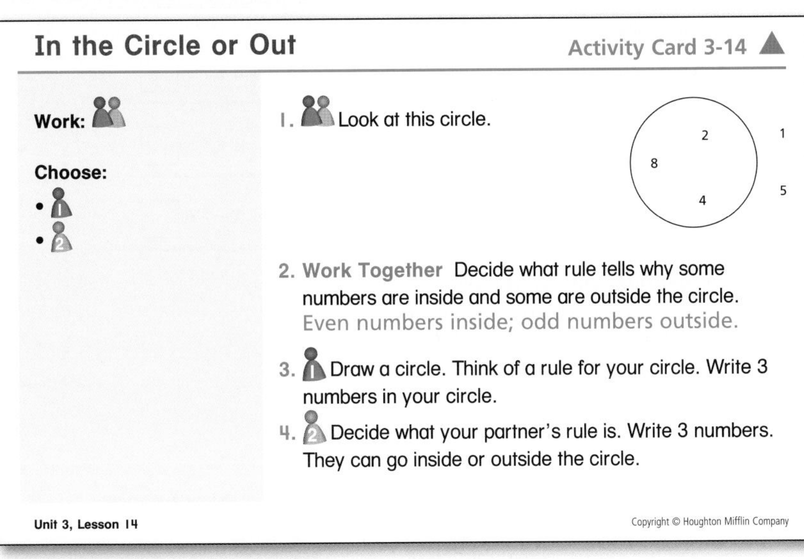

In the Circle or Out — Activity Card 3-14

Work: (pairs)

Choose:
- 1
- 2

1. Look at this circle.

2. Work Together Decide what rule tells why some numbers are inside and some are outside the circle.
Even numbers inside; odd numbers outside.
3. (1) Draw a circle. Think of a rule for your circle. Write 3 numbers in your circle.
4. (2) Decide what your partner's rule is. Write 3 numbers. They can go inside or outside the circle.

Unit 3, Lesson 14

Activity Note To extend this activity, suggest that children use a diagram to sort shapes or classroom objects.

Math Writing Prompt

The Importance of Zero Why is zero an important number?

Software Support

Use *MegaMath* for review and reinforcement of the concepts and skills presented in this lesson.

Challenge

Activity Card 3-14

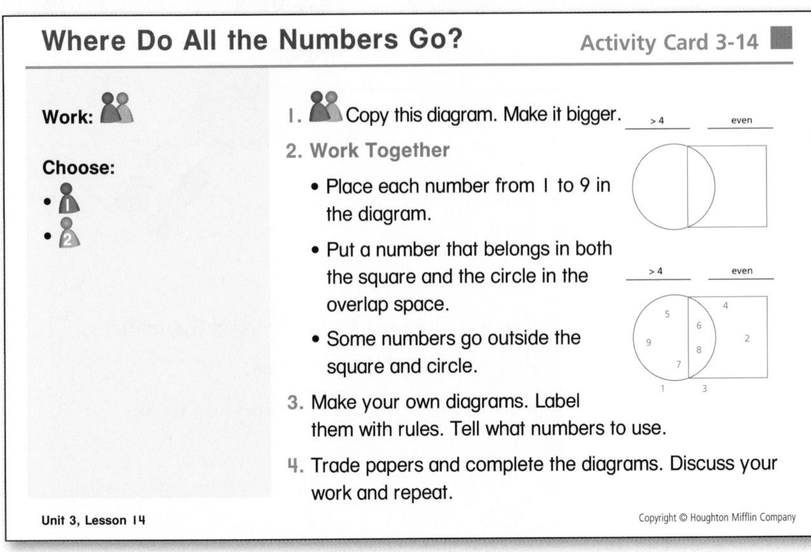

Where Do All the Numbers Go? — Activity Card 3-14

Work: (pairs)

Choose:
- 1
- 2

1. Copy this diagram. Make it bigger.
2. Work Together
   - Place each number from 1 to 9 in the diagram.
   - Put a number that belongs in both the square and the circle in the overlap space.
   - Some numbers go outside the square and circle.
3. Make your own diagrams. Label them with rules. Tell what numbers to use.
4. Trade papers and complete the diagrams. Discuss your work and repeat.

Unit 3, Lesson 14

Activity Note Caution children to consider carefully the rules and numbers they use with their diagrams so that there are not too few or too many for each section of the diagram.

Math Writing Prompt

How Did You Decide? Explain how you decided what rules and numbers you used with your diagram.

Software Support

Use *Destination Math* to take students beyond the concepts and skills presented in this lesson.

3 Homework and Spiral Review

Goal: Additional Practice

Include student's completed Homework page as part of their portfolios.

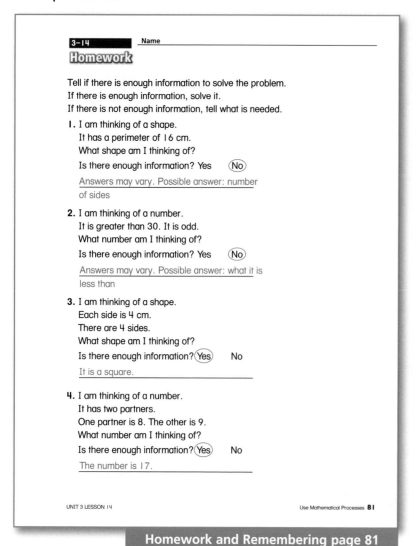

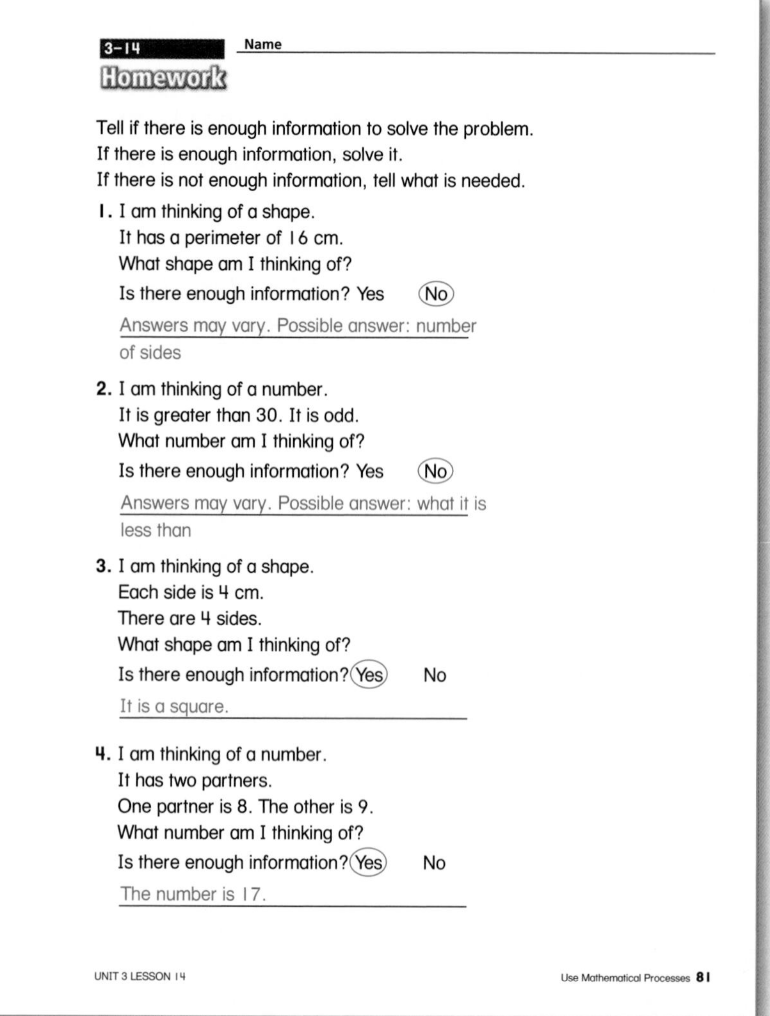

3-14 Name

Homework

Tell if there is enough information to solve the problem.
If there is enough information, solve it.
If there is not enough information, tell what is needed.

1. I am thinking of a shape.
   It has a perimeter of 16 cm.
   What shape am I thinking of?
   Is there enough information? Yes (No)
   Answers may vary. Possible answer: number of sides
2. I am thinking of a number.
   It is greater than 30. It is odd.
   What number am I thinking of?
   Is there enough information? Yes (No)
   Answers may vary. Possible answer: what it is less than
3. I am thinking of a shape.
   Each side is 4 cm.
   There are 4 sides.
   What shape am I thinking of?
   Is there enough information? (Yes) No
   It is a square.
4. I am thinking of a number.
   It has two partners.
   One partner is 8. The other is 9.
   What number am I thinking of?
   Is there enough information? (Yes) No
   The number is 17.

UNIT 3 LESSON 14 Use Mathematical Processes 81

Homework and Remembering page 81

Goal: Spiral Review

This Remembering page would be appropriate anytime after today's lesson.

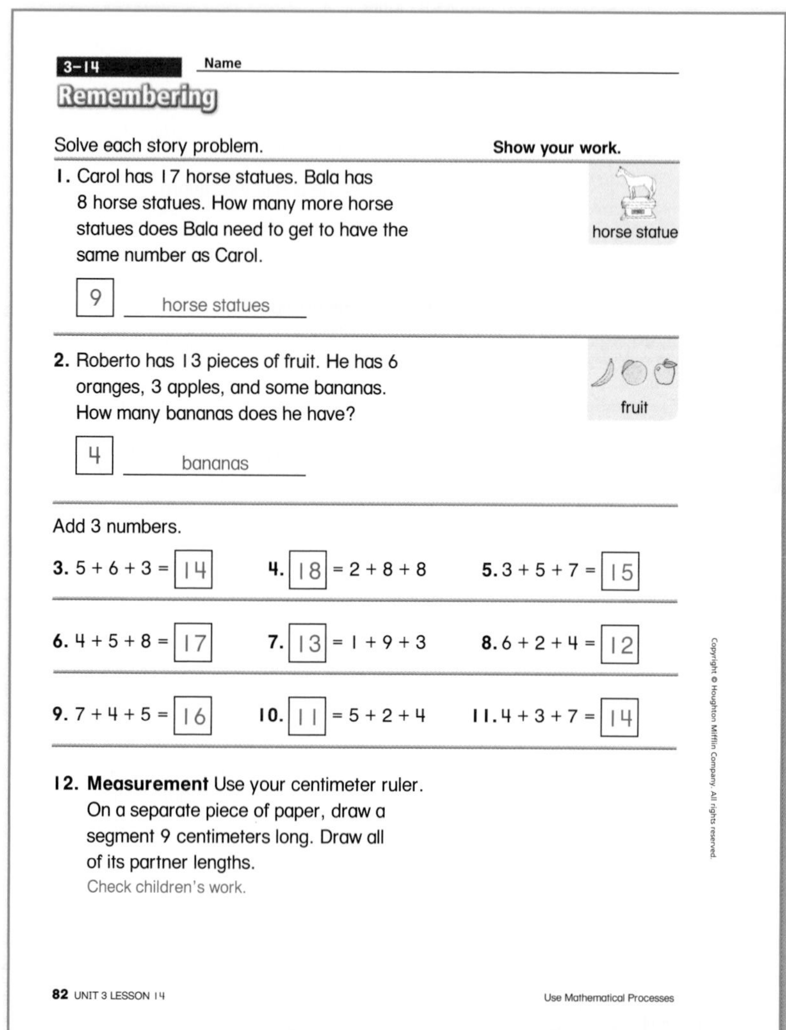

3-14 Name

Remembering

Solve each story problem. **Show your work.**

1. Carol has 17 horse statues. Bala has 8 horse statues. How many more horse statues does Bala need to get to have the same number as Carol.
   9 horse statues
   (horse statue)
2. Roberto has 13 pieces of fruit. He has 6 oranges, 3 apples, and some bananas. How many bananas does he have?
   4 bananas
   (fruit)

Add 3 numbers.

3. 5 + 6 + 3 = 14	4. 18 = 2 + 8 + 8	5. 3 + 5 + 7 = 15
6. 4 + 5 + 8 = 17	7. 13 = 1 + 9 + 3	8. 6 + 2 + 4 = 12
9. 7 + 4 + 5 = 16	10. 11 = 5 + 2 + 4	11. 4 + 3 + 7 = 14

12. **Measurement** Use your centimeter ruler. On a separate piece of paper, draw a segment 9 centimeters long. Draw all of its partner lengths.
    Check children's work.

82 UNIT 3 LESSON 14 Use Mathematical Processes

Homework and Remembering page 82

Home or School Activity

Language Arts Connection

Write a Story Ask children to think of a character they like in a book, movie, or television show. Have them write and solve a story problem about the character. Suggest that they draw a picture to illustrate the story problem.

The frog hopped 5 hops toward the princess.
Then it hopped 4 more hops.
How many hops did the frog hop in all?
9 hops

Unit Review and Test

Lesson Objectives

- **Assess children's progress on unit objectives.**

The Day at a Glance

Today's Goals	Materials
1 Assessing the Unit ▶ Assess children's progress on unit objectives. ▶ Use activities from unit lessons to reteach content. **2 Extending the Assessment** ▶ Use remediation for common errors. There is no homework assignment on a test day.	Unit 3 Test, Student Activity Book pages 123–126 Unit 3 Test, Form A or B, Assessment Guide (optional) Unit 3 Performance Assessment, Assessment Guide (optional)

Keeping Skills Sharp

Quick Practice — 5 MINUTES	
Goal: Review any skills you choose to meet the needs of your class. If you are doing a unit review day, use any of the Quick Practice activities that provide support for your class. If this is a test day, omit Quick Practice.	**Review and Test Day** You may want to choose a quiet game or other activity (reading a book or working on homework for another subject) for children who finish early.

1 Assessing the Unit

Assess Unit Objectives

3 Unit Test Name

Solve each story problem. Show your work.

1. Jenna has 11 goldfish. She gives some to her friend. Now she has only 7 goldfish. How many goldfish did she give to her friend?

goldfish

4 goldfish
label

2. There are 8 puzzle pieces on the table. Kay put 4 more on the table. How many puzzle pieces are on the table now?

table

12 puzzle pieces
label

3. Joey had a bag of peanuts. He gave 8 peanuts to his friends. Then he had 7 left. How many peanuts were in the bag?

peanuts

15 peanuts
label

UNIT 3 Test 123

Student Activity Book page 123

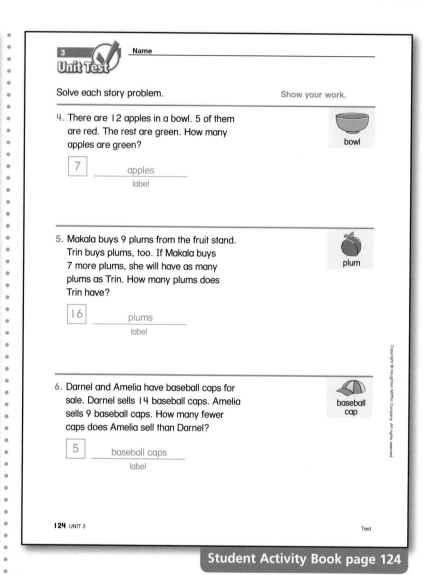

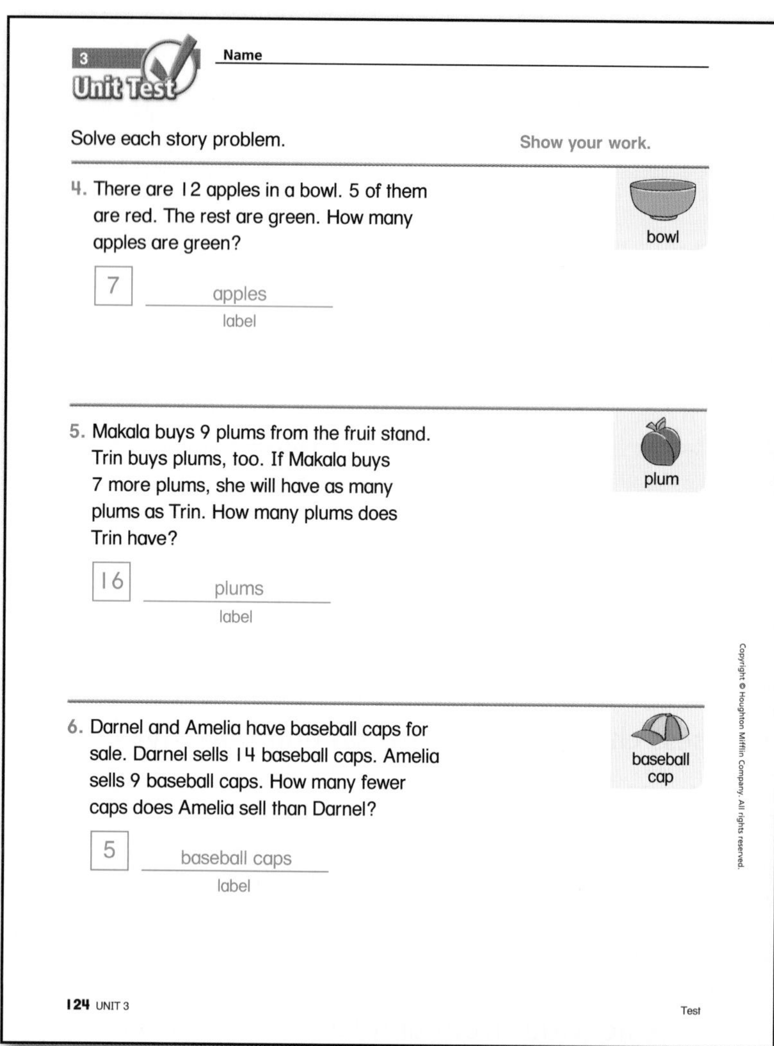

3 Unit Test Name

Solve each story problem. Show your work.

4. There are 12 apples in a bowl. 5 of them are red. The rest are green. How many apples are green?

bowl

7 apples
label

5. Makala buys 9 plums from the fruit stand. Trin buys plums, too. If Makala buys 7 more plums, she will have as many plums as Trin. How many plums does Trin have?

plum

16 plums
label

6. Darnel and Amelia have baseball caps for sale. Darnel sells 14 baseball caps. Amelia sells 9 baseball caps. How many fewer caps does Amelia sell than Darnel?

baseball cap

5 baseball caps
label

124 UNIT 3 Test

Student Activity Book page 124

45 MINUTES (more if schedule permits)

Goal: Assess children's progress on unit objectives.

Materials: Student Activity Book pages 123–126; Assessment Guide

▶ Review and Assessment

If your students are ready for assessment on the unit objectives, use either the test on the Student Activity Book pages or one of the forms of the Unit 3 Test in the Assessment Guide to assess student progress. To assign a numerical score for all of these test forms, use 10 points for each question.

The chart to the right lists the test items, the unit objectives they cover, and the lesson activities in which the objective is covered in this unit.

▶ Reteaching Resources

Unit Test Items	Unit Objectives Tested	Activities to Use for Reteaching
1–3	**3.1** Solve change plus and change minus story problems.	Lesson 1, Activity 1 Lesson 2, Activities 1-2
4	**3.2** Solve collection story problems.	Lesson 3, Activity 2
5, 6	**3.3** Solve comparison story problems.	Lesson 5, Activity 1 Lesson 6, Activities 1–2
7	**3.4** Solve story problems with extra information.	Lesson 8, Activity 2

3 Unit Test

Name

Solve each story problem.
Cross out any extra information.

Show your work.

7. Franny has 8 kittens ~~and 2 dogs.~~ 4 kittens are asleep. How many kittens are awake?

kitten

4 kittens
label

8. Evan read a book each day for a week. The next day he read 3 books. How many books did Evan read altogether?

book

10 books
label

9. There are 6 seals, a walrus, and some dolphins in the water. There are a total of 15 animals in the water. How many dolphins are in the water?

walrus

8 dolphins
label

UNIT 3 Test 125

Student Activity Book page 125

3 Unit Test

Name

10. **Extended Response** Write and solve a subtraction story problem using the numbers 9 and 6. Check children's answers.

Item 10 also addresses the Process Skills of Problem Solving and Communication.

Answer: ____ ____
label

126 UNIT 3 Test

Student Activity Book page 126

Unit Test Items	Unit Objectives Tested	Activities to Use for Reteaching
8	**3.5** Solve story problems with hidden information.	Lesson 9, Activity 2
9	**3.6** Solve two-step story problems.	Lesson 10, Activity 1
10	**3.7** Write story problems.	Lesson 12, Activity 1

▶ Assessment Resources

Free Response Tests

Form A, Free Response Test

Form B, Multiple-Choice Test

Performance Assessment

▶ Portfolio Assessment

Teacher-selected Items for Student Portfolios:

- Homework, Lessons 1, 4, and 14
- Class Activity work, Lessons 3, 6, and 12

Student-selected Items for Student Portfolios:

- Favorite Home or School Activity
- Best Writing Prompt

Extending the Assessment

Common Errors

Activities for Remediation

Unit Objective 3.1

Solve change plus and change minus story problems.

Common Error: Is Unable to Identify Whether the Unknown Is a Partner or a Total

Children may have difficulty identifying whether they need to find a partner or a total.

Remediation Have children retell the story in their own words and then make a math drawing to show the situation. Some may need help with particular language to understand the situation. A few may need to see the problem acted out or drawn by a helper.

Unit Objective 3.2

Solve collection story problems.

Common Error: Labels the Answer Incorrectly

Children may use an incorrect label for their answer in a group name problem.

Remediation Have children go back and carefully read the question, then ring what they are asked to find. Have children use this to help them label their answer.

Unit Objective 3.3

Solve comparison story problems.

Common Error: Doesn't Know Which Operation to Use

Children may not understand which operation to use to compare the objects in a story problem.

Remediation Less-advanced children should not try to think of which operation to use to solve a comparison story problem. They should concentrate on showing the story situation in a matching drawing. They can count to find the answer.

Unit Objective 3.4

Solve story problems with extra information.

Common Error: Doesn't Use Correct Information

When solving a problem with too much information, children may use the incorrect information.

Remediation Have children work backward. Have them reread the question and then determine what is needed to solve the problem. Then have children underline the information that they need to solve the story problem. What is not underlined is not needed and is the extra information and can be crossed out.

Unit Objective 3.5

Solve story problems with hidden information.

Common Error: Doesn't Recognize Words that Imply Specific Numbers

Children may not recognize words that imply specific numbers.

Remediation Have children make a list of words and phrases that have numerical meaning, such as *pair, dozen, months in a year,* and *innings in a baseball game.*

Unit Objective 3.6

Solve two-step story problems.

Common Error: Is Unable to Break a Problem into Parts

Children may have difficulty deciding when and how to break a problem into simpler parts.

Remediation Have children act out different story problems using counters. This will allow them to see concretely which steps must be performed and how to order the steps.

Triangles and Quadrilaterals

THE GOAL OF UNIT 4 is to consolidate the learning from Unit 2 about the properties of shapes and how to find the perimeter of squares, rectangles, and triangles. In this unit, parallel lines and parallelograms are introduced and children sort, name, and classify quadrilaterals. The inclusive nature of quadrilateral names will be discussed and applied to naming shapes, for instance, children will identify that a rectangle is a parallelogram and a quadrilateral. Children will also have an opportunity to draw triangles and classify them using their own criteria and informal language.

Skills Trace

Grade 1	Grade 2	Grade 3
• Relate shapes and numbers.	• Describe properties of quadrilaterals and triangles. • Classify quadrilaterals.	• Classify triangles by the lengths of sides or by the measures of their angles. • Identify and classify quadrilaterals.

Unit 4 Contents

Planning Unit 4

NCTM Standards Key: **1.** Number and Operations **2.** Algebra **3.** Geometry **4.** Measurement **5.** Data Analysis and Probability **6.** Problem Solving **7.** Reasoning and Proof **8.** Communication **9.** Connections **10.** Representation

Lesson/NCTM Standards	Resources	Materials for Lesson Activities	Materials for Going Further
4–1 **Share Observations about Geometry** NCTM Standards: 3, 8, 10	TE pp. 287–292 SAB pp. 127–130 H&R p. 83 AC 4–1 MCC 4–13	✓ 25-cm rulers or (TRB M47–M48) Geoboards Rubber bands Scissors	Straws Scissors
4–2 **Define Parallel Lines and Parallelograms** NCTM Standards: 3, 4, 7, 9	TE pp. 293–298 SAB pp. 131–134 H&R p. 85 AC 4–2 MCC 4–14	MathBoard materials ✓ 25-cm rulers Geoboards Rubber bands ✓ Pattern blocks or (TRB M58)	✓ Pattern blocks or (TRB M58) Scissors
4–3 **Relate Different Quadrilaterals** NCTM Standards: 3, 8, 9	TE pp. 299–304 SAB pp. 135–138 H&R p. 87 AC 4–3 MCC 4–15 MCC 4–16	Scissors ✓ 25-cm rulers	Straws Tangrams or (TRB M59) Centimeter Dot Paper (TRB M49)
✓ Unit Review and Test	TE pp. 305–308 SAB pp. 139–140 AG: Unit 4 tests		

Resources/Materials Key: TE: Teacher Edition SAB: Student Activity Book H&R: Homework and Remembering AC: Activity Cards MCC: Math Center Challenge AG: Assessment Guide ✓: Grade 2 kits TRB: Teacher's Resource Book

Manipulatives and Materials

Essential materials for teaching *Math Expressions* are available in the Grade 2 kits. These materials are indicated by a ✓ in these lists. At the front of this Teacher Edition is more information about kit contents, alternatives for the materials, and use of the materials.

Unit 4 Assessment

Unit Objectives Tested	Unit Test Items	Lessons
4.1 Describe properties of quadrilaterals and triangles.	1, 2, 3, 10	1, 2
4.2 Define parallel lines and parallelograms.	4, 5, 6	2
4.3 Classify quadrilaterals.	7, 8, 9	3

Assessment and Review Resources

Formal Assessment

Student Activity Book

- Unit Review and Test (pp. 139–140)

Assessment Guide

- Test A–Open Response (pp. A36–A37)
- Test B–Multiple Choice (pp. A38–A39)
- Performance Assessment (pp. A40–A42)

Test Generator CD-ROM

- Open Response Test
- Multiple Choice Test
- Test Bank Items

Informal Assessment

Teacher Edition

- Ongoing Assessment (in every lesson)
- Quick Practice (in every lesson)
- Portfolio Suggestions (p. 307)

Math Talk

- Math Talk in Action (p. 288)
- In Activities (pp. 296, 300)

Review Opportunities

Homework and Remembering

- Review of recently taught topics
- Cumulative Review

Teacher Edition

- Unit Review and Test (pp. 305–308)

Test Generator CD-ROM

- Custom Review Sheets

Independent Learning Activities

Ready-Made Math Challenge Centers

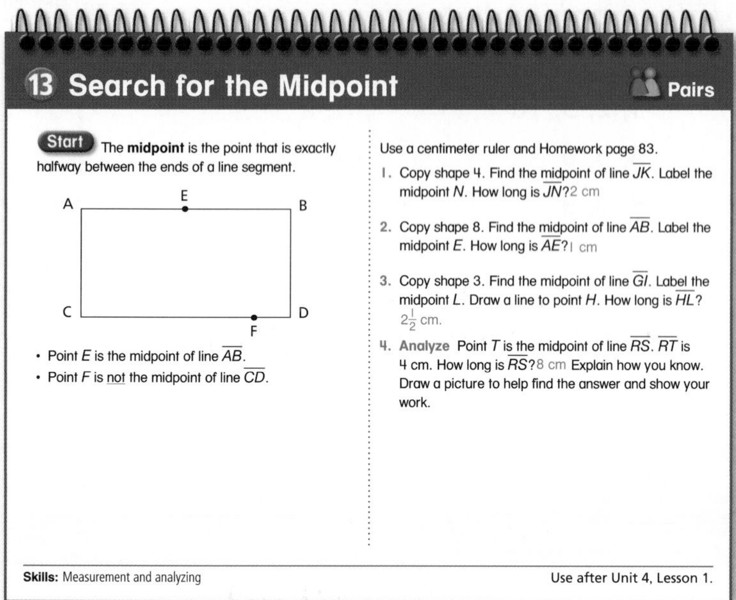

13 Search for the Midpoint

Pairs

Start The **midpoint** is the point that is exactly halfway between the ends of a line segment.

- Point *E* is the midpoint of line $\overline{AB}$.
- Point *F* is not the midpoint of line $\overline{CD}$.

Use a centimeter ruler and Homework page 83.

1. Copy shape 4. Find the midpoint of line $\overline{JK}$. Label the midpoint *N*. How long is $\overline{JN}$? 2 cm
2. Copy shape 8. Find the midpoint of line $\overline{AB}$. Label the midpoint *E*. How long is $\overline{AE}$? 1 cm
3. Copy shape 3. Find the midpoint of line $\overline{GI}$. Label the midpoint *L*. Draw a line to point *H*. How long is $\overline{HL}$? $2\frac{1}{2}$ cm.
4. **Analyze** Point *T* is the midpoint of line $\overline{RS}$. $\overline{RT}$ is 4 cm. How long is $\overline{RS}$? 8 cm Explain how you know. Draw a picture to help find the answer and show your work.

Skills: Measurement and analyzing — Use after Unit 4, Lesson 1.

Grouping Pairs

Materials Centimeter ruler or TRB M47

Objective Children measure and find the midpoint of lines.

Connections Measurement and Geometry

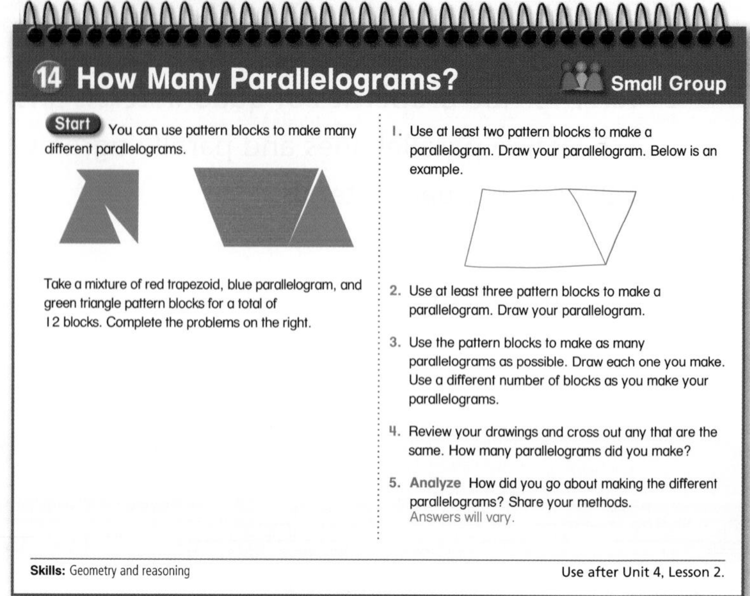

14 How Many Parallelograms?

Small Group

Start You can use pattern blocks to make many different parallelograms.

Take a mixture of red trapezoid, blue parallelogram, and green triangle pattern blocks for a total of 12 blocks. Complete the problems on the right.

1. Use at least two pattern blocks to make a parallelogram. Draw your parallelogram. Below is an example.
2. Use at least three pattern blocks to make a parallelogram. Draw your parallelogram.
3. Use the pattern blocks to make as many parallelograms as possible. Draw each one you make. Use a different number of blocks as you make your parallelograms.
4. Review your drawings and cross out any that are the same. How many parallelograms did you make?
5. **Analyze** How did you go about making the different parallelograms? Share your methods. Answers will vary.

Skills: Geometry and reasoning — Use after Unit 4, Lesson 2.

Grouping Small Group

Materials Colored pencils or crayons, and at least 12 pattern blocks for each group

Objective Children use pattern blocks to make parallelograms and analyze how they made the shapes.

Connections Geometry and Reasoning

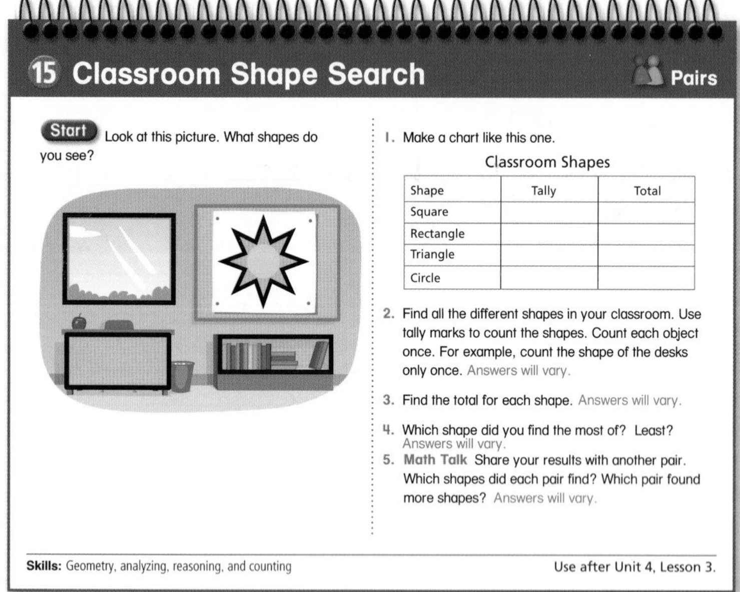

15 Classroom Shape Search

Pairs

Start Look at this picture. What shapes do you see?

1. Make a chart like this one.

Classroom Shapes

Shape	Tally	Total
Square		
Rectangle		
Triangle		
Circle		

2. Find all the different shapes in your classroom. Use tally marks to count the shapes. Count each object once. For example, count the shape of the desks only once. Answers will vary.
3. Find the total for each shape. Answers will vary.
4. Which shape did you find the most of? Least? Answers will vary.
5. **Math Talk** Share your results with another pair. Which shapes did each pair find? Which pair found more shapes? Answers will vary.

Skills: Geometry, analyzing, reasoning, and counting — Use after Unit 4, Lesson 3.

Grouping Pairs

Materials None

Objective Children identify and tally geometric shapes.

Connections Geometry and Data

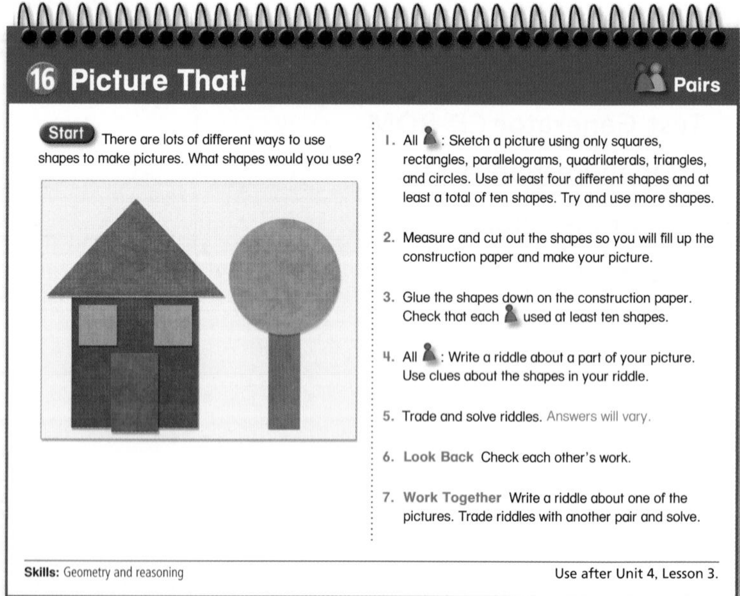

16 Picture That!

Pairs

Start There are lots of different ways to use shapes to make pictures. What shapes would you use?

1. All: Sketch a picture using only squares, rectangles, parallelograms, quadrilaterals, triangles, and circles. Use at least four different shapes and at least a total of ten shapes. Try and use more shapes.
2. Measure and cut out the shapes so you will fill up the construction paper and make your picture.
3. Glue the shapes down on the construction paper. Check that each used at least ten shapes.
4. All: Write a riddle about a part of your picture. Use clues about the shapes in your riddle.
5. Trade and solve riddles. Answers will vary.
6. **Look Back** Check each other's work.
7. **Work Together** Write a riddle about one of the pictures. Trade riddles with another pair and solve.

Skills: Geometry and reasoning — Use after Unit 4, Lesson 3.

Grouping Pairs

Materials Centimeter ruler, construction paper, glue stick

Objective Children use geometric shapes to make a picture.

Connections Geometry and Art

Ready-Made Math Resources

Technology — Tutorials, Practice, and Intervention

Use activity masters and online, individualized intervention and support to bring students to proficiency.

Help students practice skills and apply concepts through exciting math adventures.

Extend and enrich students' understanding of skills and concepts through engaging, interactive lessons and activities.

Visit **Education Place**®
www.eduplace.com

Visit www.eduplace.com/mx2t/ and find family, teacher, and student materials, activities, games, and more.

Literature Links

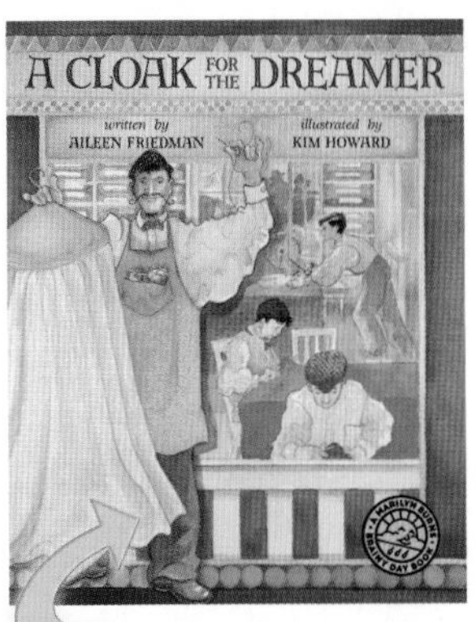

A Cloak for the Dreamer

A Cloak for the Dreamer

In the tradition of a folk tale story, Aileen Friedman's book asks the reader to follow as three sons each make a cloak for the archduke, and each is composed of different shapes.

Literature Connections

- *Shapes (Slide 'n Seek)*, by Chuck Murphy (Little Simon, 2000)
- *Shapes, Shapes, Shapes*, by Tana Hoban (HarperTrophy, 1996)

Unit 4 Teaching Resources

Differentiated Instruction

Individualizing Instruction		
	Level	Frequency
Activities	• Intervention • On Level • Challenge	All 3 in every lesson
	Level	Frequency
Math Writing Prompts	• Intervention • On Level • Challenge	All 3 in every lesson
Math Center Challenges	For advanced students	
	4 in every unit	

Reaching All Learners		
English Language Learners	Lessons	Pages
	1, 2, 3	287, 293, 299
Extra Help	Lesson	Page
	1	289

Strategies for English Language Learners

Present this activity to all children. Offer different levels of support to meet children's levels of language proficiency.

Objective Review shape vocabulary and the terms *side*, *corner*, and *angle*.

Activity Draw a square, triangle, rectangle, and circle on the board.

Newcomer

- Identify the shapes. Have children repeat and draw them in the air.
- Point to the side of a square. Say: **This is a side. A square has 4 sides.** Continue with other shapes.

Beginning

- Point and say: **This is a square. This is a side. A square has 4 sides. The sides are the same length.** Have children repeat. Continue with other shapes and vocabulary.

Intermediate

- Have children identify the shapes. Guide them to identify and count the sides and corners.
- Point to the triangle. Ask: **What is the measurement of the corner?** angle

Advanced

- Have children work in pairs. 1 partner draws a shape in the air. The other points to the sides and corners, then describes the angles.

Connections

Social Studies Connection
Lesson 2, page 298

Literature Connection
Lesson 3, page 304

Math Background

Putting Research into Practice for Unit 4

From Current Research: Classifying Shapes

Students' reasoning about classification varies during the early years. For instance, when kindergarten students sort shapes, one student may pick up a big triangular shape and say, "This one is big," and then put it with other large shapes. A friend may pick up another big triangular shape, trace its edges, and say, "Three sides—a triangle!" and then put it with other triangles. Both of these students are focusing on only one property, or attribute. By second grade, however, students are aware that shapes have multiple properties and should suggest ways of classifying that will include multiple properties.

National Council of Teachers of Mathematics. *Principles and Standards for School Mathematics.* Reston: NCTM, 2000. 123.

Pre-K–2 geometry begins with describing and naming shapes. Young students begin by using their own vocabulary to describe objects, talking about how they are alike and how they are different. Teachers must help students gradually incorporate conventional terminology into their descriptions of two-and three-dimensional shapes. However, terminology itself should not be the focus of the pre-K–2 geometry program. The goal is that early experiences with geometry lay the foundation for more-formal geometry in later grades. Using terminology to focus attention and to clarify ideas during discussions can help students build that foundation.

National Council of Teachers of Mathematics. *Principles and Standards for School Mathematics.* Reston: NCTM, 2000. 97.

Other Useful References: Classifying Quadrilaterals, Classifying Triangles

Learning Math: Geometry. Annenberg/CPB Learner.org. 1997–2004. <*www.learner.org/resources/series167.html*>.

Learning Math: Measurement. Annenberg/CPB Learner.org. 1997–2004. <*www.learner.org/resources/series184.html*>.

National Council of Teachers of Mathematics. *Teaching Children Mathematics* (Focus Issue: Geometry and Geometric Thinking) 5.6 (Feb. 1999).

National Council of Teachers of Mathematics. *Principles and Standards for School Mathematics.* Reston: NCTM, 2000.

Van de Walle, John A. "Measuring Area." *Elementary and Middle School Mathematics: Teaching Developmentally.* 4th ed. New York: Addison, 2001. 306-351.

Getting Ready to Teach Unit 4

In this unit, children classify triangles and quadrilaterals. They continue to build understanding of the concept of perimeter.

Classifying Quadrilaterals

Lessons 2 and 3

In Unit 2, children investigated attributes of squares and rectangles. In Unit 4, parallel lines and parallelograms are introduced and children look at the relationships between quadrilaterals, parallelograms, rectangles, and squares. They are introduced to the inclusive nature of these quadrilateral names. For instance, because a square has opposite sides that are equal, it is also a rectangle; because it has opposite sides that are parallel, it is also a parallelogram; and because it has four sides, it is also a quadrilateral. A square is a special rectangle with all sides equal, a rectangle is a special parallelogram with four square corners, and so on. The sorting and naming activities in this unit serve to encourage children to explore how quadrilaterals are related to each other, but at this grade level, children are not expected to master these concepts.

Classifying Triangles

Lesson 1

In Unit 2, children drew triangles and observed they had three sides and three corners. They also measured side lengths of triangles to identify that triangles can have three unique side lengths, two equal side lengths, or three equal side lengths. In this unit, children draw ten unique triangles by varying side lengths and angles. They then divide their triangles into three groups using their own criteria. Children may classify their triangles using language like "three-sides-equal" triangles or "no-big-angle" triangles. Terms like obtuse triangle, acute triangle, right triangle, equilateral, isosceles, and scalene may be introduced by teachers, but children are not expected to master these terms at this grade level.

Different Orientations

Lesson 2

In all geometry work, it is important for children to see and recognize shapes in different orientations. This helps to build their visual, spatial, as well as geometric knowledge.

Finding Perimeter

Lesson 1

In Unit 2, children calculated the perimeter of squares, rectangles, and triangles using informal methods. Class discussion included the idea that the perimeter of a square can be found using the measure of only one side. Children shared different methods of finding the perimeter of a rectangle but there was not an emphasis on finding the perimeter using the least number of measures. In this unit, children consolidate their learning by calculating the perimeter of a triangle, a square, and a rectangle and sharing their methods in class discussion. These experiences of calculating perimeter using informal methods provide the conceptual foundation for formula development in subsequent years.

Share Observations about Geometry

Lesson Objectives

- Describe properties of squares, rectangles, and triangles.
- Explain how to find the perimeter of squares, rectangles, and triangles.
- Classify triangles.

Vocabulary

square
rectangle
triangle
perimeter

The Day at a Glance

Today's Goals	Materials	
1 Teaching the Lesson **A1:** Discuss the properties of different shapes and the concept of perimeter. **A2:** Draw, compare, and classify triangles.	**Lesson Activities** Student Activity Book pp. 127–130 (includes Family Letter) Homework and Remembering pp. 83–84 25-cm rulers or 25-cm Rulers (TRB M47–M48) Geoboards and rubber bands	**Going Further** Activity Cards 4-1 Scissors Straws 25-cm rulers Math Journals
2 Going Further ▶ Differentiated Instruction		
3 Homework		

Use Math Talk today!

Keeping Skills Sharp

Daily Routines	English Language Learners
Comparing 2-Digit Quantities Using a Meter Stick, Using Number Flashes, Using the MathBoard (See pp. xxv–xxvi.) ▶ Led by Student Leaders **Money Routine** Using the 120 Poster, Using the Money Flip Chart, Using the Number Path, Using Secret Code Cards (See pp. xxiii–xxv.) ▶ Led by Student Leaders	Review the properties of a square, rectangle, and triangle. Draw each shape on the board. • **Beginning** Point to each shape. Ask simple questions. For example: **Does a square have 3 sides?** no **4 sides?** yes • **Intermediate and Advanced** Ask questions to help children describe the shapes' properties. For example: **Which shapes have parallel sides?** square, rectangle

1 Teaching the Lesson

Activity 1

Definitions and Finding Perimeter

 30 MINUTES

Goal: Discuss the properties of different shapes and the concept of perimeter.

Materials: Student Activity Book page 127, 25-cm rulers

 **NCTM Standards:**
Geometry
Communication

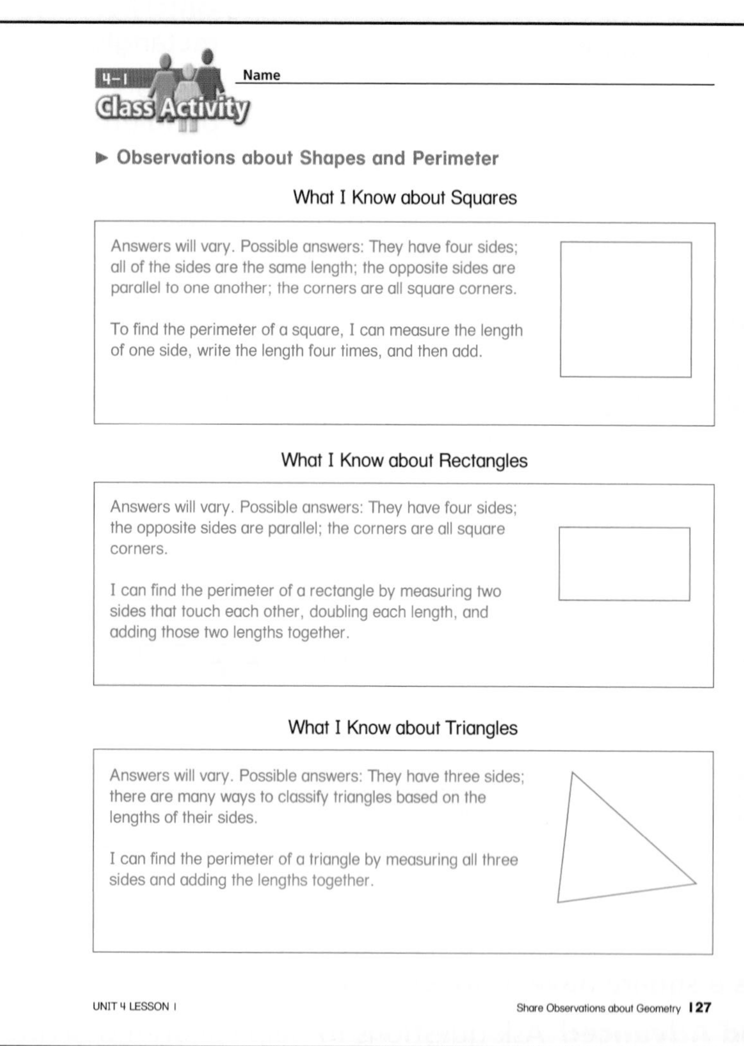
4-1 Class Activity Name

▶ Observations about Shapes and Perimeter

What I Know about Squares

Answers will vary. Possible answers: They have four sides; all of the sides are the same length; the opposite sides are parallel to one another; the corners are all square corners.

To find the perimeter of a square, I can measure the length of one side, write the length four times, and then add.

What I Know about Rectangles

Answers will vary. Possible answers: They have four sides; the opposite sides are parallel; the corners are all square corners.

I can find the perimeter of a rectangle by measuring two sides that touch each other, doubling each length, and adding those two lengths together.

What I Know about Triangles

Answers will vary. Possible answers: They have three sides; there are many ways to classify triangles based on the lengths of their sides.

I can find the perimeter of a triangle by measuring all three sides and adding the lengths together.

UNIT 4 LESSON 1 Share Observations about Geometry 127

Student Activity Book page 127

▶ Observations about Shapes and Perimeter SMALL GROUPS

Ask for Ideas Children can work in small groups to complete Student Activity Book page 127. Encourage them to include drawings in their observations about the properties of squares, rectangles, and triangles. Have them describe how they would find the perimeter of each shape. Then, ask them to work in pairs to calculate the perimeter of their shapes. Remind them to round the side measures if necessary.

When children have finished the exercise, invite them to share their observations with the rest of the class. Record key points on the board.

 Math Talk in Action

What are some of the properties of squares?

Felipa: Squares have four square corners.

Jin: Squares have four equal sides.

Jairo: Squares are special rectangles.

Tara: If you tilt a square, it is still a square.

What are some of the properties of rectangles?

Tevy: Rectangles have four square corners.

Vish: The opposite sides of a rectangle are equal in length.

What are some of the properties of triangles?

Liang: Triangles have three corners.

Victor: Triangles have three sides.

Robert: Triangles come in lots of different shapes, but they all have three corners and three sides.

What does perimeter mean?

Melanie: Perimeter is the distance around a shape. It is the total of the lengths of all of the sides.

What tool do you need to use to find the perimeter of a shape?

Aretha: You need a ruler.

How do you find the perimeter of a triangle?

Carmen: Measure all of the sides and add the lengths together.

How do you find the perimeter of a rectangle?

Ethan: You can measure all of the sides and add the lengths together, or you can measure two sides that touch each other, double each length, and add those two lengths together.

How do you find the perimeter of a square?

Nam: You can measure all of the sides and add the lengths together, or you can measure one side, write that length four times, and then add.

Activity 2

Compare and Classify Triangles

 30 MINUTES

Goal: Draw, compare, and classify triangles.

Materials: 25-cm rulers or 25-cm Rulers (TRB M47–M48) (2 per child), Student Activity Book page 128, geoboards and rubber bands, scissors

 **NCTM Standards:**
Geometry
Representation

▶ Draw and Classify Triangles PAIRS

Be sure that each child has two 25-cm rulers printed on card stock from TRB M47–M48. Demonstrate how to use two rulers to make angles of different sizes. Show children how to trace the inside of an angle and how to add a third line to create a triangle.

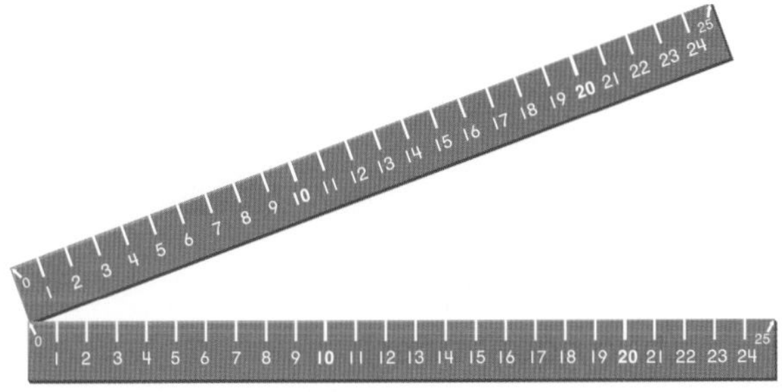

Have children use the centimeter dot paper on Student Activity Book page 128 to draw a small angle, a large angle, and a square angle.

Alternate Approach

Triangles on Geoboards Some children may benefit from using rubber bands on geoboards to help them create a wide variety of triangles.

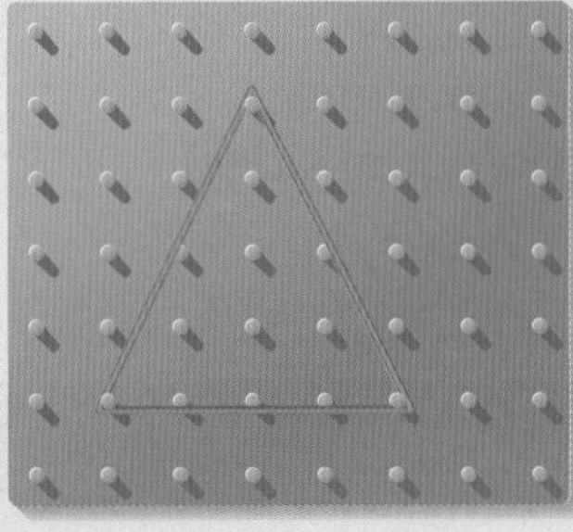

Then ask children to draw ten triangles on blank paper. Challenge them to make each triangle unique by varying the size of the angles and the number of equal sides.

When children are finished, have them cut out each of their triangles.

Invite children to work in pairs to organize their triangles into three groups according to different characteristics.

When classifying triangles, children do not need to use special labels. Children may classify the triangles by any appropriate characteristic. (See page 290.) You may, however, wish to introduce some mathematical terms at this time, such as *equilateral* and *isosceles.*

Differentiated Instruction

Extra Help If some pairs are having difficulty classifying their triangles, have them begin by looking closely at the characteristics of the triangles.

Ask them to measure all three sides of each triangle and note whether a triangle has three equal sides, two equal sides, or no equal sides.

Encourage children to move their two rulers to each angle on a triangle and to note whether the triangle has very big and very small angles, angles of equal measure, or square angles.

Activity continued ▶

❶ Teaching the Lesson (continued)

Possible Classification of Triangles

Note that terms used by children are shown above and mathematical terms are shown below.

Classify by Size of Angles

"big-angle" triangles

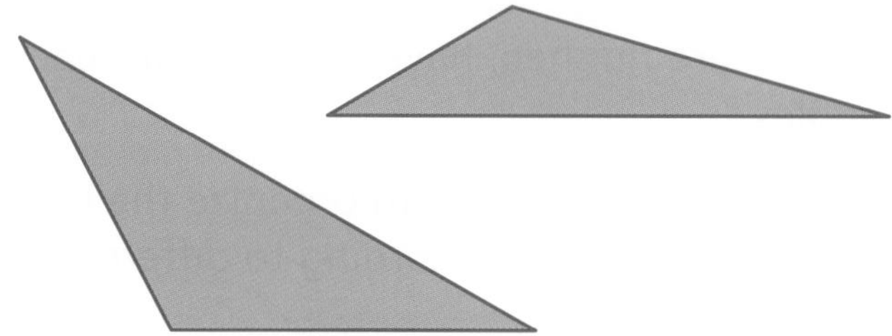

obtuse triangles
(measure of one angle > 90°)

"no-big-angle" triangles

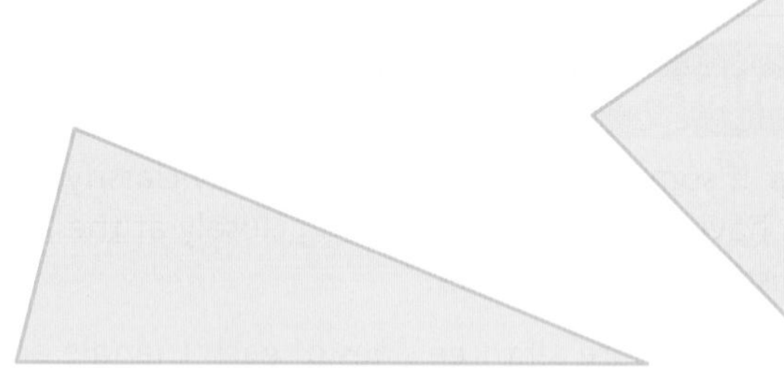

acute triangles
(measure of each angle < 90°)

"square-corner" triangles

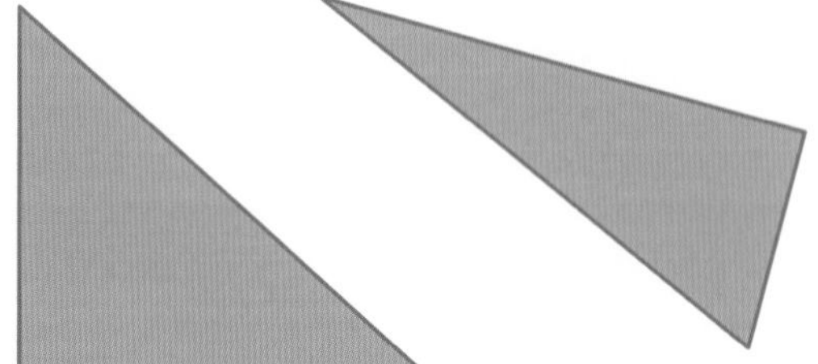

right triangles
(measure of one angle = 90° [right angle])

Classify by Number of Equal Sides

"three-sides-equal" triangles

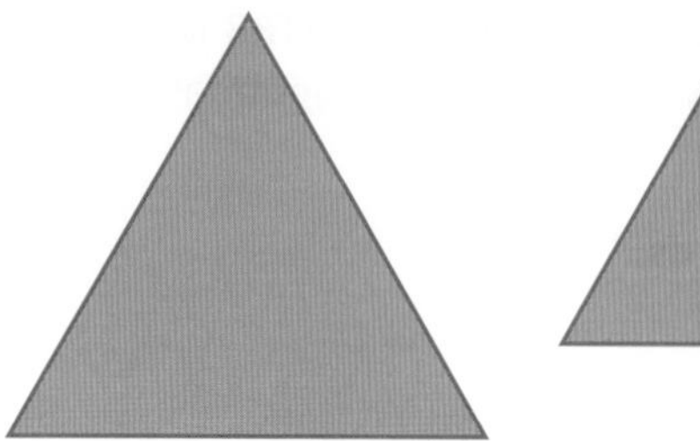

equilateral
(three equal sides)

"two-sides-equal" triangles

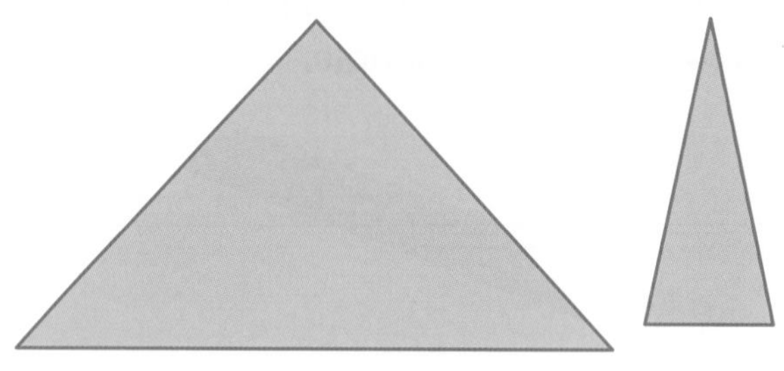

isosceles
(two equal sides)

"all-sides-different" triangles

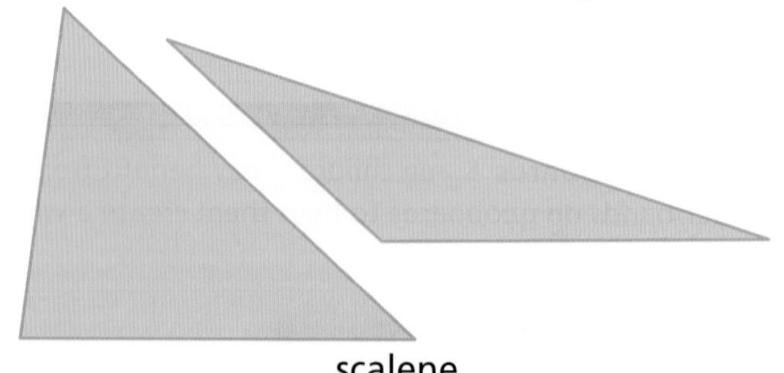

scalene
(no equal sides)

Differentiated Instruction

English Learners Have English learners record all new terminology in their math journals. Have them draw examples of each triangle and make sure that they understand how to recognize and name each.

Ongoing Assessment

Ask children to describe the triangles in each of their classification groups.

2 Going Further

Differentiated Instruction

Intervention — Activity Card 4-1

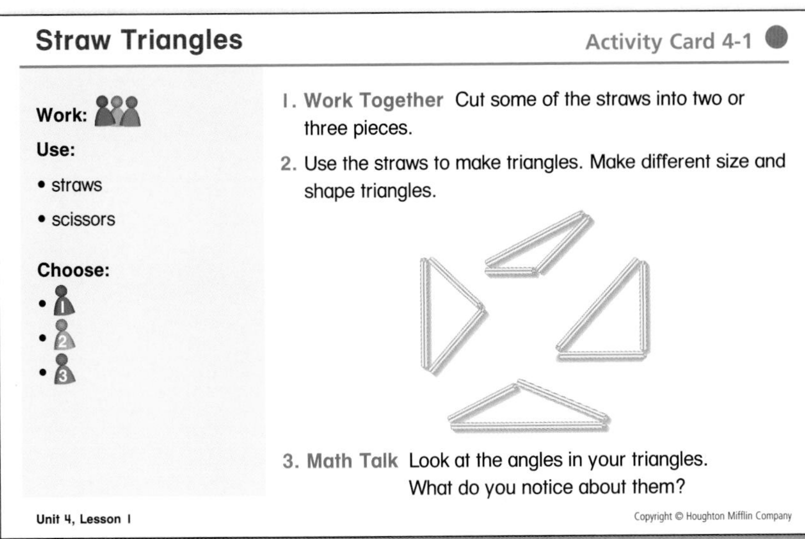
Straw Triangles — Activity Card 4-1

Work: (group)
Use:
- straws
- scissors

Choose:
- 1
- 2
- 3

1. **Work Together** Cut some of the straws into two or three pieces.
2. Use the straws to make triangles. Make different size and shape triangles.
3. **Math Talk** Look at the angles in your triangles. What do you notice about them?

Unit 4, Lesson 1 — Copyright © Houghton Mifflin Company

Activity Note Each group needs 9–12 straws and a pair of scissors. Have groups cut straws into different lengths.

Math Writing Prompt

Explain Your Prediction Two children measure the perimeter of a triangle. Each starts measuring at a different point. Will they get the same answer? Explain why or why not.

Software Support

Use *Soar to Success* for instruction of students needing targeted support for underlying skills.

On Level — Activity Card 4-1

Triangles with Equal Sides — Activity Card 4-1

Work: (pair)
Use:
- Ruler
- 9-12 Straws
- scissors

Choose:
- 1
- 2

1. Think about how you can use the straws to make three or four triangles with equal sides.
2. Cut the straws as necessary to make at least three different triangles with all the sides the same length. Use your ruler to check the lengths.
3. Compare the angles in the triangles.
4. **Math Talk** Share with your partner what you discovered about the angles in the triangles.

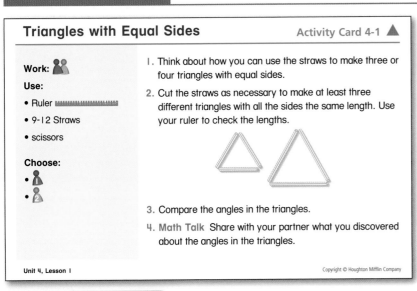

Unit 4, Lesson 1 — Copyright © Houghton Mifflin Company

Activity Note Each pair needs 25-cm ruler, 9–10 straws, and scissors. Help children understand that all the angles are equal when the three sides are the same length.

Math Writing Prompt

Investigate Math Sam says that he drew a triangle with two square corners. Is this possible? Use a picture to explain your answer.

Software Support

Use *MegaMath* for review and reinforcement of the concepts and skills presented in this lesson.

Challenge — Activity Card 4-1

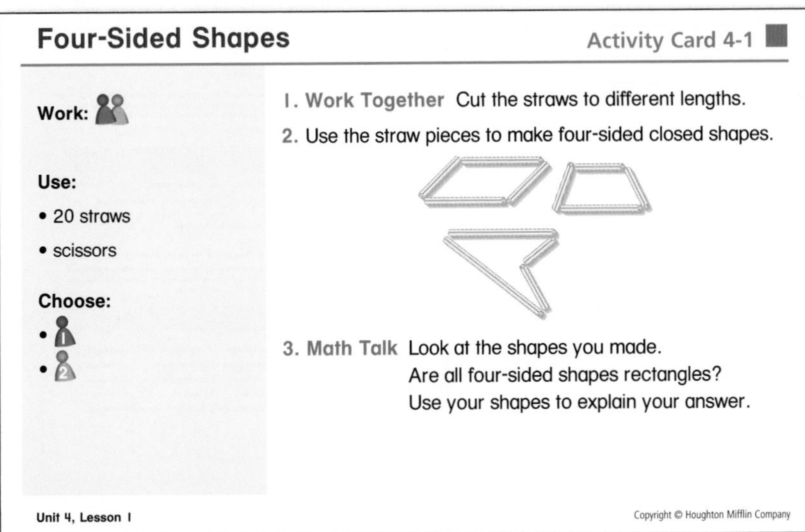
Four-Sided Shapes — Activity Card 4-1

Work: (pair)
Use:
- 20 straws
- scissors

Choose:
- 1
- 2

1. **Work Together** Cut the straws to different lengths.
2. Use the straw pieces to make four-sided closed shapes.
3. **Math Talk** Look at the shapes you made. Are all four-sided shapes rectangles? Use your shapes to explain your answer.

Unit 4, Lesson 1 — Copyright © Houghton Mifflin Company

Activity Note Each pair needs about 20 straws and scissors. Have children make different kinds of four-sided shapes.

Math Writing Prompt

Predict and Verify If the sides of a rectangle have whole-centimeter length, will the perimeter of the shape be an even or odd number? Use examples to explain your thinking.

Software Support

Use *Destination Math* to take students beyond the concepts and skills presented in this lesson.

3 Homework

Goal: Additional Practice

This Homework page allows children to practice finding perimeter.

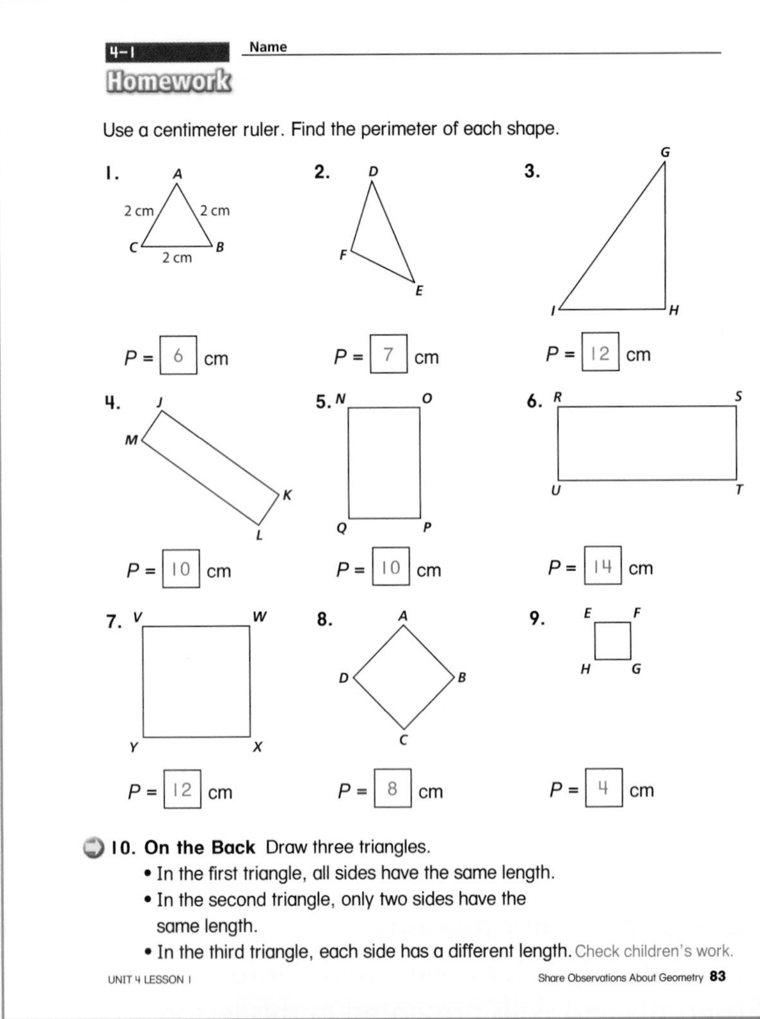

4-1 Homework Name ________________

Use a centimeter ruler. Find the perimeter of each shape.

1. A, B, C; 2 cm, 2 cm, 2 cm — $P = $ 6 cm
2. D, E, F — $P = $ 7 cm
3. G, H, I — $P = $ 12 cm
4. J, K, L, M — $P = $ 10 cm
5. N, O, P, Q — $P = $ 10 cm
6. R, S, T, U — $P = $ 14 cm
7. V, W, X, Y — $P = $ 12 cm
8. A, B, C, D — $P = $ 8 cm
9. E, F, G, H — $P = $ 4 cm

10. **On the Back** Draw three triangles.
   - In the first triangle, all sides have the same length.
   - In the second triangle, only two sides have the same length.
   - In the third triangle, each side has a different length. Check children's work.

UNIT 4 LESSON 1 Share Observations About Geometry **83**

Homework and Remembering page 83

Home and School Connection

Family Letter Have children take home the Family Letter on Student Activity Book page 129. This letter explains how the concept of quadrilaterals is developed in *Math Expressions.* It gives parents and guardians a better understanding of the learning that goes on in math class and creates a bridge between school and home. A Spanish translation of this letter is on the following page in the Student Activity Book.

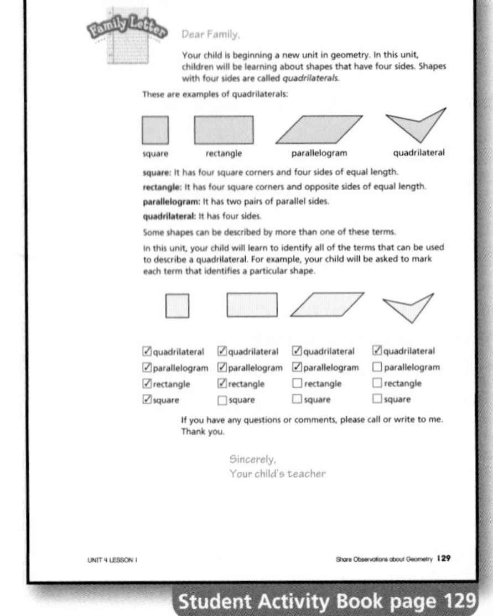

Family Letter

Dear Family,

Your child is beginning a new unit in geometry. In this unit, children will be learning about shapes that have four sides. Shapes with four sides are called *quadrilaterals.*

These are examples of quadrilaterals:

square rectangle parallelogram quadrilateral

square: It has four square corners and four sides of equal length.

rectangle: It has four square corners and opposite sides of equal length.

parallelogram: It has two pairs of parallel sides.

quadrilateral: It has four sides.

Some shapes can be described by more than one of these terms.

In this unit, your child will learn to identify all of the terms that can be used to describe a quadrilateral. For example, your child will be asked to mark each term that identifies a particular shape.

☑ quadrilateral	☑ quadrilateral	☑ quadrilateral	☑ quadrilateral
☑ parallelogram	☑ parallelogram	☑ parallelogram	☐ parallelogram
☑ rectangle	☑ rectangle	☐ rectangle	☐ rectangle
☑ square	☐ square	☐ square	☐ square

If you have any questions or comments, please call or write to me. Thank you.

Sincerely,
Your child's teacher

UNIT 4 LESSON 1 Share Observations about Geometry **129**

Student Activity Book page 129

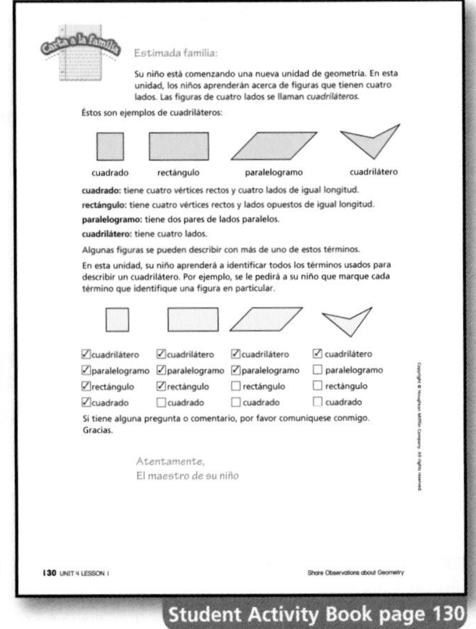

Carta a la familia

Estimada familia:

Su niño está comenzando una nueva unidad de geometría. En esta unidad, los niños aprenderán acerca de figuras que tienen cuatro lados. Las figuras de cuatro lados se llaman *cuadriláteros.*

Éstos son ejemplos de cuadriláteros:

cuadrado rectángulo paralelogramo cuadrilátero

cuadrado: tiene cuatro vértices rectos y cuatro lados de igual longitud.

rectángulo: tiene cuatro vértices rectos y lados opuestos de igual longitud.

paralelogramo: tiene dos pares de lados paralelos.

cuadrilátero: tiene cuatro lados.

Algunas figuras se pueden describir con más de uno de estos términos.

En esta unidad, su niño aprenderá a identificar todos los términos usados para describir un cuadrilátero. Por ejemplo, se le pedirá a su niño que marque cada término que identifique una figura en particular.

☑ cuadrilátero	☑ cuadrilátero	☑ cuadrilátero	☑ cuadrilátero
☑ paralelogramo	☑ paralelogramo	☑ paralelogramo	☐ paralelogramo
☑ rectángulo	☑ rectángulo	☐ rectángulo	☐ rectángulo
☑ cuadrado	☐ cuadrado	☐ cuadrado	☐ cuadrado

Si tiene alguna pregunta o comentario, por favor comuníquese conmigo. Gracias.

Atentamente,
El maestro de su niño

130 UNIT 4 LESSON 1 Share Observations about Geometry

Student Activity Book page 130

Define Parallel Lines and Parallelograms

Lesson Objectives

- Draw and explain parallel lines.
- Draw and define parallelograms.

Vocabulary
parallel
parallelogram

The Day at a Glance

Today's Goals	Materials	
1 Teaching the Lesson **A1:** Define and draw parallel lines and parallelograms. **A2:** Relate parallelograms and rectangles. **2 Going Further** ▸ Extension: Visual Thinking ▸ Differentiated Instruction **3 Homework**	**Lesson Activities** Student Activity Book pp. 131–134 Homework and Remembering pp. 85–86 MathBoard materials 25-cm rulers or 25-cm Rulers (TRB M47–M48) Geoboards and rubber bands Colored pencils or markers Scissors Pattern blocks or Pattern Blocks (TRB M58)	**Going Further** Activity Cards 4-2 Pattern blocks (TRB M58) Scissors Math Journals

Use Math Talk today!

Keeping Skills Sharp

Daily Routines	English Language Learners
Comparing 2-Digit Quantities Using a Meter Stick, Using Number Flashes, Using the MathBoard (See pp. xxv–xxvi.) ▸ Led by Student Leaders **Money Routine** Using the 120 Poster, Using the Money Flip Chart, Using the Number Path, Using Secret Code Cards (See pp. xxiii–xxv.) ▸ Led by Student Leaders	Review *parallel*. Draw intersecting lines A and B and parallel lines C and D on the board. • **Beginning** Say: ***Parallel* lines go on forever and never touch.** Point to the board. Say: **Lines C and D are parallel.** • **Intermediate and Advanced** Ask: **Do *parallel* lines ever touch?** no Point to the board. Ask: **Which lines are *parallel*?** C and D

1 Teaching the Lesson

Activity 1

Define Parallel Lines and Parallelograms

 **20 MINUTES**

Goal: Define and draw parallel lines and parallelograms.

Materials: Student Activity Book page 131, MathBoard materials, 25-cm rulers (1 per child)

✔ **NCTM Standards:**
Geometry
Reasoning and Proof

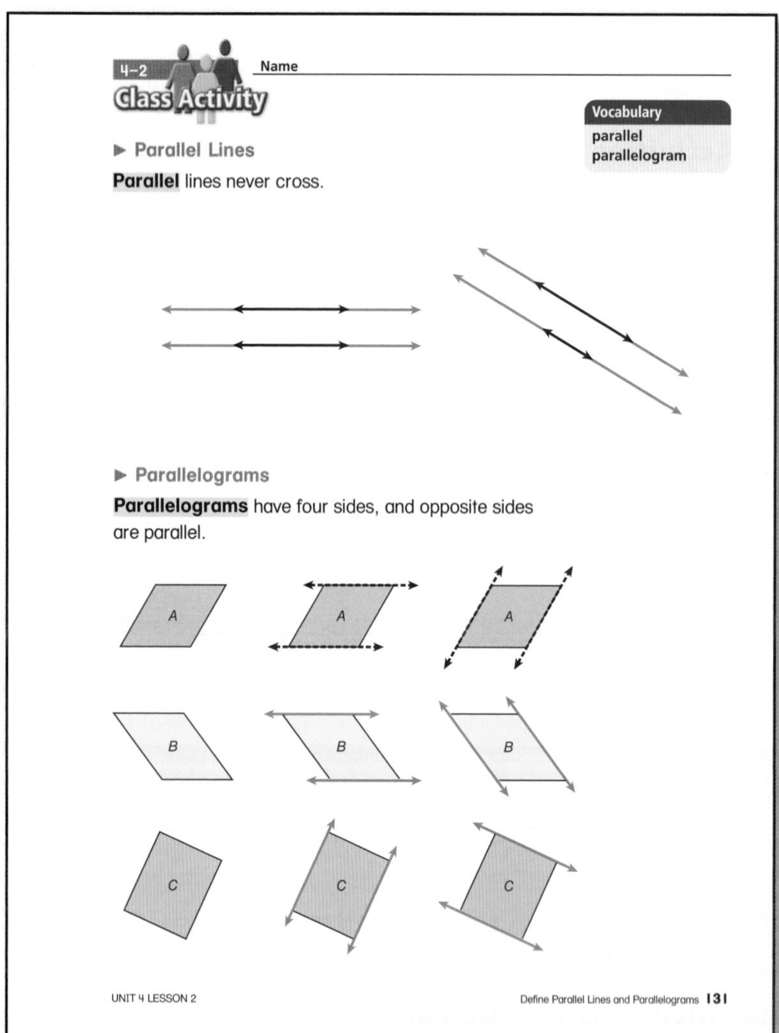
4-2 Class Activity Name

Vocabulary
parallel
parallelogram

▶ Parallel Lines

Parallel lines never cross.

▶ Parallelograms

Parallelograms have four sides, and opposite sides are parallel.

A A A

B B B

C C C

UNIT 4 LESSON 2 Define Parallel Lines and Parallelograms 131

Student Activity Book page 131

▶ Parallel Lines WHOLE CLASS

Ask for Ideas Direct children's attention to the definition of parallel lines on Student Activity Book page 131. Discuss the definition and the examples shown.

- Why do you think the arrows are shown on the lines? because the lines go on forever in each direction

Have children extend the parallel lines to demonstrate that the lines never meet. Ask them to visualize the lines going across the classroom, through the school, through their neighborhood, and beyond.

If children are having difficulty remembering what parallel means, have them write the word *parallel* on their MathBoard and ring the two "l"s in the middle of the word. This will help them remember what parallel lines look like.

Draw and Discuss Parallel Lines Have children draw more parallel lines on their MathBoards. After they've had time to practice, engage children in a discussion of parallel lines in the classroom.

- Can anyone find examples of parallel lines in the classroom? Possible responses: opposite sides of the doorway, white board, walls, tiles

▶ Parallelograms WHOLE CLASS

Read the definition of parallelogram to children. Have children measure the length of opposite sides on parallelograms A, B, and C. Ask them what they notice about the measurements of the opposite sides. Opposite sides are equal in length.

Direct their attention to the two sets of parallel lines that have been added to parallelogram A. Invite children to add similar parallel lines to parallelograms B and C. When they are finished, invite children to draw parallelograms on their MathBoards.

Engage children in a discussion of parallelograms in the classroom.

- What examples of parallelograms can you find in the classroom? Possible responses: windows, books, the top of a pencil case

Activity 2

Relate Parallelograms and Rectangles

 **25 MINUTES**

Goal: Relate parallelograms and rectangles.

Materials: Student Activity Book page 132, 25-cm rulers (1 per child), geoboards and rubber bands

 **NCTM Standards:**
Geometry
Measurement

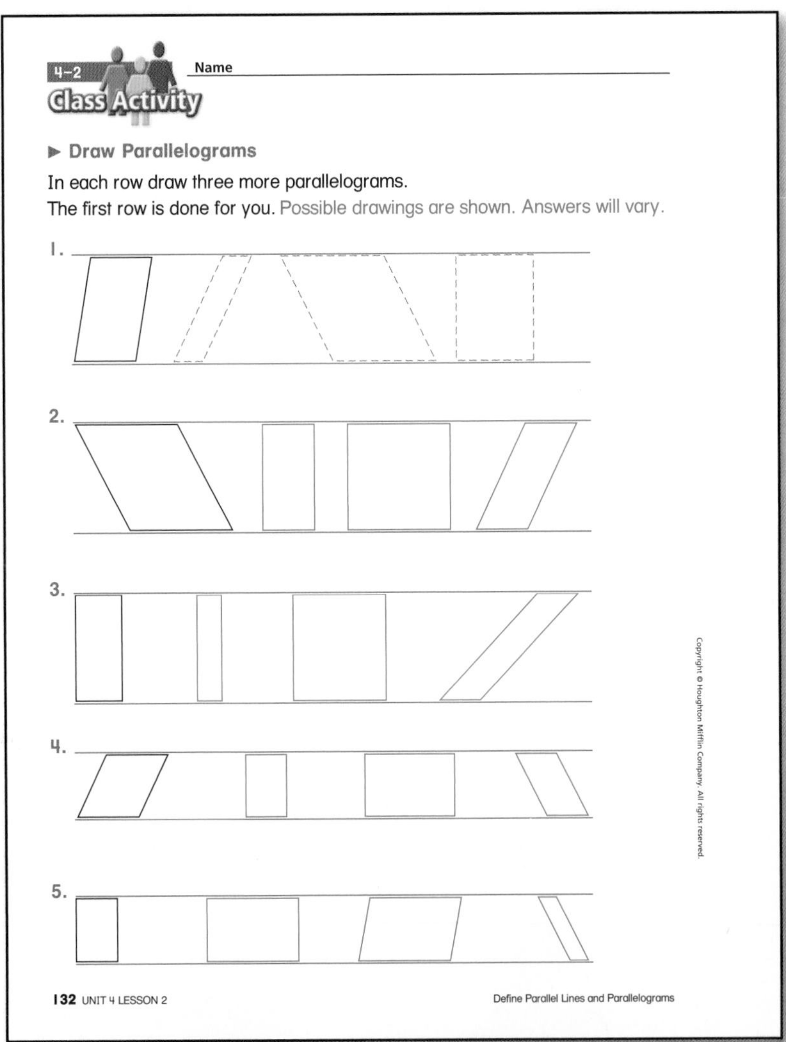

4-2 Class Activity Name

▶ Draw Parallelograms

In each row draw three more parallelograms.
The first row is done for you. Possible drawings are shown. Answers will vary.

1.

2.

3.

4.

5.

132 UNIT 4 LESSON 2 Define Parallel Lines and Parallelograms

Student Activity Book page 132

▶ Draw Parallelograms WHOLE CLASS

Have children look at Student Activity Book page 132 and discuss the first examples in each row.

- What are these shapes called? parallelograms
- Do they all look the same? no
- What makes them different from each other? Some parallelograms are almost straight up and down, others are slanted, some are skinny, and some are fat.
- Are some of these parallelograms also rectangles? yes Which ones? The parallelograms shown in exercises 3 and 5 are rectangles.
- The other parallelograms are not rectangles. How do these parallelograms differ from rectangles? They have slanted sides and their corners are not square.
- How are all parallelograms like rectangles? They have sides that are parallel.

Have children complete exercises 2–5. For each set of lines, encourage children to draw a variety of skinny and fat parallelograms that have square or non-square corners and sides that slant differently.

Alternate Approach

Geoboards To help children who are having difficulty drawing parallel lines and parallelograms, have them use a geoboard and rubber bands to construct different types of parallelograms and parallel lines.

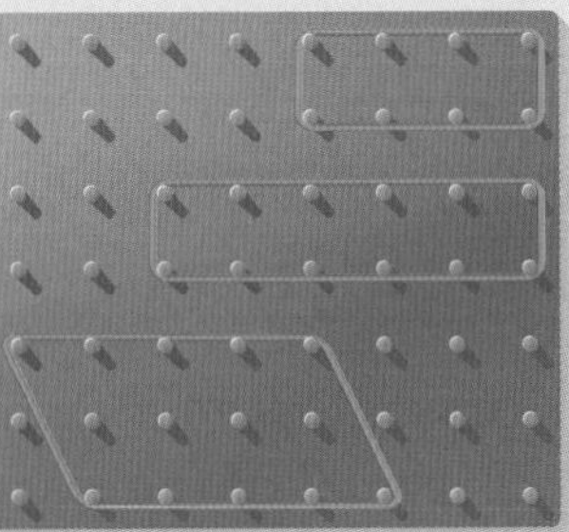

Ongoing Assessment

Ask children to complete these activities to help you assess their understanding of parallel lines and parallelograms.

- ▶ Draw four parallelograms that are different from the ones you drew in class.
- ▶ Create a list of parallelograms you might find outside your classroom.

2 Going Further

Extension: Visual Thinking

Goal: Use visual thinking and patterns to find "hidden parallelograms."

Materials: Student Activity Book page 133, colored pencils or markers, scissors (1 pair per child), pattern blocks (9 triangles, 2 parallelograms) or Pattern Blocks (TRB M58)

 **NCTM Standards:**
Geometry
Connections

▶ Hidden Parallelograms INDIVIDUALS

Before children begin to work on this page, be sure they understand what they need to do. They should color a different parallelogram inside each large triangle. Explain that there are 15 different parallelograms that they can find. Two are done for them. Do not expect most children to find them all.

If children are having difficulty getting started, point out that they can use either two or four small triangles to make a parallelogram.

▶ Compare Solutions SMALL GROUPS

When children have finished this page, have them share their answers in small groups.

You may choose to have all children in the group cut out their triangles and place duplicates in piles. This will help them find all of the possible parallelograms.

Math Talk Some children may have discovered a systematic way to show all of the parallelograms. Encourage them to share their approach with other group members or the whole class.

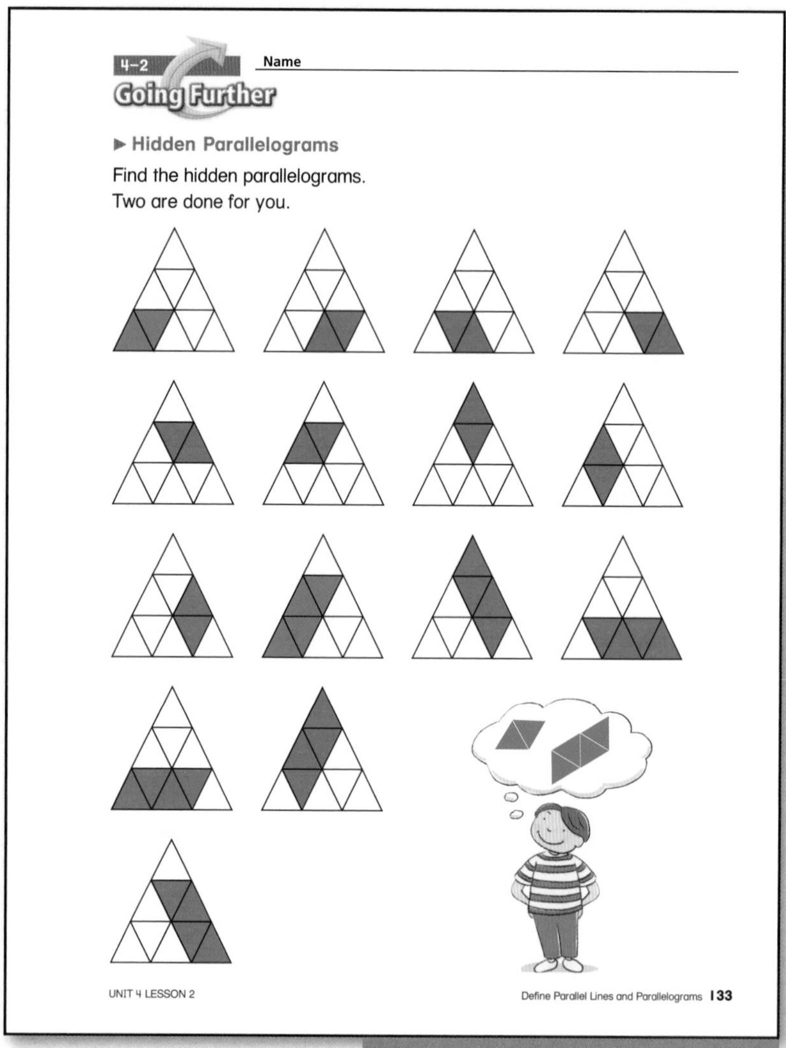
4-2 Going Further Name

▶ Hidden Parallelograms

Find the hidden parallelograms.
Two are done for you.

UNIT 4 LESSON 2 Define Parallel Lines and Parallelograms 133

Student Activity Book page 133

 **Alternate Approach**

Pattern Blocks If children are having difficulty visualizing parallelograms on paper, have them use pattern blocks or cut outs from TRB M58.

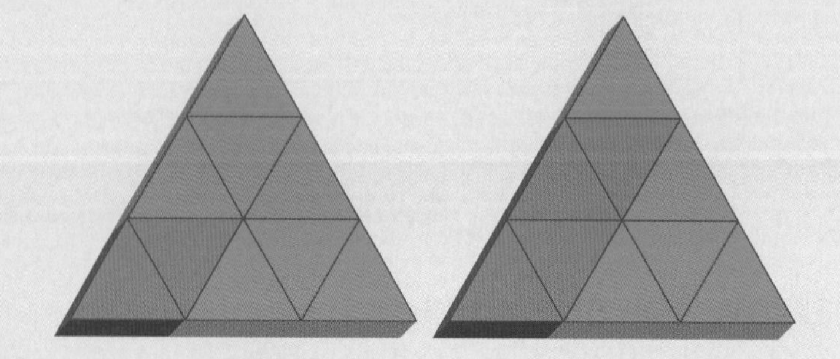

Intervention Activity Card 4-2

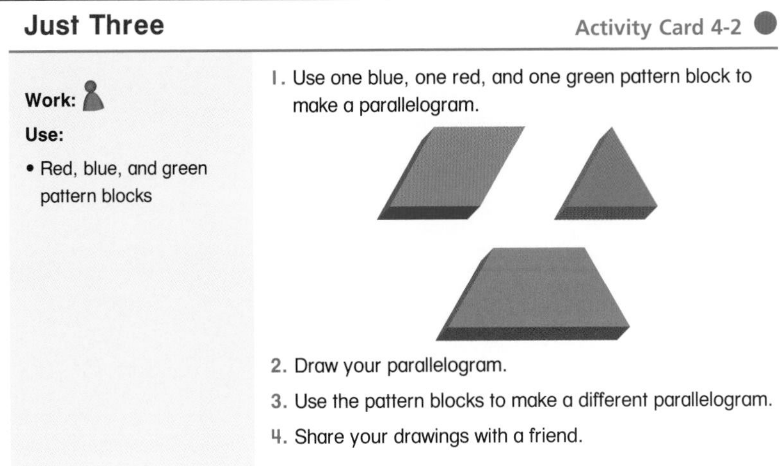

Just Three

Activity Card 4-2 ●

Work:
Use:
- Red, blue, and green pattern blocks

1. Use one blue, one red, and one green pattern block to make a parallelogram.
2. Draw your parallelogram.
3. Use the pattern blocks to make a different parallelogram.
4. Share your drawings with a friend.

Unit 4, Lesson 2

Activity Note Each child needs a red, blue, and green pattern block or TRB M58 and scissors. Help children make different parallelograms.

Math Writing Prompt

Draw and Explain Draw a pair of parallel lines and explain why they are parallel.

Software Support

Use *Soar to Success* for instruction of students needing targeted support for underlying skills.

On Level Activity Card 4-2

At Least Two

Activity Card 4-2 ▲

Work:
Use:
- 2 red, 2 blue, 2 green pattern blocks

1. Use at least two pattern blocks to make a parallelogram.

2. Draw your parallelogram.
3. Use a different number of pattern blocks to make another parallelogram.
4. Repeat to make as many parallelograms as possible.
5. Share your drawings with a friend.

Unit 4, Lesson 2

Activity Note Each child needs 2 red, 2 blue, and 2 green pattern block or TRB M58 and scissors. Help children make different parallelograms.

Math Writing Prompt

Explain Differences Draw a pair of lines that are parallel and a pair of lines that are not parallel. Explain how the pairs are different.

Software Support

Use *MegaMath* for review and reinforcement of the concepts and skills presented in this lesson.

Challenge Activity Card 4-2

All Six

Activity Card 4-2 ■

Work:
Use:
- 2 red, 2 blue, 2 green pattern blocks

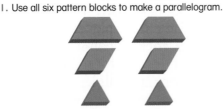

1. Use all six pattern blocks to make a parallelogram.
2. Draw your parallelogram.
3. Use your pattern blocks to make a different parallelogram.
4. Repeat to make as many parallelograms as possible.
5. Share your drawings with a friend.

Unit 4, Lesson 2

Activity Note Each child needs 2 red, 2 blue, and 2 green pattern block or TRB M58 and scissors.

Math Writing Prompt

Investigate Math Use four markers, straws, or rules that are the same length. Can you make a closed shape that is *not* a parallelogram? Use drawings to explain.

Software Support

Use *Destination Math* to take students beyond the concepts and skills presented in this lesson.

3 Homework

Goal: Additional Practice

This Homework page allows children to practice drawing parallelograms.

4–2 Homework Name

In each row draw three more parallelograms. The first row is done for you.

Possible drawings are shown. Answers will vary.

1.

2.

3.

4.

5.

6. **On the Back** Draw three different parallelograms.
Check students' parallelograms.

UNIT 4 LESSON 2 Define Parallel Lines and Parallelograms **85**

Homework and Remembering page 85

Home or School Activity

Social Studies Connection

Think About Railways Railways transport people and goods across the country.

Railway yards contain items that have many parallel lines and parallelograms.

Ask children to write about parallel lines and parallelograms found in a railway yard.

Wooden railway ties are parallelograms.
Railway ties are placed parallel to each other so that they form parallel lines.
The metal tracks form lines that never meet, so they are parallel.
Trains have square windows. Squares are parallelograms.
Trains have rectangular doors. Rectangles are parallelograms.

Relate Different Quadrilaterals

Lesson Objectives

- Describe properties of quadrilaterals, parallelograms, rectangles, and squares.
- Categorize quadrilaterals.
- Show relationships among quadrilaterals.

Vocabulary
quadrilateral
parallelogram
rectangle
right angle
square

The Day at a Glance

Today's Goals	Materials	
1 Teaching the Lesson **A1:** Observe properties of different quadrilaterals and determine how they are related to one another. **A2:** Classify quadrilaterals. **2 Going Further** ▸ Differentiated Instruction **3 Homework**	**Lesson Activities** Student Activity Book pp. 135–138 Homework and Remembering pp. 87–88 Scissors 25-cm rulers or 25-cm Rulers (TRB M47–M48)	**Going Further** Activity Cards 4-3 *Shapes (Slide 'n' Seek) by* Chuck Murphy *Shapes, Shapes, Shapes* by Tana Hoban Straws (long and short) Tangrams or Tangrams (TRB M59) Centimeter Dot Paper (TRB M49) Math Journals

123 *Use* **Math Talk** *today!*

Keeping Skills Sharp

Daily Routines	English Language Learners
Comparing 2-Digit Quantities Using a Meter Stick, Using Number Flashes, Using the MathBoard (See pp. xxv–xxvi.) ▸ Led by Student Leaders **Money Routine** Using the 120 Poster, Using the Money Flip Chart, Using the Number Path, Using Secret Code Cards (See pp. xxiii–xxv.) ▸ Led by Student Leaders	Review *quadrilateral.* Draw a square, rectangle, parallelogram, and a different quadrilateral on the board. • **Beginning** Ask: **Are these shapes the same or different?** different Have children count the sides of each shape. Say: **They all have 4 sides. They are all quadrilaterals.** Have children repeat. • **Intermediate and Advanced** Ask: **What is true about all these shapes?** They all have 4 sides. **Are they quadrilaterals?** yes

1 Teaching the Lesson

Activity 1

Observe Quadrilaterals

 40 MINUTES

Goal: Observe properties of different quadrilaterals and determine how they are related to one another.

Materials: Student Activity Book page 135, scissors (1 pair per child)

 **NCTM Standards:**
Geometry
Connections
Communication

▶ Discuss Properties of Quadrilaterals

WHOLE CLASS

Math Talk 

Teaching Note

Language and Vocabulary Use the following definitions to guide the discussion and prompt responses from children. While it is important that children are familiar with the properties of these shapes, it is not necessary for them to memorize the definitions.

Quadrilateral: A shape that has four sides.

Parallelogram: A quadrilateral that has two pairs of parallel sides.

Rectangle: A special kind of parallelogram that has four square (right-angle) corners.

Square: A special kind of rectangle with sides of equal length.

Quadrilaterals Draw a square, a rectangle, a parallelogram, and a different quadrilateral on the board.

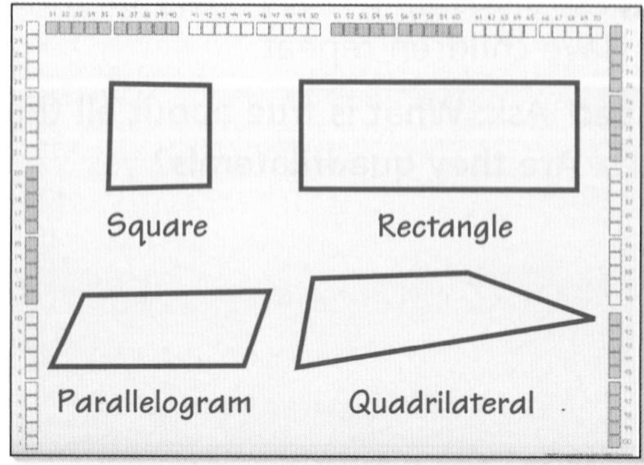

- What do all of these shapes have in common? They all have four sides and each side is a line segment.

Introduce the term *quadrilateral*. Inform children that *quadri* means "four" and *latus* means "sides," so quadrilaterals are shapes with four sides. Point out that the sides of all quadrilaterals are line segments.

Parallelograms Are Quadrilaterals Draw several different parallelograms on the board.

- What is the definition of a parallelogram? A parallelogram is a quadrilateral that has two pairs of parallel sides.
- Are all parallelograms quadrilaterals? yes Why? All parallelograms have four sides.
- Are all quadrilaterals parallelograms? No; only some quadrilaterals are parallelograms.

Rectangles Are Quadrilaterals Draw several different rectangles on the board.

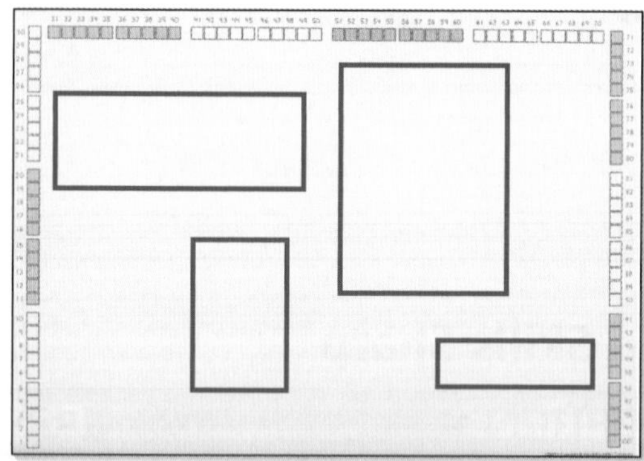

- What is the definition of a rectangle? A rectangle is a quadrilateral with four square corners (right corners, right angles).
- Are all rectangles quadrilaterals? yes Why? All rectangles have four sides.
- Are all quadrilaterals rectangles? No; only some quadrilaterals are rectangles.
- Are all rectangles parallelograms? yes Why? All rectangles have two pairs of parallel sides.
- Are all parallelograms rectangles? No; only some parallelograms are rectangles.

Squares Are Quadrilaterals Draw several different squares on the board.

- What is the definition of a square? A square is a special kind of rectangle with sides of equal length.
- Are all squares quadrilaterals? yes Why? All squares have four sides.
- Are all quadrilaterals squares? No; only some quadrilaterals are squares.
- Are all squares parallelograms? yes Why? All squares have two pairs of parallel sides.
- Are all parallelograms squares? No; only some parallelograms are squares.
- Are all squares rectangles? yes Why? All squares have four square corners.
- Are all rectangles squares? No; only some rectangles are squares.

▶ Sort Quadrilaterals WHOLE CLASS

Have children cut out the shapes on Student Activity Book page 135. Ask them to separate the shapes into two groups: quadrilaterals and not quadrilaterals.

Write the word *quadrilateral* on the board and ask children which shapes are quadrilaterals. A, B, C, D, E, F, H, I List their answers on the board.

Have children explain why all the shapes listed are quadrilaterals. They all have 4 sides.

Next, invite children to sort the quadrilaterals into two groups: parallelograms and not parallelograms. When they are finished, ask them to sort the parallelograms into two groups: rectangles and not rectangles. Finally, have them separate the rectangles into two groups: squares and not squares.

Quadrilaterals: A, B, C, D, E, F, H, I
Parallelograms: A, C, D, E, H, I
Rectangles: A, D, E, H
Squares: A, E

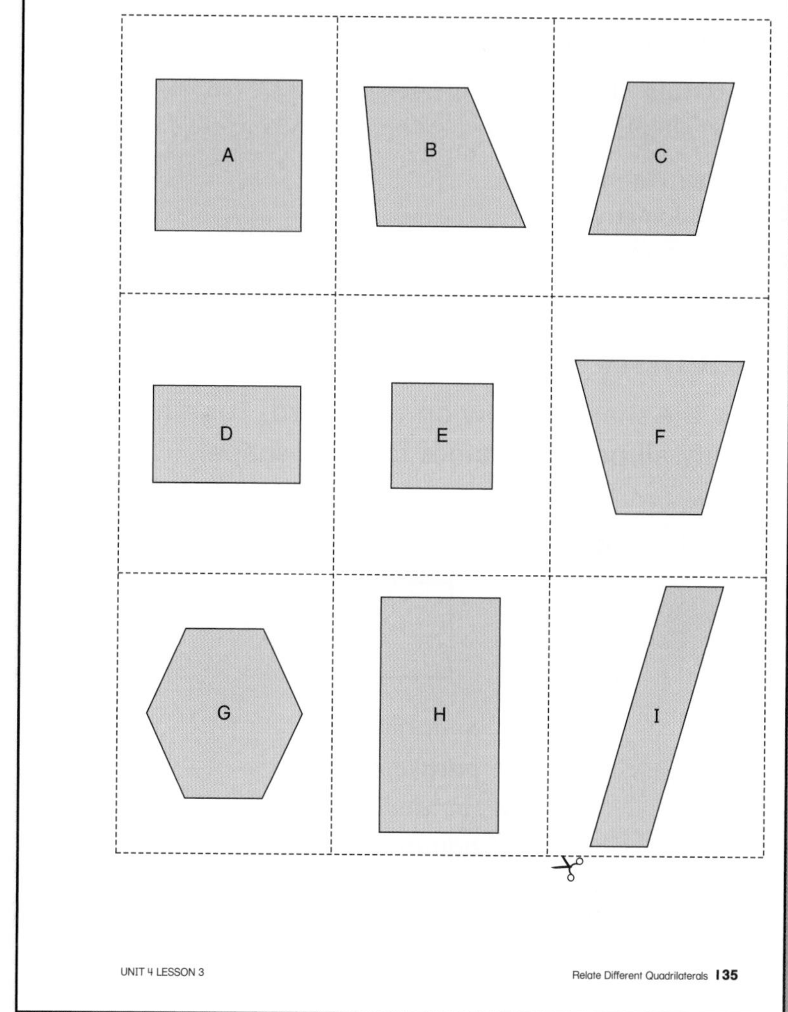

Student Activity Book page 135

Teaching Note

What to Expect from Students Class discussion on the relationships among different kinds of quadrilaterals allows children to explore new ideas. It is to be expected, however, that many children will not master these concepts at this time.

Orientation of shapes It is vital that students have experience with seeing shapes in different orientations so that they can recognize shapes when their bases are not horizontal. Have students turn their cut-out shapes and then turn their heads to make the bases horizontal to their gaze to recognize the shape. You can also rotate shapes drawn on MathBoards to provide these experiences.

Activity 2

Classify Quadrilaterals

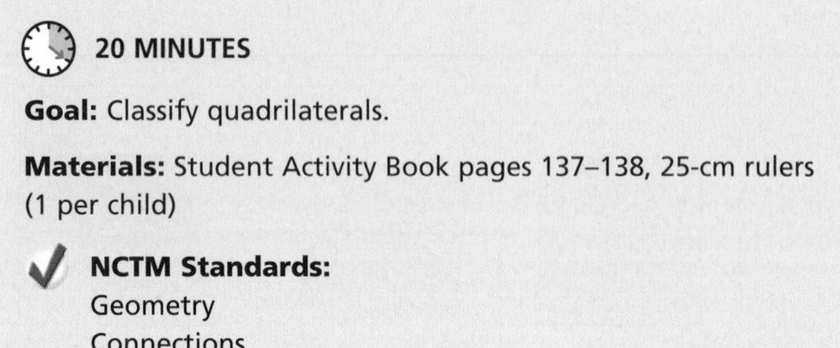

20 MINUTES

Goal: Classify quadrilaterals.

Materials: Student Activity Book pages 137–138, 25-cm rulers (1 per child)

NCTM Standards:
Geometry
Connections

► Identify Quadrilaterals WHOLE CLASS

Draw the shapes below on the board. Together, identify all possible names for each shape.

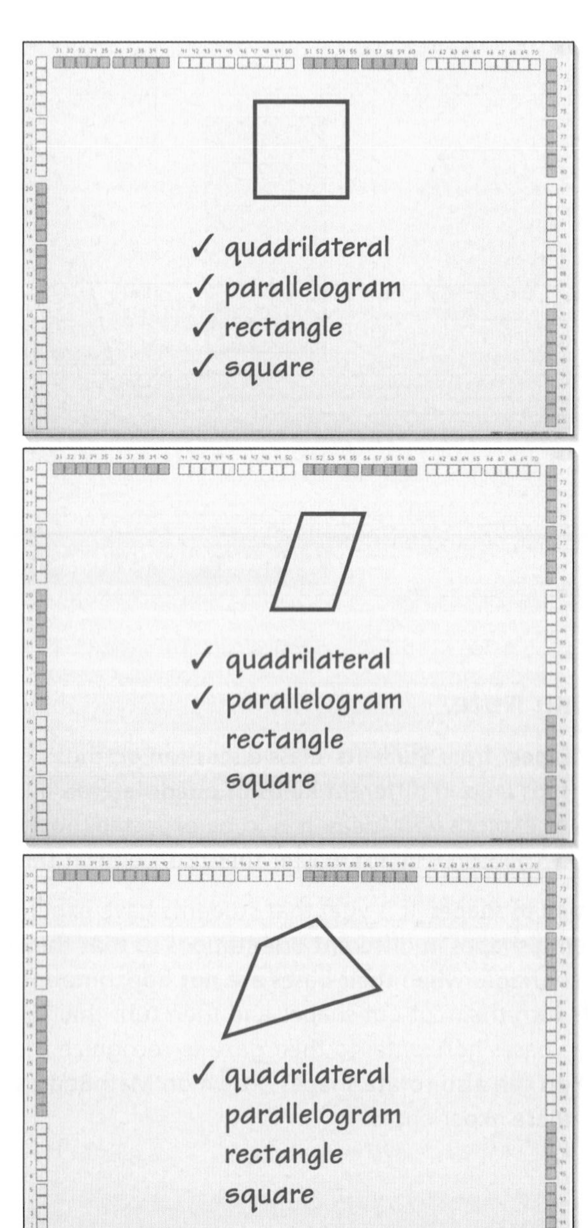

► Name Quadrilaterals INDIVIDUALS

Have children then complete exercises 1–7 independently. Assist as necessary.

4-3 Class Activity Name ____________

► Name Quadrilaterals

Place a check mark beside each word that names the shape.

1. ☑ quadrilateral ☑ parallelogram ☑ rectangle ☐ square

2. ☑ quadrilateral ☐ parallelogram ☐ rectangle ☐ square

3. ☑ quadrilateral ☑ parallelogram ☑ rectangle ☑ square

4. ☑ quadrilateral ☑ parallelogram ☐ rectangle ☐ square

5. ☑ quadrilateral ☐ parallelogram ☐ rectangle ☐ square

6. ☑ quadrilateral ☑ parallelogram ☑ rectangle ☐ square

7. **On the Back** Draw a shape that is a parallelogram but *not* a rectangle. Check students' parallelograms.

UNIT 4 LESSON 3 Relate Different Quadrilaterals 137

Student Activity Book page 137

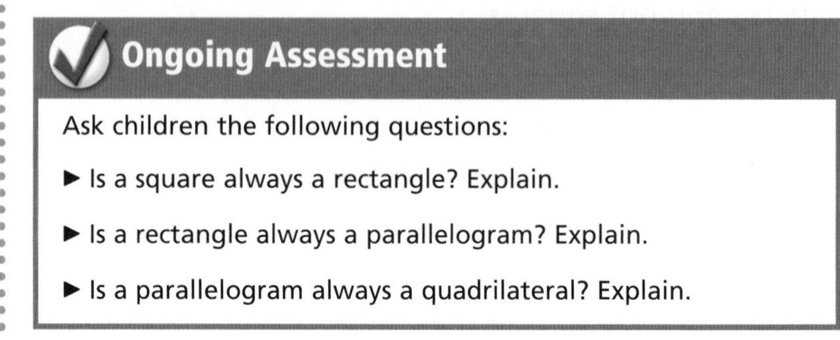

Ongoing Assessment

Ask children the following questions:

- ► Is a square always a rectangle? Explain.
- ► Is a rectangle always a parallelogram? Explain.
- ► Is a parallelogram always a quadrilateral? Explain.

Intervention Activity Card 4-3

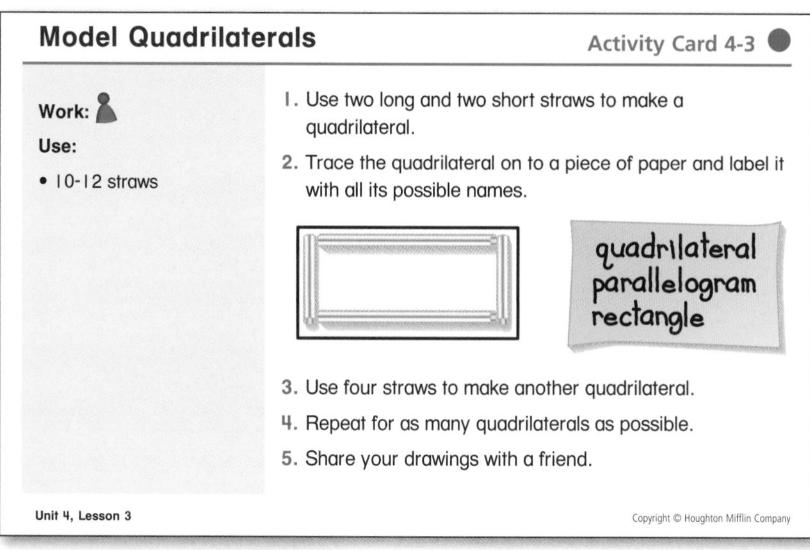

Activity Note Each child needs 10–12 short and long straws. Have children help each other label their quadrilaterals.

Math Writing Prompt

Make a Comparison Ester makes one square and one parallelogram using straws of equal length. Use words or pictures to explain how the shapes might be different.

Software Support

Use *Soar to Success* for instruction of students needing targeted support for underlying skills.

On Level Activity Card 4-3

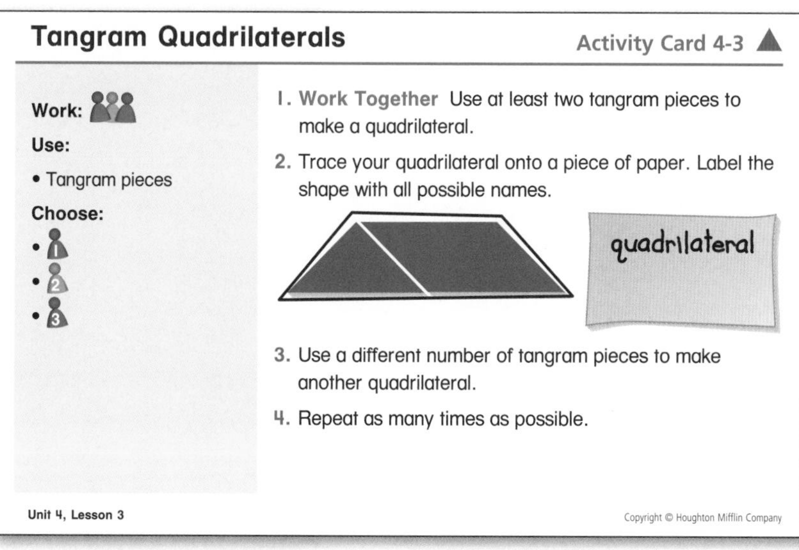

Activity Note Each group needs a set of tangrams or TRB M59. Have the group use different tangram pieces to make quadrilaterals.

Math Writing Prompt

Explain Your Thinking Jordan draws a shape and describes it as a quadrilateral, a parallelogram, and a rectangle. Is this possible? Explain your thinking.

Software Support

Use *MegaMath* for review and reinforcement of the concepts and skills presented in this lesson.

Challenge Activity Card 4-3

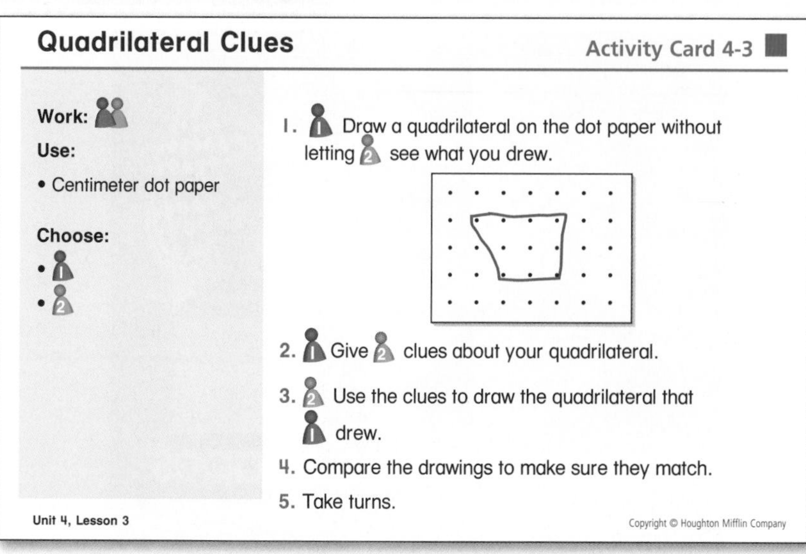

Activity Note Each pair needs several pieces of centimeter dot paper (TRB M49.) Discuss possible clues for the shapes.

Math Writing Prompt

Draw and Label a Picture Leon's shape has four sides. It has opposite sides that are parallel and corners that are not square. Draw a picture of Leon's shape and label it with all possible names.

Software Support

Use *Destination Math* to take students beyond the concepts and skills presented in this lesson.

Homework

4-3 Homework Goal: Additional Practice

✓ Include children's completed Homework page as part of their portfolios.

4-3 Homework Name ______________

Place a check mark beside each word that names the shape.

1.
- ✓ quadrilateral
- ✓ parallelogram
- ✓ rectangle
- ✓ square

2.
- ✓ quadrilateral
- ✓ parallelogram
- ☐ rectangle
- ☐ square

3.
- ✓ quadrilateral
- ☐ parallelogram
- ☐ rectangle
- ☐ square

4.
- ✓ quadrilateral
- ✓ parallelogram
- ✓ rectangle
- ☐ square

5.
- ✓ quadrilateral
- ✓ parallelogram
- ✓ rectangle
- ✓ square

6.
- ✓ quadrilateral
- ☐ parallelogram
- ☐ rectangle
- ☐ square

7. **On the Back** Draw three different quadrilaterals that have the same perimeter. Check children's work.

UNIT 4 LESSON 3 Relate Different Quadrilaterals **87**

Homework and Remembering page 87

Home or School Activity

Literature Connection

Read About Shapes Have children read these books:

Shapes (Slide 'n' Seek) by Chuck Murphy (Little Simon, 2001)

Shapes, Shapes, Shapes by Tana Hoban (HarperTrophy, 1996)

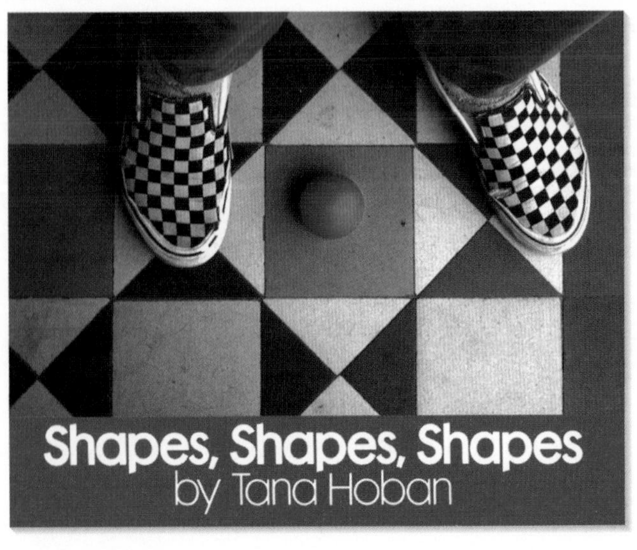

Have children then write a riddle, rhyme, or story about any type of quadrilateral.

Unit Review and Test

Lesson Objectives

- **Assess children's progress on unit objectives.**

The Day at a Glance

Today's Goals	Materials
1 Assessing the Unit ▸ Assess children's progress on unit objectives. ▸ Use activities from unit lessons to reteach content. **2 Extending the Assessment** ▸ Use remediation for common errors. There is no homework assignment on a test day.	Unit 4 Test, Student Activity Book pages 139–140 Unit 4 Test, Form A or B, Assessment Guide (optional) Unit 4 Performance Assessment, Assessment Guide (optional)

Keeping Skills Sharp

Daily Routines 5 MINUTES	
If you are doing a unit review day, go over the homework. If this is a test day, omit the homework review.	**Review and Test Day** You may want to choose a quiet game or other activity (reading a book or working on homework for another subject) for children who finish early.

 Assessing the Unit

Assess Unit Objectives

45 MINUTES (more if schedule permits)

Goal: Assess children's progress on unit objectives.

Materials: Student Activity Book pages 139–140, Assessment Guide (optional)

▶ Review and Assessment

If the children are ready for assessment on the unit objectives, you may use either the test on the Student Activity Book pages or one of the forms of the Unit 4 Test in the Assessment Guide to assess student progress.

If you feel that more review is needed first, you may use the test on the Student Activity Book pages as a review of unit content, and then use one of the forms of the Unit 4 Test in the Assessment Guide to assess student progress.

To assign a numerical score for all of these test forms, use 10 points for each question.

You may also choose to use the Unit 4 Performance Assessment. Scoring for that assessment can be found in its rubric in the Assessment Guide.

▶ Reteaching Resources

The chart lists the test items, the unit objectives they cover, and the lesson activities in which the objective is covered in this unit. You may revisit these activities with children who do not show mastery of the objectives.

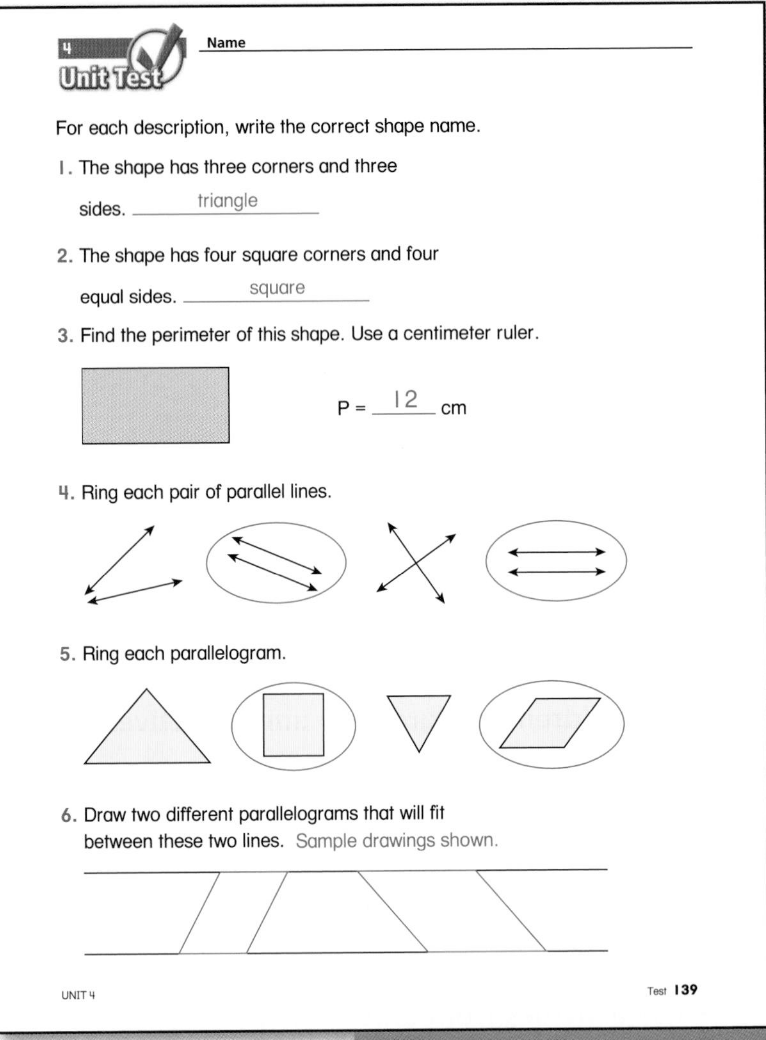
4 Unit Test Name

For each description, write the correct shape name.

1. The shape has three corners and three sides. triangle

2. The shape has four square corners and four equal sides. square

3. Find the perimeter of this shape. Use a centimeter ruler.

P = 12 cm

4. Ring each pair of parallel lines.

5. Ring each parallelogram.

6. Draw two different parallelograms that will fit between these two lines. Sample drawings shown.

UNIT 4 Test 139

Student Activity Book page 139

Unit Test Items	Unit Objectives Tested	Activities to Use for Reteaching
1, 2, 3, 10	**4.1** Describe properties of quadrilaterals and triangles.	Lesson 1, Activities 1–2
4, 5, 6	**4.2** Define parallel lines and parallelograms.	Lesson 2, Activities 1–2
7, 8, 9	**4.3** Classify quadrilaterals.	Lesson 3, Activities 1–2

4 Unit Test Name

Place a check mark beside each word that names the shape.

7.

- [x] quadrilateral
- [x] parallelogram
- [x] rectangle
- [x] square

8.

- [x] quadrilateral
- [ ] parallelogram
- [ ] rectangle
- [ ] square

9.

- [x] quadrilateral
- [x] parallelogram
- [ ] rectangle
- [ ] square

10. **Extended Response** Marco says that all triangles have sides with equal lengths. Do you agree or disagree? Explain. Include pictures and words in your answer. Explanations will vary. Sample answer given.

Disagree; Some triangles have sides with equal lengths, but not all of them. All the sides of an equilateral triangle are equal lengths. Two sides of an isosceles triangle are equal lengths. Scalene triangles do not have any sides that are equal lengths.

140 UNIT 4 Test

Student Activity Book page 140

▶ Assessment Resources

Free Response Tests
Unit 4 Test, Student Activity Book pages 139–140
Unit 4 Test, Form A, Assessment Guide

Extended Response Item
The last item in the Student Activity Book test and in the Form A test will require an extended response as an answer.

Multiple Choice Test
Unit 4 Test, Form B, Assessment Guide

Performance Assessment
Unit 4 Performance Assessment, Assessment Guide
Unit 4 Performance Assessment Rubric, Assessment Guide

▶ Portfolio Assessment

Teacher-selected Items for Student Portfolios:

- Homework, Lesson 3
- Class Activity work, Lessons 2, 3

Student-selected Items for Student Portfolios:

- Favorite Home or School Activity
- Best Writing Prompt

2 Extending the Assessment

Common Errors

Activities for Remediation

Unit Objective 4.1

Describe properties of quadrilaterals and triangles.

Common Error: **Incorrectly Identifies Shapes**

In discussing properties of quadrilaterals and triangles, children may incorrectly name shapes.

Remediation Provide children with cut outs of squares, rectangles, and triangles. Help children describe and identify each shape. Have children write the names on each shape and keep the shapes for reference. As new shapes are introduced, have children add them to their collections.

Common Error: **Doesn't Recognize That a Square Is a Rectangle**

In classifying quadrilaterals, some children may not recognize that a square is a special rectangle.

Remediation Reinforce the properties of a rectangle. Point out that in rectangles, opposite sides are parallel and congruent and that rectangles have four square (right) angles. Have students identify these properties in a square. Then explain that a square is a special rectangle having one additional property: all four sides are the same length.

Unit Objective 4.2

Define parallel lines and parallelograms.

Common Error: **Difficulty Recognizing Square Angles**

Some children may have difficulty distinguishing between a parallelogram and a rectangle because they don't recognize square (right) angles.

Remediation Demonstrate how to use the corner of a piece of paper or a ruler to help children decide if an angle is a right angle.

Common Error: **Doesn't Recognize a Rectangle as a Parallelogram**

Some children will only recognize quadrilaterals with parallel sides and non-square angles as parallelograms.

Remediation Reinforce the properties of a parallelogram. Point out that in a parallelogram opposite sides are parallel and congruent. Have students identify these properties in a rectangle. Then explain that a rectangle is a special parallelogram having one additional property: all four corners are square.

Unit Objective 4.3

Classify quadrilaterals.

Common Error: **Doesn't Classify a Square as a Rectangle, a Parallelogram, and a Quadrilateral**

Some children may have difficulty identifying that a square is a rectangle, a parallelogram, and a quadrilateral.

Remediation Draw and label a quadrilateral, parallelogram, rectangle, and square on the board. List the characteristics that are common to the previous shape in one color and then write the unique characteristic in a second color. Point out that the two attributes of quadrilaterals are listed for parallelograms, rectangles, and squares, so all of these shapes are quadrilaterals. Show them that all of the points under parallelogram are under rectangle and square, so rectangles and squares are parallelograms. Repeat the process for rectangles, pointing out how squares are also rectangles.

Quadrilateral
- 4 sides
- 4 angles

Parallelogram
- 4 sides
- 4 angles
- opposite sides are parallel

Rectangle
- 4 sides
- 4 angles
- opposite sides are parallel
- all 4 angles are square

Square
- 4 sides
- 4 angles
- opposite sides are parallel
- all 4 angles are square
- all 4 sides are equal in length

Addition to 200

THE GOAL FOR UNIT 5 is to have children grasp the concept of a new ten or a new hundred in 2-digit addition. The concept of grouping ones into a new ten, or tens into a new hundred, can be readily demonstrated with physical objects and then with sticks and circles. Through the use of these tools, children are able to understand the concept behind what they are doing when they add and can develop their own solution methods before being given any instruction.

Skills Trace

Grade 1	Grade 2	Grade 3
• Represent two-digit numbers. • Add a 2-digit number and a 1-digit number. • Solve story problems.	• Understand place value for numbers to 200. • Add 2-digit numbers with or without a new ten and a new hundred. • Solve addition story problems.	• Read, write, identify, and represent the place value of whole numbers. • Add and subtract whole numbers. • Solve a variety of word problems involving addition and subtraction.

Unit 5 Contents

Big Idea Use Place Value

Big Idea Add 2-Digit Numbers

Big Idea Money, Sequences, and 100 Matrix

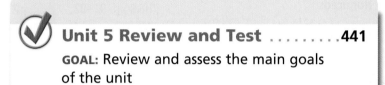

Planning Unit 5

Lesson/NCTM Standards	Resources	Materials for Lesson Activities	Materials for Going Further
5–1 **Ones, Tens, and Hundreds** NCTM Standards: 1, 8	TE pp. 309–316 SAB pp. 141–144 H&R pp. 89–90 AC 5–1	MathBoard materials (or TRB M62–M63) ✓ 120 Poster ✓ Demonstration Secret Code Cards (TRB M7–M22)	Paper Clips MathBoard materials Math Journals
5–2 **Draw Quick Tens and Quick Hundreds** NCTM Standards: 1, 8	TE pp. 317–324 SAB pp. 145–146 H&R pp. 91–92 AC 5–2	MathBoard materials Number Path (TRB M51) ✓ Secret Code Cards	MathBoard materials Number Path (TRB M51) ✓ Secret Code Cards ✓ Base-ten blocks ✓ Number cubes Math Journals
5–3 **Represent 2-Digit Numbers in Different Ways** NCTM Standards: 1	TE pp. 325–332 SAB pp. 147–148 H&R pp. 93–94 AC 5–3	MathBoard materials Number Path (TRB M51) ✓ Secret Code Cards	MathBoard materials Secret Code Cards (TRB M3–M6) Math Journals
5–4 **Add 2-Digit and 1-Digit Numbers** NCTM Standards: 1, 8, 10	TE pp. 333–340 SAB pp. 149–152 H&R pp. 95–96 AC 5–4 MCC 5–17	MathBoard materials ✓ Secret Code Cards Short piece of yarn ✓ Count-On Cards ✓ Make-a-Ten Cards	*Hippos Go Berserk!* by Sandra Boynton Homework and Remembering p. 95 MathBoard materials Number Path (TRB M51) ✓ Two-color counters Calculator Math Journals
5–5 **Find Decade Partners** NCTM Standards: 1, 8, 10	TE pp. 341–348 SAB pp. 153–154 H&R pp. 97–98 AC 5–5	MathBoard materials Number Path (TRB M51) Dot Array (TRB M63) Dry-erase markers Calculators	Student Activity Book p. 153 ✓ Base-ten blocks MathBoard materials Index cards Math Journals
5–6 **Combine Ones, Tens, and Hundreds** NCTM Standards: 1, 8, 10	TE pp. 349–354 SAB pp. 155–156 H&R pp. 99–100 AC 5–1 AG: Quick Quiz 1	✓ Secret Code Cards MathBoard materials	Student Activity Book p. 156 ✓ Counters ✓ 120 Poster Paper bag MathBoard materials Sentence strips Index cards Math Journals
5–7 **Odd and Even Numbers** NCTM Standards: 1, 2	TE pp. 355–360 SAB pp. 157–158 H&R pp. 101–102 AC 5–7	✓ Connecting cubes ✓ Number Path (TRB M51)	✓ Connecting cubes Paper bag ✓ Number Cards 1–20 Index Cards Small paper squares Math Journals

Resources/Materials Key: TE: Teacher Edition SAB: Student Activity Book H&R: Homework and Remembering AC: Activity Cards MCC: Math Center Challenge AG: Assessment Guide ✓: Grade 2 kits TRB: Teacher's Resource Book

NCTM Standards Key: 1. Number and Operations 2. Algebra 3. Geometry 4. Measurement 5. Data Analysis and Probability 6. Problem Solving 7. Reasoning and Proof 8. Communication 9. Connections 10. Representation

Lesson/NCTM Standards	Resources	Materials for Lesson Activities	Materials for Going Further
5–8 **Estimation** NCTM Standards: 1, 4, 7	TE pp. 361–366 SAB pp. 159–160 H&R pp. 103–104 AC 5–8	2 jars (same size) Marbles Paper bags Counters ✓ Pennies Paper with 55 dots Paper with 87 dots	Paper bags Small object such as macaroni ✓ Paper shapes Pennies Math Journals
5–9 **Invent 2-Digit Addition** NCTM Standards: 1, 6, 8	TE pp. 367–372 SAB pp. 161–164 H&R pp. 105–106 AC 5–9		✓ Base-ten blocks Math Journals
5–10 **Addition—Show All Totals Method** NCTM Standards: 1, 6, 10	TE pp. 373–380 SAB pp. 165–166 H&R pp. 107–108 AC 5–10	MathBoard materials ✓ Demonstration Secret Code Cards ✓ Secret Code Cards	Game Cards MathBoard materials ✓ Secret Code Cards Math Journals
5–11 **Addition—New Groups Below Method** NCTM Standards: 1, 10	TE pp. 381–386 SAB pp. 167–168 H&R pp. 109–110 AC 5–11	MathBoard materials	Homework and Remembering p. 110 ✓ Connecting cubes MathBoard materials Index cards Math Journals
5–12 **Practice Addition with Totals over 100** NCTM Standards: 1, 10	TE pp. 387–390 SAB pp. 169–170 H&R pp. 111–112 AC 5–12		Homework and Remembering p. 111 Place-Value Charts (TRB M65) MathBoard materials Math Journals
5–13 **Choose an Addition Method** NCTM Standards: 1, 10	TE pp. 391–396 SAB pp. 171–172 H&R pp. 113–114 AC 5–13 MCC 5–19	Chart paper	Spinners (TRB M27) 10 × 10 Grid (TRB M61) Paper clips Math Journals
5–14 **2-Digit Addition in Perimeter Problems** NCTM Standards: 1, 3, 4	TE pp. 397–402 SAB pp. 173–174 H&R pp. 115–116 AC 5–14 AG: Quick Quiz 2		Student Activity Book p. 174 ✓ 25-cm rulers Paper triangles and squares MathBoard materials Math Journals
5–15 **Buy with Pennies and Dimes** NCTM Standards: 1, 8, 10	TE pp. 403–408 SAB pp. 175–178 H&R pp. 117–118 AC 5–15 MCC 5–20	✓ Real or play money Coin strips Snack bags	*Get 5 Dimes* game board Number cubes Math Journals
5–16 **Buy with Pennies, Nickels, and Dimes** NCTM Standards: 1, 10	TE pp. 409–414 SAB pp. 179–180 H&R pp. 119–120 AC 5–16	✓ Real or play money ✓ Dollar bills Coin strips	Match the Coin Cards (TRB M65) Scissors Math Journals

Resources/Materials Key: TE: Teacher Edition SAB: Student Activity Book H&R: Homework and Remembering AC: Activity Cards MCC: Math Center Challenge AG: Assessment Guide ✓: Grade 2 kits TRB: Teacher's Resource Book

NCTM Standards Key: **1.** Number and Operations **2.** Algebra **3.** Geometry **4.** Measurement **5.** Data Analysis and Probability **6.** Problem Solving **7.** Reasoning and Proof **8.** Communication **9.** Connections **10.** Representation

Lesson/NCTM Standards	Resources	Materials for Lesson Activities	Materials for Going Further
5–17 **Sequences** NCTM Standards: 2, 3, 7	TE pp. 415–422 SAB pp. 181–184 H&R pp. 121–122 AC 5–17	MathBoard materials Number Path (TRB M51)	Student Activity Book p. 183 Sticky notes Math Journals
5–18 **Find 2-Digit Partners** NCTM Standards: 1, 6, 8, 10	TE pp. 423–428 SAB pp. 185–186 H&R pp. 123–124 AC 5–18	MathBoard materials	Student Activity Book pp. 185–186 ✓ Real or play money Centimeter Grid Paper (TRB M50) Scissors Math Journals
5–19 **Patterns with Objects and Numbers** NCTM Standards: 2, 3, 7	TE pp. 429–434 SAB pp. 187–188 H&R pp. 125–126 AC 5–19	✓ Pattern Blocks Classroom objects	✓ Pattern Blocks Paper strips Crayons or markers Math Journals
5–20 **Use Mathematical Processes** NCTM Standards: 6, 7, 8, 9, 10	TE pp. 435–440 SAB pp. 189–190 H&R pp. 127–128 AC 5–20	Crayons or markers Maps ✓ Play coins	MathBoard materials or Number Path (TRB M51) ✓ Secret Code Cards Math Journals
✓ Unit Review and Test	TE pp. 441–444 SAB pp. 191–194 AG: Unit 5 tests		

Resources/Materials Key: TE: Teacher Edition SAB: Student Activity Book H&R: Homework and Remembering AC: Activity Cards MCC: Math Center Challenge AG: Assessment Guide ✓: Grade 2 kits TRB: Teacher's Resource Book

Manipulatives and Materials

Essential materials for teaching *Math Expressions* are available in the Grade 2 kits. These materials are indicated by a ✓ in these lists. At the front of this Teacher Edition is more information about kit contents, alternatives for the materials, and use of the materials.

Unit 5 Assessment

Unit Objectives Tested	Unit Test Items	Lessons
5.1 Understand place value for numbers to 200.	1–4	1–6
5.2 Add 2-digit numbers with or without a new ten and a new hundred.	5–11, 20	8–13, 17
5.3 Solve addition story problems.	12–13	10-13
5.4 Determine the total value of a group of coins (pennies, nickels, and dimes).	14–15	14–15
5.5 Fill in number sequences and write a rule to describe how the numbers are generated.	16–19	16

Assessment and Review Resources

Formal Assessment

Student Activity Book

- Unit Review and Test (pp. 191–194)

Assessment Guide

- Quick Quizzes (pp. A43–A45)
- Test A–Open Response (pp. A46–A49)
- Test B–Multiple Choice (pp. A50–A53)
- Performance Assessment (pp. A54–A56)

Test Generator CD-ROM

- Open Response Test
- Multiple Choice Test
- Test Bank Items

Informal Assessment

Teacher Edition

- Ongoing Assessment (in every lesson)
- Quick Practice (in every lesson)
- Portfolio Suggestions (p. 443)

Math Talk

- Math Talk in Action (pp. 318, 369, 388, 418)
- Scenarios (pp. 406)
- In Activities (pp. 312, 326, 335, 344, 351, 377, 384, 393, 400, 410, 419, 426)

Review Opportunities

Homework and Remembering

- Review of recently taught topics
- Cumulative Review

Teacher Edition

- Unit Review and Test (pp. 441–444)

Test Generator CD-ROM

- Custom Review Sheets

Independent Learning Activities

Ready-Made Math Challenge Centers

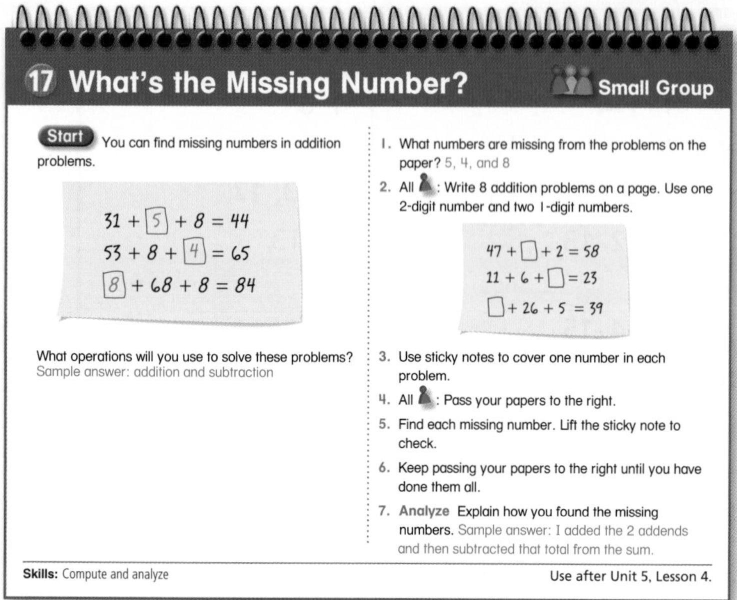

17 What's the Missing Number? Small Group

Start You can find missing numbers in addition problems.

$31 + \boxed{5} + 8 = 44$
$53 + 8 + \boxed{4} = 65$
$\boxed{8} + 68 + 8 = 84$

What operations will you use to solve these problems? Sample answer: addition and subtraction

1. What numbers are missing from the problems on the paper? 5, 4, and 8
2. All: Write 8 addition problems on a page. Use one 2-digit number and two 1-digit numbers.

$47 + \square + 2 = 58$
$11 + 6 + \square = 23$
$\square + 26 + 5 = 39$

3. Use sticky notes to cover one number in each problem.
4. All: Pass your papers to the right.
5. Find each missing number. Lift the sticky note to check.
6. Keep passing your papers to the right until you have done them all.
7. **Analyze** Explain how you found the missing numbers. Sample answer: I added the 2 addends and then subtracted that total from the sum.

Skills: Compute and analyze — Use after Unit 5, Lesson 4.

Grouping Small Group

Materials Sticky notes

Objective Children find missing digits in addition problems.

Connections Computation and Reasoning

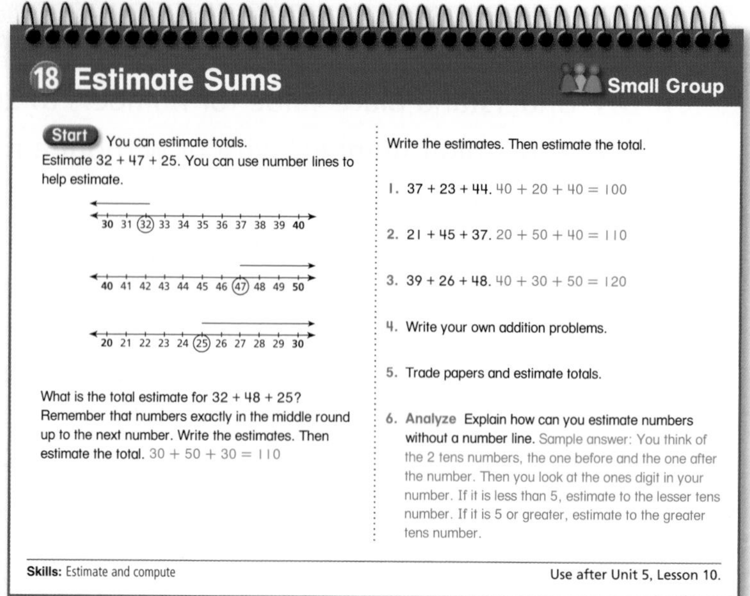

18 Estimate Sums Small Group

Start You can estimate totals.
Estimate $32 + 47 + 25$. You can use number lines to help estimate.

What is the total estimate for $32 + 48 + 25$? Remember that numbers exactly in the middle round up to the next number. Write the estimates. Then estimate the total. $30 + 50 + 30 = 110$

Write the estimates. Then estimate the total.

1. $37 + 23 + 44$. $40 + 20 + 40 = 100$
2. $21 + 45 + 37$. $20 + 50 + 40 = 110$
3. $39 + 26 + 48$. $40 + 30 + 50 = 120$
4. Write your own addition problems.
5. Trade papers and estimate totals.
6. **Analyze** Explain how can you estimate numbers without a number line. Sample answer: You think of the 2 tens numbers, the one before and the one after the number. Then you look at the ones digit in your number. If it is less than 5, estimate to the lesser tens number. If it is 5 or greater, estimate to the greater tens number.

Skills: Estimate and compute — Use after Unit 5, Lesson 10.

Grouping Small Group

Materials None

Objective Children estimate numbers to the nearest ten and then estimate sums.

Connections Estimation and Computation

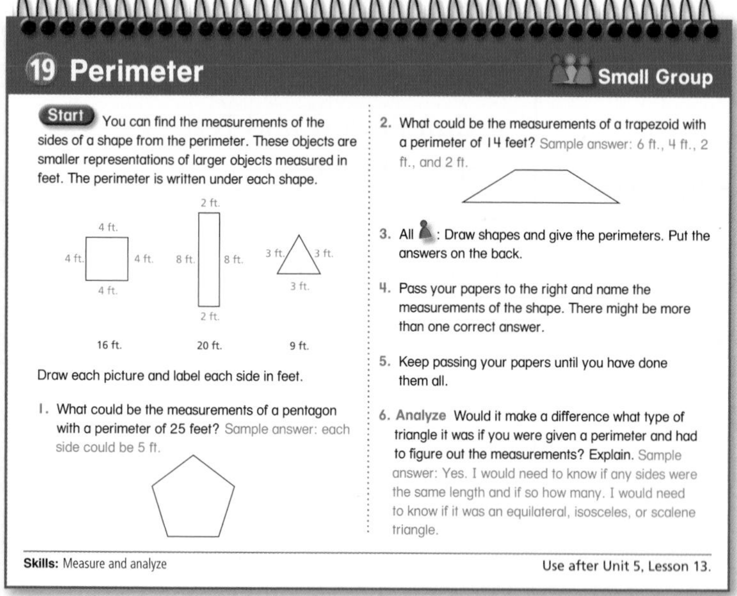

19 Perimeter Small Group

Start You can find the measurements of the sides of a shape from the perimeter. These objects are smaller representations of larger objects measured in feet. The perimeter is written under each shape.

Draw each picture and label each side in feet.

1. What could be the measurements of a pentagon with a perimeter of 25 feet? Sample answer: each side could be 5 ft.
2. What could be the measurements of a trapezoid with a perimeter of 14 feet? Sample answer: 6 ft., 4 ft., 2 ft., and 2 ft.
3. All: Draw shapes and give the perimeters. Put the answers on the back.
4. Pass your papers to the right and name the measurements of the shape. There might be more than one correct answer.
5. Keep passing your papers until you have done them all.
6. **Analyze** Would it make a difference what type of triangle it was if you were given a perimeter and had to figure out the measurements? Explain. Sample answer: Yes. I would need to know if any sides were the same length and if so how many. I would need to know if it was an equilateral, isosceles, or scalene triangle.

Skills: Measure and analyze — Use after Unit 5, Lesson 13.

Grouping Small Group

Materials None

Objective Children find measurements for sides of a shape when given the perimeter.

Connections Measurement and Analysis

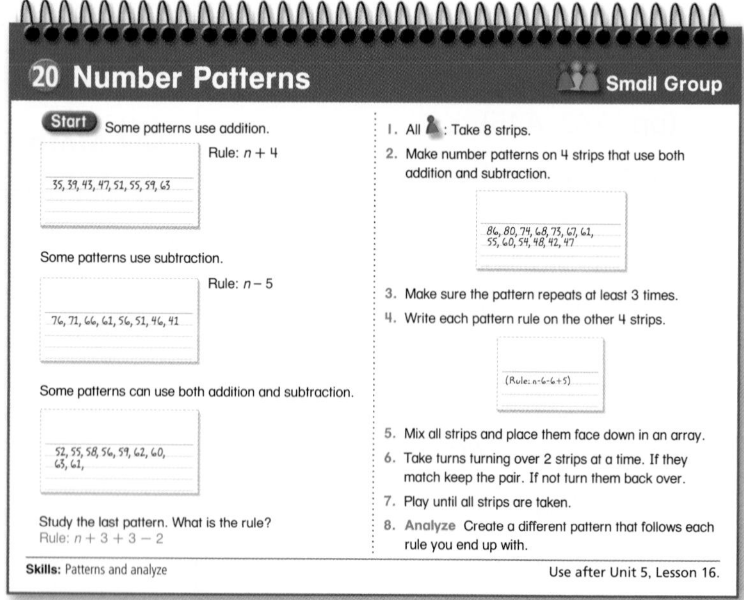

20 Number Patterns Small Group

Start Some patterns use addition.

Rule: $n + 4$

35, 39, 43, 47, 51, 55, 59, 63

Some patterns use subtraction.

Rule: $n - 5$

76, 71, 66, 61, 56, 51, 46, 41

Some patterns can use both addition and subtraction.

52, 55, 58, 56, 59, 62, 60, 63, 61,

Study the last pattern. What is the rule? Rule: $n + 3 + 3 - 2$

1. All: Take 8 strips.
2. Make number patterns on 4 strips that use both addition and subtraction.

86, 80, 74, 68, 73, 67, 61, 55, 60, 54, 48, 42, 47

3. Make sure the pattern repeats at least 3 times.
4. Write each pattern rule on the other 4 strips.

(Rule: n-6-6+5)

5. Mix all strips and place them face down in an array.
6. Take turns turning over 2 strips at a time. If they match keep the pair. If not turn them back over.
7. Play until all strips are taken.
8. **Analyze** Create a different pattern that follows each rule you end up with.

Skills: Patterns and analyze — Use after Unit 5, Lesson 16.

Grouping Small Group

Materials Paper strips

Objective Children make patterns using rules with both addition and subtraction and match patterns to their rules.

Connections Algebra and Representation

Ready-Made Math Resources

Technology — Tutorials, Practice, and Intervention

Use activity masters and online, individualized intervention and support to bring students to proficiency.

Help students practice skills and apply concepts through exciting math adventures.

Extend and enrich students' understanding of skills and concepts through engaging, interactive lessons and activities.

Visit Education Place®
www.eduplace.com

Visit www.eduplace.com/mx2t/ and find family, teacher, and student materials, activities, games, and more.

Literature Links

A Place for Zero

A Place for Zero
In this creative book, Angeline Sparanga LoPresti demonstrates the true value of zero, which if you think about it, is really quite something!

Literature Connections

- *Hippos Go Berserk!,* by Sandra Boynton (Little Simon, 2000)

Unit 5 Teaching Resources

Differentiated Instruction

Individualizing Instruction		
	Level	Frequency
Activities	• Intervention • On Level • Challenge	All 3 in every lesson
	Level	Frequency
Math Writing Prompts	• Intervention • On Level • Challenge	All 3 in every lesson
Math Center Challenges	For advanced students	
	4 in every unit	

Reaching All Learners		
	Lessons	Pages
English Language Learners	1, 2, 3, 4, 5, 6, 7, 8, 9, 10, 11, 12, 13, 14, 15, 16, 17, 18, 19, 20	310, 311, 319, 327, 334, 343, 350, 370, 375, 383, 388, 392, 398, 404, 405, 411, 416, 424
	Lessons	Pages
Extra Help	1, 4, 6, 19	312, 335, 337, 352, 432
	Lesson	Page
Advanced Learners	4	337

Strategies for English Language Learners

Present this problem to all students. Offer the different levels of support to meet children's levels of language proficiency.

Objective Help children identify the ones, tens, and hundreds place values.

Activity Write 100, 10, and 1 on the board. Have children find the Secret Code Cards for each number and count the dots on the back. Model how to show 111.

Newcomer

- Hold up each card. Point and say: **1 dot is 1 ones. 10 dots is 1 tens. 100 dots is 1 hundreds.** Have children repeat.

Beginning

- Point to each digit. Say: **In 111 there is 1 ones, 1 tens, and 1 hundreds.** Have children repeat.

Intermediate

- Point to each digit. Say: **This is the ones column. There is 1 ones.** Have children repeat. Continue with other columns

Advanced

- Identify each column. Have children repeat.
- Have children make the number 132. Point and say: **2 is in the ones column. There are 2 ___.** ones Continue with other columns.

Connections

Art Connection
Lesson 17, page 422

Language Arts Connections
Lesson 14, page 402
Lesson 15, page 408

Multicultural Connection
Lesson 16, page 414

Physical Education Connection
Lesson 2, page 324

Real-World Connections
Lesson 3, page 332
Lesson 7, page 360
Lesson 8, page 366
Lesson 11, page 386
Lesson 18, page 428
Lesson 19, page 434

Science Connections
Lesson 10, page 380
Lesson 12, page 390

Social Studies Connection
Lesson 20, page 440

Technology Connections
Lesson 5, page 438
Lesson 13, page 396

Literature Connections
Lesson 4, page 34
Lesson 6, page 354

Math Background

Putting Research into Practice for Unit 5

From Our Curriculum Research Project: 2-Digit Addition

In this unit, children will use physical objects, and then drawings, to demonstrate the concept of grouping ones into a new ten, or tens into a new hundred. From research, we see that children are able to readily comprehend the concept of new tens or new hundreds when they use models and make drawings.

Children are encouraged to develop their own methods of adding 2-digit numbers, before being given any instruction. Using models and drawings, children readily develop their own methods of adding. This unit concentrates on the addition of 2-digit numbers, with and without grouping. Children will invent their own techniques and learn other commonly used methods.

–Karen Fuson, Author
Math Expressions

From Current Research: Using Models to Represent Multi-digit Addition

Research indicates that students' experiences using physical models to represent hundreds, tens, and ones can be effective *if* the materials help them think about how to combine quantities and, eventually, how these processes connect with written procedures. . . . In order to support understanding, however, the physical models need to show tens to be collections of 10 ones and to show hundreds to be simultaneously 10 tens and 100 ones.

National Research Council: Developing Proficiency With Whole Numbers *Adding It Up: Helping Children Learn Mathematics Washington, D.C.: National Academy Press, 2001. 198.*

Other Useful References: Addition

Number and Operations Standard for Grades Pre-K–2 *Principles and Standards for School Mathematics.* Reston, VA: National Council of Teachers of Mathematics, 2000. 79–87.

Carpenter, T.P., Franke, M.L., Jacobs, V.R., Fennema, E., & Empson, S.B. "A longitudinal study of invention and understanding in children's multidigit addition and subtraction." *Journal for Research in Mathematics Education,* 29, 1998. 3–20.

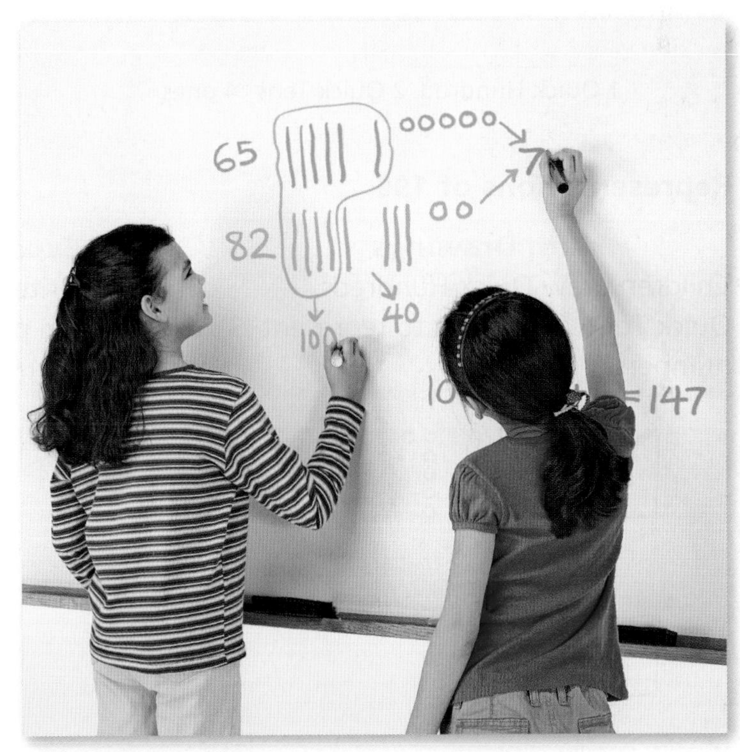

Math Expressions Vocabulary

As you teach this unit, emphasize understanding of these terms:

- decade numbers
- 100-partners
- 10-partners
- New Groups Above method
- New Groups Below method

See Glossary on pp. T7–T20.

Getting Ready to Teach Unit 5

In this unit, children extend their understanding of place value to the hundreds place, learn several methods for adding 2-digit numbers, work with money amounts over $1.00, solve problems, and continue to develop communication skills through Math Talk.

Ones, Tens, and Hundreds

Lessons 1, 2, 3, 5, and 6

Represent Numbers in Various Ways Children explore various methods of representing numbers to 200, and find the meaning of different place value positions.

Place Value Drawings for 124

Drawing of 124

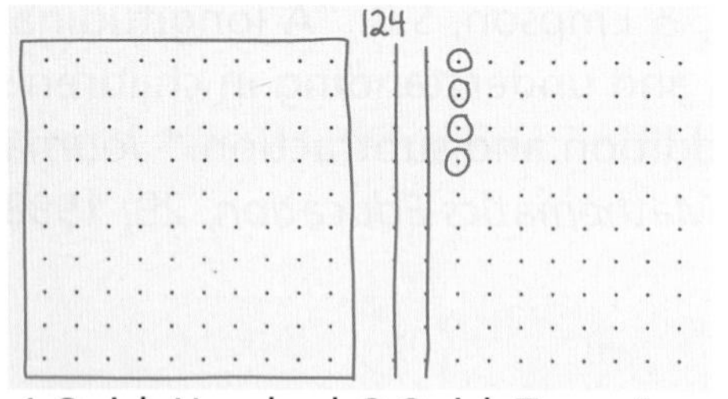

1 Quick Hundred 2 Quick Tens 4 ones

Freehand Drawing of 124

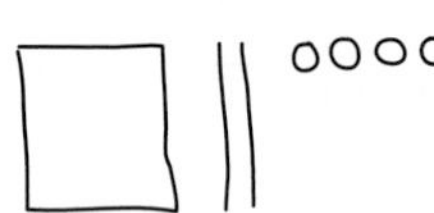

Representations of 196

Math Drawings

Children draw Quick Hundreds, Quick Tens, and circles to represent numbers.

or

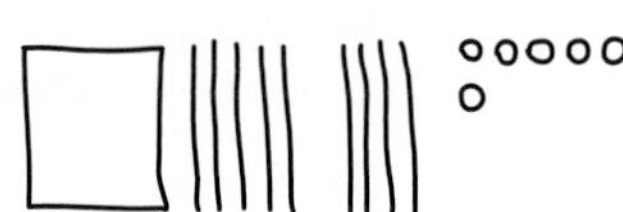

Notice the importance of using 5-groups in the tens and the ones to see each number and to be accurate.

Expanded Form

Children write the value of the digit in each place of a number in equation form.

$$196 = 100 + 90 + 6$$

Secret Code Cards

Children use the cards to show the hundreds, tens, and ones of a number. Secret Code Cards have a small number with the card's value on the top left, visible when cards are assembled.

Hundreds Card Tens Card Ones Card

Assembled Cards

Research-Based Accessible Algorithms for 2-Digit Addition

Lessons 8, 9, 10, 11, 12, and 13

Children are introduced to two methods that are mathematically general, show important mathematical features, and were found to be easily understood and used by students. These methods also relate easily to the common New Groups Above method, which is also discussed.

Show All Totals Method

Children add the tens, then add the ones, and then find the hundreds total.

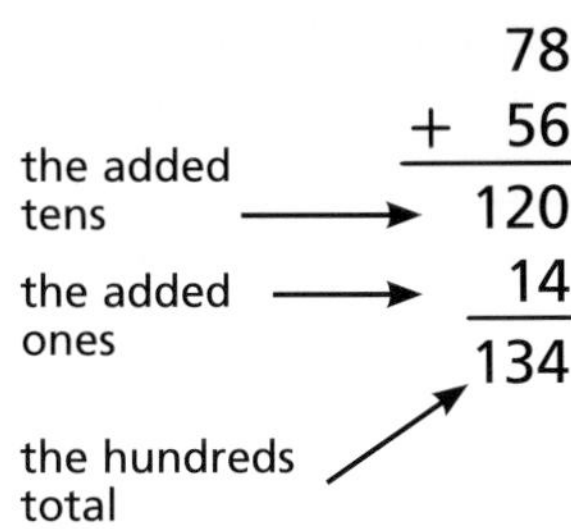

New Groups Below Method

Children write the new ten on the line below the addition example, rather than above.

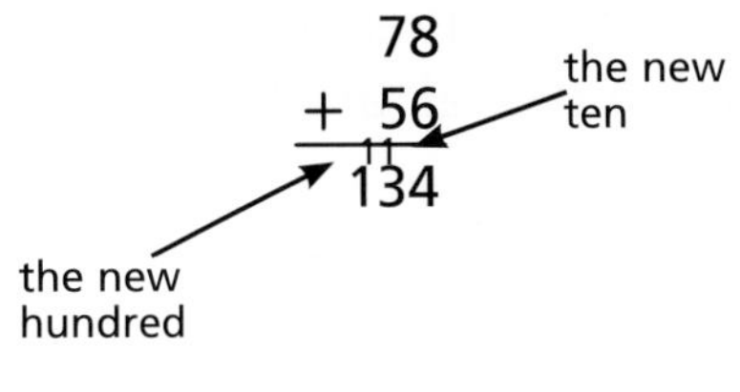

New Groups Above Method

This is the common U.S. algorithm.

$$\begin{array}{r} 78 \\ +\ 56 \\ \hline 134 \end{array}$$

New Groups Below makes the addition easier than New Groups Above because you add the 2 numbers you see and increase by 1, rather than increasing the top number by 1 and then adding the unseen result to the bottom number. Also, with New Groups Below, you can see the 14 ones and the 13 tens more easily.

Relating Math Drawings and Numerical Methods

The purpose of Proof Drawings is to make numerical methods meaningful. Therefore, each step in a drawing must be related to a step in the numerical method. Steps in this Proof Drawing can relate to each numerical method above and to others that students invent.

Problem Solving
In *Math Expressions* a research-based, algebraic problem-solving approach that focuses on problem types is used: understand the situation, represent the situation with a math drawing or an equation, solve the problem, and see that the answer makes sense. Throughout the unit, children solve a variety of problems using the graphing and comparison skills being taught in this unit.

Using Mathematical Processes

Lesson 19
The mathematical process skills of problem solving, reasoning and proof, communication, connections, and representation are pervasive in this program and underlie all the children's mathematical work. Lessons that concentrate on developing and applying process skills can be found in every unit. In this unit, Lesson 19 has activities that focus on all of the process skills. Each of these activities, and its main process skill and goal, are listed below.

Activity	Process Skill	Goal
Math and Social Studies	Connections	Investigate how many colors are needed to color a map.
Showing that Math Statements Are True	Reasoning and Proof	Explain why a math statement is true or not true.
A Dollar to Spend	Problem Solving	Find multiple solutions to a problem.
Same Value or Different Value	Representation	Use drawings to show that numbers with the same digits may not have the same value.
Classifying Triangles	Communication	Explain how to use a diagram to sort and classify triangles.

Developing Communication Skills with Math Talk

All Lessons

Explaining One Step at a Time Throughout the unit, children learn to explain their addition methods clearly and completely. This is an important goal for children in this unit—to become comfortable with explaining one step at a time. Explaining one step at a time can advance children who need extra help by allowing them to examine one aspect of the addition process at a time. Eventually, they build to an understanding of the whole. All children benefit in both their communication and process skills when they learn to hear—and eventually present—a systematic explanation of their own mathematical strategies and thinking.

Discussing and Correcting Errors
Some children may be reluctant to share their math work and thinking in public because they do not want to be incorrect. To help children change their perspective of errors, teachers can create an environment that views errors as opportunities for learning. Correcting errors models a healthy approach for children. For example, teachers can model this for children by purposely making an error, then saying, "Oh, that's OK, I see what I did." This will eventually encourage other children to recognize and correct their own errors and the errors of their classmates.

In this type of classroom, children become less hesitant to try new things and share their approaches. Children do not fear criticism when they make mistakes, and they see errors as opportunities for everyone to learn.

Ones, Tens, and Hundreds

Lesson Objectives

- Represent numbers to 200.
- Identify patterns among numbers in different place value positions.
- Relate groups of ten to decade numbers and 100.

Vocabulary

ones
tens
hundreds
decade numbers
Quick Tens

The Day at a Glance

Today's Goals	Materials	
1 Teaching the Lesson Represent numbers to 200 in various ways. Discuss the meanings of different place value positions.	**Lesson Activities** Student Activity Book pp. 141–144 (includes Family Letter) Homework and Remembering pp. 89–90 MathBoard materials (or TRB M62–M63) 120 Poster Demonstration Secret Code Cards (TRB M7–M22)	**Going Further** Activity Cards 5-1 Paper Clips MathBoard materials Math Journals
2 Going Further ▶ Differentiated Instruction		
3 Homework and Targeted Practice		

Use Math Talk today!

Keeping Skills Sharp

Quick Practice — 5 MINUTES

Goal: Count by tens to 120.

Materials: 120 Poster (See *Math Expressions* materials kits) or use TRB M60–M61 (enlarged and laminated), pointer

Count by Tens to 120 Have a Student Leader quickly sweep the pointer from the top to the bottom of each 10 column on the 120 Poster as the class counts the ten groups up to 120. As the leader reaches the decade number in each column, children should say together "10! 20! 30!" and so on. Sweeping from top to bottom emphasizes that each 10 is not the numeral 10 but the whole quantity of ten "things." Have children flash 10 fingers as they count.

1	11	21	31	41	51	61	71	81	91	101	111
2	12	22	32	42	52	62	72	82	92	102	112
3	13	23	33	43	53	63	73	83	93	103	113
4	14	24	34	44	54	64	74	84	94	104	114
5	15	25	35	45	55	65	75	85	95	105	115
6	16	26	36	46	56	66	76	86	96	106	116
7	17	27	37	47	57	67	77	87	97	107	117
8	18	28	38	48	58	68	78	88	98	108	118
9	19	29	39	49	59	69	79	89	99	109	119
10	20	30	40	50	60	70	80	90	100	110	120

Daily Routines

Math Mountains for 100 or 2-Digit Numbers Using the MathBoard, Using Dimes and Pennies
(See p. xxvi.)

▶ Led by teacher

Money Routine Using the 120 Poster, Using the Money Flip Chart, Using the Number Path, Using Secret Code Cards
(See pp. xxiii–xxv.)

▶ Led by Student Leaders

1 Teaching the Lesson

Activity

Ones, Tens, and Hundreds

50 MINUTES

Goal: Represent numbers to 200 in various ways. Discuss the meanings of different place value positions.

Materials: MathBoard materials or 10 x 10 Grid and Dot Array (TRB M61, M62), 120 Poster or TRB M60 enlarged and laminated, Demonstration Secret Code Cards (TRB M7–M22), Student Activity Book page 141

NCTM Standards:
Number and Operations
Communication

Patterns in Number Words

The "ty" stands for ten.

twen-ty	two-ty
thir-ty	three-ty
for-ty	four-ty
fif-ty	five-ty
six-ty	six-ty
seven-ty	seven-ty
eight-ty	eight-ty
nine-ty	nine-ty

The red decade words are irregular and do not sound like the ones words.

Differentiated Instruction

English Learners Make sure that English Learners understand the names of decade numbers and which ones are irregular.

▶ Write Numbers to 110 WHOLE CLASS

Have children place their MathBoards on the 10 × 10 grid side or have them use the 10 × 10 Grid and the Dot Array (TRB M61, M62).

Point to the numbers 1 through 100 on the 120 Poster as children write the numbers on their 10 × 10 grids. Write 1 ten (2 tens, 3 tens, etc.). As you finish each group of tens, say together: 10 is 1 group of ten, 20 is 2 groups of ten, 30 is 3 groups of 10 and so on. When all children have reached 100, ask what number comes next and where on the board they could write that number.

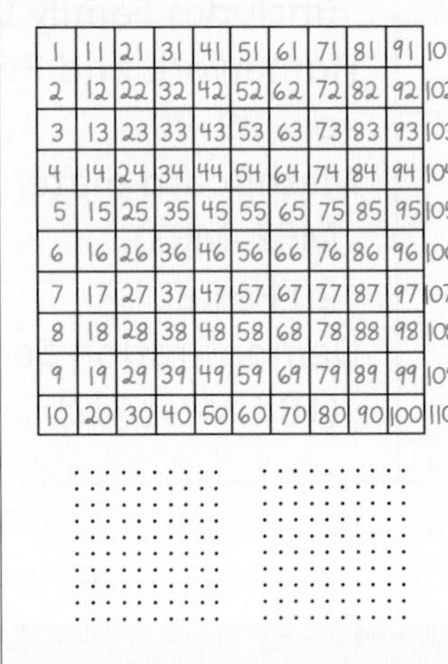

Have children write the numbers from 101 to 110 on their MathBoards as you point to the numbers on the 120 Poster. As children finish writing each new column of ten, circle that column on the 120 Poster. Use alternating colors so that children can see the groups of ten.

Count by Tens to 110 Have children flash tens as they count by tens to 110. Then have a volunteer show 100 and then 110 with the Demonstration Secret Code Cards.

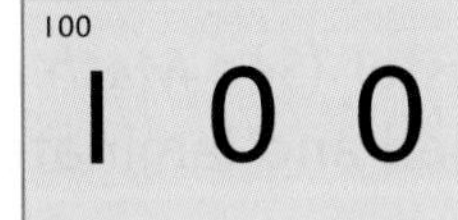

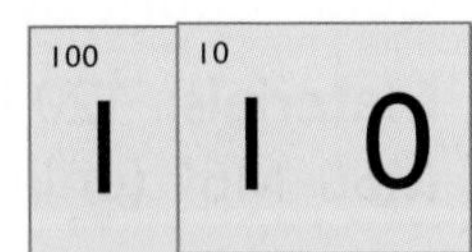

▶ Discuss Patterns WHOLE CLASS

Discuss any patterns children see in the numbers and then discuss patterns in the counting words they say. If no one mentions it, ask if they see a pattern in the tens words. If necessary, point out the pattern shown to the left.

Draw children's attention to the bottom row of the 120 Poster (10, 20, and so on). Ask the following questions:

- What does the 1 at the bottom of the left column tell us? *Point to the 1 in the number 10.* It tells how many tens there are in that number.
- What does the zero tell us? There are no ones in the number.

Repeat as needed with the numbers 20, 30, and so on, until most children understand. Do not discuss the digits in 100 yet, unless a child volunteers to explain.

▶ Understand Tens and Ones in Numbers WHOLE CLASS

Show children the 10-card from the set of Demonstration Secret Code Cards. Then put the 1-card over the zero to show 11.

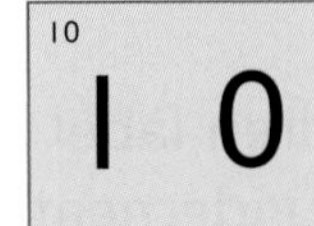

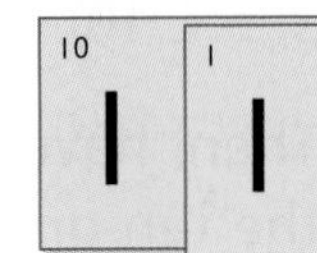

- What number am I showing now? 11
- What does this 1 tell us? Point to the 1 on the 10 card. It tells how many tens are in the number.
- What does this 1 tell us? (Point to the single-digit card.) It tells how many ones are in the number.
- What happened to the zero? It is hiding but still there, so 11 is 10 and 1.

Repeat for several more numbers, for example, 14, 22, and 58.

Now direct children's attention to the number 100 on the 120 Poster and discuss the meaning of the one and the zeros.

- Look at the hundred. There is a 1 and two zeros. Does this 1 tell us there is one 10 in this number? no
- What does it tell us? There are 10 tens, or there is 1 hundred.
- How do we know there are 10 tens and not 15 tens? The zero to the right of the 1 tells us there are no more tens.
- So this zero (*point to the zero in the tens place*) tells us there are no extra tens in this number. What does this zero (*point to the zero in the ones place*) tell us? There are no extra ones in this number.

Show 101 with the Demonstration Secret Code Cards and discuss the meaning of the ones and the zero in 101.

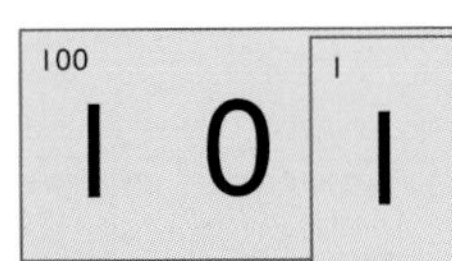

- Look at the number 101. What does the first 1 on the left tell us? There are 10 tens or 1 hundred in this number.
- What does the 1 on the right tell us? There is one extra 1.
- What does the zero tell us? There are no extra tens.

Repeat this procedure for 102 through 110 as needed.

Count by Tens and Ones to 101 Have children count by tens to 101. They should flash ten fingers for each ten and then shift from flashing tens to holding up a finger to show the 1. Repeat this procedure for 102, 103, and so on as needed.

Activity continued ▶

Teaching Note

Math Background It is very important that all children learn and use two kinds of words for each decade number 20, 30, 40, and so on. They need to be able to say 80 as *eighty* and as *eight tens. Eighty* is the counting word, and this elicits counting meanings as a word coming after *seventy-nine* and before *eighty-one. Eight tens* tells the place value meaning as one 8 written in the tens place. The Secret Code Cards help children connect these two meanings.

English Language Learners

Help children understand the difference between *counting words* and *place value*. Write 20 and *twenty* on the board. Point and say: ***Twenty is a counting word.*** Point to the 2.

- **Beginning** Say: **This means *2 tens*.** Flash ten fingers and say: **1 ten, *2 tens* is 20. *2 tens* is a *place value*.**
- **Intermediate** Say: **This means there are 2 __.** tens Ask: **Is 2 tens a counting word?** no **Is it the place value?** yes
- **Intermediate** Ask: **Is *2 tens* a counting word or place value?** place value **What is the *counting word?*** twenty

Teaching Note

Math Background The quantity in the number 101 can be expressed four ways: There is 1 hundred and an extra 1; there are 10 tens and an extra 1; there are 101 ones; or there is 1 hundred, 0 tens, and 1 one. Other 3-digit numbers can be similarly expressed.

 Teaching the Lesson (continued)

Class Management

Model how to circle dots and write numbers by drawing on the class MathBoard or on a child's MathBoard as children work on their individual boards.

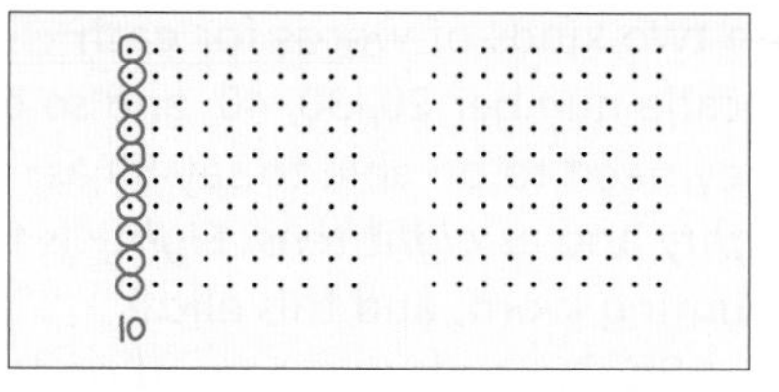

Differentiated Instruction

Extra Help Some children may have difficulty drawing lines through ten. You may wish to pair them with a child who is able to draw the lines more easily. Have the child with the better motor skills draw the lines and the other child circle the dots and write the numbers to label each column as a group of ten.

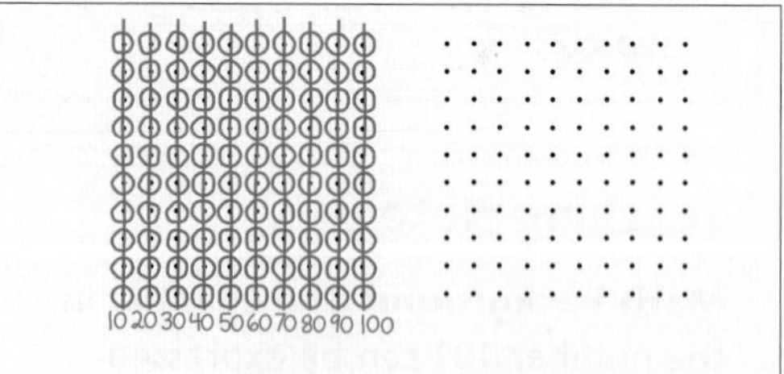

▶ Label Quantities of 10 WHOLE CLASS Math Talk

Direct the children's attention to the dots below the grid. Have them count and circle each dot in one column. Children should begin at the top of the column and count out loud as they circle the dots (1, 2, 3, . . . 10).

Then, have children label each column as a group of ten. Explain that the ten-groups underneath each column show how many groups of ten have already been counted.

- How many groups of ten are in the first column? 1 group Write 1 for the group of ten and 0 to show there are no ones left over at the bottom of the first column.
- Now let's show that 1 ten by drawing a line through all ten dots.
- Now let's circle the 10 dots in the second column. What should we write under the second column? 20 Why? Altogether we have counted 2 groups of 10; the first column has ten and the second column has ten. Together there are 20 ones or 2 groups of ten with no ones left over.
- So let's show the 2 tens by drawing a line through these ten dots. We call this a Quick Ten because it is a fast way to show the ten group.
- Why do we write 30 under the third column and make another Quick Ten? Altogether we have counted 3 groups of 10; the first column has ten, the second column has ten, and the third column has ten. Together there are 30 ones or 3 groups of ten with no ones left over.

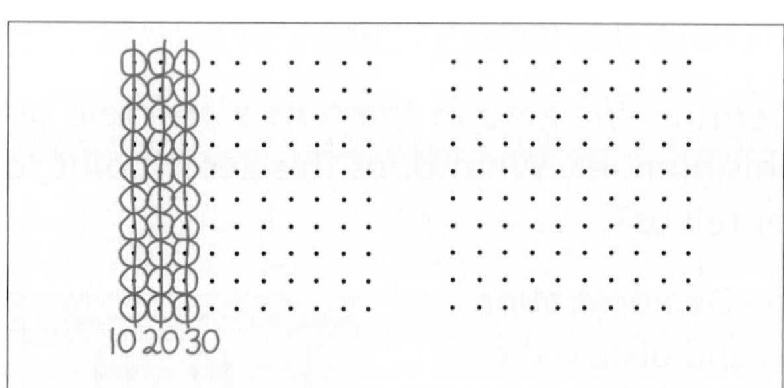

Have children write 40, 50, and so on through the 9th column, making a Quick Ten for each column. Adapt the questions above and continue to 90 (9 tens). Also, each time have children flash the accumulated groups of ten with their fingers.

▶ Visualize 100 WHOLE CLASS

When children reach the 10th column, ask the following questions:

- What will you write under the last group of ten? 100 Why? There are 10 groups of ten and no extra ones.
- What are the different ways to say 100? We can say 1 hundred, 10 groups of ten, 10 tens, or 100 ones.

▶ Discuss Numbers Greater than 100 WHOLE CLASS

Have children circle the dots in the 11th column. Point to the column and draw circles on your MathBoard as the children draw theirs.

- How many tens have you circled altogether? 11 How many hundreds in this number? 1 How many extra tens? 1 How many extra ones? none
- How do we write this number? 110

Ask a volunteer to write the number on the board. Write 110 under the 11th column.

- What does this number tell us? Possible answers: It has 1 hundred, 1 ten, and 0 ones; it has 11 tens and 0 ones; it has 1 hundred and 10 ones.

Have children circle one more dot, the first one in the 12th column. Circle the dot on your MathBoard as the children circle theirs.

- What number is that? 111 What does this number tell us? Possible answers: It has one 100, one 10, and one 1; or it has 11 tens and 1 one; or it has 111 ones.

Write the number 111 above the circled dot.

Ask volunteers to show 110 and 111 with the Demonstration Secret Code Cards. You might also have children count by tens to 111, flashing ten fingers to 110 and showing one more finger to show 111.

Write on the board: 110 = 100 + 10.

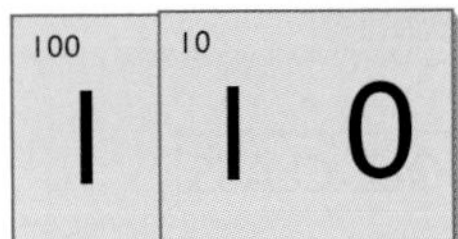

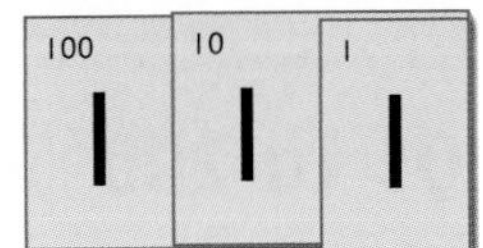

111 = 100 + 10 + 1

▶ Quick Tens and Quick Hundreds WHOLE CLASS

Draw a square around the 10 tens. Tell children that this is called a Quick Hundred.

Then explain that, from now on, it will not be necessary to circle all the dots or draw all the Quick Tens inside the Quick Hundred. (See pictures at right.)

Teaching Note

Watch For! Some children will have trouble expressing a number in more than one way. As long as they can describe the number accurately in one way, don't push them to express the number in a different way. Instead, ask if any other children can describe the same number in a different way until all the possible variations have been given. Gradually everyone will learn all ways.

Using Circles to Show 111

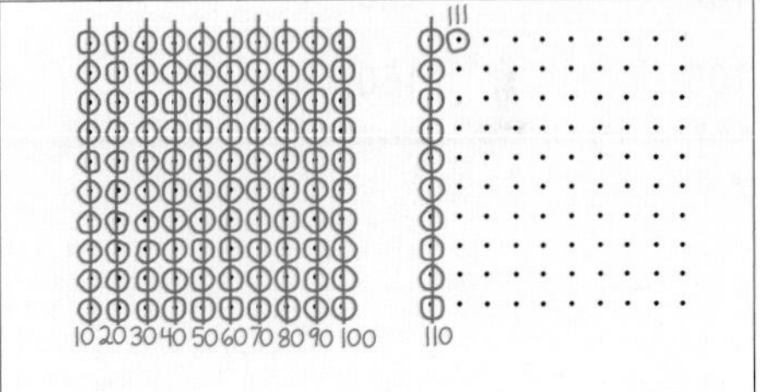

Using Quick Hundreds, Quick Tens, and Circles to Show 111

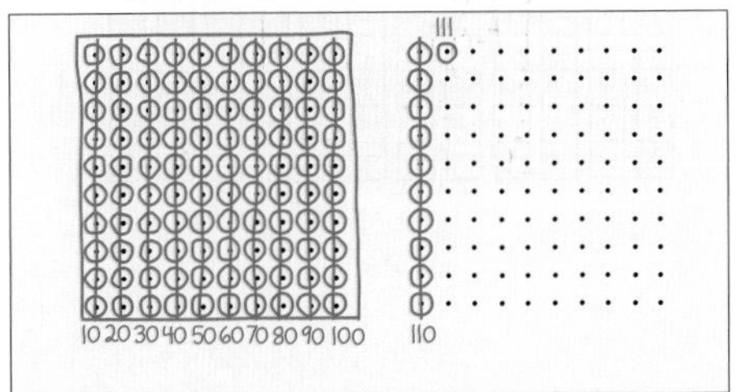

or

Teaching the Lesson (continued)

Class Management

It is important to keep going even if some children still do not seem to understand. Children are not expected to master the concepts today. Later activities in this unit will help make the concepts clear for all children.

Ongoing Assessment

Ask children to describe these numbers in as many ways as they can.

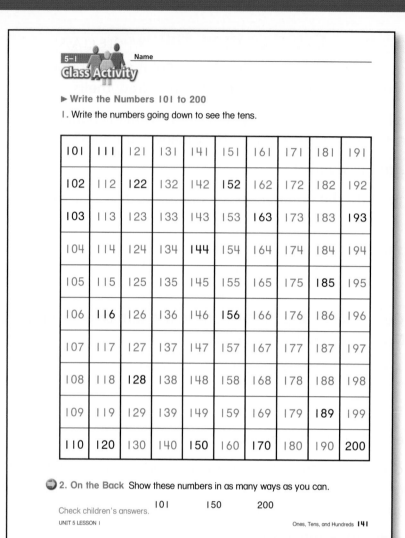

102 120

105 150

5–1 Class Activity

Name

▶ Write the Numbers 101 to 200

1. Write the numbers going down to see the tens.

101	111	121	131	141	151	161	171	181	191
102	112	122	132	142	152	162	172	182	192
103	113	123	133	143	153	163	173	183	193
104	114	124	134	144	154	164	174	184	194
105	115	125	135	145	155	165	175	185	195
106	116	126	136	146	156	166	176	186	196
107	117	127	137	147	157	167	177	187	197
108	118	128	138	148	158	168	178	188	198
109	119	129	139	149	159	169	179	189	199
110	120	130	140	150	160	170	180	190	200

2. On the Back Show these numbers in as many ways as you can.

101 150 200

Check children's answers.

UNIT 5 LESSON 1 Ones, Tens, and Hundreds 141

Student Activity Book page 141

Back of 120 Poster

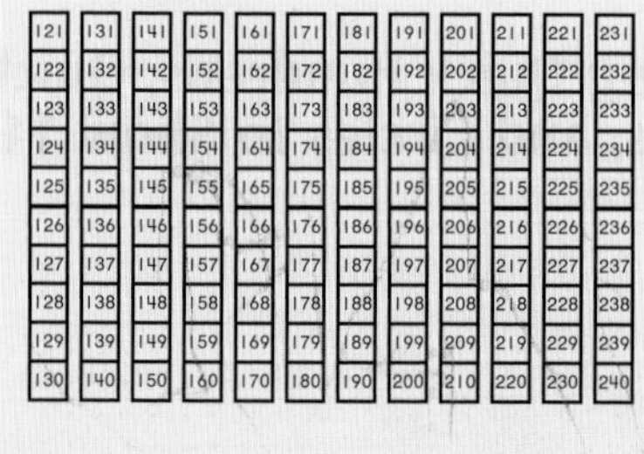

121	131	141	151	161	171	181	191	201	211	221	231
122	132	142	152	162	172	182	192	202	212	222	232
123	133	143	153	163	173	183	193	203	213	223	233
124	134	144	154	164	174	184	194	204	214	224	234
125	135	145	155	165	175	185	195	205	215	225	235
126	136	146	156	166	176	186	196	206	216	226	236
127	137	147	157	167	177	187	197	207	217	227	237
128	138	148	158	168	178	188	198	208	218	228	238
129	139	149	159	169	179	189	199	209	219	229	239
130	140	150	160	170	180	190	200	210	220	230	240

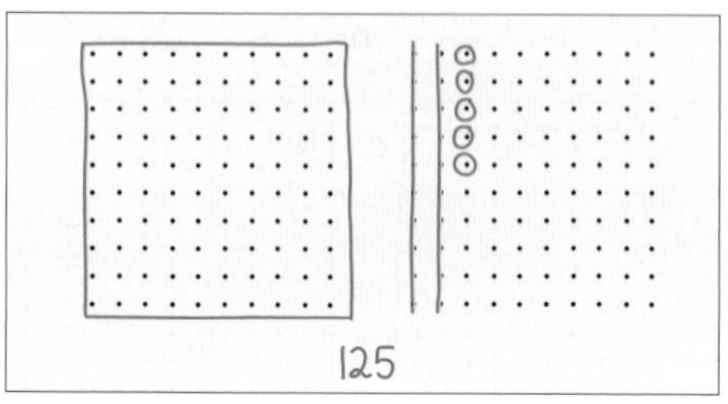

▶ Write the Numbers 101 to 200 WHOLE CLASS

Have children erase the last column (the numbers 101–110) from their 10 × 10 grids on their MathBoards. Then have them place their MathBoards (showing 1–100) to the left of Student Activity Book page 141. Have them begin to fill in the grid on the page. Help them complete the numbers through 120. Then flip the 120 Poster over, showing the numbers 121–240 and then have them complete the page independently.

Have children count together from 101 to 200, looking at the numbers they have written. Have them discuss any patterns they see. Especially focus on the bottom row of tens numbers and discuss how those numbers are 11 tens, 12 tens, 13 tens, and so on, because 10 tens make 100.

Have children represent numbers with Quick Hundreds, Quick Tens, and circles on the dot grids. (See picture on left.)

2 Going Further

Intervention — Activity Card 5-1

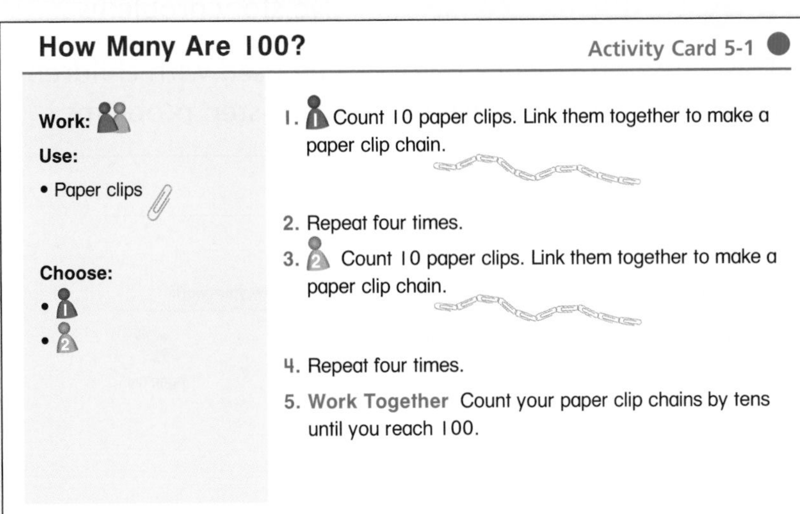
How Many Are 100? — Activity Card 5-1

Work: [pair]
Use:
- Paper clips

Choose:
- [child 1]
- [child 2]

1. Count 10 paper clips. Link them together to make a paper clip chain.
2. Repeat four times.
3. Count 10 paper clips. Link them together to make a paper clip chain.
4. Repeat four times.
5. **Work Together** Count your paper clip chains by tens until you reach 100.

Unit 5, Lesson 1

Activity Note Each pair needs 100 paper clips. Each child makes chains of 10 clips, then the pair uses the chains to count by tens to 100.

Math Writing Prompt

Explain Your Thinking Is 10 tens the same as 100? Use a Proof Drawing to explain.

Software Support

Use *Soar to Success* for instruction of students needing targeted support for underlying skills.

On Level — Activity Card 5-1

What Number Am I? — Activity Card 5-1

Work: [pair]
Use:
- MathBoard

Choose:
- [child 1]
- [child 2]

1. **Work Together** Draw Quick Hundreds, Quick Tens, and circles to solve each riddle.
   - I have 2 more tens than 140. What number am I? Answer: 160
   - I have 6 more ones than 172. What number am I? Answer: 178
   - I have 1 less ten than 127. What number am I? Answer: 117
2. Write a riddle for another pair. Then trade riddles and solve.

Unit 5, Lesson 1

Activity Note Each pair needs 25-cm ruler or TRB M47–M48. Suggest pairs draw the details of the problem.

Math Writing Prompt

Explain Your Thinking How would you use Secret Code Cards to show the number 104? Use words and pictures to explain.

Software Support

Use *MegaMath* for review and reinforcement of the concepts and skills presented in this lesson.

Challenge — Activity Card 5-1

Palindromes — Activity Card 5-1

Work: [pair]
Use:
- paper

Choose:
- [child 1]
- [child 2]

1. A palindrome is a number that is the same when read from left to right or right to left. 11 is an example. Think of other examples.
2. **Work Together** Make an organized list of all the palindromes between 11 and 200. Answer: 11, 22, 33, 44, 55, 66, 77, 88, 99, 111, 121, 131, 141, 151, 161, 171, 181, 191
3. Share your list with another pair.
4. **Math Talk** Discuss how you organized your list to find all the examples.

Unit 5, Lesson 1

Activity Note Review with children the meaning of a palindrome. Ask pairs to check and see if they found all the palindromes.

Math Writing Prompt

Explain Your Thinking Keisha has 180 stickers. She can put 10 on a page in her sticker book. How many pages does she need? Explain your answer.

Software Support

Use *Destination Math* to take students beyond the concepts and skills presented in this lesson.

3 Homework and Targeted Practice

5–1 Homework **Goal:** Additional Practice

This Homework page provides practice in writing the numbers 1–100.

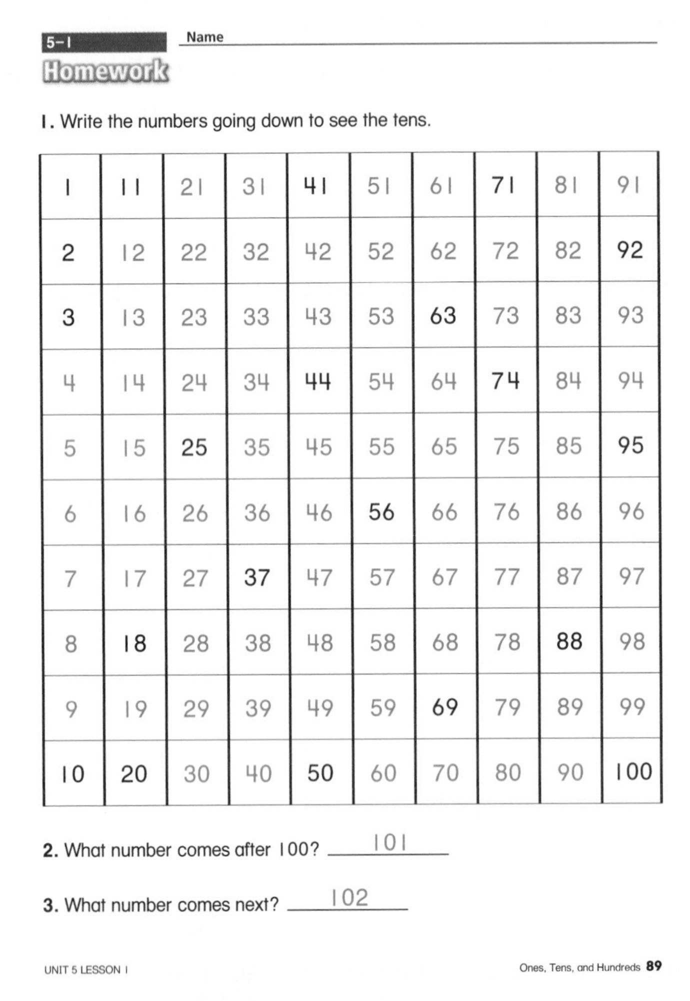

5–1 Name

Homework

1. Write the numbers going down to see the tens.

1	11	21	31	41	51	61	71	81	91
2	12	22	32	42	52	62	72	82	92
3	13	23	33	43	53	63	73	83	93
4	14	24	34	44	54	64	74	84	94
5	15	25	35	45	55	65	75	85	95
6	16	26	36	46	56	66	76	86	96
7	17	27	37	47	57	67	77	87	97
8	18	28	38	48	58	68	78	88	98
9	19	29	39	49	59	69	79	89	99
10	20	30	40	50	60	70	80	90	100

2. What number comes after 100? 101

3. What number comes next? 102

UNIT 5 LESSON 1 Ones, Tens, and Hundreds 89

Homework and Remembering page 89

5–1 Targeted Practice **Goal:** Solve story problems.

This Targeted Practice page can be used with children who need extra practice solving two-step problems.

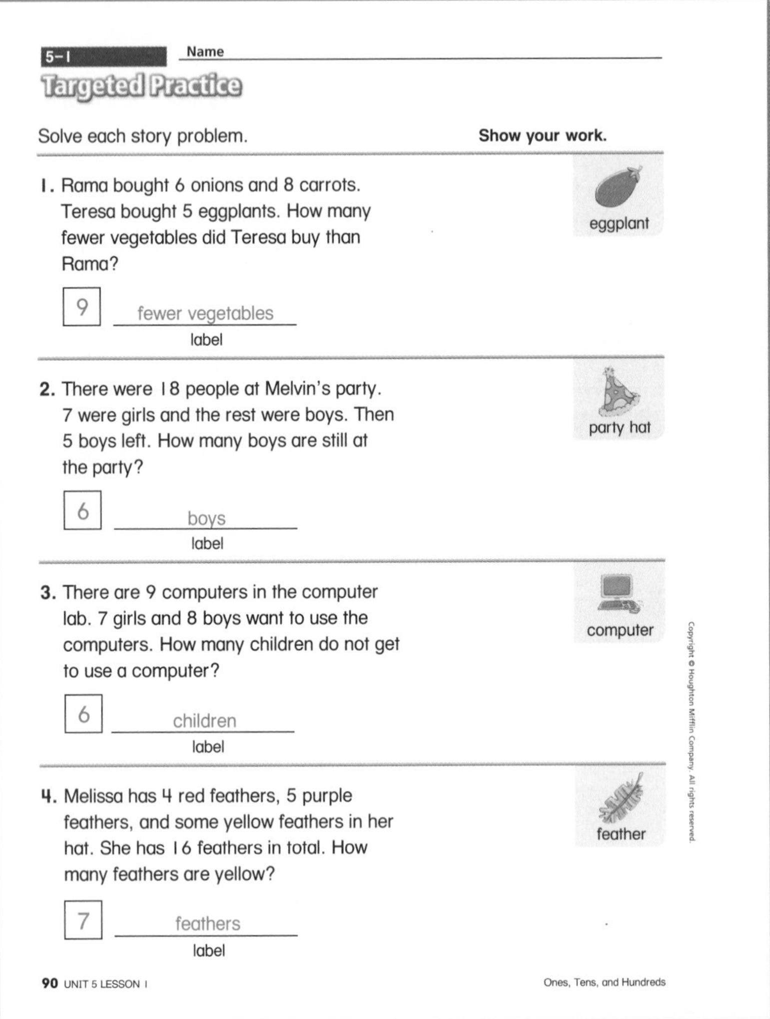

5–1 Name

Targeted Practice

Solve each story problem. **Show your work.**

1. Rama bought 6 onions and 8 carrots. Teresa bought 5 eggplants. How many fewer vegetables did Teresa buy than Rama?

   9 fewer vegetables (label)

   eggplant

2. There were 18 people at Melvin's party. 7 were girls and the rest were boys. Then 5 boys left. How many boys are still at the party?

   6 boys (label)

   party hat

3. There are 9 computers in the computer lab. 7 girls and 8 boys want to use the computers. How many children do not get to use a computer?

   6 children (label)

   computer

4. Melissa has 4 red feathers, 5 purple feathers, and some yellow feathers in her hat. She has 16 feathers in total. How many feathers are yellow?

   7 feathers (label)

   feather

Copyright © Houghton Mifflin Company. All rights reserved.

90 UNIT 5 LESSON 1 Ones, Tens, and Hundreds

Homework and Remembering page 90

Home and School Connection

Family Letter Have children take home the Family Letter on Student Activity Book page 143. This letter explains how drawings are used to show place value in *Math Expressions.* It gives parents and guardians a better understanding of the learning that goes on in math class and creates a bridge between school and home. A Spanish translation of this letter is on the following page in the Student Activity Book.

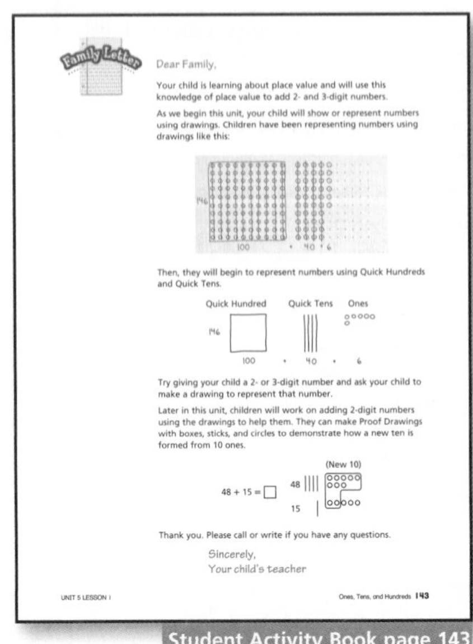

Family Letter

Dear Family,

Your child is learning about place value and will use this knowledge of place value to add 2- and 3-digit numbers.

As we begin this unit, your child will show or represent numbers using drawings. Children have been representing numbers using drawings like this:

146 — 100 + 40 + 6

Then, they will begin to represent numbers using Quick Hundreds and Quick Tens.

Quick Hundred Quick Tens Ones

146 — 100 + 40 + 6

Try giving your child a 2- or 3-digit number and ask your child to make a drawing to represent that number.

Later in this unit, children will work on adding 2-digit numbers using the drawings to help them. They can make Proof Drawings with boxes, sticks, and circles to demonstrate how a new ten is formed from 10 ones.

(New 10)

48 + 15 = □ 48 15

Thank you. Please call or write if you have any questions.

Sincerely,
Your child's teacher

UNIT 5 LESSON 1 Ones, Tens, and Hundreds 143

Student Activity Book page 143

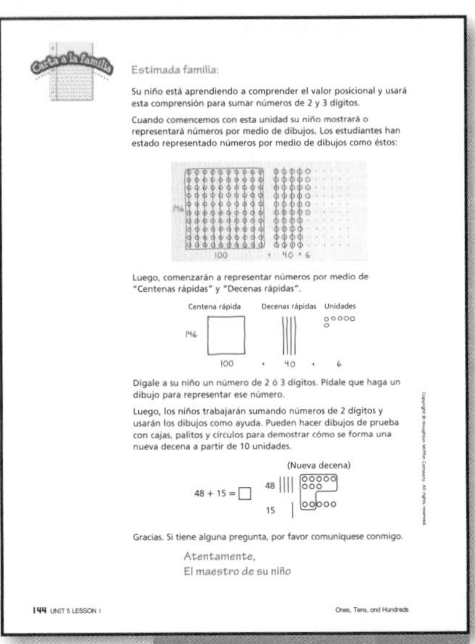

Carta a la familia

Estimada familia:

Su niño está aprendiendo a comprender el valor posicional y usará esta comprensión para sumar números de 2 y 3 dígitos.

Cuando comencemos con esta unidad su niño mostrará o representará números por medio de dibujos. Los estudiantes han estado representado números por medio de dibujos como éstos:

146 — 100 + 40 + 6

Luego, comenzarán a representar números por medio de "Centenas rápidas" y "Decenas rápidas".

Centena rápida Decenas rápidas Unidades

146 — 100 + 40 + 6

Dígale a su niño un número de 2 ó 3 dígitos. Pídale que haga un dibujo para representar ese número.

Luego, los niños trabajarán sumando números de 2 dígitos y usarán los dibujos como ayuda. Pueden hacer dibujos de prueba con cajas, palitos y círculos para demostrar cómo se forma una nueva decena a partir de 10 unidades.

(Nueva decena)

48 + 15 = □ 48 15

Gracias. Si tiene alguna pregunta, por favor comuníquese conmigo.

Atentamente,
El maestro de su niño

Copyright © Houghton Mifflin Company. All rights reserved.

144 UNIT 5 LESSON 1 Ones, Tens, and Hundreds

Student Activity Book page 144

Draw Quick Tens and Quick Hundreds

Lesson Objectives

- Represent ones, tens, and hundreds in different ways.
- Write 2- and 3-digit numbers through 200.
- Compare totals of ones and tens.

Vocabulary

ones	Number Path
tens	Quick Tens
hundreds	Quick Hundreds

The Day at a Glance

Today's Goals	Materials	
1 Teaching the Lesson **A1:** Draw Quick Tens and Quick Hundreds. **A2:** Add tens and ones and compare the totals. **2 Going Further** ▸ Differentiated Instruction **3 Homework and Spiral Review**	**Lesson Activities** Student Activity Book pp. 145–146 Homework and Remembering pp. 91–92 MathBoard materials Number Path (TRB M51) Secret Code Cards	**Going Further** Activity Cards 5-2 MathBoard materials Number Path (TRB M51) Secret Code Cards Base-ten blocks Number cubes Math Journals

Use Math Talk today!

Keeping Skills Sharp

Quick Practice — 5 MINUTES

Goal: Shift from counting by tens to counting by ones.

Materials: 120 Poster, pointer

Tens to Ones Shift Have a **Student Leader** write a 2-digit number on the board. For example, the leader might write 78.

The leader then directs the class in counting to that number by tens as they flash 10 fingers for each number. For example, "10" (flash 10 fingers), "20" (flash 10 again), "30" (flash 10 again), and so on up to 70.

When they reach "70," shift the class to counting by ones as they raise each finger by saying "freeze" and then "71, 72, 73, 74, 75, 76, 77, 78."

Repeated Quick Practice Use this Quick Practice from a previous lesson.

▸ **Count by Tens to 120**
(See Unit 5 Lesson 1.)

Daily Routines

Math Mountains for 100 or 2-Digit Numbers Using the MathBoard, Using Dimes and Pennies
(See pp. xxvi.)

▸ Led by teacher

Money Routine Using the 120 Poster, Using the Money Flip Chart, Using the Number Path, Using Secret Code Cards
(See pp. xxiii–xxv.)

▸ Led by Student Leaders

1 Teaching the Lesson

Activity 1

Draw Numbers to 200

 40 MINUTES

Goal: Draw Quick Tens and Quick Hundreds.

Materials: MathBoard materials or Number Path (TRB M51), Demonstration Secret Code Cards (TRB M7–M22)

 **NCTM Standards:**
Number and Operations
Communication

Math Talk in Action

Who can describe a way that we showed 24?

Roberto: You can use the Number Path. You can draw lines through two 10-groups and draw circles on 4 of the squares. That shows 24.

Megan: I wrote the equation $20 + 4 = 24$. That shows the two groups of 10 and the 4 ones.

Tommy: I drew sticks to show the 2 tens and circles to show the 4 ones in 24. The sticks are called Quick Tens.

▶ Draw Quick Tens and Ones WHOLE CLASS

Represent 24 Have children place their MathBoards with the Number Path facing them or have them use Number Path (TRB M51).

Explain that the Number Path has 100 squares that can be used to show the numbers from 1 to 100. Point out that the number 1 is next to the first square, the number 2 is next to the second square and so on.

Tell children that they will show the number 24 on the Number Path.

- How many groups of 10 are in 24? 2 groups

Draw Quick Tens through the first 20 squares to show the two 10-groups.

- What number does this show? 20
- How many ones are in 24? 4 Draw circles on the next four squares to show the four ones.

Write the equation $20 + 4 = 24$ on the board and have children write it on their MathBoards. Now draw Quick Tens and circles under the equation to show 24.

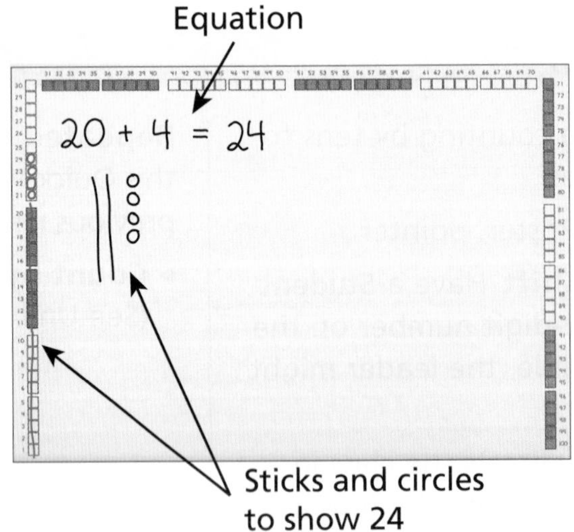

Have children discuss the different ways they represented 24. For a sample of classroom dialogue, see **Math Talk in Action** in the side column.

Then, ask a volunteer to show 24 with the Demonstration Secret Code Cards.

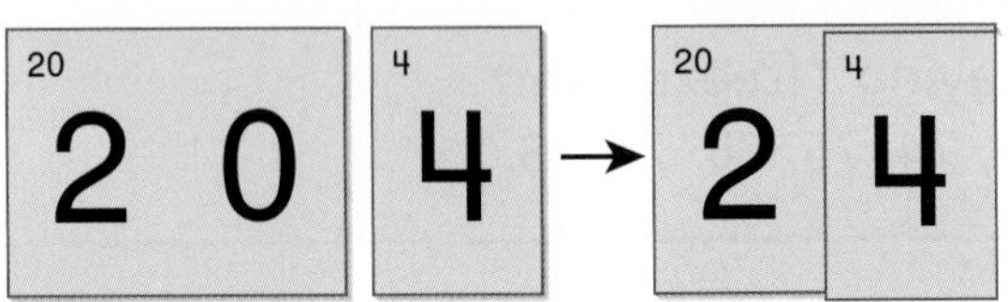

Represent 68 Have children erase their MathBoards and represent the number 68. Then draw Quick Tens and circles on the squares for the 6 tens and 8 ones in 68. Then write the equation 68 = 60 + 8 on the board and have children write it on their MathBoards.

Now, draw Quick Tens and ones under the equation to show 68. Have children do the same.

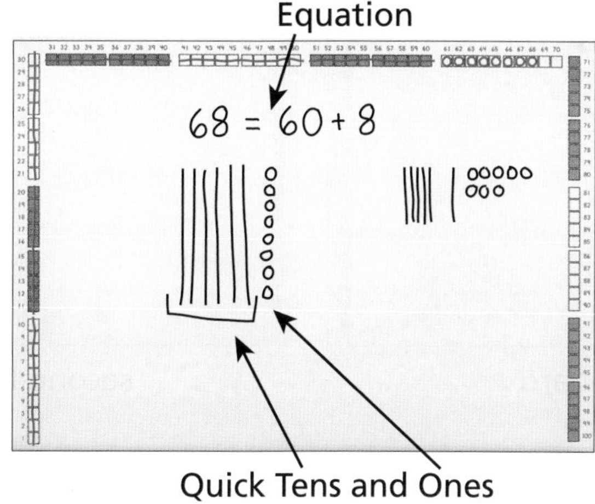

Have a volunteer show 68 with the Demonstration Secret Code Cards.

▶ Draw 5-Groups with Quick Tens and Circles

WHOLE CLASS

Explain to children that there is an easier way to draw the Quick Tens and circles.

- It is easier to see the number if you use 5-groups. Instead of having all the Quick Tens together, we want to put them in groups of 5.
- Instead of drawing all the circles in one column, we can put them in groups of 5, either across or up and down.

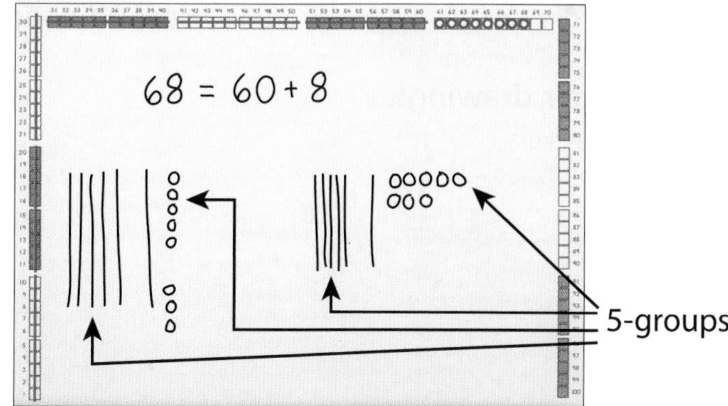

Activity continued ▶

English Language Learners

Review 5-groups with children. Draw 5 circles on the board. Say: **This is a 5-group. It has 5 circles.**

- **Beginning** Draw another circle below the 5-group. Say: **5 and 1 more is __.** 6
- **Intermediate** Draw a 5-group of Quick Tens. Say: **5 Quick Tens is __.** 50 Draw another Quick Ten. Say: **And 1 more is __.** 60
- **Advanced** Model a 5-group with Quick Tens. Have children work in pairs to show other numbers with 5-groups.

The Learning Classroom

Building Concepts It is very helpful for children to use 5-groups in their drawings. This might be difficult for some children to do, so allow them to gradually shift to using 5-groups.

Teaching Note

What to Expect from Students
Some of the children will continue to draw all of the Quick Tens together. Remind them that it is easier to count the Quick Tens if they are in 5-groups.

▶ Draw Quick Hundreds PAIRS

Have children erase their MathBoards and work in pairs, using two MathBoards. Pairs will use the first MathBoard to represent the number 100 and the second MathBoard to represent the numbers 101–200.

Have pairs use the first MathBoard to fill in the Number Path boxes with Quick Tens to show the number 100. Then have them draw 10 Quick Tens in the middle of the board to show the 10 groups of ten in 100. Draw the 10 Quick Tens on the board as the children draw them on their MathBoards.

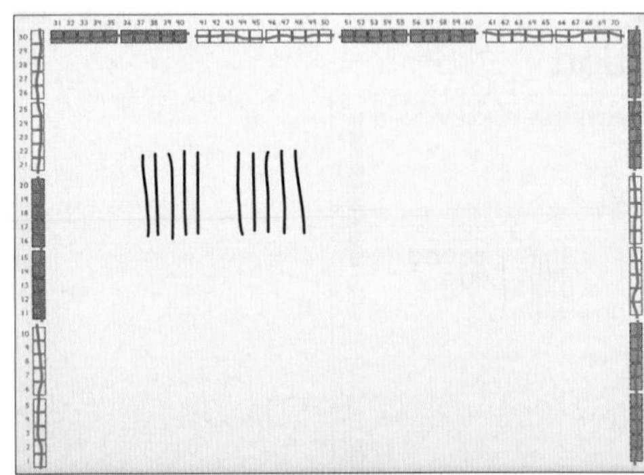

first board

second board

- There is a way to draw a Quick Hundred that is much faster than drawing 10 sticks. All you have to do is draw a box. Today have children draw a box around the 10 sticks, but next time they can just draw the box. Draw the Quick Hundred box on the board as the children draw them on their MathBoards.

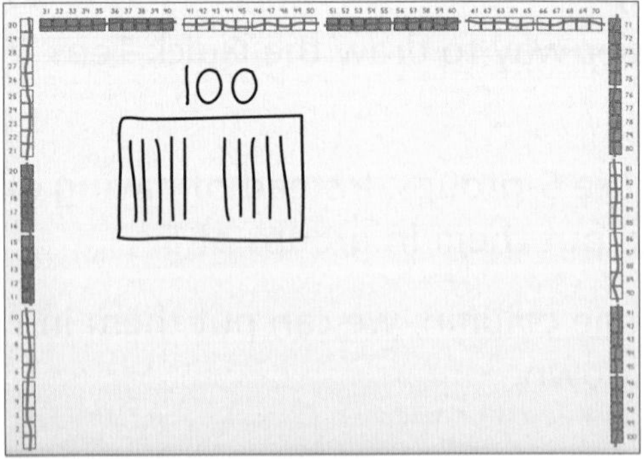

first board

second board

Have children erase their drawings.

▶ Draw Numbers to 200 PAIRS

On the second MathBoard, have children show the numbers from 101 to 200 by writing "10" in front of the numerals 1 through 9 to make the numbers 101 to 109. Then have them write "1" in front of the numerals 10 through 99 to make the numbers 110 to 199. Finally, have them change 100 to 200.

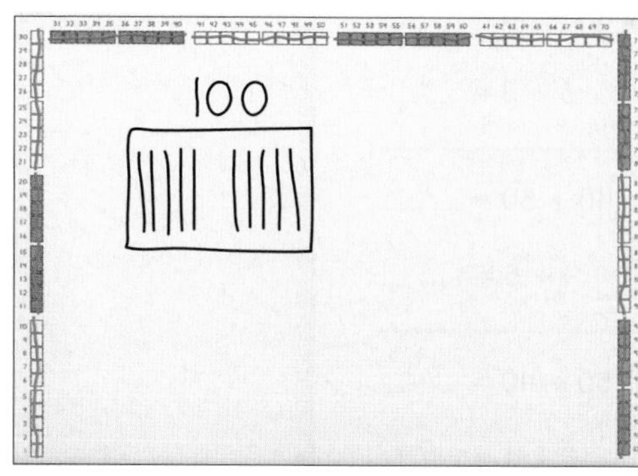

first board

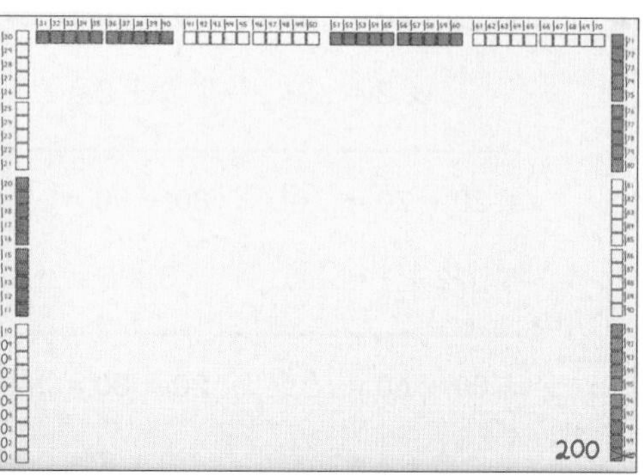

second board

Have the class count from 101 to 200 if you feel they need the practice. Then have children represent numbers on the MathBoard with Quick Hundred and Quick Ten drawings. The example shown below is for the number 166. Discuss how the children can represent the number using questions similar to those below.

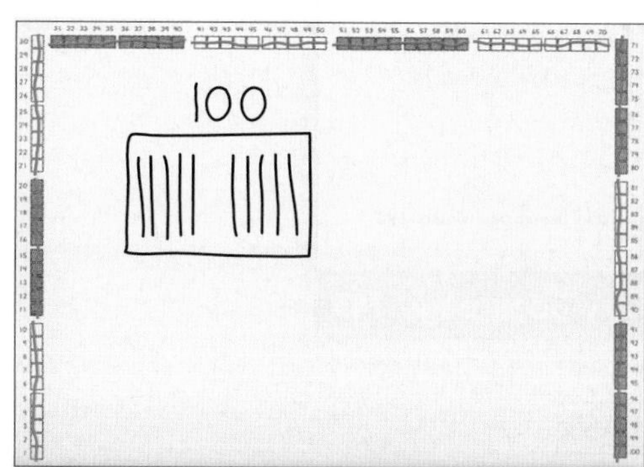

first board

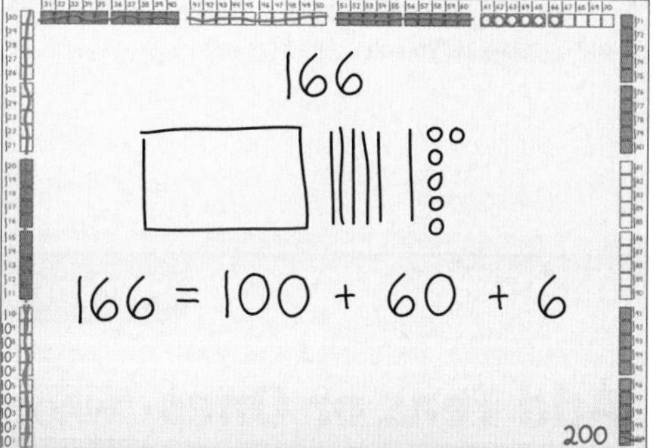

second board

- How many small squares make 166? one hundred sixty-six
- How many hundreds are in 166? 1
- How many tens are in 166? 6 or 16
- How many ones are in 166? 6 or 166

Have volunteers show 166 with the Demonstration Secret Code Cards.

Challenge children to work in pairs and show other numbers on the MathBoards and with Secret Code Cards.

Teaching Note

Watch For! To facilitate flexibility, it is important for children to understand different ways to think about a number as composed of hundreds, tens, and ones. For example, the primary meaning for 166 is 1 hundred, 6 tens, and 6 ones. But there will be times when a child will also want to think of such a number as sixteen tens and six ones or as one hundred sixty-six ones. Stressing all of these meanings will provide children with flexibility in problem solving.

Class Management

Looking Ahead Do not erase the MathBoards with numbers from 101 to 200. In Lesson 3, pairs will work together again to draw numbers below 100 on one MathBoard and then numbers between 100 and 200 on the MathBoards with those numbers.

Activity 2

Add Tens and Ones

 10 MINUTES

Goal: Add tens and ones and compare the totals.

Materials: Student Activity Book page 145

 **NCTM Standards:**
Number and Operations
Communication

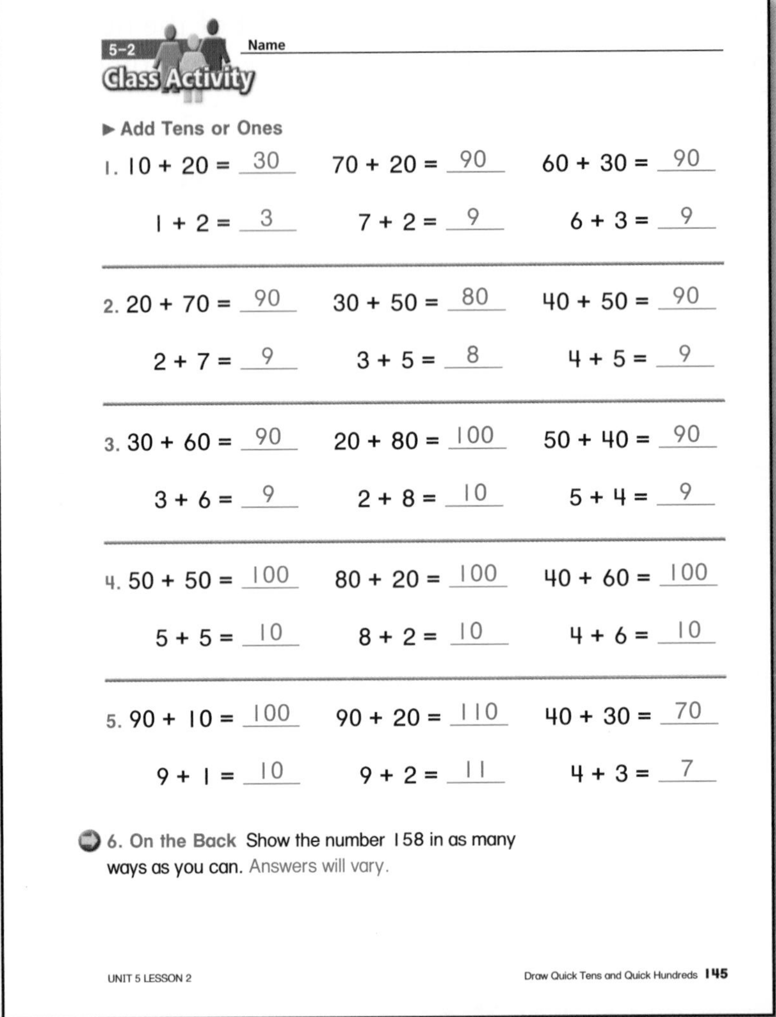
5–2 Class Activity Name

▶ Add Tens or Ones

1. 10 + 20 = 30 70 + 20 = 90 60 + 30 = 90
 1 + 2 = 3 7 + 2 = 9 6 + 3 = 9

2. 20 + 70 = 90 30 + 50 = 80 40 + 50 = 90
 2 + 7 = 9 3 + 5 = 8 4 + 5 = 9

3. 30 + 60 = 90 20 + 80 = 100 50 + 40 = 90
 3 + 6 = 9 2 + 8 = 10 5 + 4 = 9

4. 50 + 50 = 100 80 + 20 = 100 40 + 60 = 100
 5 + 5 = 10 8 + 2 = 10 4 + 6 = 10

5. 90 + 10 = 100 90 + 20 = 110 40 + 30 = 70
 9 + 1 = 10 9 + 2 = 11 4 + 3 = 7

6. On the Back Show the number 158 in as many ways as you can. Answers will vary.

UNIT 5 LESSON 2 Draw Quick Tens and Quick Hundreds 145

Student Activity Book page 145

▶ Add Tens or Ones WHOLE CLASS

Direct children's attention to Student Activity Book page 145. Do the first problem with the whole class being sure to have children solve 10 + 20 using decade words (*ten* plus *twenty*) and tens words (1 *ten* plus 2 *tens*). Discuss relationships children see between these two problems and how the second can help them solve the first [the answer is the same except that it is tens instead of ones]. Use the following questions as necessary.

- How are these answers alike? They both have 3 in them.
- How are they different? The 3 in 30 tells us there are 3 groups of 10. The 3 by itself tells us there are 3 ones.

Solve several more problems together having children describe how the problems are alike and different and how using the tens words is especially helpful here (e.g., 70 + 20 is 7 tens plus 2 tens which is 9 tens).

Circulate around the room as children complete the page and ask individual children to describe what is the same and what is different about each pair of answers.

2 Going Further

Differentiated Instruction

Intervention

Activity Card 5-2

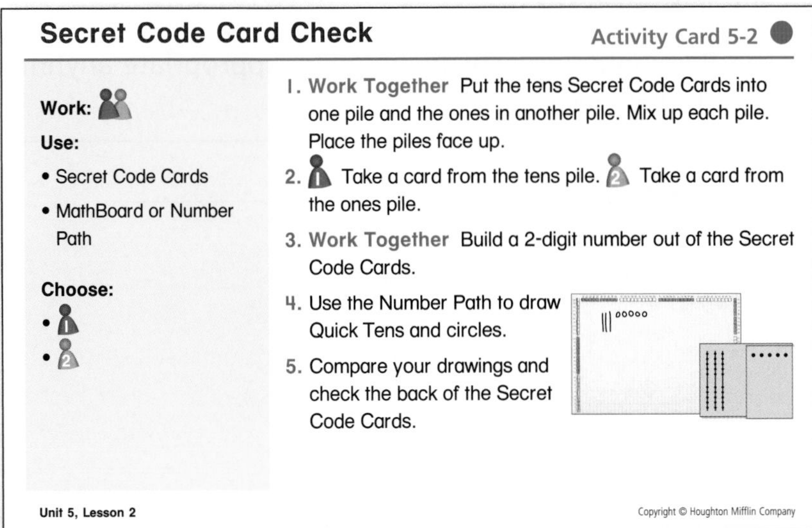

Secret Code Card Check Activity Card 5-2

Work: (pairs)

Use:

- Secret Code Cards
- MathBoard or Number Path

Choose:

- 1
- 2

1. **Work Together** Put the tens Secret Code Cards into one pile and the ones in another pile. Mix up each pile. Place the piles face up.
2. (1) Take a card from the tens pile. (2) Take a card from the ones pile.
3. **Work Together** Build a 2-digit number out of the Secret Code Cards.
4. Use the Number Path to draw Quick Tens and circles.
5. Compare your drawings and check the back of the Secret Code Cards.

Unit 5, Lesson 2 Copyright © Houghton Mifflin Company

Activity Note Each pair needs 1 set of Secret Code Cards (TRB M3–M6) and MathBoard materials or Number Path (TRB M51).

Math Writing Prompt

Draw a Picture What is the value of the 7 in the number 74? Explain by drawing Quick Tens and circles.

Software Support

Use *Soar to Success* for instruction of students needing targeted support for underlying skills.

On Level

Activity Card 5-2

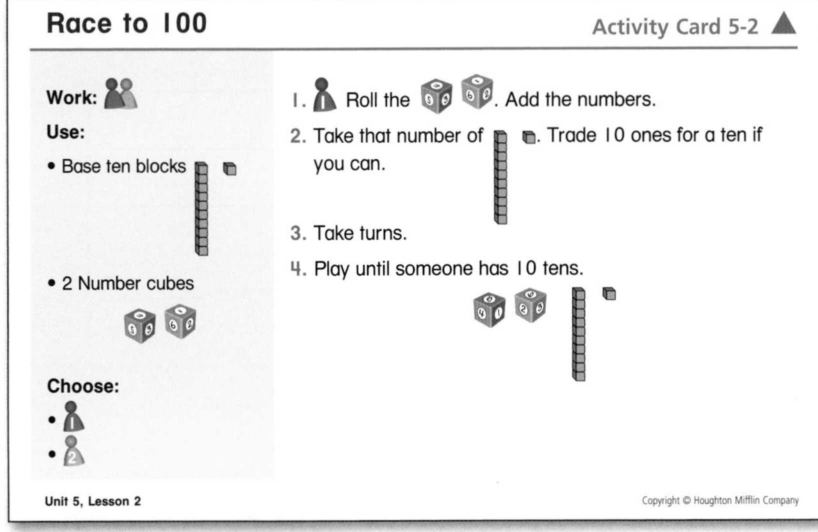

Race to 100 Activity Card 5-2

Work: (pairs)

Use:

- Base ten blocks
- 2 Number cubes

Choose:

- 1
- 2

1. (1) Roll the (cubes). Add the numbers.
2. Take that number of (tens) (ones). Trade 10 ones for a ten if you can.
3. Take turns.
4. Play until someone has 10 tens.

Unit 5, Lesson 2 Copyright © Houghton Mifflin Company

Activity Note Each pair needs 20 tens and 20 ones base ten blocks and two number cubes labeled 1–6. Review trading a 10 ones for a ten.

Math Writing Prompt

Exchange for a Dime Jan has 1 dime and 26 pennies. Can she trade some pennies for a dime? Explain. Then tell how much money Jan has.

Software Support

Use *MegaMath* for review and reinforcement of the concepts and skills presented in this lesson.

Challenge

Activity Card 5-2

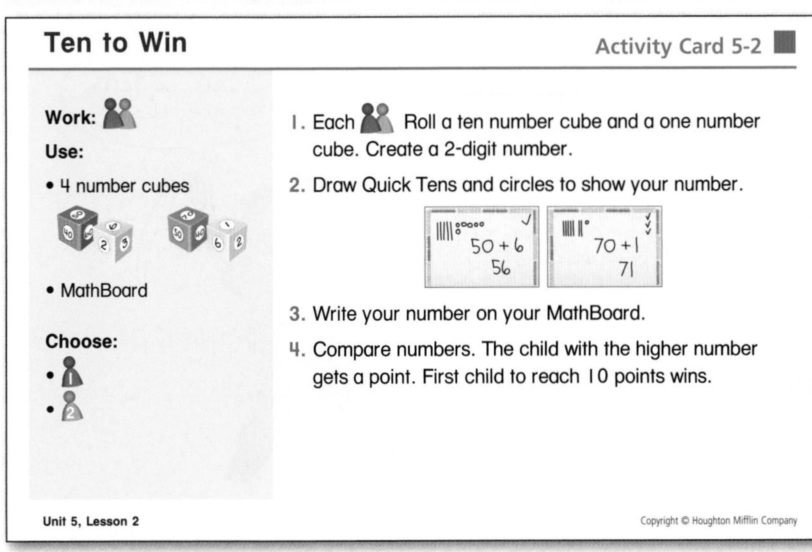

Ten to Win Activity Card 5-2

Work: (pairs)

Use:

- 4 number cubes
- MathBoard

Choose:

- 1
- 2

1. Each (pair) Roll a ten number cube and a one number cube. Create a 2-digit number.
2. Draw Quick Tens and circles to show your number.

   50 + 6 = 56   70 + 1 = 71
3. Write your number on your MathBoard.
4. Compare numbers. The child with the higher number gets a point. First child to reach 10 points wins.

Unit 5, Lesson 2 Copyright © Houghton Mifflin Company

Activity Note Each pair needs four number cubes. Two are labeled 40, 50, 60, 70, 80, 90 and two are labeled 1–6.

Math Writing Prompt

Investigate Math 10 ones = 10
10 tens = 100
What number do you think shows 10 hundreds? Explain.

DESTINATION Math® **Software Suppor**

Use *Destination Math* to take students beyond the concepts and skills presented in this lesson.

3 Homework and Spiral Review

Goal: Additional Practice

This Homework page provides practice in adding tens and ones.

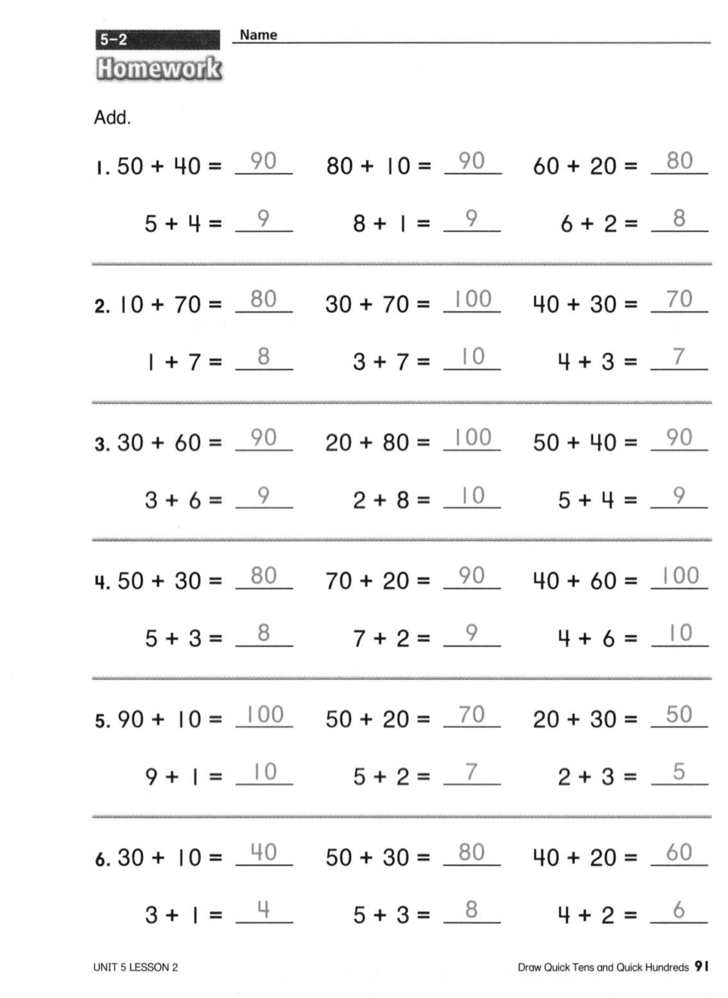

5-2 Homework

Name ______

Add.

1\. 50 + 40 = 90   80 + 10 = 90   60 + 20 = 80

5 + 4 = 9   8 + 1 = 9   6 + 2 = 8

2\. 10 + 70 = 80   30 + 70 = 100   40 + 30 = 70

1 + 7 = 8   3 + 7 = 10   4 + 3 = 7

3\. 30 + 60 = 90   20 + 80 = 100   50 + 40 = 90

3 + 6 = 9   2 + 8 = 10   5 + 4 = 9

4\. 50 + 30 = 80   70 + 20 = 90   40 + 60 = 100

5 + 3 = 8   7 + 2 = 9   4 + 6 = 10

5\. 90 + 10 = 100   50 + 20 = 70   20 + 30 = 50

9 + 1 = 10   5 + 2 = 7   2 + 3 = 5

6\. 30 + 10 = 40   50 + 30 = 80   40 + 20 = 60

3 + 1 = 4   5 + 3 = 8   4 + 2 = 6

UNIT 5 LESSON 2   Draw Quick Tens and Quick Hundreds 91

Homework and Remembering page 91

Goal: Spiral Review

This Remembering activity would be appropriate anytime after today's lesson.

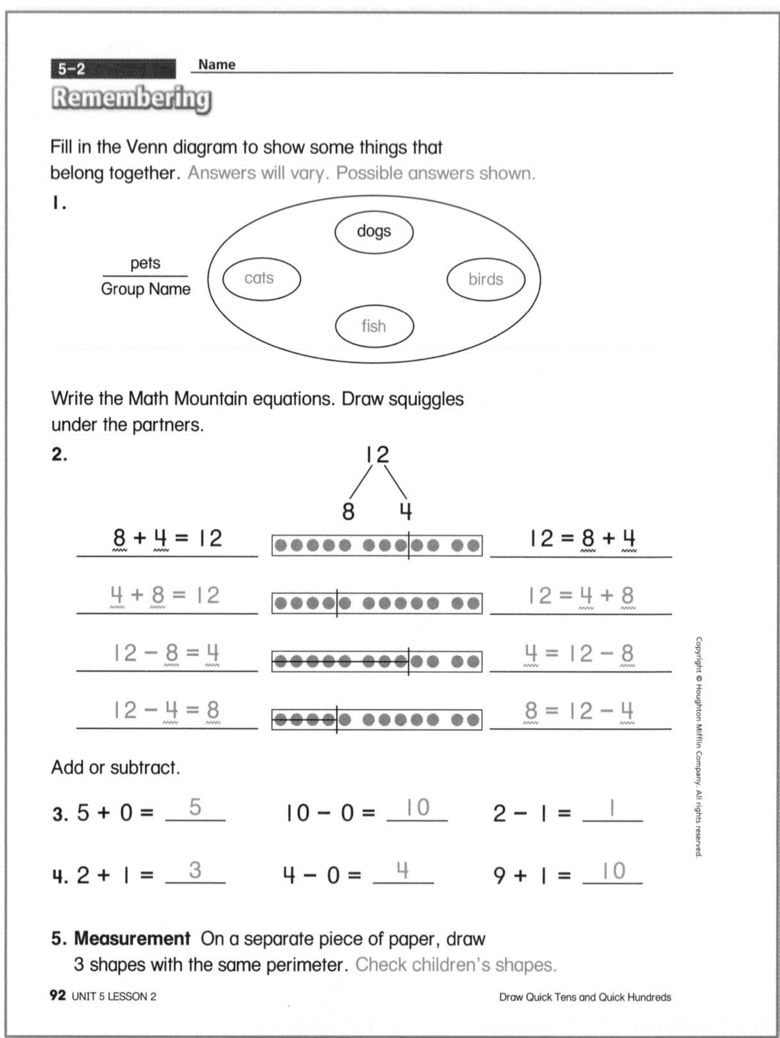

5-2 Remembering

Name ______

Fill in the Venn diagram to show some things that belong together. Answers will vary. Possible answers shown.

1\.

pets
Group Name

dogs
cats
birds
fish

Write the Math Mountain equations. Draw squiggles under the partners.

2\.

12
8 4

8 + 4 = 12	●●●●● ●●●●● ●●	12 = 8 + 4
4 + 8 = 12	●●●●● ●●●●● ●●	12 = 4 + 8
12 − 8 = 4	●●●●● ●●●●● ●●	4 = 12 − 8
12 − 4 = 8	●●●●● ●●●●● ●●	8 = 12 − 4

Add or subtract.

3\. 5 + 0 = 5   10 − 0 = 10   2 − 1 = 1

4\. 2 + 1 = 3   4 − 0 = 4   9 + 1 = 10

5\. **Measurement** On a separate piece of paper, draw 3 shapes with the same perimeter. Check children's shapes.

92 UNIT 5 LESSON 2   Draw Quick Tens and Quick Hundreds

Homework and Remembering page 92

Home or School Activity

Physical Education Connection

Jump for Tens and Clap for Ones Have children work in pairs to write 1- and 2-digit numbers on index cards.

Have children shuffle the cards and place them face down. Children take turns choosing the top card and doing jumping jacks for each ten and clapping for the ones they see in the number on the card.

For example, if the number is 46, the child does 4 jumping jacks and calls out, "1 ten, 2 tens, 3 tens, 4 tens." Then the child claps the ones and says, "1, 2, 3, 4, 5, 6."

Represent Numbers in Different Ways

Vocabulary

Quick Tens
Quick Hundreds
hundreds
tens
ones
decade numbers
word name

Lesson Objectives

- Represent 2-digit and 3-digit numbers.
- Write numbers up to 99 in word form.

The Day at a Glance

Today's Goals	Materials	
1 Teaching the Lesson A1: Review Quick Tens and ones. A2: Review and draw Quick Hundreds, Quick Tens, and ones. A3: Represent 3-digit numbers with Quick Hundreds, Quick Tens, and ones. A4: Write numbers up to 99 in word form.	**Lesson Activities** Student Activity Book pp. 147–148 Homework and Remembering pp. 93–94 MathBoard materials Number Path (TRB M51) Secret Code Cards	**Going Further** Activity Cards 5-3 MathBoard materials Secret Code Cards (TRB M3–M6) Math Journals
2 Going Further ▸ Differentiated Instruction		
3 Homework and Targeted Practice		

123 Use Math Talk today!

Keeping Skills Sharp

Quick Practice — 5 MINUTES

Goal: Count by tens to 120.

Materials: 120 Poster and pointer

Tens to Ones Shift Have a Student Leader direct the class in counting by tens and ones to a 2-digit number (for example, 48, 73, or 85) as the class flashes tens and ones. (See Unit 5 Lesson 2.)

As a variation, have children count from 100 to 200 as needed. Use the back side of the 120 Poster for the numbers greater than 120.

Repeated Quick Practice Use this Quick Practice from a previous lesson.

▸ **Count by Tens to 120** (See Unit 5 Lesson 1.)

Daily Routines

Math Mountains for 100 or 2-Digit Numbers Using the MathBoard, Using Dimes and Pennies (See pp. xxvi.)

▸ Led by teacher

Money Routine Using the 120 Poster, Using the Money Flip Chart, Using the Number Path, Using Secret Code Cards (See pp. xxiii–xxv.)

▸ Led by Student Leaders

Teaching the Lesson

Activity 1

Review Quick Tens and Ones

 **15 MINUTES**

Goal: Review Quick Tens and ones.

Materials: MathBoard materials or Number Path (TRB M51), Secret Code Cards (from Unit 1 Lesson 5 or TRB M3–M6)

 **NCTM Standard:**
Number and Operations

Teaching Note

What to Expect from Students When children draw their Quick Tens and ones, some may draw their circles (ones) horizontally instead of vertically. As long as they are drawing their tens and ones in groups of 5, allow them to draw their circles this way.

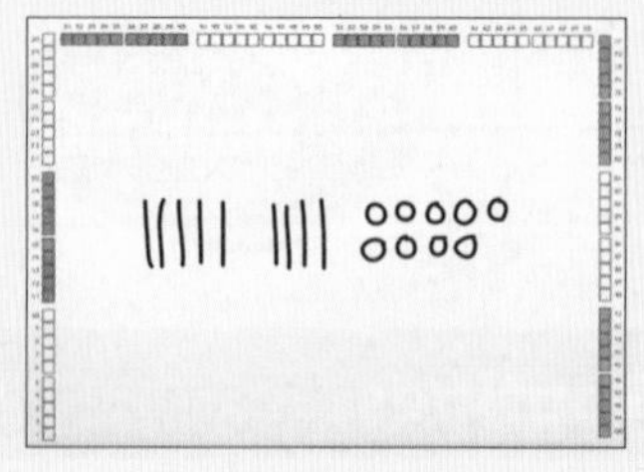

Teaching Note

Language and Vocabulary The terms *Quick Tens, 10-sticks,* and *sticks* can be used interchangeably. So can the terms *Quick Hundreds* and *boxes* or the terms *circles* and *ones.* As long as children are using the terms correctly, allow them to use any words they can understand and explain.

▶ Represent 2-Digit Numbers WHOLE CLASS Math Talk

Use the MathBoards from Lesson 2 that do not have numbers 101 to 200 written on them (you will use those in Activity 2). Have children place their MathBoards with the Number Path side up or have them use Number Path (TRB M51). Remind children that they can represent numbers on the Number Path. Select a 2-digit number for children to represent. The number 38 is used below as an example.

- How can you show 38 on your Number Path? Draw 10-sticks in 30 squares. Draw 8 circles in the next set of squares.

Have the children draw the 10-sticks and circles to show 38.

- What are other ways to show the number? Possible responses: write an equation; draw Quick Tens and ones; use Secret Code Cards.

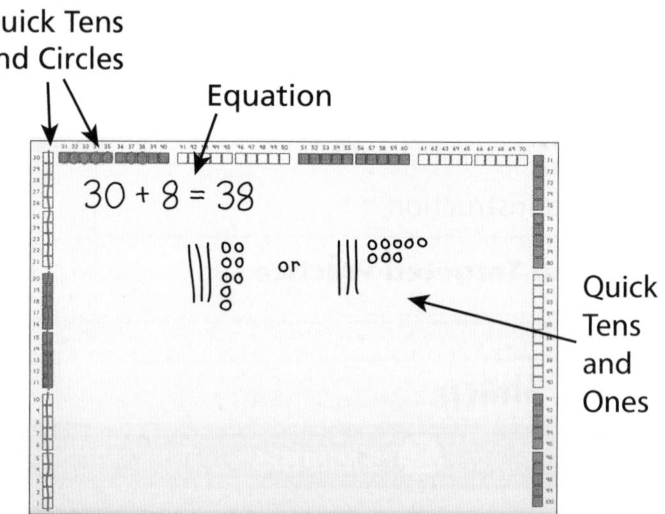

Ask children where 38 is on this board. Be aware that some children may say that just the last square is 38. Make sure that children understand that the number 38 really means 38 things—all the squares on the Number Path up to and including that square make the quantity 38.

To show that 38 is all the squares, draw a loop around the 38 squares and write 38 near the last square you counted. Demonstrate this on a child's board.

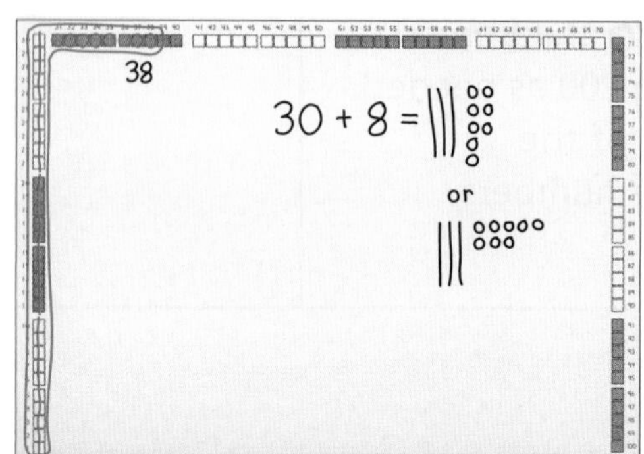

▶ Draw Quick Tens and Ones WHOLE CLASS

First, draw Quick Tens for the number 99 as shown below in the messy way. Then, draw a neater representation of the number 99 in 5-groups.

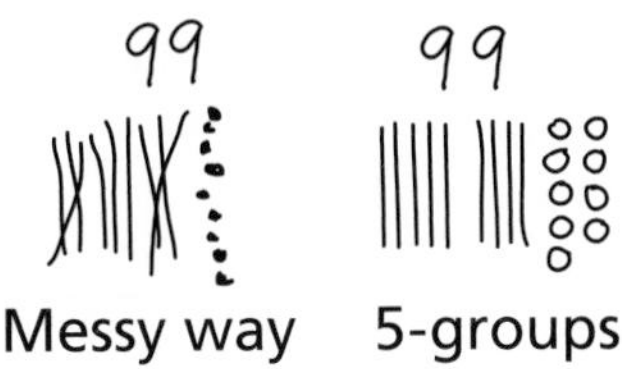

- Which drawing helps you see that the number is 99? The drawing with 5-groups. Why? You can see how many sticks and circles there are. You can see the tens and ones. You don't have to count.

English Language Learners

Use the neat representation of 99 to review *Quick Tens.*

- **Beginning** Point to a Quick Ten. Say: **Each line is a *Quick Ten.* Let's count them.** Count to 90 by tens. Have children repeat.
- **Intermediate and Advanced** Say: **Each line represents __.** 10 **They are called __.** Quick Tens

Activity 2

Review and Draw Quick Hundreds, Quick Tens, and Ones

▶ Represent Numbers between 101 and 200 PAIRS

Use the MathBoards from Lesson 2 that have numbers 101 to 200 written on them. Have pairs place their MathBoards next to each other with the Number Path side up. Point out that the board on the left will represent numbers 1 to 100, and the board on the right will represent numbers from 101 to 200.

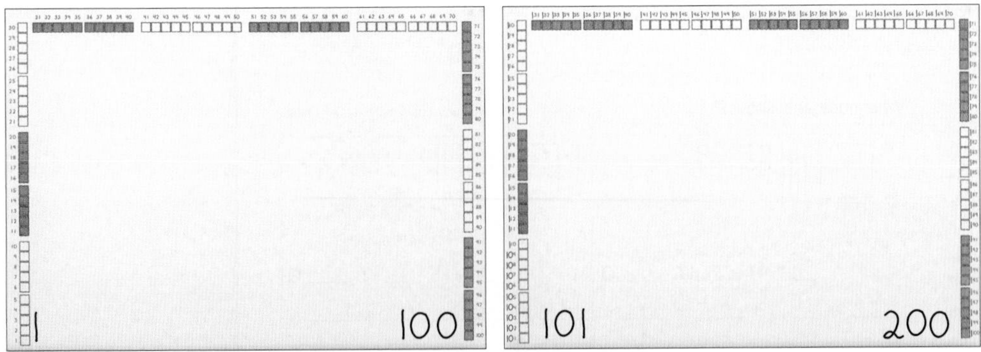

Have children work in pairs to represent 147 on their MathBoards in the same ways they represented 38. Remind children that they will need to use two boards because 147 is greater than 100.

 **15 MINUTES**

Goal: Review and draw Quick Hundreds, Quick Tens, and ones.

Materials: MathBoard materials or Number Path (TRB M51), Secret Code Cards (from Unit 1 Lesson 5 or TRB M3–M6)

 **NCTM Standard:**
Number and Operations

Activity continued ▶

Teaching Note

Do more numbers between 100 and 200 with the Secret Code Cards, Number Path, and Hundreds, Tens, and Ones drawings.

- Remember the first board shows the first 100 and the second board shows the second 100. First draw the Quick Tens and circles in the squares on the two boards.
- Then draw the Quick Tens and circles in the middle of the second board. Remember to use the Quick Hundred box to show 100.
- Finally write the equation in the middle of the second board.
- Now show the number with your Secret Code Cards.

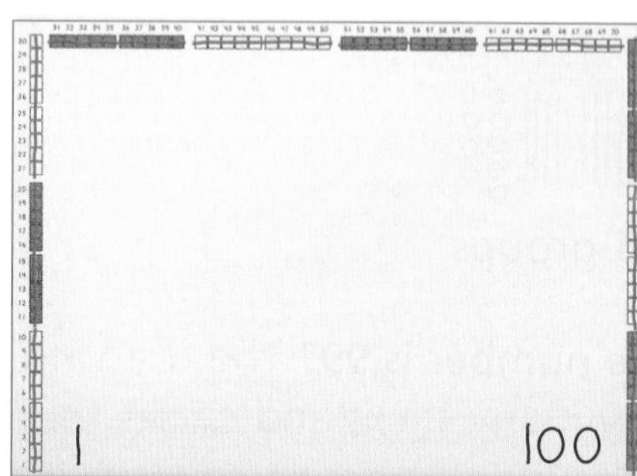

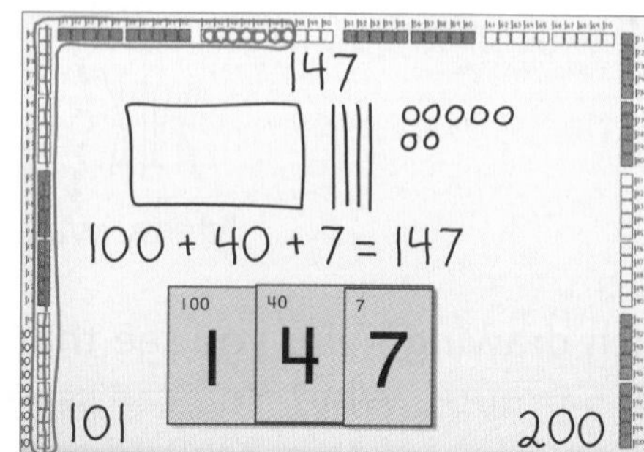

Activity 3

Practice with Hundreds, Tens, and Ones

 **10 MINUTES**

Goal: Represent 3-digit numbers with Quick Hundreds, Quick Tens, and ones.

Materials: Student Activity Book page 147

 **NCTM Standard:**
Number and Operations

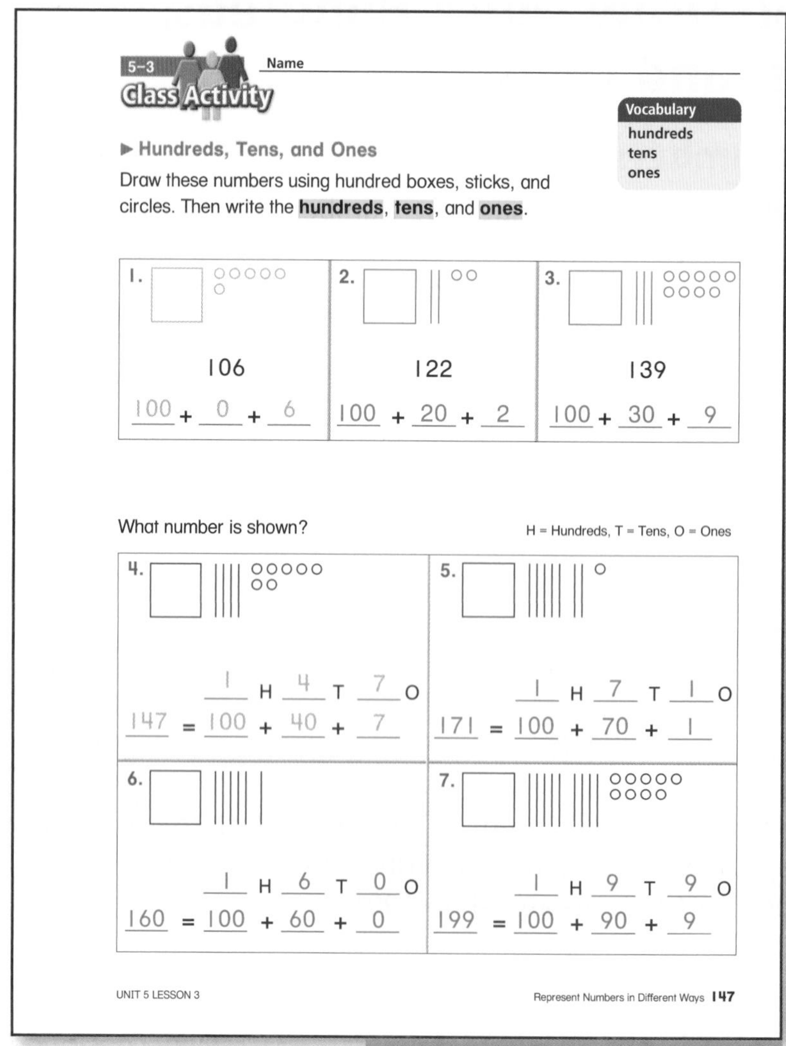

5-3 Class Activity

Name

Vocabulary
hundreds
tens
ones

▶ **Hundreds, Tens, and Ones**

Draw these numbers using hundred boxes, sticks, and circles. Then write the **hundreds**, **tens**, and **ones**.

1. 106	2. 122	3. 139
100 + 0 + 6	100 + 20 + 2	100 + 30 + 9

What number is shown?

H = Hundreds, T = Tens, O = Ones

4. 1 H 4 T 7 O
147 = 100 + 40 + 7

5. 1 H 7 T 1 O
171 = 100 + 70 + 1

6. 1 H 6 T 0 O
160 = 100 + 60 + 0

7. 1 H 9 T 9 O
199 = 100 + 90 + 9

UNIT 5 LESSON 3 — Represent Numbers in Different Ways 147

Student Activity Book page 147

▶ Hundreds, Tens, and Ones INDIVIDUALS

Direct children's attention to Student Activity Book page 147. Read aloud the directions to children and point out that two of the examples are done for them. Have children complete the page independently.

Ongoing Assessment

As you circulate around the room, ask individual children to draw one of the numbers below using boxes, sticks, and circles. Then have them represent the number by writing the hundreds, tens, and ones.

117 150 175 198

Activity 4

Word Names for Numbers to 100

▶ Review Word Names WHOLE CLASS

Write the numbers and word names for the numbers 1–9 and 11–19 on the board. Ask children to discuss patterns they see. Be sure that they discuss the reversal in the teen words where the ten is said second but written numerically first (e.g., sixteen says "six-ten" but 16 is one ten six, the reversed order).

1 one	2 two	3 three	4 four	5 five	6 six	7 seven	8 eight	9 nine
11 eleven	12 twelve	13 thirteen	14 fourteen	15 fifteen	16 sixteen	17 seventeen	18 eighteen	19 nineteen

Have children read aloud the word names together as a class. Then say one of the numbers and have children write the word name on their MathBoards. Ask children to hold up their MathBoards so that you can see what they wrote. Then repeat the activity with different numbers. Do not erase the numbers and word names from the board.

Write Word Names for the Decade Numbers Now, write the numbers and word names for the decade numbers 10–90 on the board. Discuss the patterns that children see among all 3 rows in the numerals and the number words.

10 ten	20 twenty	30 thirty	40 forty	50 fifty	60 sixty	70 seventy	80 eighty	90 ninety

Have children read aloud the word names together as a class. Then say a decade number like 40 and have children write the decade number and word name on their MathBoards. Then have them draw Quick Tens to represent the number. Ask children to hold up their MathBoards so that you can see what they wrote.

Activity continued ▶

15 MINUTES

Goal: Write numbers up to 99 in word form.

Materials: Student Activity Book page 148

NCTM Standard:
Number and Operations

Teaching Note

Watch For! Practice the irregular number words and especially the spelling variations *forty* and *fifty*.

Especially discuss the irregular words and irregular spellings that are a problem for students. Circle those (eleven, twelve, thirteen, fifteen, twenty, thirty, fifty) in color. Make a chart of these 3 rows with these irregular words circled in color. Mark the "teen" and "ty" as ten so that children see these meanings.

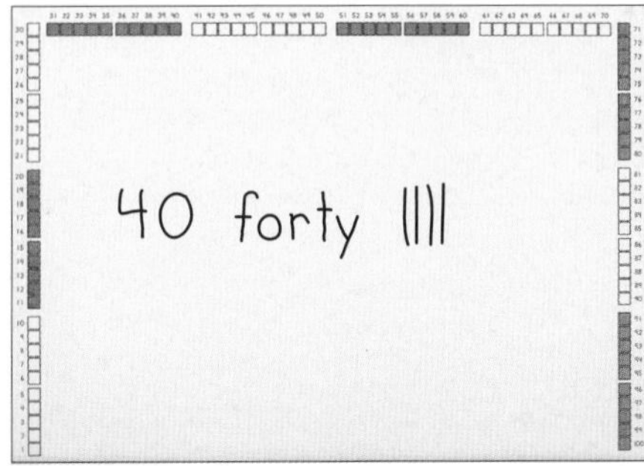

▶ Write Word Names for 2-Digit Numbers INDIVIDUALS

Write the number 58 on the board. Lead children to write the word name for 58. Write the word *fifty* on the board as children write it on their MathBoards.

- What is the word name for 5 tens? fifty

Write the word *eight* after the word *fifty* on the board as children write it on their MathBoards.

- What is the word name for 8 ones? eight

Explain that a hyphen is used between the tens and ones when you write the word name for 58. Place a hyphen between the two words on the board as children do the same thing on their MathBoards. Repeat with other examples.

▶ Recognize Word Names for Numbers INDIVIDUALS

5-3 Class Activity

Name

Vocabulary
word name

▶ Recognize Word Names for Numbers

1 one	11 eleven	10 ten	100 one hundred
2 two	12 twelve	20 twenty	
3 three	13 thirteen	30 thirty	
4 four	14 fourteen	40 forty	
5 five	15 fifteen	50 fifty	
6 six	16 sixteen	60 sixty	
7 seven	17 seventeen	70 seventy	
8 eight	18 eighteen	80 eighty	
9 nine	19 nineteen	90 ninety	

Write the number.

1. thirty-five 35
2. seventy-two 72
3. fifty-four 54
4. eighty-nine 89
5. sixty-three 63
6. ninety-one 91

Write the **word name**.

7. 47 forty-seven
8. 62 sixty-two
9. 85 eighty-five
10. 94 ninety-four
11. 28 twenty-eight
12. 86 eighty-six

Represent Write the word name and draw Quick Tens and ones in the box.

13. 60 sixty
14. 72 seventy-two

148 UNIT 5 LESSON 3 Represent Numbers in Different Ways

Student Activity Book page 148

Discuss the patterns in the number chart with children. Then have children complete Student Activity Book page 148 individually. Observe children to see that they are using hyphens correctly.

Teaching Note

Watch For Hyphens! As you circulate around the room, watch for children who are forgetting to use the hyphen between the tens and ones. Explain that all numbers from twenty-one through ninety-nine have hyphens except for the decade numbers (thirty, forty, fifty, . . .).

Watch For Irregular Words! Have children underline the *teen* and *ty* in the word name chart to focus on these phrases that mean ten. Circle the irregular words to focus attention on them and have children write these beside the chart for practice.

2 Going Further

Differentiated Instruction

Intervention — Activity Card 5-3

What's My Number? — Activity Card 5-3 ●

Work: 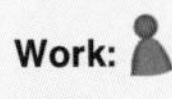

Use:

- MathBoard
- 1 set of Secret Code Cards

1. Put the tens Secret Code Cards into one pile and the ones in another pile. Mix up each pile. Place the piles face up.
2. Take one card from the tens pile and one from the ones pile.
3. Build a 2-digit number out of the Secret Code Cards.
4. Draw Quick Tens and circles to show the number. Then write the number.

5. Check the back of the Secret Code Cards.

Unit 5, Lesson 3

Activity Note Each child needs MathBoard materials and one set of Secret Code Cards (TRB M3–M6). Tell children to check their work by flipping the cards over.

Math Writing Prompt

Explain Your Thinking How is 20 different from 200? Draw a picture to show each number.

Software Support

Use *Soar to Success* for instruction of students needing targeted support for underlying skills.

On Level — Activity Card 5-3

What's My Name? — Activity Card 5-3 ▲

Work:

Use:

- paper

Choose:

- 1
- 2
- 3

1. Think of a word name for a number, like "thirty-five".
2. Write a small line for each letter in the word name. Show the lines to the other children.
3. 2 Guess a letter in the word name. 1 Write the letter if it is correct and 2 tries to guess the word name.

t _ _ _ t _ - _ _ _ _

4. 3 Guess a letter.
5. Take turns.

Unit 5, Lesson 3

Activity Note Each group member takes turn thinking of a word name for a number and then other group members try to guess the word name.

Math Writing Prompt

Compare Explain how 134 is different from 143.

Software Support

Use *MegaMath* for review and reinforcement of the concepts and skills presented in this lesson.

Challenge — Activity Card 5-3

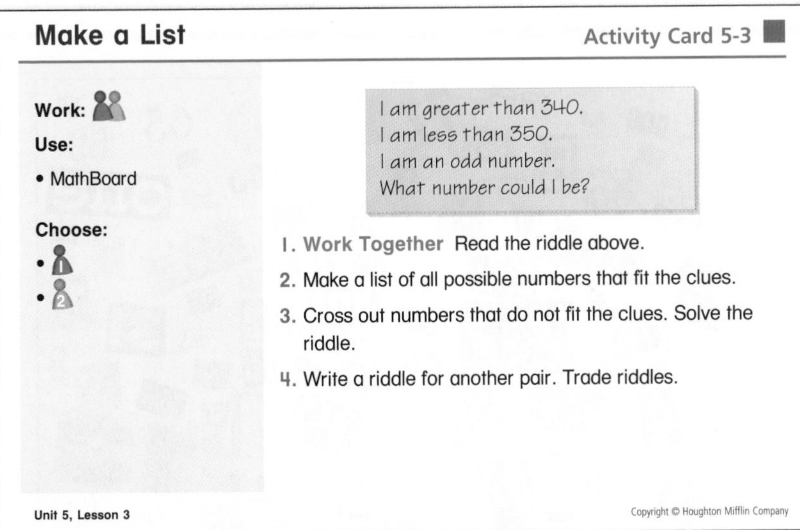

Make a List — Activity Card 5-3 ■

Work:

Use:

- MathBoard

Choose:

- 1
- 2

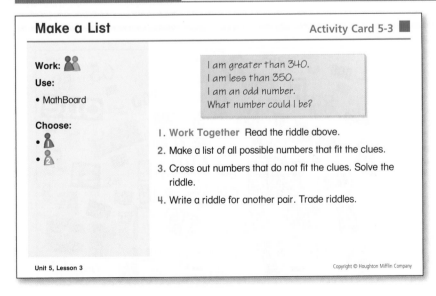

I am greater than 340.
I am less than 350.
I am an odd number.
What number could I be?

1. **Work Together** Read the riddle above.
2. Make a list of all possible numbers that fit the clues.
3. Cross out numbers that do not fit the clues. Solve the riddle.
4. Write a riddle for another pair. Trade riddles.

Unit 5, Lesson 3

Activity Note Each pair needs MathBoard materials. Have children talk about how they solve the riddle.

Math Writing Prompt

Explain Your Thinking Explain why 302 is less than 320.

Software Support

Use *Destination Math* to take students beyond the concepts and skills presented in this lesson.

3 Homework and Targeted Practice

5-3 Homework **Goal:** Additional Practice

This Homework page provides practice representing 3-digit numbers with Quick Hundreds, Quick Tens, and circles.

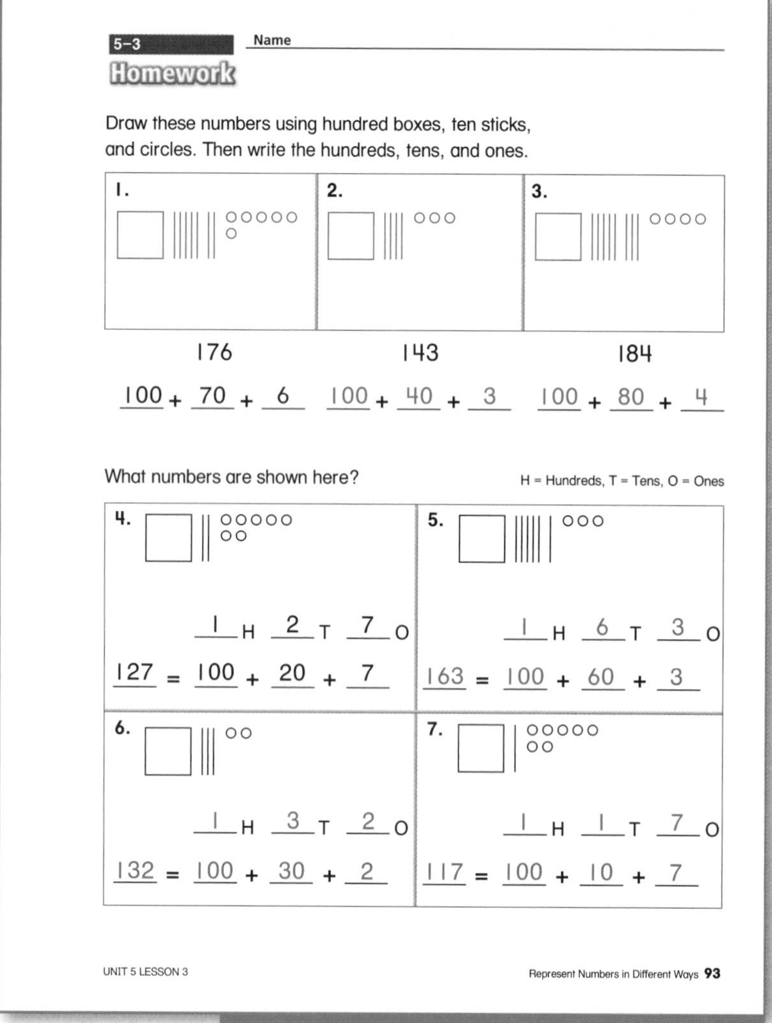

5-3 Homework Name

Draw these numbers using hundred boxes, ten sticks, and circles. Then write the hundreds, tens, and ones.

1.	2.	3.
176	143	184
100 + 70 + 6	100 + 40 + 3	100 + 80 + 4

What numbers are shown here? H = Hundreds, T = Tens, O = Ones

4.	5.
1 H 2 T 7 O	1 H 6 T 3 O
127 = 100 + 20 + 7	163 = 100 + 60 + 3

6.	7.
1 H 3 T 2 O	1 H 1 T 7 O
132 = 100 + 30 + 2	117 = 100 + 10 + 7

UNIT 5 LESSON 3 Represent Numbers in Different Ways 93

Homework and Remembering page 93

5-3 Targeted Practice **Goal:** Solve story problems.

This Targeted Practice page can be used with children who need extra practice in solving story problems.

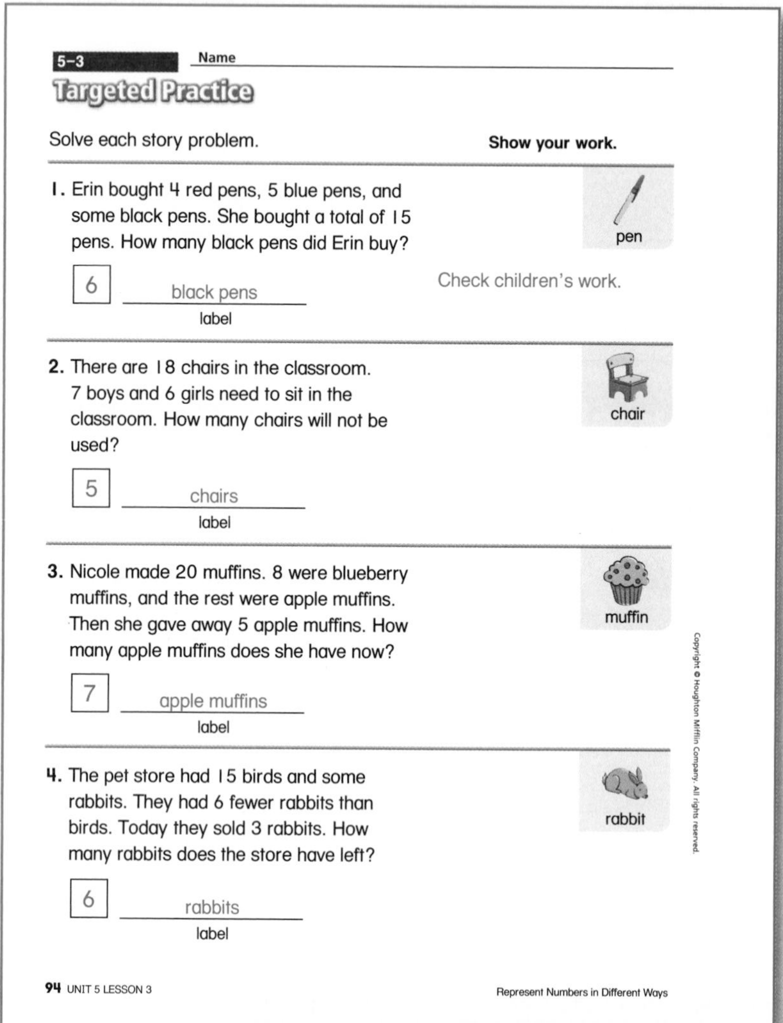

5-3 Targeted Practice Name

Solve each story problem. **Show your work.**

1. Erin bought 4 red pens, 5 blue pens, and some black pens. She bought a total of 15 pens. How many black pens did Erin buy?

6 black pens (label)

Check children's work.

2. There are 18 chairs in the classroom. 7 boys and 6 girls need to sit in the classroom. How many chairs will not be used?

5 chairs (label)

3. Nicole made 20 muffins. 8 were blueberry muffins, and the rest were apple muffins. Then she gave away 5 apple muffins. How many apple muffins does she have now?

7 apple muffins (label)

4. The pet store had 15 birds and some rabbits. They had 6 fewer rabbits than birds. Today they sold 3 rabbits. How many rabbits does the store have left?

6 rabbits (label)

94 UNIT 5 LESSON 3 Represent Numbers in Different Ways

Homework and Remembering page 94

Home or School Activity

Real-World Connection

Numbers All Around Ask children to look through magazines and newspapers and cut out examples of 1-, 2-, and 3-digit numbers. The examples can be word names, too. Children use their cutouts to make a decorative collage of numbers and word names.

Children can challenge other classmates to write as many of the word names or numbers that are on their collages.

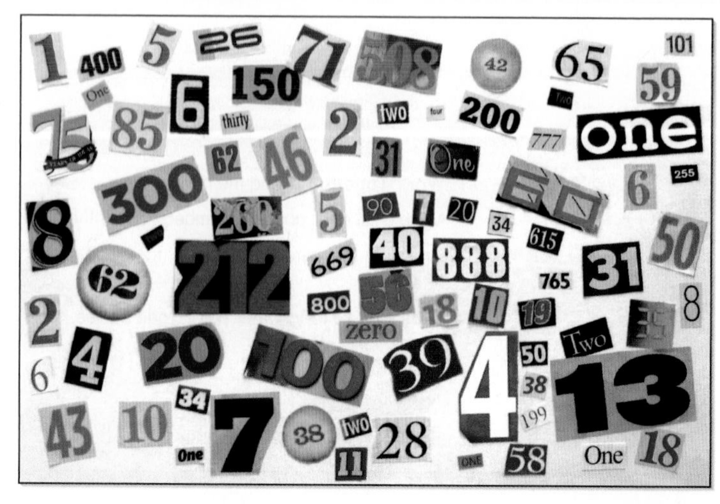

Add 2-Digit and 1-Digit Numbers

Lesson Objectives

- **Add a 1-digit number to a 2-digit number.**
- **Practice exchanging pennies for dimes.**

Vocabulary
decade number
Quick Tens

The Day at a Glance

Today's Goals	Materials	
1 Teaching the Lesson **A1:** Discuss and practice strategies for adding 1-digit numbers to 2-digit numbers. **A2:** Play a game that uses a model for adding 2-digit numbers and 1-digit numbers. **A3:** Solve addition exercises with 1- and 2-digit numbers.	**Lesson Activities** Student Activity Book pp. 149–152 (includes Dime Strips) Homework and Remembering pp. 95–96 MathBoard materials Secret Code Cards Short piece of yarn Count-on Cards Make-a-Ten Cards	**Going Further** Activity Cards 5-4 *Hippos Go Berserk!,* by Sandra Boynton Homework and Remembering p. 95 MathBoard materials Number Path (TRB M51) Two-color counters Calculator Math Journals
2 Going Further ► Differentiated Instruction		
3 Homework and Spiral Review		

Use Math Talk today!

Keeping Skills Sharp

Quick Practice — 5 MINUTES	Daily Routines
Goal: Practice addition, totals >10. **Materials:** Green Make-a-Ten Cards (addition) (from Unit 1 Lesson 13 or TRB M35–M38) **Green Make-a-Ten Cards (Addition)** Children practice with the Green Addition Make-a-Ten Cards individually or with a partner. Explain that they are practicing for Secret Code Card races and a Quick Check.	**Math Mountains for 100 or 2-Digit Numbers** Using the MathBoard, Using Dimes and Pennies (See pp. xxvi.) ► Led by Student Leaders **Money Routine** Using the 120 Poster, Using the Money Flip Chart, Using the Number Path, Using Secret Code Cards (See pp. xxiii–xxv.) ► Led by Student Leaders

 Teaching the Lesson

Activity 1

Add 1-Digit Numbers to 2-Digit Numbers

20 MINUTES

Goal: Discuss and practice strategies for adding 1-digit numbers to 2-digit numbers.

Materials: MathBoard materials, Secret Code Cards (from Unit 1 Lesson 5 or TRB M3–M6)

 **NCTM Standards:**
Number and Operations
Representation
Communication

The Learning Classroom

Building Concepts It is important for children to visualize and see the decade number inside the 2-digit number. For example, children should see 29 as 20 and 9, not 2 and 9. The Secret Code Cards reinforce this concept.

English Language Learners

Write 10, 20, 30, 40, 50, 60, 70, 80, 90, and *decade* on the board.

- **Beginning** Say: **10 is 1 *decade*.** Write and say: **10 + 10 = __.** 20 **20 is a *decade* number. 10 + 10 + 10 = __.** 30 **30 is a *decade* number.** Continue with other numbers.
- **Intermediate** Say: **10 is a *decade*. 10 + 10 = 20. 20 is the next *decade* after 10. 20 + 10 = 30. 30 is the next ___.** decade Continue with other decades.
- **Advanced** Ask: **What is the pattern in these numbers?** add 10 Say: **These numbers represent groups of 10.** Ask: **Are they *decades*.** yes

► Represent a 2-Digit Number–Decade Numbers Plus Some Ones WHOLE CLASS

Write a tens plus ones equation, such as 50 + 6 = ☐ on the board. Then ask children to represent the 2-digit number by drawing Quick Tens and ones on their MathBoards.

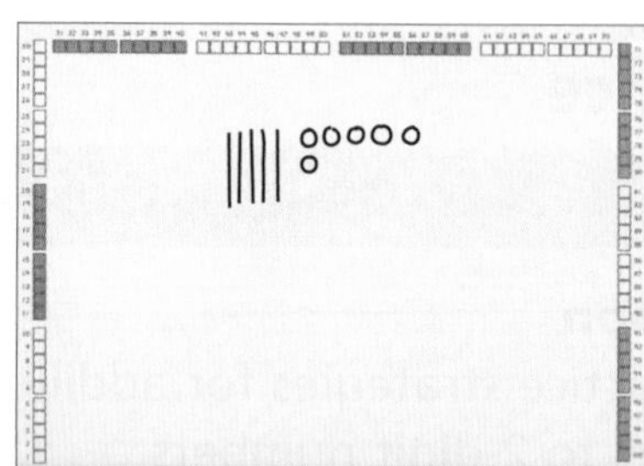

- What is the answer? 56

Now have children show the number with their Secret Code Cards. Remind children that they can think of 56 as 50 and 6 ones or as 5 tens plus 6 more ones.

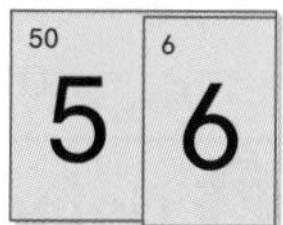

Have children use their Secret Code Cards to represent several more 2-digit numbers, for example: 20 + 9, 80 + 3, 60 + 5, and 70 + 2. Children can also represent these numbers with Quick Tens and circles.

► Add a 2-Digit and a 1-Digit Number WHOLE CLASS

Total in Same Decade Write 47 + 2 = ☐ on the board. Have children draw Quick Tens and ones for the number 47. Then have them add 2 more circles.

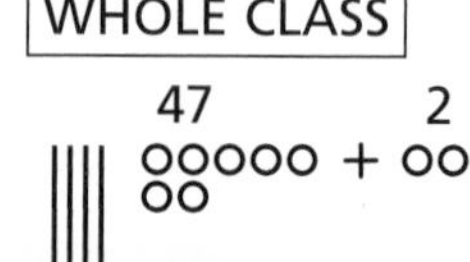

- What is the new number? 49

Have children represent the new number with their Secret Code Cards.

Discuss the strategies children used to find the new number. If no one mentions counting on, suggest it.

- Let's imagine that we already counted the 47. We can use the circles or our fingers to count on 2 more. You know there are 47 so you can just count on. Demonstrate how to count on using circles.

Have children continue counting on within one decade until they feel comfortable.

Total in Next Decade Write the equation 47 + 9 = ☐ on the board. Guide children to solve this equation. The total goes over the next decade number. Have children share their methods and strategies.

At this point, most children will just count on from 47 with their fingers or just count all the sticks and circles. Help children see that it is faster to solve this equation by making the next ten.

Math Talk On their MathBoards, have children represent 47 + 9 = ☐ with Quick Tens and circles as you work on the board.

- Look at the circles. Can we make a new ten? yes

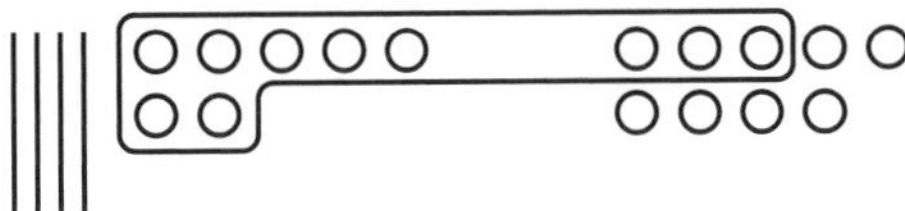

- 9 gives 3 to 47 to make a new ten. Now you have 50.
- How many ones beyond the new ten did we go? 6 What is 47 and 9? 56

Other children may solve the equation this way:

47 ○○○ ○○ ○○○○

50 + 6 = 56

It is the ultimate goal of *Math Expressions* to have *most* children making a new ten *mentally* by adding with partners. For example:

$$47 + 9 = \square$$

$$47 + 3 + 6 = 50 + 6 = 56$$

50

However, this will take many children some weeks or months. For now counting on is a good enough strategy.

Give children several more equations that involve counting on into the next decade. Help them see the process as making a new ten and then going several units (ones) beyond it.

68 + 4 = ☐ 88 + 6 = ☐ 149 + 7 = ☐ 123 + 9 = ☐

Differentiated Instruction

Extra Help Some children may be confused about when to stay in the same decade and when to move to the next decade. You can simplify the steps by having children ask the following questions to themselves.

43 + 6 = ☐

- ▶ What is the next decade number after 43? 50
- ▶ What do I have to add to 43 to get to 50? 7
- ▶ Is 7 more or less than 6? <more>

If the number you have to add to make a new ten (7) is more than the other partner (6), *stay in the decade.*

43 + 8 = ☐

- ▶ What is the next decade number after 43? 50
- ▶ What do I have to add to 43 to get to 50? 7
- ▶ Is 7 more or less than 8? less

If the number you have to add to make a ten (7) is less than the other partner (8), go to the *next decade.*

Activity 2

Get 5 Dimes

 20 MINUTES

Goal: Play a game that uses a model for adding 2-digit numbers and 1-digit numbers.

Materials: Student Activity Book page 149, 20 pennies (or Penny Strips); 5 dimes (or Dime Strips); Addition, Subtraction, and Unknown Partner Addition Count-On Cards; short piece of yarn (or pipe cleaner); Secret Code Cards

 **NCTM Standards:**
Number and Operations
Representation

▶ How to Play PAIRS

The object of the game is for a player to fill his or her game board with 5 dimes or 5 Dime Strips.

Children shuffle the Red Count-On Cards and place them in a stack with the answer side face down.

The first player looks at the top card and says the missing total or partner. The player checks the answer by turning the card over. The player then takes that number of pennies and places them on his or her game board. After they place their last penny on the game board, they should place a short piece of yarn (or pipe cleaner) to hold their place.

Red Count-On Card

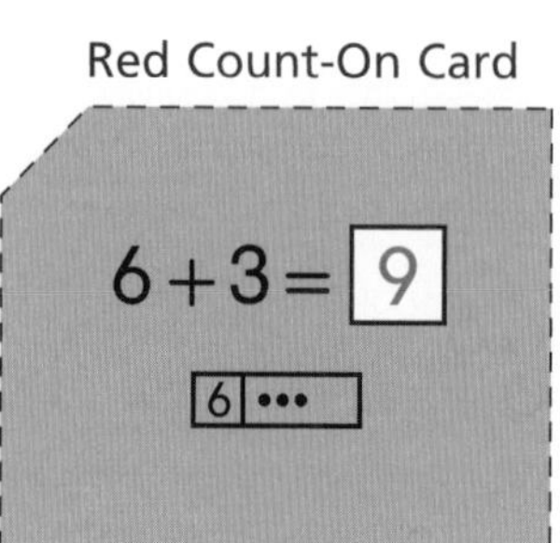

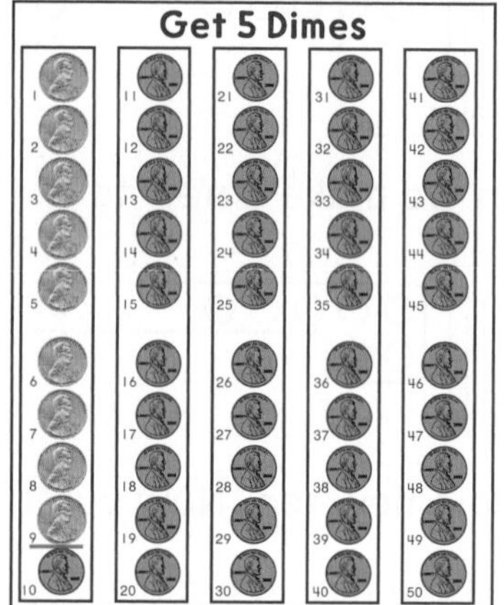

from Student Activity Book page 149

The player returns the card to the bottom of the stack.

Players alternate turns. Whenever a player has a group of ten pennies on the game board, the player trades the ten pennies for a dime or a dime strip.

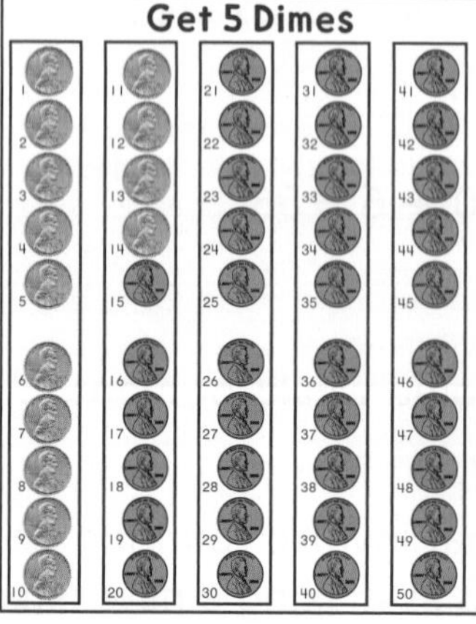

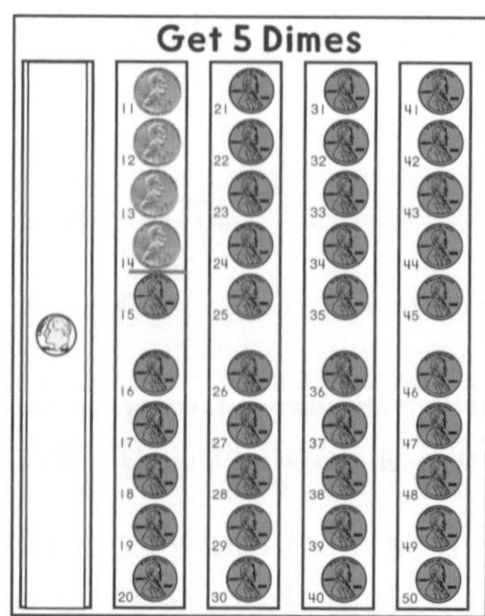

Play continues until one player has five dimes on the game board. That player is the winner.

Connect to Adding 2-Digit and 1-Digit Numbers As children play the game, they use Secret Code Cards to show their current total and they verbalize the 2-digit plus 1-digit addition they do to find the new total.

For example, suppose a player has 3 dimes and 6 pennies on the board. The player puts a short piece of yarn (or pipe cleaner) below the sixth penny.

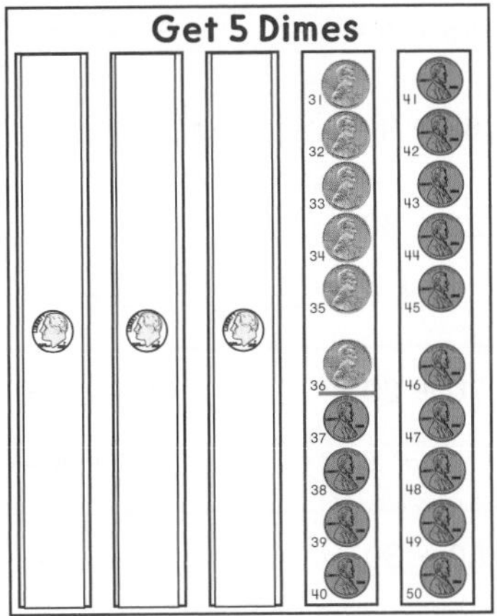

The player then takes a card that gives him or her 7 more pennies. The player places the pennies on the game board and says:

- 36 + 4 is 4 tens or 40, 40 + 3 is 43.
- I trade 10 pennies for 1 dime. Now I have 4 tens or 40. 40 and 3 is 43. My new total is 43.

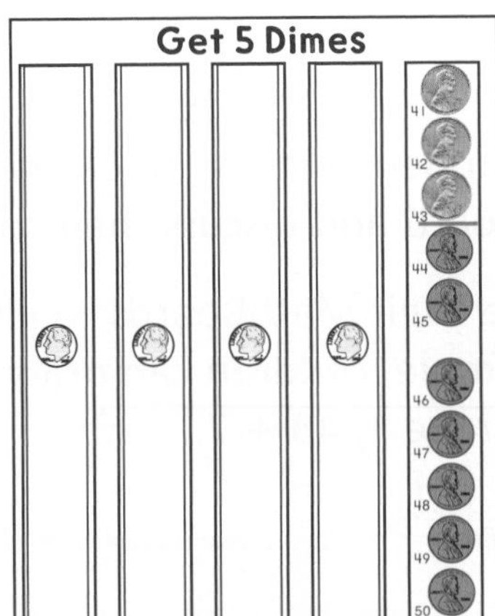

Then have children model their current total with Secret Code Cards.

You can have children repeat this game throughout the year.

Differentiated Instruction

Extra Help You may wish to introduce this game using only Red Count-On Cards (addition). Later children can play using the Orange Count-On Cards (subtraction), then the Yellow Count-On Cards (unknown partner), and eventually work up to using all three sets of cards. Students will make new dimes faster with the red cards because the answers are totals and thus larger than the unknown addends on the orange or yellow cards.

Advanced Learners Some children may be ready to play this game using both the Count-On Cards and the Blue Make-a-Ten Cards (subtraction).

Activity 3

Practice Adding 2-Digit Numbers and 1-Digit Numbers

 15 MINUTES

Goal: Solve addition exercises with 1- and 2-digit numbers

Materials: Student Activity Book page 151, MathBoard materials

 **NCTM Standards:**
Number and Operations
Communication

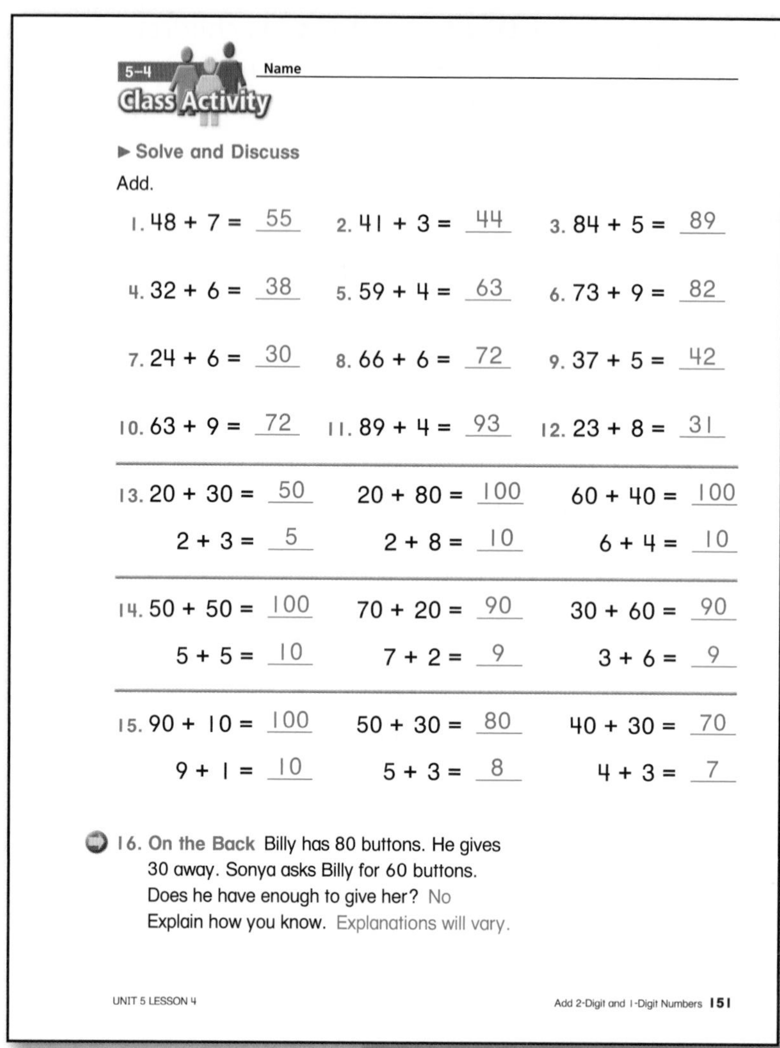

5–4 Class Activity

Name ______

▶ Solve and Discuss

Add.

1. 48 + 7 = 55
2. 41 + 3 = 44
3. 84 + 5 = 89
4. 32 + 6 = 38
5. 59 + 4 = 63
6. 73 + 9 = 82
7. 24 + 6 = 30
8. 66 + 6 = 72
9. 37 + 5 = 42
10. 63 + 9 = 72
11. 89 + 4 = 93
12. 23 + 8 = 31

13. 20 + 30 = 50   20 + 80 = 100   60 + 40 = 100
2 + 3 = 5   2 + 8 = 10   6 + 4 = 10

14. 50 + 50 = 100   70 + 20 = 90   30 + 60 = 90
5 + 5 = 10   7 + 2 = 9   3 + 6 = 9

15. 90 + 10 = 100   50 + 30 = 80   40 + 30 = 70
9 + 1 = 10   5 + 3 = 8   4 + 3 = 7

16. **On the Back** Billy has 80 buttons. He gives 30 away. Sonya asks Billy for 60 buttons. Does he have enough to give her? No
Explain how you know. Explanations will vary.

UNIT 5 LESSON 4   Add 2-Digit and 1-Digit Numbers 151

Student Activity Book page 151

▶ Solve and Discuss INDIVIDUALS

Have children complete Student Activity Book page 151. Then have volunteers come to the board and discuss their solution methods.

Encourage children to use their MathBoards to illustrate the solutions for each exercise. For example, children can draw Quick Tens and circles to find the answer to exercise 1, 48 + 7.

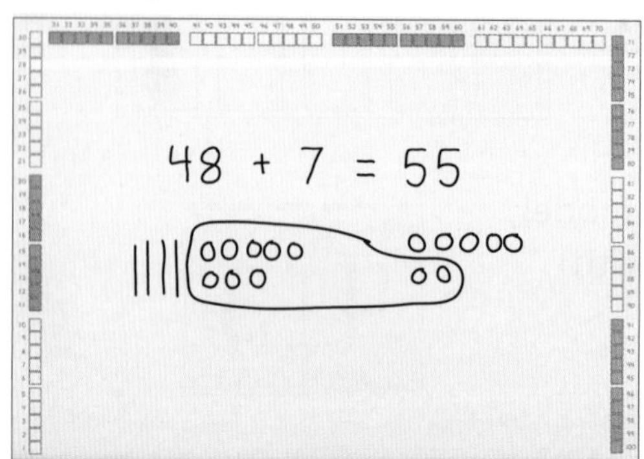

Ongoing Assessment

Ask the children to solve the following equations. Have them explain how they can use the Make a Ten strategy.

- ▶ 57 + 8 = ☐
- ▶ 72 + 9 = ☐
- ▶ 88 + 7 = ☐

2 Going Further

Differentiated Instruction

Intervention — Activity Card 5-4

Model with the Number Path — Activity Card 5-4 ●

Work: 

Use:
- MathBoard or Number Path
- Homework and Remembering page 95

Choose:
- •
- •

1. **Work Together** Look at problem 1 on Homework and Remembering page 95.
2. Find the numbered square for the 2-digit number. Draw a ring that includes that number.
3. Ring the number of squares that equal the 1-digit number. The last number is the total.
4. Repeat for problems 2–12.

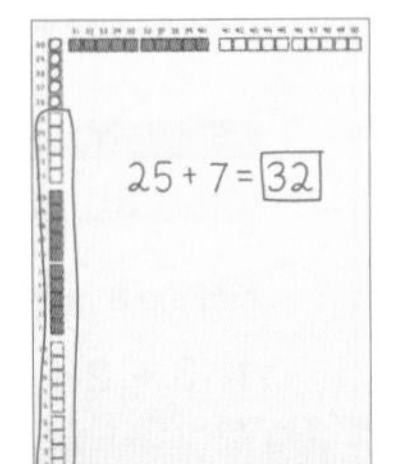

Unit 5, Lesson 4

Activity Note Each child needs MathBoard materials and Homework and Remembering p. 95. Check children's work after they complete #1.

Math Writing Prompt

Explain Your Thinking Explain how to use the Make a Ten strategy to add 27 + 5.

Software Support

Use *Soar to Success* for instruction of students needing targeted support for underlying skills.

On Level — Activity Card 5-4

Tic-Tac-Add — Activity Card 5-4 ▲

Work: 

Use:
- MathBoard
- Homework and Remembering page 95
- 10 two-color counters
- calculator

Choose:
- •
- •

1. **Work Together** Make a 3 × 3 grid on the MathBoard.
2. Copy nine equations from problems 1–12 from Homework and Remembering page 95.
3. Solve an equation. Check with the calculator. If right, place a red counter in the space.

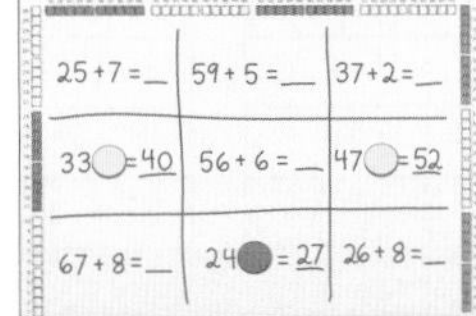

25 + 7 = __
59 + 5 = __
37 + 2 = __
33 ○ = 40
56 + 6 = __
47 ○ = 52
67 + 8 = __
24 ● = 27
26 + 8 = __

4. Take turns.
5. First person to get three in a line wins.

Unit 5, Lesson 4

Activity Note Each pair needs MathBoard materials, Homework and Remembering p. 95, 10 two-color counters, and a calculator. Partners should check each other's work.

Math Writing Prompt

You Decide Explain how you would solve $54 + 9 = \square$.

Software Support

Use *MegaMath* for review and reinforcement of the concepts and skills presented in this lesson.

Challenge — Activity Card 5-4

Three in a Line — Activity Card 5-4 ■

Work:

Use:
- MathBoard
- 10 two-color counters

Choose:
- •
- •

1. **Work Together** Make a 3 × 3 grid with the numbers shown.

8	5	9
2	1	4
6	3	7

2. Choose a number from the grid to solve the equations below.

$24 + \square = 32$	$14 + \square = 23$	$72 + \square = 78$
$51 + \square = 56$	$15 + \square = 21$	$23 + \square = 27$
$82 + \square = 83$	$59 + \square = 62$	$75 + \square = 77$

3. If your number is right, put a counter in the space with the number.
4. The first person to cover three in a line wins.

Unit 5, Lesson 4

Activity Note Each pair needs MathBoard materials and 10 two-color counters. Children use the numbers in the grid to solve the equations.

Math Writing Prompt

Math Investigation Explain how to find the unknown partner in the equation $17 + \square = 23$.

Software Support

Use *Destination Math* to take students beyond the concepts and skills presented in this lesson.

3 Homework and Spiral Review

Goal: Additional Practice

Include children's completed Homework page as part of their portfolios.

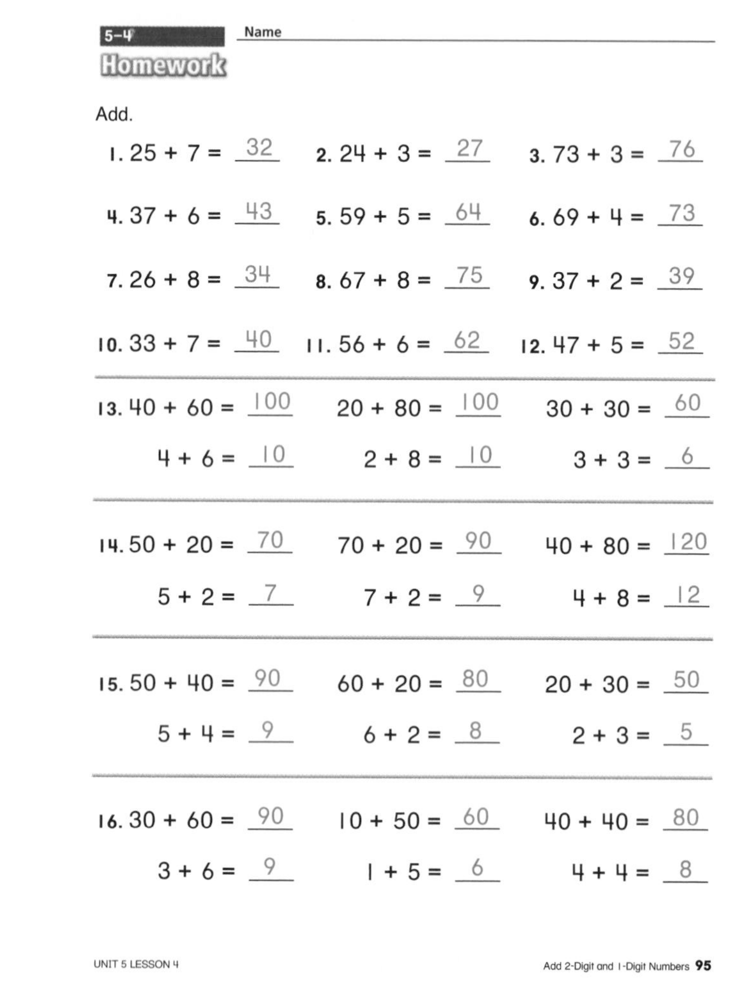

5–4 Name

Homework

Add.

1. 25 + 7 = 32   2. 24 + 3 = 27   3. 73 + 3 = 76
4. 37 + 6 = 43   5. 59 + 5 = 64   6. 69 + 4 = 73
7. 26 + 8 = 34   8. 67 + 8 = 75   9. 37 + 2 = 39
10. 33 + 7 = 40   11. 56 + 6 = 62   12. 47 + 5 = 52

13. 40 + 60 = 100   20 + 80 = 100   30 + 30 = 60
4 + 6 = 10   2 + 8 = 10   3 + 3 = 6

14. 50 + 20 = 70   70 + 20 = 90   40 + 80 = 120
5 + 2 = 7   7 + 2 = 9   4 + 8 = 12

15. 50 + 40 = 90   60 + 20 = 80   20 + 30 = 50
5 + 4 = 9   6 + 2 = 8   2 + 3 = 5

16. 30 + 60 = 90   10 + 50 = 60   40 + 40 = 80
3 + 6 = 9   1 + 5 = 6   4 + 4 = 8

UNIT 5 LESSON 4   Add 2-Digit and 1-Digit Numbers 95

Homework and Remembering page 95

Goal: Spiral Review

This Remembering activity would be appropriate anytime after today's lesson.

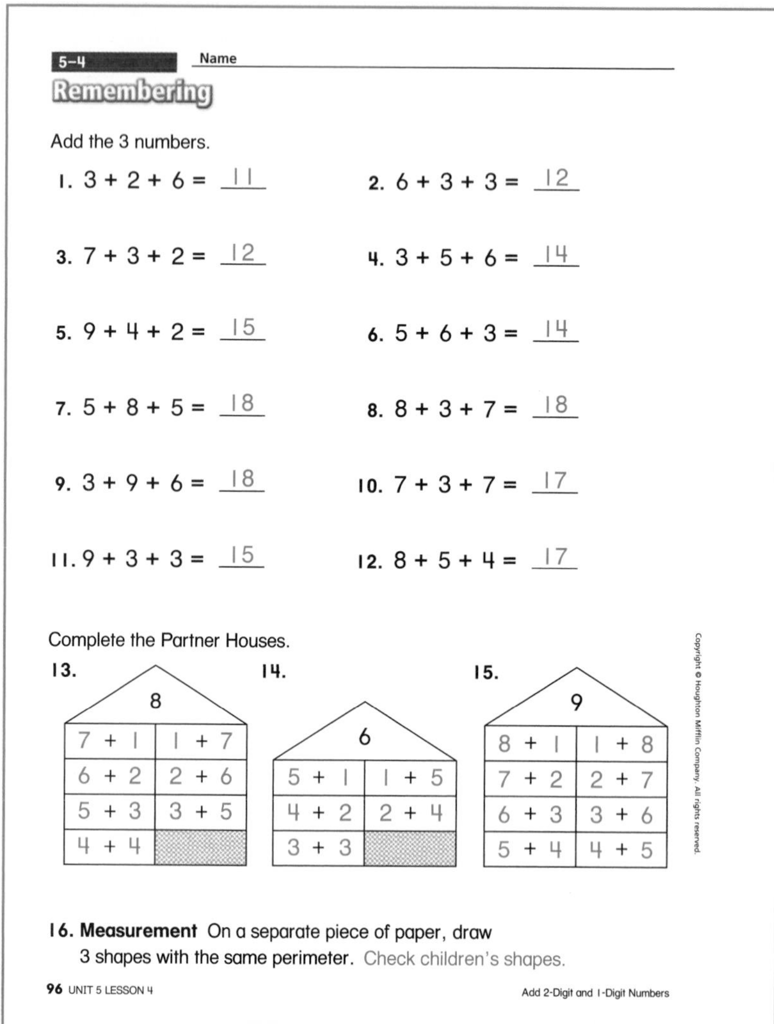

5–4 Name

Remembering

Add the 3 numbers.

1. 3 + 2 + 6 = 11   2. 6 + 3 + 3 = 12
3. 7 + 3 + 2 = 12   4. 3 + 5 + 6 = 14
5. 9 + 4 + 2 = 15   6. 5 + 6 + 3 = 14
7. 5 + 8 + 5 = 18   8. 8 + 3 + 7 = 18
9. 3 + 9 + 6 = 18   10. 7 + 3 + 7 = 17
11. 9 + 3 + 3 = 15   12. 8 + 5 + 4 = 17

Complete the Partner Houses.

13.

8	
7 + 1	1 + 7
6 + 2	2 + 6
5 + 3	3 + 5
4 + 4	

14.

6	
5 + 1	1 + 5
4 + 2	2 + 4
3 + 3	

15.

9	
8 + 1	1 + 8
7 + 2	2 + 7
6 + 3	3 + 6
5 + 4	4 + 5

16. **Measurement** On a separate piece of paper, draw 3 shapes with the same perimeter. Check children's shapes.

96 UNIT 5 LESSON 4   Add 2-Digit and 1-Digit Numbers

Homework and Remembering page 96

Home or School Activity

Literature Connection

How Many Hippos? Sandra Boynton's *Hippos Go Berserk!* (Little Simon, 2000) can be used to help children practice addition.

Children can read this book independently or it can be used as a read-aloud book. As children read or listen, they can add to find the total number of hippos. This will enable children to practice adding 1- and 2-digit numbers.

Find Decade Partners

UNIT 5 LESSON 5

Lesson Objectives

- Identify and compare 100-partners and 10-partners.
- Solve problems with tens and some ones.
- Add decade numbers over 100.

Vocabulary
100-partners
10-partners
decade numbers
round

The Day at a Glance

Today's Goals	Materials	
1 Teaching the Lesson **A1:** Draw 10-sticks to find 100-partners and draw circles to find 10-partners. Compare 100-partners and 10-partners. **A2:** Add two decade numbers. Discuss the similarities between ones plus ones and decades plus decades.	**Lesson Activities** Homework and Remembering pp. 97–98 MathBoard materials Number Path (TRB M51) Dot Array (TRB M63) Dry-erase markers Calculators	**Going Further** Activity Cards 5-5 Student Activity Book p.153 Base-ten blocks MathBoard materials Index cards Math Journals
2 Going Further ► Math Connection: Round to the Nearest Ten ► Differentiated Instruction		
3 Homework and Targeted Practice		

Use Math Talk today!

Keeping Skills Sharp

Quick Practice — 5 MINUTES

Goal: Practice addition with teen totals.

Materials: Green Make-a-Ten Cards (addition)

Teen Addition Flash Have a **Student Leader** call out two numbers that add to a teen number. The class flashes 10 and ones to show the answer. For example, the leader might call out 7 and 8. Children then flash 10 fingers and raise 5 fingers to show the total. This can help children learn the Make a Ten strategy. The Student Leader calls out 8 such pairs of numbers less than 10 that add to a teen number.

Repeated Quick Practice
Use this Quick Practice from a previous lesson.

► **Green Make-a-Ten Cards** (See Unit 5 Lesson 4.)

Daily Routines

Math Mountains for 100 or 2-Digit Numbers Using the MathBoard, Using Dimes and Pennies (See pp. xxvi.)

► Led by Student Leaders

Money Routine Using the 120 Poster, Using the Money Flip Chart, Using the Number Path, Using Secret Code Cards (See pp. xxiii–xxv.)

► Led by Student Leaders

1 Teaching the Lesson

Activity 1

Decade Partners of 100

 **30 MINUTES**

Goal: Draw 10-sticks to find 100-partners and draw circles to find 10-partners. Compare 100-partners and 10-partners.

Materials: MathBoard materials or Number Path (TRB M51)

 **NCTM Standards:**
Number and Operations
Representation
Communication

Teaching Note

What to Expect from Students The concepts presented in these activities can be difficult for children to understand. They are not expected to master the concepts by the end of the lesson. Today's activities are an introduction only. The concepts will be covered again in later lessons.

▶ Relate Decade Partners of 100 to Partners of 10

WHOLE CLASS

Guide children in finding decade partners of 100.

Draw ten 10-sticks on the board and have children do the same on the Number Path side of their MathBoards. Leave a space between the first 5 sticks and the last 5 to show the 5-groupings.

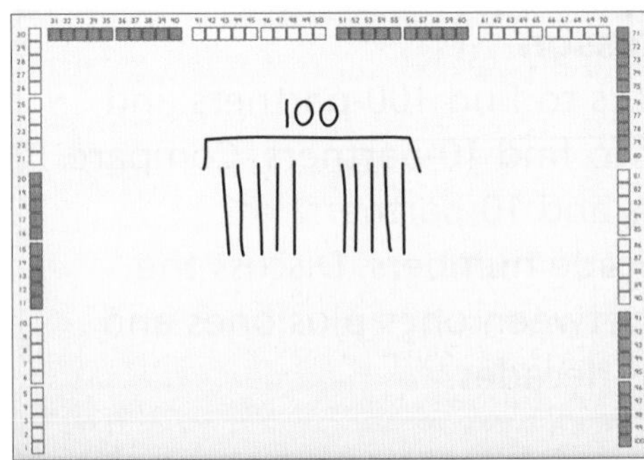

Invite children to find the decade partners of 100. Tell them that they will list tens only. Ask children to identify the first pair. 10 and 90 Write 100 = 10 + 90 on the board. Repeat this procedure until children find all of the decade partners of 100.

Now show children how to indicate the partners by drawing brackets under the appropriate number of sticks.

- Let's show one set of partners on the 10-sticks we drew. Here's how to show 100 = 10 + 90. I'll draw it on the board, while you mark it on your MathBoards.

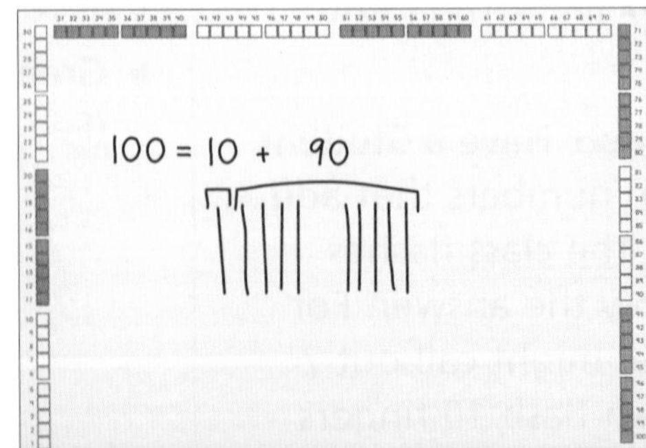

Have children use a MathBoard to mark all the 100-partners in order so that none are left out. Give the following directions.

- Write A and B the way I write them on my board. *Write A and B as shown.*
- Draw 10-sticks this way. *Draw the 10-sticks under column A. Have children draw them on their MathBoards.*
- Now show the partners 10 and 90. *Draw brackets as shown. Have children draw them on their MathBoards.*
- Write the rest of the partners. I will write them on my board.

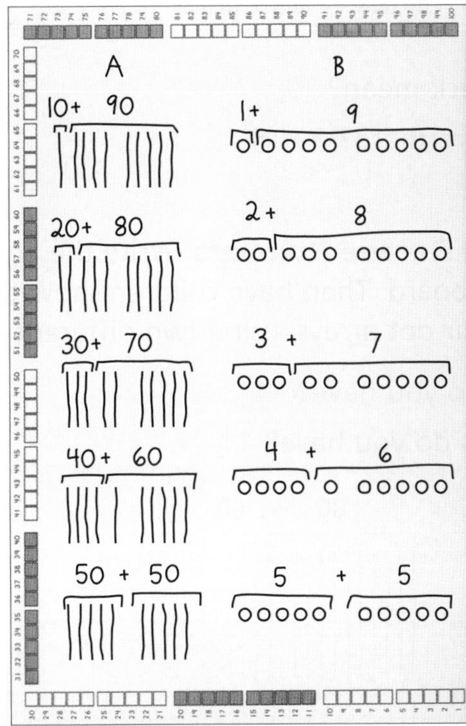

When children have completed the 100-partners in Column A, have them draw ten small circles as shown for Column B. They should then find the 10-partners by drawing brackets under groups of circles as shown.

10 = 1 + 9
o oooo ooooo

Have children discuss the similarities between 10 and 100-partners. For example, $100 = 70 + 30$ and $10 = 7 + 3$. Children should recognize that 10 *tens* = 7 *tens* + 3 *tens* in the same way that 10 *ones* = 7 *ones* + 3 *ones*.

Class Management

You may want to have Helping Pairs use two MathBoards to be sure they have plenty of room for all of the drawings for the 100-partners and 10-partners.

English Language Learners

Make sure children understand the terms *decade partners* and *100-partners*. Draw 10-sticks for 10 and 90.

- **Beginning** Say: **10 and 90 are decade numbers.** Write 10 + 90 = 100. Say: **10 and 90 are *decade partners* of 100.** Ask: **Are the *100-partners*?** yes
- **Intermediate** Say: **10 + 90 = __.** 100 Ask: **Are they *100-partners*?** yes Say: **They are *decade partners* of __.** 100
- **Advanced** Ask: **What is 10 + 90?** 100 Say: **10 and 90 are *decade partners* of __.** 100 **We also call them *100-*___.** partners

Activity 2

Add Decade Numbers over 100

 25 MINUTES

Goals: Add two decade numbers. Discuss the similarities between ones plus ones and decades plus decades.

Materials: MathBoard materials or Dot Array (TRB M63), dry-erase markers (2 different colors per child)

NCTM Standards:
Number and Operations
Representation
Communication

The Learning Classroom

Building Concepts The concept that a number such as 140 means 14 tens and that 14 tens means 140 is key to children's understanding of addition over 100. Work with children to help them see the number of tens in numbers like 130. This is not an easy concept for children to grasp, so it will take time for all of your children to understand it.

130 is 130
tens

130 = 10 tens + 3 tens = 13 tens

Drawing such numbers on the 200 dot grid in tens and making a Quick Hundred around the left 10 tens can help with this concept.

▶ Represent Two Decade Numbers

WHOLE CLASS

Math Talk 

Write 40 + 30 = ☐ on the board. Tell children that they can use the dot array on the back of their MathBoards or the Dot Array (TRB M63) to solve the equation.

Draw 4 sticks in blue to show 40. Then draw 3 sticks in red to show 30.

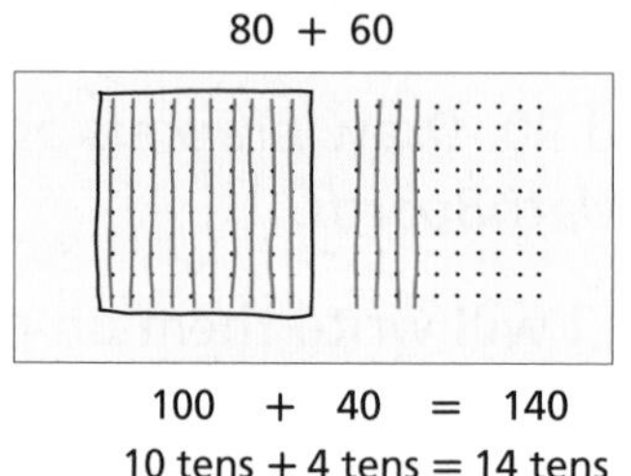

- What does each stick mean? 10
- How many sticks are there? 7 sticks
- What is 40 + 30? 70

Draw Sticks to Add Decade Numbers Write the equation 80 + 60 = ☐ on the board. Then have children show the numbers by drawing sticks on their dot arrays, using two different colored markers.

- How many sticks do you have? 14
- So, how many tens do you have? 14

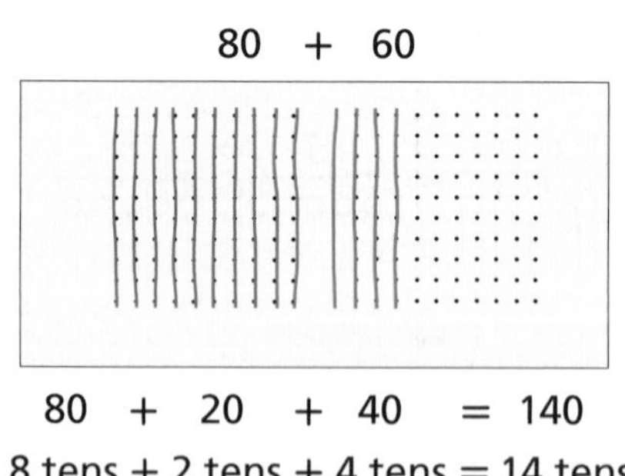

Remind children that they can draw a box around 10 tens to represent 100. Show how to do this. Point out that this makes it easier to see the 100.

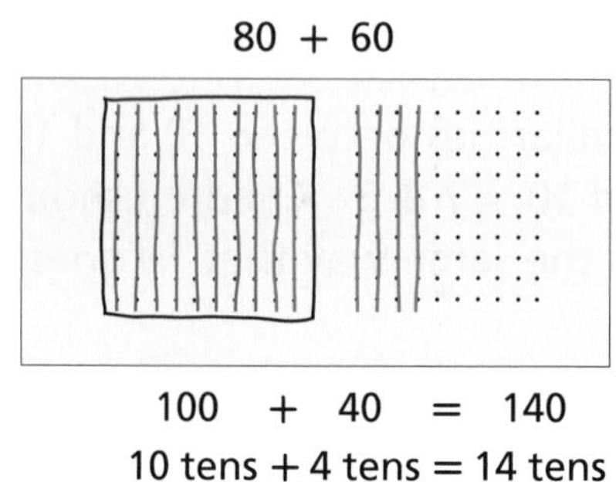

- How many tens make 100? 10
- How many more tens does 80 need to make 100? 2 tens, which is 20
- 60 gives how many tens to 80 to make 100? 2 tens, which is 20
- Let's label the box 10 tens. How many extra tens do we have? 4 Let's label them also. What is the total? 14 tens
- We can do the same thing with numbers. How many is 10 tens? 100 How many is 4 tens? 40 What is the total? 140 *Write the numbers as shown.*

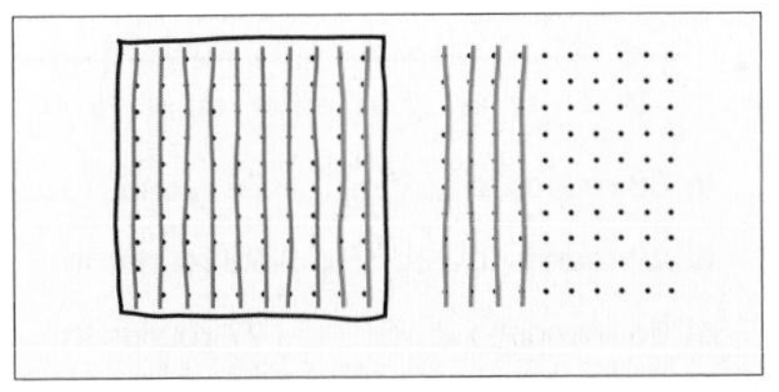

10 tens + 4 tens = 14 tens
100 + 40 = 140

Discuss Similarities Between 8 + 6 and 80 + 60 Help children see how they can use 8 + 6 = □ to help them solve 80 + 60 = □. Children should recognize that 8 *tens* + 6 *tens* = 14 *tens* in the same way that 8 *ones* + 6 *ones* = 14 *ones.* Conceptually, 8 + 6 equals 14 no matter what label is applied. The expression 8 + 6 can be solved with the Make a Ten strategy.

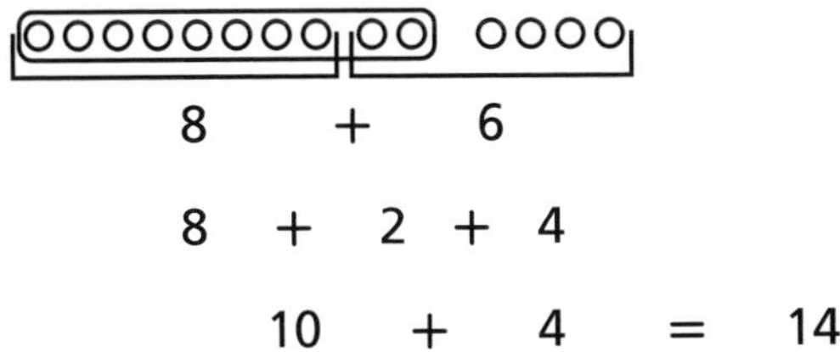

8 + 6

8 + 2 + 4

10 + 4 = 14

The expression 80 + 60 can be solved with the Make a Hundred strategy or the Make a Ten strategy used with tens.

Make a Hundred

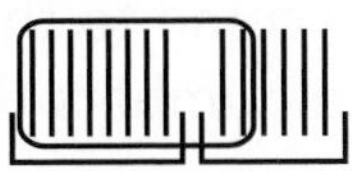

80 + 60

80 + 20 + 40

100 + 40 = 140

Make a Ten with tens

8 tens + 6 tens
8 tens + 2 tens + 4 tens
10 tens + 4 tens = 14 tens or 140

Have children solve similar equations (adding two decade numbers with a total of more than 100) in the same way. For example: 90 + 50 = □, 70 + 50 = □, 80 + 50 = □, 90 + 80 = □, and so on.

Ongoing Assessment

Have children look at the equations below with decade numbers.

► Are there easier equations you can use to help you solve these?

1. 40 + 80 = □
2. 60 + 50 = □
3. 50 + 90 = □
4. 70 + 60 = □
5. 80 + 70 = □

2 Going Further

Math Connection: Round to the Nearest Ten

Goal: Round 2-digit numbers to the nearest ten.

Materials: Student Activity Book pages 153–154

✓ **NCTM Standards:**
Number and Operations
Communication

▶ Discuss Rounding WHOLE CLASS

Draw a number line on the board showing the numbers 10 through 20. Explain that when we round a number we are estimating *about* how much it is.

- Look at the number 12. *Point to 12 on the number line and draw a dot on the number 12.*
- 12 is closer to 10 than it is to 20. So we round 12 down to 10. *Draw an arrow on the number line showing that 12 rounds down to 10.*

12 is closer to 10.
So, 12 rounds down to 10.

10 11 12 13 14 15 16 17 18 19 20

Ask volunteers to round other numbers between 11 and 19 (with the exception of the number 15) to the nearest 10. When all of the numbers have been discussed, point out that when a number is exactly in the middle of two tens, we round it up to the next highest ten. Then show how 15 rounds up to 20 on the number line.

To round 37 to the nearest 10 on a number line, look at the decade numbers before and after 37.

37 is closer to 40.
So, 37 rounds up to 40.

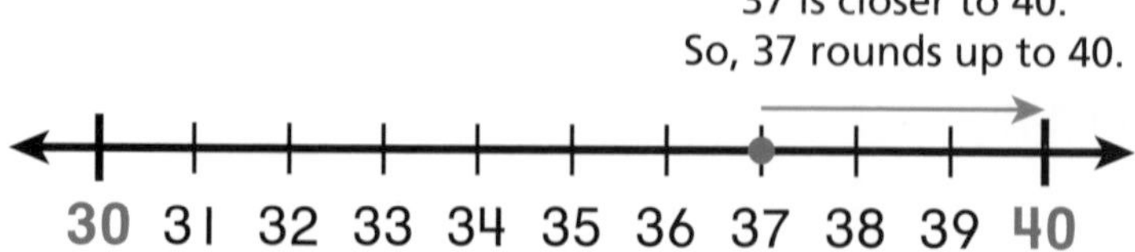

Since 37 is closer to 40, 37 rounds to 40. If a number is the same distance from each multiple of 10, it is rounded up to the next multiple of 10. So, 35 rounds up to 40.

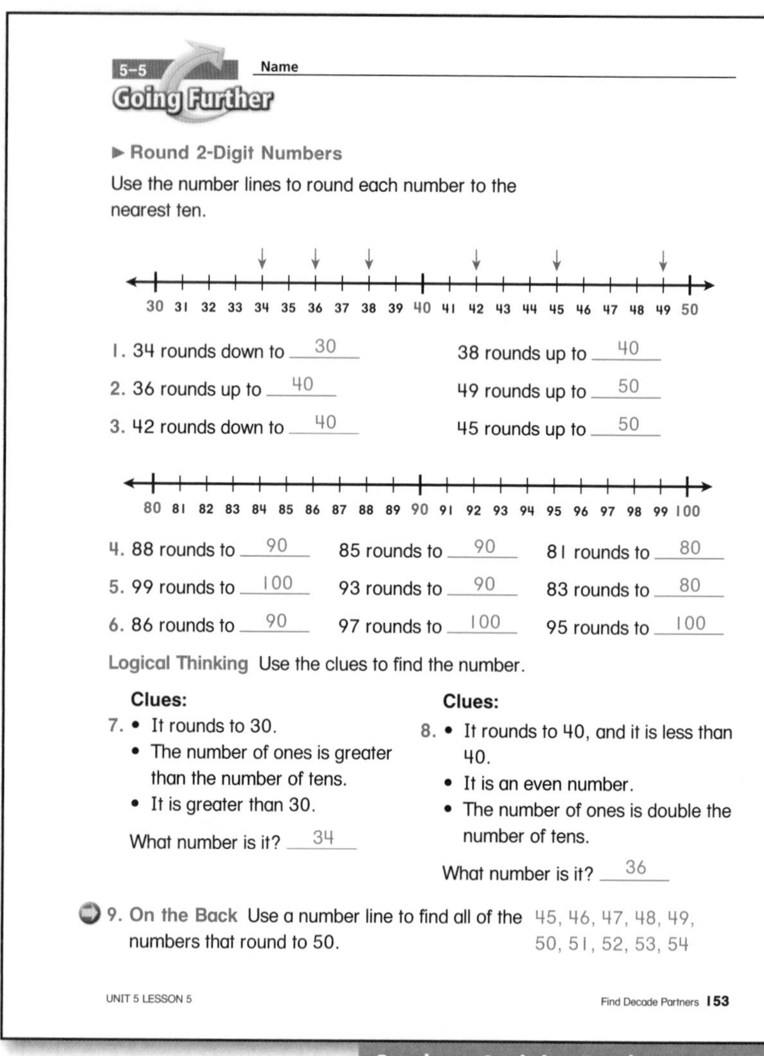

5-5 Going Further Name

▶ Round 2-Digit Numbers

Use the number lines to round each number to the nearest ten.

30 31 32 33 34 35 36 37 38 39 40 41 42 43 44 45 46 47 48 49 50

1. 34 rounds down to 30 — 38 rounds up to 40
2. 36 rounds up to 40 — 49 rounds up to 50
3. 42 rounds down to 40 — 45 rounds up to 50

80 81 82 83 84 85 86 87 88 89 90 91 92 93 94 95 96 97 98 99 100

4. 88 rounds to 90 — 85 rounds to 90 — 81 rounds to 80
5. 99 rounds to 100 — 93 rounds to 90 — 83 rounds to 80
6. 86 rounds to 90 — 97 rounds to 100 — 95 rounds to 100

Logical Thinking Use the clues to find the number.

7. Clues:
- It rounds to 30.
- The number of ones is greater than the number of tens.
- It is greater than 30.

What number is it? 34

8. Clues:
- It rounds to 40, and it is less than 40.
- It is an even number.
- The number of ones is double the number of tens.

What number is it? 36

9. On the Back Use a number line to find all of the numbers that round to 50. 45, 46, 47, 48, 49, 50, 51, 52, 53, 54

UNIT 5 LESSON 5 — Find Decade Partners 153

Student Activity Book page 153

▶ Round 2-Digit Numbers INDIVIDUALS

Have children work independently or with a partner to complete Student Activity Book page 153.

After children have completed the page, ask them to discuss how they found the unknown numbers for exercises 7 and 8. Then ask volunteers to come to the board to show how they found all of the numbers that round to 50 in exercise 9.

Intervention — Activity Card 5-5

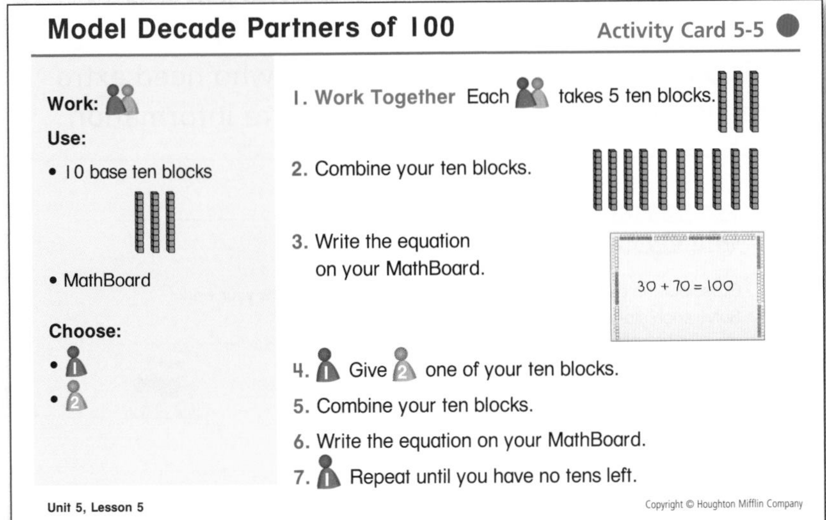

Model Decade Partners of 100

Activity Card 5-5

Work: pairs

Use:
- 10 base ten blocks
- MathBoard

Choose:
- 1
- 2

1. **Work Together** Each takes 5 ten blocks.
2. Combine your ten blocks.
3. Write the equation on your MathBoard. 30 + 70 = 100
4. 1 Give 2 one of your ten blocks.
5. Combine your ten blocks.
6. Write the equation on your MathBoard.
7. 1 Repeat until you have no tens left.

Unit 5, Lesson 5

Activity Note Each pair needs 10 tens base ten blocks and MathBoard materials. The pair starts with 50 + 50 and makes other decade problems.

Math Writing Prompt

Explain Your Thinking Explain how knowing that 8 + 2 = 10 can help you to find the total of 80 + 20.

Software Support

Use *Soar to Success* for instruction of students needing targeted support for underlying skills.

On Level — Activity Card 5-5

Partners of 100

Activity Card 5-5

Work: pairs

Use:
- 9 index cards

Choose:
- 1
- 2

1. **Work Together** Write one decade number 10 – 90 on each of the index cards.
2. Place the cards face down.
3. 1 Turn over two cards. If the cards are partners of 100, keep the cards.
4. If the cards are not partners of 100, return the cards.
5. Take turns.
6. The person with the most pairs wins.

Unit 5, Lesson 5

Activity Note Each pair needs nine index cards. Make sure children write only one number on each card, but write all the numbers. Suggest partners check their addition.

Math Writing Prompt

Compare How are partners of 10 like decade partners of 100? Explain.

Software Support

Use *MegaMath* for review and reinforcement of the concepts and skills presented in this lesson.

Challenge — Activity Card 5-5

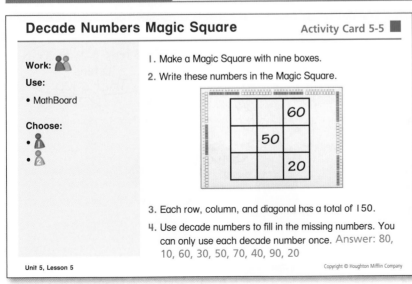

Decade Numbers Magic Square

Activity Card 5-5

Work: pairs

Use:
- MathBoard

Choose:
- 1
- 2

1. Make a Magic Square with nine boxes.
2. Write these numbers in the Magic Square.

		60
	50	
		20

3. Each row, column, and diagonal has a total of 150.
4. Use decade numbers to fill in the missing numbers. You can only use each decade number once. Answer: 80, 10, 60, 30, 50, 70, 40, 90, 20

Unit 5, Lesson 5

Activity Note Each pair needs MathBoard materials. Review the properties of Magic Squares.

Math Writing Prompt

Use a Simpler Equation Explain how you would solve this equation.

70 + □ = 160

Software Support

Use *Destination Math* to take students beyond the concepts and skills presented in this lesson.

3 Homework and Targeted Practice

Goal: Additional Practice

This Homework page provides practice in representing 10-partners and 100-partners and adding tens and ones.

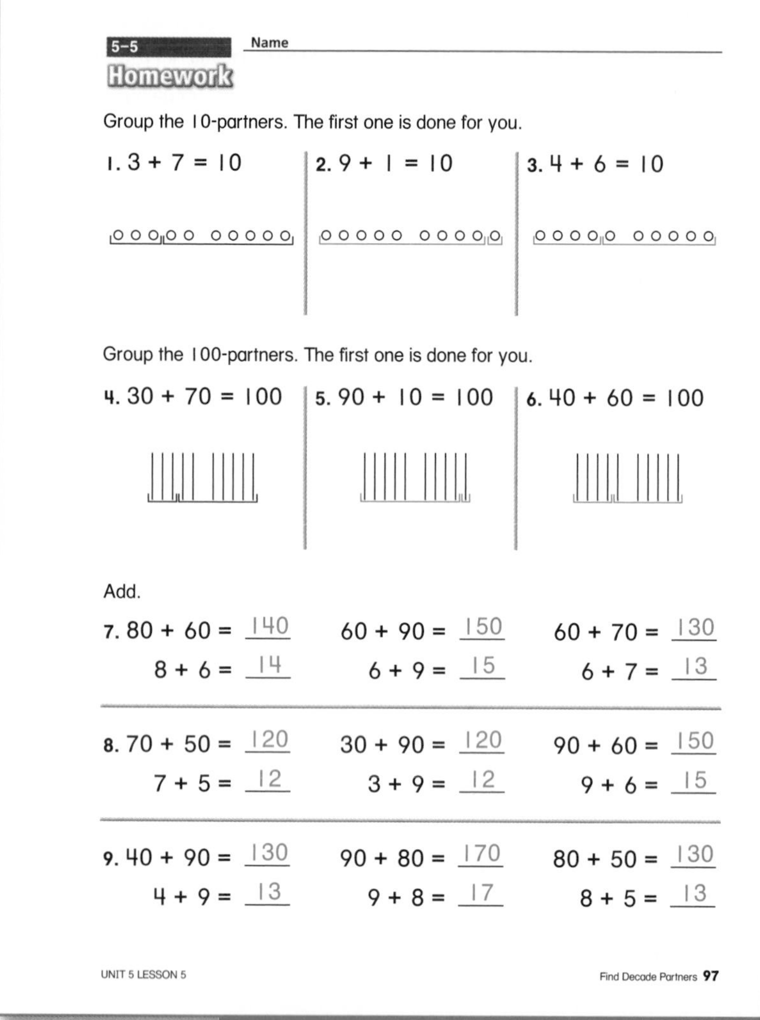

5–5 Homework Name ____________

Group the 10-partners. The first one is done for you.

1. 3 + 7 = 10
2. 9 + 1 = 10
3. 4 + 6 = 10

Group the 100-partners. The first one is done for you.

4. 30 + 70 = 100
5. 90 + 10 = 100
6. 40 + 60 = 100

Add.

7. 80 + 60 = 140 | 60 + 90 = 150 | 60 + 70 = 130
   8 + 6 = 14 | 6 + 9 = 15 | 6 + 7 = 13
8. 70 + 50 = 120 | 30 + 90 = 120 | 90 + 60 = 150
   7 + 5 = 12 | 3 + 9 = 12 | 9 + 6 = 15
9. 40 + 90 = 130 | 90 + 80 = 170 | 80 + 50 = 130
   4 + 9 = 13 | 9 + 8 = 17 | 8 + 5 = 13

UNIT 5 LESSON 5 Find Decade Partners 97

Homework and Remembering page 97

Goal: Solve story problems.

This page can be used with children who need extra practice in solving problems with extra information.

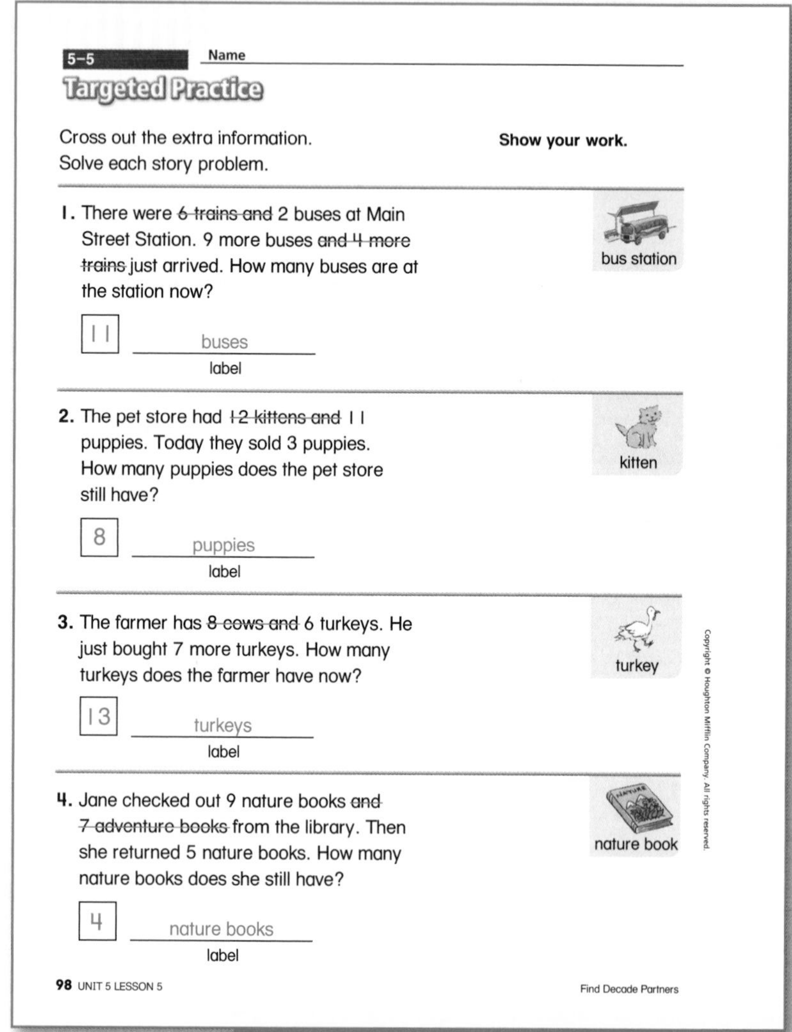

5–5 Targeted Practice Name ____________

Cross out the extra information.
Solve each story problem.

Show your work.

1. There were ~~6 trains and~~ 2 buses at Main Street Station. 9 more buses ~~and 4 more trains~~ just arrived. How many buses are at the station now?
   11 buses (label)
   bus station
2. The pet store had ~~12 kittens and~~ 11 puppies. Today they sold 3 puppies. How many puppies does the pet store still have?
   8 puppies (label)
   kitten
3. The farmer has ~~8 cows and~~ 6 turkeys. He just bought 7 more turkeys. How many turkeys does the farmer have now?
   13 turkeys (label)
   turkey
4. Jane checked out 9 nature books ~~and 7 adventure books~~ from the library. Then she returned 5 nature books. How many nature books does she still have?
   4 nature books (label)
   nature book

98 UNIT 5 LESSON 5 Find Decade Partners

Homework and Remembering page 98

Home or School Activity

Technology Connection

Mental Math or Calculator Give pairs of children decade addition exercises such as 60 + 40 = ☐.

One child uses a calculator and the other uses mental math. Once they have finished, have them discuss whether using a calculator was quicker. The children may be surprised to learn that mental math can often be quicker than using a calculator.

Combine Ones, Tens, and Hundreds

Vocabulary

ones
tens
hundreds
estimate

Lesson Objectives

- Add 1- and 2-digit numbers to 100.
- Solve ten-based story problems.

The Day at a Glance

Today's Goals	Materials	
1 Teaching the Lesson **A1:** Add 100 and a 1-digit or 2-digit number. **A2:** Make groups of ten to solve story problems.	**Lesson Activities** Student Activity Book p. 155 Homework and Remembering pp. 99–100 Secret Code Cards MathBoard materials Quick Quiz 1 (Assessment Guide)	**Going Further** Activity Cards 5-6 Student Activity Book p. 156 Counters 120 Poster Paper bag MathBoard materials Sentence strips Index cards Math Journals
2 Going Further ► Math Connection: Estimate Using Ten ► Differentiated Instruction		
3 Homework and Spiral Review		

Use Math Talk today!

Keeping Skills Sharp

Quick Practice — 5 MINUTES

Goal: Addition with teen totals.

Materials: Secret Code Cards, Parachute Drop–Teen Totals (from Unit 3 Lesson 7 or TRB M46)

Secret Code Card Addition Race, Teens Have children quickly arrange their Secret Code Cards across their desks from 1 to 10. Introduce the race and demonstrate what the Student Leader and the class should do. Have **Student Leaders** call out addition problems, reading from the bottom of the first column of Parachute Drop–Teen Totals. As quickly as possible, children hold up a 1-digit card and a 10-to show the answer.

Repeated Quick Practice
Use this Quick Practice from a previous lesson.

► **Teen Addition Flash**
(See Unit 5 Lesson 4.)

Daily Routines

Math Mountains for 100 or 2-Digit Numbers Using the MathBoard, Using Dimes and Pennies
(See pp. xxvi.)

► Led by Student Leaders

Money Routine Using the 120 Poster, Using the Money Flip Chart, Using the Number Path, Using Secret Code Cards
(See pp. xxiii–xxv.)

► Led by Student Leaders

1 Teaching the Lesson

Activity 1

Add Ones, Tens, and a Hundred

 30 MINUTES

Goal: Add 100 and a 1-digit or 2-digit number.

Materials: Secret Code Cards (from Unit 1 Lesson 5 or TRB M3–M6), MathBoard materials

 **NCTM Standards:**
Number and Operations
Representation

Teaching Note

What to Expect from Students
Equations like 100 + 1 = ☐ are often difficult for children. Watch to see that they are representing the number amounts correctly as they find the answer. For example, children should use a box (or 10-sticks enclosed in a box) for 100, a stick for-10, and a circle for 1. Both the MathBoards and the Secret Code Cards will help children visualize the addition.

English Language Learners

Help children identify ones, tens, and hundreds. Write 123 on the board. Have children build it with their Secret Code Cards.

- **Beginning** Point and say: **3 is in the ones column. 2 is in the tens column. 1 is in the hundreds column.** Have children repeat.
- **Intermediate** Ask: **Is 3 in the ones or tens column?** ones Continue with other columns.
- **Advanced** Ask: **What number is in the ones column?** 3 **Tens?** 2 **Hundreds?** 1

▶ 100 Plus a Number WHOLE CLASS

Write 100 + 1 = ☐ on the board. Have children represent the equation on their MathBoards. They can use either a Quick Hundred or draw 10-sticks with a box around them.

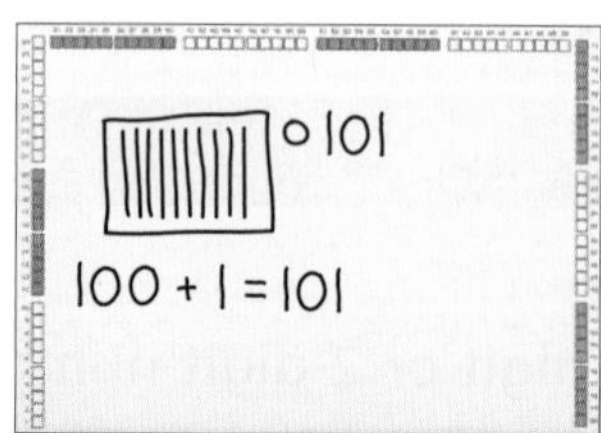

Then have children represent the equation with Secret Code Cards. If there is any confusion about the correct card to use, ask children if they added a 10 or a 1 to the hundred.

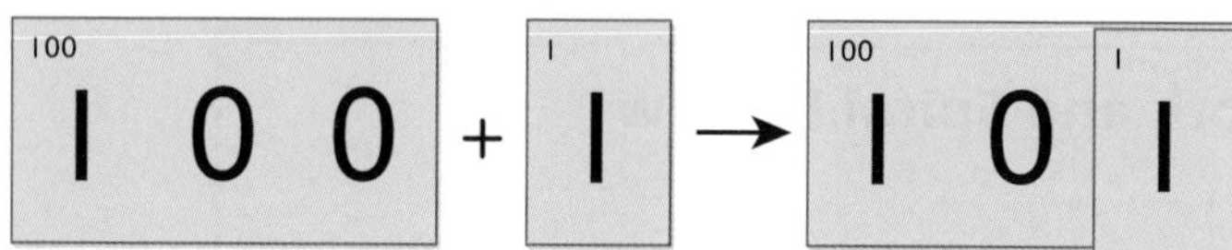

Since the backs of the Secret Code Cards contain a graphic representation of the number with the appropriate number of boxes, sticks, or circles, children may check their work by turning the cards over to see 100 plus 1.

Have the children practice by adding any number (up to 20) to 100. See examples at the right. Children should draw the solution on their MathBoards (either on the dot side or the Number Path side) and then check their answer with Secret Code Cards. Repeat this process with a few more numbers to 20.

100 + 10 = ☐
100 + 8 = ☐
100 + 15 = ☐
100 + 2 = ☐
100 + 20 = ☐

Then have children solve the sets of related problems shown below. As before, they should draw the solutions and check the answers with their Secret Code Cards.

100 + 5 = ☐	100 + 26 = ☐
10 + 5 = ☐	10 + 26 = ☐
1 + 5 = ☐	1 + 26 = ☐

Activity 2

Ten-Based Story Problems

5-6 Class Activity Name

▶ Story Problems with Groups of Ten

Solve each story problem.

1. Remah has 34 stickers. Only 10 stickers fit on a page in her scrapbook. How many pages can she fill with stickers? How many stickers will be left over? Check children's work.

[3] pages [4] stickers left over

2. David has 42 beads. He wants to make some necklaces that take 10 beads each. How many necklaces can he make? How many beads will be left over?

[4] necklaces [2] beads left over

3. The team wants to buy T-shirts that cost 10 dollars each. They have 57 dollars. How many shirts can they buy? How many dollars will be left over?

[5] T-shirts [7] dollars left over

4. The store has 63 apples. Each basket can hold 10 apples. How many baskets can they fill with apples? How many apples will be left over?

[6] baskets [3] apples left over

UNIT 5 LESSON 6 Combine Ones, Tens, and Hundreds 155

Student Activity Book page 155

▶ Story Problems with Groups of Ten WHOLE CLASS

Read aloud the first problem on Student Activity Book page 155. Discuss with children how they might solve the problem and allow time for them to solve it. Encourage children to make a proof drawing with sticks and circles. Invite some children to work at the board while the rest of the class works at their seats.

Math Talk **Share Problem-Solving Strategies** Many children will already know that there are 3 tens in 34. Others will use sticks and circles or some other suitable method to see the tens.

- How many pages of 10 can Remah make? 3 How do you know? I found 3 groups of ten. How many stickers will be left over? 4 Yes, 34 means 3 groups of ten and 4 left over.

Have children complete the page independently or with a partner.

25 MINUTES

Goal: Make groups of ten to solve story problems.

Materials: Student Activity Book page 155

NCTM Standards:
Number and Operations
Representation
Communication

Teaching Note

Math Background Even if some children are able to answer these problems without making a drawing, explain to them that this is a *Proof Drawing*—a drawing that proves the answer to others. They should make drawings that show the 10-groups in ways that do not involve drawing all 42 objects. For example:

Necklaces with 10 beads each

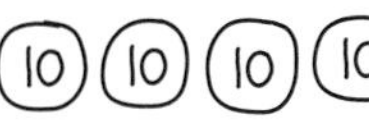

Quick Quiz

See Assessment Guide for Unit 5 Quick Quiz 1.

Ongoing Assessment

Have children solve the story problem below.

▶ I have 58 peanuts that I want to put into cups. If I can put 10 peanuts in each cup, how many cups can I fill? How many peanuts are left over?

2 Going Further

Math Connection: Estimate Using Tens

Goal: Estimate amounts using 10 as a benchmark.

Materials: Counters (about 100 per group), Student Activity Book page 156

NCTM Standards:
Number and Operations
Communication

▶ Introduce Ten-Benchmarks SMALL GROUPS

Give each group of children a collection of counters. Ask children to make a group of 10 with some of the counters. Then challenge them to estimate the total number of counters left on their desks, without actually counting them. Have them write their estimates on a piece of paper.

Remind children that an estimate is a thoughtful guess and not an exact answer. They should use the group of 10 counters to help them make their estimate.

After children have made their estimates, have them count the counters to see how close their estimates were to the exact number of counters.

Repeat the activity a few times (using a different number of counters) until the children seem comfortable using 10 as a benchmark for making estimates.

▶ Estimate with Ten-Benchmarks

WHOLE CLASS

Complete exercise 1 on Student Activity Book page 156 as a class. Then have children complete the page independently.

Circulate around the room, checking that no one is forgetting to count the circled group of 10 in their estimate. If necessary, remind children that they are estimating the whole group, which includes the 10 they circled.

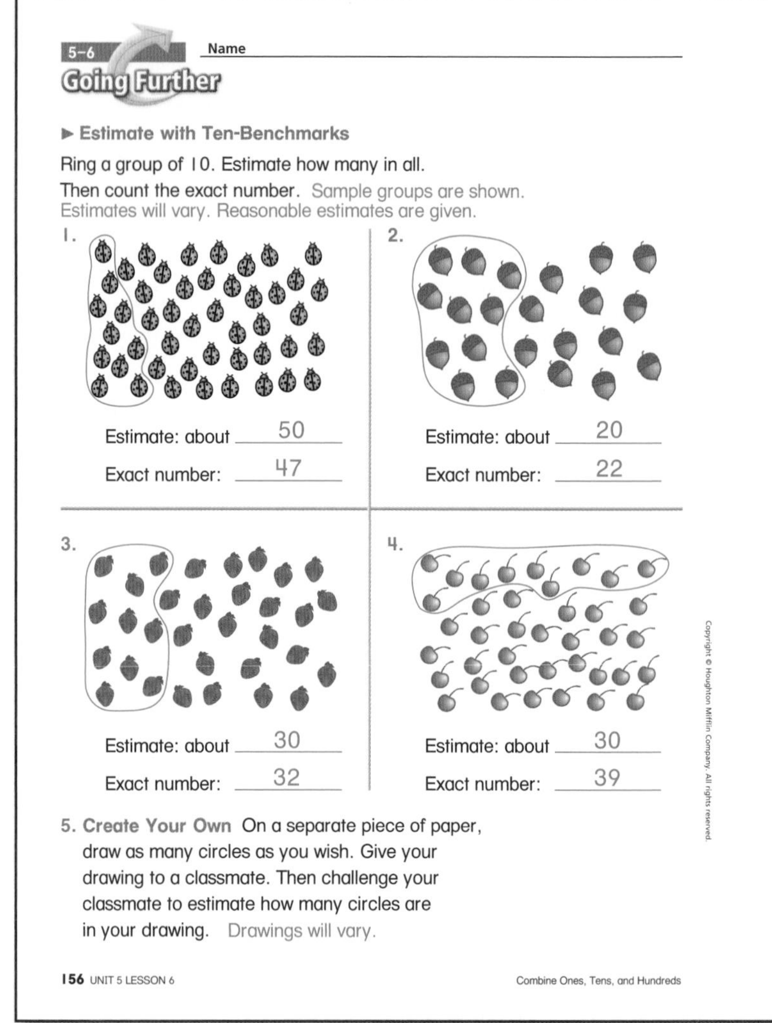

5–6 Going Further Name

▶ Estimate with Ten-Benchmarks

Ring a group of 10. Estimate how many in all.
Then count the exact number. Sample groups are shown.
Estimates will vary. Reasonable estimates are given.

1. Estimate: about 50
Exact number: 47

2. Estimate: about 20
Exact number: 22

3. Estimate: about 30
Exact number: 32

4. Estimate: about 30
Exact number: 39

5. **Create Your Own** On a separate piece of paper, draw as many circles as you wish. Give your drawing to a classmate. Then challenge your classmate to estimate how many circles are in your drawing. Drawings will vary.

156 UNIT 5 LESSON 6 Combine Ones, Tens, and Hundreds

Copyright © Houghton Mifflin Company. All rights reserved.

Student Activity Book page 156

Differentiated Instruction

Extra Help Some children need to see how estimation relates to everyday life to better understand the concept. Discuss situations where knowing an exact number is necessary, and situations where giving an estimate is enough.

Differentiated Instruction

English Learners Make sure that English Learners understand the difference in meaning and pronunciation of *estimate* as both a noun and a verb.

Intervention — Activity Card 5-6

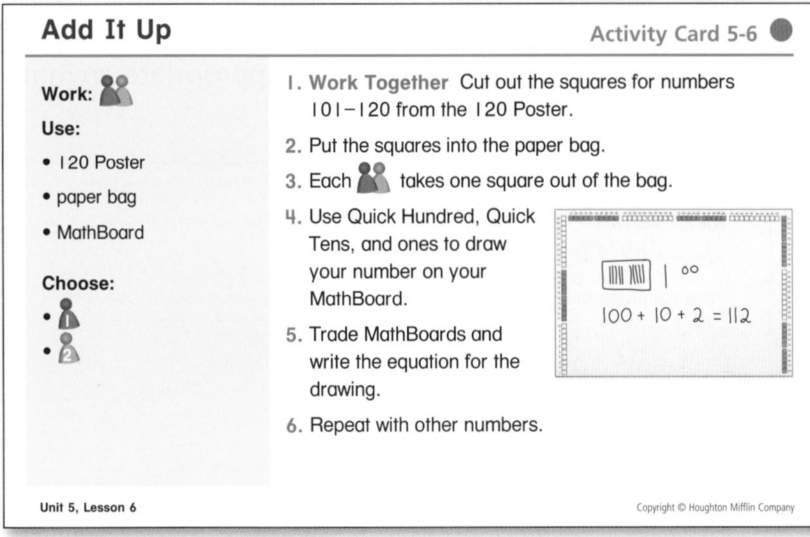

Add It Up — Activity Card 5-6

Work: (pairs)

Use:

- 120 Poster
- paper bag
- MathBoard

Choose:

- 1
- 2

1. **Work Together** Cut out the squares for numbers 101–120 from the 120 Poster.
2. Put the squares into the paper bag.
3. Each (child) takes one square out of the bag.
4. Use Quick Hundred, Quick Tens, and ones to draw your number on your MathBoard.
5. Trade MathBoards and write the equation for the drawing.
6. Repeat with other numbers.

100 + 10 + 2 = 112

Unit 5, Lesson 6 — Copyright © Houghton Mifflin Company

Activity Note Each pair needs a 120 Poster (TRB M60), a paper bag, and MathBoard materials. Check children's drawings.

Math Writing Prompt

How Many Beads? Meg had 100 gold beads. Her sister gave her some blue beads. Meg now has 119 beads in all. How many blue beads did Meg's sister give her? Explain how you found your answer.

Software Support

Use *Soar to Success* for instruction of students needing targeted support for underlying skills.

On Level — Activity Card 5-6

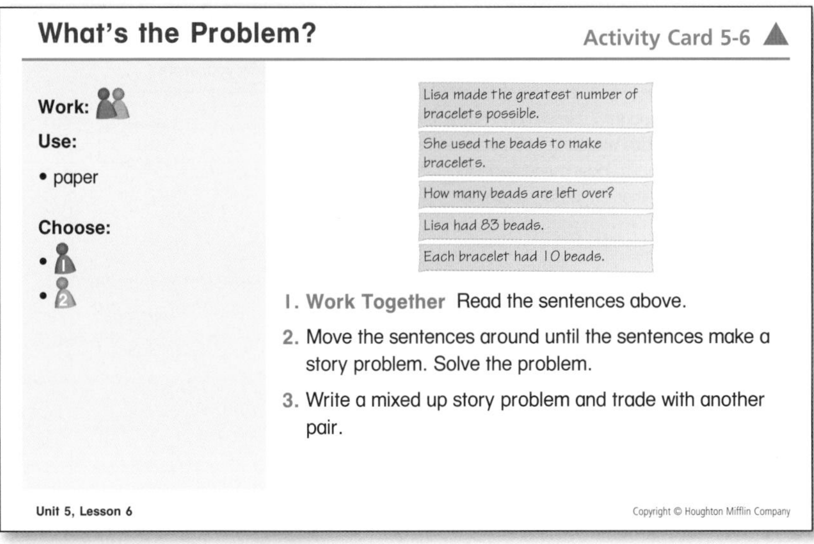

What's the Problem? — Activity Card 5-6

Work: (pairs)

Use:

- paper

Choose:

- 1
- 2

Lisa made the greatest number of bracelets possible.

She used the beads to make bracelets.

How many beads are left over?

Lisa had 83 beads.

Each bracelet had 10 beads.

1. **Work Together** Read the sentences above.
2. Move the sentences around until the sentences make a story problem. Solve the problem.
3. Write a mixed up story problem and trade with another pair.

Unit 5, Lesson 6 — Copyright © Houghton Mifflin Company

Activity Note Each pair needs to rearrange the sentences to make a story problem. You may want to put each sentence on a sentence strip to make it easier to rearrange.

Math Writing Prompt

Complete and Solve Rick had 47 trading cards. He put them in stacks of 10. Add a question to make these sentences into a story problem. Solve the problem.

Software Support

Use *MegaMath* for review and reinforcement of the concepts and skills presented in this lesson.

Challenge — Activity Card 5-6

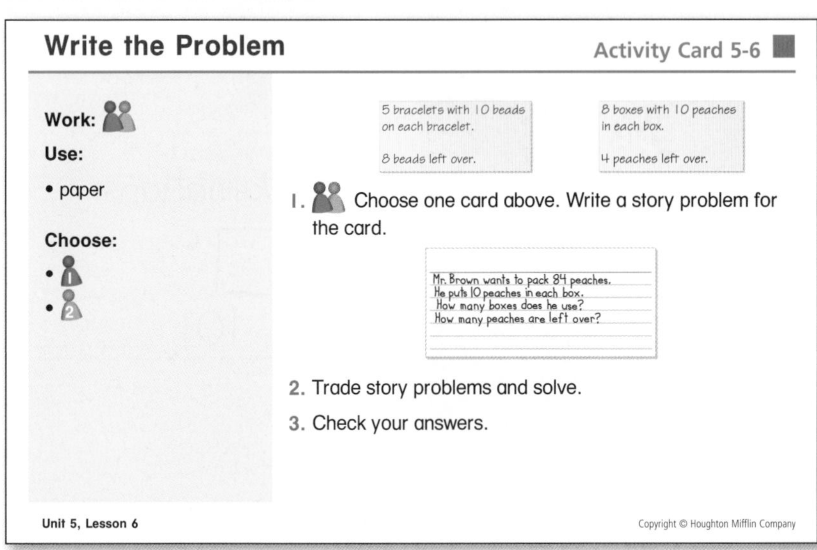

Write the Problem — Activity Card 5-6

Work: (pairs)

Use:

- paper

Choose:

- 1
- 2

5 bracelets with 10 beads on each bracelet.
8 beads left over.

8 boxes with 10 peaches in each box.
4 peaches left over.

1. (pairs) Choose one card above. Write a story problem for the card.

Mr. Brown wants to pack 84 peaches.
He puts 10 peaches in each box.
How many boxes does he use?
How many peaches are left over?

2. Trade story problems and solve.
3. Check your answers.

Unit 5, Lesson 6 — Copyright © Houghton Mifflin Company

Activity Note Each pair needs two index cards. Have each child choose a different set of facts and write a story problem.

Math Writing Prompt

What's the Problem? Answer: 7 bags with 10 marbles in each bag and 3 marbles left over. Write a story problem for this answer. Describe the steps you followed to write your problem.

Software Support

Use *Destination Math* to take students beyond the concepts and skills presented in this lesson.

3 Homework and Spiral Review

Goal: Additional Practice

This Homework page provides practice in making groups of ten to solve story problems.

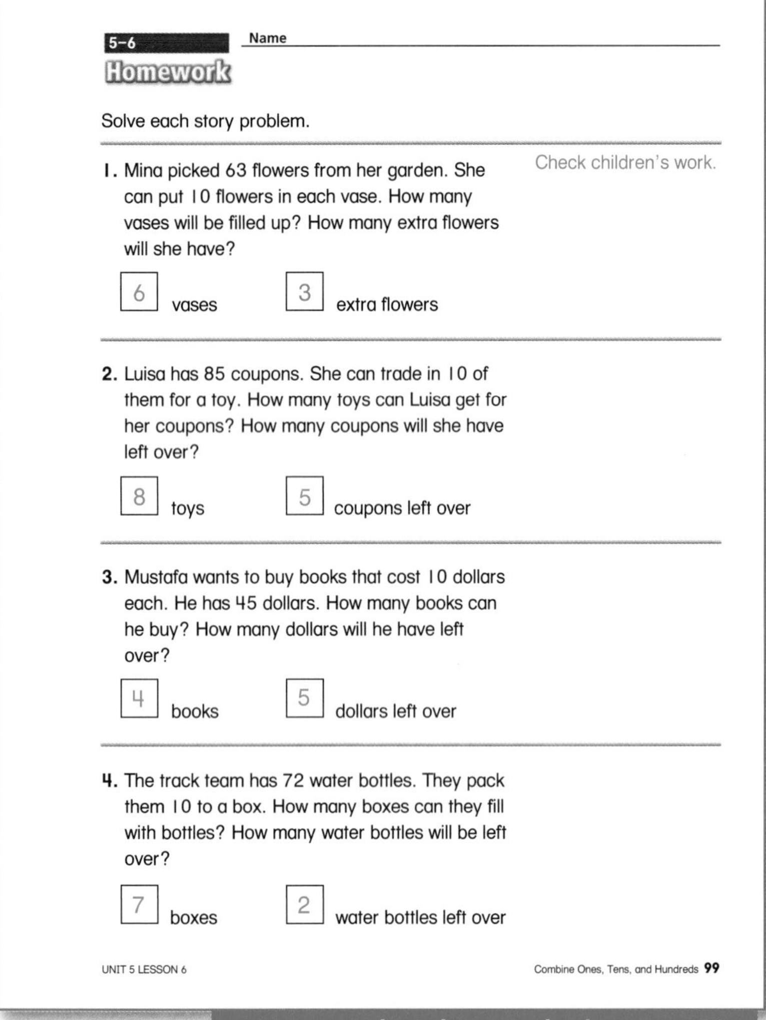

5-6 Homework Name

Solve each story problem.

1. Mina picked 63 flowers from her garden. She can put 10 flowers in each vase. How many vases will be filled up? How many extra flowers will she have? Check children's work.

6 vases 3 extra flowers

2. Luisa has 85 coupons. She can trade in 10 of them for a toy. How many toys can Luisa get for her coupons? How many coupons will she have left over?

8 toys 5 coupons left over

3. Mustafa wants to buy books that cost 10 dollars each. He has 45 dollars. How many books can he buy? How many dollars will he have left over?

4 books 5 dollars left over

4. The track team has 72 water bottles. They pack them 10 to a box. How many boxes can they fill with bottles? How many water bottles will be left over?

7 boxes 2 water bottles left over

UNIT 5 LESSON 6 Combine Ones, Tens, and Hundreds 99

Homework and Remembering page 99

Goal: Spiral Review

This Remembering activity would be appropriate anytime after today's lesson.

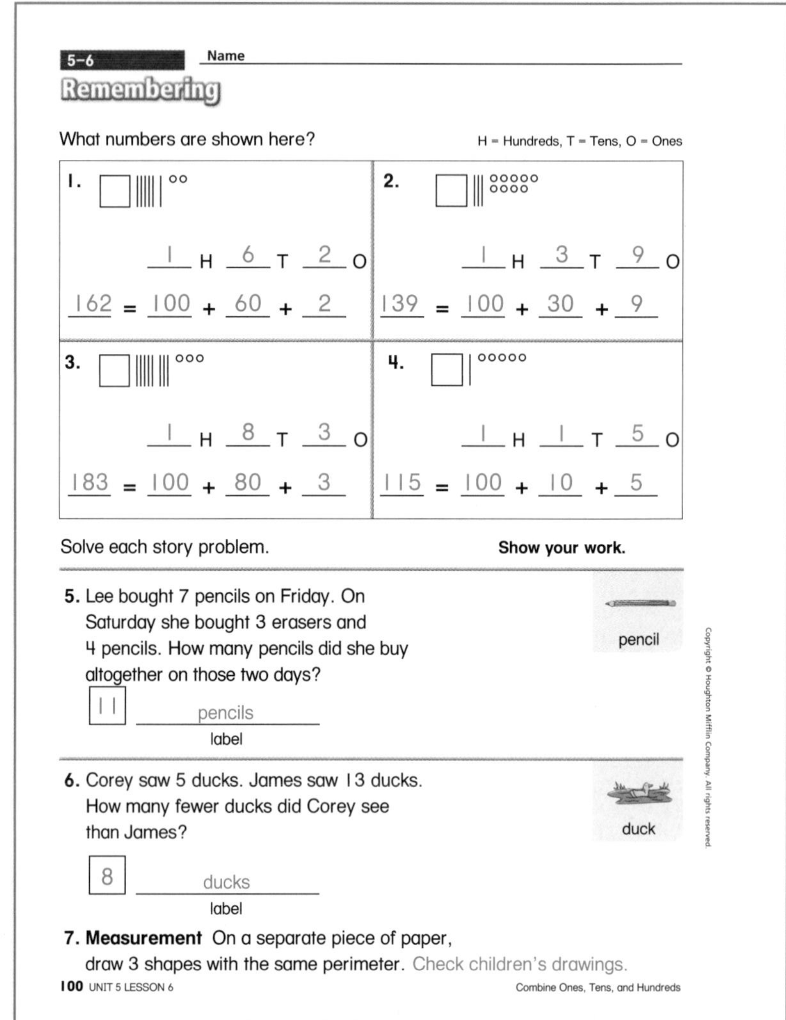

5-6 Remembering Name

What numbers are shown here? H = Hundreds, T = Tens, O = Ones

1. 1 H 6 T 2 O
162 = 100 + 60 + 2

2. 1 H 3 T 9 O
139 = 100 + 30 + 9

3. 1 H 8 T 3 O
183 = 100 + 80 + 3

4. 1 H 1 T 5 O
115 = 100 + 10 + 5

Solve each story problem. **Show your work.**

5. Lee bought 7 pencils on Friday. On Saturday she bought 3 erasers and 4 pencils. How many pencils did she buy altogether on those two days?

11 pencils (label)

6. Corey saw 5 ducks. James saw 13 ducks. How many fewer ducks did Corey see than James?

8 ducks (label)

7. **Measurement** On a separate piece of paper, draw 3 shapes with the same perimeter. Check children's drawings.

100 UNIT 5 LESSON 6 Combine Ones, Tens, and Hundreds

Homework and Remembering page 100

Home or School Activity

Literature Connection

Numbers in Books Have children look for book titles that have numbers less than 200. Children can write the title and then show the number using Quick Hundreds, Quick Tens, and ones.

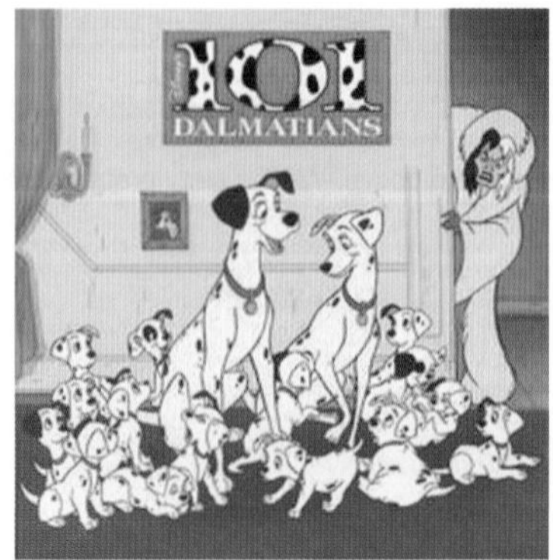

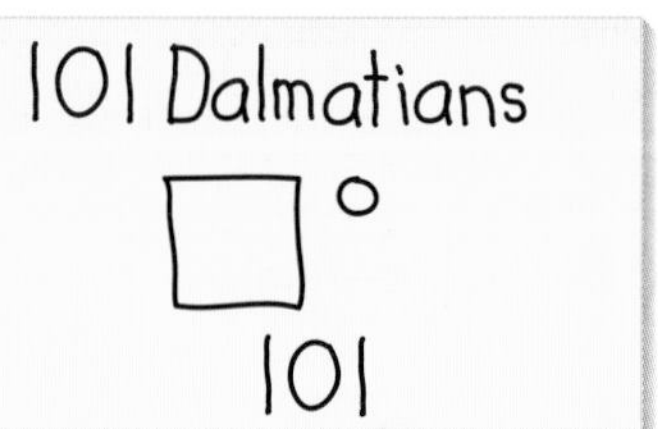

Odd and Even Numbers

Lesson Objectives

- Identify sets as odd or even.
- Identify numbers as odd or even.

Vocabulary
odd
even

The Day at a Glance

Today's Goals	Materials	
1 Teaching the Lesson **A1:** Classify sets as odd or even. **A2:** Identify numbers as odd or even.	**Lesson Activities** Student Activity Book pp. 157–158 Homework and Remembering pp. 101–102 Connecting Cubes Number Path (TRB M51)	**Going Further** Activity Cards 5-7 Connecting cubes Paper Bag Number Cards 1–20 Index Cards Small paper squares Math Journals
2 Going Further ▶ Differentiated Instruction		
3 Homework and Spiral Review		

Use Math Talk today!

Keeping Skills Sharp

Quick Practice 5 MINUTES	Daily Routines
Goal: Addition with teen totals. **Materials:** Secret Code Cards, Parachute Drop–Teen Totals (from Unit 3 Lesson 7 or TRB M46) **Secret Code Card Addition Race, Teens** Have children quickly arrange their Secret Code Cards across their desks from 1 to 10. Introduce the race and demonstrate what the Student Leader and the class should do. Have **Student Leaders** call out addition problems, reading from the bottom of the first column of Parachute Drop–Teen Totals. As quickly as possible, children hold up a 1-digit card and a 10 to show the answer.	**Math Mountains for 100 or 2-Digit Numbers** Using the MathBoard, Using Dimes and Pennies (See pp. xxvi.) ▶ Led by Student Leaders **Money Routine** Using the 120 Poster, Using the Money Flip Chart, Using the Number Path, Using Secret Code Cards (See pp. xxiii–xxv.) ▶ Led by Student Leaders

1 Teaching the Lesson

Activity 1

Classify Sets as Odd or Even

 35 MINUTES

Goal: Make pairs to determine if sets of cubes are odd or even.

Materials: Student Activity Book page 157; connecting cubes (20 per group)

 **NCTM Standards:**
Number and Operation
Algebra

English Language Learners

Draw 2 shoes on the board. Write *pair*. Say: **This is a *pair* of shoes.**

- **Beginning** Say: ***Pair* means two.** Have children repeat.
- **Intermediate** Ask: **Are there 3 in a *pair*?** no **Are there 2 in a *pair*?** yes
- **Advanced** Have children name something that comes in a *pair*.

▶ Make Pairs WHOLE CLASS

Introduce the words *odd* and *even*. Explain that when pairs can be made with none left over the group is even and when there is a leftover the group is odd. Remind children that a pair is two.

- Have children take one cube. Ask if they can make a pair. Explain that since a pair cannot be made, and there is just 1 the group of 1 is odd. Draw 1 circle on the board and write the number 1 and the word odd.

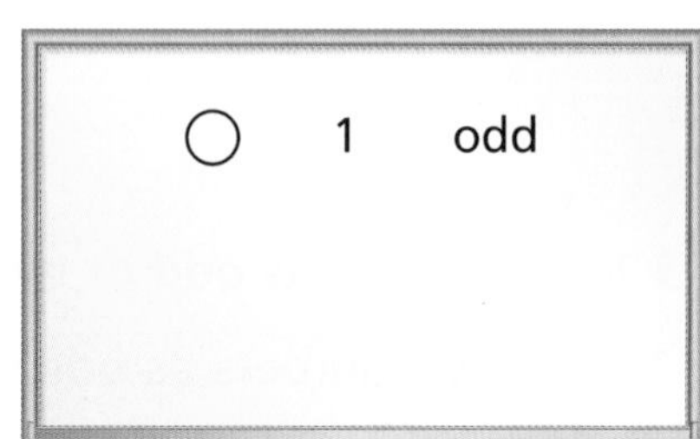

- Have children take 2 cubes and ask if a pair can be made. If yes have them click cubes to make pairs. Explain that since after pairs are made there are none left it means that 2 is even. Draw 2 circles on the board and write the number 2 and the word even.

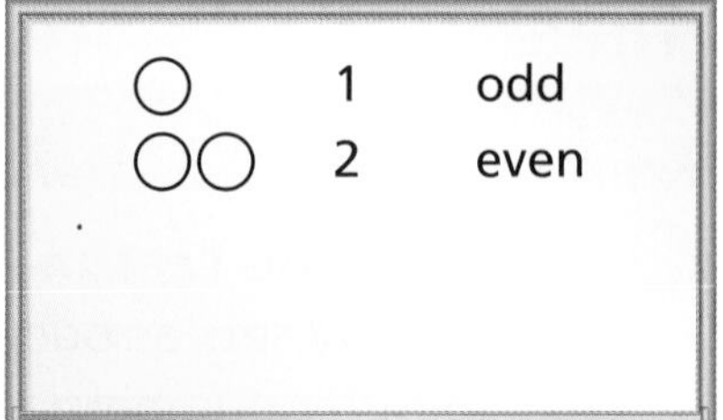

- Have children take 3 cubes. Tell them to make as many pairs as they can. Ask if there are any left over. Since there is a leftover the number 3 is odd. Draw 3 circles on the board and write the number 3 and the word odd.

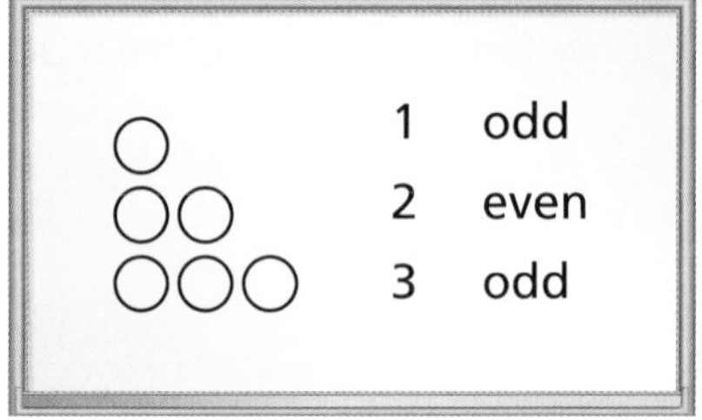

- Have children take 4 cubes. Tell them to make as many pairs as they can. Ask if there are any left over. Since there are none leftover the number 4 is even. Draw 4 circles on the board and write the number 4 and the word even.

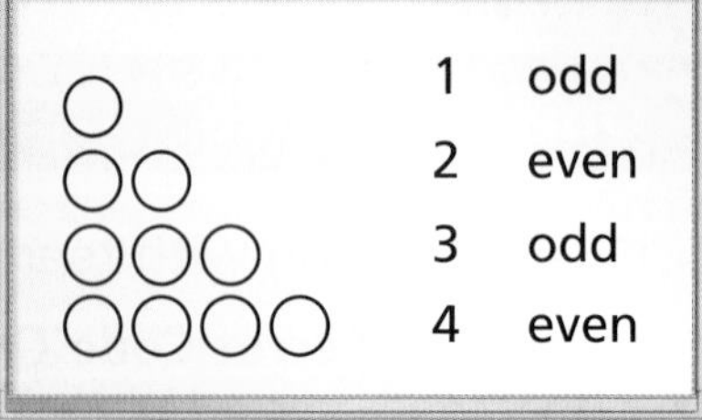

- Continue with similar questioning for the numbers 5–10.

▶ Sort Odd and Even

Sort the numbers in 2 columns on the board titled *odd* and *even*.

- Which numbers are odd? 1, 3, 5, 7, and 9
- Which numbers are even? 0, 2, 4, 6, and 8

Explain that numbers ending with 1, 3, 5, 7, and 9 are always odd and numbers ending with 0, 2, 4, 6, and 8 are always even.

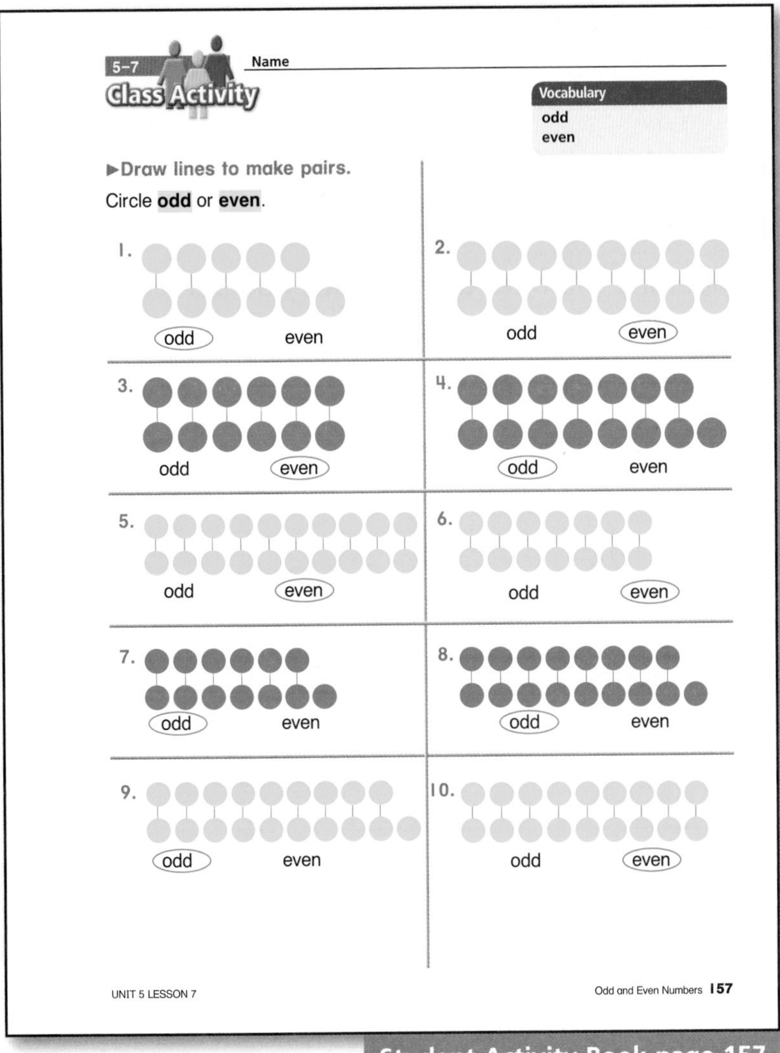
5-7
Class Activity

Name ____________

Vocabulary
odd
even

▶Draw lines to make pairs.
Circle **odd** or **even**.

1. odd even (odd circled)
2. odd even (even circled)
3. odd even (even circled)
4. odd even (odd circled)
5. odd even (even circled)
6. odd even (even circled)
7. odd even (odd circled)
8. odd even (odd circled)
9. odd even (odd circled)
10. odd even (even circled)

UNIT 5 LESSON 7

Odd and Even Numbers 157

Student Activity Book page 157

▶ Make Pairs SMALL GROUPS

Refer children to Student Activity Book page 157. Children will work in small groups to complete the page.

Instruct children to look at Exercise 1. Draw their attention to the two rows of counters. Have them draw lines to connect pairs of dots from the top row to the bottom as possible. Also provide connecting cubes to model the sets shown. Then have children click as many pairs together as they can.

- Are there any leftovers? yes
- What does it mean if there are leftovers? It means the set is odd.
- What does it mean if there are no leftovers? It means the set is even.

Instruct children to complete the page with their group.

1 Teaching the Lesson (continued)

Activity 2

Odd or Even

 15 MINUTES

Goal: Determine if a number is odd or even.

Materials: Student Activity Book page 158, Number Path (TRB M51)

 **NCTM Standards:**
Number and Operations
Algebra

Alternate Approach

Odd and Even Give pairs of children a number path, TRB M51. Have one child go around the number path and circle all odd numbers. Have the other child put an X on all even numbers. Have the children discuss the pattern they see.

Ongoing Assessment

Assess children's understanding of odd and even. Ask questions such as:

- Is 51 odd or even? odd
- Is 47 odd or even? odd
- Is 36 odd or even? even
- Is 82 odd or even? even

▶ Odd or Even Numbers INDIVIDUALS

Refer children to Student Activity Book page 158. Children will work individually to complete the page. Tell children that they will now determine if a number is odd or even.

- Numbers ending with which digits are odd? 1, 3, 5, 7, and 9
- Numbers ending with which digits are even? 0, 2, 4, 6, and 8

Instruct children to underline the ones digit in each number. Have them use it to determine if the number is odd or even.

5–7 Class Activity — Name

Write odd or even for each number.

1. 8 even	2. 25 odd
3. 39 odd	4. 13 odd
5. 57 odd	6. 96 even
7. 41 odd	8. 32 even
9. 84 even	10. 70 even

158 UNIT 5 LESSON 7 — Odd and Even Numbers

Student Activity Book page 158

Math Talk Write the number 4,859 on the board. **Can you tell if this number is odd or even? Explain how you know.** Yes, it is odd. I know because I looked at the ones digit and it is 9. Numbers ending with the digit 9 are odd.

2 Going Further

Differentiated Instruction

Intervention — Activity Card 5-7

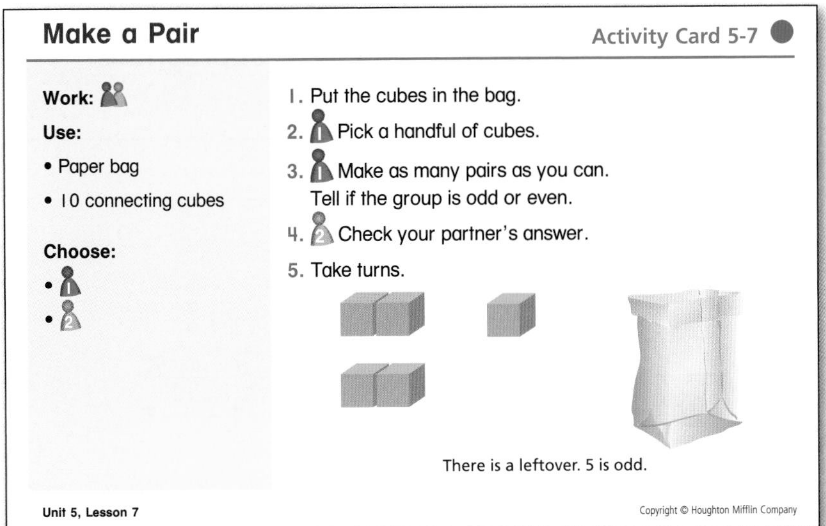

Make a Pair — Activity Card 5-7

Work: (pairs)
Use:
- Paper bag
- 10 connecting cubes

Choose:
- 1
- 2

1. Put the cubes in the bag.
2. (1) Pick a handful of cubes.
3. (1) Make as many pairs as you can. Tell if the group is odd or even.
4. (2) Check your partner's answer.
5. Take turns.

There is a leftover. 5 is odd.

Unit 5, Lesson 7

Copyright © Houghton Mifflin Company

Activity Note For each pair, prepare a paper bag and 20 connecting cubes. Remind children groups that make pairs with no leftovers are even and that groups with a leftover are odd.

Math Writing Prompt

Draw and Explain Have children draw an example of an odd group and an even group and explain how they know which is which.

Software Support

Use *Soar to Success* for instruction of students needing targeted support for underlying skills.

On Level — Activity Card 5-7

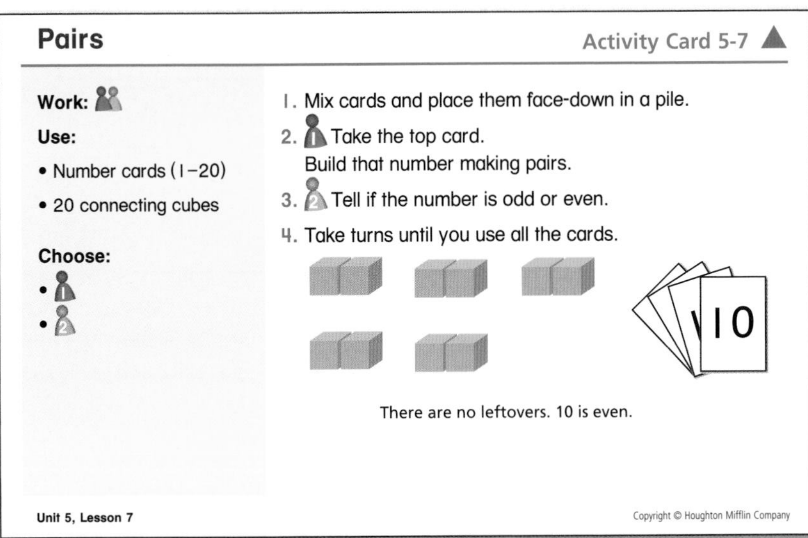

Pairs — Activity Card 5-7

Work: (pairs)
Use:
- Number cards (1–20)
- 20 connecting cubes

Choose:
- 1
- 2

1. Mix cards and place them face-down in a pile.
2. (1) Take the top card. Build that number making pairs.
3. (2) Tell if the number is odd or even.
4. Take turns until you use all the cards.

10

There are no leftovers. 10 is even.

Unit 5, Lesson 7

Copyright © Houghton Mifflin Company

Activity Note For each pair prepare number cards 1–20. Have children list the ending digits for odd numbers and the ending digits for even numbers.

Math Writing Prompt

Explain Your Thinking Explain how you would determine if the following numbers were odd or even: 13, 26, 71, and 50.

Software Support

Use *MegaMath* for review and reinforcement of the concepts and skills presented in this lesson.

Challenge — Activity Card 5-7

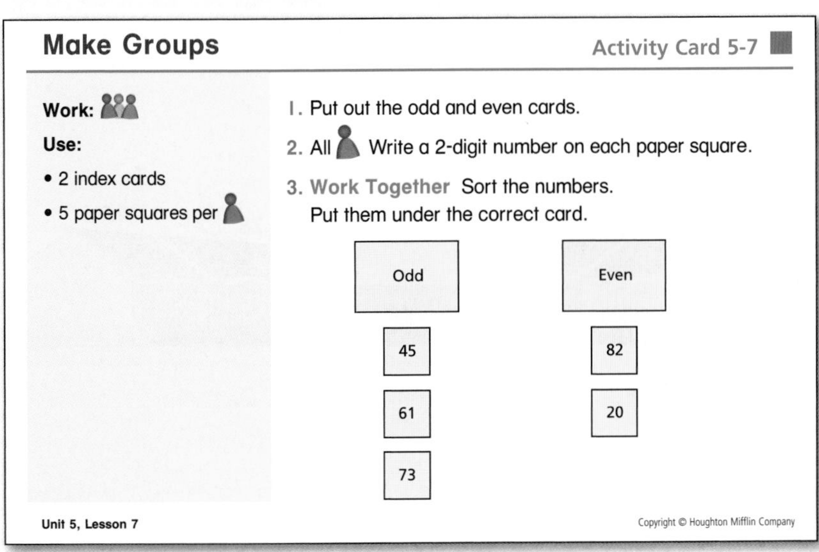

Make Groups — Activity Card 5-7

Work: (small groups)
Use:
- 2 index cards
- 5 paper squares per (child)

1. Put out the odd and even cards.
2. All (children) Write a 2-digit number on each paper square.
3. Work Together Sort the numbers. Put them under the correct card.

Odd	Even
45	82
61	20
73	

Unit 5, Lesson 7

Copyright © Houghton Mifflin Company

Activity Note For each group provide 2 index cards, one labeled *Odd* and the other labeled *Even*. To give a greater challenge you may then have children use 3 or 4-digit numbers.

Math Writing Prompt

Investigate Math How long would it take to figure if an 8-digit number was odd or even. Explain your answer.

DESTINATION Math® **Software Support**

Use *Destination Math* to take students beyond the concepts and skills presented in this lesson.

3 Homework and Spiral Review

Goal: Additional Practice

Use this homework activity to provide children more practice with odd and even numbers.

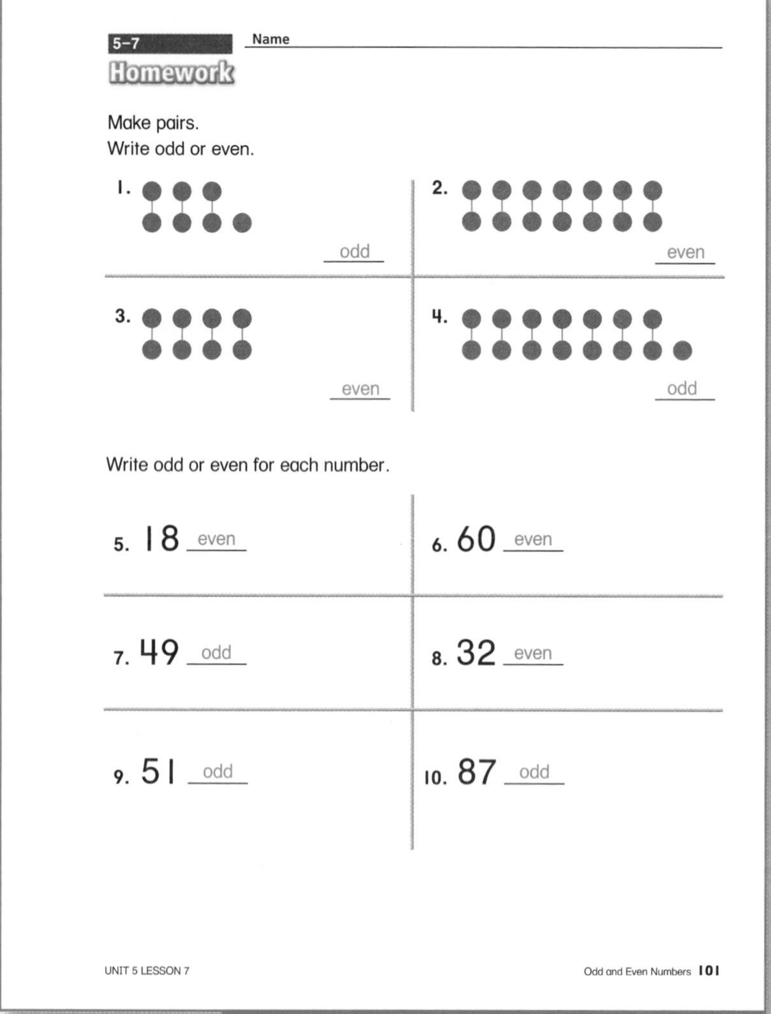

5-7 Name

Homework

Make pairs.
Write odd or even.

1. odd
2. even
3. even
4. odd

Write odd or even for each number.

5. 18 even
6. 60 even
7. 49 odd
8. 32 even
9. 51 odd
10. 87 odd

UNIT 5 LESSON 7 Odd and Even Numbers 101

Homework and Remembering page 101

Goal: Spiral Review

This Remembering activity would be appropriate anytime after today's lesson.

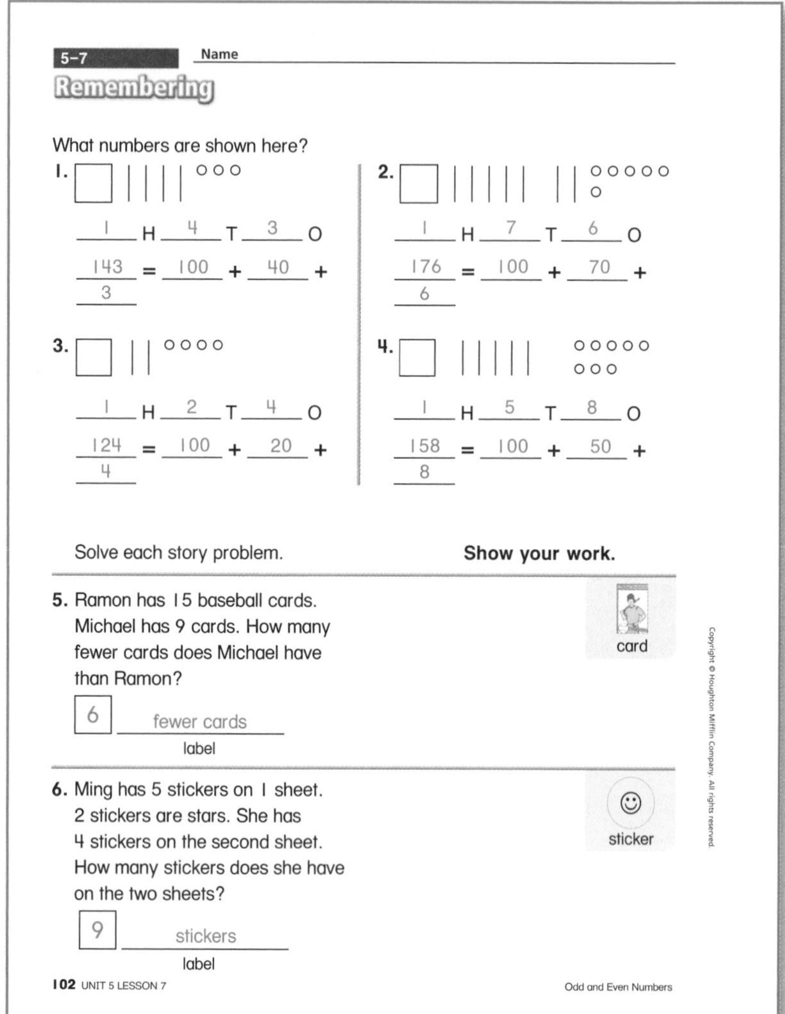

5-7 Name

Remembering

What numbers are shown here?

1. 1 H 4 T 3 O
143 = 100 + 40 + 3

2. 1 H 7 T 6 O
176 = 100 + 70 + 6

3. 1 H 2 T 4 O
124 = 100 + 20 + 4

4. 1 H 5 T 8 O
158 = 100 + 50 + 8

Solve each story problem. **Show your work.**

5. Ramon has 15 baseball cards. Michael has 9 cards. How many fewer cards does Michael have than Ramon?
card
6 fewer cards
label

6. Ming has 5 stickers on 1 sheet. 2 stickers are stars. She has 4 stickers on the second sheet. How many stickers does she have on the two sheets?
sticker
9 stickers
label

102 UNIT 5 LESSON 7 Odd and Even Numbers

Homework and Remembering page 102

Home or School Activity

Real-World Connection

House Numbers Ask children to do this activity after school. Instruct them look at and write down the numbers in order on one side of their street and then do the same for the other side of the street. Have them write down what they notice about the numbers on each side of the street.

Estimation

Lesson Objectives

- Estimate how many of an object is shown.
- Estimate how many of an object will fit in a given space.

Vocabulary
estimate

The Day at a Glance

Today's Goals	Materials	
1 Teaching the Lesson **A1:** Estimate the number of objects that will fit in a jar. **A2:** Estimate the number of objects shown. **A3:** Estimate the number of pennies that will fit in a given space.	**Lesson Activities** Student Activity Book pp. 159–160 Homework and Remembering pp. 103–104 2 jars (same size) marbles paper bags counters pennies paper with 55 dots paper with 87 dots	**Going Further** Activity Cards 5-8 Paper bags small object such as macaroni paper shapes pennies Math Journals Use Math Talk today!
2 Going Further ▶ Differentiated Instruction		
3 Homework and Spiral Review		

Keeping Skills Sharp

Quick Practice 5 MINUTES	Daily Routines
Goal: Practice addition, totals >10. **Materials:** Green Make-a-Ten Cards (addition) (from Unit 1 Lesson 13 or TRB M35–M38) **Green Make-a-Ten Cards (Addition)** Children practice with the Green Addition Make-a-Ten Cards individually or with a partner. Explain that they are practicing for Secret Code Card races and a Quick Check.	**Math Mountains for 100 or 2-Digit Numbers** Using the MathBoard, Using Dimes and Pennies (See pp. xxvi.) ▶ Led by Student Leaders **Money Routine** Using the 120 Poster, Using the Money Flip Chart, Using the Number Path, Using Secret Code Cards (See pp. xxiii–xxv.) ▶ Led by Student Leaders

1 Teaching the Lesson

Activity 1

How Many Marbles?

 **15 MINUTES**

Goal: Estimate the number of objects in a jar.

Materials: marbles, 2 jars (same size), macaroni (optional), pennies (optional)

 **NCTM Standards:**
Number and Operations
Measurement
Reasoning and Proof

English Language Learners

Write *estimate* on the board.
Hold up a jar of pennies Say: **Let's *estimate* how many pennies there are.**

- **Beginning** Say: **An *estimate* is a guess.** Have children repeat.
- **Intermediate** Ask: **Is an *estimate* a guess?** yes **Do we count the pennies to *estimate*?** no
- **Advanced** Say: **An *estimate* isn't exact, it's a good __.** guess

▶ How Many? WHOLE CLASS

Prepare 2 jars, one with 10 marbles and at least 100 in the other. Show children the jar filled 100 plus marbles. Ask the following question and get answers from many volunteers.

- How many marbles do you think are in the jar?

Then show the jar with 10 marbles. Call on a volunteer to come up and count the marbles in that jar. Put the 2 jars next to each other.

- Now that you know 10 marbles are in the second jar, does that help you make a better guess for the number of marbles in the first jar?
- You may change your guess or estimate if you would like.

Introduce the word estimate and explain that an estimate is a guess, but they should use what they know to have the best guess or estimate possible. After children have come up with new estimates call on volunteers to count the number of marbles in the first jar.

- Was your second estimate closer than your first? Why?

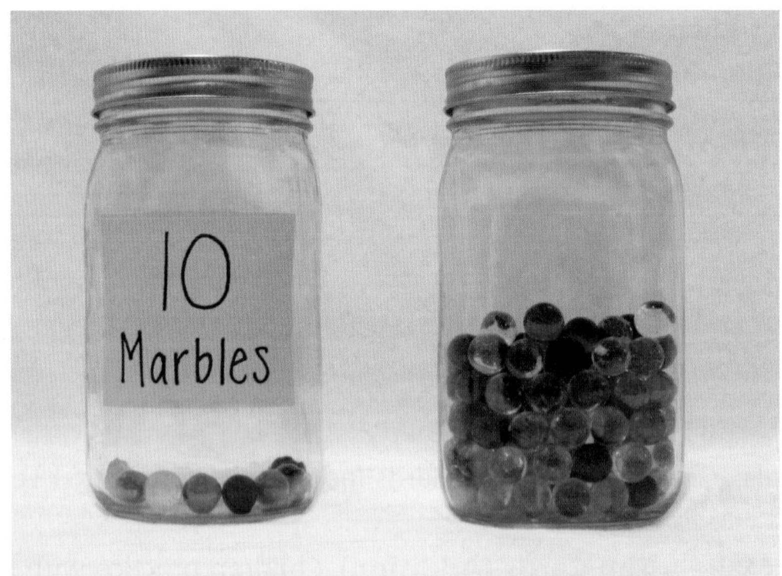

You may take this opportunity to repeat the activity with different small objects such as macaroni or pennies.

Math Talk How would you estimate the number of students in the school? What might you use to help make a better estimate? Possible answer: I would count how many children are in one class and think about how many classes there are in all.

Activity 2

Estimate How Many

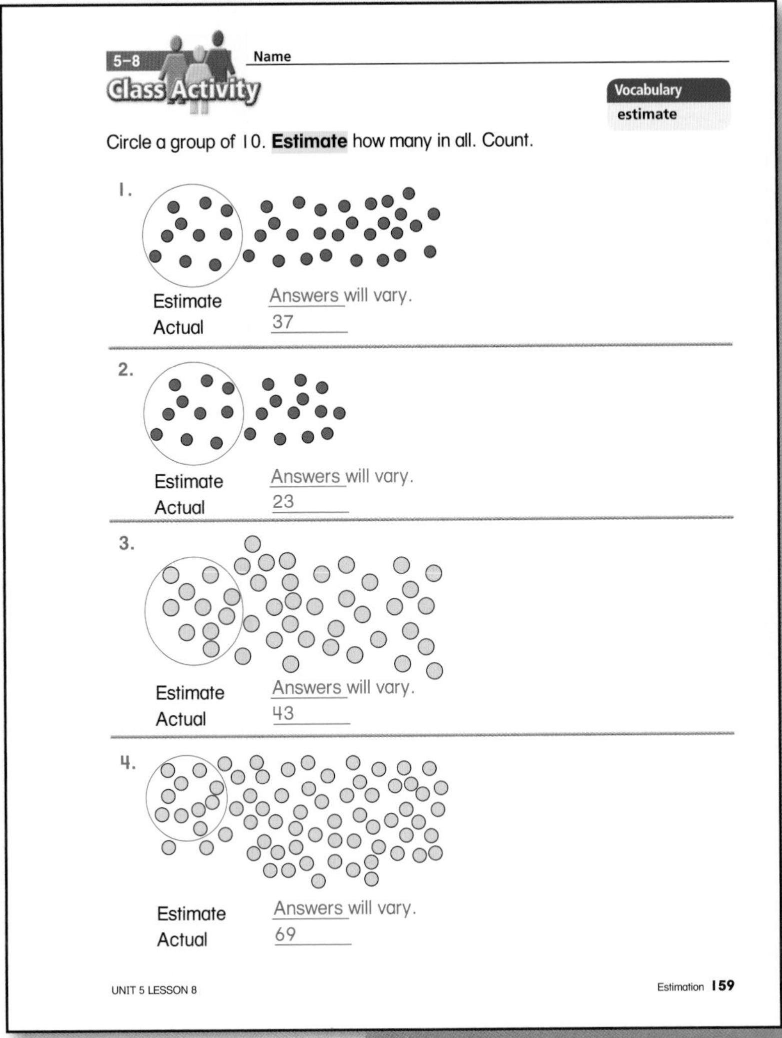

5-8 Class Activity

Name

Vocabulary
estimate

Circle a group of 10. **Estimate** how many in all. Count.

1. Estimate Answers will vary.
Actual 37

2. Estimate Answers will vary.
Actual 23

3. Estimate Answers will vary.
Actual 43

4. Estimate Answers will vary.
Actual 69

UNIT 5 LESSON 8

Estimation 159

Student Activity Book page 159

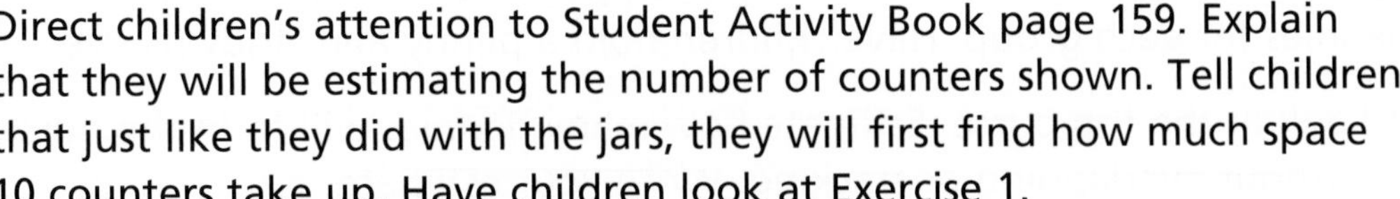

▶ Estimate Counters WHOLE CLASS

Math Talk

Direct children's attention to Student Activity Book page 159. Explain that they will be estimating the number of counters shown. Tell children that just like they did with the jars, they will first find how much space 10 counters take up. Have children look at Exercise 1.

- Count out and circle 10 counters using 1 large circle.
- Write your estimate.
- Count the counters. Put an X on each one as your count to help. Write the actual number.
- Was your estimate close?

Complete this page together. Discuss if children's estimate got better as they did the exercises.

15 MINUTES

Goal: Estimate the number of objects shown.

Materials: Student Activity Book page 159, paper bags, counters

NCTM Standards:
Number and Operations
Reasoning and Proof

Alternate Approach

How Many Prepare bags of counters each with 35–70. Give pairs of children a bag. Instruct children to spill out the bag of counters and estimate how many. Then have children count out 10 of the counters. Inform children they can then change their estimates. Tell children to count all the counters and discuss their estimates. Children may trade bags and repeat the activity.

Activity 3

Estimate Space

 15 MINUTES

Goal: Estimate the number of objects that will fit in a given space.

Materials: Student Activity Book page 160, pennies, paper with 55 dots, paper with 87 dots

 **NCTM Standards:**
Number and Operations
Reasoning and Proof

Ongoing Assessment

Assess children's estimation skills. Show a piece of paper with 55 dots on it.

- Estimate the number of dots. Do you think it is about 20, about 50 or about 100?

Show a paper with 87 dots on it.

- Estimate the number of dots. Do you think it is about 20, about 50 or about 100?

► How Many Will Fit? SMALL GROUPS

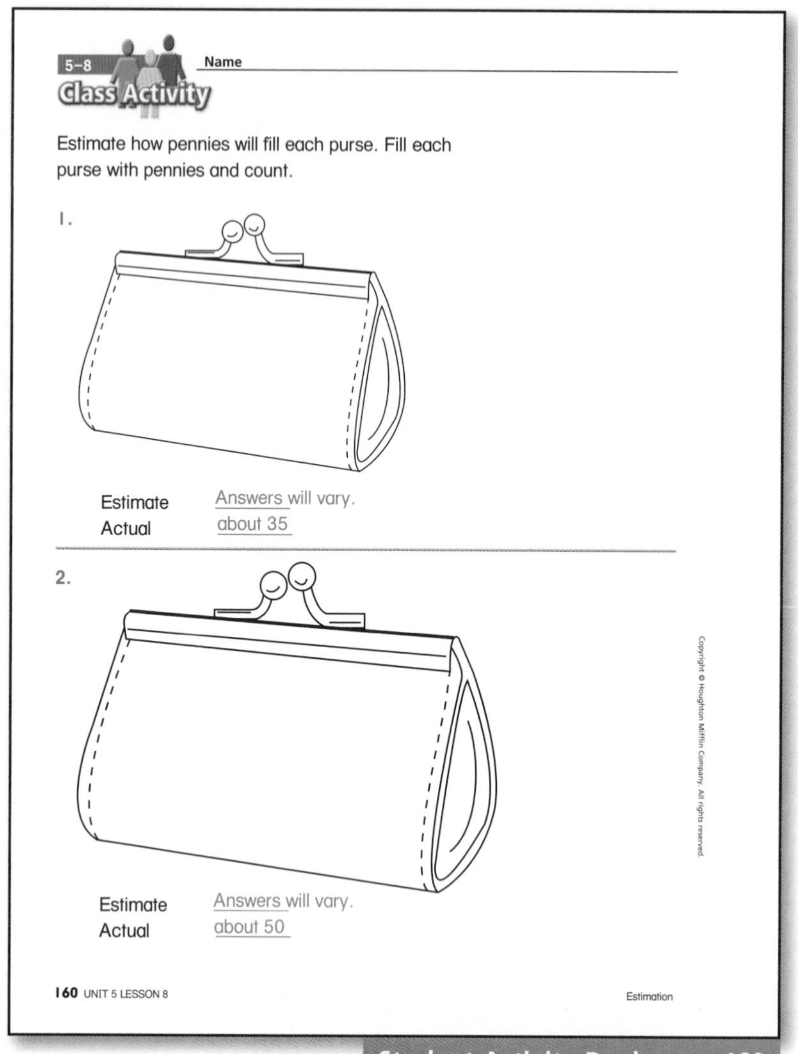
5-8 Class Activity Name

Estimate how pennies will fill each purse. Fill each purse with pennies and count.

1.

Estimate Answers will vary.
Actual about 35

2.

Estimate Answers will vary.
Actual about 50

160 UNIT 5 LESSON 8 Estimation

Copyright © Houghton Mifflin Company. All rights reserved.

Student Activity Book page 160

Have children find Student Activity Book page 160. Provide about 60 pennies for each group. Have children hold a penny and study its size.

- Look at the top purse. Estimate how many pennies will fit in the purse without overlapping or stacking. Write your estimate.
- Have children fill the purse with pennies. Have them fit as many as they can without overlapping or going outside the line. Instruct them to count as they put each penny in.
- How many pennies fit in the purse?

Repeat for the second purse.

To end this activity, have each child draw a shape and estimate the number of pennies that would fit inside. Then have children place the pennies to see how close their estimates were.

2 Going Further

Differentiated Instruction

Intervention — Activity Card 5-8

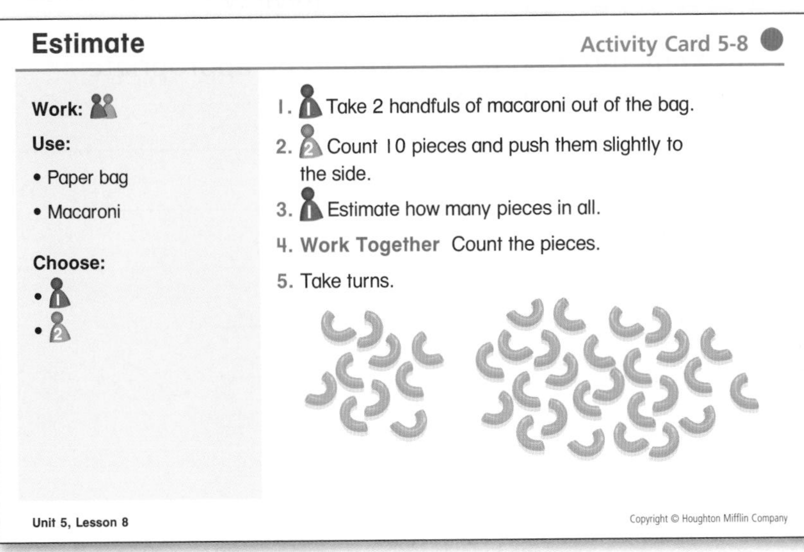

Estimate — Activity Card 5-8

Work: pairs
Use:
- Paper bag
- Macaroni

Choose:
- 1
- 2

1. Take 2 handfuls of macaroni out of the bag.
2. Count 10 pieces and push them slightly to the side.
3. Estimate how many pieces in all.
4. **Work Together** Count the pieces.
5. Take turns.

Unit 5, Lesson 8 — Copyright © Houghton Mifflin Company

Activity Note For each pair, prepare paper bags with about 80 pieces of macaroni.

Math Writing Prompt

Explain Your Thinking How does looking at the 10 pieces help you make a better estimate?

Software Support

Use *Soar to Success* for instruction of students needing targeted support for underlying skills.

On Level — Activity Card 5-8

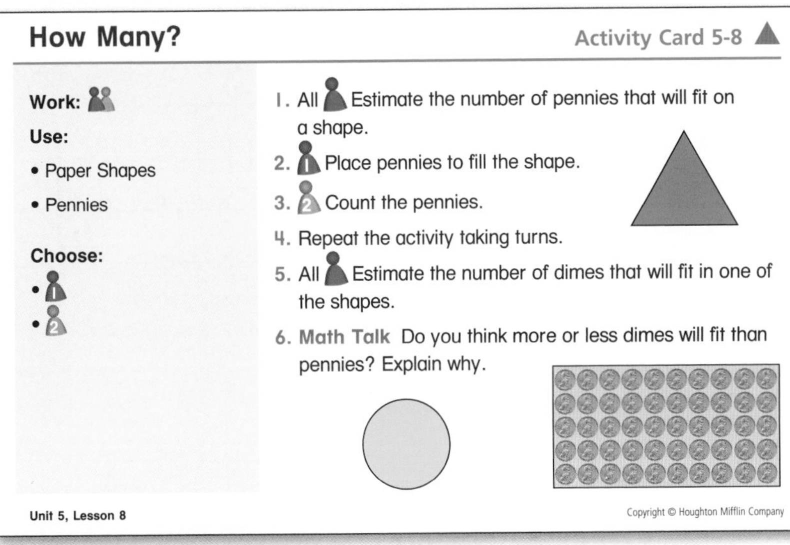

How Many? — Activity Card 5-8

Work: pairs
Use:
- Paper Shapes
- Pennies

Choose:
- 1
- 2

1. All Estimate the number of pennies that will fit on a shape.
2. Place pennies to fill the shape.
3. Count the pennies.
4. Repeat the activity taking turns.
5. All Estimate the number of dimes that will fit in one of the shapes.
6. **Math Talk** Do you think more or less dimes will fit than pennies? Explain why.

Unit 5, Lesson 8 — Copyright © Houghton Mifflin Company

Activity Note For each pair prepare 3–5 construction paper cut-out shapes that would hold 30–80 pennies. Give each group 90 pennies.

Math Writing Prompt

Explain Would you use more or less quarters than pennies to fill a shape? Explain.

Software Support

Use *MegaMath* for review and reinforcement of the concepts and skills presented in this lesson.

Challenge — Activity Card 5-8

Draw the Space — Activity Card 5-8

Work: groups of 3
Use:
- Crayons or markers
- Pennies

Choose:
- 1
- 2
- 3

1. Draw a shape that you think will fit exactly 10 pennies.
2. Fill the shape with pennies.
3. Count the pennies. Was it close to 10?
4. Take turns making shapes for 30 and 50 pennies.
5. **Math Talk** Was it harder to make the shape for more pennies or less pennies? Why do you think so?

Unit 5, Lesson 8 — Copyright © Houghton Mifflin Company

Activity Note Provide 60 pennies for each group. Tell children to think about the shape that held 10 to help them draw shapes to hold 30 and 50.

Math Writing Prompt

Explain Your Thinking If you needed to find a box to hold 500 crayons explain how to choose what size box to use.

Software Support

Use *Destination Math* to take students beyond the concepts and skills presented in this lesson.

3 Homework and Spiral Review

Goal: Additional Practice

Use this homework activity to provide children more practice with estimation.

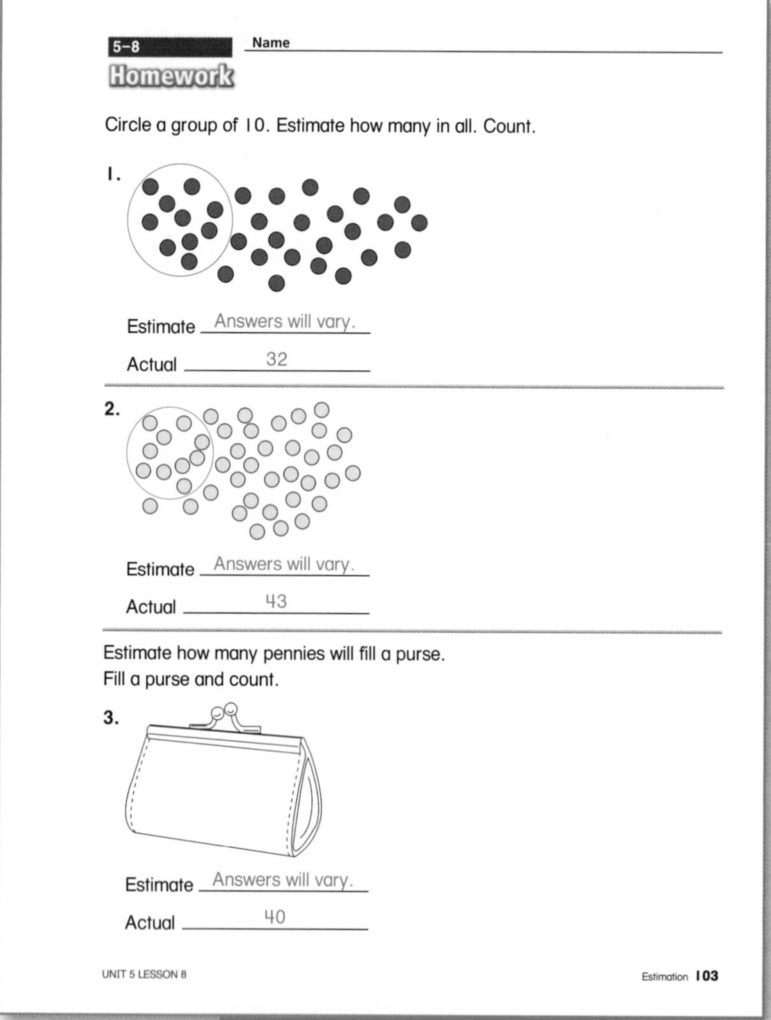

5-8 Homework

Name ____________

Circle a group of 10. Estimate how many in all. Count.

1.

Estimate Answers will vary.

Actual 32

2.

Estimate Answers will vary.

Actual 43

Estimate how many pennies will fill a purse.
Fill a purse and count.

3.

Estimate Answers will vary.

Actual 40

UNIT 5 LESSON 8 Estimation 103

Homework and Remembering page 103

Goal: Spiral Review

This Remembering activity would be appropriate anytime after today's lesson.

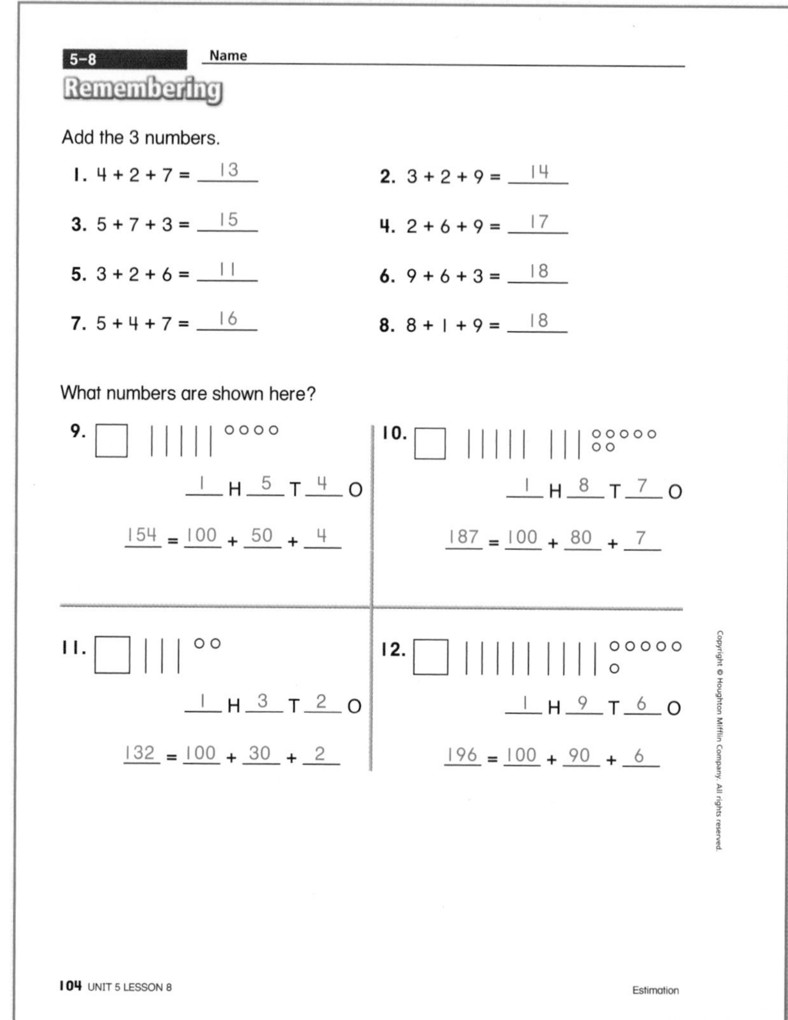

5-8 Remembering

Name ____________

Add the 3 numbers.

1. 4 + 2 + 7 = 13
2. 3 + 2 + 9 = 14
3. 5 + 7 + 3 = 15
4. 2 + 6 + 9 = 17
5. 3 + 2 + 6 = 11
6. 9 + 6 + 3 = 18
7. 5 + 4 + 7 = 16
8. 8 + 1 + 9 = 18

What numbers are shown here?

9. 1 H 5 T 4 O
154 = 100 + 50 + 4

10. 1 H 8 T 7 O
187 = 100 + 80 + 7

11. 1 H 3 T 2 O
132 = 100 + 30 + 2

12. 1 H 9 T 6 O
196 = 100 + 90 + 6

104 UNIT 5 LESSON 8 Estimation

Homework and Remembering page 104

Home or School Activity

Real-World Connection

How Many? Tell children to estimate the number of small household items, such as a handful of macaroni or pennies in storage containers. If they have a large group remind them to put 10 aside and use it to help with their estimations.

Invent 2-Digit Addition

Lesson Objectives

- Invent a method of solving 2-digit addition problems.
- Group ones to make a new ten; group tens to make a new hundred.

Vocabulary

New Groups Above method
New Groups Below method
Show All Totals method

The Day at a Glance

Today's Goals	Materials	
① **Teaching the Lesson** Solve story problems that involve making a new ten or a new hundred.	**Lesson Activities** Student Activity Book pp. 161–164 (includes Family Letter) Homework and Remembering pp. 105–106	**Going Further** Activity Cards 5-9 Base-ten blocks Math Journals
② **Going Further** ▸ Differentiated Instruction		
③ **Homework and Targeted Practice**		

Use Math Talk today!

Keeping Skills Sharp

Quick Practice — 5 MINUTES

Goal: Practice saying hundreds numbers as groups of 10.

Tens Talking Write the multiples of 10 from 110 through 190 on the board in random order. (A sample list appears at the right.)

160
110
120
150
140
130
170
190
180

Have two Student Leaders take turns pointing to a number. The class responds, on a given signal, by saying the number, then the number of tens.

Student Leader 1 (pointing to 160): How many tens?
Class: One hundred sixty is 16 tens.

Student Leader 2 (pointing to 160): How many ones?
Class: 16 tens is one hundred sixty.

Use the same procedure for each number on the board.

Daily Routines

Math Mountains for 100 or 2-Digit Numbers Using the MathBoard, Using Dimes and Pennies
(See pp. xxvi.)

▸ Led by Student Leaders

Money Routine Using the 120 Poster, Using the Money Flip Chart, Using the Number Path, Using Secret Code Cards
(See pp. xxiii–xxv.)

▸ Led by Student Leaders

1 Teaching the Lesson

Activity

Stock the Shelves at the Grocery Store

 50 MINUTES

Goal: Solve story problems that involve making a new ten or a new hundred.

Materials: MathBoard materials, Student Activity Book page 161

 **NCTM Standards:**
Number and Operations
Problem Solving
Communication

Teaching Note

Solving on MathBoards When using the **Solve and Discuss** structure to solve problems, it is useful to have children at their seats solve their early problems on MathBoards and their later problems on their student page. Solving on MathBoards allows them to have plenty of space to connect a proof drawing to a numerical method. Also, if you see an interesting method done on a MathBoard, you can ask that child to take the MathBoard to the front and explain that method. Solving on the student page allows you to collect the papers and quickly review children's methods and errors so that you can address them the following day.

5-9 Class Activity Name ______

▶ The New Ten

Solve each story problem. Show your work.

1. Mr. Green put 56 red peppers in the vegetable bin. Mrs. Green put 28 yellow peppers in the bin. How many peppers did they put in the bin altogether?

84 peppers
label

2. Mrs. Green stacked 43 tomatoes. Mr. Green added 39 more. How many tomatoes are stacked now?

82 tomatoes
label

3. Mr. Green counted 65 cans. Mrs. Green counted 82 cans. How many cans did they count in all?

147 cans
label

4. Mrs. Green counted 57 bags of beans. Mr. Green counted 71 bags of beans. How many bags of beans did they count in all?

128 bags
label

On the Back Use the back of the page if you need more room for your work.

UNIT 5 LESSON 9 Invent 2-Digit Addition 161

Student Activity Book page 161

▶ The New Ten WHOLE CLASS

Introduce Mr. and Mrs. Green, the grocers on Student Activity Book page 161.

- Mr. and Mrs. Green own a grocery store. They work very hard in their store. There are many boxes, cans, bags, and bottles to count. On this page there are story problems about some of the things they count in their store.

Ask children why Mr. and Mrs. Green need to count the items in their grocery store. Answers may vary. Possible responses: They have to keep track of what they sell; they need to know when to order more items; they need to know what people like to buy.

Read aloud problem 1 on Student Activity Book page 161. Have a few volunteers represent the numbers 56 and 28 with sticks and circles on the board as the rest of the class works at their seats.

Have children write the problem in numbers on the board. Be sure they show both the horizontal and vertical format.

$$56 + 28 = \square \qquad \begin{array}{r} 56 \\ +\ 28 \\ \hline \square \end{array}$$

Invite children to invent and explain a method for finding the total number of peppers Mr. and Mrs. Green put in the bin.

- How can we add 56 + 28? Possible response: We could think of a way to add with sticks and circles, and then show it with numbers too.

Have children at the board share their methods and answers with the class. Be sure children use correct tens and ones language in their explanations. Some children may use methods they learned last year, such as New Groups Below, New Groups Above, or Show All Totals. These methods will be discussed formally in subsequent lessons. For possible classroom discussion, see **Math Talk in Action** in the side column.

Now invite children to consider the "mystery" this problem evokes, if it did not come up in the previous discussion. Explain that, if they count the sticks they drew, they will find there are 7 sticks, representing 7 tens. The problem has 5 tens and 2 tens. Yet the answer is 84. Have the class discuss where the extra ten in the answer came from. The extra ten came from the ones.

Ask children to suggest ways to show the new ten so they don't forget it is there. (It is important for children to consider ways to show the new ten, as that is the key to solving multi-digit addition problems correctly. This issue will be addressed more systematically in subsequent lessons.)

Have children solve problem 2 on Student Activity Book page 161 using any method they wish. Those who use a numeric method should create a proof drawing with sticks and circles.

It is also vital that those who make a proof drawing should also write a numerical method. Using proof drawings should give meaning to a numeric method, not stand alone as an answer-getting device. So Miguel in the Math Talk in Action example to the right needs to be encouraged to develop or adopt a numeric method to record his proof drawing.

Activity continued ▶

Math Talk in Action

Miguel: I used sticks and circles. I drew my proof drawing and then I looked to see if I could group a new ten or new hundred. 56 and 28 is 84.

Anya: I used a Counting On strategy. I started with 56 and added 2 tens. Then I added 8 ones.

56 → 66, 76 77, 78, 79, 80, 81, 82, 83, 84

Add 2 tens. Then add 8 ones.

Timothy: I used the New Groups Below Strategy. I added 6 plus 8 to get 14. That's 4 ones and 1 ten. So I wrote 4 in the ones place, and I wrote the new ten below the 5 tens and 2 tens.

$$\begin{array}{r} 56 \\ +\ 28 \\ \hline 84 \end{array}$$ New Groups Below

Gwen: I used the Show All Totals Strategy. First I found the tens total. Then I found the ones total. Then I added them together.

$$\begin{array}{r} 56 \\ +\ 28 \\ \hline 70 \\ +\ 14 \\ \hline 84 \end{array}$$ Show All Totals

Children in your class may invent other strategies. Any method that children can explain and that make accurate use of tens and ones language is acceptable.

① Teaching the Lesson (continued)

Teaching Note

Language and Vocabulary Be sure that children use correct hundreds, tens, and ones language in their explanations.

English Language Learners

Provide support with vocabulary to solve problems. Point to a proof drawing on the board.

- **Beginning** Ask: **Is this a *Proof Drawing?*** yes **Are these circles ones or tens?** ones **Are these sticks tens or hundreds?** tens
- **Intermediate** Say: **This is a *Proof* ___.** Drawing **The circles are ___.** ones **The sticks are ___.** tens **Ten sticks equal 1 ___.** hundred
- **Advanced** Have children work in pairs to tell about their Proof Drawings. Walk around and make sure they use correct ones, tens, and hundreds language.

Ongoing Assessment

Observe children as they solve problems 2 and 4.

- ▶ Will there be 7 tens or 8 tens after you add the numbers of tomatoes? How do you know?
- ▶ Will there be a new hundred after you add the numbers of bags? How do you know?

▶ The Hundred WHOLE CLASS

Have a volunteer read aloud problem 3 on Student Activity Book page 161. Invite a few children to the board to solve the problem and have the other children work at their seats. Ask several children to share their methods with the class.

- Who thought of a good way to solve this problem? Answers will vary. Possible response: First, I drew a proof drawing. Then I added the 5 ones and 2 ones and got 7 ones. Then I added 6 tens and 8 tens and got 14 tens. That's the same as 1 hundred and 4 tens.

65 |||||| ooooo → 7
82 |||||||| oo
100 40

$100 + 40 + 7 = 147$

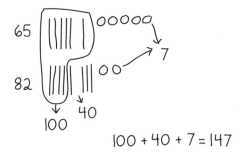

Most children will probably adapt a sticks and circles method like the one above. Those who use numeric methods like the ones below should also create a proof drawing with sticks and circles, and children only making proof drawings need to develop a numeric method.

$65 + 82 = 147$

$$\begin{array}{r} 65 \\ +\,82 \\ \hline 147 \end{array}$$

Have the class discuss where the hundred in the answer came from. Point out that if they count the sticks they drew they will find there are 14 sticks, representing 14 tens. But the answer is expressed as a hundred, some tens, and some ones.

- Something doesn't seem right. Look at the sticks you drew. I see 14 sticks, but our answer is 147.

Discuss where the hundred came from. Be sure children notice that 14 tens is 140 and that the hundred came from 10 of those tens. Have children draw a box around 10 tens and explain that this is how we can show 100.

Have children solve problem 4 on Student Activity Book page 161 using any method they wish. Those who use a numeric method should create a proof drawing with sticks and circles, and children only making proof drawings need to develop a numeric method.

Differentiated Instruction

Intervention — Activity Card 5-9

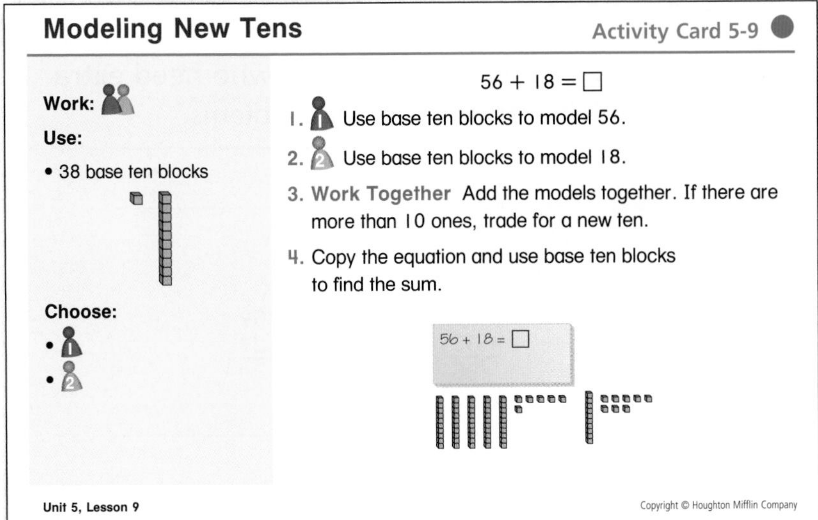

Modeling New Tens — Activity Card 5-9

Work: (pairs)
Use:
- 38 base ten blocks

Choose:
- 1
- 2

56 + 18 = □

1. Use base ten blocks to model 56.
2. Use base ten blocks to model 18.
3. **Work Together** Add the models together. If there are more than 10 ones, trade for a new ten.
4. Copy the equation and use base ten blocks to find the sum.

56 + 18 = □

Unit 5, Lesson 9

Activity Note Each pair needs 18 tens and 18 ones base ten blocks. Review with children when to trade 10 ones for a new ten.

Math Writing Prompt

Explain Your Thinking What does it mean to make a new ten when you add two numbers?

Software Support

Use *Soar to Success* for instruction of students needing targeted support for underlying skills.

On Level — Activity Card 5-9

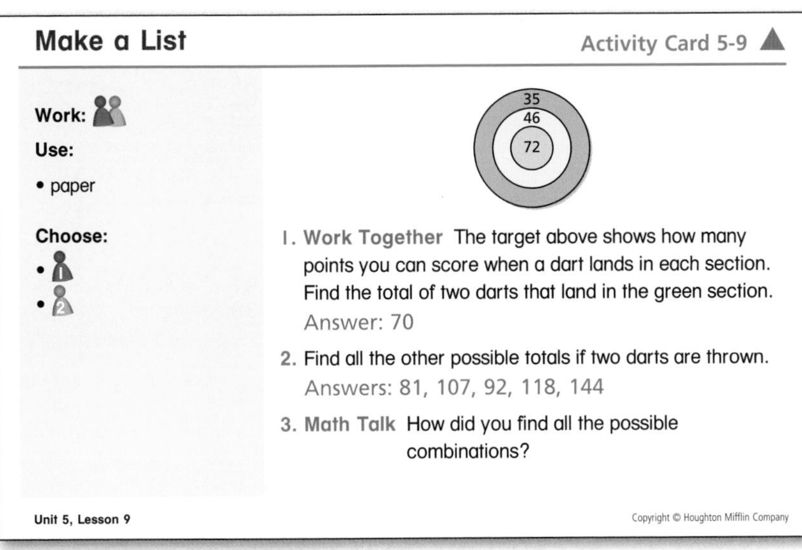

Make a List — Activity Card 5-9

Work: (pairs)
Use:
- paper

Choose:
- 1
- 2

35, 46, 72

1. **Work Together** The target above shows how many points you can score when a dart lands in each section. Find the total of two darts that land in the green section. Answer: 70
2. Find all the other possible totals if two darts are thrown. Answers: 81, 107, 92, 118, 144
3. **Math Talk** How did you find all the possible combinations?

Unit 5, Lesson 9

Activity Note Review the game of darts for children and explain that they want to find all the possible combinations of two darts.

Math Writing Prompt

Write About It Write your own story problem about counting items in a grocery store. Use the numbers 38 and 54. Explain how you solved your problem.

Software Support

Use *MegaMath* for review and reinforcement of the concepts and skills presented in this lesson.

Challenge — Activity Card 5-9

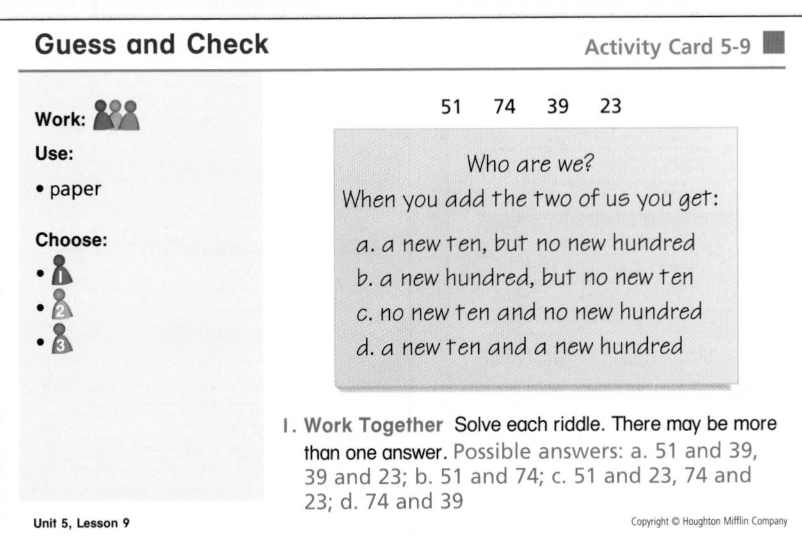

Guess and Check — Activity Card 5-9

Work: (groups)
Use:
- paper

Choose:
- 1
- 2
- 3

51 74 39 23

Who are we?
When you add the two of us you get:
a. a new ten, but no new hundred
b. a new hundred, but no new ten
c. no new ten and no new hundred
d. a new ten and a new hundred

1. **Work Together** Solve each riddle. There may be more than one answer. Possible answers: a. 51 and 39, 39 and 23; b. 51 and 74; c. 51 and 23, 74 and 23; d. 74 and 39

Unit 5, Lesson 9

Activity Note Each group needs to use the four numbers to solve the riddles. Remind children that there may be more than one answer for some riddles.

Math Writing Prompt

Critical Thinking Will there always be a new ten when you add two numbers? Will there ever be two new tens? Explain with examples.

Software Support

Use *Destination Math* to take students beyond the concepts and skills presented in this lesson.

3 Homework and Targeted Practice

Goal: Additional Practice

✓ Include children's completed Homework page as part of their portfolios.

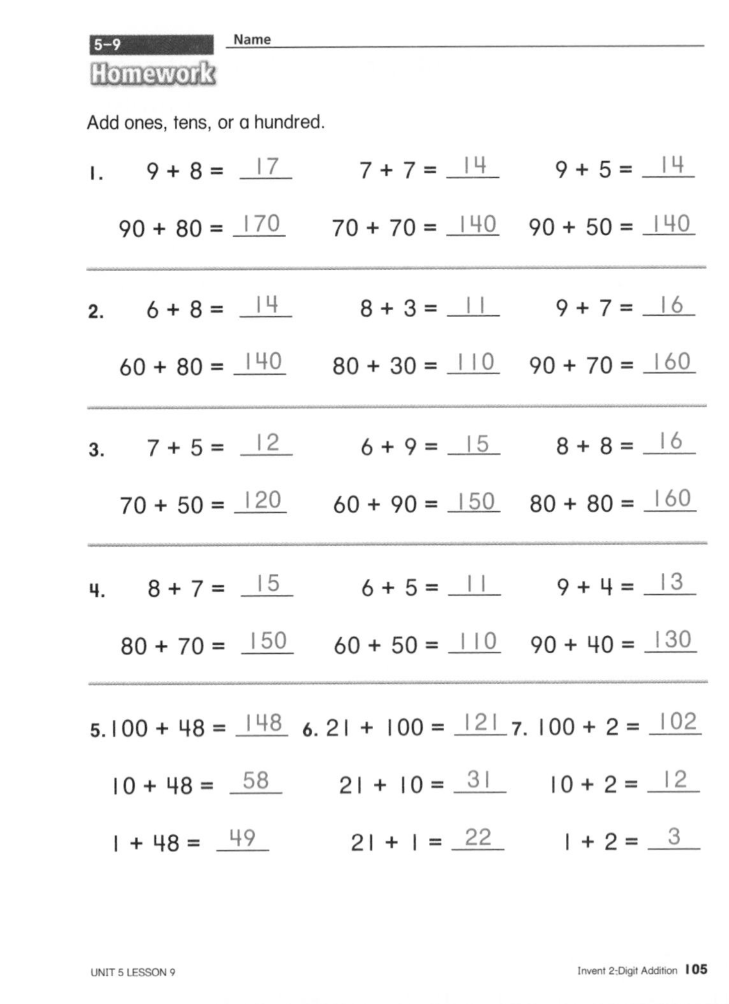

5–9 Homework Name

Add ones, tens, or a hundred.

1. 9 + 8 = 17   7 + 7 = 14   9 + 5 = 14
   90 + 80 = 170   70 + 70 = 140   90 + 50 = 140
2. 6 + 8 = 14   8 + 3 = 11   9 + 7 = 16
   60 + 80 = 140   80 + 30 = 110   90 + 70 = 160
3. 7 + 5 = 12   6 + 9 = 15   8 + 8 = 16
   70 + 50 = 120   60 + 90 = 150   80 + 80 = 160
4. 8 + 7 = 15   6 + 5 = 11   9 + 4 = 13
   80 + 70 = 150   60 + 50 = 110   90 + 40 = 130
5. 100 + 48 = 148   10 + 48 = 58   1 + 48 = 49
6. 21 + 100 = 121   21 + 10 = 31   21 + 1 = 22
7. 100 + 2 = 102   10 + 2 = 12   1 + 2 = 3

UNIT 5 LESSON 9   Invent 2-Digit Addition 105

Homework and Remembering page 105

Goal: Solve story problems.

This page can be used with children who need extra practice in solving addition story problems.

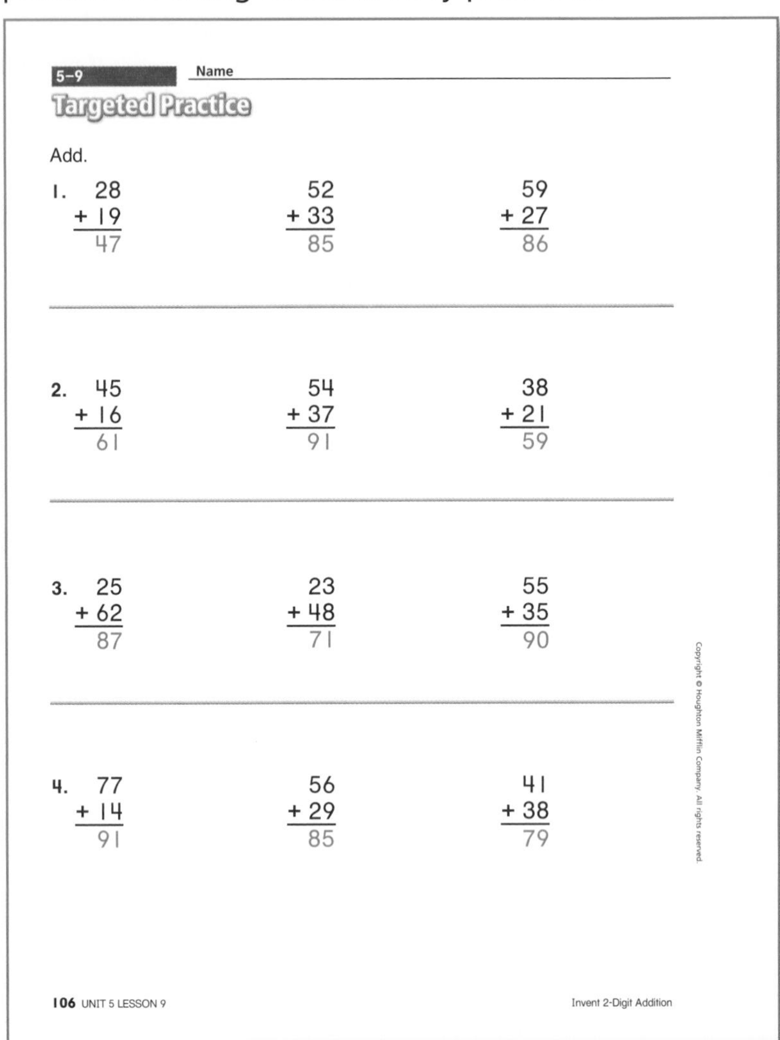

5–9 Targeted Practice Name

Add.

1. 28 + 19 = 47   52 + 33 = 85   59 + 27 = 86
2. 45 + 16 = 61   54 + 37 = 91   38 + 21 = 59
3. 25 + 62 = 87   23 + 48 = 71   55 + 35 = 90
4. 77 + 14 = 91   56 + 29 = 85   41 + 38 = 79

106 UNIT 5 LESSON 9   Invent 2-Digit Addition

Homework and Remembering page 106

Home and School Connection

Family Letter Have children take home the Family Letter on Student Activity Book page 163. This letter explains how the concept of adding 2-digit numbers is developed in *Math Expressions.* It gives parents and guardians a better understanding of the learning that goes on in math class and creates a bridge between school and home. A Spanish translation of this letter is on the following page in the Student Activity Book.

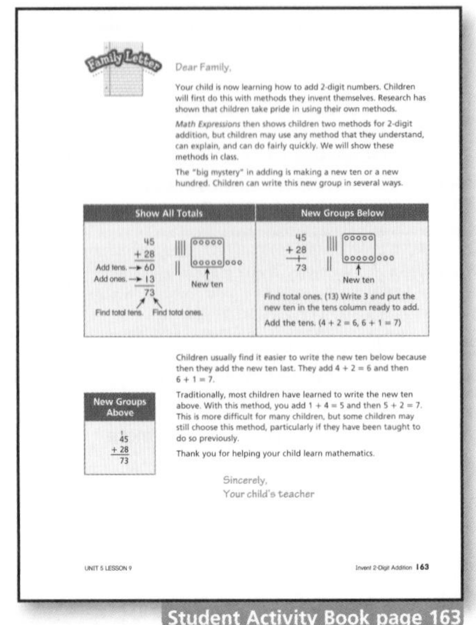

Family Letter

Dear Family,

Your child is now learning how to add 2-digit numbers. Children will first do this with methods they invent themselves. Research has shown that children take pride in using their own methods.

Math Expressions then shows children two methods for 2-digit addition, but children may use any method that they understand, can explain, and can do fairly quickly. We will show these methods in class.

The "big mystery" in adding is making a new ten or a new hundred. Children can write this new group in several ways.

Show All Totals	New Groups Below
45 + 28; Add tens. → 60; Add ones. → 13; 73. Find total tens. Find total ones. New ten	45 + 28 = 73. New ten. Find total ones. (13) Write 3 and put the new ten in the tens column ready to add. Add the tens. (4 + 2 = 6, 6 + 1 = 7)

Children usually find it easier to write the new ten below because then they add the new ten last. They add 4 + 2 = 6 and then 6 + 1 = 7.

New Groups Above: 45 + 28 = 73

Traditionally, most children have learned to write the new ten above. With this method, you add 1 + 4 = 5 and then 5 + 2 = 7. This is more difficult for many children, but some children may still choose this method, particularly if they have been taught to do so previously.

Thank you for helping your child learn mathematics.

Sincerely,
Your child's teacher

UNIT 5 LESSON 9   Invent 2-Digit Addition 163

Student Activity Book page 163

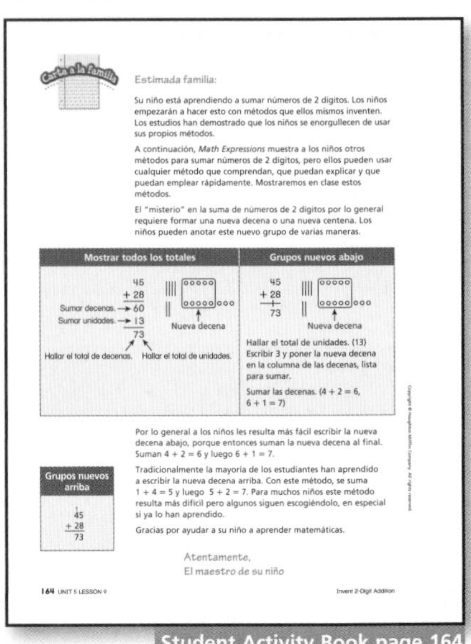

Carta a la familia

Estimada familia:

Su niño está aprendiendo a sumar números de 2 dígitos. Los niños empezarán a hacer esto con métodos que ellos mismos inventen. Los estudios han demostrado que los niños se enorgullecen de usar sus propios métodos.

A continuación, *Math Expressions* muestra a los niños otros métodos para sumar números de 2 dígitos, pero ellos pueden usar cualquier método que comprendan, que puedan explicar y que puedan emplear rápidamente. Mostraremos en clase estos métodos.

El "misterio" en la suma de números de 2 dígitos por lo general requiere formar una nueva decena o una nueva centena. Los niños pueden anotar este nuevo grupo de varias maneras.

Mostrar todos los totales	Grupos nuevos abajo
45 + 28; Sumar decenas. → 60; Sumar unidades. → 13; 73. Hallar el total de decenas. Hallar el total de unidades. Nueva decena	45 + 28 = 73. Nueva decena. Hallar el total de unidades. (13) Escribir 3 y poner la nueva decena en la columna de las decenas, lista para sumar. Sumar las decenas. (4 + 2 = 6, 6 + 1 = 7)

Por lo general a los niños les resulta más fácil escribir la nueva decena abajo, porque entonces suman la nueva decena al final. Suman 4 + 2 = 6 y luego 6 + 1 = 7.

Grupos nuevos arriba: 45 + 28 = 73

Tradicionalmente la mayoría de los estudiantes han aprendido a escribir la nueva decena arriba. Con este método, se suma 1 + 4 = 5 y luego 5 + 2 = 7. Para muchos niños este método resulta más difícil pero algunos siguen escogiéndolo, en especial si ya lo han aprendido.

Gracias por ayudar a su niño a aprender matemáticas.

Atentamente,
El maestro de su niño

164 UNIT 5 LESSON 9   Invent 2-Digit Addition

Student Activity Book page 164

Addition – Show All Totals Method

Lesson Objectives

- Apply addition concepts and strategies to a real-world situation.
- Solve 2-digit addition problems using the Show All Totals method.
- Differentiate between tens and ones in 2-digit addition.

Vocabulary
addends
sum
Show All Totals method

The Day at a Glance

Today's Goals	Materials	
1 Teaching the Lesson Use the Show All Totals method to solve addition story problems that have 2-digit addends and 2- or 3-digit sums. **2 Going Further** ▸ Extra Practice ▸ Differentiated Instruction **3 Homework and Spiral Review**	**Lesson Activities** Student Activity Book pp. 165–166 Homework and Remembering pp. 107–108 MathBoard materials Demonstration Secret Code Cards Secret Code Cards	**Going Further** Activity Cards 5-10 Game Cards MathBoard materials Secret Code Cards Math Journals

Use Math Talk today!

Keeping Skills Sharp

Quick Practice — 5 MINUTES

Goal: Practice counting on or making a ten or hundred to find an unknown partner.

Over a Hundred Write an unknown addition equation on the board. The first partner should be in the nineties. The total should be between 100 and 111. The class explains the two steps to find the unknown partner.

97 + □ = 109

Class: Add 3 to get to 100; then add 9 to get to 109. The unknown partner is 12 because 3 and 9 are 12.

Repeated Quick Practice
Use this Quick Practice from a previous lesson.

- **Tens Talking** (See Unit 5 Lesson 9.)

Daily Routines

Math Mountains for 100 or 2-Digit Numbers Using the MathBoard, Using Dimes and Pennies
(See p. xxvi.)

- Led by Student Leaders

Money Routine Using the 120 Poster, Using the Money Flip Chart, Using the Number Path, Using Secret Code Cards
(See pp. xxiii–xxv.)

- Led by Student Leaders

1 Teaching the Lesson

Activity

The Grocery Store

50 MINUTES

Goal: Use the Show All Totals method to solve addition story problems that have 2-digit addends and 2- or 3-digit sums.

Materials: MathBoard materials, Secret Code Cards (from Unit 1 Lesson 5 or TRB M3–M6), Student Activity Book page 165

NCTM Standards:
Number and Operations
Problem Solving
Representation

Teaching Note

Math Background Many children will invent their own methods for adding 2-digit numbers. Doing so will help their conceptual understanding of addition. Children may continue to use their own methods, but most children, however, benefit from seeing other methods. The two methods shown in this unit help children understand important concepts regarding place value and multi-digit addition.

In the method called Show All Totals, children record the tens and ones separately. Refer to the Secret Code Cards as necessary during this activity (and anytime later). You can use the Demonstration Secret Code Cards at anytime, and some children may need to continue to use their cards.

5-10 Class Activity Name

▶ Show All Totals Method

1. Mr. Green will order 25 jars of grape jelly and 48 jars of strawberry jelly. How many jars of jelly will he order?

73 jars
label

2. Mrs. Green ordered 65 pounds of bananas. That was not enough. So she ordered 29 more pounds. How many pounds did she order altogether?

94 pounds
label

3. Mrs. Green ordered 78 pounds of white rice and 57 pounds of brown rice. How many pounds of rice did she order?

135 pounds
label

4. Mr. Green ordered 49 jars of plain peanut butter and 86 jars of chunky peanut butter. How many jars of peanut butter did he order in all?

135 jars
label

On the Back Use the back of the page to make proof drawings for problems 1–4. Check students' proof drawings.

UNIT 5 LESSON 10 Addition – Show All Totals Method 165

Student Activity Book page 165

▶ Show All Totals Method WHOLE CLASS

Read aloud problem 1 on Student Activity Book page 165. Write the addends in vertical form on the board and direct children to do the same on their MathBoards. Tell children that they will now learn how Mr. Green solves the problem without Secret Code Cards and without drawing sticks and circles.

$$\begin{array}{r} 25 \\ +48 \\ \hline \end{array}$$

Work through the steps at the board as children work on their MathBoards.

Show All Totals Method with Proof Drawings

Step 1: Add the Tens

$$\begin{array}{r} 25 \\ +\ 48 \\ \hline 60 \end{array}$$

- I see 20 inside 25 and 40 inside 48. I add 20 and 40. I add 2 tens and 4 tens.
- There are 2 tens plus 4 tens. How many is that? 6 tens That is the same as saying that 20 and 40 are 60.

60

Step 2: Add the Ones

$$\begin{array}{r} 25 \\ +\ 48 \\ \hline 60 \\ 13 \end{array}$$

- Now I add the ones: 5 plus 8 equals 13.
- What are 5 ones and 8 ones? 13 ones

$3 + 10 = 13$

Step 3: Find the Tens Total

$$\begin{array}{r} 25 \\ +\ 48 \\ \hline 60 \\ 13 \\ \hline 7 \end{array}$$

- Now I add my two totals. First I add the tens: 6 tens and 1 ten are 7 tens.

3 1 ten

6 tens

6 tens + 1 ten = 7 tens
or $60 + 10 = 70$

Step 4: Find the Ones Total

$$\begin{array}{r} 25 \\ +48 \\ \hline 60 \\ 13 \\ \hline 73 \end{array}$$

- Then I add the ones: 0 ones and 3 ones equals 3 ones.

3

0 ones + 3 ones = 3 ones

- The answer is 73, or 7 tens and 3 ones.

Activity continued ▶

Teaching Note

Language and Vocabulary The words *partner* and *total* are child-friendly words that help children relate addition and subtraction. This especially helps with story problems in reducing the confusion between *some* (a partner) and *sum* (the total), especially with **English learners.** However, you should also be using the math terms *addend* and *sum* enough so that children will learn them and be able to use them.

English Language Learners

Tell children that *addend* is another word for partner and *sum* is another word for total. Write 15 + 23 = 38 on the board.

- **Beginning** Ask: **Are 15 and 23 the *addends*?** yes **Is 38 the *sum*?** yes
- **Intermediate** Ask: **Is 15 an *addend* or the *sum*?** addend **What it the *sum*?** 38 Say: **23 is an ___.** addend
- **Advanced Have children tell what the addends and sums are in different equations.**

Teaching the Lesson (continued)

The Learning Classroom

Math Talk

Step by Step at the Board Read, or have a volunteer read problem 2 on Student Activity Book page 165. Invite five children to each present one of the steps of the Show All Totals method to solve the problem. As each child presents and explains a step, the rest of class should follow along at their desks. If the child who is explaining is having difficulty, classmates should offer to help.

Alternate Approach

Add Ones First Children can also show all totals working from right to left, as shown below. However, most children start on the left. Some teachers find that children experiencing difficulty do well with this method.

$$\begin{array}{r} 78 \\ +\ 57 \\ \hline 15 \\ 120 \\ \hline 135 \end{array}$$

Adding Larger Numbers Have a volunteer read aloud problem 3 on Student Activity Book page 165. Write the addends in vertical form on the board and have children to do the same on their MathBoards.

$$\begin{array}{r} 78 \\ +57 \\ \hline \end{array}$$

- The numbers in this problem are greater than those in the first two problems. Do you think Mr. Green's Show All Totals method will work with larger numbers?

Mr. Green's Method: Show All Totals

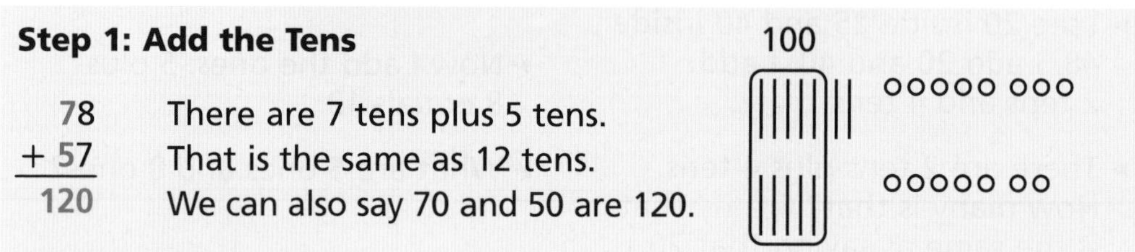

Step 1: Add the Tens

$$\begin{array}{r} 78 \\ +\ 57 \\ \hline 120 \end{array}$$

There are 7 tens plus 5 tens. That is the same as 12 tens. We can also say 70 and 50 are 120.

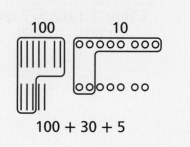

Step 2: Add the Ones

$$\begin{array}{r} 78 \\ +\ 57 \\ \hline 120 \\ 15 \end{array}$$

8 ones and 7 ones are 15 ones.

Step 3: Find the Hundreds Total

$$\begin{array}{r} 78 \\ +\ 57 \\ \hline 120 \\ 15 \\ \hline 1 \end{array}$$

1 hundred and 0 hundreds is 1 hundred.

Step 4: Find the Tens Total

$$\begin{array}{r} 78 \\ +\ 57 \\ \hline 120 \\ 15 \\ \hline 13 \end{array}$$

2 tens and 1 ten are 3 tens, or 20 plus 10 is 30.

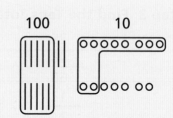

Step 5: Find the Ones Total

$$\begin{array}{r} 78 \\ +\ 57 \\ \hline 120 \\ 15 \\ \hline 135 \end{array}$$

0 ones plus 5 ones equals 5 ones.

Discuss the Show All Totals Method Discuss the advantages of the Show All Totals method. Point out how this method solves the mysterious new ten or new hundred problem.

Copy the addition example as shown below on the board and ask children what is wrong with the way the totals are written.

$$\begin{array}{r} 78 \\ +57 \\ \hline 120 \\ 15\ \ \end{array}$$

To facilitate the discussion, have children explain what each number means in terms of place value. For example, 15 equals 1 ten and 5 ones. Help children realize the importance of putting ones in the ones place, tens in the tens place, and the hundred in the hundreds place.

To further illustrate this point, some children may find it helpful to make the numbers with their Secret Code Cards. When aligned at the right, the cards automatically show place value correctly. Children can count the number of hundreds, tens, and ones to see the correct total.

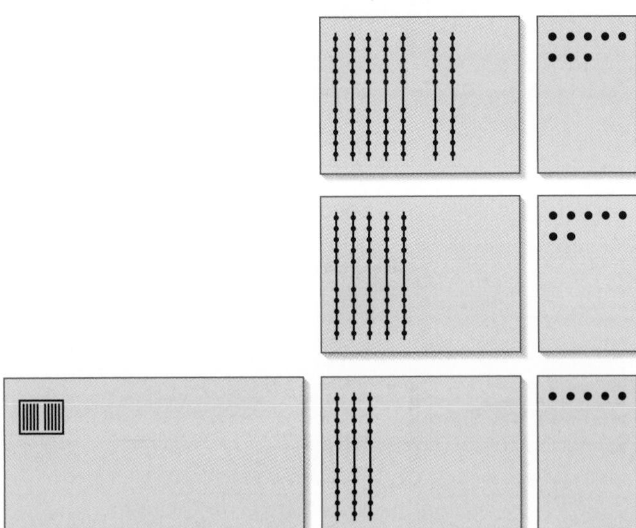

Alternate Approach

Show All Totals Horizontally The Show All Totals method can also be presented horizontally. This involves more writing, but it does allow children to see how a number can be expressed in tens and ones. This method is sometimes called the Expanded Method.

$$\begin{array}{rcrcr} 25 & = & 20 & + & 5 \\ +48 & = & 40 & + & 8 \\ \hline & & 60 & + & 13 = 73 \end{array}$$

$$\begin{array}{rcrcr} 78 & = & 70 & + & 8 \\ +57 & = & 50 & + & 7 \\ \hline & & 120 & + & 15 = 135 \end{array}$$

Ongoing Assessment

Observe children as they solve problem 4. Check that they are representing the digits 4 and 8 as 4 tens and 8 tens, or 40 and 80. Be sure children understand that the digits 9 and 6 represent 9 ones and 6 ones.

- ► We know that 4 plus 8 equals 12. So why do we write the total in this problem as 120?
- ► When we add 9 plus 6, why don't we write the total as 150?

2 Going Further

Extra Practice

Goals: Practice addition (totals to 100), practice mystery addition and subtraction (totals ≤ 18).

Materials: MathBoard materials, Addition, Subtraction, and Mystery Addition Count-On cards, Addition and Subtraction Make-a-Ten Cards

NCTM Standards:
Number and Operations
Representation

▶ How to Play the *Number Path Race* PAIRS

The object of the game is to be the first player to go completely around the Number Path on the MathBoard.

Choose which sets of cards (from the Count-On and Make-a-Ten cards) that you would like the children to use. Children shuffle the cards and place them in a stack with the answer side face down.

Each player has a game board—his or her own Number Path. Players alternate turns. The player looks at the top card and says the missing total or partner. The player then checks the answer by turning the card over. If the player is correct, the player adds that number of circles to his or her Number Path. The child writes the horizontal addition: Starting Number + Number from Card = New Number. The child then draws a bar after the new number. The 10-groups on the Number Path help children see the make-a-ten process. (If a player does not give the correct answer to the exercise on the front of the card, play passes to the other player.)

The example below shows how a player's game board might look after four turns.

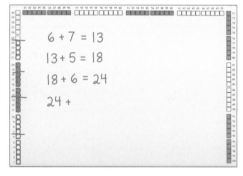

After each turn, the player returns the card to the bottom of the stack. The first player to get a total of 100 or more is the winner.

You can have children repeat this game throughout the year.

▶ Using a Variation of the *Number Path Race* PAIRS

Before beginning the game, each player designs a game board for the other player. They do this by placing the following *hazards* and *helps* on their opponent's game board.

− T	Lose 1 turn.
+ T	Take an extra turn.
+ 10	Go ahead 10.
− 10	Go back 10.

First Player's Game Board

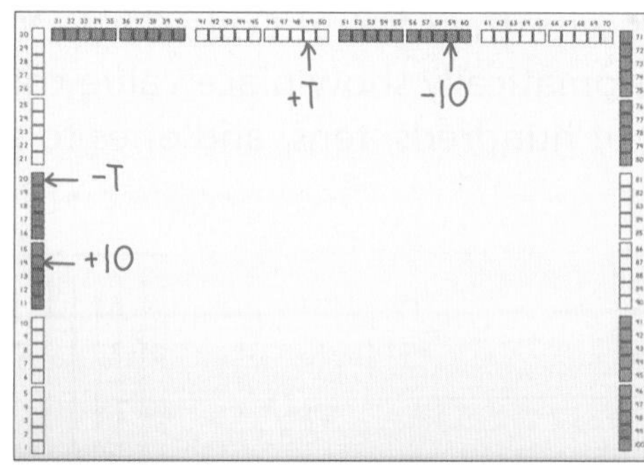

Second Player's Game Board

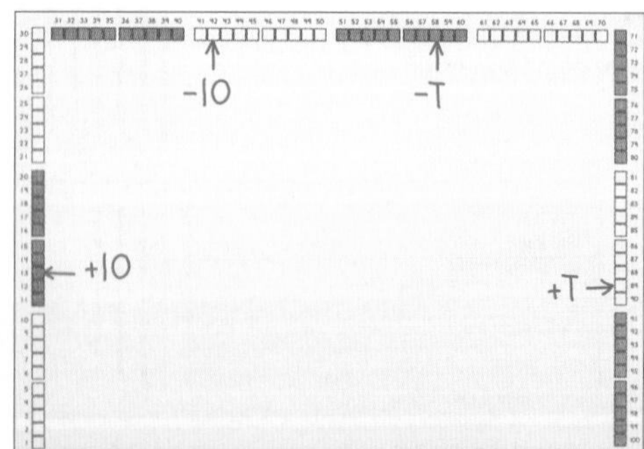

The game is then played in the same way as the original game except that if a player's total is on a *hazard* or a *help*, the player loses or gains a turn, or goes ahead or back 10.

After children have played the game several times, you may wish to suggest other *hazards* and *helps* such as +9 or −9.

Intervention Activity Card 5-10

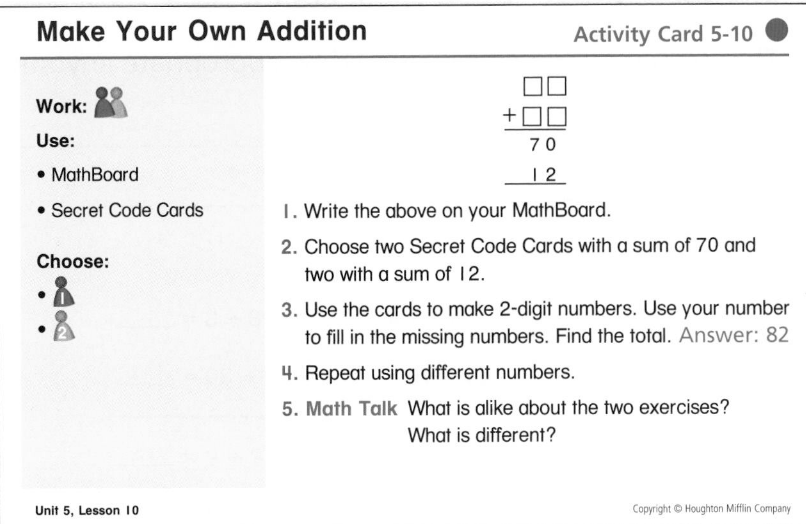

Make Your Own Addition Activity Card 5-10 ●

Work: pairs
Use:
- MathBoard
- Secret Code Cards

Choose:
- 1
- 2

□□
+□□
70
12

1. Write the above on your MathBoard.
2. Choose two Secret Code Cards with a sum of 70 and two with a sum of 12.
3. Use the cards to make 2-digit numbers. Use your number to fill in the missing numbers. Find the total. Answer: 82
4. Repeat using different numbers.
5. Math Talk What is alike about the two exercises? What is different?

Unit 5, Lesson 10

Activity Note Each pair needs MathBoard materials and one set of Secret Code Cards (TRB M3–M6). Remind children to check their work.

Math Writing Prompt

Explain Your Thinking Explain the steps you would take to add 35 and 47.

Software Support

Use *Soar to Success* for instruction of students needing targeted support for underlying skills.

On Level Activity Card 5-10

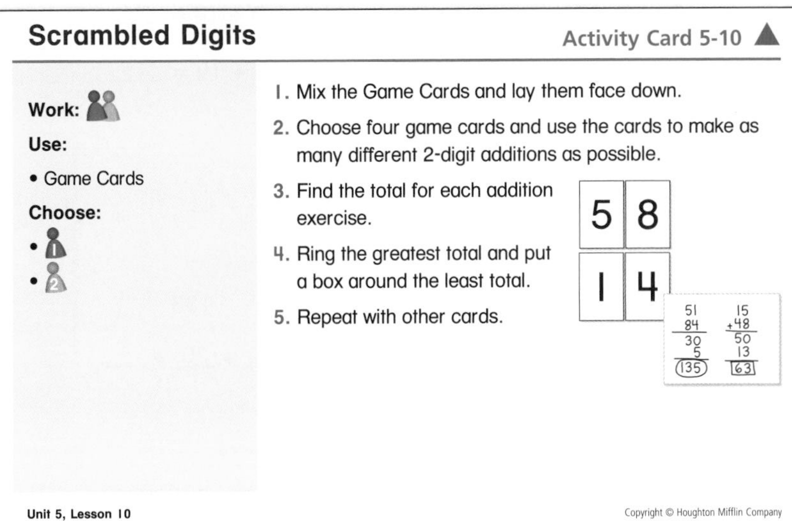

Scrambled Digits Activity Card 5-10 ▲

Work: pairs
Use:
- Game Cards

Choose:
- 1
- 2

1. Mix the Game Cards and lay them face down.
2. Choose four game cards and use the cards to make as many different 2-digit additions as possible.
3. Find the total for each addition exercise.
4. Ring the greatest total and put a box around the least total.
5. Repeat with other cards.

5 8
1 4

51 + 84: 30, 5, (135)
15 + 48: 50, 13, [63]

Unit 5, Lesson 10

Activity Note Each pair needs 1 set of Game Cards (TRB M23). Ask children how they know they found all possible 2-digit numbers.

Math Writing Prompt

Predict Tell how to predict whether 26 + 57 will be more or less than 100. Don't find the exact total.

Software Support

Use *MegaMath* for review and reinforcement of the concepts and skills presented in this lesson.

Challenge Activity Card 5-10

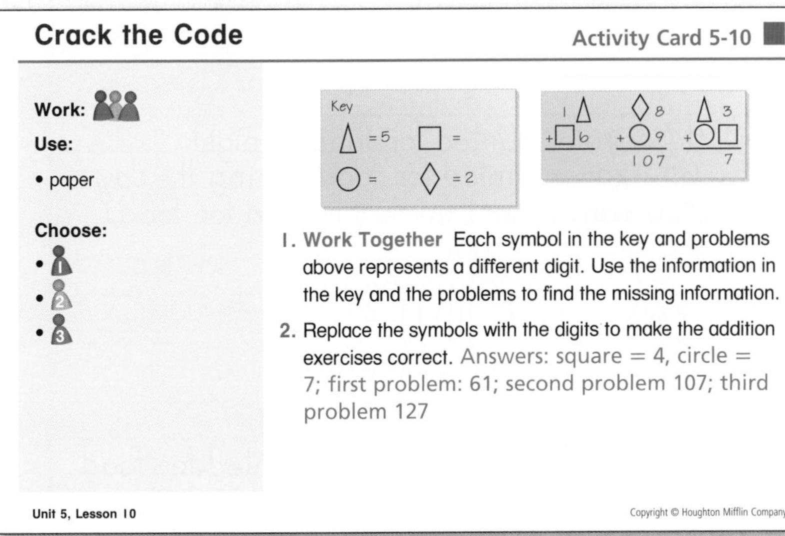

Crack the Code Activity Card 5-10 ■

Work: groups
Use:
- paper

Choose:
- 1
- 2
- 3

Key: △ = 5, □ =, ○ =, ◇ = 2

1△ + □6; ◇8 + ○9 = 107; △3 + ○□ = 7

1. Work Together Each symbol in the key and problems above represents a different digit. Use the information in the key and the problems to find the missing information.
2. Replace the symbols with the digits to make the addition exercises correct. Answers: square = 4, circle = 7; first problem: 61; second problem 107; third problem 127

Unit 5, Lesson 10

Activity Note Groups need to try different combinations until they solve all three problems.

Math Writing Prompt

Predict and Verify Which two of these totals will be equal? Explain how you can predict without finding all three totals. Then check.
67 + 84, 68 + 74, 55 + 87.

Software Support

Use *Destination Math* to take students beyond the concepts and skills presented in this lesson.

3 Homework and Spiral Review

Goal: Additional Practice

✓ Include children's completed Homework page as part of their portfolios.

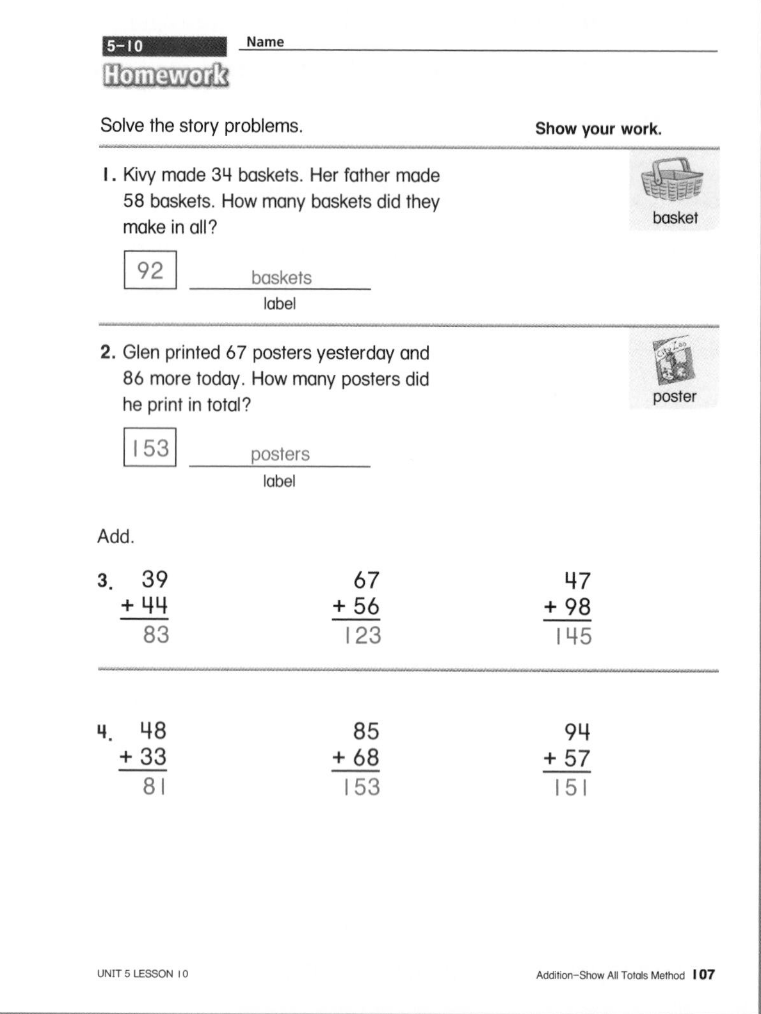

5–10 Homework Name

Solve the story problems. **Show your work.**

1. Kivy made 34 baskets. Her father made 58 baskets. How many baskets did they make in all?

basket

92 baskets
label

2. Glen printed 67 posters yesterday and 86 more today. How many posters did he print in total?

poster

153 posters
label

Add.

3. 39 + 44 = 83 67 + 56 = 123 47 + 98 = 145

4. 48 + 33 = 81 85 + 68 = 153 94 + 57 = 151

UNIT 5 LESSON 10 Addition–Show All Totals Method **107**

Homework and Remembering page 107

Goal: Spiral Review

This Remembering activity would be appropriate anytime after today's lesson.

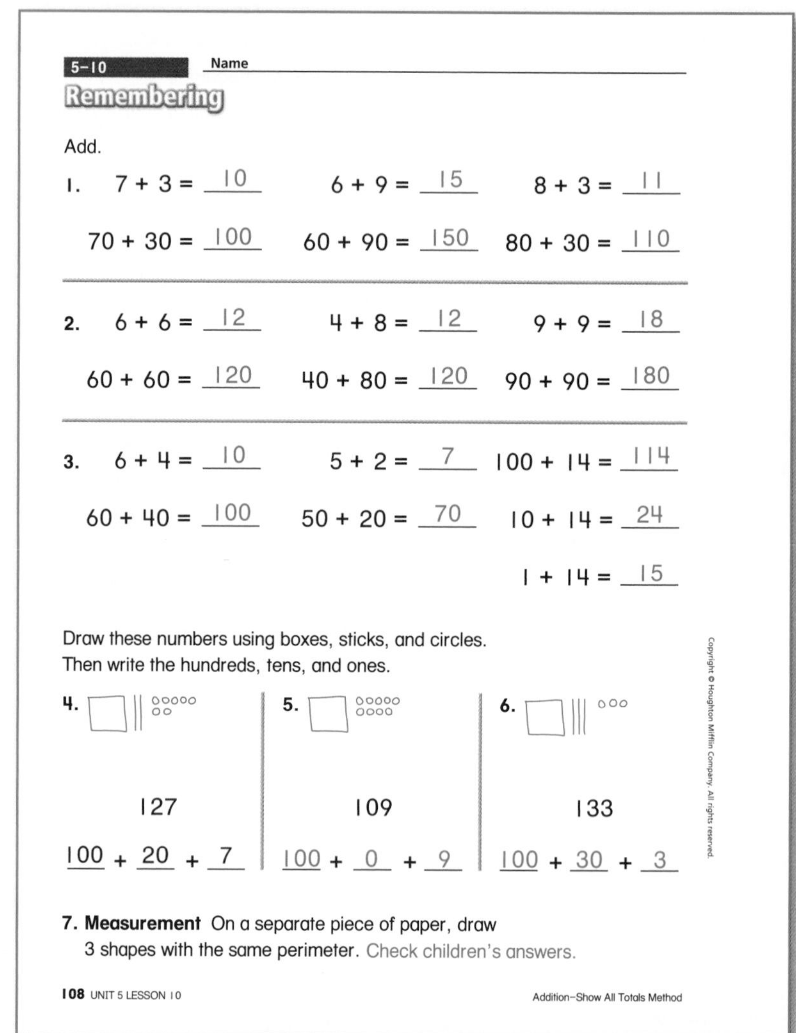

5–10 Remembering Name

Add.

1. 7 + 3 = 10 6 + 9 = 15 8 + 3 = 11
70 + 30 = 100 60 + 90 = 150 80 + 30 = 110

2. 6 + 6 = 12 4 + 8 = 12 9 + 9 = 18
60 + 60 = 120 40 + 80 = 120 90 + 90 = 180

3. 6 + 4 = 10 5 + 2 = 7 100 + 14 = 114
60 + 40 = 100 50 + 20 = 70 10 + 14 = 24
1 + 14 = 15

Draw these numbers using boxes, sticks, and circles. Then write the hundreds, tens, and ones.

4. 127
100 + 20 + 7

5. 109
100 + 0 + 9

6. 133
100 + 30 + 3

7. **Measurement** On a separate piece of paper, draw 3 shapes with the same perimeter. Check children's answers.

108 UNIT 5 LESSON 10 Addition–Show All Totals Method

Homework and Remembering page 108

Home or School Activity

Science Connection

Animals in the Desert Have children research animals that live in the desert. Then have them use the information to write and illustrate an addition story problem about desert animals. The total for the story problem should be greater than 100.

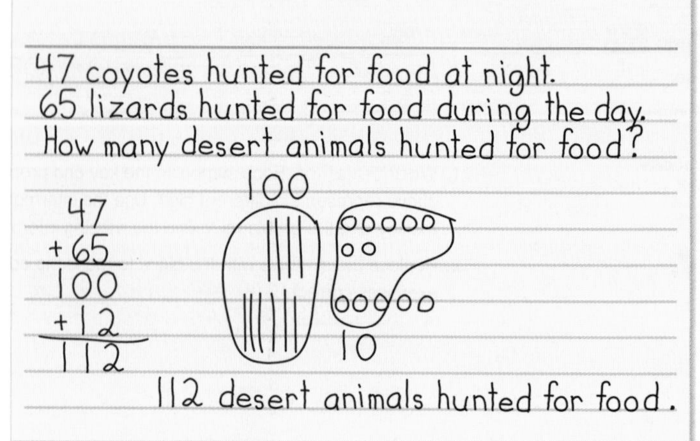

47 coyotes hunted for food at night.
65 lizards hunted for food during the day.
How many desert animals hunted for food?
47
+65
100
+12
112
100
10
112 desert animals hunted for food.

Addition – New Groups Below Method

Lesson Objectives

- Solve 2-digit addition exercises using the New Groups Below method.
- Differentiate tens and ones in 2-digit addition.

Vocabulary

New Groups Below method

The Day at a Glance

Today's Goals	Materials	
1 Teaching the Lesson **A1:** Introduce the New Groups Below method. **A2:** Practice the New Groups Below method.	**Lesson Activities** Student Activity Book pp. 167–168 Homework and Remembering pp. 109–110 MathBoard materials	**Going Further** Activity Cards 5-11 Homework and Remembering p. 110 Connecting cubes MathBoard materials Index cards Math Journals
2 Going Further ► Math Connection: Round to Estimate Sums ► Differentiated Instruction		
3 Homework and Targeted Practice		

Use Math Talk today!

Keeping Skills Sharp

Quick Practice — 5 MINUTES

Goals: Find unknown partners for teen totals. Practice addition (totals >10).

Materials: Green Make-a-Ten Cards (addition) (from Unit 1 Lesson 13 or TRB M35–M38)

Teen Unknown Addition Flash While the Make-a-Ten Cards are being distributed at the beginning of Quick Practice and collected at the end, have a **Student Leader** direct the class in Teen Unknown Addition Flash. Have a Student Leader call out a teen total and one partner. The class then flashes the unknown partner. (See Unit 5 Lesson 4.)

Addition Make-a-Ten Cards Children practice with the Green Make-a-Ten Cards (addition) individually or with a partner. Explain that they are practicing for Secret Code Card races and a Quick Check.

Repeated Quick Practice Use this Quick Practice from a previous lesson.

- **Over a Hundred** (See Unit 5 Lesson 10.)

Daily Routines

Math Mountains for 100 or 2-Digit Numbers Using the MathBoard, Using Dimes and Pennies (See p. xxvi.)

- Led by Student Leaders

Money Routine Using the 120 Poster, Using the Money Flip Chart, Using the Number Path, Using Secret Code Cards (See pp. xxiii–xxv.)

- Led by Student Leaders

1 Teaching the Lesson

Activity 1

Introduce the New Groups Below Method

 25 MINUTES

Goal: Introduce the New Groups Below method.

Materials: MathBoard materials

 **NCTM Standards:**
Number and Operations
Representation

Teaching Note

Research The New Groups Below method of 2-digit addition is a clear and understandable approach that is a minor variation of the common U.S. algorithm New Groups Above. The only difference is that the new ten is written below the tens column rather than above. This makes addition easier because children can add the 1 extra ten after they have totaled the other numbers in the tens column. When the new ten is written above, children usually add it to the top number, remember that number, and add the new unseen number to the bottom number. Writing the new ten below also makes it easier to see the teen total. For instance, in Step 1 of the class example, you can see the 15 that is the total of 6 and 9.

If children have not done this method in class before, be sure to show and discuss it at the end of the day. Ask children to compare it to the New Groups Below. Be sure that they see how much easier it is to add with New Groups Below. On the other hand, if children already can use New Groups Above and can explain it, allow them to continue using it.

$$\begin{array}{r} {\scriptstyle 1} \\ 36 \\ +\ 49 \\ \hline \mathbf{85} \end{array}$$

▶ Addition with Totals Less than 100 WHOLE CLASS

Introduce Mrs. Green's addition method, called the New Groups Below method.

- Mrs. Green likes to add numbers a different way from Mr. Green. She likes to start on the right. She adds the ones first and then adds the tens on the left. Let's do an addition exercise together to show how she does it.

New Groups Below Method

Step 1: Add the Ones

$$\begin{array}{r} 36 \\ +\ 4\underset{1}{}9 \\ \hline 5 \end{array}$$

Add the ones first. There are 6 ones and 9 ones. That is 15. We know 15 is 1 ten and 5 ones. Write the 1 ten on the line in the tens column. It will be waiting when we get to the tens. Write the 5 ones in the ones column where it belongs.

Mrs. Green's Proof Drawings

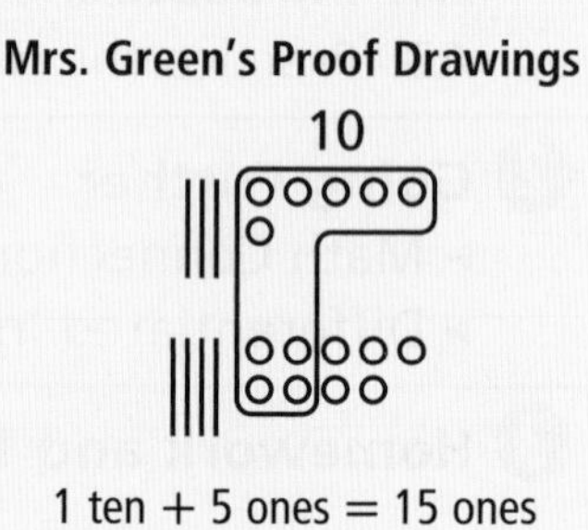

1 ten + 5 ones = 15 ones

Step 2: Add the Tens

$$\begin{array}{r} 36 \\ +\ 4\underset{1}{}9 \\ \hline 85 \end{array}$$

Now add the tens. There are 3 tens and 4 tens. That is 7 tens. And one more ten below to make 8 tens. The answer is 85.

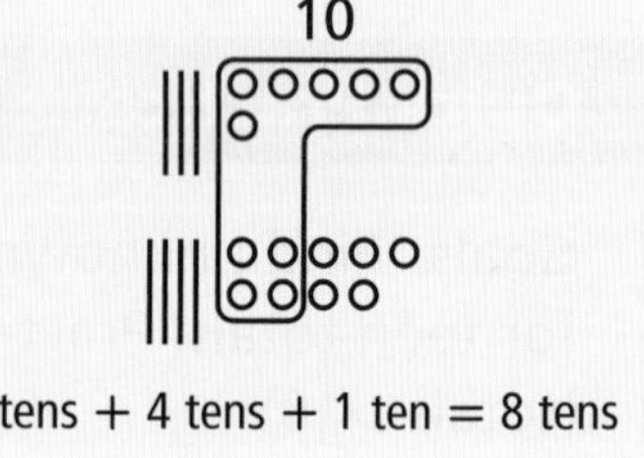

3 tens + 4 tens + 1 ten = 8 tens

Discuss how the New Groups Below method solves the problem of the "mysterious new ten."

Step-by-Step at the Board Invite two children to come to the board. Present a new addition exercise that requires grouping, such as 26 + 58. Each child at the board should explain one step. The rest of the class should do the indicated step on their MathBoards at their seats.

Then have children add two numbers that do not require grouping, such as 32 + 54, and have them discuss how the steps differ this time.

▶ Addition with Totals Greater than 100 WHOLE CLASS

Now present children with an example that will have a total greater than 100. Discuss how to add these numbers using the New Groups Below method. Be sure children keep the places aligned and that their explanations include correct hundreds, tens, and ones language. They should make a Proof Drawing for each step.

Step 1: Add the Ones

$$\begin{array}{r} 89 \\ +\ 64 \\ \hline {}^{1}\ \\ 3 \end{array}$$

Proof Drawing

1 ten + 3 ones = 13 ones

Step 2: Add the Tens

$$\begin{array}{r} 89 \\ +\ 64 \\ \hline {}^{1\,1} \\ 53 \end{array}$$

Proof Drawing

8 tens + 6 tens + 1 ten = 15 tens = 1 hundred and 5 tens

Step 3: Add the Hundreds

$$\begin{array}{r} 89 \\ +\ 64 \\ \hline {}^{1\,1} \\ 153 \end{array}$$

Proof Drawing

1 hundred plus 0 hundred = 1 hundred
The answer is 153.

Discuss how the New Groups Below method solves the problem of the "mysterious new hundred."

Ongoing Assessment

Have children look at the following example.

$$\begin{array}{r} 28 \\ +\ 45 \\ \hline {}^{1}\ \\ 73 \end{array}$$

▶ Why do we write a 1 below the 4?

▶ We know that 2 tens plus 4 tens is 6 tens, so why do we write a 7 in the tens place of the answer?

English Language Learners

Review *above* and *below*. Point to things around the classroom.

- **Beginning** Ask: **Is the clock *above* or *below* your desks?**
- **Intermediate and Advanced** Have children say what things in the classroom are *above* and *below* their desks/heads/knees.

Activity 2

Practice the New Groups Below Method

▶ Work Together to Find Totals PAIRS

Write the examples on the board. Have children work in **Helping Pairs** on their MathBoards. Have pairs explain their methods.

$$\begin{array}{r} 57 \\ +\ 38 \\ \hline \end{array} \qquad \begin{array}{r} 67 \\ +\ 87 \\ \hline \end{array} \qquad \begin{array}{r} 73 \\ +\ 21 \\ \hline \end{array} \qquad \begin{array}{r} 87 \\ +\ 62 \\ \hline \end{array}$$

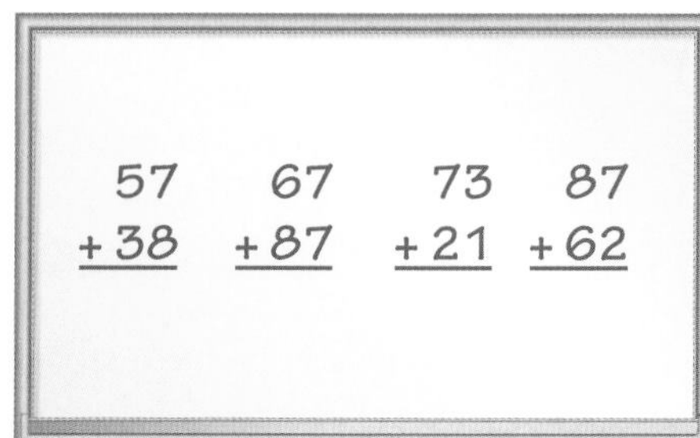

Some examples do not require children to make a new ten or a new hundred. Discuss these if these exercises cause difficulty.

25 MINUTES

Goal: Practice the New Groups Below method.

Materials: MathBoard materials

NCTM Standard:
Number and Operations

2 Going Further

Math Connection: Round to Estimate Sums

Goal: Estimate the total of 2-digit numbers by rounding to the nearest ten.

Materials: Student Activity Book pages 167–168

 **NCTM Standards:**
Number and Operations
Representation

▶ Introduce Estimating Sums WHOLE CLASS

Have children look at the number lines at the top of Student Activity Book page 167. Briefly review how to round numbers to the nearest ten. Remind children that they must round up if a number is exactly in the middle of two tens. (See Going Further, Unit 5 Lesson 5.)

Discuss the example in the blue box. Point out to children that they are being asked for an estimate. Be sure they understand this means that their answer will not be the exact total of 41 and 25. Their answer will be a decade number that tells *about* how much the total is.

▶ Practice Estimating Sums

 PAIRS **Math Talk** 

Have children work individually to find the estimates in exercises 1–6. Then pairs should take turns explaining to each other how they rounded the numbers and then added them to estimate the total.

Critical Thinking

- When you round two numbers and then find the total, is the answer always the same as when you add the numbers then round the total? Sample response: No. For example, 34 + 24 = 58, which rounds to 60. But when you round the numbers first, the estimate is 30 + 20 = 50.
- When you round two numbers up, how does the estimate compare to the exact total? The estimate is greater than the total. What if you round two numbers down? The estimate is less than the total. What if you round one number up and the other number down? The estimate might be greater than, less than, or equal to the total.

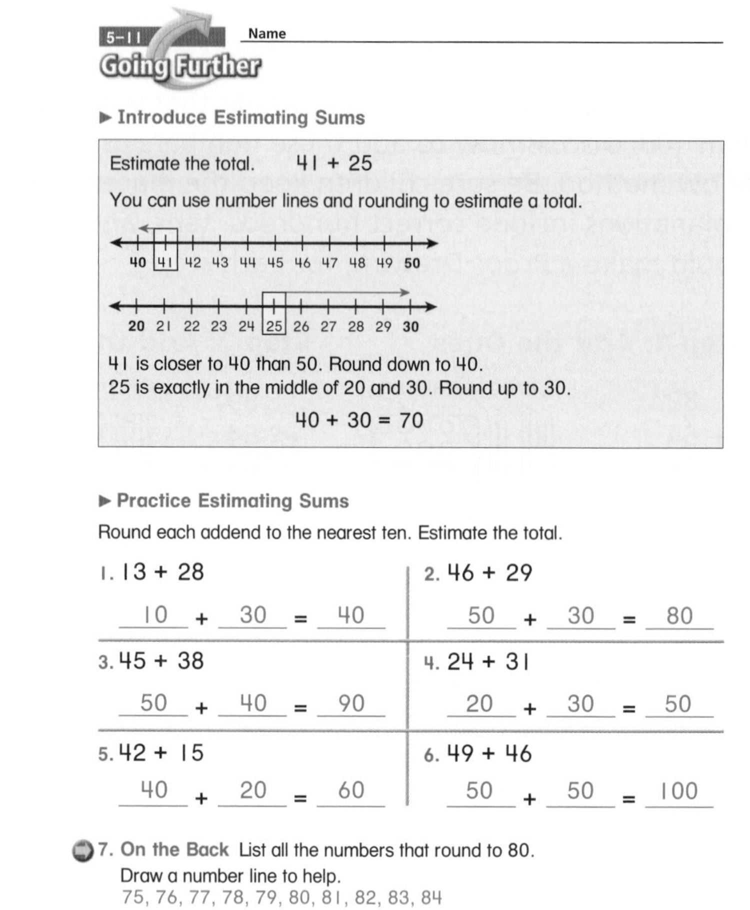
5-11 Going Further Name

▶ Introduce Estimating Sums

Estimate the total. 41 + 25

You can use number lines and rounding to estimate a total.

41 is closer to 40 than 50. Round down to 40.
25 is exactly in the middle of 20 and 30. Round up to 30.

40 + 30 = 70

▶ Practice Estimating Sums

Round each addend to the nearest ten. Estimate the total.

1. 13 + 28 — 10 + 30 = 40
2. 46 + 29 — 50 + 30 = 80
3. 45 + 38 — 50 + 40 = 90
4. 24 + 31 — 20 + 30 = 50
5. 42 + 15 — 40 + 20 = 60
6. 49 + 46 — 50 + 50 = 100
7. On the Back List all the numbers that round to 80. Draw a number line to help. 75, 76, 77, 78, 79, 80, 81, 82, 83, 84

UNIT 5 LESSON 11 Addition – New Groups Below Method 167

Student Activity Book page 167

Teaching Note

Math Background When it is not necessary to find the exact total of two numbers, an estimate can be used. There are several ways to estimate a total, but the most commonly used method is to round each number to a specific place and add the rounded numbers.

Intervention Activity Card 5-11

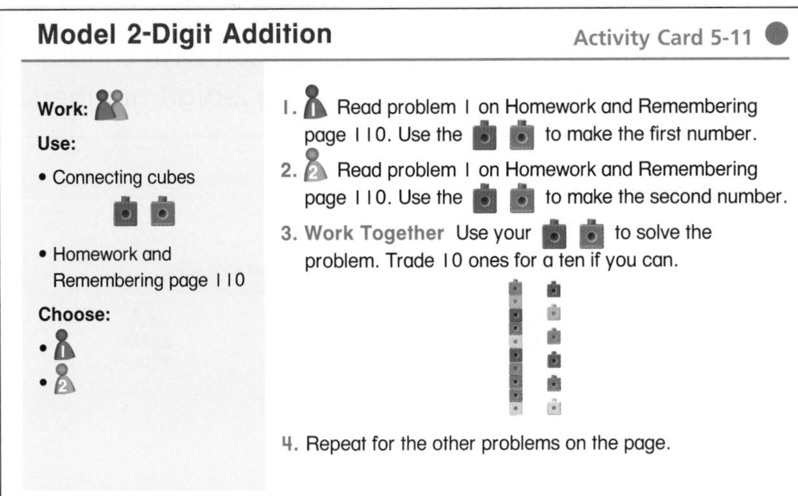

Model 2-Digit Addition

Activity Card 5-11

Work: Pairs

Use:

- Connecting cubes
- Homework and Remembering page 110

Choose:

- Student 1
- Student 2

1. Student 1 Read problem 1 on Homework and Remembering page 110. Use the cubes to make the first number.
2. Student 2 Read problem 1 on Homework and Remembering page 110. Use the cubes to make the second number.
3. **Work Together** Use your cubes to solve the problem. Trade 10 ones for a ten if you can.
4. Repeat for the other problems on the page.

Unit 5, Lesson 11

Activity Note Each pair needs 20 single connecting cubes, 3 towers of ten cubes, and Homework and Remembering p. 110. Review trading ones for a ten.

Math Writing Prompt

Write a Rule How can you tell by looking at two numbers that there will be a new ten in their total? Write a rule.

Software Support

Use *Soar to Success* for instruction of students needing targeted support for underlying skills.

On Level Activity Card 5-11

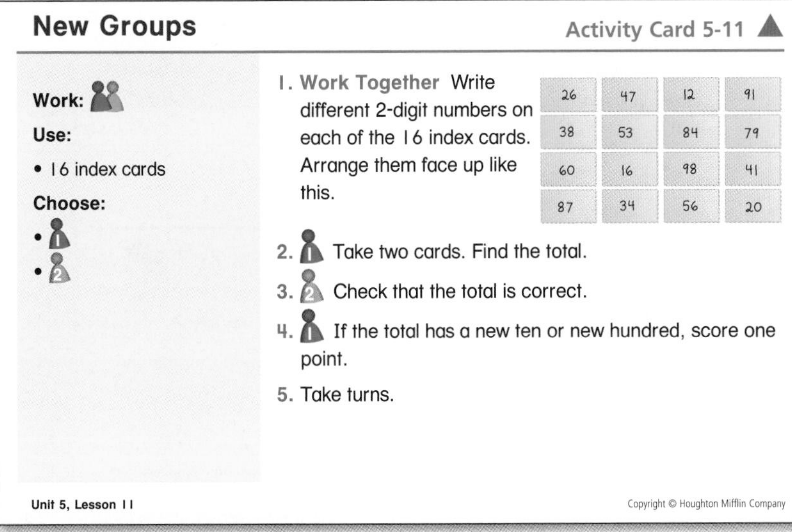

New Groups

Activity Card 5-11

Work: Pairs

Use:

- 16 index cards

Choose:

- Student 1
- Student 2

1. **Work Together** Write different 2-digit numbers on each of the 16 index cards. Arrange them face up like this.

26	47	12	91
38	53	84	79
60	16	98	41
87	34	56	20

2. Student 1 Take two cards. Find the total.
3. Student 2 Check that the total is correct.
4. Student 1 If the total has a new ten or new hundred, score one point.
5. Take turns.

Unit 5, Lesson 11

Activity Note Each pair needs 16 index cards. Check that children write different 2-digit numbers on each index card. You may want to have calculators available.

Math Writing Prompt

Explain Your Thinking You add a number with 9 ones and a number with 4 ones. Will there always be a new ten or a new hundred? Use an example to explain.

Software Support

Use *MegaMath* for review and reinforcement of the concepts and skills presented in this lesson.

Challenge Activity Card 5-11

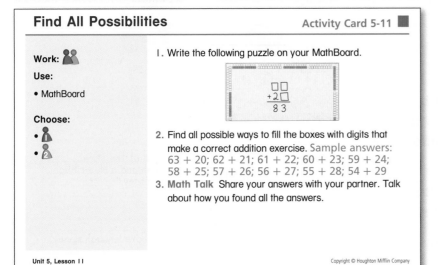

Find All Possibilities

Activity Card 5-11

Work: Pairs

Use:

- MathBoard

Choose:

- Student 1
- Student 2

1. Write the following puzzle on your MathBoard.

$$\begin{array}{r} \square\square \\ +2\square \\ \hline 83 \end{array}$$

2. Find all possible ways to fill the boxes with digits that make a correct addition exercise. Sample answers: 63 + 20; 62 + 21; 61 + 22; 60 + 23; 59 + 24; 58 + 25; 57 + 26; 56 + 27; 55 + 28; 54 + 29
3. **Math Talk** Share your answers with your partner. Talk about how you found all the answers.

Unit 5, Lesson 11

Activity Note Each pair needs MathBoard materials. Have children work independently to find all possible combinations that work in the puzzle.

Math Writing Prompt

Mental Math You know that 28 + 40 = 68. How can you use what you know to quickly add 28 + 39? Explain.

Software Support

Use *Destination Math* to take students beyond the concepts and skills presented in this lesson.

Homework and Targeted Practice

5-11 **Homework** **Goal:** Additional Practice

Include children's completed Homework page as part of their portfolio.

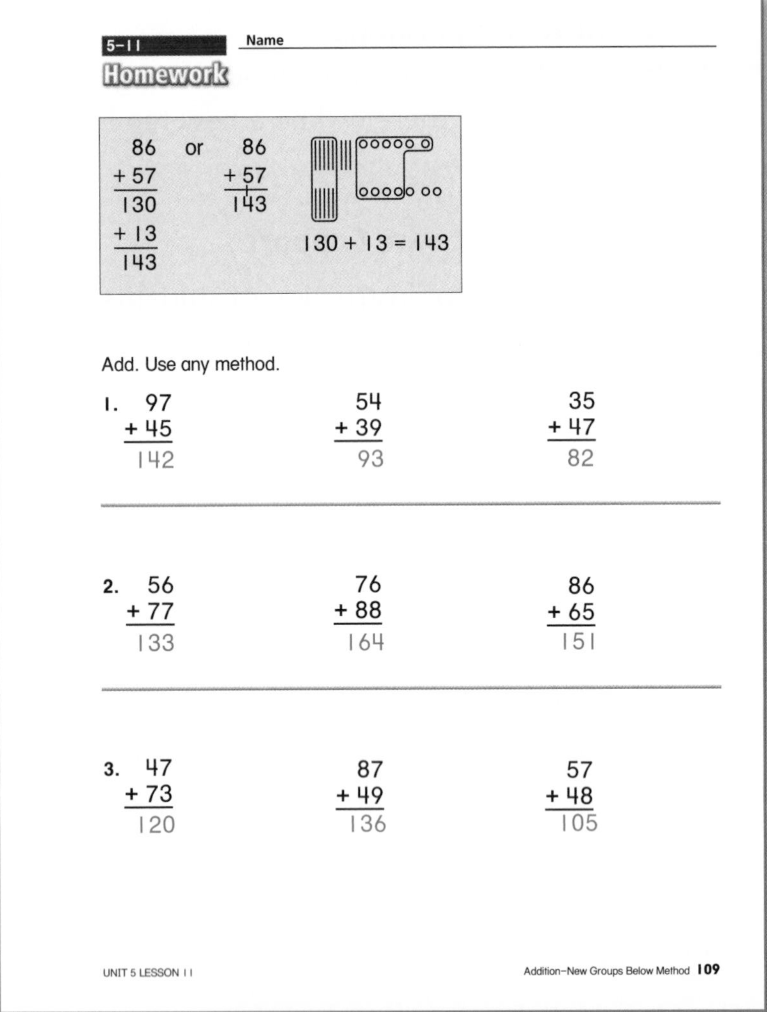

5-11 Homework Name

86 + 57 = 130, 130 + 13 = 143 or 86 + 57 = 143

130 + 13 = 143

Add. Use any method.

1. 97 + 45 = 142   54 + 39 = 93   35 + 47 = 82

2. 56 + 77 = 133   76 + 88 = 164   86 + 65 = 151

3. 47 + 73 = 120   87 + 49 = 136   57 + 48 = 105

UNIT 5 LESSON 11   Addition–New Groups Below Method **109**

Homework and Remembering page 109

5-11 **Targeted Practice** **Goal:** Add 2-digit numbers.

This Targeted Practice page can be used with children who need extra practice with adding 2-digit numbers.

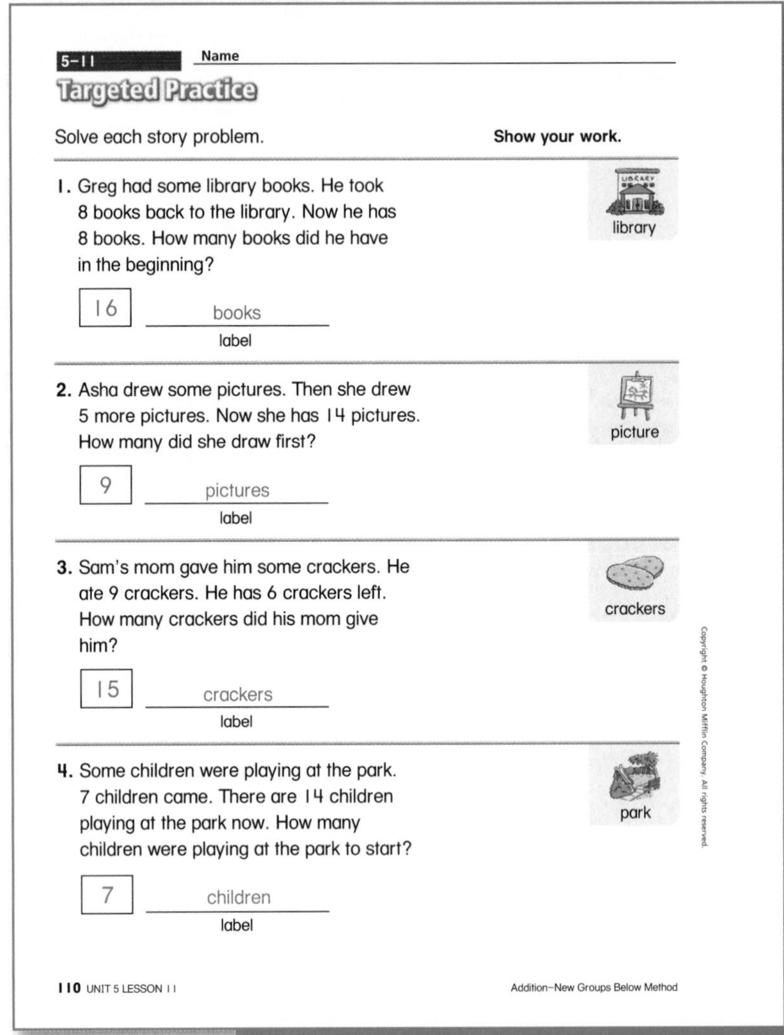

5-11 Targeted Practice Name

Solve each story problem. **Show your work.**

1. Greg had some library books. He took 8 books back to the library. Now he has 8 books. How many books did he have in the beginning?

16 books (label)

2. Asha drew some pictures. Then she drew 5 more pictures. Now she has 14 pictures. How many did she draw first?

9 pictures (label)

3. Sam's mom gave him some crackers. He ate 9 crackers. He has 6 crackers left. How many crackers did his mom give him?

15 crackers (label)

4. Some children were playing at the park. 7 children came. There are 14 children playing at the park now. How many children were playing at the park to start?

7 children (label)

110 UNIT 5 LESSON 11   Addition–New Groups Below Method

Homework and Remembering page 110

Home or School Activity

Real-World Connection

Items for Sale Gather several small items, such as a comb, button, or plant. Have children label each item with a price tag. The amount written on each tag should be a 2-digit number less than 45¢.

Have children select two of the items. Children then write and solve an addition story problem about the two items they chose.

Children can repeat the activity using two different items.

I have 75¢ to spend at the store.
I want to buy a brush and a blue ribbon.
Do I have enough money?

37¢ + 15¢ = 52¢ Yes, I have enough money.

Practice Addition with Totals over 100

Lesson Objectives

- Use a preferred method to solve 2-digit addition exercises.
- Differentiate between ones, tens, and hundreds in 2-digit addition exercises.
- Add 2-digit numbers with totals greater than 100.

The Day at a Glance

Today's Goals	Materials	
1 Teaching the Lesson Use a preferred method to solve 2-digit addition exercises.	**Lesson Activities** Student Activity Book pp. 169–170 Homework and Remembering pp. 111–112	**Going Further** Activity Cards 5-12 Homework and Remembering p. 111 Place Value Charts (TRB M65) MathBoard materials Math Journals
2 Going Further ▶ Differentiated Instruction		
3 Homework and Spiral Review		

Use Math Talk today!

Keeping Skills Sharp

Quick Practice — 5 MINUTES

Goal: Find unknown partners for teen totals. Practice addition (totals >10).

Materials: Green Make-a-Ten Cards (addition) (from Unit 1 Lesson 13 or TRB M35–M38)

Teen Unknown Partner Addition Flash While the Make-a-Ten Cards are being distributed at the beginning of Quick Practice and collected at the end, have a **Student Leader** direct the class in Teen Unknown Partner Addition Flash. The procedure is the same as for Teen Addition Flash. (See Unit 5 Lesson 4.)

Have a Student Leader call out a teen total and one partner. The class then flashes the unknown partner.

Addition Make-a-Ten Cards Children practice with the Green Make-a-Ten Cards (addition) individually or with a partner. Explain that they are practicing for Secret Code Card races and a Quick Check.

Repeated Quick Practice Use this Quick Practice from a previous lesson.

- ▶ **Over a Hundred** (See Unit 5 Lesson 10.)

Daily Routines

Math Mountains for 100 or 2-Digit Numbers Using the MathBoard, Using Dimes and Pennies (See p. xxvi.)

- ▶ Led by Student Leaders

Money Routine Using the 120 Poster, Using the Money Flip Chart, Using the Number Path, Using Secret Code Cards (See pp. xxiii–xxv.)

- ▶ Led by Student Leaders

1 Teaching the Lesson

Activity

Solve and Discuss

 **50 MINUTES**

Goal: Use a preferred method to solve 2-digit addition exercises.

Materials: Student Activity Book page 169

 **NCTM Standards:**
Number and Operations
Representation

Math Talk in Action

How did you solve the problem?

Will: I used the New Groups Below method.

```
  39
+ 97
 11
 136
```

Daria: I used the same method. Then I made a proof drawing to check my work.

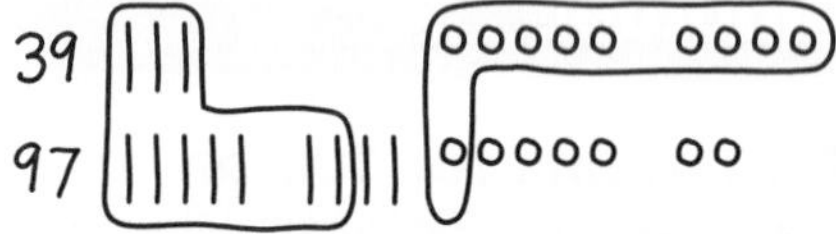

English Language Learners

Review the terms for the 3 addition methods. Write an example of each method on the board. Point to each one and ask: **Did I write the new groups above or below? Did I show all totals? What method is this?** Make sure children correctly name each method.

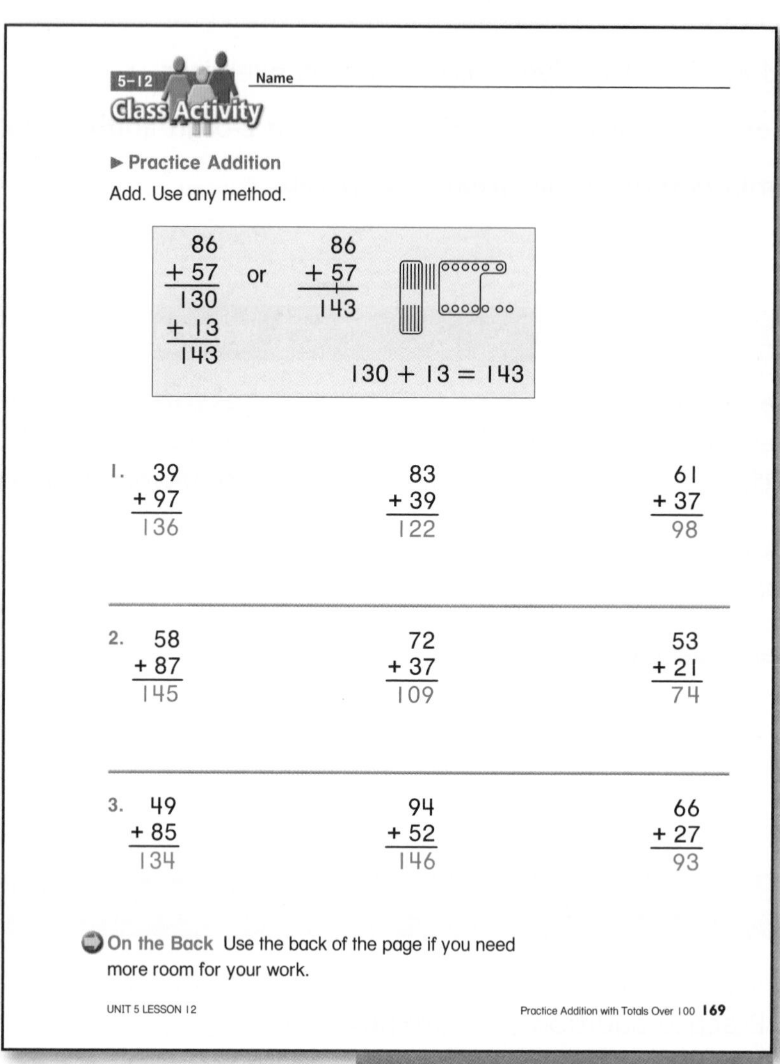

5-12 Class Activity Name

▶ Practice Addition

Add. Use any method.

86 + 57 = 130, 130 + 13 = 143 or 86 + 57 = 143

130 + 13 = 143

1. 39 + 97 = 136	83 + 39 = 122	61 + 37 = 98
2. 58 + 87 = 145	72 + 37 = 109	53 + 21 = 74
3. 49 + 85 = 134	94 + 52 = 146	66 + 27 = 93

On the Back Use the back of the page if you need more room for your work.

UNIT 5 LESSON 12 Practice Addition with Totals Over 100 **169**

Student Activity Book page 169

▶ Practice and Share WHOLE CLASS

Elicit word problems for the problem 86 + 57. Using the **Solve and Discuss** structure, have children find the totals in exercise 1 on Student Activity Book page 169. Send to the board children who will use different methods so all can be discussed. Then have children solve the rest of the problems in some combination of working independently, in **Helping Partners,** or **Small Groups.**

For at least 2 problems, have children explain their method to a partner or small group. Their listeners should help them explain clearly. Children can use any method they can explain.

While children share story problems, you might want to work at the board with a group of children who need help on exercises 2 and 3.

2 Going Further

Differentiated Instruction

Intervention — Activity Card 5-12

Use a Place Value Chart

Activity Card 5-12 ●

Work: 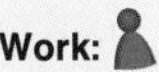

Use:

- Place Value Charts
- Homework and Remembering page 111

1. Look at problem 1 on Homework and Remembering page 111.
2. Write the numbers in the first place value chart on the Place Value Charts page.

	Hundreds	Tens	Ones
		8	3
+		7	9
	1	6	2

3. Use the place value chart to help you find the answer.
4. Copy the answer onto Homework and Remembering page 111.
5. Repeat for other problems.

Unit 5, Lesson 12

Activity Note Each child needs Place Value Charts (TRB M65) and Homework and Remembering p. 111. Help children use the place value charts to solve problems.

Math Writing Prompt

Write a Rule When you look at two numbers, how do you know if the total will be greater than 100?

Software Support

Use *Soar to Success* for instruction of students needing targeted support for underlying skills.

On Level — Activity Card 5-12

Make 100

Activity Card 5-12 ▲

Work: (group)

Use:

- paper

Choose:

- 1
- 2
- 3

□□ + □□ = 100

1. **Work Together** Find at least ten different ways to fill in the boxes using the digits 1–9. You can use the same digit more than once. Sample answers: 32 + 68; 82 + 18; 47 + 53; 22 + 78; 64 + 36; 15 + 85; 79 + 21; 61 + 39; 58 + 42; 35 + 65
2. Write a rule that tells how to use the digits 1–9 to make two 2-digit numbers with a total of exactly 100. Sample answer: Make the total of the ones digits equal 10. Make the total of the tens digits equal 9.

Unit 5, Lesson 12

Activity Note Each group needs to work together to find ten ways to use the digits 1–9 to make 100.

Math Writing Prompt

Create a Problem Write a story problem that you can solve by using this addition exercise. 97 + 86. Show how to solve your problem.

Software Support

Use *MegaMath* for review and reinforcement of the concepts and skills presented in this lesson.

Challenge — Activity Card 5-12

Addition Tic Tac Toe

Activity Card 5-12 ■

Work: (pair)

Use:

- MathBoard

Choose:

- 1
- 2

Side			
53, 85	147	173	132
94, 68	179	153	138
79	164	121	162

1. Copy the Tic Tac Toe game onto the MathBoard.
2. (1) Add two numbers from the side. If the total is on the board, mark an X on the space. If the total is not there, do nothing.
3. (2) Add two numbers from the side. If the total is on the board, mark an O on the space, if there is no mark there. If the total is not there, do nothing.
4. Play until one player gets three totals in a line. If no one gets three in a row, no one wins.

Unit 5, Lesson 12

Activity Note Each pair needs MathBoard materials. Explain that children can only put a mark on an empty space.

Math Writing Prompt

Mental Math You know that 100 + 57 = 157. How can you use what you know to add 57 + 98? Explain.

Software Support

Use *Destination Math* to take students beyond the concepts and skills presented in this lesson.

3 Homework and Spiral Review

Goal: Additional Practice

This Homework page provides practice in 2-digit addition.

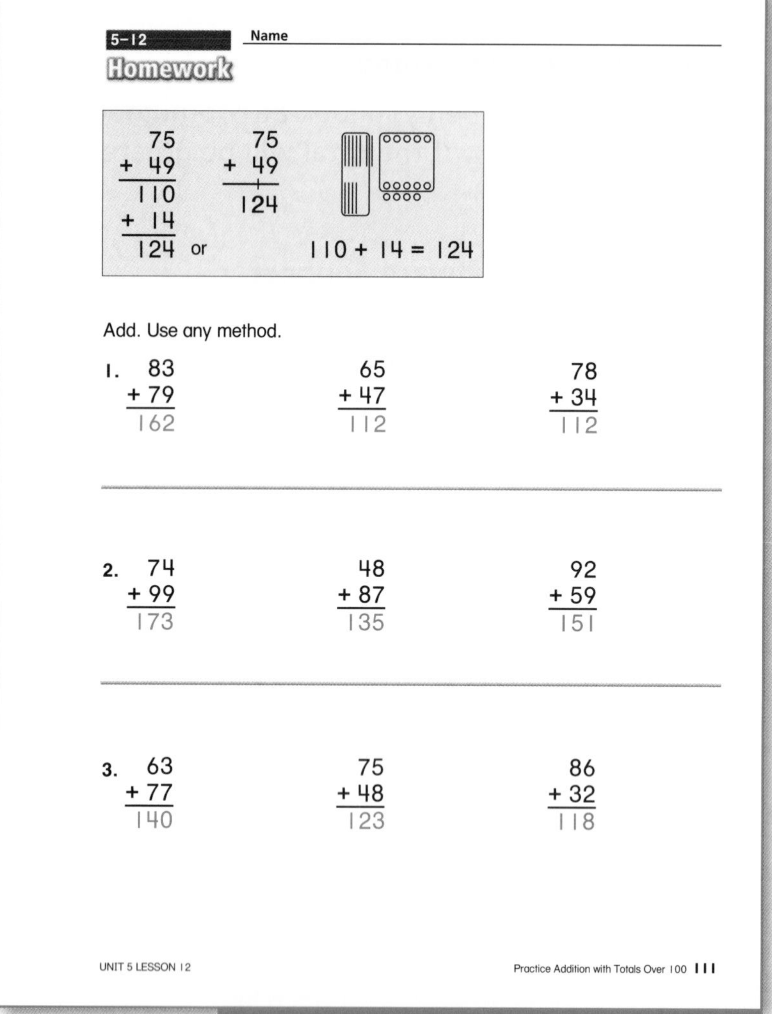

5-12 Homework

Name

75 + 49 = 110, 110 + 14 = 124 or	75 + 49 = 124	110 + 14 = 124

Add. Use any method.

1. 83 + 79 = 162   65 + 47 = 112   78 + 34 = 112

2. 74 + 99 = 173   48 + 87 = 135   92 + 59 = 151

3. 63 + 77 = 140   75 + 48 = 123   86 + 32 = 118

UNIT 5 LESSON 12   Practice Addition with Totals Over 100   111

Homework and Remembering page 111

Goal: Spiral Review

This Remembering activity would be appropriate anytime after today's lesson.

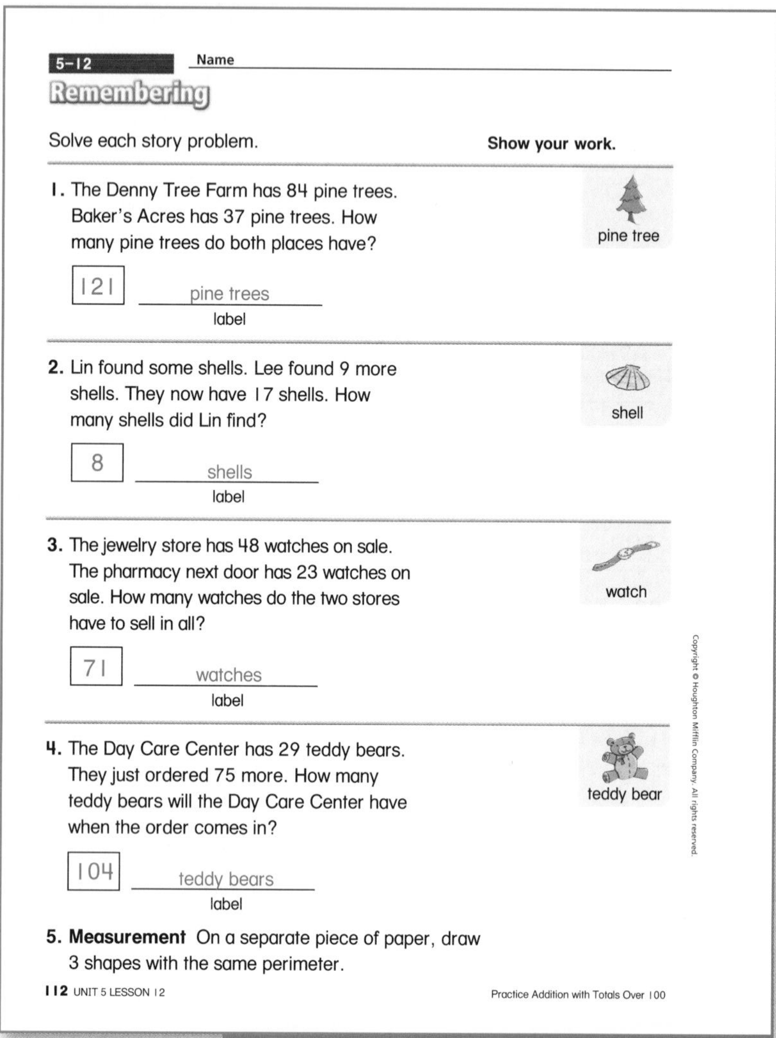

5-12 Remembering

Name

Solve each story problem. **Show your work.**

1. The Denny Tree Farm has 84 pine trees. Baker's Acres has 37 pine trees. How many pine trees do both places have?
   121 pine trees (label)
2. Lin found some shells. Lee found 9 more shells. They now have 17 shells. How many shells did Lin find?
   8 shells (label)
3. The jewelry store has 48 watches on sale. The pharmacy next door has 23 watches on sale. How many watches do the two stores have to sell in all?
   71 watches (label)
4. The Day Care Center has 29 teddy bears. They just ordered 75 more. How many teddy bears will the Day Care Center have when the order comes in?
   104 teddy bears (label)
5. **Measurement** On a separate piece of paper, draw 3 shapes with the same perimeter.

112 UNIT 5 LESSON 12   Practice Addition with Totals Over 100

Homework and Remembering page 112

Home or School Activity

Science Connection

Ant Habitat Have children research information about ants and draw an underground habitat for over 100 ants.

Have the child choose two partners with a total greater than 100 and draw an ant group to represent each partner. (Children may draw black dots to represent each ant and should loop each group of 10.)

Children then write an addition equation to match their drawing.

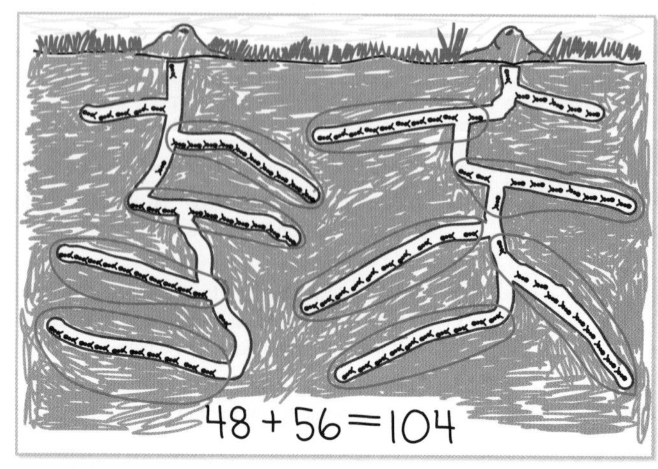

Choose an Addition Method

Lesson Objectives

- Compare and contrast various solution methods for 2-digit addition.
- Recognize, discuss, and correct common 2-digit addition errors.

Vocabulary

error

The Day at a Glance

Today's Goals	Materials	
1 Teaching the Lesson **A1:** Find totals for 1-digit partners. **A2:** Discuss advantages and disadvantages of the various ways to add. **A3:** Find and correct addition errors and discuss ways to avoid making errors.	**Lesson Activities** Student Activity Book pp. 171–172 Homework and Remembering pp. 113–114 Chart paper	**Going Further** Activity Cards 5-13 Spinners (TRB M27) 10 × 10 Grid (TRB M61) Paper clips Math Journals
2 Going Further ▶ Differentiated Instruction		
3 Homework and Targeted Practice		

123 Use Math Talk today!

Keeping Skills Sharp

Quick Practice — 5 MINUTES

Goals: Find unknown partners for teen totals. Practice addition (totals >10).

Materials: Green Make-a-Ten Cards (addition)

Teen Unknown Addition Flash While the Make-a-Ten Cards are being distributed at the beginning of the Quick Practice and collected at the end, have a Student Leader call out a teen total and one addend. The class then flashes the unknown addend. (See Unit 5 Lesson 11.)

Student Leader: 7 and 15!
Children: (flash 8 fingers)

Addition Make-a-Ten Cards Children practice with the Green Make-a-Ten Cards (addition) individually or with a partner. Explain that they are practicing for Secret Code Card races and a Quick Check.

Repeated Quick Practice
Use this Quick Practice from a previous lesson.

▶ **Over a Hundred** (See Unit 5 Lesson 10.)

Daily Routines

Math Mountains for 100 or 2-Digit Numbers Using the MathBoard, Using Dimes and Pennies
(See p. xxvi.)

▶ Led by Student Leaders

Money Routine Using the 120 Poster, Using the Money Flip Chart, Using the Number Path, Using Secret Code Cards
(See pp. xxiii–xxv.)

▶ Led by Student Leaders

1 Teaching the Lesson

Activity 1

Addition Sprint

 5 MINUTES

Goal: Find totals for 1-digit partners.

Materials: Student Activity Book page 171

 **NCTM Standard:**
Number and Operations

English Language Learners

Children may not understand the word *sprint*. Provide examples and act out if necessary.

- **Beginning** Say: **A *sprint* is very fast but short run.**
- **Intermediate** Say: ***Sprint* is another word for run. When you *sprint* you run very fast but not very far.**
- **Advanced** Give children the definition above for *sprint*. Say: **Now we will do a math *sprint*. Is this activity going to take a long time?** no

Class Management

There are many ways to administer the Addition Sprint, and procedures should vary according to specific classroom needs. You may choose to allow children an unlimited amount of time to complete the activity.

Teaching Note

Write 39 + 46 vertically on the board. Ask a child to explain the Make-a-Ten method for adding 9 + 6. Discuss how thinking of 9 + 6 as 10 + 5 gives you the new ten to write somewhere in your problem and the 5 ones to write in the ones column. Suggest that using Make-a-Ten when you're adding multi-digit numbers can be faster than counting on.

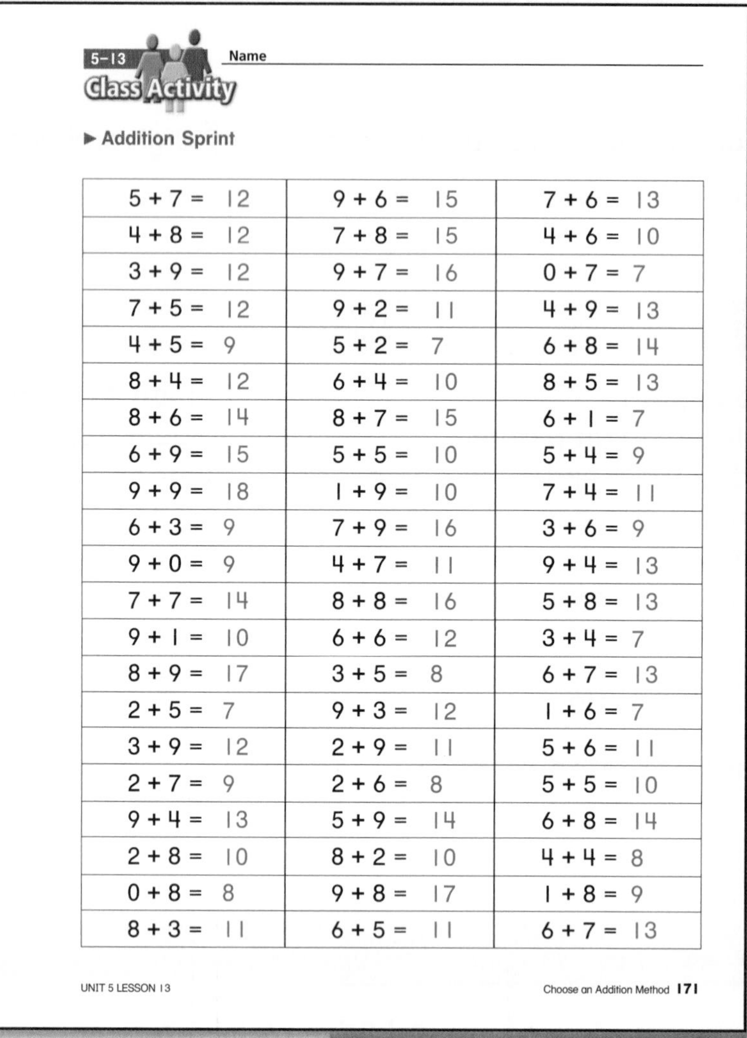
5-13 Class Activity Name

▶ Addition Sprint

5 + 7 = 12	9 + 6 = 15	7 + 6 = 13
4 + 8 = 12	7 + 8 = 15	4 + 6 = 10
3 + 9 = 12	9 + 7 = 16	0 + 7 = 7
7 + 5 = 12	9 + 2 = 11	4 + 9 = 13
4 + 5 = 9	5 + 2 = 7	6 + 8 = 14
8 + 4 = 12	6 + 4 = 10	8 + 5 = 13
8 + 6 = 14	8 + 7 = 15	6 + 1 = 7
6 + 9 = 15	5 + 5 = 10	5 + 4 = 9
9 + 9 = 18	1 + 9 = 10	7 + 4 = 11
6 + 3 = 9	7 + 9 = 16	3 + 6 = 9
9 + 0 = 9	4 + 7 = 11	9 + 4 = 13
7 + 7 = 14	8 + 8 = 16	5 + 8 = 13
9 + 1 = 10	6 + 6 = 12	3 + 4 = 7
8 + 9 = 17	3 + 5 = 8	6 + 7 = 13
2 + 5 = 7	9 + 3 = 12	1 + 6 = 7
3 + 9 = 12	2 + 9 = 11	5 + 6 = 11
2 + 7 = 9	2 + 6 = 8	5 + 5 = 10
9 + 4 = 13	5 + 9 = 14	6 + 8 = 14
2 + 8 = 10	8 + 2 = 10	4 + 4 = 8
0 + 8 = 8	9 + 8 = 17	1 + 8 = 9
8 + 3 = 11	6 + 5 = 11	6 + 7 = 13

UNIT 5 LESSON 13 Choose an Addition Method 171

Student Activity Book page 171

▶ Addition Sprint INDIVIDUALS

Direct children's attention to Student Activity Book page 171. Decide how much time to give them to complete the Addition Sprint. Explain the procedure and time limit to them.

Children will do this Sprint several more times during the year. You may want to have children save their papers and make note of their progress.

Watch your less-advanced children as they solve the sprint to see if any of them are still counting all. If so, work with them later to move them to use counting on instead. Discuss at the end of the sprint how many children are starting to use Make-a-Ten when they are adding in multi-digit addition.

Activity 2

Favorite Addition Methods

▶ Discuss 2-Digit Addition Methods WHOLE CLASS

Lead a discussion on the advantages and disadvantages of addition methods. Ask children to compile a list of all the 2-digit addition methods they know. List the methods on the board, along with an example if necessary (See a sample list in the side column). You may need to assign a name to each method. If children have created their own methods, use a descriptive name, or name them after the children themselves. For example, you might refer to Sam's method or Rosa's method.

As children compare methods, have them consider how well each method helps them see the new ten and new hundred.

Math Talk

- Here we have our list of methods to use when we solve 2-digit addition. Each method has advantages. Those are the good things about it. A method might have disadvantages too. Those are the things that are not good, or things that cause problems.
- What are the advantages of using the first method on our list? Does the method have any disadvantages or things you don't like about it? What are they? Answers may vary. Accept all appropriate answers that children can explain.

Favorite 2-Digit Addition Methods Take a brief survey of the class, polling the children to see which methods they can actually do. Children should raise their hands for every method they can use and explain.

Now, take another survey and read down the list and have children vote for their *favorite* method. Each child should only vote once. Determine which method received the most votes and help children explain the reasons.

 **20 MINUTES**

Goal: Discuss advantages and disadvantages of the various ways to add.

Materials: Chart paper

✓ **NCTM Standards:**
Number and Operations
Representation

Possible 2-Digit Addition Methods

1. Show All Totals
2. New Groups Below
3. New Groups Above

Activity 3

Recognize and Correct Errors

▶ Discuss Common Errors in 2-Digit Addition

WHOLE CLASS

Discuss the kinds of errors children might make as they add 2-digit numbers. If children have trouble generating a list of common errors, you may wish to present yourself as Mrs. (or Ms. or Mr.) Mistake. Add two numbers on the board and make an error you have observed

Activity continued ▶

 **30 MINUTES**

Goal: Find and correct addition errors and discuss ways to avoid making errors.

 **NCTM Standards:**
Number and Operations
Representation

The Learning Classroom

Building Concepts Children may find it helpful to give each error a short, descriptive name so they can refer to it easily in their discussions. For example, making an unnecessary ten (see chart to the right) might be called the extra ten error because the ten is not really there.

Emphasize using Proof Drawings to check the answer and to show any new ten or hundred that was created as a result of grouping.

Notice the last 3 drawings on the right. Some children make their new ten by connecting their ones with a short stick. They say it looks like another ten so it is easier to count their new ten. For children who forget to count their new ten group, suggest this way of making their ten group to see if it helps.

Ongoing Assessment

Have children look at the following addition exercises.

$$\begin{array}{r} 95 \\ +\ 68 \\ \hline 153 \end{array} \qquad \begin{array}{r} 95 \\ +\ 62 \\ \hline 157 \end{array}$$

- ▶ One of the totals is not correct. Which one is it?
- ▶ What mistake do you think was made?
- ▶ How can you find the correct total?

children making. Children should recognize the error and suggest ways to correct it. Have them pay special attention to what went wrong and how they may avoid the problem in the future. (See the chart below for common 2-digit addition errors.)

Recognize Common Errors The chart below shows the most common errors children make when learning 2-digit addition. The examples given here show totals under 100, but the principles apply to all such problems. Address these and any other errors you have noticed in the class activities or homework.

Common 2-Digit Addition Errors

Make an unnecessary new ten

$$\begin{array}{r} 32 \\ +\ 25 \\ \hline 67 \end{array}$$

There are not enough loose ones to make a new ten, but a ten is recorded nonetheless.

Ignore the new ten

$$\begin{array}{r} 38 \\ +\ 25 \\ \hline 53 \end{array}$$

There are enough loose ones to make a new ten, but it is ignored and not recorded.

Put the tens in the answer

$$\begin{array}{r} 38 \\ +\ 25 \\ \hline 513 \end{array}$$

There are enough loose ones to make a new ten. The new ten gets written as part of the answer.

Confuse the tens and ones

$$\begin{array}{r} {}^{3}\ \ \\ 38 \\ +\ 25 \\ \hline 81 \end{array}$$

There are enough loose ones to make a ten. The ones, however, are added to the tens column, and the ten is recorded below the ones column.

Record the tens with the ones

$$\begin{array}{r} {}^{1} \\ 38 \\ +\ 25 \\ \hline 54 \end{array}$$

There are enough loose ones to make a ten. The new ten is recorded in the ones column and added to the ones.

Samples of Correct Proof Drawings

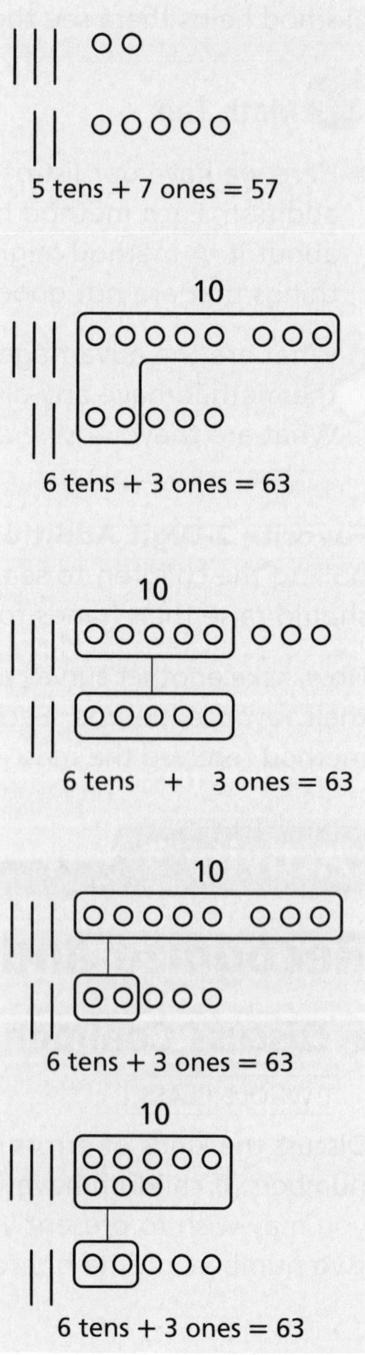

2 Going Further

Differentiated Instruction

Intervention — Activity Card 5-13

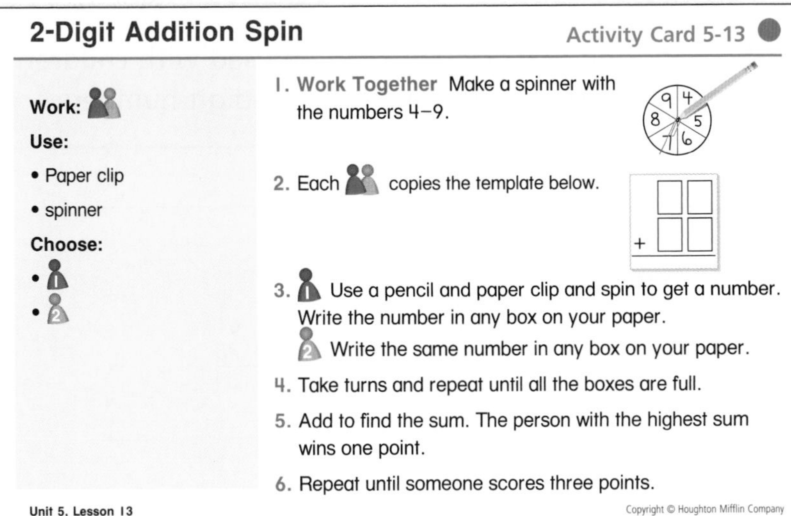

2-Digit Addition Spin — Activity Card 5-13

Work: pairs
Use:
- Paper clip
- spinner

Choose:
- 1
- 2

1. **Work Together** Make a spinner with the numbers 4–9.
2. Each copies the template below.
3. 1 Use a pencil and paper clip and spin to get a number. Write the number in any box on your paper.
   2 Write the same number in any box on your paper.
4. Take turns and repeat until all the boxes are full.
5. Add to find the sum. The person with the highest sum wins one point.
6. Repeat until someone scores three points.

Unit 5, Lesson 13

Activity Note Each pair needs a paper clip and Spinner (TRB M27). Tell children that once a number is written down, it can't be moved in that round.

Math Writing Prompt

Find the Error Cory says that the total of 67 and 85 is 142. Explain Cory's mistake.

Software Support

Use *Soar to Success* for instruction of students needing targeted support for underlying skills.

On Level — Activity Card 5-13

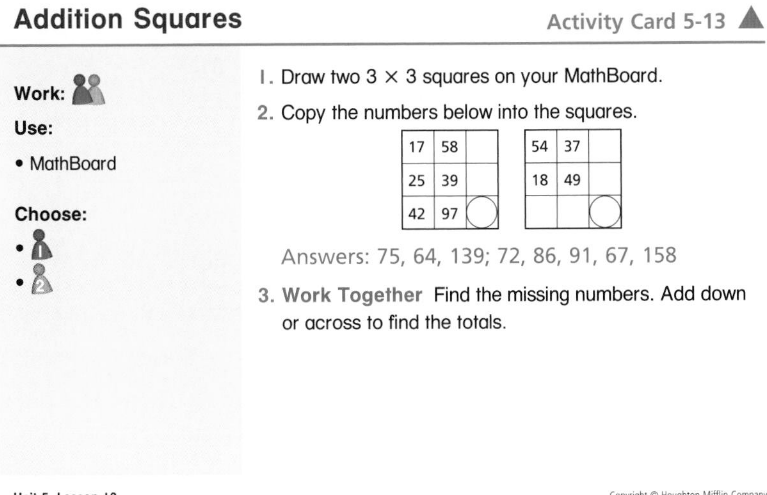

Addition Squares — Activity Card 5-13

Work: pairs
Use:
- MathBoard

Choose:
- 1
- 2

1. Draw two 3 × 3 squares on your MathBoard.
2. Copy the numbers below into the squares.

17	58	
25	39	
42	97	○

54	37	
18	49	
		○

Answers: 75, 64, 139; 72, 86, 91, 67, 158

3. **Work Together** Find the missing numbers. Add down or across to find the totals.

Unit 5, Lesson 13

Activity Note Each pair needs MathBoard materials. You may want to provide calculators for children to use to check the sums.

Math Writing Prompt

Explain Your Thinking What is your favorite method for adding 2-digit numbers? Explain why you like that method.

Software Support

Use *MegaMath* for review and reinforcement of the concepts and skills presented in this lesson.

Challenge — Activity Card 5-13

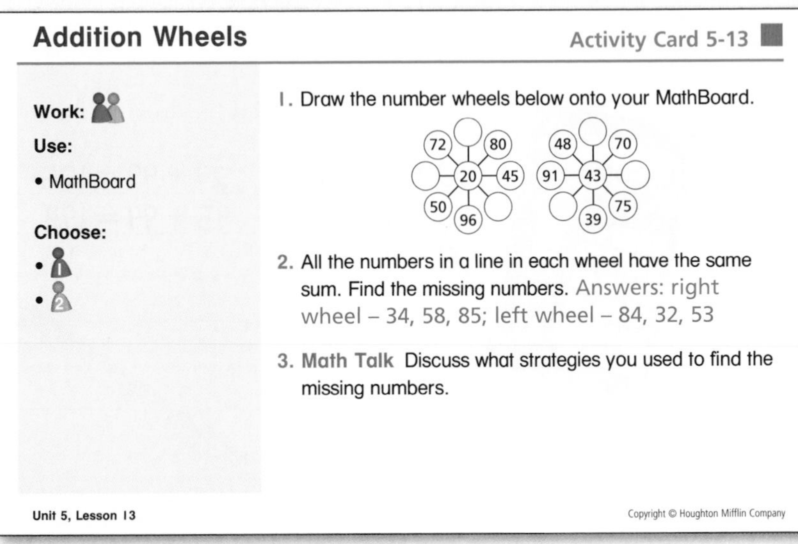

Addition Wheels — Activity Card 5-13

Work: pairs
Use:
- MathBoard

Choose:
- 1
- 2

1. Draw the number wheels below onto your MathBoard.
2. All the numbers in a line in each wheel have the same sum. Find the missing numbers. Answers: right wheel – 34, 58, 85; left wheel – 84, 32, 53
3. **Math Talk** Discuss what strategies you used to find the missing numbers.

Unit 5, Lesson 13

Activity Note Each pair needs MathBoard materials. Suggest that children find one total for each wheel and then find the missing numbers.

Math Writing Prompt

Estimation How do you know that the total of 67 and 85 is greater than 140? Is the total greater than 150? Explain how you know.

Software Support

Use *Destination Math* to take students beyond the concepts and skills presented in this lesson.

 Homework and Targeted Practice

5-13 Homework **Goal:** Additional Practice

This Homework page provides practice recognizing and correcting 2-digit addition errors.

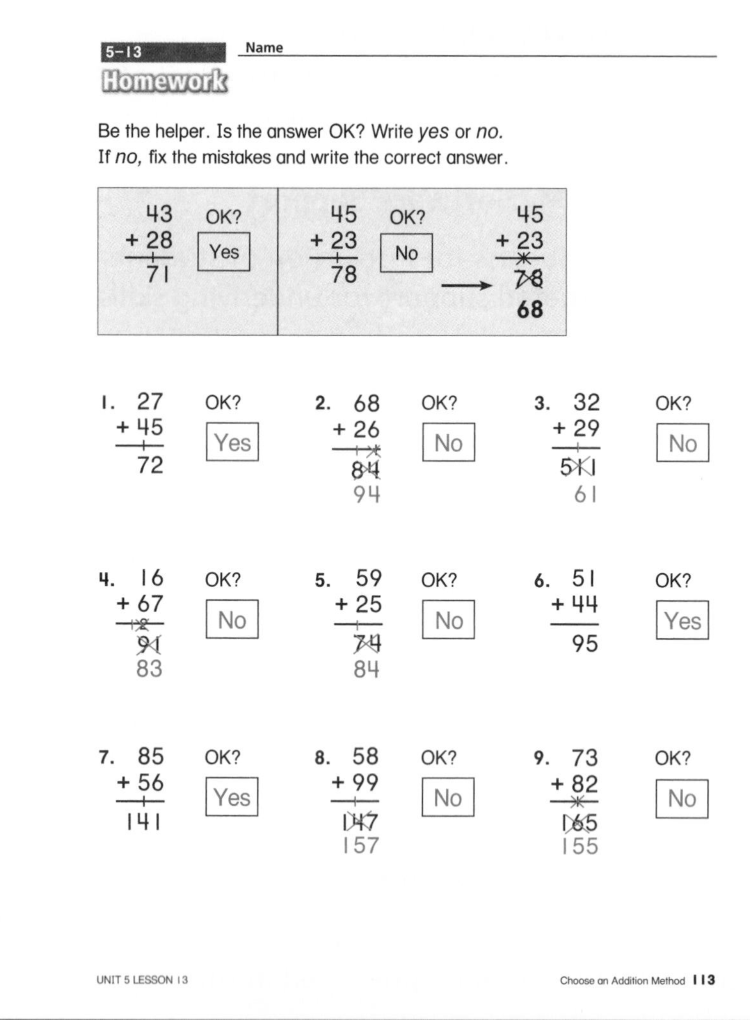

5-13 Homework Name ____________

Be the helper. Is the answer OK? Write *yes* or *no*.
If *no*, fix the mistakes and write the correct answer.

43 + 28 = 71	OK? Yes	
45 + 23 = 78	OK? No	45 + 23 = ~~78~~ **68**

1. 27 + 45 = 72 OK? Yes	2. 68 + 26 = ~~84~~ 94 OK? No	3. 32 + 29 = ~~51~~ 61 OK? No
4. 16 + 67 = ~~91~~ 83 OK? No	5. 59 + 25 = ~~74~~ 84 OK? No	6. 51 + 44 = 95 OK? Yes
7. 85 + 56 = 141 OK? Yes	8. 58 + 99 = ~~147~~ 157 OK? No	9. 73 + 82 = ~~165~~ 155 OK? No

UNIT 5 LESSON 13 Choose an Addition Method **113**

Homework and Remembering page 113

5-13 Targeted Practice **Goal:** Practice addition.

This Targeted Practice page can be used with children who need extra practice in adding 2-digit numbers.

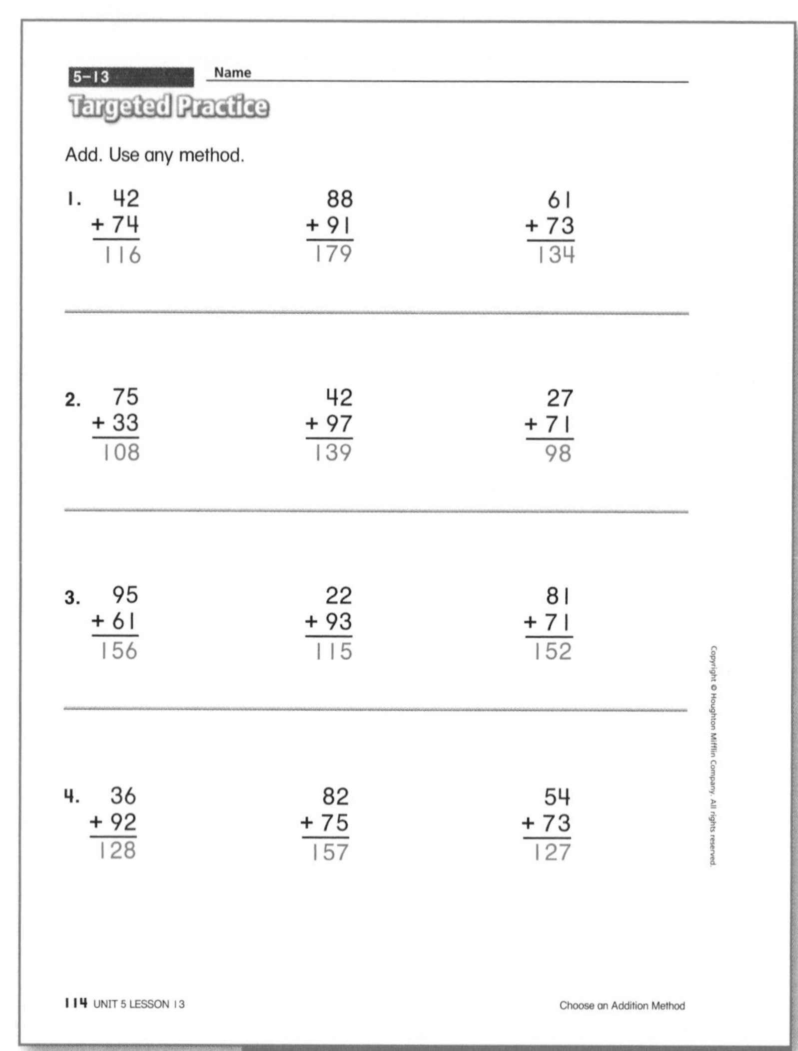

5-13 Targeted Practice Name ____________

Add. Use any method.

1.	42 + 74 = 116	88 + 91 = 179	61 + 73 = 134
2.	75 + 33 = 108	42 + 97 = 139	27 + 71 = 98
3.	95 + 61 = 156	22 + 93 = 115	81 + 71 = 152
4.	36 + 92 = 128	82 + 75 = 157	54 + 73 = 127

114 UNIT 5 LESSON 13 Choose an Addition Method

Homework and Remembering page 114

Home or School Activity

 Technology Connection

Predict and Verify Have children make a list of five 2-digit numbers. Then have them use a calculator to add 99 to each number on their list. Encourage children to look for patterns they see.

Have children predict the answer for 56 + 99, then use a calculator to verify their prediction. Have children write a rule for these exercises.

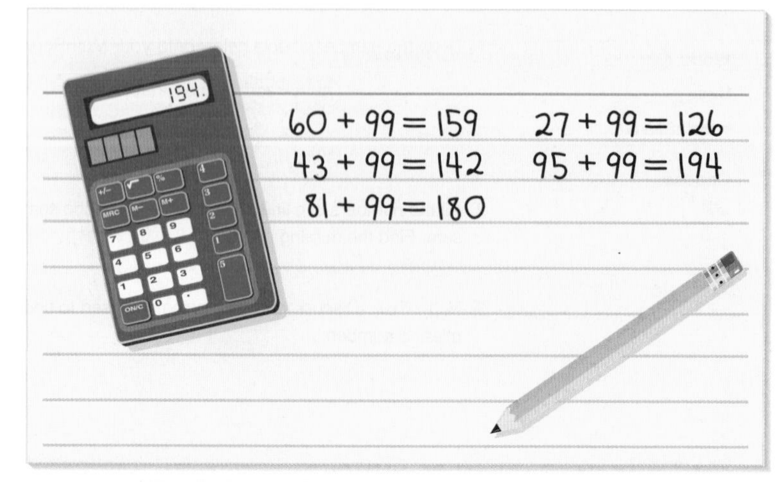

2-Digit Addition in Perimeter Problems

Lesson Objectives

- Solve 2-digit addition problems.
- Review the definition of perimeter.
- Measure the perimeter of regular and irregular shapes.

Vocabulary
perimeter

The Day at a Glance

Today's Goals	Materials	
1 Teaching the Lesson Solve perimeter problems. **2 Going Further** ▸ Math Connection: More Than One Answer ▸ Differentiated Instruction **3 Homework and Spiral Review**	**For Lesson Activities** Student Activity Book p. 173 Homework and Remembering pp. 115–116 Quick Quiz 2 (Assessment Guide)	**Going Further** Activity Cards 5-14 Student Activity Book p. 174 25-cm rulers Paper triangles and squares

123 Use Math Talk today!

Keeping Skills Sharp

Quick Practice — 5 MINUTES

Goal: Monitor progress in adding 2-digit numbers.

Quick Check Write the following exercises on the board for children to solve. Remind children to work independently. This activity should help identify children who are having difficulty with 2–digit addition. Walk around and see how children are doing so you know whether you need a basic review to start the day. You can check details of children's errors later.

$$\begin{array}{r} 35 \\ +\ 47 \\ \hline 82 \end{array} \qquad \begin{array}{r} 74 \\ +\ 59 \\ \hline 133 \end{array}$$

Daily Routines

Math Mountains for 100 or 2-Digit Numbers Using the MathBoard, Using Dimes and Pennies
(See p. xxvi.)

▸ Led by Student Leaders

Money Routine Using the 120 Poster, Using the Money Flip Chart, Using the Number Path, Using Secret Code Cards
(See pp. xxiii–xxv.)

▸ Led by Student Leaders

1 Teaching the Lesson

Activity

Solve Perimeter Problems

 50 MINUTES

Goal: Solve perimeter problems.

Materials: Student Activity Book page 173

 **NCTM Standards:**
Number and Operations
Measurement
Geometry

Teaching Note

What to Expect from Students If children add two numbers at a time to solve the perimeter problems, they will not need to make more than one new ten (see Example 1). More capable children may add three or four numbers successively to get totals in the twenties as shown in Example 2. They will create two new tens in the process.

Example 1

$$\begin{array}{r} 26 \\ +27 \\ \hline 53 \end{array} \nearrow \begin{array}{r} 53 \\ +28 \\ \hline 81 \end{array}$$

Example 2

$$\begin{array}{r} 26 \\ 27 \\ +28 \\ \hline 81 \end{array}$$

English Language Learners

Review the term *perimeter*. Model how to find the perimeter of a desk.

- **Beginning** Say: **I measure each side. I add the lengths. The total is the ___.** perimeter
- **Intermediate and Advanced** Have children use short sentences to tell the steps for finding *perimeter.*

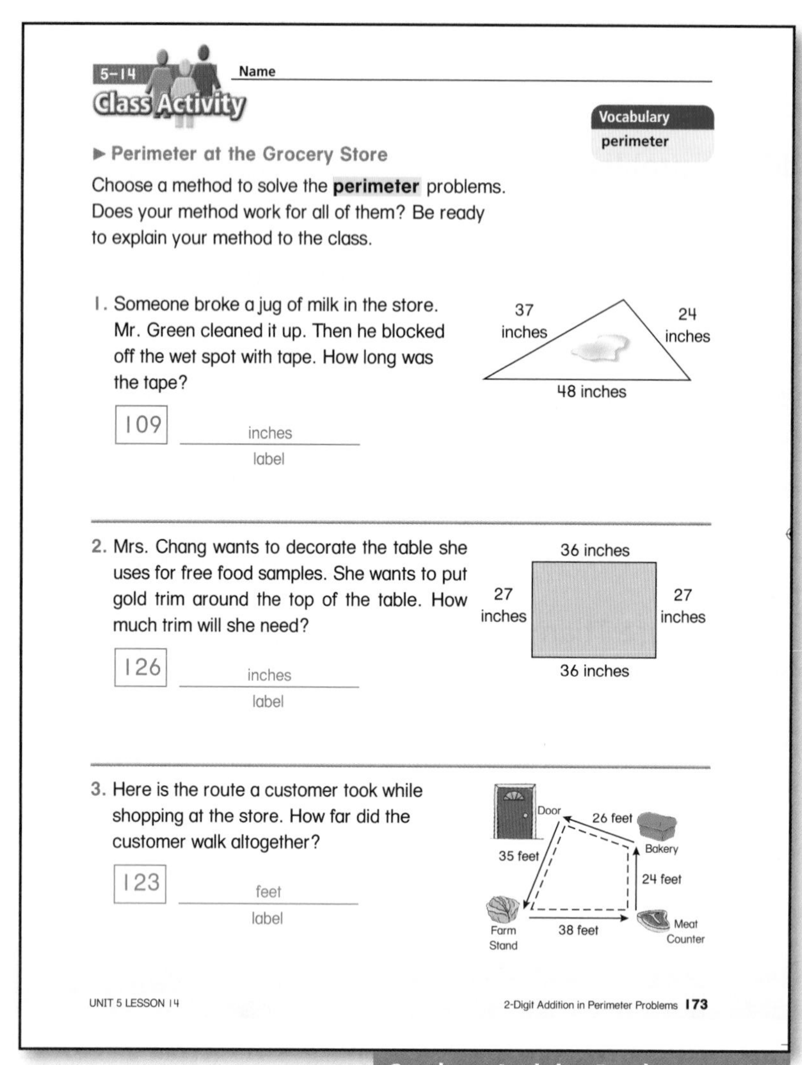

5-14 Class Activity Name

Vocabulary
perimeter

▶ Perimeter at the Grocery Store

Choose a method to solve the **perimeter** problems. Does your method work for all of them? Be ready to explain your method to the class.

1. Someone broke a jug of milk in the store. Mr. Green cleaned it up. Then he blocked off the wet spot with tape. How long was the tape?

109 inches
label

2. Mrs. Chang wants to decorate the table she uses for free food samples. She wants to put gold trim around the top of the table. How much trim will she need?

126 inches
label

3. Here is the route a customer took while shopping at the store. How far did the customer walk altogether?

123 feet
label

UNIT 5 LESSON 14 2-Digit Addition in Perimeter Problems 173

Student Activity Book page 173

▶ Perimeter at the Grocery Store WHOLE CLASS

Use Solve and Discuss for the perimeter problems on Student Activity Book page 173. It may be helpful for children to work in **Helping Pairs** or small groups. Tell children that there are several different ways to solve these problems, and they will be trying to figure out all of the different ways they can solve them. Children who do not need to make proof drawings do not need to do so for these problems unless a classmate asks them to do so.

Methods for Finding Perimeter Two methods for solving problem 3 are shown below. Children may also add all 4 numbers in one column. Encourage your more-advanced children to try that so that you can discuss how sometimes you get more than one new ten (26 + 35 + 38 + 24 will give 2 new tens in the ones total in 23).

Add Another Side to the On-Going Total

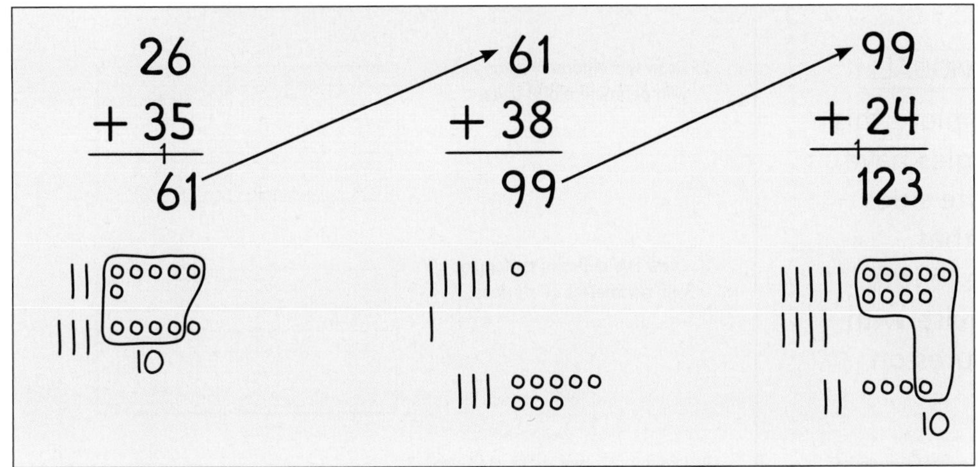

Add 2 Sides, Add the Other 2 Sides, and Add those Totals

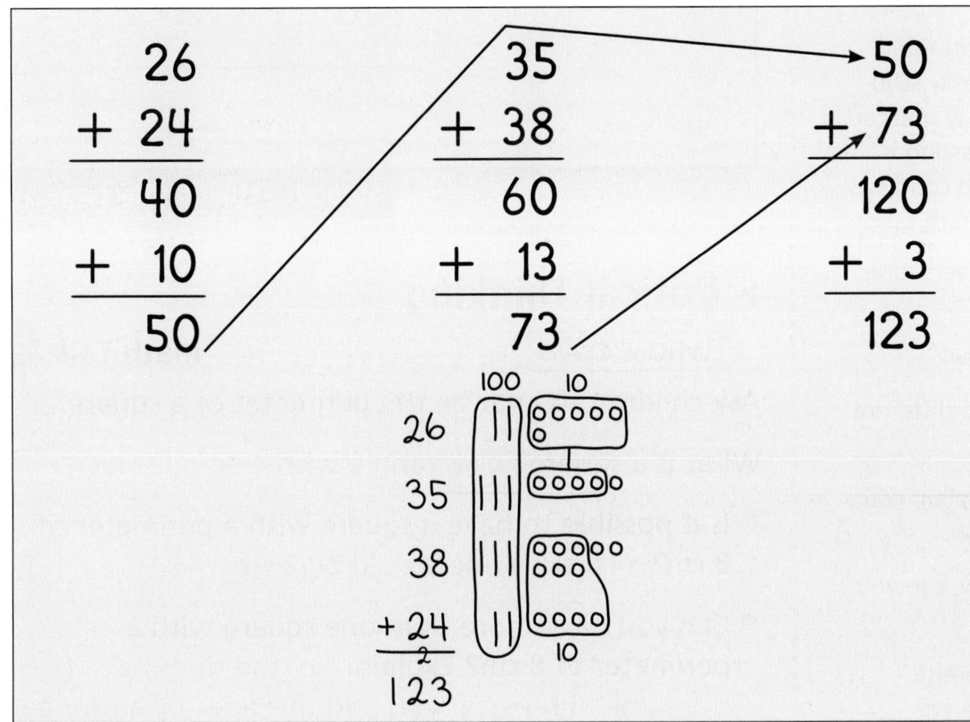

▶ Write Perimeter Problems INDIVIDUALS

Children who finish early can write and solve a 2-digit perimeter problem of their own. The perimeter should be between 100 and 200 units.

The Learning Classroom

Math Talk Encourage children to question each other constructively. Constructive questions help clarify issues, provide insight into children's thinking, and are phrased in a way that the whole class can understand. Some questions appropriate for the activities in this lesson include:

- ▶ Did you get a new ten (or hundred) when you added?
- ▶ How did you show the new ten (or hundred)?

Ongoing Assessment

Draw and label the sides of a triangle with 2-digit lengths. Ask children questions, such as:

- ▶ What is the perimeter?
- ▶ What numbers do you add to find the perimeter of this triangle?
- ▶ How would you add these three numbers?

See Assessment Guide for Unit 5 Quick Quiz 2.

2 Going Further

Math Connection: More Than One Answer

Goal: Draw two different shapes with the same perimeter.

Materials: 25-cm rulers, Student Activity Book page 174

✓ **NCTM Standards:**
Number and Operations
Geometry
Measurement

▶ Find the Different Shapes INDIVIDUALS

Review the definition for a rectangle. To complete this page, children will need to know that rectangles have 4 sides, 4 square corners, and that the opposite sides are the same length. They should also know that squares are rectangles with all sides the same length. You may want to work through the first exercise with children so they understand how to draw figures on the grid and how to count units.

The Learning Classroom

Math Talk You can create math conversations by eliciting multiple strategies for solving problems. When you ask, "Did anyone do this problem differently?" children will pay greater attention because they will be comparing and contrasting it with their own math strategies. The comparisons and contrasts that result can naturally springboard to significant math talk.

Here are some questions you may ask to get the conversation going:

- ▶ Did anyone think of this problem in a different way?
- ▶ Does anyone have the same answer, but got it in a different way?
- ▶ Does anyone have a different answer? Will you explain your solution to us?
- ▶ Now that you have solved the problem in that way, can you think of another way to work on this problem?
- ▶ Does it really make sense for there to be two different answers to this problem? Is that okay? So, how can we decide which answer is mathematically correct?
- ▶ How is your way of solving like _________'s way?
- ▶ How is your way of solving different from _________'s way?

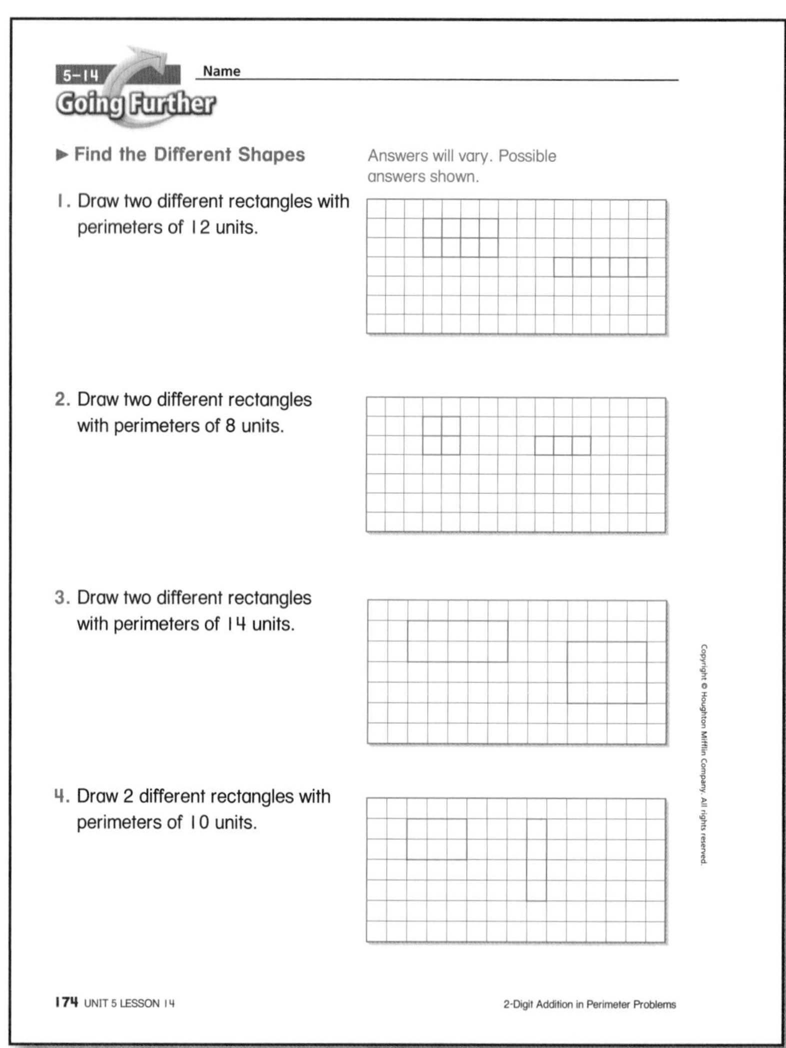
5-14 Going Further Name ______________

▶ Find the Different Shapes

Answers will vary. Possible answers shown.

1. Draw two different rectangles with perimeters of 12 units.

2. Draw two different rectangles with perimeters of 8 units.

3. Draw two different rectangles with perimeters of 14 units.

4. Draw 2 different rectangles with perimeters of 10 units.

Copyright © Houghton Mifflin Company. All rights reserved.

174 UNIT 5 LESSON 14 2-Digit Addition in Perimeter Problems

Student Activity Book page 174

▶ Critical Thinking

WHOLE CLASS **Math Talk** 

Ask children to analyze the perimeter of a square.

What is a square? a rectangle with 4 equal sides

- Is it possible to have a square with a perimeter of 8 cm? Yes, each side would be 2 cm.
- Can you have more than one square with a perimeter of 8 cm? Explain. No, the sides have to be the same number. If you add the sides by a number other than 2, the total would be more or less than 8 cm.

Intervention Activity Card 5-14

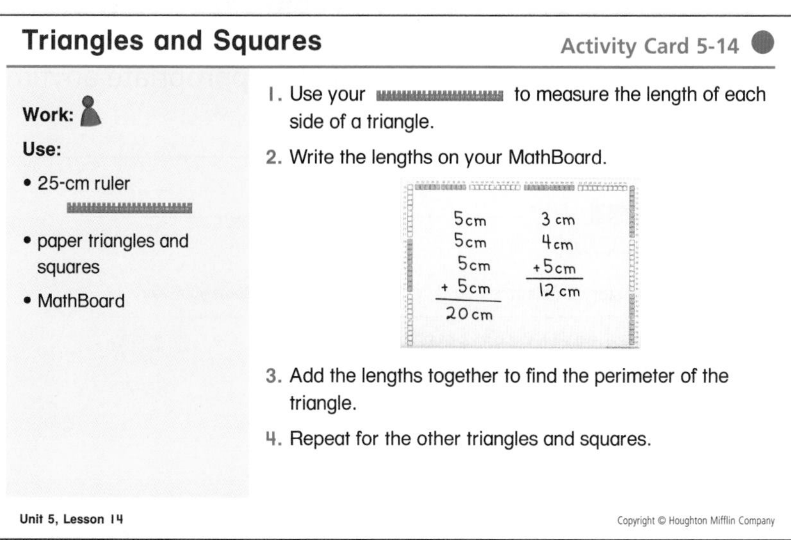

Triangles and Squares Activity Card 5-14

Work:
Use:
- 25-cm ruler
- paper triangles and squares
- MathBoard

1. Use your ruler to measure the length of each side of a triangle.
2. Write the lengths on your MathBoard.

5 cm + 5 cm + 5 cm + 5 cm = 20 cm
3 cm + 4 cm + 5 cm = 12 cm

3. Add the lengths together to find the perimeter of the triangle.
4. Repeat for the other triangles and squares.

Unit 5, Lesson 14

Activity Note Cut out several triangles and squares cut to exact centimeter lengths per child. Each child also needs 25-cm ruler and MathBoard materials.

Math Writing Prompt

Explain Your Thinking Draw a triangle. Label each side with a 2-digit number of centimeters. Add to find the perimeter. Show your work.

Software Support

Use *Soar to Success* for instruction of students needing targeted support for underlying skills.

On Level Activity Card 5-14

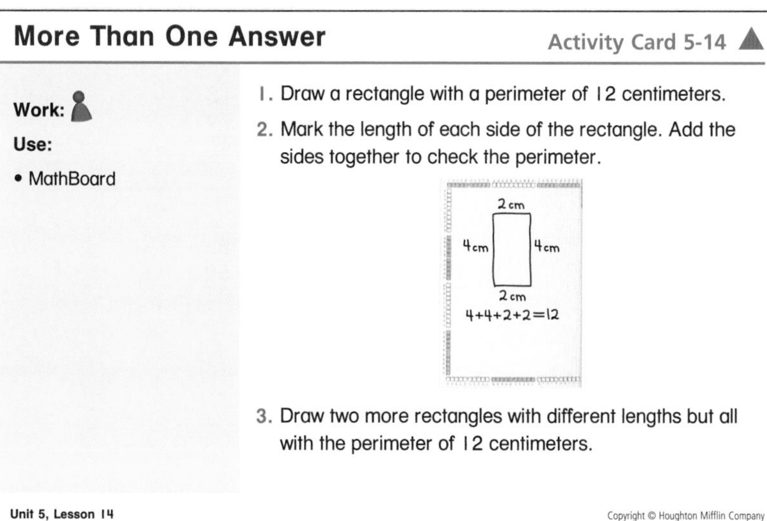

More Than One Answer Activity Card 5-14

Work:
Use:
- MathBoard

1. Draw a rectangle with a perimeter of 12 centimeters.
2. Mark the length of each side of the rectangle. Add the sides together to check the perimeter.

2 cm, 4 cm, 4 cm, 2 cm
4+4+2+2=12

3. Draw two more rectangles with different lengths but all with the perimeter of 12 centimeters.

Unit 5, Lesson 14

Activity Note Each child needs MathBoard materials. Tell children that all sides should be whole numbers.

Math Writing Prompt

Side of a Triangle Draw a triangle. Label the three sides so that the perimeter is 54 centimeters. Explain how you decided which numbers to use.

Software Support

Use *MegaMath* for review and reinforcement of the concepts and skills presented in this lesson.

Challenge Activity Card 5-14

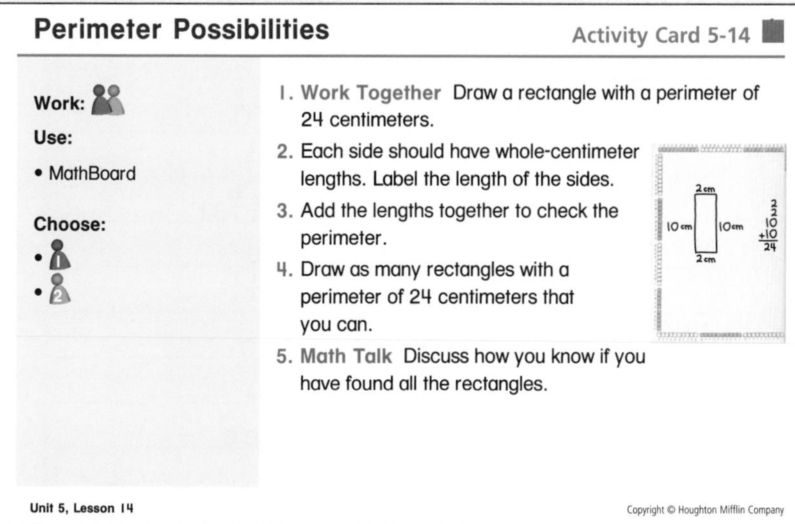

Perimeter Possibilities Activity Card 5-14

Work:
Use:
- MathBoard

Choose:
- 1
- 2

1. **Work Together** Draw a rectangle with a perimeter of 24 centimeters.
2. Each side should have whole-centimeter lengths. Label the length of the sides.
3. Add the lengths together to check the perimeter.
4. Draw as many rectangles with a perimeter of 24 centimeters that you can.
5. **Math Talk** Discuss how you know if you have found all the rectangles.

2 cm, 10 cm, 10 cm, 2 cm
2 + 2 + 10 + 10 = 24

Unit 5, Lesson 14

Activity Note Each child needs MathBoard materials. Tell children that all sides should be whole numbers. Have pairs compare their work.

Math Writing Prompt

Investigate Math A square has a perimeter of 48 centimeters. How long is each side? Explain how you found the answer.

Software Support

Use *Destination Math* to take students beyond the concepts and skills presented in this lesson.

3 Homework and Spiral Review

5–14 Homework **Goal:** Additional Practice

✓ Include children's completed Homework page as part of their portfolios.

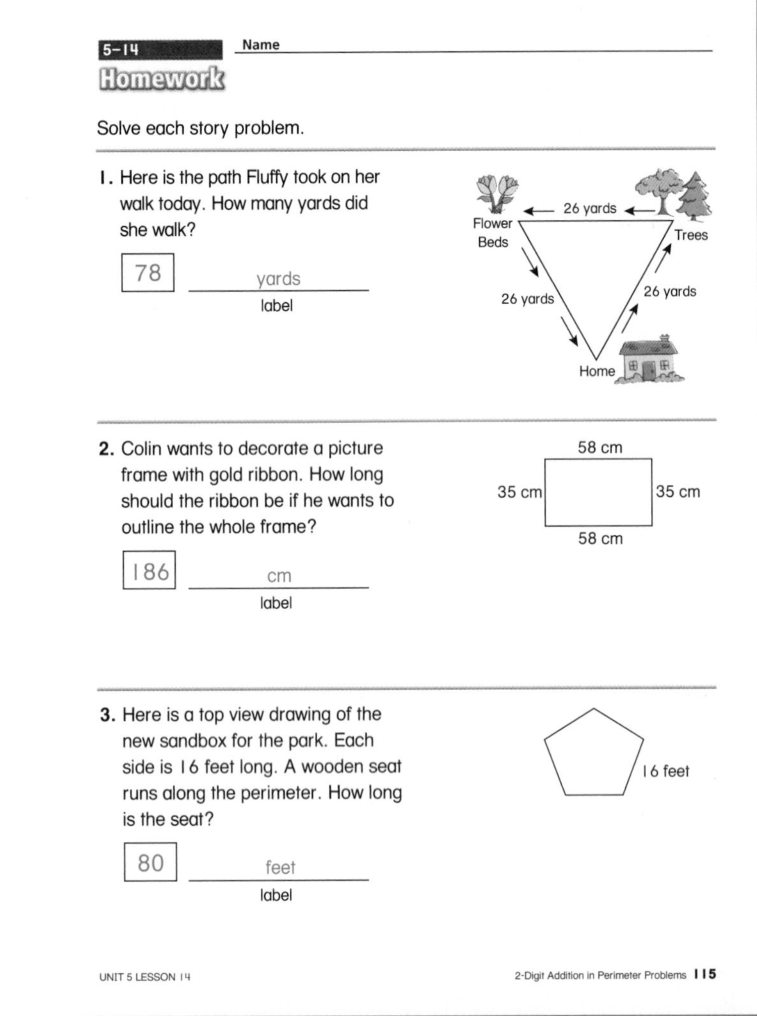

5–14 Homework Name

Solve each story problem.

1. Here is the path Fluffy took on her walk today. How many yards did she walk?

78 yards
label

2. Colin wants to decorate a picture frame with gold ribbon. How long should the ribbon be if he wants to outline the whole frame?

186 cm
label

3. Here is a top view drawing of the new sandbox for the park. Each side is 16 feet long. A wooden seat runs along the perimeter. How long is the seat?

80 feet
label

UNIT 5 LESSON 14 2-Digit Addition in Perimeter Problems 115

Homework and Remembering page 115

5–14 Remembering **Goal:** Spiral Review

This Remembering activity would be appropriate anytime after today's lesson.

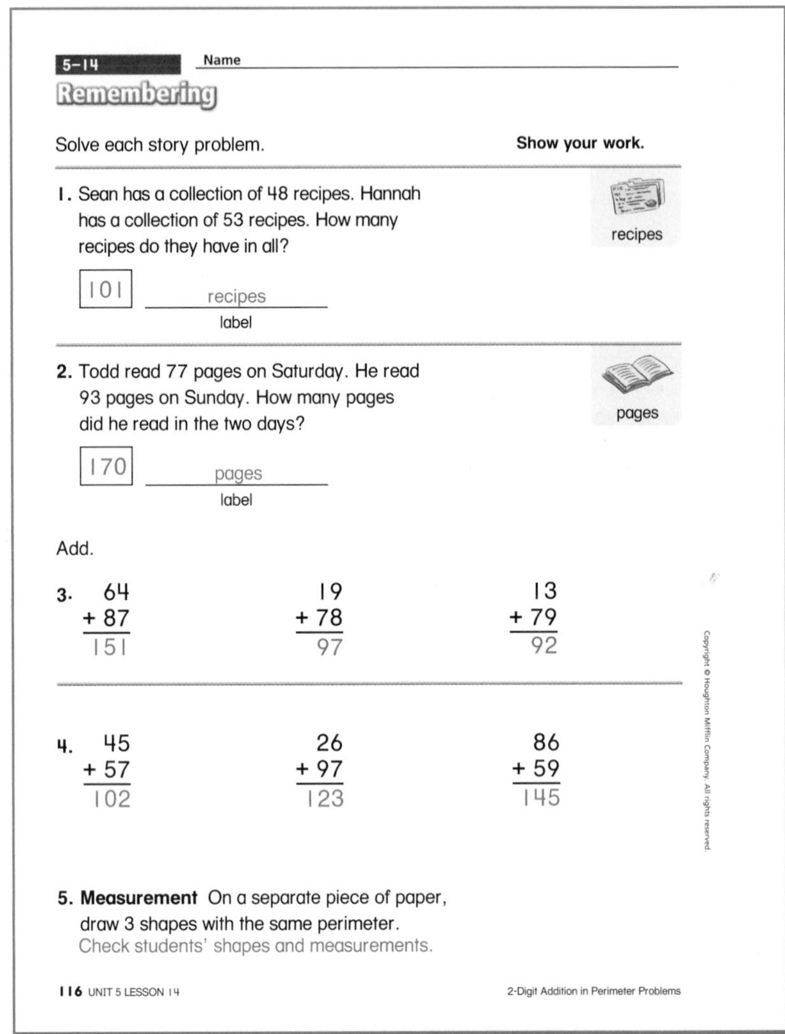

5–14 Remembering Name

Solve each story problem. **Show your work.**

1. Sean has a collection of 48 recipes. Hannah has a collection of 53 recipes. How many recipes do they have in all?

101 recipes
label

2. Todd read 77 pages on Saturday. He read 93 pages on Sunday. How many pages did he read in the two days?

170 pages
label

Add.

3. $64 + 87 = 151$ $19 + 78 = 97$ $13 + 79 = 92$

4. $45 + 57 = 102$ $26 + 97 = 123$ $86 + 59 = 145$

5. **Measurement** On a separate piece of paper, draw 3 shapes with the same perimeter.
Check students' shapes and measurements.

116 UNIT 5 LESSON 14 2-Digit Addition in Perimeter Problems

Homework and Remembering page 116

Home or School Activity

Language Arts Connection

Word List Write the word *math.* Show children how they can use the letters in the word *math* to find other words such as *ham, hat,* and *mat.* Then write the word *perimeter*. Have children make a list of the words they can make using the letters in the word *perimeter.*

perimeter

- rim
- pet
- meter
- me
- pit
- rip
- tip
- tree

Buy with Pennies and Dimes

Lesson Objectives

- Represent 2- and 3-digit money amounts using dollars, dimes, and pennies.
- Apply addition concepts and strategies to real-world situations.

Vocabulary

penny
dime
dollar
Quick Ten
Quick Hundred

The Day at a Glance

Today's Goals	Materials	
1 Teaching the Lesson **A1:** Represent money amounts with dollars, dimes, and pennies. **A2:** Make exact money amounts to purchase items.	**Lesson Activities** Student Activity Book pp. 175–178 (Includes Dollar Bills) Homework and Remembering pp. 117–118 Real or play money Coin strips Snack bags	**Going Further** Activity Cards 5-15 *Get 5 Dimes* game board Number cubes Math Journals
2 Going Further ▸ Differentiated Instruction		
3 Homework and Targeted Practice		

Use Math Talk today!

Keeping Skills Sharp

Quick Practice — 5 MINUTES

Goals: Use place-value patterns to add. Practice adding single-digit and decade numbers.

Trios Have a **Student Leader** write the three exercises shown below on the board. The leader reads aloud the exercises, one at a time, giving a hand signal to indicate when the class should respond with the answer.

59 + 1 = ☐ 59 + 10 = ☐ 59 + 100 = ☐

Add Tens or Ones On the board, write equations similar to the ones on the right. Have a Student Leader direct the class in adding tens or ones. The class should then say the answer.

6 + 6 = ☐ 4 + 3 = ☐

60 + 60 = ☐ 40 + 30 = ☐

Daily Routines

Math Mountains for 100 or 2-Digit Numbers Using the MathBoard, Using Dimes and Pennies
(See p. xxvi.)

▸ Led by Student Leaders

Money Routine Using the 120 Poster, Using the Money Flip Chart, Using the Number Path, Using Secret Code Cards
(See pp. xxiii–xxv.)

▸ Led by Student Leaders

1 Teaching the Lesson

Activity 1

Money Amounts with Dollars, Dimes, and Pennies

 30 MINUTES

Goal: Represent money amounts with dollars, dimes, and pennies.

Materials: Real or play money (dollars, dimes, and pennies), Coin Strips (1 Penny Strip, 1 Dime Strip per child), Dollar Bill (TRB M67– M68), snack bags, Student Activity Book page 175

 **NCTM Standards:**
Number and Operations
Communication
Representation

 **Class Management**

Looking Ahead Children will use the dollars again in Lesson 15, so they should store them in a snack bag at the end of today's activities. It may be helpful to have children store the dollars in a snack bag as well as the coins from Student Activity Book page 175.

English Language Learners

Make sure children can identify coins and their values. Give them play money to show different amounts.

- **Beginning** Have children hold up a penny. Ask: **Is a *penny* 1¢ or 10¢?** 1¢ Hold up a dime. Ask: **Is a *dime* 5¢ or 10¢?** 10¢
- **Intermediate** Hold up each coin. Say: **This is a ___.** penny, dime Ask: **How many cents is a *penny*?** 1 **A *dime*?** 10
- **Advanced** Have children identify each coin and its value. Ask: **How many *pennies* equal 1 *dime*?** 10 **How many *dimes* equal 1 *dollar*?** 10

Getting Ready Before you begin this activity, place 3 dimes and 5 pennies in your pocket.

▶ Represent Money Amounts with Dimes and Pennies WHOLE CLASS

- Imagine that I have 35¢ in my pocket. How many tens are in 30? 3 tens How many ones are in 5? 5 ones 30 and 5 equals 35.
- I have **only** pennies and dimes in my pocket and they add up to 35¢.

Distribute play money to children and have children represent 35¢ with dimes and pennies. If they are using Penny Strips, they may tear or cut off individual pennies. They may turn over an intact Penny Strip to represent each dime.

Allow time for children to represent the money amount and then reveal the coins in your pocket.

▶ Represent with Dollars, Dimes, and Pennies

WHOLE CLASS

Have children cut out the dollar bills from Student Activity Book page 175.

Write these 2-digit money amounts on the board: 52¢ and 73¢. Ask children to represent each amount with dimes and pennies or Penny and Dime Strips. If necessary, review the use of the cents symbol (¢). Circulate around the room to see that everyone is able to represent the amounts correctly.

Next, present children with a money amount over one dollar, but less than two dollars. Write 124¢ on the board.

Have them represent the amount with a dollar, dimes, and pennies. Be sure children know that 10 dimes equal one dollar, 100 pennies equal one dollar, and 10 pennies equal one dime.

- How can we make 124¢ with a dollar, dimes, and pennies? 1 dollar, 2 dimes, and 4 pennies

You may wish to sketch the money on the board as children suggest the answer.

124¢ = [1 dollar] (10¢) (10¢) (1¢) (1¢) (1¢) (1¢)

Help children relate the dollars and dimes to Quick Hundreds and Quick Tens. Then have them draw Quick Hundreds and Quick Tens to show the number 124.

124 = □ | | ○○○○

Repeat this procedure for 178¢ and 157¢.

Activity 2

Exact Money Amounts

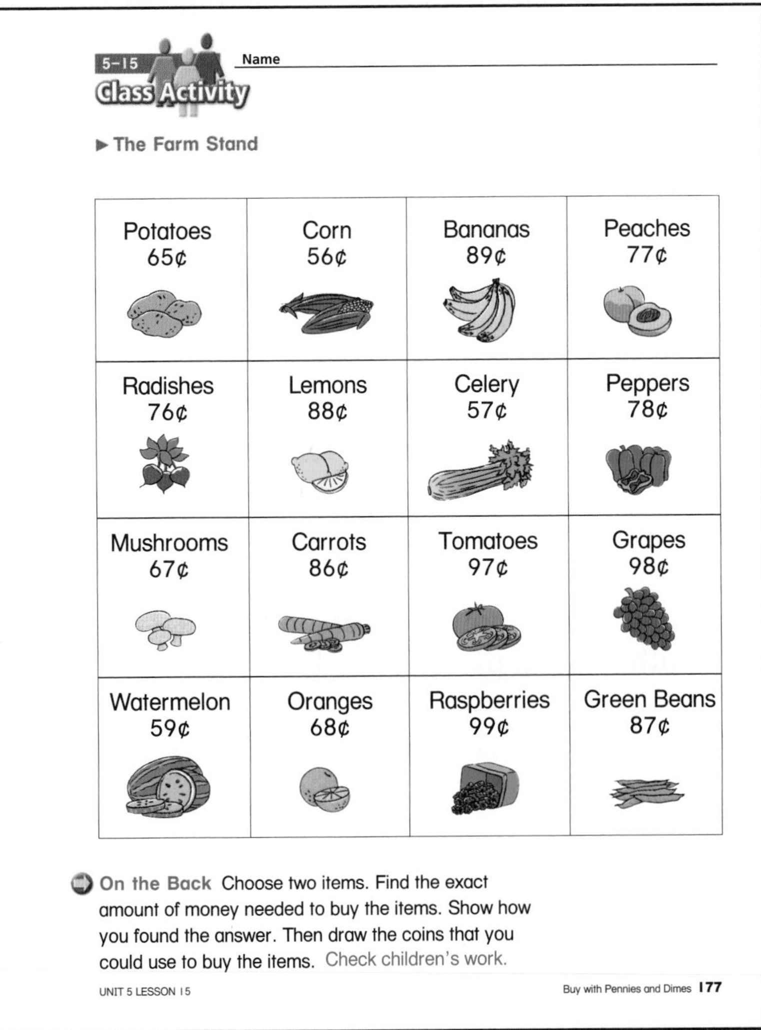

5-15 Class Activity

Name

▶ The Farm Stand

Potatoes 65¢	Corn 56¢	Bananas 89¢	Peaches 77¢
Radishes 76¢	Lemons 88¢	Celery 57¢	Peppers 78¢
Mushrooms 67¢	Carrots 86¢	Tomatoes 97¢	Grapes 98¢
Watermelon 59¢	Oranges 68¢	Raspberries 99¢	Green Beans 87¢

On the Back Choose two items. Find the exact amount of money needed to buy the items. Show how you found the answer. Then draw the coins that you could use to buy the items. Check children's work.

UNIT 5 LESSON 15 Buy with Pennies and Dimes 177

Student Activity Book page 177

 **20 MINUTES**

Goal: Make exact money amounts to purchase items.

Materials: Real or play money (dollars, dimes, pennies), Coin Strips (1 Penny Strip, 1 Dime Strip per child), Dollar Bill (TRB M67–M68), snack bag, Student Activity Book page 177

 **NCTM Standards:**
Number and Operations
Communication
Representation

Differentiated Instruction

English Learners Preview Student Activity Book page 177 with children. Point out that the title in each box tells the name of the fruit or vegetable shown in the picture. Allow time for children to practice saying the names of the fruits and vegetables so that they can better participate in the class activity. You can also use the page for children to practice reading prices, such as 65¢ as "sixty-five cents."

Activity continued ▶

▶ The Farm Stand WHOLE CLASS

Have children look at Student Activity Book page 177. Explain to children that in this activity they are going to buy food items at an imaginary farm stand.

Have children imagine they are at the Farm Stand in Mr. and Mrs. Green's grocery store. There are fresh fruits and vegetables there. Tell them to choose two items they would like to buy. Using dimes and pennies, have children show the exact money amount for each item they chose. Then have them add the two money amounts together. Encourage children to change 10 pennies for a dime and 10 dimes for a dollar, if they can. Finally, have children add the prices using numbers. The coins should match their totals.

Work through an example from Student Activity Book page 177 with the class. Have volunteers choose two different items and show the amounts using dimes and pennies. Then have a volunteer add the amounts to determine how much it will cost to buy both items. Finally, show how to add the prices using the New Groups Below Method and the Expanded Method.

Tomatoes	97¢	or	Tomatoes	97¢
Bananas	89¢ (new group: 1)		Bananas	89¢
	186¢			170¢
				16¢
				186¢

▶ Act It Out PAIRS

Math Talk 

Scenarios Have children form **Helping Pairs** and work together on this activity. Have pairs record their purchases by writing the names of the items they bought, the prices, and the total cost. Drawing bills and coins is optional.

Circulate around the room to make sure that everyone understands what to do. You might work with a group of children who are having difficulty.

Teaching Note

Critical Thinking No matter which two items children choose from the farm stand, the total cost will be greater than one dollar. Ask the following:

- Before you add the numbers, how do you know that the total price of the lemons (88¢) and celery (57¢) will be more than one dollar (100¢)? Possible answer: Both items cost more than 50¢ and 50¢ + 50¢ = 100¢

Ongoing Assessment

Ask children to use dimes and pennies or Coin Strips to represent 52¢.

The Learning Classroom

Scenarios This structure can be used to demonstrate mathematical concepts in a visual and memorable way. A group of children is called to the front of the classroom to act out a particular situation. Scenarios are especially useful when a concept is introduced for the first time, and they are particularly helpful to English learners.

2 Going Further

Differentiated Instruction

Intervention

Activity Card 5-15

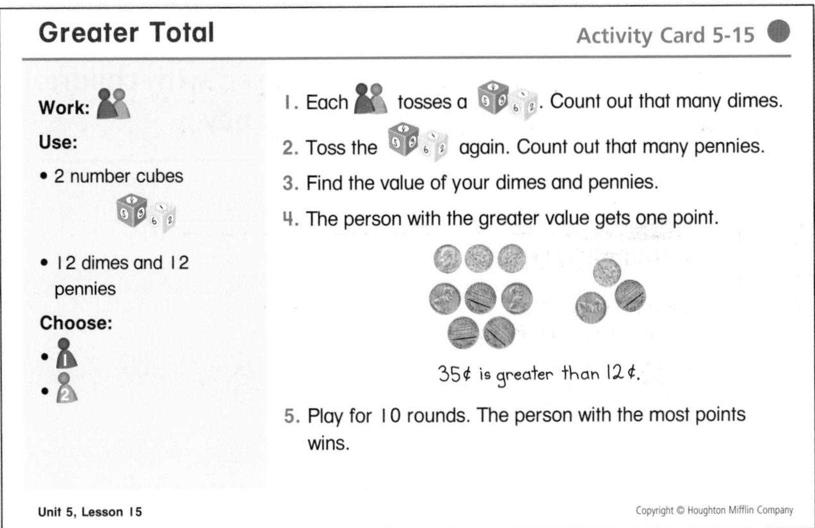

Greater Total — Activity Card 5-15 ●

Work: [pair]

Use:
- 2 number cubes
- 12 dimes and 12 pennies

Choose:
- [person 1]
- [person 2]

1. Each [pair] tosses a [number cube]. Count out that many dimes.
2. Toss the [number cube] again. Count out that many pennies.
3. Find the value of your dimes and pennies.
4. The person with the greater value gets one point.

35¢ is greater than 12¢.

5. Play for 10 rounds. The person with the most points wins.

Unit 5, Lesson 15

Activity Note Each pair needs two number cubes labeled 1–6, 12 real or play dimes, and 12 real or play pennies. Have children check each other's work.

Math Writing Prompt

Dimes and Pennies Draw the coins you would use to pay for a snack that cost 83¢. Explain how you found your answer.

Software Support

Use *Soar to Success* for instruction of students needing targeted support for underlying skills.

On Level

Activity Card 5-15

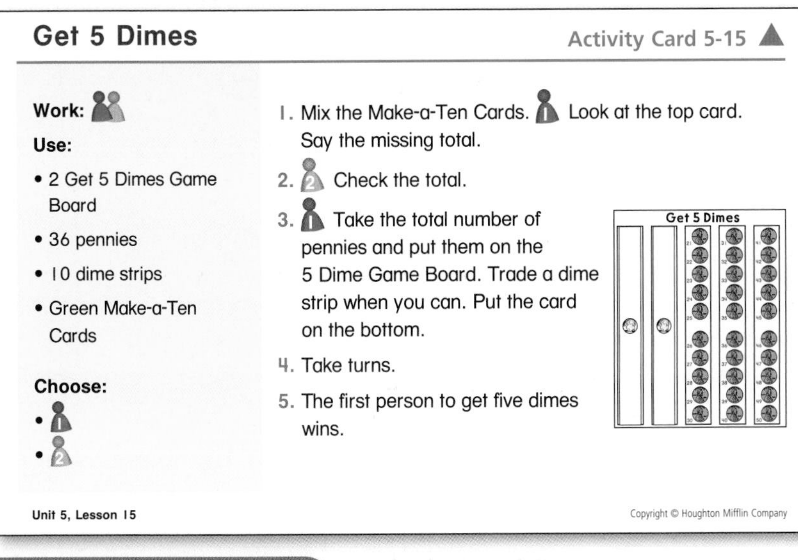

Get 5 Dimes — Activity Card 5-15 ▲

Work: [pair]

Use:
- 2 Get 5 Dimes Game Board
- 36 pennies
- 10 dime strips
- Green Make-a-Ten Cards

Choose:
- [person 1]
- [person 2]

1. Mix the Make-a-Ten Cards. [person 1] Look at the top card. Say the missing total.
2. [person 2] Check the total.
3. [person 1] Take the total number of pennies and put them on the 5 Dime Game Board. Trade a dime strip when you can. Put the card on the bottom.
4. Take turns.
5. The first person to get five dimes wins.

Get 5 Dimes

Unit 5, Lesson 15

Activity Note Each pair needs two Get 5 Dimes game boards (TRB M64), 36 pennies, 10 Dime Strips (TRB M1), and Green Make-a-Ten Cards (TRB M35–M38). Review Unit 5, Lesson 4, Activity 2 with children.

Math Writing Prompt

Connected Math Explain how you can use dimes and pennies to add 24 and 19.

Software Support

Use *MegaMath* for review and reinforcement of the concepts and skills presented in this lesson.

Challenge

Activity Card 5-15

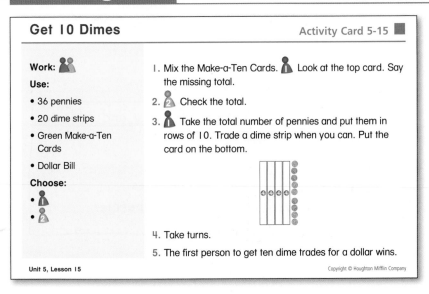

Get 10 Dimes — Activity Card 5-15 ■

Work: [pair]

Use:
- 36 pennies
- 20 dime strips
- Green Make-a-Ten Cards
- Dollar Bill

Choose:
- [person 1]
- [person 2]

1. Mix the Make-a-Ten Cards. [person 1] Look at the top card. Say the missing total.
2. [person 2] Check the total.
3. [person 1] Take the total number of pennies and put them in rows of 10. Trade a dime strip when you can. Put the card on the bottom.
4. Take turns.
5. The first person to get ten dime trades for a dollar wins.

Unit 5, Lesson 15

Activity Note Each pair needs 36 pennies, 20 Dime Strips (TRB M1), and Green Make-a-Ten Cards (TRB M35–M38), and a dollar bill (TRB M67).

Math Writing Prompt

Explain Your Thinking How many combinations of dimes and pennies can you use to make 83¢. Explain how you found your answer.

Software Support

Use *Destination Math* to take students beyond the concepts and skills presented in this lesson.

3 Homework and Targeted Practice

5-15 Homework **Goal:** Additional Practice

This Homework page provides practice finding exact money amounts to purchase items.

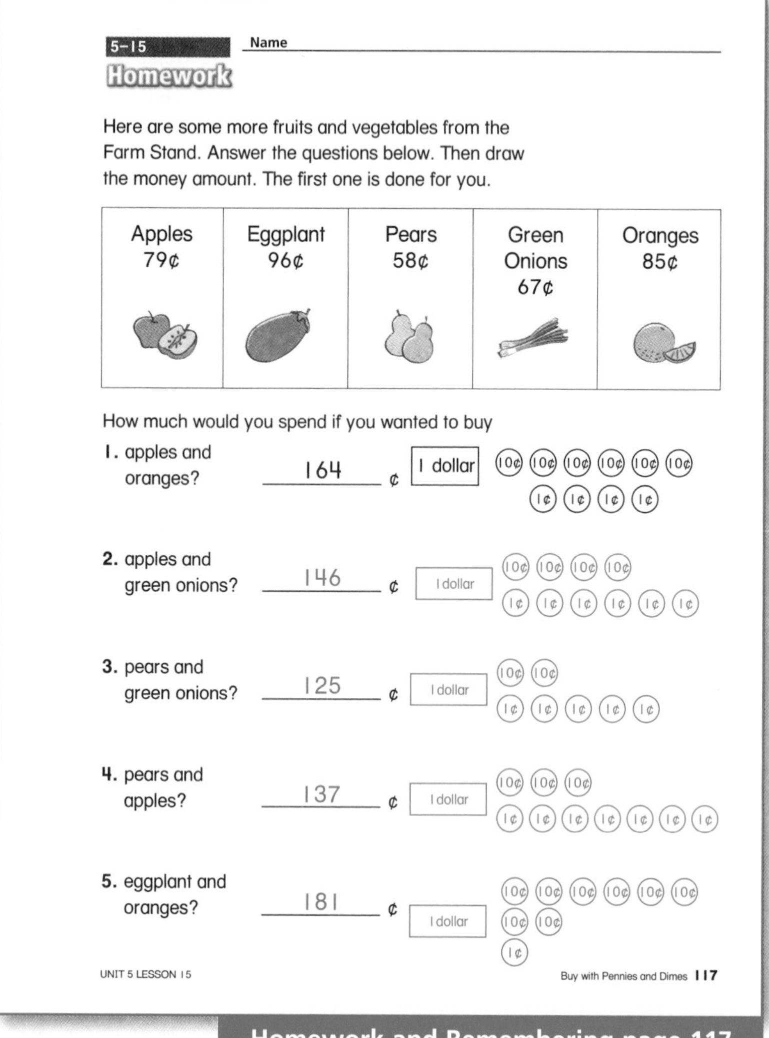

5-15 Homework

Name ________________

Here are some more fruits and vegetables from the Farm Stand. Answer the questions below. Then draw the money amount. The first one is done for you.

Apples 79¢	Eggplant 96¢	Pears 58¢	Green Onions 67¢	Oranges 85¢

How much would you spend if you wanted to buy

1. apples and oranges? 164 ¢ — 1 dollar, 10¢ 10¢ 10¢ 10¢ 10¢ 10¢, 1¢ 1¢ 1¢ 1¢
2. apples and green onions? 146 ¢ — 1 dollar, 10¢ 10¢ 10¢ 10¢, 1¢ 1¢ 1¢ 1¢ 1¢ 1¢
3. pears and green onions? 125 ¢ — 1 dollar, 10¢ 10¢, 1¢ 1¢ 1¢ 1¢ 1¢
4. pears and apples? 137 ¢ — 1 dollar, 10¢ 10¢ 10¢, 1¢ 1¢ 1¢ 1¢ 1¢ 1¢ 1¢
5. eggplant and oranges? 181 ¢ — 1 dollar, 10¢ 10¢ 10¢ 10¢ 10¢ 10¢, 10¢ 10¢, 1¢

UNIT 5 LESSON 15 — Buy with Pennies and Dimes 117

Homework and Remembering page 117

5-15 Targeted Practice **Goal:** Count coins to find the total.

This Targeted Practice page can be used with children who need extra practice counting money.

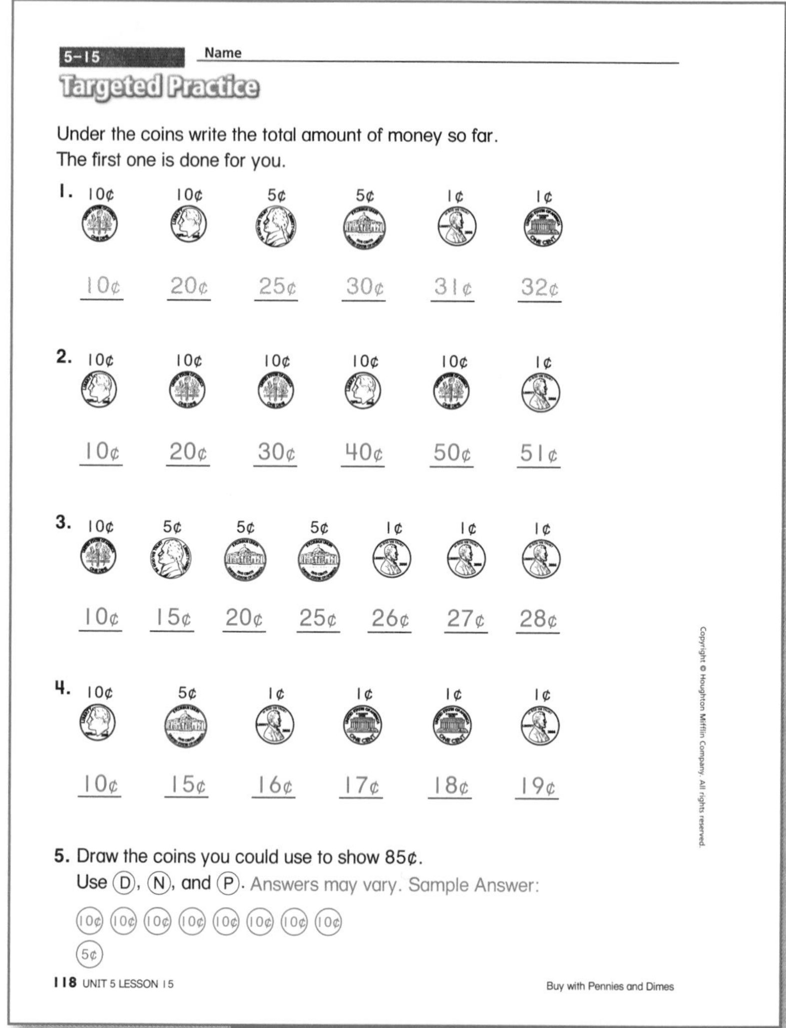

5-15 Targeted Practice

Name ________________

Under the coins write the total amount of money so far. The first one is done for you.

1. 10¢, 10¢, 5¢, 5¢, 1¢, 1¢ — 10¢, 20¢, 25¢, 30¢, 31¢, 32¢
2. 10¢, 10¢, 10¢, 10¢, 10¢, 1¢ — 10¢, 20¢, 30¢, 40¢, 50¢, 51¢
3. 10¢, 5¢, 5¢, 5¢, 1¢, 1¢, 1¢ — 10¢, 15¢, 20¢, 25¢, 26¢, 27¢, 28¢
4. 10¢, 5¢, 1¢, 1¢, 1¢, 1¢ — 10¢, 15¢, 16¢, 17¢, 18¢, 19¢
5. Draw the coins you could use to show 85¢. Use (D), (N), and (P). Answers may vary. Sample Answer: 10¢ 10¢ 10¢ 10¢ 10¢ 10¢ 10¢ 10¢ 5¢

Copyright © Houghton Mifflin Company. All rights reserved.

118 UNIT 5 LESSON 15 — Buy with Pennies and Dimes

Homework and Remembering page 118

Home or School Activity

Language Arts Connection

Make It Plural Introduce or review the initial rules for forming plural words. Show how the word *dime* becomes plural by adding an –s at the end. Then, show how *penny* becomes plural by dropping the –y and adding –ies. Have children list as many words as they can think of that fit into these two categories for forming plural words.

Word	Add–s	Drop–y and add–ies
dime	dimes	
pen	pens	
penny		pennies
strawberry		strawberries
nickel	nickels	

Buy with Pennies, Nickels, and Dimes

Vocabulary
- penny
- nickel
- dime
- dollar
- cents

Lesson Objectives

- **Add coins to amounts between $1.00 and $2.00.**
- **Combine pennies, nickels, and dimes to make different money amounts.**
- **Add money amounts to purchase two items between $1.00 and $2.00.**

The Day at a Glance

Today's Goals	Materials	
1 Teaching the Lesson **A1:** Find equivalencies of nickels. Represent money amounts Dime and Nickel Strips and pennies. **A2:** Make exact money totals with dollars, dimes, nickels, and pennies.	**Lesson Activities** Student Activity Book pp. 179–180 Homework and Remembering pp. 119–120 Real or play money Dollar bills Coin strips	**Going Further** Activity Cards 5-16 Match the Coin Cards (TRB M65) Scissors Math Journals
2 Going Further ▸ Differentiated Instruction		
3 Homework and Spiral Review		

Use Math Talk today!

Keeping Skills Sharp

Quick Practice — 5 MINUTES

Goal: Monitor progress in adding 2-digit numbers.

Quick Check Write the following exercises on the board for children to solve. Remind children to work independently. This activity should help identify children who are having difficulty with 2-digit addition. Walk around and see how children are doing so you know whether you need a basic review to start the day. You can check details of children's errors later.

$$\begin{array}{r} 53 \\ +\ 75 \\ \hline 128 \end{array} \qquad \begin{array}{r} 83 \\ +\ 64 \\ \hline 147 \end{array}$$

Daily Routines

Math Mountains for 100 or 2-Digit Numbers Using the MathBoard, Using Dimes and Pennies
(See p. xxvi.)

▸ Led by Student Leaders

Money Routine Using the 120 Poster, Using the Money Flip Chart, Using the Number Path, Using Secret Code Cards
(See pp. xxiii–xxv.)

▸ Led by Student Leaders

Teaching the Lesson

Activity 1

Review the Nickel

 30 MINUTES

Goal: Find equivalencies of nickels. Represent money amounts with Dime and Nickel Strips and pennies.

Materials: Real or play money (pennies, nickels, dimes, and dollars) or Coin Strips (1 Penny Strip, 1 Dime Strip per child), Dollar Bill (TRB M67–M68), Student Activity Book pages 175–176, 179

 **NCTM Standards:**
Number and Operations
Representation

 **Alternate Approach**

Relate 5 Pennies to 5 Fingers Relate the fingers of one hand to pennies and a nickel. Have children count the number of fingers (including the thumb) on one hand. Point out that there are 5 fingers on 1 hand just like there are 5 pennies in 1 nickel. Encourage children to use their hand to remember this equivalency.

5 pennies = 1 nickel

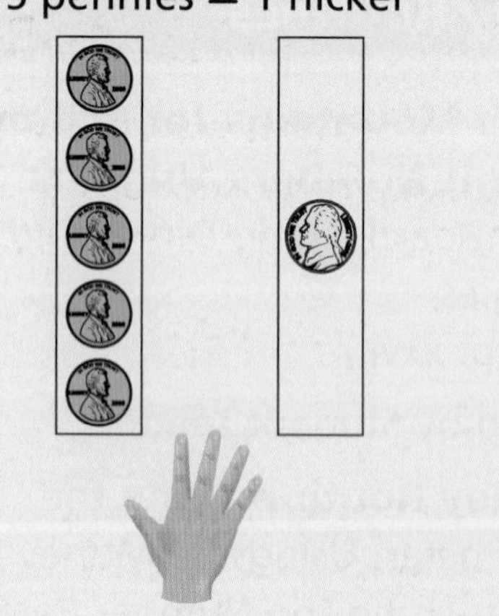

▶ The Value of a Nickel

WHOLE CLASS

Math Talk

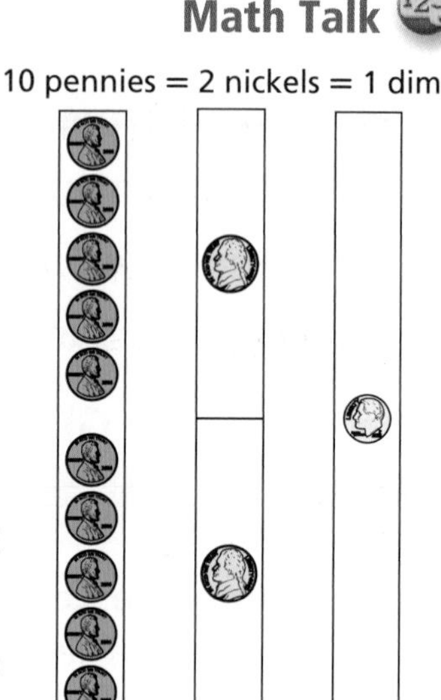

Allow children to examine some nickels so they see that a nickel is worth 5 pennies and 2 nickels are worth 10 pennies or a dime. Have children look at Dime and Nickel Strips to see these equivalent relationships. Use the Dime and Nickel Strips, and some pennies to find coin equivalencies.

- What coin is worth 5 pennies? a nickel
- I have 10 pennies. How many nickels is that? 2
- I have 1 dime. How many nickels is that? 2
- I have 2 nickels. How many pennies is that? 10
- How many dimes is 10 pennies? 1

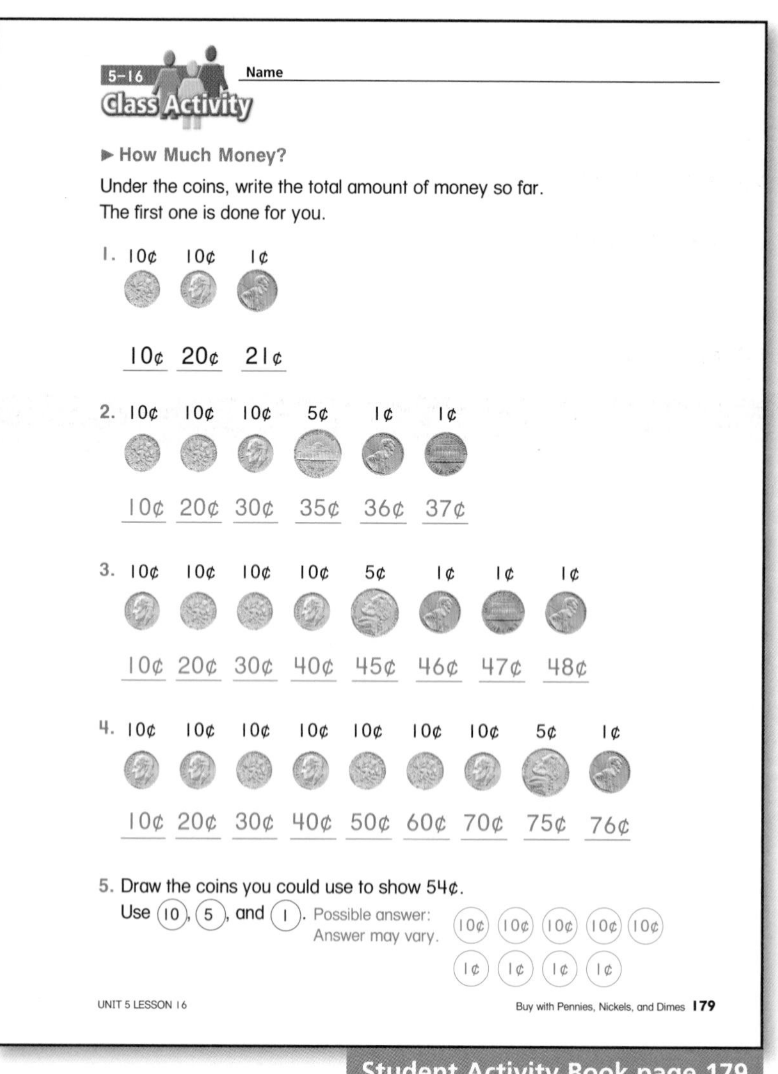

5-16 Class Activity Name ____

▶ How Much Money?

Under the coins, write the total amount of money so far. The first one is done for you.

1. 10¢ 10¢ 1¢
10¢ 20¢ 21¢

2. 10¢ 10¢ 10¢ 5¢ 1¢ 1¢
10¢ 20¢ 30¢ 35¢ 36¢ 37¢

3. 10¢ 10¢ 10¢ 10¢ 5¢ 1¢ 1¢ 1¢
10¢ 20¢ 30¢ 40¢ 45¢ 46¢ 47¢ 48¢

4. 10¢ 10¢ 10¢ 10¢ 10¢ 10¢ 10¢ 5¢ 1¢
10¢ 20¢ 30¢ 40¢ 50¢ 60¢ 70¢ 75¢ 76¢

5. Draw the coins you could use to show 54¢.
Use (10), (5), and (1). Possible answer: Answer may vary. (10¢) (10¢) (10¢) (10¢) (10¢) (1¢) (1¢) (1¢) (1¢)

UNIT 5 LESSON 16 Buy with Pennies, Nickels, and Dimes 179

Student Activity Book page 179

▶ How Much Money? WHOLE CLASS

Present children with a money amount up to 99¢. Have them represent the amount with dimes, nickels, and pennies (or Coin Strips). Challenge them to represent the amount with the fewest number of coins.

- How can we show 57¢ with dimes, nickels, and pennies? Try and find the way that uses the fewest coins. 5 dimes, 1 nickel, and 2 pennies
- What other way can we show 57¢? Accept various solutions.

Repeat this activity for other money amounts under one dollar, and then for amounts between one and two dollars. Have children show each amount with the dollar, dimes, nickels, and pennies. You may wish to sketch the money on the board as children suggest answers.

Have children complete Student Activity Book page 179 with a partner or individually.

English Language Learners

Provide children with more practice identifying coins and telling their values. Hold up a penny, nickel, then dime. Say: **This is a __.** Ask: **How many cents is it?** Have children tell the value and hold up the correct number of fingers.

Activity 2

Make Money Amounts

▶ The Snack Bar PAIRS

Direct children's attention to Student Activity Book page 180.

Mr. and Mrs. Green's Snack Bar Tell children they are going to visit Mr. and Mrs. Green's store again today. Inside the store is a snack bar where people can buy things for a snack or a light lunch.

Have each pair choose two items to purchase from the snack bar. Then have them add the prices together and show the exact money total using a dollar, dimes, nickels, and pennies.

Work through an example with the class. Have volunteers choose two different items and show each amount using dimes, nickels, and pennies. Encourage children to exchange five pennies for a nickel whenever they can.

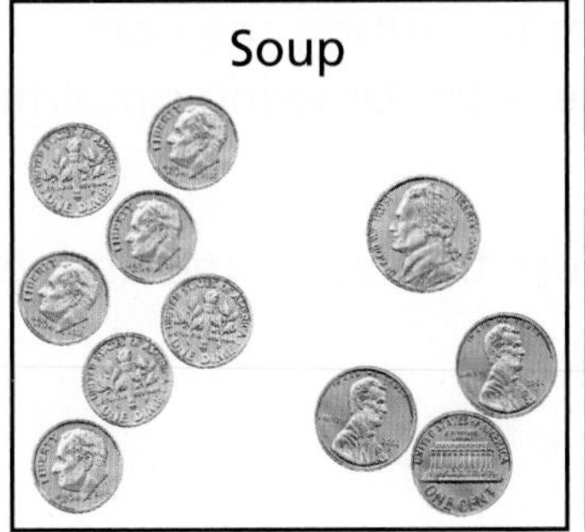

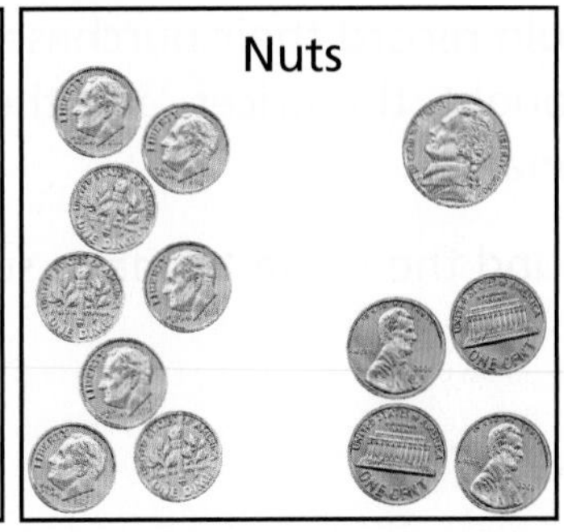

Activity continued ▶

20 MINUTES

Goal: Make exact money totals with dollars, dimes, nickels, and pennies.

Materials: Real or play money (pennies, nickels, dimes, and dollars) or Coin Strips (1 Penny Strip, 1 Dime Strip per child), Dollar Bill (TRB M67–M68), Student Activity Book pages 175–176, 180

 **NCTM Standards:**
Number and Operations
Representation

❶ Teaching the Lesson (continued)

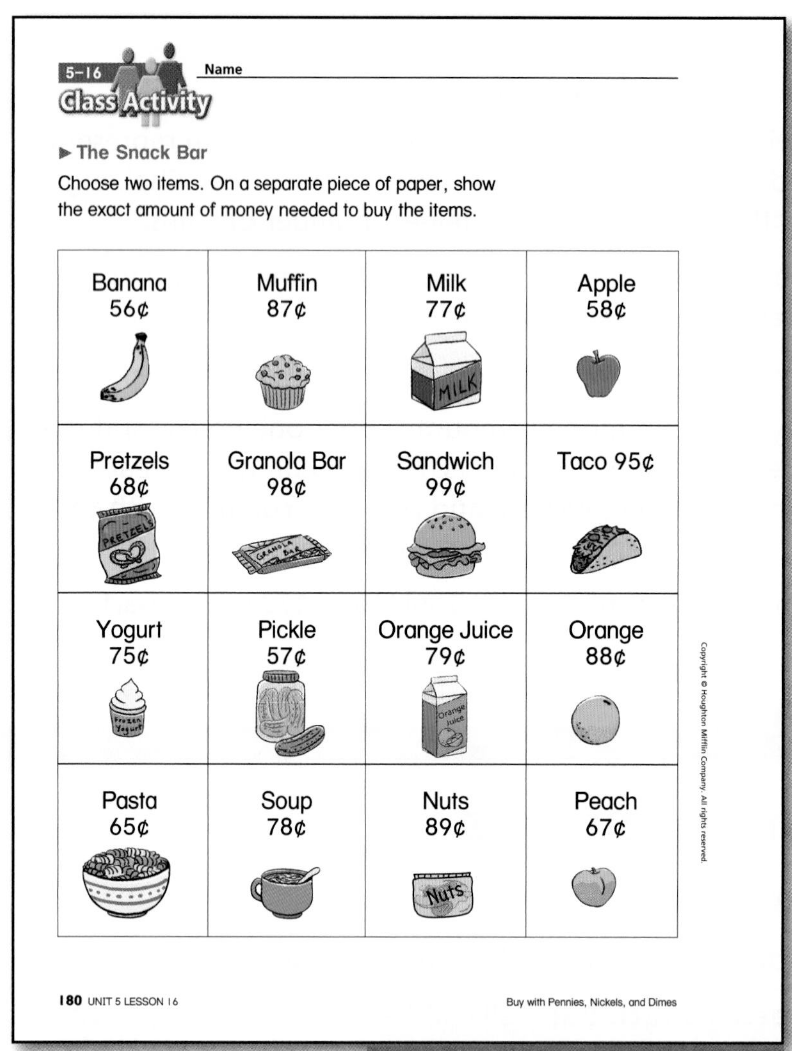

5-16 **Class Activity** Name

▶ **The Snack Bar**

Choose two items. On a separate piece of paper, show the exact amount of money needed to buy the items.

Banana 56¢	Muffin 87¢	Milk 77¢	Apple 58¢
Pretzels 68¢	Granola Bar 98¢	Sandwich 99¢	Taco 95¢
Yogurt 75¢	Pickle 57¢	Orange Juice 79¢	Orange 88¢
Pasta 65¢	Soup 78¢	Nuts 89¢	Peach 67¢

180 UNIT 5 LESSON 16 Buy with Pennies, Nickels, and Dimes

Student Activity Book page 180

Then have a volunteer add the amounts together to determine how much it will cost to buy both items. Finally, show how to add the prices using numbers.

Soup	78¢
Nuts	89¢
	167¢

Children should record their purchases by writing the names of the snack items they bought, the prices, and the total. Drawing simplified bills and coins is optional.

Circulate around the room to make sure that everyone understands what to do.

Teaching Note

Math Symbols Write the cents symbol (¢), and the word *cents* on the board. Point out that the cents symbol stands for the word *cents.* Children should understand that something labeled 78¢ costs 78 cents. Ask children to suggest ways to remember the meaning of the cents symbol. They may notice, for example, that the symbol looks like the letter *c*, the first letter in the word *cents*.

Teaching Note

What to Expect from Students Some children may add the two prices numerically first, then use the dollar, dimes, nickels, and pennies to represent that total. Children who are having difficulty, however, should show each money amount separately, and then combine the two groups to find the total. They can exchange 5 pennies for a nickel, 2 nickels for a dime, 10 pennies for a dime, and 10 dimes for a dollar to reduce and simplify the number of coins.

Ongoing Assessment

Give each child 20 pennies.

▶ How many pennies are in a nickel?

▶ You have 20 pennies. How many nickels is that? How many dimes?

2 Going Further

Differentiated Instruction

Intervention

Activity Card 5-16

Match the Coins Activity Card 5-16

Work:
Use:
- Match the Coins Cards
- scissors

Choose:
-
-

1. **Work Together** Cut the Match the Coins Cards apart.
2. Put the cards face down in two equal rows.
3. Turn over two cards. If the cards show the same amounts, keep the cards. If the cards don't match, turn them back over.
4. Take turns. Play until all the matches have been made. The player with the most cards wins.

Unit 5, Lesson 16

Activity Note Each pair needs Match the Coins Cards (TRB M66) and scissors. Have partners count the coins to check that the cards match.

Math Writing Prompt

Name the Coins Rachel has five coins in her pocket. The total of the coins is 40¢. Name the coins in Rachel's pocket. Explain how you found the answer.

Software Support

Use *Soar to Success* for instruction of students needing targeted support for underlying skills.

On Level

Activity Card 5-16

Dimes, Nickels, and Pennies Activity Card 5-16

Work:
Use:
- paper

1. Start with 1 dime, 1 nickel, and 1 penny. Write down how much money this is. Answer: 16¢
2. Find other amounts up to 100¢ that you can make with an equal number of dimes, nickels, and pennies.
3. For each amount, write the amount and what coins you used.

   Answers: 32¢ = 2 dimes, 2 nickels, 2 pennies; 48¢ = 3 dimes, 3 nickels, 3 pennies; 64¢ = 4 dimes, 4 nickels, 4 pennies; 80¢ = 5 dimes, 5 nickels, 5 pennies; and 96¢ = 6 dimes, 6 nickels, 6 pennies
4. Check your work with a classmate.

Unit 5, Lesson 16

Activity Note Review with children that they want to find the value of equal number of coins. Have children check each other's work.

Math Writing Prompt

Coin Trade Explain why you can trade 3 nickels for 1 dime and 5 pennies.

Software Support

Use *MegaMath* for review and reinforcement of the concepts and skills presented in this lesson.

Challenge

Activity Card 5-16

Money Combinations Activity Card 5-16

Work:
Use:
- paper

Choose:
-
-

1. **Work Together** Think of one way to show 20¢ using dimes, nickels, and pennies.
2. Record the coins you used.

3. Find eight more ways to show 20¢. Answer: 2 dimes; 1 dime, 2 nickels; 1 dime, 1 nickel, 5 pennies; 1 dime, 10 pennies; 4 nickels; 3 nickels, 5 pennies; 2 nickels, 10 pennies; 1 nickel, 15 pennies
4. Write each way.
5. Compare your list with another pair.

Unit 5, Lesson 16

Activity Note Each pair works together to find nine ways to make 20¢ using dimes, nickels, and pennies. You may want to provide coins for children to work with.

Math Writing Prompt

Show the Fewest Coins Explain how you would show 77¢ using dimes, nickels, and pennies. Use the fewest coins you can. Explain.

Software Support

Use *Destination Math* to take students beyond the concepts and skills presented in this lesson.

❸ Homework and Spiral Review

Goal: Additional Practice

✓ Include children's completed Homework page as part of their portfolios.

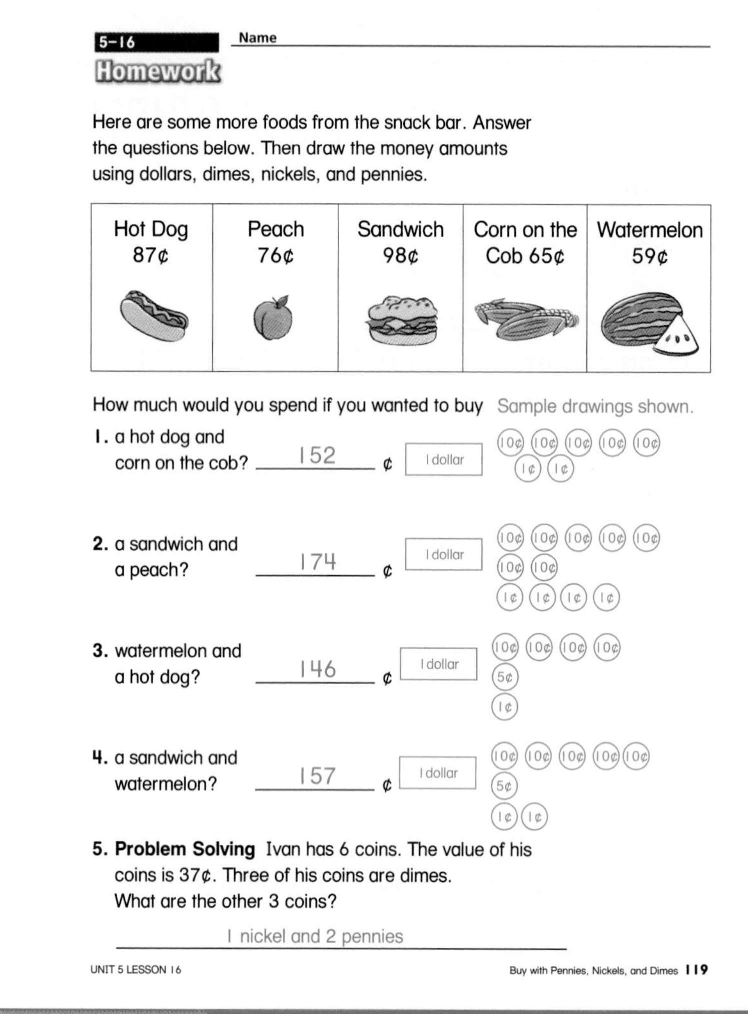

5-16 Homework Name

Here are some more foods from the snack bar. Answer the questions below. Then draw the money amounts using dollars, dimes, nickels, and pennies.

Hot Dog 87¢	Peach 76¢	Sandwich 98¢	Corn on the Cob 65¢	Watermelon 59¢

How much would you spend if you wanted to buy Sample drawings shown.

1. a hot dog and corn on the cob? 152 ¢ 1 dollar 10¢ 10¢ 10¢ 10¢ 10¢ 1¢ 1¢
2. a sandwich and a peach? 174 ¢ 1 dollar 10¢ 10¢ 10¢ 10¢ 10¢ 10¢ 10¢ 1¢ 1¢ 1¢ 1¢
3. watermelon and a hot dog? 146 ¢ 1 dollar 10¢ 10¢ 10¢ 10¢ 5¢ 1¢
4. a sandwich and watermelon? 157 ¢ 1 dollar 10¢ 10¢ 10¢ 10¢ 10¢ 5¢ 1¢ 1¢
5. **Problem Solving** Ivan has 6 coins. The value of his coins is 37¢. Three of his coins are dimes. What are the other 3 coins?

   1 nickel and 2 pennies

UNIT 5 LESSON 16 Buy with Pennies, Nickels, and Dimes **119**

Homework and Remembering page 119

5-16 Remembering **Goal:** Spiral Review

This Remembering activity would be appropriate anytime after today's lesson.

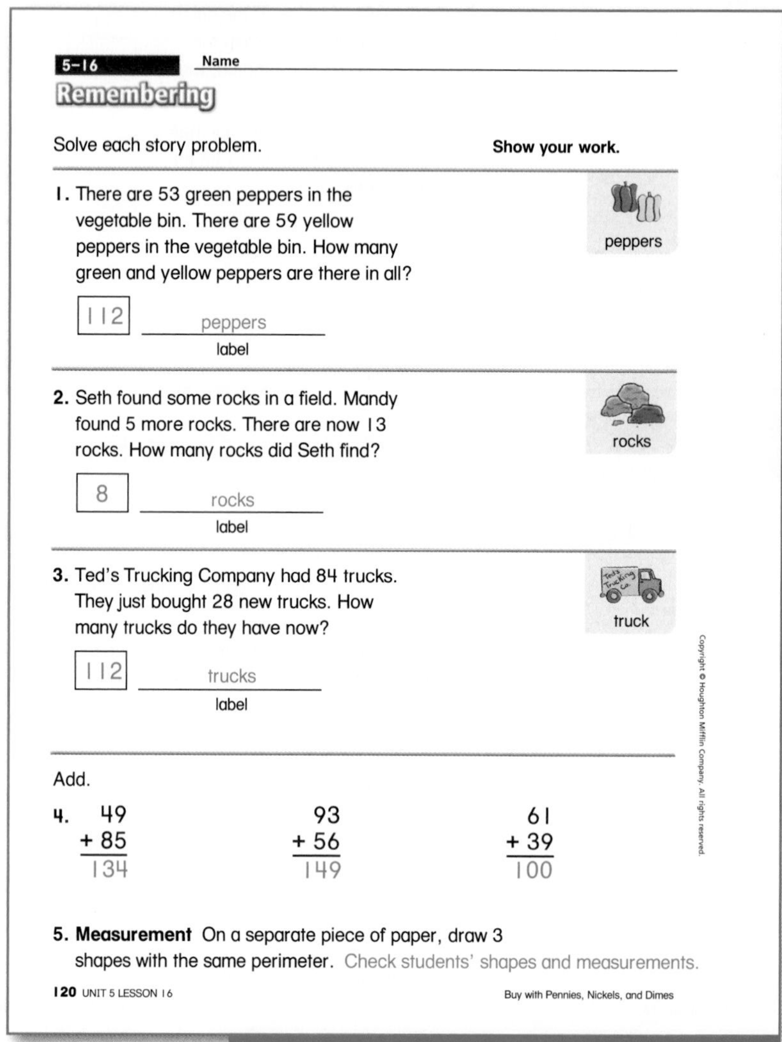

5-16 Remembering Name

Solve each story problem. **Show your work.**

1. There are 53 green peppers in the vegetable bin. There are 59 yellow peppers in the vegetable bin. How many green and yellow peppers are there in all?

   112 peppers (label)

2. Seth found some rocks in a field. Mandy found 5 more rocks. There are now 13 rocks. How many rocks did Seth find?

   8 rocks (label)

3. Ted's Trucking Company had 84 trucks. They just bought 28 new trucks. How many trucks do they have now?

   112 trucks (label)

Add.

4. 49 + 85 = 134 93 + 56 = 149 61 + 39 = 100

5. **Measurement** On a separate piece of paper, draw 3 shapes with the same perimeter. Check students' shapes and measurements.

120 UNIT 5 LESSON 16 Buy with Pennies, Nickels, and Dimes

Homework and Remembering page 120

Home or School Activity

Multicultural Connection

Coins from Different Countries Have children research coins from different countries. Encourage children to bring in coins or pictures of coins to share with their classmates.

Sequences

Lesson Objectives

- Skip count forward and backward.
- Analyze relationships between numbers in sequences.
- Discuss patterns in a horizontal hundred grid.
- Solve addition exercises.

Vocabulary

skip count
forward sequence
backward sequence
rule

The Day at a Glance

Today's Goals	Materials	
1 Teaching the Lesson **A1:** Skip count, write rules for number sequences, and fill in missing numbers in sequences. **A2:** Write the numbers 1 to 100 in a horizontal grid. **A3:** Practice addition.	**Lesson Activities** Student Activity Book pp. 181–184 Homework and Remembering pp. 121–122 MathBoard materials Number Path (TRB M51)	**Going Further** Activity Cards 5-17 Student Activity Book p. 183 Sticky notes Math Journals
2 Going Further ► Differentiated Instruction		
3 Homework and Targeted Practice		

Use Math Talk today!

Keeping Skills Sharp

Quick Practice — 5 MINUTES

Goals: Use place-value patterns to add. Identify tens and ones to solve addition problems.

Trios Have a **Student Leader** write the three problems shown below on the board. The leader reads the problems aloud, one at a time, giving a hand signal to indicate when the class should respond with the answer. (See Unit 5 Lesson 15.)

42 + 1 = ☐ 42 + 10 = ☐
42 + 100 = ☐

Repeated Quick Practice
Use this Quick Practice from a previous lesson.

► **Add Tens or Ones** (See Unit 5 Lesson 15.)

Daily Routines

Math Mountains for 100 or 2-Digit Numbers Using the MathBoard, Using Dimes and Pennies (See p. xxvi.)

► Led by Student Leaders

Money Routine Using the 120 Poster, Using the Money Flip Chart, Using the Number Path, Using Secret Code Cards (See pp. xxiii–xxv.)

► Led by Student Leaders

1 Teaching the Lesson

Activity 1

Forward and Backward Sequences

 **30 MINUTES**

Goal: Repeatedly add or subtract, write rules for number sequences, and fill in missing numbers in sequences.

Materials: MathBoard materials or Number Path (TRB M51), Student Activity Book page 181

 **NCTM Standards:**
Number and Operations
Algebra
Representation

English Language Learners

Have children stand and march forward then backward 5 steps. Write example sequences on the board. Label them *forward* and *backward*.

- **Beginning** Say: **A *sequence* is a number pattern. The numbers get bigger. In a *backward sequence* the numbers get smaller.** Have children repeat.
- **Intermediate** Say: **These are *sequences*.** Ask: **Are *sequences* like number patterns?** yes **Which sequence gets bigger?** forward **Smaller?** backward
- **Advanced** Have children use short sentences to describe the sequences.

▶ Introduce Sequences WHOLE CLASS

Forward Sequences Tell the class that forward sequences involve adding the same number over and over. Write the following sequence on the board.

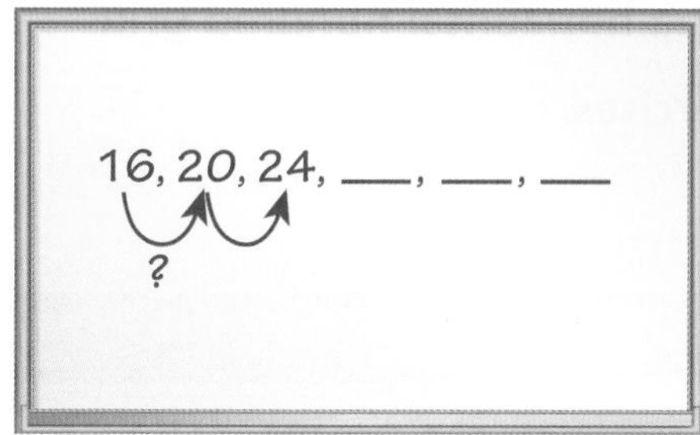

Ask children if they can figure out what numbers go on the lines once they find the rule for what number they are adding over and over.

- What is the rule? add 4
- How do you know? 16 + 4 = 20 and 20 + 4 = 24
- What are the unknown numbers? 28, 32, and 36
- How do you know? 24 + 4 = 28; 28 + 4 = 32; 32 + 4 = 36

Sequences on the Number Path Write 47 on the board. Have children find 47 on their Number Paths. Then count by 3s starting at 47. Count by saying **47** loudly, then 48, 49 softly, then **50** loudly, and so on.

Have children circle groups of 3 on their boards and write +3 under each group. Explain that the 3 tells how many there are in each group they counted.

- When you add the same number over and over, you write every third number. What is the third number after 50? 53 and after that? 56
- What is the rule for this sequence? Add 3.

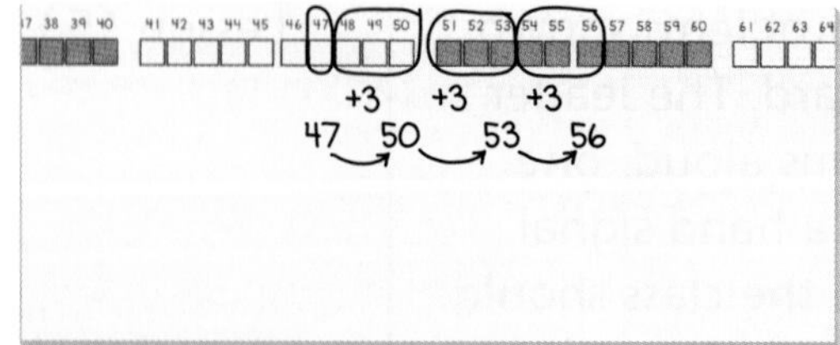

Write this sequence on the board and find more numbers in it, first by adding, and then by circling groups of 3 on the Number Path to check.

47, 50, 53, 56, ___, ___, ___, ___

Do more forward sequences by finding the rule, adding the same number, and checking on the Number Path.

35, 37, 39, ___, ___, ___, ___

64, 69, 74, ___, ___, ___, ___

Backward Sequences Explain that backward sequences involve subtraction. Write the following sequence and have children determine the rule so they can fill in the unknown numbers.

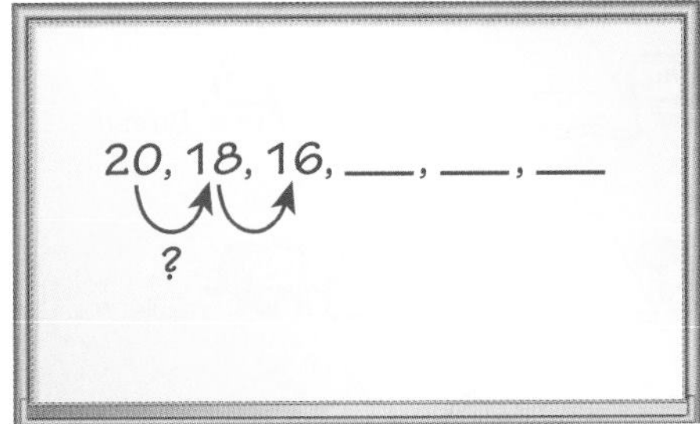

- What is the rule? subtract 2
- How do you know? $20 - 2 = 18$
- What are the next three numbers? 14, 12, and 10

Give more backward sequences, finding the rule, and then checking the sequence on the Number Path by circling groups before the starting number.

64, 61, 58, ___, ___, ___, ___

51, 46, 41, ___, ___, ___, ___

Activity continued ▶

The Learning Classroom

Building Concepts As children repeatedly add or subtract by different numbers, remind them to look at the number paths on their MathBoards. These paths provide a visual reference that children can use until they become more familiar with repeated addition or subtraction by 2s and 3s. Repeated addition or subtraction is often referred to as skip counting.

Teaching the Lesson (continued)

Teaching Note

Math Background Using a letter such as *n* to represent a number introduces children to algebraic concepts. Letters used in place of numbers are called variables or unknowns. Any letter can be a variable, though the letters *x, y,* and *n* are commonly used.

Math Talk in Action

Kaya: Name a sequence with numbers between 100 and 200.

Greg: 120, 122, 124, 126, ...

Kaya: What is the rule in this sequence?

Greg: 120 + 2 is 122 so I add 2 to go from 120 to 122, and from 122 to 124 and also from 124 to 126. The pattern is to skip count by 2s.

Kaya: How can you write this rule using the letter *n*?

Greg: The letter *n* stands for a number. The rule is to add 2 to a number to get the next number. So the rule is $n + 2$.

Kaya: What are the next three numbers in this sequence?

Greg: I can skip count by 2s to find the next numbers. The last number in the sequence is 126, so the next number after that is 126 + 2 or 128. After 128 comes 130 and 132.

Kaya: So the sequence is 120, 122, 124, 126, 128, 130, 132.

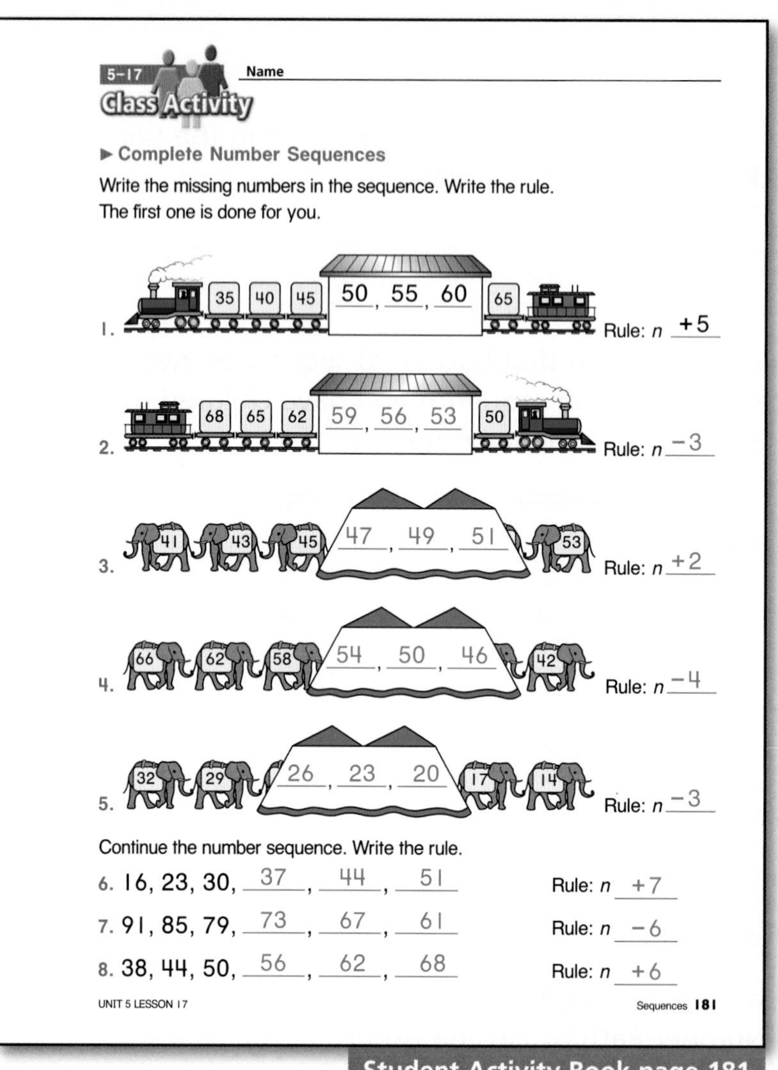

5-17 Class Activity

Name

► Complete Number Sequences

Write the missing numbers in the sequence. Write the rule. The first one is done for you.

1. 35, 40, 45, 50, 55, 60, 65 Rule: n +5
2. 68, 65, 62, 59, 56, 53, 50 Rule: n −3
3. 41, 43, 45, 47, 49, 51, 53 Rule: n +2
4. 66, 62, 58, 54, 50, 46, 42 Rule: n −4
5. 32, 29, 26, 23, 20, 17, 14 Rule: n −3

Continue the number sequence. Write the rule.

6. 16, 23, 30, 37, 44, 51 Rule: n +7
7. 91, 85, 79, 73, 67, 61 Rule: n −6
8. 38, 44, 50, 56, 62, 68 Rule: n +6

UNIT 5 LESSON 17 Sequences 181

Student Activity Book page 181

► Complete Number Sequences WHOLE CLASS

Discuss how to state rules for sequences using *n* to stand for *number.* Explain that if we need to add 4, we can say: "The rule is *n* plus 4." If the rule is to subtract 2, we can say: "The rule is *n* minus 2."

Direct children's attention to Student Activity Book page 181. Do the first row on the page as a class and then have children complete the page independently.

If time allows, invite children to create sequences for classmates to continue and to write the rule using *n.* For sample classroom dialogue, see **Math Talk in Action** in the side column.

Activity 2

Count to 100

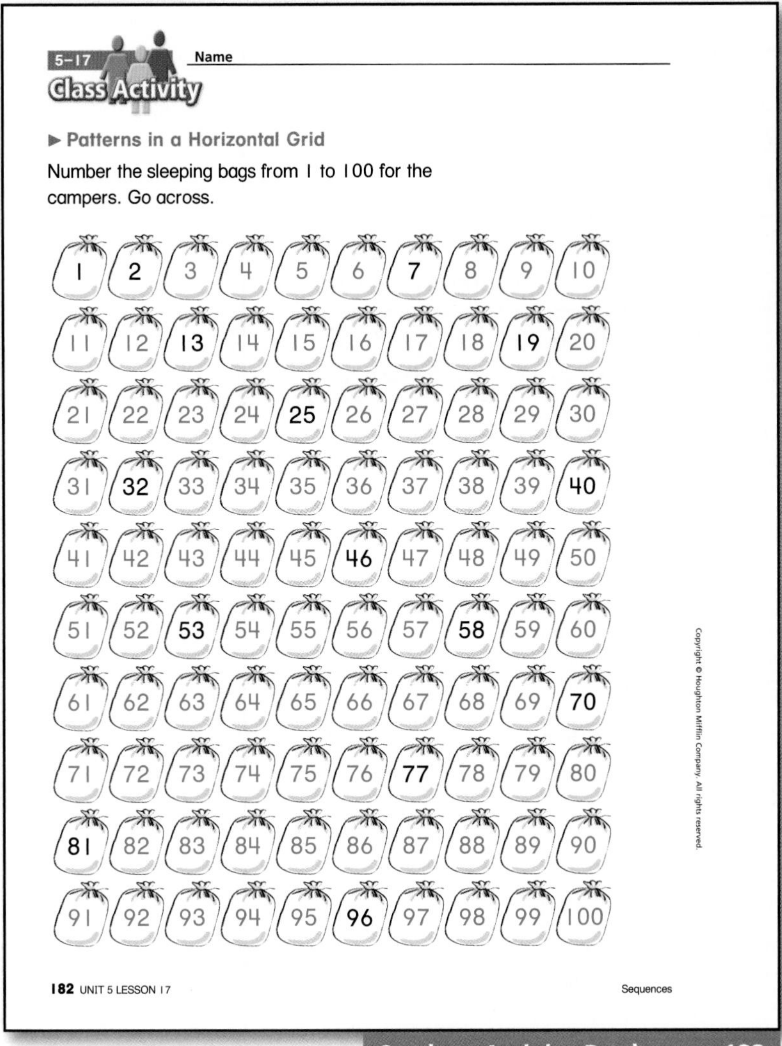
5-17 Class Activity Name

► Patterns in a Horizontal Grid

Number the sleeping bags from 1 to 100 for the campers. Go across.

1	2	3	4	5	6	7	8	9	10
11	12	13	14	15	16	17	18	19	20
21	22	23	24	25	26	27	28	29	30
31	32	33	34	35	36	37	38	39	40
41	42	43	44	45	46	47	48	49	50
51	52	53	54	55	56	57	58	59	60
61	62	63	64	65	66	67	68	69	70
71	72	73	74	75	76	77	78	79	80
81	82	83	84	85	86	87	88	89	90
91	92	93	94	95	96	97	98	99	100

182 UNIT 5 LESSON 17 Sequences

Student Activity Book page 182

► Patterns in a Horizontal Grid INDIVIDUALS

Have children look at Student Activity Book page 182. Explain to children that they need to number the sleeping bags in order from 1 to 100. Point out that the numbers begin in the upper left corner with the number 1. Explain that the numbers go across rather then down. Work with children to fill in the first three rows.

After children finish filling in the chart, name numbers between 10–90. Have the children state what numbers are 10 more and 10 less than the named number.

Discuss Patterns Invite children to share patterns they see in the grid. Have them also compare this grid to other grids they have seen.

Activity continued ►

 **10 MINUTES**

Goal: Write the numbers 1 to 100 in a horizontal grid.

Materials: Student Activity Book page 182

 **NCTM Standards:**
Number and Operations
Representation

Teaching Note

Watch For! Some children may start to write the numbers down in columns rather than across the rows. Be sure each child starts the activity correctly by checking the first three rows before children continue the activity on their own. Some children may skip a number or make another error as they write the numbers from 1 to 100.

Have children think about and discuss possible checkpoints they can use to make sure they have completed each row correctly. They can, for example, be sure they write a decade numbering the last space of each row or check that each number in a column ends in the same digit. Children should notice that the page includes the numbers 32, 70, and 96 at the appropriate sleeping bag. If children's numbers do match these checkpoints, they should go back and check their work.

1 Teaching the Lesson (continued)

Activity 3 OPTIONAL

Addition Practice

15 MINUTES

Goal: Practice addition.

Materials: Student Activity Book page 183

NCTM Standard:
Number and Operations

Teaching Note

Language and Vocabulary When children talk about adding the numbers that correspond to the letters in their names, they may benefit from knowing the terms "addend" and "sum." Explain that the numbers being added in an addition problem are called the *addends* and the answer or "total" is the *sum*. For the name Ray, the addends are 18, 1, and 25 and the sum is 44.

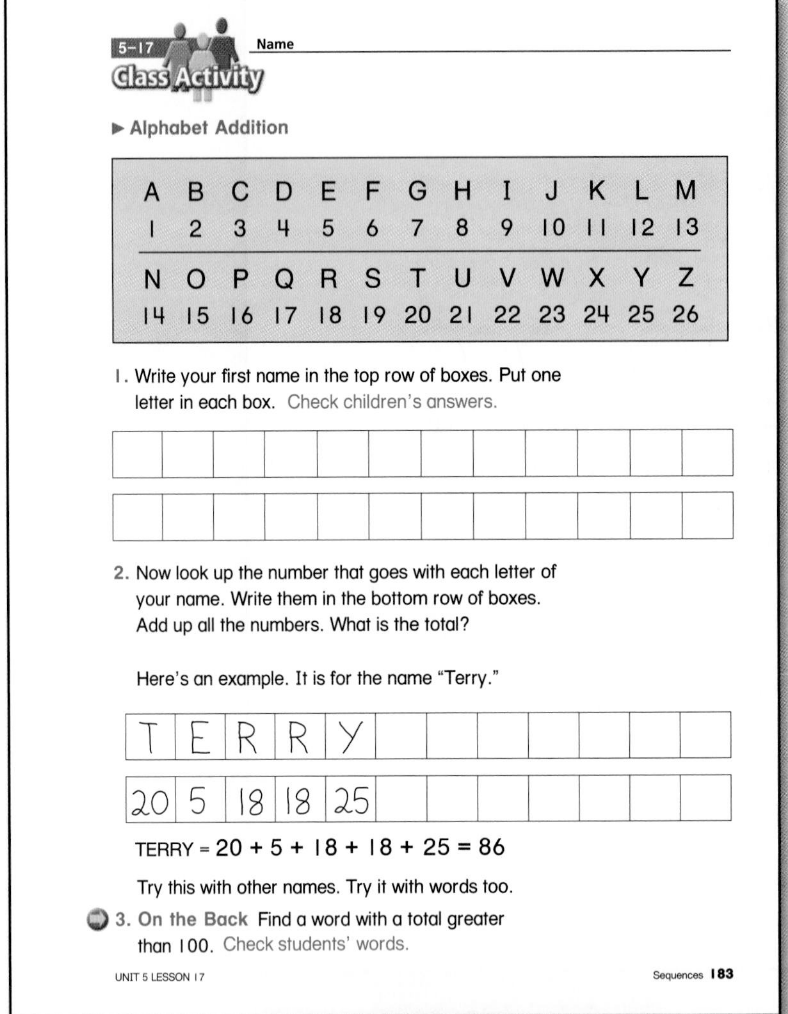

5–17 Class Activity Name ____________

▶ Alphabet Addition

A	B	C	D	E	F	G	H	I	J	K	L	M
1	2	3	4	5	6	7	8	9	10	11	12	13
N	O	P	Q	R	S	T	U	V	W	X	Y	Z
14	15	16	17	18	19	20	21	22	23	24	25	26

1. Write your first name in the top row of boxes. Put one letter in each box. Check children's answers.

2. Now look up the number that goes with each letter of your name. Write them in the bottom row of boxes. Add up all the numbers. What is the total?

Here's an example. It is for the name "Terry."

T	E	R	R	Y							
20	5	18	18	25							

TERRY = 20 + 5 + 18 + 18 + 25 = 86

Try this with other names. Try it with words too.

3. On the Back Find a word with a total greater than 100. Check students' words.

UNIT 5 LESSON 17 Sequences 183

Student Activity Book page 183

▶ Alphabet Addition INDIVIDUALS

Refer children to the Student Activity Book page 183. Make sure children understand that they need to figure out the total of their names by giving a number value to each letter. The letters are assigned values according to their order in the alphabet. For example, A = 1, B = 2, C = 3, and so on.

After children figure out the total of their name, have them determine which classmate's name has the greatest total.

- Who would like to say their total?
- Does anyone have a greater total?

Have children complete the pages independently or in **Helping Pairs**. For the On the Back activity, tell children to fold their papers up so they can write on the back and still look at the values for each letter.

Ongoing Assessment

Write 3, 6, 9, 12, ___, ___, ___ on the board. Ask children to write a rule for the sequence using the letter *n* and identify the next numbers.

2 Going Further

Differentiated Instruction

Intervention — Activity Card 5-17

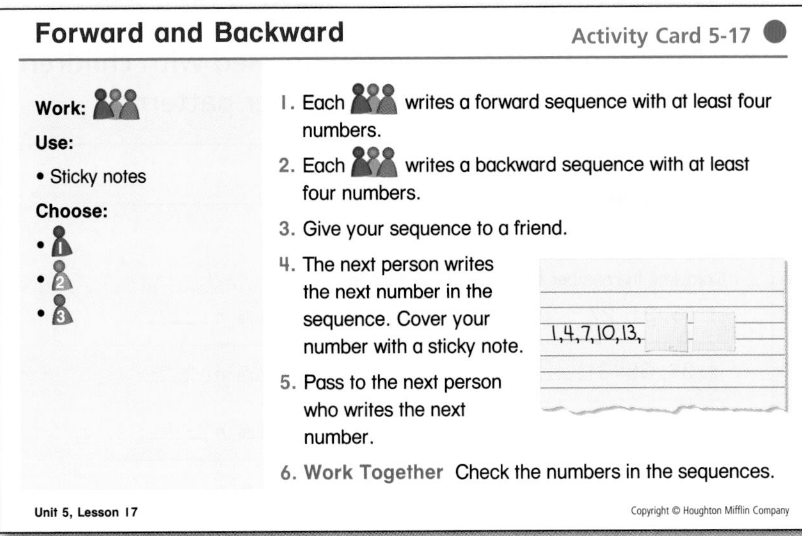

Forward and Backward — Activity Card 5-17

Work: (group)
Use:
- Sticky notes

Choose:
- 1
- 2
- 3

1. Each (group member) writes a forward sequence with at least four numbers.
2. Each (group member) writes a backward sequence with at least four numbers.
3. Give your sequence to a friend.
4. The next person writes the next number in the sequence. Cover your number with a sticky note.
5. Pass to the next person who writes the next number.
6. **Work Together** Check the numbers in the sequences.

Unit 5, Lesson 17

Activity Note Each group needs sticky notes. Each child writes a forward and backward sequence. Then other group members figure out the sequence and write the next number.

Math Writing Prompt

Explain Your Thinking Explain how you find the missing number in the sequence 2, 6, 10, 14, 18, ___.

Software Support

Use *Soar to Success* for instruction of students needing targeted support for underlying skills.

On Level — Activity Card 5-17

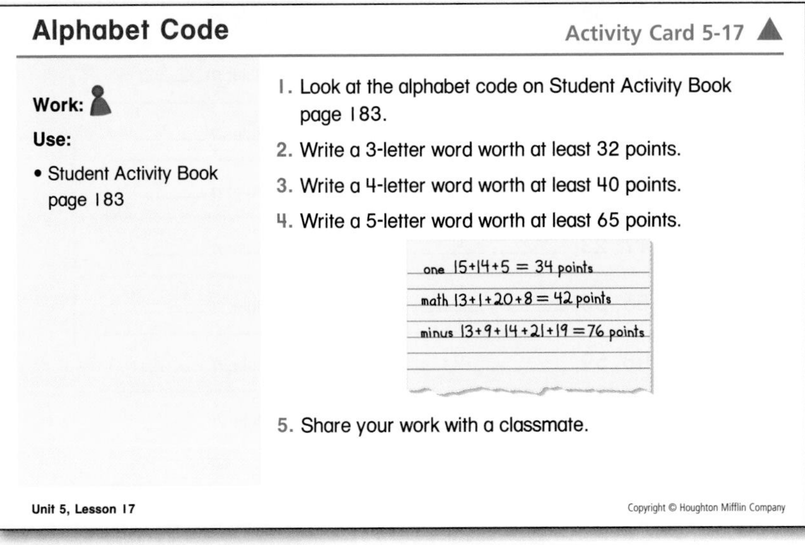

Alphabet Code — Activity Card 5-17

Work: (individual)
Use:
- Student Activity Book page 183

1. Look at the alphabet code on Student Activity Book page 183.
2. Write a 3-letter word worth at least 32 points.
3. Write a 4-letter word worth at least 40 points.
4. Write a 5-letter word worth at least 65 points.

5. Share your work with a classmate.

Unit 5, Lesson 17

Activity Note Each child needs the alphabet code on Student Activity Book p. 183. Show children how to find the point value of a word. Have children write different words from the samples on their cards.

Math Writing Prompt

Different Ways to Add Describe two different ways to add 14 + 11 + 28.

Software Support

Use *MegaMath* for review and reinforcement of the concepts and skills presented in this lesson.

Challenge — Activity Card 5-17

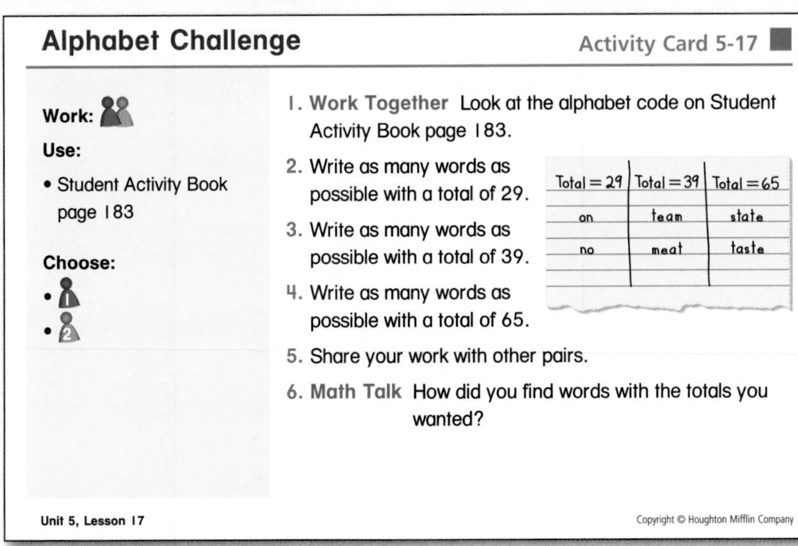

Alphabet Challenge — Activity Card 5-17

Work: (pair)
Use:
- Student Activity Book page 183

Choose:
- 1
- 2

1. **Work Together** Look at the alphabet code on Student Activity Book page 183.
2. Write as many words as possible with a total of 29.
3. Write as many words as possible with a total of 39.
4. Write as many words as possible with a total of 65.
5. Share your work with other pairs.
6. **Math Talk** How did you find words with the totals you wanted?

Total = 29	Total = 39	Total = 65
on	team	state
no	meat	taste

Unit 5, Lesson 17

Activity Note Each pair needs the alphabet code on Student Activity Book p. 183. Review how to use the code to find the value of words. Have children find different words from the sample.

Math Writing Prompt

Compare and Contrast Explain how the rule $n + 3$ is alike and different from the rule $n - 3$.

DESTINATION Math® **Software Support**

Use *Destination Math* to take students beyond the concepts and skills presented in this lesson.

3 Homework and Targeted Practice

5–17 Homework **Goal:** Additional Practice

This Homework page provides practice in completing number sequences.

5–17 Homework Name ______

Complete the number sequence. Write the rule.

1. 12, 14, 16, 18, 20, 22, 24 Rule: n + 2
2. 25, 30, 35, 40, 45, 50, 55 Rule: n + 5
3. 49, 52, 55, 58, 61, 64, 67 Rule: n + 3
4. 80, 90, 100, 110, 120, 130, 140 Rule: n + 10
5. 46, 56, 66, 76, 86, 96, 106 Rule: n + 10
6. 58, 56, 54, 52, 50, 48, 46 Rule: n − 2
7. 39, 36, 33, 30, 27, 24, 21 Rule: n − 3
8. 48, 42, 36, 30, 24, 18, 12 Rule: n − 6
9. 70, 65, 60, 55, 50, 45, 40 Rule: n − 5
10. 126, 130, 134, 138, 142, 146, 150 Rule: n + 4
11. 135, 140, 145, 150, 155, 160, 165 Rule: n + 5
12. **Explain Your Thinking** Which takes less time? Explain.
    - Skip count by 2s from 2 to 100.
    - Skip count by 5s from 5 to 100.

    Answers will vary.

UNIT 5 LESSON 17 Sequences **121**

Homework and Remembering page 121

5–17 Targeted Practice **Goal:** Number sequences.

This Targeted Practice page can be used with children who need extra practice with number patterns.

5–17 Targeted Practice Name ______

Complete the number sequence. Write the rule.

1. 15, 21, 27, 33, 39, 45 Rule: n + 6
2. 39, 35, 31, 27, 23, 19 Rule: n − 4
3. 29, 34, 39, 44, 49, 54 Rule: n + 5
4. 43, 39, 35, 31, 27, 23 Rule: n − 4
5. 66, 69, 72, 75, 78, 81 Rule: n + 3
6. 43, 35, 27, 19, 11, 3 Rule: n − 8
7. 84, 86, 88, 90, 92, 94 Rule: n + 2
8. 52, 46, 40, 34, 28, 22 Rule: n − 6
9. 21, 29, 37, 45, 53, 61 Rule: n + 8
10. 90, 87, 84, 81, 78, 75 Rule: n − 3
11. 11, 17, 23, 29, 35, 41 Rule: n + 6
12. 49, 56, 63, 70, 77, 84 Rule: n + 7
13. 37, 48, 59, 70, 81, 92 Rule: n + 11
14. 84, 75, 66, 57, 48, 39 Rule: n − 9

122 UNIT 5 LESSON 17 Sequences

Homework and Remembering page 122

Home or School Activity

Art Connection

Create a Pattern Have children use Student Activity Book page 182 to create a pattern using skip-counting. Children should choose a rule and then color the appropriate bags to match the rule. For example, if the rule is to skip count by 5s, the child can color bags 1–5 one color, bags 6–10 a second color, bags 11–15 the first color, bags 16–20 the second color, and so on.

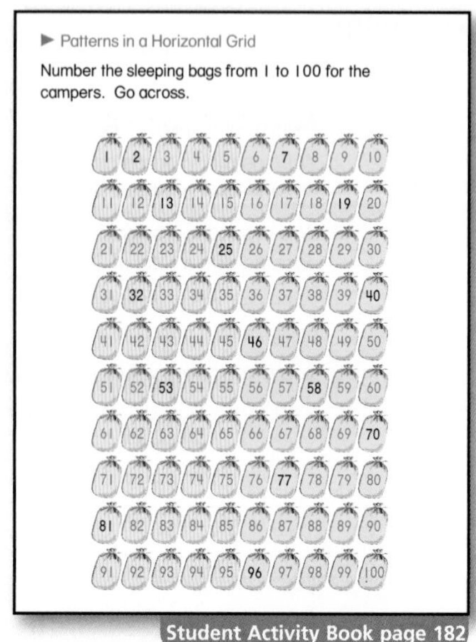

► Patterns in a Horizontal Grid

Number the sleeping bags from 1 to 100 for the campers. Go across.

1	2	3	4	5	6	7	8	9	10
11	12	13	14	15	16	17	18	19	20
21	22	23	24	25	26	27	28	29	30
31	32	33	34	35	36	37	38	39	40
41	42	43	44	45	46	47	48	49	50
51	52	53	54	55	56	57	58	59	60
61	62	63	64	65	66	67	68	69	70
71	72	73	74	75	76	77	78	79	80
81	82	83	84	85	86	87	88	89	90
91	92	93	94	95	96	97	98	99	100

Student Activity Book page 182

Find 2-Digit Partners

Vocabulary
partners
break-apart
Math Mountains

Lesson Objective

- **Find partners of 2-digit numbers and partners of 100.**

The Day at a Glance

Today's Goals	Materials	
1 Teaching the Lesson **A1:** Find partners of 100. **A2:** Find partners of 2-digit numbers. **2 Going Further** ► Problem-Solving Strategy: Estimate to Solve Story Problems ► Differentiated Instruction **3 Homework and Spiral Review**	**Lesson Activities** Homework and Remembering pp. 123–124 MathBoard materials Quick Quiz 3 (Assessment Guide)	**Going Further** Activity Cards 5-18 Student Activity Book pp. 185–186 Real or play money Centimeter Grid Paper (TRB M50) Scissors Math Journals

Use Math Talk today!

Keeping Skills Sharp

Quick Practice — 5 MINUTES

Goals: Use place-value patterns to add. Practice adding ones or adding tens.

Trios Have a **Student Leader** write the three exercises shown below on the board. The leader reads the exercises aloud, one at a time, giving a hand signal to indicate when the class should respond with the answer. (See Unit 5 Lesson 15.)

26 + 3 = ☐ 26 + 30 = ☐ 26 + 300 = ☐

Add Tens or Ones Write examples like the ones below on the board. Have a Student Leader direct the class as they say whether they are adding tens or ones. The class should then say the answer. (See Unit 5 Lesson 15.)

8 + 1 = ☐ 4 + 5 = ☐
80 + 10 = ☐ 40 + 50 = ☐

Daily Routines

Math Mountains for 100 or 2-Digit Numbers Using the MathBoard, Using Dimes and Pennies
(See p. xxvi.)

► Led by Student Leaders

Money Routine Using the 120 Poster, Using the Money Flip Chart, Using the Number Path, Using Secret Code Cards
(See pp. xxiii–xxv.)

► Led by Student Leaders

1 Teaching the Lesson

Activity 1

Find Partners of One Hundred

 30 MINUTES

Goal: Find partners of 100.

Materials: MathBoard materials

 **NCTM Standards:**
Number and Operations
Communication
Representation

 **Class Management**

Looking Ahead Children will practice the skills from this lesson on the Remembering pages in Unit 7. On those pages, children will find one unknown partner for a total between 20 and 100. Children can add up, count on, or draw sticks and circles. These experiences prepare them for 2-digit subtraction in Unit 9.

English Language Learners

Help children with vocabulary in the story problem. Draw a parking lot with some empty spaces on the board.

- **Beginning** Point to the picture as you say: **This is a *parking lot*. Every car goes in a *space*. This *space* does not have a car. It is *empty*.**
- **Intermediate** Ask: **Is this a parking lot or a garage?** parking lot Point to the picture. Say: **This *space* has a car in it.** Ask: **Is it *empty?*** no Point to an empty space. Ask: **Is this *space* empty?** yes
- **Advanced** Ask: **What is this?** parking lot Say: **Some of the *spaces* have cars in them. Some are ___.** empty

▶ Break Apart One Hundred WHOLE CLASS

Write this story problem on the board and read it aloud to the class.

There are 100 spaces in the parking lot. 32 of them have cars. How many spaces are empty?

Invite a few volunteers to work at the board, while the rest of the class works on their MathBoards at their seats. Ask children to discuss different solution methods for this problem.

Count on Using 10-Sticks and Circles	Add Up to 100	Break Apart 100
|||○○ ○○○○○ ○○○ |||||| 32 + 8 + 60 8 + 60 is 40 is 100 = 68	32 + 8 is 40 +60 is 100 so 68	32 2 8 60 68 100 32 68

Relate the problem to break-apart partners and to the Secret Code Cards: 100 has 32 and 68 hiding inside it. Change the problem to 100 spaces and 49 cars.

There are 100 spaces in the parking lot. 49 of them have cars. How many spaces are empty?

Explain to children that they may use previously learned methods to solve the problem. They may also just know that 50 + 50 = 100, so they can move 1 from 50 to the other 50 to make the partners 49 and 51.

Do one or two more problems breaking apart 100 into 76 and a partner and into 69 and a partner. Use the parking lot problem or have children make up another problem.

Activity 2

Find Partners of 2-Digit Numbers

▶ Break Apart 2-Digit Numbers PAIRS

You may use the following light bulb problem, the parking lot problem from Activity 1, or have children make up their own problem. Have them solve, describe, and compare their solution methods.

There are 43 light bulbs on the baseball scoreboard. 28 burned out. How many are still working?

Possible Solution Methods

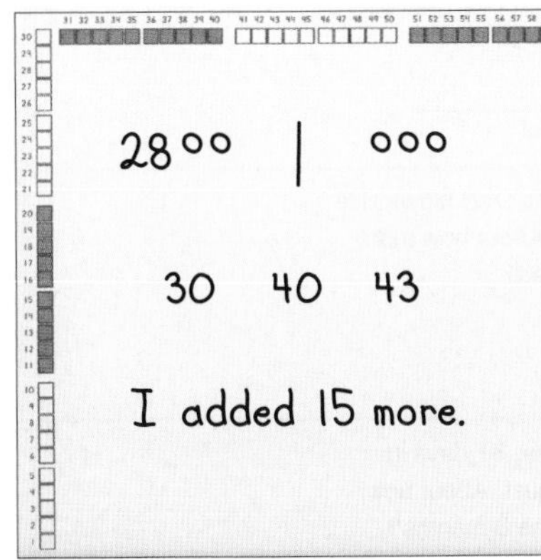

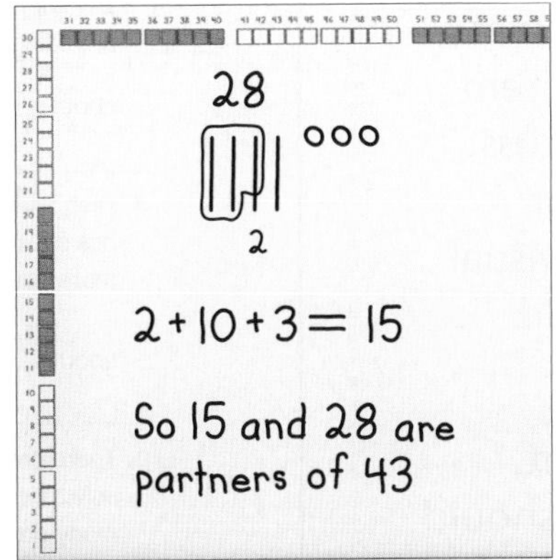

Encourage children to count on or add on using tens as well as ones.

If they write:

28 + ooooooooooooooo = 43

Then encourage them to use tens:

28 oo | ooo
30 40 43

or

28 | ooooo
38 43

Have children relate their results to Math Mountains.

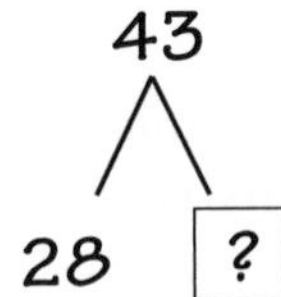

- 43 has partners 28 and what number? 15

Solve two or three more problems as time permits. Have student helpers work with classmates experiencing difficulty.

 **25 MINUTES**

Goal: Find partners of 2-digit numbers.

Materials: MathBoard materials

 **NCTM Standards:**
Number and Operations
Communication
Representation

The Learning Classroom

Building Concepts As children solve similar problems on the Remembering pages in Unit 7, check their methods. Challenge children to find the unknown partner in more than one way.

Ongoing Assessment

Ask children to solve the following problems:

- ▶ A parking lot has 100 spaces. 41 have cars. How many spaces are empty?
- ▶ A parking lot has 57 spaces. 33 are empty. How many spaces have cars?

Quick Quiz

See the Assessment Guide for Unit 5 Quick Quiz 3.

2 Going Further

Problem-Solving Strategy: Estimate to Solve Story Problems

Goal: Round addends to solve story problems.

Materials: Student Activity Book page 185

 **NCTM Standards:**
Number and Operations
Problem Solving

▶ Round and Estimate WHOLE CLASS

Write the number 43 on the board. Discuss what it means to round and how rounding gives an estimate, rather than an exact answer. Elicit as many different methods for rounding as children can offer. Discuss how the last digit shows whether to round up or down. You may wish to use a number line as a visual aid. Then ask children to explain how they would round the number. (See Unit 5 Lesson 5.)

Have children complete the problems on Student Activity Book page 185. For exercise 5, children should understand that estimates help give you an idea of what the actual answer should be.

▶ Critical Thinking

WHOLE CLASS

Math Talk 

Ask children to think about the answer to this question.

- If I round two partners to the nearest ten, will my estimate be the same as the exact total rounded to the nearest ten?

Allow children to think about the answer to this question. If children seem to agree that the answer is "yes," have them consider rounding to estimate 46 + 25. If one estimates the total by rounding, the estimate is 50 + 30, or 80. The exact total, however, is 71, which rounds to 70. Children should keep this in mind when using estimation to check their totals.

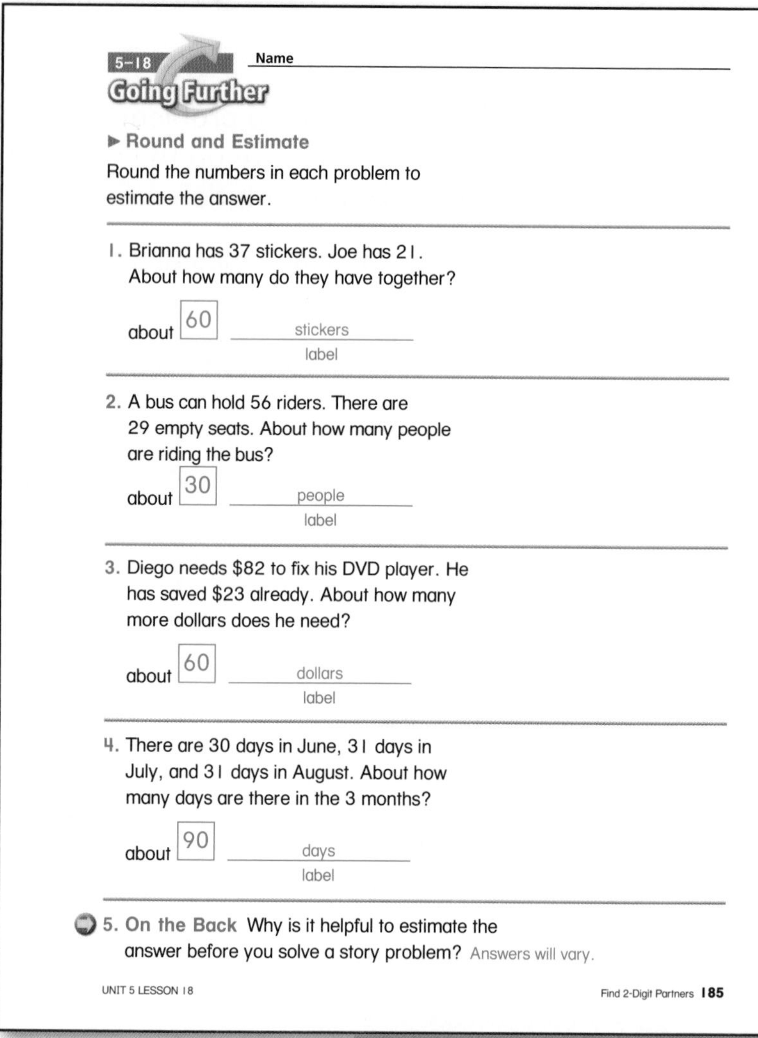
5-18 Going Further Name

▶ Round and Estimate

Round the numbers in each problem to estimate the answer.

1. Brianna has 37 stickers. Joe has 21. About how many do they have together?

about 60 stickers (label)

2. A bus can hold 56 riders. There are 29 empty seats. About how many people are riding the bus?

about 30 people (label)

3. Diego needs $82 to fix his DVD player. He has saved $23 already. About how many more dollars does he need?

about 60 dollars (label)

4. There are 30 days in June, 31 days in July, and 31 days in August. About how many days are there in the 3 months?

about 90 days (label)

5. On the Back Why is it helpful to estimate the answer before you solve a story problem? Answers will vary.

UNIT 5 LESSON 18 Find 2-Digit Partners 185

Student Activity Book page 185

The Learning Classroom

Math Talk Have children practice explaining one another's work in their own words from their seats, or have them go to the board and point to the parts of the first child's work as you or another child explain the first child's work.

Intervention — Activity Card 5-18

Use Coins to Find Partners of 100

Activity Card 5-18 ●

Work: 
Use:
- 9 dimes
- 10 pennies

Choose:
- 1
- 2

1. **Work Together** Use the coins to make a partner of 100.

$32 + 68 = 100$

2. Write your partners of 100 on the paper.
3. Use the coins to find other partners of 100. Record them.
4. How many partners did you find? Share what you found with other pairs.

Unit 5, Lesson 18

Activity Note Each pair needs 9 dimes and 10 pennies of real or play money or 1 Penny Strip and 9 Dime Strips (TRB M1). Ask pairs to think of partners of 100 and try and make the numbers with the money.

Math Writing Prompt

Find the Partner You have 68¢. How much more do you need to make a dollar? Explain, using a drawing.

Soar to Success Math Software Support

Use *Soar to Success* for instruction of students needing targeted support for underlying skills.

On Level — Activity Card 5-18

Use Grids to Find Partners of 100

Activity Card 5-18 ▲

Work: 
Use:
- Centimeter Grid Paper
- scissors

1. Cut two 10 × 10 grids from the Centimeter Grid Paper.
2. Cut one 10 × 10 grid into two pieces to show partners of 100.
3. Write the partners of 100 you made with the grid.
4. Cut the other 10 × 10 grid into two pieces to show another partner of 100. Write the partners you made.
5. Share the partners you made with other pairs.

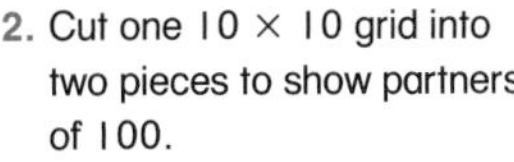

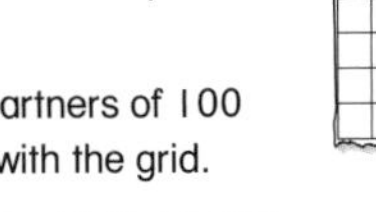

$24 + 76 = 100$

Unit 5, Lesson 18

Activity Note Each pair needs Centimeter Grid Paper (TRB M50) and scissors. Ask pairs to compare different partners they made.

Math Writing Prompt

Partners Use a Proof Drawing to explain that 28 and 33 are partners of 61.

MegaMath Software Support

Use *MegaMath* for review and reinforcement of the concepts and skills presented in this lesson.

Challenge — Activity Card 5-18

Find the Partners

Activity Card 5-18 ■

Work: 
Use:
- MathBoard
- Index cards with 2-digit numbers

Choose:
- 1
- 2

1. **Work Together** Pick an index card. Use the number to make a Math Mountain. Record the Math Mountain on your MathBoard.

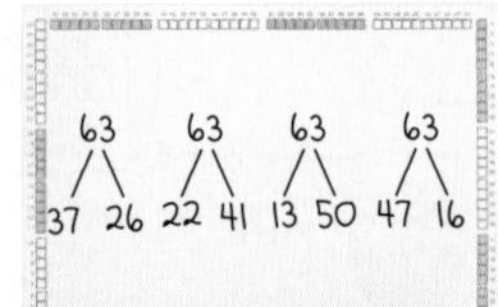

2. Find as many other Math Mountains as you can for the number on the index card.
3. Repeat with another index card.
4. **Math Talk** Discuss how you found partners for your number.

Unit 5, Lesson 18

Activity Note Each pair needs MathBoard materials and two index cards with a 2-digit number on each card. Remind children to check the Math Mountains.

Math Writing Prompt

Make a Ten How do you use the Make a Ten strategy to find partners of 100?

Destination Math Software Support

Use *Destination Math* to take students beyond the concepts and skills presented in this lesson.

3 Homework and Spiral Review

Goal: Additional Practice

This Homework page provides practice in solving story problems.

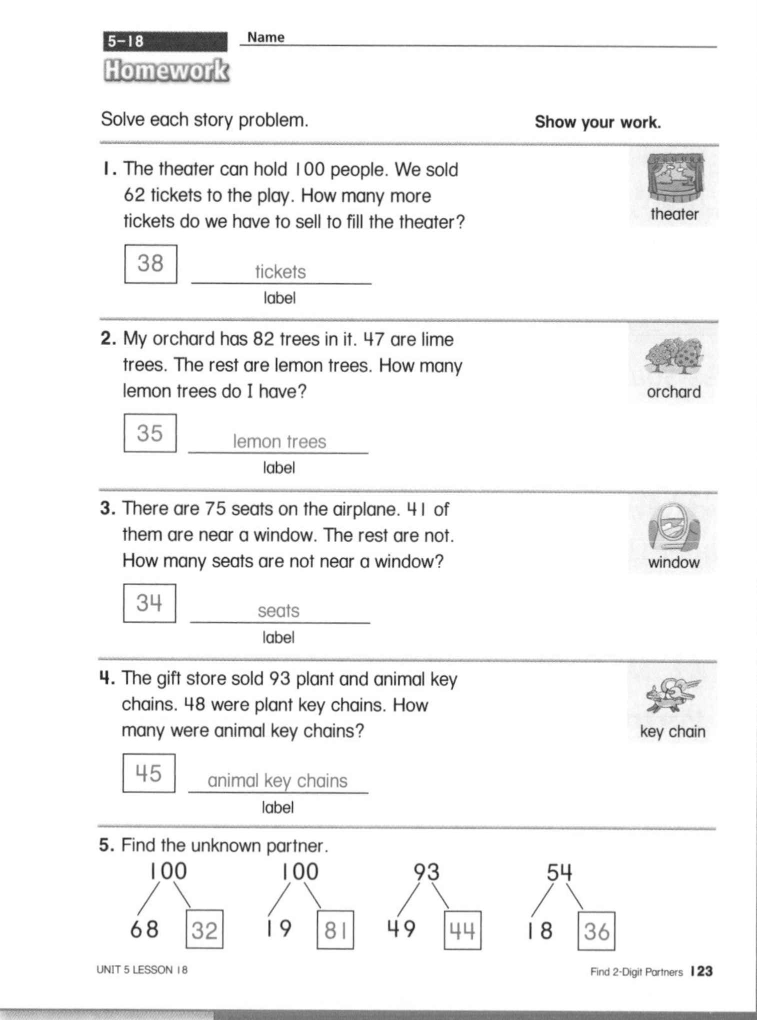

5–18 Homework Name

Solve each story problem. **Show your work.**

1. The theater can hold 100 people. We sold 62 tickets to the play. How many more tickets do we have to sell to fill the theater? (theater)
   38 tickets (label)

2. My orchard has 82 trees in it. 47 are lime trees. The rest are lemon trees. How many lemon trees do I have? (orchard)
   35 lemon trees (label)

3. There are 75 seats on the airplane. 41 of them are near a window. The rest are not. How many seats are not near a window? (window)
   34 seats (label)

4. The gift store sold 93 plant and animal key chains. 48 were plant key chains. How many were animal key chains? (key chain)
   45 animal key chains (label)

5. Find the unknown partner.
   100: 68, 32 100: 19, 81 93: 49, 44 54: 18, 36

UNIT 5 LESSON 18 Find 2-Digit Partners 123

Homework and Remembering page 123

Goal: Spiral Review

This Remembering activity would be appropriate anytime after today's lesson.

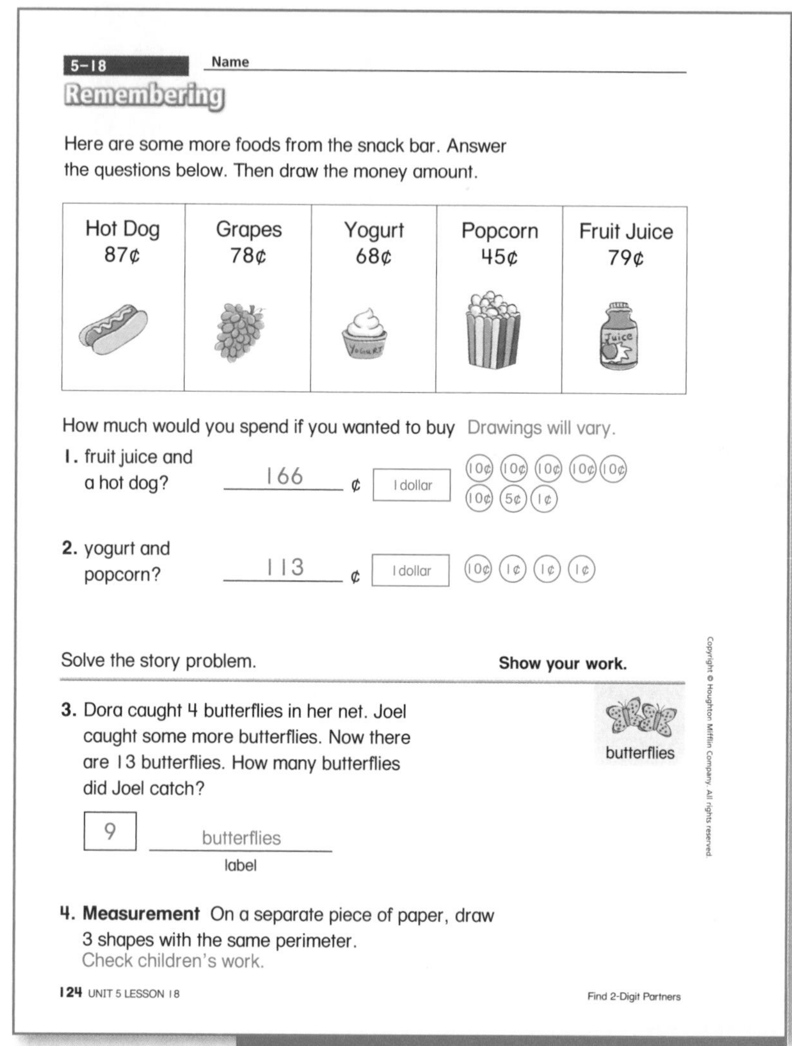

5–18 Remembering Name

Here are some more foods from the snack bar. Answer the questions below. Then draw the money amount.

Hot Dog 87¢	Grapes 78¢	Yogurt 68¢	Popcorn 45¢	Fruit Juice 79¢

How much would you spend if you wanted to buy Drawings will vary.

1. fruit juice and a hot dog? 166 ¢ [1 dollar] 10¢ 10¢ 10¢ 10¢ 10¢ 10¢ 5¢ 1¢
2. yogurt and popcorn? 113 ¢ [1 dollar] 10¢ 1¢ 1¢ 1¢

Solve the story problem. **Show your work.**

3. Dora caught 4 butterflies in her net. Joel caught some more butterflies. Now there are 13 butterflies. How many butterflies did Joel catch? (butterflies)
   9 butterflies (label)

4. **Measurement** On a separate piece of paper, draw 3 shapes with the same perimeter.
   Check children's work.

124 UNIT 5 LESSON 18 Find 2-Digit Partners

Homework and Remembering page 124

Home or School Activity

Real-World Connection

Change from $1.00 Have children look through newspaper flyers to find a picture of an item that costs less than a dollar. Have children cut and paste the picture of the item (and the price) and show the amount of change a person would receive if he or she paid for the item with a dollar.

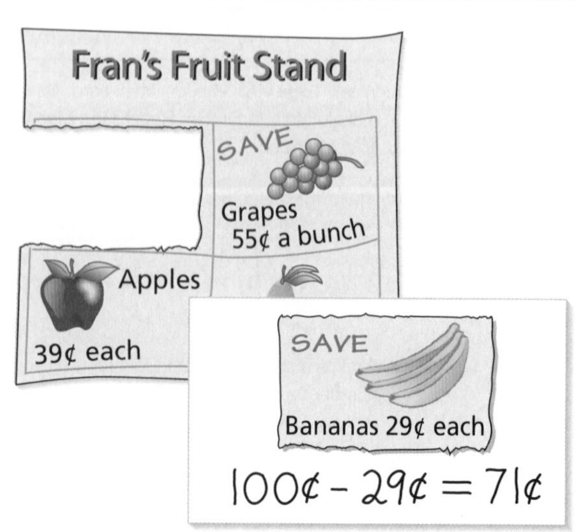

Patterns with Objects and Numbers

Lesson Objectives

- Represent and analyze repeating patterns.
- Extend object and number patterns.
- Describe missing units in a pattern.

Vocabulary
pattern

The Day at a Glance

Today's Goals	Materials	
1 Teaching the Lesson **A1:** Identify people patterns. **A2:** Create pattern block patterns. **A3:** Extend the pattern. **A4:** Find missing units.	**Lesson Activities** Student Activity Book pp. 187–188 Homework and Remembering pp. 125–126 Pattern Blocks Classroom objects	**Going Further** Activity Cards 5-19 Pattern blocks Paper strips Crayons or markers Math Journals
2 Going Further ▸ Differentiated Instruction		
3 Homework and Spiral Review		

Use Math Talk today!

Keeping Skills Sharp

Quick Practice — 5 MINUTES

Goals: Use place-value patterns to add. Practice adding ones or adding tens.

Trios Have a **Student Leader** write the three exercises shown below on the board. The leader reads the exercises aloud, one at a time, giving a hand signal to indicate when the class should respond with the answer. (See Unit 5 Lesson 15.)

$26 + 3 = \square$ $26 + 30 = \square$ $26 + 300 = \square$

Add Tens or Ones Write examples like the ones below on the board. Have a Student Leader direct the class as they say whether they are adding tens or ones. The class should then say the answer. (See Unit 5 Lesson 15.)

$8 + 1 = \square$ $4 + 5 = \square$

$80 + 10 = \square$ $40 + 50 = \square$

Daily Routines

Math Mountains for 100 or 2-Digit Numbers Using the MathBoard, Using Dimes and Pennies (See pp. xxvi.)

▸ Led by Student Leaders

Money Routine Using the 120 Poster, Using the Money Flip Chart, Using the Number Path, Using Secret Code Cards (See pp. xxiii–xxv.)

▸ Led by Student Leaders

1 Teaching the Lesson

Activity 1

Identify People Patterns

 10 MINUTES

Goal: Identify patterns in a line of children.

 **NCTM Standards:**
Algebra
Reasoning and Proof
Communication

▶ Find the Pattern WHOLE CLASS

Introduce the word pattern. Explain that a pattern is how objects or numbers relate to each other. Explain that some patterns repeat.

Choose 5 girls and 5 boys. Line them up in front of the room in a boy, girl pattern.

- Do you see a part that keeps repeating? yes
- Explain the pattern. The pattern keeps switching from boy to girl and back again.

Activity 2

Create Pattern Block Patterns

 15 MINUTES

Goal: Create patterns using pattern blocks.

Materials: pattern blocks

 **NCTM Standards:**
Geometry
Algebra
Reasoning and Proof

▶ Pattern Blocks PAIRS

Provide 3 different types of pattern blocks for each pair. Write ABCABCABC on the board. Tell children that each letter stands for a different pattern block. For example A could be triangle, B could be parallelogram, and C could be a hexagon. Have children create a repeating pattern using 3 different types of pattern blocks. Explain that the pattern should repeat at least 3 times.

- What pattern did you make? Possible answer: a square, hexagon, triangle pattern

       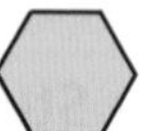 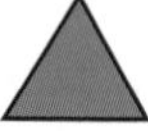

Write the pattern AABAABAAB on the board and have children create this pattern using pattern blocks.

- How many types of blocks will you use? 2
- What pattern did you make? Possible answer: parallelogram, parallelogram, hexagon pattern

After children create the pattern block patterns have them use the ABC pattern and AAB pattern to create a rhythmic pattern such as clap, snap, stomp or clap clap, snap.

English Language Learners

Point to patterns in different things in the classroom (tiles, on clothing, in artwork).

- **Beginning** Say: **This has a *pattern*. The colors/shapes repeat.** Point and tell how the colors/shapes repeat. Have children repeat.
- **Intermediate and Advanced** Ask: **Do the colors repeat? Do the shapes repeat? Is this a *pattern*?**

Activity 3

Extend the Pattern

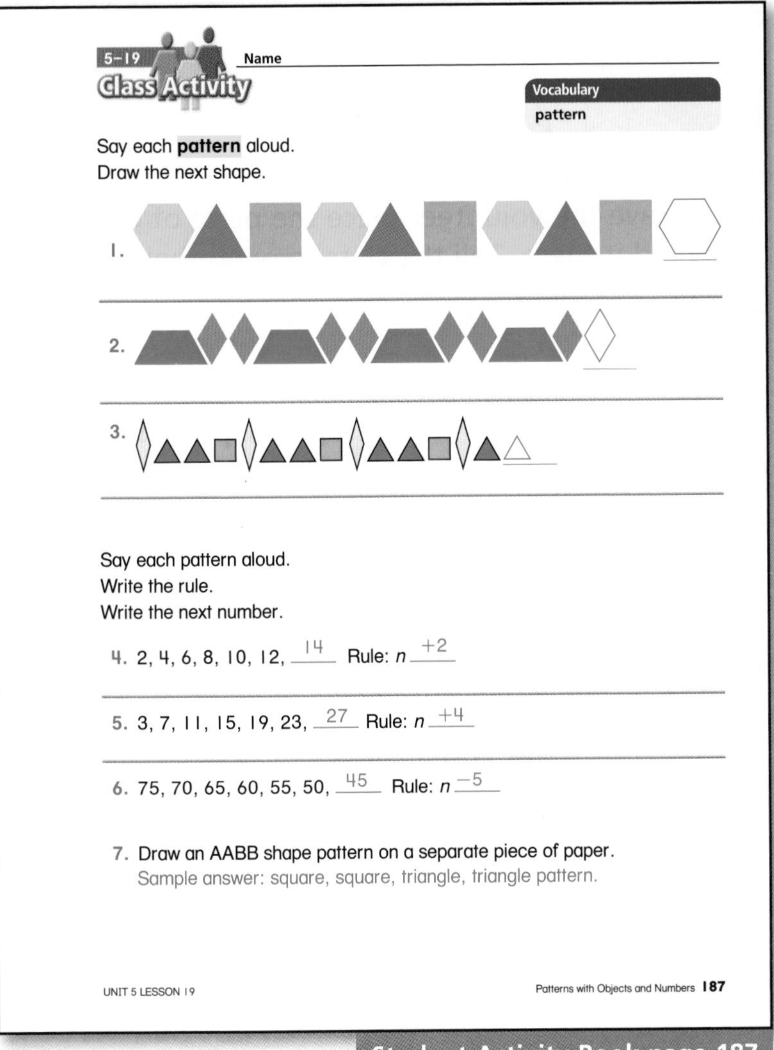

5-19 Class Activity

Name

Vocabulary
pattern

Say each **pattern** aloud.
Draw the next shape.

1.

2.

3.

Say each pattern aloud.
Write the rule.
Write the next number.

4. 2, 4, 6, 8, 10, 12, 14 Rule: n +2

5. 3, 7, 11, 15, 19, 23, 27 Rule: n +4

6. 75, 70, 65, 60, 55, 50, 45 Rule: n −5

7. Draw an AABB shape pattern on a separate piece of paper.
Sample answer: square, square, triangle, triangle pattern.

UNIT 5 LESSON 19 — Patterns with Objects and Numbers 187

Student Activity Book page 187

▶ Introduce Extend the Pattern WHOLE CLASS

Direct children's attention to Student Activity Book page 187. Instruct children to look at the pattern for Exercise 1.

- Say the pattern. hexagon, triangle, square, hexagon, triangle, square, hexagon, triangle, square
- What part keeps repeating? hexagon, triangle, square
- What is the next shape after the square? hexagon

Use similar questioning for Exercises 2 and 3.

Math Talk Have children discuss how they could make a pattern using coins. Have them give 2 examples of an ABB pattern using coins.

 **15 MINUTES**

Goal: Extend object and number patterns.

Materials: Student Activity Book page 187, pattern blocks

 **NCTM Standards:**
Algebra
Geometry
Reasoning and Proof

Teaching Note

Pattern Unit You may wish to have children circle the repeating part in each pattern. They can then use that pattern for reference to see which shape or number comes next.

Teaching Note

Explain that numbers can also be used to show a pattern. Instruct children to look at the pattern for Exercise 4.

- Say the pattern? 2, 4, 6, 8, 10, 12
- What is happening to the numbers or what is the rule? add 2
- What number comes after 12? 14

Use similar questioning for Exercises 5 and 6.

For Exercise 7 have children draw an AABB shape pattern.

- How many different shapes will you use? 2

Teaching the Lesson (continued)

Activity 4

Find Missing Units

 15 MINUTES

Goal: Find the missing unit of a pattern.

Materials: Student Activity Book page 188

 **NCTM Standards:**
Algebra
Geometry
Reasoning and Proof

 **Ongoing Assessment**

Assess children's understanding of patterns. Ask questions such as:

- What is next in this pattern? triangle, triangle, rectangle, triangle, triangle, rectangle, triangle, triangle, rectangle triangle
- What is next in this pattern? 1, 3, 5, 7, 9, 11 13

Differentiated Instruction

Extra Help Instruct children to look at the pattern for Exercise 1. Have them read the pattern aloud and say *blank* for the write on line.

- Do you notice a part that repeats? If so what is it? hexagon, trapezoid, parallelogram.
- The write on line is after the trapezoid. What comes after the trapezoid in the repeating part? parallelogram.

Have children work independently for Exercises 2–4. Instruct children to look at the pattern for Exercise 5. Have them read the numbers aloud and say *blank* for the write on line.

- Say the pattern. 14, 24, 34, blank, 54, 64, 74
- What is the rule? add 10
- What number comes after 34? 44

Use similar questioning for Exercises 6–8

▶ Find the Missing Shape WHOLE CLASS

Draw on the board.

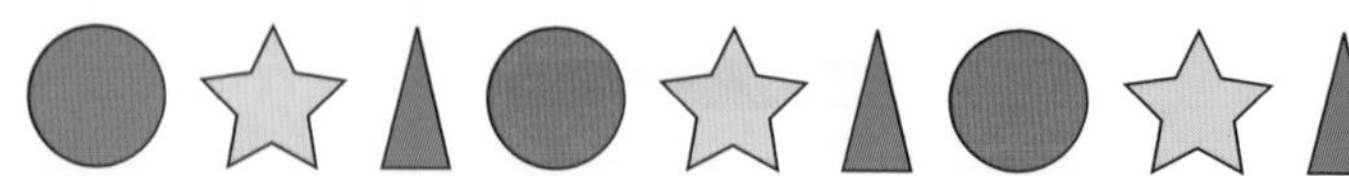

Choose a volunteer. Give the volunteer a piece of paper. Instruct the class to close their eyes. Have the volunteer place the piece of paper over one of the shapes and hold it there. Tell the class to open their eyes.

- What shape is covered?

Math Talk **Discuss how you can find the missing shape.** Make sure children realize they should be looking for the repeating pattern unit and use it to determine the missing part of the pattern.

5-19 Class Activity Name

Use pattern blocks and classroom objects to model the pattern.
Draw the missing shape.

1\.

2\.

3\.

4\. Make an AAB shape pattern. Draw it. Patterns will vary.

Write the missing number in each pattern.

5\. 14, 24, 34, 44 54, 64, 74 Rule: *n* +10

6\. 100 97, 94, 91, 88, 85, 82, 79 Rule: *n* −3

7\. 74, 72, 70, 68 66, 64, 62, 60 Rule: *n* −2

8\. 27, 33, 39, 45, 51 57, 63, 69 Rule: *n* +6

188 UNIT 5 LESSON 19 Patterns with Objects and Numbers

Student Activity Book page 188

Have children complete Student Activity Book page 188.

2 Going Further

Differentiated Instruction

Intervention

Activity Card 5-19

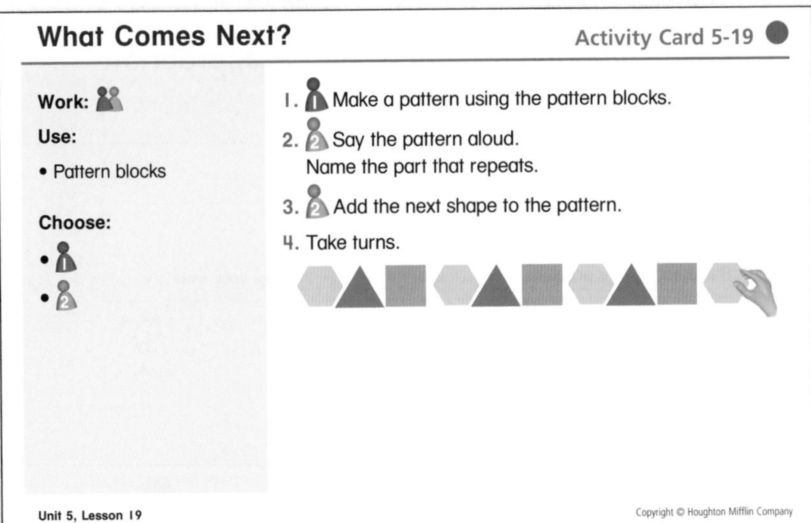

What Comes Next? Activity Card 5-19 ●

Work: [pair]
Use:
- Pattern blocks

Choose:
- 1
- 2

1. Make a pattern using the pattern blocks.
2. Say the pattern aloud. Name the part that repeats.
3. Add the next shape to the pattern.
4. Take turns.

Unit 5, Lesson 19

Copyright © Houghton Mifflin Company

Activity Note For each pair, prepare a group of 3 different types of pattern blocks (at least 6 of each type). Remind children to repeat the pattern unit at least 3 times.

Math Writing Prompt

Explain Tell your partner how you knew which pattern block was next in the pattern.

Software Support

Use *Soar to Success* for instruction of students needing targeted support for underlying skills.

On Level

Activity Card 5-19

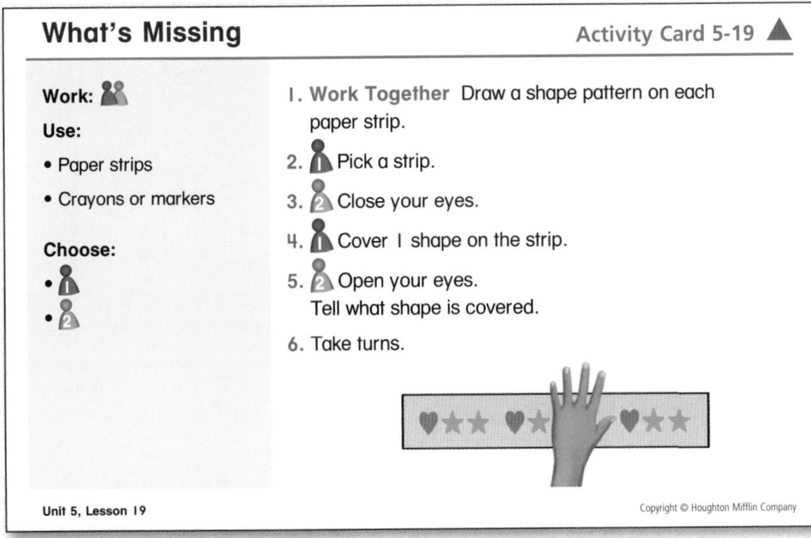

What's Missing Activity Card 5-19 ▲

Work: [pair]
Use:
- Paper strips
- Crayons or markers

Choose:
- 1
- 2

1. **Work Together** Draw a shape pattern on each paper strip.
2. Pick a strip.
3. Close your eyes.
4. Cover 1 shape on the strip.
5. Open your eyes. Tell what shape is covered.
6. Take turns.

Unit 5, Lesson 19

Copyright © Houghton Mifflin Company

Activity Note For each pair prepare 8 paper strips. Remind children to repeat the pattern unit at least 3 times when drawing the patterns.

Math Writing Prompt

Explain Your Thinking Explain how you were able to find the missing shape.

Software Support

Use *MegaMath* for review and reinforcement of the concepts and skills presented in this lesson.

Challenge

Activity Card 5-19

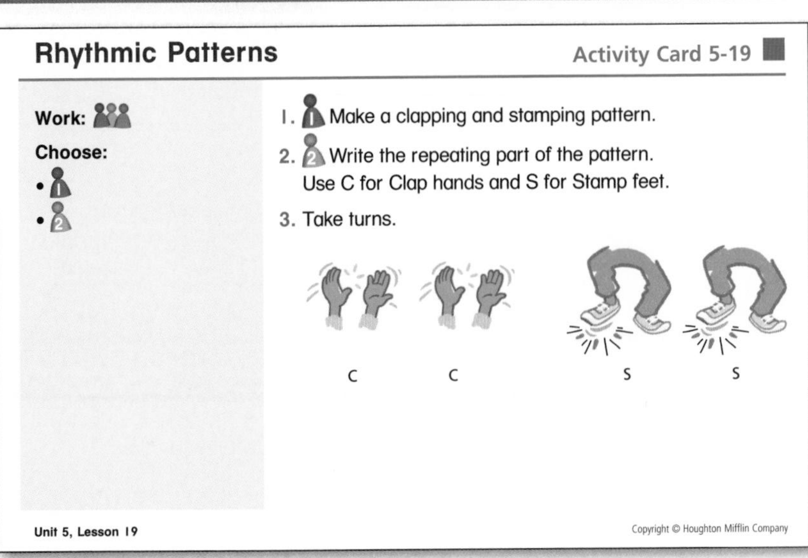

Rhythmic Patterns Activity Card 5-19 ■

Work: [group of 3]

Choose:
- 1
- 2

1. Make a clapping and stamping pattern.
2. Write the repeating part of the pattern. Use C for Clap hands and S for Stamp feet.
3. Take turns.

C C S S

Unit 5, Lesson 19

Copyright © Houghton Mifflin Company

Activity Note Explain to children that they should first think of the clapping and stomping part that is going to repeat.

Math Writing Prompt

Investigate Math What other things could you do to make a rhythmic pattern?

Software Support

Use *Destination Math* to take students beyond the concepts and skills presented in this lesson.

Homework and Spiral Review

Goal: Additional Practice

Use this homework activity to provide children more practice with patterns.

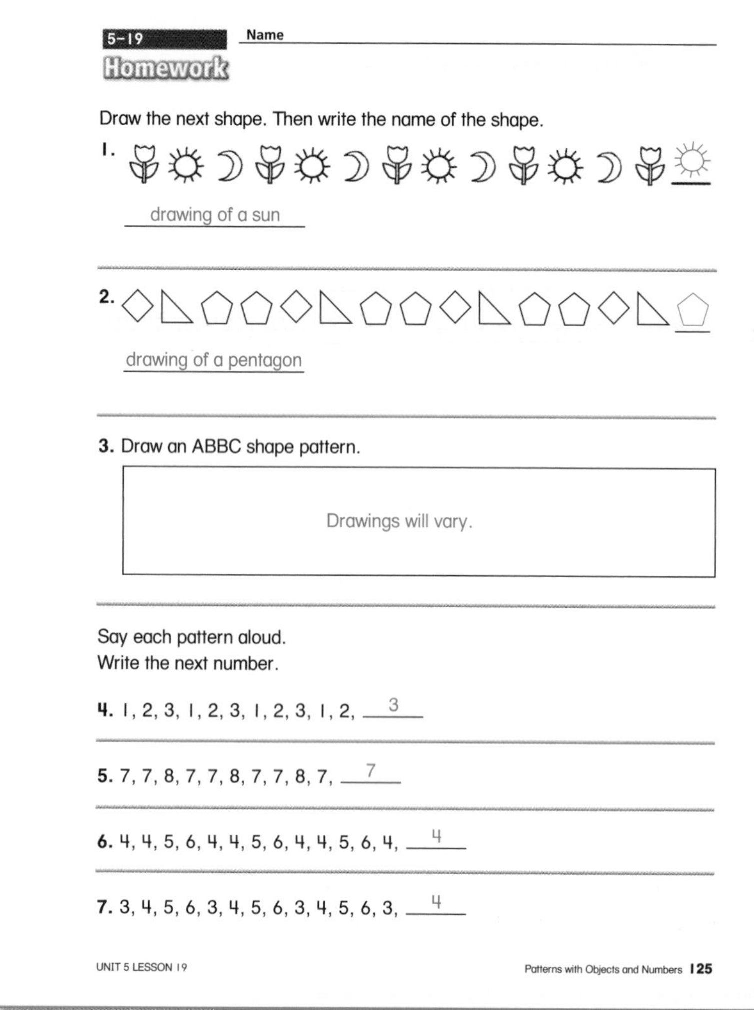

5-19 Homework Name

Draw the next shape. Then write the name of the shape.

1. drawing of a sun

2. drawing of a pentagon

3. Draw an ABBC shape pattern.

Drawings will vary.

Say each pattern aloud.
Write the next number.

4. 1, 2, 3, 1, 2, 3, 1, 2, 3, 1, 2, 3

5. 7, 7, 8, 7, 7, 8, 7, 7, 8, 7, 7

6. 4, 4, 5, 6, 4, 4, 5, 6, 4, 4, 5, 6, 4, 4

7. 3, 4, 5, 6, 3, 4, 5, 6, 3, 4, 5, 6, 3, 4

UNIT 5 LESSON 19 Patterns with Objects and Numbers 125

Homework and Remembering page 125

Goal: Spiral Review

This Remembering activity would be appropriate anytime after today's lesson.

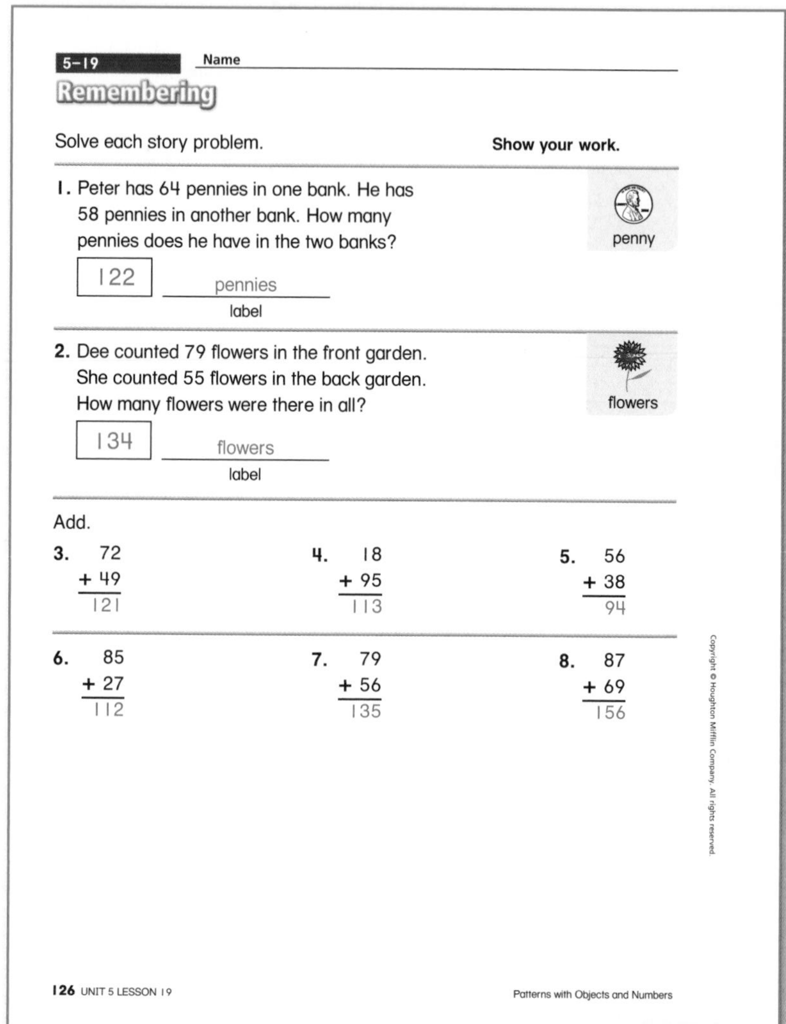

5-19 Remembering Name

Solve each story problem. **Show your work.**

1. Peter has 64 pennies in one bank. He has 58 pennies in another bank. How many pennies does he have in the two banks?

122 pennies (label)

penny

2. Dee counted 79 flowers in the front garden. She counted 55 flowers in the back garden. How many flowers were there in all?

134 flowers (label)

flowers

Add.

3. 72 + 49 = 121

4. 18 + 95 = 113

5. 56 + 38 = 94

6. 85 + 27 = 112

7. 79 + 56 = 135

8. 87 + 69 = 156

126 UNIT 5 LESSON 19 Patterns with Objects and Numbers

Homework and Remembering page 126

Home or School Activity

Real-World Connection

Find Patterns Have children look around at school or home to find patterns. Explain that they may see patterns on clothing, on boarders of bulletin boards, game boards or many other places. They may make a list to share with classmates.

Use Mathematical Processes

Lesson Objectives

- **Solve a variety of problems using mathematical concepts and skills.**
- **Use mathematical processes in the context of problem solving, connections, reasoning and proof, communication, and representation.**

The Day at a Glance

Today's Goals	Materials	
1 Teaching the Lesson **A1: Social Studies Connection** Make a prediction; color a map with the least number of colors possible. **A2: Reasoning and Proof** Decide whether a mathematical statement is true or not true; invent and support a mathematical statement. **A3: Problem Solving** Find multiple solutions to a problem. **A4: Representation** Use drawings to show why numbers with the same digits may not have the same value. **A5: Communication** Classify shapes with a diagram; explain decisions.	**Lesson Activities** Student Activity Book pp. 189–190 Homework and Remembering pp. 127–128 Crayons or markers Maps Play coins	**Going Further** Activity Cards 5-20 MathBoard materials or Number Path (TRB M51) Secret Code Cards Math Journals
2 Going Further ▸ Differentiated Instruction		
3 Homework and Spiral Review		

Use Math Talk today!

Keeping Skills Sharp

Quick Practice/Daily Routines	
No Quick Practice or Daily Routines are recommended. If you choose to do some, use those that provide extra practice that meets the needs of your class.	**Class Management** Use this lesson to provide more understanding of the NCTM process standards. Depending on how you choose to carry out the activities, this lesson may take two or more days of teaching.

1 Teaching the Lesson

Activity 1

Connections

Math and Social Studies

 **45 MINUTES**

Goals: Make a prediction; color a map with the least number of colors possible.

Materials: Student Activity Book page 189, crayons or markers, maps (Note: You may want to make some extra copies of page 189 so you will have extra maps for those who may want to try again.)

 **NCTM Standards:**

Problem Solving	Connections
Communication	Reasoning

Name ____________________

▶ Math and Social Studies

Many maps have parts that show places. Each part is a different color from all other parts that touch it. Map makers try to use as few colors as possible.

1. Look at the map below. How many colors do you think are needed to color it?

Predict I will use Possible answer: 5 colors.

2. Color the map so that the color of each part is different from all other parts that touch it. Try to use the least number of colors possible.

The Western United States

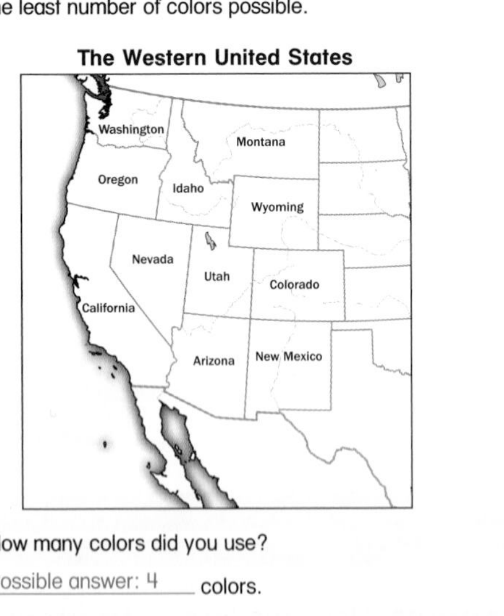

3. How many colors did you use?

Possible answer: 4 colors.

UNIT 5 LESSON 20 Use Mathematical Processes 189

Student Activity Book page 189

▶ Making Maps

Ask for Ideas Show children some maps and have them share what they know about maps. Discuss what kinds of information can be found on maps and how people use maps. Guide children to notice how colors are used on the maps.

Explain that map makers usually color the parts of a map that show places so that people can tell one place from another. They do it in such a way that two parts of the same color never touch at all. They may also try to use the least number of colors possible. Look back at the maps and discuss how many different colors are used.

Tasks 1 and 2 Then have children look at the map on Student Activity Book page 189 and tell what is on the map. states in the western United States Tell them that their job is to color this map using the least number of colors possible and that before they begin they will predict how many colors they will need.

▶ Check Predictions

Math Talk 

Task 3 Have children count the number of colors they used and compare that number with their prediction.

▶ How many colors did you need to use?

▶ How close was your prediction to the number of colors you actually used?

▶ Compare your map with the map of someone near you. Are they the same or different?

English Language Learners

Show 3 red and 2 blue cubes. Put them in a bag. Say: **Let's *predict* what color I'll take out first.**

- **Beginning** Say: ***Predict* means guess what will happen.** Have children repeat.
- **Intermediate and Advanced** Ask: **Does *predict* mean guess what will happen?** yes

Showing that Math Statements are True

 45 MINUTES

Goals: Decide whether a mathematical statement is true or not true; invent and support a mathematical statement.

Materials: Student Activity Book page 190

 **NCTM Standards:**
Problem Solving
Reasoning and Proof
Communication

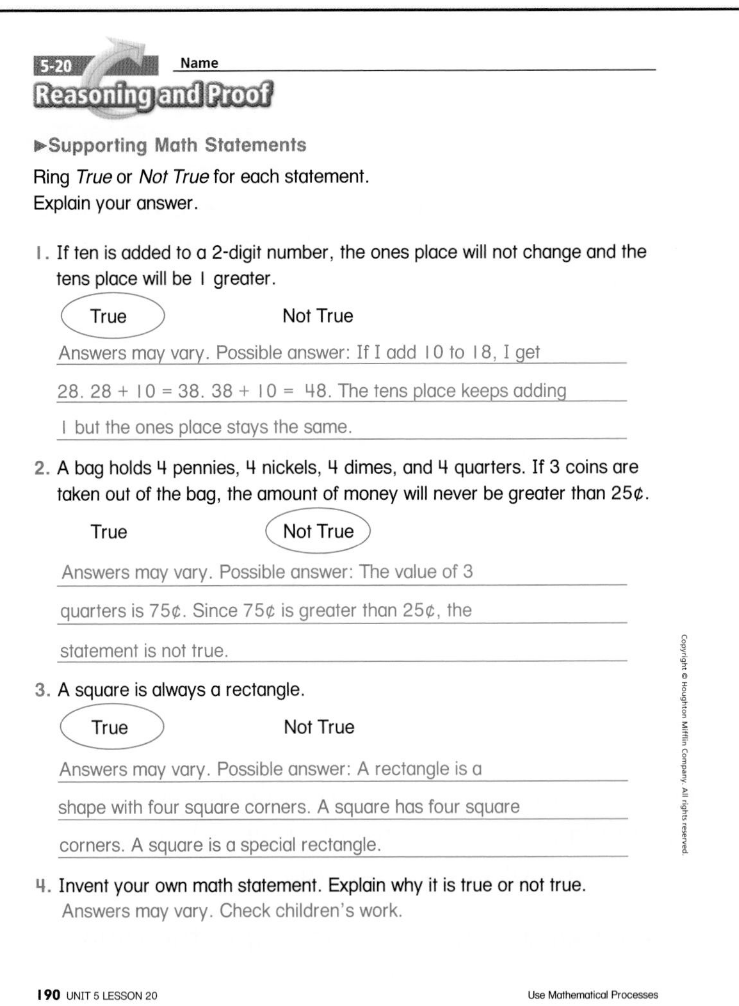
5-20 Name

Reasoning and Proof

▶Supporting Math Statements

Ring *True* or *Not True* for each statement.
Explain your answer.

1. If ten is added to a 2-digit number, the ones place will not change and the tens place will be 1 greater.
(True) Not True
Answers may vary. Possible answer: If I add 10 to 18, I get 28. 28 + 10 = 38. 38 + 10 = 48. The tens place keeps adding 1 but the ones place stays the same.

2. A bag holds 4 pennies, 4 nickels, 4 dimes, and 4 quarters. If 3 coins are taken out of the bag, the amount of money will never be greater than 25¢.
True (Not True)
Answers may vary. Possible answer: The value of 3 quarters is 75¢. Since 75¢ is greater than 25¢, the statement is not true.

3. A square is always a rectangle.
(True) Not True
Answers may vary. Possible answer: A rectangle is a shape with four square corners. A square has four square corners. A square is a special rectangle.

4. Invent your own math statement. Explain why it is true or not true.
Answers may vary. Check children's work.

190 UNIT 5 LESSON 20 Use Mathematical Processes

Student Activity Book page 190

Teaching Note

Math Background A *conjecture* is a mathematical statement that has not been formally proven true or not true. Outside of mathematics, people often use the term for an educated guess. A *counterexample* is an example that shows a conjecture or other mathematical statement is not true.

▶ Checking Mathematical Statements

Tasks 1–3 Tell children that there are three mathematical statements on their student page. They may be true or not true. Their job will be to decide whether each statement is true or not true and to explain their decision with words, drawings, or both.

You may want to talk about the idea that only one example is needed to show that a statement is not true. If there is one example that does not follow the statement, then the statement is not always true. Some children may be interested to learn the words *conjecture* and *counterexample.* (See the Teaching Note below.)

▶ Making and Testing a Statement

Math Talk 

Task 3 Ask volunteers to present their responses to the three statements. After children share their explanations for each of the statements, guide the discussion to include questions like the following:

▶ Did the explanation you just heard show that the statement is true (or not true)? Answers may vary. Possible answer: I am not sure that all shapes with 4 square corners are rectangles.

▶ If a statement is not true, why is it easy to show that? Answers may vary. Possible answer: You only need one example that shows the opposite of the statement.

Then have children make up their own statement, decide whether it is true or not true, and write an explanation. When everyone is finished, continue asking volunteers to present their statements and explanations for class discussion.

❶ Teaching the Lesson (continued)

Activity 3

Problem Solving

A Dollar to Spend

 **15 MINUTES**

Goal: Find multiple solutions to a problem.

 **NCTM Standards:**
Problem Solving
Connections

Kavi has $1.00 to spend. He wants to buy some stickers. The stickers and their prices are: butterfly for 25¢, eagle for 35¢, elephant for 50¢, and dinosaur for 75¢. He does not want to buy more than one of each sticker. Which stickers can he buy with one dollar? Answers will vary. See next column.

Discuss approaches and answers for this problem.

- ► How did you decide which stickers Kavi could buy? Answers may vary.
- ► Let's list all the possibilities. the 75¢ dinosaur and the 25¢ butterfly; the 35¢ eagle and the 25¢ butterfly; the 50¢ elephant and the 25¢ butterfly; the 50¢ elephant and the 35¢ eagle
- ► Why is there more than one answer to this problem? Answers may vary.

Activity 4

Representation

Same Value or Different Value?

 **15 MINUTES**

Goal: Use drawings to show why numbers with the same digits may not have the same value.

 **NCTM Standards:**
Problem Solving
Communication
Representation

Do numbers with the same digits have the same value? Does 173 equal 137? Use a drawing to explain your answer. No. Check children's drawings.

Have children share their drawings of this situation.

- ► How did you use a drawing to show that 137 and 173 do not have the same value? Answers may vary.
- ► Do you need to make a drawing to show that 137 and 173 do not have the same value? Answers may vary.

Activity 5

Communication

Classifying Triangles

 **15 MINUTES**

Goal: Classify shapes with a diagram; explain decisions.

 **NCTM Standards:**
Communication
Representation
Reasoning

Draw this diagram on the board. Ask children to copy it.

Triangles

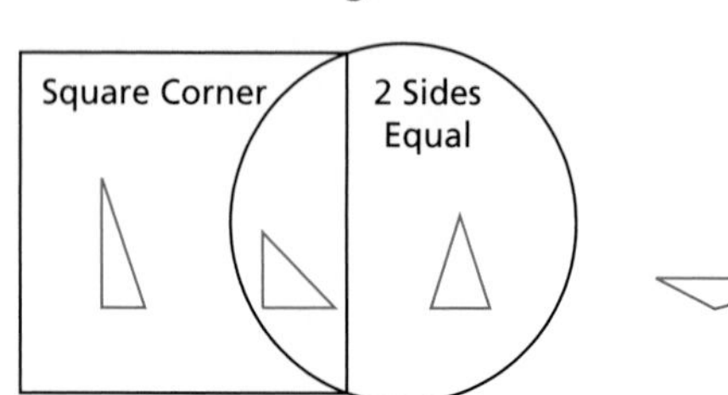

Then ask them to draw a triangle in each section and explain how they decided what kind of triangle to put in each section.

- ► What kind of triangles belong in the square? triangles that have a square corner
- ► What belongs in the circle? triangles with 2 sides equal
- ► What belongs in the overlap section? triangles with 2 sides equal and a square corner
- ► What belongs outside the square and circle? triangles that don't have 2 sides equal or a square corner

2 Going Further

Differentiated Instruction

Intervention — Activity Card 5-20

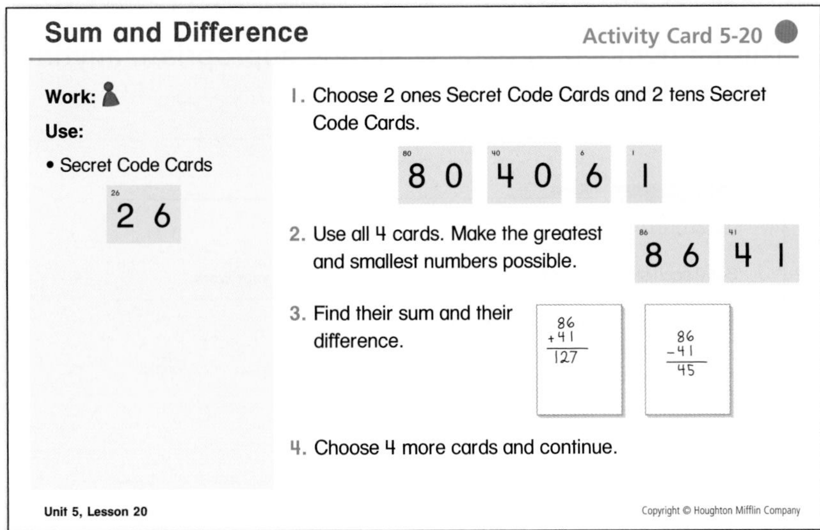

Sum and Difference — Activity Card 5-20

Work: (individual)
Use:
- Secret Code Cards

2 6

1. Choose 2 ones Secret Code Cards and 2 tens Secret Code Cards.

   8 0 4 0 6 1

2. Use all 4 cards. Make the greatest and smallest numbers possible.

   8 6 4 1

3. Find their sum and their difference.

   86 + 41 = 127   86 − 41 = 45

4. Choose 4 more cards and continue.

Unit 5, Lesson 20 — Copyright © Houghton Mifflin Company

Activity Note Although this activity provides independent practice with place value concepts, addition, and subtraction, children may also benefit from working with a Helping Partner.

Math Writing Prompt

Make the Greatest Number You have these cards: 7 tens, 3 tens, 9 ones, and 5 ones. Explain how to choose two cards to make the greatest possible number.

Software Support

Use *Soar to Success* for instruction of students needing targeted support for underlying skills.

On Level — Activity Card 5-20

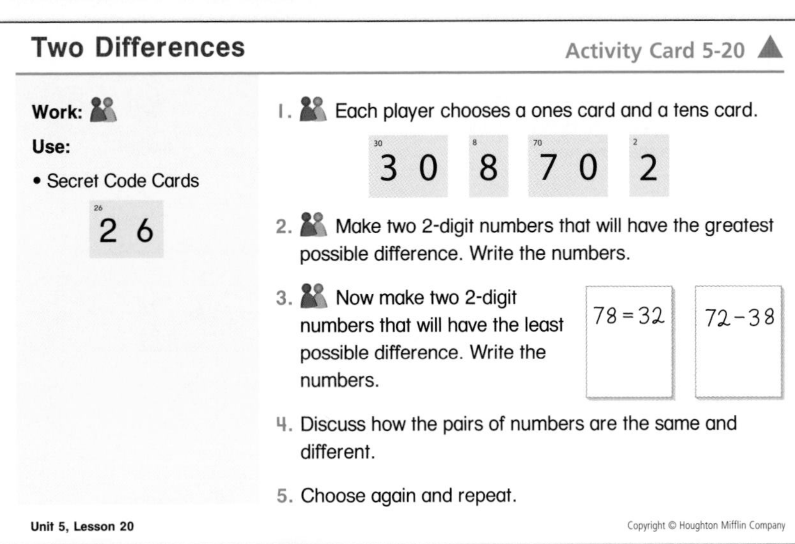

Two Differences — Activity Card 5-20

Work: (pairs)
Use:
- Secret Code Cards

2 6

1. Each player chooses a ones card and a tens card.

   3 0 8 7 0 2

2. Make two 2-digit numbers that will have the greatest possible difference. Write the numbers.
3. Now make two 2-digit numbers that will have the least possible difference. Write the numbers.

   78 − 32   72 − 38

4. Discuss how the pairs of numbers are the same and different.
5. Choose again and repeat.

Unit 5, Lesson 20 — Copyright © Houghton Mifflin Company

Activity Note This activity is a chance for students to practice the problem solving process skill of communication.

Math Writing Prompt

Make the Least Difference You have cards for 8 tens, 4 tens, 9 ones, and 2 ones. Explain how you decide how to make two 2-digit numbers with the least difference.

Software Support

Use *MegaMath* for review and reinforcement of the concepts and skills presented in this lesson.

Challenge — Activity Card 5-20

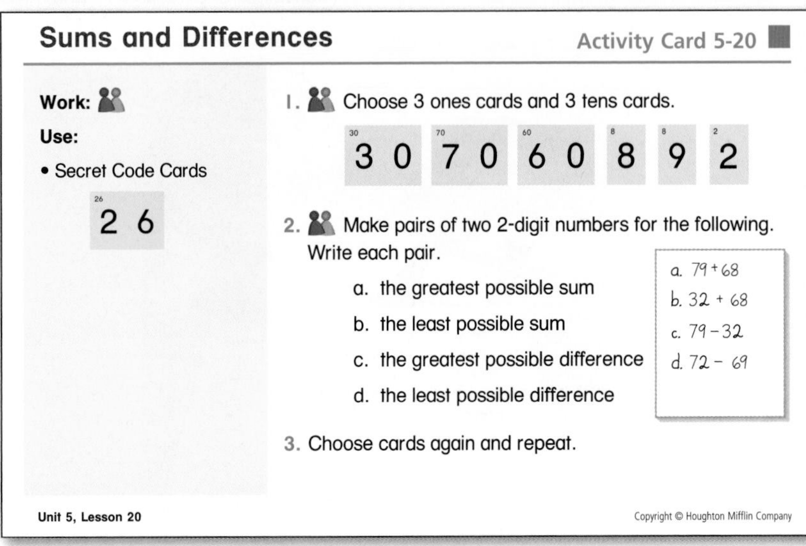

Sums and Differences — Activity Card 5-20

Work: (pairs)
Use:
- Secret Code Cards

2 6

1. Choose 3 ones cards and 3 tens cards.

   3 0 7 0 6 0 8 9 2

2. Make pairs of two 2-digit numbers for the following. Write each pair.
   a. the greatest possible sum
   b. the least possible sum
   c. the greatest possible difference
   d. the least possible difference

   a. 79 + 68
   b. 32 + 68
   c. 79 − 32
   d. 72 − 69

3. Choose cards again and repeat.

Unit 5, Lesson 20 — Copyright © Houghton Mifflin Company

Activity Note To extend the activity, have children select 4 tens and 4 ones cards from which to make the sums and differences.

Math Writing Prompt

Describe Your Strategy Tell what strategy you used to make the least sum and the greatest difference.

Software Support

Use *Destination Math* to take students beyond the concepts and skills presented in this lesson.

Homework and Spiral Review

Goal: Additional Practice

Include student's completed Homework page as part of their portfolios.

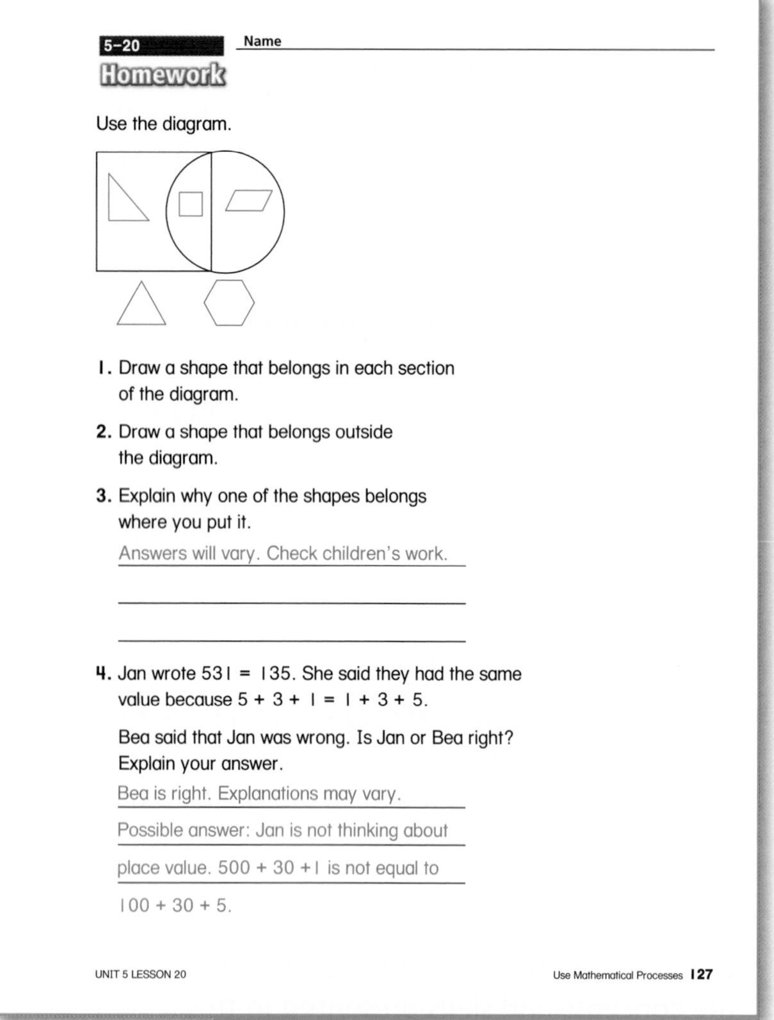

5–20 Name

Homework

Use the diagram.

1. Draw a shape that belongs in each section of the diagram.
2. Draw a shape that belongs outside the diagram.
3. Explain why one of the shapes belongs where you put it.
   Answers will vary. Check children's work.
4. Jan wrote 531 = 135. She said they had the same value because 5 + 3 + 1 = 1 + 3 + 5.
   Bea said that Jan was wrong. Is Jan or Bea right? Explain your answer.
   Bea is right. Explanations may vary. Possible answer: Jan is not thinking about place value. 500 + 30 + 1 is not equal to 100 + 30 + 5.

UNIT 5 LESSON 20 Use Mathematical Processes 127

Homework and Remembering page 127

Goal: Spiral Review

This Remembering page would be appropriate anytime after today's lesson.

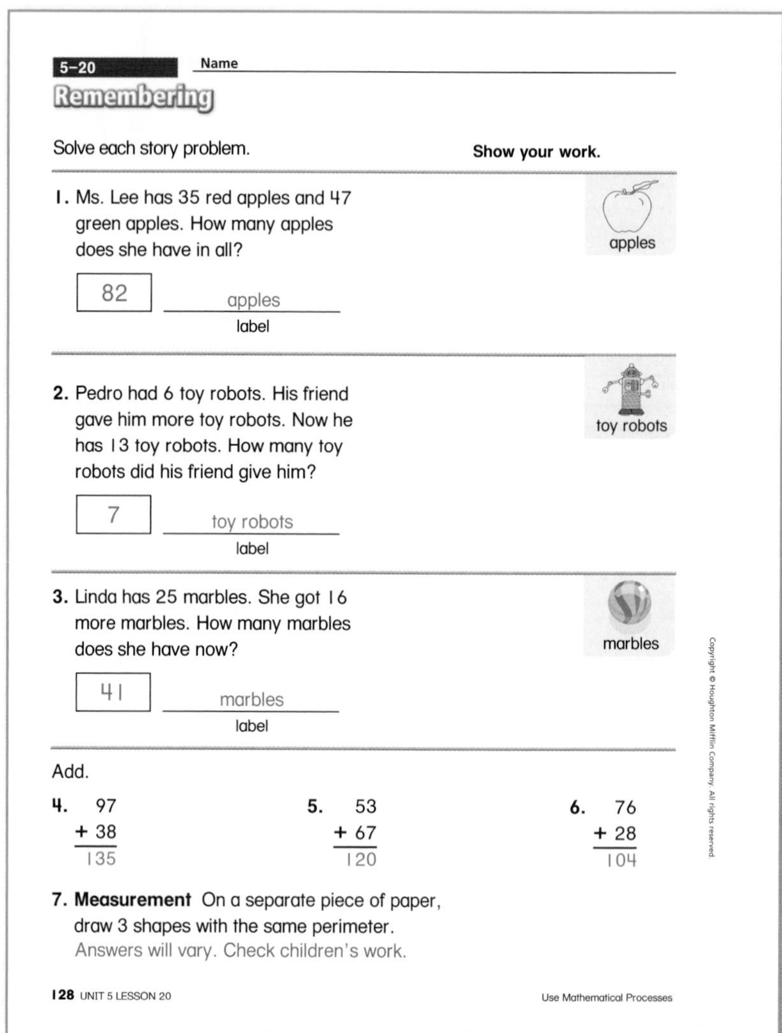

5–20 Name

Remembering

Solve each story problem. **Show your work.**

1. Ms. Lee has 35 red apples and 47 green apples. How many apples does she have in all?
   82 apples (label)
2. Pedro had 6 toy robots. His friend gave him more toy robots. Now he has 13 toy robots. How many toy robots did his friend give him?
   7 toy robots (label)
3. Linda has 25 marbles. She got 16 more marbles. How many marbles does she have now?
   41 marbles (label)

Add.

4. 97 + 38 = 135
5. 53 + 67 = 120
6. 76 + 28 = 104

7. **Measurement** On a separate piece of paper, draw 3 shapes with the same perimeter.
   Answers will vary. Check children's work.

128 UNIT 5 LESSON 20 Use Mathematical Processes

Copyright © Houghton Mifflin Company. All rights reserved.

Homework and Remembering page 128

Home or School Activity

Social Studies Connection

A Survey of Maps Have children look at home or in the library for different kinds of maps and to count the colors used in each map. Ask them to make a chart of the kinds of maps, where they found the maps, and the number of colors in the maps.

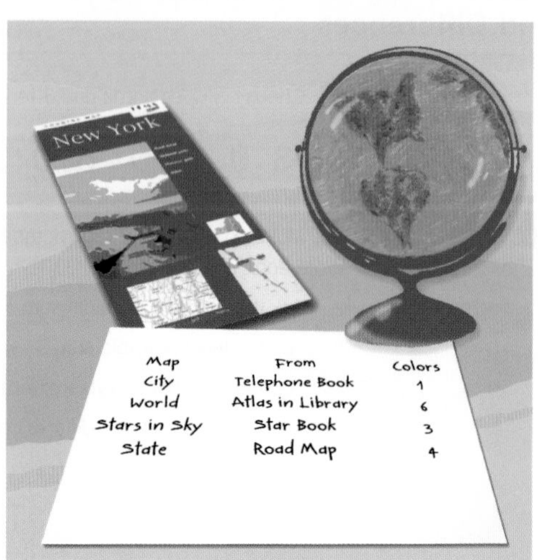

UNIT 5

Unit Review and Test

Lesson Objectives

- **Assess children's progress on unit objectives.**

The Day at a Glance

Today's Goals	Materials
1 Assessing the Unit ▶ Assess children's progress on unit objectives. ▶ Use activities from unit lessons to reteach content.	Unit 5 Test, Student Activity Book pages 191–194 Unit 5 Test, Form A or B, Assessment Guide (optional) Unit 5 Performance Assessment, Assessment Guide (optional)
2 Extending the Assessment ▶ Use remediation for common errors.	
There is no homework assignment on a test day.	

Keeping Skills Sharp

Quick Practice 5 MINUTES	
Goal: Review any skills you choose to meet the needs of your class. If you are doing a unit review day, use any of the Quick Practice activities that provide support for your class. If this is a test day, omit Quick Practice.	**Review and Test Day** You may want to choose a quiet game or other activity (reading a book or working on homework for another subject) for children who finish early.

1 Assessing the Unit

Assess Unit Objectives

5 Unit Test

Name

Draw each number using hundred boxes, ten sticks, and circles.

1. 148

2. 163

What number is shown?
Write the number and write the number in words.

3.

124

one hundred twenty-four

4.

103

one hundred three

Add.

5. 83 + 6 = 89

6. 80 + 10 = 90

7. 60 + 40 = 100

UNIT 5 Test 191

Student Activity Book page 191

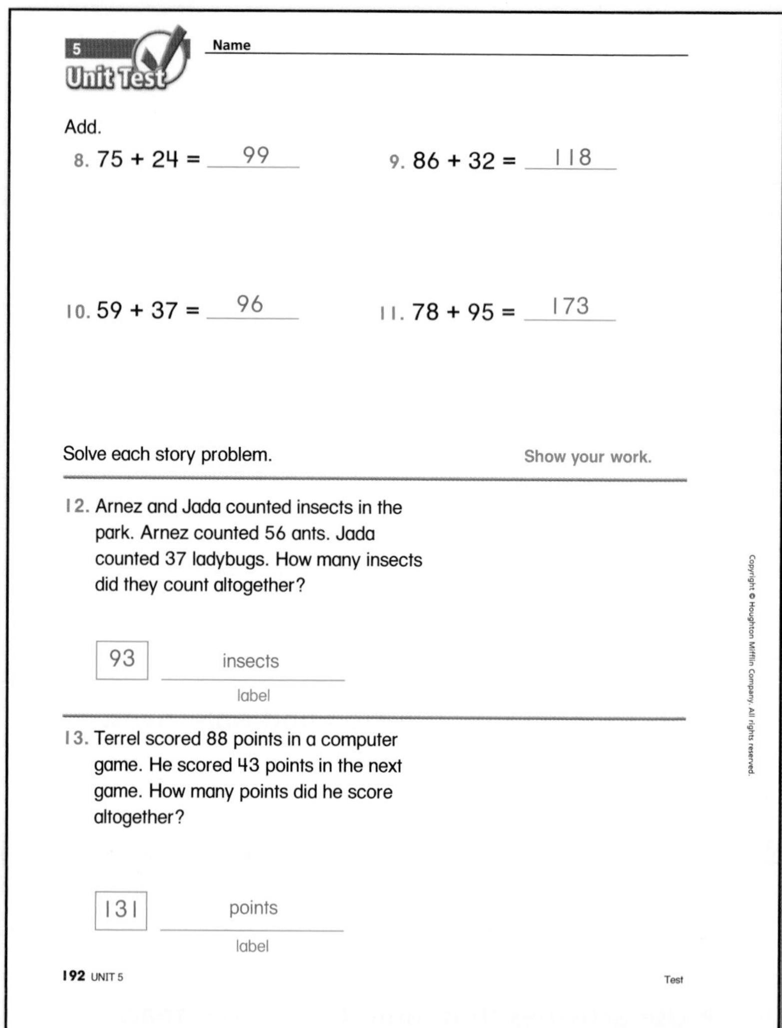

5 Unit Test

Name

Add.

8. 75 + 24 = 99

9. 86 + 32 = 118

10. 59 + 37 = 96

11. 78 + 95 = 173

Solve each story problem. Show your work.

12. Arnez and Jada counted insects in the park. Arnez counted 56 ants. Jada counted 37 ladybugs. How many insects did they count altogether?

93 insects
label

13. Terrel scored 88 points in a computer game. He scored 43 points in the next game. How many points did he score altogether?

131 points
label

192 UNIT 5 Test

Student Activity Book page 192

45 MINUTES (more if schedule permits)

Goal: Assess children's progress on unit objectives.

Materials: Student Activity Book pages 191–194; Assessment Guide

▶ Review and Assessment

If your students are ready for assessment on the unit objectives, use either the test on the Student Activity Book pages or one of the forms of the Unit 5 Test in the Assessment Guide to assess student progress. To assign a numerical score for all of these test forms, use 5 points for each question.

The chart to the right lists the test items, the unit objectives they cover, and the lesson activities in which the objective is covered in this unit.

▶ Reteaching Resources

Unit Test Items	Unit Objectives Tested	Activities to Use for Reteaching
1–4	**5.1** Understand place value for numbers to 200.	Lesson 1, Activity 1 Lesson 2, Activity 1 Lesson 3, Activity 3
5–11, 20	**5.2** Add 2-digit numbers with or without a new ten and a new hundred.	Lesson 4, Activity 1 Lesson 10, Activity 1 Lesson 11, Activity 1 Lesson 12, Activity 1 Lesson 13, Activity 3
12, 13	**5.3** Solve addition story problems.	Lesson 9, Activity 1

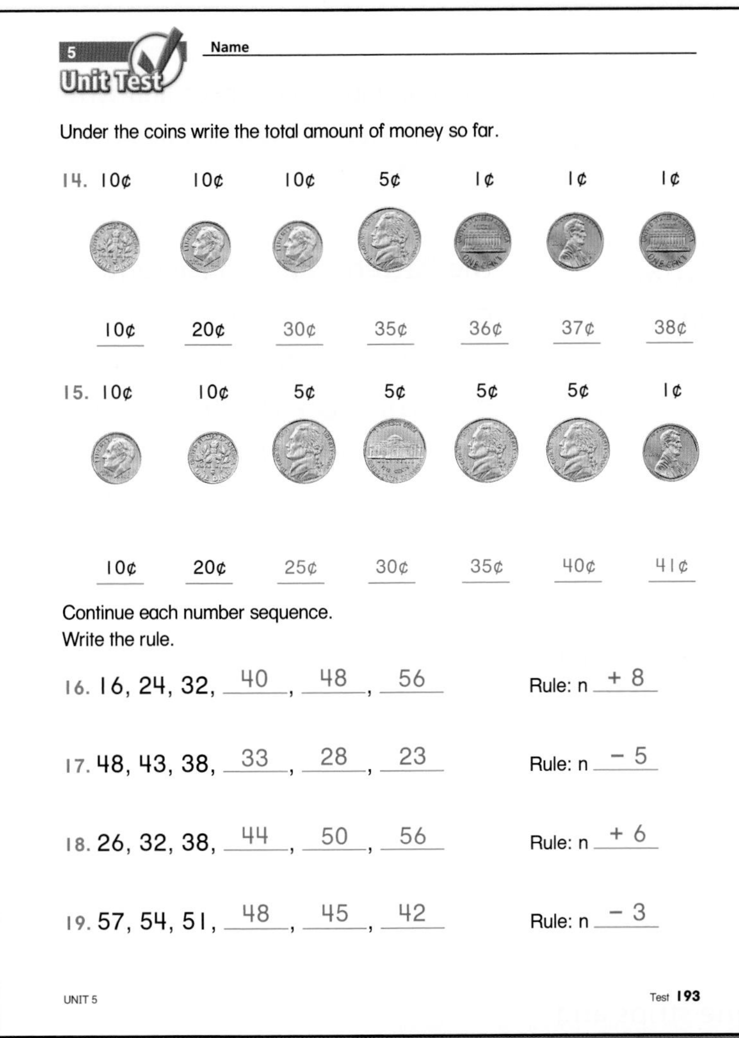
5 Unit Test

Name ______

Under the coins write the total amount of money so far.

14. 10¢ 10¢ 10¢ 5¢ 1¢ 1¢ 1¢

10¢ 20¢ 30¢ 35¢ 36¢ 37¢ 38¢

15. 10¢ 10¢ 5¢ 5¢ 5¢ 5¢ 1¢

10¢ 20¢ 25¢ 30¢ 35¢ 40¢ 41¢

Continue each number sequence.
Write the rule.

16. 16, 24, 32, 40, 48, 56 Rule: n + 8

17. 48, 43, 38, 33, 28, 23 Rule: n − 5

18. 26, 32, 38, 44, 50, 56 Rule: n + 6

19. 57, 54, 51, 48, 45, 42 Rule: n − 3

UNIT 5 Test 193

Student Activity Book page 193

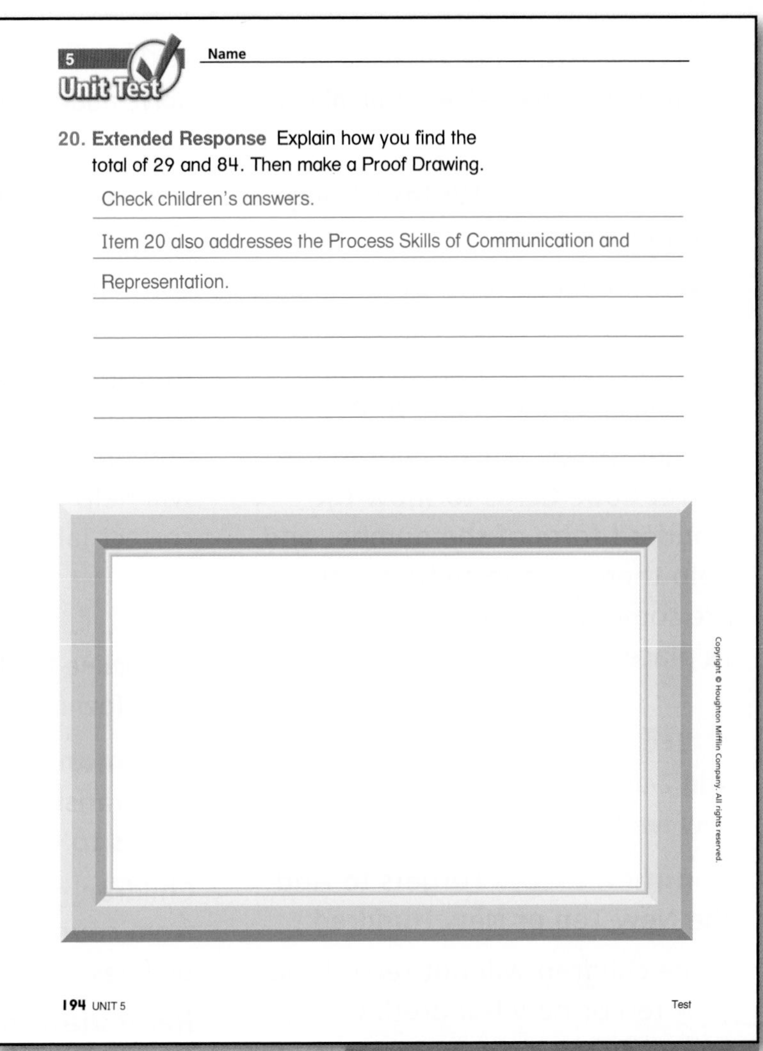
5 Unit Test

Name ______

20. **Extended Response** Explain how you find the total of 29 and 84. Then make a Proof Drawing.

Check children's answers.

Item 20 also addresses the Process Skills of Communication and Representation.

194 UNIT 5 Test

Student Activity Book page 194

Unit Test Items	Unit Objectives Tested	Activities to Use for Reteaching
14, 15	**5.4** Determine the total value of a group of coins (pennies, nickels, and dimes).	Lesson 15, Activity 1
16–19	**5.5** Fill in number sequences and write a rule to describe how the numbers are generated.	Lesson 17, Activity 1

▶ Assessment Resources

Free Response Tests

Form A, Free Response Test

Form B, Multiple-Choice Test

Performance Assessment

▶ Portfolio Assessment

Teacher-selected Items for Student Portfolios:

- Homework, Lessons 4, 10, and 20
- Class Activity work, Lessons 3, 6, and 12

Student-selected Items for Student Portfolios:

- Favorite Home or School Activity
- Best Writing Prompt

2 Extending the Assessment

Common Errors

Activities for Remediation

Unit Objective 5.1

Understand place value for numbers to 200.

Common Error: Writes Wrong Number of Zeros

Given the word form of a number, children may sometimes omit or add extra zeros when writing the standard form of the number.

Remediation Have children use Secret Code Cards to show the standard form of the number and help them recognize that zeros are sometimes needed to be used as placeholders.

Unit Objective 5.2

Add 2-digit numbers with or without a new ten and a new hundred.

Common Error: Forgets to Add the New Ten or New Hundred

Some children will not record the new ten or new hundred. Others will write the new ten or new hundred so small, they will not see it when they add the tens column.

Remediation Emphasize that children must write the new ten or new hundred large enough so that they can see it when adding tens. You may even want them to write the new ten in a bright color.

Unit Objective 5.3

Solve addition story problems.

Common Error: Does Not Label the Answer Correctly

Children may not label the answer correctly. This error occurs most often in group name problems.

Remediation Have children carefully read the story problem and underline the question. This will help them determine the correct label for the answer.

Unit Objective 5.4

Determine the total value of a group of coins (pennies, nickels, and dimes).

Common Error: Fails to Make the Transition from Counting Dimes to Counting Nickels

Children must be able to switch from counting by tens to counting by fives.

Remediation Use dime strips and nickel strips and have children practice the shift from counting by tens to counting by fives. First, make sure they can do each separately. Then count by tens, say "freeze" and ask them to think about what they are counting by next, and continue the count by fives. This may take repeated practice with a Helping Partner.

Unit Objective 5.5

Fill in number sequences and write a rule to describe how the numbers are generated.

Common Error: Doesn't Apply the Pattern Rule Consistently

Children may not apply the pattern rule consistently.

Remediation Use the Number Path and circle the groups that are being added or subtracted over and over.

Unit 6 Overview

Time

UNIT 6 BEGINS WITH telling time to the hour. As the unit progresses, children extend their skills to telling time to 5 minutes and then to 1 minute. Activities include drawing hands on clocks, observing how the hour hand moves with the minute hand, and telling time as before and after the hour. Once children are comfortable reading time on a clock, they work with the concept of elapsed time. Calendars and ordinal numbers for dates are also introduced in this unit and children learn to extend function tables. Although time is introduced in this unit, children continue to practice telling time in the Daily Routines in later units.

Skills Trace

Grade 1	Grade 2	Grade 3
• Tell time to the hour and half-hour. • Recognize days, weeks, and months.	• Tell time to one minute. • Determine elapsed time (hours and half-hours). • Read a calendar.	• Read and write time to the hour, half-hour, quarter-hour, 5 minutes, and 1 minute. • Solve real-world problems involving elapsed time.

Unit 6 Contents

Big Idea Time

Planning Unit 6

NCTM Standards Key: 1. Number and Operations 2. Algebra 3. Geometry 4. Measurement 5. Data Analysis and Probability 6. Problem Solving 7. Reasoning and Proof 8. Communication 9. Connections 10. Representation

Lesson/NCTM Standards	Resources	Materials for Lesson Activities	Materials for Going Further
6–1 **Understand Hours on the Clock** NCTM Standards: 4, 9	TE pp. 445–452 SAB pp. 195–202 H&R pp. 129–130 AC 6–1 MCC 6–21	Paper Clock (TRB M69) Demonstration clock or Time Poster Scissors, paper plates Prong fasteners	MathBoard materials Math Journals
6–2 **Hours and Minutes** NCTM Standards: 4, 9	TE pp. 453–458 SAB pp. 203–204 H&R pp. 131–132 AC 6–2	Handmade clock from Lesson 1 Demonstration Clock or Time Poster MathBoard materials Sticky notes	Handmade clock from Unit 6 Lesson 1 Math Journals
6–3 **More on Telling Time** NCTM Standards: 4, 9	TE pp. 459–466 SAB pp. 205–206 H&R pp. 133–134 AC 6–3 MCC 6–22	Handmade clock from Lesson 1 Demonstration clock or Time Poster MathBoard materials	Index cards Math Journals
6–4 **Elapsed Time** NCTM Standards: 1, 4	TE pp. 467–474 SAB pp. 207–210 H&R pp. 135–136 AC 6–4 MCC 6–23	A current calendar Demonstration clock or Time Poster Newspapers and magazines Minute timer	Handmade clock from Lesson 1 Math Journals
6–5 **Calendars and Function Tables** NCTM Standards: 1, 5	TE pp. 475–482 SAB pp. 211–214 H&R pp. 137–138 AC 6–5 MCC 6–24	A current calendar	Math Journals
✓ Unit Review and Test	TE pp. 483–486 SAB pp. 212–214 AG: Unit 6 tests		

Resources/Materials Key: TE: Teacher Edition SAB: Student Activity Book H&R: Homework and Remembering AC: Activity Cards MCC: Math Center Challenge AG: Assessment Guide ✓: Grade 2 kits TRB: Teacher's Resource Book

Manipulatives and Materials

Essential materials for teaching Math Expressions are available in the Grade 2 kits. These materials are indicated by a ✓ in these lists. At the front of this Teacher Edition is more information about kit contents, alternatives for the materials, and use of the materials.

Unit 6 Assessment

Unit Objectives Tested	Unit Test Items	Lessons
6.1 Tell time to 1 minute.	1, 2, 3, 4, 5, 20	1, 2 ,3
6.2 Read the time as after the hour and before the hour.	6, 7	3
6.3 Use A.M. and P.M.	8, 9	1
6.4 Choose the most appropriate units to measure time.	10, 11	4
6.5 Determine elapsed time (hours and half-hours).	12, 13	4
6.6 Read a calendar.	15, 16	5
6.7 Use ordinal numbers.	17, 18, 19	5
6.8 Complete function tables.	14	5

Assessment and Review Resources

Formal Assessment

Student Activity Book

- Unit Review and Test (pp. 215–218)

Assessment Guide

- Test A–Open Response (pp. A57–A60)
- Test B–Multiple Choice (pp. A61–A65)
- Performance Assessment (pp. A66–A68)

Test Generator CD-ROM

- Open Response Test
- Multiple Choice Test
- Test Bank Items

Informal Assessment

Teacher Edition

- Ongoing Assessment (in every lesson)
- Quick Practice (in every lesson)
- Portfolio Suggestions (p. 485)

Math Talk

- In Activities (pp. 456, 461, 480)

Review Opportunities

Homework and Remembering

- Review of recently taught topics
- Cumulative Review

Teacher Edition

- Unit Review and Test (pp. 483–486)

Test Generator CD-ROM

- Custom Review Sheets

Unit 6 Teaching Resources

Differentiated Instruction

Individualizing Instruction		
Activities	Level	Frequency
	• Intervention • On Level • Challenge	All 3 in every lesson
Math Writing Prompts	Level	Frequency
	• Intervention • On Level • Challenge	All 3 in every lesson
Math Center Challenges	For advanced students	
	4 in every unit	

Reaching All Learners		
English Language Learners	Lessons	Pages
	1, 2, 3, 4, 5, 6, 7, 8, 9, 10, 11, 12, 13, 14, 15	445, 453, 459, 463, 467, 469, 475, 477
Extra Help	Lesson	Page
	5	480
Advanced Learners	Lessons	Pages
	1, 3, 4, 5	450, 461, 469, 480

Strategies for English Language Learners

Present this problem to all children. Offer different levels of support to meet student's levels of language proficiency.

Objective To identify clocks as a way to tell time.

Problem Show a *clock*. Ask: **What do you use a *clock* for?** to tell time **What are the numbers on the *clock*?** 1-12 **What are the numbers used for?** to read the time

Newcomer

- Point to the clock. Say: **This is a *clock*.** Have children repeat.
- Say: **Let's read the numbers on the clock.** Provide number words as needed.

Beginning

- Point to the clock and say: **This is a *clock*. We use *clocks* to tell time.** Have children repeat.
- Say: **Let's read the numbers on the clock.** Have children say numbers as you point to them.

Intermediate

- Point to the clock. Ask: **What are *clocks* used for?** to tell time **What do you read on the clock to tell the time?** the numbers **Are *clocks* used at school?** yes **Do *clocks* tell us what time to go home?** yes

Advanced

- Have children tell about how clocks are used at school for telling time.

Connections

Art Connection
Lesson 2, page 458

Real-World Connection
Lesson 4, page 474

Technology Connection
Lesson 5, page 482

Literature Connection
Lesson 3, page 466

Independent Learning Activities

Ready-Made Math Challenge Centers

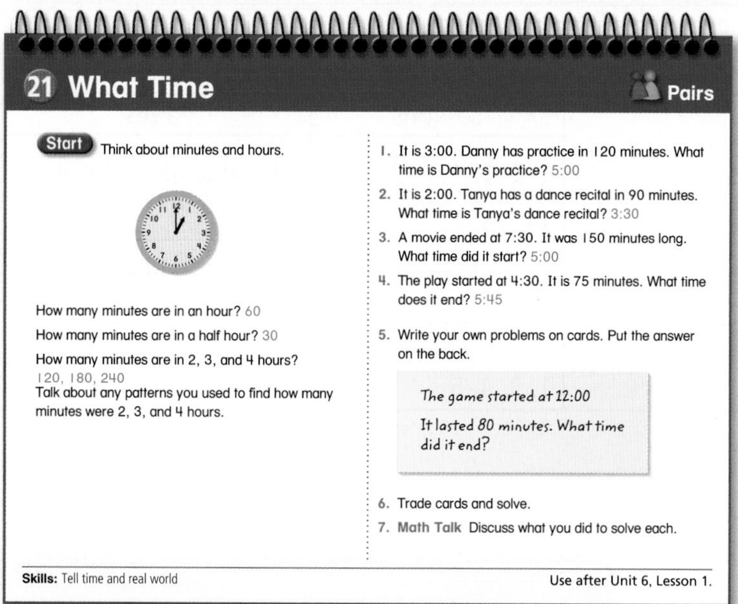

21 What Time Pairs

Start Think about minutes and hours.

How many minutes are in an hour? 60

How many minutes are in a half hour? 30

How many minutes are in 2, 3, and 4 hours? 120, 180, 240

Talk about any patterns you used to find how many minutes were 2, 3, and 4 hours.

1. It is 3:00. Danny has practice in 120 minutes. What time is Danny's practice? 5:00
2. It is 2:00. Tanya has a dance recital in 90 minutes. What time is Tanya's dance recital? 3:30
3. A movie ended at 7:30. It was 150 minutes long. What time did it start? 5:00
4. The play started at 4:30. It is 75 minutes. What time does it end? 5:45
5. Write your own problems on cards. Put the answer on the back.

   The game started at 12:00
   It lasted 80 minutes. What time did it end?

6. Trade cards and solve.
7. **Math Talk** Discuss what you did to solve each.

Skills: Tell time and real world — Use after Unit 6, Lesson 1.

Grouping Pairs

Materials Index cards

Objective Children convert minutes to hours and hours to minutes.

Connections Measurement and Real World

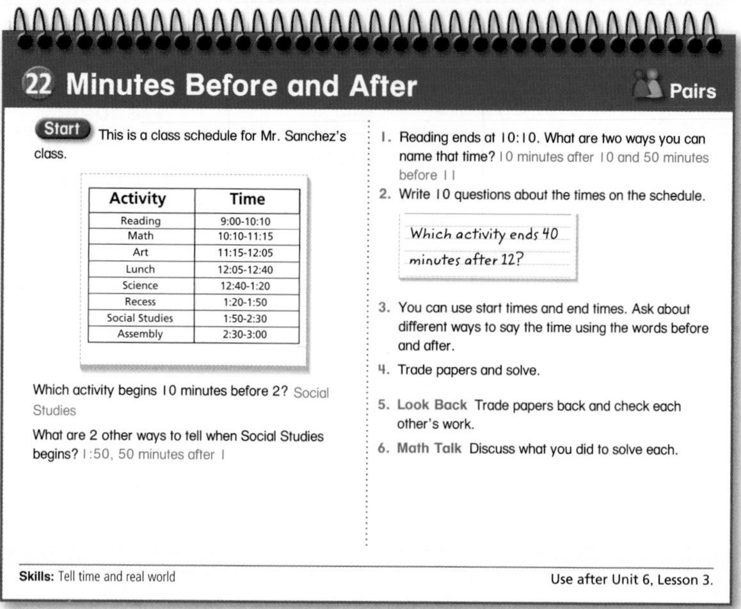

22 Minutes Before and After Pairs

Start This is a class schedule for Mr. Sanchez's class.

Activity	Time
Reading	9:00-10:10
Math	10:10-11:15
Art	11:15-12:05
Lunch	12:05-12:40
Science	12:40-1:20
Recess	1:20-1:50
Social Studies	1:50-2:30
Assembly	2:30-3:00

Which activity begins 10 minutes before 2? Social Studies

What are 2 other ways to tell when Social Studies begins? 1:50, 50 minutes after 1

1. Reading ends at 10:10. What are two ways you can name that time? 10 minutes after 10 and 50 minutes before 11
2. Write 10 questions about the times on the schedule.

   Which activity ends 40 minutes after 12?

3. You can use start times and end times. Ask about different ways to say the time using the words before and after.
4. Trade papers and solve.
5. **Look Back** Trade papers back and check each other's work.
6. **Math Talk** Discuss what you did to solve each.

Skills: Tell time and real world — Use after Unit 6, Lesson 3.

Grouping Pairs

Materials None

Objective Children tell times different ways using the words before and after.

Connections Measurement and Real World

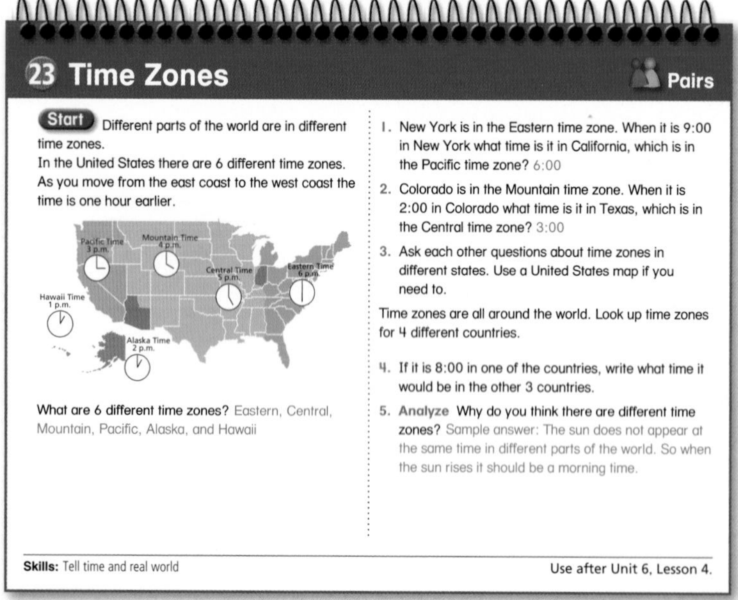

23 Time Zones Pairs

Start Different parts of the world are in different time zones.

In the United States there are 6 different time zones. As you move from the east coast to the west coast the time is one hour earlier.

What are 6 different time zones? Eastern, Central, Mountain, Pacific, Alaska, and Hawaii

1. New York is in the Eastern time zone. When it is 9:00 in New York what time is it in California, which is in the Pacific time zone? 6:00
2. Colorado is in the Mountain time zone. When it is 2:00 in Colorado what time is it in Texas, which is in the Central time zone? 3:00
3. Ask each other questions about time zones in different states. Use a United States map if you need to.

Time zones are all around the world. Look up time zones for 4 different countries.

4. If it is 8:00 in one of the countries, write what time it would be in the other 3 countries.
5. **Analyze** Why do you think there are different time zones? Sample answer: The sun does not appear at the same time in different parts of the world. So when the sun rises it should be a morning time.

Skills: Tell time and real world — Use after Unit 6, Lesson 4.

Grouping Pairs

Materials Resource materials for time zones (such as books or the Internet)

Objective Children identify times for places in different time zones.

Connections Measurement and Real World

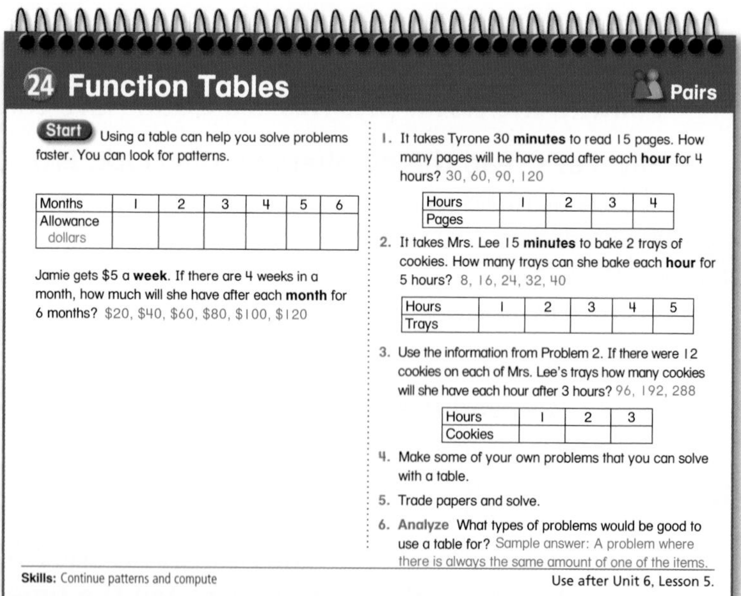

24 Function Tables Pairs

Start Using a table can help you solve problems faster. You can look for patterns.

Months	1	2	3	4	5	6
Allowance dollars						

Jamie gets $5 a **week**. If there are 4 weeks in a month, how much will she have after each **month** for 6 months? $20, $40, $60, $80, $100, $120

1. It takes Tyrone 30 **minutes** to read 15 pages. How many pages will he have read after each **hour** for 4 hours? 30, 60, 90, 120

Hours	1	2	3	4
Pages				

2. It takes Mrs. Lee 15 **minutes** to bake 2 trays of cookies. How many trays can she bake each **hour** for 5 hours? 8, 16, 24, 32, 40

Hours	1	2	3	4	5
Trays					

3. Use the information from Problem 2. If there were 12 cookies on each of Mrs. Lee's trays how many cookies will she have each hour after 3 hours? 96, 192, 288

Hours	1	2	3
Cookies			

4. Make some of your own problems that you can solve with a table.
5. Trade papers and solve.
6. **Analyze** What types of problems would be good to use a table for? Sample answer: A problem where there is always the same amount of one of the items.

Skills: Continue patterns and compute — Use after Unit 6, Lesson 5.

Grouping Pairs

Materials None

Objective Children solve and write problems using function tables.

Connections Algebra and Problem Solving

Ready-Made Math Resources

Technology — Tutorials, Practice, and Intervention

Use activity masters and online, individualized intervention and support to bring students to proficiency.

Help students practice skills and apply concepts through exciting math adventures.

Extend and enrich students' understanding of skills and concepts through engaging, interactive lessons and activities.

Visit **Education Place**®
www.eduplace.com

Visit www.eduplace.com/mx2t/ and find family, teacher, and student materials, activities, games, and more.

Literature Links

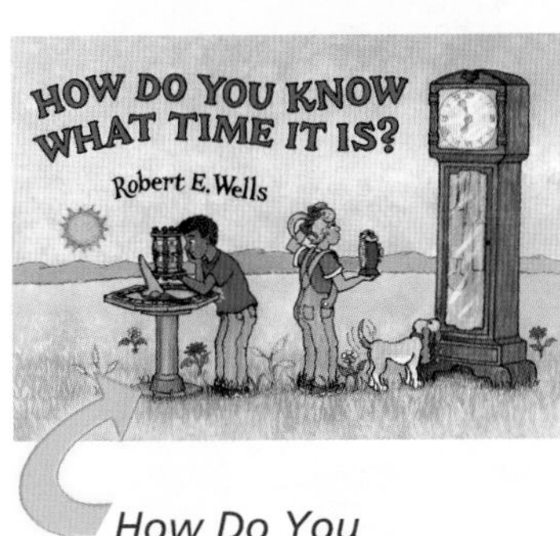

How Do You Know What Time It Is?

How Do You Know What Time It Is?
The telling of time has a unique history as Robert E. Well's book chronicles. Use the book as an introduction to this Unit study or as an enrichment study during the Unit.

Literature Connections

- *Clocks and More Clocks*, by Pat Hutchins (Aladdin Paperbacks, Simon & Schuster, 1970)
- *My Grandmother's Clock*, by Geraldine McCaughrean, illustrated by Stephen Lambert (Clarion Books, 2002)

Putting Research into Practice for Unit 6

From Current Research: Reading Time K–2

Another emphasis at this level should be on developing concepts of time and the ways it is measured. When children use calendars or sequence events in stories, they are using measures of time in a real context. Opportunities arise throughout the school day for teachers to focus on time and its measurement through short conversations with their children. A teacher might say, for example, "Look at the clock. It's one o'clock—time for gym! It is just like the picture of the clock on our schedule." As teachers call attention to the clock, many young children will learn to tell time. However, this is less important than their understanding patterns of minutes, hours, days, weeks, and months.

National Council of Teachers of Mathematics. *Principles and Standards for School Mathematics.* Reston: NCTM, 2000. 104.

The study of measurement is crucial in the school mathematics curriculum because of its practicality and pervasiveness in so many aspects of life. The Measurement Standard includes understanding the attributes, units, systems, and processes of measurement as well as applying the techniques, tools, and formulas to determine measurements. Measurement can serve as a way to integrate the different strands of mathematics because it offers opportunities to learn about and apply other areas of mathematics such as number, geometry, functions, and statistical ideas.

National Council of Teachers of Mathematics. "Executive Summary." *Principles and Standards for School Mathematics.* Reston: NCTM, 2000. 3–4.

Other Useful References: Calendars, Function Tables

Barger, Rita H., Cynthia G. Bryant. "Calendar Capers." *Mathematics Teaching in the Middle School* 8.6 (Feb. 2003): 316 (includes history of calendars).

Greenes, Carole, Mary Cavanagh, Linda Dacey, Carol Findell, Marian Small. *Navigating Through Algebra in Prekindergarten–Grade 2*. Navigations series. Reston: NCTM, 2001.

Shreero, Betsy, Cindy Sullivan, Alicia Urbano. "Calendar Math." *Teaching Children Mathematics* 9.2 (Oct. 2002): 96.

Stump, Sheryl, Joyce Bishop, Barbara Britton. "Building a Vision of Algebra for Preservice Teachers." *Teaching Children Mathematics* 10.3 (Nov. 2003): 180.

Getting Ready to Teach Unit 6

In Unit 6, children discuss the features and functions of clocks, see how clocks are tools for measuring time in hours, minutes, and seconds, use a calendar, and solve problems.

Telling Time
Lessons 1, 2, and 3

By labeling the numbers on an analog clock face, children see that clocks, like all measuring tools, are comprised of iterated units. Children begin developing their skills in telling time by reading time to the hour and drawing hands on clock faces for times to the hour. Children then examine how we use the numbers on a clock face to tell the number of minutes after the hour. The scale for minutes is different from that of hours; each sector represents 5 minutes. Using their 5s count-bys, children tell time to 5 minutes and draw hands on clock faces for times to 5 minutes. They observe that the hour hand moves with the minute hand, though at this grade they are not expected to note exact placement of the hour hand for times after the hour. They also learn the relationship between seconds and minutes. In Lesson 3, children's skills are extended to reading time to the minute and reading times as before and after the hour. Throughout the unit, children link times to daily activities.

Elapsed Time
Lesson 4

After several lessons of reading time to the nearest hour, 5 minutes, and minute, children are introduced to finding elapsed time from a start time and an end time. In this unit, children measure elapsed time in hours and half-hours and apply these skills to real-world problems. To find elapsed time, they count the sectors through which the clock hands travel, thereby reinforcing the principle that clocks are comprised of iterated units.

Math Expressions Vocabulary

As you teach this unit, emphasize understanding of this term:

- Time Poster

See Glossary on pp. T7–T20.

Using a Calendar
Lessons 5 and 6

In Lesson 5, children use a calendar to explore how a year is divided into months, weeks, and days. They use ordinal words to say dates and to refer to days, weeks, or months in position; for instance, they are asked to name the day of the week as the third Tuesday of the month. To help consolidate their understanding of calendars, children identify number patterns on calendars.

Function Tables
Lesson 6

In the final activity of this unit, children use function tables to continue patterns and solve problems. This work provides an important foundation for future algebraic thinking.

Hours on the Clock

Lesson Objectives

- Describe analog and digital clocks.
- Define A.M. and P.M.
- Link times to daily activities.
- Tell time to the hour.

Vocabulary	
clock	minute hand
analog clock	A.M.
digital clock	P.M.
hour hand	Time Poster

The Day at a Glance

Today's Goals	Materials	
1 Teaching the Lesson **A1:** Discuss the features and functions of clocks. **A2:** Show the time by drawing hands on a clock and read time to the hour.	**Lesson Activities** Student Activity Book pp. 195–202 (includes Clock, Family Letter) Homework and Remembering pp. 129–130 Paper Clock (TRB M69) Demonstration clock or Time Poster Scissors, paper plates Prong fasteners	**Going Further** Activity Cards 6-1 MathBoard materials Math Journals
2 Going Further ▸ Differentiated Instruction		
3 Homework		

Use Math Talk today!

Keeping Skills Sharp

Daily Routines	English Language Learners
Math Mountains for 100 or 2-Digit Numbers Using the MathBoard, Using Dimes and Pennies (See p. xxvi.) ▸ Led by Student Leaders **Money Routine** Using the 120 Poster, Using the Money Flip Chart, Using the Number Path, Using Secret Code Cards (See pp. xxiii–xxv.) ▸ Led by Student Leaders	Draw an analog clock that shows 10:00. Write *analog* on the board. • **Beginning** Say: ***Analog* clocks have hands. This *analog* clock has 2 hands.** Have children repeat. • **Intermediate** Say: ***Analog* clocks have hands.** Ask: **How many hands does this *analog* clock have?** 2 • **Advanced** Have children tell about a place they have seen an analog clock.

1 Teaching the Lesson

Activity 1

Introduce Time and Clocks

 **25 MINUTES**

Goal: Discuss the features and functions of clocks.

Materials: Student Activity Book pages 195–196, demonstration clock or Time Poster and dry-erase markers

 **NCTM Standards:**
Measurement
Connections

▶ Features of Clocks WHOLE CLASS

Begin a class discussion about the purpose of clocks.

- Why do we have clocks? Answers will vary. Possible answers: Clocks tell us when to get up in the morning; they tell us when to go to school.
- How is a clock like a ruler or a scale? Clocks are used to measure.
- What do clocks measure? They measure time in hours and minutes, and sometimes in seconds.

Have children complete exercise 1 on Student Activity Book page 195. When they are finished, discuss their answers together. Be sure that children identify that analog clocks have faces, hands, and numbers, and that digital clocks have only numbers.

Draw a large circle on the board. Point out that people often say that analog clocks have faces.

- How many numbers are on the face of an analog clock? 12 numbers

Encourage children to guide you as you add the numbers to the clock on the board.

- Where should I place the number 12? at the top of the clock
- Where should I place the number 1? to the right of number 12

Continue until you have filled in all of the numbers on the clock face.

Have children complete exercises 2–4 to practice labeling a clock face with numbers.

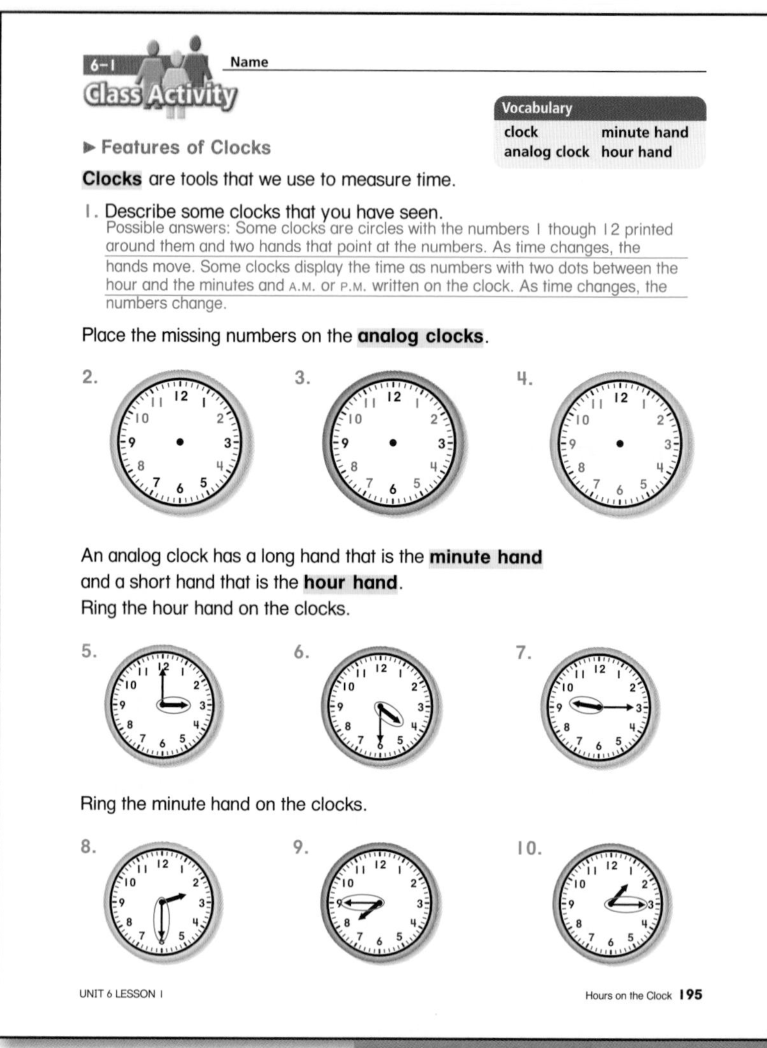
6-1 Class Activity Name

Vocabulary
clock minute hand
analog clock hour hand

▶ Features of Clocks

Clocks are tools that we use to measure time.

1. Describe some clocks that you have seen.
Possible answers: Some clocks are circles with the numbers 1 though 12 printed around them and two hands that point at the numbers. As time changes, the hands move. Some clocks display the time as numbers with two dots between the hour and the minutes and A.M. or P.M. written on the clock. As time changes, the numbers change.

Place the missing numbers on the **analog clocks**.

2. 3. 4.

An analog clock has a long hand that is the **minute hand** and a short hand that is the **hour hand**.
Ring the hour hand on the clocks.

5. 6. 7.

Ring the minute hand on the clocks.

8. 9. 10.

UNIT 6 LESSON 1 Hours on the Clock 195

Student Activity Book page 195

Add an hour hand and a minute hand to the clock on the board. Point to the hour hand and ask children to tell you its name. Answers will vary. Possible answers: short hand, small hand, hour hand

Point to the minute hand and ask children to tell you its name. Answers will vary. Possible answers: long hand, big hand, minute hand

Have children practice identifying the minute hand and the hour hand by completing exercises 5–10.

Teaching Note

What to Expect from Students In your discussion about the hands on a clock, some children may mention the second hand on an analog clock.

▶ Times of Daily Activities INDIVIDUALS

Display 6:00 on a demonstration clock or draw clock hands on the Time Poster. Tell children that we say this time as "6 o'clock."

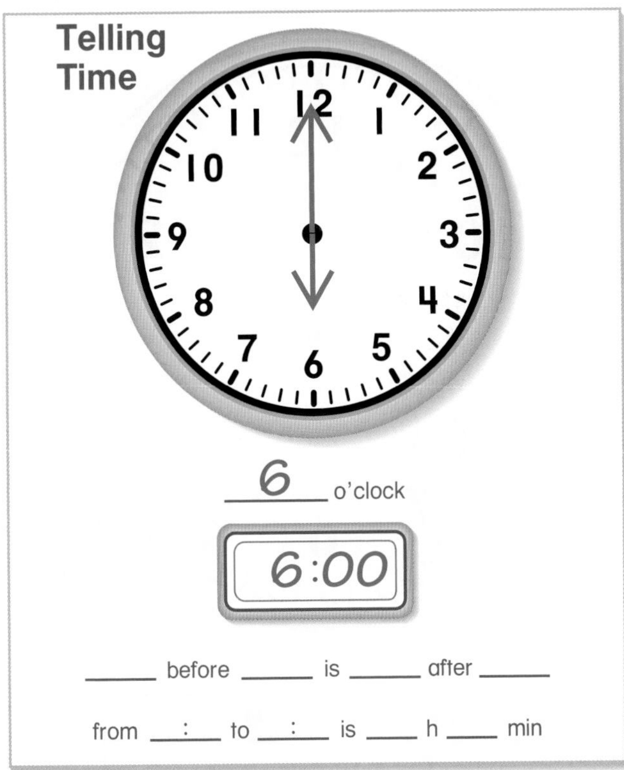

- When you look at the clock, can you tell whether it is 6 o'clock in the morning or 6 o'clock in the evening? no

Explain to children that the clock's hour hand moves in a complete circle twice each day. Tell them that we say A.M. for times after midnight and before noon (morning) and P.M. for times after noon and before midnight (afternoon and evening).

Refer children to Student Activity Book page 196. Ask them to complete exercise 11 on their own and discuss their answers as a class.

Teaching Note

Language and Vocabulary The abbreviation A.M. stands for *ante meridiem* and the abbreviation P.M. stands for *post meridiem.* These are Latin words: *ante* means "before," *post* means "after," and *meridiem* means "noon." Note that we do not use either A.M. or P.M. for midnight or noon.

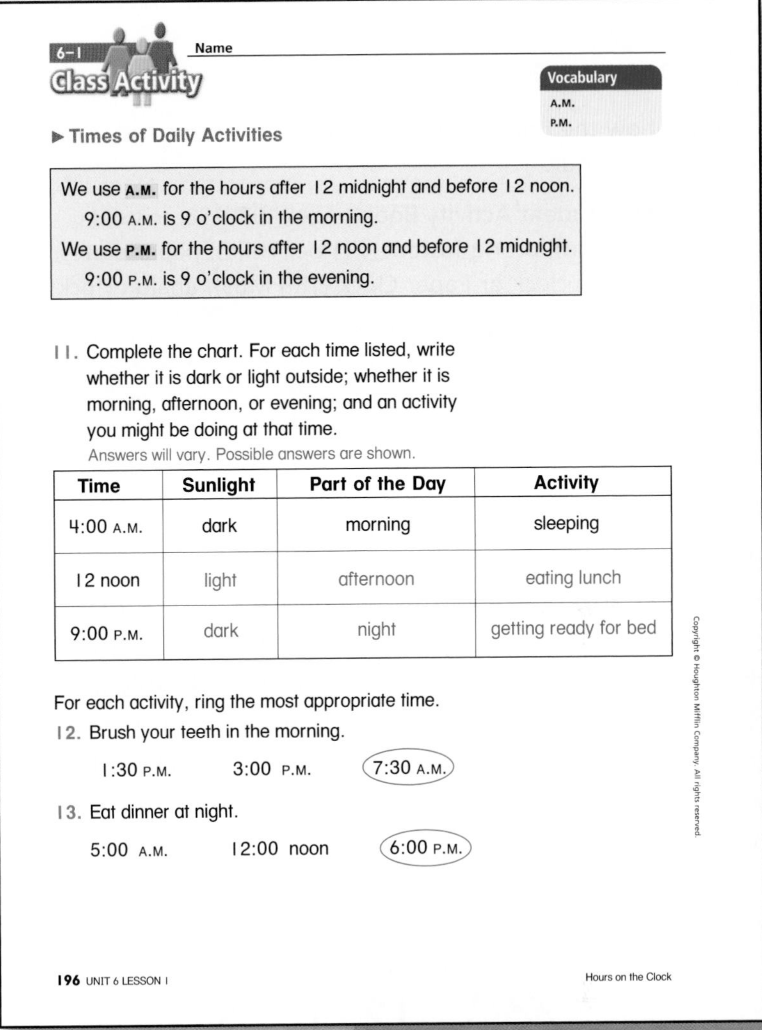

6–1 Class Activity Name

Vocabulary
A.M.
P.M.

▶ Times of Daily Activities

We use A.M. for the hours after 12 midnight and before 12 noon.
9:00 A.M. is 9 o'clock in the morning.
We use P.M. for the hours after 12 noon and before 12 midnight.
9:00 P.M. is 9 o'clock in the evening.

11. Complete the chart. For each time listed, write whether it is dark or light outside; whether it is morning, afternoon, or evening; and an activity you might be doing at that time.
Answers will vary. Possible answers are shown.

Time	Sunlight	Part of the Day	Activity
4:00 A.M.	dark	morning	sleeping
12 noon	light	afternoon	eating lunch
9:00 P.M.	dark	night	getting ready for bed

For each activity, ring the most appropriate time.

12. Brush your teeth in the morning.
1:30 P.M. 3:00 P.M. (7:30 A.M.)

13. Eat dinner at night.
5:00 A.M. 12:00 noon (6:00 P.M.)

196 UNIT 6 LESSON 1 Hours on the Clock

Student Activity Book page 196

Ongoing Assessment

Ask children these questions:

- ▶ Is 8 o'clock in the morning 8:00 A.M. or 8:00 P.M.?
- ▶ What might you be doing at that time of day?

Activity 2

Time to the Hour

30 MINUTES

Goal: Show the time by drawing hands on a clock and read time to the hour.

Materials: Student Activity Book pages 197–198, scissors (1 pair per child), prong fasteners (1 per child), paper plates, demonstration clock or Paper Clock (TRB M69), analog clock

 **NCTM Standards:**
Measurement
Connections

▶ Make a Clock WHOLE CLASS

Have student helpers distribute scissors, prong fasteners, and paper plates to children and refer the class to Student Activity Book page 197. Have them use this page to create their own analog clock. Assist children as necessary, particularly in attaching the clock to the paper plate and then attaching the clock hands with the prong fastener. Tell children that they will be using their clocks in many of the upcoming activities.

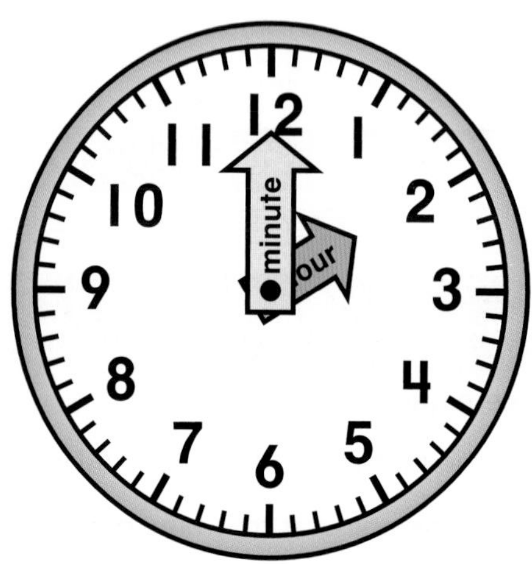

Student Activity Book page 197

Class Management

Looking Ahead Have children store their analog clocks in a safe place. They will be using their clocks in activities throughout this unit. If necessary, children can create another clock using Paper Clock TRB M69.

▶ Tell Time to the Hour WHOLE CLASS

Display 7:00 on a demonstration clock or on the Time Poster. Invite children to set this time on their own analog clocks. Write 7 o'clock and the digital notation on the poster.

- How does the clock show that it is 7 o'clock? The hour hand points to the 7 and the minute hand points to the 12.

Change the time on the clock to 8 o'clock, and ask children to do the same on their clocks.

- What time is it now? 8 o'clock
- How do you know? The hour hand is pointing to 8.
- How much time has passed since 7 o'clock? 1 hour

Point out to children that the hour hand moves from one number to the next during the time it takes the minute hand to travel around the clock once. Use a demonstration clock or one of the children's clocks to demonstrate this concept. Move the minute hand in one complete circle so the hour hand travels from 8 to 9.

- Do both hands on a clock move in the same direction? yes

Sketch a circle with arrows pointing in a clockwise direction on the board.

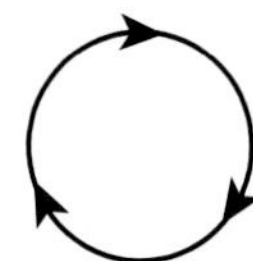

Emphasize for children that the hands on a clock move in the same direction as the numbers on the face increase.

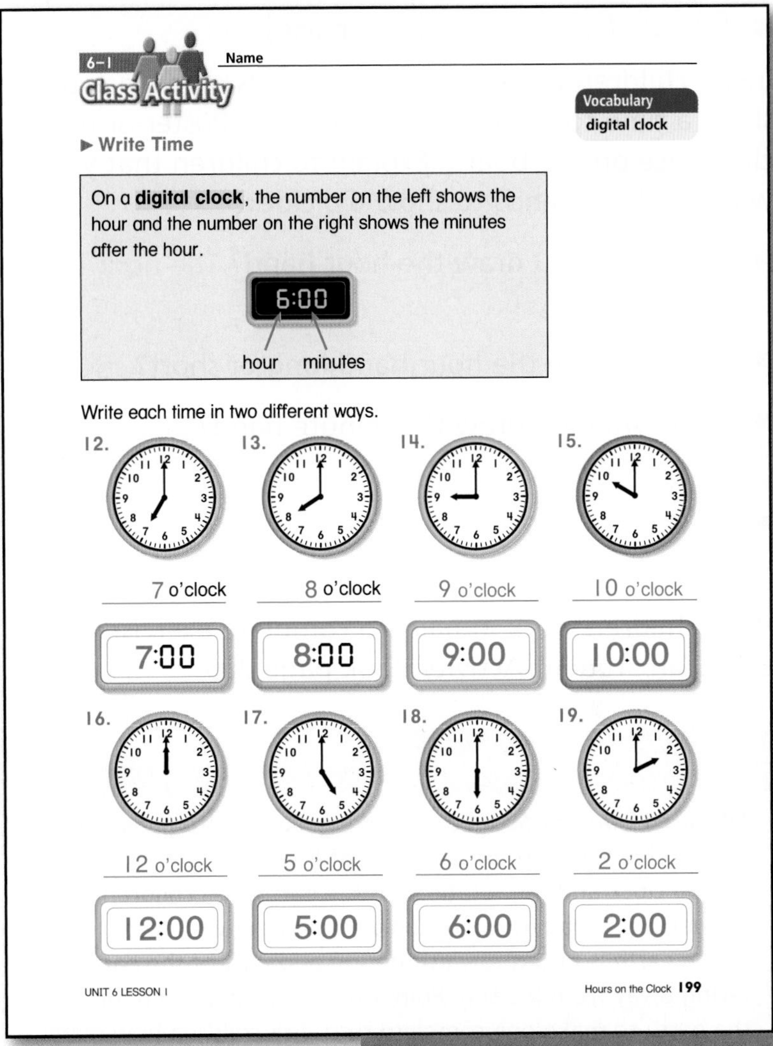

6-1 Class Activity

Name

Vocabulary
digital clock

▶ Write Time

On a **digital clock**, the number on the left shows the hour and the number on the right shows the minutes after the hour.

6:00
hour minutes

Write each time in two different ways.

12. 7 o'clock 7:00
13. 8 o'clock 8:00
14. 9 o'clock 9:00
15. 10 o'clock 10:00
16. 12 o'clock 12:00
17. 5 o'clock 5:00
18. 6 o'clock 6:00
19. 2 o'clock 2:00

UNIT 6 LESSON 1 Hours on the Clock 199

Student Activity Book page 199

Alternate Approach

Analog Clocks Some children will benefit from moving the hands of a real analog clock to see that as they rotate the minute hand in a complete circle, the hour hand moves to the next number.

▶ Write Time INDIVIDUALS

Refer children to Student Activity Book page 199 and discuss as a class how time appears on a digital clock.

Invite children to complete exercises 12–19 individually.

Activity continued ▶

► Draw Clock Hands PAIRS

Invite children to help you draw hands on a clock to show a time to the hour. Use the Time Poster or draw a clock face on the board. Explain to children that you want to draw hands to show 6 o'clock.

- Where should I draw the hour hand? The hour hand should point to 6.
- Should I make the hour hand long or short? short
- Where should I draw the minute hand? The minute hand should point to 12.
- Why? At 6 o'clock, there are no minutes past the hour.

Have children work in pairs to complete exercises 20–25 on Student Activity Book page 200.

Differentiated Instruction

Advanced Learners Some children may benefit from making a connection between the rotations of the hour hand on an analog clock and the rotations of the earth. Tell children that the earth is always turning. Explain that at any moment, part of the earth is facing toward the sun and part of the earth is facing away from the sun. Point out that it takes 24 hours for the earth to make one complete turn. Ask children how many times the hour hand goes around the clock in 24 hours.

Tell children that some countries tell time using 24 hours instead of 12 hours twice a day. Discuss what the afternoon hours would be called on a 24-hour clock.

6-1 Class Activity Name

► Draw Clock Hands

Draw the hands on each analog clock and write the time on each digital clock below.

20. 7 o'clock 7:00

21. 11 o'clock 11:00

22. 2 o'clock 2:00

23. 3 o'clock 3:00

24. 5 o'clock 5:00

25. 10 o'clock 10:00

Copyright © Houghton Mifflin Company. All rights reserved.

200 UNIT 6 LESSON 1 Hours on the Clock

Student Activity Book page 200

Teaching Note

Language and Vocabulary Help children remember that the short hand is the hour hand and the long hand is the minute hand by drawing a short arrow around the shorter word *hour* and a long arrow around the longer word *minute*.

2 Going Further

Differentiated Instruction

Intervention — Activity Card 6-1

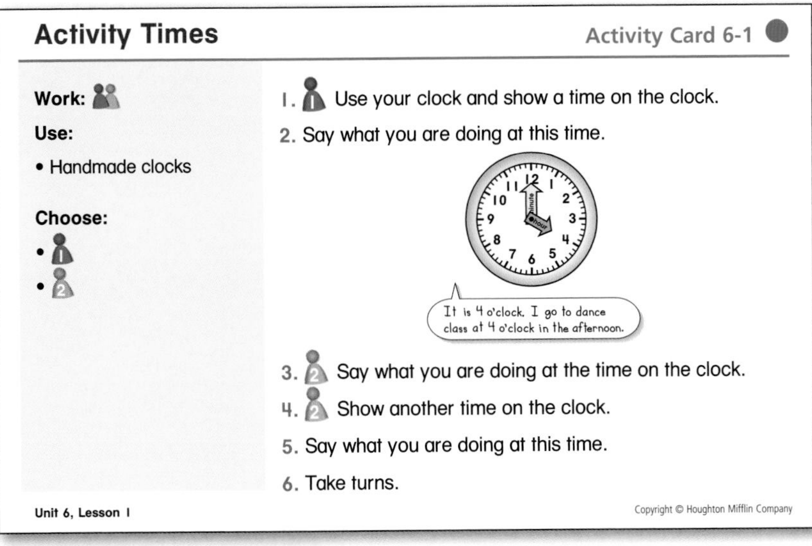

Activity Times — Activity Card 6-1 ●

Work:
Use:
- Handmade clocks

Choose:
- 1
- 2

1. Use your clock and show a time on the clock.
2. Say what you are doing at this time.

It is 4 o'clock. I go to dance class at 4 o'clock in the afternoon.

3. Say what you are doing at the time on the clock.
4. Show another time on the clock.
5. Say what you are doing at this time.
6. Take turns.

Unit 6, Lesson 1

Activity Note Each pair needs the homemade clock from Activity 2 or Student Activity Book page 197. Check that children set their clocks to the hour.

Math Writing Prompt

Draw a Picture How is a digital clock like an analog clock? How is it different? Include drawings in your answer.

Software Support

Use *Soar to Success* for instruction of students needing targeted support for underlying skills.

On Level — Activity Card 6-1

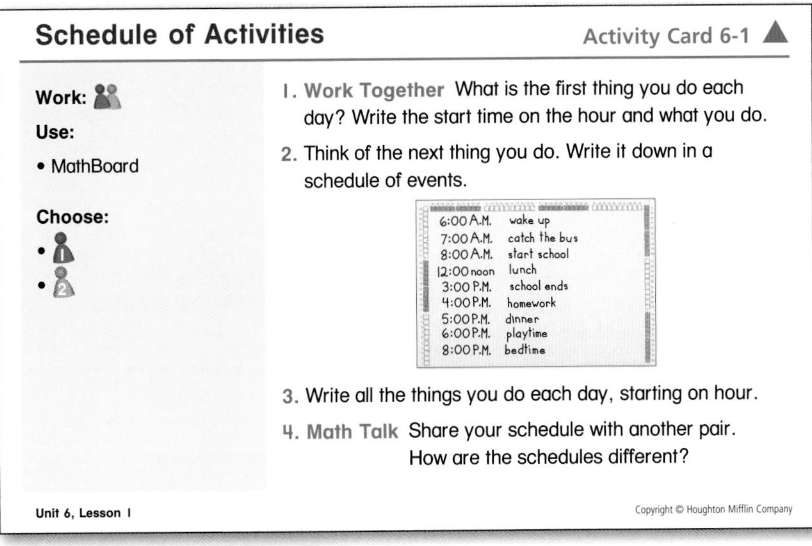

Schedule of Activities — Activity Card 6-1 ▲

Work:
Use:
- MathBoard

Choose:
- 1
- 2

1. **Work Together** What is the first thing you do each day? Write the start time on the hour and what you do.
2. Think of the next thing you do. Write it down in a schedule of events.

6:00 A.M.	wake up
7:00 A.M.	catch the bus
8:00 A.M.	start school
12:00 noon	lunch
3:00 P.M.	school ends
4:00 P.M.	homework
5:00 P.M.	dinner
6:00 P.M.	playtime
8:00 P.M.	bedtime

3. Write all the things you do each day, starting on hour.
4. **Math Talk** Share your schedule with another pair. How are the schedules different?

Unit 6, Lesson 1

Activity Note Each pair needs MathBoard materials. Remind children to start each activity on the hour. You may want to have pairs type their schedule on a computer.

Math Writing Prompt

Write a Story Write a story that shows why it is important to include A.M. or P.M. when you say a time.

Software Support

Use *MegaMath* for review and reinforcement of the concepts and skills presented in this lesson.

Challenge — Activity Card 6-1

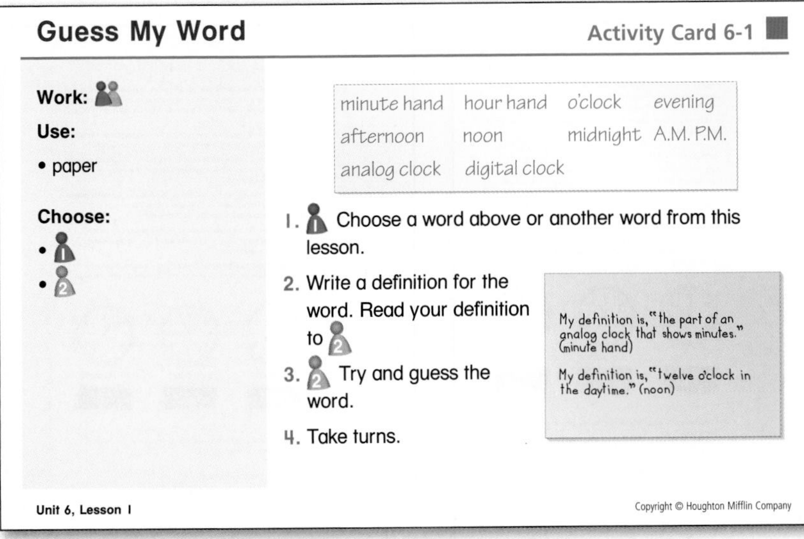

Guess My Word — Activity Card 6-1 ■

Work:
Use:
- paper

Choose:
- 1
- 2

minute hand	hour hand	o'clock	evening
afternoon	noon	midnight	A.M. P.M.
analog clock	digital clock		

1. Choose a word above or another word from this lesson.
2. Write a definition for the word. Read your definition to 2.
3. Try and guess the word.
4. Take turns.

My definition is, "the part of an analog clock that shows minutes." (minute hand)
My definition is, "twelve o'clock in the daytime." (noon)

Unit 6, Lesson 1

Activity Note Each child writes a definition for a word from the lesson. The other child tries and guess the word from the definition.

Math Writing Prompt

Explain Your Thinking Which hand moves faster on a clock, the hour hand or the minute hand? Explain your thinking.

Software Support

Use *Destination Math* to take students beyond the concepts and skills presented in this lesson.

Homework

6–1 Homework Goal: Additional Practice

This Homework page allows children to practice filling in numbers on clock faces and writing the time.

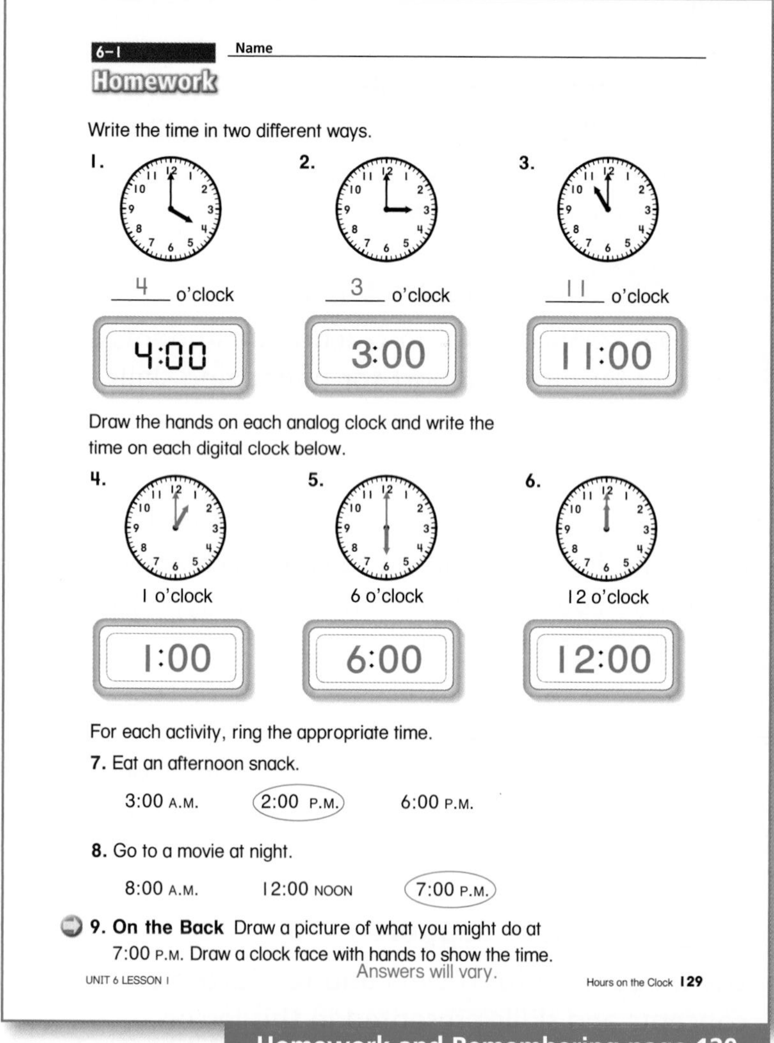

6–1 Homework Name ______

Write the time in two different ways.

1. 4 o'clock 4:00
2. 3 o'clock 3:00
3. 11 o'clock 11:00

Draw the hands on each analog clock and write the time on each digital clock below.

4. 1 o'clock 1:00
5. 6 o'clock 6:00
6. 12 o'clock 12:00

For each activity, ring the appropriate time.

7. Eat an afternoon snack.

3:00 A.M. (2:00 P.M.) 6:00 P.M.

8. Go to a movie at night.

8:00 A.M. 12:00 NOON (7:00 P.M.)

9. **On the Back** Draw a picture of what you might do at 7:00 P.M. Draw a clock face with hands to show the time.
Answers will vary.

UNIT 6 LESSON 1 Hours on the Clock **129**

Homework and Remembering page 129

Home and School Connection

Family Letter Have children take home the Family Letter on Student Activity Book page 201. This letter explains how the concept of time is developed in *Math Expressions.* It gives parents and guardians a better understanding of the learning that goes on in math class and creates a bridge between school and home. A Spanish translation of this letter is on the following page in the Student Activity Book.

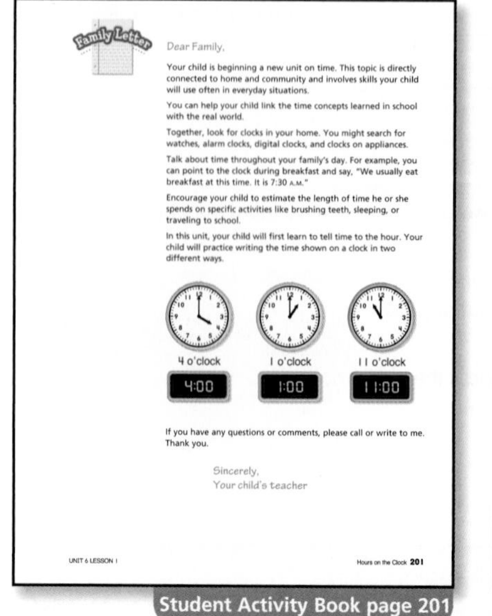

Family Letter

Dear Family,

Your child is beginning a new unit on time. This topic is directly connected to home and community and involves skills your child will use often in everyday situations.

You can help your child link the time concepts learned in school with the real world.

Together, look for clocks in your home. You might search for watches, alarm clocks, digital clocks, and clocks on appliances.

Talk about time throughout your family's day. For example, you can point to the clock during breakfast and say, "We usually eat breakfast at this time. It is 7:30 A.M."

Encourage your child to estimate the length of time he or she spends on specific activities like brushing teeth, sleeping, or traveling to school.

In this unit, your child will first learn to tell time to the hour. Your child will practice writing the time shown on a clock in two different ways.

4 o'clock 4:00 1 o'clock 1:00 11 o'clock 11:00

If you have any questions or comments, please call or write to me. Thank you.

Sincerely,
Your child's teacher

UNIT 6 LESSON 1 Hours on the Clock 201

Student Activity Book page 201

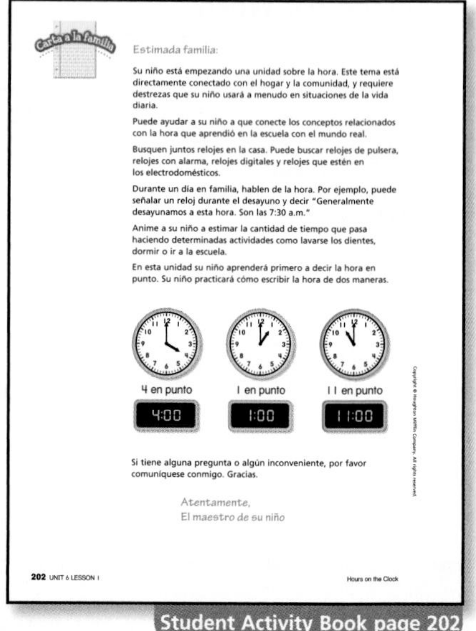

Carta a la familia

Estimada familia:

Su niño está empezando una unidad sobre la hora. Este tema está directamente conectado con el hogar y la comunidad, y requiere destrezas que su niño usará a menudo en situaciones de la vida diaria.

Puede ayudar a su niño a que conecte los conceptos relacionados con la hora que aprendió en la escuela con el mundo real.

Busquen juntos relojes en la casa. Puede buscar relojes de pulsera, relojes con alarma, relojes digitales y relojes que estén en los electrodomésticos.

Durante un día en familia, hablen de la hora. Por ejemplo, puede señalar un reloj durante el desayuno y decir "Generalmente desayunamos a esta hora. Son las 7:30 a.m."

Anime a su niño a estimar la cantidad de tiempo que pasa haciendo determinadas actividades como lavarse los dientes, dormir o ir a la escuela.

En esta unidad su niño aprenderá primero a decir la hora en punto. Su niño practicará cómo escribir la hora de dos maneras.

4 en punto 4:00 1 en punto 1:00 11 en punto 11:00

Si tiene alguna pregunta o algún inconveniente, por favor comuníquese conmigo. Gracias.

Atentamente,
El maestro de su niño

202 UNIT 6 LESSON 1 Hours on the Clock

Student Activity Book page 202

Hours and Minutes

Lesson Objectives

- **Experience how long a minute is.**
- **Define an hour.**
- **Tell time to 5 minutes.**

Vocabulary

analog clock	hour hand
digital clock	5-minute interval
minute hand	

The Day at a Glance

Today's Goals	Materials	
1 Teaching the Lesson **A1:** Time 1-minute activities and mark numbers for 5-minute intervals on a clock. **A2:** Read and show time to 5 minutes.	**Lesson Activities** Student Activity Book pp. 203–204 Homework and Remembering pp. 131–132 Handmade clock from Lesson 1 Demonstration Clock or Time Poster MathBoard materials Sticky notes	**Going Further** Activity Cards 6-2 Handmade clock from Unit 6 Lesson 1 Math Journals
2 Going Further ▸ Differentiated Instruction		
3 Homework		

Use Math Talk today!

Keeping Skills Sharp

Daily Routines	English Language Learners
Math Mountains for 100 or 2-Digit Numbers Using the MathBoard, Using Dimes and Pennies (See p. xxvi.) ▸ Led by Student Leaders **Money Routine** Using the 120 Poster, Using the Money Flip Chart, Using the Number Path, Using Secret Code Cards (See pp. xxiii–xxv.) ▸ Led by Student Leaders	Draw a digital clock that shows 7:15. Write *digital* on the board. Say: ***Digital* clocks don't have hands. *Digital* clocks have numbers only.** • **Beginning** Say: **The *digital* clock shows the numbers 7 and 15.** Have children repeat. • **Intermediate** Ask: **What numbers does the *digital clock* show?** 7 and 15 • **Advanced** Have children say where at home they might have a digital clock.

1 Teaching the Lesson

Activity 1

Hours and Minutes

 25 MINUTES

Goal: Time 1-minute activities and mark numbers for 5-minute intervals on a clock.

Materials: Demonstration clock or Time Poster, handmade clocks from Lesson 1 or Paper Clock (TRB M69), Student Activity Book page 203, sticky notes, MathBoard materials

 **NCTM Standards:**
Measurement
Connections

▶ How Long Are 1 Minute and 1 Hour?

WHOLE CLASS

Ask for Ideas Have children do different activities for a minute to help them develop a sense of the duration of 1 minute.

Ask children to jump up and down for 1 minute. Indicate exactly when they should start and stop. Invite them to then sit quietly for 1 minute.

- Does a minute seem like a long time or a short time? Answers will vary. Possible answers are shown. When I was busy jumping, the minute went by quickly. When I was sitting quietly, the minute seemed to take a longer time.

Ask children to think about how an hour feels.

- What are some activities you do that take 1 hour to finish? Answers will vary. Possible answers are shown. play at lunchtime, watch a television show, do my homework

▶ Hours and Minutes on a Clock

WHOLE CLASS

Display 1 o'clock on a demonstration clock or on the Time Poster. You can ask children to follow along using their handmade clocks from Lesson 1. Write 1 o'clock and the digital notation on the poster.

- Which hand on an analog clock tells the hour? short hand, hour hand
- Which number or numbers on a digital clock tell the hour? number(s) on the left

Advance the hands on the analog clock to show 2:00.

- When the minute hand goes all the way around the clock, what happens to the hour hand? It moves ahead by 1 number.

Show 2:20 on the analog clock and digital clock.

- Which numbers on a digital clock tell the minutes after the hour? numbers on the right
- Which hand on an analog clock tells the minutes after the hour? long hand, minute hand

Emphasize for children that on a digital clock we read "20 minutes after 2"; on an analog clock, we can see that the minute hand points to the number 4.

Tell children that most analog clocks don't show the number for each minute. Explain that clocks typically show the number for each hour, but we can use these numbers and the tick marks to help tell the number of minutes after the hour as well.

▶ 5-Minute Intervals WHOLE CLASS

Refer children to Student Activity Book page 203. Explain that the small numbers shown around the outside of the clock face tell the number of minutes after the hour.

- How many minutes are there between 12 and 1 on the clock face? 5 minutes
- How many minutes are there between 12 and 2 on the clock face? 10 minutes

Have children fill in the boxes with the number of minutes after the hour in 5-minute intervals.

When they are finished, ask them how many minutes are on the clock. 60 minutes

- How many minutes are in 1 hour? 60 minutes

Alternate Approach

Clock Poster Display the Time Poster in the classroom and have children help you label the 5-minute intervals with sticky notes.

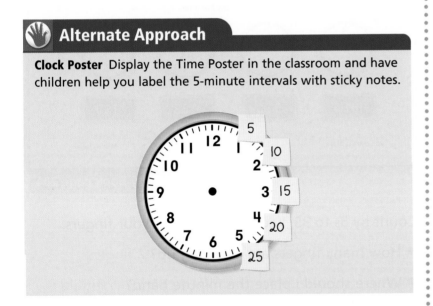

Encourage children to practice counting by 5s by reading the minutes on a clock. Ask how many minutes pass when the minute hand moves from 12 to 1. 5 minutes

- How many minutes pass when the minute hand moves from 12 to 2? 10 minutes
- How many minutes pass when the minute hand moves from 12 to 3? 15 minutes

Continue until you reach 12 again.

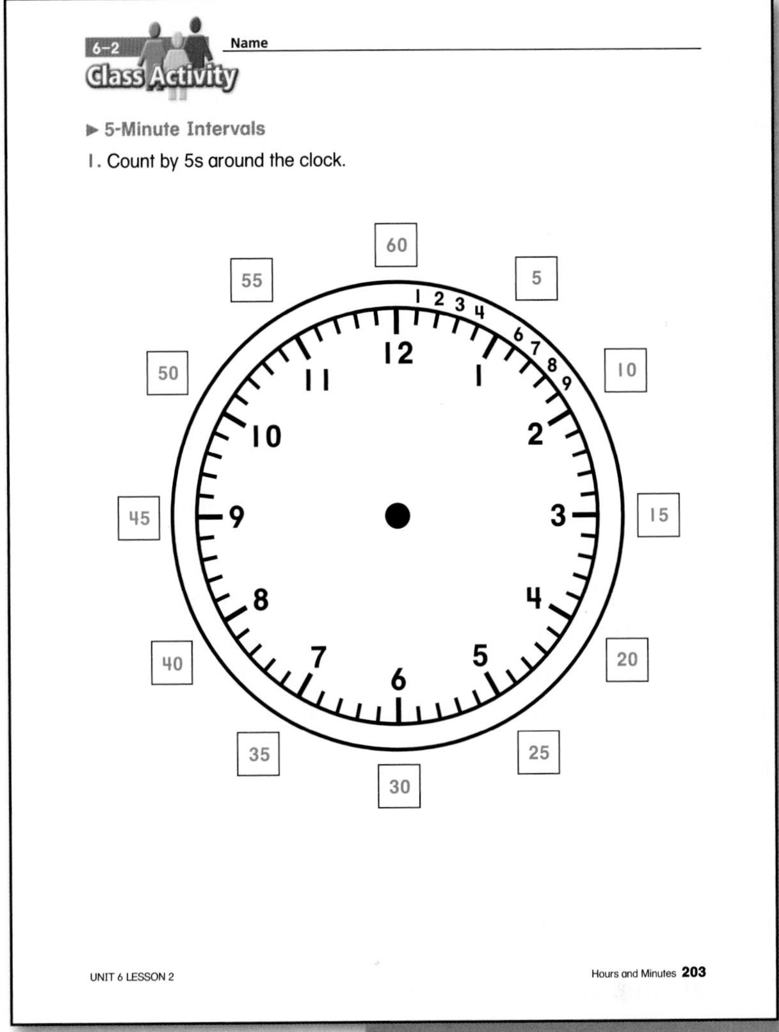

6–2 Class Activity Name

▶ 5-Minute Intervals

1. Count by 5s around the clock.

UNIT 6 LESSON 2

Hours and Minutes 203

Student Activity Book page 203

Ask for Ideas Discuss with children what they already know about the relationship between seconds and minutes and between hours and days.

- How many seconds are in 1 minute? 60 seconds
- How many minutes are in 1 hour? 60 minutes
- How many hours are in 1 day? 24 hours

Ongoing Assessment

Ask children to draw an analog clock on their MathBoards and to include numbers from 1 to 12. Have them write the number of minutes after the hour in 5-minute intervals around the outside of the clock.

Activity 2

Tell Time to 5 Minutes

30 MINUTES

Goal: Read and show time to 5 minutes.

Materials: Demonstration clock or Time Poster, Student Activity Book page 204

NCTM Standards:
Measurement
Connections

▶ Read and Show Time to 5 Minutes

Math Talk

Work through several examples of reading time to 5 minutes. Emphasize the minute hand in your discussion, but keep in mind that children need to understand that the hour hand moves between two numbers as the minute hand travels around the clock.

Show 4:25 on a demonstration clock.

- When the minute hand points to 5, how many minutes after the hour is it? 25 minutes

Have the class count by 5s to 25 minutes. 5, 10, 15, 20, 25

- What time does this clock show? 4:25
- Where is the hour hand? between 4 and 5

Repeat this series of questions with 5:00 and 6:30. Then have children complete exercises 2–9 on Student Activity Book page 204.

Teaching Note

Watch For! Some children may mistakenly read a time like 4:55 as 5:55 because the hour hand is so close to 5. Explain that when the hour hand is between two numbers, the hour is always the smaller number. Other children may not know the direction in which the clock hands move. Remind children that the clock hands travel in the same direction as the numbers on the clock increase.

Draw Hands on a Clock Write 10:35 on the board and show how to position the hands on a clock face.

- How many minutes after the hour is this time? 35 minutes

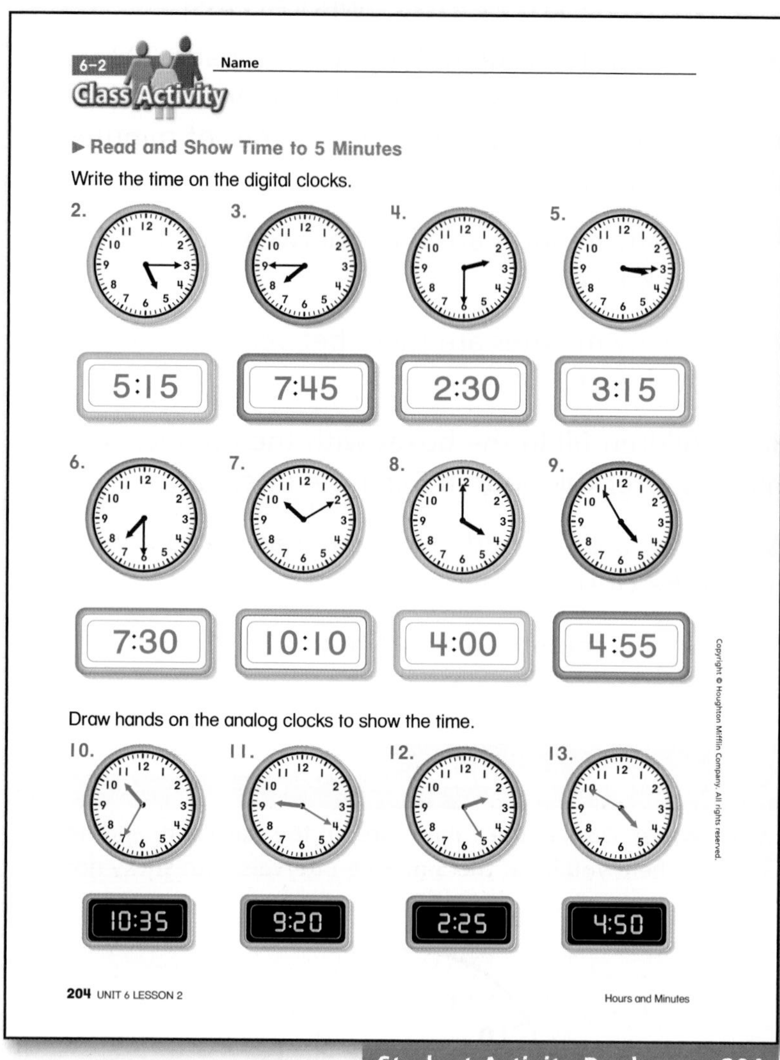

6-2 Class Activity

Name

▶ Read and Show Time to 5 Minutes

Write the time on the digital clocks.

2. 5:15
3. 7:45
4. 2:30
5. 3:15
6. 7:30
7. 10:10
8. 4:00
9. 4:55

Draw hands on the analog clocks to show the time.

10. 10:35
11. 9:20
12. 2:25
13. 4:50

204 UNIT 6 LESSON 2 — Hours and Minutes

Student Activity Book page 204

Count by 5s to 35, keeping track with your fingers.

- How many fingers am I holding up? 7 fingers
- Where should I place the minute hand? It should point to 7.
- Between which two numbers should I place the hour hand? between 10 and 11
- How do you know? 10:35 is between 10 and 11 o'clock.

Have children work through exercises 10–13 in pairs. Note that some children may not place the hour hand in an exactly accurate position. At this point, simply ensure that they position the hour hand between the correct two numbers.

2 Going Further

Intervention — Activity Card 6-2

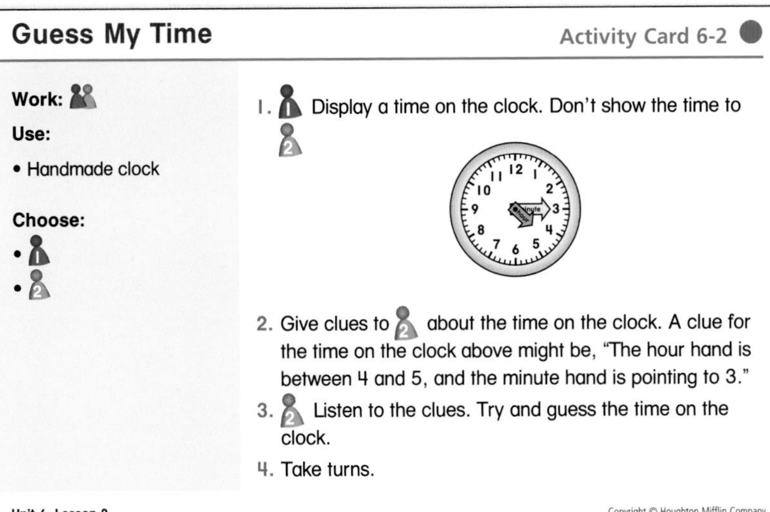

Guess My Time — Activity Card 6-2 ●

Work: (pair)
Use:
- Handmade clock

Choose:
- 1
- 2

1. (1) Display a time on the clock. Don't show the time to (2).
2. Give clues to (2) about the time on the clock. A clue for the time on the clock above might be, "The hour hand is between 4 and 5, and the minute hand is pointing to 3."
3. (2) Listen to the clues. Try and guess the time on the clock.
4. Take turns.

Unit 6, Lesson 2

Activity Note Each pair needs the handmade clock from Lesson 1 or Student Activity Page 197. Check children's clues.

Math Writing Prompt

Draw a Picture On an analog clock, how do you know the time is between 8:00 and 9:00? Draw a picture to help explain your answer.

Software Support

Use *Soar to Success* for instruction of students needing targeted support for underlying skills.

On Level — Activity Card 6-2

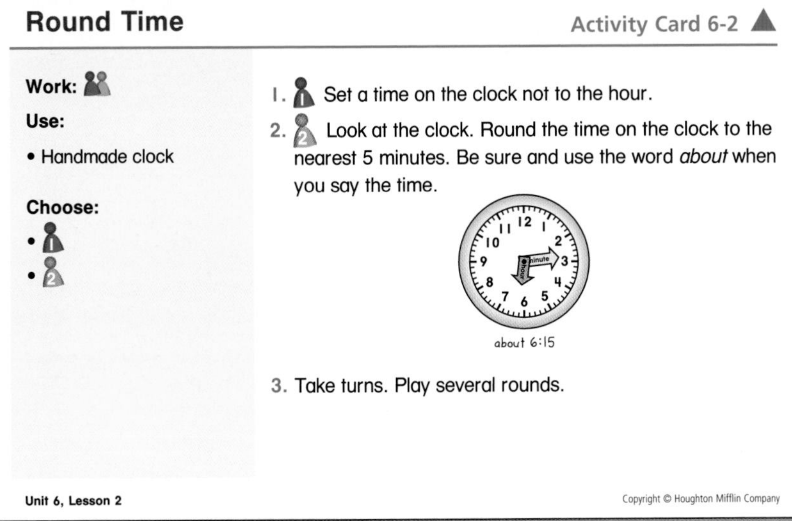

Round Time — Activity Card 6-2 ▲

Work: (pair)
Use:
- Handmade clock

Choose:
- 1
- 2

1. (1) Set a time on the clock not to the hour.
2. (2) Look at the clock. Round the time on the clock to the nearest 5 minutes. Be sure and use the word *about* when you say the time.

about 6:15

3. Take turns. Play several rounds.

Unit 6, Lesson 2

Activity Note Each pair needs the handmade clock from Lesson 1 or Student Activity Page 197. Suggest that children set the time on the clock to a non-exact time.

Math Writing Prompt

Explain Your Thinking How does an analog clock show that there are 60 minutes in 1 hour? Explain your thinking.

Software Support

Use *MegaMath* for review and reinforcement of the concepts and skills presented in this lesson.

Challenge — Activity Card 6-2

Time Equations — Activity Card 6-2 ■

Work: (individual)
Use:
- MathBoard

1 hour = ____ minutes
180 minutes = ____ hours
2 hours = ____ minutes
30 minutes = ____ hour

1. Copy the equations above onto your MathBoard.
2. Complete each equation. Answers: 60 minutes, 3 hours, 120 minutes, $\frac{1}{2}$ hour
3. **Math Talk** Compare your equations with a friend. Do you have the same answers? Talk about how you found your answers.

Unit 6, Lesson 2

Activity Note Each child needs MathBoard materials. Have children check their answers and share how they found the answers.

Math Writing Prompt

You Decide Would a clock ever show 8:64? Explain your reasoning.

Software Support

Use *Destination Math* to take students beyond the concepts and skills presented in this lesson.

3 Homework

Goal: Additional Practice

This Homework page allows children to work with 5-minute intervals as they read and write time.

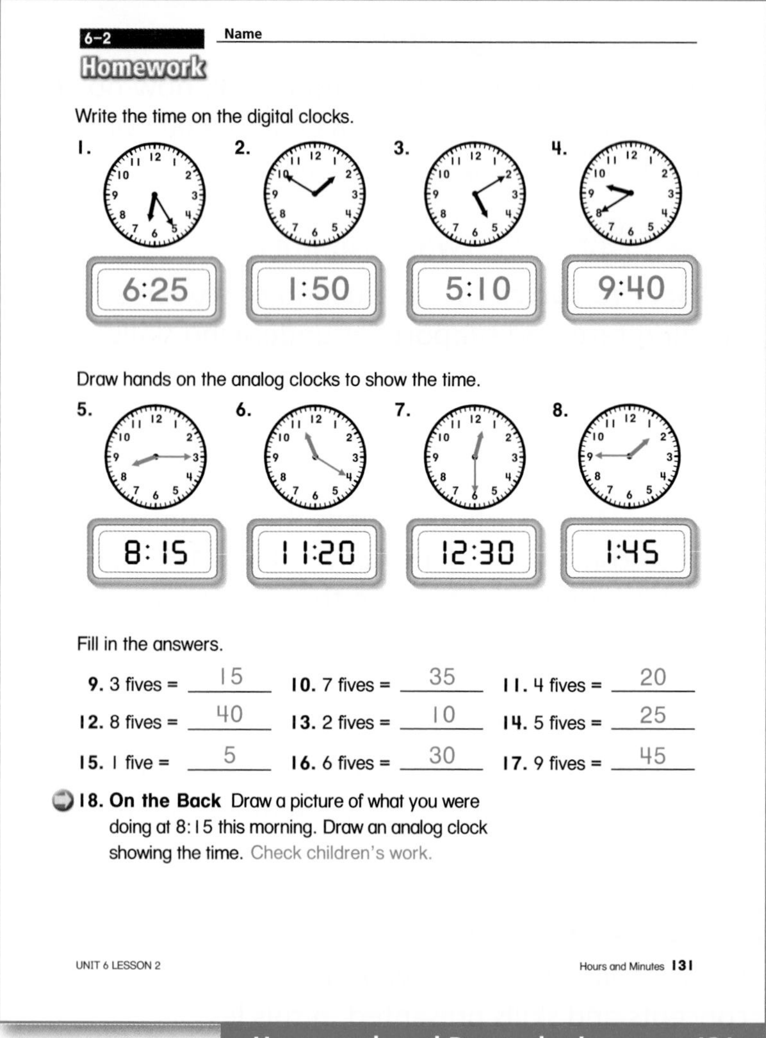

6–2 Homework

Name ____________

Write the time on the digital clocks.

1. 6:25
2. 1:50
3. 5:10
4. 9:40

Draw hands on the analog clocks to show the time.

5. 8:15
6. 11:20
7. 12:30
8. 1:45

Fill in the answers.

9. 3 fives = 15	10. 7 fives = 35	11. 4 fives = 20
12. 8 fives = 40	13. 2 fives = 10	14. 5 fives = 25
15. 1 five = 5	16. 6 fives = 30	17. 9 fives = 45

18. **On the Back** Draw a picture of what you were doing at 8:15 this morning. Draw an analog clock showing the time. Check children's work.

UNIT 6 LESSON 2 Hours and Minutes 131

Homework and Remembering page 131

Home or School Activity

Art Connection

Activity Times Invite children to cut out pictures of different activities from magazines, newspapers, or flyers. They might also draw or paint pictures. Have them draw an analog clock and write the digital time for each activity.

More on Telling Time

Lesson Objectives

- Observe how the hour hand moves with the minute hand.
- Position the hour hand to reflect the number of minutes after the hour.
- Tell time to 1 minute.
- Read time as after the hour and before the hour.

Vocabulary
half-hour
after the hour
before the hour

The Day at a Glance

Today's Goals	Materials	
1 Teaching the Lesson **A1:** Observe how the hour hand moves with the minute hand. **A2:** Read and show time to 1 minute. Read time as before and after the hour.	**Lesson Activities** Student Activity Book pp. 205–206 Homework and Remembering pp. 133–134 Handmade clock from Lesson 1 Demonstration Clock or Time Poster MathBoard materials	**Going Further** Activity Cards 6-3 Index cards Math Journals
2 Going Further ► Differentiated Instruction		
3 Homework		

Use Math Talk today!

Keeping Skills Sharp

Daily Routines

Math Mountains for 100 or 2-Digit Numbers Using the MathBoard, Using Dimes and Pennies (See p. xxvi.)

► Led by Student Leaders

Money Routine Using the 120 Poster, Using the Money Flip Chart, Using the Number Path, Using Secret Code Cards (See pp. xxiii–xxv.)

► Led by Student Leaders

English Language Learners

Draw 2 analog clocks, one showing 11:00 and the other showing 11:30. Write *half-hour.*

- **Beginning** Say: **A *half-hour* is 30 minutes. The times on the clocks are a *half-hour* apart.** Have children repeat.
- **Intermediate** Say: **A *half-hour* is 30 minutes.** Ask: **Are the clocks a *half-hour* apart?** yes
- **Advanced** Have children tell how 30 minutes and half-hour can be used to describe time.

1 Teaching the Lesson

Activity 1

The Hour Hand

 20 MINUTES

Goal: Observe how the hour hand moves with the minute hand.

Materials: Handmade clocks from Lesson 1 or Paper Clock (TRB M69), Student Activity Book page 205

 **NCTM Standards:**
Measurement
Connections

▶ Act It Out WHOLE CLASS

Scenarios Invite five volunteers to stand in a line at the front of the class with the analog clocks they made in Lesson 1 or they can use Paper Clock (TRB M69). Ask the first volunteer to show 4:00.

- What time does Pam's clock show? 4 o'clock
- Where is the hour hand? It is pointing to 4.

Invite the second volunteer to step forward and show 4:15 on his or her clock. Assist children as necessary, especially in positioning the hour hand on their clocks.

- How many minutes after 4:00 does Harper's clock show? 15 minutes
- How do you know by looking at the clock? I counted by 5s to 3, which is 15.
- Where is the hour hand? The hour hand is a little bit past 4.

Have the third volunteer show 4:30.

- How many minutes after 4:00 does Manoj's clock show? 30 minutes
- How do you know by looking at the clock? I counted by 5s to 6, which is 30.
- Where is the hour hand? The hour hand is exactly halfway between 4 and 5.

Emphasize for children the way in which the hour hand moves with the minute hand around the clock. Explain that 30 minutes is exactly halfway between 0 minutes and 60 minutes, so at 4:30 the hour hand is right in the middle, between 4 and 5.

Continue the activity for 4:45 and 5:00.

Have the fourth volunteer show 4:45 and the fifth volunteer show 5:00 on their clocks. Continue asking similar questions like the ones before. It will help children see how the clock hands move around the clock.

The Learning Classroom

Scenarios This structure can be used to demonstrate mathematical concepts in a visual and memorable way. A group of children is called to the front of the classroom to act out a particular situation. Scenarios are especially useful when a concept is introduced for the first time, and they are particularly helpful to English learners.

 **Math Talk**

Once you have completed the five clocks to 5:00, invite children to consider how the position of the hour hand changes as the minute hand travels around the clock.

- When the minute hand is 15 minutes past the hour, where is the hour hand? just after 4
- When the minute hand is 30 minutes past the hour, where is the hour hand? exactly halfway between 4 and 5
- When the minute hand is 45 minutes past the hour, where is the hour hand? closer to 5
- Where would you place the hour hand for 4:55? just before 5

Differentiated Instruction

Advanced Learners You might introduce the terms *quarter past the hour* and *half past the hour* to advanced children in your class (unless your state or district specifies this topic as a required goal for all learners). You can connect time with fractions by linking these terms to a quarter-hour and half-hour by showing a clock face divided into fourths.

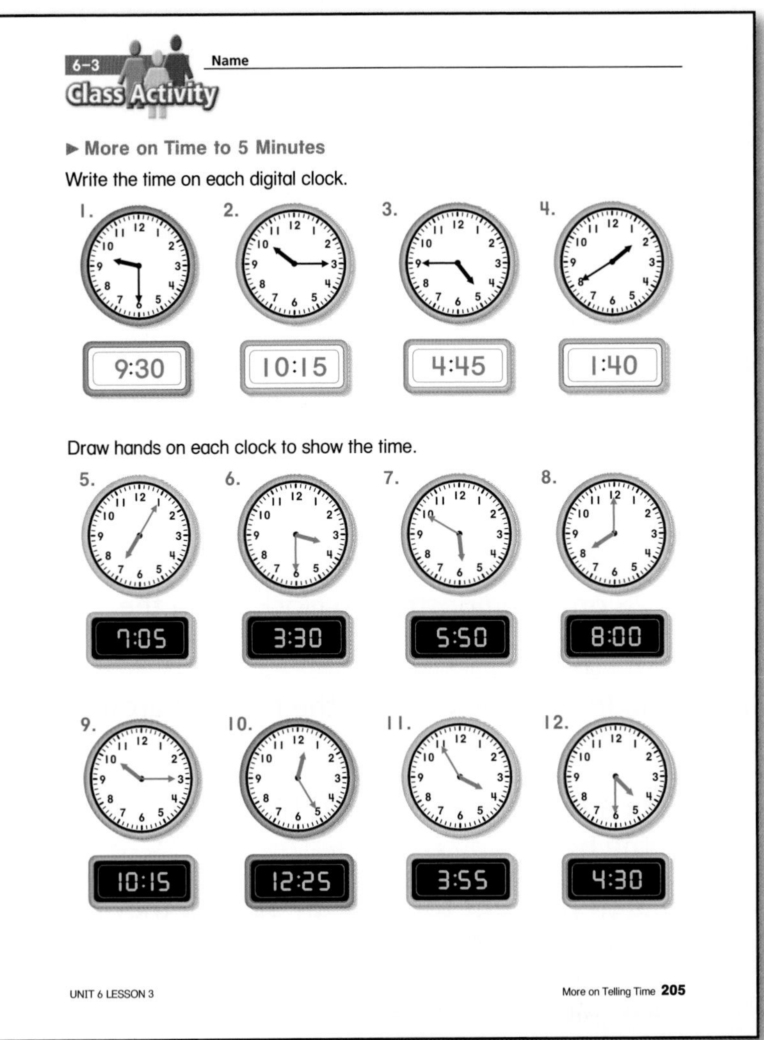
6–3 Class Activity

Name

► More on Time to 5 Minutes

Write the time on each digital clock.

1. 9:30
2. 10:15
3. 4:45
4. 1:40

Draw hands on each clock to show the time.

5. 7:05
6. 3:30
7. 5:50
8. 8:00
9. 10:15
10. 12:25
11. 3:55
12. 4:30

UNIT 6 LESSON 3

More on Telling Time 205

Student Activity Book page 205

► More on Time to 5 Minutes INDIVIDUALS

Have children complete exercises 1–12 on Student Activity Book page 205.

Teaching Note

What to Expect from Students Children should recognize that the hour hand moves with the minute hand. Knowing the exact position of the hour hand, however, is not a goal for this grade.

1 Teaching the Lesson (continued)

Activity 2

Different Ways to Read Time

 **35 MINUTES**

Goals: Read and show time to 1 minute. Read time as before and after the hour.

Materials: Demonstration clock or Time Poster, Student Activity Book page 206

 **NCTM Standards:**
Measurement
Connections

▶ Read and Show Time to 1 Minute

WHOLE CLASS

Show 9:28 on a demonstration clock or on the Time Poster.

Invite children to count aloud the minutes around the clock. 1, 2, 3, 4, 5 ... 28

- Is there a faster way to count the number of minutes after the hour? You can count by 5s.

Ask children to count together by 5s until they reach the 5-minute interval before 28. 5, 10, 15, 20, 25

Then have children count by 1s to 28. 26, 27, 28

Together, work through several examples to allow children further opportunity to practice counting the minutes by 5s and 1s.

- How do you know when to stop counting by 5s and start counting by 1s? I know to stop counting by 5s when I get to the last 5-minute interval before the minute hand.

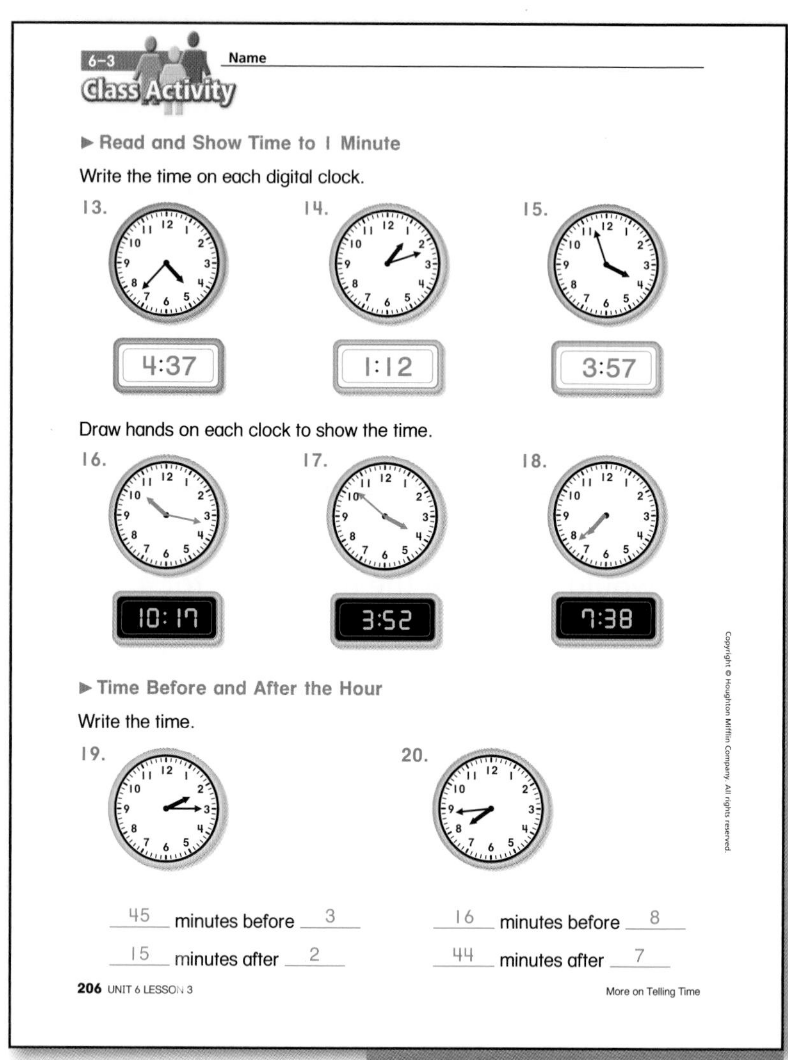

6-3 Class Activity   Name ____________

▶ Read and Show Time to 1 Minute

Write the time on each digital clock.

13. 4:37   14. 1:12   15. 3:57

Draw hands on each clock to show the time.

16. 10:17   17. 3:52   18. 7:38

▶ Time Before and After the Hour

Write the time.

19. 45 minutes before 3
15 minutes after 2

20. 16 minutes before 8
44 minutes after 7

206 UNIT 6 LESSON 3   More on Telling Time

Student Activity Book page 206

Refer children to Student Activity Book page 206 and have them complete exercises 13–15.

When children are finished, write the time 6:17 on the board, and demonstrate how to show time to 1 minute on an analog clock. Work together as a class to correctly position the hands.

- Where do I place the hour hand? Place the hour hand between 6 and 7 but closer to 6.

Count aloud by 5s to determine the number of 5-minute intervals after the hour. 5, 10, 15

Point to 3 on the clock and together count on by 1s to 17. Position the minute hand at 17 minutes after the hour.

Ask children to complete exercises 16–18 on their own.

▶ Time Before and After the Hour

WHOLE CLASS

Display 1:40 on a demonstration clock or on the Time Poster and write the time digitally.

Explain to children that they can read this time as the time after the hour or as the time before the next hour. Draw an arrow from 12 to 8 to outline the minutes after the hour. Draw a second arrow in the opposite direction from 12 back to 8 to outline the minutes before the next hour.

- What is the time after the hour? 40 minutes after 1
- How do you know that it is 40 minutes after the hour? I counted by 5s from 12 to 8. That's 5, 10, 15, 20, 25, 30, 35, 40 minutes.

Write the time "40 minutes after 1" on the board.

Demonstrate how to read the time as before the hour. Explain to children that when you read time as before the hour, you start at 12 and count back by 5-minute intervals. For 1:40, you count by 5s from 12 to 11, 11 to 10, 10 to 9, and 9 to 8 for a total of 20 minutes.

Write the time "20 minutes before 2" on the board.

Differentiated Instruction

English Learners Some children may not know that the words *past* and *passed* have different meanings even though they sound the same. Explain that *past* means "after" while *passed* means "moved by." When we read time, we say "20 minutes past 2" or "20 minutes after 2."

Activity continued ▶

❶ Teaching the Lesson (continued)

Time to the Minute Before and After the Hour
On a demonstration clock or the Time Poster show how to read the time 3:38 as before the hour and after the hour. Begin by reading the time after the hour.

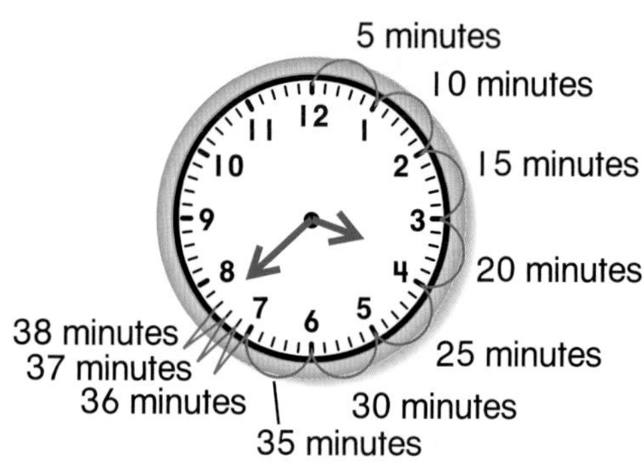

Write "38 minutes after 3" on the board.

Next, read the time before the hour.

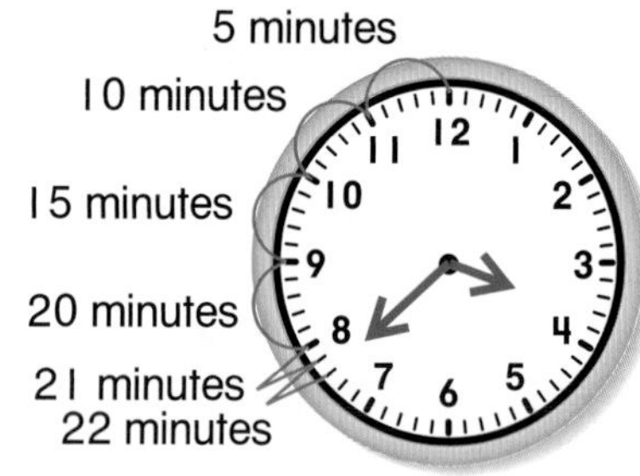

Point out for children that you can read time to the minute before the hour just as you do after the hour, counting by 5s and 1s. The only difference is that to read time to the minute before the hour, you count back from 12.

Write "22 minutes before 4" on the board.

Work through several examples together, until children are comfortable counting on from 12 for time after the hour and back from 12 for time before the hour.

Provide further opportunity for practice by writing four different times on the board and having children work in pairs to write each time as before the hour and after the hour on their MathBoards.

Then have children complete exercises 19 and 20 on Student Activity Book page 194.

Teaching Note

Watch For! Some children may not use the correct hour when telling time before and after the hour. Remind them to use the previous hour when they tell minutes after the hour and the next hour when they tell minutes before the hour.

Ongoing Assessment

Write these times on the board:

9:50 1:55 4:37

Have children show each time on a clock. Then, ask them to read each time as before the hour and after the hour.

2 Going Further

Differentiated Instruction

Intervention

Activity Card 6-3

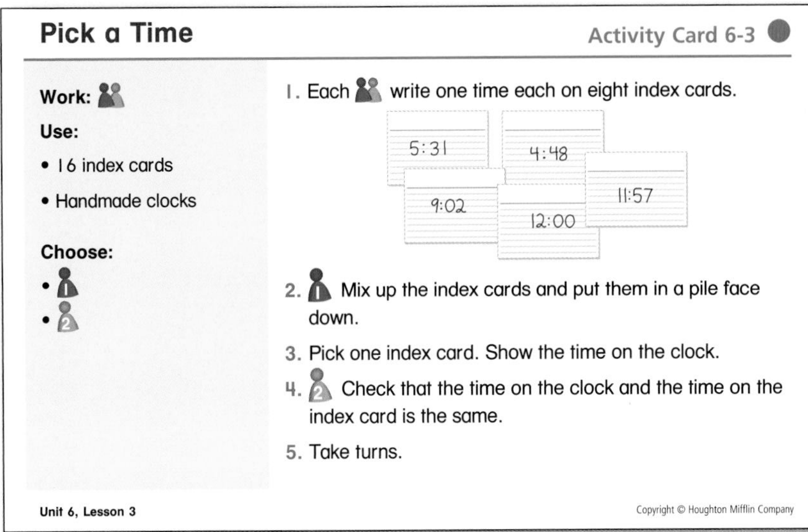

Pick a Time Activity Card 6-3

Work: pairs
Use:
- 16 index cards
- Handmade clocks

Choose:
- 1
- 2

1. Each pair write one time each on eight index cards.

2. (1) Mix up the index cards and put them in a pile face down.
3. Pick one index card. Show the time on the clock.
4. (2) Check that the time on the clock and the time on the index card is the same.
5. Take turns.

Unit 6, Lesson 3

Activity Note Each pair needs 18 index cards and the handmade clock from Lesson 1 or Student Activity Page 197. Remind children to check each other's work.

Math Writing Prompt

Explain a Method Lim Sing counted by 1s to 47 in order to read the time 1:47. Can you explain a faster way to find the number of minutes past the hour?

Software Support

Use *Soar to Success* for instruction of students needing targeted support for underlying skills.

On Level

Activity Card 6-3

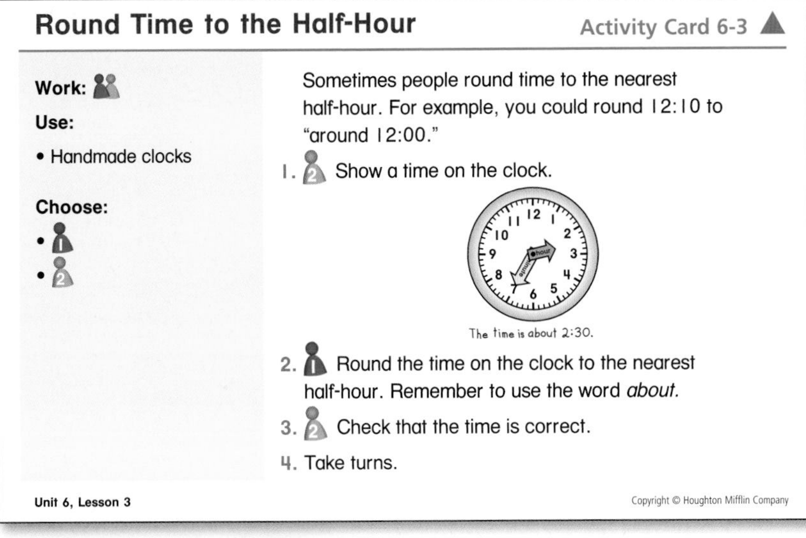

Round Time to the Half-Hour Activity Card 6-3

Work: pairs
Use:
- Handmade clocks

Choose:
- 1
- 2

Sometimes people round time to the nearest half-hour. For example, you could round 12:10 to "around 12:00."

1. (2) Show a time on the clock.

The time is about 2:30.

2. (1) Round the time on the clock to the nearest half-hour. Remember to use the word *about*.
3. (2) Check that the time is correct.
4. Take turns.

Unit 6, Lesson 3

Activity Note Each pair needs the handmade clock from Lesson 1 or Student Activity Page 197. Review rounding time to the nearest half-hour.

Math Writing Prompt

Explain Your Thinking Why is 45 minutes after 5 the same time as 15 minutes before 6? Explain your thinking.

Software Support

Use *MegaMath* for review and reinforcement of the concepts and skills presented in this lesson.

Challenge

Activity Card 6-3

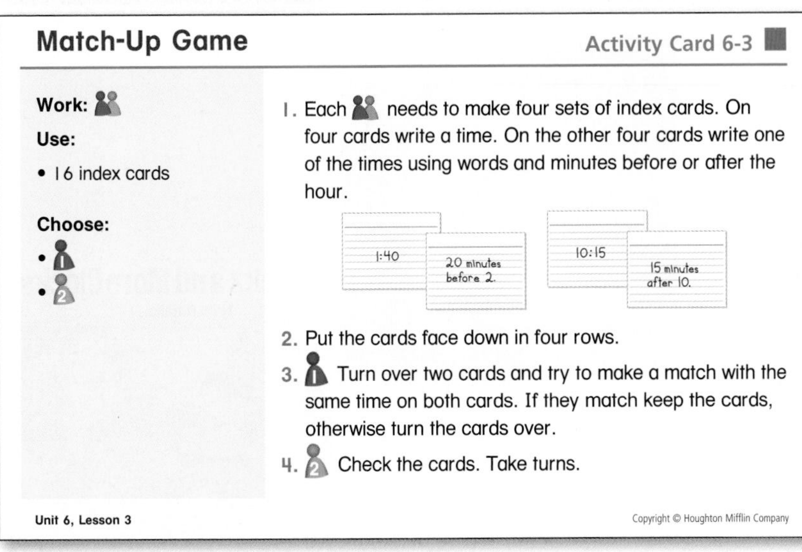

Match-Up Game Activity Card 6-3

Work: pairs
Use:
- 16 index cards

Choose:
- 1
- 2

1. Each pair needs to make four sets of index cards. On four cards write a time. On the other four cards write one of the times using words and minutes before or after the hour.

2. Put the cards face down in four rows.
3. (1) Turn over two cards and try to make a match with the same time on both cards. If they match keep the cards, otherwise turn the cards over.
4. (2) Check the cards. Take turns.

Unit 6, Lesson 3

Activity Note Each pair needs 16 index cards. Have children check that they wrote the time with words that matches a time on the other cards.

Math Writing Prompt

You Decide If you had a clock with only one hand, which hand would you want it to have? Why?

Software Support

Use *Destination Math* to take students beyond the concepts and skills presented in this lesson.

3 Homework

Goal: Additional Practice

Include children's completed Homework page as part of their portfolios.

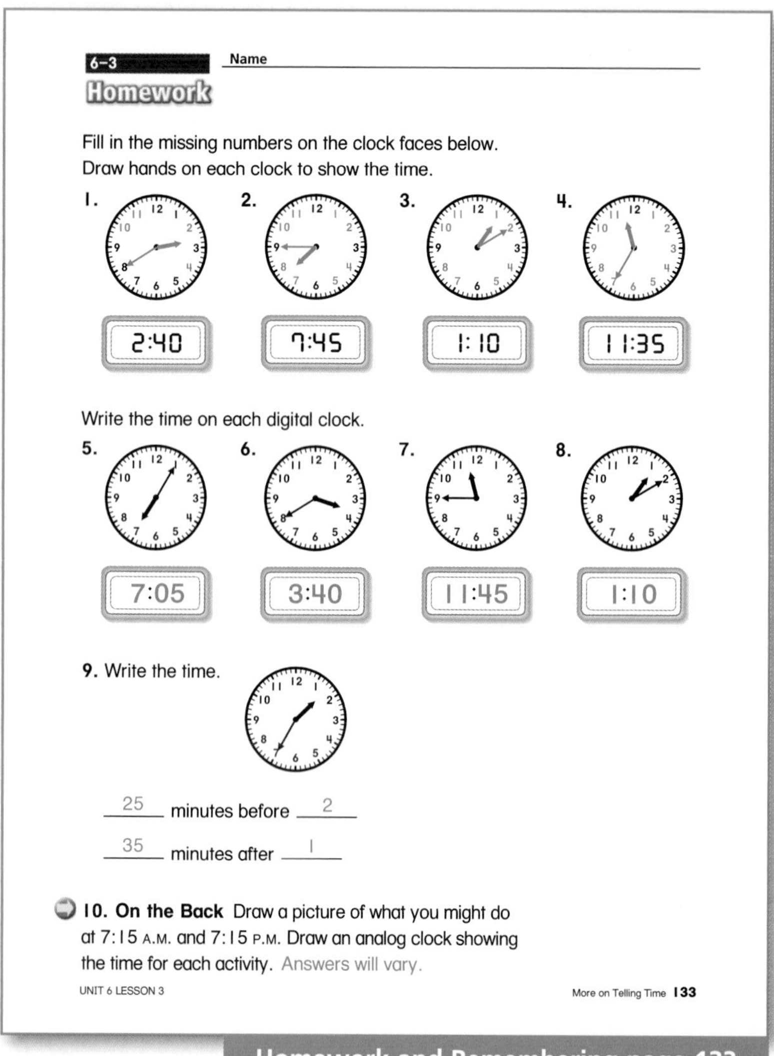

6–3 Homework Name ________

Fill in the missing numbers on the clock faces below.
Draw hands on each clock to show the time.

1. 2:40
2. 7:45
3. 1:10
4. 11:35

Write the time on each digital clock.

5. 7:05
6. 3:40
7. 11:45
8. 1:10

9. Write the time.

25 minutes before 2

35 minutes after 1

10. On the Back Draw a picture of what you might do at 7:15 A.M. and 7:15 P.M. Draw an analog clock showing the time for each activity. Answers will vary.

UNIT 6 LESSON 3 More on Telling Time 133

Homework and Remembering page 133

Home or School Activity

Literature Connection

Measure Time Have children read *Clocks and More Clocks* by Pat Hutchins (Aladdin Paperbacks, Simon & Schuster, 1970). In this story, Mr. Higgins discovers that clocks show time passing. Have children draw clock faces to show the times mentioned in the book.

Children can also read *My Grandmother's Clock* by Geraldine McCaughrean (Clarion Books, 2002). In this story, a girl and her grandmother explore many ways to measure time, not all of them with a clock.

Elapsed Time

Vocabulary

minute
hour
day
half-hour

Lesson Objectives

- **Use appropriate units to measure time.**
- **Determine elapsed time.**

The Day at a Glance

Today's Goals	Materials	
1 Teaching the Lesson **A1:** Choose the most appropriate unit to measure time. **A2:** Determine how much time has passed in hours. **A3:** Determine how much time has passed in hours and half-hours.	**Lesson Activities** Student Activity Book pp. 207–210 Homework and Remembering pp. 135–136 A current calendar Demonstration clock or Time Poster Newspapers and magazines Minute timer	**Going Further** Activity Cards 6-4 Handmade clock from Lesson 1 Math Journals
2 Going Further ► Differentiated Instruction		
3 Homework		

Use Math Talk today!

Keeping Skills Sharp

Daily Routines	English Language Learners
Math Mountains for 100 or 2-Digit Numbers Using the MathBoard, Using Dimes and Pennies (See p. xxvi.) ► Led by Student Leaders **Money Routine** Using the 120 Poster, Using the Money Flip Chart, Using the Number Path, Using Secret Code Cards (See pp. xxiii–xxv.) ► Led by Student Leaders	Write *minute* and *hour* on the board. • **Beginning** Say: **An *hour* is 60 minutes. *Hours* are longer than *minutes*.** Have children repeat. • **Intermediate** Say **An *hour* is 60 *minutes*.** Ask: **Are an *hour* and a *minute* the same?** no **Which is longer?** hour • **Advanced** Have children tell about the difference between hours and minutes.

1 Teaching the Lesson

Activity 1

Choose the Appropriate Unit

 15 MINUTES

Goal: Choose the most appropriate unit to measure time.

Materials: A current calendar, demonstration clock or the Time Poster, newspapers and magazines, Student Activity Book page 207, minute timer

 **NCTM Standards:**
Measurement
Number and Operations

▶ Measure Time WHOLE CLASS

Hold up a calendar for the current year and a demonstration clock or the Time Poster. Use these tools to begin a class discussion about different units for measuring time.

- What units of time can you find in a calendar? day, week, month, year
- What units of time do clocks measure? minute, hour
- Which is the smallest of these units: day, hour, or minute? minute
- How many seconds are in 1 minute? 60 seconds
- Which is the largest of those units? day
- How many hours are in 1 day? 24 hours
- Which unit would you use to describe the length of a vacation? Possible answers: day, week, month

Teaching Note

What to Expect from Students Some children may mention *seconds* as a unit of time. Acknowledge that they are correct, but explain that you will not be using seconds in this lesson.

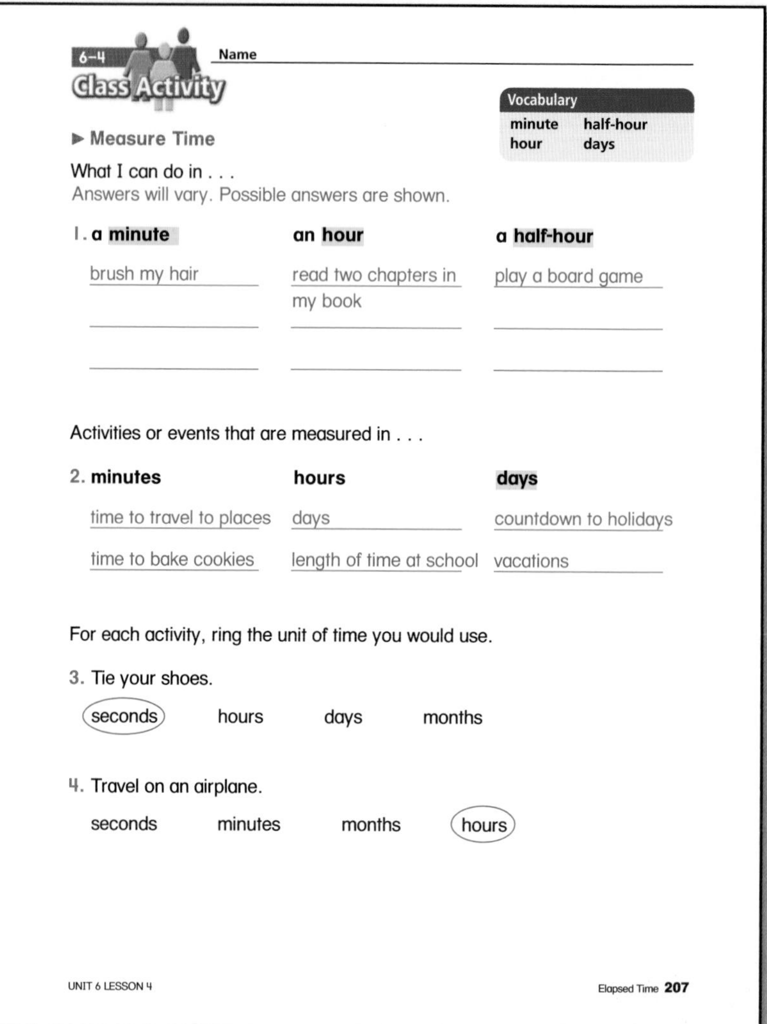
6–4 Class Activity Name

Vocabulary: minute, half-hour, hour, days

▶ Measure Time

What I can do in . . .
Answers will vary. Possible answers are shown.

1. a **minute** — brush my hair
an **hour** — read two chapters in my book
a **half-hour** — play a board game

Activities or events that are measured in . . .

2. **minutes** — time to travel to places; time to bake cookies
hours — days; length of time at school
days — countdown to holidays; vacations

For each activity, ring the unit of time you would use.

3. Tie your shoes.
(seconds) hours days months

4. Travel on an airplane.
seconds minutes months (hours)

UNIT 6 LESSON 4 Elapsed Time 207

Student Activity Book page 207

 Alternate Approach

Photographs from Newspapers and Magazines Invite children to look through newspapers and magazines for photographs of people doing different activities. Have them estimate the time it takes to complete each activity in minutes, hours, days, weeks, or months.

Before having children complete the exercises on Student Activity Book page 207, discuss activities that take different periods of time. Answers will vary. Possible answers are shown.

- Tell me what you can do in less than a minute. I can print my name, sketch a picture, drink a glass of juice.
- Tell me what you do that takes about an hour. I can do homework, eat lunch, watch a television program.
- Tell me what you do that takes about a half-hour. I can get ready for school, eat dinner, finish a puzzle.
- Name some activities or events that you might measure in days. taking a vacation, completing a big project, recovering from sickness, driving across the country

Then discuss how long certain activities may take to complete. Encourage children to think about the units they select in their responses. Answers will vary. Possible answers are shown.

- How long does it take you to brush your teeth? 2 minutes
- About how much time do you spend on your homework? 1 hour
- About how much sleep do you get each night? 10 hours
- How much time do you spend in school each week? 30 hours
- About how much school time did you miss last year because you were sick? 5 days

Have children complete exercises 1–4 and then have them share their answers.

Alternate Approach

Use a Timer Use a minute timer, such as a sand timer, and invite children to predict and test what they can do in 1 minute.

- ▶ How many times can you write your name in 1 minute?
- ▶ How many stars can you draw in 1 minute?
- ▶ How many times can you clap your hands in 1 minute?
- ▶ How many jumping jacks can you do in 1 minute?

Differentiated Instruction

Advanced Learners Invite children to compare times with different units. Ask questions like the following:

- ▶ Which is longer, 1 month or 3 weeks?
- ▶ Which is shorter, 1 hour or 45 minutes?
- ▶ Which is longer, 1 day or 22 hours?

Activity 2

Elapsed Time in Hours

 **20 MINUTES**

Goal: Determine how much time has passed in hours.

Materials: Handmade clocks from Lesson 1 or Paper Clock (TRB M69), Student Activity Book page 208

 **NCTM Standards:**
Measurement
Number and Operations

▶ Time in Hours PAIRS

Ask children a question involving elapsed time in hours.

- If a movie starts at 4:00 P.M. and lasts 2 hours, at what time does it end? 6:00 P.M.

Have children work in pairs using the analog clock they made in Lesson 1. Continue to ask questions involving elapsed time. Have one partner show the start time and the other partner show the end time. Ask several questions to allow children to experiment with different elapsed times. Use the same example, but this time on a digital clock. Show how time elapses on a digital clock.

When they are comfortable with the concept of elapsed time, have children complete the chart on Student Activity Book page 208.

If children finish their work early, have them draw an activity that might take a certain amount of time and have other children try to guess how long the activity would take. This allows you to see the reasonableness of children's guesses.

Teaching Note

Watch For! Some children may include the start time in their calculation of elapsed time. Emphasize that an hour is equal to the time it takes for the hour hand to travel from one number to the next. Demonstrate how to find elapsed time by moving the hour hand from the start time to the end time and counting aloud each elapsed hour.

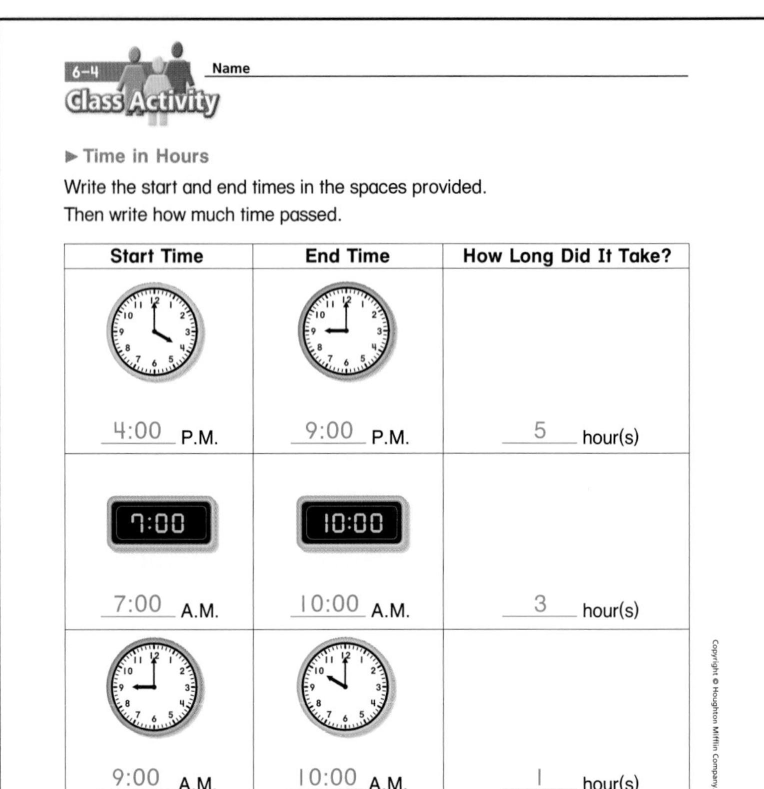
6–4 Class Activity Name

▶ Time in Hours

Write the start and end times in the spaces provided.
Then write how much time passed.

Start Time	End Time	How Long Did It Take?
4:00 P.M.	9:00 P.M.	5 hour(s)
7:00 A.M.	10:00 A.M.	3 hour(s)
9:00 A.M.	10:00 A.M.	1 hour(s)
1:00 P.M.	8:00 P.M.	7 hour(s)

208 UNIT 6 LESSON 4 Elapsed Time

Student Activity Book page 208

The Learning Classroom

Building Concepts Challenge children to find elapsed time involving an A.M. start time and a P.M. end time. Ask these questions:

- ▶ If a friend arrives at your house for a sleepover at 3:00 P.M. and leaves at 9:00 A.M., how long did he or she stay?
- ▶ If you went to the zoo at 10:00 A.M. and left at 4:00 P.M., how long did you spend at the zoo?

Activity 3

Elapsed Time in Half-Hours

 20 MINUTES

Goal: Determine how much time has passed in hours and half-hours.

Materials: Demonstration clock or handmade clock from Lesson 1, Student Activity Book pages 209–210

 **NCTM Standards:**
Measurement
Number and Operations
Problem Solving

▶ Time in Half-Hours PAIRS

Show 4:00 on a demonstration clock or on a handmade clock from Lesson 1.

- How many minutes are in 1 hour? 60 minutes

Move the clock hands to show 4:30.

- What time is it now? 4:30
- Why is a time period of 30 minutes called a half-hour? 30 minutes is halfway around the clock and once around the clock is 1 hour.
- If a movie starts at 4:30 and ends at 6:00, how long is the movie? The movie is 1 hour and 30 minutes, or an hour and a half.

If children seem to have difficulty with this concept, show the passage of time around the clock.

- How long is it from 4:30 to 5:30? 1 hour
- How long is it from 5:30 to 6:00? 30 minutes or a half-hour
- How much time passed altogether? 1 hour and 30 minutes, or an hour and a half

Show how the time progresses on a digital clock. Have children work in pairs to complete the chart on Student Activity Book page 209.

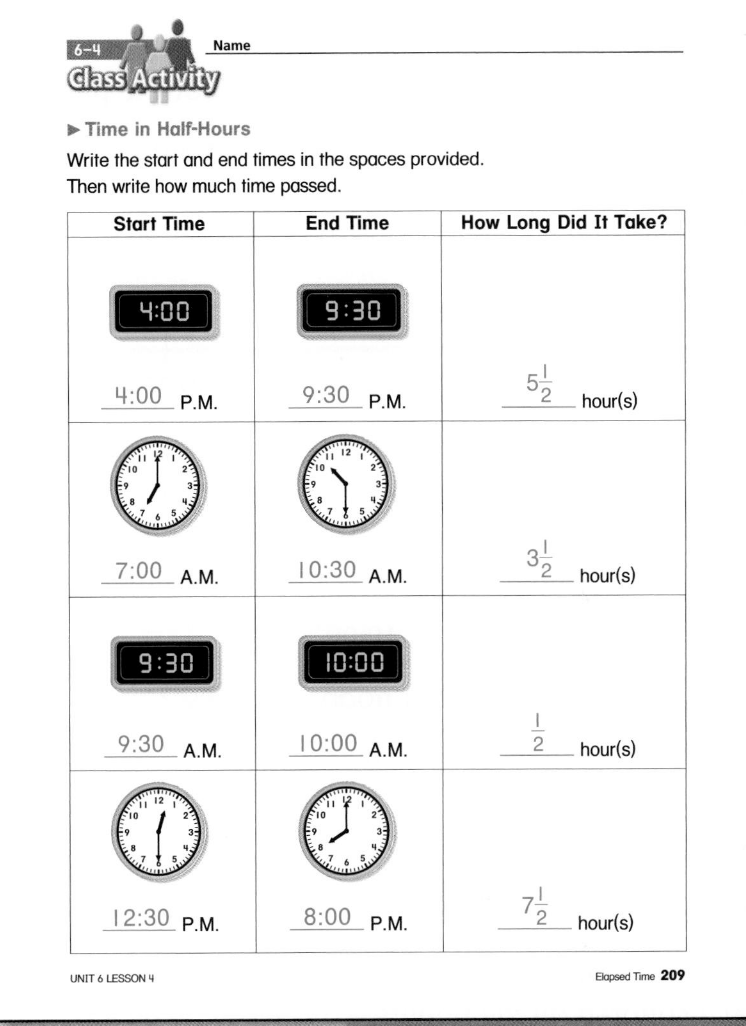
6–4 Class Activity Name

▶ Time in Half-Hours

Write the start and end times in the spaces provided.
Then write how much time passed.

Start Time	End Time	How Long Did It Take?
4:00 P.M.	9:30 P.M.	$5\frac{1}{2}$ hour(s)
7:00 A.M.	10:30 A.M.	$3\frac{1}{2}$ hour(s)
9:30 A.M.	10:00 A.M.	$\frac{1}{2}$ hour(s)
12:30 P.M.	8:00 P.M.	$7\frac{1}{2}$ hour(s)

UNIT 6 LESSON 4 Elapsed Time 209

Student Activity Book page 209

Activity continued ▶

1 Teaching the Lesson (continued)

▶ Solve Problems WHOLE CLASS

Pose this question to the class:

- Suppose you go to the park at 10:00 A.M. and come home at 3:00 P.M. How long were you at the park?

Draw a time line on the board and elicit a discussion about how to find elapsed time from the morning to the afternoon. See **Math Talk in Action** for an example of this discussion.

Once children understand and can find elapsed time, discuss with them that they can use the timeline to sequence events. You might ask what they think might have been happening at each hour in this timeline.

- What happened *first* at 10:00 A.M.?
- What happened *next* at noon, 12:00 P.M.?
- What happened *last* at 3:00 P.M.?

Math Talk in Action

How can you find out how much time has passed at the park?

Sal: I counted on my fingers. I started at 10:00 A.M. and counted 11, 12, 1, 2, 3. I had five fingers up so I spent 5 hours at the park.

Did anyone use a different strategy or method?

Sonia: I used the time line and added noon to it. I figured that there are 2 hours between 10 and noon, and 3 hours between noon and 3; 2 + 3 equals 5, so the answer is 5 hours.

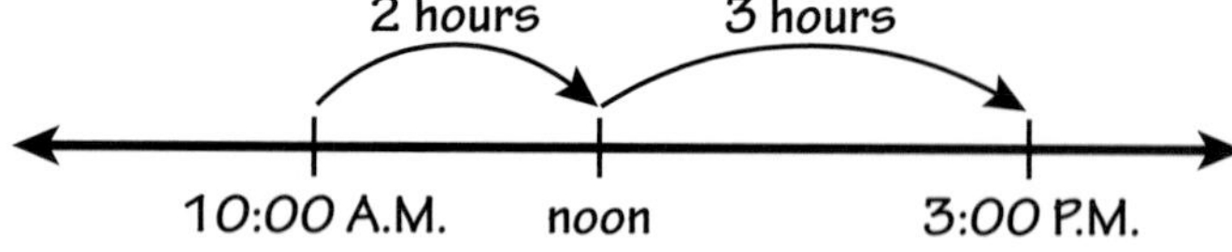

Ask children to complete problems 1–4 on Student Activity Book page 210.

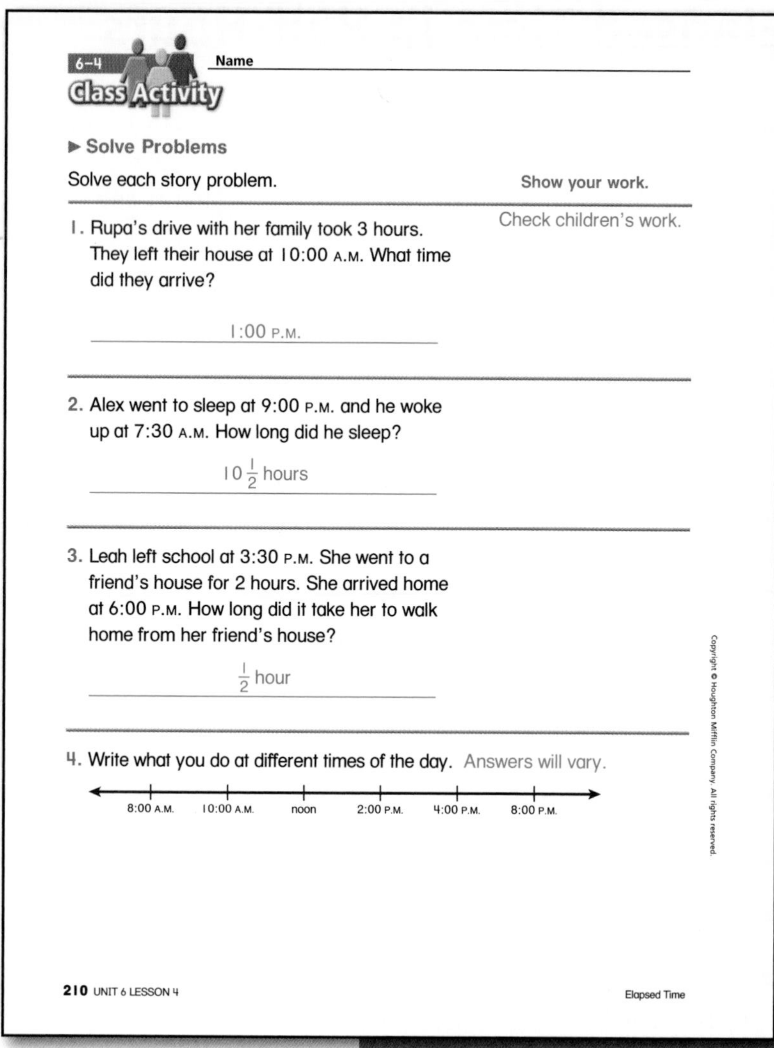

6–4 Class Activity Name

▶ Solve Problems

Solve each story problem. Show your work.

Check children's work.

1. Rupa's drive with her family took 3 hours. They left their house at 10:00 A.M. What time did they arrive?

1:00 P.M.

2. Alex went to sleep at 9:00 P.M. and he woke up at 7:30 A.M. How long did he sleep?

$10\frac{1}{2}$ hours

3. Leah left school at 3:30 P.M. She went to a friend's house for 2 hours. She arrived home at 6:00 P.M. How long did it take her to walk home from her friend's house?

$\frac{1}{2}$ hour

4. Write what you do at different times of the day. Answers will vary.

8:00 A.M. 10:00 A.M. noon 2:00 P.M. 4:00 P.M. 8:00 P.M.

210 UNIT 6 LESSON 4 Elapsed Time

Student Activity Book page 210

Ongoing Assessment

Ask questions about the passing of time throughout the school day.

▶ How much time passes between the start of the school day and lunchtime? Explain how you found your answer.

2 Going Further

Differentiated Instruction

Intervention Activity Card 6-4

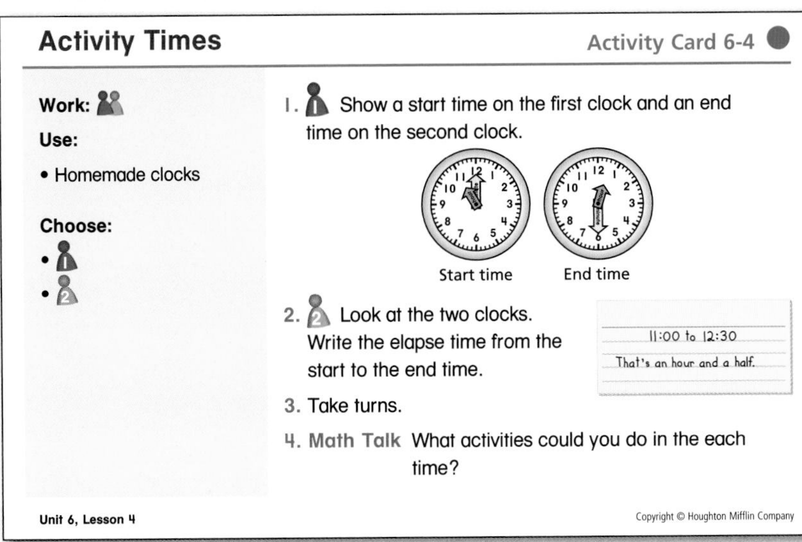

Activity Times Activity Card 6-4

Work: pairs

Use:

- Homemade clocks

Choose:

- 1
- 2

1. 1 Show a start time on the first clock and an end time on the second clock.

2. 2 Look at the two clocks. Write the elapse time from the start to the end time.

3. Take turns.
4. **Math Talk** What activities could you do in the each time?

Unit 6, Lesson 4

Activity Note Each pair the handmade clock from Lesson 1 or Student Activity Page 197. Make sure the second time is after the time on the first clock.

Math Writing Prompt

Write About It Describe an activity or event that takes about 3 hours. Include a start and end time in your description.

Software Support

Use *Soar to Success* for instruction of students needing targeted support for underlying skills.

On Level Activity Card 6-4

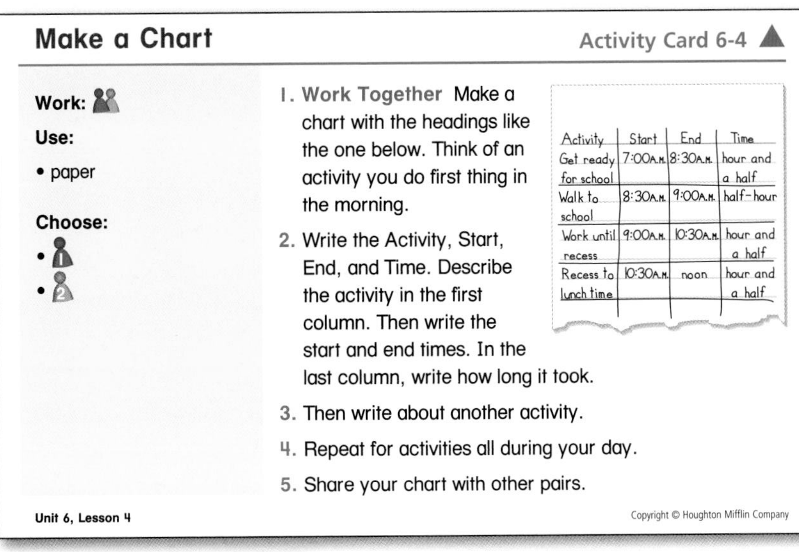

Make a Chart Activity Card 6-4

Work: pairs

Use:

- paper

Choose:

- 1
- 2

1. **Work Together** Make a chart with the headings like the one below. Think of an activity you do first thing in the morning.
2. Write the Activity, Start, End, and Time. Describe the activity in the first column. Then write the start and end times. In the last column, write how long it took.
3. Then write about another activity.
4. Repeat for activities all during your day.
5. Share your chart with other pairs.

Activity	Start	End	Time
Get ready for school	7:00 A.M.	8:30 A.M.	hour and a half
Walk to school	8:30 A.M.	9:00 A.M.	half-hour
Work until recess	9:00 A.M.	10:30 A.M.	hour and a half
Recess to lunch time	10:30 A.M.	noon	hour and a half

Unit 6, Lesson 4

Activity Note Each pair needs to make a timetable of activities for their day. Have children check their work carefully.

Math Writing Prompt

Write a Problem Describe an activity that you can do that takes more than an hour. Then write a story problem about the time it takes to complete the activity. Include an answer with your problem.

Software Support

Use *MegaMath* for review and reinforcement of the concepts and skills presented in this lesson.

Challenge Activity Card 6-4

Draw a Time Line Activity Card 6-4

Work: pairs

Use:

- paper

Choose:

- 1
- 2

1. **Work Together** You want to make a time line for your school day. Draw a line from the top of a page to the bottom.
2. Write what time school starts.
3. Then write what time different activities start all during the school day.
4. Take turns asking questions about the school day. Use the time line to help you answer each question.

9:00 A.M. — school starts
10:00 A.M. — recess
10:15 A.M. — math lesson
11:15 A.M. — science lesson
noon — lunch
1:00 P.M. — gym
2:00 P.M. — reading
3:30 P.M. — school ends

Unit 6, Lesson 4

Activity Note Help children identify when activities during the day occur and how long they last.

Math Writing Prompt

Explain Your Thinking A soccer car wash on Tuesday started at 11:00 A.M. and ended at 6:00 P.M. How many hours did it last altogether? Show how you found your answer.

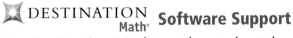

DESTINATION Math®

Software Support

Use *Destination Math* to take students beyond the concepts and skills presented in this lesson.

3 Homework

6–4 Homework **Goal:** Additional Practice

On this Homework page, children determine how much time has elapsed between different start and end times.

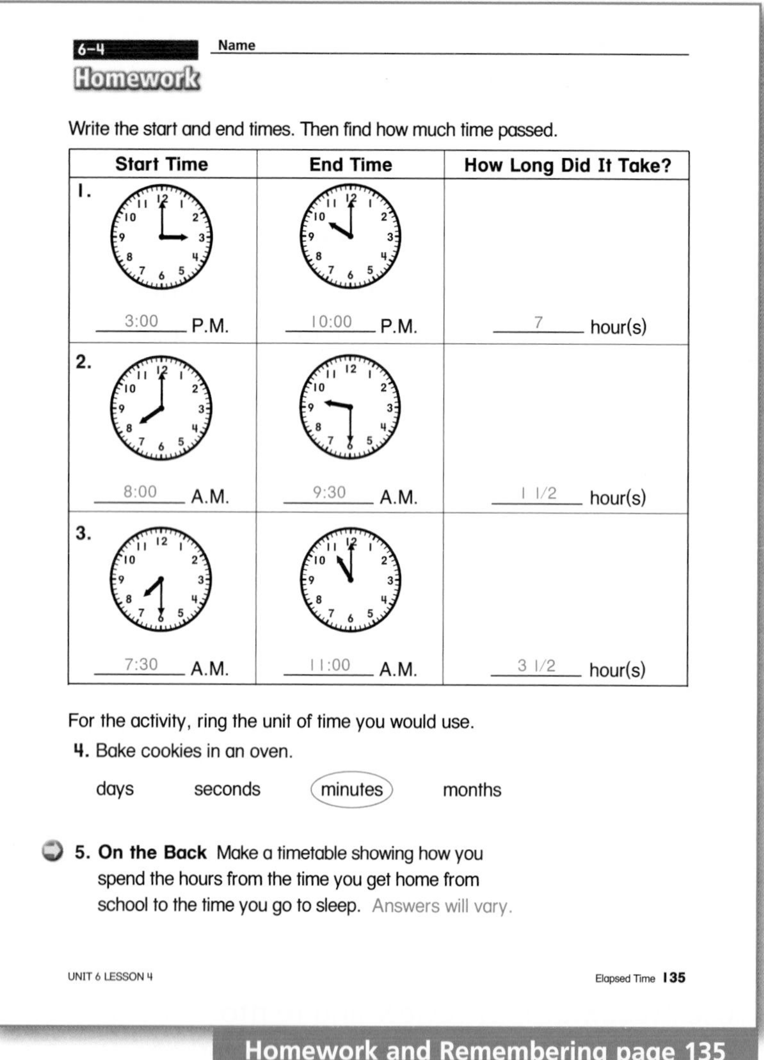

6–4 Homework Name

Write the start and end times. Then find how much time passed.

	Start Time	End Time	How Long Did It Take?
1.	3:00 P.M.	10:00 P.M.	7 hour(s)
2.	8:00 A.M.	9:30 A.M.	1 1/2 hour(s)
3.	7:30 A.M.	11:00 A.M.	3 1/2 hour(s)

For the activity, ring the unit of time you would use.

4. Bake cookies in an oven.

days seconds (minutes) months

5. **On the Back** Make a timetable showing how you spend the hours from the time you get home from school to the time you go to sleep. Answers will vary.

UNIT 6 LESSON 4 Elapsed Time 135

Homework and Remembering page 135

Home or School Activity

Real-World Connection

Reading Schedules Have children use the movie listings online or in the newspaper to find the time between the start of one screening and the start of the next screening.

The newspaper says that the first show in the afternoon starts at 2:00 P.M. and the next show starts at 4:00 P.M. The movie is 2 hours long.

Calendars and Function Tables

Lesson Objectives

- Read and understand calendars.
- Use ordinal numbers.
- Describe and extend patterns in a function table.

Vocabulary
calendar
month
ordinal number

The Day at a Glance

Today's Goals	Materials	
1 Teaching the Lesson **A1:** Learn how a year is divided into months, weeks, and days. **A2:** Use patterns to extend a table.	**Lesson Activities** Student Activity Book pp. 211–214 Homework and Remembering pp. 137–138 A current calendar	**Going Further** Activity Cards 6-5 Student Activity Book p. 211 Math Journals
2 Going Further ▶ Differentiated Instruction		
3 Homework		

Use Math Talk today!

Keeping Skills Sharp

Daily Routines	English Language Learners
Math Mountains for 100 or 2-Digit Numbers Using the MathBoard, Using Dimes and Pennies (See p. xxvi.) ▶ Led by Student Leaders **Money Routine** Using the 120 Poster, Using the Money Flip Chart, Using the Number Path, Using Secret Code Cards (See pp. xxiii–xxv.) ▶ Led by Student Leaders	Draw a calendar for May. Write the word *calendar* on the board. • **Beginning** Say: **This is a May *calendar*. A *calendar* shows all of the days in a month.** Have children repeat. • **Intermediate** Say: **This is a May *calendar*.** Ask: **What does the calendar show?** the days in May • **Advanced** Have children tell about what the May calendar shows.

1 Teaching the Lesson

Activity 1

Days, Weeks, Months, and Years

 35 MINUTES

Goal: Learn how a year is divided into months, weeks, and days.

Materials: Student Activity Book pages 211–214, a calendar for the current year

 **NCTM Standards:**
Measurement
Number and Operations

▶ Make a Calendar INDIVIDUALS

Have children look at the calendar on Student Activity Book page 211 and tell them the name of the current month and the day of the week when the first of the month occurred.

- The first day of this month was on a ________. Place a 1 in the first row of your calendar under that day of the week.
- How many days are in this month? Answers will vary. Possible answers: 28, 29, 30, or 31

Have children fill in the numbers on the calendar to the last day of the month.

Ask for Ideas Ask children what they already know about the relationship between weeks and years.

- How many days are in 1 week? 7 days
- How many weeks are in 1 year? 52 weeks

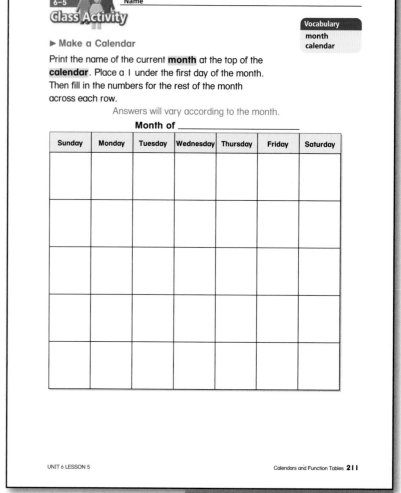

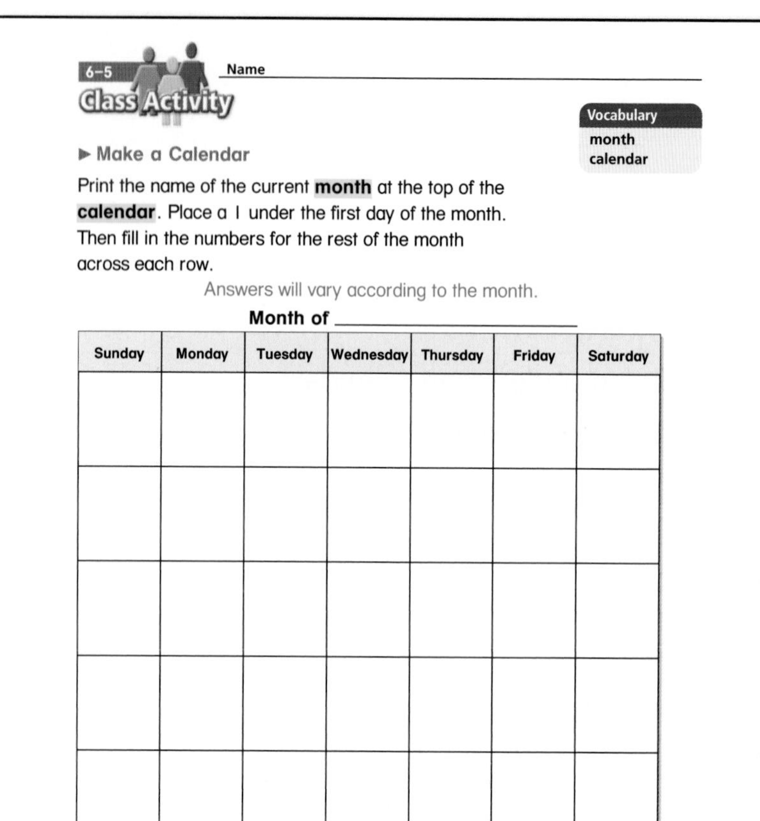
6–5 Class Activity Name ____________

Vocabulary
month
calendar

▶ Make a Calendar

Print the name of the current **month** at the top of the **calendar**. Place a 1 under the first day of the month. Then fill in the numbers for the rest of the month across each row.

Answers will vary according to the month.

Month of ____________

Sunday	Monday	Tuesday	Wednesday	Thursday	Friday	Saturday

UNIT 6 LESSON 5 Calendars and Function Tables 211

Student Activity Book page 211

▶ Use Ordinal Numbers WHOLE CLASS

Introduce ordinal numbers by writing *first, second, third, fourth ... twelfth* on the board. Explain to children that ordinal numbers describe the position or sequence of objects or events, not the quantity of them. Together, discuss how we use ordinal numbers.

- Where have you seen or heard ordinal numbers used? Possible responses: street names, floors of a building, position in a line-up, dates, standings in sports, games, or other competitions

Record the abbreviations *1st, 2nd, 3rd,* and *4th* on the board. Tell children that you can show all other ordinal numbers up to 20th by adding "th" after the numeral: 5th, 6th, 7th, and so on.

Discuss as a class how we use ordinal numbers to express dates.

- We use ordinal numbers to say dates, like the first of the month or January 1st. Recite the numbers in your calendar aloud using ordinal numbers. 1st, 2nd, 3rd, 4th, and so on

Next, discuss the days of the week.

- Each row on your calendar page is 1 week. How many days are in 1 week? 7 days

Name several dates using ordinal numbers and ask children to refer to their calendars and to identify the day of the week of each date.

- What day of the week is the fifth? the seventeenth? the twenty-third?

Be sure your examples include dates that fall on each of the seven days of the week.

Differentiated Instruction

English Learners Have English learners record the names of ordinal numbers in their math journal. Make sure that they understand when the different ways or saying numbers are used. Examples:
"Twentieth place"
"Fifteenth anniversary"
"October eighth"

Review other ways to say numbers and their uses:
5 = "Five"
50 = "Fifty"
5th = "Fifth"

Ask several questions, like the following, that will encourage children to closely examine their calendars. Answers will vary depending on the month.

- How many Tuesdays are there in this month?
- How many school days are in this month? How many weekend days?
- What is the date of the third Saturday of the month?
- Is there a holiday this month? What date is it?
- On what day does the next month begin? On what day did the last month end?

Look for Patterns Invite children to look for patterns in their calendar. Answers will vary according to the month.

- Look at the first column where you can see the first of the month. What numbers do you see in this column? 1, 8, 15, 22, (29)
- What pattern can you see in these numbers? If you add 7 to each number, you'll get the next number in the column.
- Do you see this pattern in every column? yes
- Why is this so? There are 7 days in a week and each week has a row in the calendar.

Month of ____________

Sunday	Monday	Tuesday	Wednesday	Thursday	Friday	Saturday

Activity continued ▶

1 Teaching the Lesson (continued)

▶ Learn About Months INDIVIDUALS

Display a class calendar or distribute individual calendars to each child. Ask children to use the year calendar as a reference and to fill in the number of days below the name of each month on Student Activity Book page 212.

Then have children complete exercises 2–11 on their own or work together as a class.

When children are finished, invite them to share their answers. You can continue the discussion by asking children to complete these sentences.

- One week before July 14 is ________. July 7
- Ten days after March 30 is ________. April 9
- Ten days before December 2 is ________. November 22
- Three weeks after April 15 is ________. May 6

Teaching Note

Language and Vocabulary Ask children whether they can define *leap year.* If the current year is a leap year, ask children to describe what is special about the month of February during this year. Alternatively, tell children when the next leap year will be and explain that the month of February will have 29, not 28, days that year. Explain to children that although we say a year is 365 days, this number is not exact. It takes a little more than 365 days for Earth to revolve around the Sun. So every 4 years, February has an extra day to balance the part-days in the previous years.

Class Management

You might teach children this familiar rhyme to help them remember the number of days in each month. The following is one of many different versions. Post the rhyme on chart paper or on the board until children can recite it from memory.

Thirty days hath September,
April, June, and November;
February has twenty-eight alone,
All the rest have thirty-one,
Excepting leap year, that's the time
When February's days are twenty-nine.

6–5 Name ________

▶ Learn About Months

This chart shows the months in a year.

1. Write the number of days in each month.

January 31	February 28 or 29	March 31	April 30
May 31	June 30	July 31	August 31
September 30	October 31	November 30	December 31

Answer the questions below about the months of the year.

2. How many months are in 1 year? 12 months
3. What is the name of the seventh month? July
4. What month comes 5 months after February? July
5. What month comes 6 months before November? May
6. What month comes 4 months after November? March

List the months.

7. Months with 30 days: April June September November
8. Months with 31 days: January March May July August October December
9. Which month has fewer than 30 days? February

Write each date.

10. One week after June 16 is June 23.
11. One week after September 24 is October 1.

Student Activity Book page 212

Ongoing Assessment

Have children use a calendar to determine the day of the week on which these events will or did occur this year: July 4, New Year's Day, and their birthday.

Activity 2

Change Over Time (Function Tables)

20 MINUTES

Goal: Use patterns to extend a table.

Materials: Student Activity Book pages 213–214

NCTM Standards:
Measurement
Algebra

▶ Continue the Pattern PAIRS

Refer children to exercise 12 on Student Activity Book page 213.

- What number was added to 7 to get the number of days in 2 weeks? 7
- What number do you need to add to 14 to find the number of days in 3 weeks? 7
- How can you fill in the rest of the table? I can keep adding 7 to the number above.

Have children work in pairs to complete exercises 12–15. Encourage them to discuss with one another their strategies for completing each table.

6–5  Name

▶ Continue the Pattern

Complete each table for exercises 12–14.

12.

Number of Weeks	Number of Days
1	7
2	14
3	21
4	28
5	35
6	42
7	49

13.

Number of Years	Number of Months
1	12
2	24
3	36
4	48
5	60
6	72
7	84

14.

Number of Weeks	Number of School Days
1	5
2	10
3	15
4	20
5	25
6	30
7	35

15. How many days are in 11 weeks? 77 days

How many months are in 8 years? 96 months

How many school days are in 9 weeks? 45 school days

UNIT 6 LESSON 5 Calendars and Function Tables 213

Student Activity Book page 213

Teaching Note

Math Background In mathematics, a function is defined as a set of ordered pairs of numbers that follow this rule: for any first number there is only one possible second number. Each of the tables in these problems represents a function.

Activity continued ▶

▶ Solve Problems with Patterns

WHOLE CLASS

Math Talk 

Write this story problem on the board.

The flower shop sells lily bulbs in packages of 3. How many bulbs will Maria have if she buys 5 packages?

Draw a table on the board with these headings: Number of Packages and Number of Bulbs. Write numbers 1 to 5 in the row labeled Number of Packages.

Number of Packages	1	2	3	4	5
Number of Bulbs					

- How many lily bulbs are in one package? 3

Write 3 below the number 1 in the table.

- What number will you add to 3 to find the number of bulbs in two packages? 3
- So, how many bulbs are in two packages? 6

Write 6 below the number 2 in the table.

Continue until you have completed the table together.

- How many bulbs will Maria have if she buys five packages? 15

Have children solve problems 16–19 by completing the tables on Student Activity Book page 214.

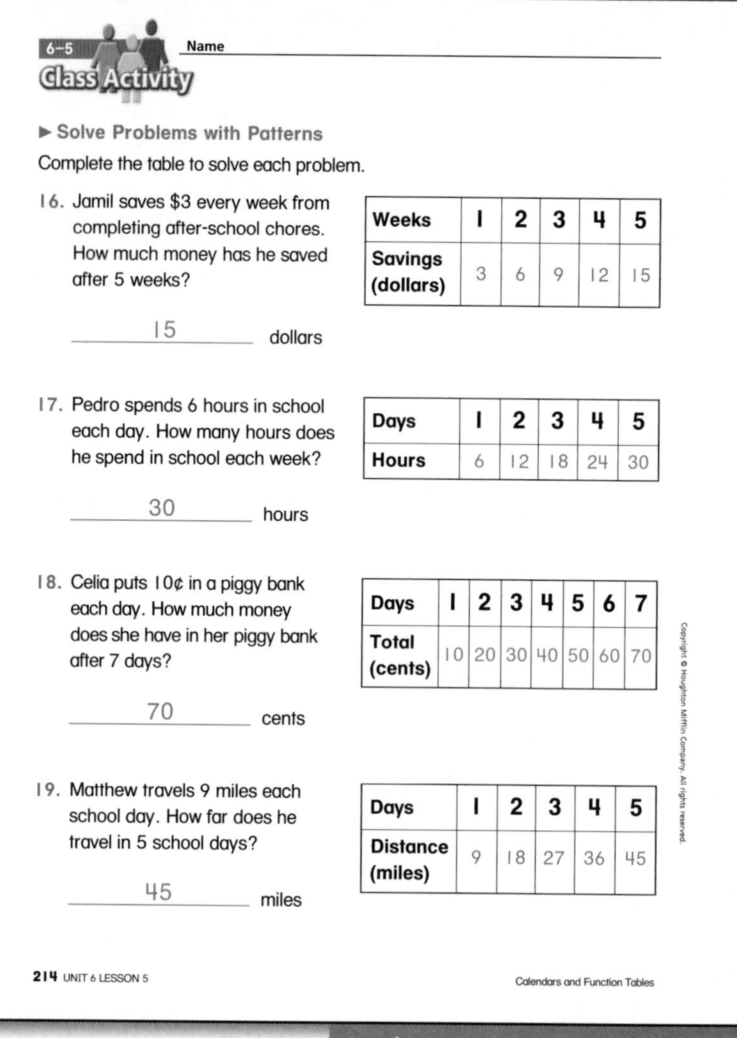

6–5 Class Activity Name

▶ Solve Problems with Patterns

Complete the table to solve each problem.

16. Jamil saves $3 every week from completing after-school chores. How much money has he saved after 5 weeks?

Weeks	1	2	3	4	5
Savings (dollars)	3	6	9	12	15

15 dollars

17. Pedro spends 6 hours in school each day. How many hours does he spend in school each week?

Days	1	2	3	4	5
Hours	6	12	18	24	30

30 hours

18. Celia puts 10¢ in a piggy bank each day. How much money does she have in her piggy bank after 7 days?

Days	1	2	3	4	5	6	7
Total (cents)	10	20	30	40	50	60	70

70 cents

19. Matthew travels 9 miles each school day. How far does he travel in 5 school days?

Days	1	2	3	4	5
Distance (miles)	9	18	27	36	45

45 miles

214 UNIT 6 LESSON 5 Calendars and Function Tables

Student Activity Book page 214

Differentiated Instruction

Extra Help Encourage children who are having difficulty to read the problems carefully and to work through each table one box at a time. Have them choose the number that belongs in the first part of the table. Ask questions to assist their thinking:

- ▶ How much money does Jamil have after 1 week? $3
- ▶ Where will you place 3 in the table? I'll put 3 in the box underneath 1 for 1 week.
- ▶ What number do you add to 3 to get the total after 2 weeks? 3

Differentiated Instruction

Advanced Learners Challenge children to solve this story problem using a table: Tiwa is making ladybugs with glass beads for eyes. She uses 2 beads for each ladybug. How many beads will she need to make 7 ladybugs?

Ask questions to help children create a table:

- ▶ How many columns will be in your table?
- ▶ How many rows will be in your table?
- ▶ What will you name the top and bottom rows?

Intervention Activity Card 6-5

Examine a Calendar
Activity Card 6-5

Work: (groups)
Use:
- Completed calendar

Choose:
- 1
- 2
- 3

1. **Work Together** Look at your calendar. Which day or days of the week occur five or more times during this month? Answer will vary depending on the month used.
2. Use the calendar. How many times do the other days of week occur during this month? Answer will vary depending on the month used.
3. Use the calendar to write a riddle about the month for another group. Trade riddles.

Unit 6, Lesson 5

Activity Note Each group needs a completed calendar from Activity 1 or Student Activity Book page 211. Remind children to agree on their answers.

Math Writing Prompt

Explain Your Thinking What is the date 1 week from today. Tell how you found your answer.

Software Support

Use *Soar to Success* for instruction of students needing targeted support for underlying skills.

On Level Activity Card 6-5

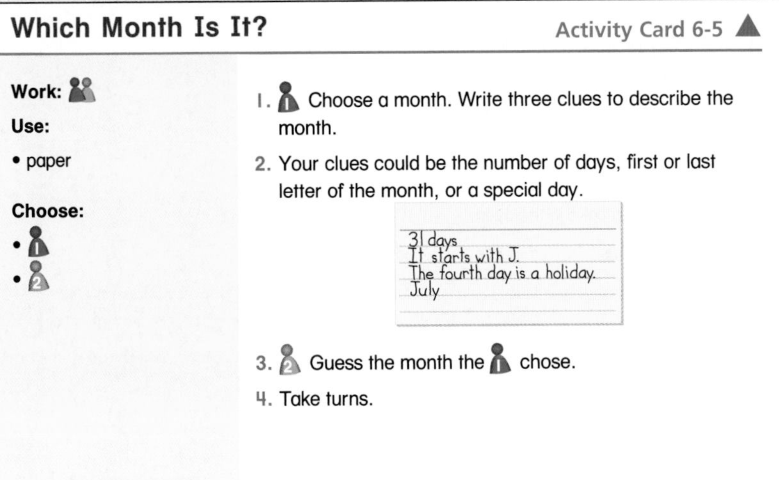

Which Month Is It?
Activity Card 6-5

Work: (pairs)
Use:
- paper

Choose:
- 1
- 2

1. (1) Choose a month. Write three clues to describe the month.
2. Your clues could be the number of days, first or last letter of the month, or a special day.

31 days
It starts with J.
The fourth day is a holiday.
July

3. (2) Guess the month the (1) chose.
4. Take turns.

Unit 6, Lesson 5

Activity Note Each pair takes turns writing clues about the months. Tell kids that the clues should apply to several months. Avoid clues like "28 days" or "starts with D."

Math Writing Prompt

Use Ordinal Numbers Use ordinal numbers to tell about the day of the month and the month of the year in which you were born.

Software Support

Use *MegaMath* for review and reinforcement of the concepts and skills presented in this lesson.

Challenge Activity Card 6-5

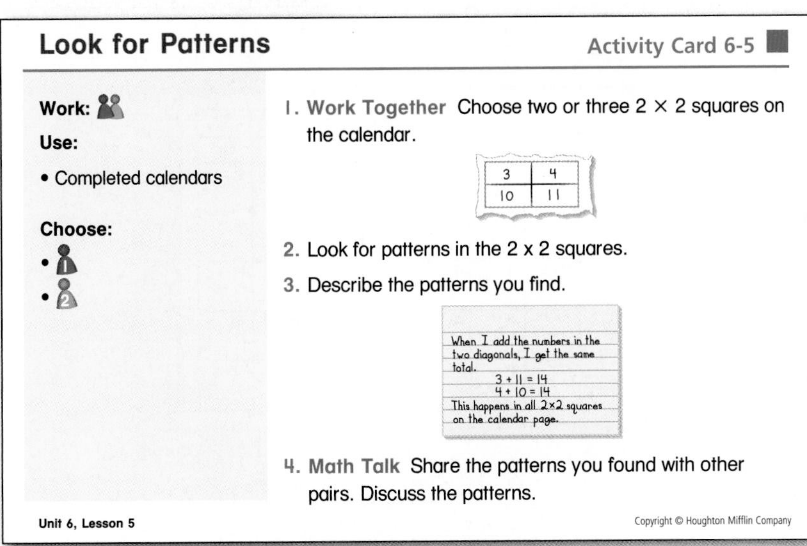

Look for Patterns
Activity Card 6-5

Work: (pairs)
Use:
- Completed calendars

Choose:
- 1
- 2

1. **Work Together** Choose two or three 2 × 2 squares on the calendar.

3	4
10	11

2. Look for patterns in the 2 x 2 squares.
3. Describe the patterns you find.

When I add the numbers in the two diagonals, I get the same total.
3 + 11 = 14
4 + 10 = 14
This happens in all 2×2 squares on the calendar page.

4. **Math Talk** Share the patterns you found with other pairs. Discuss the patterns.

Unit 6, Lesson 5

Activity Note Each pair needs a completed calendar from Activity 1 or Student Activity Book page 211. Show children a 2 × 2 square.

Math Writing Prompt

Predict and Verify If January 1 is a Monday, predict the day of the week for the first of each month of the year. Use a calendar to check your predictions.

Software Support

Use *Destination Math* to take students beyond the concepts and skills presented in this lesson.

3 Homework

Goal: Additional Practice

This Homework page allows children to solve problems by extending patterns in a table.

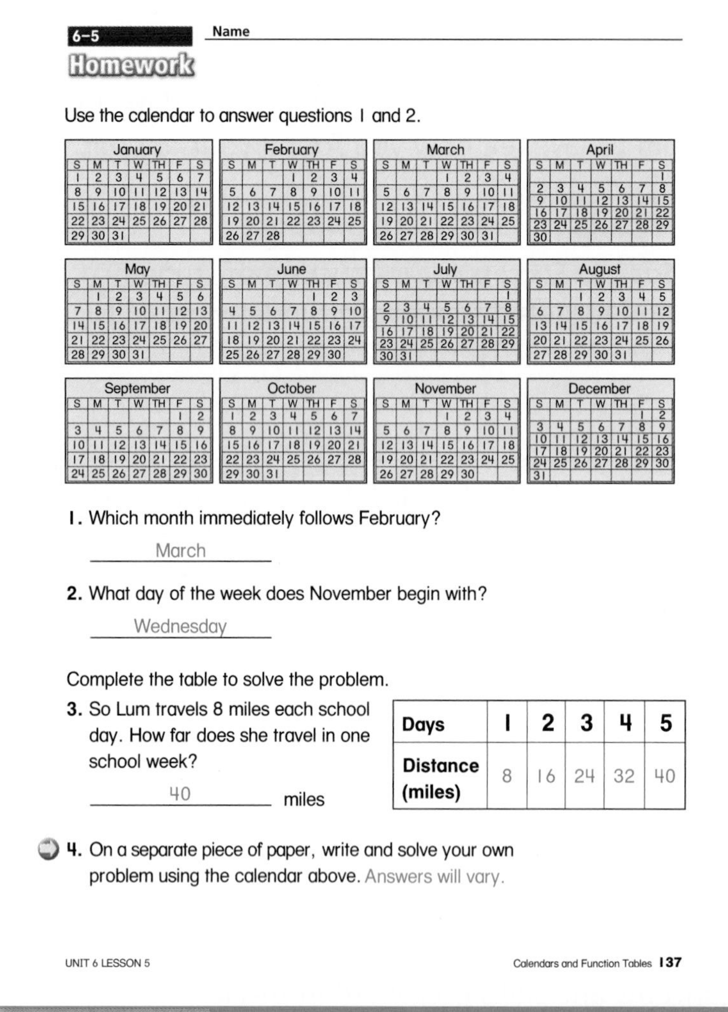

6-5 Homework

Name ____________________

Use the calendar to answer questions 1 and 2.

January						
S	M	T	W	TH	F	S
1	2	3	4	5	6	7
8	9	10	11	12	13	14
15	16	17	18	19	20	21
22	23	24	25	26	27	28
29	30	31				

February						
S	M	T	W	TH	F	S
			1	2	3	4
5	6	7	8	9	10	11
12	13	14	15	16	17	18
19	20	21	22	23	24	25
26	27	28				

March						
S	M	T	W	TH	F	S
			1	2	3	4
5	6	7	8	9	10	11
12	13	14	15	16	17	18
19	20	21	22	23	24	25
26	27	28	29	30	31	

April						
S	M	T	W	TH	F	S
						1
2	3	4	5	6	7	8
9	10	11	12	13	14	15
16	17	18	19	20	21	22
23	24	25	26	27	28	29
30						

May						
S	M	T	W	TH	F	S
	1	2	3	4	5	6
7	8	9	10	11	12	13
14	15	16	17	18	19	20
21	22	23	24	25	26	27
28	29	30	31			

June						
S	M	T	W	TH	F	S
				1	2	3
4	5	6	7	8	9	10
11	12	13	14	15	16	17
18	19	20	21	22	23	24
25	26	27	28	29	30	

July						
S	M	T	W	TH	F	S
						1
2	3	4	5	6	7	8
9	10	11	12	13	14	15
16	17	18	19	20	21	22
23	24	25	26	27	28	29
30	31					

August						
S	M	T	W	TH	F	S
		1	2	3	4	5
6	7	8	9	10	11	12
13	14	15	16	17	18	19
20	21	22	23	24	25	26
27	28	29	30	31		

September						
S	M	T	W	TH	F	S
					1	2
3	4	5	6	7	8	9
10	11	12	13	14	15	16
17	18	19	20	21	22	23
24	25	26	27	28	29	30

October						
S	M	T	W	TH	F	S
1	2	3	4	5	6	7
8	9	10	11	12	13	14
15	16	17	18	19	20	21
22	23	24	25	26	27	28
29	30	31				

November						
S	M	T	W	TH	F	S
			1	2	3	4
5	6	7	8	9	10	11
12	13	14	15	16	17	18
19	20	21	22	23	24	25
26	27	28	29	30		

December						
S	M	T	W	TH	F	S
					1	2
3	4	5	6	7	8	9
10	11	12	13	14	15	16
17	18	19	20	21	22	23
24	25	26	27	28	29	30
31						

1. Which month immediately follows February?

   March

2. What day of the week does November begin with?

   Wednesday

Complete the table to solve the problem.

3. So Lum travels 8 miles each school day. How far does she travel in one school week?

   40 miles

Days	1	2	3	4	5
Distance (miles)	8	16	24	32	40

4. On a separate piece of paper, write and solve your own problem using the calendar above. Answers will vary.

UNIT 6 LESSON 5 Calendars and Function Tables 137

Homework and Remembering page 137

Goal: Sprial Review

This Remembering activity would be appropriate anytime after today's lesson.

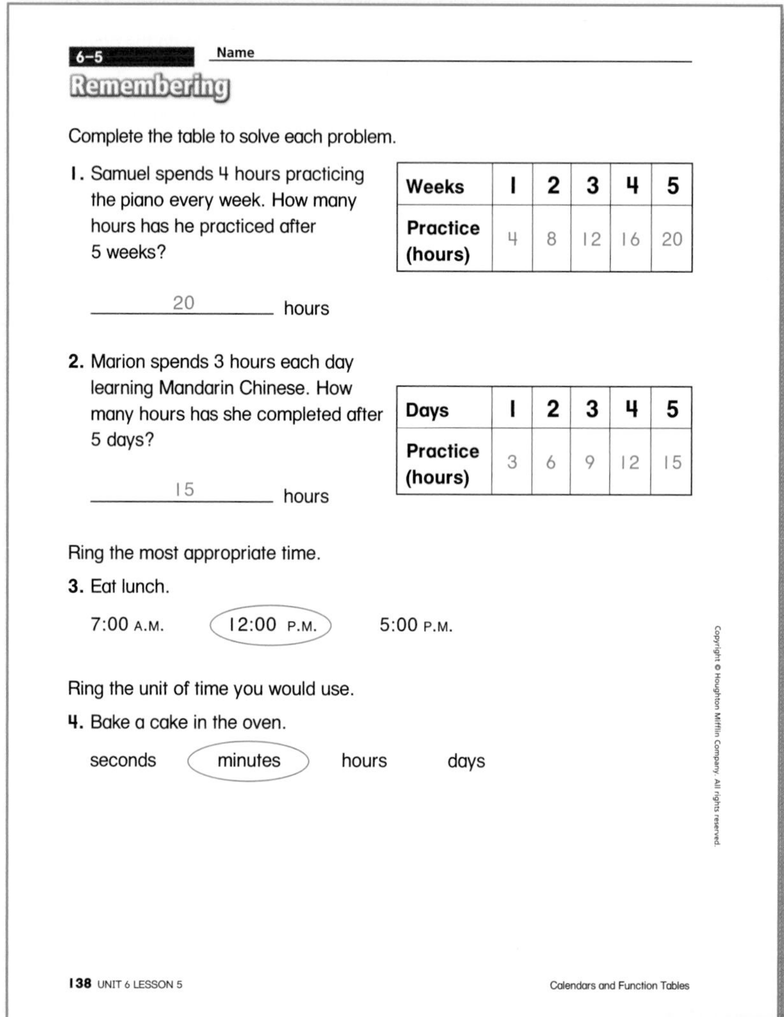

6-5 Remembering

Name ____________________

Complete the table to solve each problem.

1. Samuel spends 4 hours practicing the piano every week. How many hours has he practiced after 5 weeks?

   20 hours

Weeks	1	2	3	4	5
Practice (hours)	4	8	12	16	20

2. Marion spends 3 hours each day learning Mandarin Chinese. How many hours has she completed after 5 days?

   15 hours

Days	1	2	3	4	5
Practice (hours)	3	6	9	12	15

Ring the most appropriate time.

3. Eat lunch.

   7:00 A.M. (12:00 P.M.) 5:00 P.M.

Ring the unit of time you would use.

4. Bake a cake in the oven.

   seconds (minutes) hours days

Copyright © Houghton Mifflin Company. All rights reserved.

138 UNIT 6 LESSON 5 Calendars and Function Tables

Homework and Remembering page 138

Home or School Activity

Technology Connection

Special Days Have children list four special days that occur this year, such as birthdays, national holidays, and favorite family days. Children can research special days on the Internet and use a program on the computer to create a calendar to mark the special days.

Unit Review and Test

Lesson Objectives

- **Assess children's progress on unit objectives.**

The Day at a Glance

Today's Goals	Materials
1 Assessing the Unit ▶ Assess children's progress on unit objectives. ▶ Use activities from unit lessons to reteach content.	Unit 6 Test, Student Activity Book pages 215–218 Unit 6 Test, Form A or B, Assessment Guide (optional) Unit 6 Performance Assessment, Assessment Guide (optional)
2 Extending the Assessment ▶ Use remediation for common errors.	
There is no homework assignment on a test day.	

Keeping Skills Sharp

Daily Routines 5 MINUTES	
If you are doing a unit review day, go over the homework. If this is a test day, omit the homework review.	**Review and Test Day** You may want to choose a quiet game or other activity (reading a book or working on homework for another subject) for children who finish early.

Assessing the Unit

Assess Unit Objectives

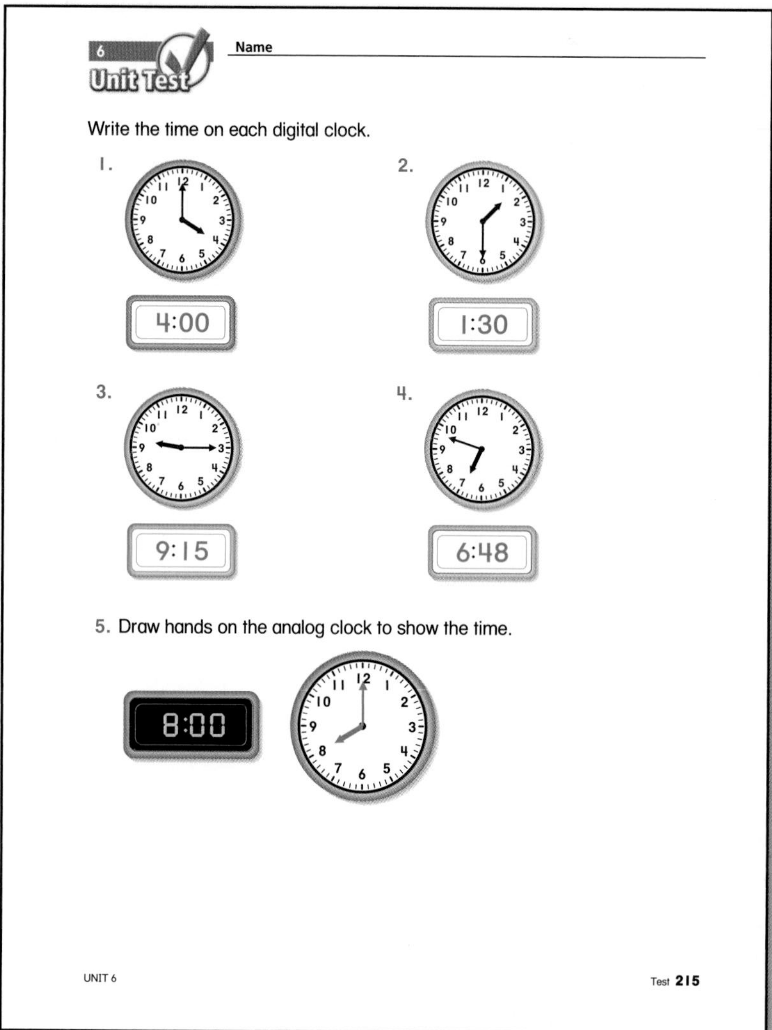
6 Unit Test
Name

Write the time on each digital clock.

1. 4:00
2. 1:30
3. 9:15
4. 6:48
5. Draw hands on the analog clock to show the time.

8:00

UNIT 6 Test 215

Student Activity Book page 215

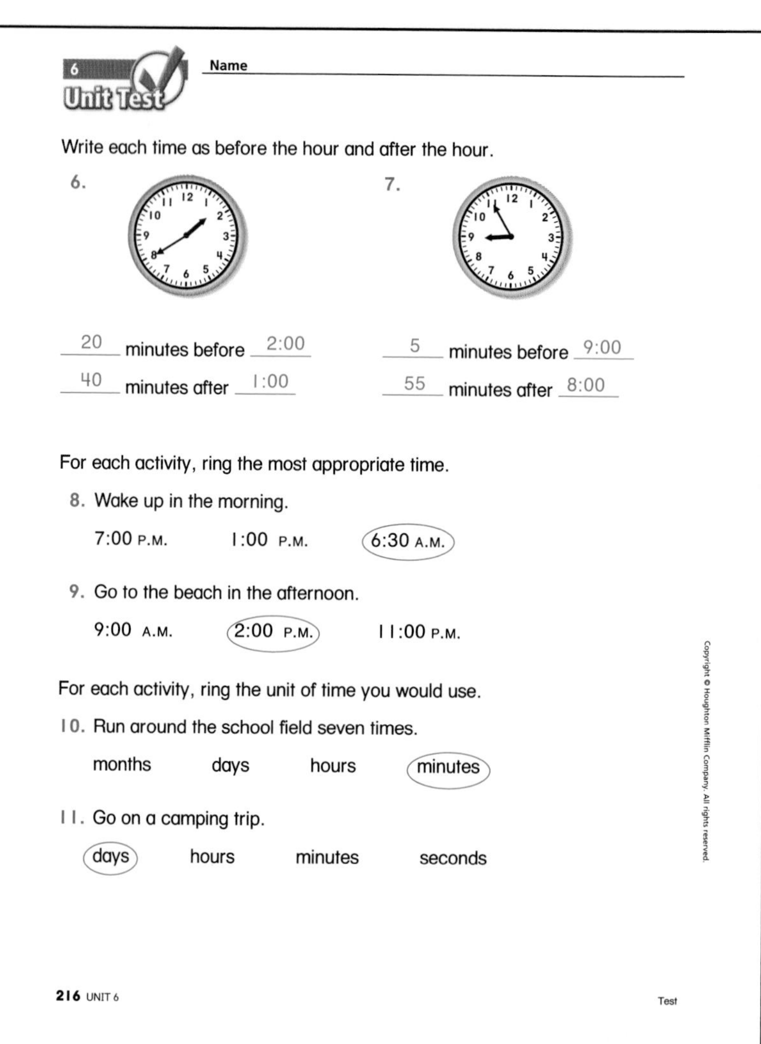
6 Unit Test
Name

Write each time as before the hour and after the hour.

6. 20 minutes before 2:00
40 minutes after 1:00

7. 5 minutes before 9:00
55 minutes after 8:00

For each activity, ring the most appropriate time.

8. Wake up in the morning.
7:00 P.M. 1:00 P.M. 6:30 A.M.

9. Go to the beach in the afternoon.
9:00 A.M. 2:00 P.M. 11:00 P.M.

For each activity, ring the unit of time you would use.

10. Run around the school field seven times.
months days hours minutes

11. Go on a camping trip.
days hours minutes seconds

216 UNIT 6 Test

Student Activity Book page 216

45 MINUTES (more if schedule permits)

Goal: Assess children's progress on unit objectives.

Materials: Student Activity Book pages 215–218, Assessment Guide (optional)

▶ Review and Assessment

If your students are ready for assessment on the unit objectives, use either the test on the Student Activity Book pages or one of the forms of the Unit 6 Test in the Assessment Guide to assess student progress. To assign a numerical score for all of these test forms, use 5 points for each question.

The chart to the right lists the test items, the unit objectives they cover, and the lesson activities in which the objective is covered in this unit.

▶ Reteaching Resources

Unit Test Items	Unit Objectives Tested	Activities to Use for Reteaching
1, 2, 3, 4, 5, 20	**6.1** Tell time to 1 minute.	Lesson 3, Activity 2
6, 7	**6.2** Read time as after the hour and before the hour.	Lesson 3, Activity 3
8, 9	**6.3** Use A.M. and P.M.	Lesson 1, Activity 1

Name

Write the start time and end time. Then find how much time passed.

12.

Start Time	End Time	How long did it take?
2:00 P.M.	6:00 P.M.	4 hours

13.

Start Time	End Time	How long did it take?
7:00 A.M.	10:30 A.M.	$3\frac{1}{2}$ or 3 and one half

14. Complete the table.

Number of Weeks	Number of Days
1	7
2	14
3	21
4	28
5	35
6	42
7	49

UNIT 6 Test **217**

Student Activity Book page 217

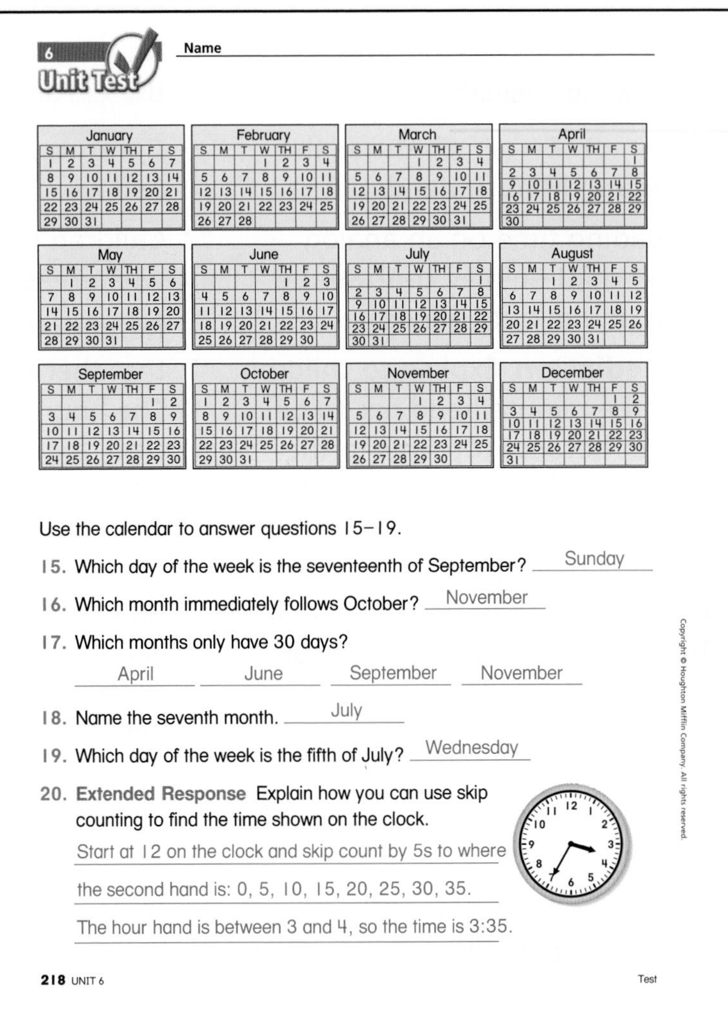

Name

January						
S	M	T	W	TH	F	S
1	2	3	4	5	6	7
8	9	10	11	12	13	14
15	16	17	18	19	20	21
22	23	24	25	26	27	28
29	30	31				

February						
S	M	T	W	TH	F	S
			1	2	3	4
5	6	7	8	9	10	11
12	13	14	15	16	17	18
19	20	21	22	23	24	25
26	27	28				

March						
S	M	T	W	TH	F	S
			1	2	3	4
5	6	7	8	9	10	11
12	13	14	15	16	17	18
19	20	21	22	23	24	25
26	27	28	29	30	31	

April						
S	M	T	W	TH	F	S
						1
2	3	4	5	6	7	8
9	10	11	12	13	14	15
16	17	18	19	20	21	22
23	24	25	26	27	28	29
30						

May						
S	M	T	W	TH	F	S
	1	2	3	4	5	6
7	8	9	10	11	12	13
14	15	16	17	18	19	20
21	22	23	24	25	26	27
28	29	30	31			

June						
S	M	T	W	TH	F	S
				1	2	3
4	5	6	7	8	9	10
11	12	13	14	15	16	17
18	19	20	21	22	23	24
25	26	27	28	29	30	

July						
S	M	T	W	TH	F	S
						1
2	3	4	5	6	7	8
9	10	11	12	13	14	15
16	17	18	19	20	21	22
23	24	25	26	27	28	29
30	31					

August						
S	M	T	W	TH	F	S
		1	2	3	4	5
6	7	8	9	10	11	12
13	14	15	16	17	18	19
20	21	22	23	24	25	26
27	28	29	30	31		

September						
S	M	T	W	TH	F	S
					1	2
3	4	5	6	7	8	9
10	11	12	13	14	15	16
17	18	19	20	21	22	23
24	25	26	27	28	29	30

October						
S	M	T	W	TH	F	S
1	2	3	4	5	6	7
8	9	10	11	12	13	14
15	16	17	18	19	20	21
22	23	24	25	26	27	28
29	30	31				

November						
S	M	T	W	TH	F	S
			1	2	3	4
5	6	7	8	9	10	11
12	13	14	15	16	17	18
19	20	21	22	23	24	25
26	27	28	29	30		

December						
S	M	T	W	TH	F	S
					1	2
3	4	5	6	7	8	9
10	11	12	13	14	15	16
17	18	19	20	21	22	23
24	25	26	27	28	29	30
31						

Use the calendar to answer questions 15–19.

15. Which day of the week is the seventeenth of September? Sunday

16. Which month immediately follows October? November

17. Which months only have 30 days?
April June September November

18. Name the seventh month. July

19. Which day of the week is the fifth of July? Wednesday

20. **Extended Response** Explain how you can use skip counting to find the time shown on the clock.
Start at 12 on the clock and skip count by 5s to where the second hand is: 0, 5, 10, 15, 20, 25, 30, 35.
The hour hand is between 3 and 4, so the time is 3:35.

218 UNIT 6 Test

Student Activity Book page 218

Unit Test Items	Unit Objectives Tested	Activities to Use for Reteaching
10, 11	**6.4** Choose the most appropriate units to measure time.	Lesson 4, Activity 1
12, 13	**6.5** Determine elapsed time (hours and half-hours).	Lesson 4, Activities 2 and 3
15,16	**6.6** Read a calendar.	Lesson 5, Activity 1
17,18,19	**6.7** Use ordinal numbers.	Lesson 5, Activity 1
14	**6.8** Complete function tables.	Lesson 5, Activity 2

▶ Assessment Resources

Free Response Tests

Form A, Free Response Test

Form B, Multiple Choice Test

Performance Assessment

▶ Portfolio Assessment

Teacher-selected Items for Student Portfolios:

- Homework, Lesson 3
- Class Activity work, Lessons 2, 4, and 5

Student-selected Items for Student Portfolios:

- Favorite Home or School Activity
- Best Writing Prompt

2 Extending the Assessment

Common Errors

Activities for Remediation

Unit Objective 6.1

Tell time to 1 minute.

Common Error: Confuses the Hour and Minute Hands

In reading time on an analog clock, children may confuse the hour and minute hands.

Remediation Explain to children that the minute hand has to be longer because it points to the tiny marks between the numbers; otherwise, we would not be able to easily read the minutes past the hour. It is easy to see which mark the hour hand points to, so the hour hand is shorter.

Unit Objective 6.2

Read time as after the hour and before the hour.

Common Error: Identifies the Previous Hour When Telling Time before the Hour

In telling time before the hour, children may use the number that the hour hand has just passed.

Remediation Explain to children that when they are reading the time as before or after the hour, they must examine the position of the hour hand. Remind them of the direction that the hour hand moves and that the time will always be later than the hour that the hand has just passed. When they are reading a time before the hour, they must look at the next hour.

Unit Objective 6.3

Use A.M. and P.M.

Common Error: Confuses A.M. and P.M.

Children may confuse A.M. and P.M. when reading time.

Remediation Remind children that there are 24 hours in one day. The hour hand goes around the clock twice each day: 12 hours + 12 hours = 24 hours. Tell children that we use A.M. for times between midnight and noon and P.M. for times between noon and midnight. Set up a 24-hour time line in the classroom with the times between midnight and noon labeled A.M., and the times between noon and midnight labeled P.M.

Unit Objective 6.5

Determine elapsed time (hours and half-hours).

Common Error: Includes Start Time in Count of Elapsed Time

In finding elapsed time, children may count the start time as the first hour.

Remediation Reinforce that an hour is a unit of measurement, like a centimeter. Demonstrate on a clock that one hour is the time it takes for the hour hand to move from one number to the next. Explain to children that when they are finding elapsed time, they are counting the number of hour units that have passed. Likewise, when they measure length in centimeters, they count to the end of each centimeter unit on a ruler.

Unit Objective 6.6

Read a calendar.

Common Error: Thinks Months Always Begin on the Same Day of the Week

Some children may think that a month, like a week, always starts on the same day.

Remediation Remind children that different months have different numbers of days. Have them look at a month on a calendar. Ask them to identify the day of the week for the first day and the last day of the month. Then have them look at the next month and see the day of the week on which it begins. Continue with each month of the year.

Unit Objective 6.7

Use ordinal numbers.

Common Error: Confuses Cardinal and Ordinal Numbers

When working with dates and calendars, children may confuse cardinal and ordinal numbers.

Remediation Explain to children that cardinal numbers (one, two, three, etc.) tell how many while ordinal numbers (first, second, third, etc.) tell which one or which position. Draw a series of groups of circles on the board. Point to a group and ask how many circles are in the group. Then tell the ordinal number that describes the group's position on the board.

Tables and Graphs

THE GOAL FOR UNIT 7 is to introduce the graphical representation of information. Graphing provides children with a powerful tool to make comparisons and to represent the numeric information extracted from a story problem. Children will read and create picture graphs to record and analyze data as the first step in learning about comparisons. As children collect data for use in a class project, they will create data tables, picture graphs, and bar graphs to understand the data. Finally, they will be introduced to circle graphs. Through the use of these tools, children will explore comparison situations.

Skills Trace		
Grade 1	**Grade 2**	**Grade 3**
• Read, make, and use tables and picture graphs to compare data.	• Read and interpret information from a table, picture graph, bar graph, or circle graph.	• Interpret data in a table or graph; make bar graphs, and complete tables.

Unit 7 Contents

Big Idea Picture Graphs and Comparing

Big Idea Tables, Data, and Picture Graphs

Big Idea Bar Graphs, Circle Graphs, and Word Problems

Unit 7 Assessment

Unit Objectives Tested	Unit Test Items	Lessons
7.1 Read and interpret information from a picture graph.	1	1–3
7.2 Solve comparison story problems.	2–3	3–4
7.3 Read and interpret information from a table.	4–5	5–6, 14
7.4 Convert information from a table to a picture graph.	6	6–8
7.5 Read and interpret information from a bar graph.	7–8	8–10, 13, 14
7.6 Read and interpret information from a circle graph.	9–10	11–12, 14

Assessment and Review Resources

Formal Assessment

Student Activity Book

- Unit Review and Test (pp. 253–265)

Assessment Guide

- Quick Quizzes (pp. A69–A71)
- Test A–Open Response (pp. A72–A74)
- Test B–Multiple Choice (pp. A75–A78)
- Performance Assessment (pp. A79–A81)

Test Generator CD-ROM

- Open Response Test
- Multiple Choice Test
- Test Bank Items

Informal Assessment

Teacher Edition

- Ongoing Assessment (in every lesson)
- Quick Practice (in every lesson)
- Portfolio Suggestions (p. 583)

Math Talk

- Math Talk in Action (pp. 540, 552)
- In Activities (pp. 489, 496, 500, 507, 513, 523, 530, 535, 548, 565)

Review Opportunities

Homework and Remembering

- Review of recently taught topics
- Cumulative Review

Teacher Edition

- Unit Review and Test (pp. 581–584)

Test Generator CD-ROM

- Custom Review Sheets

Planning Unit 7

Lesson/NCTM Standards	Resources	Materials for Lesson Activities	Materials for Going Further
7–1 **Introduce Picture Graphs** NCTM Standards: 1, 5, 8	TE pp. 487–492 SAB pp. 219–220 H&R pp. 139–140 AC 7–1	MathBoard materials or 10 × 10 Grid (TRB M62) ✓ Real or play money Large piece of paper or posterboard	Index cards Shoes Chart paper Construction paper Tape Math Journals
7–2 **Read Picture Graphs** NCTM Standards: 1, 5, 8	TE pp. 493–498 SAB pp. 221–222 H&R pp. 141–142 AC 7–2 MCC 7–25	MathBoard materials or 10 × 10 Grid (TRB M62) Chart paper	Sticky notes Reading book Connecting cubes Math Journals
7–3 **The Language of Comparison** NCTM Standards: 1, 5, 8	TE pp. 499–504 SAB pp. 223–224 H&R pp. 143–144 AC 7–3	MathBoard materials or 10 × 10 Grid (TRB M62)	3 oz paper cup ✓ Real or play money Small cup Number cubes Math Journals
7–4 **Pose and Solve Comparison Story Problems** NCTM Standards: 1, 5, 8	TE pp. 505–510 SAB pp. 225–226 H&R pp. 145–146 AG: Quick Quiz 1 AC 7–4	MathBoard materials or 10 × 10 Grid (TRB M62)	✓ Connecting cubes Large bowl ✓ Real or play money Small container Math Journals
7–5 **Tables** NCTM Standards: 1, 5, 8	TE pp. 511–516 SAB pp. 227–228 H&R pp. 147–148 AC 7–5	MathBoard materials Tally list from Lesson 2	Small colored paper clips Spinners Crayons or colored pencils Math Journals
7–6 **Convert Tables to Picture Graphs** NCTM Standards: 5, 8	TE pp. 517–520 SAB pp. 229–230 H&R pp. 149–150 AC 7–6		Chart paper Book of nursery rhymes Math Journals
7–7 **Graph Data** NCTM Standards: 1, 5, 8	TE pp. 521–526 SAB pp. 231–232 H&R pp. 151–152 AG: Quick Quiz 2 AC 7–7 MCC 7–26	Completed tally list from Lesson 6 Blank transparency (optional)	Class list Construction paper Crayons or colored pencils Paper plates Math Journals
7–8 **Introduce Bar Graphs** NCTM Standards: 5	TE pp. 527–532 SAB pp. 233–234 H&R pp. 153–154 AC 7–8	MathBoard materials or 10 x 10 Grid (TRB M62)	Real or play money Math Journals
7–9 **Read Bar Graphs** NCTM Standards: 1, 5, 6, 9, 10	TE pp. 533–538 SAB pp. 235–236 H&R pp. 155–156 AC 7–9	Blank transparency (optional) Ruler MathBoard materials (optional)	Student Activity Book p. 235 Index cards Inch Grid Paper (TRB M70) Math Journals

Resources/Materials Key: TE: Teacher Edition SAB: Student Activity Book H&R: Homework and Remembering AC: Activity Cards MCC: Math Center Challenge AG: Assessment Guide ✓: Grade 2 kits TRB: Teacher's Resource Book

NCTM Standards Key: 1. Number and Operations 2. Algebra 3. Geometry 4. Measurement 5. Data Analysis and Probability 6. Problem Solving 7. Reasoning and Proof 8. Communication 9. Connections 10. Representation

Lesson/NCTM Standards	Resources	Materials for Lesson Activities	Materials for Going Further
7–10 **Analyze Information in Bar Graphs** NCTM Standards: 1, 5, 6, 9, 10	TE pp. 539–544 SAB pp. 237–238 H&R pp. 157–158 AC 7–10 MCC 7–27	Transparency of Student Activity Book p. 237 (optional)	✓ Connecting cubes Inch Grid Paper (TRB M70) Ruler Math Journals
7–11 **Introduce Circle Graphs** NCTM Standards: 1, 5, 6, 9, 10	TE pp. 545–550 SAB pp. 239–240 H&R pp. 159–160 AC 7–11	Transparency of Student Activity Book p. 239 (optional)	Homework and Remembering p. 159 MathBoard materials Inch Grid Paper (TRB M70) Colored pencils or markers ✓ Connecting cubes Paper bag Math Journals
7–12 **Explore Circle Graphs** NCTM Standards: 1, 5, 6, 9, 10	TE pp. 551–556 SAB pp. 241–244 H&R pp. 161–162 AC 7–12		*Tiger Math: Learning to Graph from a Baby Tiger* by Ann Whitehead Nagda and Cindy Bickel Student Activity Book p. 243 Construction paper Glue stick Colored pencils MathBoard materials Math Journals
7–13 **Talk About Graphs** NCTM Standards: 1, 5, 6, 9, 10	TE pp. 557–562 SAB pp. 245–246 H&R pp. 163–164 AC 7–13 MCC 7–28	MathBoard materials	Index cards Crayons or colored pencils ✓ Connecting cubes Inch Grid Paper (TRB M70) Math Journals
7–14 **2-Digit Addition with Tables and Graphs** NCTM Standards: 1, 5, 6, 9, 10	TE pp. 563–568 SAB pp. 247–248 H&R pp. 165–166 AC 7–14	Transparency of Student Activity Book p. 247 (optional) ✓ Cubes (2 colors) or real or play money (2 different coins)	Index cards Inch Grid Paper (TRB M70) Math Journals
7–15 **Use Data to Predict** NCTM Standards: 5, 6, 7, 8	TE pp. 569–574 SAB pp. 249–250 H&R pp. 167–168 AC 7–15	✓ Connecting cubes ✓ Number Cubes	✓ Pattern Blocks Paper strips Crayons or markers Math Journals
7–16 **Use Mathematical Processes** NCTM Standards: 6, 7, 8, 9, 10	TE pp. 702–707 SAB pp. 251–252 H&R pp. 169–170 AC 7–16	Rectangular sheets of paper Scissors 10 × 10 Grid (TRB M62)	✓ Two-Color Counters Crayons Spinner (TRB M27) Paper clip ✓ Number Cubes (1–6) Math Journals
✓ Unit Review and Test	TE pp. 581–584 SAB pp. 253–256 AG: Unit 7 tests		

Manipulatives and Materials

Essential materials for teaching Math Expressions are available in the Grade 2 kits. These materials are indicated by a ✓ in these lists. At the front of this Teacher Edition is more information about kit contents, alternatives for the materials, and use of the materials.

Independent Learning Activities

Ready-Made Math Challenge Centers

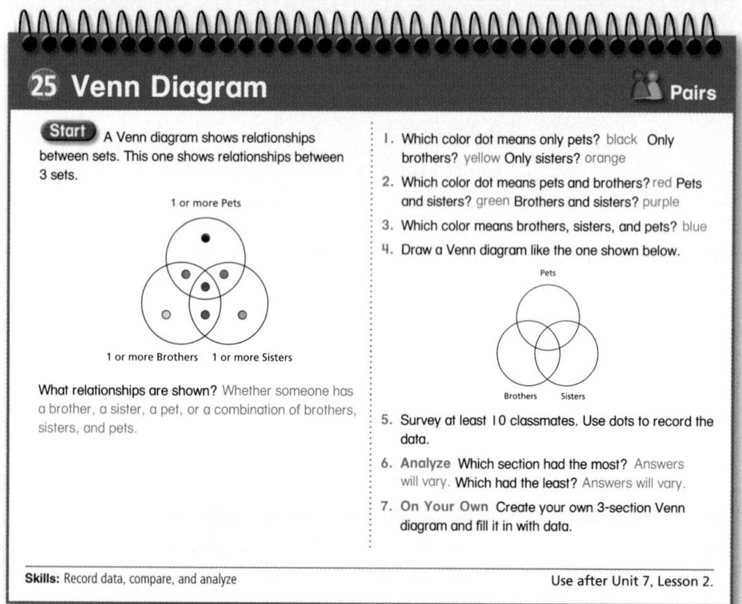

25 Venn Diagram — Pairs

Start A Venn diagram shows relationships between sets. This one shows relationships between 3 sets.

What relationships are shown? Whether someone has a brother, a sister, a pet, or a combination of brothers, sisters, and pets.

1. Which color dot means only pets? black Only brothers? yellow Only sisters? orange
2. Which color dot means pets and brothers? red Pets and sisters? green Brothers and sisters? purple
3. Which color means brothers, sisters, and pets? blue
4. Draw a Venn diagram like the one shown below.

5. Survey at least 10 classmates. Use dots to record the data.
6. Analyze Which section had the most? Answers will vary. Which had the least? Answers will vary.
7. On Your Own Create your own 3-section Venn diagram and fill it in with data.

Skills: Record data, compare, and analyze — Use after Unit 7, Lesson 2.

Grouping Pairs

Materials None

Objective Children analyze a Venn diagram and then create one on their own.

Connections Data and Representation

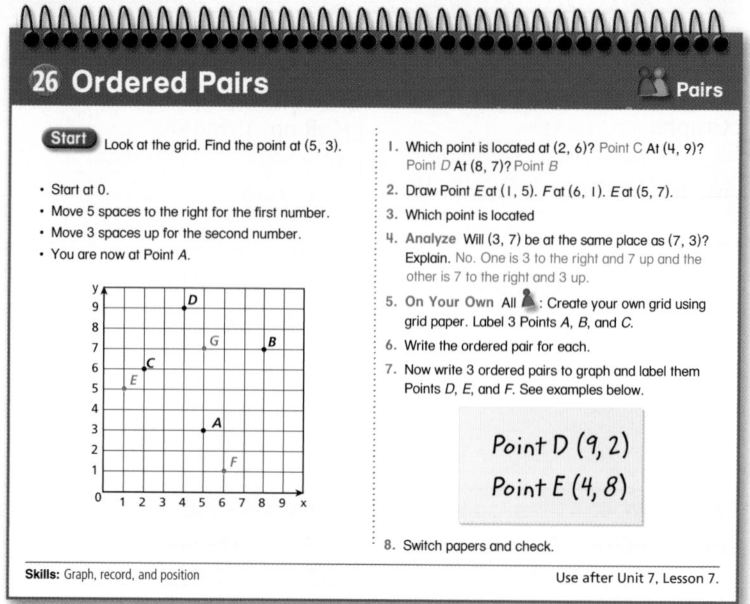

26 Ordered Pairs — Pairs

Start Look at the grid. Find the point at (5, 3).

- Start at 0.
- Move 5 spaces to the right for the first number.
- Move 3 spaces up for the second number.
- You are now at Point *A*.

1. Which point is located at (2, 6)? Point C At (4, 9)? Point *D* At (8, 7)? Point *B*
2. Draw Point *E* at (1, 5). *F* at (6, 1). *E* at (5, 7).
3. Which point is located
4. Analyze Will (3, 7) be at the same place as (7, 3)? Explain. No. One is 3 to the right and 7 up and the other is 7 to the right and 3 up.
5. On Your Own All: Create your own grid using grid paper. Label 3 Points *A*, *B*, and *C*.
6. Write the ordered pair for each.
7. Now write 3 ordered pairs to graph and label them Points *D*, *E*, and *F*. See examples below.

8. Switch papers and check.

Skills: Graph, record, and position — Use after Unit 7, Lesson 7.

Grouping Pairs

Materials 10 × 10 Grid Paper (M62)

Objective Children identify points for ordered pairs on a coordinate grid and will identify ordered pairs for points on a coordinate grid.

Connections Data and Representation

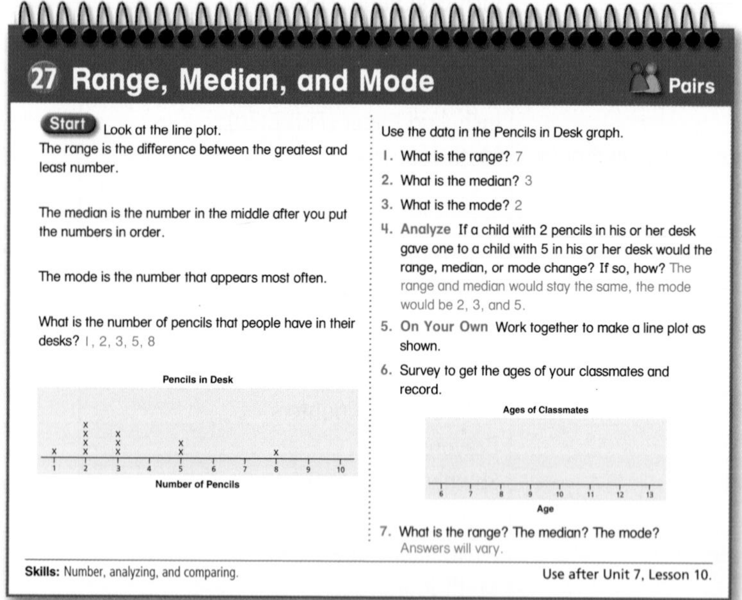

27 Range, Median, and Mode — Pairs

Start Look at the line plot.

The range is the difference between the greatest and least number.

The median is the number in the middle after you put the numbers in order.

The mode is the number that appears most often.

What is the number of pencils that people have in their desks? 1, 2, 3, 5, 8

Use the data in the Pencils in Desk graph.

1. What is the range? 7
2. What is the median? 3
3. What is the mode? 2
4. Analyze If a child with 2 pencils in his or her desk gave one to a child with 5 in his or her desk would the range, median, or mode change? If so, how? The range and median would stay the same, the mode would be 2, 3, and 5.
5. On Your Own Work together to make a line plot as shown.
6. Survey to get the ages of your classmates and record.

7. What is the range? The median? The mode? Answers will vary.

Skills: Number, analyzing, and comparing. — Use after Unit 7, Lesson 10.

Grouping Pairs

Materials None

Objective Children identify the range, median, and mode of a given set of data and then repeat with data they collect and record on their own.

Connections Data and Representation

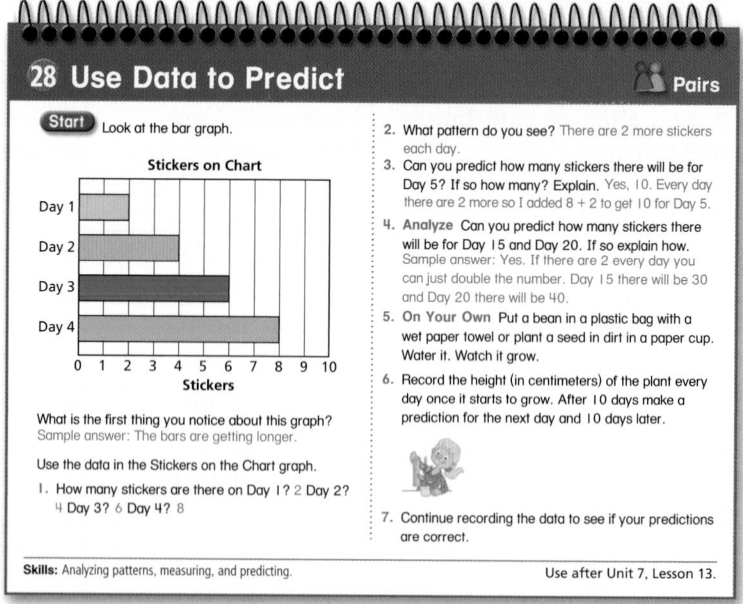

28 Use Data to Predict — Pairs

Start Look at the bar graph.

What is the first thing you notice about this graph? Sample answer: The bars are getting longer.

Use the data in the Stickers on the Chart graph.

1. How many stickers are there on Day 1? 2 Day 2? 4 Day 3? 6 Day 4? 8
2. What pattern do you see? There are 2 more stickers each day.
3. Can you predict how many stickers there will be for Day 5? If so how many? Explain. Yes, 10. Every day there are 2 more so I added 8 + 2 to get 10 for Day 5.
4. Analyze Can you predict how many stickers there will be for Day 15 and Day 20. If so explain how. Sample answer: Yes. If there are 2 every day you can just double the number. Day 15 there will be 30 and Day 20 there will be 40.
5. On Your Own Put a bean in a plastic bag with a wet paper towel or plant a seed in dirt in a paper cup. Water it. Watch it grow.
6. Record the height (in centimeters) of the plant every day once it starts to grow. After 10 days make a prediction for the next day and 10 days later.
7. Continue recording the data to see if your predictions are correct.

Skills: Analyzing patterns, measuring, and predicting. — Use after Unit 7, Lesson 13.

Grouping Pairs

Materials Bean, plastic bag, and paper towel or paper cup, dirt, and seed; centimeter ruler

Objective Children analyze patterns to make predictions from given data and data students collect.

Connections Data and Measurement

Ready-Made Math Resources

Technology — Tutorials, Practice, and Intervention

Use activity masters and online, individualized intervention and support to bring students to proficiency.

Help students practice skills and apply concepts through exciting math adventures.

Extend and enrich students' understanding of skills and concepts through engaging, interactive lessons and activities.

Visit **Education Place®**
www.eduplace.com

Visit www.eduplace.com/mx2t/ and find family, teacher, and student materials, activities, games, and more.

Literature Links

Fair is Fair

Fair is Fair

Marco sets out to prove his three-dollar allowance isn't fair when compared to that which classmates receive, and his proof is documented in graphs! What father wouldn't be impressed!

Literature Connections

Tiger Math: Learning to Graph from a Baby Tiger, by Ann Whitehead Nagda and Cindy Bickel (Henry Holt and Company, 2000)

Unit 7 Teaching Resources

Differentiated Instruction

Individualizing Instruction		
Activities	**Level**	**Frequency**
	• Intervention • On Level • Challenge	All 3 in every lesson
Math Writing Prompts	**Level**	**Frequency**
	• Intervention • On Level • Challenge	All 3 in every lesson
Math Center Challenges	**For advanced students**	
	4 in every unit	

Reaching All Learners		
English Language Learners	**Lessons**	**Pages**
	1, 2, 3, 4, 5, 6, 7, 8, 9, 10, 11, 12, 13, 14, 15	489, 494, 500, 506, 512, 518, 522, 529, 534, 535, 541, 546, 547, 553, 559, 565
Extra Help	**Lesson**	**Page**
	10	540
Advanced Learners	**Lesson**	**Page**
	523	

Strategies for English Language Learners

Present this problem to all children. Offer the different levels of support to meet children's levels of language proficiency.

Objective To compare quantities of two groups

Problem Give children 6 red and 4 blue cubes. Ask: **How many red cubes are there?** 6 **Blue cubes?** 4 **How many groups of cubes are there?** 2 **What are the groups?** red, blue

Newcomer

- Have children count the number of cubes in each group. Say: **Let's count the red/blue group.**

Beginning

- Point and say: **There are 2 groups. There are 6 cubes in the red group and 4 cubes in the blue group.** Have children repeat.
- Line the cubes up to compare them. Say: **There are 2 more red cubes than blue cubes.** Have children repeat.

Intermediate

- Point to the groups. Ask: **How many groups are there?** 2 **What are they?** red, blue **How many cubes are in the red group?** 6 **The blue group?** 4
- Guide children to line up the cubes to compare them. Ask: **Which group has more cubes?** red **How many more red cubes are there than blue cubes?** 2

Advanced

- Have children explain how the cubes can be grouped.
- Have children tell about how to compare the groups.

Connections

Art Connection
Lesson 5, page 516

Language Arts Connection
Lesson 7, page 526

Physical Education Connection
Lesson 14, page 568

Real-World Connections
Lesson 2, page 498
Lesson 10, page 544
Lesson 11, page 550
Lesson 15, page 574
Lesson 16, page 580

Science Connections
Lesson 3, page 504
Lesson 8, page 532
Lesson 9, page 538
Lesson 13, page 562

Sports Connection
Lesson 4, page 510

Technology Connection
Lesson 6, page 520

Literature Connection
Lesson 12, page 556

Math Background

Putting Research into Practice for Unit 7

From Our Curriculum Research Project: Tables and Graphs

The goal of this unit is for children to describe, organize, and represent data in tables and graphs. Children are introduced to the concept that some information, whether it be written or spoken, can be shown in a visual way. When presented as a graph, the information becomes readily accessible to children because they can study the relationships of the quantities depicted, either as parts of a whole or as separate entities to compare.

Children learn how to read picture graphs, tables, and bar and circle graphs, and they answer questions about them. They create picture graphs, tables, and bar graphs. They also consider the advantages and disadvantages of each form of data presentation.

–Karen Fuson, Author
Math Expressions

From Current Research: Statistics and Learning to Use Data

Processes like organizing data and conventions like labeling and scaling are crucial to data representation and are strongly connected to the concepts and processes of measurement. Given the difficulties students experience, instruction might need to differentiate these processes and conventions more sharply. Fundamental concepts . . . such as the conventions of scaling in graphs . . . need more careful attention in initial instruction.

National Research Council. "Developing Proficiency with Whole Numbers." *Adding It Up: Helping Students Learn Mathematics.* Washington, D.C.: National Academy Press, 2001. 288–294.

Other Useful References: Tables and Graphs

Jones, G.A., C.A. Thornton, C.W. Langrall, E.S Mooney, B. Perry, and I.J. Putt. "A Framework for Characterizing Children's Statistical Thinking." *Mathematical Thinking and Learning,* 2 (2000): 269–307.

Jones, G.A., C.A. Thornton, C.W. Langrall, E.S. Mooney, A. Wares, B. Perry, and I.J. Putt. "Using Students' Statistical Thinking to Inform Instruction." *Paper presented at the research pre-session of the meeting of the National Council of Teachers of Mathematics,* San Francisco. 1999.

Mullis, I.V.S., M.O. Martin, A.E. Beaton, E.J. Gonzalez, D.L. Kelly, and T.A. Smith. "Mathematics Achievement in the Primary School Years." *IEA's Third International Mathematics and Science Study* (TIMSS). Chestnut Hill, MA: Boston College, 1997.

Zawojewski, J.S., and D.S. Heckman. "What Do Students Know About Data Analysis, Statistics, and Probability?" *Results from the Sixth Mathematics Assessment of the National Assessment of Educational Progress,* Eds. P.A. Kenney & E.A. Silver. Reston, VA: National Council of Teachers of Mathematics, 1997. 195–223.

Getting Ready to Teach Unit 7

Throughout the unit, children will represent information in the form of pictures, numbers, and bars, as they create graphs and tables. They will be able to see that the same information can be shown in different ways—one important aspect of representation. As they work with various types of graphs, children continue to develop their skills with comparison situations and use them to solve problems.

Picture Graphs
Lessons 1, 2, 6, 7, and 14

Children begin learning how to make a picture graph by drawing one circle to represent each penny that two friends in a story problem have. Children learn how to label their graphs with the first initial of the friends' names and how to give the graph a title. Children then pose and answer questions about the data in the graph. Organizing information into a graph and describing the information are key processes in learning to work with data.

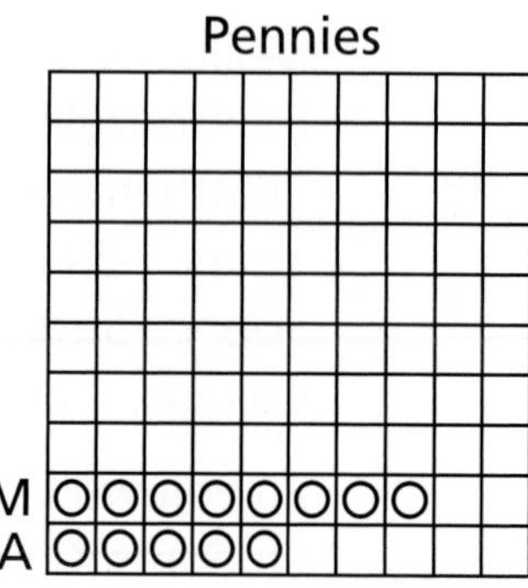

Using Comparison Language
Lessons 3, 4, 13, and 14

Children solve comparison problems depicted in picture graphs. They use the comparative terms *same, more,* and *fewer,* as well as the >, <, and = symbols, to compare the information in the graphs. Because the pictures in the rows or columns of a picture graph are aligned, they can be easily compared to find how many more or how many fewer items would equalize the groups.

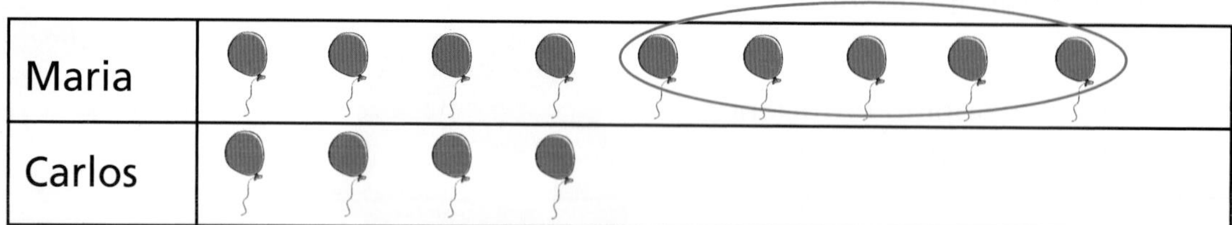

Maria has 5 more balloons than Carlos.
Carlos has 5 fewer balloons than Maria.
Carlos needs 5 balloons to have as many as Maria.

Introducing Tables
Lessons 5, 6, 7, 14, and 15

Children will construct tables with rows, columns, headings, and numbers. Children will see how they can easily compare information when it is organized into a table. They will also have an opportunity to convert tables to picture graphs and pose and answer questions about all of these data formats.

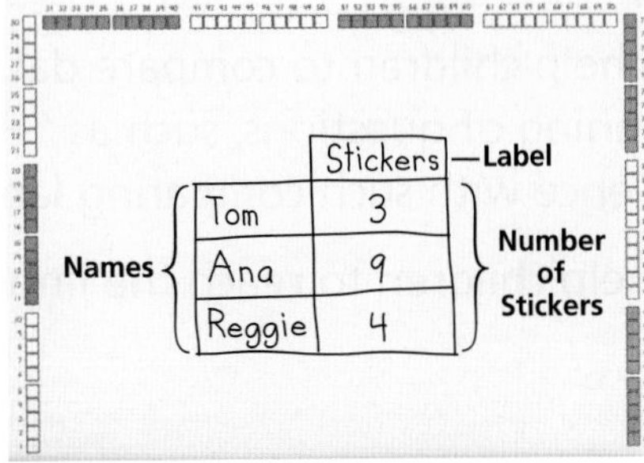

Bar Graphs
Lessons 8, 9, 10, 13, 14, and 15

Children move from picture graphs to bar graphs as they learn to convert a picture graph to a bar graph by shading the squares that have pictures in them. They change the numerical scale to the number line length model with numbers at the end of each square telling how many so far.

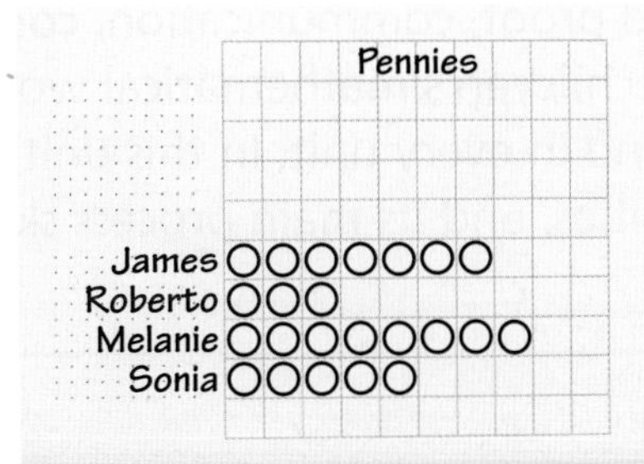

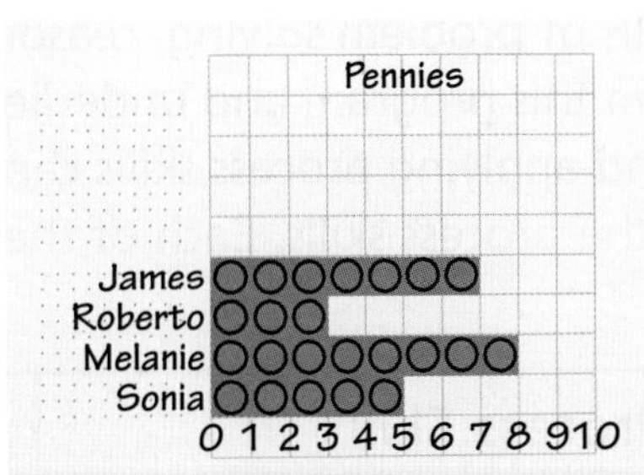

Children will read information in bar graphs and pose and solve problems using information in the bar graphs. They will use bar graphs in both horizontal and vertical form.

Circle Graphs
Lessons 11, 12, and 14

Children learn how parts of a circle and the size of the parts can represent different information and values. They complete a circle graph using information from a bar graph. They compare bar graphs and circle graphs and find how each can be used for different purposes.

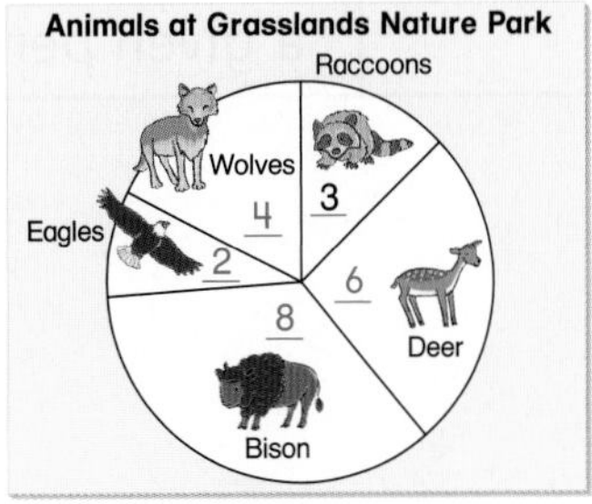

Class Data Project
Lessons 1, 2, and 7

Children will also be involved in a class project in which they will gather, organize, and display data. As the children decide how to display the data in a graph, they will develop their judgment about best ways to represent information. Meanwhile, children will learn graphing conventions, such as how to label and make a scale so that others can understand the data.

Representing information in graphs will also help children to compare data easily. Seeing the information in a visual way helps children understand the meaning of questions, such as "How many more?" and "How many fewer?" Children have a great deal of experience with such comparing language in this unit.

This systematic focus on representation can help children to reach the important mathematical goal of learning to use data.

Problem Solving
In *Math Expressions* a research-based, algebraic problem-solving approach that focuses on problem types is used: understand the situation, represent the situation with a math drawing or an equation, solve the problem, and see that the answer makes sense. Throughout the unit, children solve a variety of problems using the graphing and comparison skills being taught in this unit.

Using Mathematical Processes
Lessons 16

The mathematical process skills of problem solving, reasoning and proof, communication, connections, and representation are pervasive in this program and underlie all the children's mathematical work. Lessons that concentrate on developing and applying process skills can be found in every unit. In this unit, Lesson 16 has activities that focus on all of the process skills. Each of these activities, and its main process skill and goal, are listed below.

Activity	Process Skill	Goal
Math and Art	Connections	Use paper folding to explore symmetry in shapes.
Are Survey Results Always the Same?	Problem Solving	Observe that data collected from different populations may vary.
Predict and Verify	Reasoning and Proof	Make and check a prediction.
Lupe's Painting	Representation	Make and support a statement about a problem with multiple solutions.
How to Make a Square	Communication	Give directions for generating a square with a given perimeter.

Introduce Picture Graphs

Lesson Objectives

- Construct and interpret picture graphs.
- Plan a data collection project.

Vocabulary

picture graph	less
scale	vertical
fewer	data
tally marks	

The Day at a Glance

Today's Goals	Materials	
1 Teaching the Lesson **A1:** Construct and interpret picture graphs. **A2:** Plan a data collection project.	**Lesson Activities** Student Activity Book pp. 219–220 (includes Family Letter) Homework and Remembering pp. 139–140 MathBoard materials or 10 × 10 Grid (TRB M62) Real or play money Large piece of paper or posterboard	**Going Further** Activity Cards 7-1 Index cards Shoes Chart paper Construction paper Tape Math Journals
2 Going Further ▸ Differentiated Instruction		
3 Homework and Targeted Practice		

Use Math Talk today!

Keeping Skills Sharp

Quick Practice 5 MINUTES

Goal: Practice addition with teen totals.

Materials: Green Make-a-Ten Cards (addition) (from Unit 1 Lesson 13 or TRB M35-M38)

Make-a-Ten Cards: Addition Have children practice addition with teen totals using the Green Make-a-Ten Cards. Children look at the front of the card and say the answer to themselves and then turn over the card to check their answer. (If they miss an answer, they should look at the small numbers and dots on the back of the card to see how making a ten can help them find the teen total.) (See Unit 1 Lesson 13.)

Daily Routines

Telling Time Naming the Hands, Telling Time on the Time Poster (See pp. xxv–xxvi.)

▸ Led by Student Leaders

Money Routine Using the 120 Poster, Using the Money Flip Chart, Using the Number Path, Using Secret Code Cards (See pp. xxiii–xxv.)

▸ Led by Student Leaders

1 Teaching the Lesson

Activity 1

Introduce Picture Graphs

 40 MINUTES

Goals: Construct and interpret picture graphs.

Materials: MathBoard materials or 10 × 10 Grid (TRB M62), real or play money (13 pennies), blank transparency (optional)

 **NCTM Standards:**
Data Analysis and Probability
Number and Operations
Communication

 **Class Management**

You may wish to make a transparency of a blank 10 ×10 grid for use with an overhead projector. You can then use the transparency to show children how to draw the picture graphs. Otherwise you can make simple sketches on a child's MathBoard or on the classroom board (without grid lines).

Teaching Note

Math Background In this unit, children make picture graphs using very simple drawings. Some picture graphs use more detailed pictures and may use pictures that are not all the same.

Picture graphs do not usually have numbers. Numbers are used in this program to create a bridge from picture graphs to bar graphs.

▶ Activate Prior Knowledge WHOLE CLASS

Ask for Ideas Explain to the class that they are beginning a unit on graphs. Draw this web graphic organizer on the board or on chart paper and ask children to brainstorm what they already know about graphs.

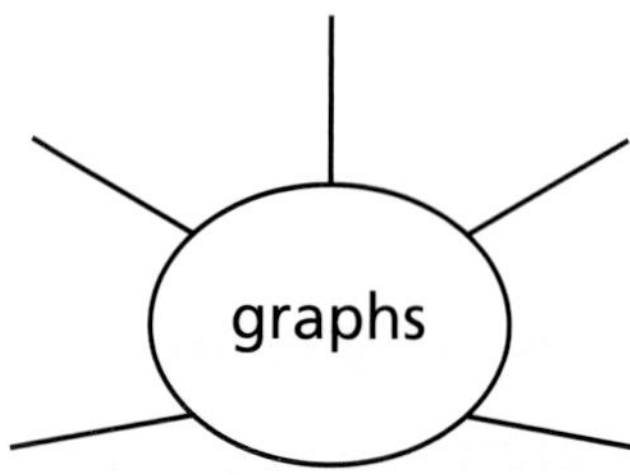

Activating prior knowledge is especially helpful for **English Learners**. You may wish to keep this model posted throughout the unit. Picture graphs are the first type of graphs introduced.

▶ Record Information Using a Picture Graph

WHOLE CLASS

Have children turn their MathBoards so the 10 × 10 Grid is at the bottom as shown. If MathBoards are unavailable, use the 10 × 10 Grid (TRB M62).

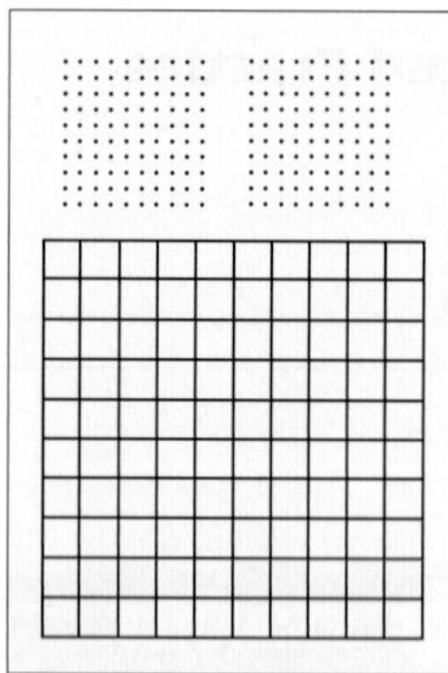

Give 8 pennies to one child (Maya) and 5 pennies to another child (Anthony). Then invite the class to record this by making a graph on their MathBoards. Have children hold up their MathBoards so that their classmates can see them. Discuss which drawings best represent all the information given. (Children's graphs may vary depending upon their prior experience with graphing.)

Formalize what children have done on their own by introducing the picture graph as a way to represent information.

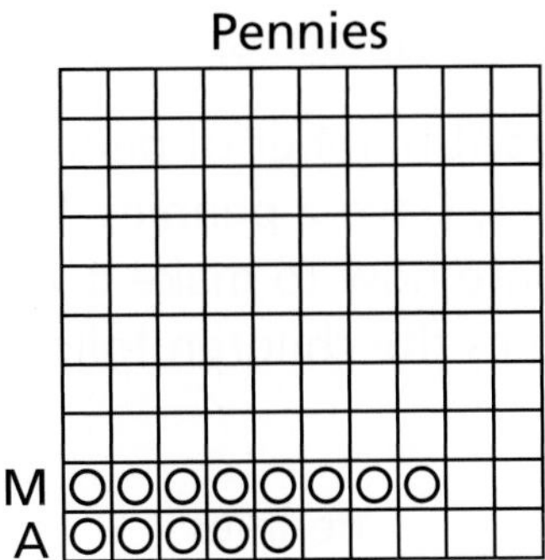

Be sure that children label their own graphs as you draw the graph shown.

- We can use a picture graph to show that Maya has 8 pennies and Anthony has 5 pennies.
- We can write the initials of the children on the left side. *Write "M" and "A" as shown.*
- We can draw the pennies that each one has. *Draw the pennies.* Then we can give the graph a title: "Pennies." *Write the title at the top.*

▶ Ask Questions About Picture Graphs

WHOLE CLASS

Math Talk 

Invite volunteers to ask questions about information in the picture graph. Have the class answer the questions. Then invite children who are holding the pennies to rephrase the answers from their own point of view. See the examples of children's questions and responses below.

- Who has more pennies? Maya *Invite Maya to say, "I have more pennies than Anthony."*
- Who has fewer pennies? Anthony *Invite Anthony to say, "I have fewer pennies than Maya."*
- How many more pennies does Maya have than Anthony? 3 pennies *Invite Maya to say, "I have 3 more pennies than Anthony."*
- How many fewer pennies does Anthony have than Maya? 3 pennies *Invite Anthony to say, "I have 3 fewer pennies than Maya."*
- How many pennies do Maya and Anthony have together? 13 pennies *Invite both children to say, "We have 13 pennies together."*
- I'm going to give one child (Jenny) 7 pennies and another child (Rosa) 3 pennies. Let's show this on our graphs.

If children spontaneously ask equalizing questions such as, "How many more pennies must Anthony get to have as many as Maya?" you may have children answer them as they are able. Questions of this type will be introduced in Lesson 3, which discusses the language of comparisons.

Activity continued ▶

Teaching Note

Language and Vocabulary
Understanding the distinction between *fewer* and *less* is difficult for many people. Instead of attempting to teach the children the difference between the two words, model correct use of these words as much as possible. The important thing at this point is to make sure children are familiar with both words.

As a rule, the word *fewer* is used with plurals or things that can be itemized: *fewer words, fewer hats,* or *fewer grapes. Less* is used for singular words and words that represent entities such as: *less* money, *less* trust, or *less* imagination.

There are also a few conventions governing the use of less.

- ▶ Use *less* when the difference is only one: I have one *less* book than you do.
- ▶ Use *less* with "bare" numbers: 23 is *less* than 28.
- ▶ Use *less* for money amounts: 25 dollars is *less* than 30 dollars.

English Language Learners

Draw 4 As, 3 Bs, and 2 Cs. Write *fewer* and *less*.

- **Beginning** Say: **There is 1 *less* B than As. There are 2 *fewer* Cs than As.** Have children repeat.
- **Intermediate** Say: **There is 1 *less* B than A.** Ask: **Is there 1 *less* C than Bs?** no Say: **There are 2 *fewer* Cs than Bs.**
- **Advanced** Have children use *less* and *fewer* to describe the number of As, Bs, and Cs.

1 Teaching the Lesson (continued)

► Draw a Vertical Picture Graph WHOLE CLASS

Have children erase their MathBoards. Then tell children that they will draw the graph a different way. Explain that it will be a vertical graph. It will go up and down rather than across.

Give four children a different number of pennies less than 10. For example, give Pat 4 pennies, Dave 2 pennies, Lloyd 5 pennies, and Carla 9 pennies. Then demonstrate how to make a vertical picture graph to represent the information as the children follow along making their own graphs.

Pennies

			O
			O
			O
			O
		O	O
O		O	O
O		O	O
O	O	O	O
O	O	O	O
P	D	L	C

Ongoing Assessment

After children have made their vertical picture graphs, ask questions such as

- ► Who has the most pennies?
- ► Who has the least pennies?
- ► How many pennies do Pat and Dave have altogether?
- ► How many more pennies does Carla have than Lloyd?

Activity 2

Data Collection Project

 10 MINUTES

Goal: Plan a data collection project.

Materials: large piece of paper or poster board

 **NCTM Standards:**
Data Analysis
Number and Operations
Communication

► Explain the Data Collection Project WHOLE CLASS

Tell children that for the next few days they will collect information for a given purpose. Today they will create and plan a survey in order to collect the information. Then after they have collected all the information they will make a picture graph to display the information.

- The first thing we need to do is to think about what our picture graph will show.
- We want something in our picture graph that is interesting to us. It should be fun to talk about. What do you think we should show in our graph?

Have children decide on a subject for their data collection project. Some suggestions to spark discussion are: favorite colors, favorite foods, favorite games, or favorite animals. Write the chosen topic on the board or on a large piece of paper or poster board. Then tell children that they will begin working on the data collection project in the next lesson.

 **Class Management**

As children collect the information over the next few days, you may wish to keep the findings posted prominently on the board or on a large piece of paper or poster board. They will be using this information to make a picture graph in Lesson 7.

2 Going Further

Differentiated Instruction

Intervention — Activity Card 7-1

It's a Shoe-In — Activity Card 7-1

Work: 

Use:

- 14 index cards
- 1 shoe for each child

Choose:

1. On separate index cards, write *Lace, Slip-On, Other,* and *Our Shoes.*
2. On other index cards, write 1-10 on separate cards.
3. Use the index cards to set up a picture graph on the floor or on a table.
4. Work with other groups. Each takes off one shoe. Place it on the right row on the graph.
5. Ask one question about the graph.
6. Answer the question using the graph. Take turns.

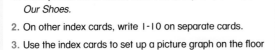

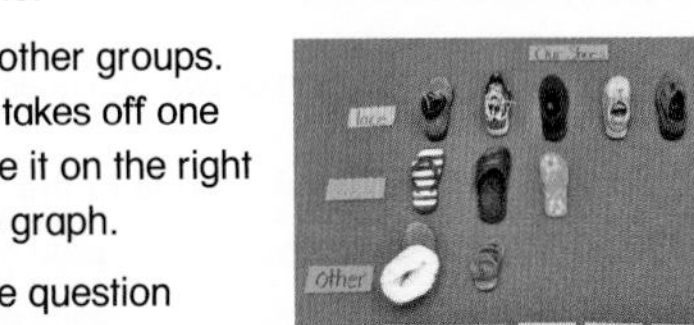

Unit 7, Lesson 1 — Copyright © Houghton Mifflin Company

Activity Note Each group needs 14 index cards and one shoe per child. Discuss with children how to set up the graph. You may want to have the whole class help make the graph.

Math Writing Prompt

Draw It Draw a picture graph that shows that Ron has 3 books and Mario has 5 books.

Software Support

Use *Soar to Success* for instruction of students needing targeted support for underlying skills.

On Level — Activity Card 7-1

Make a Picture Graph — Activity Card 7-1

Work: 

Use:

- chart paper
- construction paper
- tape

Choose:

1. **Work Together** Make a graph on the chart paper. The title is *Favorite Subject.* Along the left side, use the subjects *Reading, Math,* and *Science.*
2. Make 10-12 smiley faces on the construction paper. Cut the smiley faces out.
3. Ask your group and other groups which is their favorite subject. Tape a smiley face for each choice.
4. Take turns asking and answering questions about the picture graph.

Unit 7, Lesson 1 — Copyright © Houghton Mifflin Company

Activity Note Each group needs chart paper, construction paper, and tape. Help groups set up their picture graph. You may want to have groups work together.

Math Writing Prompt

More Than One Answer Draw a picture graph that matches this statement. Henry has 2 more books than Antonio.

Software Support

Use *MegaMath* for review and reinforcement of the concepts and skills presented in this lesson.

Challenge — Activity Card 7-1

What's for Lunch? — Activity Card 7-1

Work: 

Use:

- MathBoard or 10 × 10 Grid

Choose:

1. **Work Together** Ask classmates which sandwich they like most. Give three choices such as turkey, cheese, and peanut butter and jelly or any sandwiches your friends like.
2. Make tally marks to show each choice.
3. Use the tally marks to make a picture graph.
4. Write two questions about the graph for others to answer.
5. Try and answer other's questions.

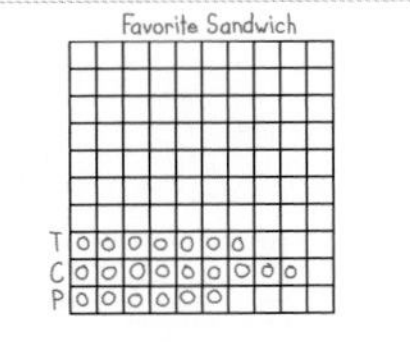

Unit 7, Lesson 1 — Copyright © Houghton Mifflin Company

Activity Note Each group needs MathBoard materials or 10 × 10 grid (TRB M62).

Math Writing Prompt

Stretch Your Thinking Draw a picture graph that matches these statements. Jamie has 3 more books than Arlene. Vince has 5 fewer books than Jamie. Brad has 2 more books than Arlene.

DESTINATION Math® **Software Support**

Use *Destination Math* to take students beyond the concepts and skills presented in this lesson.

③ Homework and Targeted Practice

7-1 **Homework** **Goal:** Additional Practice

This Homework page provides practice in reading picture graphs.

7-1 Name ______________________

Homework

Use the picture graph to answer the questions.

Book Sales

Peter									
Tammy									
Shana									

1. Who sold the most books? Shana
2. Who sold the fewest books? Tammy
3. How many more books did Shana sell than Tammy?
   5 more books
   label
4. How many fewer books did Peter sell than Shana?
   4 fewer books
   label
5. How many more books did Peter sell than Tammy?
   1 more book
   label
6. How many books did the children sell altogether?
   18 books
   label
7. **Write Your Own** Write and solve your own question about the graph.
   Answers will vary.

UNIT 7 LESSON 1 Introduce Picture Graphs **139**

Homework and Remembering page 139

7-1 **Targeted Practice** **Goal:** Read picture graphs

This Targeted Practice page can be used with children who need extra practice reading picture graphs.

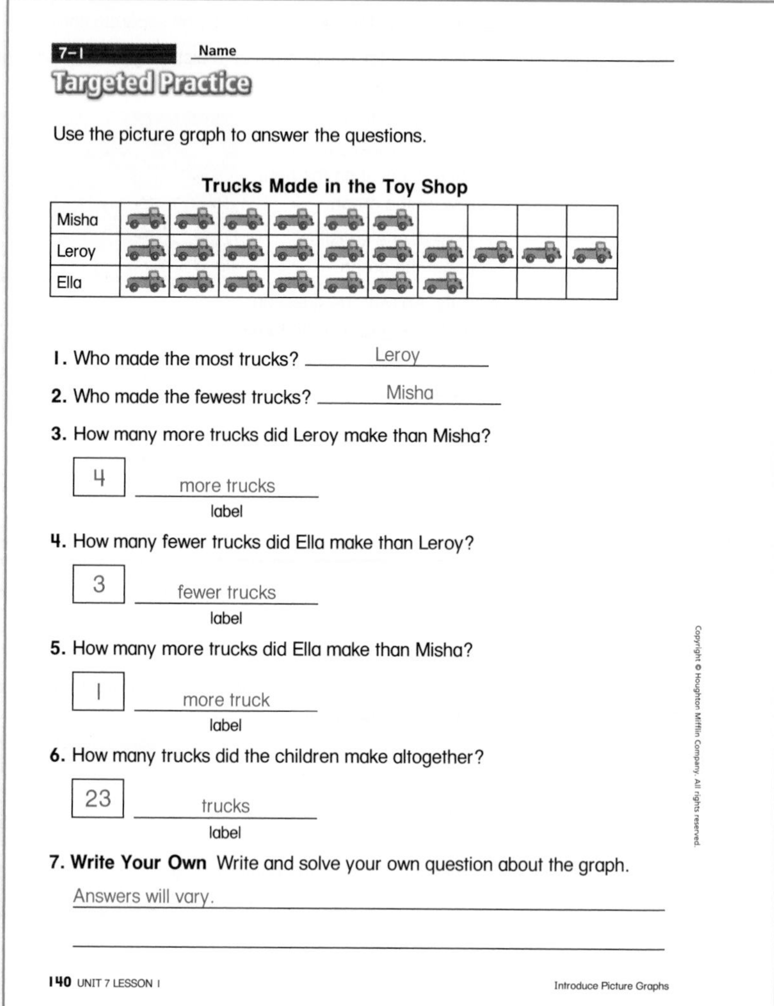

7-1 Name ______________________

Targeted Practice

Use the picture graph to answer the questions.

Trucks Made in the Toy Shop

Misha										
Leroy										
Ella										

1. Who made the most trucks? Leroy
2. Who made the fewest trucks? Misha
3. How many more trucks did Leroy make than Misha?
   4 more trucks
   label
4. How many fewer trucks did Ella make than Leroy?
   3 fewer trucks
   label
5. How many more trucks did Ella make than Misha?
   1 more truck
   label
6. How many trucks did the children make altogether?
   23 trucks
   label
7. **Write Your Own** Write and solve your own question about the graph.
   Answers will vary.

140 UNIT 7 LESSON 1 Introduce Picture Graphs

Homework and Remembering page 140

Home or School Connection

Family Letter Have children take home the Family Letter on Student Activity Book page 219. This letter explains how the concept of reading and creating graphs is developed in *Math Expressions.* It gives parents and guardians a better understanding of the learning that goes on in math class and creates a bridge between school and home. A Spanish translation of this letter is on the following page in the Student Activity Book.

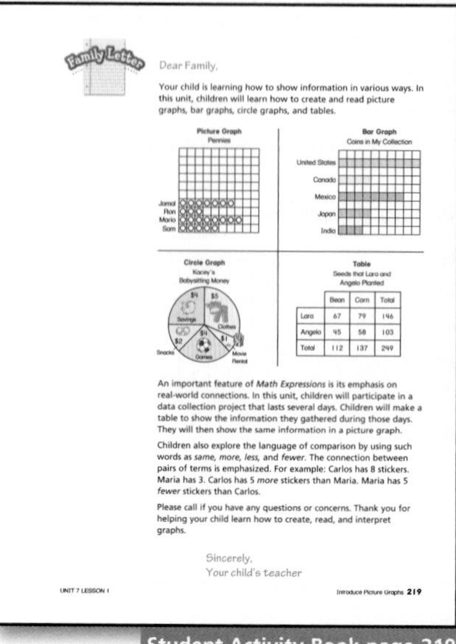

Family Letter

Dear Family,

Your child is learning how to show information in various ways. In this unit, children will learn how to create and read picture graphs, bar graphs, circle graphs, and tables.

Picture Graph Pennies — Jamal, Ron, Mario, Sam

Bar Graph Coins in My Collection — United States, Canada, Mexico, Japan, India

Circle Graph Kacey's Babysitting Money — $4 Savings, $5 Clothes, $1 Movie Rental, $4 Games, $2 Snacks

Table Seeds that Lara and Angelo Planted

	Bean	Corn	Total
Lara	67	79	146
Angelo	45	58	103
Total	112	137	249

An important feature of *Math Expressions* is its emphasis on real-world connections. In this unit, children will participate in a data collection project that lasts several days. Children will make a table to show the information they gathered during those days. They will then show the same information in a picture graph.

Children also explore the language of comparison by using such words as *same, more, less,* and *fewer.* The connection between pairs of terms is emphasized. For example: Carlos has 8 stickers. Maria has 3. Carlos has 5 *more* stickers than Maria. Maria has 5 *fewer* stickers than Carlos.

Please call if you have any questions or concerns. Thank you for helping your child learn how to create, read, and interpret graphs.

Sincerely,
Your child's teacher

UNIT 7 LESSON 1 Introduce Picture Graphs **219**

Student Activity Book page 219

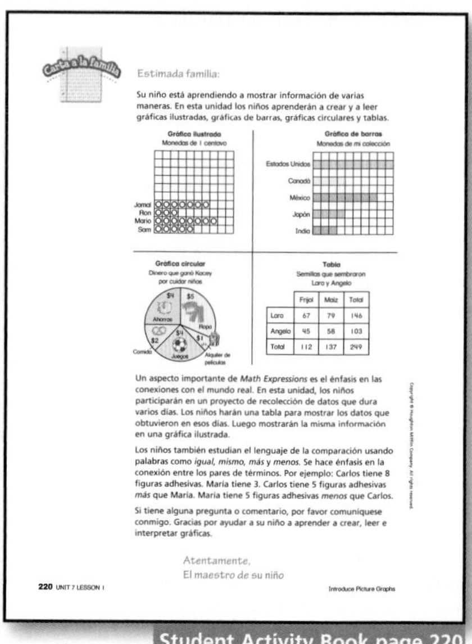

Carta a la familia

Estimada familia:

Su niño está aprendiendo a mostrar información de varias maneras. En esta unidad los niños aprenderán a crear y a leer gráficas ilustradas, gráficas de barras, gráficas circulares y tablas.

Gráfica ilustrada Monedas de 1 centavo — Jamal, Ron, Mario, Sam

Gráfica de barras Monedas de mi colección — Estados Unidos, Canadá, México, Japón, India

Gráfica circular Dinero que ganó Kacey por cuidar niños — $4 Ahorros, $5 Ropa, $1 Alquiler de películas, $4 Juegos, $2 Comida

Tabla Semillas que sembraron Lara y Angelo

	Frijol	Maíz	Total
Lara	67	79	146
Angelo	45	58	103
Total	112	137	249

Un aspecto importante de *Math Expressions* es el énfasis en las conexiones con el mundo real. En esta unidad, los niños participarán en un proyecto de recolección de datos que dura varios días. Los niños harán una tabla para mostrar los datos que obtuvieron en esos días. Luego mostrarán la misma información en una gráfica ilustrada.

Los niños también estudian el lenguaje de la comparación usando palabras como *igual, mismo, más* y *menos.* Se hace énfasis en la conexión entre los pares de términos. Por ejemplo: Carlos tiene 8 figuras adhesivas. María tiene 3. Carlos tiene 5 figuras adhesivas *más* que María. María tiene 5 figuras adhesivas *menos* que Carlos.

Si tiene alguna pregunta o comentario, por favor comuníquese conmigo. Gracias por ayudar a su niño a aprender a crear, leer e interpretar gráficas.

Atentamente,
El maestro de su niño

220 UNIT 7 LESSON 1 Introduce Picture Graphs

Student Activity Book page 220

Read Picture Graphs

Lesson Objectives

- Analyze information in picture graphs to create and solve problems.
- Use the comparative terms *same*, *more*, and *fewer* to talk about information in picture graphs.
- Collect data for a class project.

Vocabulary

picture graph	tally
more	tally marks
fewer	key
data	

The Day at a Glance

Today's Goals	Materials	
1 Teaching the Lesson **A1:** Create and solve problems based on information in picture graphs. **A2:** Collect data for a class project. **2 Going Further** ▶ Math Connection: Pictographs ▶ Differentiated Instruction **3 Homework and Spiral Review**	**Lesson Activities** Student Activity Book p. 221 Homework and Remembering pp. 141–142 MathBoard materials or 10 × 10 Grid (TRB M62) Chart paper	**Going Further** Activity Cards 7-2 Student Activity Book p. 222 Sticky notes Reading book Connecting cubes Math Journals

Use Math Talk today!

Keeping Skills Sharp

Quick Practice — 5 MINUTES

Goal: Practice addition with teen totals.

Materials: Green Make-a-Ten Cards (addition) (from Unit 1 Lesson 13 or TRB M35–M38)

Teen Addition Flash Have a Student Leader call out two numbers that add up to a teen number. The class flashes 10 and ones to show the answer. (See Unit 5 Lesson 4.)

Make-a-Ten Cards: Addition Have children practice addition with teen totals using the Green Make-a-Ten Cards. (See Unit 7 Lesson 1.)

Daily Routines

Telling Time Naming the Hands, Telling Time on the Time Poster (See p. xxvii.)

▶ Led by teacher

Money Routine Using the 120 Poster, Using the Money Flip Chart, Using the Number Path, Using Secret Code Cards (See pp. xxiii–xxv.)

▶ Led by Student Leaders

1 Teaching the Lesson

Activity 1

Solve Story Problems from a Graph

 40 MINUTES

Goal: Create and solve problems based on information in picture graphs.

Materials: MathBoard materials or 10 × 10 Grid (TRB M62), Student Activity Book page 221

 **NCTM Standards:**
Data Analysis and Probability
Number and Operations
Communication

The Learning Classroom

Building Concepts Whenever possible, have children state the comparisons from both perspectives. For example:

- Ana has 5 more stickers than Reggie.
- Reggie has 5 fewer stickers than Ana.

English Language Learners

Show a horizontal graph. Say: **This is a *horizontal* graph. *Horizontal* means across.** Show a vertical graph.

- **Beginning** Say: **This is a *vertical* graph. *Vertical* means up and down.** Have children repeat.
- **Intermediate** Ask: **Is this a *horizontal* graph?** no Say: **This is a *vertical* graph.**
- **Advanced** Have children tell how *horizontal* and *vertical* graphs are different.

▶ Make Picture Graphs WHOLE CLASS

Write the information below on the board and read it aloud.

Tom has 3 stickers.
Ana has 9 stickers.
Reggie has 4 stickers.

Then challenge children to display the information in a graph, using their MathBoards or 10 × 10 Grid (TRB M62).

Half the class should make a horizontal graph while the other half makes a vertical graph to represent the data. (Children may use any picture to represent a sticker. The graphs below use circles.)

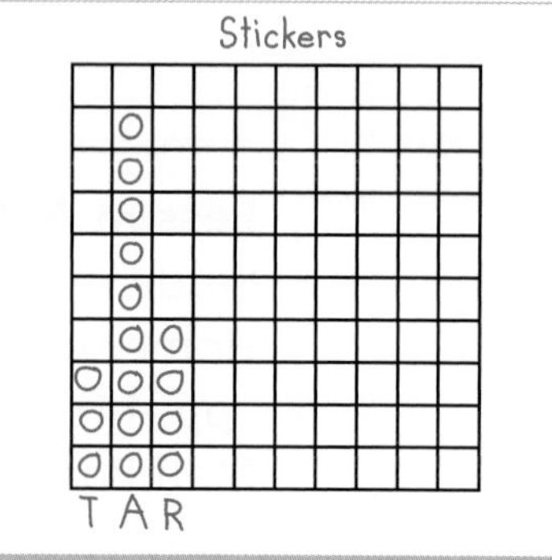

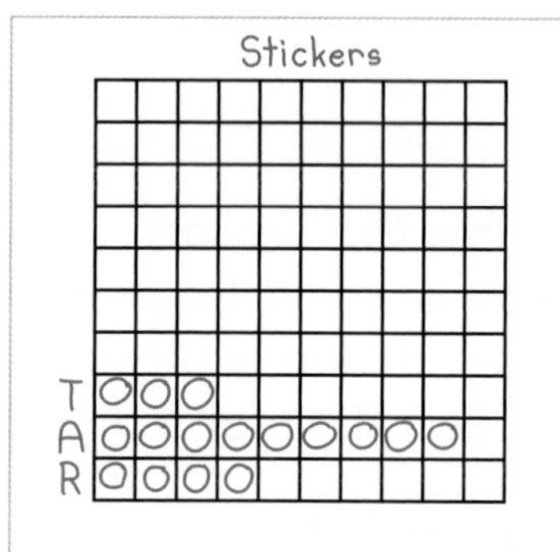

Then using two children's graphs as examples (one horizontal and one vertical), point out the information that should be displayed on the graphs.

- Here are the names or initials of the children at the bottom of the graph or the left side of the graph. *Indicate on the children's graphs.*
- Here are pictures to show the stickers each of the children have. *Indicate on the children's graphs.*
- Finally, here is the title for the graph. *Indicate on the children's graphs.*

Create and Solve Problems Review how to interpret graphs and ask questions as necessary. Then have children create and share story problems using information from the graph.

- How many more stickers does Ana have than Reggie? 5 more stickers
- How many fewer stickers does Tom have than Ana? 6 fewer stickers

Then have children discuss how to solve each problem. Encourage some children to take the roles of the children in the graph if they wish.

▶ Use Picture Graphs to Compare Amounts INDIVIDUALS

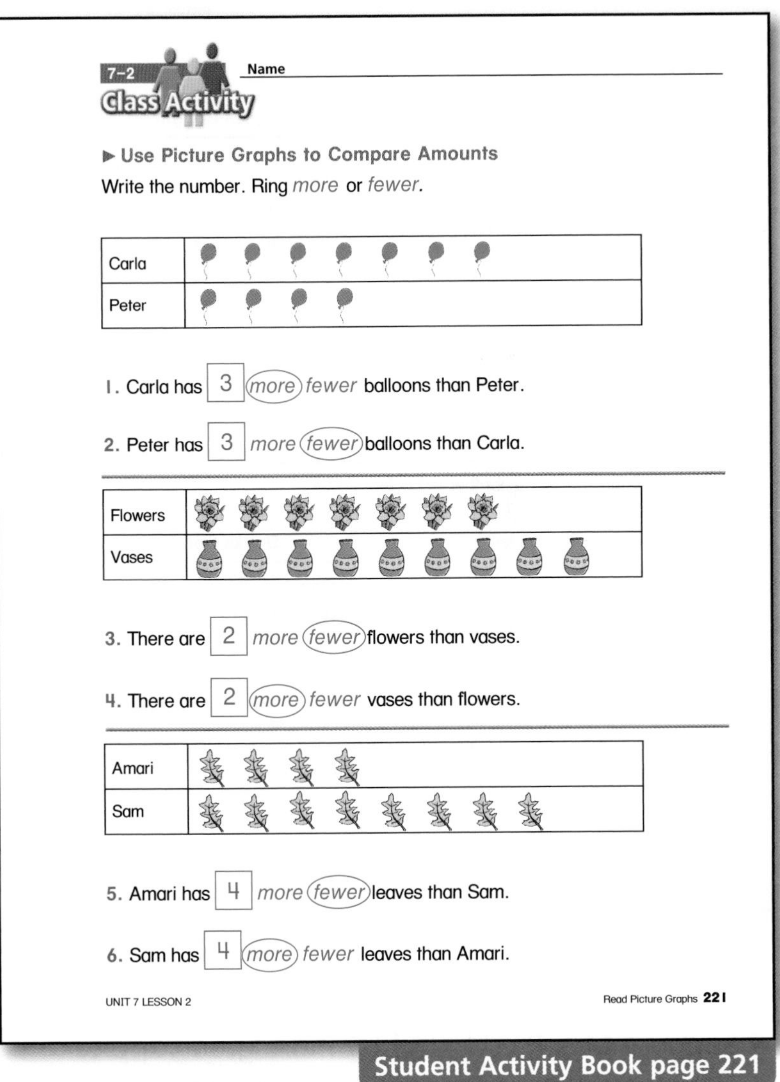
7-2 Class Activity

Name

▶ Use Picture Graphs to Compare Amounts

Write the number. Ring *more* or *fewer*.

Carla	7 balloons
Peter	4 balloons

1. Carla has 3 *more* *fewer* balloons than Peter. (more circled)
2. Peter has 3 *more* *fewer* balloons than Carla. (fewer circled)

Flowers	7 flowers
Vases	9 vases

3. There are 2 *more* *fewer* flowers than vases. (fewer circled)
4. There are 2 *more* *fewer* vases than flowers. (more circled)

Amari	4 leaves
Sam	8 leaves

5. Amari has 4 *more* *fewer* leaves than Sam. (fewer circled)
6. Sam has 4 *more* *fewer* leaves than Amari. (more circled)

UNIT 7 LESSON 2 Read Picture Graphs 221

Student Activity Book page 221

Ongoing Assessment

Circulate around the room while children complete Student Activity Book page 221. You may wish to have Student Leaders circulate as well. If anyone seems confused by a comparison problem, ask, "Who has more?" After that is established, children may find it easier to determine how many more or how many fewer.

Activity 2

Collect Data for a Class Project

Begin collecting data for a class project. You will collect data over a period of time and use the data in Lesson 7. The topic of favorite color is used here as an example.

Ask a third of the children to tell the class their favorite color. Record their answers with tally marks.

Favorite Color
Yellow |
Red ||
Green |
Blue ||||

15 MINUTES

Goal: Collect data for a class project.

Materials: chart paper

NCTM Standards:
Data Analysis and Probability
Communication

2 Going Further

Math Connection: Pictographs

Goal: Read and make a pictograph.

Materials: Student Activity Book page 222

NCTM Standards:
Data Analysis and Probabilty
Number and Operations
Communication

▶ Introduce Pictographs WHOLE CLASS

Draw the following pictograph on the board.

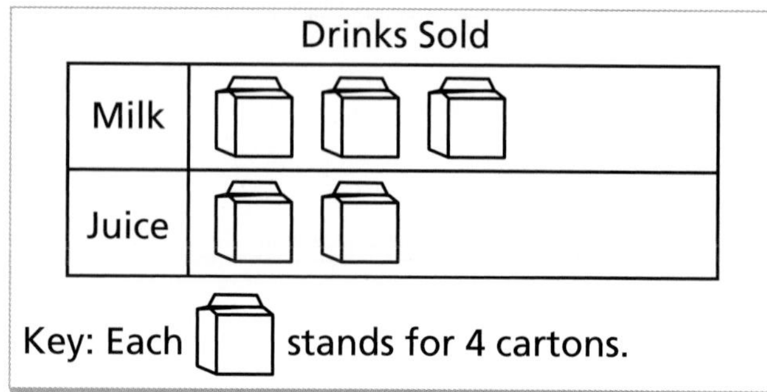

Ask for Ideas Elicit from the children how this graph is different from other picture graphs. Each symbol stands for 4 cartons. Explain the difference between picture graphs and pictographs. In a picture graph, each picture stands for 1. In pictographs, the symbol can stand for more than 1. So, it is important to read the key. Then ask questions such as the following:

- How much milk was sold? 12 cartons
- How much juice was sold? 8 cartons

Have children work independently to complete Student Activity Book page 222. Remind children that each symbol for the first graph equals 2 and each symbol for the second graph equals 5.

▶ Critical Thinking

Math Talk 

- What color are most of the apples? red
- How can you find the answer without counting? Look for the longest row of symbols.

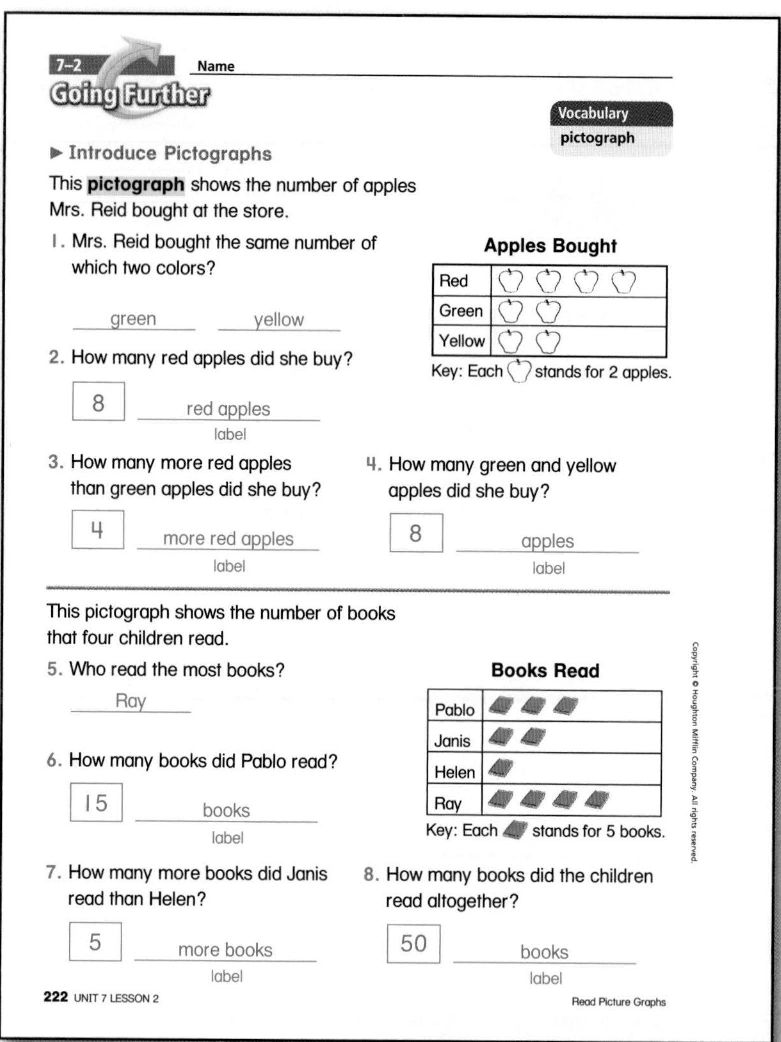

7–2 Going Further Name

Vocabulary
pictograph

▶ Introduce Pictographs

This **pictograph** shows the number of apples Mrs. Reid bought at the store.

Apples Bought

Red	4 apples
Green	2 apples
Yellow	2 apples

Key: Each apple stands for 2 apples.

1. Mrs. Reid bought the same number of which two colors?
green yellow

2. How many red apples did she buy?
8 red apples
label

3. How many more red apples than green apples did she buy?
4 more red apples
label

4. How many green and yellow apples did she buy?
8 apples
label

This pictograph shows the number of books that four children read.

Books Read

Pablo	3 books
Janis	2 books
Helen	1 book
Ray	4 books

Key: Each book stands for 5 books.

5. Who read the most books?
Ray

6. How many books did Pablo read?
15 books
label

7. How many more books did Janis read than Helen?
5 more books
label

8. How many books did the children read altogether?
50 books
label

222 UNIT 7 LESSON 2 Read Picture Graphs

Student Activity Book page 222

- Suppose Mrs. Reid bought 2 more green apples. How would you change the pictograph? Draw one more apple in the row that shows green apples.
- Suppose Mrs. Reid bought 9 red apples. How would you change the pictograph? Draw half of an apple in the row that shows the red apples.

▶ Draw Pictographs PAIRS

Have children use the information in the first picture graph on Student Activity Book page 221 to make a pictograph. Have a balloon stand for 2 balloons. Be sure children include a key.

Differentiated Instruction

Intervention — Activity Card 7-2

Breakfast Foods — Activity Card 7-2 ●

Work: [group]

Use:

- Sticky notes
- Picture graph outline

Choose:

- 1
- 2
- 3

1. **Work Together** Look at the three choices on the picture graph. Which one do you like best for breakfast?
2. Put a sticky note in the row that names the food you like best for breakfast.
3. Each [group] writes a sentence describing the data on the graph.
4. Share your sentences with others.

Favorite Breakfast Foods

Hot Cereal
Cold Cereal
Pancakes

2 children like hot cereal.

3 more children like cold cereal than pancakes.

Unit 7, Lesson 2

Activity Note Each group needs one sticky note per child and a picture graph outline. The graph title is *Favorite Breakfast Foods* and the *rows* are *Hot Cereal, Cold Cereal,* and *Pancakes.*

Math Writing Prompt

Write a Problem Look at the picture graphs on Homework and Remembering page 141. Write and answer a question about the first picture graph.

Software Support

Use *Soar to Success* for instruction of students needing targeted support for underlying skills.

On Level — Activity Card 7-2

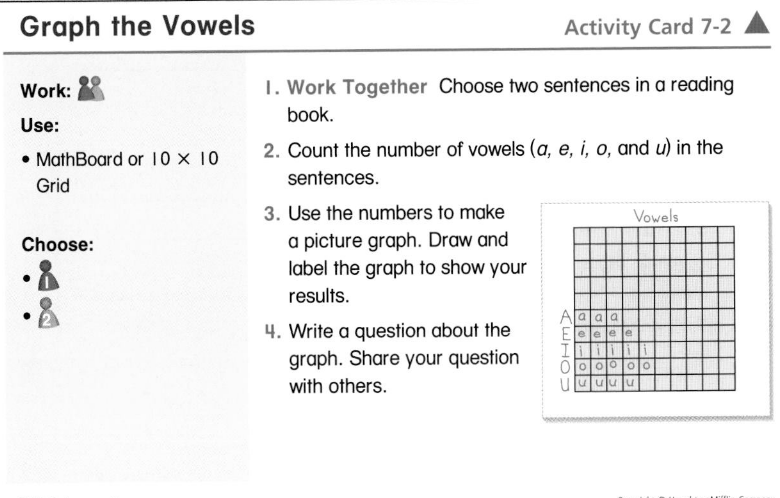

Graph the Vowels — Activity Card 7-2 ▲

Work: [pair]

Use:

- MathBoard or 10 × 10 Grid

Choose:

- 1
- 2

1. **Work Together** Choose two sentences in a reading book.
2. Count the number of vowels (*a, e, i, o,* and *u*) in the sentences.
3. Use the numbers to make a picture graph. Draw and label the graph to show your results.
4. Write a question about the graph. Share your question with others.

Vowels

A	a	a	a		
E	e	e	e	e	
I	i	i	i	i	i
O	o	o	o	o	o
U	u	u	u	u	

Unit 7, Lesson 2

Activity Note Each pair needs MathBoard materials or 10 × 10 Grid (TRB M62). Help children find two sentences to count the vowels.

Math Writing Prompt

Explain Your Thinking Explain how to make and count tally marks when conducting a survey.

Software Support

Use *MegaMath* for review and reinforcement of the concepts and skills presented in this lesson.

Challenge — Activity Card 7-2

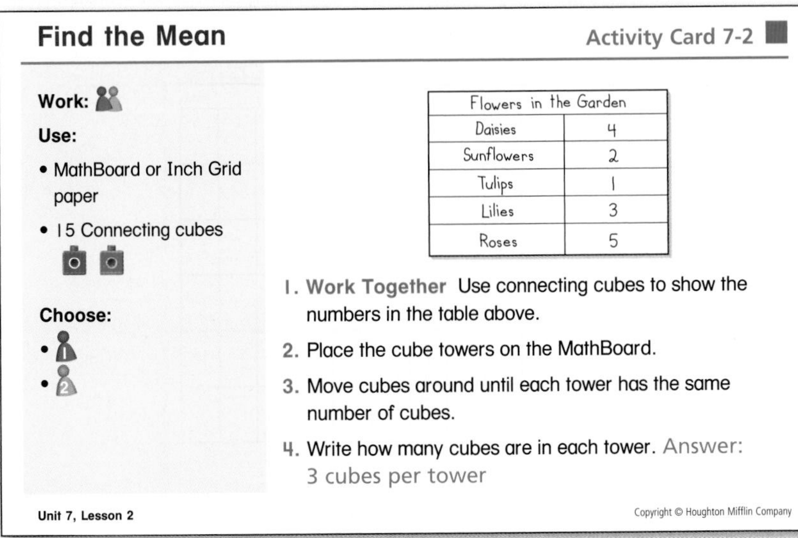

Find the Mean — Activity Card 7-2 ■

Work: [pair]

Use:

- MathBoard or Inch Grid paper
- 15 Connecting cubes

Choose:

- 1
- 2

Flowers in the Garden	
Daisies	4
Sunflowers	2
Tulips	1
Lilies	3
Roses	5

1. **Work Together** Use connecting cubes to show the numbers in the table above.
2. Place the cube towers on the MathBoard.
3. Move cubes around until each tower has the same number of cubes.
4. Write how many cubes are in each tower. Answer: 3 cubes per tower

Unit 7, Lesson 2

Activity Note Each pair needs MathBoard materials or Inch Grid Paper (TRB M70). Explain average to children.

Math Writing Prompt

Make a Graph Curtis has 4 apples. Ming has 2 apples. Linda has 6 apples. Make and label a picture graph to show the information. Then write two comparison sentences.

DESTINATION Math®

Software Support

Use *Destination Math* to take students beyond the concepts and skills presented in this lesson.

3 Homework and Spiral Review

7–2 Homework **Goal:** Additional Practice

This Homework page provides practice in reading picture graphs to compare data.

7–2 Homework Name ____________

Compare to find how many **more** or **fewer**.
Write the number. Ring *more* or *fewer*.

Hats	🎉 🎉
Horns	📯 📯 📯 📯 📯 📯

1. There are 4 *more* (*fewer*) hats than horns.

2. There are 4 (*more*) *fewer* horns than hats.

Mina	🐟 🐟 🐟 🐟
Emily	🐟 🐟 🐟 🐟 🐟 🐟 🐟

3. Mina has 3 *more* (*fewer*) goldfish than Emily.

4. Emily has 3 (*more*) *fewer* goldfish than Mina.

Dan	🔔 🔔 🔔 🔔 🔔 🔔 🔔 🔔
Tani	🔔 🔔 🔔

5. Dan has 5 (*more*) *fewer* bells than Tani.

6. Tani has 5 *more* (*fewer*) bells than Dan.

UNIT 7 LESSON 2 Read Picture Graphs 141

Homework and Remembering page 141

7–2 Remembering **Goal:** Spiral Review

This Remembering activity would be appropriate anytime after today's lesson.

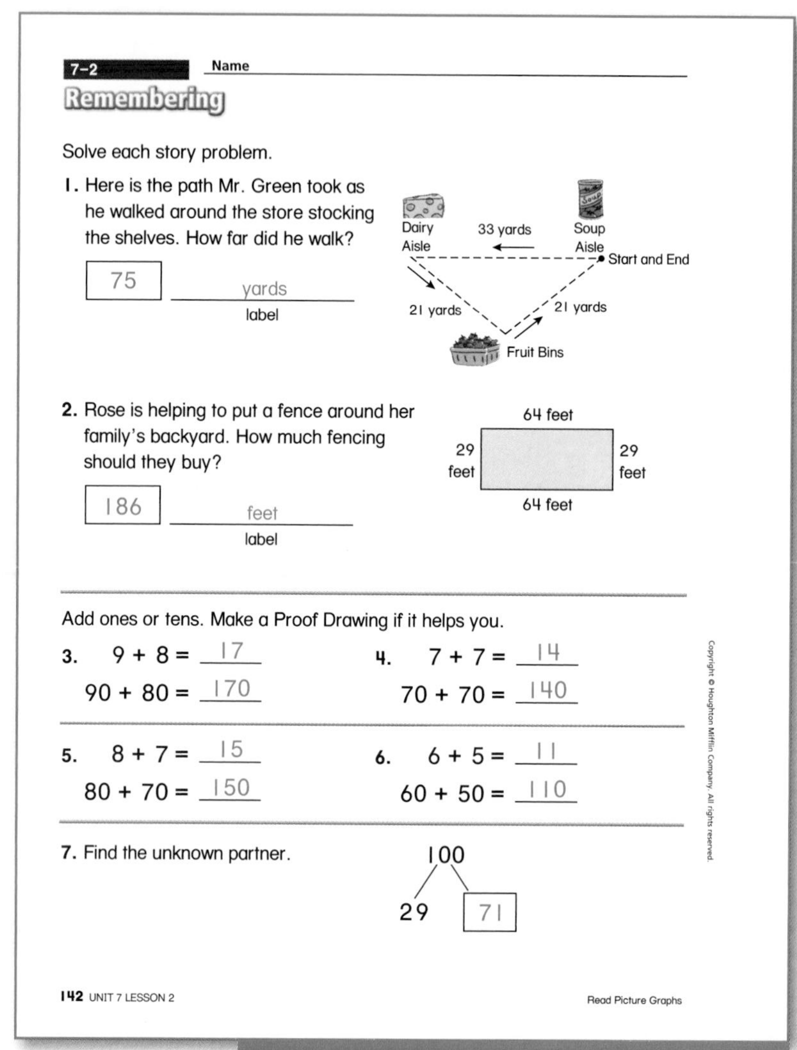

7–2 Remembering Name ____________

Solve each story problem.

1. Here is the path Mr. Green took as he walked around the store stocking the shelves. How far did he walk?

75 yards
label

2. Rose is helping to put a fence around her family's backyard. How much fencing should they buy?

186 feet
label

Add ones or tens. Make a Proof Drawing if it helps you.

3. 9 + 8 = 17
90 + 80 = 170

4. 7 + 7 = 14
70 + 70 = 140

5. 8 + 7 = 15
80 + 70 = 150

6. 6 + 5 = 11
60 + 50 = 110

7. Find the unknown partner.

100
29 71

142 UNIT 7 LESSON 2 Read Picture Graphs

Homework and Remembering page 142

Home or School Activity

Real-World Connection

Count the Letters Have children write the first names of the members of their family. Then have them make a picture graph that compares the numbers of letters in the first names of each person in their family.

Names of Family Members

Enrico	E	N	R	I	C	O			
Juan	J	U	A	N					
Nicole	N	I	C	O	L	E			
Chanel	C	H	A	N	E	L			
Elizabeth	E	L	I	Z	A	B	E	T	H
Michelle	M	I	C	H	E	L	L	E	

The Language of Comparison

Lesson Objectives

- **Solve comparison problems depicted in picture graphs.**
- **Use the comparative terms *same, more,* and *fewer* to talk about information in picture graphs.**
- **Review the *is greater than* and *is less than* comparison symbols.**

Vocabulary	
picture graph	**same**
more	**is greater than (>)**
fewer	**is less than (<)**

The Day at a Glance

Today's Goals	Materials	
1 Teaching the Lesson **A1:** Solve comparison problems and discuss information in picture graphs. **A2:** Describe comparisons in two ways, using the words *more* and *fewer*. **A3:** Review the comparison symbols for is *greater than* and is *less than* (> and <).	**Lesson Activities** Student Activity Book pp. 223–224 Homework and Remembering pp. 143–144 MathBoard materials of 10 × 10 Grid (TRB M62)	**Going Further** Activity Cards 7-3 3 oz paper cup Real or play money Small cup Number cubes Math Journals
2 Going Further ► Differentiated Instruction		
3 Homework and Targeted Practice		

123 Use Math Talk today!

Keeping Skills Sharp

Quick Practice 5 MINUTES	Daily Routines
Goal: Practice addition with teen totals. **Materials:** Green Make-a-Ten Cards (addition) (from Unit 1 Lesson 13 or TRB M35–M38) **Teen Addition Flash** Have a Student Leader call out two numbers that add to a teen number. The class flashes 10 and ones to show the answer. (See Unit 5 Lesson 4.) **Make-a-Ten Cards: Addition** Have children practice addition with teen totals using the Green Make-a-Ten Cards. (See Unit 7 Lesson 2.)	**Telling Time** Naming the Hands, Telling Time on the Time Poster (See p. xxvii.) ► Led by teacher **Money Routine** Using the 120 Poster, Using the Money Flip Chart, Using the Number Path, Using Secret Code Cards (See pp. xxiii–xxv.) ► Led by Student Leaders

1 Teaching the Lesson

Activity 1

Same, More, and Fewer

 **20 MINUTES**

Goals: Solve comparison problems and discuss information in picture graphs.

Materials: Student Activity Book page 223

 **NCTM Standards:**
Data Analysis and Probability
Number and Operations
Communication

Teaching Note

What to Expect from Students
Comparison problems may be difficult because some children do not clearly understand the situation or the language. To minimize the difficulty, use a wide variety of words and phrases that children may encounter in such problems. Picture graphs provide a clear visual representation of a comparison situation and allow for discussion of troublesome words.

English Language Learners

Draw the sample graph of Maria and Carlos on the board. Write the word *same*.

- **Beginning** Say: **Maria and Carlos each have 4. They have the *same* amount.** Have children repeat.
- **Intermediate** Ask: **Maria and Carlos both have how many?** 4 **Do they have the *same* amount?** yes
- **Advanced** Have children tell about what it means to have the *same* amount.

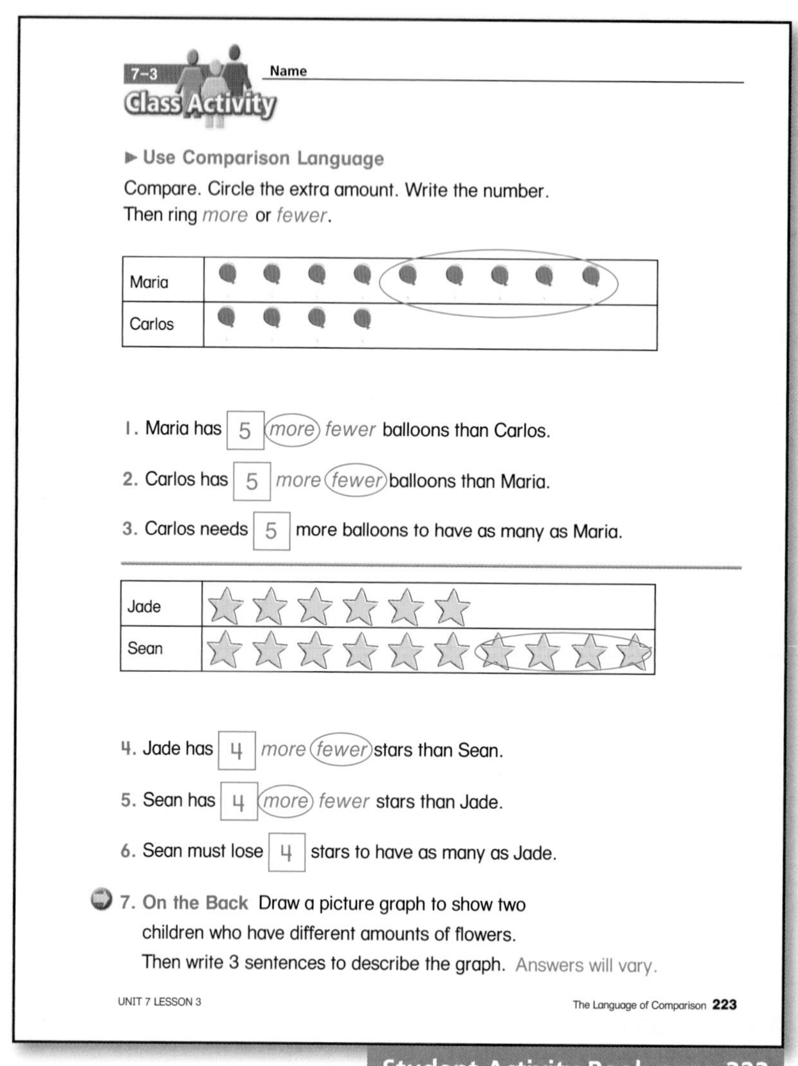

7-3 Class Activity Name

▶ Use Comparison Language

Compare. Circle the extra amount. Write the number.
Then ring *more* or *fewer*.

Maria	● ● ● ● ● ● ● ● ●
Carlos	● ● ● ●

1. Maria has 5 (more) fewer balloons than Carlos.
2. Carlos has 5 more (fewer) balloons than Maria.
3. Carlos needs 5 more balloons to have as many as Maria.

Jade	☆ ☆ ☆ ☆ ☆ ☆
Sean	☆ ☆ ☆ ☆ ☆ ☆ ☆ ☆ ☆ ☆

4. Jade has 4 more (fewer) stars than Sean.
5. Sean has 4 (more) fewer stars than Jade.
6. Sean must lose 4 stars to have as many as Jade.
7. On the Back Draw a picture graph to show two children who have different amounts of flowers. Then write 3 sentences to describe the graph. Answers will vary.

UNIT 7 LESSON 3 The Language of Comparison 223

Student Activity Book page 223

▶ Use Comparison Language WHOLE CLASS Math Talk 

Draw a graph on the board like the one to the left and use it to review the concept of *same*.

- Who has more balloons? no one Who has fewer? no one So both children have the **same** number of balloons.
- We can put a line to mark that they both have the same amount. *Draw a vertical line through the graph as shown.*
- Now, I'll give 5 more balloons to Maria. *Draw 5 circles on the graph.*

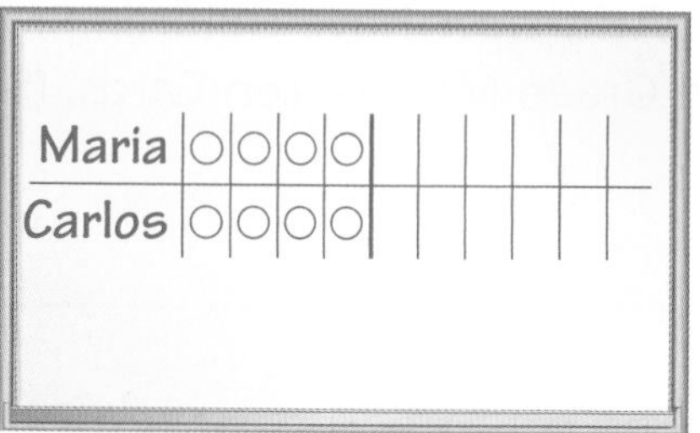

- Who has more now? Maria How many more? 5 more Let's circle the extra amount that Maria has. Circle the extra amount and have the children do the same on the first graph on Student Activity Book page 223. See the sample to the right for an example.
- Now let's compare using the word *fewer*. Who has fewer balloons? Carlos So we can say: "Carlos has fewer balloons than Maria has."

Equalize Questions These questions ask how many more or fewer one of the children needs in order to have the same number as the other.

- We can also ask how many more balloons one child needs in order to have as many as the other. Or ask how many balloons one child would have to lose in order to have as many as the other. Who would like to ask a question like that? How many more balloons does Carlos need to have as many as Maria? (5 balloons) How many balloons does Maria need to lose to have as many as Carlos? (5 balloons)

Work together as a class to complete the exercises on the page, if necessary. Otherwise, allow children to complete the page in Helping Pairs. Be sure children understand that they must decide who has more and who has fewer. Remind them that comparisons can be said in two ways and that they should say both of the comparisons aloud to each other.

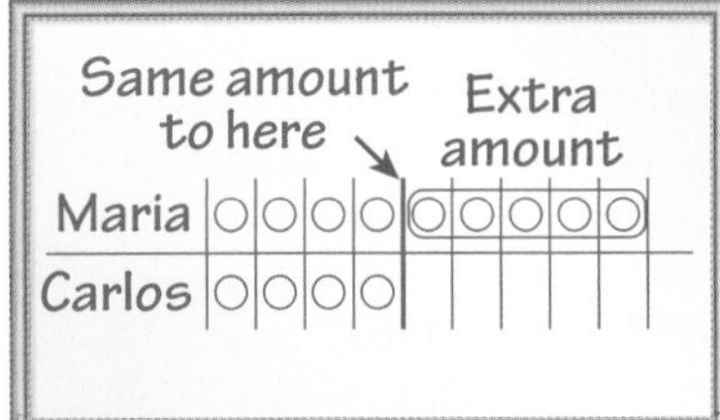

Ongoing Assessment

Marta has 8 pencils and Reni has 5 pencils.

- ▶ Who has more pencils?
- ▶ Who has fewer pencils?
- ▶ How many more pencils does Reni need to have the same number as Marta?
- ▶ How many pencils does Marta need to lose so that she has the same number as Reni?

Activity 2

More Comparison Statements from a Graph

▶ Make Up Numbers of Things to Compare

WHOLE CLASS

Invite children to make up two things to compare and then show the information on a picture graph. Have some children draw at the board while the other children make graphs on their MathBoards or on the 10 × 10 Grid (TRB M62).

Have children use their graphs to write two comparison statements, one using *more* and one using *fewer.*

 **15 MINUTES**

Goal: Describe comparisons in two ways, using the words *more* and *fewer.*

Materials: MathBoard materials or 10 × 10 Grid (TRB M62)

 **NCTM Standards:**
Data Analysis and Probability
Number and Operations
Communication

Activity 3

Comparison Symbols

 20 MINUTES

Goal: Review the comparison symbols for *is greater than* and *is less than* (> and <).

 **NCTM Standards:**
Number and Operations
Communication

 **Class Management**

If you have been doing the Daily Routines, this activity can be used as a review of the *is greater than* and *is less than* symbols.

Teaching Note

Language and Vocabulary Many children have difficulty remembering which symbol means *is greater than* and which means *is less than.* You may need to work with children to develop a way of distinguishing the two. One simple method is to remember that the small end of each symbol points to the smaller number in the pair, and the large end points to the larger number. For example, $2 < 7$ (2 is less than 7) and $7 > 2$ (7 is greater than 2).

▶ Review the > and the < Symbols WHOLE CLASS

Ask for Ideas Remind children that in math we can also use symbols to show if something is more than or less than another thing. Demonstrate the use of the symbols by illustrating the problem below on the board.

- Let's say that Lydia has 5 candles and Harry has 8 candles.

5 8

- Which number is less? 5 Let's say it in a sentence. 5 is less than 8.
- Remember there is a symbol that stands for *is less than.* I'll write it so that the numbers read 5 is less than 8. *Write the symbol.* Let's say it together: "Five is less than eight."

$5 < 8$

Have children replace the 5 with other numbers that are less than 8.

- I'm going to erase the 5. What would be another number we could put in its place? *Erase the 5 and write in a number less than 8 suggested by one of the children.* Let's say it together: "two is less than eight."

Reverse the order of the numbers and have children state which number is greater.

- Remember Lydia has 5 candles and Harry has 8 candles. Now I want to talk about the greater number first. Which number is greater? 8 Let's say it in a sentence. "Eight is greater than five." I'll write 8 and 5 on the board.

8 5

- There is a symbol that stands for *is greater than.* I'll write it so that the numbers read that 8 is greater than 5. *Write the symbol.*

$8 > 5$

- Let's replace the 5 with other numbers that complete the statement. I'm going to erase the 5. What would be another number we could put in its place? *Erase the 5 and write in a number that a child suggests.* Let's say it together: "Eight is greater than four."

Have children generate and write more statements using *is greater than* and *is less than.*

Intervention Activity Card 7-3

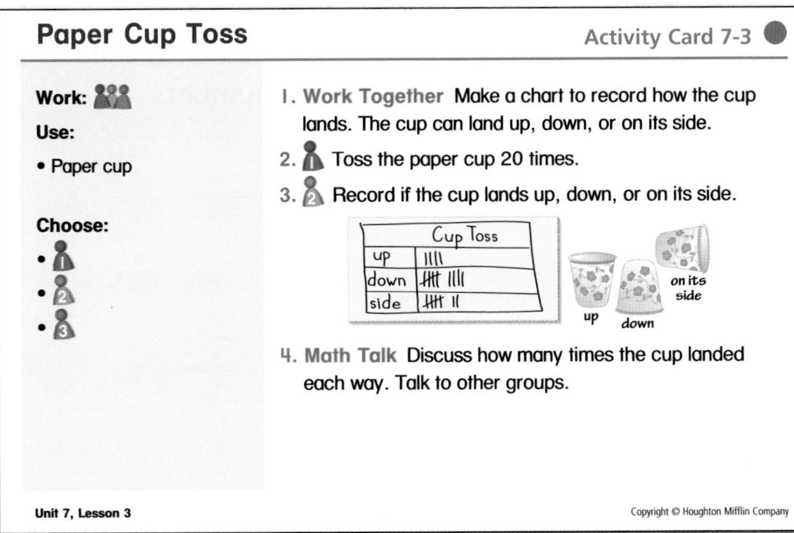

Paper Cup Toss Activity Card 7-3 ●

Work: (group)
Use:
- Paper cup

Choose:
- 1
- 2
- 3

1. **Work Together** Make a chart to record how the cup lands. The cup can land up, down, or on its side.
2. Toss the paper cup 20 times.
3. Record if the cup lands up, down, or on its side.

Cup Toss	
up	||||
down	卌 ||||
side	卌 ||

4. **Math Talk** Discuss how many times the cup landed each way. Talk to other groups.

Unit 7, Lesson 3 Copyright © Houghton Mifflin Company

Activity Note Each pair needs one 3 oz paper cup. Explain that the result that occurred the greatest number of times is the *mode*.

Math Writing Prompt

Apply Write the comparison sentence for 8 > 4.

Software Support

Use *Soar to Success* for instruction of students needing targeted support for underlying skills.

On Level Activity Card 7-3

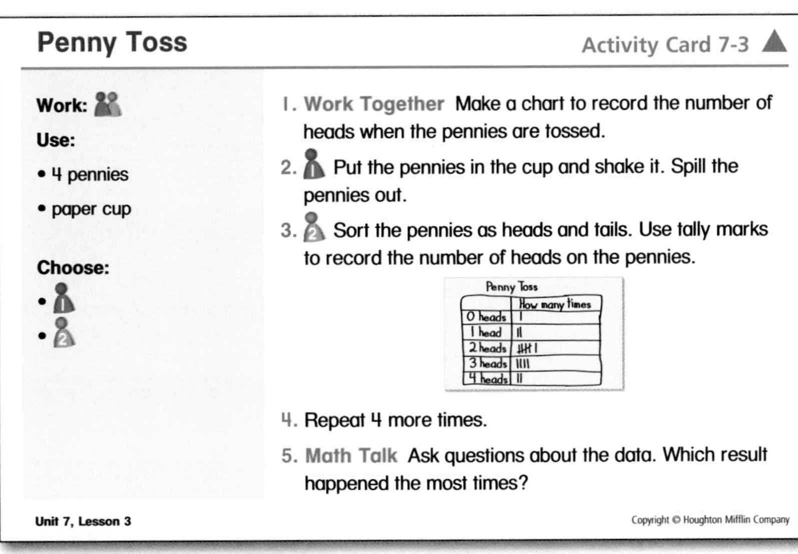

Penny Toss Activity Card 7-3 ▲

Work: (pair)
Use:
- 4 pennies
- paper cup

Choose:
- 1
- 2

1. **Work Together** Make a chart to record the number of heads when the pennies are tossed.
2. Put the pennies in the cup and shake it. Spill the pennies out.
3. Sort the pennies as heads and tails. Use tally marks to record the number of heads on the pennies.

Penny Toss

	How many times
0 heads	|
1 head	||
2 heads	卌 |
3 heads	||||
4 heads	||

4. Repeat 4 more times.
5. **Math Talk** Ask questions about the data. Which result happened the most times?

Unit 7, Lesson 3 Copyright © Houghton Mifflin Company

Activity Note Each pair needs four pennies and a 3 oz paper cup. Explain that the result that occurred the greatest number of times is the *mode*.

Math Writing Prompt

Write Your Own Write the two different comparison sentences for 5 < 8.

Software Support

Use *MegaMath* for review and reinforcement of the concepts and skills presented in this lesson.

Challenge Activity Card 7-3

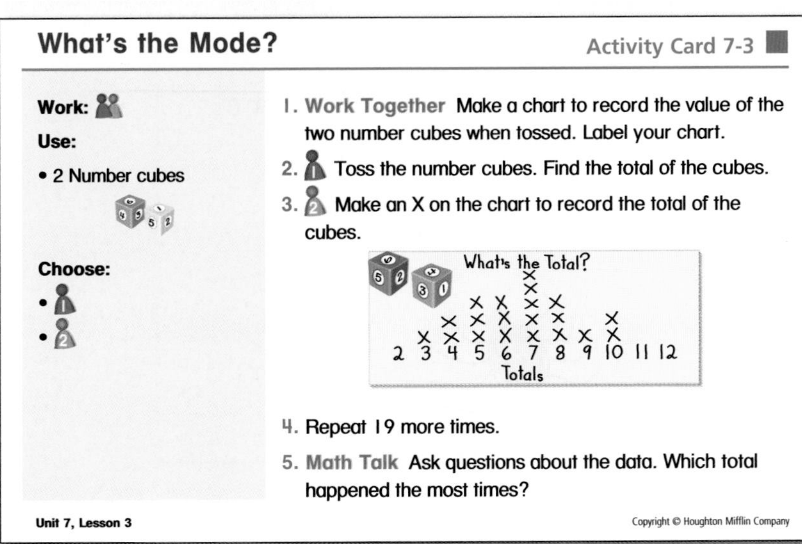

What's the Mode? Activity Card 7-3 ■

Work: (pair)
Use:
- 2 Number cubes

Choose:
- 1
- 2

1. **Work Together** Make a chart to record the value of the two number cubes when tossed. Label your chart.
2. Toss the number cubes. Find the total of the cubes.
3. Make an X on the chart to record the total of the cubes.

4. Repeat 19 more times.
5. **Math Talk** Ask questions about the data. Which total happened the most times?

Unit 7, Lesson 3 Copyright © Houghton Mifflin Company

Activity Note Each pair needs two number cubes labeled 1–6. Explain that the total that occurred the most times is the *mode*.

Math Writing Prompt

Comparison Strategies In your own words, explain how you remember the difference between the < or > symbols and when to use them.

DESTINATION Math®

Software Support

Use *Destination Math* to take students beyond the concepts and skills presented in this lesson.

Homework and Targeted Practice

7-3 Homework **Goal:** Additional Practice

This Homework page provides practice in comparing numbers.

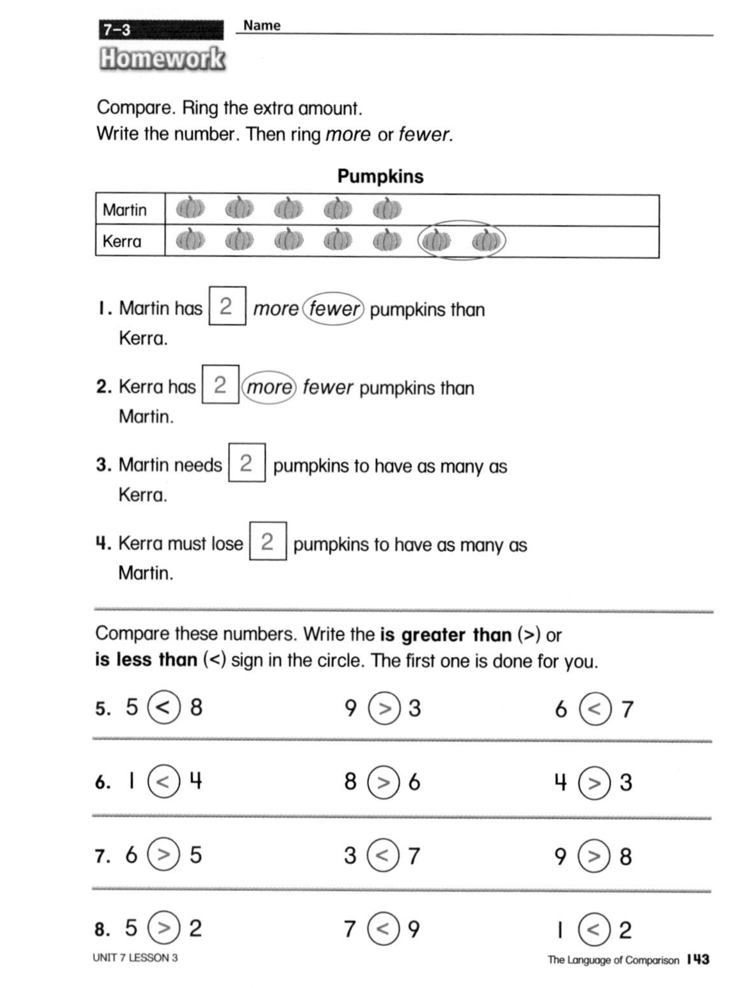

7-3 Homework

Name

Compare. Ring the extra amount.
Write the number. Then ring *more* or *fewer*.

Pumpkins

Martin	5 pumpkins
Kerra	7 pumpkins (2 ringed)

1. Martin has 2 *more* (*fewer*) pumpkins than Kerra.
2. Kerra has 2 (*more*) *fewer* pumpkins than Martin.
3. Martin needs 2 pumpkins to have as many as Kerra.
4. Kerra must lose 2 pumpkins to have as many as Martin.

Compare these numbers. Write the **is greater than** (>) or **is less than** (<) sign in the circle. The first one is done for you.

5. 5 < 8 9 > 3 6 < 7
6. 1 < 4 8 > 6 4 > 3
7. 6 > 5 3 < 7 9 > 8
8. 5 > 2 7 < 9 1 < 2

UNIT 7 LESSON 3 The Language of Comparison 143

Homework and Remembering page 143

7-3 Targeted Practice **Goal:** Compare numbers

This Targeted Practice page can be used with children who need extra practice comparing numbers.

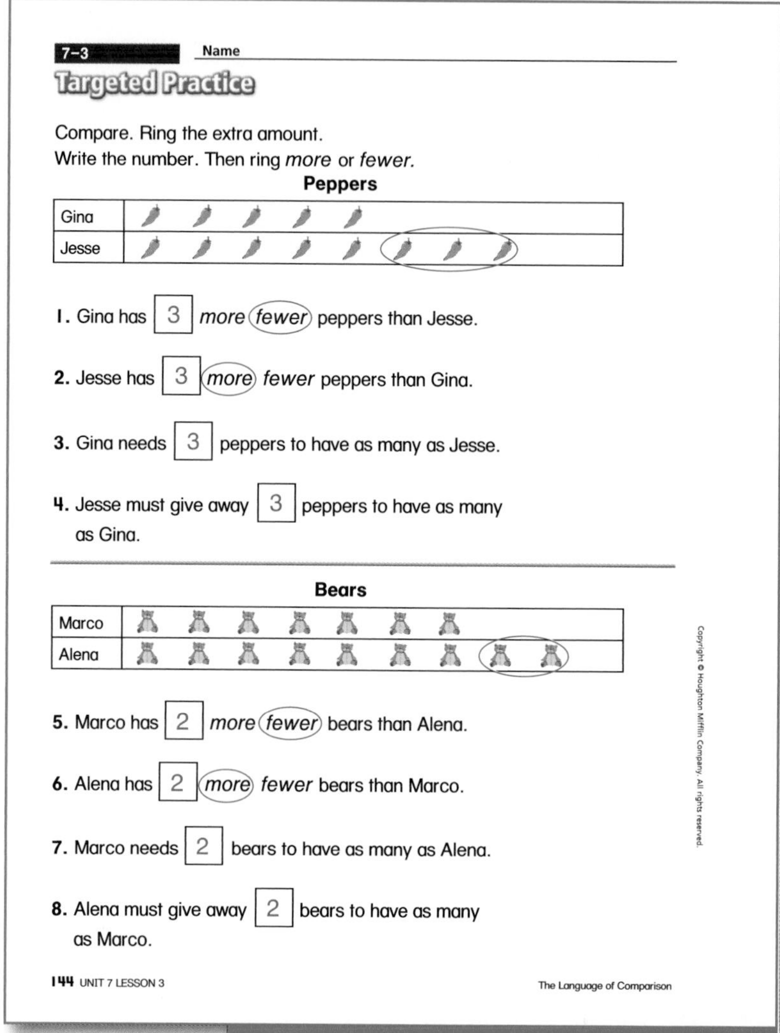

7-3 Targeted Practice

Name

Compare. Ring the extra amount.
Write the number. Then ring *more* or *fewer*.

Peppers

Gina	5 peppers
Jesse	8 peppers (3 ringed)

1. Gina has 3 *more* (*fewer*) peppers than Jesse.
2. Jesse has 3 (*more*) *fewer* peppers than Gina.
3. Gina needs 3 peppers to have as many as Jesse.
4. Jesse must give away 3 peppers to have as many as Gina.

Bears

Marco	7 bears
Alena	9 bears (2 ringed)

5. Marco has 2 *more* (*fewer*) bears than Alena.
6. Alena has 2 (*more*) *fewer* bears than Marco.
7. Marco needs 2 bears to have as many as Alena.
8. Alena must give away 2 bears to have as many as Marco.

144 UNIT 7 LESSON 3 The Language of Comparison

Homework and Remembering page 144

Home or School Activity

Science Connection

Animal Legs Some animals, like spiders, have eight legs, while others, like dogs, have four legs. To help children practice using comparison sentences and symbols, have them choose two animals and research the number of legs they have on the Internet or in books. Then have children write a comparison sentence involving the legs on those two animals and compare the numbers using the correct comparison symbol.

Spiders have 2 more legs than ladybugs.
8 > 6

Pose and Solve Comparison Story Problems

Lesson Objectives

- Create, represent, and solve comparison story problems.
- Represent information in story problems in a simple picture graph.
- Use comparative terms *more, fewer,* and *same*.

Vocabulary

comparison story problems
picture graph
more
fewer
same

The Day at a Glance

Today's Goals	Materials	
1 Teaching the Lesson **A1:** Draw picture graphs to represent comparison story problems and solve the problems in two ways. **A2:** Create comparison problems for other children to solve.	**Lesson Activities** Student Activity Book pp. 225–226 Homework and Remembering pp. 145–146 MathBoard materials of 10 × 10 Grid (TRB M62) Quick Quiz 1 (Assessment Guide)	**Going Further** Activity Cards 7-4 Connecting cubes Large bowl Real or play money Small container Math Journals
2 Going Further ► Differentiated Instruction		
3 Homework and Spiral Review		

123 Use Math Talk today!

Keeping Skills Sharp

Quick Practice — 10 MINUTES

Goal: Find totals for 1-digit partners.

Materials: Student Activity Book page 225

Addition Sprint Direct children's attention to Student Activity Book page 225. This sprint is the same as the one from Unit 5 Lesson 12 (Activity 1). See page 392 for more information.

7-4 Class Activity Name

► Addition Sprint

5 + 7 = 12	9 + 6 = 15	7 + 6 = 13
4 + 8 = 12	7 + 8 = 15	4 + 6 = 10
3 + 9 = 12	9 + 7 = 16	0 + 7 = 7
7 + 5 = 12	9 + 2 = 11	4 + 9 = 13
4 + 5 = 9	5 + 2 = 7	6 + 8 = 14
8 + 4 = 12	6 + 4 = 10	8 + 5 = 13
8 + 6 = 14	8 + 7 = 15	6 + 1 = 7
6 + 9 = 15	5 + 5 = 10	5 + 4 = 9
9 + 9 = 18	1 + 9 = 10	7 + 4 = 11
6 + 3 = 9	7 + 9 = 16	3 + 6 = 9
9 + 0 = 9	4 + 7 = 11	9 + 4 = 13
7 + 7 = 14	8 + 8 = 16	5 + 8 = 13
9 + 1 = 10	6 + 6 = 12	3 + 4 = 7
8 + 9 = 17	3 + 5 = 8	6 + 7 = 13
2 + 5 = 7	9 + 3 = 12	1 + 6 = 7
3 + 9 = 12	2 + 9 = 11	5 + 6 = 11
2 + 7 = 9	2 + 6 = 8	5 + 5 = 10
9 + 4 = 13	5 + 9 = 14	6 + 8 = 14
2 + 8 = 10	8 + 2 = 10	4 + 4 = 8
0 + 8 = 8	9 + 8 = 17	1 + 8 = 9
8 + 3 = 11	6 + 5 = 11	6 + 7 = 13

UNIT 7 LESSON 4 Addition Sprint 225

Student Activity Book Page 225

Daily Routines

Telling Time Naming the Hands, Telling Time on the Time Poster (See p. xxvii.)

► Led by Student Leaders

Money Routine Using the 120 Poster, Using the Money Flip Chart, Using the Number Path, Using Secret Code Cards (See pp. xxiii–xxv.)

► Led by Student Leaders

1 Teaching the Lesson

Activity 1

Graph Comparison Story Problems

 30 MINUTES

Goals: Draw picture graphs to represent comparison story problems and solve the problems in two ways.

Materials: MathBoard materials or 10 × 10 Grid (TRB M62), Student Activity Book page 226

 **NCTM Standards:**
Data Analysis and Probability
Problem Solving
Communication

Alternate Approach

Model Word Problems Some children may benefit from modeling story problems with connecting cubes.

Carrie
Dave

English Language Learners

Write the following problem: *Sue has 2 fish. Jose has 4 more fish than Sue. How many fish does Jose have?* Read the problem. Say: **This is a *comparison* problem.**

- **Beginning** Say: **We are *comparing* the number of fish Sue and Jose have.** Have children repeat.
- **Intermediate** Ask: **We are *comparing* the number of Sue's and Jose's what?** fish
- **Advanced** Have children tell about what is being compared.

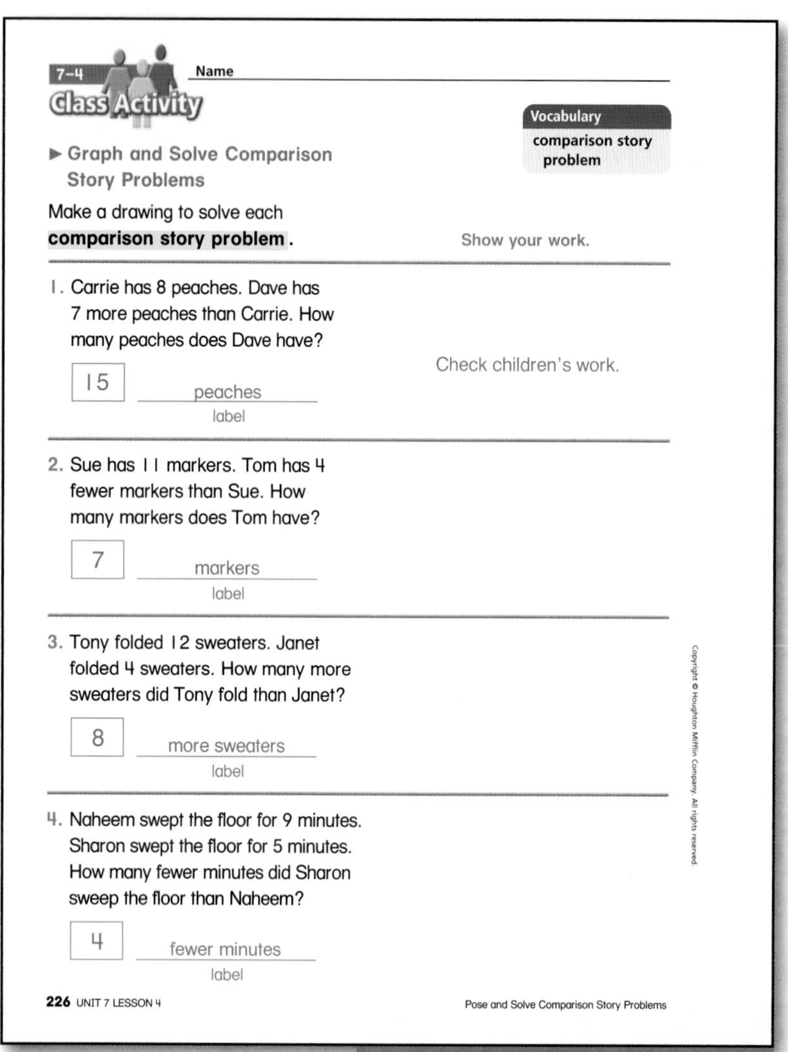

7-4 Class Activity Name

Vocabulary
comparison story problem

▶ Graph and Solve Comparison Story Problems

Make a drawing to solve each **comparison story problem**.

Show your work.

1. Carrie has 8 peaches. Dave has 7 more peaches than Carrie. How many peaches does Dave have?

15 peaches
label

Check children's work.

2. Sue has 11 markers. Tom has 4 fewer markers than Sue. How many markers does Tom have?

7 markers
label

3. Tony folded 12 sweaters. Janet folded 4 sweaters. How many more sweaters did Tony fold than Janet?

8 more sweaters
label

4. Naheem swept the floor for 9 minutes. Sharon swept the floor for 5 minutes. How many fewer minutes did Sharon sweep the floor than Naheem?

4 fewer minutes
label

226 UNIT 7 LESSON 4 Pose and Solve Comparison Story Problems

Student Activity Book page 226

▶ Solve Comparison Story Problems WHOLE CLASS

Read, or have a volunteer read aloud the first problem on Student Activity Book page 226. Discuss how to represent the problem with a drawing.

You may want to have several children work at the board while others draw on their MathBoards or 10 × 10 Grid (TRB M62). When children use their MathBoards, they should position them so the dots are to the children's right. That way they can keep going to the right without running out of room.

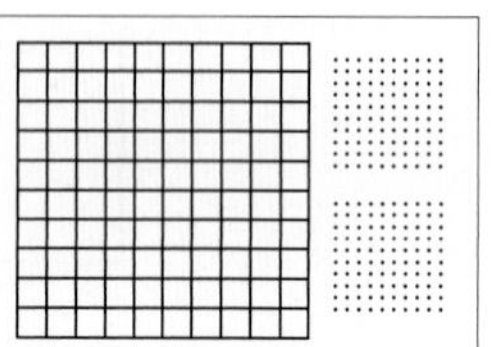

▶ Solve the First Problem WHOLE CLASS

Math Talk 

Draw a 10 × 10 grid on the board and use it to demonstrate how to solve the first problem. Be sure children label their own drawings.

- What do we know? Carrie has 8 peaches. Dave has 7 more.
- Do we know yet how many peaches Dave has? no
- How can we show what Carrie has? We can make circles in 8 squares. *Demonstrate on your grid as the children do the same on their grids.*
- How can we show what Dave has? He has more than Carrie, so he has to have at least 8.
- We can start by drawing circles for the 8 we know he has. *Demonstrate on your grid as the children do the same on their grids.*
- What do we do next? Draw the extras that Dave has.
- How many extra peaches does Dave have? 7 extra peaches So we need to draw 7 more circles on the grid.
- We don't have enough room on our MathBoard graph to show all of Dave's extra peaches. But you can make more columns over the dots on your MathBoard.
- How many peaches does Dave have? 15 peaches

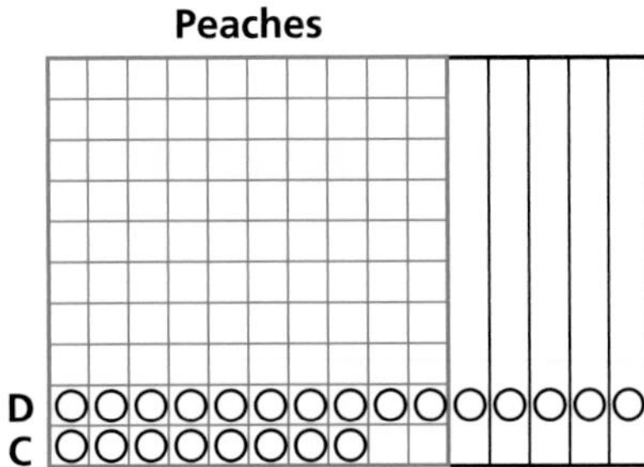

Now have children reword the problem so that it tells who has fewer peaches.

- The way the problem is worded, we are told who has more peaches. How can we say the problem so we know who has fewer peaches? Possible answer: Carrie has 8 peaches in her basket. She has 7 fewer peaches than Dave. How many peaches does Dave have in his basket?

Activity continued ▶

The Learning Classroom

Building Concepts After solving the first problem, you may wish to have children write equations for both forms of the problem.

▶ What would be an equation for the way the problem is written in the book?

$8 + 7 = \square$ So $8 + 7 = \boxed{15}$

Carrie Dave C D

▶ What would be an equation for:

Carries has 8 peaches in her basket. She has 7 fewer peaches than Dave. How many peaches does Dave have in his basket?

$\square - 7 = 8$ $\boxed{15} - 7 = 8$

D C D C

Don't be concerned if many of the children are not able to write these equations. This is an optional activity and it is not for mastery.

Ongoing Assessment

Ask individual children to solve comparison story problems like the ones below.

▶ Jaret has 14 toy cars. His brother has 6 fewer toy cars than Jaret has. How many toy cars does Jaret's brother have?

▶ Yesterday Dana rode her bike for 10 minutes. Today she rode it 5 minutes longer than yesterday. How long did Dana ride her bike today?

Teaching the Lesson (continued)

Quick Quiz

See Assessment Guide for Unit 7 Quick Quiz 1.

▶ Solve the Second Problem WHOLE CLASS

Draw a 10 × 10 grid on the board. Use it to model the solution to problem 2.

- What should we draw first on the grid? It should be something we know from the information in the problem. We know Sue has 11 markers so we can draw that.
- You don't have to draw actual markers. That would take too long. Just draw circles. *Demonstrate on your grid as the children do the same on their grids.*
- What do we know about Tom's markers? He has 4 fewer than Sue has.
- How do we show that on the grid? We can take 4 away from 11.
- How do we know to do that? If Tom had the same amount of markers that Sue has, he would have 11. So we have to take 4 away from 11.
- How many markers does Tom have? 7

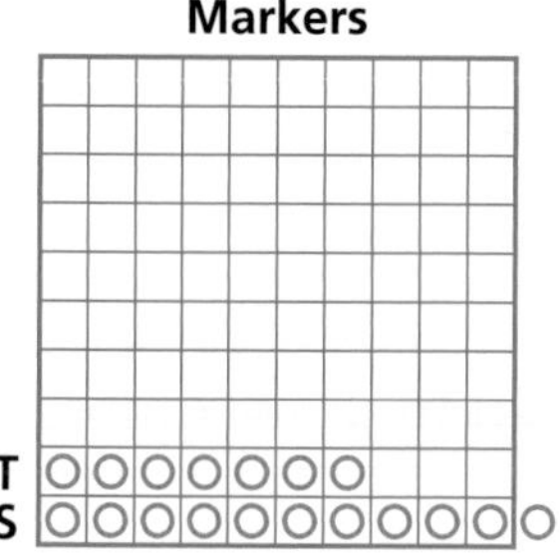

Now have children state the problem another way. Sue has 11 markers. She has 4 more markers than Tom. How many markers does Tom have?

Have children complete the rest of the problems.

Activity 2

Create Comparison Problems

25 MINUTES

Goal: Create comparison problems for other children to solve.

NCTM Standards:
Number and Operations
Problem Solving
Communication

▶ Write and Share Comparison Problems WHOLE CLASS

Invite children to write their own comparison story problems. Remind them that the problems can be about things other than people.

Point out that some comparison problems ask for one of the amounts, which is more or less than the known amount. Other comparison problems ask about the difference between the two amounts (how many more or how many fewer).

Have children share their story problems with the class. Have other children come to the board and explain how to solve each problem.

2 Going Further

Differentiated Instruction

Intervention — Activity Card 7-4

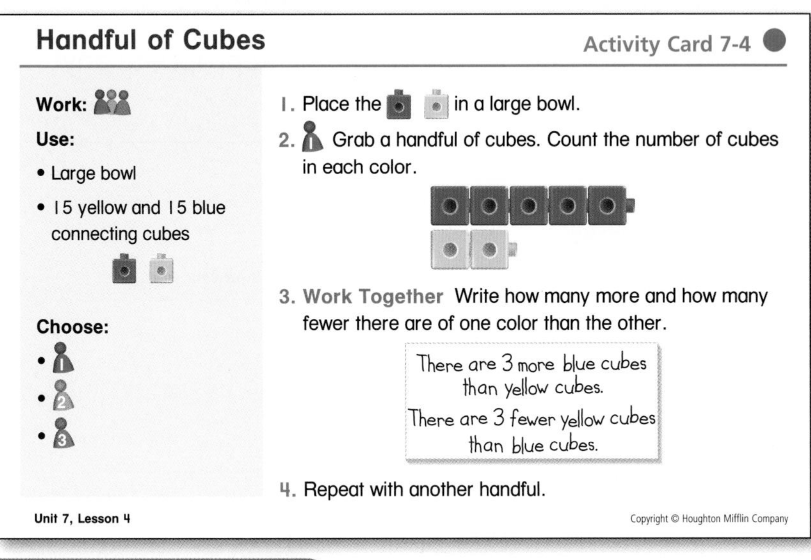

Handful of Cubes — Activity Card 7-4

Work: [group]
Use:
- Large bowl
- 15 yellow and 15 blue connecting cubes

Choose:
- 1
- 2
- 3

1. Place the [blue cubes] [yellow cubes] in a large bowl.
2. [1] Grab a handful of cubes. Count the number of cubes in each color.
3. Work Together Write how many more and how many fewer there are of one color than the other.

There are 3 more blue cubes than yellow cubes.
There are 3 fewer yellow cubes than blue cubes.

4. Repeat with another handful.

Unit 7, Lesson 4

Copyright © Houghton Mifflin Company

Activity Note Each group needs 15 blue and 15 yellow connecting cubes and a large bowl. Help groups compare the number of cubes and write about the comparison.

Math Writing Prompt

Write Your Own Write a comparison story problem using 5 black cars and 7 blue cars.

Software Support

Use *Soar to Success* for instruction of students needing targeted support for underlying skills.

On Level — Activity Card 7-4

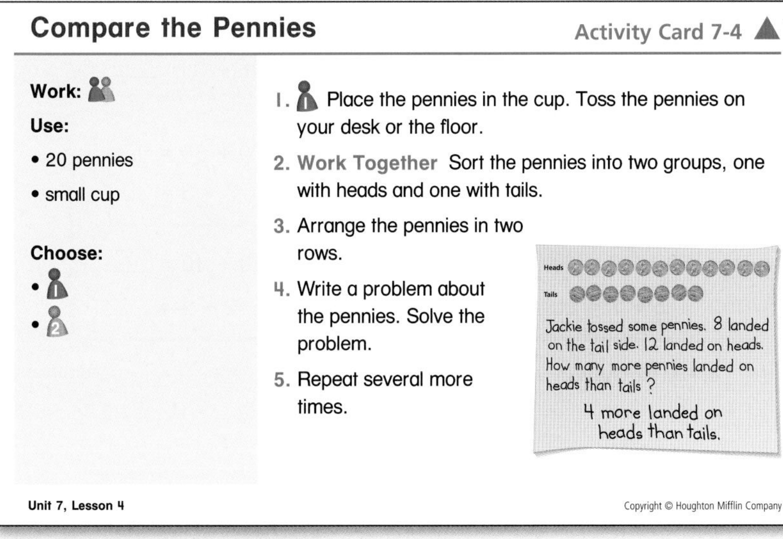

Compare the Pennies — Activity Card 7-4

Work: [pair]
Use:
- 20 pennies
- small cup

Choose:
- 1
- 2

1. [1] Place the pennies in the cup. Toss the pennies on your desk or the floor.
2. Work Together Sort the pennies into two groups, one with heads and one with tails.
3. Arrange the pennies in two rows.
4. Write a problem about the pennies. Solve the problem.
5. Repeat several more times.

Heads
Tails

Jackie tossed some pennies. 8 landed on the tail side. 12 landed on heads. How many more pennies landed on heads than tails?
4 more landed on heads than tails.

Unit 7, Lesson 4

Copyright © Houghton Mifflin Company

Activity Note Each pair needs 20 pennies (real or play) and a small cup. You may want to have each child write a comparison story problem for his or her partner.

Math Writing Prompt

Work Backward Write a comparison story problem that has the answer *8 carrots*.

Software Support

Use *MegaMath* for review and reinforcement of the concepts and skills presented in this lesson.

Challenge — Activity Card 7-4

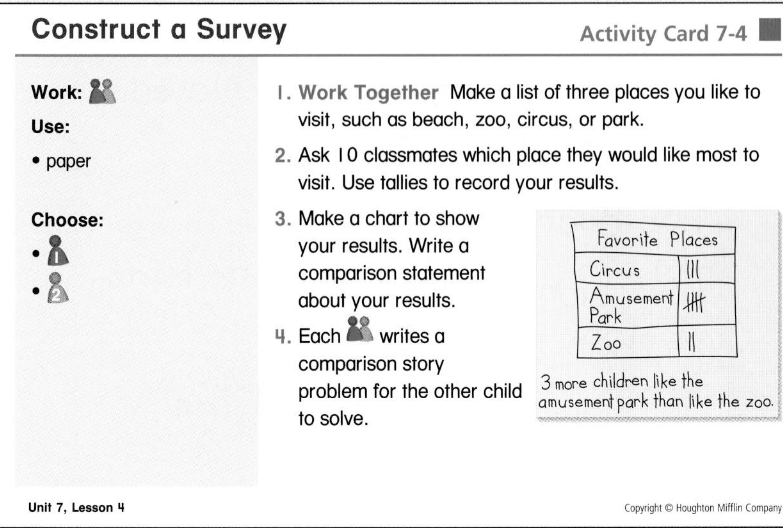

Construct a Survey — Activity Card 7-4

Work: [pair]
Use:
- paper

Choose:
- 1
- 2

1. Work Together Make a list of three places you like to visit, such as beach, zoo, circus, or park.
2. Ask 10 classmates which place they would like most to visit. Use tallies to record your results.
3. Make a chart to show your results. Write a comparison statement about your results.
4. Each [partner] writes a comparison story problem for the other child to solve.

Favorite Places	
Circus	III
Amusement Park	~~IIII~~
Zoo	II

3 more children like the amusement park than like the zoo.

Unit 7, Lesson 4

Copyright © Houghton Mifflin Company

Activity Note Have pairs write comparison problems to share with other pairs. You may want to combine all the results and have children write comparison story problems.

Math Writing Prompt

Two Different Ways Write a comparison story problem. Show two different drawings that could help you solve the problem.

Software Support

Use *Destination Math* to take students beyond the concepts and skills presented in this lesson.

3 Homework and Spiral Review

Goal: Additional Practice

This Homework page provides practice solving comparison story problems.

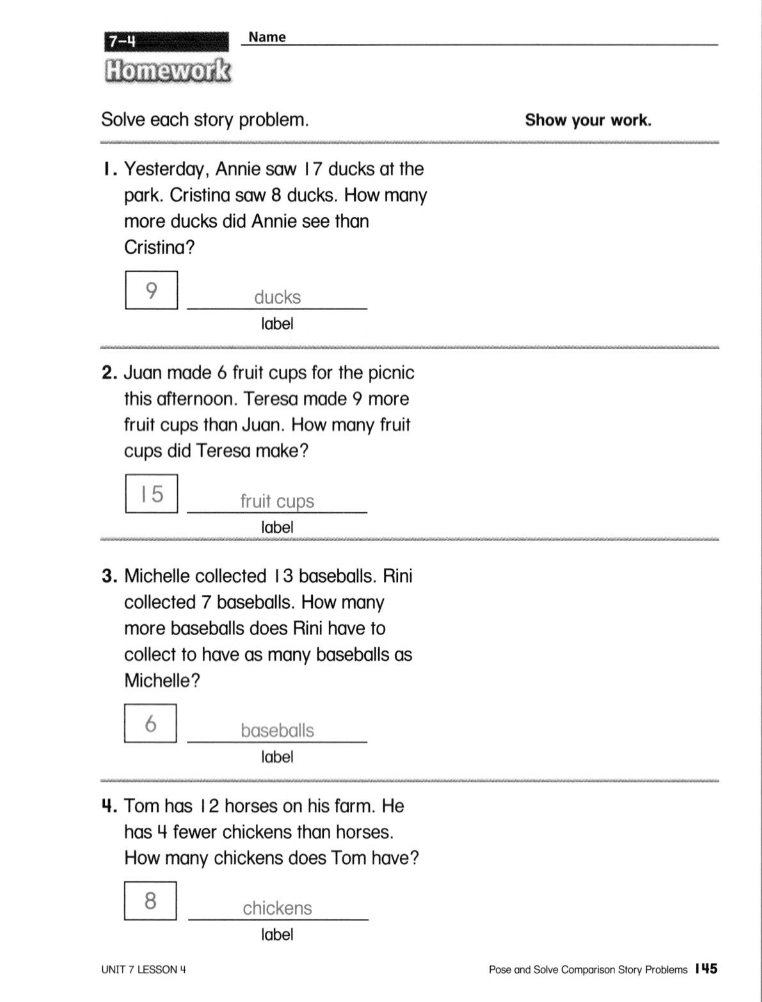

7–4 Homework Name ______

Solve each story problem. **Show your work.**

1. Yesterday, Annie saw 17 ducks at the park. Cristina saw 8 ducks. How many more ducks did Annie see than Cristina?

   9 ducks (label)

2. Juan made 6 fruit cups for the picnic this afternoon. Teresa made 9 more fruit cups than Juan. How many fruit cups did Teresa make?

   15 fruit cups (label)

3. Michelle collected 13 baseballs. Rini collected 7 baseballs. How many more baseballs does Rini have to collect to have as many baseballs as Michelle?

   6 baseballs (label)

4. Tom has 12 horses on his farm. He has 4 fewer chickens than horses. How many chickens does Tom have?

   8 chickens (label)

UNIT 7 LESSON 4 Pose and Solve Comparison Story Problems 145

Homework and Remembering page 145

Goal: Spiral Review

This Remembering activity would be appropriate anytime after today's lesson.

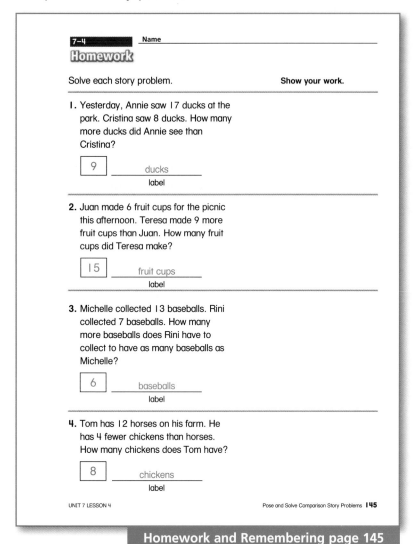

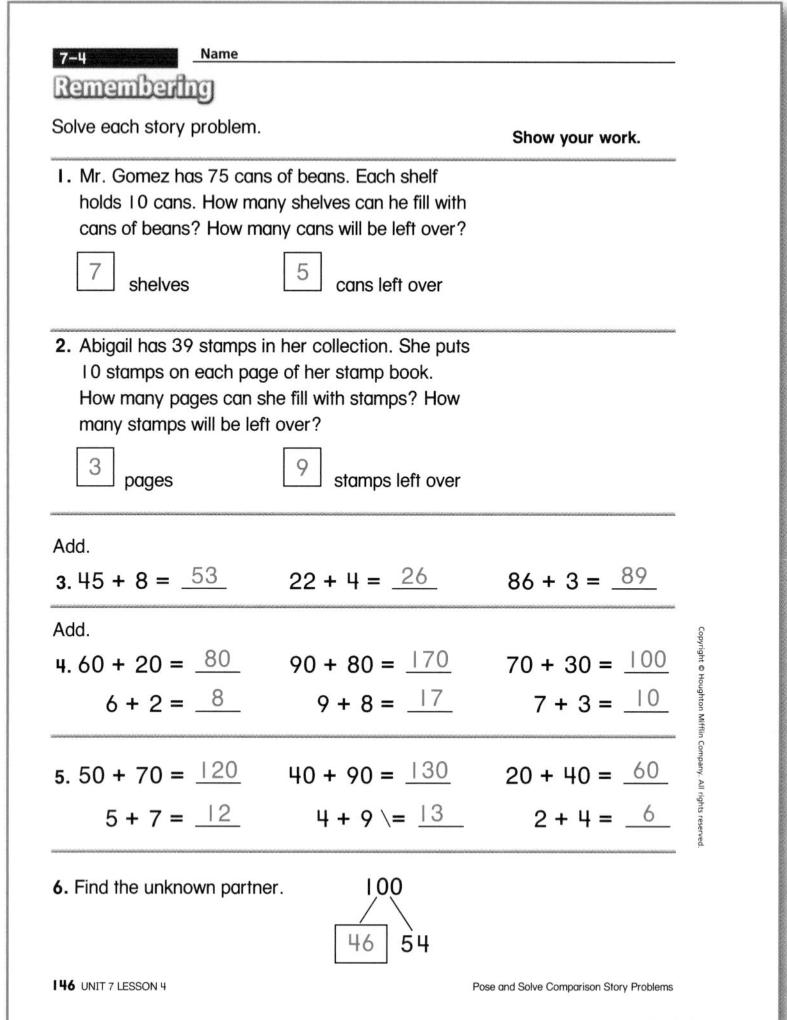

7–4 Remembering Name ______

Solve each story problem. **Show your work.**

1. Mr. Gomez has 75 cans of beans. Each shelf holds 10 cans. How many shelves can he fill with cans of beans? How many cans will be left over?

   7 shelves 5 cans left over

2. Abigail has 39 stamps in her collection. She puts 10 stamps on each page of her stamp book. How many pages can she fill with stamps? How many stamps will be left over?

   3 pages 9 stamps left over

Add.

3. 45 + 8 = 53 22 + 4 = 26 86 + 3 = 89

Add.

4. 60 + 20 = 80 90 + 80 = 170 70 + 30 = 100
   6 + 2 = 8 9 + 8 = 17 7 + 3 = 10

5. 50 + 70 = 120 40 + 90 = 130 20 + 40 = 60
   5 + 7 = 12 4 + 9 = 13 2 + 4 = 6

6. Find the unknown partner.

   100
   46 54

146 UNIT 7 LESSON 4 Pose and Solve Comparison Story Problems

Homework and Remembering page 146

Home or School Activity

Sports Connection

What's the Score? Have children work in pairs to find information about two sports teams. For example, they could find the number of runs scored by two different baseball teams during a game. Then have them write and solve a comparison story problem using the information they found.

The Bears and the Lions played baseball last night.
The Bears scored 8 runs.
The Lions scored 2 more runs than the Bears.
How many runs did the Lions score?

Tables

Lesson Objectives

- Construct tables for comparison situations.
- Ask and answer comparison questions using information in a table.
- Continue collecting data for a class project.

Vocabulary
table
more
fewer
data

The Day at a Glance

Today's Goals	Materials	
1 Teaching the Lesson **A1:** Construct tables for comparison situations. **A2:** Read information in a table. **A3:** Collect data for a class project. **2 Going Further** ▸ Differentiated Instruction **3 Homework and Targeted Practice**	**Lesson Activities** Student Activity Book pp. 227–228 Homework and Remembering pp. 147–148 MathBoard materials Tally list from Lesson 2	**Going Further** Activity Cards 7-5 Small colored paper clips Spinners Crayons or colored pencils Math Journals

Keeping Skills Sharp

Quick Practice — 5 MINUTES

Goal: Practice subtraction with teen totals.

Materials: Blue Make-a-Ten Cards (Subtraction) (from Unit 1 Lesson 15 or TRB M39–M42)

Teen Subtraction Flash Have a **Student Leader** call out a teen total and one of its partners. The class flashes the other partner with their fingers. Example: The Student Leader says: "14 take away 5 equals something." The children flash nine fingers to show the unknown addend.

Make-a-Ten Cards: Subtraction Have children practice subtraction with teen totals using the Blue Make-a-Ten Cards. Children look at the front of the card and say the answer to themselves and then turn the card over to check the answer.

Daily Routines

Telling Time Naming the Hands, Telling Time on the Time Poster (See p. xxvii.)

▸ Led by Student Leaders

Money Routine Using the 120 Poster, Using the Money Flip Chart, Using the Number Path, Using Secret Code Cards (See pp. xxiii–xxv.)

▸ Led by Student Leaders

1 Teaching the Lesson

Activity 1

Construct a Table

 25 MINUTES

Goal: Construct tables for comparison situations.

Materials: MathBoard materials

 **NCTM Standards:**
Data Analysis and Probability
Number and Operations

Differentiated Instruction

English Learners Some children may be confused by the use of the word *table*. Point out that although the word *table* often refers to a piece of furniture, in this lesson we are talking about a different kind of table.

Explain to children that in math, a *table* is an orderly arrangement of information in columns and rows. Tables are used to organize information so that it is easier to read and understand.

English Language Learners

Draw the table showing Julio and Crystal's flowers. Write the word *table*.

- **Beginning** Say: **This is a *table*. A *table* shows data.** Have children repeat.
- **Intermediate** Say: **This is a *table*.** Ask: **What does the *table* show?** data
- **Advanced** Have children make a table and tell about the data it shows.

▶ Construct a Table for Comparison Situations

WHOLE CLASS

Write the following situation on the board. Read it aloud, or have a volunteer read it.

Julio has 3 flowers. Crystal has 7 flowers.

Show children how to display the information in a table. If children are familiar with tables, elicit as much help from them as possible.

- We can use a table to show how many flowers each person has. I'll draw a table on the board while you draw one on your MathBoards.
- We can write the names of children at the left side of the table. Instead of drawing flowers, we can write the word *flowers* to show what the children have. That is our label. *Demonstrate on your table as the children do the same on their tables.*
- How many flowers does Julio have? 3 flowers *Write the number on your table as the children do the same on their tables.*
- How many flowers does Crystal have? 7 flowers *Write the number on your table as the children do the same on their tables.*

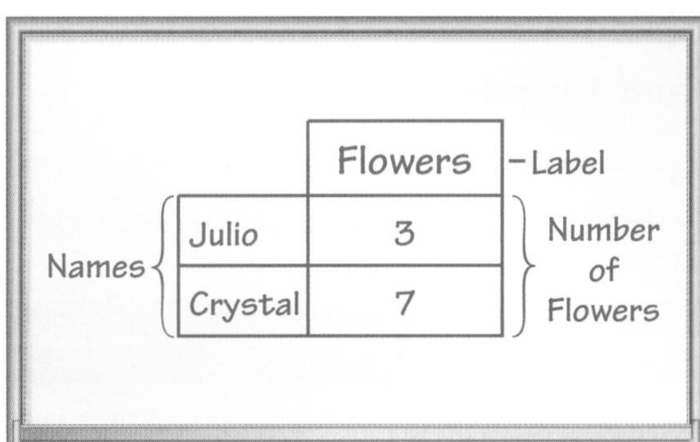

	Flowers
Julio	3
Crystal	7

▶ Construct Another Table for a Comparison Situation

WHOLE CLASS

Remind children of the sticker problem they solved in Lesson 2 and explain that the information in that problem can also be organized in a table.

- Here is a story we've seen before:

  Tom has 3 stickers, Ana has 9 stickers, and Reggie has 4 stickers.

- Last time, we made a picture graph with these numbers. Now we can use a table to show the same information.

Have children create a table that shows the number of stickers each child in the problem has. This may be done as a class on the board, or individually on MathBoards.

If children draw their tables on MathBoards, you might ask a few volunteers to display their boards to the rest of the class. Invite other children to comment and ask questions.

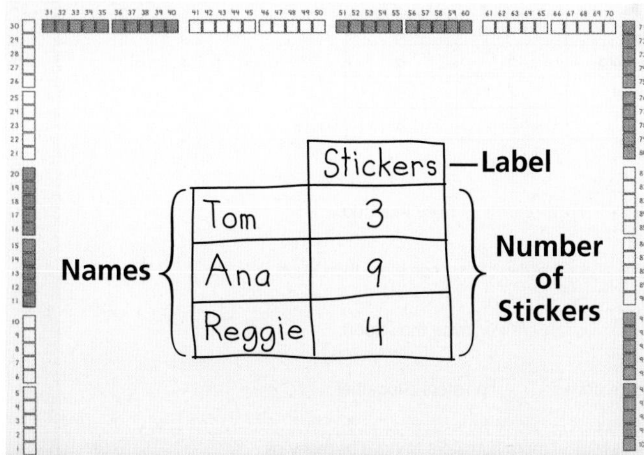

▶ Ask and Answer Questions Using a Table

WHOLE CLASS

Math Talk 

Invite children to use the table they just made to make up questions for the rest of the class to answer. Be sure children ask comparison questions using the words *more* and *fewer.* Remind them that the questions should be expressed both ways. For example:

- How many more stickers does Ana have than Tom?
- How many fewer stickers does Tom have than Ana?

If children do not spontaneously ask equalizing questions (For example: "How many more stickers does Tom need to have as many as Ana?" or "How many stickers does Ana have to lose to have as many as Tom?") you might want to ask some yourself.

After each question is asked, invite children to come to the board and explain how to answer the question. Encourage other children to comment and ask questions as needed.

Teaching Note

Watch For! Circulate around the room as children are constructing their tables. Make sure they are making their tables correctly and are not forgetting to include any of the parts. Specifically, check that everyone remembers to include a label on their table.

Ongoing Assessment

To check children's understanding of tables, ask questions like these:

- ▶ How many more stickers does Ana have than Reggie?
- ▶ How many more stickers does Reggie need to have as many as Ana?
- ▶ How many fewer stickers does Tom have than Reggie?
- ▶ How many stickers does Reggie have to lose to have as many as Tom?

Activity 2

Read Information from a Table

 15 MINUTES

Goal: Read information in a table.

Materials: Student Activity Book page 227

 **NCTM Standards:**
Data Analysis and Probability
Number and Operations
Communication

The Learning Classroom

Helping Community Some children may have difficulty finding the correct information in the table on Student Activity Book page 227. Have them work in Helping Pairs to decide which numbers to use to answer each question.

▶ More Comparisons INDIVIDUALS

Have children complete Student Activity Book page 227.

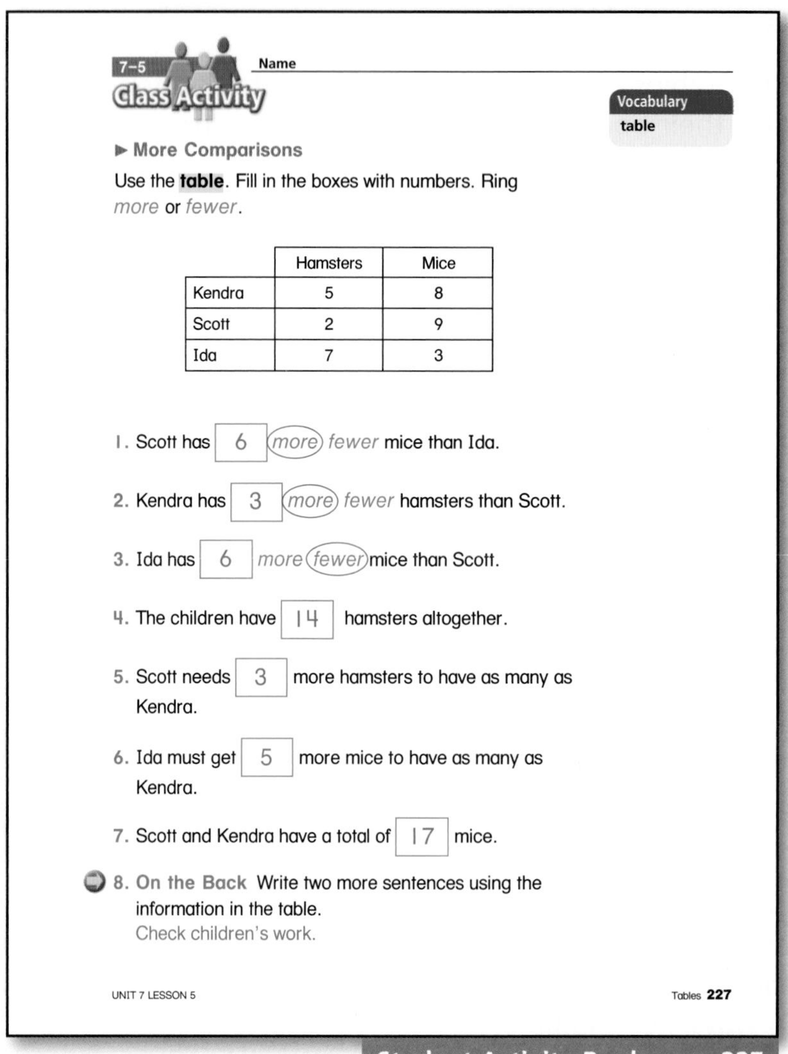

7–5 Class Activity

Name

Vocabulary
table

▶ More Comparisons

Use the **table**. Fill in the boxes with numbers. Ring *more* or *fewer*.

	Hamsters	Mice
Kendra	5	8
Scott	2	9
Ida	7	3

1. Scott has 6 (more) fewer mice than Ida.
2. Kendra has 3 (more) fewer hamsters than Scott.
3. Ida has 6 more (fewer) mice than Scott.
4. The children have 14 hamsters altogether.
5. Scott needs 3 more hamsters to have as many as Kendra.
6. Ida must get 5 more mice to have as many as Kendra.
7. Scott and Kendra have a total of 17 mice.
8. On the Back Write two more sentences using the information in the table.
Check children's work.

UNIT 7 LESSON 5 Tables 227

Student Activity Book page 227

Activity 3

Collect Data for the Class Project

 10 MINUTES

Goal: Collect data for a class project.

Materials: tally list from Lesson 2

 **NCTM Standard**
Data Analysis and Probability

▶ Data Collection Project WHOLE CLASS

Explain to children that today another third of the class will be giving information for the class project. (See page 495.) As you record the data, remind children how to make tally marks.

- Remember we show four tally marks like this: ||||
- Then when we get to five, we use the fifth mark to cross through the other four: Now, we have a group of five marks. 

2 Going Further

Intervention — Activity Card 7-5

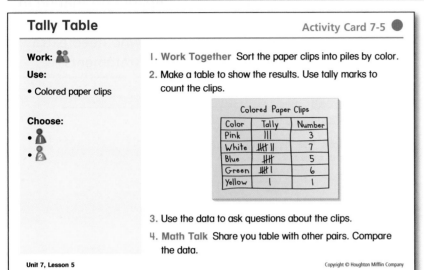

Tally Table — Activity Card 7-5

Work: pairs

Use:

- Colored paper clips

Choose:

- 1
- 2

1. **Work Together** Sort the paper clips into piles by color.
2. Make a table to show the results. Use tally marks to count the clips.

Colored Paper Clips

Color	Tally	Number
Pink	|||	3
White	𝍸 ||	7
Blue	𝍸	5
Green	𝍸 |	6
Yellow	|	1

3. Use the data to ask questions about the clips.
4. **Math Talk** Share you table with other pairs. Compare the data.

Unit 7, Lesson 5

Activity Note Each pair needs a handful of small colored paper clips or other small objects. Help children make the table to record the results.

Math Writing Prompt

Compare the Data Jill has 8 marbles and Kevin has 6 marbles. Make a table to show the results. Write a comparison statement.

Software Support

Use *Soar to Success* for instruction of students needing targeted support for underlying skills.

On Level — Activity Card 7-5

Spin the Spinner — Activity Card 7-5

Work: pairs

Use:

- Spinner
- Paper clip
- Crayons or markers

Choose:

- 1
- 2

1. **Work Together** Color each section of the spinner a different color.
2. Use a pencil and paper clip to spin the spinner 20 times.
3. Record the number of times the paper clip landed on each color. Make and label a table to record the results.
4. Write two statements about the information in the table.

	Spinner
Red	3
Blue	7
Green	5
Yellow	5

We spun blue the greatest number of times.

We spun green and yellow the same number of times.

Unit 7, Lesson 5

Activity Note Each pair needs a spinner (TRB M27), paper clip, and crayons or markers. Have pairs compare their results.

Math Writing Prompt

Compare and Contrast How are a tally table and a picture graph alike? How are they different?

Software Support

Use *MegaMath* for review and reinforcement of the concepts and skills presented in this lesson.

Challenge — Activity Card 7-5

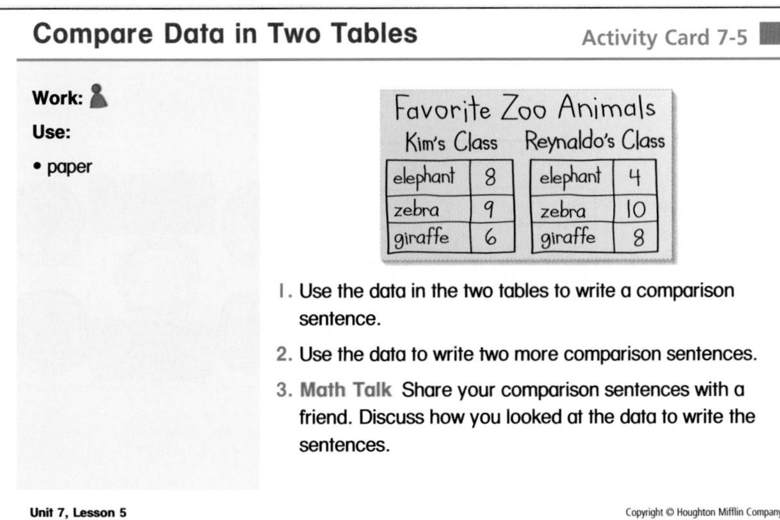

Compare Data in Two Tables — Activity Card 7-5

Work: individual

Use:

- paper

Favorite Zoo Animals

Kim's Class		Reynaldo's Class	
elephant	8	elephant	4
zebra	9	zebra	10
giraffe	6	giraffe	8

1. Use the data in the two tables to write a comparison sentence.
2. Use the data to write two more comparison sentences.
3. **Math Talk** Share your comparison sentences with a friend. Discuss how you looked at the data to write the sentences.

Unit 7, Lesson 5

Copyright © Houghton Mifflin Company

Activity Note You may want to have children write comparison story problems to share with other children to solve.

Math Writing Prompt

Explore Your Data In Mr. Lee's class, 8 children like corn, 3 like carrots, and 7 like peas. Write three comparison statements about the data.

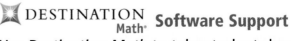

Software Support

Use *Destination Math* to take students beyond the concepts and skills presented in this lesson.

3 Homework and Targeted Practice

Goal: Additional Practice

This Homework page provides practice answering comparison questions from a table.

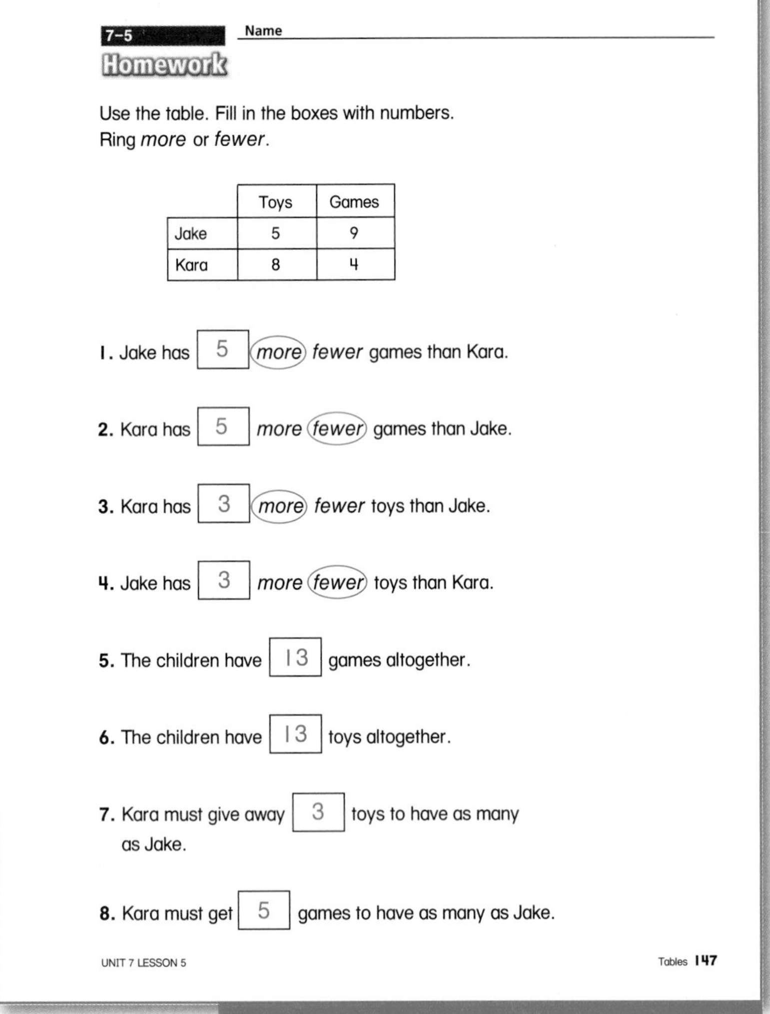

7–5 Homework Name ______

Use the table. Fill in the boxes with numbers.
Ring *more* or *fewer*.

	Toys	Games
Jake	5	9
Kara	8	4

1. Jake has [5] (*more*) *fewer* games than Kara.
2. Kara has [5] *more* (*fewer*) games than Jake.
3. Kara has [3] (*more*) *fewer* toys than Jake.
4. Jake has [3] *more* (*fewer*) toys than Kara.
5. The children have [13] games altogether.
6. The children have [13] toys altogether.
7. Kara must give away [3] toys to have as many as Jake.
8. Kara must get [5] games to have as many as Jake.

UNIT 7 LESSON 5 Tables 147

Homework and Remembering page 147

Goal: Compare information in a table.

This page can be used with children who need extra practice with tables and comparison statements.

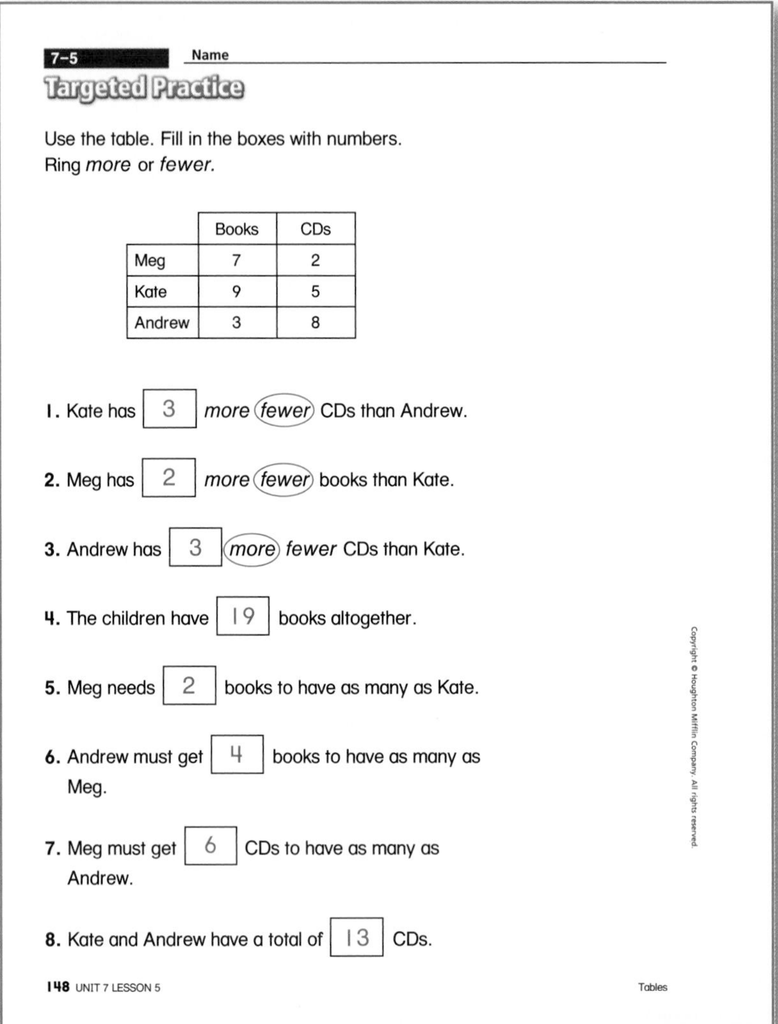

7–5 Targeted Practice Name ______

Use the table. Fill in the boxes with numbers.
Ring *more* or *fewer*.

	Books	CDs
Meg	7	2
Kate	9	5
Andrew	3	8

1. Kate has [3] *more* (*fewer*) CDs than Andrew.
2. Meg has [2] *more* (*fewer*) books than Kate.
3. Andrew has [3] (*more*) *fewer* CDs than Kate.
4. The children have [19] books altogether.
5. Meg needs [2] books to have as many as Kate.
6. Andrew must get [4] books to have as many as Meg.
7. Meg must get [6] CDs to have as many as Andrew.
8. Kate and Andrew have a total of [13] CDs.

148 UNIT 7 LESSON 5 Tables

Homework and Remembering page 148

Home or School Activity

Art Connection

Abstract Art Discuss abstract art with children. Point out that sometimes artists use geometric shapes in their drawings. If possible, show children a few examples of Pablo Picasso's, Georges Braque's, Wassily Kandinsky's, or Piet Mondrian's work and have them point out the different shapes they see.

Challenge children to draw a design using only circles, triangles, and rectangles. Have a partner make a table indicating how many of each shape appear in the drawing.

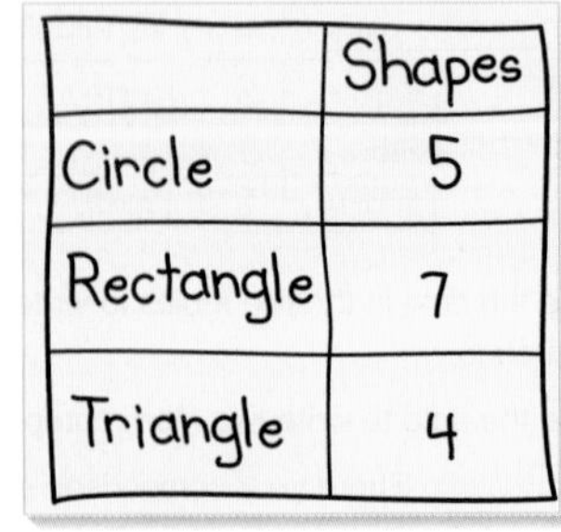

	Shapes
Circle	5
Rectangle	7
Triangle	4

Convert Tables to Picture Graphs

Lesson Objectives

- Construct tables and convert them to picture graphs.
- Record data collected for a class project.

Vocabulary
table
picture graph
data

The Day at a Glance

Today's Goals	Materials	
1 Teaching the Lesson **A1:** Construct tables and convert them to picture graphs. **A2:** Record data for a class project.	**Lesson Activities** Student Activity Book pp. 229–230 Homework and Remembering pp. 149–150	**Going Further** Activity Cards 7-6 Chart paper Book of nursery rhymes Math Journals
2 Going Further ▸ Differentiated Instruction		
3 Homework and Spiral Review		

123 Use Math Talk today!

Keeping Skills Sharp

Quick Practice — 5 MINUTES

Goal: Practice subtraction with teen totals.

Materials: Blue Make-a-Ten Cards (Subtraction) (from Unit 1 Lesson 15 or TRB M39–M42)

Make-a-Ten Cards: Subtraction Have children practice subtraction with teen totals using the Blue Make-a-Ten Cards. Children look at the front of the card and say the answer to themselves and then turn the card over to check the answer. (If they miss an answer, they should look at the small numbers on the card to see how making a ten can help them with subtraction from teen numbers.) Children put the cards they answered quickly in one pile, the cards they know accurately but slowly in another pile, and the ones they missed in a third pile. Then they practice the ones they missed or answered slowly. (See Unit 7 Lesson 5.)

Repeated Quick Practice
Use this Quick Practice from a previous lesson.

▸ **Teen Subtraction Flash** (See Unit 7 Lesson 5.)

Daily Routines

Telling Time Naming the Hands, Telling Time on the Time Poster (See p. xxvii.)

▸ Led by Student Leaders

Money Routine Using the 120 Poster, Using the Money Flip Chart, Using the Number Path, Using Secret Code Cards (See pp. xxiii–xxv.)

▸ Led by Student Leaders

1 Teaching the Lesson

Activity 1

Construct a Picture Graph

40 MINUTES

Goals: Construct tables and convert them to picture graphs.

Materials: Student Activity Book page 229

NCTM Standards:
Data Analysis and Probability
Communication

English Language Learners

Draw a table and picture graph that both show the same data.

- **Beginning** Say: **A *table* shows data using numbers and words. A *picture graph* shows data using pictures.** Have children repeat.
- **Intermediate** Ask: **Do *tables* use numbers and words to show data?** yes **What do *picture graphs* use to show data?** pictures
- **Advanced** Have children tell how tables and picture graphs show data differently.

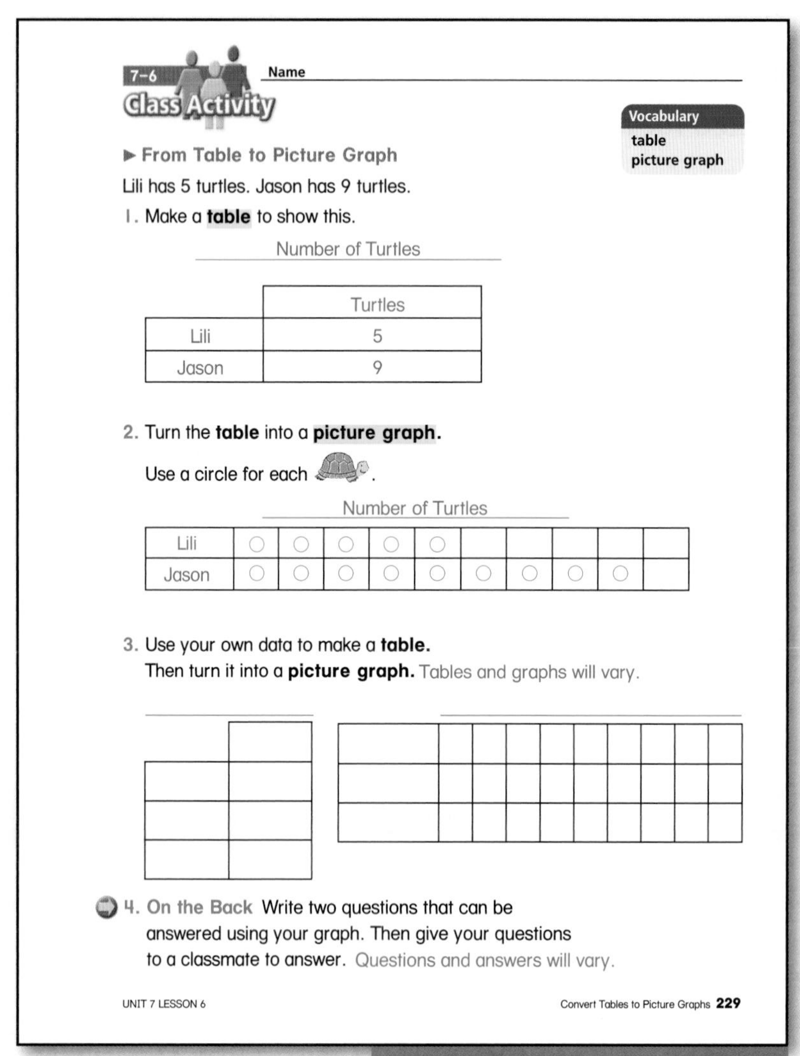

7-6 Class Activity

Name

Vocabulary
table
picture graph

▶ From Table to Picture Graph

Lili has 5 turtles. Jason has 9 turtles.

1. Make a **table** to show this.

Number of Turtles

	Turtles
Lili	5
Jason	9

2. Turn the **table** into a **picture graph**.

Use a circle for each turtle.

Number of Turtles

Lili	○	○	○	○	○					
Jason	○	○	○	○	○	○	○	○	○	

3. Use your own data to make a **table**.
Then turn it into a **picture graph.** Tables and graphs will vary.

4. On the Back Write two questions that can be answered using your graph. Then give your questions to a classmate to answer. Questions and answers will vary.

UNIT 7 LESSON 6 Convert Tables to Picture Graphs 229

Student Activity Book page 229

▶ From Table to Picture Graph WHOLE CLASS

Work through exercises 1 and 2 as a class. Have children complete exercises 3 and 4 independently and then share their work.

Activity 2

Data Collection

15 MINUTES

Goal: Record data for a class project.

Materials: tally list from Lesson 5

▶ Complete Collecting Data for the Class Project

Review the use of tally marks as necessary. Finish collecting data from the rest of the class. Keep the data posted for the next lesson. (See page 495.)

2 Going Further

Differentiated Instruction

Intervention — Activity Card 7-6

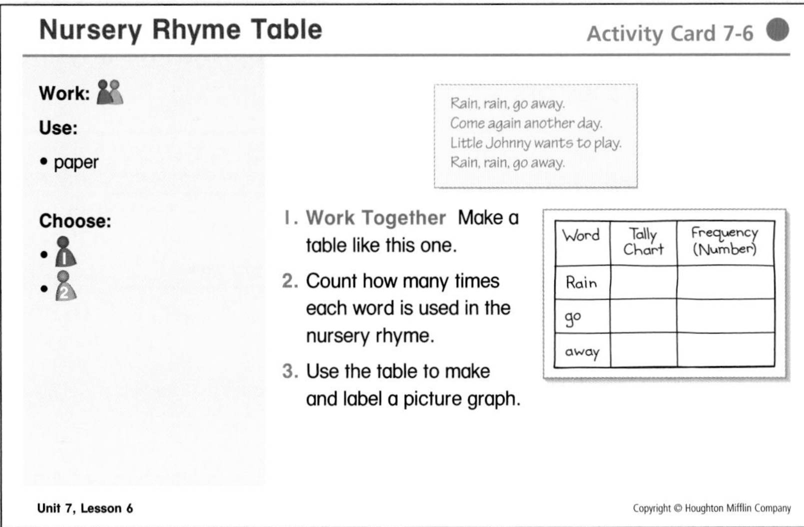

Nursery Rhyme Table — Activity Card 7-6

Work: (pairs)
Use:
- paper

Choose:
- 1
- 2

Rain, rain, go away.
Come again another day.
Little Johnny wants to play.
Rain, rain, go away.

1. **Work Together** Make a table like this one.
2. Count how many times each word is used in the nursery rhyme.
3. Use the table to make and label a picture graph.

Word	Tally Chart	Frequency (Number)
Rain		
go		
away		

Unit 7, Lesson 6 — Copyright © Houghton Mifflin Company

Activity Note Each pair needs to make a table to count the words in the nursery rhyme and then make a picture graph.

Math Writing Prompt

How Many in Your Class? Write a problem that can be solved with a picture graph that shows the number of boys and girls in your class.

Software Support

Use *Soar to Success* for instruction of students needing targeted support for underlying skills.

On Level — Activity Card 7-6

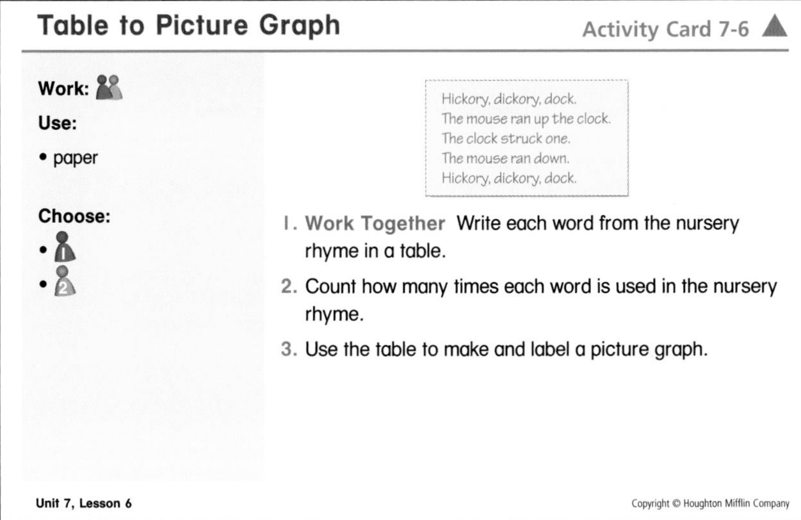

Table to Picture Graph — Activity Card 7-6

Work: (pairs)
Use:
- paper

Choose:
- 1
- 2

Hickory, dickory, dock.
The mouse ran up the clock.
The clock struck one.
The mouse ran down.
Hickory, dickory, dock.

1. **Work Together** Write each word from the nursery rhyme in a table.
2. Count how many times each word is used in the nursery rhyme.
3. Use the table to make and label a picture graph.

Unit 7, Lesson 6 — Copyright © Houghton Mifflin Company

Activity Note Check that pairs are counting each different word. Children should check each other's work.

Math Writing Prompt

Write a Letter Write a letter to a friend explaining how to use a table to make a picture graph.

Software Support

Use *MegaMath* for review and reinforcement of the concepts and skills presented in this lesson.

Challenge — Activity Card 7-6

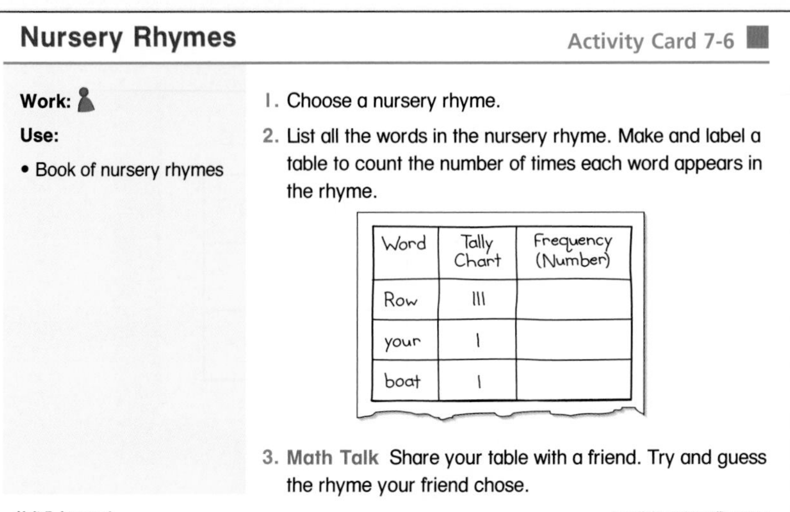

Nursery Rhymes — Activity Card 7-6

Work: (individual)
Use:
- Book of nursery rhymes

1. Choose a nursery rhyme.
2. List all the words in the nursery rhyme. Make and label a table to count the number of times each word appears in the rhyme.

Word	Tally Chart	Frequency (Number)
Row	III	
your	I	
boat	I	

3. **Math Talk** Share your table with a friend. Try and guess the rhyme your friend chose.

Unit 7, Lesson 6 — Copyright © Houghton Mifflin Company

Activity Note Have several books of nursery rhymes available. Display the tables and have children guess the rhymes.

Math Writing Prompt

Make a Picture Graph In a table, record how many windows and doors are in your classroom. Then make a picture graph. Use pictures and words to explain your graph.

DESTINATION Math®

Software Support

Use *Destination Math* to take students beyond the concepts and skills presented in this lesson.

3 Homework and Spiral Review

Goal: Additional Practice

✓ Include children's completed Homework page as part of their portfolios.

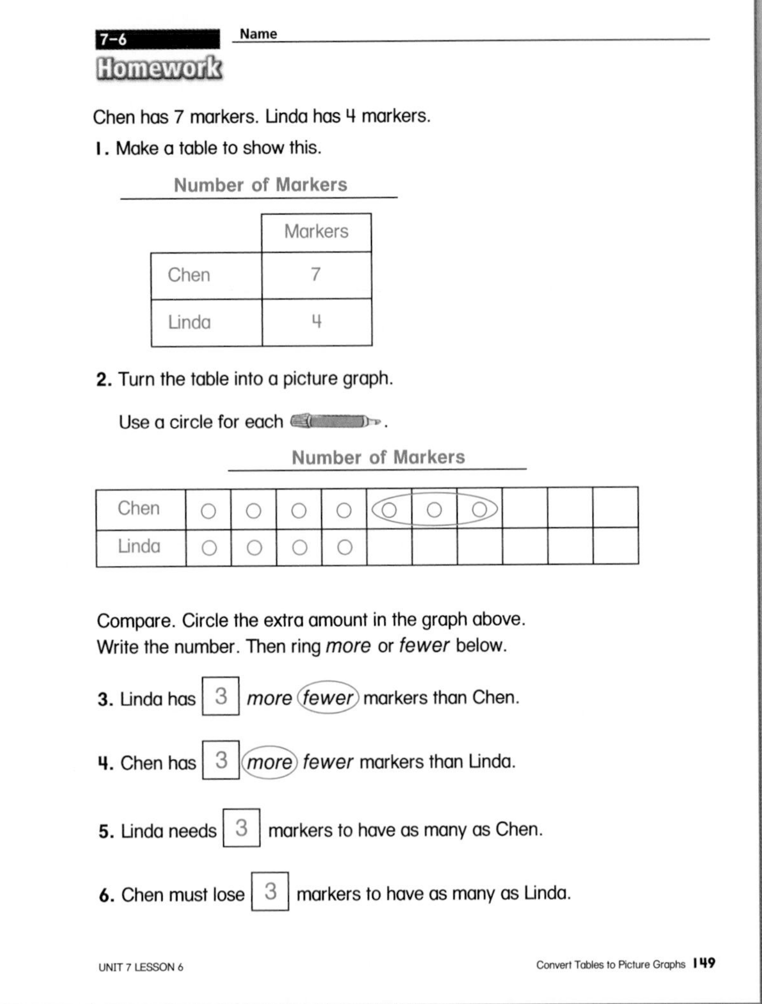

7–6 Homework
Name ______

Chen has 7 markers. Linda has 4 markers.

1. Make a table to show this.

Number of Markers

	Markers
Chen	7
Linda	4

2. Turn the table into a picture graph.

Use a circle for each marker.

Number of Markers

Chen	○	○	○	○	○	○	○			
Linda	○	○	○	○						

Compare. Circle the extra amount in the graph above.
Write the number. Then ring *more* or *fewer* below.

3. Linda has 3 *more* *fewer* markers than Chen.

4. Chen has 3 *more* *fewer* markers than Linda.

5. Linda needs 3 markers to have as many as Chen.

6. Chen must lose 3 markers to have as many as Linda.

UNIT 7 LESSON 6 Convert Tables to Picture Graphs 149

Homework and Remembering page 149

Goal: Spiral Review

This Remembering activity would be appropriate anytime after today's lesson.

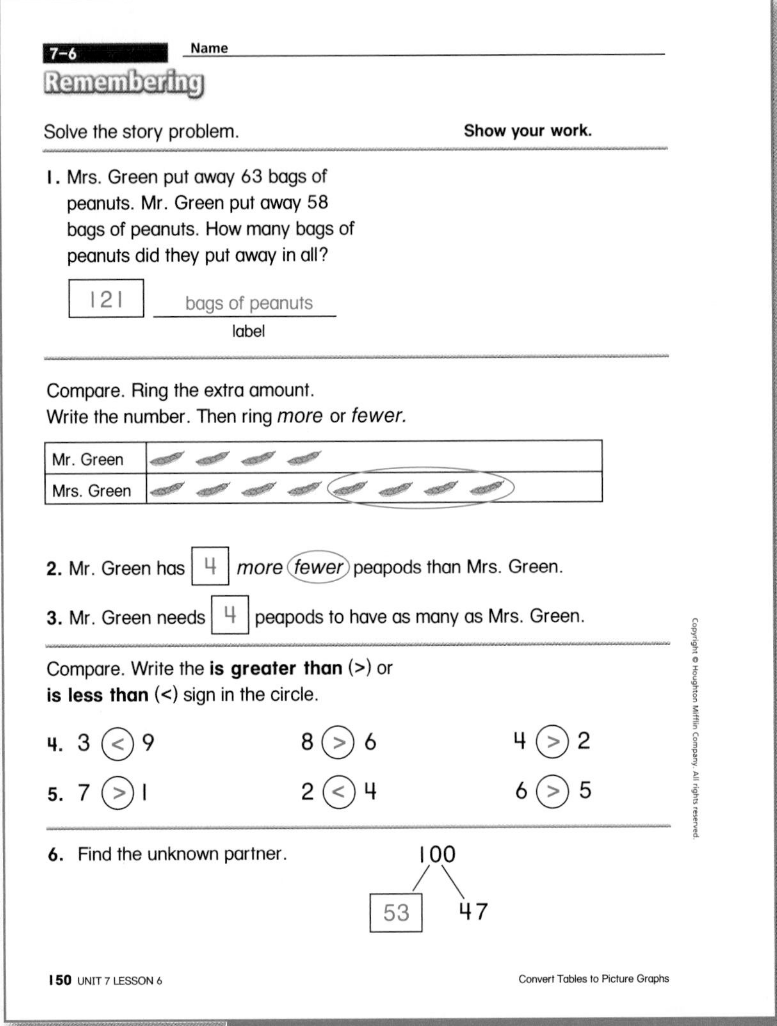

7–6 Remembering
Name ______

Solve the story problem. **Show your work.**

1. Mrs. Green put away 63 bags of peanuts. Mr. Green put away 58 bags of peanuts. How many bags of peanuts did they put away in all?

121 bags of peanuts
label

Compare. Ring the extra amount.
Write the number. Then ring *more* or *fewer.*

Mr. Green	4 peapods
Mrs. Green	8 peapods

2. Mr. Green has 4 *more* *fewer* peapods than Mrs. Green.

3. Mr. Green needs 4 peapods to have as many as Mrs. Green.

Compare. Write the **is greater than** (>) or **is less than** (<) sign in the circle.

4. 3 < 9 8 > 6 4 > 2

5. 7 > 1 2 < 4 6 > 5

6. Find the unknown partner.

100
53 47

150 UNIT 7 LESSON 6 Convert Tables to Picture Graphs

Copyright © Houghton Mifflin Company. All rights reserved.

Homework and Remembering page 150

Home or School Activity

Technology Connection

Use a Computer Have children use a word processing program to create the table at the top of Student Activity Book page 229.

Number of Turtles

	Turtles
Lili	5
Jason	9

Graph Data

Lesson Objectives

- Convert data from a tally list to a summary table.
- Convert a table to a picture graph and ask questions based on the data.

Vocabulary

data	picture graph
tally list	survey
table	tally marks

The Day at a Glance

Today's Goals	Materials	
1 Teaching the Lesson A: Convert data from a tally list to a table. Convert the table to a picture graph and ask questions based on the data.	**Lesson Activities** Student Activity Book p. 231 Homework and Remembering pp. 151–152 Completed tally list from Lesson 6 Blank transparency (optional) Quick Quiz 2 (Assessment Guide)	**Going Further** Activity Cards 7-7 Student Activity Book p. 232 Class list Construction paper Crayons or colored pencils Paper plates Math Journals
2 Going Further ► Extension: Independent Data Project ► Differentiated Instruction		
3 Homework and Targeted Practice		

Use Math Talk today!

Keeping Skills Sharp

Quick Practice — 5 MINUTES	Daily Routines
Goal: Practice subtraction with teen totals. **Materials:** Blue Make-a-Ten Cards (subtraction) (from Unit 1 Lesson 15 or TRB M39–M42.) **Teen Subtraction Flash** The Student Leader calls out a teen total and one of its partners. The class flashes the other partner with their fingers. (See Unit 7 Lesson 5.) **Make-a-Ten Cards: Subtraction** Have children practice subtraction with teen totals using the Blue Make-a-Ten Cards. Children look at the front of the card and say the answer to themselves and then turn the card over to check the answer. (If they miss an answer, they should look at the small numbers on the card to see how making a ten can help them with subtraction from teen numbers.) (See Unit 7 Lesson 6.)	**Telling Time** Naming the Hands, Telling Time on the Time Poster (See p. xxvii.) ► Led by Student Leaders **Money Routine** Using the 120 Poster, Using the Money Flip Chart, Using the Number Path, Using Secret Code Cards (See pp. xxiii–xxv.) ► Led by Student Leaders

1 Teaching the Lesson

Activity

Present Collected Data

 **55 MINUTES**

Goals: Convert data from a tally list to a table. Convert the table to a picture graph and ask questions based on the data.

Materials: completed tally list from Lesson 6, Student Activity Book page 231, blank transparency (optional)

 **NCTM Standards:**
Data Analysis and Probability
Number and Operations
Communication

Teaching Note

What to Expect from Students Some children might still be confused about how to count tally marks for groups of 5. If necessary provide practice on drawing and counting tally marks for 5, 10, and 15.

English Language Learners

Survey the class about their favorite color. Draw an example of a tally list. Write *tally list* on the board.

- **Beginning** Say: **This is a *tally list*.** Point to the *tally marks*. **A *tally list* is a list of *tally marks*.** Have children repeat.
- **Intermediate** Say: **This is a *tally list*.** Ask: **What is a *tally list* a list of?** tally marks
- **Advanced** Have children tell about a time they might use a tally list.

▶ Class Data WHOLE CLASS

Display the completed tally list from Lesson 6 and have children count the tally marks for each category. Use the data collected from your class. Favorite color is used as an example below.

Favorite Color
Yellow ||||
Red 𝍸 ||
Green 𝍸 |
Blue 𝍸 𝍸 |

▶ Record the Collected Data WHOLE CLASS

Direct children's attention to Student Activity Book page 231. Guide them in recording the information from the tally list into a table.

You may want to make a transparency of Student Activity Book page 231 or draw a blank table on the board. Have children select a title for the table. Ask a volunteer to read the results to the class. Then have children work together to complete the table.

Create a Picture Graph Refer children to the blank grid on Student Activity Book page 231. You may want to draw a blank grid like the one shown, on the board. Explain to children this grid will be used to create a picture graph. If you are drawing the graph on the board, do not spend time drawing each dividing line. A simple sketch will be fine. Guide children in using the data in the table to make a picture graph.

- Our next step is to make a picture graph using the information in the table. I'll draw a blank picture graph on the board while you fill in the blank graph in exercise 2.
- How should we start? Who would like to come to the board and begin our graph?

Invite different children to come to the board to fill in parts of the graph. Have other children make comments and suggestions on how to draw the graph. Children should make corrections as needed. As a group, the class should agree on how to graph the information from the table. Explain to children that they can use smiley faces to represent each child in the picture graph.

7-7 **Class Activity** Name

Vocabulary
table
picture graph
data

► **Record the Collected Data** Answers will vary. Sample answers shown.

1. Fill in the **table**. Your teacher will help you.

Favorite Colors

	Number of Children
Yellow	4
Red	7
Green	6
Blue	11

2. Fill in the **picture graph**. Your teacher will help you.

Our Favorite Colors

Yellow	☺	☺	☺	☺								
Red	☺	☺	☺	☺	☺	☺	☺					
Green	☺	☺	☺	☺	☺	☺						
Blue	☺	☺	☺	☺	☺	☺	☺	☺	☺	☺	☺	

3. Write two questions about the **data** in the graph. Questions will vary. Sample questions shown.

Which color was chosen the most?

How many more children chose red than yellow?

UNIT 7 LESSON 7 Graph Data 231

Student Activity Book page 231

Our Favorite Colors

Yellow	☺	☺	☺	☺								
Red	☺	☺	☺	☺	☺	☺	☺					
Green	☺	☺	☺	☺	☺	☺						
Blue	☺	☺	☺	☺	☺	☺	☺	☺	☺	☺	☺	

Math Talk **Ask Questions About the Data** Have children take turns asking questions about the graph. For variety, you may also have children make statements based on the information found in the graph. For example:

- In our class, 11 children like blue. That's 5 more than like green.

If time allows, you may wish to have the children make a vertical bar graph on a separate sheet of paper. Have children discuss how the vertical and horizontal graphs are the same and how they are different.

Differentiated Instruction

Advanced Learners You might wish to have some of your advanced children make pictographs to show the data in the table. After they have completed their pictographs, encourage them to share and discuss them with the class.

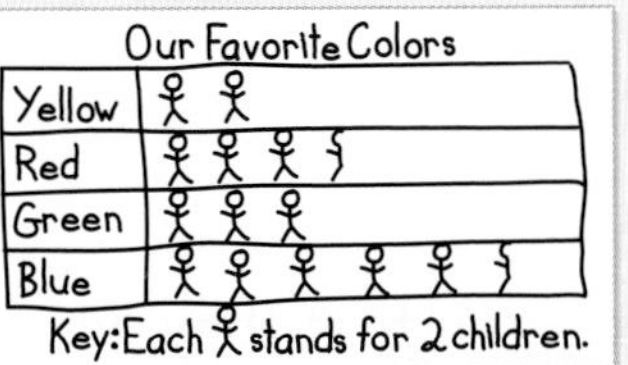

Ongoing Assessment

Ask questions about the information in the graph similar to the ones below.

- ► How many more children like blue than red?
- ► How many children like green or yellow?
- ► How many children like red or blue?

Quick Quiz

See Assessment Guide for Unit 7 Quick Quiz 2.

2 Going Further

Extension: Independent Data Project

Goals: Create and plan a survey. Take a survey, make tables, and create a picture graph.

Materials: Student Activity Book page 232, class list (1 copy per pair)

NCTM Standards:
Data Analysis and Probability
Number and Operations
Communication

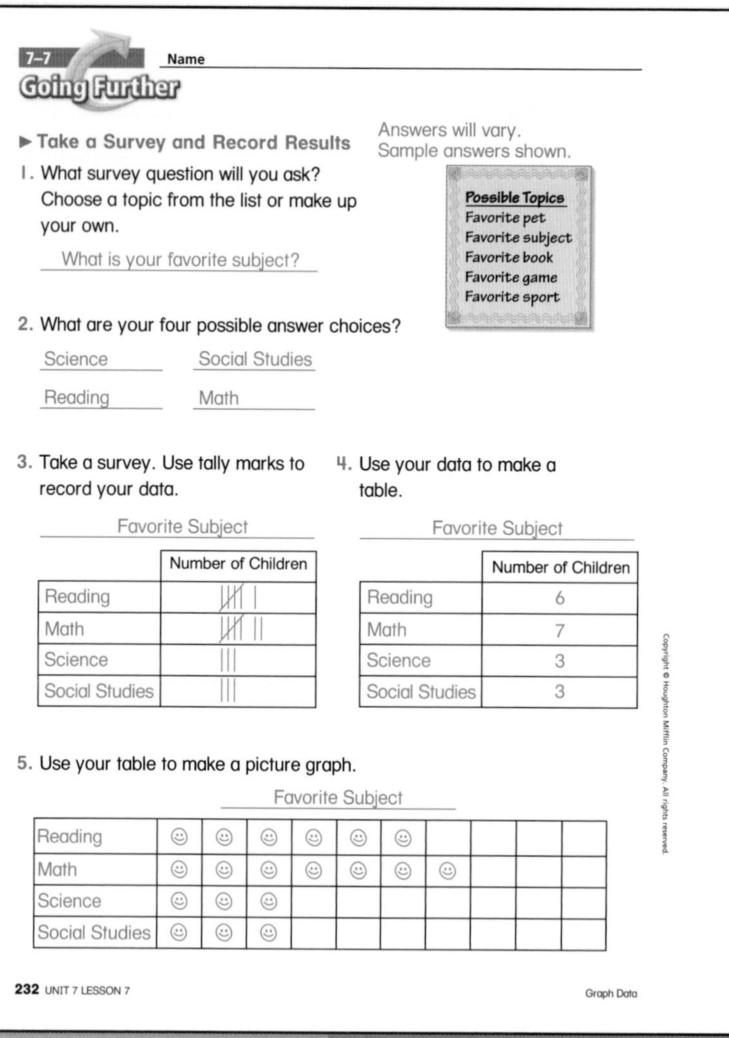

7–7 Going Further Name ____________

▶ Take a Survey and Record Results

Answers will vary.
Sample answers shown.

1. What survey question will you ask? Choose a topic from the list or make up your own.

What is your favorite subject?

Possible Topics
Favorite pet
Favorite subject
Favorite book
Favorite game
Favorite sport

2. What are your four possible answer choices?

Science Social Studies
Reading Math

3. Take a survey. Use tally marks to record your data.

Favorite Subject

	Number of Children
Reading	~~||||~~	
Math	~~||||~~ ||
Science	|||
Social Studies	|||

4. Use your data to make a table.

Favorite Subject

	Number of Children
Reading	6
Math	7
Science	3
Social Studies	3

5. Use your table to make a picture graph.

Favorite Subject

Reading	☺	☺	☺	☺	☺	☺				
Math	☺	☺	☺	☺	☺	☺	☺			
Science	☺	☺	☺							
Social Studies	☺	☺	☺							

232 UNIT 7 LESSON 7 Graph Data

Student Activity Book page 232

▶ Take a Survey and Record Results

PAIRS

Tell children that they will be working in pairs to collect information for the purpose of making a table and a picture graph.

Create and Plan a Survey Have children decide on a topic for their data project. Tell them to choose a topic from the list on Student Activity Book page 232 or to make up one of their own.

After the pair has chosen a topic, have them write their survey question at the top of the page. Then, underneath the survey question, have them write four possible answer choices for that question. For example, a question like, "What is your favorite subject?" could have choices such as Reading, Math, Science, and Social Studies.

Take a Survey After children have decided on their question and possible answer choices, have them meet with other children in the class to conduct their survey. Remind them to use tally marks to record the results. You may wish to provide children with a class list to help them keep track of the children they have surveyed.

Make a Table and Graph Once the surveys are complete, have children use their data to make a table. Then have them use the table to make a picture graph to display the data. Remind children to use a smiley face or stick figure to represent children who voted in the picture graph.

Class Management

Walk around the room and observe as the children use their tally lists to create tables and picture graphs. Watch for children who omit labels or use incorrect labels on their graphs. Use questioning to help them display the data from the tally list in a picture graph.

- ▶ What are the answer choices in your tally list?
- ▶ Where are the answer choices on your table?
- ▶ Where are the answer choices on your graph?
- ▶ Which answer choice was chosen the most?
- ▶ Which answer choice was chosen the least?
- ▶ How do you know how many circles to draw on the picture graph for each answer choice?

Intervention

Activity Card 7-7

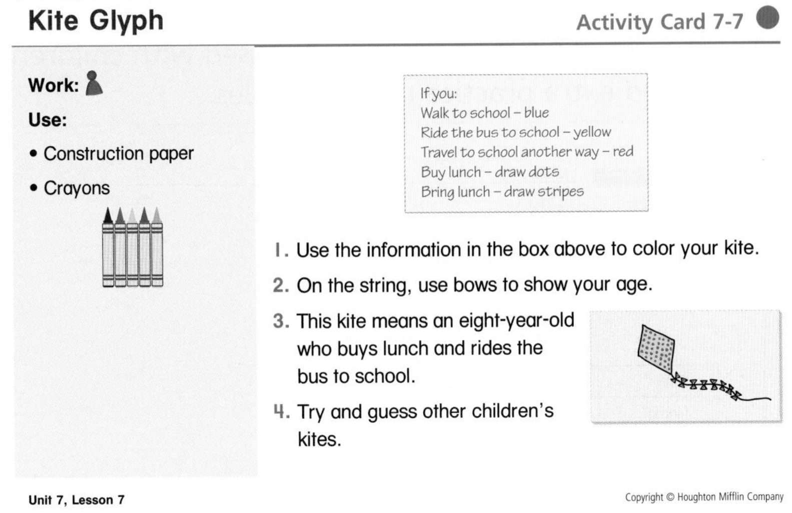

Kite Glyph Activity Card 7-7 ●

Work:

Use:

- Construction paper
- Crayons

If you:
Walk to school – blue
Ride the bus to school – yellow
Travel to school another way – red
Buy lunch – draw dots
Bring lunch – draw stripes

1. Use the information in the box above to color your kite.
2. On the string, use bows to show your age.
3. This kite means an eight-year-old who buys lunch and rides the bus to school.
4. Try and guess other children's kites.

Unit 7, Lesson 7

Copyright © Houghton Mifflin Company

Activity Note Explain to children that a glyph is another way to show information. Draw an outline of a kite on the construction paper.

Math Writing Prompt

Interpret Data Complete the table on Homework and Remembering page 151. Write two comparison statements about the table.

Software Support

Use *Soar to Success* for instruction of students needing targeted support for underlying skills.

On Level

Activity Card 7-7

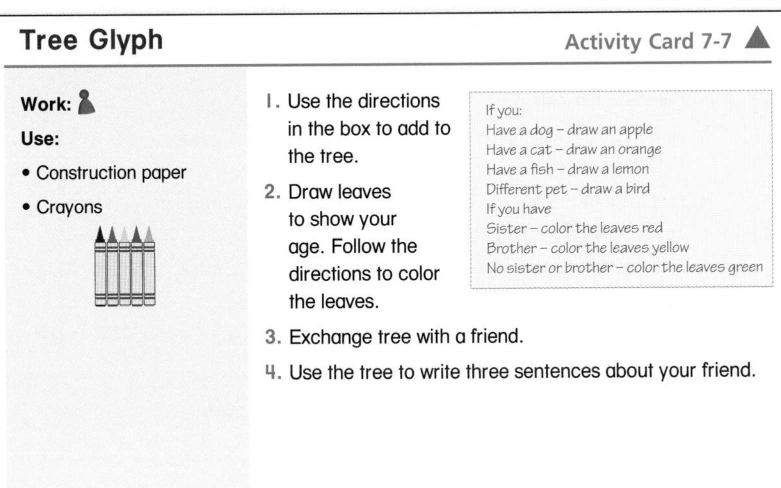

Tree Glyph Activity Card 7-7 ▲

Work:

Use:

- Construction paper
- Crayons

1. Use the directions in the box to add to the tree.
2. Draw leaves to show your age. Follow the directions to color the leaves.
3. Exchange tree with a friend.
4. Use the tree to write three sentences about your friend.

If you:
Have a dog – draw an apple
Have a cat – draw an orange
Have a fish – draw a lemon
Different pet – draw a bird
If you have
Sister – color the leaves red
Brother – color the leaves yellow
No sister or brother – color the leaves green

Unit 7, Lesson 7

Copyright © Houghton Mifflin Company

Activity Note Explain to children that a glyph is another way to show information. Draw an outline of a tree on the construction paper.

Math Writing Prompt

Write About It Write about when you think a picture graph may be helpful to use.

Software Support

Use *MegaMath* for review and reinforcement of the concepts and skills presented in this lesson.

Challenge

Activity Card 7-7

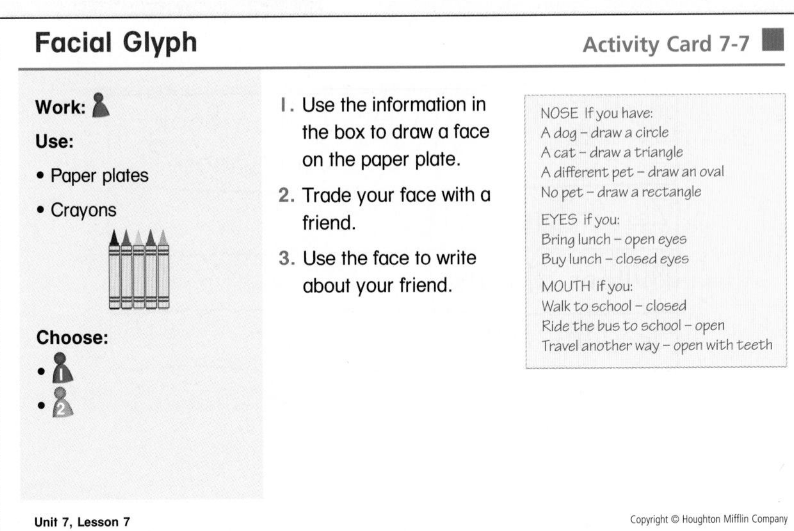

Facial Glyph Activity Card 7-7 ■

Work:

Use:

- Paper plates
- Crayons

Choose:

-
-

1. Use the information in the box to draw a face on the paper plate.
2. Trade your face with a friend.
3. Use the face to write about your friend.

NOSE If you have:
A dog – draw a circle
A cat – draw a triangle
A different pet – draw an oval
No pet – draw a rectangle

EYES If you:
Bring lunch – open eyes
Buy lunch – closed eyes

MOUTH If you:
Walk to school – closed
Ride the bus to school – open
Travel another way – open with teeth

Unit 7, Lesson 7

Copyright © Houghton Mifflin Company

Activity Note Explain to children that a glyph is another way to show information. Have children use the glyph to write about their friends.

Math Writing Prompt

Make a Table Ed found 14 rocks. Al found 5 more rocks than Ed. Robin found 3 fewer rocks than Al. Make a table to show how many rocks each child found.

Software Support

Use *Destination Math* to take students beyond the concepts and skills presented in this lesson.

3 Homework and Targeted Practice

Goal: Additional Practice

This Homework page provides practice making a table and picture graph and interpreting data.

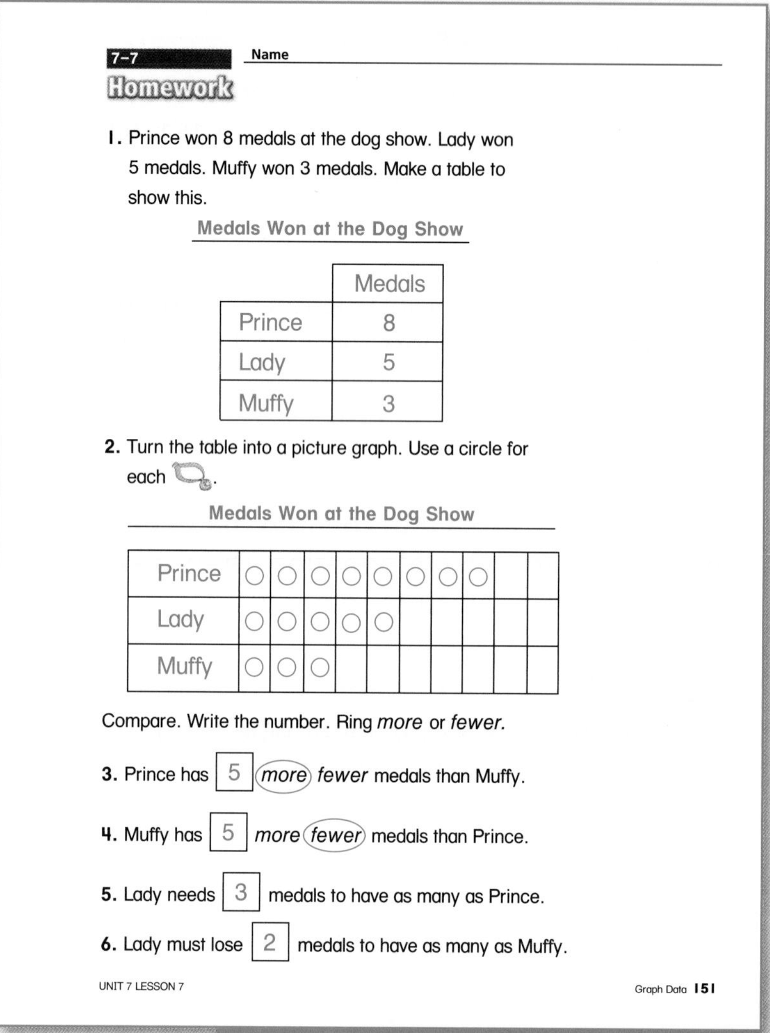

7–7 Homework Name ____________

1. Prince won 8 medals at the dog show. Lady won 5 medals. Muffy won 3 medals. Make a table to show this.

Medals Won at the Dog Show

	Medals
Prince	8
Lady	5
Muffy	3

2. Turn the table into a picture graph. Use a circle for each .

Medals Won at the Dog Show

Prince	○	○	○	○	○	○	○	○		
Lady	○	○	○	○	○					
Muffy	○	○	○							

Compare. Write the number. Ring *more* or *fewer.*

3. Prince has [5] (*more*) *fewer* medals than Muffy.

4. Muffy has [5] *more* (*fewer*) medals than Prince.

5. Lady needs [3] medals to have as many as Prince.

6. Lady must lose [2] medals to have as many as Muffy.

UNIT 7 LESSON 7 Graph Data **151**

Homework and Remembering page 151

7–7 Targeted Practice

Goal: Read information from a table.

This Targeted Practice page can be used with children who need extra practice reading tables.

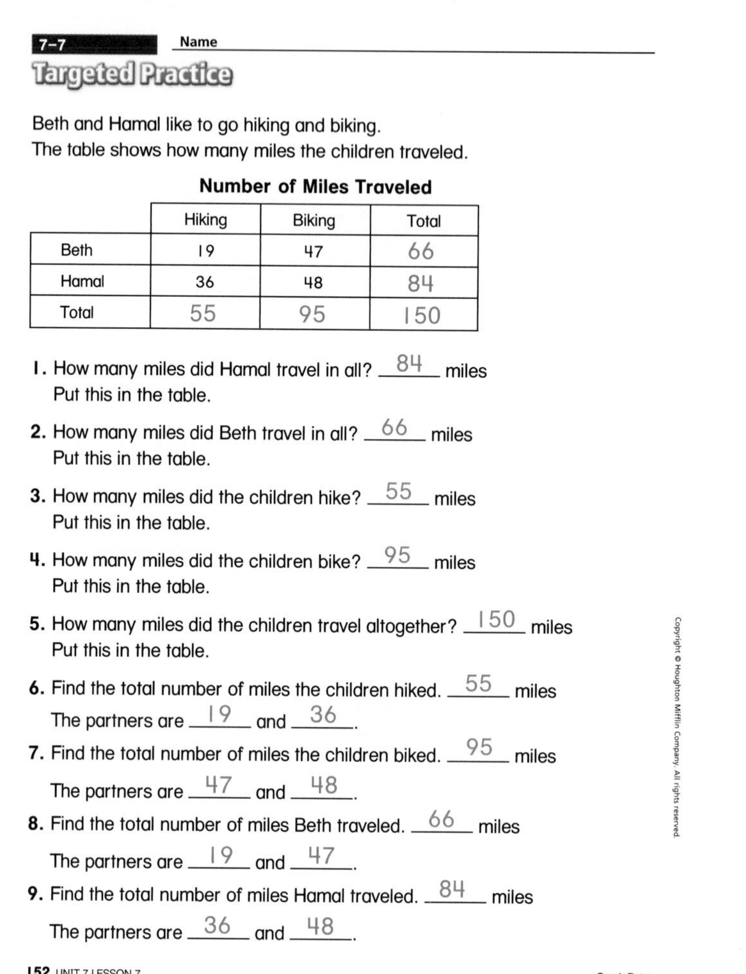

7–7 Targeted Practice Name ____________

Beth and Hamal like to go hiking and biking.
The table shows how many miles the children traveled.

Number of Miles Traveled

	Hiking	Biking	Total
Beth	19	47	66
Hamal	36	48	84
Total	55	95	150

1. How many miles did Hamal travel in all? 84 miles
Put this in the table.
2. How many miles did Beth travel in all? 66 miles
Put this in the table.
3. How many miles did the children hike? 55 miles
Put this in the table.
4. How many miles did the children bike? 95 miles
Put this in the table.
5. How many miles did the children travel altogether? 150 miles
Put this in the table.
6. Find the total number of miles the children hiked. 55 miles
The partners are 19 and 36.
7. Find the total number of miles the children biked. 95 miles
The partners are 47 and 48.
8. Find the total number of miles Beth traveled. 66 miles
The partners are 19 and 47.
9. Find the total number of miles Hamal traveled. 84 miles
The partners are 36 and 48.

152 UNIT 7 LESSON 7 Graph Data

Homework and Remembering page 152

Home or School Activity

Language Arts Connection

Fiction Books Explain to children that fiction books are books about people and things that are not real. Have children check out three fiction books from the library and then survey 15 people to find out which book they would most like to read. Have children record the data using tallies and then show the data in a table or a picture graph.

	Which Fiction Book Would You Choose?
Zen Shorts	5
Millions of Cats	8
Tea With Milk	2

Introduce Bar Graphs

Lesson Objectives

- Distinguish bar graphs from picture graphs.
- Convert picture graphs into bar graphs.

Vocabulary

picture graph
bar graph

The Day at a Glance

Today's Goals	Materials	
1 Teaching the Lesson **A1:** Introduce bar graphs. **A2:** Convert a picture graph into a bar graph.	**Lesson Activities** Student Activity Book pp. 233–234 Homework and Remembering pp. 153–154 MathBoard materials or 10 × 10 Grid (TRB M62)	**Going Further** Activity Cards 7-8 Real or play money Math Journals
2 Going Further ▶ Differentiated Instruction		
3 Homework and Spiral Review		

Use Math Talk today!

Keeping Skills Sharp

Quick Practice — 5 MINUTES

Goal: Find totals for 1-digit partners.

Materials: Student Activity Book page 233

Addition Sprint Direct children's attention to Student Activity Book page 233. Decide how much time to give them to complete the Sprint. Explain the procedure and time limit to them. (See Unit 7, Lesson 4.)

7-8 Class Activity Name ________

▶ Addition Sprint

5 + 7 = 12	9 + 6 = 15	7 + 6 = 13
4 + 8 = 12	7 + 8 = 15	4 + 6 = 10
3 + 9 = 12	9 + 7 = 16	0 + 7 = 7
7 + 5 = 12	9 + 2 = 11	4 + 9 = 13
4 + 5 = 9	5 + 2 = 7	6 + 8 = 14
8 + 4 = 12	6 + 4 = 10	8 + 5 = 13
8 + 6 = 14	8 + 7 = 15	6 + 1 = 7
6 + 9 = 15	5 + 5 = 10	5 + 4 = 9
9 + 9 = 18	1 + 9 = 10	7 + 4 = 11
6 + 3 = 9	7 + 9 = 16	3 + 6 = 9
9 + 0 = 9	4 + 7 = 11	9 + 4 = 13
7 + 7 = 14	8 + 8 = 16	5 + 8 = 13
9 + 1 = 10	6 + 6 = 12	3 + 4 = 7
8 + 9 = 17	3 + 5 = 8	6 + 7 = 13
2 + 5 = 7	9 + 3 = 12	1 + 6 = 7
3 + 9 = 12	2 + 9 = 11	5 + 6 = 11
2 + 7 = 9	2 + 6 = 8	5 + 5 = 10
9 + 4 = 13	5 + 9 = 14	6 + 8 = 14
2 + 8 = 10	8 + 2 = 10	4 + 4 = 8
0 + 8 = 8	9 + 8 = 17	1 + 8 = 9
8 + 3 = 11	6 + 5 = 11	6 + 7 = 13

UNIT 7 LESSON 8 Addition Sprint 233

Student Activity Book page 233

Daily Routines

Telling Time Naming the Hands, Telling Time on the Time Poster (See p. xxvii.)

▶ Led by Student Leaders

Money Routine Using the 120 Poster, Using the Money Flip Chart, Using the Number Path, Using Secret Code Cards (See pp. xxiii–xxv.)

▶ Led by Student Leaders

1 Teaching the Lesson

Activity 1

Bar Graphs

 **25 MINUTES**

Goal: Introduce bar graphs.

Materials: MathBoard materials or 10 × 10 Grid (TRB M62)

 **NCTM Standard:**
Data Analysis and Probability

▶ Convert a Picture Graph into a Bar Graph

WHOLE CLASS

Be sure children have their MathBoard materials or 10 × 10 Grid (TRB M62). On the board, create the following picture graph for children to copy. Remind children that this graph is similar to the picture graph they created in Lesson 1 with the pennies. It shows how many pennies each of the 4 people have.

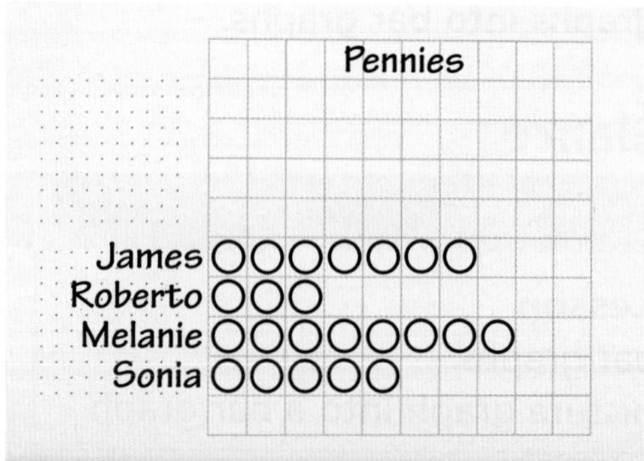

▶ Create a Bar Graph

WHOLE CLASS

Demonstrate to children how to turn their picture graph into a bar graph. While you shade the squares that have pictures in them, have children do the same on their MathBoards. Have children explain why bar graphs are easier to make than picture graphs. You don't have to draw all the pictures.

Demonstrate how to add numbers on the bar graph. Have children do the same on their graphs. Emphasize that bar graphs are like rulers; the numbers are at the end of the lines marking the length. Be sure to include a zero.

Teaching Note

Watch For! Some children may have difficulty understanding the shift of numbers when converting a picture graph to a bar graph. Keep reminding children that numbers are in the middle of the square in picture graphs, and at the end of the line in bar graphs. This is because bar graphs show *lengths*, and picture graphs show *things*. Walk around the classroom to make sure children are constructing the graphs correctly.

Activity 2

Make Graphs from a Table

▶ Create a Data Table WHOLE CLASS

Create a data table of the classroom's favorite pizza on the board. Survey the children and record results in the table. Explain to the class that they will make a picture graph and a bar graph from the table.

Here is an example of a data table of favorite kinds of pizza.

Favorite Kinds of Pizza

Mushroom	𝍸 II	7
Plain Cheese	𝍸 IIII	9
Chicken	III	3
Green Pepper	𝍸	5

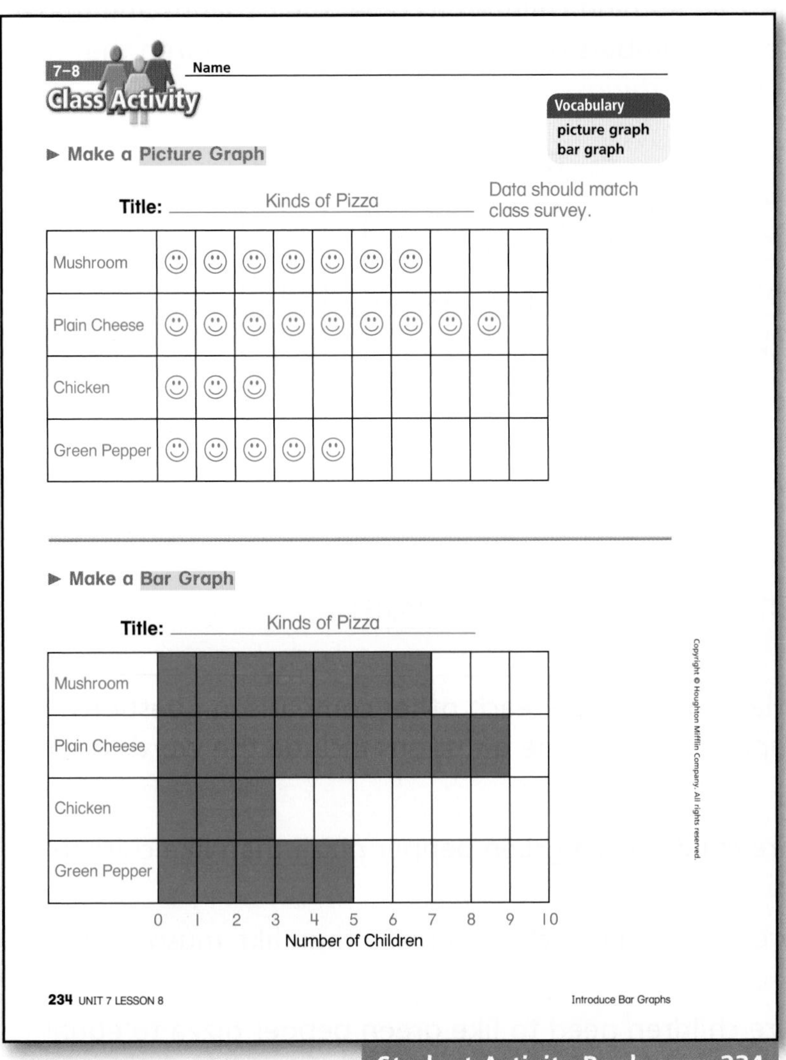

7–8 Class Activity

Name

Vocabulary
picture graph
bar graph

▶ Make a Picture Graph

Title: Kinds of Pizza Data should match class survey.

Mushroom	☺	☺	☺	☺	☺	☺	☺			
Plain Cheese	☺	☺	☺	☺	☺	☺	☺	☺	☺	
Chicken	☺	☺	☺							
Green Pepper	☺	☺	☺	☺	☺					

▶ Make a Bar Graph

Title: Kinds of Pizza

Mushroom
Plain Cheese
Chicken
Green Pepper

0 1 2 3 4 5 6 7 8 9 10
Number of Children

Student Activity Book page 234

Activity continued ▶

 **25 MINUTES**

Goal: Convert a picture graph into a bar graph.

Materials: Student Activity Book, page 234

 **NCTM Standard:**
Data Analysis and Probability

English Language Learners

Draw the example data table Favorite Kinds of Pizza on p. 529. Write *bar graph* and *picture graph*. Have children look at Student Activity Book p. 234.

- **Beginning** Say: **A *bar graph* uses bars to show data. A *picture graph* uses pictures to show data.** Have children repeat.
- **Intermediate** Ask: **Does a *bar graph* use bars or pictures to show data?** bars Say: **A *picture graph* uses ___.** pictures
- **Advanced** Have children tell how a *bar graph* and *picture graph* show data.

▶ Make a Picture Graph INDIVIDUALS

Have children use their data table to make a picture graph on Student Activity Book page 234. For the pictures in the graph have children use smiley faces.

Title: Favorite Kinds of Pizza

Mushroom	☺	☺	☺	☺	☺	☺	☺			
Plain Cheese	☺	☺	☺	☺	☺	☺	☺	☺	☺	
Chicken	☺	☺	☺							
Green Pepper	☺	☺	☺	☺	☺					

▶ Make a Bar Graph INDIVIDUALS

Have children make a bar graph from their picture graph on Student Activity Book page 234. Remind children to label their graphs and make sure children place the numbers on the graph. Remind children that bar graphs show *lengths*, not *things*.

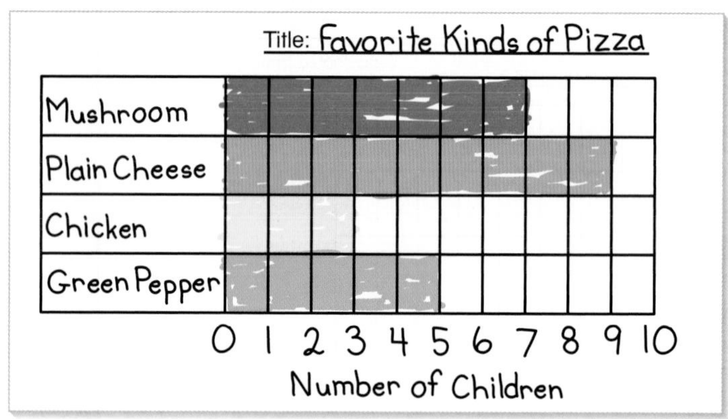

▶ Ask Comparison Questions PAIRS

Math Talk Have children ask each other comparison questions based on their graphs. Be sure some questions include the words *more* and *fewer.*

- How many more children like green pepper pizza than like chicken pizza? 2 more children
- How many fewer children like chicken pizza than like mushroom pizza? 4 fewer children
- How many more children need to like green pepper pizza to equal the number of children who like plain cheese pizza? 4 more children

Ongoing Assessment

To check children's understanding of picture graphs and bar graphs, ask these questions:

- ▶ How is a bar graph different from a picture graph?
- ▶ Explain how the numbers on a picture graph are different from the numbers on a bar graph.

2 Going Further

Differentiated Instruction

Intervention

Activity Card 7-8

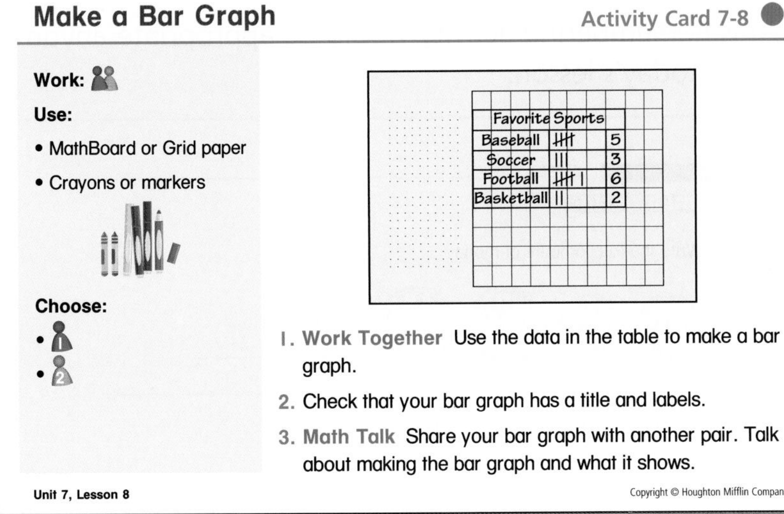

Make a Bar Graph Activity Card 7-8

Work:

Use:

- MathBoard or Grid paper
- Crayons or markers

Choose:

1. **Work Together** Use the data in the table to make a bar graph.
2. Check that your bar graph has a title and labels.
3. **Math Talk** Share your bar graph with another pair. Talk about making the bar graph and what it shows.

Unit 7, Lesson 8

Activity Note Each pair needs MathBoard Materials or 10 × 10 Grid (TRB M62) and crayons or markers. Review the data with children as they make bar graphs.

Math Writing Prompt

Explain Use your own words to describe a bar graph.

Software Support

Use *Soar to Success* for instruction of students needing targeted support for underlying skills.

On Level

Activity Card 7-8

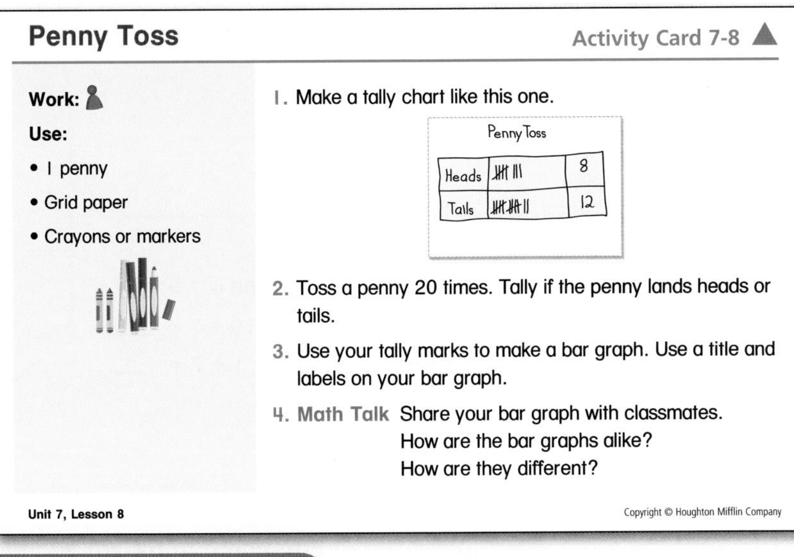

Penny Toss Activity Card 7-8

Work:

Use:

- 1 penny
- Grid paper
- Crayons or markers

1. Make a tally chart like this one.

2. Toss a penny 20 times. Tally if the penny lands heads or tails.
3. Use your tally marks to make a bar graph. Use a title and labels on your bar graph.
4. **Math Talk** Share your bar graph with classmates. How are the bar graphs alike? How are they different?

Unit 7, Lesson 8

Activity Note Each child needs 1 penny (real or play), 10 × 10 Grid (TRB M62), and crayons or markers. Review with children that the bar graph should show the information from the tally chart.

Math Writing Prompt

Compare and Contrast What is the same about a bar graph and a picture graph? What is different?

Software Support

Use *MegaMath* for review and reinforcement of the concepts and skills presented in this lesson.

Challenge

Activity Card 7-8

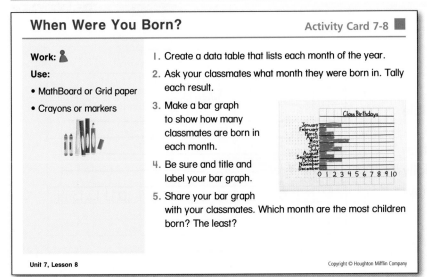

When Were You Born? Activity Card 7-8

Work:

Use:

- MathBoard or Grid paper
- Crayons or markers

1. Create a data table that lists each month of the year.
2. Ask your classmates what month they were born in. Tally each result.
3. Make a bar graph to show how many classmates are born in each month.
4. Be sure and title and label your bar graph.
5. Share your bar graph with your classmates. Which month are the most children born? The least?

Class Birthdays: January, February, March, April, May, June, July, August, September, October, November, December; 0 1 2 3 4 5 6 7 8 9 10

Unit 7, Lesson 8

Activity Note Each child needs MathBoard Materials or 10 × 10 Grid (TRB M62) and crayons or markers. You may want to display the bar graphs when children are done.

Math Writing Prompt

Write the Steps Explain to a friend the steps you take to make a bar graph.

Software Support

Use *Destination Math* to take students beyond the concepts and skills presented in this lesson.

3 Homework and Spiral Review

7-8 Homework **Goal:** Additional Practice

✓ Include children's completed Homework page as part of their portfolios.

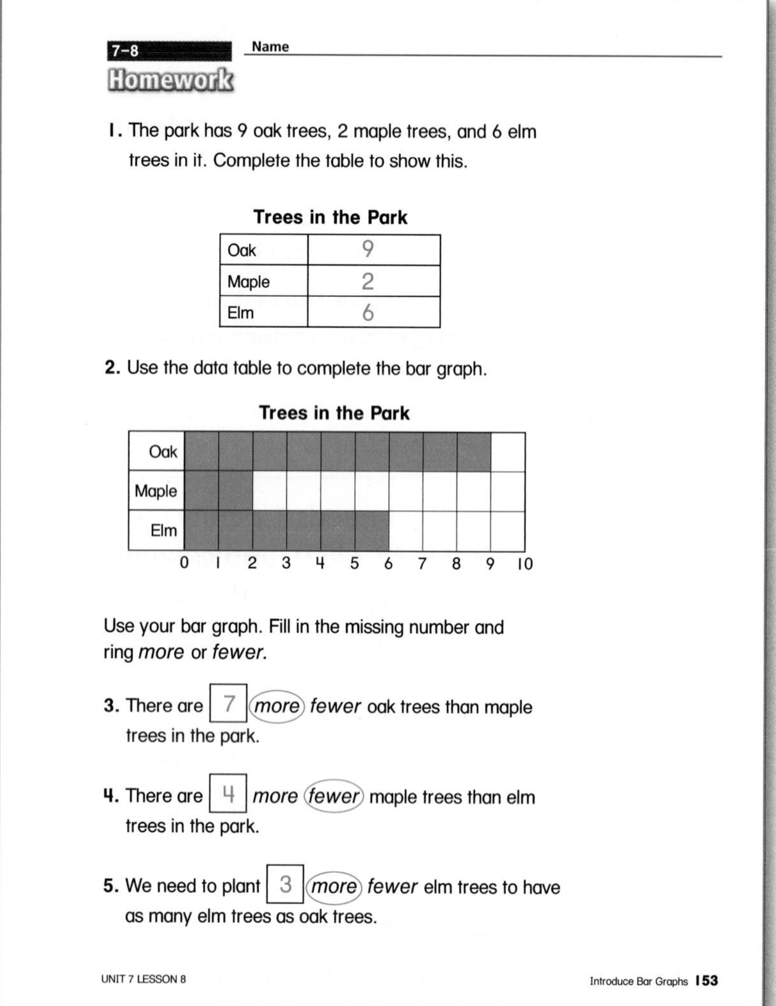

7-8 Homework Name ____________

1. The park has 9 oak trees, 2 maple trees, and 6 elm trees in it. Complete the table to show this.

Trees in the Park

Oak	9
Maple	2
Elm	6

2. Use the data table to complete the bar graph.

Trees in the Park

Use your bar graph. Fill in the missing number and ring *more* or *fewer*.

3. There are [7] (*more*) *fewer* oak trees than maple trees in the park.

4. There are [4] *more* (*fewer*) maple trees than elm trees in the park.

5. We need to plant [3] (*more*) *fewer* elm trees to have as many elm trees as oak trees.

UNIT 7 LESSON 8 Introduce Bar Graphs **153**

Homework and Remembering page 153

7-8 Remembering **Goal:** Spiral Review

This Remembering activity would be appropriate anytime after today's lesson.

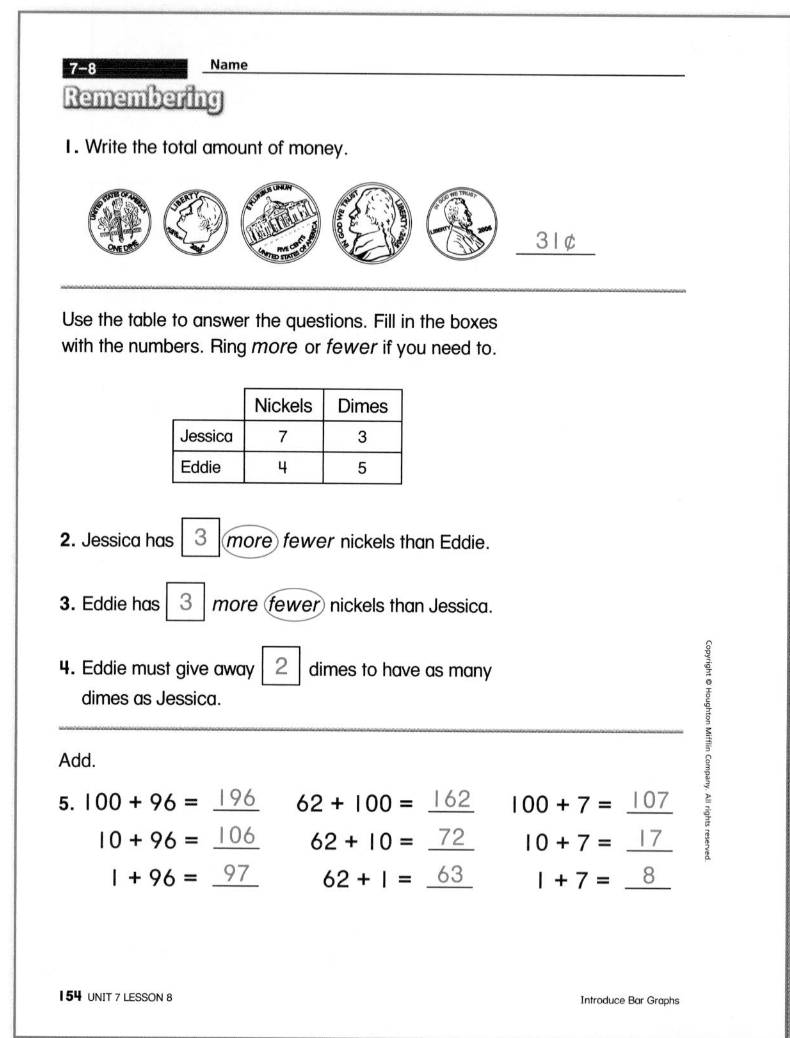

7-8 Remembering Name ____________

1. Write the total amount of money.

31¢

Use the table to answer the questions. Fill in the boxes with the numbers. Ring *more* or *fewer* if you need to.

	Nickels	Dimes
Jessica	7	3
Eddie	4	5

2. Jessica has [3] (*more*) *fewer* nickels than Eddie.

3. Eddie has [3] *more* (*fewer*) nickels than Jessica.

4. Eddie must give away [2] dimes to have as many dimes as Jessica.

Add.

5. 100 + 96 = 196 62 + 100 = 162 100 + 7 = 107
10 + 96 = 106 62 + 10 = 72 10 + 7 = 17
1 + 96 = 97 62 + 1 = 63 1 + 7 = 8

154 UNIT 7 LESSON 8 Introduce Bar Graphs

Homework and Remembering page 154

Home or School Activity

Science Connection

How's the Weather? Brainstorm with the class a list of possible adjectives to describe the weather. Children will observe the weather and choose the adjective they think best describes the weather each day. Have children record their observations daily in a tally list. After 25 days, children create a bar graph to show the data they collected.

Weather

Clear
Cloudy
Rainy
Snowy
0 1 2 3 4 5 6 7 8 9 10 11 12 13 14

Read Bar Graphs

Lesson Objectives

- Read and analyze information in a bar graph.
- Use a bar graph to ask and answer comparison questions.

Vocabulary
bar graph
horizontal
vertical

The Day at a Glance

Today's Goals	Materials	
1 Teaching the Lesson A: Read and answer questions about a horizontal or vertical bar graph. **2 Going Further** ▶ Differentiated Instruction **3 Homework and Targeted Practice**	**Lesson Activities** Student Activity Book pp. 235–236 Homework and Remembering pp. 155–156 Blank transparency (optional) Ruler MathBoard materials (optional)	**Going Further** Activity Cards 7-9 Student Activity Book p. 235 Index cards Inch Grid Paper (TRB M70) Math Journals

Use Math Talk today!

Keeping Skills Sharp

Quick Practice — 5 MINUTES

Goals: Add by regrouping ones. Solve addition exercises by identifying tens and ones.

Add Over Ten Write the five equations below on the board. Have a Student Leader point to them one at a time. On a given signal, the class says the total.

$45 + 7 = \square$ $37 + 6 = \square$
$57 + 8 = \square$ $78 + 3 = \square$
$63 + 9 = \square$

Add Tens or Ones On the board write similar equations like the ones below. Have a Student Leader direct the class in adding tens or ones. The class then says the answer as a group. (See Unit 3 Lesson 13.)

$8 + 6 = \square$ $9 + 7 = \square$
$80 + 60 = \square$ $90 + 70 = \square$

Daily Routines

Telling Time Naming the Hands, Telling Time on the Time Poster (See p. xxvii.)

▶ Led by Student Leaders

Money Routine Using the 120 Poster, Using the Money Flip Chart, Using the Number Path, Using Secret Code Cards (See pp. xxiii–xxv.)

▶ Led by Student Leaders

1 Teaching the Lesson

Activity

Horizontal and Vertical Bar Graphs

 55 MINUTES

Goal: Read and answer questions about a horizontal or vertical bar graph.

Materials: Student Activity Book page 235, blank transparency (optional), ruler, MathBoard materials (optional)

 **NCTM Standards:**
Number and Operations
Data Analysis and Probability
Problem Solving
Connections
Representation

Teaching Note

Watch For! Some children may have difficulty determining the length of a bar when a longer bar is covering the lines on the number scale. Show children how to use their fingers to follow the line from the end of a bar to the correct number on the number scale. Other children may need to complete the lines by drawing straight across a bar.

Differentiated Instruction

English Learners Have children describe the coins in their native language and compare and contrast them to coins in the United States.

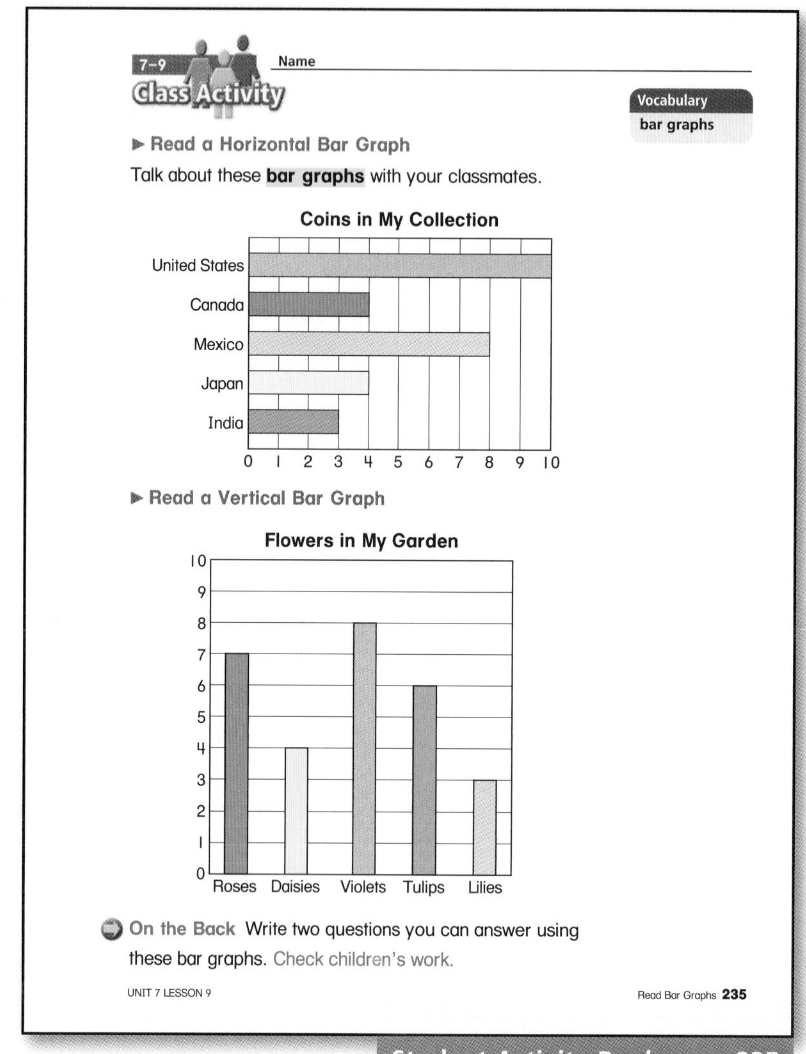
7–9 Class Activity Name

Vocabulary
bar graphs

▶ Read a Horizontal Bar Graph

Talk about these **bar graphs** with your classmates.

▶ Read a Vertical Bar Graph

On the Back Write two questions you can answer using these bar graphs. Check children's work.

UNIT 7 LESSON 9 Read Bar Graphs 235

Student Activity Book page 235

▶ Read a Horizontal Bar Graph WHOLE CLASS

Direct children's attention to the bar graph at the top of Student Activity Book page 235. Sketch the same graph on the board or you may wish to use a transparency of the page.

- This graph shows the number of coins in my coin collection. I have coins from the United States, Canada, Mexico, Japan, and India.

Have children discuss how they can figure out how many coins of each kind there are.

- How many coins from the United States do I have? 10
- How do you know? We can look at the length of the bar.

- How many coins from Canada do I have? I have 4 coins from Canada.

Have children write the number of coins next to each bar. Explain that this will make it easier to ask and answer questions about the graph.

Math Talk **Discuss Information in a Bar Graph** Have children make comparisons using the information in the graph, and then reword their comparison sentences.

- There are four more coins from Mexico than from Japan.
- You can say the same thing using *fewer:* There are four *fewer* coins from Japan than from Mexico.

Have other children share comparison sentences using data from the graph. Challenge children to reword their comparisons.

▶ Convert a Horizontal Bar Graph into a Vertical Bar Graph WHOLE CLASS

Explain that some bar graphs are drawn vertically instead of horizontally. Begin drawing a vertical graph of the coin collection graph, on the board or on an overhead transparency. Have children consider the changes that must be made to the graph if it is to be shown that way. For example:

- Where should the numbers be? along the left side of the graph
- Where should the labels be? along the bottom of the graph

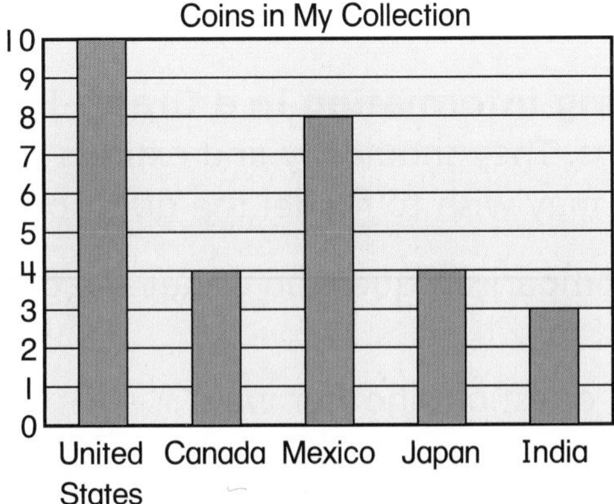

You may wish to have children recreate the vertical bar graph shown above, on their MathBoards or on paper.

Activity continued ▶

Teaching Note

Language and Vocabulary Review the meanings of *horizontal* and *vertical* with children. Explain that the term horizontal relates to the horizon or the line where the land or sea seems to meet the sky. Have them write *horizontal* horizontally. Then explain that vertical means "up and down" and have children write the term vertically:

v
e
r
t   h o r i z o n t a l
i
c
a
l

English Language Learners

Draw a vertical and horizontal bar graph on the board. Write *vertical bar graph* and *horizontal bar graph*.

- **Beginning** Gesture up and down as you say: ***Vertical* means up and down. In a *vertical bar graph* the bars go___.** up and down Continue with *horizontal bar graph*.
- **Intermediate and Advanced** Point and say: ***Vertical bar graphs* have bars going ___.** up and down Ask: **Which way to the bars in a horizontal bar graph go?** right and left

Teaching the Lesson (continued)

▶ Read a Vertical Bar Graph WHOLE CLASS

Ask children to look at the vertical bar graph at the bottom of Student Activity Book page 235.

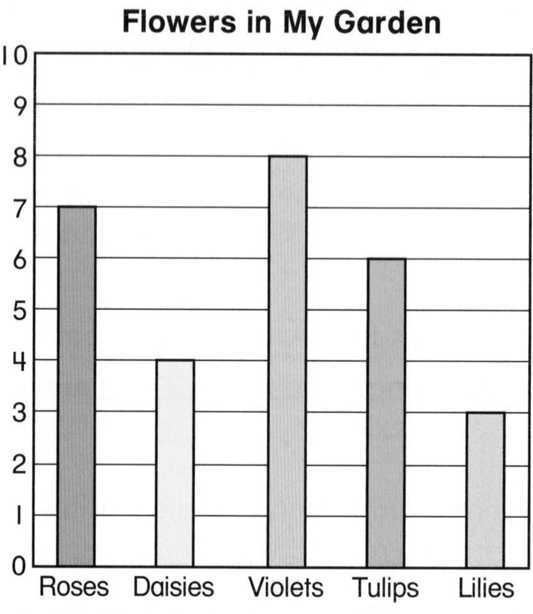

Read the title of the graph and be sure children can read the information.

Have children read the graph to find out how many of each flower there are. Then have them write the number at the top of each bar. This will make the graph easier to read as they ask and answer questions.

- How many violets are there? 8 violets
- How do you know? We can look at the height of the bar.

Have several children explain how they figured out how many flowers of each type are in the garden. They may draw lines across or hold a piece of paper or a pencil to check that they are correct.

Pose Problems Using Information in a Graph Have children ask comparison questions. They should try and express their questions in different ways. You may wish to model the questions for them.

- Who can ask a comparison question about the graph? How many *more* violets are there than lilies?
- Who can ask the question another way? How many *fewer* lilies are there than violets?
- How many more daisies should I get if I want to have as many as I have violets? 4 more daisies

Examples of Other Questions

- How many roses and lilies are in my garden?
- Are there more daisies and lilies than violets?
- Of which kind of flower do I have the most?

Ongoing Assessment

As children use bar graphs to solve problems, ask questions such as:

- ▶ How can you use the bars in the graph to solve the problem?
- ▶ Can you show me how you used the number scale to solve the problem?

2 Going Further

Differentiated Instruction

Intervention — Activity Card 7-9

Comparison Statements — Activity Card 7-9

Work: pairs

Use:
- 5 index cards
- word cube
- Student Activity Book page 235

Choose:
- 1
- 2

1. **Work Together** Write one flower name from the bar graph on Student Activity Book page 235 on each index card.
2. Place the index cards face down.
3. (1) Turn two index cards face up.
4. (2) Toss the word cube.
5. **Work Together** Use the word on the cube and the flowers on the index cards to make a comparison statement.
6. Take turns.

violets
roses
more
fewer
There are fewer roses than violets.

Unit 7, Lesson 9

Activity Note Each pair needs five index cards, a number cube labeled *more* on three sides and *fewer* on three sides, and Student Activity Book p. 235.

Math Writing Prompt

More and Fewer Doug has 3 fewer dogs than cats.

How can you rewrite this sentence using the word *more*?

Software Support

Use *Soar to Success* for instruction of students needing targeted support for underlying skills.

On Level — Activity Card 7-9

Horizontal to Vertical — Activity Card 7-9

Work: individual

Use:
- Ruler
- Homework and Remembering page 155
- Inch Grid paper

1. Look at the bar graph on Homework and Remembering page 155.
2. Use the ruler to make a vertical bar graph to show the same information.
3. Make a vertical bar graph of the horizontal graph.
4. **Math Talk** Share your bar graph with a classmate. Discuss what the bar graph shows.

Instruments My Friends Play
10 9 8 7 6 5 4 3 2 1 0
Piano Drums Guitar Violin

Unit 7, Lesson 9

Activity Note Each child needs a 25-cm ruler, Homework and Remembering p. 155, and Inch Grid paper (TRB M70).

Math Writing Prompt

Compare How are horizontal and vertical bar graphs alike? How are they different?

Software Support

Use *MegaMath* for review and reinforcement of the concepts and skills presented in this lesson.

Challenge — Activity Card 7-9

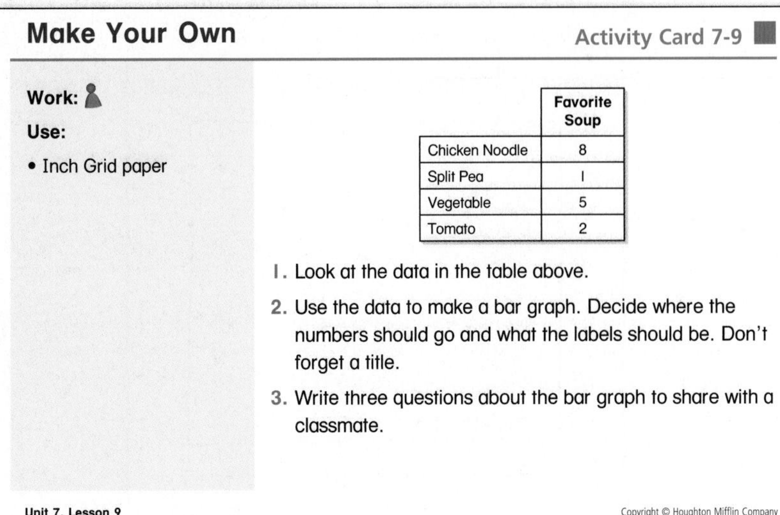

Make Your Own — Activity Card 7-9

Work: individual

Use:
- Inch Grid paper

	Favorite Soup
Chicken Noodle	8
Split Pea	1
Vegetable	5
Tomato	2

1. Look at the data in the table above.
2. Use the data to make a bar graph. Decide where the numbers should go and what the labels should be. Don't forget a title.
3. Write three questions about the bar graph to share with a classmate.

Unit 7, Lesson 9

Activity Note Each child needs Inch Grid paper (TRB M70). Display the questions children write.

Math Writing Prompt

Draw a Picture Create a bar graph that has three bars. The first bar shows 5 cars. The second bar is twice as long as the first bar. The third bar is the same length as the second bar. How many cars do the three bars show?

Software Support

Use *Destination Math* to take students beyond the concepts and skills presented in this lesson.

3 Homework and Targeted Practice

Goal: Additional Practice

This Homework page provides practice in reading bar graphs.

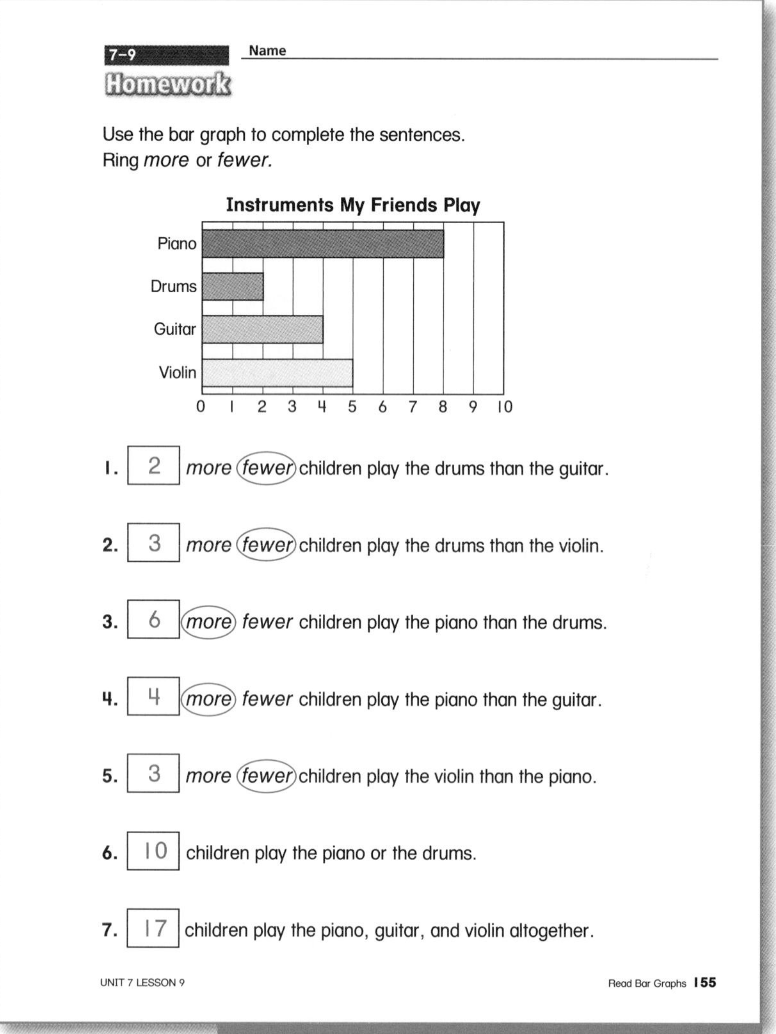

7–9 Homework Name

Use the bar graph to complete the sentences.
Ring *more* or *fewer*.

Instruments My Friends Play

Piano
Drums
Guitar
Violin
0 1 2 3 4 5 6 7 8 9 10

1. [2] *more* (*fewer*) children play the drums than the guitar.
2. [3] *more* (*fewer*) children play the drums than the violin.
3. [6] (*more*) *fewer* children play the piano than the drums.
4. [4] (*more*) *fewer* children play the piano than the guitar.
5. [3] *more* (*fewer*) children play the violin than the piano.
6. [10] children play the piano or the drums.
7. [17] children play the piano, guitar, and violin altogether.

UNIT 7 LESSON 9 Read Bar Graphs **155**

Homework and Remembering page 155

7–9 Targeted Practice **Goal:** Read bar graphs

This Targeted Practice page can be used with children who need extra practice in reading bar graphs.

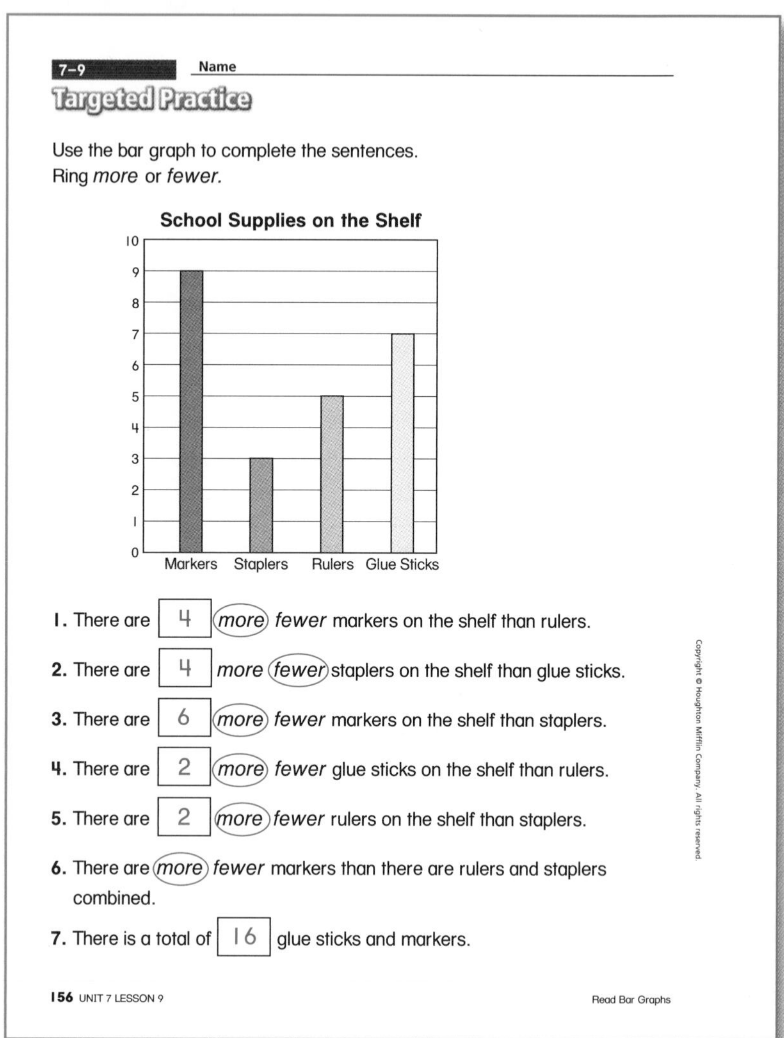

7–9 Targeted Practice Name

Use the bar graph to complete the sentences.
Ring *more* or *fewer*.

School Supplies on the Shelf

10 9 8 7 6 5 4 3 2 1 0
Markers Staplers Rulers Glue Sticks

1. There are [4] (*more*) *fewer* markers on the shelf than rulers.
2. There are [4] *more* (*fewer*) staplers on the shelf than glue sticks.
3. There are [6] (*more*) *fewer* markers on the shelf than staplers.
4. There are [2] (*more*) *fewer* glue sticks on the shelf than rulers.
5. There are [2] (*more*) *fewer* rulers on the shelf than staplers.
6. There are (*more*) *fewer* markers than there are rulers and staplers combined.
7. There is a total of [16] glue sticks and markers.

156 UNIT 7 LESSON 9 Read Bar Graphs

Homework and Remembering page 156

Home or School Activity

Science Connection

Nature Walk Walk around the neighborhood or a park and have children collect several small objects, such as leaves, rocks, or flowers.

Discuss ways in which the objects can be grouped. Then have children make a bar graph to show the objects they collected. You may also wish to have children make two bar graphs, one horizontal and the other vertical.

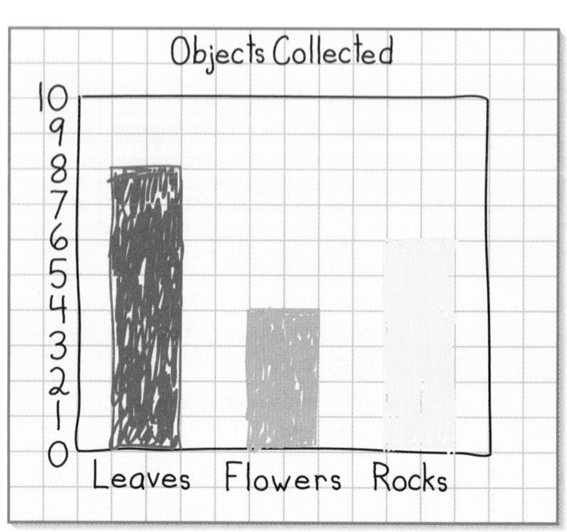

Analyze Information in Bar Graphs

Lesson Objectives

- Analyze information in bar graphs to answer questions.
- Select a way to categorize and display raw data.
- Create bar graphs to display data.

Vocabulary

bar graph
horizontal
vertical
scale
title

The Day at a Glance

Today's Goals	Materials	
1 Teaching the Lesson **A1:** Solve problems based on information in a bar graph. **A2:** Sort shapes and make a bar graph showing the information.	**Lesson Activities** Student Activity Book pp. 237–238 Homework and Remembering pp. 157–158 Transparency of Student Activity Book 237 (optional)	**Going Further** Activity Cards 7-10 Connecting cubes Inch Grid Paper (TRB M70) Ruler Math Journals
2 Going Further ▸ Differentiated Instruction		
3 Homework and Spiral Review		

123 Use Math Talk today!

Keeping Skills Sharp

Quick Practice — 5 MINUTES

Goals: Add by regrouping ones.

Add Over Ten Write the five equations below on the board. Have a Student Leader point to them one at a time. On a given signal, the class says the total. (See Unit 7 Lesson 9.)

77 + 5 = ☐ 24 + 7 = ☐
46 + 2 = ☐ 38 + 4 = ☐
89 + 2 = ☐

Repeated Quick Practice Use this Quick Practice from a previous lesson.

▸ **Add Tens or Ones** (See Unit 7 Lesson 9.)

Daily Routines

Telling Time Naming the Hands, Telling Time on the Time Poster (See p. xxvii.)

▸ Led by Student Leaders

Money Routine Using the 120 Poster, Using the Money Flip Chart, Using the Number Path, Using Secret Code Cards (See pp. xxiii–xxv.)

▸ Led by Student Leaders

1 Teaching the Lesson

Activity 1

Read Bar Graphs

 25 MINUTES

Goal: Solve problems based on information in a bar graph.

Materials: Student Activity Book page 237, transparency of Student Activity Book page 237 (optional)

 **NCTM Standards:**
Number and Operations
Data Analysis and Probability
Problem Solving
Connections
Representation

Differentiated Instruction

Extra Help To help children use the graph to answer questions, they can write the numbers at the end of each bar for a quick reference.

Math Talk in Action

How did you use the graph to decide if there were *more* or *fewer* tigers than bears?

Jun: I looked at the lengths of the bars.

Laura: So did I. The bar for bears is longer than the bar for tigers. There are *more* bears than tigers.

Did anyone use a different strategy?

Bob: Yes, I found the answer a different way. I looked at the number of tigers and the number of bears.

Ali: So did I. The graph shows that there are 2 tigers and 4 bears.

Jerome: Right. Four is more than two so there are more bears.

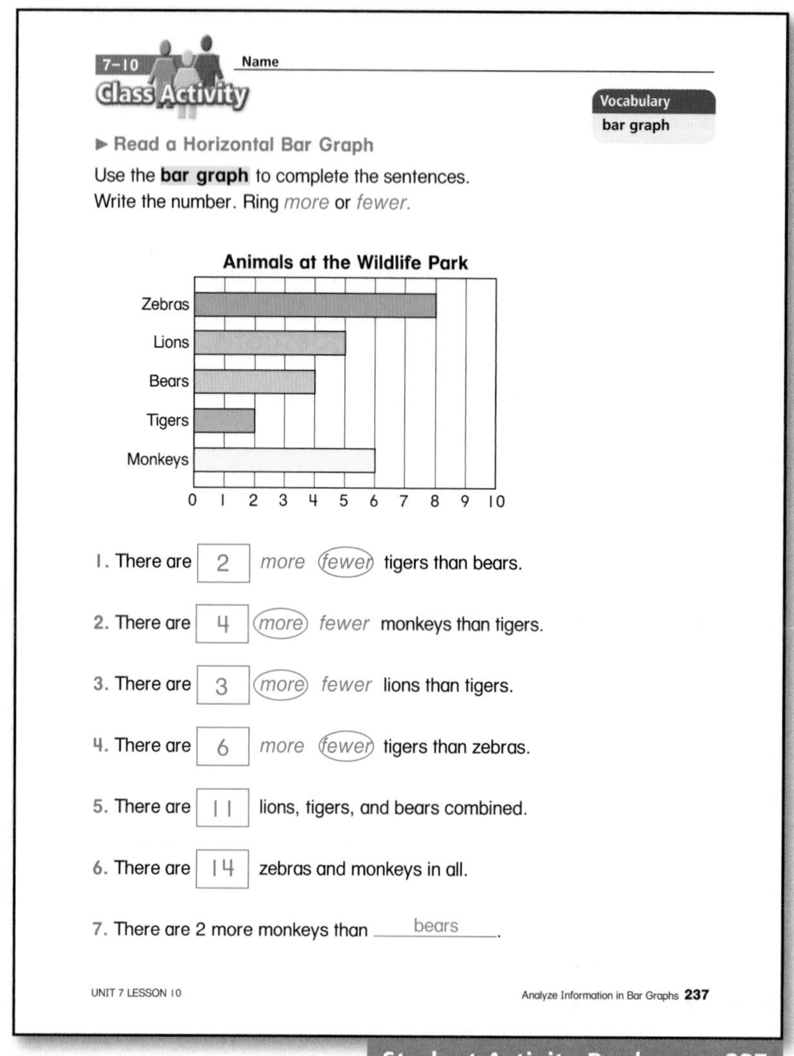

7-10 Class Activity Name ______

Vocabulary
bar graph

▶ Read a Horizontal Bar Graph

Use the **bar graph** to complete the sentences.
Write the number. Ring *more* or *fewer*.

1. There are [2] more (fewer) tigers than bears.
2. There are [4] (more) fewer monkeys than tigers.
3. There are [3] (more) fewer lions than tigers.
4. There are [6] more (fewer) tigers than zebras.
5. There are [11] lions, tigers, and bears combined.
6. There are [14] zebras and monkeys in all.
7. There are 2 more monkeys than bears.

UNIT 7 LESSON 10 Analyze Information in Bar Graphs 237

Student Activity Book page 237

▶ Read a Horizontal Bar Graph INDIVIDUALS

Direct children's attention to Student Activity Book page 237 or display the graph about animal populations on the overhead projector. Explain to the children that the graph represents the populations of different animals at the wildlife park.

Have children complete the page independently or with a partner and then explain how they found their answers. See the **Math Talk in Action** in the side column for an example of classroom dialogue.

As part of their explanations, the children should make comparisons.

You may want to have children create new questions about the graph.

Activity 2

Sort Information

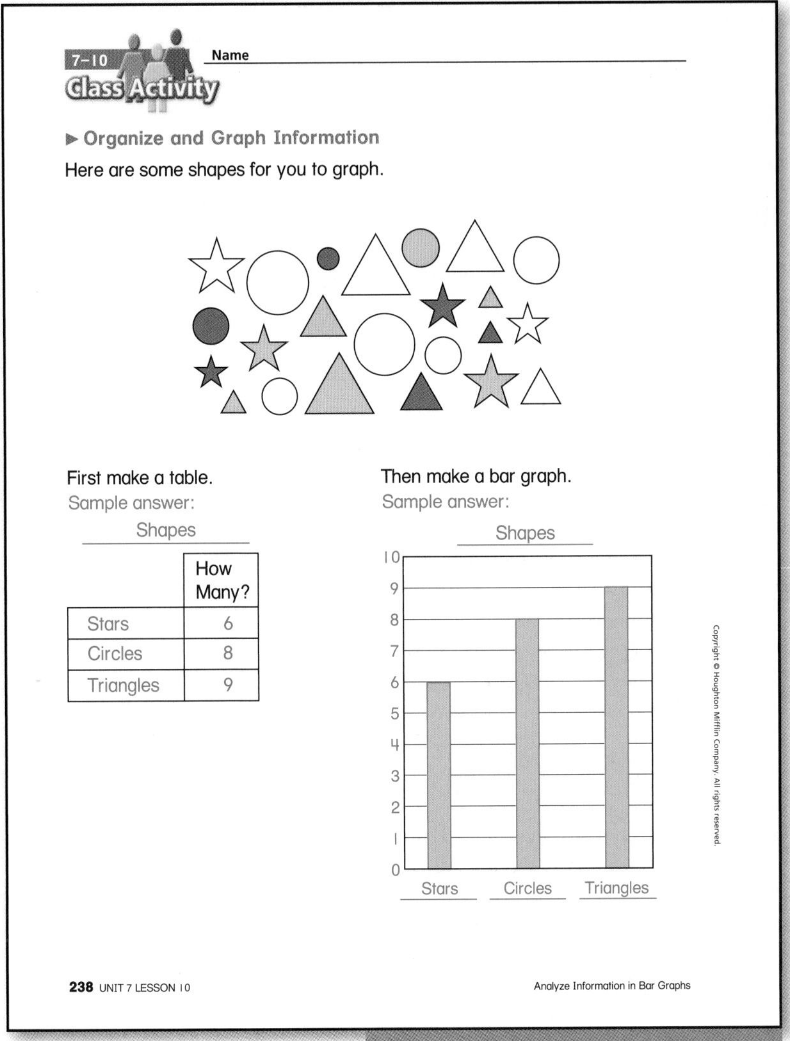

7-10 Class Activity Name

▶ Organize and Graph Information

Here are some shapes for you to graph.

First make a table.

Sample answer:

Shapes

	How Many?
Stars	6
Circles	8
Triangles	9

Then make a bar graph.

Sample answer:

Student Activity Book page 238

▶ Organize and Graph Information WHOLE CLASS

Ask children to look at the shapes at the top of Student Activity Book page 238. Discuss how the information might be categorized or grouped.

- First we have to decide what we want to graph. We can graph these shapes by their name. What are the shapes? stars, circles, triangles
- Is there any other way we could graph these instead? The shapes can be grouped by color. They can also be grouped by size.

Activity continued ▶

 **30 MINUTES**

Goal: Sort shapes and make a bar graph showing the information.

Materials: Student Activity Book page 238

 **NCTM Standards:**

Number and Operations
Data Analysis and Probability
Problem Solving
Connections
Representation

Differentiated Instruction

Extra Help It may help children to cut out and sort the shapes rather than count the shapes they see on the page.

English Language Learners

Draw ○ O ◆ • ◆ ○ O ▭ □ ◆ on the board: Say: ***Sort*** **means to group things that are alike.**

- **Beginning** Say: **We can *sort* these shapes into groups of circles, diamonds, and rectangles.** Have children repeat.
- **Intermediate** Ask: **What groups can we *sort* these shapes into?** circles, diamonds, rectangles
- **Advanced** Have children work in pairs to sort the shapes. Invite volunteers tell how they *sorted* the shapes.

1 Teaching the Lesson (continued)

Class Management

For this activity, you can also divide the class into Helping Pairs or small groups. Some of the groups could graph by color, others by size, and others by shape.

Ongoing Assessment

Ask children to write and answer a question about the information in one of their graphs.

Make a Table and Bar Graph Have the class select an attribute to graph. You could have the children decide as a class. The example here is for shape name.

- What shapes do we find? stars, circles, and triangles
- How many stars do we have? 6 stars
- How many circles? 8 circles
- How many triangles? 9 triangles
- Let's make a table and a bar graph.

Help children properly label the graph with a title and a correct number scale.

Let children work for 10 minutes. Circulate around the class to make sure groups understand the task. On a separate piece of paper, have children make a different table and graph from the same information (sort by color or size).

In the last few minutes, have groups share and discuss their graphs with the rest of the class.

2 Going Further

Differentiated Instruction

Intervention — Activity Card 7-10

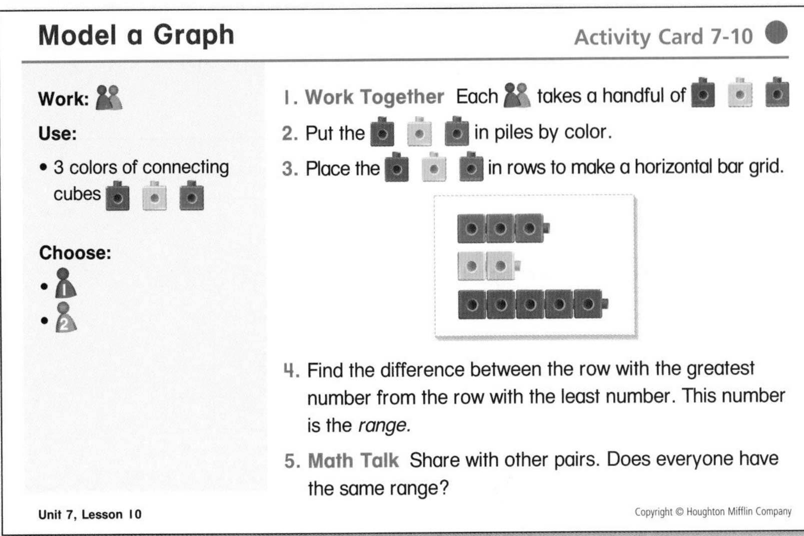

Model a Graph — Activity Card 7-10 ●

Work: (pair)
Use:
- 3 colors of connecting cubes

Choose:
- 1
- 2

1. **Work Together** Each pair takes a handful of cubes.
2. Put the cubes in piles by color.
3. Place the cubes in rows to make a horizontal bar grid.
4. Find the difference between the row with the greatest number from the row with the least number. This number is the *range*.
5. **Math Talk** Share with other pairs. Does everyone have the same range?

Unit 7, Lesson 10

Activity Note Place connecting cubes (3 colors) in a bowl. Each child takes a handful of cubes and the pair makes a bar graph. Review what *range* means with children.

Math Writing Prompt

Summarize Tell how you would explain to a friend what a bar graph is.

Software Support

Use *Soar to Success* for instruction of students needing targeted support for underlying skills.

On Level — Activity Card 7-10

Garden Graph — Activity Card 7-10 ▲

Work: (individual)
Use:
- Ruler
- Inch Grid paper

1. In the garden there are 3 more roses than tulips and 2 fewer violets than roses.
2. Make a bar graph to show how many flowers are in the garden. Decide where to put your number scale and labels. Don't forget a title. Use numbers different from this bar graph.
3. Find the difference between the greatest number and least number. This number is the *range*.
4. **Math Talk** Look at other bar graphs. Do all graphs have the same range?

Flowers in the Garden (0–10; Roses, Tulips, Violets)

Unit 7, Lesson 10

Activity Note Each child needs Inch Grid paper (TRB M70). Review what *range* means and how to find it with children.

Math Writing Prompt

The Look of a Graph What would a bar graph about different coins in a piggy bank look like, if there were fewer nickels than dimes, and more pennies than dimes in the bank? Draw an example.

Software Support

Use *MegaMath* for review and reinforcement of the concepts and skills presented in this lesson.

Challenge — Activity Card 7-10

Investigate Range — Activity Card 7-10 ■

Work: (individual)
Use:
- Inch Grid paper
- Ruler

1. A garden has 3 more roses than tulips and 2 fewer violets than roses.
2. Make a bar graph to show how many flowers are in the garden. Use different numbers from this graph.
3. Find the difference between the greatest number and least number. This number is the *range*.
4. **Math Talk** Look at other bar graphs. Do all graphs have the same range? What do you think the results mean? What have you learned about range?

Flowers in the Garden (0–10; Roses, Tulips, Violets)

Unit 7, Lesson 10

Activity Note Each child needs Inch Grid paper (TRB M70). Guide children to conclude that if the difference between numbers remains the same, the range is the same.

Math Writing Prompt

Which is Easier? Which is easier to make—a graph showing ages or heights of your classmates? Explain.

Software Support

Use *Destination Math* to take students beyond the concepts and skills presented in this lesson.

Homework and Spiral Review

7–10 Homework Goal: Additional Practice

This Homework page provides practice in reading bar graphs.

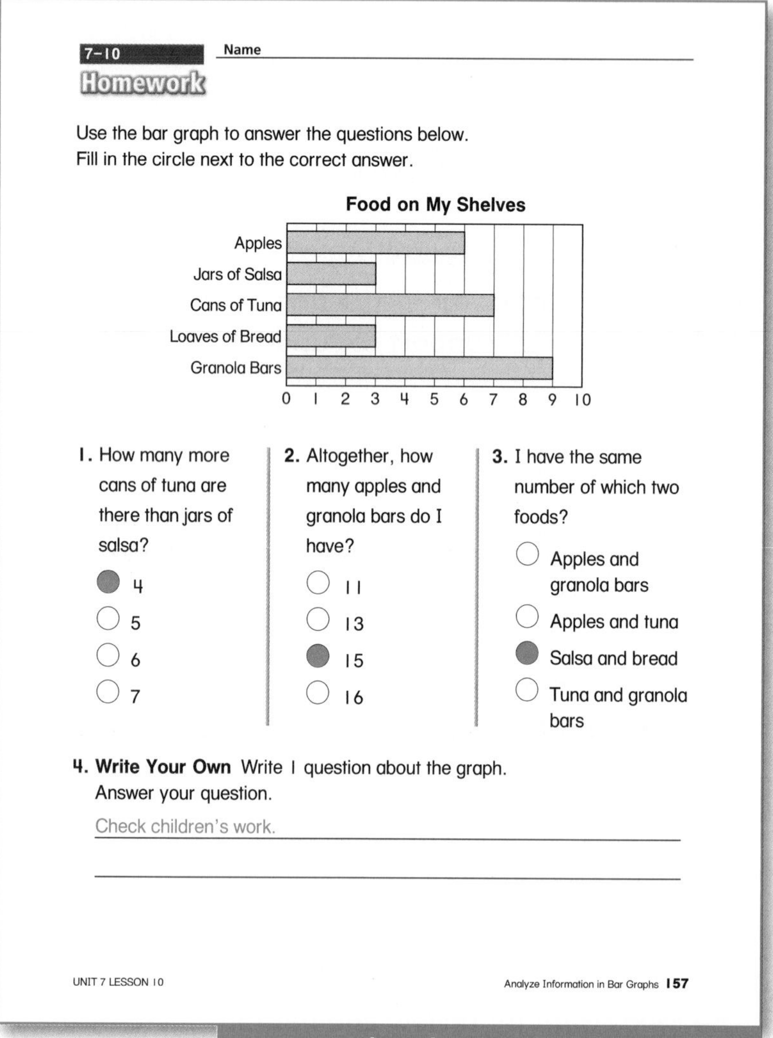

7–10 Homework Name ______

Use the bar graph to answer the questions below.
Fill in the circle next to the correct answer.

Food on My Shelves

Apples
Jars of Salsa
Cans of Tuna
Loaves of Bread
Granola Bars

0 1 2 3 4 5 6 7 8 9 10

1. How many more cans of tuna are there than jars of salsa?
   - ● 4
   - ○ 5
   - ○ 6
   - ○ 7

2. Altogether, how many apples and granola bars do I have?
   - ○ 11
   - ○ 13
   - ● 15
   - ○ 16

3. I have the same number of which two foods?
   - ○ Apples and granola bars
   - ○ Apples and tuna
   - ● Salsa and bread
   - ○ Tuna and granola bars

4. **Write Your Own** Write 1 question about the graph. Answer your question.
   Check children's work.

UNIT 7 LESSON 10 Analyze Information in Bar Graphs **157**

Homework and Remembering page 157

7–10 Remembering Goal: Spiral Review

This Remembering activity would be appropriate anytime after today's lesson.

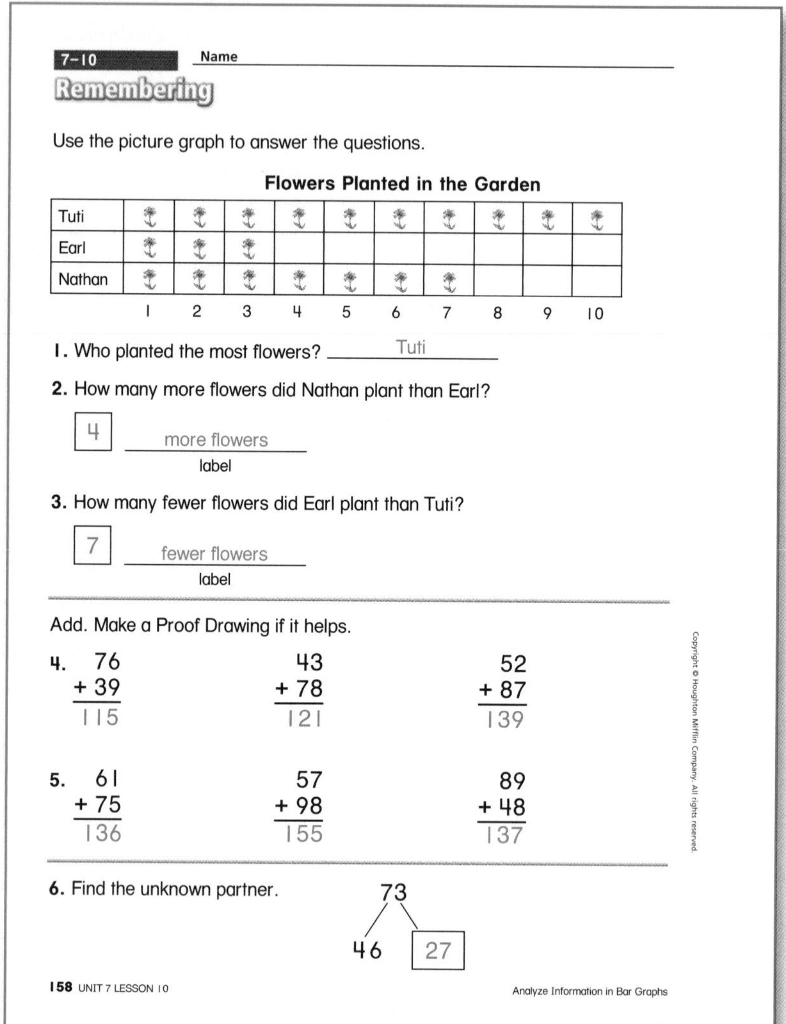

7–10 Remembering Name ______

Use the picture graph to answer the questions.

Flowers Planted in the Garden

Tuti	✿	✿	✿	✿	✿	✿	✿	✿	✿	✿
Earl	✿	✿	✿							
Nathan	✿	✿	✿	✿	✿	✿	✿			
	1	2	3	4	5	6	7	8	9	10

1. Who planted the most flowers? Tuti
2. How many more flowers did Nathan plant than Earl?
   4 more flowers (label)
3. How many fewer flowers did Earl plant than Tuti?
   7 fewer flowers (label)

Add. Make a Proof Drawing if it helps.

4. 76 + 39 = 115   43 + 78 = 121   52 + 87 = 139
5. 61 + 75 = 136   57 + 98 = 155   89 + 48 = 137
6. Find the unknown partner.
   73 → 46 and 27

158 UNIT 7 LESSON 10 Analyze Information in Bar Graphs

Homework and Remembering page 158

Home or School Activity

Real-World Connection

Jobs to Grow On Have each child survey 10 friends about jobs they might like to have when they grow up. Then have each child make a bar graph to display the survey results.

Introduce Circle Graphs

Lesson Objectives

- Analyze information to create bar graphs.
- Compare bar graphs and circle graphs.
- Convert bar graphs into circle graphs.

Vocabulary
bar graph
circle graph
pie graph

The Day at a Glance

Today's Goals	Materials	
1 Teaching the Lesson A: Compare bar graphs and circle graphs. **2 Going Further** ► Differentiated Instruction **3 Homework and Targeted Practice**	**Lesson Activities** Student Activity Book pp. 239–240 Homework and Remembering pp. 159–160 Transparency of Student Activity Book p. 239 (optional)	**Going Further** Activity Cards 7-11 Homework and Remembering p. 159 MathBoard materials Inch Grid Paper (TRB M70) Colored pencils or markers Connecting cubes Paper bag Math Journals

Use Math Talk today!

Keeping Skills Sharp

Quick Practice — 5 MINUTES

Goal: Add by regrouping ones. Identify tens and ones to solve addition equations.

Add Over Ten Write the five equations below on the board. Have a Student Leader point to them one at a time. On a given signal, the class says the total. (See Unit 4 Lesson 9.)

59 + 5 = ☐   23 + 8 = ☐   48 + 3 = ☐   44 + 9 = ☐   77 + 7 = ☐

Add Tens or Ones Write equations like the ones below on the board. Have a Student Leader direct the class in first telling whether they are adding tens or ones, and then saying the total. (See Unit 4 Lesson 9.)

3 + 8 = ☐   30 + 80 = ☐   7 + 4 = ☐   70 + 40 = ☐

Daily Routines

Telling Time Naming the Hands, Telling Time on the Time Poster (See p. xxvii.)

► Led by Student Leaders

Money Routine Using the 120 Poster, Using the Money Flip Chart, Using the Number Path, Using Secret Code Cards (See pp. xxiii–xxv.)

► Led by Student Leaders

1 Teaching the Lesson

Activity

Bar Graphs and Circle Graphs

 55 MINUTES

Goal: Compare bar graphs and circle graphs.

Materials: Student Activity Book page 239, transparency of Student Activity Book page 239 *(optional)*

 **NCTM Standards:**
Number and Operations
Data Analysis and Probability
Problem Solving
Connections
Representation

English Language Learners

Draw a circle graph on the board showing favorite colors.

- **Beginning** Trace the circle with a finger. Say: **This is a *circle graph*. It is in the shape of a circle.** Point to the sections. Say: **We also call it a *pie graph*. Each part is like a piece of pie.** Have children repeat.
- **Intermediate** Say: **This is a *pie graph*.** Ask: **What shape is it?** circle Say: **We also call it a *circle graph*.**
- **Advanced** Have children tell about the *circle graph* and its sections.

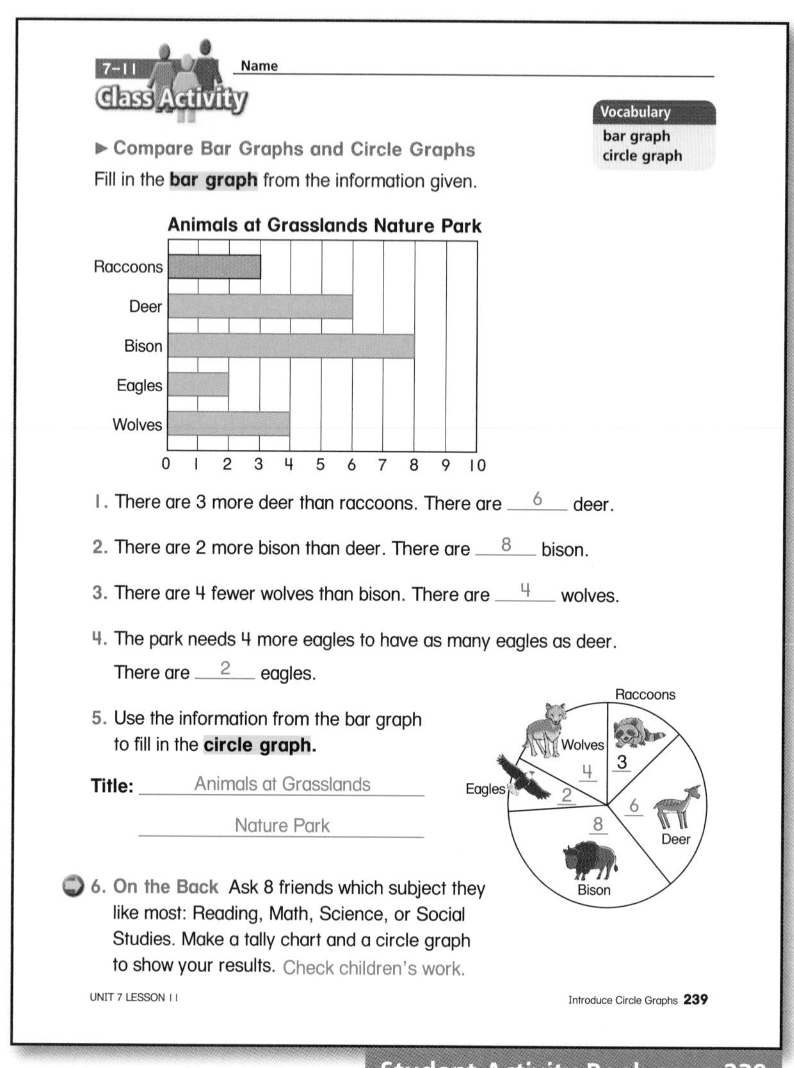

7-11 Class Activity Name

Vocabulary
bar graph
circle graph

► Compare Bar Graphs and Circle Graphs

Fill in the **bar graph** from the information given.

1. There are 3 more deer than raccoons. There are 6 deer.
2. There are 2 more bison than deer. There are 8 bison.
3. There are 4 fewer wolves than bison. There are 4 wolves.
4. The park needs 4 more eagles to have as many eagles as deer. There are 2 eagles.
5. Use the information from the bar graph to fill in the **circle graph**.

Title: Animals at Grasslands Nature Park

6. On the Back Ask 8 friends which subject they like most: Reading, Math, Science, or Social Studies. Make a tally chart and a circle graph to show your results. Check children's work.

UNIT 7 LESSON 11 Introduce Circle Graphs 239

Student Activity Book page 239

► Compare Bar Graphs and Circle Graphs WHOLE CLASS

Direct children's attention to Student Activity Book page 239. Sketch the bar graph on the board or project a transparency of the page.

- This graph will display the number of animals that live in Grasslands Nature Park. We can figure out the number of each type of animal from the information given below the graph.
- The bar for raccoons is already drawn on the graph. It shows that there are 3 raccoons. Exercise 1 says that there are 3 more deer than raccoons. How many deer are there? 6 deer *Draw in the bar for the deer.*
- Exercise 2 says that there are 2 more bison than deer. Are there more deer or more bison? bison

- Who can tell us how to find the number of bison? There are 6 deer. Two more makes 8. There are 8 bison.
- Exercise 3 says that there are 4 fewer wolves than bison. Let's think about this. Which animal will have the smaller number? wolves
- How many bison are there? 8
- What number is four fewer than eight? 4
- How many wolves are there then? 4 wolves

Help children determine the number of eagles in the park.

- The last bar we need to fill in is for the eagles. The park needs 4 more eagles to have as many eagles as there are deer. Does the park have more deer or eagles? deer
- How many more? 4 more deer
- Now who can explain how to find the number of eagles? Possible response: There are 6 deer. If the eagles need 4 more to have as many as the deer, they only have 2 right now.

The children should go back and check their work by reviewing all of the statements. Each statement should be true based on the completed bar graph.

Introduce Circle Graphs Have children look at the circle graph at the bottom of Student Activity Book page 239. Discuss the term *circle graph.* Point out that a circle graph is sometimes called a *pie graph.*

- We just did an activity with a bar graph. Look at this new kind of graph. What would you call a graph like this? Possible responses: circle graph, orange slice graph, pie graph
- It is called a circle graph or sometimes a pie graph. Why would it be called those names? It is a circle. It looks like a pie cut up into parts.
- This circle graph looks very different from the bar graph we just saw. Do you think it could show the same information? How can we tell? One number is given, so we could compare it to the bar graph. We can compare the sizes of the slices to see if they fit the information we know.

Activity continued ▶

Teaching Note

Math Background Circle graphs are best suited to representing the parts of a whole, in this case, the various types of animals constituting a larger population of animals. Bar graphs are best suited to showing amounts to be compared because most people find it easier to perceive length than area.

Differentiated Instruction

English Learners Encourage children to use the pictures of the animals in the circle graph to compare the information between the bar graph and the circle graph. You may wish to sketch or tape the same animal pictures to the labels on the bar graph to reinforce the relationship.

Teaching the Lesson (continued)

Alternate Approach

Visual Learners After completing the entire circle graph activity, have children cut out the slices of the graph to see how they compare in size to each other. Children should notice that the greater the number of animals in a category, the larger the size of the slice. Some children may figure out that when the number of animals is double, the slice is twice as large.

Ongoing Assessment

Refer children to the completed bar graph and circle graph on Student Activity Book page 239. Ask the following questions:

- How do you know from the bar graph that the bison is the most common animal? How can you tell on the circle graph?
- How can you tell on each graph that there are 6 deer?
- Explain one way bar graphs and circle graphs are alike and one way they are different.

Complete the Circle Graph Have children write the numbers for the animals in the circle graph using information from the bar graph. They may use the same title for the circle graph.

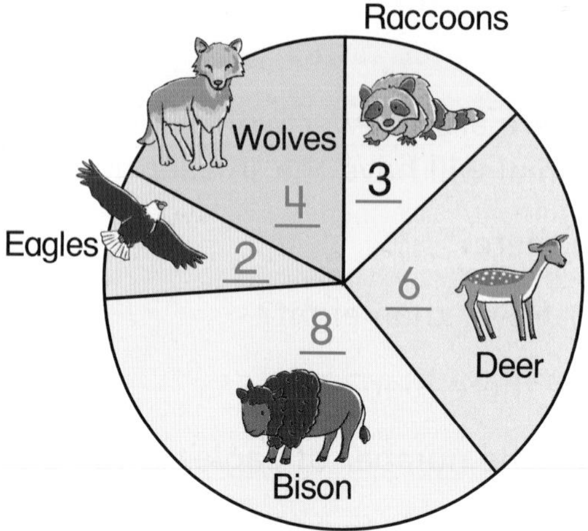

Math Talk Lead a discussion about circle graphs.

- Why are some of the slices in the circle graph bigger than others? Possible response: They stand for larger numbers, the way the longer bars stand for larger numbers.

Have children compare and contrast the circle graph and bar graph.

- In what ways is the circle graph different from the bar graph? It is a circle; it doesn't have bars; there's no number scale to read.
- In what ways is the circle graph like the bar graph? They both show the same information, just in a different way. They both have titles.

Help children understand the purpose of circle graphs.

- Circle graphs are used for showing the parts of a whole or the parts of a whole group.

2 Going Further

Differentiated Instruction

Intervention — Activity Card 7-11

Circle Graph to Bar Graph — Activity Card 7-11

Work:
Use:
- MathBoard
- Homework and Remembering page 159
- 25-cm ruler

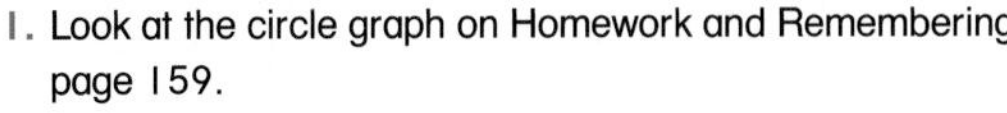

1. Look at the circle graph on Homework and Remembering page 159.
2. Use the circle graph to make a bar graph.
3. Remember to use labels, number scale, and a title.

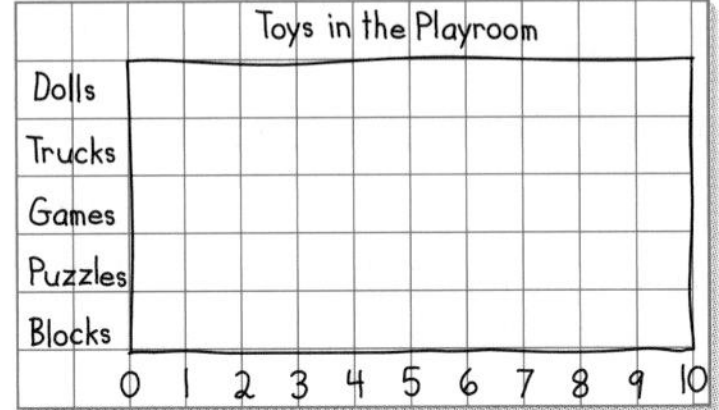

4. Check your work with a friend.

Unit 7, Lesson 11

Activity Note Each child needs MathBoard materials or Inch Grid paper (TRB M70) and 25-cm ruler. You may want to have children work in pairs to make the graph.

Math Writing Prompt

Compare Explain how bar graphs and circle graphs are alike and how they are different.

Software Support

Use *Soar to Success* for instruction of students needing targeted support for underlying skills.

On Level — Activity Card 7-11

Make a Circle Graph — Activity Card 7-11

Work:
Use:
- connecting cubes

- crayons or markers

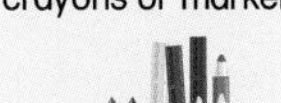

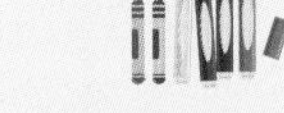

- paper bag
- blank circle graph

1. Take 8 from the bag.
2. Group the by color.
3. Color one part of the circle graph to show each .
4. Label each color section.

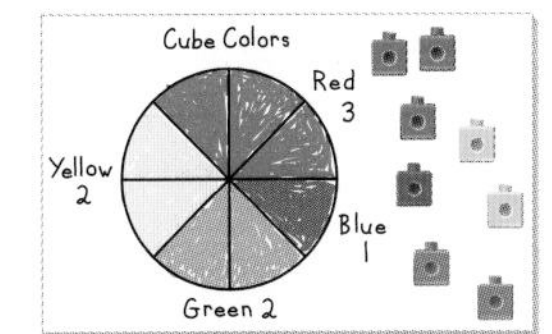

5. **Math Talk** Share your circle graph with classmates. How are they different? How are they the same?

Unit 7, Lesson 11

Activity Note Prepare a circle graph with 8 sections for each child. Each child needs 20 connecting cubes in four colors and crayons in colors to match.

Math Writing Prompt

You Decide Do you think a bar graph or a circle graph is easier to read? Explain your thinking.

Software Support

Use *MegaMath* for review and reinforcement of the concepts and skills presented in this lesson.

Challenge — Activity Card 7-11

Show Survey Results — Activity Card 7-11

Work:
Use:
- MathBoard
- Ruler

Choose:
- 1
- 2

1. **Work Together** Make a circle on your MathBoard and divide the circle into 8 equal sections.
2. Ask eight friends which is their favorite hobby: reading, playing sports, listening to music, or arts and crafts. Tally the results.
3. Use the results to make a circle graph.
4. Write a question about your circle graph. Trade questions with another pair and answer their question.

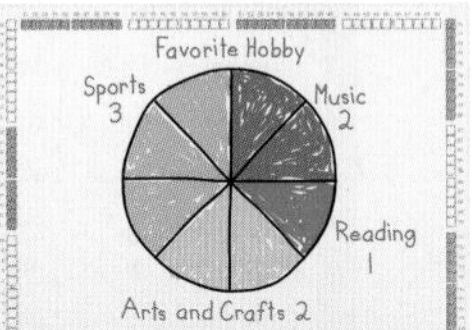

Unit 7, Lesson 11

Activity Note Help pairs make a circle graph on their MathBoard. Ask children to compare their results with pairs who surveyed different classmates.

Math Writing Prompt

Real-World Applications Explain a few situations in which you might use a circle graph to show data. Explain why a circle graph might be a good way to show data.

DESTINATION Math® **Software Support**

Use *Destination Math* to take students beyond the concepts and skills presented in this lesson.

3 Homework and Targeted Practice

Goal: Additional Practice

This Homework page provides practice in reading circle graphs.

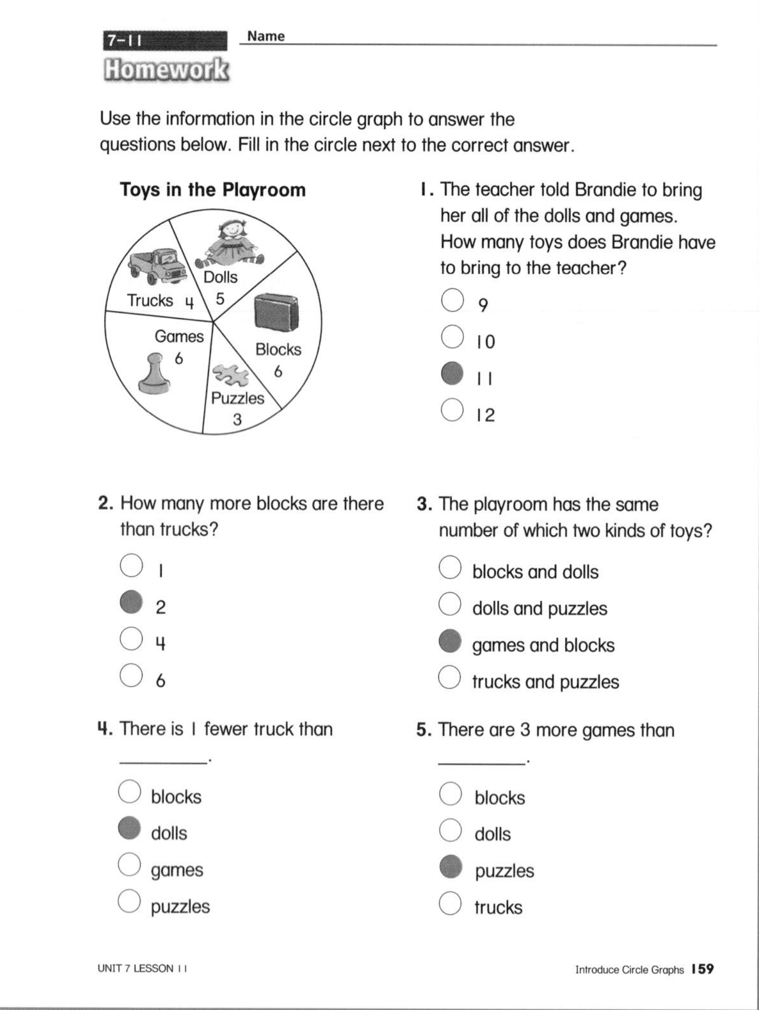

7-11 Homework Name ______________________

Use the information in the circle graph to answer the questions below. Fill in the circle next to the correct answer.

1. The teacher told Brandie to bring her all of the dolls and games. How many toys does Brandie have to bring to the teacher?
   - ○ 9
   - ○ 10
   - ● 11
   - ○ 12

2. How many more blocks are there than trucks?
   - ○ 1
   - ● 2
   - ○ 4
   - ○ 6

3. The playroom has the same number of which two kinds of toys?
   - ○ blocks and dolls
   - ○ dolls and puzzles
   - ● games and blocks
   - ○ trucks and puzzles

4. There is 1 fewer truck than ________.
   - ○ blocks
   - ● dolls
   - ○ games
   - ○ puzzles

5. There are 3 more games than ________.
   - ○ blocks
   - ○ dolls
   - ● puzzles
   - ○ trucks

UNIT 7 LESSON 11 Introduce Circle Graphs **159**

Homework and Remembering page 159

7-11 Targeted Practice **Goal:** Read a circle graph

This Targeted Practice page can be used with children who need extra practice in reading circle graphs.

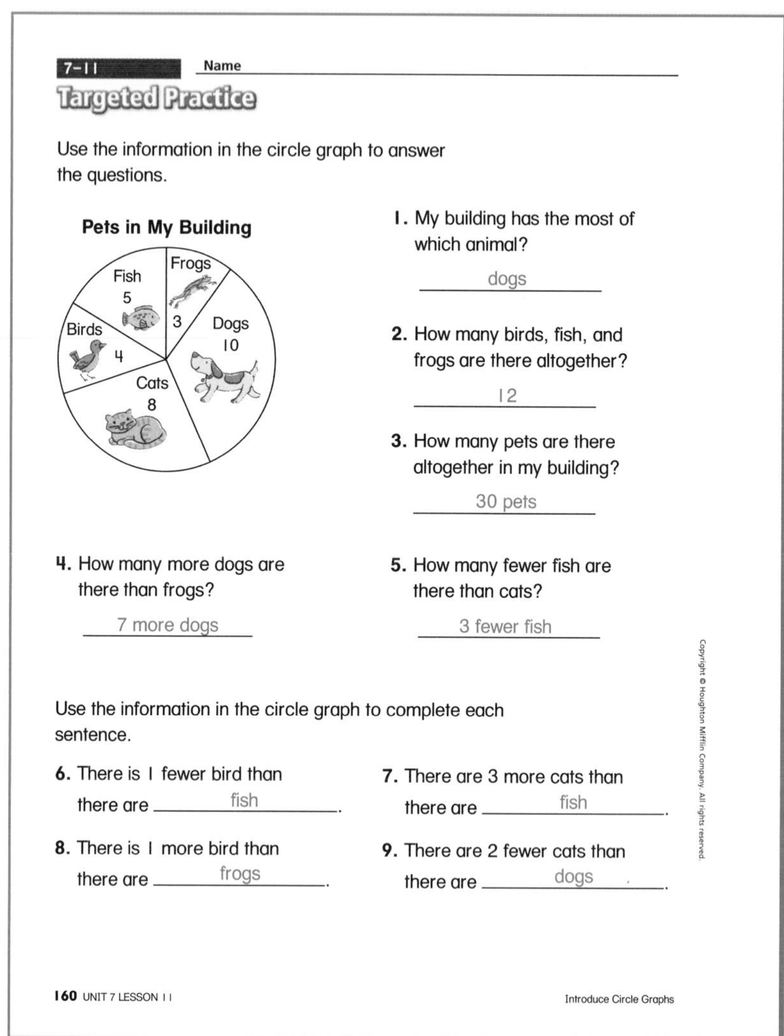

7-11 Targeted Practice Name ______________________

Use the information in the circle graph to answer the questions.

1. My building has the most of which animal? dogs
2. How many birds, fish, and frogs are there altogether? 12
3. How many pets are there altogether in my building? 30 pets
4. How many more dogs are there than frogs? 7 more dogs
5. How many fewer fish are there than cats? 3 fewer fish

Use the information in the circle graph to complete each sentence.

6. There is 1 fewer bird than there are fish.
7. There are 3 more cats than there are fish.
8. There is 1 more bird than there are frogs.
9. There are 2 fewer cats than there are dogs.

160 UNIT 7 LESSON 11 Introduce Circle Graphs

Homework and Remembering page 160

Home or School Activity

Real-World Connection

Graphs and Tables in Print Give children old magazines or newspapers. Have them look through the materials to find examples of graphs and tables.

Display the graphs and tables on a bulletin board.

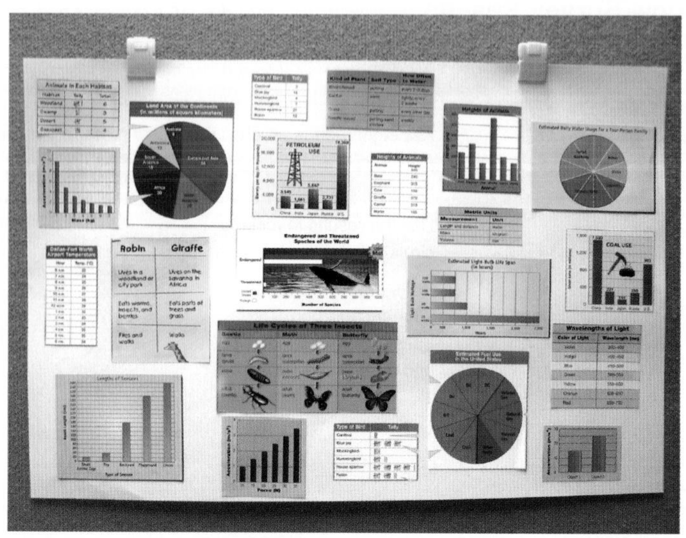

Explore Circle Graphs

Lesson Objectives

- Read information from a circle graph.
- Generate and solve problems based on a given circle graph.

Vocabulary
- ordered pair
- coordinate grid
- circle graph

The Day at a Glance

Today's Goals	Materials	
1 Teaching the Lesson A: Create and answer questions about information in a circle graph. **2 Going Further** ▶ Extension: Graph Ordered Pairs ▶ Differentiated Instruction **3 Homework and Spiral Review**	**Lesson Activities** Student Activity Book pp. 241–244 Homework and Remembering pp. 161–162	**Going Further** Activity Cards 7-12 *Tiger Math: Learning to Graph from a Baby Tiger* by Ann Whitehead Nagda and Cindy Bickel Student Activity Book p. 243 Construction paper Glue stick Colored pencils MathBoard materials Math Journals

Use Math Talk today!

Keeping Skills Sharp

Quick Practice — 5 MINUTES

Goal: Find totals for 1-digit partners.

Materials: Student Activity Book page 241

Addition Sprint Direct children's attention to Student Activity Book page 241. Decide how much time to give them to complete the Sprint. Explain the procedure and time limit to them (See Unit 7 Lesson 4.)

7-12 Class Activity Name ____

▶ Addition Sprint

5 + 7 = 12	9 + 6 = 15	7 + 6 = 13
4 + 8 = 12	7 + 8 = 15	4 + 6 = 10
3 + 9 = 12	9 + 7 = 16	0 + 7 = 7
7 + 5 = 12	9 + 2 = 11	4 + 9 = 13
4 + 5 = 9	5 + 2 = 7	6 + 8 = 14
8 + 4 = 12	6 + 4 = 10	8 + 5 = 13
8 + 6 = 14	8 + 7 = 15	6 + 1 = 7
6 + 9 = 15	5 + 5 = 10	5 + 4 = 9
9 + 9 = 18	1 + 9 = 10	7 + 4 = 11
6 + 3 = 9	7 + 9 = 16	3 + 6 = 9
9 + 0 = 9	4 + 7 = 11	9 + 4 = 13
7 + 7 = 14	8 + 8 = 16	5 + 8 = 13
9 + 1 = 10	6 + 6 = 12	3 + 4 = 7
8 + 9 = 17	3 + 5 = 8	6 + 7 = 13
2 + 5 = 7	9 + 3 = 12	1 + 6 = 7
3 + 9 = 12	2 + 9 = 11	5 + 6 = 11
2 + 7 = 9	2 + 6 = 8	5 + 5 = 10
9 + 4 = 13	5 + 9 = 14	6 + 8 = 14
2 + 8 = 10	8 + 2 = 10	4 + 4 = 8
0 + 8 = 8	9 + 8 = 17	1 + 8 = 9
8 + 3 = 11	6 + 5 = 11	6 + 7 = 13

UNIT 7 LESSON 12 Addition Sprint 241

Student Activity Book page 241

Daily Routines

Telling Time Naming the Hands, Telling Time on the Time Poster (See p. xxvii.)

▶ Led by Student Leaders

Money Routine Using the 120 Poster, Using the Money Flip Chart, Using the Number Path, Using Secret Code Cards (See pp. xxiii–xxv.)

▶ Led by Student Leaders

1 Teaching the Lesson

Activity

Read and Interpret a Circle Graph

 45 MINUTES

Goal: Create and answer questions about information in a circle graph.

Materials: Student Activity Book page 242

 **NCTM Standards:**
Number and Operations
Data Analysis and Probability
Problem Solving
Connections
Representation

Math Talk in Action

What does the circle graph show?

Greta: There are five slices in the circle graph so the graph shows what five things Kacey did with her money.

Who can tell us one thing Kacey did with her money?

Marco: One slice of the circle graph has a shirt and pants and shows the word *clothes.* Kacey spent some money on clothes.

What else did she buy?

Anya: The soccer ball section shows that she also spent money on games.

Lupe: She also spent money on snacks. That's the section with the pretzel.

Cameron: And on a movie rental.

Eddie: The last section is for savings. I guess that means she kept some of the money for the future.

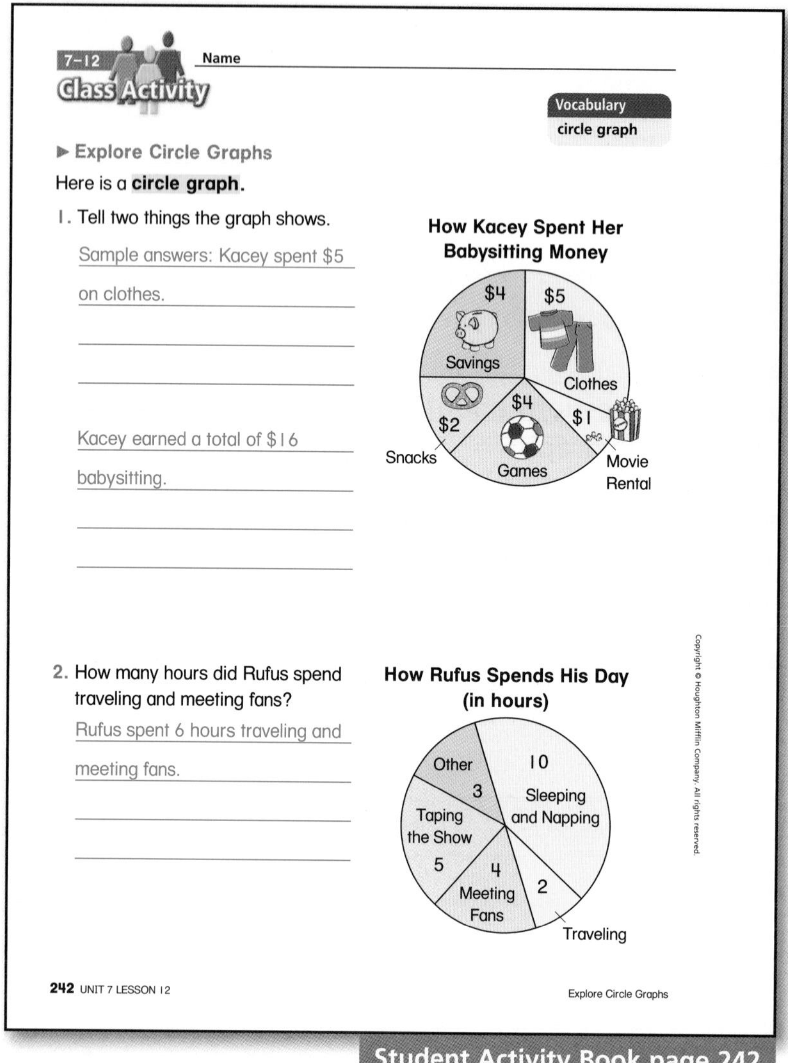
7-12 Class Activity Name

Vocabulary
circle graph

▶ Explore Circle Graphs

Here is a **circle graph.**

1. Tell two things the graph shows.

Sample answers: Kacey spent $5 on clothes.

Kacey earned a total of $16 babysitting.

2. How many hours did Rufus spend traveling and meeting fans?

Rufus spent 6 hours traveling and meeting fans.

242 UNIT 7 LESSON 12 Explore Circle Graphs

Student Activity Book page 242

▶ Explore Circle Graphs WHOLE CLASS

Kacey's Babysitting Money Have children look at Student Activity Book page 242. Explain that the circle graph at the top of the page represents what Kacey did with her babysitting money.

Draw the graph on the board if necessary, omitting the pictures.

Begin by having children read the information from the graph.

- Who can tell us one thing Kacey did with her money? What else did she buy?

Continue until each of the categories has been mentioned.

See **Math Talk in Action** in the side column for possible classroom discussion.

Suggest a few comparison questions for children to answer. Encourage them to think of problems of their own for the class to solve.

- What did Kacey spend the most money on? clothes
- What did she spend the least on? movie rental
  Did she spend more on snacks or on games? games
  How much more? $2
- How much less did she spend on movie rental than on games? $3
- Kacey spent the same amount of money on which two things? savings and games

Then have children complete exercise 1. Encourage them to make statements about the information found directly on the graph, as well as statements which make use of one or more pieces of data on the graph. For example: Kacey earned a total of $16 babysitting.

Rufus, the Television Dog Have children look at the circle graph at the bottom of Student Activity Book page 242. Introduce the scenario about Rufus, a dog actor with his own television show. Ask the class what the graph shows about Rufus. How he spends his day.

Have children work independently or in Helping Pairs to create and answer three questions about the circle graph. The problems should contain comparing language.

Sample Questions

How many more hours does Rufus spend sleeping than taping the show? 5 hours

How many fewer hours does Rufus spend meeting fans and taping the show than sleeping? 1 hour

How many more hours would Rufus have to travel to spend as much time as taping the show? 3 hours

Present children with a circle graph, either a new one or one they have seen before. Ask them a comparison question they can answer using the information in the graph. Then ask them to create their own question about the information in the graph.

English Language Learners

Draw the circle graph below:

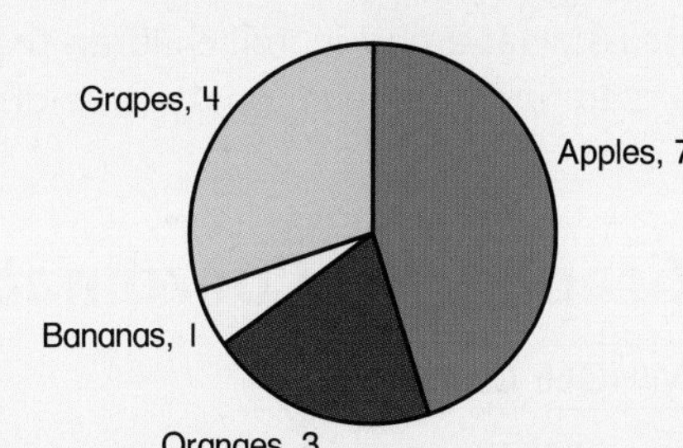

- **Beginning** Say: **The *circle graph* shows that apples were the fruit the children ate the *most*.** Have children repeat. Continue with *least*.
- **Intermediate** Ask: **Which fruit did the children eat the most—apples or grapes?** apples **The *least*?** bananas
- **Advanced** Have children tell what fruit was eaten the *most* and *least*.

2 Going Further

Extension: Graph Ordered Pairs

Goal: Name and graph ordered pairs on a grid.

Materials: Student Activity Book page 243

✓ **NCTM Standards:**
Number and Operations
Data Analysis and Probability
Problem Solving
Connections
Representation

Teaching Note

Language and Vocabulary Display or sketch a blank grid on the board. Explain to children that this it is called a *grid.* Tell them that they will use a grid to locate different things. Write (2, 4) next to the grid. Explain that it is called an *ordered pair.* Discuss what a pair is. Tell children that they will use ordered pairs to find and name points on a grid.

▶ Graph on a Coordinate Grid

WHOLE CLASS

Direct children's attention to the coordinate grid on Student Activity Book page 243. Tell children that they need to locate the object at the ordered pair (1, 4). Explain that the first number in an ordered pair tells you how many spaces to move to the right. The second number tells you how many spaces to move up. Model how to move on the grid. Be sure children understand that you should start at the zero.

- What object is at (1, 4)? the square

Have children complete exercises 1–6 independently or in **Helping Pairs.**

Now explain that sometimes you will need to find the ordered pair for a location. Have children focus on the heart. To find the ordered pair, explain that you start at the zero and count the number of spaces to the right, stopping on the line of the object. Then you count the number of spaces you moved up.

- How many spaces did we move to the right? 3
- How many spaces did we move up? 3

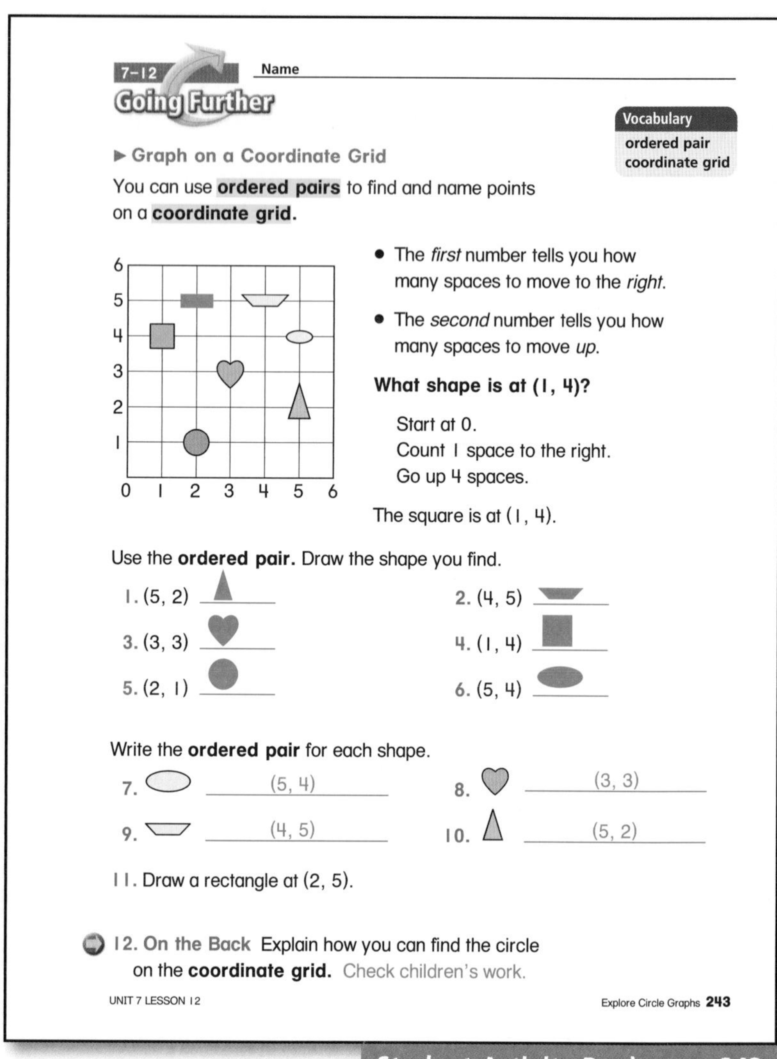

7–12 Going Further Name

Vocabulary
ordered pair
coordinate grid

▶ Graph on a Coordinate Grid

You can use **ordered pairs** to find and name points on a **coordinate grid.**

- The *first* number tells you how many spaces to move to the *right.*
- The *second* number tells you how many spaces to move *up.*

What shape is at (1, 4)?

Start at 0.
Count 1 space to the right.
Go up 4 spaces.

The square is at (1, 4).

Use the **ordered pair.** Draw the shape you find.

1. (5, 2)
2. (4, 5)
3. (3, 3)
4. (1, 4)
5. (2, 1)
6. (5, 4)

Write the **ordered pair** for each shape.

7. (5, 4)
8. (3, 3)
9. (4, 5)
10. (5, 2)
11. Draw a rectangle at (2, 5).

12. On the Back Explain how you can find the circle on the **coordinate grid.** Check children's work.

UNIT 7 LESSON 12 Explore Circle Graphs 243

Student Activity Book page 243

- What is the ordered pair for the triangle? (5, 2)

Have children complete exercises 7–12 independently or in Helping Pairs.

Teaching Note

Critical Thinking Have children consider what happens if they use the ordered pairs as "directions," but do not start at zero. Ask them to make conclusions about what happens if they count up first and then right, rather than right first, and then up.

Intervention — Activity Card 7-12

Create a Circle Graph — Activity Card 7-12

Work: 

Use:

- Circle graph parts
- Construction Paper
- Glue stick
- Crayons or markers

Choose:

- 1
- 2

Fruit Basket
There are 3 oranges in the basket.
There are 4 bananas in the basket.
There is 1 pear in the basket.

1. **Work Together** Decide how many pieces of fruit there are in the fruit basket.
2. Match each part of the circle to a type of fruit. Sample answer: $\frac{1}{8}$ pear, $\frac{3}{8}$ orange, $\frac{4}{8}$ banana
3. Label the parts. Glue the circle parts onto the construction paper to make a circle graph.
4. Put a title on your circle graph.

Unit 7, Lesson 12

Activity Note For each pair, prepare the parts of a circle graph. The parts need to be $\frac{1}{8}$, $\frac{3}{8}$, and $\frac{4}{8}$. Children glue the parts onto paper to make a circle graph.

Math Writing Prompt

What Does the Graph Show? Look at the circle graph on Homework and Remembering page 161. Explain what the graph shows. Write two sentences that compare.

Software Support

Use *Soar to Success* for instruction of students needing targeted support for underlying skills.

On Level — Activity Card 7-12

Alternate Questions — Activity Card 7-12

Work:

Use:

- Homework and Remembering page 161.

Choose:

- 1
- 2

1. Look at the circle graph on Homework and Remembering page 161.
2. 1 Use the circle graph to ask a comparison question. Use the words *fewer* or *more*.

How many fewer buses are there than airplanes?

3. 2 Answer the question. Then ask your own question.
4. Repeat. Ask equalizing questions this time.

Unit 7, Lesson 12

Activity Note Each pair needs Homework and Remembering page 161. You may want to have each pair write a question for another pair.

Math Writing Prompt

You Decide Tell whether you think a tally chart or a circle graph is easier to read and why.

Software Support

Use *MegaMath* for review and reinforcement of the concepts and skills presented in this lesson.

Challenge — Activity Card 7-12

Make a Circle Graph — Activity Card 7-12

Work:

Use:

- MathBoard

Carolyn has more ribbons than Jessica.
Erin has fewer ribbons than Patricia and Jessica.
Jessica has more ribbons than Patricia.
Patricia has 3 ribbons.

1. Use the information in the box to make a circle graph. Use numbers that make sense for the information in the box.
2. Be sure and label and title your bar graph.
3. Write three questions about your bar graph. Give your questions to a classmate.
4. Solve the questions your classmate wrote.

Unit 7, Lesson 12

Activity Note Each child needs MathBoard materials. Explain that there is more than one circle graph for this problem.

Math Writing Prompt

Write Your Own Write a problem about favorite fruits that can be solved using a circle graph. Draw the graph and explain how you got your answer.

DESTINATION Math®

Software Support

Use *Destination Math* to take students beyond the concepts and skills presented in this lesson.

3 Homework and Spiral Review

Goal: Additional Practice

This Homework page provides practice in reading circle graphs.

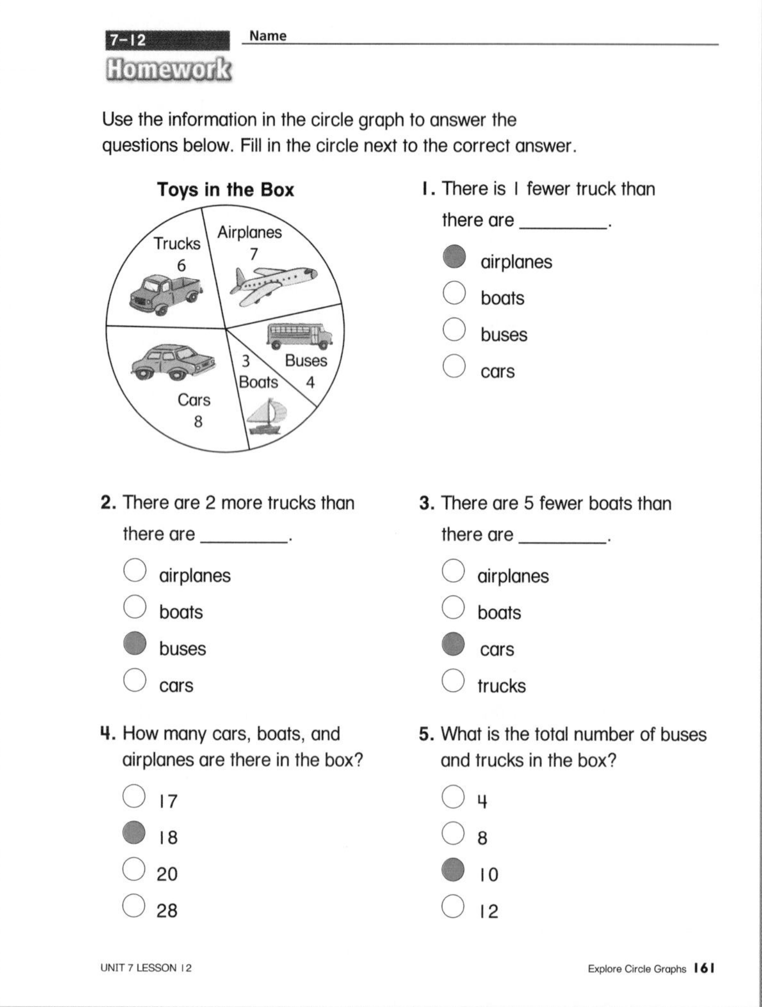

7–12 Homework Name ____________

Use the information in the circle graph to answer the questions below. Fill in the circle next to the correct answer.

Toys in the Box

Trucks 6, Airplanes 7, Buses 4, Boats 3, Cars 8

1. There is 1 fewer truck than there are ________.
   - ● airplanes
   - ○ boats
   - ○ buses
   - ○ cars

2. There are 2 more trucks than there are ________.
   - ○ airplanes
   - ○ boats
   - ● buses
   - ○ cars

3. There are 5 fewer boats than there are ________.
   - ○ airplanes
   - ○ boats
   - ● cars
   - ○ trucks

4. How many cars, boats, and airplanes are there in the box?
   - ○ 17
   - ● 18
   - ○ 20
   - ○ 28

5. What is the total number of buses and trucks in the box?
   - ○ 4
   - ○ 8
   - ● 10
   - ○ 12

UNIT 7 LESSON 12 Explore Circle Graphs **161**

Homework and Remembering page 161

7–12 Remembering **Goal:** Spiral Review

This Remembering activity would be appropriate anytime after today's lesson.

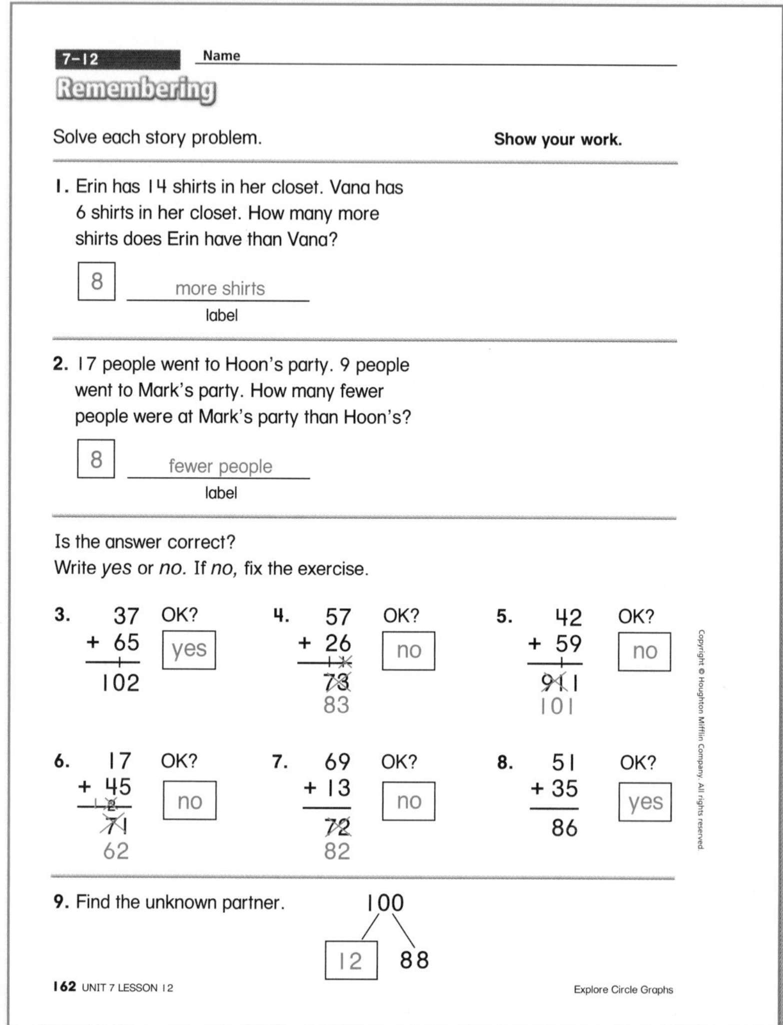

7–12 Remembering Name ____________

Solve each story problem. **Show your work.**

1. Erin has 14 shirts in her closet. Vana has 6 shirts in her closet. How many more shirts does Erin have than Vana?

   8 more shirts (label)

2. 17 people went to Hoon's party. 9 people went to Mark's party. How many fewer people were at Mark's party than Hoon's?

   8 fewer people (label)

Is the answer correct?
Write *yes* or *no*. If *no*, fix the exercise.

3. 37 + 65 = 102 OK? yes
4. 57 + 26 = 73 OK? no — 83
5. 42 + 59 = 911 OK? no — 101
6. 17 + 45 = 71 OK? no — 62
7. 69 + 13 = 72 OK? no — 82
8. 51 + 35 = 86 OK? yes

9. Find the unknown partner. 100 → 12 and 88

162 UNIT 7 LESSON 12 Explore Circle Graphs

Copyright © Houghton Mifflin Company. All rights reserved.

Homework and Remembering page 162

Home or School Activity

Literature Connection

Tiger Math Read aloud or have children read *Tiger Math: Learning to Graph from a Baby Tiger* by Ann Whitehead Nagda and Cindy Bickel (Henry Holt and Company, 2000). This book reinforces how to make and read bar graphs and circle graphs in a real-world and engaging way.

Have children write and solve comparison and equalizing questions for at least three of the graphs.

Talk About Graphs

Lesson Objectives

- Create questions and make comparison statements based on a given graph.
- Convert horizontal graphs to vertical graphs.

Vocabulary

is greater than	horizontal bar graph
is less than	vertical bar graph

The Day at a Glance

Today's Goals	Materials	
1 Teaching the Lesson A: Create comparison questions based on a bar graph. Change a horizontal bar graph to a vertical bar graph.	**Lesson Activities** Student Activity Book pp. 245–246 Homework and Remembering pp. 163–164 MathBoard materials	**Going Further** Activity Cards 7-13 Index cards Crayons or colored pencils Connecting cubes Inch Grid Paper (TRB M70) Math Journals
2 Going Further ► Extension: Double Bar Graphs ► Differentiated Instruction		
3 Homework and Spiral Review		

Use Math Talk today!

Keeping Skills Sharp

Quick Practice 5 MINUTES

Goals: Find partners for teen numbers. Practice addition and subtraction.

Materials: Blue Math Mountain Cards (from Unit 1 Lesson 16 or TRB M43–44)

Teen Flash–Unknown Addends The Student Leader calls out a teen total and one of its partners. The class flashes the other partner with their fingers. Example: The Student Leader says: "8 plus something equals 14." The children flash six fingers to show the unknown addend.

Blue Math Mountain Cards Have children practice addition and subtraction with their Math Mountain Cards. Remind them that there are four equations to practice on each card. (See page 113.)

Daily Routines

Telling Time Naming the Hands, Telling Time on the Time Poster (See p. xxvii.)

► Led by Student Leaders

Money Routine Using the 120 Poster, Using the Money Flip Chart, Using the Number Path, Using Secret Code Cards (See pp. xxiii–xxv.)

► Led by Student Leaders

1 Teaching the Lesson

Activity

Review Bar Graphs

 **45 MINUTES**

Goals: Create comparison questions based on a bar graph. Change a horizontal bar graph to a vertical bar graph.

Materials: Student Activity Book page 245, MathBoard materials

 **NCTM Standards:**
Number and Operations
Data Analysis and Probability
Problem Solving
Connections
Representation

Teaching Note

Math Background Graphs help make comparison statements in two ways. The lengths of the bars in a bar graph and the sizes of the "slices" in a circle graph give a general picture of how categories compare: more or less, greater than or less than. Encourage children to use the visual clues provided in a graph to get an overview of the relationships, and then to use the numbers to work out the details.

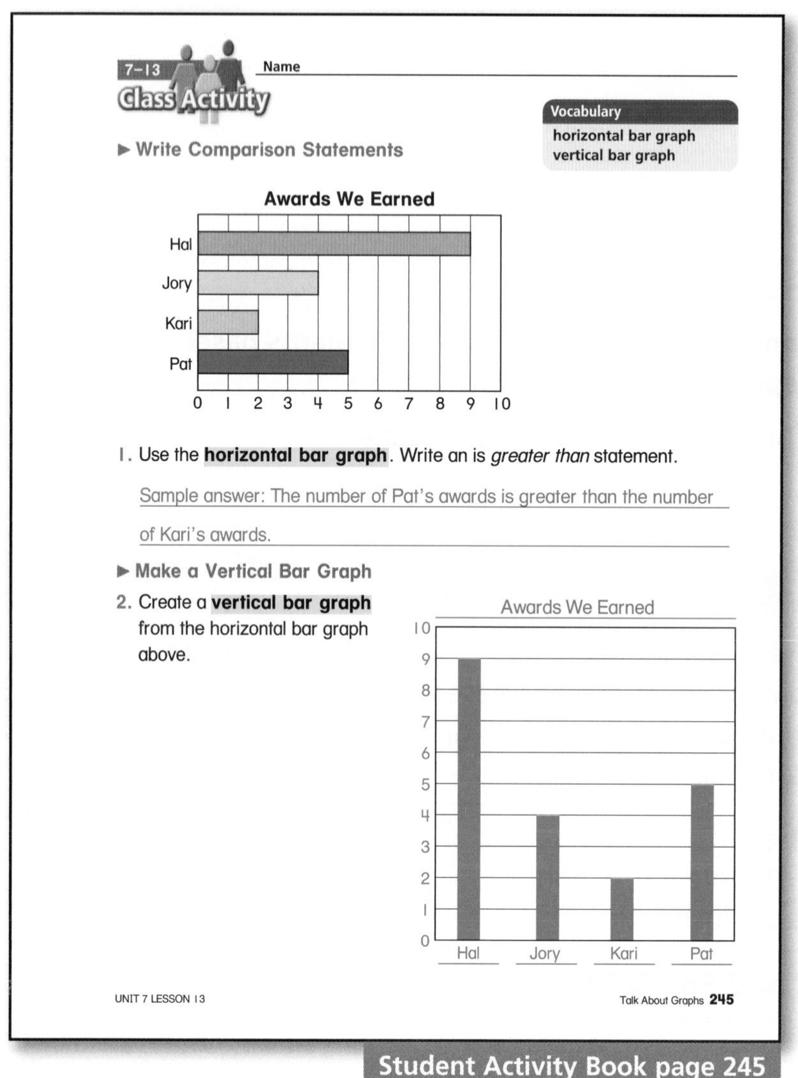
7-13 Class Activity Name

Vocabulary
horizontal bar graph
vertical bar graph

▶ Write Comparison Statements

1. Use the **horizontal bar graph**. Write an is *greater than* statement.

Sample answer: The number of Pat's awards is greater than the number of Kari's awards.

▶ Make a Vertical Bar Graph

2. Create a **vertical bar graph** from the horizontal bar graph above.

UNIT 7 LESSON 13 Talk About Graphs 245

Student Activity Book page 245

▶ Write Comparison Questions WHOLE CLASS

Refer children to Student Activity Book page 245. Have them write comparison questions for the graph on their MathBoards. If their questions tend to be simple or of the same type, model more sophisticated or diverse examples (for example, equalize questions) for children to imitate.

▶ Write Comparison Statements WHOLE CLASS

Compare with Words Have children complete exercise 1 on Student Activity Book page 245.

Compare with Numbers and Symbols Lead children through this process to translate their statements from exercise 1 into comparison statements that include numbers and symbols.

- The number of Pat's awards is greater than the number of Kari's awards.
- Pat has 5. Kari has 2.
- 5 is greater than 2.
- 5 > 2.

Repeat the process, but this time start from Kari's point of view.

- Kari has fewer awards than Pat.
- Kari has 2. Pat has 5.
- 2 is less than 5.
- 2 < 5.

▶ Make a Vertical Bar Graph WHOLE CLASS

Explain to children that they are going to change the horizontal bar graph at the top of Student Activity Book page 245 into a vertical bar graph. Review the similarities and differences between the two kinds of graphs.

- What changes would you need to make to the graph so that the bars could be vertical instead of horizontal? The number scale will go on the left side of the graph, and the names of the children will go along the bottom.
- What are the names of the children on the vertical bar graph? Hal, Jory, Kari, Pat
- Where will the names be written on the graph? along the bottom of the graph
- What is the number scale on the vertical bar graph? 0 to 10
- Where and how will the numbers be written? along the left side of the graph with 0 at the bottom and 10 at the top

In the space provided on Student Activity Book page 245, have children redraw the graph as a vertical bar graph.

Class Management

Children may prefer to draw on their MathBoards instead of on page 245. You may wish to have some children work at the classroom board.

Differentiated Instruction

English Learners Children learning a second language greatly benefit from visual clues to help them get the meaning of things. Visual clues like charts, pictures, and graphs should be incorporated with as many lessons as possible even after this graphing unit is completed.

English Language Learners

Draw a horizontal bar graph. Identify the scale and its location. Draw a vertical bar graph.

- **Beginning** Point to the scale. Ask: **Is the *scale* on the bottom?** no **Is it on the left side.** yes
- **Intermediate** Ask: **Is the *scale* on a vertical bar graph across the bottom or on the left side?** left side
- **Advanced** Have children locate the *scale* on a vertical bar graph.

Ongoing Assessment

Have each child make a comparison statement and then write and answer a comparing or equalizing question using the graph on Student Activity Book page 245.

2 Going Further

Extension: Double Bar Graphs

Goal: Read information in a double bar graph.

Materials: Student Activity Book page 246

 **NCTM Standards:**
Number and Operations
Data Analysis and Probability
Problem Solving
Connections
Representations

▶ Introduce Double Bar Graphs

WHOLE CLASS

Direct children's attention to the double bar graph on Student Activity Book page 246. Explain that a double bar graph compares two sets of information. Review and identify the different features of the graph. Point out the labeled shaded boxes on the double bar graph and explain that they are called the *key*. Discuss the purpose of a door or car key to unlock something. Explain that a key on a graph unlocks the meaning of the bars.

Discuss why it might be useful to have two bars in each category. Explain that the graph shows the same kind of information for two different cities, and that placing the bars on the same graph makes it easier to compare the data.

▶ Critical Thinking

Math Talk 

- What does the key show? Why does the key use different shades?
- Is a double bar graph a good way to show how much a puppy weighs each month for 6 months? Why or why not?

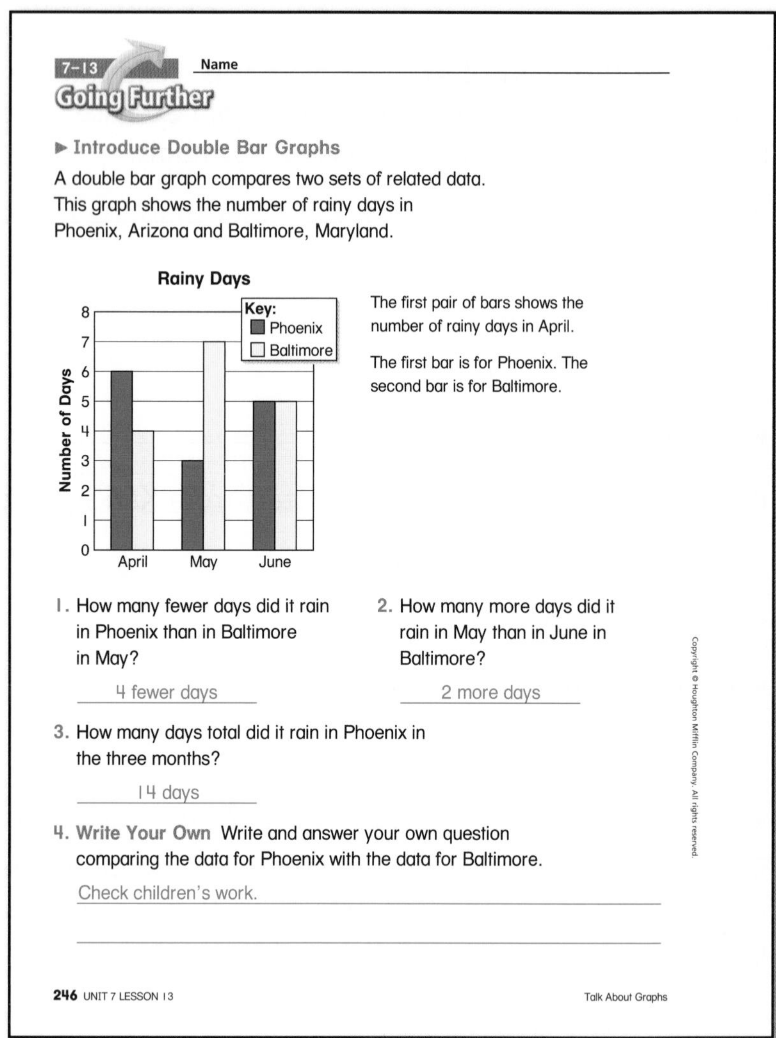

7-13 Going Further Name

▶ Introduce Double Bar Graphs

A double bar graph compares two sets of related data. This graph shows the number of rainy days in Phoenix, Arizona and Baltimore, Maryland.

The first pair of bars shows the number of rainy days in April.

The first bar is for Phoenix. The second bar is for Baltimore.

1. How many fewer days did it rain in Phoenix than in Baltimore in May?
   4 fewer days
2. How many more days did it rain in May than in June in Baltimore?
   2 more days
3. How many days total did it rain in Phoenix in the three months?
   14 days
4. **Write Your Own** Write and answer your own question comparing the data for Phoenix with the data for Baltimore.
   Check children's work.

246 UNIT 7 LESSON 13 Talk About Graphs

Student Activity Book page 246

- Could you make a vertical double bar graph into a horizontal double bar graph? If so, what would you do?
- Could you make the information in a double bar graph into a circle graph? Explain.

The Learning Classroom

Math Talk Have children discuss how a double bar graph is different from a single bar graph. Then have them explain how the features of both graphs are alike and how they are different.

Intervention — Activity Card 7-13

Human Bar Graph

Activity Card 7-13 ●

Work: [group]

Use:

- 3 index cards
- Crayons or markers

Choose:

- 1
- 2
- 3

1. **Work Together** Write *Mystery*, *Comedy*, and *Science Fiction* on the index cards.
2. Place the index cards on the floor. Have group members or class members stand behind the index card for their favorite type of movie.
3. Count how many children are behind each index card.
4. Use the information to make a vertical bar graph.

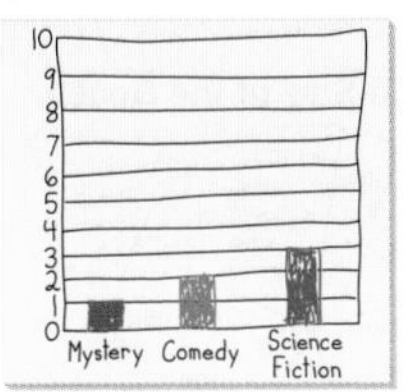

Unit 7, Lesson 13

Activity Note Each group needs three index cards. You may want to have groups put their numbers together.

Math Writing Prompt

Use Symbols Rewrite the sentences below using numbers and symbols.

Five is greater than three.
Six is less than nine.

Software Support

Use *Soar to Success* for instruction of students needing targeted support for underlying skills.

On Level — Activity Card 7-13

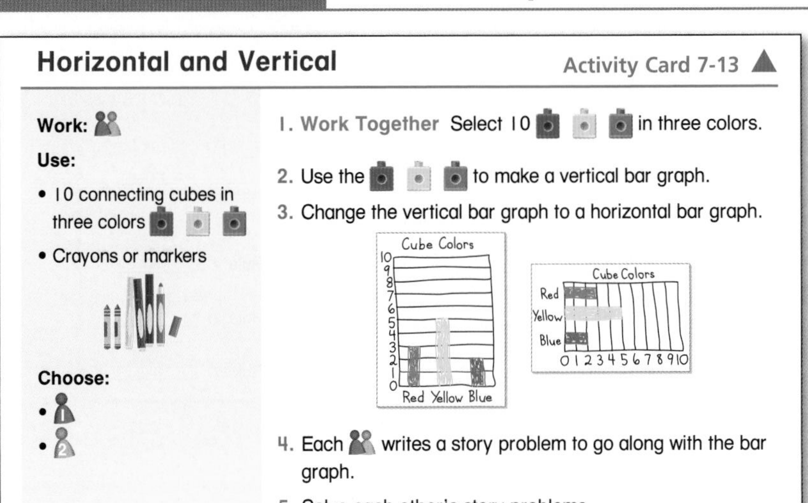

Horizontal and Vertical

Activity Card 7-13 ▲

Work: [pair]

Use:

- 10 connecting cubes in three colors
- Crayons or markers

Choose:

- 1
- 2

1. **Work Together** Select 10 [cubes] in three colors.
2. Use the [cubes] to make a vertical bar graph.
3. Change the vertical bar graph to a horizontal bar graph.

Cube Colors (10 9 8 7 6 5 4 3 2 1 0; Red Yellow Blue)

Cube Colors (Red, Yellow, Blue; 0 1 2 3 4 5 6 7 8 9 10)

4. Each [pair] writes a story problem to go along with the bar graph.
5. Solve each other's story problems.

Unit 7, Lesson 13

Activity Note Each pair needs 10 connecting cubes in three different colors. Remind children to label and title their bar graphs.

Math Writing Prompt

Summarize Explain two differences between a horizontal and a vertical bar graph.

Software Support

Use *MegaMath* for review and reinforcement of the concepts and skills presented in this lesson.

Challenge — Activity Card 7-13

Make a Horizontal and Vertical Bar Graph

Activity Card 7-13 ■

Work: [pair]

Use:

- Inch Grid paper
- Crayons or markers

Choose:

- 1
- 2

Fish in the Aquarium
There are fewer angelfish than goldfish.
There are more angelfish than neons.
There are more neons than mollies.

1. Each [pair] should draw a horizontal bar graph so that each statement above is true.

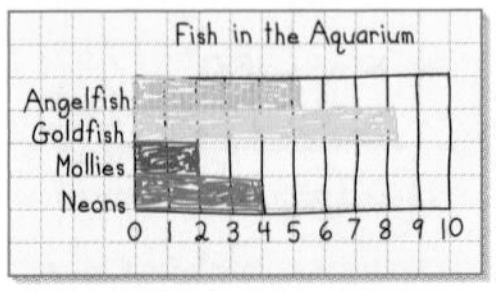

Fish in the Aquarium (Angelfish, Goldfish, Mollies, Neons; 0 1 2 3 4 5 6 7 8 9 10)

2. Compare your horizontal bar graphs to be sure they are correct.
3. Change the horizontal bar graphs to vertical bar graphs.

Unit 7, Lesson 13

Activity Note Each pair needs four sheets of Inch Grid paper (TRB M70). Discuss how the numbers in the graphs may vary.

Math Writing Prompt

Make a List You asked 10 friends about their favorite color: red, blue, or yellow. Six friends picked yellow. List all possible combinations of votes for red and blue.

Software Support

Use *Destination Math* to take students beyond the concepts and skills presented in this lesson.

3 Homework and Spiral Review

Goal: Additional Practice

This Homework page provides practice in reading bar graphs and comparing numbers.

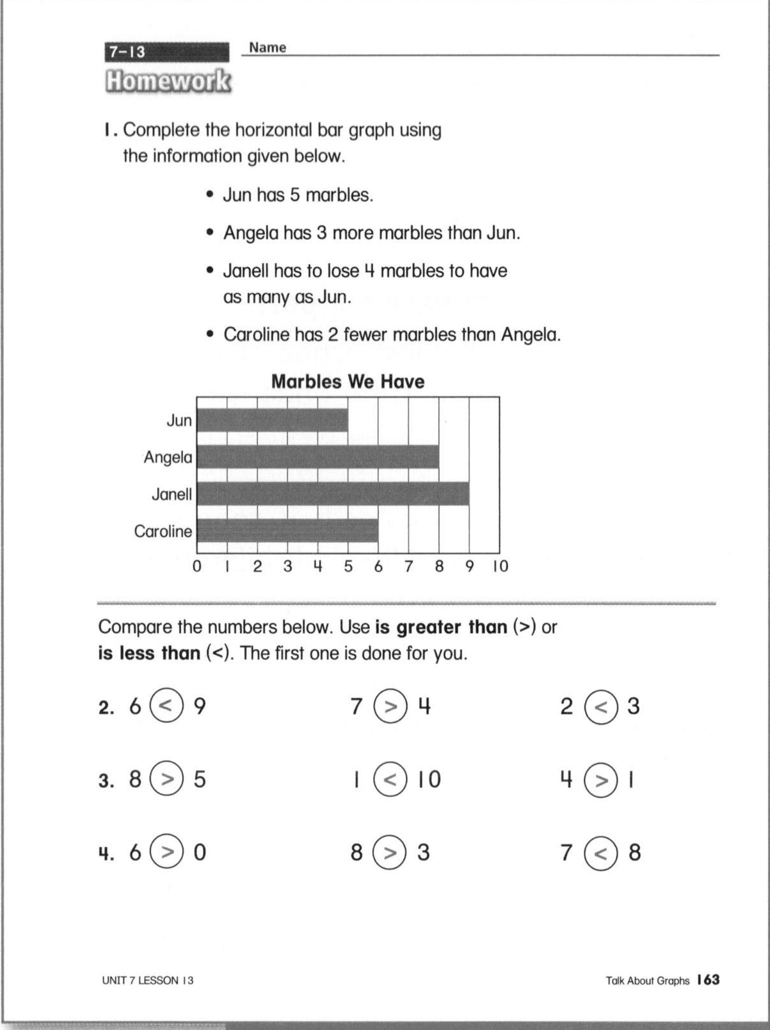

7-13 Name

Homework

1. Complete the horizontal bar graph using the information given below.

- Jun has 5 marbles.
- Angela has 3 more marbles than Jun.
- Janell has to lose 4 marbles to have as many as Jun.
- Caroline has 2 fewer marbles than Angela.

Compare the numbers below. Use **is greater than** (>) or **is less than** (<). The first one is done for you.

2. 6 (<) 9   7 (>) 4   2 (<) 3

3. 8 (>) 5   1 (<) 10   4 (>) 1

4. 6 (>) 0   8 (>) 3   7 (<) 8

UNIT 7 LESSON 13   Talk About Graphs **163**

Homework and Remembering page 163

Goal: Spiral Review

This Remembering activity would be appropriate anytime after today's lesson.

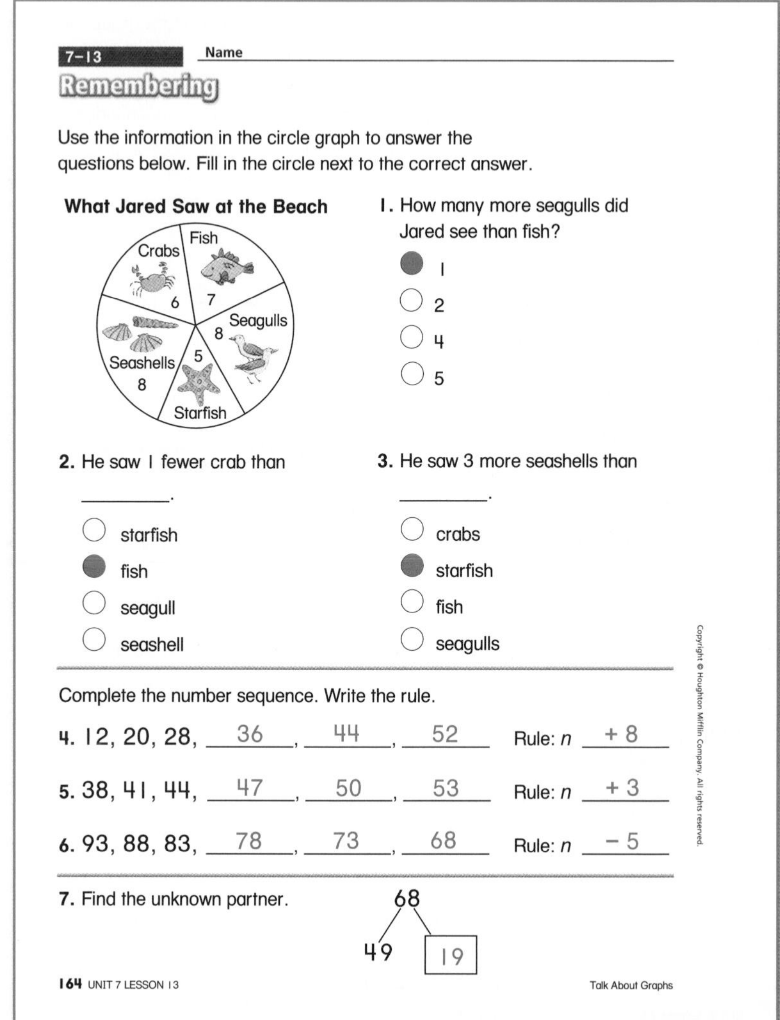

7-13 Name

Remembering

Use the information in the circle graph to answer the questions below. Fill in the circle next to the correct answer.

1. How many more seagulls did Jared see than fish?
   - ● 1
   - ○ 2
   - ○ 4
   - ○ 5

2. He saw 1 fewer crab than ________.
   - ○ starfish
   - ● fish
   - ○ seagull
   - ○ seashell

3. He saw 3 more seashells than ________.
   - ○ crabs
   - ● starfish
   - ○ fish
   - ○ seagulls

Complete the number sequence. Write the rule.

4. 12, 20, 28, 36, 44, 52   Rule: n + 8

5. 38, 41, 44, 47, 50, 53   Rule: n + 3

6. 93, 88, 83, 78, 73, 68   Rule: n − 5

7. Find the unknown partner.

68
49   19

164 UNIT 7 LESSON 13   Talk About Graphs

Homework and Remembering page 164

Home or School Activity

Science Connection

Rock-a-Bye Baby Some animals sleep longer than others. Help children research the number of hours various animals sleep each night. Have them make a table and then create a horizontal or vertical bar graph using the information they found. Then have children write and solve three comparison questions.

Animal	Hours of Sleep Each Night
Elephant	4
Giraffe	2
Goat	5

2-Digit Addition with Tables and Graphs

Lesson Objectives

- **Read and answer questions about information in tables, bar graphs, and circle graphs.**
- **Find number partners in tables.**
- **Write equation chains.**

Vocabulary
table
bar graph
circle graph

The Day at a Glance

Today's Goals	Materials	
1 Teaching the Lesson **A1:** Answer questions based on information in a table. **A2:** Interpret a bar graph and a circle graph. **A3:** Facilitate equation building and mastery of 1-digit addition. **2 Going Further** ▶ Differentiated Instruction **3 Homework and Spiral Review**	**Lesson Activities** Student Activity Book pp. 247–248 Homework and Remembering pp. 165–166 Transparency of Student Activity Book p. 247 (optional) Cubes (2 colors) or real or play money (2 different coins) Quick Quiz 3 (Assessment Guide)	**Going Further** Activity Cards 7-14 Index cards Inch Grid Paper (TRB M70) Math Journals

123 Use Math Talk today!

Keeping Skills Sharp

Quick Practice — 5 MINUTES

Goals: Find partners for teen numbers.

Teen Flash–Unknown Addends
The **Student Leader** calls out a teen total and one of its partners. The class flashes the other partner with their fingers. Example: The Student Leader says: "4 plus something equals 13." The children flash nine fingers to show the unknown addend. (See page 113.)

Repeated Quick Practice
Use this Quick Practice from a previous lesson.

- **Blue Math Mountain Cards** (See Unit 7 Lesson 13.)

Daily Routines

Telling Time Naming the Hands, Telling Time on the Time Poster (See p. xxvii.)

- Led by Student Leaders

Money Routine Using the 120 Poster, Using the Money Flip Chart, Using the Number Path, Using Secret Code Cards (See pp. xxiii–xxv.)

- Led by Student Leaders

1 Teaching the Lesson

Activity 1

Plant Seeds

 25 MINUTES

Goal: Answer questions based on information in a table.

Materials: Student Activity Book page 247; transparency of Student Activity Book page 247 (optional)

 **NCTM Standards:**
Number and Operations
Problem Solving
Representation

 **Class Management**

It may be helpful to draw the table about planting seeds on the board or make a transparency of Student Activity Book page 247.

 **Ongoing Assessment**

Provide pairs with a container filled with red and green cubes or pennies and dimes, or any two different objects. Have each child select a large handful of the objects and then sort and count the number of each object. They should display their information in a table like the one shown below. After children complete the table, ask them to find partners for one of the totals.

	Red	Green	*Total*
Gil	16	11	27
Toya	14	18	32
Total	30	29	59

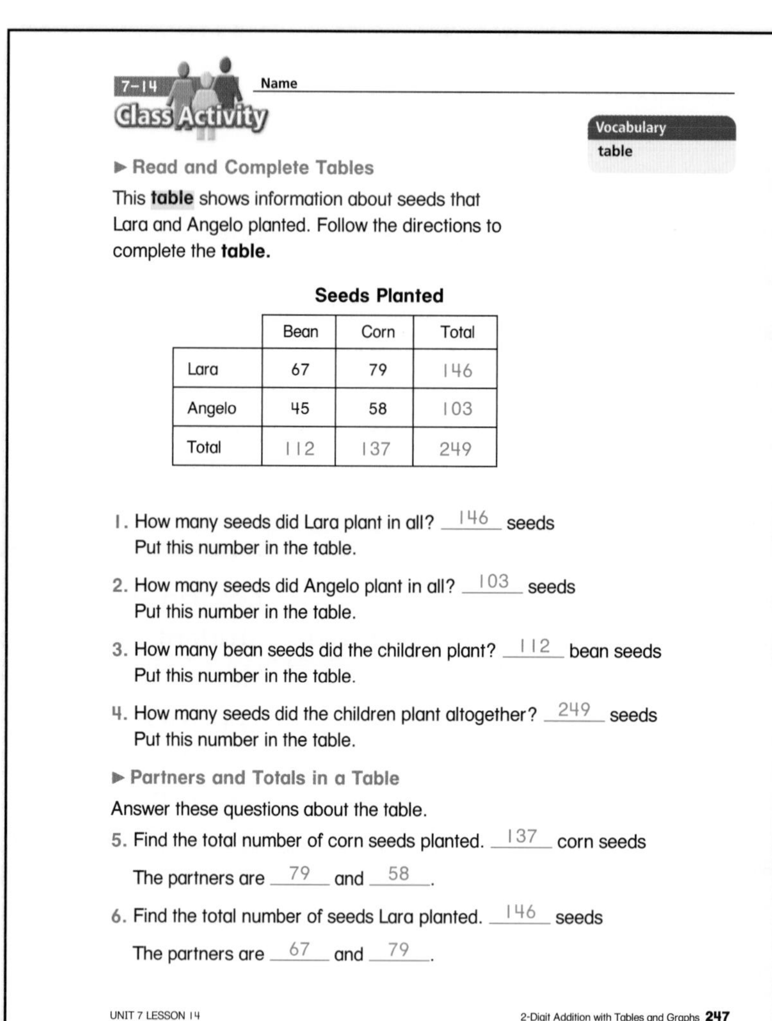

7-14 Class Activity

Name

Vocabulary
table

▶ Read and Complete Tables

This **table** shows information about seeds that Lara and Angelo planted. Follow the directions to complete the **table.**

Seeds Planted

	Bean	Corn	Total
Lara	67	79	146
Angelo	45	58	103
Total	112	137	249

1. How many seeds did Lara plant in all? 146 seeds
Put this number in the table.
2. How many seeds did Angelo plant in all? 103 seeds
Put this number in the table.
3. How many bean seeds did the children plant? 112 bean seeds
Put this number in the table.
4. How many seeds did the children plant altogether? 249 seeds
Put this number in the table.

▶ Partners and Totals in a Table

Answer these questions about the table.

5. Find the total number of corn seeds planted. 137 corn seeds
The partners are 79 and 58.
6. Find the total number of seeds Lara planted. 146 seeds
The partners are 67 and 79.

UNIT 7 LESSON 14 — 2-Digit Addition with Tables and Graphs 247

Student Activity Book page 247

▶ Read and Complete Tables PAIRS

Direct children's attention to the table at the top of Student Activity Book page 247, or the Student Activity Book page 247 transparency. Point out that there are two different places where the total is listed. Tell children that they will need to find the total for each column and each row for this table.

Have children work in **Helping Pairs** to complete exercises 1–4.

- You will read the table on page 247 and answer questions about it. The table is about the seeds that Lara and Angelo planted.

Have children explain how they answered the questions.

▶ Partners and Totals in a Table

In exercises 5 and 6, have children find the smaller numbers hiding inside the larger totals on the table.

Activity 2

Practice with Bar Graphs and Circle Graphs

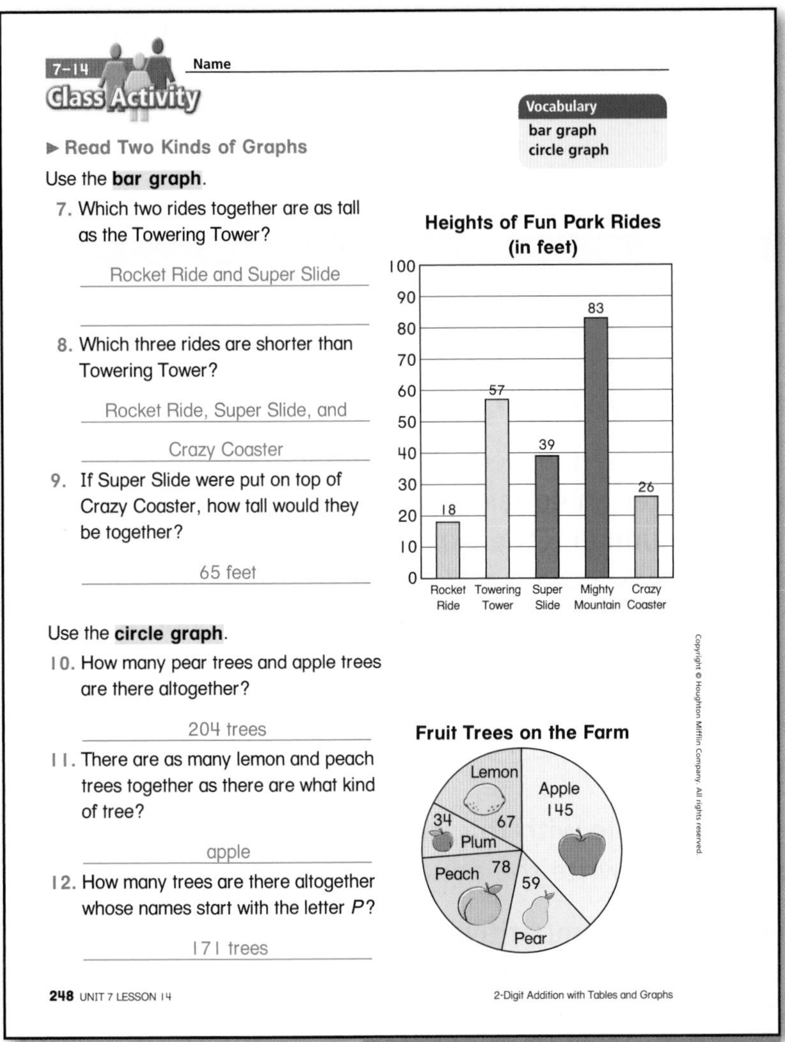

7-14 Class Activity

Name ______

Vocabulary
bar graph
circle graph

▶ Read Two Kinds of Graphs

Use the **bar graph**.

7. Which two rides together are as tall as the Towering Tower?

Rocket Ride and Super Slide

8. Which three rides are shorter than Towering Tower?

Rocket Ride, Super Slide, and Crazy Coaster

9. If Super Slide were put on top of Crazy Coaster, how tall would they be together?

65 feet

Heights of Fun Park Rides (in feet)

100
90
80
70
60
50
40
30
20
10
0

Rocket Ride 18
Towering Tower 57
Super Slide 39
Mighty Mountain 83
Crazy Coaster 26

Use the **circle graph**.

10. How many pear trees and apple trees are there altogether?

204 trees

11. There are as many lemon and peach trees together as there are what kind of tree?

apple

12. How many trees are there altogether whose names start with the letter *P*?

171 trees

Fruit Trees on the Farm

Lemon 67
Apple 145
Plum 34
Peach 78
Pear 59

248 UNIT 7 LESSON 14 2-Digit Addition with Tables and Graphs

Student Activity Book page 248

15 MINUTES

Goal: Interpret a bar graph and a circle graph.

Materials: Student Activity Book page 248

NCTM Standards:
Number and Operations
Data Analysis and Probability
Problem Solving
Representation

▶ Read Two Kinds of Graphs PAIRS

Math Talk 

Bar Graph Have children take a minute or two to look at the bar graph at the top of Student Activity Book page 248 and decide what information it contains.

- This page shows us two graphs—a bar graph and a circle graph. We'll start with the bar graph at the top. What does the bar graph show us? Possible responses: the heights of the rides at a park; how tall the different rides are
- How are the numbers on the scale of this bar graph different from other bar graph scales we have seen? Possible responses: they are decade numbers; they increase by ten

Activity continued ▶

Teaching Note

Watch For! Some children may have difficulty reading basic information from either the bar graph or the circle graph. Children may be challenged in this activity to add 2-digit numbers or solve more complicated problems, but they should be able to answer basic questions such as "How high is the Super Slide?" If children have difficulty completing the exercises on Student Activity Book page 248, check that the source of the problem is not finding information in the graphs.

English Language Learners

Draw a bar graph about pets on the board. Write *data* and *information.*

- **Beginning** Say: **The bar graph shows *data* about pets. *Data* is the *information* on a graph.** Have children repeat.
- **Intermediate** Ask: **Does the bar graph show *data* about colors?** no **Pets?** yes Say: **There is pet *data*, or *information*, on the graph.**
- **Advanced** Have children tell about the *data/information* on the graph.

Have children work in Helping Pairs to answer questions 7–9 on the page, and then discuss as many questions as time permits.

Circle Graph Point out that the circle graph shows the kinds of fruit trees on a farm. Have children solve problems 10–12 and then explain how they solved them.

Activity 3

Equation Chains

 **15 MINUTES**

Goal: Facilitate equation building and mastery of 1-digit addition

 **NCTM Standards:**
Number and Operations
Problem Solving
Connections

See Assessment Guide for Unit 7 Quick Quiz 3.

▶ How to Play *Equation Chains* WHOLE CLASS

One child goes to the board and writes a teen number. Another child goes to the board and writes an equals sign and an addition expression that is equal to the teen number. (The expression may have two or more addends.) A third child draws a chain and writes another addition expression with the same total. Other children continue, trying to make the chain as long as possible.

13 = 8 + 2 + 3 ⚭ = 8 + 5 ⚭ = 9 + 3 + 1 ⚭ = 6 + 6 + 1

When children are comfortable with this, they may begin to omit the picture of the chain and just write the equals sign and the expression.

If children are interested in a competitive game, the class can be divided into two teams. Each team receives one point for every correct expression generated before a mistake is made or there are no more possible expressions.

Children can also play a variation of the *Equation Chains* game (*Inequality Chains*) by using < or > symbols. You may wish to demonstrate this variation first with a Student Leader and the example shown here:

$8 + 2 + 3 > 6 + 5 > 2 + 2 + 4 + 2 > \dots$

2 Going Further

Differentiated Instruction

Intervention — Activity Card 7-14

Totals and Partners

Activity Card 7-14 ●

Work: pairs

Use:

- paper

Choose:

- Student 1
- Student 2

	Raspberries	Blueberries	Total
Jada	47	39	86
Tyler	34	58	92
Total	81	97	178

1. **Work Together** Copy the table onto a piece of paper.
2. Find the totals for each row and column. Answers: Jada – 86, Tyler – 92, Raspberries – 81, Blueberries – 97, Total – 178
3. Student 1: Use the information in the table to write a comparison question. Use the words *more* and *fewer*.
4. Student 2: Solve the comparison question.
5. Take turns.

Unit 7, Lesson 14

Activity Note You may want to provide a blank table for children to fill in. Have pairs share their questions.

Math Writing Prompt

Compare and Contrast How are bar graphs and tables the same? How are they different? Explain.

Software Support

Use *Soar to Success* for instruction of students needing targeted support for underlying skills.

On Level — Activity Card 7-14

Sort Partners

Activity Card 7-14 ▲

Work: pairs

Use:

- 6 index cards

Choose:

- Student 1
- Student 2

1. **Work Together** Write the numbers 17, 34, 51, 62, 79, and 85 on the index cards.
2. Sort the index cards into two piles. In each pile, two of the numbers should be partners for the third number.
3. Make a table to show the partners and totals. The table should look like this one.

Partner	Partner	Total

Unit 7, Lesson 14

Activity Note Each pair needs six index cards. Have pairs share their tables with others to check their work.

Math Writing Prompt

Guess and Check Explain how to find the unknown partner for 43 + □ = 91.

Software Support

Use *MegaMath* for review and reinforcement of the concepts and skills presented in this lesson.

Challenge — Activity Card 7-14

Make a Double Bar Graph

Activity Card 7-14 ■

Work: pairs

Use:

- Student Activity Book page 247
- Inch Grid paper
- Crayons or markers

Choose:

- Student 1
- Student 2

1. **Work Together** Look at the table at the top of Student Activity Book page 247.
2. Remember, a double bar graph compares two sets of information.
3. Use the information in the table on Student Activity Book page 247 to make a double bar graph.
4. **Math Talk** Discuss how a double bar graph is a good way to compare two sets of data.

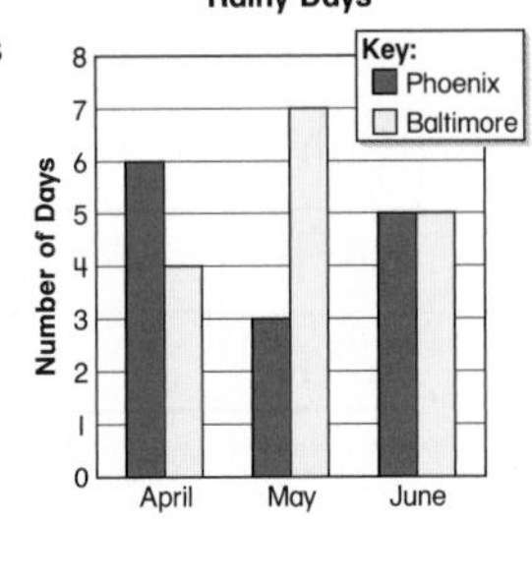

Unit 7, Lesson 14

Activity Note Each pair needs Student Activity Book page 247, Inch Grid paper (TRB M70), and crayons or markers. Review double bar graphs with children.

Math Writing Prompt

Explain Your Thinking Some number and 56 are partners of 102. Explain how you can find the unknown partner.

DESTINATION Math®

Software Support

Use *Destination Math* to take students beyond the concepts and skills presented in this lesson.

3 Homework and Spiral Review

Goal: Additional Practice

This Homework page provides practice in reading tables and graphs.

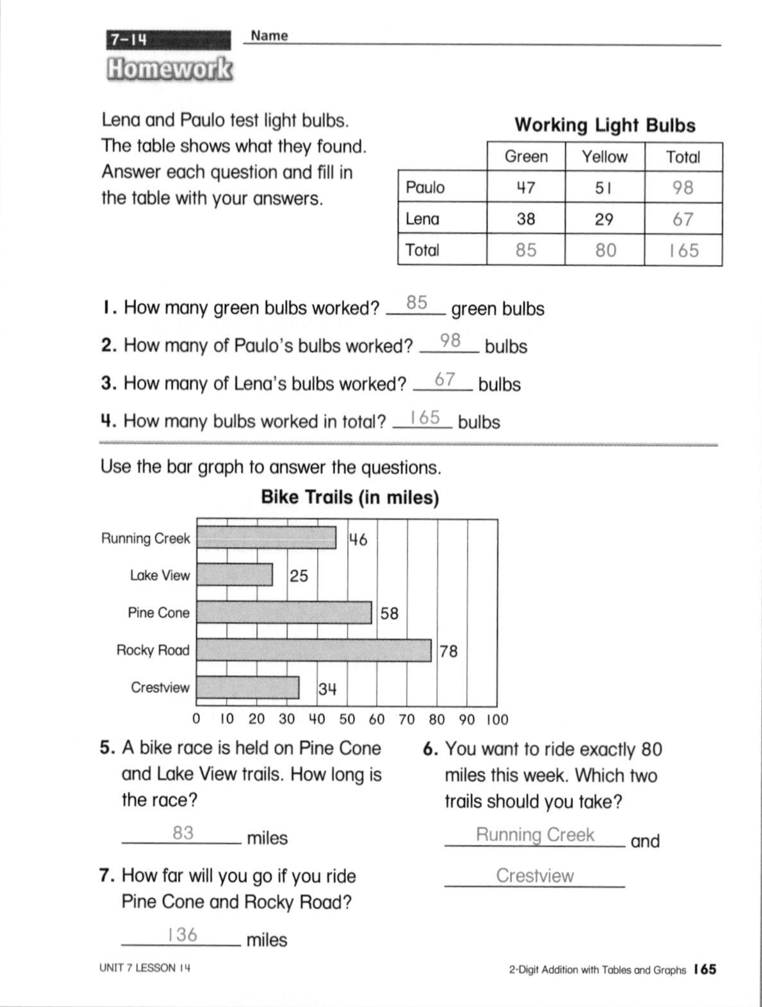
7–14 Homework Name ______

Lena and Paulo test light bulbs. The table shows what they found. Answer each question and fill in the table with your answers.

Working Light Bulbs

	Green	Yellow	Total
Paulo	47	51	98
Lena	38	29	67
Total	85	80	165

1. How many green bulbs worked? 85 green bulbs
2. How many of Paulo's bulbs worked? 98 bulbs
3. How many of Lena's bulbs worked? 67 bulbs
4. How many bulbs worked in total? 165 bulbs

Use the bar graph to answer the questions.

Bike Trails (in miles)

Running Creek 46
Lake View 25
Pine Cone 58
Rocky Road 78
Crestview 34
0 10 20 30 40 50 60 70 80 90 100

5. A bike race is held on Pine Cone and Lake View trails. How long is the race? 83 miles
6. You want to ride exactly 80 miles this week. Which two trails should you take? Running Creek and Crestview
7. How far will you go if you ride Pine Cone and Rocky Road? 136 miles

UNIT 7 LESSON 14 2-Digit Addition with Tables and Graphs 165

Homework and Remembering page 165

Goal: Spiral Review

This Remembering activity would be appropriate anytime after today's lesson.

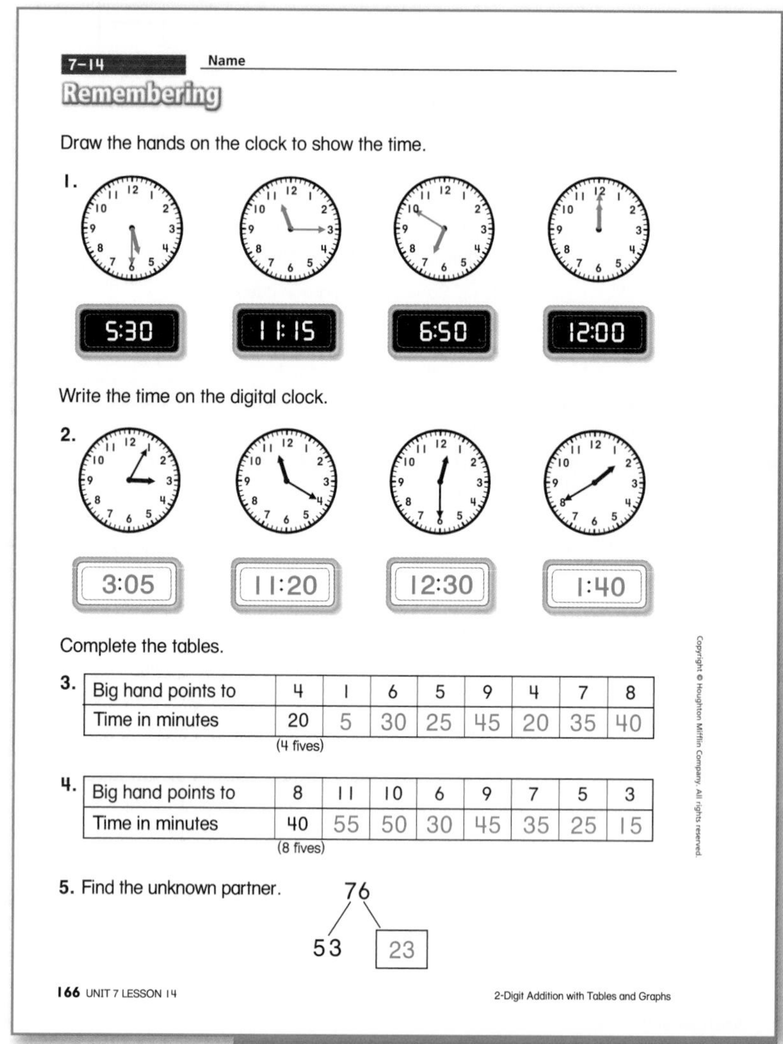
7–14 Remembering Name ______

Draw the hands on the clock to show the time.

1. 5:30 11:15 6:50 12:00

Write the time on the digital clock.

2. 3:05 11:20 12:30 1:40

Complete the tables.

3.

Big hand points to	4	1	6	5	9	4	7	8
Time in minutes	20 (4 fives)	5	30	25	45	20	35	40

4.

Big hand points to	8	11	10	6	9	7	5	3
Time in minutes	40 (8 fives)	55	50	30	45	35	25	15

5. Find the unknown partner. 76: 53 and 23

166 UNIT 7 LESSON 14 2-Digit Addition with Tables and Graphs

Homework and Remembering page 166

Home or School Activity

Physical Education Connection

Balancing Act Have children count the number of times in a row they can hop on one foot (first right, then left). Then have them count the number of times they can bounce a ball using one hand (first right, then left). Children record the data in a table and then find the totals and look for patterns. Do they get higher numbers using the right (or left) foot and right (or left) hand?

	Number of hops	Number of bounces	Total
Right			
Left			
Total			

Use Data to Predict

Lesson Objectives

- **Make predictions from simple data.**
- **Discuss conclusions and make predictions from graphs.**
- **Infer trends from data.**

Vocabulary
predict

The Day at a Glance

Today's Goals	Materials	
1 Teaching the Lesson **A1:** Draw conclusions from data. **A2:** Use bar graphs to predict. **A3:** Collect data and make predictions.	**Lesson Activities** Student Activity Book pp. 249–250 Homework and Remembering pp. 167–168 Connecting cubes Number cubes	**Going Further** Activity Cards 7–15 Pattern blocks Paper strips Crayons or markers Math Journals
2 Going Further ▶ Differentiated Instruction		
3 Homework and Spiral Review		

Use Math Talk today!

Keeping Skills Sharp

Quick Practice — 5 MINUTES	Daily Routines
Goals: Find partners for teen numbers. **Teen Flash–Unknown Addends** The **Student Leader** calls out a teen total and one of its partners. The class flashes the other partner with their fingers. Example: The Student Leader says: "4 plus something equals 13." The children flash nine fingers to show the unknown addend. (See page 113.)	**Telling Time** Naming the Hands, Telling Time on the Time Poster (See p. xxvii.) ▶ Led by Student Leaders **Money Routine** Using the 120 Poster, Using the Money Flip Chart, Using the Number Path, Using Secret Code Cards (See pp. xxiii–xxv.) ▶ Led by Student Leaders

1 Teaching the Lesson

Activity 1

How Long Does it Take?

 **10 MINUTES**

Goal: Predict how long an event will take based on previous data.

 **NCTM Standards:**
Data Analysis and Probability
Problem Solving
Reasoning and Proof
Communication

English Language Learners

Write and ask: ***How long*** **are we in school?** Underline *How long*.

- **Beginning** Say: ***How long*** **means how much time.** Have children repeat.
- **Intermediate** Ask: **Does *how long* mean how much time?** yes **How long is your birthday?** 1 day
- **Advanced** Have children tell *how long* they waited to get something they really wanted.

▶ Write Your Name WHOLE CLASS

Think about how long it take to write your name. Think about how long it will take to write your name 10 times. Explain that the children will be timing how long it takes to write their names 5 times. Have children number a paper 1–5.

- When I say, "Go" you will write your first and last name 5 times. I will count off the time as you are writing. Count off every five seconds.
- When you finish write the number of seconds I just said as you finished.

Discuss that children will not all have the same time due to writing speeds and lengths of names.

Repeat the same activity having children write their names 10, 15, and 20 times. Count off time by 5-second increments and use minutes and seconds when needed.

- Look at the times you wrote down each time you did the activity. What do you notice? Sample answer: The time it took increased each time we did the activity.
- Why did the time keep increasing? Sample answer: Each time we did the same activity but we had to do more of it so it would take longer.
- Can you make any predictions about how long it would take to write your name 25 times? Sample answer: It would take longer than writing it 20 times.
- What other predictions can you make? Sample answer: The more times we write our name the longer it will take.

1. Amy Brown
2. Amy Brown
3. Amy Brown
4. Amy Brown
5. Amy Brown
6. Amy Brown
7. Amy Brown
8. Amy Brown
9. Amy Brown
10. Amy Brown

You may take this opportunity to compare the times of children with long names and children with short names. Then you can give a short and long name example and ask children to predict which name would take longer to write.

Activity 2

Predictions from a Bar Graph

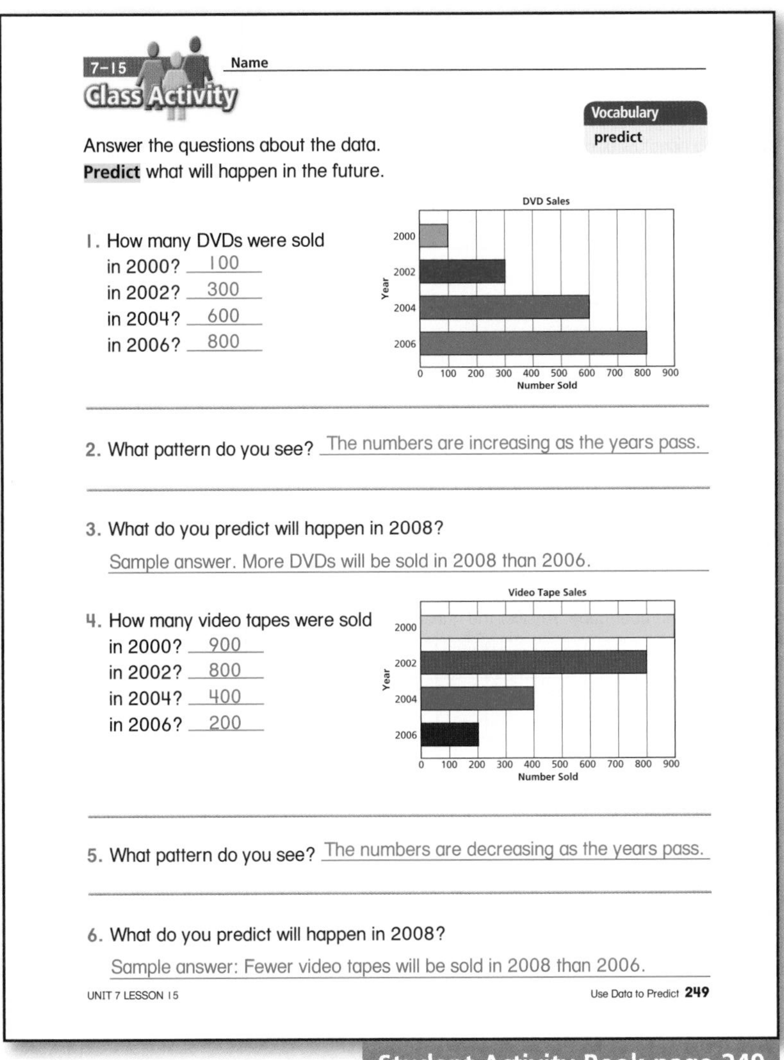

7-15 Class Activity

Name ______

Vocabulary
predict

Answer the questions about the data.
Predict what will happen in the future.

1. How many DVDs were sold
   in 2000? 100
   in 2002? 300
   in 2004? 600
   in 2006? 800

2. What pattern do you see? The numbers are increasing as the years pass.

3. What do you predict will happen in 2008?
   Sample answer. More DVDs will be sold in 2008 than 2006.

4. How many video tapes were sold
   in 2000? 900
   in 2002? 800
   in 2004? 400
   in 2006? 200

5. What pattern do you see? The numbers are decreasing as the years pass.

6. What do you predict will happen in 2008?
   Sample answer: Fewer video tapes will be sold in 2008 than 2006.

UNIT 7 LESSON 15 Use Data to Predict 249

Student Activity Book page 249

▶ Make Predictions WHOLE CLASS

Direct children's attention to Student Activity Book page 249.

- What does this graph show? the number of DVD sales
- What years of sales are shown on the graph? 2000, 2002, 2004, 2006
- What do the numbers on the bottom of the graph represent? number of DVDs sold

Complete this page together. Explain that to make a prediction for Exercises 3 and 7 they should use what they know about the data they have to determine what will happen in the future.

Math Talk Have children discuss why they think the sales keep increasing in the top graph and keep decreasing in the bottom graph. Children should talk about the trend and what they believe will happen to the sales over the next 5 years and why.

 **15 MINUTES**

Goal: Use data from bar graphs to make predictions.

Materials: Student Activity Book page 249

 **NCTM Standards:**
Data Analysis and Probability
Problem Solving
Reasoning and Proof

Teaching Note

Math Background Children will be making predictions based on bar graphs showing DVD sales rising as video sales falling. A trend is shown by this example. The trend of watching movies has changed over time. Other trends are fewer sales of records as CD sales rise. Trends can help us draw conclusions and make predictions.

 Teaching the Lesson (continued)

Activity 3

Collect Data and Predict

 20 MINUTES

Goal: Collect data and make predictions.

Materials: Student Activity Book page 250, connecting cubes, number cube

 **NCTM Standards:**
Data Analysis and Probability
Problem Solving
Reasoning and Proof

 **Ongoing Assessment**

Assess children's understanding of predicting using data. Have children think about their heights at age 1, 3, 5, and 7.

- ► What pattern do you notice about your height? I get taller each year.
- ► What prediction can you make about your height at age 10? I will be taller than I am now.

► Collect Data SMALL GROUPS

7-15 Class Activity

Name ____________

Collect and record the data using handfuls of counters. Answer the questions.

Number of Handfuls	Number of Counters
1	
2	
3	
4	

1. Fill in the chart.
2. How many counters in 1 handful? ______ in 2 handfuls? ______ in 3 handfuls? ______ in 4 handfuls? Answers will vary but should increase.
3. What pattern do you see?
The numbers increase as the number of handfuls increase.
4. What do you predict will happen with 5 handfuls?
Sample answer: There will be more counters than with 4 handfuls.

Collect and record data by rolling a number cube. Answer the questions.

Turn	1	2	3	4	5	6	7	8	9	10
Number Rolled										

5. Fill in the table.
6. Do you see a pattern?
Answers will vary, but most likely there will be no pattern.
7. Can you accurately predict what will happen with the next turn? Explain.
Sample answer: No. There is no pattern, any of the 6 numbers can turn up.

250 UNIT 7 LESSON 15 Use Data to Predict

Student Activity Book page 250

Put children in small groups and pass out 6 handfuls of counters to each group. Have children find Student Activity Book page 250. Tell children to have 1 child take a handful of counters and count and record them in the chart. Then have 2 other children each take a handful to find the number of counters for 2 handfuls. Continue with 3 and 4 handfuls. Have children discuss the pattern they see and use it to make a prediction for 5 handfuls.

Give each group a number cube and have them take turns rolling it and recording the number it lands on.

- Do you see a pattern? no
- Can you accurately predict what the next roll will be? Why or why not? No, since there is no pattern. The data is random. Any of the 6 numbers can turn up.

Explain that sometimes data can be random and therefore an accurate prediction cannot be made.

2 Going Further

Differentiated Instruction

Intervention — Activity Card 7-15

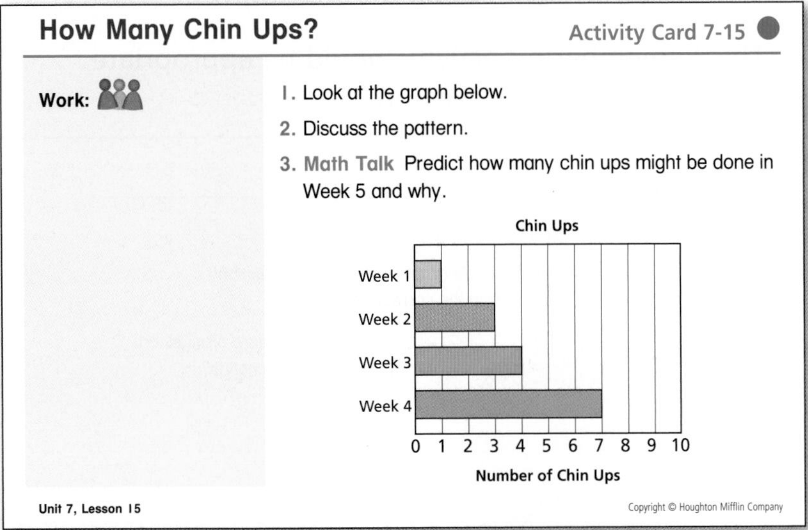

How Many Chin Ups? — Activity Card 7-15 ●

Work: 👥

1. Look at the graph below.
2. Discuss the pattern.
3. Math Talk Predict how many chin ups might be done in Week 5 and why.

Unit 7, Lesson 15

Activity Note Put children in small groups. Remind children to use the pattern they see to help them make a prediction.

Math Writing Prompt

Explain Your Thinking Explain why a prediction of 4 for Week 5 would not be a good prediction.

Software Support

Use *Soar to Success* for instruction of students needing targeted support for underlying skills.

On Level — Activity Card 7-15

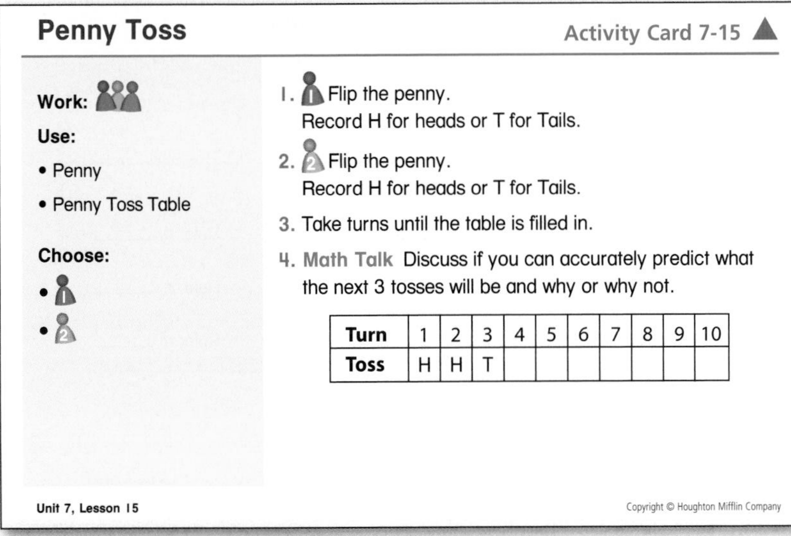

Penny Toss — Activity Card 7-15 ▲

Work: 👥

Use:
- Penny
- Penny Toss Table

Choose:
- 1
- 2

1. Flip the penny. Record H for heads or T for Tails.
2. Flip the penny. Record H for heads or T for Tails.
3. Take turns until the table is filled in.
4. Math Talk Discuss if you can accurately predict what the next 3 tosses will be and why or why not.

Turn	1	2	3	4	5	6	7	8	9	10
Toss	H	H	T							

Unit 7, Lesson 15

Activity Note For each pair prepare a table. Make sure children understand the tosses are random and therefore an accurate prediction cannot be made.

Math Writing Prompt

Explain Which would give a prediction of a higher number: the data for the height of a new plant during 4 weeks or for the height of a snowman in the sun for 4 hours? Explain.

Software Support

Use *MegaMath* for review and reinforcement of the concepts and skills presented in this lesson.

Challenge — Activity Card 7-15

Predict Data — Activity Card 7-15 ■

Work: 👥

Use:
- Crayons or markers

Choose:
- 1
- 2
- 3

1. Make a set of data that would show a prediction for a greater number following the data.
2. Make a set of data that would show a prediction for a lesser number following the data.
3. Make a set of data that you would not be able to make an accurate prediction following the data.
4. Work Together Share your data. Check each other's work.

Snow on Ground

Week 1
Week 2
Week 3
Week 4

0 1 2 3 4 5 6 7 8 9 10

Inches

Unit 7, Lesson 15

Activity Note Provide graph paper. Help children realize that a growing pattern will predict an increase while a decreasing pattern will predict a decrease in the data.

Math Writing Prompt

Explain Your Thinking What type of data would you use to make a set of data that you could not make a prediction from? Explain.

Use *Destination Math* to take students beyond the concepts and skills presented in this lesson.

3 Homework and Spiral Review

Goal: Additional Practice

Use this homework activity to provide children more practice using data to predict.

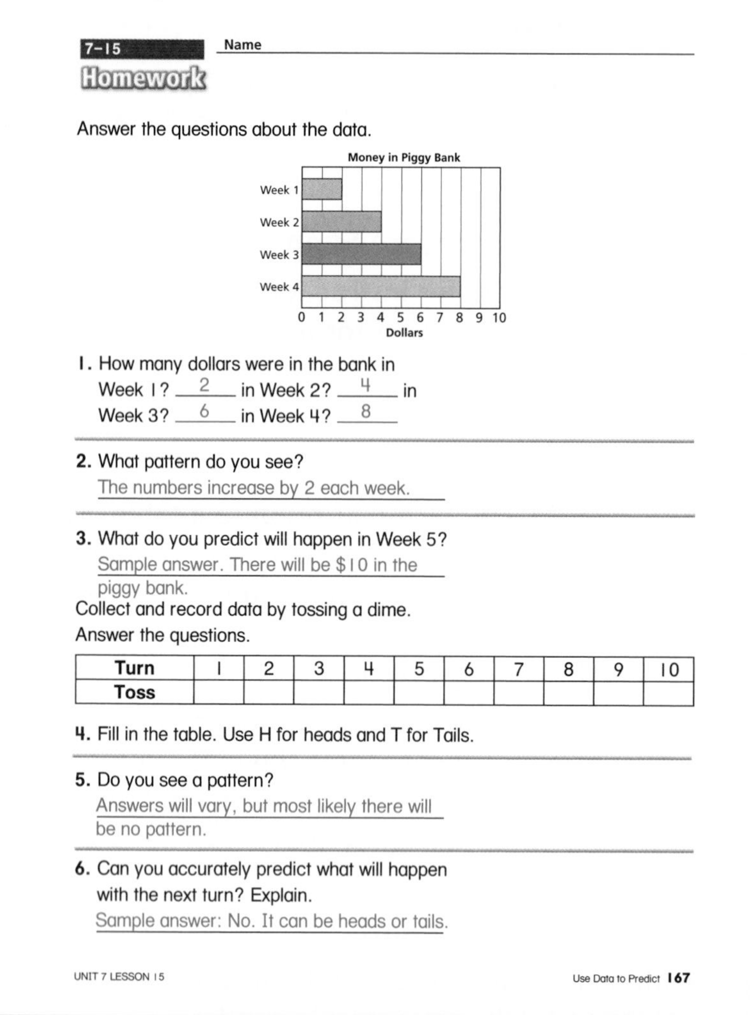

7-15 Name

Homework

Answer the questions about the data.

Money in Piggy Bank

Week 1
Week 2
Week 3
Week 4

0 1 2 3 4 5 6 7 8 9 10
Dollars

1. How many dollars were in the bank in Week 1? 2 in Week 2? 4 in Week 3? 6 in Week 4? 8

2. What pattern do you see?
The numbers increase by 2 each week.

3. What do you predict will happen in Week 5?
Sample answer. There will be $10 in the piggy bank.

Collect and record data by tossing a dime.
Answer the questions.

Turn	1	2	3	4	5	6	7	8	9	10
Toss										

4. Fill in the table. Use H for heads and T for Tails.

5. Do you see a pattern?
Answers will vary, but most likely there will be no pattern.

6. Can you accurately predict what will happen with the next turn? Explain.
Sample answer: No. It can be heads or tails.

UNIT 7 LESSON 15 Use Data to Predict 167

Homework and Remembering page 167

Goal: Spiral Review

This Remembering activity would be appropriate anytime after today's lesson.

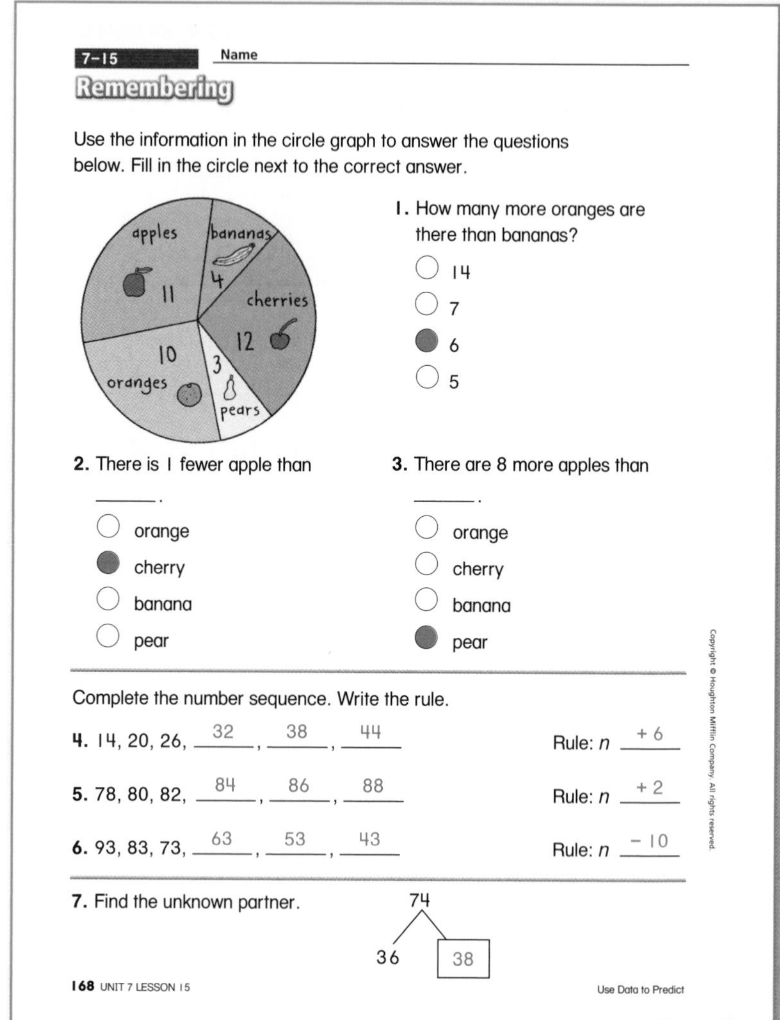

7-15 Name

Remembering

Use the information in the circle graph to answer the questions below. Fill in the circle next to the correct answer.

apples 11
bananas 4
cherries 12
oranges 10
pears 3

1. How many more oranges are there than bananas?
○ 14
○ 7
● 6
○ 5

2. There is 1 fewer apple than ____.
○ orange
● cherry
○ banana
○ pear

3. There are 8 more apples than ____.
○ orange
○ cherry
○ banana
● pear

Complete the number sequence. Write the rule.

4. 14, 20, 26, 32, 38, 44 Rule: n + 6

5. 78, 80, 82, 84, 86, 88 Rule: n + 2

6. 93, 83, 73, 63, 53, 43 Rule: n − 10

7. Find the unknown partner.
74
36 38

168 UNIT 7 LESSON 15 Use Data to Predict

Homework and Remembering page 168

Home or School Activity

Real-World Connection

Age in a Grade Tell children to find out the age of a child in Kindergarten. Then have children find the age of a child in first through fourth grades. Instruct children to graph the ages and grades that they find. Tell student to write patterns they see and predict what they think would happen to the graph if they continued it through grade 6?

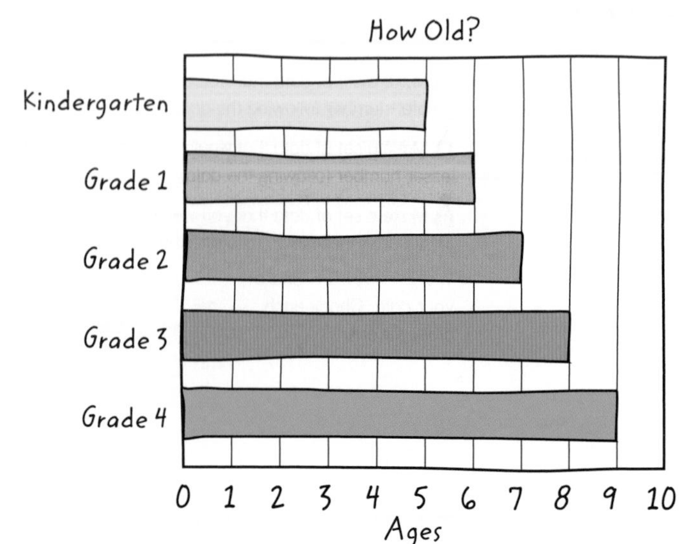

Use Mathematical Processes

Lesson Objectives

- Solve a variety of problems using mathematical concepts and skills.
- Use mathematical processes in the contest of problem solving, connections, reasoning and proof, communication, and representation.

The Day at a Glance

Today's Goals	Materials	
1 Teaching the Lesson **A1: Art Connection** Explore shapes with paper folding. **A2: Problem Solving** Survey two different groups of people; record and compare the results; recognize that data may vary from one population to another. **A3: Reasoning and Proof** Make and check a prediction. **A4: Representation** Make and support a statement about a situation. **A5: Communication** Write directions for drawing a figure.	**Lesson Activities** Student Activity Book pp. 251–252 Homework and Remembering pp. 169–170 Rectangular sheets of paper (8 1/2 by 11 is fine but smaller rectangles may be easier to fold) Scissors 10 x 10 Grid (TRB M62)	**Going Further** Activity Cards 7–16 Two-Color Counters Crayons Spinner (TRB M27) Paperclip Number cubes (1–6) Math Journals
2 Going Further ▸ Differentiated Instruction		
3 Homework and Spiral Review		

123 Use Math Talk today!

Keeping Skills Sharp

Quick Practice/Daily Routines	
No Quick Practice or Daily Routines are recommended. If you choose to do some, use those that provide extra practice that meets the needs of your class.	**Class Management** Use this lesson to provide more understanding of the NCTM process standards. Depending on how you choose to carry out the activities, this lesson may take two or more days of teaching.

1 Teaching the Lesson

Activity 1

Connections

Math and Art

 45 MINUTES

Goal: Explore shapes with paper folding.

Materials: Student Activity Book page 251–252, rectangular sheets of paper (8 1/2 by 11 or smaller), scissors

 **NCTM Standards:**

Problem Solving	Connections
Communication	Representation

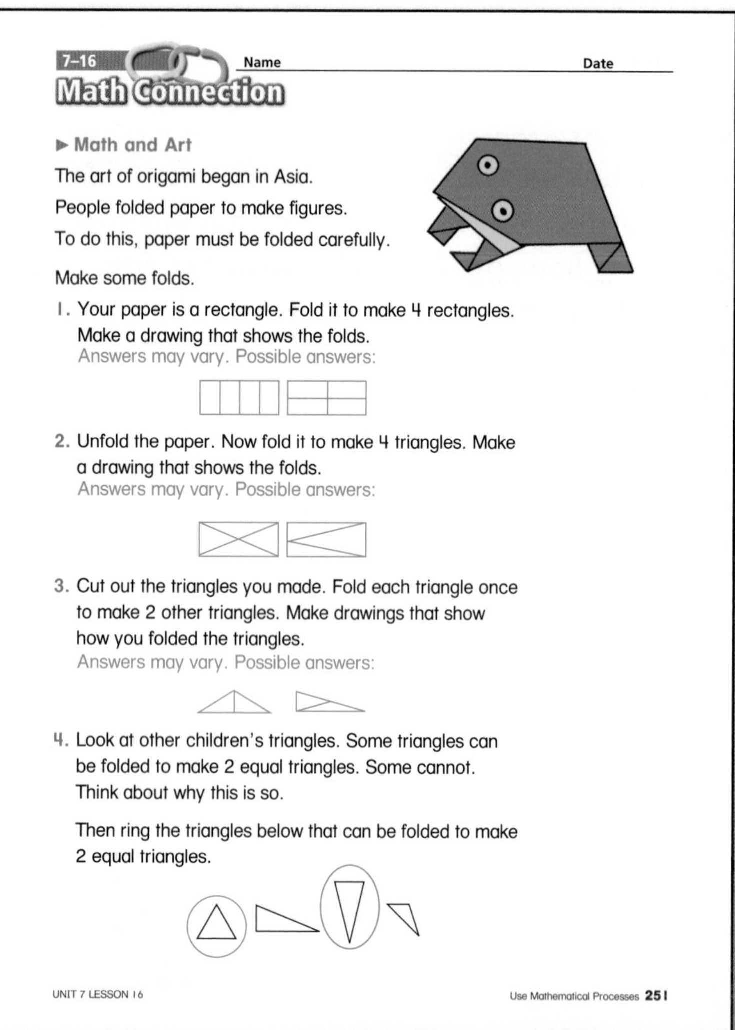

7-16 Math Connection Name Date

▶ Math and Art

The art of origami began in Asia.

People folded paper to make figures.

To do this, paper must be folded carefully.

Make some folds.

1. Your paper is a rectangle. Fold it to make 4 rectangles. Make a drawing that shows the folds.
Answers may vary. Possible answers:

2. Unfold the paper. Now fold it to make 4 triangles. Make a drawing that shows the folds.
Answers may vary. Possible answers:

3. Cut out the triangles you made. Fold each triangle once to make 2 other triangles. Make drawings that show how you folded the triangles.
Answers may vary. Possible answers:

4. Look at other children's triangles. Some triangles can be folded to make 2 equal triangles. Some cannot. Think about why this is so.

Then ring the triangles below that can be folded to make 2 equal triangles.

UNIT 7 LESSON 16 Use Mathematical Processes 251

Student Activity Book page 251

Teaching Note

Math Background Symmetry will not be taught until Unit 13. This informal exposure to the concept will be helpful to children, especially if this concept is on your state or local annual test. If you want to introduce the concept of congruence early, this is a good opportunity to do that. The shapes formed by a line of symmetry are congruent shapes.

▶ The Art of Paper Folding

Have children look at the origami animals at the top of the page. Tell them that origami, the art of paper folding, was developed in Asia many years ago and is popular today in many countries around the world. In Japan, children fold paper figures as part of the celebration of special holidays. To make folded figures from paper, it is important to make folds that are sharply creased and very exact.

Tasks 1–3 Tell children that as they do some paper folding activities today they will explore how shapes can be made from other shapes. Give children paper and scissors and have them follow the instructions in items 1–3.

▶ Look at Shapes

Math Talk

Have children share different ways of folding the paper. Each time, ask what shapes were formed and whether the folded shapes are all the same or different. Guide children to see that not all triangles can be folded to make two triangles that are the same. You might explain that a fold that makes two shapes that are the same is called a line of symmetry.

Task 4 Have children complete item 4. Then ask them to explain their answers.

▶ Which triangles can be folded to make 2 triangles that are the same? Explain why. Answers may vary. Possible answer: The first and third, because they are the same on both sides.

▶ Which triangles can't be folded to make 2 triangles that are the same? Answers may vary. Possible answer: The second and fourth because there is no way that they overlap.

Activity 2 **Problem Solving**

Are Survey Results Always the Same?

 45 MINUTES

Goals: Survey two different groups of people; record and compare the results; recognize that data may vary from one population to another

Materials: Student Activity Book page 252, 10 x 10 Grid (TRB M62)

 **NCTM Standards:**

Problem Solving
Representation
Communication
Connections

7–16 Problem Solving Name Date

▶ Are Survey Results Always the Same?

Survey Question: Which sandwich would you rather eat?

chicken salad grilled cheese
peanut butter and jelly roast beef

1. Do you think that children and adults will answer the question the same way? Why?

Answers may vary. Possible answer: They will be different. I love peanut butter and jelly sandwiches but my parents don't.

2. Use the survey question with 2 groups of people. One group should be only children. The other group should be only adults. Ask 10 or more people in each group.

3. Record your results in the chart below. Answers will vary.

Type of Sandwich	Children	Adults
Chicken salad		
Grilled cheese		
Peanut butter and jelly		
Roast beef		

4. Did both groups have about the same results? Explain how they are different.

Answers may vary. Possible answer: No, adults liked the meat sandwiches more than children did.

5. Write another question that children and adults would answer differently. Answers may vary. Possible answer: What is your favorite game?

252 UNIT 7 LESSON 16 Use Mathematical Processes

Student Activity Book page 252

▶ Discuss Surveys

Tell the class that you are going to carry out a survey about them.

- ▶ What do you most like to do after you eat supper? Answers will vary.
- ▶ If you asked a group of children and a group of adults that question, do you think the groups give the same answers? Answers will vary.

Tasks 1–3 Tell children that they are going to do a survey about sandwiches with 2 different groups of people. One group will be children. The other group will be adults. Explain that they will survey 10 or more in each group.

▶ Compare Results  

Math Talk

Use questions like the following to discuss the results.

- ▶ Did the two groups choose the same sandwich?
- ▶ Why do you think the different groups chose different sandwiches?
- ▶ Was the answer that was chosen the least the same for both groups?
- ▶ Were you surprised at the results?

Task 4 Check understanding of the idea that survey results may vary depending on who answers the question by asking children to write another question for which children and adults will likely give different responses. Have children share their questions with the class.

English Language Learners

Write *What is your favorite sport: basketball, football, or tennis?* on the board. Write *survey*.

- **Beginning** Say: ***Survey* means ask different people the same question.** Have children repeat.
- **Intermediate and Advanced** Ask: **Is this *survey* about foods?** no **Is this *survey* about sports?** yes

Activity 3

Reasoning and Proof

Predict and Verify

 15 MINUTES

Goal: Make and check a prediction.

 **NCTM Standards:**
Reasoning and Proof
Communication

Predict the fewest number of measurements needed to find the perimeter of a rectangle. Then explain your answer. 2 measurements are needed. Explanations may vary. Possible response: You need to measure two sides of the rectangle. Since opposite sides are the same length, you can figure out the lengths of the other sides.

Then ask this question:

Suppose the rectangle is a square. How would your answer change? Explain. Only 1 measurement is needed. Explanations may vary. Possible response: You need to measure one side of the square. Since all sides are the same length, you can figure out the lengths of the other sides.

Activity 4

Representation

Lupe's Painting

 15 MINUTES

Goal: Make and support a statement about a situation.

 **NCTM Standards:**
Problem Solving
Representation
Connections

Lupe has a painting. It is in the shape of a rectangle and its perimeter is 18 inches. Write a statement about what the actual shape of Lupe's painting might be. Use a drawing to support your statement. Answers may vary. Possible answer: It is a rectangle that is 6 inches by 3 inches. (A drawing shows a labeled 6 in. by 3 in. rectangle and the equation: $6 + 6 + 3 + 3 = 18$)

You might use **Solve and Discuss** for this problem. Have children share different ways that the painting could look.

- Why are there many different ways to show the answer to this problem? Answers may vary. Possible answer: We do not know enough about the shape to draw it exactly. We can only try different possibilities.

Activity 5

Communication

How to Make a Square

 15 MINUTES

Goal: Tell how to make a square with a given perimeter.

 **NCTM Standards:**
Problem Solving
Communication

James wants to make a square with a perimeter of 32 inches. Write a set of directions to tell him how he can do that. Answers may vary.

Use a **Scenario** approach to discussing children's answers. Have children volunteer to be James and have others read their directions for James to follow. Ask questions such as:

- Is the drawing that James made a square with a perimeter of 32 inches?
- What is clear about these directions?
- What is not clear about these directions?

Encourage children to ask other questions.

2 Going Further

Intervention — Activity Card 7-16

Make a Survey — Activity Card 7-16 ●

Work: (pairs)
Use:
- 10 × 10 Grid

1. **Work Together** Think of a question. Make a table.
   Do you like ice cream or fruit for dessert?
2. Ask 10 people. Record the results.

Ice Cream	||||
Fruit	~~||||~~ |

3. Describe the results.
   4 people like ice cream and 6 people like fruit for dessert.

Unit 7, Lesson 16

Activity Note You may want each child to carry out his or her own survey. If so, have pairs compare their results when they finish.

Math Writing Prompt

Ask the Teachers Suppose you could use one question to survey all the teachers in your school. Write what that question would be.

Software Support

Use *Soar to Success* for instruction of students needing targeted support for underlying skills.

On Level — Activity Card 7-16

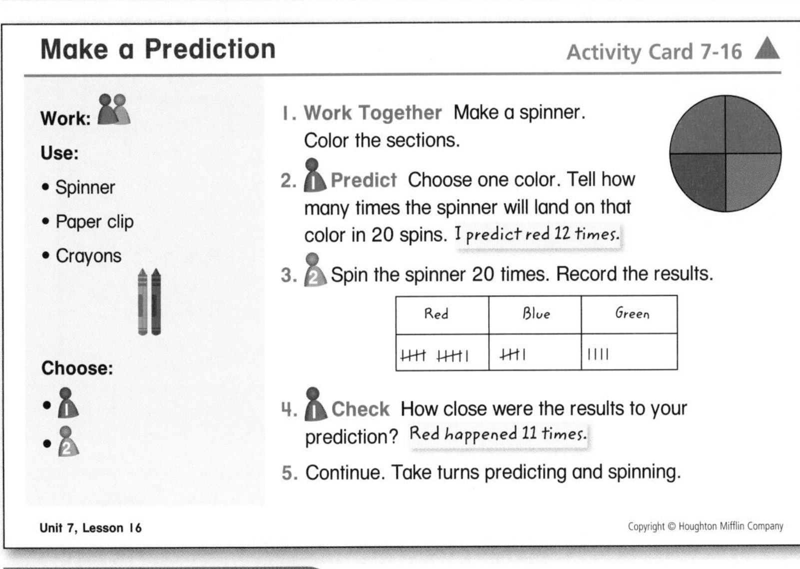

Make a Prediction — Activity Card 7-16 ▲

Work: (pairs)
Use:
- Spinner
- Paper clip
- Crayons

Choose:
- Student 1
- Student 2

1. **Work Together** Make a spinner. Color the sections.
2. **Predict** Choose one color. Tell how many times the spinner will land on that color in 20 spins. *I predict red 12 times.*
3. Spin the spinner 20 times. Record the results.

Red	Blue	Green
~~||||~~ ~~||||~~ |	~~||||~~ |	||||

4. **Check** How close were the results to your prediction? *Red happened 11 times.*
5. Continue. Take turns predicting and spinning.

Unit 7, Lesson 16

Activity Note Help children understand that to make a prediction, they use what they know to make a good guess. It is not important that their prediction is exactly the same as the actual results, just that it is close.

Math Writing Prompt

Coloring a Spinner How could you color a spinner to make red show up more than blue? Write or draw two different ways.

Software Support

Use *MegaMath* for review and reinforcement of the concepts and skills presented in this lesson.

Challenge — Activity Card 7-16

Number Cube Toss — Activity Card 7-16 ■

Work: (pairs)
Use:
- 10 × 10 Grid
- 2 Number cubes labeled 1–6

Choose:
- Student 1
- Student 2

You will toss both cubes 20 times. Each time you will find the sum of the numbers.

1. First each student predicts what sum will be made most often. *I predict 6.*
2. Toss the cubes 20 times. Find the sums.
3. Display the results in a bar graph. 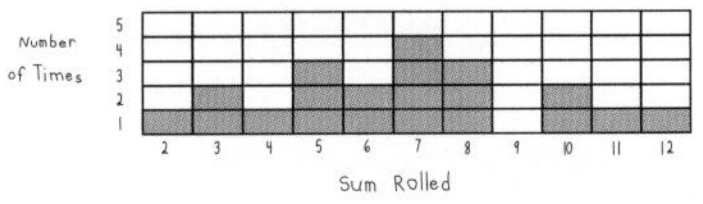
   (Graph: Number of Times 1–5; Sum Rolled 2–12)
4. Check which prediction was closer to the sum with the tallest bar. Try again.

Unit 7, Lesson 16

Activity Note The most likely sum is 7. There are 6 ways to roll a sum of 7, 5 ways for a sum of 6 or 8, 4 ways for a sum of 5 or 9, 3 ways for a sum of 4 or 10, 2 ways for a sum of 3 or 11, and only 1 way for a sum of 2 or 12.

Math Writing Prompt

The Most Frequent Sum Which sum did you find most often? Why do you think that is?

Software Support

Use *Destination Math* to take students beyond the concepts and skills presented in this lesson.

Homework and Spiral Review

Goal: Additional Practice

Include student's completed Homework page as part of their portfolios.

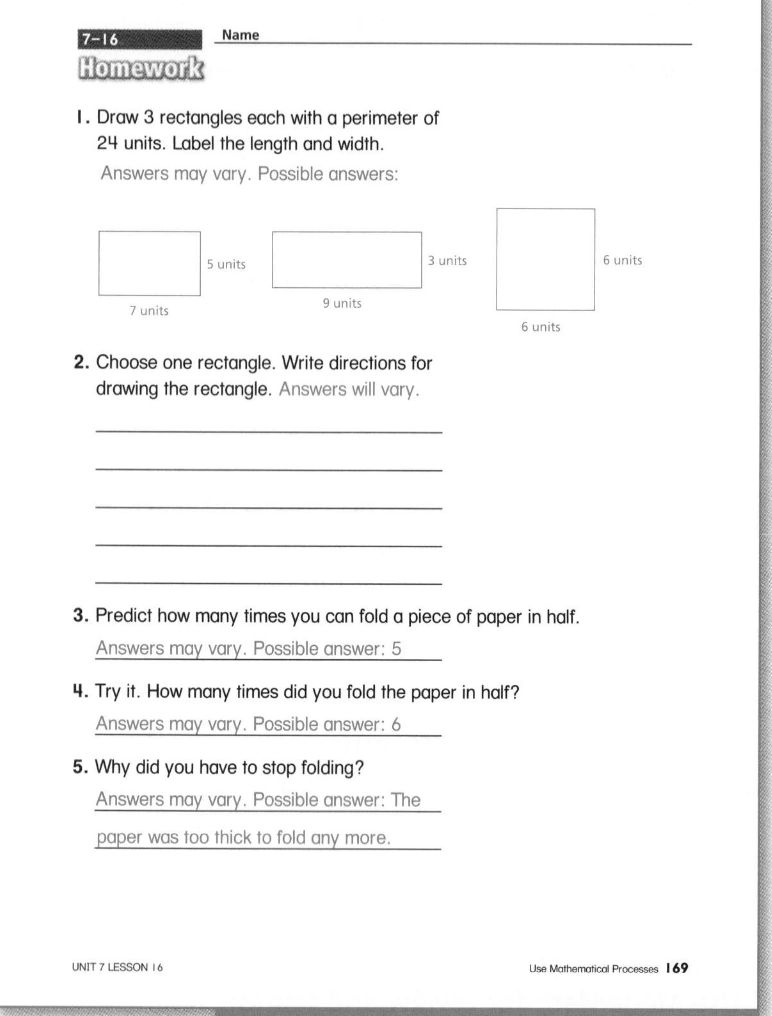

7–16 Homework

Name ______

1. Draw 3 rectangles each with a perimeter of 24 units. Label the length and width.
   Answers may vary. Possible answers:

2. Choose one rectangle. Write directions for drawing the rectangle. Answers will vary.

3. Predict how many times you can fold a piece of paper in half.
   Answers may vary. Possible answer: 5
4. Try it. How many times did you fold the paper in half?
   Answers may vary. Possible answer: 6
5. Why did you have to stop folding?
   Answers may vary. Possible answer: The paper was too thick to fold any more.

UNIT 7 LESSON 16 — Use Mathematical Processes 169

Homework and Remembering page 169

Goal: Spiral Review

This Remembering page would be appropriate anytime after today's lesson.

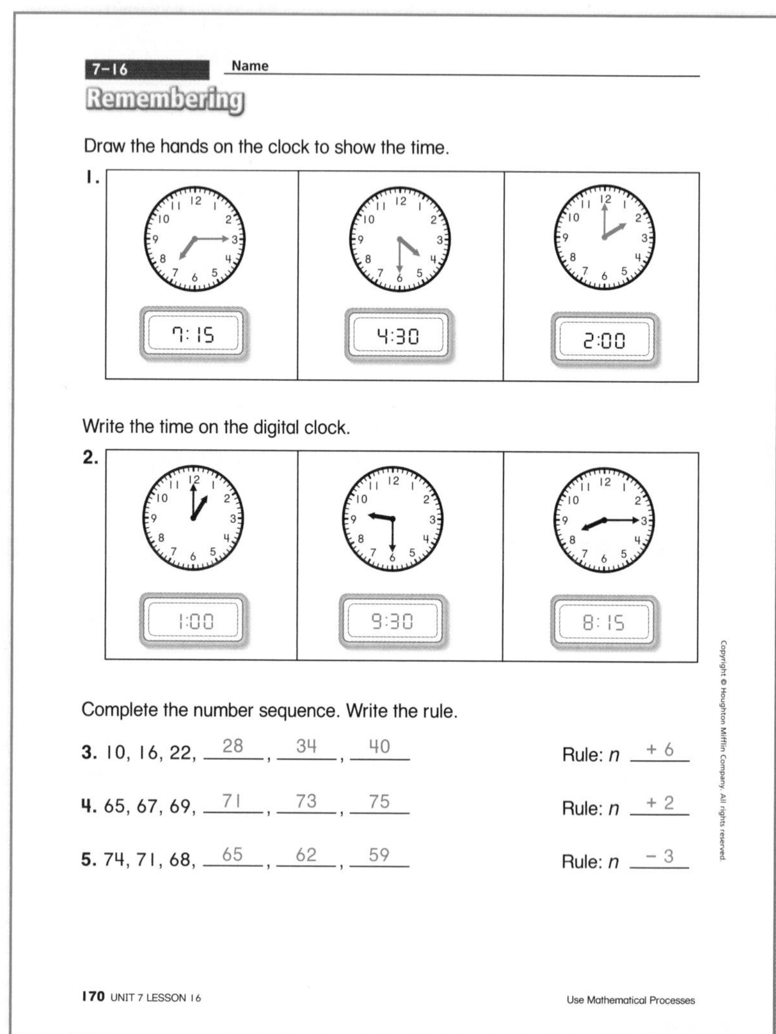

7–16 Remembering

Name ______

Draw the hands on the clock to show the time.

1. 7:15 | 4:30 | 2:00

Write the time on the digital clock.

2. 1:00 | 9:30 | 8:15

Complete the number sequence. Write the rule.

3. 10, 16, 22, 28, 34, 40 — Rule: n + 6
4. 65, 67, 69, 71, 73, 75 — Rule: n + 2
5. 74, 71, 68, 65, 62, 59 — Rule: n − 3

170 UNIT 7 LESSON 16 — Use Mathematical Processes

Homework and Remembering page 170

Home or School Activity

Real-World Connection

Favorite Movies Ask children to survey their friends and older family members to find out what kind of movie they like best. Have them create and complete a table like the one to the right.

Suggest that they write a report of the results. Some children may want to see whether children and adults responded differently to the question.

Kind of Movie	Friends	Family
Cartoon	III	I
Western	IIII	IIII
Action	I	IIII
Comedy	IIII	I

Unit Review and Test

Lesson Objectives

- **Assess children's progress on unit objectives.**

The Day at a Glance

Today's Goals	Materials
1 Assessing the Unit ▶ Assess children's progress on unit objectives. ▶ Use activities from unit lessons to reteach content. **2 Extending the Assessment** ▶ Use remediation for common errors. There is no homework assignment on a test day.	Unit 7 Test, Student Activity Book pages 253–256 Unit 7 Test, Form A or B, Assessment Guide (optional) Unit 7 Performance Assessment, Assessment Guide (optional)

Keeping Skills Sharp

Quick Practice — 5 MINUTES	
Goal: Review any skills you choose to meet the needs of your class. If you are doing a unit review day, use any of the Quick Practice activities that provide support for your class. If this is a test day, omit Quick Practice.	**Review and Test Day** You may want to choose a quiet game or other activity (reading a book or working on homework for another subject) for children who finish early.

1 Assessing the Unit

Assess Unit Objectives

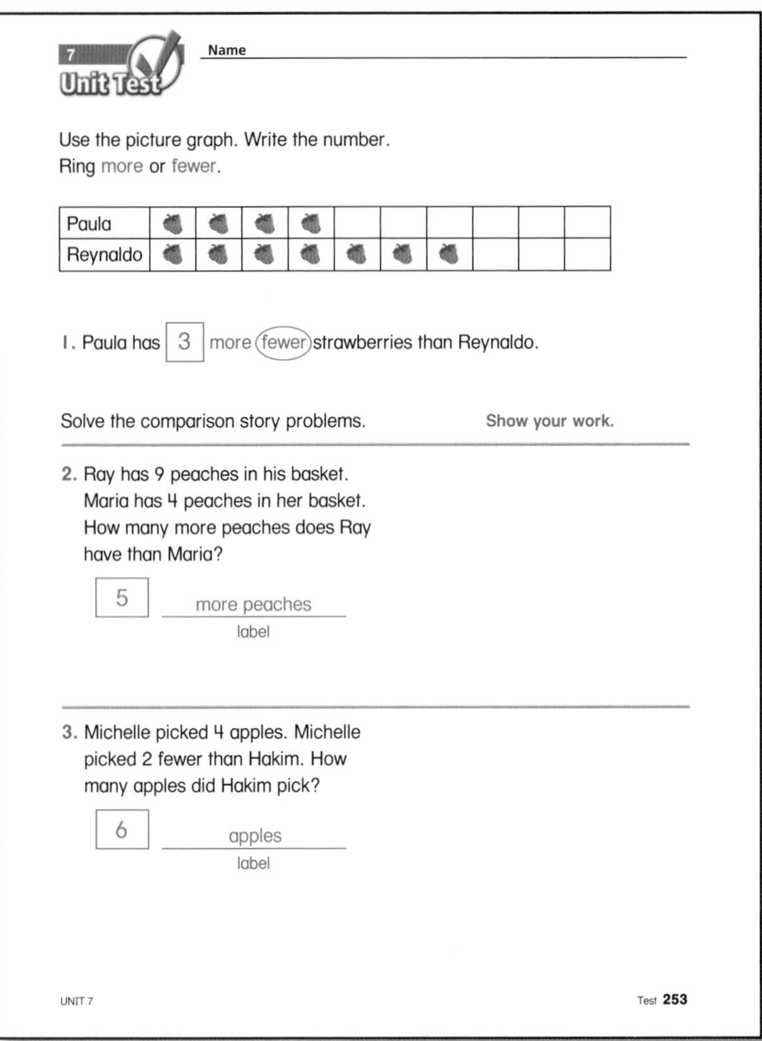
7 Unit Test

Name

Use the picture graph. Write the number.
Ring more or fewer.

Paula										
Reynaldo										

1. Paula has [3] more (fewer) strawberries than Reynaldo.

Solve the comparison story problems. **Show your work.**

2. Ray has 9 peaches in his basket. Maria has 4 peaches in her basket. How many more peaches does Ray have than Maria?

[5] more peaches
label

3. Michelle picked 4 apples. Michelle picked 2 fewer than Hakim. How many apples did Hakim pick?

[6] apples
label

UNIT 7 Test **253**

Student Activity Book page 253

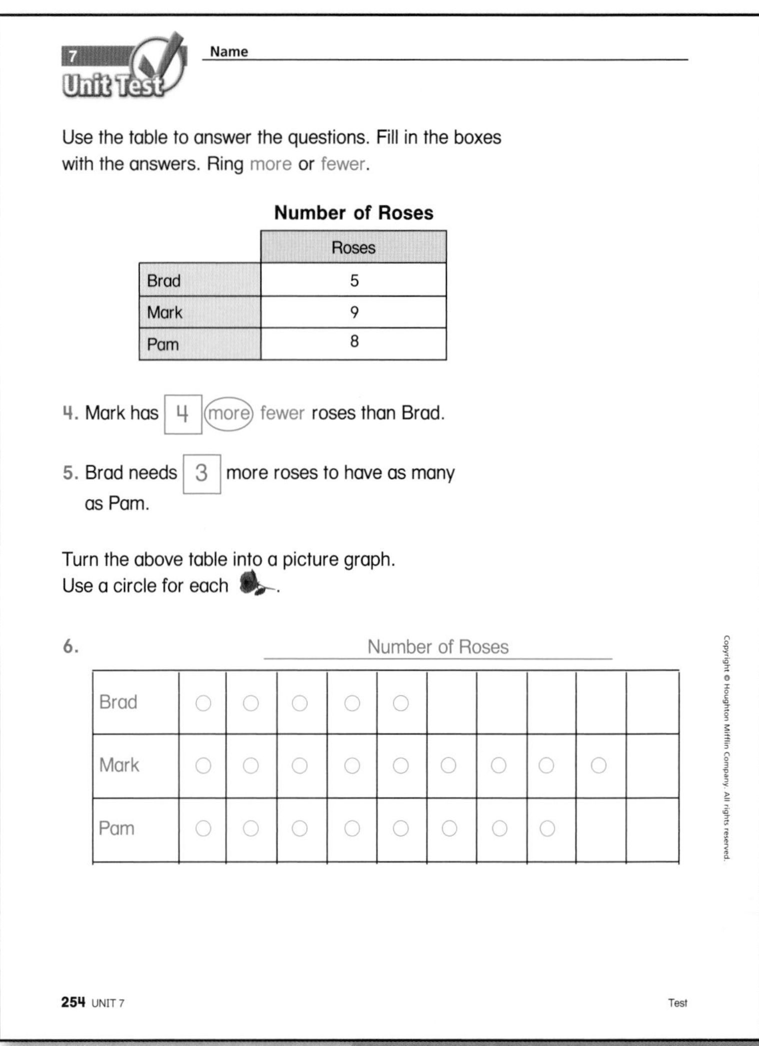
7 Unit Test

Name

Use the table to answer the questions. Fill in the boxes with the answers. Ring more or fewer.

Number of Roses

	Roses
Brad	5
Mark	9
Pam	8

4. Mark has [4] (more) fewer roses than Brad.

5. Brad needs [3] more roses to have as many as Pam.

Turn the above table into a picture graph.
Use a circle for each rose.

6. Number of Roses

Brad	○	○	○	○	○					
Mark	○	○	○	○	○	○	○	○	○	
Pam	○	○	○	○	○	○	○	○		

254 UNIT 7 Test

Student Activity Book page 254

45 MINUTES (more if schedule permits)

Goal: Assess children's progress on unit objectives.

Materials: Student Activity Book pages 253–256, Assessment Guide (optional)

▶ Review and Assessment

If your students are ready for assessment on the unit objectives, use either the test on the Student Activity Book pages or one of the forms of the Unit 7 Test in the Assessment Guide to assess student progress. To assign a numerical score for all of these test forms, use 10 points for each question.

The chart to the right lists the test items, the unit objectives they cover, and the lesson activities in which the objective is covered in this unit.

▶ Reteaching Resources

Unit Test Items	Unit Objectives Tested	Activities to Use for Reteaching
1	**7.1** Read and interpret information from a picture graph.	Lesson 1, Activity 1 Lesson 2, Activity 1 Lesson 3, Activity 1
2–3	**7.2** Solve comparison story problems.	Lesson 3, Activity 1 Lesson 4, Activity 1
4–5	**7.3** Read and interpret information from a table.	Lesson 5, Activity 1 Lesson 14, Activity 1

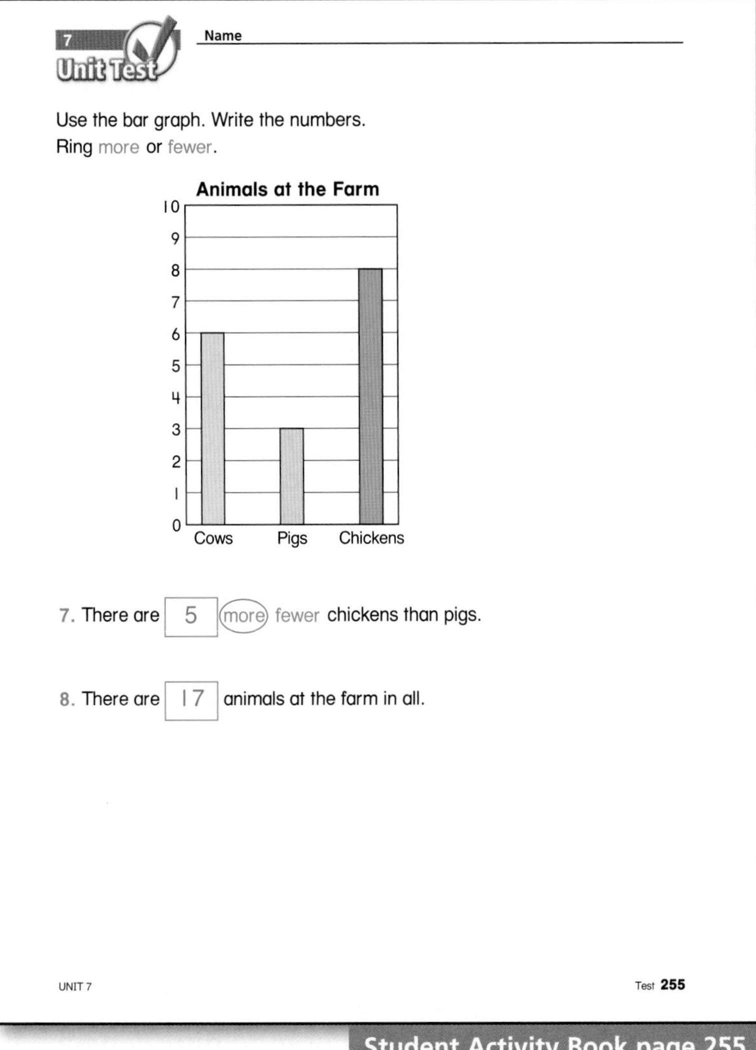
7 Unit Test

Name

Use the bar graph. Write the numbers.
Ring more or fewer.

7. There are 5 (more) fewer chickens than pigs.

8. There are 17 animals at the farm in all.

UNIT 7 Test 255

Student Activity Book page 255

7 Unit Test

Name

Use the circle graph to answer the question.

9. How many more tomatoes than carrots are in the vegetable garden?

7 more tomatoes

Vegetables in the Garden

Heads of Lettuce 5
Tomatoes 9
2 Carrots
Ears of Corn 7

10. **Write Your Own** Write and solve a comparison problem about things in the circle graph. Answers will vary.

*Item 10 also assesses the Process Skills of Problem Solving and Communication.

256 UNIT 7 Test

Student Activity Book page 256

Unit Test Items	Unit Objectives Tested	Activities to Use for Reteaching
6	**7.4** Convert information from a table to a picture graph.	Lesson 6, Activity 1 Lesson 7, Activity 1 Lesson 8, Activity 2
7–8	**7.5** Read and interpret information from a bar graph.	Lesson 8, Activity 1 Lesson 9, Activity 1 Lesson 10, Activity 1 Lesson 13, Activity 1 Lesson 14, Activity 2
9–10	**7.6** Read and interpret information from a circle graph.	Lesson 11, Activity 1 Lesson 12, Activity 1 Lesson 14, Activity 2

▶ Assessment Resources

Form A, Free Response Test (Assessment Guide)
Form B, Multiple-Choice Test (Assessment Guide)
Performance Assessment (Assessment Guide)

▶ Portfolio Assessment

Teacher-selected Items for Student Portfolios:

- Homework, Lessons 6, 8, and 16
- Class Activity work, Lessons 4, 6, 12, and 13

Student-selected Items for Student Portfolios:

- Favorite Home or School Activity
- Best Writing Prompt

2 Extending the Assessment

Common Errors

Activities for Remediation

Unit Objective 7.1

Read and interpret information from a picture graph.

Common Error: **Refers to the Wrong Row on a Picture Graph**

Some children may refer to the wrong row when answering questions.

Remediation Have children identify the row in which they can find the answer to the question being asked. Children can use the words *top, middle,* or *bottom* to describe the rows. Children may also use a strip of paper to help them focus on the designated row.

Unit Objective 7.2

Solve comparison story problems.

Common Error: **Chooses the Wrong Operation to Solve Problems**

Children may add when they should subtract or subtract when they should add.

Remediation Have children use counters or pictures to model the problem. Then have them use the answer to the problem to help them decide whether the problem required addition or subtraction.

Unit Objective 7.3

Read and interpret information from a table.

Common Error: **Does Not Understand the Meaning of the Numbers in a Table**

Children may choose the wrong number when gathering information.

Remediation Have children practice reading the information from the table before asking them to interpret the information. Ask questions such as "How many roses does Brandon have?"

Unit Objective 7.4

Convert information from a table to a picture graph.

Common Error: **Transfers Data Incorrectly**

Children may not write the labels or draw the correct number of pictures in the correct places.

Remediation Have children draw a small dot in each space of the graph as they count to the number shown in the table. Then have children look back at the table to be sure they used the correct number and that the labels match before drawing the pictures in the graph.

Unit Objective 7.5

Read and interpret information from a bar graph.

Common Error: **Misreads the Bar Graph**

Children may read the length of the bars incorrectly.

Remediation Have children use a paper strip, a ruler, or their finger to follow the line from the end of a bar to the correct number on the number scale.

Unit Objective 7.6

Read and interpret information from a circle graph.

Common Error: **Has Difficulty Interpreting Circle Graphs**

Children may not understand how to read a circle graph.

Remediation Have children make their own simple circle graphs to reinforce that circle graphs are used to display data that represent parts of a total amount.

Give children a circle divided equally into eight parts. Have children make a circle graph showing the colors of a set of eight cubes of varying color.

Student Glossary

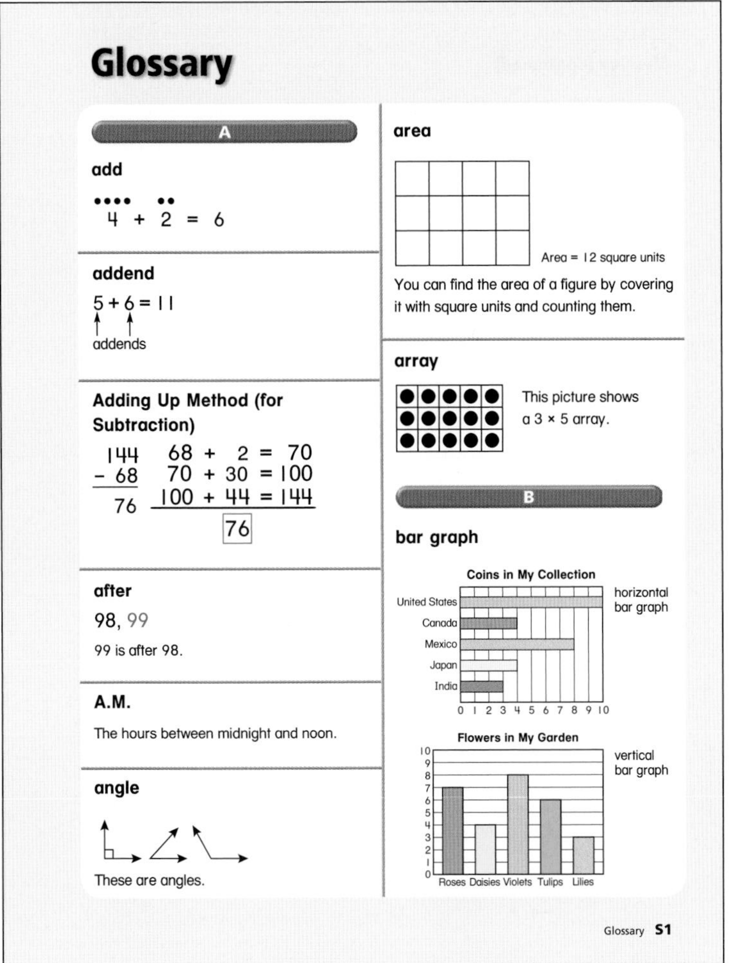

Glossary

A

add

4 + 2 = 6

addend

5 + 6 = 11

addends

Adding Up Method (for Subtraction)

144 − 68 = 76

68 + 2 = 70

70 + 30 = 100

100 + 44 = 144

76

after

98, 99

99 is after 98.

A.M.

The hours between midnight and noon.

angle

These are angles.

area

Area = 12 square units

You can find the area of a figure by covering it with square units and counting them.

array

This picture shows a 3 × 5 array.

B

bar graph

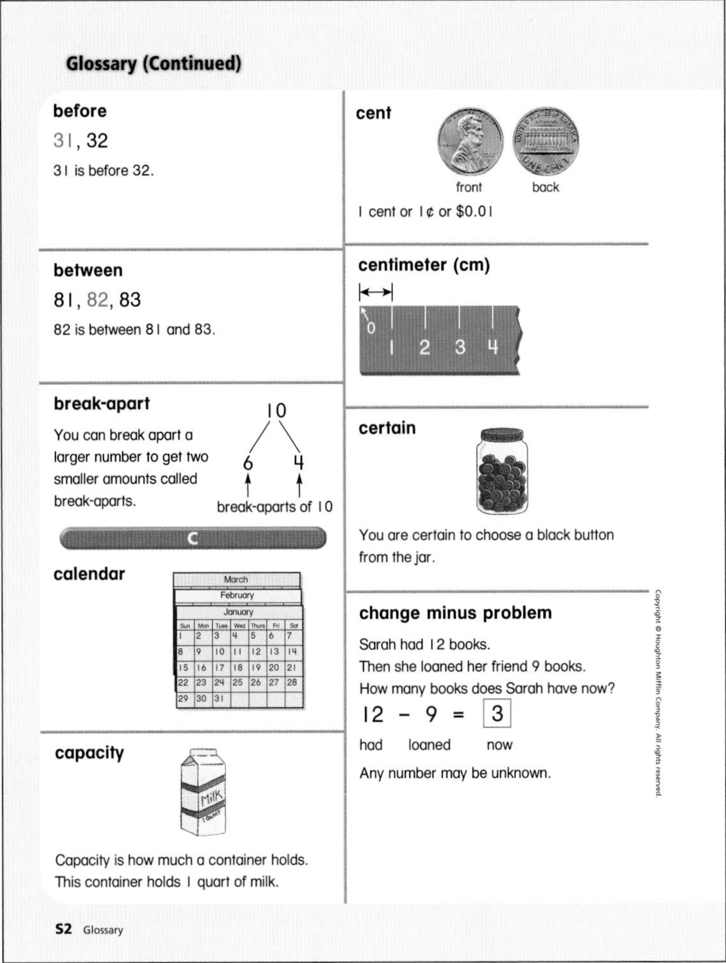

Glossary (Continued)

before

31, 32

31 is before 32.

between

81, 82, 83

82 is between 81 and 83.

break-apart

You can break apart a larger number to get two smaller amounts called break-aparts.

10 → 6, 4

break-aparts of 10

C

calendar

capacity

Capacity is how much a container holds. This container holds 1 quart of milk.

cent

front back

1 cent or 1¢ or $0.01

centimeter (cm)

certain

You are certain to choose a black button from the jar.

change minus problem

Sarah had 12 books.
Then she loaned her friend 9 books.
How many books does Sarah have now?

12 − 9 = 3

had loaned now

Any number may be unknown.

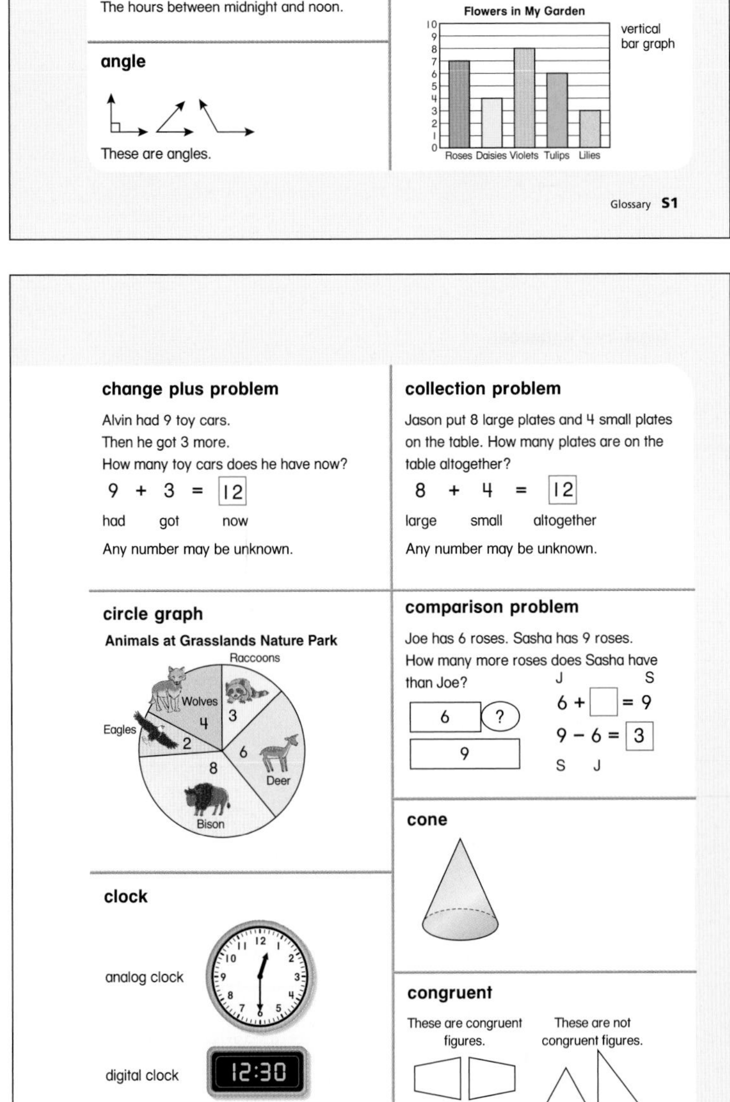

change plus problem

Alvin had 9 toy cars.
Then he got 3 more.
How many toy cars does he have now?

9 + 3 = 12

had got now

Any number may be unknown.

circle graph

Animals at Grasslands Nature Park

clock

analog clock

digital clock

collection problem

Jason put 8 large plates and 4 small plates on the table. How many plates are on the table altogether?

8 + 4 = 12

large small altogether

Any number may be unknown.

comparison problem

Joe has 6 roses. Sasha has 9 roses. How many more roses does Sasha have than Joe?

cone

congruent

These are congruent figures. These are not congruent figures.

Congruent figures have the same size and shape.

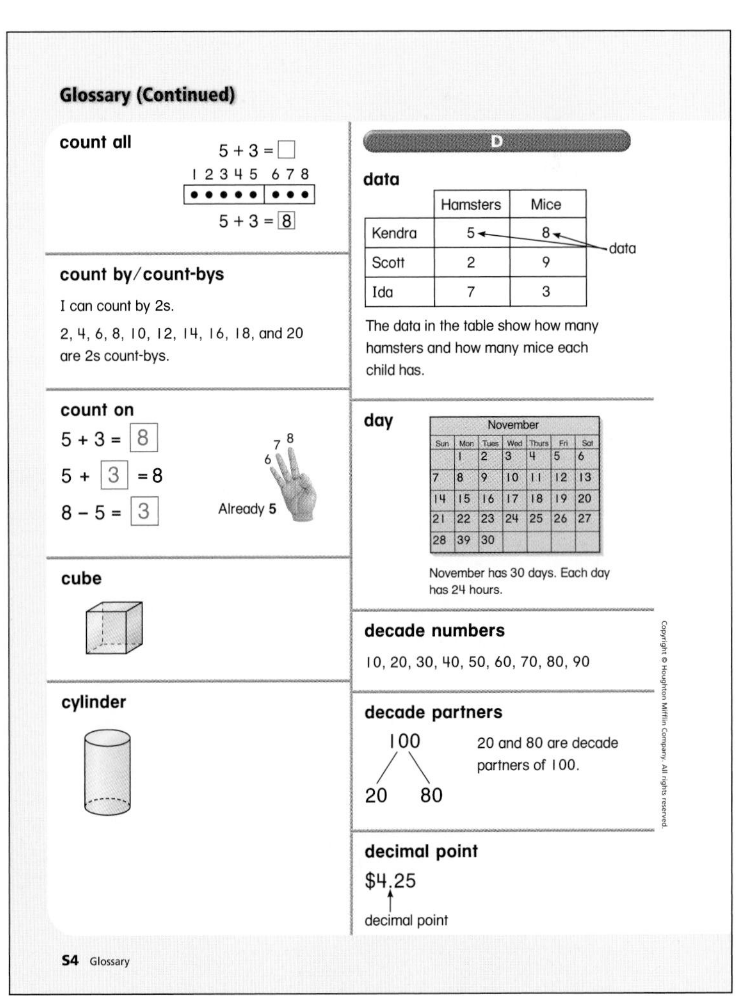

Glossary (Continued)

count all

5 + 3 = ☐

1 2 3 4 5 6 7 8

5 + 3 = 8

count by/count-bys

I can count by 2s.

2, 4, 6, 8, 10, 12, 14, 16, 18, and 20 are 2s count-bys.

count on

5 + 3 = 8

5 + 3 = 8

8 − 5 = 3

Already 5

cube

cylinder

D

data

	Hamsters	Mice
Kendra	5	8
Scott	2	9
Ida	7	3

data

The data in the table show how many hamsters and how many mice each child has.

day

November has 30 days. Each day has 24 hours.

decade numbers

10, 20, 30, 40, 50, 60, 70, 80, 90

decade partners

100 → 20, 80

20 and 80 are decade partners of 100.

decimal point

$4.25

decimal point

Student Glossary (Continued)

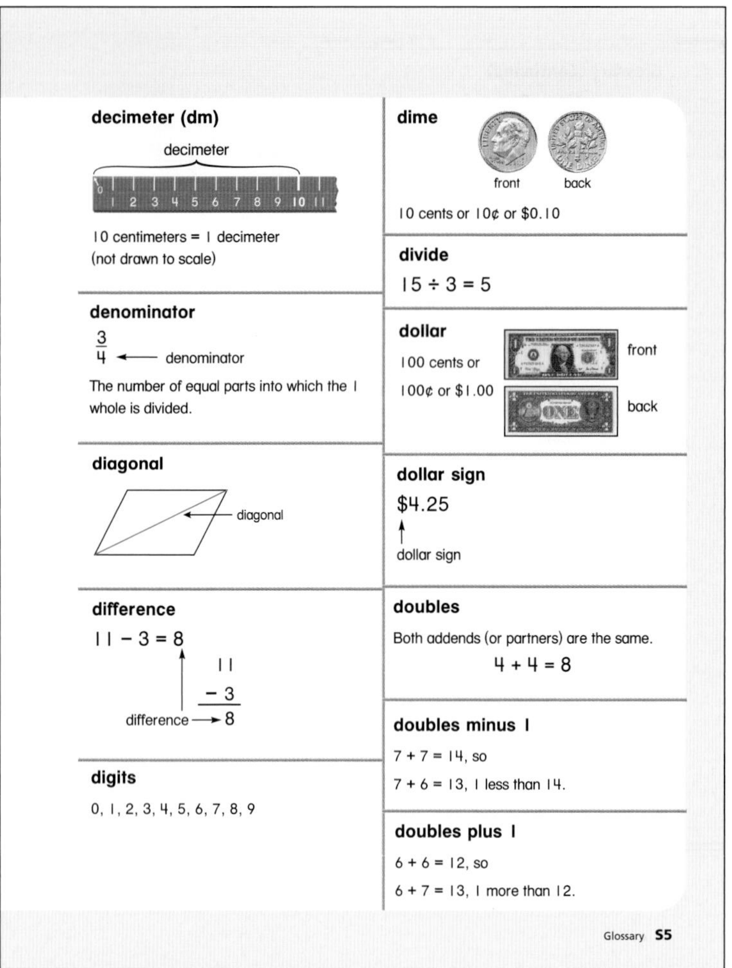

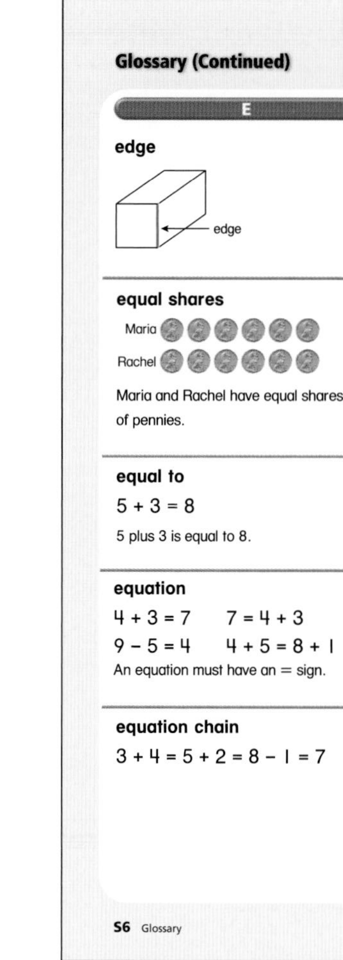

decimeter (dm)

decimeter

10 centimeters = 1 decimeter
(not drawn to scale)

denominator

$\frac{3}{4}$ ← denominator

The number of equal parts into which the 1 whole is divided.

diagonal

diagonal

difference

11 − 3 = 8

11
− 3
difference → 8

digits

0, 1, 2, 3, 4, 5, 6, 7, 8, 9

dime

front back

10 cents or 10¢ or $0.10

divide

15 ÷ 3 = 5

dollar

100 cents or 100¢ or $1.00

front

back

dollar sign

$4.25
↑
dollar sign

doubles

Both addends (or partners) are the same.

4 + 4 = 8

doubles minus 1

7 + 7 = 14, so
7 + 6 = 13, 1 less than 14.

doubles plus 1

6 + 6 = 12, so
6 + 7 = 13, 1 more than 12.

Glossary **S5**

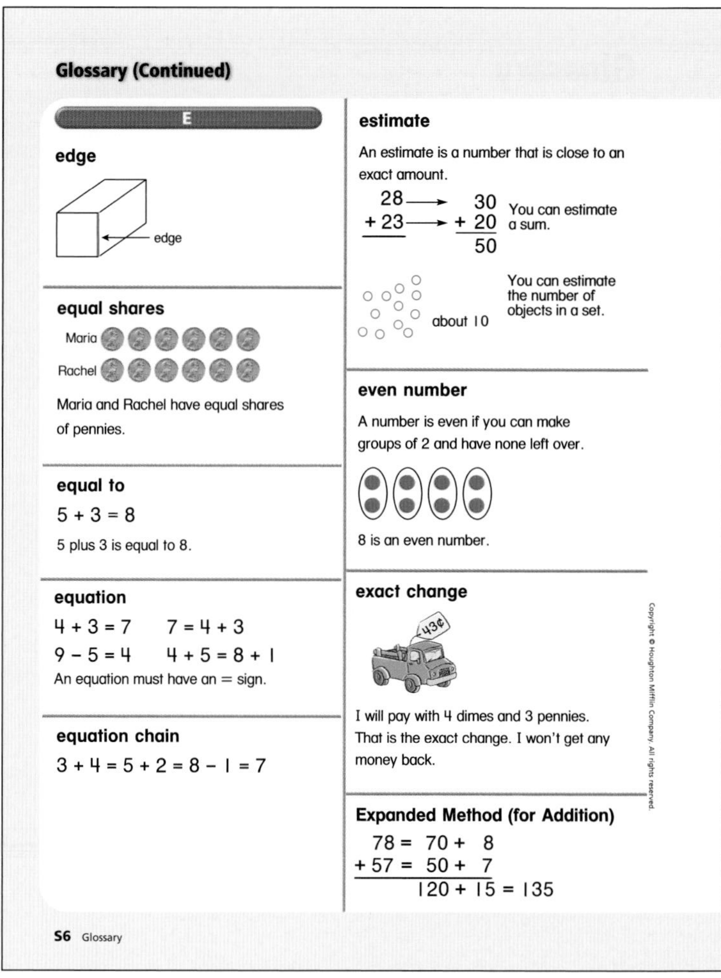

Glossary (Continued)

E

edge

edge

equal shares

Maria

Rachel

Maria and Rachel have equal shares of pennies.

equal to

5 + 3 = 8

5 plus 3 is equal to 8.

equation

4 + 3 = 7   7 = 4 + 3
9 − 5 = 4   4 + 5 = 8 + 1

An equation must have an = sign.

equation chain

3 + 4 = 5 + 2 = 8 − 1 = 7

estimate

An estimate is a number that is close to an exact amount.

28 → 30
+ 23 → + 20
50

You can estimate a sum.

about 10

You can estimate the number of objects in a set.

even number

A number is even if you can make groups of 2 and have none left over.

8 is an even number.

exact change

43¢

I will pay with 4 dimes and 3 pennies. That is the exact change. I won't get any money back.

Expanded Method (for Addition)

78 = 70 + 8
+ 57 = 50 + 7
120 + 15 = 135

Copyright © Houghton Mifflin Company. All rights reserved.

S6 Glossary

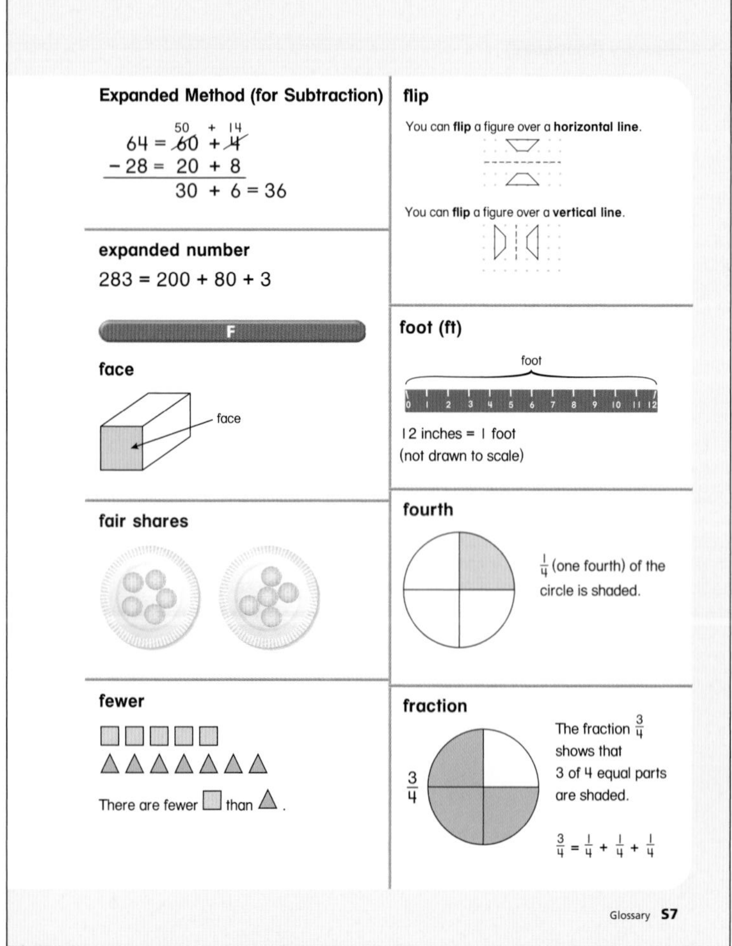

Expanded Method (for Subtraction)

50 + 14
64 = 60 + 4
− 28 = 20 + 8
30 + 6 = 36

expanded number

283 = 200 + 80 + 3

F

face

face

fair shares

fewer

There are fewer □ than △.

flip

You can **flip** a figure over a **horizontal line**.

You can **flip** a figure over a **vertical line**.

foot (ft)

foot

12 inches = 1 foot
(not drawn to scale)

fourth

$\frac{1}{4}$ (one fourth) of the circle is shaded.

fraction

$\frac{3}{4}$

The fraction $\frac{3}{4}$ shows that 3 of 4 equal parts are shaded.

$\frac{3}{4} = \frac{1}{4} + \frac{1}{4} + \frac{1}{4}$

Glossary **S7**

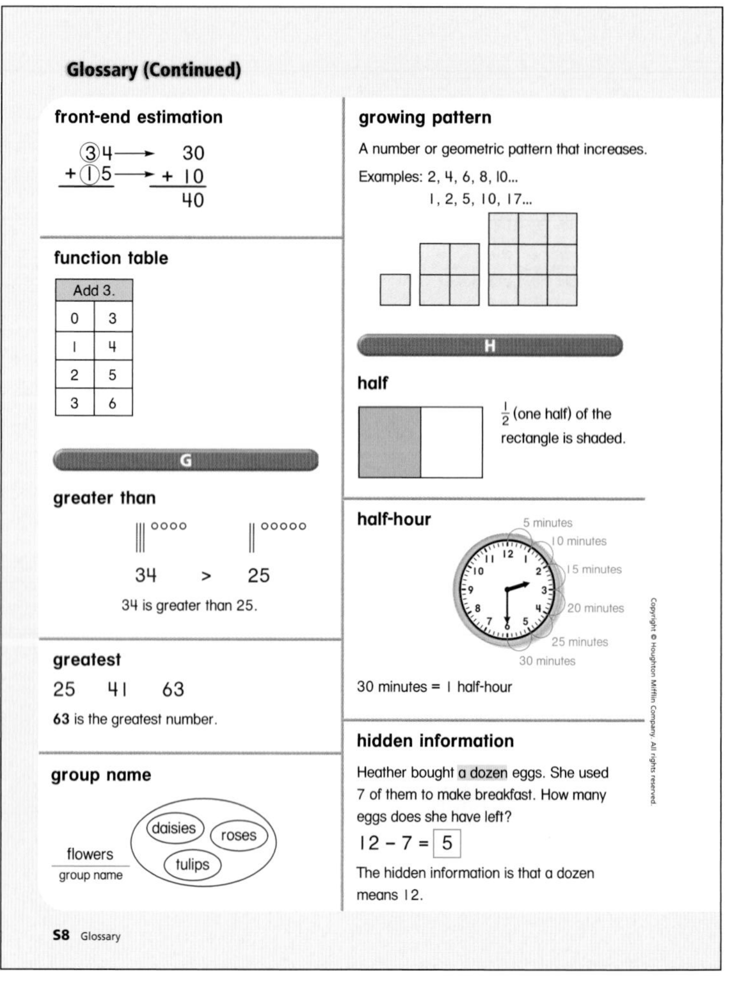

Glossary (Continued)

front-end estimation

(3)4 → 30
+ (1)5 → + 10
40

function table

Add 3.	
0	3
1	4
2	5
3	6

G

greater than

34 > 25

34 is greater than 25.

greatest

25 41 63

63 is the greatest number.

group name

flowers
group name

daisies roses tulips

growing pattern

A number or geometric pattern that increases.

Examples: 2, 4, 6, 8, 10...
1, 2, 5, 10, 17...

H

half

$\frac{1}{2}$ (one half) of the rectangle is shaded.

half-hour

5 minutes
10 minutes
15 minutes
20 minutes
25 minutes
30 minutes

30 minutes = 1 half-hour

hidden information

Heather bought a dozen eggs. She used 7 of them to make breakfast. How many eggs does she have left?

12 − 7 = 5

The hidden information is that a dozen means 12.

Copyright © Houghton Mifflin Company. All rights reserved.

S8 Glossary

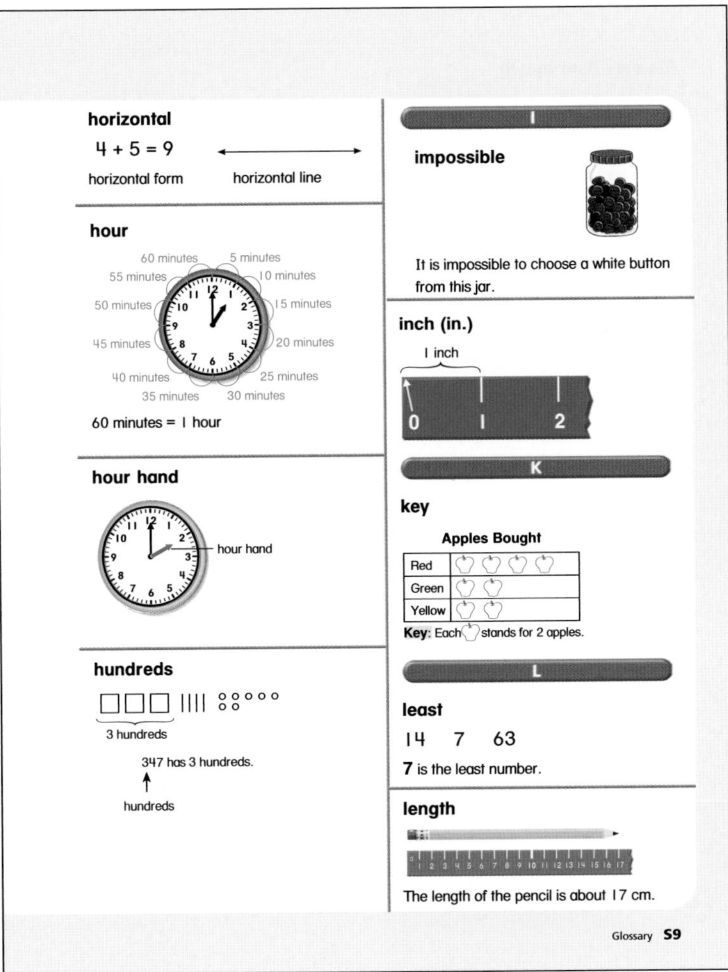

horizontal

4 + 5 = 9

horizontal form — horizontal line

hour

60 minutes = 1 hour

hour hand

hundreds

3 hundreds

347 has 3 hundreds.

hundreds

I

impossible

It is impossible to choose a white button from this jar.

inch (in.)

K

key

Apples Bought

Red	🍎 🍎 🍎 🍎
Green	🍎 🍎
Yellow	🍎 🍎

Key: Each 🍎 stands for 2 apples.

L

least

14 7 63

7 is the least number.

length

The length of the pencil is about 17 cm.

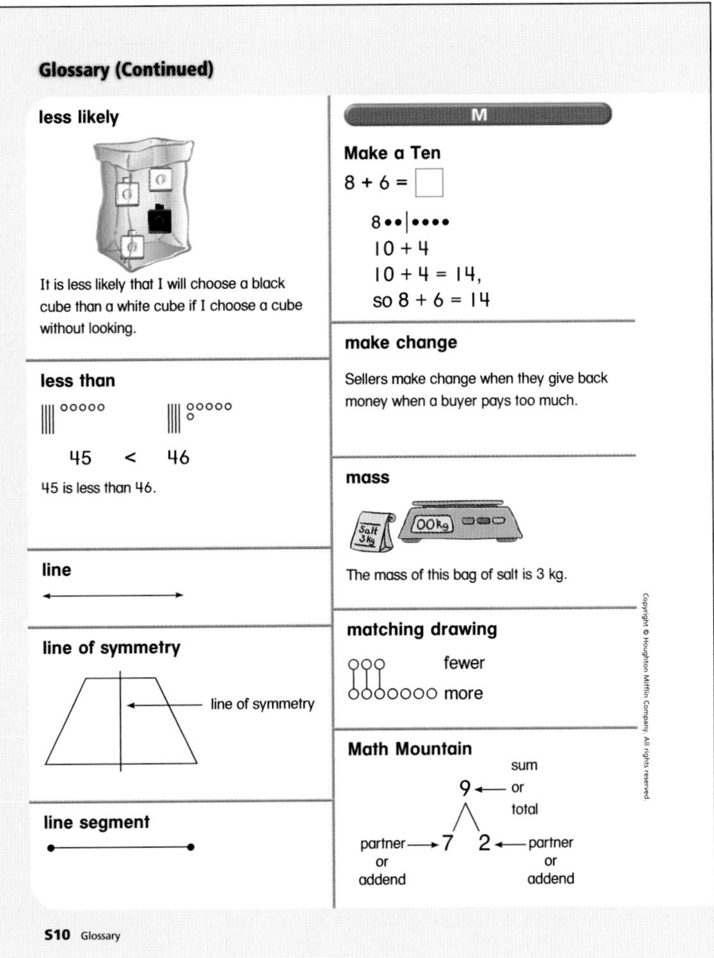

Glossary (Continued)

less likely

It is less likely that I will choose a black cube than a white cube if I choose a cube without looking.

less than

45 < 46

45 is less than 46.

line

line of symmetry

line segment

M

Make a Ten

8 + 6 = ☐

8 •• | ••••

10 + 4

10 + 4 = 14,

so 8 + 6 = 14

make change

Sellers make change when they give back money when a buyer pays too much.

mass

The mass of this bag of salt is 3 kg.

matching drawing

fewer

more

Math Mountain

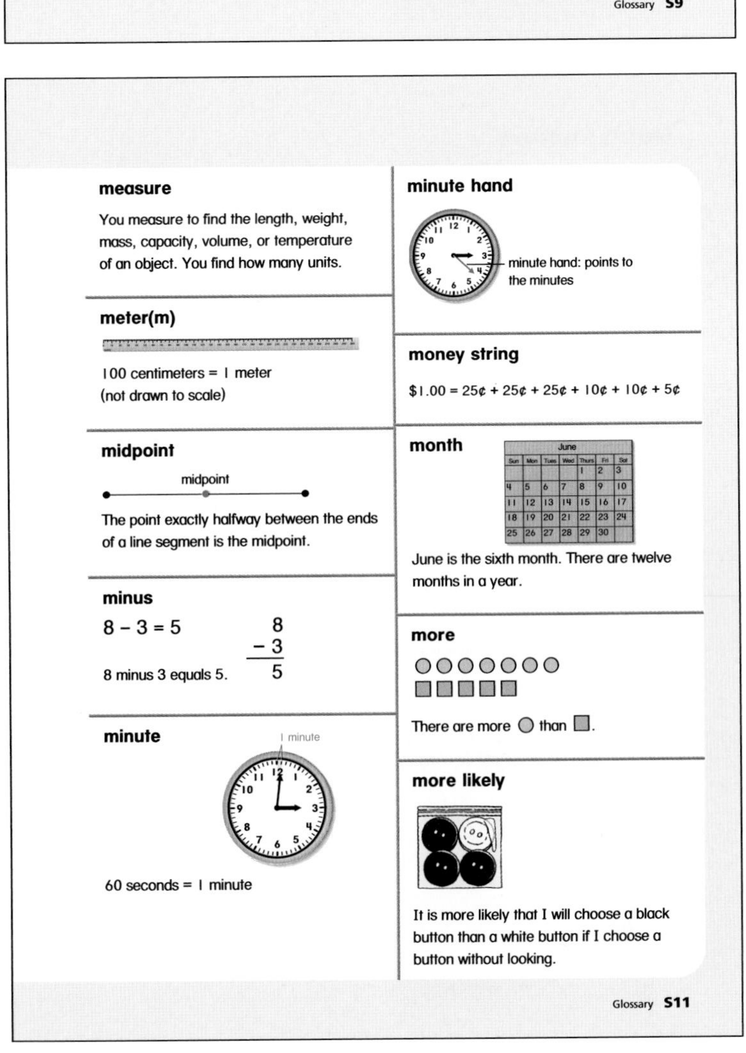

measure

You measure to find the length, weight, mass, capacity, volume, or temperature of an object. You find how many units.

meter(m)

100 centimeters = 1 meter

(not drawn to scale)

midpoint

The point exactly halfway between the ends of a line segment is the midpoint.

minus

8 − 3 = 5

$\begin{array}{r} 8 \\ -\ 3 \\ \hline 5 \end{array}$

8 minus 3 equals 5.

minute

60 seconds = 1 minute

minute hand

money string

\$1.00 = 25¢ + 25¢ + 25¢ + 10¢ + 10¢ + 5¢

month

June

Sun	Mon	Tues	Wed	Thurs	Fri	Sat
				1	2	3
4	5	6	7	8	9	10
11	12	13	14	15	16	17
18	19	20	21	22	23	24
25	26	27	28	29	30	

June is the sixth month. There are twelve months in a year.

more

There are more ◯ than ▢.

more likely

It is more likely that I will choose a black button than a white button if I choose a button without looking.

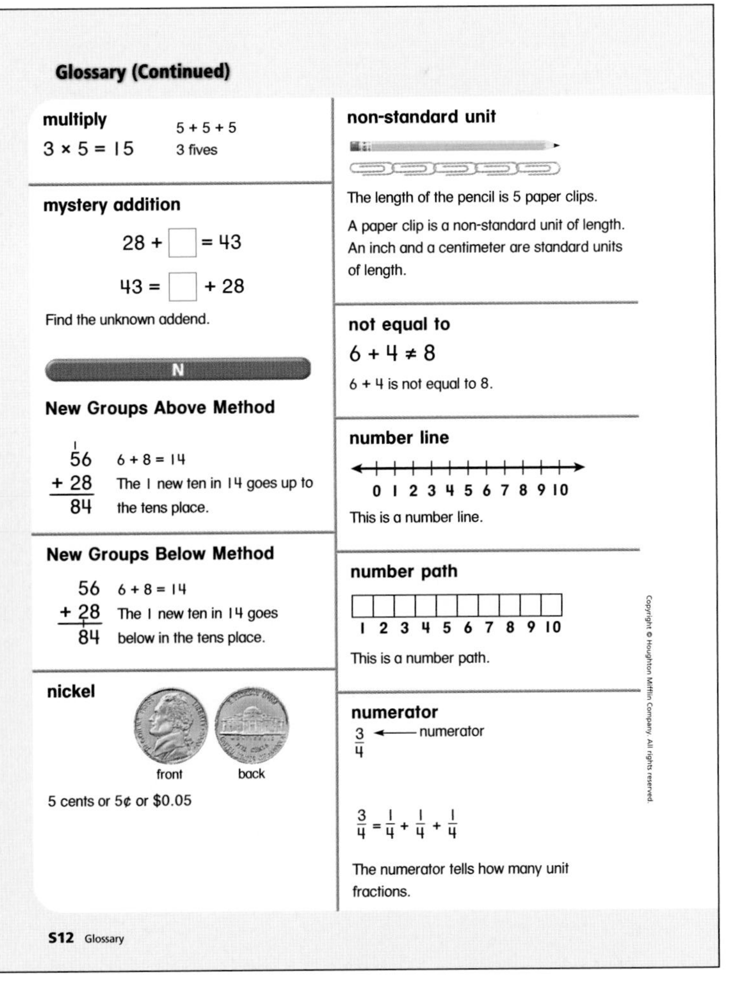

Glossary (Continued)

multiply

3 × 5 = 15

5 + 5 + 5

3 fives

mystery addition

28 + ☐ = 43

43 = ☐ + 28

Find the unknown addend.

N

New Groups Above Method

$\begin{array}{r} ^{1}\ \ \\ 56 \\ +\ 28 \\ \hline 84 \end{array}$

6 + 8 = 14

The 1 new ten in 14 goes up to the tens place.

New Groups Below Method

$\begin{array}{r} 56 \\ +\ 28 \\ \hline 84 \end{array}$

6 + 8 = 14

The 1 new ten in 14 goes below in the tens place.

nickel

front — back

5 cents or 5¢ or \$0.05

non-standard unit

The length of the pencil is 5 paper clips.

A paper clip is a non-standard unit of length. An inch and a centimeter are standard units of length.

not equal to

6 + 4 ≠ 8

6 + 4 is not equal to 8.

number line

This is a number line.

number path

This is a number path.

numerator

$\frac{3}{4}$ ← numerator

$\frac{3}{4} = \frac{1}{4} + \frac{1}{4} + \frac{1}{4}$

The numerator tells how many unit fractions.

Student Glossary (Continued)

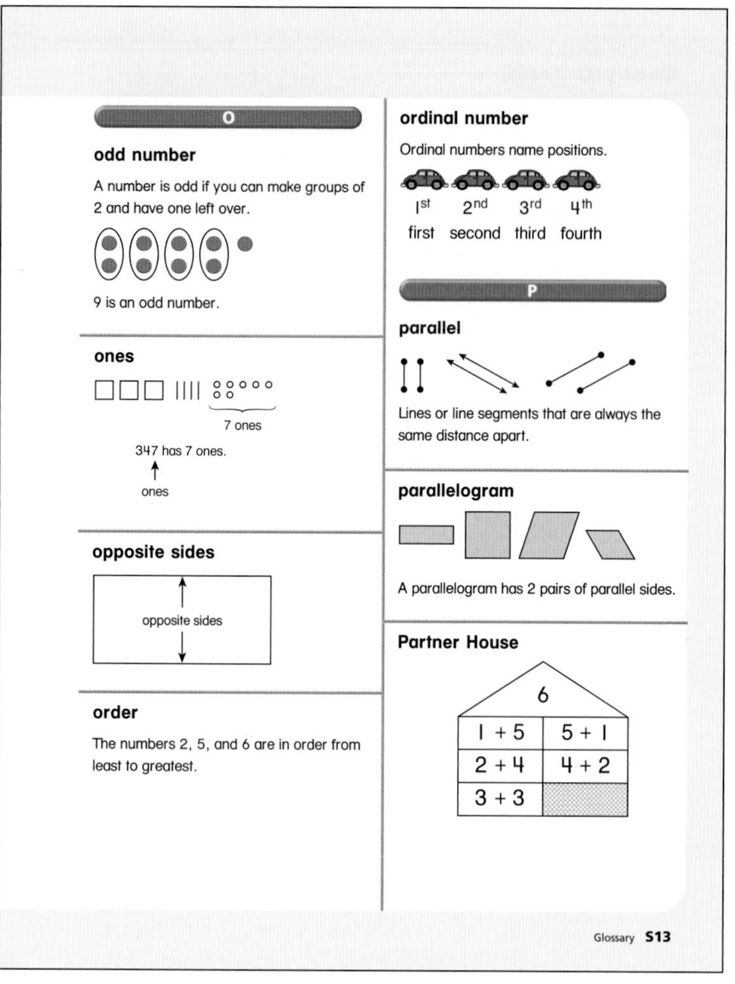

O

odd number

A number is odd if you can make groups of 2 and have one left over.

9 is an odd number.

ones

7 ones

347 has 7 ones.

ones

opposite sides

opposite sides

order

The numbers 2, 5, and 6 are in order from least to greatest.

ordinal number

Ordinal numbers name positions.

1st 2nd 3rd 4th

first second third fourth

P

parallel

Lines or line segments that are always the same distance apart.

parallelogram

A parallelogram has 2 pairs of parallel sides.

Partner House

6	
1 + 5	5 + 1
2 + 4	4 + 2
3 + 3	

Glossary S13

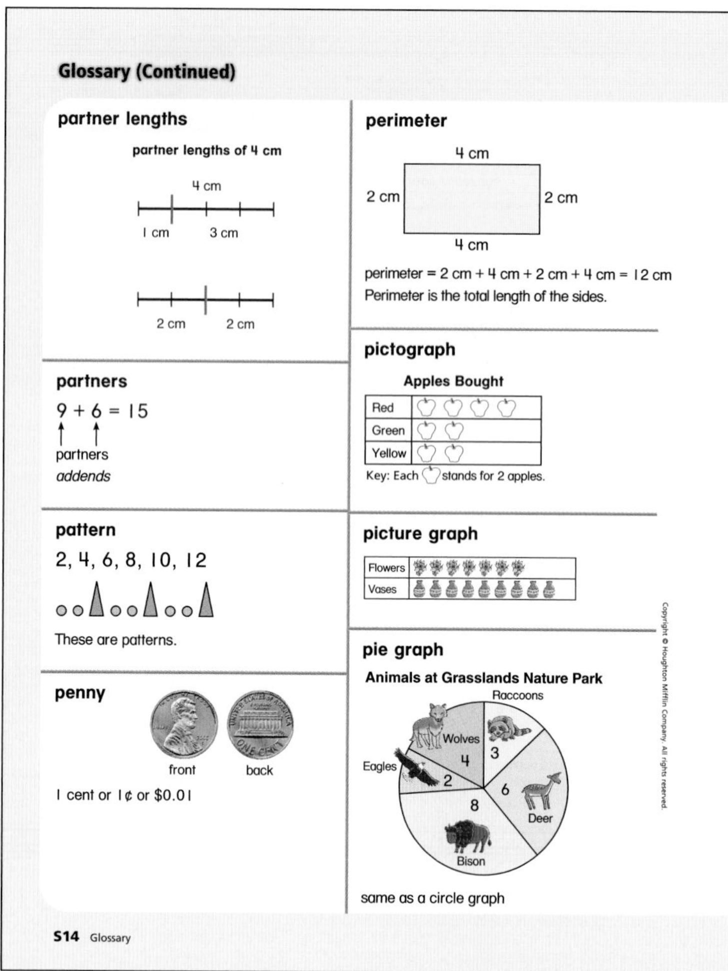

Glossary (Continued)

partner lengths

partner lengths of 4 cm

4 cm

1 cm 3 cm

2 cm 2 cm

partners

9 + 6 = 15

partners

addends

pattern

2, 4, 6, 8, 10, 12

These are patterns.

penny

front back

1 cent or 1¢ or $0.01

perimeter

4 cm

2 cm 2 cm

4 cm

perimeter = 2 cm + 4 cm + 2 cm + 4 cm = 12 cm

Perimeter is the total length of the sides.

pictograph

Apples Bought

Red

Green

Yellow

Key: Each stands for 2 apples.

picture graph

Flowers

Vases

pie graph

Animals at Grasslands Nature Park

Raccoons 3, Wolves 4, Eagles 2, Deer 6, Bison 8

same as a circle graph

Copyright © Houghton Mifflin Company. All rights reserved.

S14 Glossary

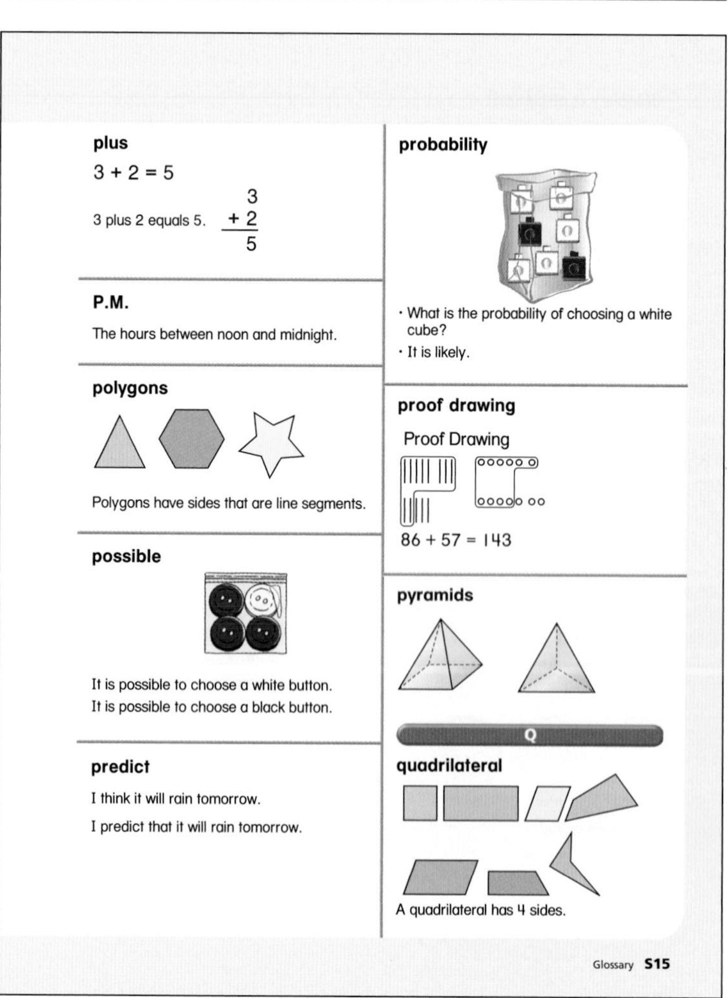

plus

3 + 2 = 5

3 plus 2 equals 5.

$$\begin{array}{r} 3 \\ +\ 2 \\ \hline 5 \end{array}$$

P.M.

The hours between noon and midnight.

polygons

Polygons have sides that are line segments.

possible

It is possible to choose a white button.

It is possible to choose a black button.

predict

I think it will rain tomorrow.

I predict that it will rain tomorrow.

probability

- What is the probability of choosing a white cube?
- It is likely.

proof drawing

Proof Drawing

86 + 57 = 143

pyramids

Q

quadrilateral

A quadrilateral has 4 sides.

Glossary S15

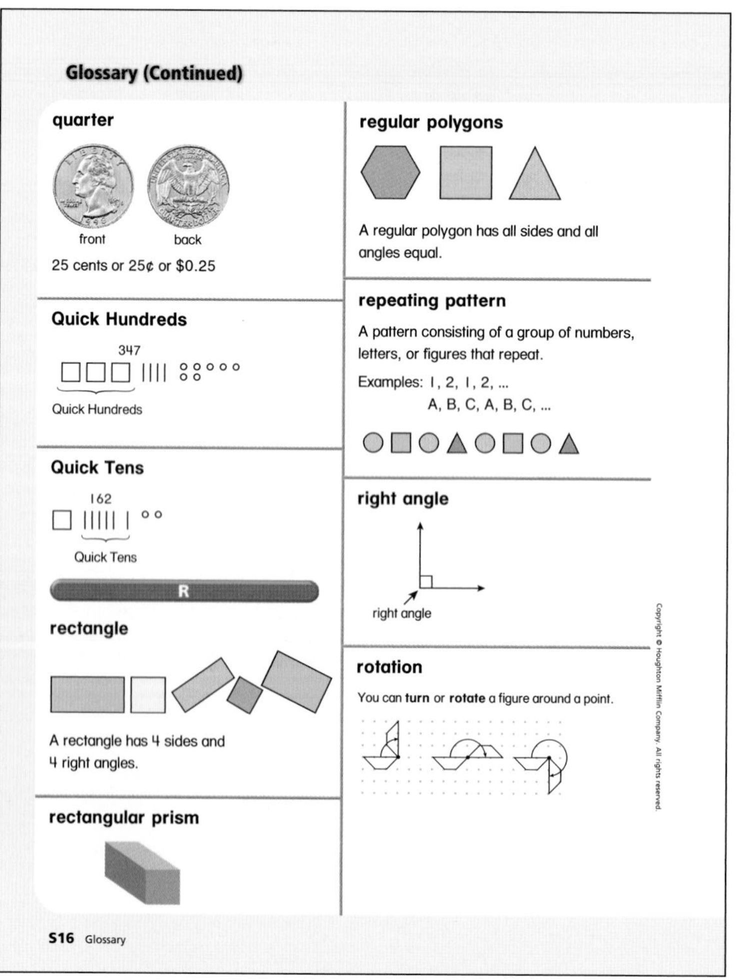

Glossary (Continued)

quarter

front back

25 cents or 25¢ or $0.25

Quick Hundreds

347

Quick Hundreds

Quick Tens

162

Quick Tens

R

rectangle

A rectangle has 4 sides and 4 right angles.

rectangular prism

regular polygons

A regular polygon has all sides and all angles equal.

repeating pattern

A pattern consisting of a group of numbers, letters, or figures that repeat.

Examples: 1, 2, 1, 2, ...

A, B, C, A, B, C, ...

right angle

right angle

rotation

You can **turn** or **rotate** a figure around a point.

Copyright © Houghton Mifflin Company. All rights reserved.

S16 Glossary

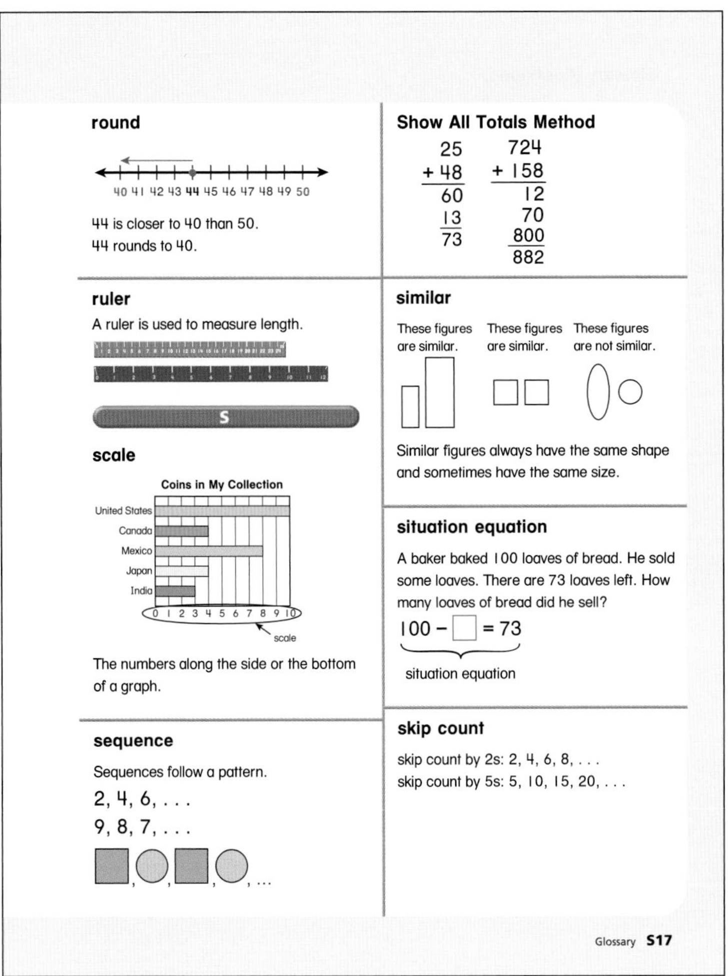

round

44 is closer to 40 than 50.
44 rounds to 40.

ruler

A ruler is used to measure length.

S

scale

The numbers along the side or the bottom of a graph.

sequence

Sequences follow a pattern.

2, 4, 6, . . .

9, 8, 7, . . .

Show All Totals Method

$$\begin{array}{r} 25 \\ +48 \\ \hline 60 \\ 13 \\ \hline 73 \end{array} \qquad \begin{array}{r} 724 \\ +158 \\ \hline 12 \\ 70 \\ 800 \\ \hline 882 \end{array}$$

similar

These figures are similar. These figures are similar. These figures are not similar.

Similar figures always have the same shape and sometimes have the same size.

situation equation

A baker baked 100 loaves of bread. He sold some loaves. There are 73 loaves left. How many loaves of bread did he sell?

100 − ☐ = 73

situation equation

skip count

skip count by 2s: 2, 4, 6, 8, . . .
skip count by 5s: 5, 10, 15, 20, . . .

Glossary **S17**

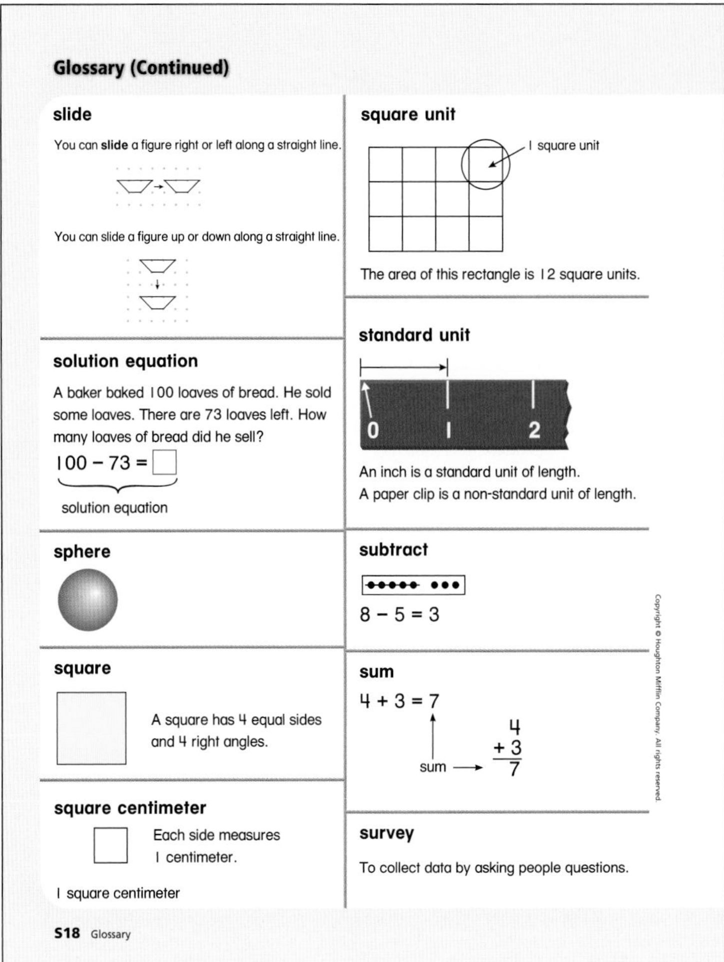

Glossary (Continued)

slide

You can **slide** a figure right or left along a straight line.

You can slide a figure up or down along a straight line.

solution equation

A baker baked 100 loaves of bread. He sold some loaves. There are 73 loaves left. How many loaves of bread did he sell?

100 − 73 = ☐

solution equation

sphere

square

A square has 4 equal sides and 4 right angles.

square centimeter

Each side measures 1 centimeter.

1 square centimeter

square unit

The area of this rectangle is 12 square units.

standard unit

An inch is a standard unit of length.
A paper clip is a non-standard unit of length.

subtract

8 − 5 = 3

sum

4 + 3 = 7

$$\begin{array}{r} 4 \\ +3 \\ \hline 7 \end{array}$$

sum

survey

To collect data by asking people questions.

S18 Glossary

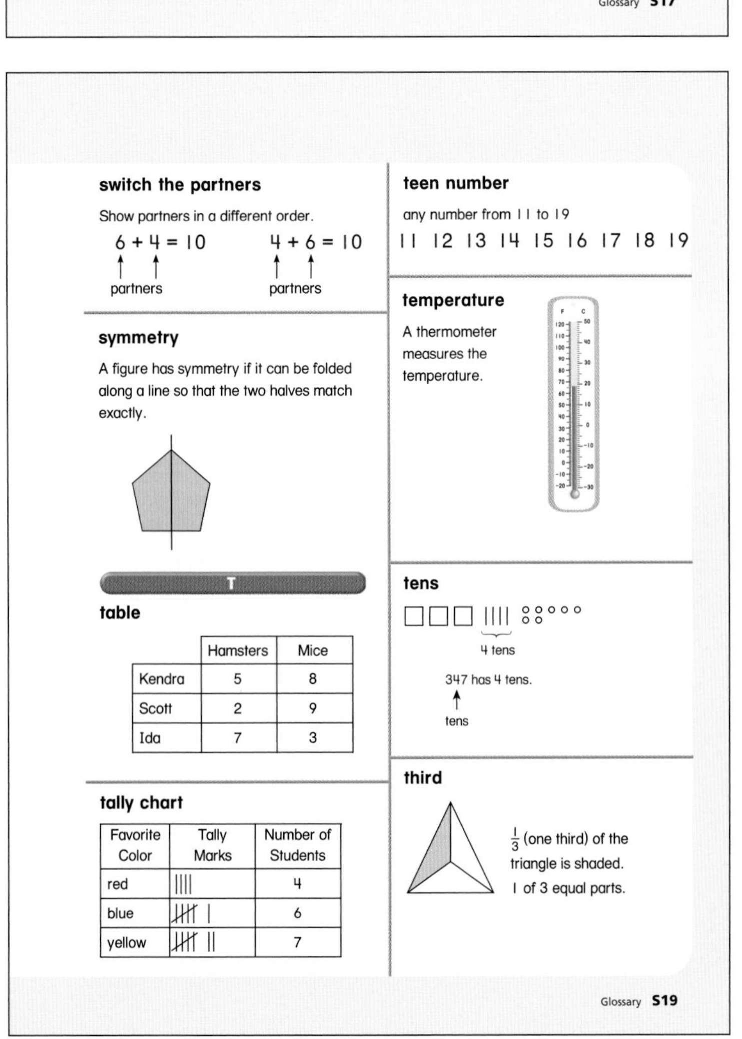

switch the partners

Show partners in a different order.

6 + 4 = 10 4 + 6 = 10

partners partners

symmetry

A figure has symmetry if it can be folded along a line so that the two halves match exactly.

T

table

	Hamsters	Mice
Kendra	5	8
Scott	2	9
Ida	7	3

tally chart

Favorite Color	Tally Marks	Number of Students
red	||||	4
blue	~~||||~~ |	6
yellow	~~||||~~ ||	7

teen number

any number from 11 to 19

11 12 13 14 15 16 17 18 19

temperature

A thermometer measures the temperature.

tens

4 tens

347 has 4 tens.

tens

third

$\frac{1}{3}$ (one third) of the triangle is shaded.
1 of 3 equal parts.

Glossary **S19**

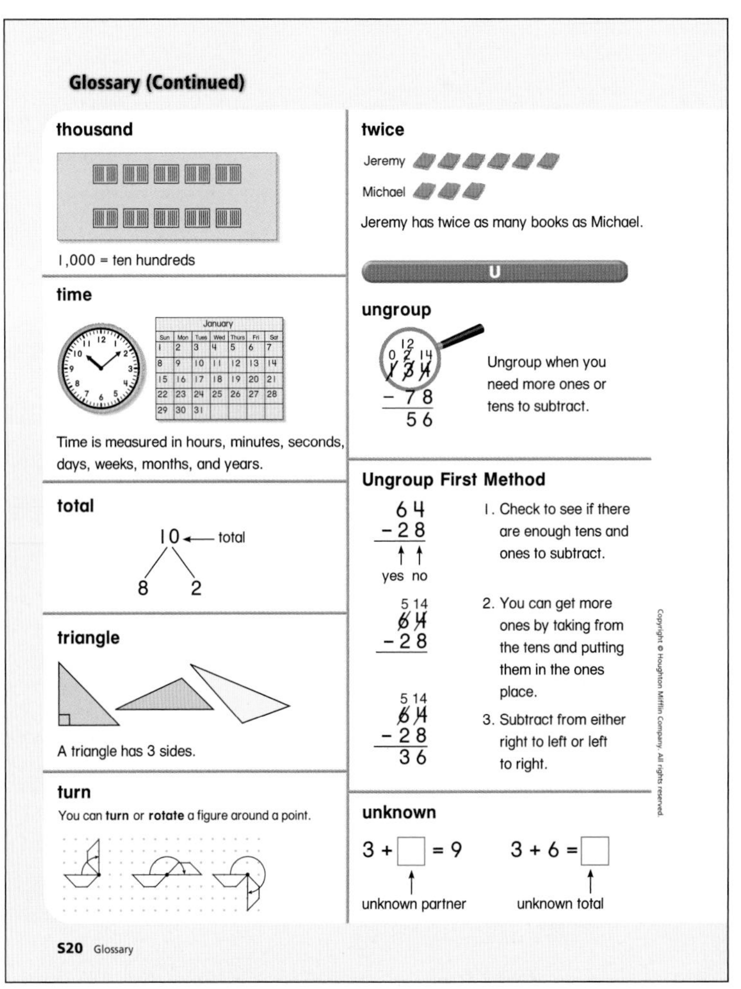

Glossary (Continued)

thousand

1,000 = ten hundreds

time

Time is measured in hours, minutes, seconds, days, weeks, months, and years.

total

triangle

A triangle has 3 sides.

turn

You can **turn** or **rotate** a figure around a point.

twice

Jeremy
Michael

Jeremy has twice as many books as Michael.

U

ungroup

Ungroup when you need more ones or tens to subtract.

Ungroup First Method

1. Check to see if there are enough tens and ones to subtract.
2. You can get more ones by taking from the tens and putting them in the ones place.
3. Subtract from either right to left or left to right.

unknown

3 + ☐ = 9 3 + 6 = ☐

unknown partner unknown total

S20 Glossary

Student Glossary (Continued)

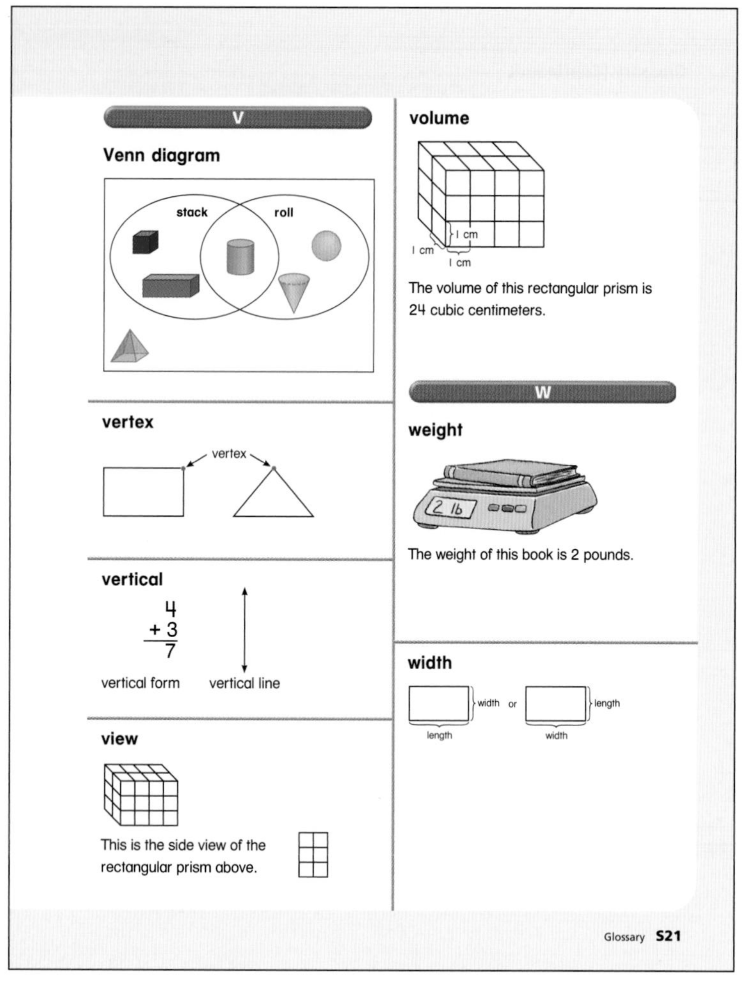

V
Venn diagram
stack
roll
vertex
vertex
vertical
4
+ 3
7
vertical form
vertical line
view
This is the side view of the rectangular prism above.
volume
1 cm
1 cm
1 cm
The volume of this rectangular prism is 24 cubic centimeters.
W
weight
2 lb
The weight of this book is 2 pounds.
width
width
or
length
length
width
Glossary S21

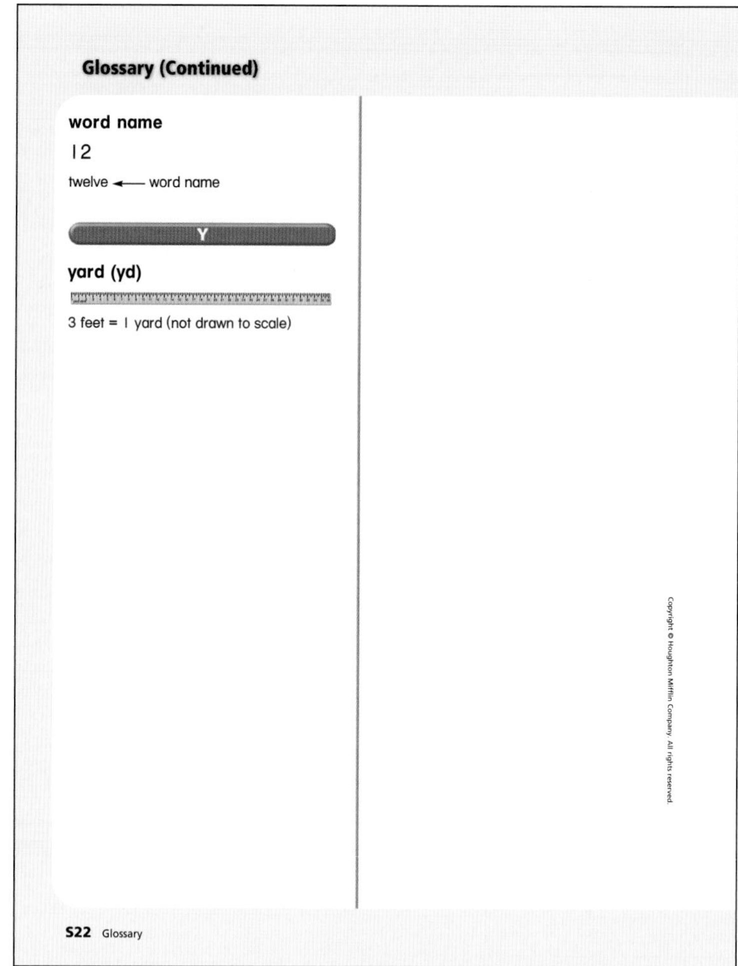

Glossary (Continued)
word name
12
twelve ← word name
Y
yard (yd)
3 feet = 1 yard (not drawn to scale)
Copyright © Houghton Mifflin Company. All rights reserved.
S22 Glossary

Teacher Glossary

A

actual amount The exact amount. Often found by counting or calculating after an estimate has been made.

acute angle An angle that measures less than 90°.

acute triangle A triangle in which each of the three angles is acute.

addend A number to be added in an addition equation. In the equation 7 + 4 + 8 = ☐, the numbers 7, 4 and 8 are addends.

Adding Up Method A method of finding an unknown partner or unknown addend in which children add up from the known partner until they reach the total.

34 + ☐ = 73

73 − 34 = ☐

Start at 34 and add up to 73.

34 + 6 = 40
40 + 30 = 70
70 + 3 = 73
39

after the hour The most common way of reading time where minutes are counted forward from the hour as in "38 minutes after 3 o'clock."

A.M. The abbreviation for *ante meridiem,* Latin for "before noon". Used to indicate a time between midnight and noon.

analog clock A clock displaying time by using hour and minute hands and the numbers 1 through 12.

angle A figure formed by two rays with a common endpoint.

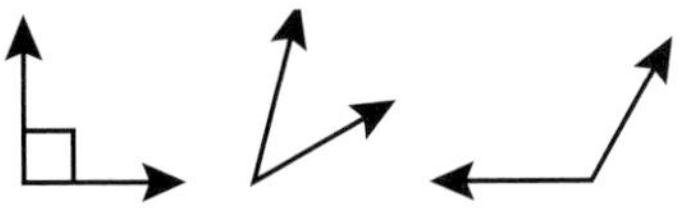

area The measure in square units of the surface of a plane figure.

array An arrangement of objects, pictures or numbers in columns and rows.

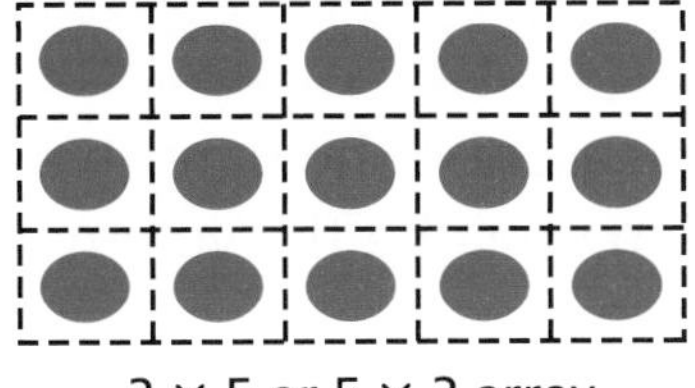

3 × 5 or 5 × 3 array

B

backward sequence A sequence of numbers that uses a subtraction rule to determine the next number.

20, 18, 16, 14, 12, 10 . . . Rule: $n - 2$

bar graph A graph that shows information using rectangular bars, either horizontally or vertically. The bars may be horizontal or vertical.

base ten blocks Blocks measured in metric units that can be used in measuring or place value. The ones block is a one centimeter cube; the tens block is one centimeter wide, 10 centimeters long, and one centimeter thick (made up of 10 ones). The hundreds block is 10 centimeters long, 10 centimeters wide, and 1 centimeter thick (made up of 100 ones).

before the hour A way of reading time where minutes are counted backward from the hour as in "20 minutes before 3 o'clock."

Blue Make-a-Ten Cards Cards used to help children become fluent in the Make a Ten strategy for subtraction.

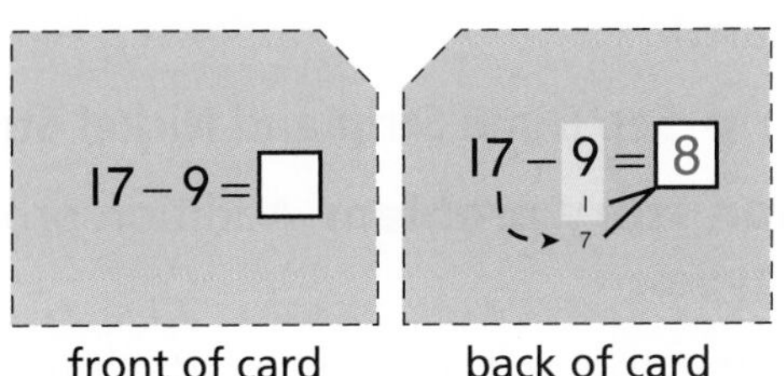

front of card   back of card

Teacher Glossary (Continued)

break-apart (noun or verb) You can break apart (verb) a larger number to get two smaller amounts called break-aparts (noun) or partners.

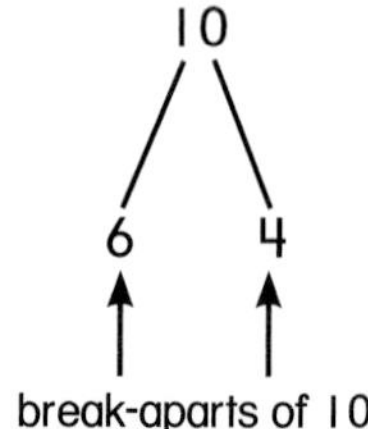

C

capacity A measure of how much a container can hold. Used to describe the volume of fluids such as water or sand.

cent The smallest unit of U.S. currency; the value of a penny; $.01.

centimeter (cm) A metric unit of length equal to 0.01 ($\frac{1}{100}$) meter.

certain Describes a probability outcome that is sure to happen.

change minus story problem A problem that begins with a given quantity which is then modified by a change—something is subtracted—that results in a new quantity.

Sarah had 12 books. She loaned her friend 9 books. How many books does Sarah have now?

Any of the three quantities can be unknown.

change plus story problem A problem that begins with a given quantity which is then modified by a change—something is added—that results in a new quantity.

Alvin had 9 toy cars. He received 3 more for his birthday. How many toy cars does Alvin have now?

Any of the three quantities can be unknown.

circle graph A graph used to display data that make up a whole. (Also called a pie graph or a pie chart.)

Coin Strip See **Dime Strip** and **Nickel Strip.**

collection story problem Addition problem of three types:

1) putting things together (putting two kinds of flowers in a vase);
2) separating a collection of things (putting some books on a shelf and some on a desk);
3) static, no action occurs (some windows are open, some windows are closed).

combine To put together; to form one group from many groups.

comparison bars A visual representation of the numbers in an additive comparison story problem; children draw different length bars to represent each number.

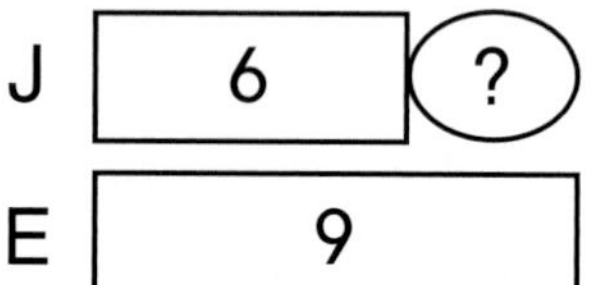

comparison drawing A drawing children make to illustrate the numbers in an additive comparison story problem.

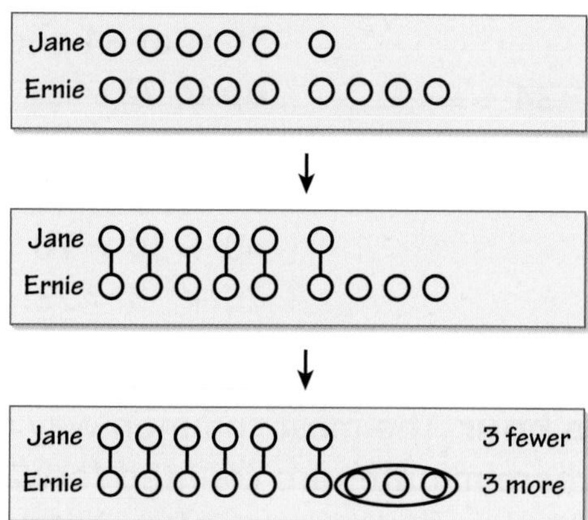

comparison language Having the same size and the same shape.

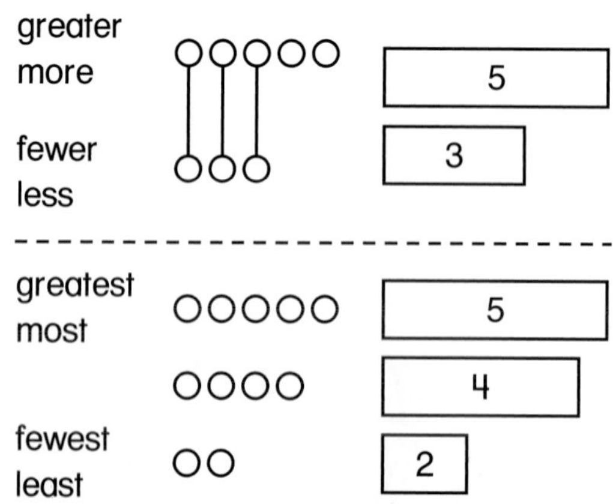

comparison story problem (additive) A problem that involves someone or something that has "more" or "less" of something than someone or something else. Comparison problems may require addition or subtraction to solve.

comparison story problem (additive) continued

Types of additive comparison problems:

1) More/Fewer Language
Manny has 5 roses. Asha has 8 roses. How many more roses does Asha have than Manny?
2) Equalizing Language
Manny has 5 roses. Asha has 8 roses. How many roses does Manny need to get to have the same amount of roses as Asha?

compose Put together.

congruent Having the same size and shape.

count all An addition strategy where children count all of something (for example, fingers on their hands or the dots on two Secret Code Cards) to find the total.

1 2 3 4 5 6 7 8
● ● ● ● ● | ● ● ● $5 + 3 = \boxed{8}$

count-bys Numbers that are found by counting by a particular number; 5s count-bys would be 5, 10, 15, 20, 25, and so on; 3s count-bys would be 3, 6, 9, 12, and so on.

count on An addition or subtraction strategy in which children begin with one partner and count on to the total. This strategy can be used to find an unknown partner or an unknown total.

$5 + 3 = \boxed{8}$

$5 + \boxed{3} = 8$

$8 - 5 = \boxed{3}$

6 7 8

Already **5**

D

data Pieces of information.

data table A list of data in rows and columns.

decade numbers Numbers that are multiples of 10: 10, 20, 30, 40, 50, 60, 70, 80, 90.

decade partners Decade numbers that have a sum of 100. 40 and 60 are decade partners; 30 and 70 are decade partners.

decimal notation for money A method of writing monetary values using the dollar sign symbol ($) and a decimal point (.). Fifty cents is written in decimal notation as $0.50.

decimal point In dollar notation, the symbol (.) used to separate the dollars position from the cents position; in decimal notation, the symbol used to separate the whole number position from the decimal fraction position.

decimeter (dm) A metric unit of length equal to 0.1 ($\frac{1}{10}$) meter.

decompose Take apart.

degrees Celsius (°C) The metric unit of temperature.

degrees Fahrenheit (°F) The customary unit of temperature.

Demonstration Secret Code Cards A larger version of the Secret Code Cards, for classroom use. (See **Secret Code Cards.**)

denominator In a fraction, the number below the bar. It tells the number of equal parts into which a whole is divided.

diagonal A line segment that connects two corners of a polygon and is not a side of the polygon.

difference The result of subtraction. In the subtraction equation, $5 - 2 = 3$, 3 is the difference.

digit Any one of these 10 symbols: 0, 1, 2, 3, 4, 5, 6, 7, 8, 9.

digital clock A clock displaying time in hours and minutes separated by a colon.

dime A coin that has a value of 10 cents or $0.10. Ten dimes are equal to one dollar.

Dime Strip A double-sided strip of paper or cardboard displaying a dime on one side and 10 pennies on the other side.

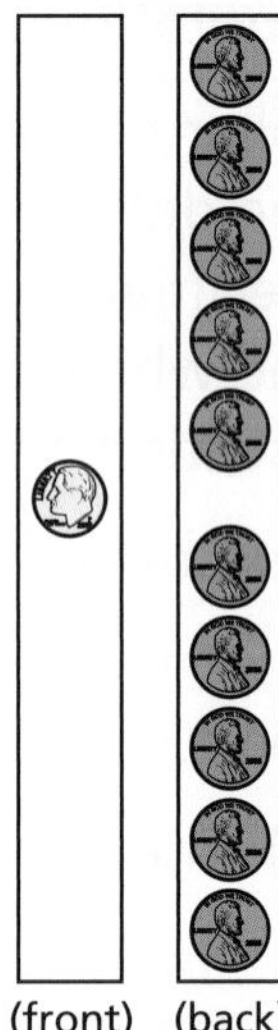

Dive the Deep A student activity used to practice subtraction with teen totals. Using columns of completed equations, children cover the answers with a strip of paper and slowly move the paper up or down the column to uncover and check the answer after solving each exercise.

Dive the Deep

11 − 6 = 5	12 − 6 = 6	13 − 8 = 5
12 − 7 = 5	17 − 8 = 9	15 − 6 = 9
12 − 9 = 3	13 − 5 = 8	11 − 9 = 2
13 − 4 = 9	14 − 6 = 8	13 − 9 = 4
11 − 5 = 6	17 − 9 = 8	15 − 7 = 8
14 − 9 = 5	11 − 8 = 3	14 − 8 = 6
14 − 7 = 7	12 − 4 = 8	12 − 5 = 7
16 − 7 = 9	16 − 8 = 8	11 − 3 = 8
11 − 7 = 4	15 − 7 = 8	13 − 6 = 7
12 − 3 = 9	16 − 9 = 7	18 − 9 = 9
13 − 7 = 6	11 − 4 = 7	12 − 8 = 4

UNIT 5 LESSON 5 Two Methods of Subtraction 265

dollar notation A method of writing monetary values using the dollar sign symbol ($) and a decimal point (.). Two dollars and fifty cents is written in dollar notation as $2.50.

dollar The basic unit of U.S. currency. One dollar is equal to four quarters, ten dimes, twenty nickels or one hundred pennies.

dollar sign The symbol ($) used to show dollar notation.

Double Minus 1 An addition strategy using doubles (two of the same addend). Used when one addend is decreased by 1. Since $5 + \mathbf{5} = 10$, $5 + \mathbf{4} = 9$, 1 less than 10.

Double Plus 1 An addition strategy using doubles (two of the same addend) in which one addend is increased by 1. Since $5 + \mathbf{5} = 10$, $5 + \mathbf{6} = 11$, 1 more than 10.

doubles Two of the same addend. In the equation $5 + 5 = 10$, the two fives are doubles.

E

equal shares Describes groups of equal size.

Equal Shares Drawing A drawing which children create that represents factors and products.

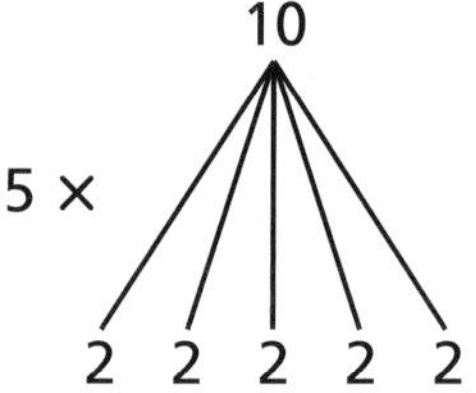

Equal Shares Drawing for $5 \times 2 = 10$

equation A mathematical sentence that uses an equals sign to show that two expressions are equal.

$12 - 5 = 7$ $3 + 1 = 4$ $5 = 2 + 3$
$6 = 8 - 2$ $6 + 2 = 4 + 4$

equation chain A series of expressions that equal the same number.

$5 = 2 + 3 = 3 + 2 = 4 + 1 = 1 + 4 = 1 + 1 + 1 + 1 + 1 = 6 - 1$

equilateral Describes a geometric figure that has all sides of equal length.

estimate (noun) A number close to an exact amount. An estimate tells *about* how much or *about* how many.

estimate (verb) To make a thoughtful guess or to tell *about* how much or *about* how many.

even number A number that is a multiple of 2. The ones digit of an even number is 0, 2, 4, 6 or 8. Even numbers are those that can be divided into two equal groups.

exact change The exact amount needed to purchase an item.

Expanded Method A method of subtraction in which children show the place value of each digit.

$$\begin{array}{rl} & \ 50 + 14 \\ 64 & = \cancel{60} + \cancel{4} \\ \underline{-\ 28} & = \underline{20 + 8} \\ & \ 30 + 6 = 36 \end{array}$$

expanded numbers or expanded notation Numbers written in a form that shows the place value of the digits.

254 = 2 hundreds + 5 tens + 4 ones or
254 = 200 + 50 + 4

expression A number, a variable, or any combination of numbers, variables, operation signs and grouping symbols.

F

face A flat surface of a solid figure.

fair game A game in which the likelihood of winning is equally likely for all players.

fair shares Describes groups of equal shares.

fewer Fewer is used to compare two quantities that can be counted. There are fewer red books than blue books. Less is used to compare two quantities that can be measured. There is less water than juice. *See* comparison language.

fewest Fewest is used to compare three or more quantities. (See fewer.)

flash ten A way for children to display the value of ten by opening and closing both hands at the same time. Flashing ten twice would represent 20.

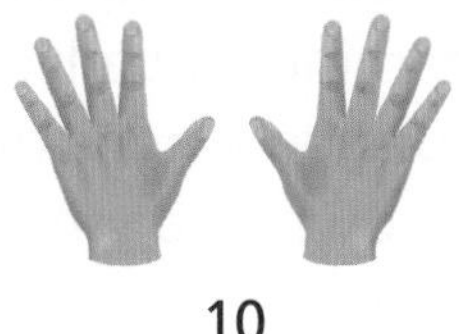

10

flip To turn a figure over a line so that the moved figure is a mirror image of the original; also referred to as a reflection.

You can **flip** a figure over a horizontal line.

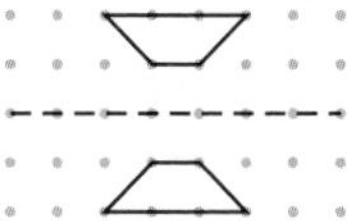

You can **flip** a figure over a vertical line.

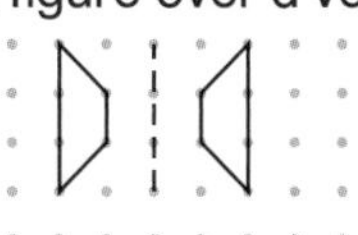

foot A customary unit of length equal to 12 inches.

forward sequence A sequence of numbers that uses an addition rule to determine the next number.

16, 20, 24, 28, 32, 36 . . . Rule: $n + 4$

fraction A number used to describe part of a whole, a whole, or more than one whole. $\frac{1}{2}$, $\frac{4}{4}$, and $\frac{6}{5}$ are fractions.

front-end estimation A method of estimation accomplished by computing with the digits in the greatest place.

$$\begin{array}{rcr} 49 & \rightarrow & 40 \\ \underline{+\ 27} & \rightarrow & \underline{+\ 20} \\ & & 60 \end{array} \leftarrow \text{front-end estimate}$$

function A relationship between two sets of numbers in which each number in the first set is paired with exactly one number in the second set.

function table A table that shows a function.

Subtract 4.	
9	5
10	6
7	3
8	4

G

Game Cards Cards displaying the numerals 0–9. These are on Copymaster M23.

geoboards Pegboards (usually plastic) that children use to construct geometric shapes by placing elastic bands on the pegs.

greater Larger or more than. Used to compare two quantities or numbers.

greatest Largest or most. Used to compare three or more quantities or numbers.

Green Make-a-Ten Cards Cards used to help children become fluent in the Make a Ten strategy for addition.

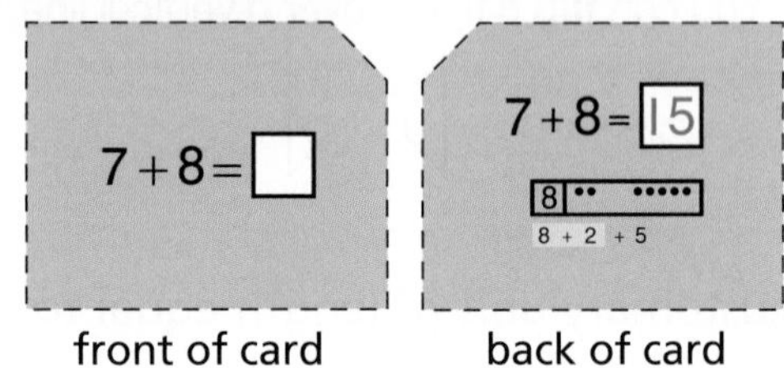

front of card back of card

group (verb) To combine ones to form tens, to combine tens to form hundreds, and so on.

group name A name used as a category or classification. Flowers is the group name for daisies and roses.

Grouping Drawing A drawing which children create that represents factors and products.

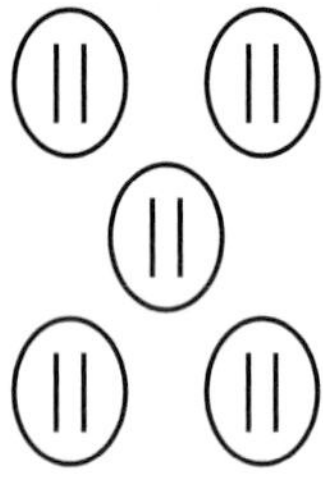

Grouping Drawing for $5 \times 2 = 10$

growing pattern A number or geometric pattern that increases.
Examples: 2, 4, 6, 8, 10 ...
1, 2, 5, 10, 17 ...

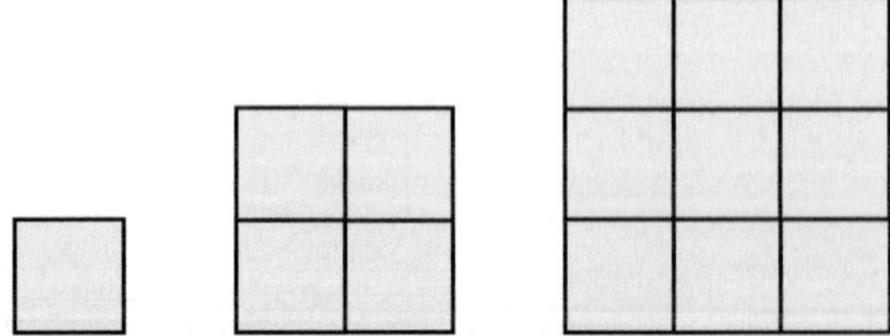

H

hidden information An implied number or implied information in a story problem: pair, dozen, double the amount.

horizontal Parallel to the horizon; going straight across.

horizontal bar graph A bar graph in which data are displayed using horizontal bars.

hundreds The name given to the third position from the right when describing whole number place value. In the number 312, 3 is in the hundreds position.

I

impossible Not able to happen (as in a particular outcome in a probability experiment).

inch A customary unit of length equal to $\frac{1}{12}$ foot.

inverse operations Opposite or reverse operations that undo each other. Addition and subtraction are inverse operations. Multiplication and division are inverse operations.

is equal to (=) Having the same value as that of another quantity or expression.

is greater than (>) Having a value that is more than that of another quantity or expression.

is less than (<) Having a value that is less than that of another quantity or expression.

is not equal to (≠) Having a value that is not the same as another quantity or expression.

isosceles triangle A triangle that has at least two sides of equal length.

K

key A part of a map, graph or chart that explains what symbols mean.

L

least Smallest amount or fewest.

length The measure of how long something is or one dimension of a two-dimensional figure.

less Word used to show a quantity smaller than another. Less is used to compare quantities that cannot be counted individually: less milk, less traffic; less is also used when comparing numbers on their own and when comparing amounts of money.

less likely Having less of a chance of happening than something else (as in an outcome in a probability experiment).

line of symmetry The line along which a figure can be folded so that the two halves match exactly.

line plot A way to show data using a number line.

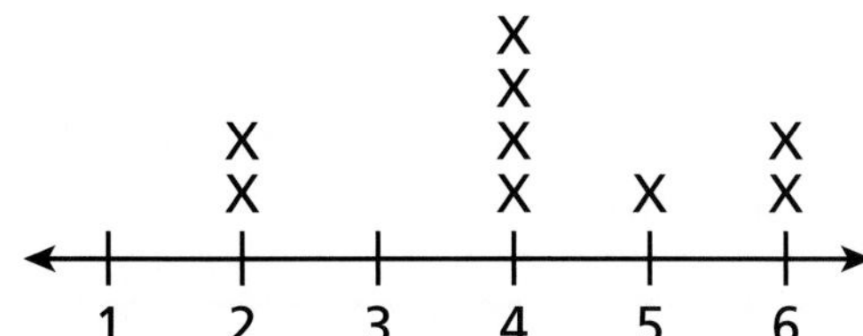

line segment A part of a line that has two endpoints.

line symmetry A property that pertains to a figure that can be folded to make two parts that are mirror images. Also called reflectional symmetry.

M

Make a Ten strategy An addition or subtraction strategy in which children count on to ten to add or subtract.

making change Finding the amount of money that needs to be returned to the buyer when the amount of money given to the seller is more than the cost of the purchase.

mass The amount of matter in an object. (Mass is constant; weight varies because weight is the effect of gravity on matter.)

matching drawing (See **comparison drawing.**)

Math Mountain A visual representation of the partners and totals of a number. The total (*sum*) appears at the top and the two partners (*addends*) that are added to produce the larger number are below to the left and right.

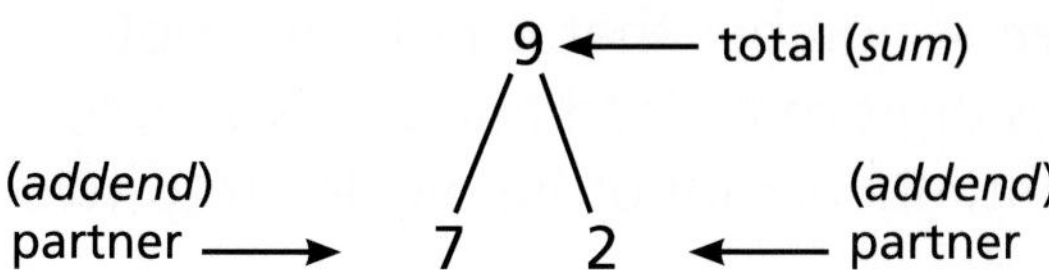

Math Mountain Cards Triangular-shaped cards used to practice addition and subtraction. Each card shows a total at the top and a pair of partners at the bottom. Yellow cards have totals of 10 or less; blue cards have teen totals.

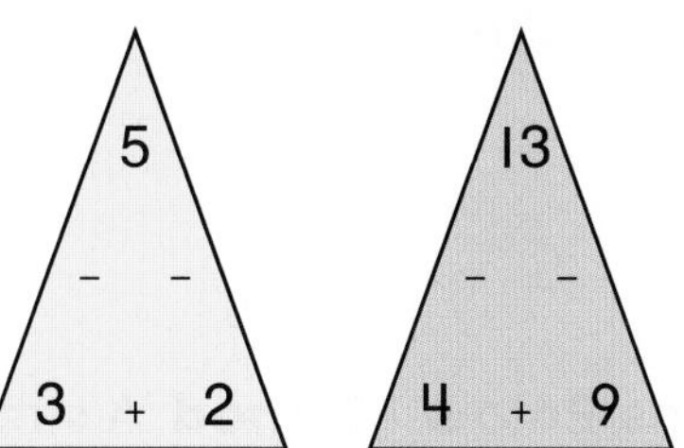

meter In the metric system, the basic unit of length or distance.

midpoint The point that divides a line segment into two congruent parts.

money string Combinations of dollars and/or coins that equal an amount.

$1.29 = $1 + 25¢ + 1¢ + 1¢ + 1¢ + 1¢ = 25¢ + 25¢ + 25¢ + 10¢ + 10¢ + 10¢ + 5¢ + 5¢ + 5¢ + 5¢ + 1¢ + 1¢ + 1¢ +1¢

more Describes an amount or quantity greater than another. *See* comparison language.

more likely Having more of a chance of happening than something else (as in an outcome in a probability experiment).

most Greatest amount or quantity.

multiple Number which is the product of a given number and any whole number. 4 is a multiple of 4 because it is the product of 4 and whole number 1; 8 is a multiple of 4 because it is the product of 4 and the whole number 2. (See **count-bys**.)

multiplication The operation of repeated addition of the same number. 3 x 5 is the same as 5 + 5 + 5.

mystery addition An addition problem in which children are asked to find an unknown addend.

$6 + \square = 10$

mystery multiplication A multiplication problem in which children are asked to find an unknown factor.

$\square \times 7 = 28$

N

New Groups Above Method A strategy for multi-digit addition. The new groups are placed above the existing groups. This is a common method of addition.

```
  1 1
  298
+ 177
  475
```

New Groups Below Method A strategy for multi-digit addition. The new groups are placed below the existing groups on the line waiting to be added.

```
  298
+ 177
  1 1
  475
```

nickel A coin with a value of 5 cents or $0.05. A nickel is equal to five pennies.

Nickel Strip A double-sided strip of paper or cardboard displaying a nickel on one side and 5 pennies on the other side.

(front) (back)

non-standard unit A unit of measure not commonly recognized, such as a paper clip. An inch and a centimeter are standard units of measure.

number The word used to describe value or quantity (cardinal number: 1, 2, 3) or order (ordinal number: 1st, 2nd, 3rd).

number flash A way for children to display the value of a number by holding up the appropriate number of fingers and/or hands (See also **flash ten.**) A child would flash two by holding up two fingers; a child would flash eleven by flashing ten (opening and closing both hands once at the same time) and then moving both hands to the right, closing both and then putting up just one finger to the right. Eleven is ten and one.

number line A diagram that represents numbers as lengths on a line.

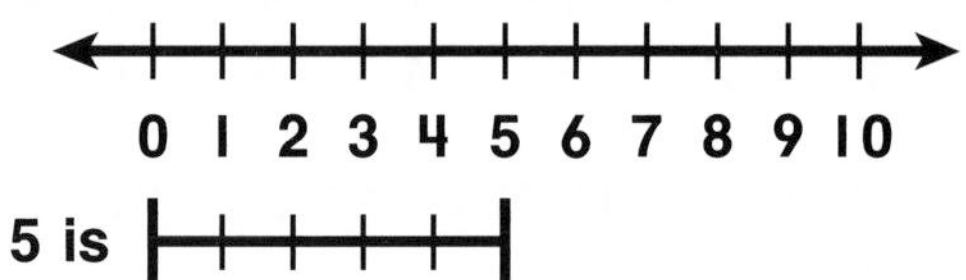

Number Path A display of the numbers 1 through 100 in groups of ten, found on the outside edge of the MathBoard or Copymaster M51.

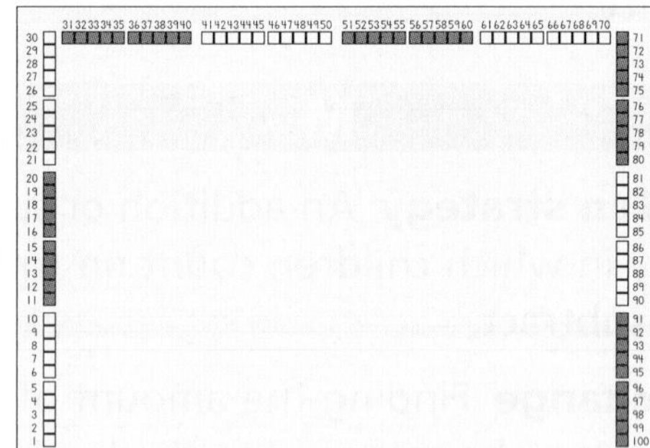

numeral A symbol used to represent a number. 7 is the numeral for seven.

numerator In a fraction, the number above the bar. The numerator tells the number of equal parts being described.

O

obtuse angle An angle that measures more than 90° and less than 180°.

obtuse triangle A triangle with one angle that measures more than 90°.

odd number A number that is not a multiple of 2. The ones digit of an odd number is 1, 3, 5, 7, or 9. Odd numbers cannot be divided into two equal groups.

ones The name given to the position furthest to the right when describing whole number place value. In the number 12, 2 is in the ones position.

Orange Count-On Cards Cards used to practice the Counting On strategy for subtraction. One side of the card shows a subtraction equation. The other side shows the answer and a counting-on drawing.

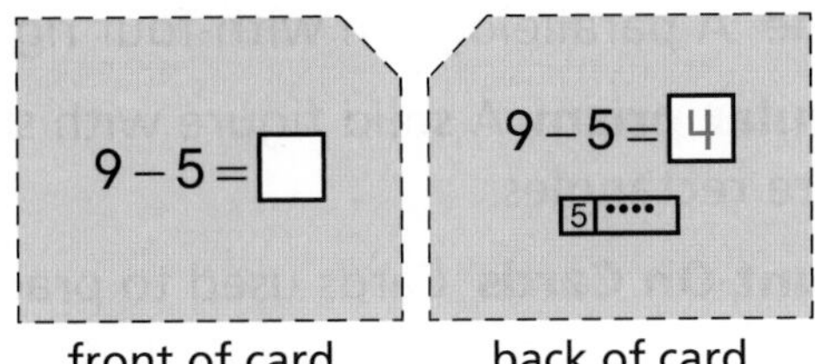

front of card back of card

ordinal number A number that describes the position in an ordered sequence of objects or events, not the quantity of them. 1st, 2nd, 3rd and 4th are ordinal numbers.

P

Parachute Drop A student activity to practice addition and subtraction with totals ≤ 10. Using columns of completed equations, children cover the answers with a strip of paper and slowly move the paper up or down the column to check their answers after solving each exercise.

Parachute Drop

5 + 3 = 8	5 + 3 = 8	8 – 5 = 3
6 + 2 = 8	6 + 2 = 8	8 – 6 = 2
4 + 5 = 9	4 + 5 = 9	9 – 4 = 5
3 + 6 = 9	3 + 6 = 9	9 – 3 = 6
2 + 4 = 6	2 + 4 = 6	6 – 2 = 4
6 + 4 = 10	6 + 4 = 10	10 – 6 = 4
4 + 3 = 7	4 + 3 = 7	7 – 4 = 3
3 + 7 = 10	3 + 7 = 10	10 – 3 = 7
8 + 2 = 10	8 + 2 = 10	10 – 8 = 2
3 + 2 = 5	3 + 2 = 5	5 – 2 = 3
4 + 4 = 8	4 + 4 = 8	8 – 4 = 4

parallel A word used to describe lines or line segments that do not intersect. The distance between the lines or line segments is the same at every point.

parallelogram A quadrilateral in which both pairs of opposite sides are parallel and opposite angles are congruent.

Partner House A pictorial representation of all the sets of partners for a total. The total is shown on the roof of the house. Each floor of the house shows a set of partners. Pairs of partners that can be "switched" are shown twice on the same floor in different order. A pair of doubles is shown only once on a floor.

6	
1 + 5	5 + 1
2 + 4	4 + 2
3 + 3	

partner lengths Two lengths that add up to another length.

5 cm + 1 cm = 6 cm; 5 cm and 1 cm are partner lengths of 6 cm.

partners A pair of numbers in a break-apart.

When 10 is broken apart into 10 = 3 + 7, 3 and 7 are partners (addends).

pattern A way in which numbers or drawings are related to one another that allows predictions about the next number or drawing.

pattern blocks Small geometric shapes that children use to build other geometric shapes or to form patterns.

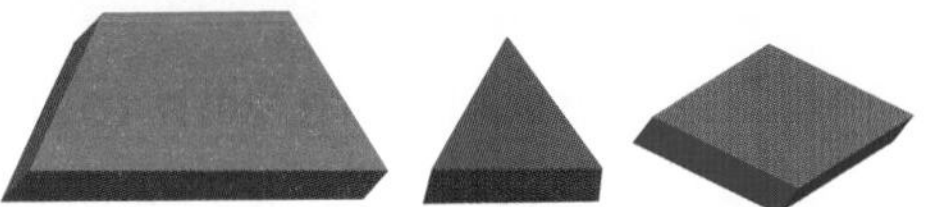

penny A coin with a value of 1 cent or $0.01.

perimeter The distance around a figure.

picture graph A graph in which data are displayed using pictures. Each picture represents one of whatever is being displayed.

pie graph or pie chart Another name for a circle graph. (See **circle graph**.)

plane A flat surface that extends in all directions without end.

plane figure A geometric figure that lies entirely in one plane.

P.M. The abbreviation for post meridiem, Latin for after noon. Used to indicate a time after noon.

point symmetry Property that pertains to a figure that can be turned less than a full turn (360°) and still look the same as it did before the turn. Also called rotational symmetry.

polygon A closed plane (two-dimensional) figure made up of three or more line segments.

possible Able to happen (as in a particular outcome in a probability experiment).

predict To think about what might happen; to guess; to anticipate what will come next.

probability The mathematical science of measuring and estimating predictability.

Proof Drawing A math drawing children create to show how to solve a problem, including the solution. It is not a formal proof.

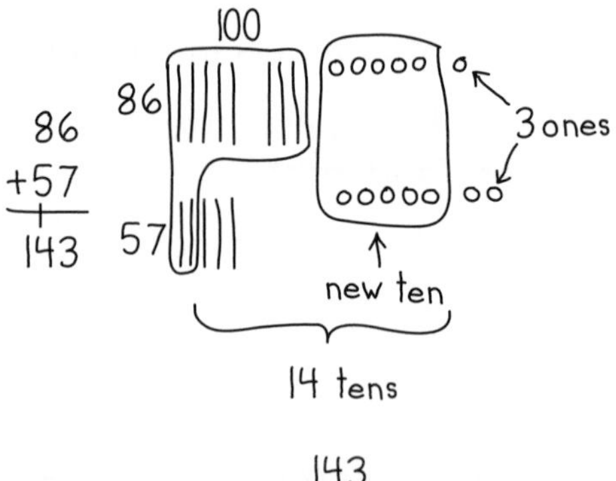

Q

quadrilateral A closed figure with four sides.

quarter A coin that has a value of twenty-five cents or $0.25.

Quick Hundred A box children draw to represent 100. The children will have first drawn 10 Quick Tens inside the box but will subsequently use only the box to represent 100.

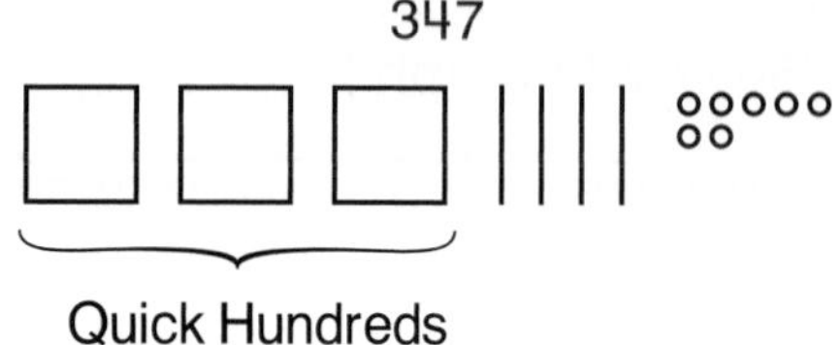

Quick Ten A vertical line children draw to represent 10.

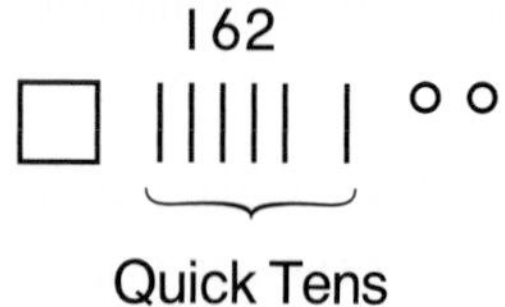

R

rectangle A parallelogram with four right angles.

rectangular prism A solid figure with six faces that are rectangles.

Red Count-On Cards Cards used to practice the Counting-On strategy for addition. One side of the card shows an addition equation with unknown total ≤ 10. The other side gives the same equation with the total. It also shows a counting-on drawing.

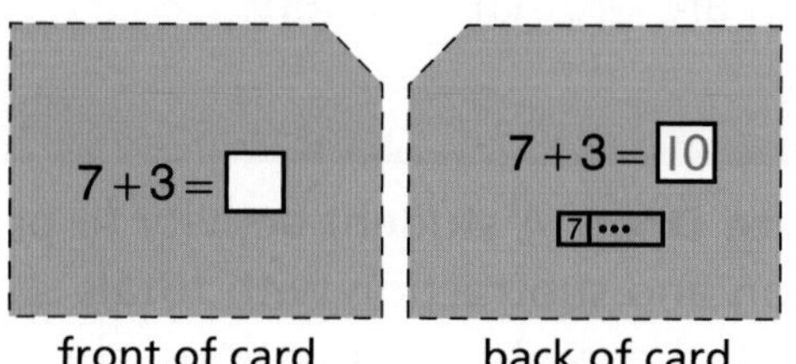

reflection A transformation that produces a mirror image of a figure on the opposite side of a line; also referred to as a flip.

reflectional symmetry See **line symmetry.**

regular polygon A polygon with all sides having the same length and all angles having the same measure.

repeating pattern A pattern consisting of a group of numbers, letters, or figures that repeat.
Examples: 1, 2, 1, 2, ...
A, B, C, A, B, C, ...

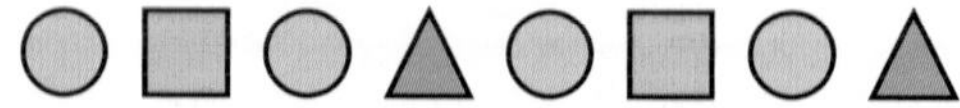

right angle An angle that measures 90°.

right triangle A triangle with one right angle.

rotation A transformation that involves a turning movement of a figure about a point, also referred to as a turn.

You can **turn** or **rotate** a figure around a point.

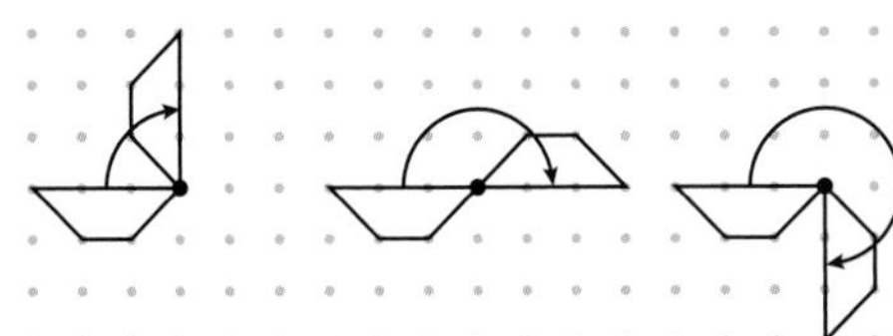

rotational symmetry See **point symmetry.**

rounding The process of finding *about* how many or *about* how much by expressing a number to the nearest unit, ten, hundred, thousand, etc.

rule In a pattern such as a function table or number sequence, what is done to the first number to get to the second number and so on. The rule *Add 3* is shown in the function table and the rule $n + 7$ is shown for the number sequence.

Function Table

Add 3.	
0	3
1	4
2	5
3	6

Number Sequence 16, 23, 30, 37, 44, 51 Rule: $n + 7$

S

scale On a graph, the numbers along the axes. The numbers are arranged in order with equal intervals.

scalene triangle A triangle whose sides are all different lengths.

Secret Code Cards Cards printed with the digits 0 through 9, multiples of 10 from 10 through 90 and multiples of 100 from 100 through 1,000. The number is represented on the back of the card by dots, sticks, or boxes. The cards are used to teach place value.

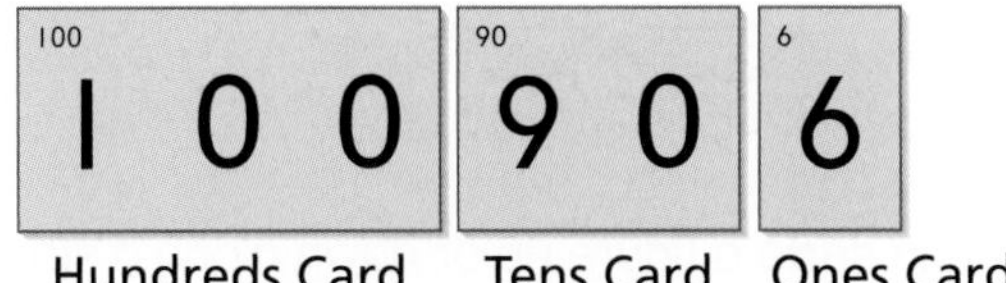

Hundreds Card Tens Card Ones Card

100 + 90 + 6

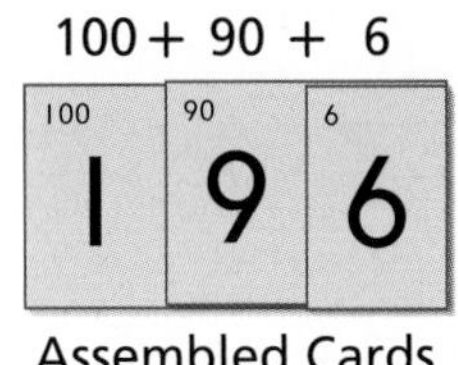

Assembled Cards

Show All Totals Method A method for finding a total of multi-digit numbers.

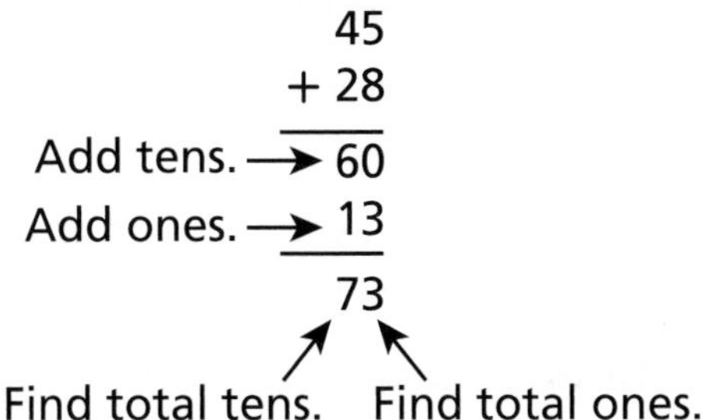

similar figures Figures that are the same shape but not necessarily the same size.

situation equation An equation children write to represent a story problem. It represents a literal translation of the problem. It may or may not have the unknown isolated on one side of the equals sign.

skip count To say the count-bys of a number. (See **count-bys.**)

Teacher Glossary (Continued)

slide A transformation in which a figure is moved along a line; also referred to as a translation. The size and shape of the figure remain the same.

You can **slide** a figure right or left along a straight line.

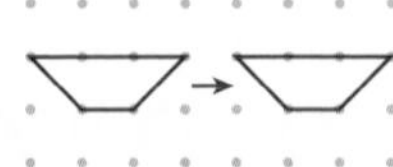

You can **slide** a figure up or down along a straight line.

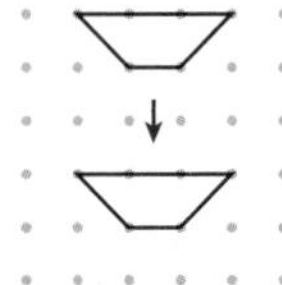

solution equation A situation equation that has been rewritten so that the unknown is on the right side of the equals sign. It is related to the operation needed to solve the problem rather than to a literal translation of the story problem.

square A figure with four right angles and four congruent sides.

square centimeter A standard metric unit for measuring area that is 1 cm on each side.

square rectangle Since a square has opposite sides parallel and four right angles, a square is also a rectangle, so it is sometimes called a square rectangle.

square unit Unit used to measure area that is 1 unit on each side. A square unit can refer to a standard or non-standard unit.

standard unit A recognized unit of measure, such as an inch or a centimeter. A non-standard unit of measure might be a paper clip.

sticks and circles A visual representation of groups of tens, as sticks and individual ones, as circles. The numbers 64 and 28 are shown.

story problem A math problem using topics from daily life and the math that is being studied.

sum The result of addition. In the addition equation, $3 + 2 = 5$, 5 is the sum.

survey (noun) A method of collecting information.

survey (verb) To collect information.

Switch the Partners To change the order of the partners in an addition equation. Used to demonstrate the Commutative Property of Addition.

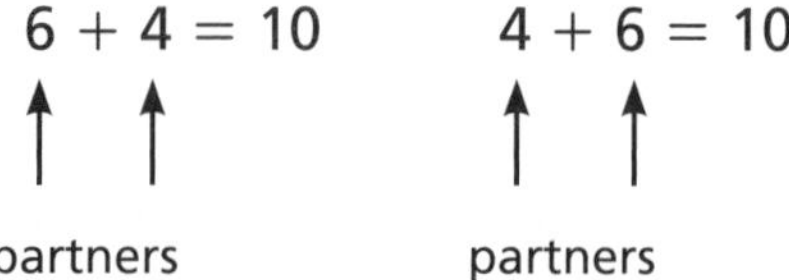

symmetry See **line symmetry** and **point symmetry.**

T

table A list of data organized in rows and columns.

tally (verb or noun) To count/record data or the type of mark that represents an individual item of data.

Colored Paper Clips

Color	Tally	Number
Pink	|||	3
White	~~||||~~ ||	7
Blue	~~||||~~	5
Green	~~||||~~ |	6
Yellow	|	1

teen numbers Numbers made up of one ten and some ones. In this program, the numbers 11 through 19 are referred to as teen numbers.

Ten Frame A diagram showing two rows of 5 squares that children use to practice making a ten.

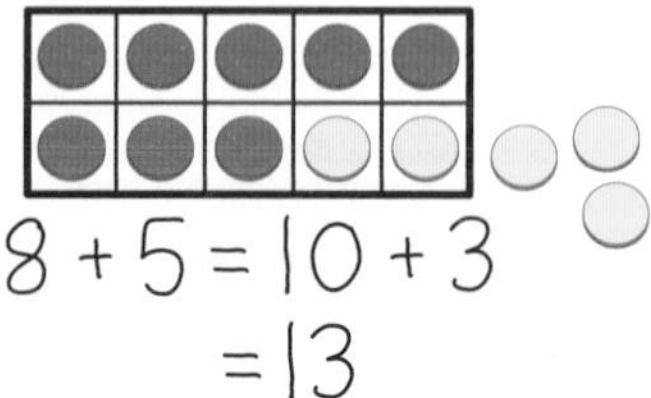

tens The name given to the second position from the right when describing whole number place value. In the number 12, 1 is in the tens position.

Time Poster

three-dimensional (3-D) Having three dimensions: length, width and height.

three-dimensional figure A figure with three dimensions.

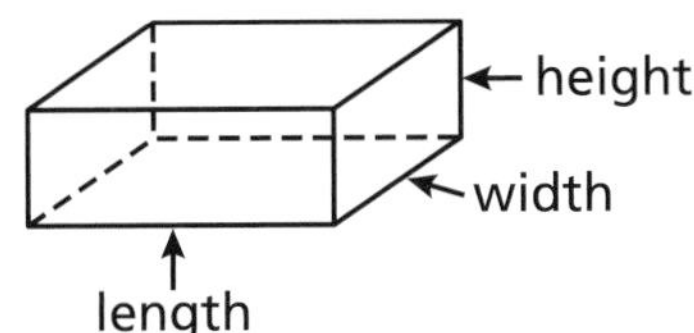

total A number that represents the combined amount of all the items added. A term used in *Math Expressions* to refer to the sum of two partners.

transformation A geometric change in the position of a figure. Transformations include slides (translations), flips (reflections) and turns (rotations).

translation See **slide.**

triangle A polygon with three sides.

turn A figure that is rotated around a point or axis; also referred to as a rotation. The size and shape of the figure remain the same. (See **rotation.**)

two-dimensional (2-D) Having two dimensions: length and width.

two-step story problem A story problem requiring two steps to arrive at the solution.

U

unfair game A game in which the likelihood of winning is not equally likely for each player.

ungroup To break into a new group in order to subtract. For example, 1 hundred can be ungrouped into 10 tens and 1 ten can be ungrouped into 10 ones.

ungrouping In subtraction, the process of breaking a number into a new group. Children may also refer to ungrouping as *trading, borrowing,* or *unpacking.*

Ungrouping First Method A method of subtraction in which children check each place to see if they need to ungroup in order to subtract. Children then complete all necessary ungrouping before they subtract.

unit fraction A fraction that is one equal part of a whole. $\frac{1}{3}$ and $\frac{1}{4}$ are unit fractions.

unknown addend

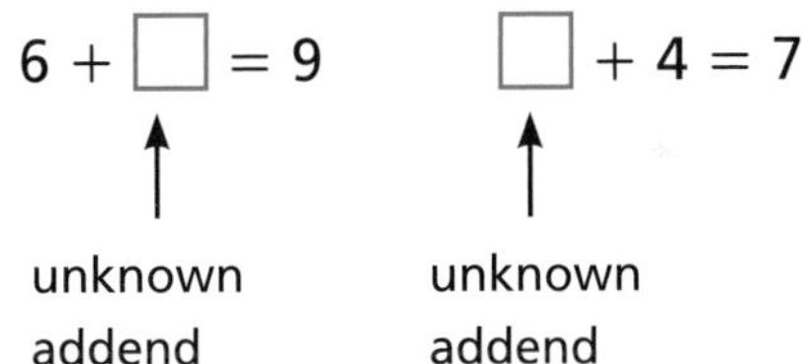

unknown partner

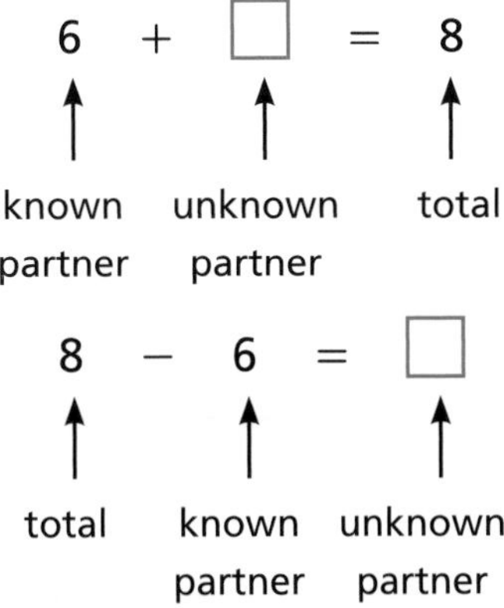

unknown start problem A change plus or change minus problem in which the starting number is the unknown number.

V

Venn diagram A pictorial way to represent relationships between sets.

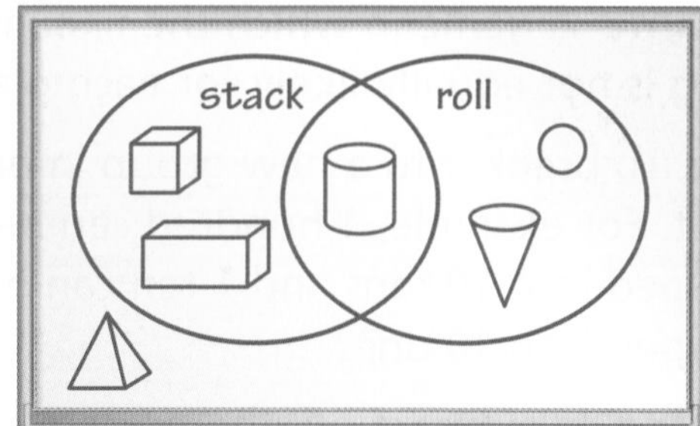

vertical Straight up and down.

vertical bar graph A bar graph in which data are displayed using vertical bars.

vertical form A way to position numbers in a problem in an up and down format.

$$\begin{array}{r} 7 \\ +\ 4 \\ \hline 11 \end{array}$$

volume The number of cubic units it takes to fill a solid.

W

word name A number represented as a word; the word name for 19 is *nineteen.*

Y

yard A customary unit for measuring length. One yard is equal to three feet; one yard is equal to thirty-six inches.

Yellow Count-On Cards Cards used to practice the Counting On strategy for addition. One side of the card shows an addition equation with an unknown partner. The other side shows the partner with a counting-on drawing.

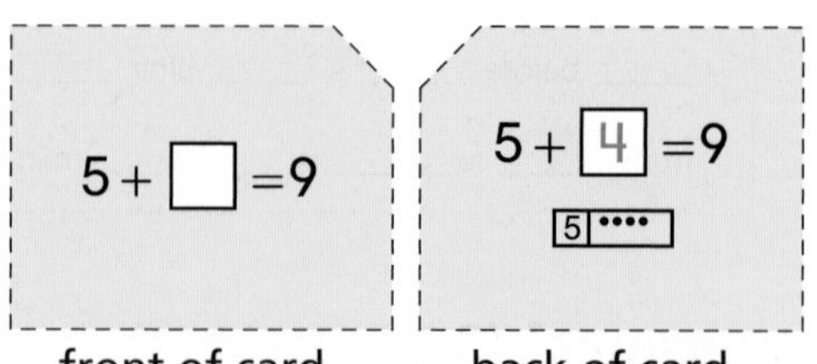

front of card back of card

Recommended Books

Unit 1

Oliver's Party, by Jenny Fry and Angela Jolliffe (Barron's Educational Series, Inc., 2002)

Jelly Beans for Sale, by Bruce McMillan (Scholastic, 1996)

Domino Addition, by Lynette Long (Charlesbridge, 1996)

Unit 2

Racing Around, by Stuart J. Reed, illustrated by Chuck Murphy (HarperTrophy, 2001)

Keep Your Distance, by Gail Herman, illustrated by Jerry Smath (The Kane Press, 2001)

Unit 3

Even Steven and Odd Todd, by Kathryn Cristaldi, illustrated by Henry Morehouse (Cartwheel, 1996)

Count on Pablo, by Barbara deRubertis, illustrated by Rebecca Thornburgh (Kane Press, 1999)

Unit 4

Shapes (Slide 'n Seek), by Chuck Murphy (Little Simon, 2001)

Shapes, Shapes, Shapes, by Tana Hoban (HarperTrophy, 1996)

A Cloak for a Dreamer, by Aileen Friedman, illustrated by Kim Howard (Scholastic, 1994)

Unit 5

Hippos Go Berserk!, by Sandra Boynton (Little Simon, 2000)

A Place for Zero, Angeline Sparanga LoPresti, illustrated by Phyllis Hornung (Charlesbridge, 2003)

Unit 6

Clocks and More Clocks, by Pat Hutchins (Aladdin Paperbacks, Simon & Schuster, 1970)

My Grandmother's Clock, by Geraldine McCaughrean, illustrated by Stephen Lambert (Clarion Books, 2002)

How Do You Know What Time It Is?, by Robert E. Wells (Albert Whitman & Company, 2002)

Unit 7

Tiger Math: Learning to Graph from a Baby Tiger, by Ann Whitehead Nagda and Cindy Bickel (Henry Holt and Company, 2000)

Fair is Fair, by Jennifer Dussling, illustrated by Diane Palmisciano (The Kane Press, 2003)

Recommended Books (Continued)

Unit 8

A Cloak for a Dreamer, by Aileen Friedman, illustrated by Kim Howard (Scholastic, 1994)

Unit 9

Tightwad Tod, by Daphne Skinner, illustrated by John A. Nez (Disney Press, 2005)

100th Day Worries, by Margery Cuyler, illustrated by Arthur Howard (Simon & Schuster Children's Publishing, 2000)

Pigs Will Be Pigs: Fun with Math and Money, by Amy Axelrod, illustrated by Sharon McGinley-Nally (Aladdin Picture Books, 1997)

Henry Hikes to Fitchburg, by D.B. Johnson (Houghton Mifflin Company, 2006)

Unit 10

Patterns in Nature, by Jennifer Rozines Roy and Gregory Roy (Benchmark Books, 2005)

Unit 11

Earth Day-Hooray!, by Stuart J. Murphy (Harper Trophy, 2004)

The 329th Friend, by Marjorie Weinman Sharmat (Four Winds Press, 1979)

Hannah's Collections, by Marthe Jocelyn (Dutton Children's Books, 2000)

One Grain of Rice, by Demi (Scholastic, 1997)

Unit 12

Tell Me How Far It Is, by Shirley Willis, (Gardners Books, 2005)

Millions to Measure by David M. Schwartz, illustrated by Steven Kellogg (HarperCollins, 2003)

Measuring Penny, by Loreen Leedy (Henry Holt and company, 1997)

Unit 13

Each Orange Had 8 Slices: A Counting Book, by Paul Giaganti (HarperTrophy, 1999)

The Doorbell Rang, by Pat Hutchins (HarperTrophy, 1989)

Let's Fly a Kite, by Stuart J. Murphy (HarperTrophy, 2000)

The Grapes of Math, by Greg Tang (Scolastic, 2004)

Unit 14

Henry Hikes to Fitchburg, by D.B. Johnson (Houghton Mifflin Company, 2006)

Index

Index (Continued)

Index (Continued)

N

O

P